GLOBAL INSIGHTS
People & Cultures

Hantula • Flickema • Farah • Karls
Johnson • Thuermer • Resnick • Kane

PUBLISHING COMPANY

Columbus, Ohio

Authors

James Neil Hantula is an Associate Professor in the Department of Teaching at the University of Northern Iowa, where he teaches at the Malcolm Price Laboratory School. He is an active member of the National Council for Geographic Education, the American Historical Association, the Organization of American Historians, the National Education Association, and Phi Delta Kappa.

Dr. Thomas O. Flickema is Vice President for Academic Affairs at Northern State College in Aberdeen, South Dakota. Formerly Dean of the Graduate School at Kearney State College in Nebraska, and Chairman of the History Department and Director of Latin American Studies at California State University, Fullerton, he has authored several articles on historical research and written reviews for *The Hispanic-American Historical Review* and *The Américas*.

Dr. Mounir A. Farah is Department Chairman of Social Studies in the Monroe, Connecticut public schools and an adjunct lecturer at Western Connecticut State University and New York University. Past President of the Connecticut Council for Social Studies and a member of the Middle East Institute, the Middle East Studies Association, and the National Council for Social Studies, he is senior author of Merrill's world history textbook, *The Human Experience*.

Andrea Berens Karls is a freelance writer and coauthor of *The Human Experience*. Formerly a Program Associate at Global Perspectives in Education, Inc., she has taught at both the elementary and secondary levels. She is a member of the National Council of Social Studies and the American Historical Association.

Ellen C.K. Johnson is Outreach Coordinator for the Program in South and West Asian Studies at University of Illinois, Urbana, and a social studies teacher in the Urbana, Illinois public schools. Past International Coordinator for The University High School in Urbana, she is an active member of the Council on Anthropology and Education and the Advisory Council of the Committee on Teaching about Asia in the Association for Asian Studies.

Katherine A. Thuermer is a curriculum specialist in African Studies at Michigan State University, where she coordinates the community and school outreach program. A member of the African Studies Association, she has lived and worked in Ghana, Mali, Madagascar, and Tanzania, as a Peace Corps volunteer, in public health with Catholic Relief Services, and with Operation Crossroads Africa.

Dr. Abraham Resnick is a Professor of Education at Jersey City State College, New Jersey, and for many years was Director of The Instructional Materials Center at the Rutgers University Graduate School of Education. The author of several text and trade books for children, he has conducted educational field research as the guest of the Bulgarian, Romanian, Soviet, and Japanese governments.

Paul W. Kane is a Professor of Education and Acting Dean of the School of Human Development and Community Service at California State University, Fullerton, where he was formerly the Chairman of the Division of Teacher Education. A past member of the California Social Science Framework Committee, he is active in the California Council for Social Studies.

ISBN 0-675-02004-2
Published by
MERRILL PUBLISHING COMPANY

Columbus, Ohio 43216

Copyright © 1980, 1987 by Merrill Publishing Company
All rights reserved. No part of this book may be reproduced in any form, electronic or mechanical, including photocopy, recording, or any information storage or retrieval system, without permission in writing from the publisher.
Printed in the United States of America

6 7 8 9 10 11 12 13 14 15 VH 00 99 98 97 96 95 94 93 92 91 90

PREFACE

The behavior of an individual is determined not by his racial affiliation, but by the character of . . . ancestry and . . . cultural environment.

Franz Boas

For Franz Boas, a German-born American anthropologist, ancestry and cultural environment were all important. If Boas was right about these two elements determining behavior, what better way to gain knowledge and understanding of a people—any people—than by learning about their history, geography, beliefs, values, and traditions?

The intent of *Global Insights* is to provide that knowledge and understanding by having the peoples of eight different geographical regions speak for themselves about the elements that have shaped their lives and made them the way they are today. The text is divided into eight units—Africa, China, Japan, India, Latin America, the Middle East, the Soviet Union, and Western Europe. Each unit opens with a descriptive photograph, a brief rationale, and a unit table of contents. Each unit concludes with a two-page Unit Review that includes a brief summary of the unit content; review questions; suggestions for individual and group activities; and a one-page feature called "Comparing Cultures" that compares an element of the unit culture with a like element of the American culture of the United States.

Each unit is divided into six or seven chapters, beginning with a chapter on geography and the environment and then covering such topics as history, religion, the arts, family, government, and daily life. Each chapter opens with a theme-related photograph, two questions that emphasize the theme of the chapter, a primary or secondary source that sets the tone for the chapter theme or topic, and a brief narrative that leads into or reinforces that theme or topic. Throughout the chapter, author narrative is interwoven with an abundance of primary and secondary source readings. To promote ease of reading and comprehension, the chapter is divided into sections and subsections, the headings of which serve as a content outline. Following each major section is a series of recall questions. In addition, concept terms and foreign words and phrases appear in boldface type and are immediately defined, explained, or exemplified. Concluding each chapter is a Chapter Review that consists of a listing of key points; comprehensive review questions, many of which invite the reader's personal viewpoint on a particular concept or action; vocabulary words to identify or define; and an activity that develops a skill by teaching, defining, and applying it, all in relation to chapter content.

Supplementing the basic chapter and unit content are three types of special features—Insights on People, Case Study, and Exploration—each of which is color-coded according to type of feature. The Insights features consist of one-page profiles of key individuals or groups. The Case Studies, also one page in length, focus on a particular aspect, event, or issue integral to the history or development of the culture under study. The Explorations, which vary in length (either one or two pages), serve to put the chapter topic or theme into perspective and show how it fits into the overall picture of the culture.

Throughout *Global Insights,* there is a wide variety of photographs and full-color illustrations, maps, charts, graphs, and diagrams designed to support, reinforce, and supplement the written word. The text concludes with an appendix that contains additional elements designed to broaden the reader's horizons even further. These include a full-color atlas; a glossary that provides pronunciations for and definitions of all terms that are boldfaced in the text; a comprehensive, cross-referenced index; and a listing of suggested resources for both teachers and students.

REVIEWERS

Pete Bellesis
Social Studies Department Chairperson
Bloomington South High School
Bloomington, Indiana

Lloyd Chorley
Chairperson, Social Sciences
C.K. McClatchy High School
Sacramento, California

Dr. Hunter Draper
Social Studies Coordinator
Charleston County School District
Charleston, South Carolina

Judy Dubé
Social Studies Teacher
Bathurst, New Brunswick
Canada

Consultant
Robert Hatton

Al Johnston
Teacher
Shoreline High School
Seattle, Washington

Dr. Walter S. Polka
Coordinator, Social Studies and Science K-12
Williamsville Central School
East Amhurst, New York

John A. Roy
Social Studies Department Chairperson
Savona Central School
Savona, New York

Dr. Regina T. White
Assistant Superintendent
  for Curriculum and Instruction
Wyandanch School District
Wyandanch, New York

STAFF

Project Editor Myra Immell; *Assistant Editors* Robert Kohan, Donna Roxey, Joyce White, Veronica Goolsby, Joan Nieto; *Project Designers* Scott Sommers, Patricia Cohan; *Project Artist* Barbara White; *Artists* Kenneth E. Stevenson, Lucia Condo, Jeff Kobelt; *Illustrator* Karen Tafoya; *Graphic/Map Illustrators* Intergraphics; *Charts and Graphs* David Germon; *Production Editors* Jan Wagner, Vicki Althoff; *Photo Editor* Aaron Haupt; *Permissions Editor* Jack Borchers; *Indexer* Schroeder Editorial Services

CONTENTS

UNIT ONE
AFRICA

Chapter 1
Adapting To The Environment — 6
   The African Continent — 8
   Working The Land — 10
   Urbanization — 16

Chapter 2
African Heritage — 22
   Early African Societies — 24
   From Colonialism To Nationalism — 30

Chapter 3
Nigeria — 38
   The People — 40
   Historical Perspective — 42
   Nigeria Today — 45

Chapter 4
South Africa — 54
   The Early Years — 56
   Apartheid — 58
   A Future In Question — 65

Chapter 5
Kenya — 70
   From Foreign Rule To Independence — 72
   The Way Of Life — 75
   Patterns Of Change — 78

Chapter 6
The Arts In Daily Life — 86
   Music — 88
   Oral Literature — 91

   Visual Arts — 93
   Masks — 94
   Films — 96

Chapter 7
Challenges To Development — 102
   The Need To Develop — 104
   Facing The Challenges — 109

UNIT TWO
CHINA

Chapter 8
The Land Under Heaven — 122
- Variety Of The Land — 124
- Mountains — 124
- Desert, Steppe, And Plain — 125
- Rivers — 128
- Cities And Villages — 131

Chapter 9
The Mandate Of Heaven — 140
- Dynastic Government — 142
- Dynastic Change — 144
- China And The Outside World — 147
- The End Of Dynastic Rule — 151

Chapter 10
The Few And The Many — 156
- The Upper Class — 158
- The Lower Classes — 161
- Women — 165
- The Arts — 166

Chapter 11
The Chinese Heritage — 172
- Traditional Chinese Beliefs — 174
- Daoism — 175
- Confucianism — 177
- Other Faiths And Viewpoints — 180

Chapter 12
The Chinese Revolution — 186
- Beginnings — 188
- A Divided China — 190
- Guomindang, Communists, And The Japanese — 192
- The People's Republic — 195

Chapter 13
China After Mao — 202
- Political Change — 204
- Agriculture — 205
- Industry — 207
- Science, Technology, And The Military — 211
- Foreign Policy — 212

Chapter 14
Daily Life In Modern China — 218
- The Communist Party — 220
- In The Countryside And The City — 221
- Young People — 224

UNIT THREE
JAPAN

Chapter 15
The Great Island Country — 236
- In The Beginning — 238
- Mountains — 238
- The Sea — 240
- The Plains — 242

Chapter 16
Traditional Japan — 252
- An Emerging Civilization — 254
- The Heian Period — 255
- The *Shoguns* — 257
- Contact With The West — 261

Chapter 17
Modern Japan — 268
- A New Era — 270
- Drift To War — 272
- Japanese Expansion — 275

Chapter 18
Religion And The Arts — 284
- Religion — 286
- Celebrations And Festivals — 289
- The Written And Spoken Word — 291
- Crafts And Other Arts — 294

Chapter 19
Japanese Society — 300
- Marriage — 302
- Family Life — 303
- Women — 305
- Young People — 306

Chapter 20
Work And Leisure — 314
- Work—A Way Of Life — 316
- Urban Life Styles — 319
- Rural Life Styles — 321
- Recreation — 323

UNIT FOUR
INDIA

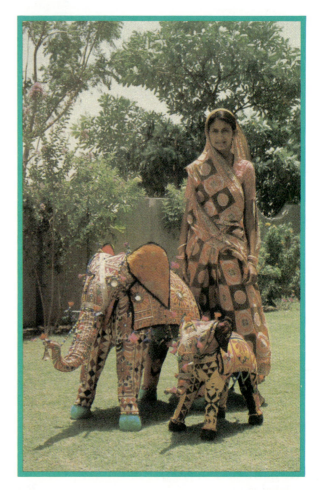

Chapter 21
Land And Water — 332
   The Himalayas — 334
   The Indo-Gangetic Plains — 335
   The Peninsula — 337
   Water—The Key To Life — 339

Chapter 22
The Indian People — 348
   Marriage — 350
   Family Life — 352
   Indian Women — 355
   Village Life — 356
   City Life — 359

Chapter 23
Religions of India — 366
   Hinduism — 368
   Islam — 375
   Other Religions — 377

Chapter 24
An Old And New Land — 382
   Early India — 384
   Muslim India — 386
   British India — 387
   Independent India — 391

Chapter 25
Developing India — 400
   Agriculture — 402
   Industry — 404
   Natural Resources — 406
   The Quality Of Life — 407

Chapter 26
The Arts — 414
   Architecture, Painting, And Sculpture — 416
   The Written Word — 419
   The Performing Arts — 423

UNIT FIVE
LATIN AMERICA

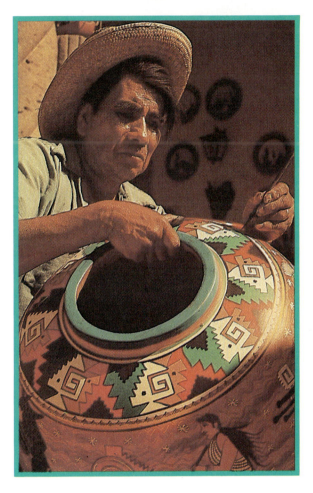

Chapter 27
Vast And Varied Environment — 434
   Mountains — 436
   Plains — 439
   Rivers — 441
   Rain Forests And Deserts — 443

Chapter 28
The Human Diversity — 450
   Indians — 452
   The Europeans — 457
   The Africans — 459
   The Asians — 460

Chapter 29
The Social Fabric — 464
   Social Class — 466
   The Family — 472
   Living Life To The Fullest — 474

Chapter 30
Prayer And Politics — 482
   The Church In The New World — 484
   The National Period — 486
   The Catholic Church Today — 488

Chapter 31
Change Takes Many Forms — 496
   The People Explosion — 498
   In The Countryside — 502
   The State Of Development — 507
   The State Of Education — 509

Chapter 32
Dictatorships And Democracies — 516
   The Old Tradition — 518
   The New Tradition — 520
   Reaction To Change — 522

UNIT SIX
MIDDLE EAST

Chapter 33
Environment And People   536
- The Region   538
- On The Deserts   540
- On Watered Lands   542
- In The Cities   545

Chapter 34
A Mosaic Of Peoples   554
- The Arabs   556
- The Iranians And The Turks   557
- The Israelis   560
- The Palestinians   561
- The Armenians And The Kurds   563

Chapter 35
The Way Of Life   568
- The Family   570
- Social Life   573
- Breaking With Tradition   576

Chapter 36
Religion And State   584
- Three Religions   586
- A Divine Chain   589
- The Islamic State   593
- Impact And Achievements   598

Chapter 37
The Great Bitterness   602
- Syria And Lebanon   604
- The Suez Canal   606
- The Arab-Israeli Conflict   609
- The Persian Gulf   611

Chapter 38
The Middle East Today   616
- The Arab-Israeli Conflict Today   618
- Civil War   623
- Revolution And War   625
- A Land In Transition   629

UNIT SEVEN
SOVIET UNION

Chapter 39
Giant Among The Gigantics — 638
- The Factor Of Size — 640
- Global Position And Climate — 640
- The Lay Of The Land — 644

Chapter 40
The Russian Past — 654
- Early Russia — 656
- The First Tsars — 658
- The "Reforming" Romanovs — 661
- The Last Of The Romanovs — 664

Chapter 41
The Soviet Era — 672
- The Double Revolution — 674
- The Communist State — 677
- A New Superpower — 682

Chapter 42
Peoples Of The Soviet Union — 688
- Slavs — 690
- Lithuanians, Latvians, And Estonians — 692
- Georgians, Armenians, And Azerbaijanians — 694
- Central Asians — 696
- Russification — 698

Chapter 43
City And Country — 704
- City Life — 706
- Rural Life — 712

Chapter 44
The All-Powerful State — 720
- The Party — 722
- The Economy — 723
- The Arts — 724
- Religion And Dissent — 729

Chapter 45
Soviet Life — 734
- Family — 736
- Women — 737
- Youth And Education — 739
- Leisure — 742

xi

UNIT EIGHT
WESTERN EUROPE

Chapter 46
Variety In A Small Space — 752
- The Western Fringe Of Eurasia — 754
- Coastline And Islands — 756
- Mountain Areas — 757
- Plains And Rivers — 761
- Dry Lands — 763

Chapter 47
Roots Of Western Europe — 770
- The Greeks — 773
- The Romans — 776
- The Middle Ages — 780

Chapter 48
Rise Of Western Europe — 790
- Rebirth And Reform — 792
- Age Of Discovery — 794
- Rise Of The Nation-State — 797
- From Reason To Revolution — 799
- The Industrial Revolution — 800
- The Turmoil Of World War — 804

Chapter 49
A Sense Of Themselves — 810
- Family — 812
- Social Class — 813
- Place — 815
- Language — 818
- Religion — 820
- History And Tradition — 822

Chapter 50
Arts And Thought — 828
- From The Greeks To Dickens — 830
- Artistic Trends — 834
- Scientific And Political Thought — 840

Chapter 51
The Ways Of Life — 848
- The Way Of The City — 850
- The Way Of The Countryside — 854
- Education — 857
- Leisure Activities — 859

APPENDIX — 869
ATLAS — 870
GLOSSARY — 879
INDEX — 889
SUGGESTED RESOURCES — 909

SPECIAL FEATURES

CASE STUDY

Environmental Awareness	11
The Atlantic Slave Trade	29
The Whites of Africa	59
Women and Development	110
North, South, East, West, and Center	130
Yang and Yin	133
Women and the Revolution	193
China's Revolutionary Drama	210
The Other China	227
Earthquakes in Japan	243
The Japan Expedition	265
My Restaurant, My Life	307
Service Industries	318
"Mother Earth"	341
The Old and the New	360
A Hindu Holy City	371
The Diminishing Rain Forests	445
The Indian Today	456
Women	473
Unresolved Problems	506
The Green Patrols	649
Long-Lifers	695
Soviet Rock Fans	743
Land from the Sea	765
The Crusades	785
The Holocaust	807
The Art of Eating	819
The Americanization of Western Europe	841
Bullfighting	863

EXPLORATION

for Adapting to the Environment	18
for African Heritage	34
for South Africa	67
for Kenya	82
for The Arts In Daily Life	98
for Challenges to Development	114
for The Land Under Heaven	136
for The Mandate of Heaven	153
for The Few and the Many	169
for The Chinese Heritage	182
for The Chinese Revolution	198
for China After Mao	214
for Daily Life in Modern China	228
for The Great Island Country	248
for Modern Japan	280
for Japanese Society	311
for Land and Water	344
for Religions of India	379
for Developing India	411
for Vast and Varied Environment	446
for The Social Fabric	479
for Prayer and Politics	492
for Change Takes Many Forms	512
for Dictatorships and Democracies	529
for Environment and People	550
for A Mosaic of Peoples	565
for The Way of Life	580
for Religion and State	599
for The Great Bitterness	613
for Giant Among the Gigantics	650
for The Russian Past	668
for The Soviet Era	684
for Peoples of the Soviet Union	700
for City and Country	717
for The All-Powerful State	731
for Variety in a Small Space	766
for Roots of Western Europe	787
for A Sense of Themselves	825

INSIGHTS ON PEOPLE

Flora Nwapa	51	Moctezuma	453
Miriam Makeba	90	Al-Idrīsī	594
Kang Xi	148	Maimonides	596
The Wang Clan	160	Anwar el-Sadat	619
Tokugawa Ieyasu	259	Golda Meir	620
Hokusai	297	Eugenia Ginzburg	680
Mohandas K. Gandhi	392	Charlemagne	781
Indira Gandhi	395	Napoleon Bonaparte	801
Ravi Shankar	424	Wolfgang Amadeus Mozart	835

SKILLS

Reading a Chapter	21	Writing Descriptively	449
Recognizing Ethnocentric Statements	37	Supporting Generalizations	463
Creating a Time Line	53	Preparing a Research Report	481
Recognizing Fallacies in a Line of Reasoning	69	Summarizing	495
Recognizing Unstated Assumptions	85	Interviewing	515
Classifying Information	101	Distinguishing Between Fact and Opinion	531
Identifying the Main Idea	117	Narrative Writing	553
Taking Notes	139	Distinguishing Between Warranted and Unwarranted Claims	567
Identifying Cause and Effect	155	Analyzing Photographs	583
Identifying the Values of a Culture	171	Using Persuasive Arguments	601
Hypothesizing	185	Interpreting Historical Documents	615
Using a Time Line	201	Interpreting Biographical Accounts	633
Making Generalizations	217	Gaining Understanding Through Context	653
Analyzing Primary and Secondary Sources	231	Using Literature as a Cultural Source	671
Reading for Detail	251	Determining the Reliability of a Source	687
Interpreting Point of View	267	Determining the Strength of an Argument	703
Expressing and Supporting a Viewpoint	283	Identifying Ambiguous or Equivocal Statements	719
Making Inferences	299	Identifying Evidence	733
Identifying Trends and Making Forecasts	313	Using Reference Works in Research	747
Preparing Note Cards for a Research Report	327	Asking Effective Questions	769
Reading Thematic Maps	347	Identifying Valid Assumptions	789
Distinguishing Relevant Information from Irrelevant Information	365	Analyzing Editorial Cartoons	809
Developing a Global Point of View	381	Making Comparisons	827
Determining Factual Accuracy	399	Analyzing Art as a Primary Source	847
Placing Information in Order of Significance	413	Making Decisions	865
Detecting Bias	429		

MAPS

Africa
Landforms	9
Relative Size	18
Food Supply	18
Population Density	19
Early Africa	24
Colonialism, 1914	30
Nigeria	46
Republic of South Africa	62
South African Homelands	62
Kenya	75
African Independence	104
The Kiswahili Language	115

China
Natural Regions	136
Climate	136
Land Use	137
Population Density	137
Chinese Dynasties 1994 BC–1912 AD	146
Spheres of Influence	153
The Long March 1934–35	194

Japan
Climate	248
Population Density	248
Landforms and Natural Resources	249
Average Annual Rainfall	249
Russo-Japanese War 1904–1905	271

India
Landforms	344
Wet Seasons	344
Average Annual Rainfall	345
Agricultural Resources	345
Major Cities of India	359
Indian States and Territories	397

Latin America
Landforms	446
Climate	446
Land Use and Resources	447
Population Density	447

Middle East
Agricultural Resources	542
Population Density	550
Population Patterns	551
Culture-Language Groups	565
Major Religions	588
Gulf States	612
Sykes-Picot Agreement, 1916	613
The Mandate System, 1920	613

Soviet Union
Natural Resources	650
Natural Regions	651
Russian Expansion 1000 AD–Present	658
Union of Soviet Socialist Republics	690
Moscow	706
Major Soviet Cities	711

Western Europe
Climate	766
Industry	766
Population Density	767

CHARTS AND DIAGRAMS

Africa
Traditional Dress	42
Literacy Chart	111

China
Cardinal Directions	130
Royal City	131
Major Chinese Dynasties	143
Five Zones of Chinese Culture	147
Chinese Characters	167
The Chinese Zodiac	175
Characteristics of the Major Philosophies/Religions of China	183
The Chinese Revolution	192
Population Growth	214
Family Planning Options 1980–2080	215
Political Structure of the People's Republic of China	220

Japan
Leaders of Traditional Japan	254
Characteristics of the Major Religions of Japan	287

India
Indian Empires	385

Latin America
Ethnic Diversity in Latin America	454
Population of Central America	498
Population of South America	499

Middle East
English Words of Arabic Origin	598

Soviet Union
Russian Proverbs	663
Romanov Tsars of Russia 1801–1917	666
Cultural Figures	726
Political Structure of the Soviet Union	749
Political Structure of the United States	749

Western Europe
Greek Contributions	772
A Roman Banquet Menu	778
Renaissance Manners	792
Explorers	795
Western European Inventors	803
Greek Gods and Goddesses	830
Cultural Figures	836
Science and Technology	843

PROLOGUE

A sixteenth-century French intellectual named François Rabelais once commented, "Then I began to think, that it is very true which is commonly said, that the one-half of the world knoweth not how the other half liveth." Centuries later, what Rabelais said still held true for many. There was a difference, however. In Rabelais' time, not only did most people not know about much of the rest of the world, but, perhaps more importantly, they did not think that they had to know about it. For the most part, events that took place among a "strange people" in a "faraway land" had little or no effect on the day-to-day life of most people in other lands, near or far.

Part of what held true in the time of Rabelais, however, no longer holds true today. In one way or another, to a small extent or to a great one, what happens in one part of the globe may very well influence what happens both near and far away. A twentieth-century French author-philosopher named Albert Camus once said that "civilization does not lie in a greater or lesser degree of refinement, but in an awareness shared by a whole people." During an inaugural address in 1945, given while his country was in the midst of a world war, American President Franklin Delano Roosevelt said much the same thing when he declared the following:

> We have learned that we cannot live alone, at peace; that our own well-being is dependent on the well-being of other nations, far away. We have learned that we must live as men, and not as ostriches, nor as dogs in the manger. We have learned to be citizens of the world, members of the human community.

People of the twentieth century have the benefits of many means of communication that were not available or, in some cases, even dreamed of, just a few generations ago. Newspapers, magazines, radio, television, and satellites tell people a great many things about what is going on in the world around them. Based on what they learn from these and other sources, individuals say they "know" about events and happenings not only at home but in places whose names most cannot even pronounce correctly. For example, most people "know" that Communist governments rule the Soviet Union and the People's Republic of China. They "know" that people in Ethiopia and some other areas of Africa are starving and that the practice of apartheid is being violently challenged in South Africa. They "know" that peace still eludes Arabs and Israelis in the Middle East.

There is a great difference, however, between knowing and understanding. The dictionary defines the term "know" as "to be acquainted or familiar with." It defines the term "understand" as "to perceive or comprehend the nature and significance of." When, for example, one says that he or she knows that the People's Republic of China and the Soviet Union are under Communist rule, that some Africans are starving and others are subject to apartheid, or that in the Middle East Arabs and Israelis have not settled their differences, what does that individual actually mean?

Does that person have any idea why the People's Republic of China and the Soviet Union are under Communist rule or how Soviet and Chinese citizens feel about that rule? Does he or she know why some Africans are starving or what needs to be done to reverse the situation, or how apartheid came about and why the whites and blacks of South Africa regard it as they do? Does he or she know why the Arabs and Israelis cannot come to terms and how the people of the

Middle East feel about the conflict under which they must live? Even for those who can answer these questions, do they merely know, or do they truly understand?

All of us are a small part of that "whole people" of which Camus spoke, and, as such, we should have an awareness not only of ourselves and our ways, but also of the lands and cultures with which we share the world. The world is peopled by many different cultures, each of which is basically a group of people who share common beliefs, social forms, behavior patterns, institutions, and historical background and traditions. These cultures may be grouped or classified socially, racially, religiously, or geographically. How they are grouped, however, has little or no bearing on how they develop or progress. Most often, the groupings or classifications are artificial ones generally made for others for purposes of research. In order for any culture to carry on its basic functions, it develops its own political and economic systems. How a culture develops is influenced by many different factors, including geography and environment; religious values and beliefs; and past experience, which people call history. Since no culture remains static, all of these factors work together to produce change. Today that change not only affects the culture itself but other cultures as well.

The view many of us have today about other cultures is based on images, or mental pictures, that have been created not only by what has been said or shown about that culture, but also by what has not been said or shown. These images become lasting ones when they are repeated over and over again. Repetition of an image, however, does not always mean that the image is a true one. An image, no matter how often it is repeated, may give only part of the picture. The reality may be far different and far more complex.

Many images have grown up over the years, created from tales told by traders, soldiers, missionaries, travelers, stories, books, or songs. Consider, for example, these excerpts written in the 1800's by two different visitors to the Middle East. The first was written by a British traveler, the second by an American.

Here the head is shaved, the beard not shaved; the men wear petticoats of cloth; the women trousers of silk or cotton. Instead of a hat, a piece of muslim is twisted round the head; instead of surtout [overcoat], a blanket is thrown around the shoulders; a carpet serves for a bed; a wooden bowl for a plate; a pewter tray for a table-cloth; fingers do for forks, and swords for carving knives. A man salutes without stooping, sits down without a chair. If you inquire after the health of his wife, it is at the hazard of your head; if you praise the beauty of his children, he suspects you of the evil eye. The name of the Prophet [Allah] is in every man's mouth, and the fear of God in few men's hearts.*

One who has never met an Arab in the desert can have no idea of his terrible appearance. The worse pictures of the Italian bandits or Greek mountain robbers I ever saw are tame in comparison. I have seen Gasperini, who ten years ago kept in terror the whole country between Rome and Naples, and who was so strong as to make a treaty with the pope. I saw him surrounded by nearly twenty of his comrades; and when he told me he could not remember how many murders he had committed, he looked civil and harmless compared with a Bedouin of the desert. The dark complexion of the Bedouin, his long beard, his piercing coal-black eyes, half-naked figure, an enormous sword slung over his back, and a rusty matchlock [musket with a gunlock in which powder is ignited by a match] in his hand, make the best figure for a painter I ever saw; but, happily, he is not so bad as he looks to be.†

What images do you think were created by these writings? If you lived in the 1800's and were reading them, what image would you

---

*Adapted from *Travels in Turkey, Egypt, Nubia, and Palestine, Vol. I*, by R.R. Madden, 1829, Henry Colburn, p. 307.

†Adapted from *Incidents of Travel in Egypt, Arabia, Petraea, and the Holy Land, Vol. I*, by John L. Stephens, 1837, Harper & Brothers, p. 82.

form of the Middle East and of the Arabs? Existing images, some like these, have been added to in more recent times by movies, television programs, newspaper reports, photographs, cartoons, and advertisements. Modern transportation has made it possible for more people to travel today than in the past, be it on business trips or on vacations. To convince these people to visit certain places, it is not uncommon for travel posters and brochures to make statements like these:

What warm people. Weather, beaches, shopping, everything—perfect. What a tough life, eh? Feel the warmth of Mexico.

The haunting atmosphere of a village street unchanged since Biblical times. Great cities spiked with minarets and bud-like domes. The endless, flowing sea of sand.

Just when you start to feel winter closing in, the fun starts heating up in Holland. The divas and ballerinas and bassoonists are all warmed up. The chefs are cooking. The jazz sizzling.

These advertisements and others like them are designed to create an image. What they have in common with many other image-creating materials is that they focus on the exotic, the different, and ignore the common, the similar.

Yet, in order for people to share peacefully the same world, what is important is not similarities or differences, but understanding. Without understanding, there can be little progress or development. For this reason, many people believe there is a need to learn more about others and have others learn about them and, most importantly, to put that learning in the proper perspective. As an official of UNICEF from Sri Lanka explains, it is time for change:

There are times in the life of a human being when what one has been is no longer an adequate indication of what one could become. The past—so familiar, for some even comfortable—is then no longer a reliable pad from which the future may be be launched, but an intricate though superficial structure of habit, condition, thought, and reflex, which make the past the prison of the future. It is so with individual living beings, with the human collective we call nations, and with the world of nations.

But, because the present is largely the product, the repository of the past, and we must think and act today, in the here and now, we look over our shoulders towards the past, to where we have been, to find the methods, the instruments, the ideas and values which must guide us into the future . . . .

The age we are passing into calls for a fundamental change . . . . *

**"Time for Change,"* speech by Tarzie Vittachi, quoted in "Third World Women: Understanding Their Role in Development," in *A Training Resource Manual, Peace Corps,* 1981, Office of Programming and Training Coordination, pp. 1, 2.

Unit One

The continent of Africa has a long and rich historical tradition. For centuries, however, very little was actually known about this vast continent or its peoples. Eventually, Africa's wealth of natural resources captured the interest of European powers. The result was a period of western domination, brought to an end in many cases only after years of resistance and struggle. Today, Africa is made up of more than 50 independent nations. Each has its own ethnic, religious, linguistic, and cultural traditions, and each is working to develop and achieve a better standard of living for its peoples. At the same time, as a cooperative unit, these nations have become an increasingly important voice in the world arena, determined to secure Africa's future without completely forsaking its past.

CONTENTS

1	ADAPTING TO THE ENVIRONMENT	6
2	AFRICAN HERITAGE	22
3	NIGERIA	38
4	SOUTH AFRICA	54
5	KENYA	70
6	THE ARTS IN DAILY LIFE	86
7	CHALLENGES TO DEVELOPMENT	102

AFRICA

CHAPTER 1
ADAPTING TO THE ENVIRONMENT

1. How has climate shaped the physical features and vegetation of the African continent?
2. In what ways have people from African nations adapted to their environment?

... In a hoarse voice Muti ... began singing the song of Africa, and not one Muti sang but a hundred Mutis, ten thousand Mutis, and they all sang the song that was Africa.

And as they sang there was a deep calm.
And this is what they sang.
Nkosi Sikele' Afrika ...

which means God bless Africa. God bless the sun-scorched Karoo [the Great Karoo plateau] and the green of the Valley of a Thousand Hills. God bless the mountain streams that chatter impudently when they are high in the hills and are young, but roll lazily from side to side like old women in the Great Plains. And the dry pans which twist their tortured bosoms to the hot skies. And the mighty waters that hurl themselves against her shores and mockingly retreat only to come again with a new energy as if to engulf the mielies [corn] and the land and the villages and the towns, even great Africa itself. God bless the cataracts that taunt the solemn rocks and the African sky that spits blood in the evening. And the timeless hills where the shy roebuck rears its tragic eyes and the dassie [rabbit] sips in silent pools. And the blue krantzes [cliffs] where man has still to breathe. God bless this Africa of heat and cold, and laughter and tears, and deep joy and bitter sorrow. God bless this Africa of blue skies and brown veld [grassland], and black and white and love and hatred, and friend and enemy.

God bless this Africa, this Africa which is part of us. God protect this Africa. God have mercy upon Africa.
And still they sang.
Maluphakonyisw' Upshondo Lwayo. ... *

Africa is many things to many people. To the people who fought for independence, it is a continent demanding its rightful voice in world affairs. To the peanut farmer of Mali and the businesswoman of Zimbabwe, it is home. To them and others like them, the "deep joy" of knowing the history of their people, of sharing communal life and family values, is balanced by the "bitter sorrow" of hard times. Africa finds its population growing faster than its ability to feed itself. To the black people of South Africa and Namibia, Africa is proof that the struggle to attain justice will not stop until the entire continent is free. To Richard Rive, the black South African who wrote the opening words of this chapter, it is the land that defines "great Africa itself."

*"African Song" by Richard Rive in *Black African Voices*, 1970, Scott Foresman & Co., p. 300.

THE AFRICAN CONTINENT

Lying astride the equator, the enormous landmass of Africa, situated in both the northern and southern hemispheres, stretches over 11,685,000 square miles (30.4 million square kilometers). If one were to fly from the northernmost point in Tunisia to the Cape of Good Hope in South Africa, the distance would be the same as traveling from New York to San Francisco—and back.

The continent, which accounts for 20 percent of the world's land area and is home to 11.1 percent of its population, is made up of 54 nations. Included are several island states, the largest of which is Madagascar. The borders of the countries were marked out by Europeans during Africa's colonial period.

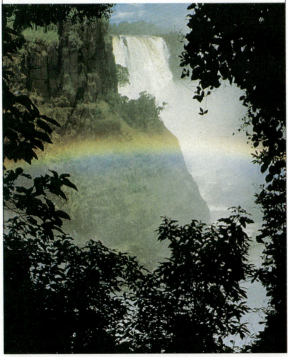

Victoria Falls, located on the Zambezi River, was discovered in 1855 by explorer David Livingstone. The falls measure 343 feet (105 meters) in height. What two African nations are divided by the Zambezi River?

Because the borders were chosen without regard to the unity of the different peoples living in the area, today each country is home to a variety of ethnic groups, languages, religions, and customs.

Most of Africa consists of a large, rolling plateau that ranges from 500 to 4500 feet (152.4 to 1371.6 meters) above sea level. A narrow coastal belt encircles the continent. There are few inlets, large bays, gulfs, or natural harbors. The mountains that do exist are relatively small, having been worn away by hundreds of millions of years of erosion. The tallest peak still standing is Mount Kilimanjaro in Tanzania. It is 19,340 feet (5803.2 meters) high. Breaking the monotony of the plateau is the Great Rift Valley—a long, narrow break in the earth's surface that runs for over 3000 miles (4800 kilometers) through the eastern highlands of Ethiopia and Kenya.

The variety of vegetation and the extreme physical features of the African landscape—scorching deserts, lush rain forests, and even snowcapped mountains on the equator—can be linked to the climate. Of vital importance is the amount and distribution of rainfall a region receives each year. In fact, Africa's major climatic zones can be roughly identified by the amount of rainfall each region receives.

The area that receives the most rainfall is the **rain forest,** or a heavily wooded area found in warm, humid regions mostly near the equator. In Africa, the rain forest is a large zone that stretches across equatorial Africa from the Atlantic to the Great Rift Valley. To the north and south of this zone lies the less watered **savanna,** or grasslands. Further north and south of the savanna are the semiarid lands and the deserts. Finally, at the northernmost part and southernmost tip of the continent, the people enjoy a Mediterranean-type climate.

Africa also has extensive river systems. The rivers have played an important role in the continent's history and development. The Zambezi River, in southern Africa, divides the nations of Zambia and Zimbabwe. The Niger, in West Africa, helps water the parched, semiarid Sahel that stretches from Mauritania to the edge of the Sudan. The Nile, which flows from Uganda and Ethiopia into Egypt, creates fertile farmland along its banks for thousands of miles. It is the longest river in the world.

Still another river is the Zaire, which used to be known as the Congo. It is Africa's second longest river. Below, one writer talks about the river, the people of Zaire who live along it, and the land through which it winds:

> The river rises in southeastern central Africa.... This is flat, open country, a highland savanna thinly covered in scrub and twisted thorn trees, solitary silver baobabs and yellow elephant grass, and spotted with those giant sandcastle-like structures that the driver ants build....
>
> This was once a land of great herds of wild game ... but it is no longer. For this plateau ... lies in the continent's copper belt and contains astonishingly rich deposits of malachite ore. The Baluba and Balunda ... of this region mined and smelted it, using the giant ant hills for their ovens, as long ago as the fourteenth century.... But in the twentieth century the European colonizers of the plateau ... scarred the savanna into an ugly moonscape with their huge open-pit mines and killed or drove off the magnificent herds....
>
> Plumes of dust, whipped off the charred and cracked earth by sudden gusts of hot wind, blow hard against you in the dry season, tearing at your eyes and choking in your mouth. And, in the rainy season, ferocious thunderstorms lash across this ruined highland plain, flooding its lakes and rivers and turning huge tracts of it into swamp....
>
> The river's descent from the highland savanna to the rain forests occurs over a

LANDFORMS

> distance of some 500 miles [800 kilometers].... The descent is perceptible mainly by the steadily increasing richness of the vegetation. The grass becomes thicker; stands of acacia trees form into shady woods, in which weaverbirds nest in great chattering flocks; the baobabs put out broad shiny leaves; and one begins to see palms and lotus and the mangos of the old slave trails....
>
> But at Kongolo the river suddenly funnels into the Portes d'Enfer, the Gates of Hell, a startling gorge in the floor of the savanna ... where the waters boil up alarmingly and turn into impassable rapids....
>
> It is seemingly endless.... The river, fed by dozens of tributaries, has widened now ... and, rolling ever northward, has taken on the glinting, greasy-gray color of the heavy, lowering sky....
>
> The villages along the river now belong mostly to the Lokele.... They are famous for their "talking" drums, which one hears day and night sending messages of boats' progress downriver, so that at every

Shown here, in Zambia, is one of many river markets in central and southeastern Africa. Canoes and barges transport goods and small businesses, bringing buyers and sellers together. Why do floating markets prosper in Africa?

village we pass the Lokele are expecting us and come out in their canoes loaded with goods to trade....

This trade is the chief occupation and entertainment of the journey. The lower decks and cargo barges turn into thriving market places, floating bazaars. Stalls are set up to barter or sell manufactured goods, barbers go into business, laundries materialize, butchers prepare the animals and fish brought aboard, restaurants serve meals from open fires, beer parlors spring into existence complete with brassy music from transistor radios, and the buying and selling goes on around the clock....

But one morning you wake up and go on deck and you discover that... there are high, rugged yellow limestone hills rearing up on both banks. These are the Crystal Mountains....

The only way down this stretch of the river is by the road or railway the Belgians built around it at the beginning of this century....

From Matadi to Banana, the river... steadily widens... and once again we find sizable islands standing in its stream. Its banks are heavily forested, now mainly with palm trees and mangroves and... giant water ferns.

Two sandy peninsulas, some 15 miles [24 kilometers] apart and arcing out into the Atlantic like the opposing jaws of a giant crab's claw, form the... mouth. The river... rushes to it and through it and then well beyond it.... And we can see the river's waters, in their unrelenting flow, staining the ocean's surface for scores of miles offshore with the mud and vegetation carried down on the long journey from the savanna highlands.*

1. Where is the African continent located? Of how many nations does it consist?
2. What are the major climatic regions of Africa?
3. What are some of the major rivers of Africa?

WORKING THE LAND

Some people think of the African continent as a tropical paradise. But geography and climate have long made it a challenge to human settlement. Many parts suffer from

---

*Abridged from pages 3 to 16 of *The River Congo* by Peter Forbath. Copyright ©1977 by Peter Forbath. Reprinted by permission of Harper & Row, Publishers, Inc., and Martin Secker & Warburg Ltd., London.

CASE STUDY
AFRICA

ENVIRONMENTAL AWARENESS

In recent years, people all over the world have become more aware of their environment and the need to preserve and protect it. In Africa, sensitivity to the environment has long been important. Below, the head of the Science Education Program for Africa, in Ghana, describes some of the ways in which people in rural areas of Africa show respect for their environment:

"*Umhlaba yimpilo yethu, wonge*" is . . . printed on government stationery in Swaziland. It calls on people to preserve the land because it is the source of our health and livelihood. In that part of Africa as well as in West Africa, sensitivity to, and action on behalf of, the environment is not a recent phenomenon. Before the arrival of Europeans, Africans in Southern Africa had practised strip mining but they always refilled the stripped area. . . . In the semidesert areas in Chad, Somalia, and Botswana traditional rural inhabitants were not only very knowledgeable about the flora and fauna found in their environment but were also acutely sensitive to the needs of their tender existence.

In the Kalahari (Kgalagadi) region [in southern Africa], to select just one example, an outsider might be struck only by the sun's heat, the wind, dry acacia and grass, and by the absence of a large variety of animals. But the inhabitants know in detail the interdependence of living things in the semidesert environment—the "honey diviner," a local bird, is never attacked or killed because through its song it leads the people to beehives, and the inhabitants always reward it by giving it a portion of the honey which is essential to its livelihood. . . .

Today's African rural settlements illustrate not just action on behalf of the environment but simultaneous benefits to human beings . . . [such as] . . . the use of materials from the local environment extended to the construction of homesteads e.g., use of stones, local earth mixtures and plant hedges, of reed stems or palm ribs or bamboo or eucalyptus wood or other types of materials. . . . In the savannah areas thatched roofs were also useful in keeping indoor temperatures low during the hot season and comparatively warm in the cold season. . . .

In forest areas, for example, sacred woods serve as a nature reserve as well as a learning resource in the education of the youth in nondestructive ways of utilizing the environment and in balancing human needs against environmental requirements.

As information on useful conservation principles and practises becomes available from the rural dwellers themselves, it could be taken into account in policy issues relating to development and could be incorporated into environmental studies courses in the formal school system. Such action is underway in several African countries where the role of the school as a powerful vehicle in the retrieval of African skills and values is recognized.*

1. What are some of the ways in which Africans show respect for their environment?
2. What role can be played by schools in helping protect the environment?

*"Environmental Awareness in Rural Africa" by Hubert M. Dyasi, in *Curriculum Materials for Teachers 1983*, University of Illinois, pp. 83–84. Reprinted by permission.

poor soils and erosion. Other areas receive too little or too much rainfall. Those with dense vegetation attract parasites that make it impossible to raise livestock. And the river systems often are interrupted by waterfalls that reduce their navigability.

Despite the obstacles, however, the people of many parts of Africa have adapted to, or changed, their environment to meet their needs. Today, about one-third of the total land area of Africa is under cultivation, and more than three-quarters of the working population is engaged in farming activities. Senegalese in West Africa cultivate peanuts and millet. Their Algerian neighbors to the north grow wheat. In the Kenyan highlands, the people pick tea. In Zimbabwe, they grow corn; and in the Sudan, cotton.

In addition to farmers, there are many herders, fishers, miners, and manufacturers. In Mauritania, herders tend cattle, sheep, camels, and goats. In the great lakes areas of Central Africa, fishermen and women catch, dry, and market fish. In South Africa, black miners extract diamonds from one of the richest deposits on earth. In Zambia and Zaire, miners work the largest concentration of copper and cobalt in the world. Geography and climate clearly influence the ways of life of the people.

LIVING IN THE RAIN FOREST

The third largest rain forest in the world is found in Central Africa. Like those of South America and Southeast Asia, it is made up of three layers of vegetation—a ground cover of plants and ferns, a dense layer of trees and climbers, and a canopy of giant broad-leaved evergreen trees, some as high as 150 feet (45.7 meters).

As in other climatic zones of Africa, the rain forest, even with its dense vegetation, supports agriculture. In some parts of the rain forest, small communities of farmers cultivate such root crops as cassava and sweet potatoes. As one scholar explains, theirs is a difficult task because they "are not

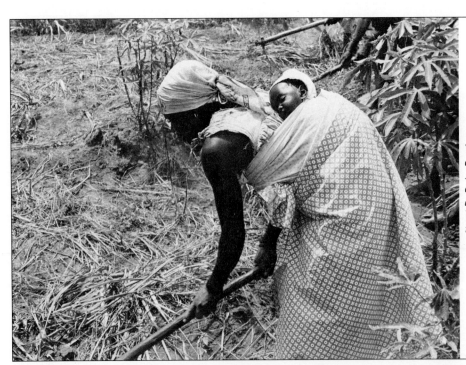

This woman is cultivating cassava, a major crop in Angola. Bananas, coffee, corn, and sugar cane are also produced in Angola. What major crops are grown in other African nations?

content to take what the forest offers them, but they change it. . . . For them the forest is . . . the enemy force against which they struggle to wrest and keep the earth in the clearings."

Below, an anthropologist who lived in the Ituri forest of Zaire talks about the forest and the people who live in it:

> Many people who have visited the Ituri . . . , and many who have lived there, feel . . . overpowered by the heaviness of everything—the damp air, the gigantic water-laden trees that are constantly dripping, never quite drying out between the violent storms that come with monotonous regularity, the very earth itself heavy and cloying after the slightest shower. And, above all, such people feel overpowered by the seeming silence and the age-old remoteness and loneliness of it all.
>
> But these are the feelings of outsiders, of those who do not belong to the forest. If you *are* of the forest it is a very different place. What seems to other people to be eternal and depressing gloom becomes a cool, restful, shady world with light filtering lazily through the treetops that meet high overhead and shut out the direct sunlight—the sunlight that dries up the non-forest world of the outsiders and makes it hot and dusty and dirty. . . .
>
> . . . The villagers are friendly and hospitable to strangers, offering them the best of whatever food and drink they have, and always clearing out a house where the traveler can rest in comfort and safety. But these villages are set among plantations in great clearings cut from the heart of the forest around them. It is from the plantations that the food comes, not from the forest, and for the villagers life is a constant battle to prevent their plantations from being overgrown. . . .
>
> . . . The Bambuti are the real people of the forest . . . [They] have been in the forest for many thousands of years. It is their world, and in return for their affection and trust it supplies them with all their needs.

> They do not have to cut the forest down to build plantations, for they know how to hunt the game of the region and gather the wild fruits. . . . They know how to distinguish the innocent-looking *itaba* vine from the many others it resembles so closely, and they know how to follow it until it leads them to a cache of nutritious, sweet-tasting roots. They know the tiny sounds that tell where the bees have hidden their honey; they recognize the kind of weather that brings a multitude of different kinds of mushrooms springing to the surface; and they know what kinds of wood and leaves often disguise this food. . . . They know the secret language that is denied all outsiders and without which life in the forest is an impossibility.*

FARMING THE SAVANNA

Savanna covers more than one-third of the African continent and is home to many farmers and herders. Below, a Senegalese writer relates how the seasons can shape the life of a savanna farmer:

> According to Oumar's calculations, the rainy season would be coming in a matter of days. A few puffs of wind, laden with heat, were all that stirred in the air. The clouds had stopped moving. The young man continued his long walks across the savanna. . . . Now days and weeks mattered little. Only the seasons ordered his existence.
>
> The rainy season began. Nature seemed painted on a deep green canvas with a sea-blue sky.
>
> The rain fell unremittingly, persistently. Even as she drank it in, the earth, spewing up water, flooded the rich fields where water birds flocked down. . . .
>
> In the bush, hunting was becoming difficult; the animals had abandoned the streams, now that they found pasture and water everywhere. . . .

The Forest People by Colin M. Turnbull, Copyright ©1961, by Colin M. Turnbull, pp. 12–14. Reprinted by permission of Simon & Schuster, Inc.

The strongest animals of the forest . . . could no longer easily track down their prey, and at nightfall began to approach the villages where the herds were kept. The hyena took a terrible toll there and some of the large beasts were able to carry off oxen or cattle from inside the enclosures.

Little by little the landscape changed color; from deep green it became grayish. The clouds piled up and remained motionless for long periods. Nights became long for the peasants. Knots of birds emigrated towards the east. While awaiting the harvest, people devoted themselves to their favorite games, and the merchants restocked their cloth. . . .

The life of the farmer is not always restful: he sows, he weeds, he struggles, then he waits for the harvest. But when he feels the joy of seeing his work completed, his field ripening before his eyes, the fine sprigs standing up, . . . a man forgets that he is tired; he wishes he had given even more of this strength, and his heart fills with pride and joy. Yes, life, this life of labor, is a good one.

"Oh my land, my beautiful people!" sang Oumar as he trod this ground.

He walked alone through the fields, dreaming who knows what? He stopped in front of a ground-nut plant to straighten its leaves, freed a fly caught by a spider, avoided stepping on a beetle; a little further on he separated two millet stems, propped up a heavy corn stalk. . . .

He had constructed an immense granary, propped up on stilts to avoid the moisture. With very simple tools he had widened the stream; the *fayats*, big boats that could carry ten or twelve people, were moored side by side. Wild vines wound all through the palm-grove. The wide leaves of the water lilies covered the sleepy surface of the water.

The harvest was at hand.

Following in the wake of the hot season, the clouds were returning. The clear blue sky and the gray green earth foretold renewal; the trees and all the greenery seemed freshly painted once again.

The end of the bad season drew the farmers away from their distractions, and the festivities ended. Holiday clothes were returned to the bottom of the wooden trunks. People had spent all they had and had gone into debt during the inactive period. Nothing was left in the granaries

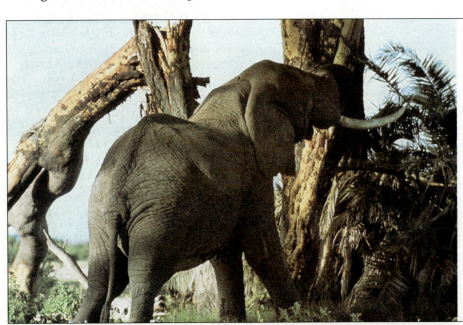

Many wild animals in Africa feed on fruits, leaves, and other vegetation of their habitats. Here, an elephant is eating bark from a tree in Kenya. Why do animals compete with people for savanna land in Africa?

and everyone hoped for a good crop—if God willed it.

Oumar had sold half of his crop; he hoped to sell the rest at a high price to the large companies. He resumed his work, enlarging his fields, increasing the number of his rice-paddies, and even taking up growing cassava. He had become severe and hard like all those who work the earth and live off it.*

The savanna also supports a large wildlife population. To prevent the many different species of wildlife from becoming extinct, a number of African governments have established national game parks, particularly in countries in east and southern Africa. This has led many people to associate these areas chiefly with wildlife even though domestic farm herds greatly outnumber the wildlife population.

In recent years, the competition for savanna land between humans and animals has become critical in some smaller nations. In Rwanda, for example, farmers have had to encroach on forest highlands which traditionally were the home of the now rare mountain gorillas. The demand for pastureland and firewood also have taken their toll. This has led many African countries to pass laws to help protect the natural environment and to prevent rural areas from becoming unproductive wastelands.

THE NEED FOR RAIN

Much of Africa north of the Equator receives very little rainfall. In this area is the world's largest tropical desert—the Sahara. It stretches over 3.2 million square miles (8.3 million square kilometers). A great many years ago, the desert was a fertile region that supported a thriving civilization. Today, most of it is uninhabitable. Some nomads,

---

O Pays, Mon Beau Peuple by Sembene Ousmane as cited in *Palaver: Modern African Writings* by Wilfred Cartey, 1970, E. P. Dutton, Inc., pp. 116–118. Reprinted by permission.

Pictured here is an oasis in Algeria. Saharan oases are watered by springs from underground streams and rains that result from air currents blown from nearby mountains. Why are oases important to the Tuareg?

such as the Tuareg, however, continue to live there as they have for centuries. Although camel caravans traditionally used for transportation are still common, they are being replaced by trucks. As a camel driver from Timbuktu, Mali, observed, "One truck alone can carry a hundred camel loads of salt and do in a few days what it takes a camel 16."

On the southern border of the Sahara is the Sahel, which in Arabic means "coastal land." Between 1968 and 1974, the Sahel experienced a drought that destroyed thousands of livestock and caused many people of West Africa to starve.

In the mid-1980's, many African countries again began to feel the destructive effects of little or no rain. Below, an American journalist visiting Africa describes what he observed in one of those countries—the Islamic Republic of Mauritania:

"We are beginning our descent toward Nouakchott," the steward of Air Mauritania's flight from Dakar barked over the loudspeaker system. As the Fokker-28 began its approach to Nouakchott airport, the pristine blue sky suddenly gave way to a sepia cloud of windblown sand. The plane continued what seemed like an interminable descent and my Mauritanian neighbor . . . began to get extremely nervous for it was impossible to see the ground.

The next thing we knew the plane had successfully landed. . . . However, these sandstorms, which make civilian aviation hazardous, are even more devastating for agriculture and livestock. . . . Last year a sad record was set: Nouakchott registered over 200 days of sandstorms.

In the capital the effects of the windblown sand are specially noticeable in the outlying quarters where mini-sand dunes gradually engulf houses. In the countryside, the situation is more dramatic. The northern oases of Chinguetti and Ouadane are literally being suffocated by the advancing sand, with their once flourishing palm groves now drying up. The population, deprived of its traditional livelihood, has fled to urban areas. . . .

During a recent 1,500 kilometre [900 mile] trip into the central and southern part of the country . . . I was able to witness at first hand the devastation. . . . In traditional agro-pastural areas in the Trarza, Brakna and Tagant regions . . . the tough acacia trees were losing the battle against the lack of water and windblown sand. There was practically no pastureland and a marked absence of the herds which once were the pride of local populations. It was only around a few *cuvettes* (depressions) and behind some makeshift earthen dams that the farmers tried to eke out a bare living from agriculture. . . .

This trip through rural Mauritania drove home to me what an agricultural expert had said in Nouakchott: "From a Sahelian state, Mauritania is rapidly becoming a Saharan country." . . .

Tagant in Berber [Afro-Asiatic language] means forest. Traveling through this region today it is hard to imagine that older inhabitants can still remember when vegetation was plentiful and game abundant. "When I first came to Moudjeria in 1948," remarked an old-time resident, "the sand dune which is advancing on the town was inexistent and the palm grove yielded plentiful crops of dates." He went on to add: "Pastureland was abundant and herds well stocked, and gazelles and other game were present all over the area. Then in Moudjeria, believe me, it was paradise."*

1. Why do farmers in the rain forest face a difficult task?
2. Why is the change of seasons important on the savanna?
3. What can happen when drought occurs?

URBANIZATION

African history is rich with evidence of ancient cities that once were great centers of learning and of trade. Later, during the colonial periods, cities were created to serve the economic needs of the European powers. In South Africa, for example, a tax was imposed on Africans that had to be paid each year in cash. This forced many African men to leave their families in the countryside while they went to the cities and mining areas in search of the jobs they needed to earn the money to pay the tax.

Today, although nearly three-fourths of the population remains rural, Africa is the fastest urbanizing continent in the world. The bright lights of Nairobi (Kenya), Lagos (Nigeria), and Harare (Zimbabwe) are attracting so many people that experts predict that the population of many African cities will double every 10 years. In the following reading, a Kenyan author shows the mixed emotions a move to the city can evoke:

---
*"Praying for Rain" by Howard Schissel in *West Africa*, 12 March, 1984, pp. 551–553. Reprinted by permission.

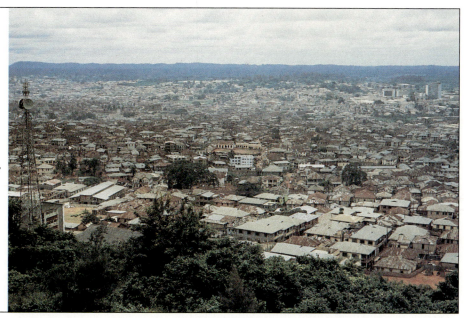

Since the 1960's many African cities have become increasingly crowded as people move from the rural areas. Shown is Ibadan, Nigeria's second largest city, an example of rapid urbanization. How has the growth of cities affected African agriculture?

It was a dark night. Njoroge and Kamau stood on the "hill". . . .

"Do you see those distant lights?"

"Yes."

"That's Nairobi isn't it?" Njoroge's voice trembled slightly.

"Yes," Kamau answered dreamily.

Njoroge peered through the darkness and looked beyond. Far away a multitude of lights could be seen. Above the host of lights was the grey haze of the sky. Njoroge let his eyes dwell on the scene. Nairobi, the big city, was a place of mystery that had at last called away his brothers from the family circle. The attraction of this strange city that was near and yet far weakened him. He sighed. He could not yet understand why his brothers had just decided to go. Like that.

"Do you think that they've found jobs?"

"Kori said that jobs there are plenty."

"I see."

"It is a big city. . . ."

"Yes-it-is-a-big-city."

"Mr. Howlands often goes there."

"And Jacobo too. . . . Do you think they'll forget home?"

"I'm sure they won't. None can forget home."

"Why couldn't they work here?"

"Do you think they didn't want to? You know this place. Even there where they go, they will learn that mere salary without a piece of land to cultivate is nothing. Look at Howlands. He is not employed by anybody. Yet he is very rich and happy. It's because he has land."*

Cities in Africa today have the same critical problems as other cities around the world—overcrowding, slum areas with inadequate sanitation, crime from unemployment, and pollution of the air and nearby rivers. In addition, as more young people move to the city in search of better opportunities and education, fewer remain in the rural areas to grow food for the rapidly expanding urban population.

1. Why did many young Africans leave the countryside during the colonial periods?
2. With what does Kamau equate wealth and happiness?
3. What problems can arise when people move to the cities in great numbers?

Weep Not, Child by Ngugi wa Thiong'o, 1974, Heinemann Educational Books Ltd., pp. 40–41. Reprinted by permission.

Exploration
Africa

"Eating is the right of everybody."
—Swahili proverb

At present, many African nations are experiencing a severe food crisis. There are many reasons for this, including drought and a fall in the price of African export products. The main reason, however, is that the production of food cannot keep up with the needs of the growing population. Below, Ayele Foly, a health and agricultural extension trainer from Togo, discusses the problem with a reporter. After reading the interview and studying the maps that follow it, write a short paper on the food crisis in Africa. Include information on the status and the causes of the crisis as well as possible solutions for it.

[Reporter] There's very much written in the news media about the problem of hunger in Africa, and in particular about declining food production. It appears that a lot of money is being spent on this, but without satisfactory results. How would you set spending priorities on agricultural development?

[Foly] . . . I would say that many farming projects make a mistake in urging people to clear great tracts of land and to cut down the trees. In a great number of instances this . . . contributes to the problem of desertification. So reforestation is important. . . . And so is teaching people to use available . . . materials for fertilizer. . . .

Another matter . . . is public health and sanitation. When a people lack clean water to drink they suffer from a variety of sicknesses and they can't be productive. This affects agricultural potential. . . .

I should mention cash crops, too. Sometimes governments promote cash crops which are not food crops. And the farmers grow too much of that and not enough food.

I would also like to see more money spent on training women. Usually when they start these farming projects they train only men. But we found

RELATIVE SIZE

FOOD SUPPLY

AFRICA UNIT 1

CHAPTER 1 REVIEW

POINTS TO REMEMBER

1. The continent of Africa, which lies astride the Equator, is made up of 54 nations, including several island states. Each of the states has a variety of ethnic groups, languages, religions, and customs.
2. The amount and distribution of rainfall a region receives each year is of vital importance. The greatest amount falls in the rain forest, a lesser amount in the savanna, and the least in the semiarid lands and deserts.
3. Africa's extensive river systems have played a major role in its history and development. Often a thriving culture based on trade grows up along the banks of the rivers.
4. About one-third of Africa's total land area is devoted to agriculture with three-quarters of the work force engaged in farming activities.
5. Both rain forest and savanna support agriculture. The savanna also is home to herders and, in parts of Africa, to a large wildlife population.
6. A recurrence of drought in the semiarid Sahel and other parts of Africa, caused by the lack of seasonal rains, has had a destructive effect on agriculture, livestock, and people.
7. Africa is the fastest urbanizing continent in the world. This rapid growth in cities has led to overcrowding, slums, inadequate sanitation, crime, and pollution.

VOCABULARY

Identify

Mount Kilimanjaro
Great Rift Valley
Zambezi
Niger
Nile
Zaire
Lokele
Sahara
Sahel
Nouakchott

Define

rain forest
savanna

DISCUSSING IMPORTANT IDEAS

1. Why are Africa's rivers so important?
2. In what ways do geography and climate influence the life styles of people in different African nations?
3. What kinds of problems do herders in the Sahel and farmers in the rain forest have to overcome?
4. Do you think it is better to live in the city and risk not finding a job or to stay in the countryside and farm your own plot of land? Explain your answer.
5. What impact do you think there is on a region when its people migrate in large numbers from the countryside to cities?

that women spend a full 80% of their time in agriculture. . . . Yet . . . they not only neglect to train women and give them land, they actually take away land the women were using to plant vegetable gardens.
[Reporter] So you would say that a lack of involvement of women is one of the major mistakes that is made?
[Foly] Yes. Women ought to be given training in growing these new crops because they can use the money and they will use it to improve the quality of life. . . .

In farming, you can use a small amount of money to train farmers to use manure as fertilizer on their crops. But a big agency will spend a lot of money to get a tractor that doesn't have spare parts. And then that sits neglected, because there is no driver or else the driver cannot repair it.*

*"Foly: A Grassroots Approach to Progress" in *Africa News*, Vol. XXIII, No. 11–12, September 24, 1984, pp. 9–10. Reprinted by permission.

POPULATION DENSITY

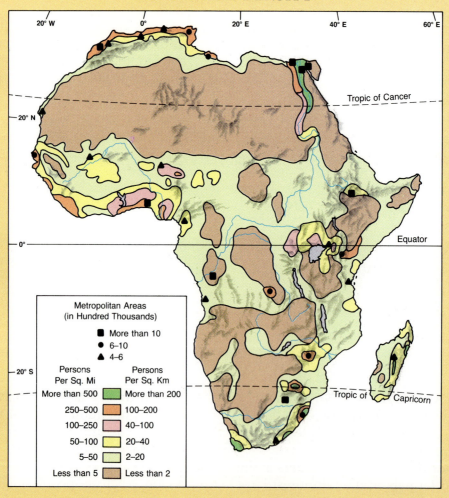

Developing Skills

READING A CHAPTER

Every book you read is organized in a special way. This book is organized to present certain factual material in a way that is interesting, informative, and not too difficult to understand. To accomplish this, it is divided into units and chapters, each of which focuses on a specific theme and the topics related to it. Each unit is devoted to a different region, and each chapter within a unit focuses on a particular aspect or element related to that region and its peoples.

Knowing how to read a chapter systematically will help you learn as much as possible in the shortest amount of time. One way to do this is to follow these steps:

1. Survey the chapter to get an overview of it. In this text, the key to what aspect or element of the culture is being featured can be found on the first page of the chapter, on which appears the chapter title, a photograph, and two questions. The title of this chapter, for example, is "Adapting to the Environment." The photograph is of Mount Kilimanjaro, the highest mountain in Africa. The first question asks about the relationship between climate and the physical features and vegetation of Africa. The second asks how Africans have adapted to their environment. The chapter, then, is basically about the geography of Africa and how Africans have adapted to it.
2. Go through the chapter, and pull out the section and subsection headings. Each heading appears on a line by itself in capital letters. All of these headings are related in one way or another to geography or to the ways in which Africans have adapted to it. This will give you not only have a better idea of the chapter theme, but you have an outline of the topics covered as well.

In this chapter, the headings are as follows.

 I. The African Continent

 II. Working the Land

   A. Living in the Rain Forest

   B. Farming the Savanna

   C. The Need for Rain

 III. Urbanization

3. Read the chapter introduction, which appears on the second page of the chapter, opposite the chapter title, opening photograph, and questions.
4. On a sheet of paper, write the name of the chapter title. Make a question out of the first section head, and write it on the paper. For example, a question for the first section head, "The African Continent," might be *What features make up the African continent?* Keeping in mind that you want to find an answer to the question, read the section, writing down subheads and noting key phrases as you come across them. When you have finished reading the section, restate the question to yourself, and recite the answer you have determined.
5. Repeat these steps for each section of the chapter. When you have completed all of the sections, review your notes. Refresh your memory by listing each section head and the main points of the section. As additional review, work through the Chapter Review that appears at the end of the chapter.

For further practice in this skill, follow the same procedure as you study each chapter of the text.

CHAPTER 2
AFRICAN HERITAGE

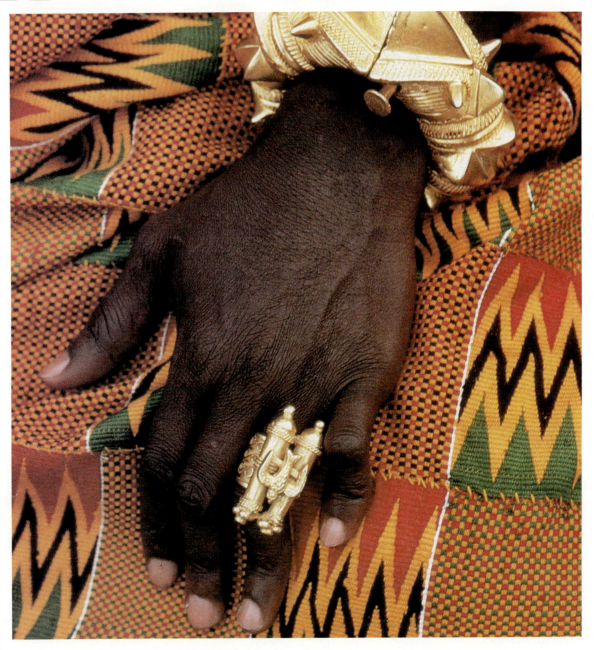

1. What were the major characteristics of early African societies?
2. What was the European role in Africa?

—Before most Europeans had even thought of building cities, Africa had thriving metropolises that were centers of trade and technology.

—Before northern Europe had universities, Africa had centers of learning at Timbuktu and Jenne that drew students from as far away as Rome and Greece.

—When Europe was still a collection of clans fighting to stay alive, Africa had great kingdoms with courts of law.

—When the Normans invaded a little-known island called England in 1066 A.D., they could muster an army of only 15,000 soldiers. In the same year the West African state of Ghana could put 200,000 warriors in the field.

—When the Arabs invaded Europe in the eighth century A.D., they were able to push all the way through Spain into France. When they invaded West Africa, they were stopped.

—When the Europeans were still pagans, in the fourth century A.D., the ancient kingdom of Ethiopia (then called Aksum) was a center of Christianity. In fact, Ethiopia is the oldest Christian empire in the world; its stone churches, built centuries ago, are among the wonders of the world.*

The above comments may surprise many Westerners, who over the years have come to believe that Africa was "discovered" by Europeans, that before the Europeans penetrated Africa it was a desolate continent inhabited by fantastic and mythical creatures. But the truth of the matter is that the African continent is the home of humankind's earliest known ancestors. Recently discovered fossils show that humans lived in its eastern and southern savannas 4 million years ago.

*The African Past and the Coming of the European, Unit III of Through African Eyes: Cultures in Change by Leon E. Clark, © by The Conference on World Affairs, Inc., The Center for International Training and Education (CITE), pp. 3–4. Reprinted by permission.

Over the past 25 years or so, many new sources of information have become available about the African continent, especially about the daily life of the people and the rise of great states. Written accounts left by early Arab and African travelers and scholars have been discovered. Language studies, satellite photography, and archaeology are supplying new data. In addition, historians are beginning to recognize the value of African **oral traditions,** the legends and history of a society passed by word of mouth from one generation to the next. From all these sources, a picture of Africa as a continent with a rich and diverse past and heritage has emerged.

EARLY AFRICAN SOCIETIES

The earliest African societies were bands of people who moved from place to place, living by hunting game and gathering wild plants. Several thousand years ago, the development of agriculture changed their way of life. As the knowledge of agriculture spread, small villages began to grow up on the African continent.

Within these agricultural communities were people who specialized in crafts. Ironsmiths, for example, made tools that they traded for items produced by neighboring societies. This trade took place not only within Africa but with nations across the sea. In parts of Africa, it was trade that led to the development of large states and empires.

One of the earliest African states was that of ancient Egypt, which grew up along the Nile River. Other early northeast African states were Kush and Meroë, which were early centers of iron working. Another was Ghana. The first West African state to gain control of the gold-salt trade established by North African Arab merchants, it dominated West Africa for nearly 1000 years. Still another was Monomotapa in southeastern Africa. It traded with the Asian empires of the East. The ancient Monomotapan city of Great Zimbabwe, the largest city of its time in Africa, has gained worldwide recognition for its architecture.

Great Zimbabwe, however, was not the only major city, state, or empire of early Africa. Equally important were Axum, Mali, Timbuktu, Sofala, Kilwa, and Mombasa.

AXUM

Axum's importance was due to its strategic location on the trade route between Asia and the Mediterranean world. Through Adulis, Axum's main port on the Red Sea, were exported gold, ivory, rhinoceros horn, tortoise shell, and spices. The gold was obtained from the people of Sasu, who lived far to the southwest of Adulis. Below, a Greek traveler visiting the king of Axum in 525 AD describes how the Axumites obtained the gold, a process that later came to be known as "the silent gold trade:"

EARLY AFRICA

> . . . The King . . . every other year . . . sends thither [to Sasu] special agents to bargain for the gold, and these are accompanied by many other traders—upwards, say, of five hundred—bound on the same errand as themselves. They take along with them to the mining district oxen, lumps of salt, and iron, and when they reach its neighbourhood they make a halt at a certain spot and form an encampment, which they fence round with a great hedge of thorns. Within this they live, and

Only ruins remain of Great Zimbabwe, once the largest city in Monomotapa, an ancient African state. Noted for its architecture, Great Zimbabwe was built of slabs of granite fitted without mortar. How did improved agriculture contribute to the development of early African societies?

having slaughtered the oxen, cut them in pieces, and lay the pieces on the top of the thorns, along with the lumps of salt and the iron. Then come the natives bringing gold in nuggets like peas . . . and lay one or two more of these upon what pleases them—the pieces of flesh or the salt or the iron, and then they retire to some distance off. Then the owner of the meat approaches, and if he is satisfied he takes the gold away, and upon seeing this its owner comes and takes the flesh or the salt or the iron. If, however, he is not satisfied, he leaves the gold, when the native seeing that he has not taken it, comes and either puts down more gold, or takes up what he had laid down, and goes away. Such is the mode in which business is transacted with the people of that country, because their language is different and interpreters are hardly to be found. The time they stay in that country is five days more or less. . . . The space of six months is taken up with this trading expedition, including both the going and the returning.*

***The Christian Topography of Cosmas, an Egyptian Monk,* translated and edited by J. W. McCrindle, 1897, Bedford Press, pp. 52–53. Reprinted by permission.

MALI

In the 1200's, one of the most powerful empires of Africa was Mali in West Africa. Under the rule of Mansa Musa, it became an **Islamic Empire,** a nation-state whose official religion is Islam. Beautiful **mosques,** Muslim houses of worship, were built in the important towns. Before long, Mali became known as a great center of learning, and scholars came from many lands to live and study in its large commercial centers. Below, Ibn Battuta, a North African scholar who set out in the 1300's to visit all the Muslim nations of the world, gives his view of Mali and its people:

> When I decided to make the journey to Mállí [Mali], . . . I hired a guide . . . and set out with three of my companions. . . .
> We . . . came to the river of Sansara, which is about ten miles (16 kilometers) from Mállí. It is their custom that no persons except those who have attained permission are allowed to enter the city. I had already written to the white [North African] community [there] requesting them to

hire a house for me, so when I arrived at this river, I crossed by the ferry without interference. Thus I reached the city of Mállí, the capital of the king of the blacks. . . .

I was at Mállí during the two festivals of the sacrifice and the fast-breaking. On these days the sultan takes his seat . . . after the midafternoon prayer. The armour-bearers bring in magnificent arms —quivers of gold and silver, swords ornamented with gold and with golden scabbards, gold and silver lances, and crystal maces. At his head stand four amirs [princes] driving off the flies. . . . The commanders, qádí, and preacher sit in their usual places. . . . A chair is placed for Dugha [the interpreter] to sit on. He plays on an instrument made of reeds . . . and chants a poem in praise of the sultan. . . .

The negroes possess some admirable qualities. They are seldom unjust, and have a greater [hatred] of injustice than any other people. Their sultan shows no mercy to anyone who is guilty of the least act of it. There is complete security in their country. Neither traveller nor inhabitant in it has anything to fear from robbers or men of violence. They do not [take] the property of any white man who dies in their country. . . . On the contrary, they give it into the charge of some trustworthy person among the whites, until the rightful heir takes possession of it. They are careful to observe the hours of prayer, and assiduous in attending them in congregations, and in bringing their children to them. On Fridays, if a man does not go early to the mosque, he cannot find a corner to pray in, on account of the crowd. . . .

Another of their good qualities is their habit of wearing clean white garments on Fridays. . . . Yet another is their zeal for learning the Koran.*

TIMBUKTU

In 1468, another empire, the Songhai, took over the Malian city of Timbuktu. Less than 10 years later, Songhai controlled nearly all of Mali's empire. Under Songhai rule, Timbuktu continued to thrive. On the next page,

*Ibn Battuta: Travels in Asia and Africa, 1325–1354, translated by H. A. R. Gibb, 1929, Routledge & Kegan Paul PLC, pp. 321–322, 323, 328–330. Reprinted by permission.

Abraham Cresques was the first European to draw a map of North Africa. His map, drawn in 1375, is shown here. At lower right of the map is a sketch of Mansa Musa, a wealthy and powerful Muslim leader of Mali. How did Islam affect life in medieval Mali?

Leo Africanus, a North African scholar and traveler, describes Timbuktu and its people as he saw them in the 1500's:

. . . there is a most stately temple to be seen, the walls whereof are made of stone and lime; and a princely palace. . . . Here are many shops of artisans, and merchants, and especially of such as weave linen and cotton cloth. And hither do the Barbary [North African] merchants bring cloth of Europe. All the women of this region except maid-servants go with their faces covered, and sell all necessary food. The inhabitants, and especially strangers there residing, are exceeding rich, insomuch, that the king married both his daughters unto two rich merchants. Here are many wells, containing most sweet water; and so often as the river Niger overflows, they convey the water thereof by certain channels into the town. Corn, cattle, milk, and butter this region yields in great abundance: but salt is very scarce here. . . . The rich king has many plates and scepters of gold, some of which weigh 1300 pounds [585 kilograms]: and he keeps a magnificent and well furnished court.

. . . Whosoever will speak unto this king must first fall down before his feet, and then taking up earth must sprinkle it upon his own head and shoulders: which custom is ordinarily observed by them that never saluted the king before, or come as ambassadors from other princes. He has always three thousand horsemen, and a great number of footmen that shoot poisoned arrows, attending upon him. They have often skirmishes with those that refuse to pay tribute, and so many as they take, they sell unto the merchants of Timbuktu. . . . Here are great store of doctors, judges, priests, and other learned men that are bountifully maintained at the king's cost and charges. And hither are brought diverse manuscripts or written books out of Barbary, which are sold for more money than any other merchandise. The coin of Timbuktu is of gold without any stamp or inscription: but in matters of small value they use certain shells brought hither out of the kingdom of Persia.*

---

*Adapted from *The Historie and Description of Africa* by Leo Africanus, translated by John Pory in 1600 and edited by Dr. Robert Brown, 1896, Hakluyt Society, Vol. III, pp. 824–825. Reprinted by permission.

SOFALA, KILWA, AND MOMBASA

Between the 1100's and 1300's, African peoples who came to be known as the Swahili built large trading cities along Africa's east coast and on several offshore islands. Each city was independent with its own ruler. Below, a Portuguese sailor who went to Africa in the early 1500's tells what he observed in three of the cities—Sofala, Kilwa, and Mombasa:

> The Moors [Swahili] of Sofala kept these wares [goods brought by traders from other kingdoms] and sold them afterwards to the heathen of the Kingdom of Benametapa, who came thither laden with gold which they gave in exchange for the said cloths without weighing it. These Moors collect also great store of ivory which they find hard by Sofala, and this also they sell in the [Indian] kingdom of Cambay. . . . These Moors are black, and some of them tawny; some of them speak Arabic, but the more part use the language of their country. They clothe themselves from the waist down with cotton and silk cloths, and other cloths they wear over their shoulders like capes, and turbans on their heads. Some of them wear small caps dyed in grain . . . and other woolen clothes in many tints. . . .
>
> Their food is millet, rice, [meat], and fish. In this river as far as the sea are many sea horses, which come out on the land to graze . . . ; they have tasks like those of small elephants. . . .
>
> In this same Sofala now of late they make great store of cotton and weave it, and from it they make much white cloth, and as they know not how to dye it, . . . they take the Cambray cloths, blue or otherwise colored, and unravel them and make them up again, so that it becomes a new thing. With this thread and their own white they make much colored cloth, and from it they gain much gold. . . .
>
> Going along the coast . . . , there is an island . . . called Kilwa, in which is a Moorish town with many fair houses of stones and mortar, with many windows after our fashion, very well arranged in streets, with many flat roofs. The doors are of wood, well carved. . . . Around it are streams and orchards and fruit-gardens with many channels of sweet water. It has a Moorish king over it. From this place they trade with Sofala, whence they bring back gold. . . .
>
> Further on, an advance along the coast towards India, there is an isle . . . on which is a town called Mombasa. It is a very fair place, with lofty stone and mortar houses well aligned in streets after the fashion of Kilwa. . . . It has its own king, himself a Moor. The men are in color either tawny, black or white and also their women go very bravely attired with many fine garments of silk and gold in abundance. This is a place of great traffic, and has a good harbor, in which are always moored craft of many kinds and also great ships. . . .
>
> This Mombasa is a land very full of food. Here are found many very fine sheep . . . , cows and other cattle in great plenty, and many fowls. . . . There is much millet and rice, sweet and bitter oranges, lemons, pomegranates, Indian figs, vegetables . . . , and much sweet water. The men thereof are oftentimes at war but seldom at peace with those of the mainland, and they carry on trade with them, bringing thence great store of honey, wax and ivory.*

1. What led to the development of many early African states and empires?
2. How did the people of Axum obtain gold? What was the process called?
3. What were some characteristics of Mali? Timbuktu? The Swahili cities?

---

*From *The Book of Duarte Barbosa*, translated by Mansel Longworth Dames as cited in *The African Past: Chronicles from Antiquity to Modern Times* by Basil Davidson. Copyright ©1964, by Basil Davidson. By permission of Little, Brown and Company in association with the Atlantic Monthly Press.

CASE STUDY
AFRICA

THE ATLANTIC SLAVE TRADE

Out of the Portuguese explorations of the African coasts in the 1400's grew what came to be known as the Atlantic slave trade. Over the next four centuries, Europeans transported millions of African slaves to the New World. The European trade in slaves, however, did not cause African slavery. Africans traded slaves across the Sahara to Asia and Europe long before the Portuguese arrived.

The forced removal of several million people from one side of the ocean to the other caused tremendous suffering. In 1756, an 11-year-old Ibo from Nigeria named Olaudah Equiano was captured and sold into slavery. Below, he tells his story:

. . . One day, when . . . only I and my dear sister were left to mind the house, two men and a woman got over our walls, and in a moment seized us both, and . . . they stopped our mouths and ran off with us into the nearest wood. Here they tied our hands and continued to carry us as far as they could. . . . [The] only comfort we had was in being in one another's arms . . . and bathing each other with our tears. . . . The next day . . . my sister and I were separated while we lay clasped in each other's arms. . . . She was torn from me and immediately carried away. . . .

. . . I continued to travel, sometimes by land, sometimes by water, through different countries and various nations, till at the end of six or seven months . . . I arrived at the sea coast.

The first object which saluted my eyes when I arrived . . . was the sea, and a slave ship . . . waiting for its cargo. These filled me with astonishment, which was converted into terror. . . . I no longer doubted of my fate; and quite overpowered with horror and anguish, I fell motionless on the deck and fainted. When I recovered a little I found some black people around me. . . .

I was put down under the decks, and there . . . with the loathsomeness of the stench and crying together, I became so sick and low that I was not able to eat. . . . [On] my refusing to eat, one [white man] held me fast by the hands and laid me across I think the windlass, and tied my feet while the other flogged me severely. . . . I inquired . . . what was to be done with us; they gave me to understand we were to be carried to these white people's country to work for them. . . . At last, when the ship we were in had got in all her cargo, they made ready [to sail] . . . , and we were all put under deck. . . .

The closeness of the place and the heat of the climate, added to the number in the ship . . . almost suffocated us. This produced copious perspiration, so that the air soon became unfit for respiration . . . , and brought on a sickness among the slaves. . . . The shrieks of the women and the groans of the dying rendered the whole a scene of horror. . . . In this manner we continued to undergo more hardships than I can now relate, hardships which are inseparable from this accursed trade.*

1. What was the Atlantic slave trade?
2. How would you have reacted had you been Olaudah Equiano?

---

*The Interesting Narrative of the Life of Olaudah Equiano, or Gustavus Vassa the African, Written by Himself, abridged and edited by Paul Edwards as Equiano's Travels, 1967, Heinemann Educational Books Ltd., pp. 16, 24, 25–30. Reprinted by permission.

From Colonialism to Nationalism

For many years, European colonies in Africa were limited to those of the Dutch and British in southern Africa and the French and British military outposts in North Africa. But beginning in the late 1800's, European explorers found in the interior of Africa vast lands and huge amounts of raw materials.

By setting up colonies, the Europeans could supply raw materials to their factories at home and provide new markets for their products. It did not take them long to determine that African possessions could be very important to their economic and political goals. The "Scramble for Africa," the rush by European powers to claim African territory, had begun.

By 1914, Britain, France, Germany, Portugal, Spain, and Italy had **partitioned,** or divided, nearly all of Africa among themselves. Only Liberia, which had been founded by freed slaves from the United States, and Ethiopia, remained solely under African control.

THE EUROPEANS

During the colonial era, the Europeans made many attempts to justify colonialism. Most Europeans would have agreed with the views expressed below by a British colonial officer:

> Let it be admitted at the outset that European brains, capital, and energy have not, and never will be, expended in developing the resources of Africa from motives of pure philanthropy; that Europe is in Africa for the mutual benefit of her own industrial classes, and of the native races in their progress to a higher plane. . . .
>
> By railways and roads, by reclamation of swamps and deserts, and by a system of fair trade and competition, we have added to the prosperity and wealth of these lands, and checked famine and disease. . . . We are endeavoring to teach the native races to conduct their own affairs with justice and humanity, and to educate them alike in letters and in industry. . . .
>
> As Roman imperialism laid the foundations of modern civilisation, and led the wild barbarians . . . along the path of progress, so in Africa today we are repaying the debt, and bringing to the dark places of the earth . . . the torch of culture and progress. . . . British methods have not perhaps in all cases produced ideal results, but I am profoundly convinced that there can be no question but that British rule has promoted the happiness and welfare of the primitive races. . . . If there is unrest, and a desire for independence, . . . it is because we have taught the value of liberty and freedom. . . . Their very discontent is a measure of their progress.

COLONIALISM, 1914

This print shows negotiations between an African leader and a British soldier, regarding colonial rule. European nations forced their laws on colonized African states. What European nations colonized Africa?

We hold these countries because it is the genius of our race to colonise, to trade, and to govern.*

THE AFRICANS

Most Africans, however, did not share this view. Below, Patrice Lumumba, a Congolese independence-fighter who later became the first prime minister of the independent Republic of the Congo, recalls what it was like to live under Belgian rule:

> We have known the back-breaking work exacted from us in exchange for salaries which permitted us neither to eat enough to satisfy our hunger, nor to dress and lodge ourselves decently, nor to raise our children as the beloved creatures that they are.
>
> We have known the mockery, the insults, the blows submitted to morning, noon and night because we were "negres [black]." Who will forget that to a Negro one used the familiar term of address; not, certainly, as to a friend, but because the more dignified forms were reserved for Whites alone?
>
> We have known that our lands were despoiled in the name of supposedly legal texts, which in reality recognized only the right of the stronger.
>
> We have known the law was never the same, whether dealing with a White or a Negro; that it was accommodating for the one, cruel and inhuman to the other.
>
> We have known the atrocious suffering of those who were imprisoned for political opinion or religious beliefs: exiles in their own country. . . .
>
> We have known that in the cities there were magnificent houses for the Whites and crumbling hovels for the Negroes, that a Negro was not admitted to movie theaters or restaurants, that he was not allowed to enter so-called "European"

The Dual Mandate in British Tropical Africa by Sir F. D. Lugard, 1929, William Blackwood & Sons, Ltd., pp. 617–619.

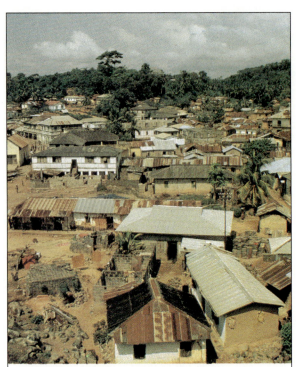

The closely spaced houses in this western Ghanaian town are made of mud or block walls and have metal roofs. How does this typical town and village housing compare to the housing shown in the photo below?

stores, that when the Negro traveled, it was on the lowest level of a boat, at the feet of the White man in his deluxe cabin.

And, finally, who will forget the hangings or the firing squads where so many . . . perished, or the cells into which were brutally thrown those who escaped the soldiers' bullets—the soldiers whom the colonialists made the instruments of their domination?

From all this, my brothers, have we deeply suffered.*

In many parts of Africa, Africans fiercely resisted colonization and colonial rule. An example is Zaire, which King Leopold of Belgium established as his own personal colony in the late 1800's. He called the colony the Congo Free State. The Congolese were forced to work for the colony, and many died of disease and malnutrition. Resistance was met with torture or death. By 1907, world opinion forced the Belgian government to seize the colony from Leopold. Meanwhile, however, no single war or revolt in colonial Africa cost more lives than the first 24 years of colonial rule in the Congo. Nearly 1.5 million Congolese—nearly one-half of the population—died.

Although all African efforts did not meet with success, the Africans did not give up. Between the outbreak of World War I in 1914 and the start of World War II in 1939, the seeds of **nationalism,** a people's demand for

This stately home in Zimbabwe reflects the privileged life style enjoyed by whites during colonial rule in some African countries. What were some characteristics of colonial rule in Zaire?

---

*"The Independence of the Congo" by Patrice Lumumba in *Africa Speaks*, edited by James Duffy and Robert A. Manner, 1961, D. Van Nostrand Company, Inc., pp. 90–91.

Led by Kwame Nkrumah, above, the Gold Coast was the first British African colony to gain independence. It became Ghana. How did European colonial education aid African nationalist movements?

independence, grew. A generation of young educated Africans, determined to see their countries free from colonial rule, wrote about independence and became leaders of nationalist movements.

Most nationalists agreed with Kwame Nkrumah, who later became the first president of independent Ghana, when he declared: "We want to be able to govern ourselves in this country of ours without outside interference, and we are going to see that it is done!" Below, another nationalist leader, Nnamdi Azikiwe of Nigeria, challenges British colonizers to explain why African soldiers should fight for the British for freedom and democracy when there was none for them at home:

> . . . It is very significant that in the last two world wars, African peoples were inveigled into participating in the destruction of their fellow human beings on the ground that . . . the world should be made safe for democracy—a political theory which seems to be an exclusive property of the good peoples of Europe and America, whose rulers appear to find war a profitable mission and enterprise. . . .
>
> Today, in Nigeria, thousands of ex-servicemen are unemployed; they are disillusioned and frustrated, while some of them have been maimed for life. . . . In spite of their war efforts, the people of Nigeria and the Cameroons have been denied political freedom, economic security, and social emancipation. Our national identity has been stifled to serve the selfish purposes of alien rule. We are denied elementary human rights. We are sentenced to political servitude, and we are committed to economic serfdom. Only those who accept slavery as their destiny would continue to live under such humiliating conditions without asserting their right to life and the pursuit of freedom, and joining forces with progressive movements for peace.*

1. Why were the Europeans interested in establishing colonies in Africa?
2. What caused the "Scramble for Africa?"
3. How did some Europeans justify colonialism in Africa?
4. How did many Africans react to European colonization? Why did they react this way?
5. What was the goal of the nationalists?

*Zik: A Selection from the Speeches of Nnamdi Azikiwe by Nnamdi Azikiwe, 1961, Cambridge University Press, pp. 61–63. Reprinted by permission.

EXPLORATION
AFRICA

The quotes that follow present different views of the European role in Africa. Based on the statements made in the quotes, answer the following:

1. How did Europeans perceive their role in Africa?
2. How did Africans perceive the European role in Africa?
3. Put yourself first in the place of an African and then of a European, and explain why you might have objected to or been in favor of European colonialism.

What use is missionary teaching? The white men can read and write, but it doesn't make them good.

When the whites came to our country, we had the land and they had the Bible; now we have the Bible and they have the land.

I contend that we are the first race in the world and that the more of the world we inhabit the better it is for the human race. I contend that every acre added to our territory provides for the birth of more of the English race, who otherwise would not be brought into existence. . . . I believe it to be my duty to God, my Queen and my Country to paint the whole map of Africa red. . . . That is my creed, my dream and my mission.*

The White Man killed my father,
My father was proud.
The White Man seduced my mother,
My mother was beautiful.
The White Man burnt my brother beneath the
    noonday sun.
My brother was strong.
His hands red with black blood
The White Man turned to me;
And in the Conqueror's voice said,
"Boy! a chair, a napkin, a drink."†

---

*Cecil Rhodes as quoted in *A Plague of Europeans* by David Killingray, 1973, Penguin Education, p. 84. Reprinted by permission of Penguin Books Ltd

†"Martyr" by David Diop as cited in *An Anthology of West African Verse,* edited and translated by Olumbe Bassir, 1957, Ibadan University Press, p. 53. Reprinted by permission.

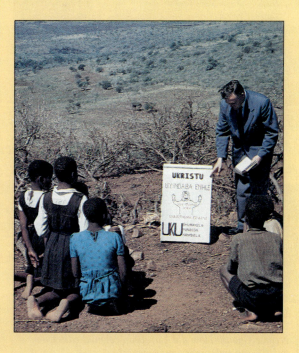

I got into a rickshaw, locally called a go-cart. It was pulled in front by two government negroes and pushed behind by another pair, all neatly attired in white jackets and knee breeches, and crimson cummerbunds yards long, bound round their middles. Now it is an ingrained characteristic of the uneducated negro, that he cannot keep on a neat and complete garment of any kind. It does not matter what that garment may be; so long as it is whole, off it comes.*

**Travels in West Africa* by Mary Kingsley, 1897, Virago Press, p. 31.

... my object is to open up traffic along the banks of the Zambesi, and also to preach the Gospel. The natives of Central Africa are very desirous of trading, but their only traffic is at present in slaves . . . : it is therefore most desirable to encourage the former principle, and thus open the way for the consumption of free productions, and the introduction of Christianity and commerce. By encouraging the native propensity for trade, the advantages that might be derived in a commercial point of view are [great]; nor should we lose sight of the [many] blessings it is in our power to bestow upon the unenlightened African, by giving him the light of Christianity. Those two pioneers of civilization —Christianity and commerce—should ever be inseparable.*

In an evening in the bush I always wore a long evening dress to keep up my morale but also one had to wear mosquito boots; there were mosquitoes and sand-flies everywhere and the long dress was a great help. . . . [The] Development Officer would come along and have dinner with me—he in a dinner suit and I in an evening dress—and we would walk along the bush path talking and everyone gathered to see us. . . . I think they wondered why we got all dressed up and covered ourselves when it was so frightfully hot. In an evening I would often play my . . . records. . . . All the village would come. We'd sit round and we would have these records on and then always there was a drummer with his drum and he would start drumming. . . . And it was absolutely beautiful, . . . and I can't tell you how friendly they were. And although I was often on my own I was safer there than I would have ever been anywhere in England today.†

We have been engaged in drawing lines upon maps where no whiteman's foot ever trod; we have been giving away mountains and rivers and lakes to each other, only hindered by the small impediment that we never knew exactly where the mountains and rivers and lakes were.

I look back with deep gratitude to my early years, which I spent at Lubwa, a mission station of the Church of Scotland in the Northern Province of Northern Rhodesia [Zambia]. My father was an evangelist. . . . My mother . . . is a woman of deep spiritual understanding, and what I know of the Christian faith I learned from her. I think I can say in all honesty that the one thing which influenced me more than any other in the first years of my life was the deep Christian faith of my parents, and the fact that I was living in a community on the Mission Station which was based on love, friendship and kindness. I think it is important to emphasize this point because it was a spiritual and psychological shock to me when I left my home and the Mission Station and found myself facing the hard realities of society in Northern Rhodesia.*

---

*Lecture at Cambridge University by David Livingstone in 1857 as quoted in *Africa* by Phyllis M. Martin and Patrick O'Meara, 1977, Indiana University Press, p. 126. Reprinted by permission.

†Catherine Dinnick-Parr as quoted in *Tales From the Dark Continent* by Charles Allen, 1979, Andre Deutsch, pp. 155–156. Reprinted by permission.

*"Reflections of a Leader" by Kenneth Kaunda as quoted in *Through African Eyes: The Rise of Nationalism: Freedom Regained* by Leon Clark, 1970, © The Conference on World Affairs, Inc., The Center for International Training and Education (CITE), p. 75. Reprinted by permission.

AFRICA UNIT 1

CHAPTER 2 REVIEW

POINTS TO REMEMBER

1. The earliest African societies were nomadic bands of hunters and gatherers. As the knowledge of agriculture spread, small villages grew up on the African continent. These villages traded with other villages and nations, which in turn led to the development of large states and empires.
2. The Monomotapan city of Great Zimbabwe was the largest city of its time in Africa. Great Zimbabwe was also known for its architecture.
3. The kingdom of Axum was important due to its strategic location on the trade route between Asia and the Mediterranean world. The Axumites obtained gold through a process known as "the silent gold trade."
4. In the 1200's, one of the most powerful empires of Africa was Mali in West Africa. Under the rule of Mansa Musa, it became an Islamic Empire and a great center of learning.
5. In the 1400's, another empire, the Songhai, captured the Malian city of Timbuktu. Under the Songhai, Timbuktu became a wealthy agriculture and dairy producing area ruled over by a powerful king.
6. Between the 1100's and the 1300's, African peoples known as the Swahili built large trading cities along Africa's east coast and on several offshore islands. These cities included Sofala, Kilwa, and Mombasa.
7. In the late 1800's, European explorers found in the interior of Africa vast lands for settlement and huge amounts of raw materials. By 1914, Britain, France, Germany, Portugal, Spain, and Italy had partitioned nearly all of the African continent among themselves.
8. The Europeans made many attempts to justify colonialism. In many parts of Africa, however, Africans fiercely resisted colonization and colonial rule.
9. Between the outbreaks of World War I in 1914 and World War II in 1939, the seeds of nationalism grew more intensely all over Africa. Young educated Africans worked to see their countries free from colonial rule.

VOCABULARY

Identify

Great Zimbabwe
Axum
Adulis
Mali
Mansa Musa
Ibn Battuta
Timbuktu
Songhai
Leo Africanus
Sofala
Kilwa
Mombasa
Swahili
Patrice Lumumba
Zaire
King Leopold
Kwame Nkrumah
Nnamdi Azikiwe
Atlantic slave trade
Olaudah Equiano

Define

oral traditions
Islamic Empire
mosques
partitioned
nationalism

DISCUSSING IMPORTANT IDEAS

1. Many historians say that African history has long been presented in a distorted manner. Why do you think this was the case?
2. What role did trade play in the development of Africa?
3. How do you think Europe would be different if the Europeans had never colonized Africa? How do you think Africa would be different?
4. If you were African, would you have become a nationalist? Explain.

DEVELOPING SKILLS

RECOGNIZING ETHNOCENTRIC STATEMENTS

Some people believe that their own racial, ethnic, or cultural group is superior to any other. In their view, their group is "Number One" or "The Best" in every way that they consider important. This leads them to view and base their judgment of the behavior and attitudes of others on their own values and standards. If something is right—or wrong—for them, it is right—or wrong—for everyone else. For example, Westerners tend to view dogs as pets. In some areas of Asia, however, dogs are considered food. The Westerner who says that the Asian is wrong to eat dog is judging the Asian by a Western standard. This is known as *ethnocentrism*. Ethnocentrism may be found to some degree in almost every racial, ethnic, or cultural group.

Ethnocentric statements often appear in written material. It is especially important to be able to recognize such statements when studying about global issues or events. Study the following example, which will provide you with steps to help you develop this skill:

1. Read the written statement.

    I contend that we are the first race in the world and that the more of the world we inhabit the better it is for the human race. I contend that every acre added to our territory provides for the birth of more of the English race, who otherwise would not be brought into existence. . . . I believe it is my duty to God, my Queen and my country to paint the whole map of Africa red. . . .

2. Ask yourself the following questions: What is the speaker's racial, ethnic, or cultural group? (*English, Western European*) To whom does the speaker feel superior? (*Africans*)

3. Determine which statements appear to be ethnocentric. (*. . . we are the first race in the world. . . .; . . . the more of the world we inhabit the better it is for the human race.; . . . I believe it to be my duty to God, my Queen and my country to paint the whole map of Africa red. . . .*)

4. Reread the statements you think may be ethnocentric, asking yourself:

    (a) Can the information in this statement be proven or verified? (*If the answer is no, the statement is ethnocentric.*)

    (b) By whose standards is the judgment being made? (*If the answer is "those of the speaker," and the speaker is of a different culture, chances are that the statement may be ethnocentric.*)

For further practice in this skill, using these steps, consider the comments by the British officer on pages 30 and 31.

CHAPTER 3
NIGERIA

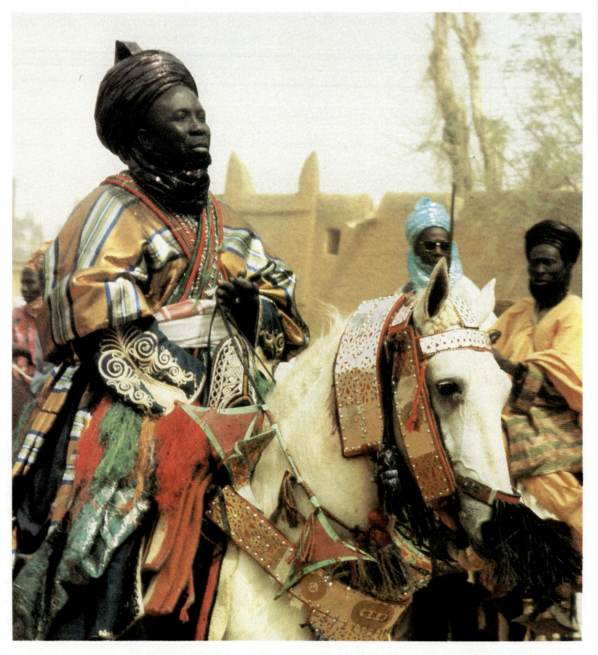

1. Why is Nigeria considered the "giant of Africa?"
2. What are some traditional and new elements of Nigerian history and culture?

The last time I visited Nigeria . . . , a night storm felled a large tree across a road in my home village. The following morning, a cluster of people formed beside the tree—men and women on . . . some early morning errand, children on their way to school. Some of the people were dressed to travel a distance. Others were in ragged house or work clothes, and their faces were streaked with sleep.

The scene made me shimmer with nostalgia. I was forty years old and had been away from the village for more than twenty, but I could recall countless such scenes from my childhood. . . .

Many things had changed since I had been a child in this village, but many things had also stayed the same. In composition and age, in manners and speech, in clothes' style and interpersonal relationships, the crowd was eternal. A few things had been updated, but all of the old archetypes were there. Something, though, had changed in a radical way—the cohesion and collective spirit of the people. Had this been thirty years before, the elders on the scene would have declared that all personal and private work in the village had to cease, until the obstruction was removed from the road. The men who were standing about . . . would have been ordered to go to their houses and return promptly with machetes, axes, and saws. Everyone would have hacked or whacked . . . until the tree was out of the way.

However, no elder spoke up on this occasion. . . . The unspoken consensus seemed to be that the obstructed road was now a government road, and not the village's responsibility. . . .

When I left home two weeks later, the tree was still there. . . .

Back in the United States, I have been continually saddened by this episode. . . . I realise that my home village is quickly becoming "mass". Family compounds, which used to contain more than twenty grown men and twice as many wives, are now disbanding into one-man compounds. . . . The tom-tom no longer sounds for Community Work Day, a day of the week set aside for such things as cleaning the village paths, repairing the market stalls, and doing whatever needed to be done on the premises of the local primary school. Not long ago these were accorded unquestioned precedence over the private labours of every villager. . . . As for the elders who used to dictate what had to be done, they have been rendered irrelevant by new circumstances.*

These observations by a Nigerian who teaches in the United States reflect the reaction of many Nigerians who return home for a visit after having spent a long time away from their country.

Nigeria, which is located along West Africa's Gulf of Guinea, consists of 19 states and makes up 3 percent of Africa's landmass. With over 91 million people—almost 17 percent of the population of Africa—it is the continent's most populous state. Nigeria's rich historical tradition, strong economy, and the determination of its people have made it a natural leader on the continent and earned it a reputation as the "giant of Africa."

---

*"Meditations beside a fallen tree" by T. Obinkaram Echewa in *West Africa*, 30 April 1984, pp. 928–929.

THE PEOPLE

Nigeria's population is as diverse as it is large. Over 250 different peoples, or ethnic groups, live in Nigeria. The Hausa kola-nut trader, the Fulani cattle herder, the Benin chief, and the Abuja potter all call themselves Nigerians. The four largest groups, however, are the Hausa and the Fulani in the north of the country, the Ibo in the southeast, and the Yoruba in the southwest.

Even though Nigeria has sought to forge a national identity over the years, ethnic identity still remains important. Today's Nigerians are proud of who they are and where their origins lie. As one specialist noted, "ethnicity . . . remains strong because it is a means of identifying people, of categorizing strangers, of obtaining favors, and of acquiring help in times of insecurity."

The diversity of the people is reflected in many ways—from ways of earning a living to art to language to customs to tradition to choice of religion. Although Islam and Christianity are the major religions, other religious beliefs also thrive, often combined with Christian ones. Some of the more traditional religions are characterized by the worship of gods and spirits that represent the natural elements and which, in the view of the believers, protect them from destructive forces. Followers of these religions often express their beliefs in dance, music, works of art, and ceremonies to honor ancestors.

Christianity and Islam have led to a move away from many of the traditional ways. Christianity is especially strong among the Ibos. Christian churches are a familiar sight in many parts of the country, especially in the east in Iboland. Yorubas, on the other hand, tend to belong to independent African churches or to be strong followers of the Muslim religion. The Hausas and the Fulanis also tend to be Muslim.

Much of Nigeria's power lies in the talent and versatility of its people. Below, a black American educator who visited Nigeria relates her experiences with and impressions of that talent and versatility:

> . . . I have for many years dreamed of visiting the land of my forefathers. . . . I have always felt a need, a yearning to

For centuries, the Fulani have been nomadic cattle herders, moving their livestock between wet-season and dry-season grazing areas. Because the Fulani measure wealth in terms of how many cattle they own, even the many who have become settled village farmers will keep large herds. The Fulani live among what ethnic group in northern Nigeria?

come "full circle," and touch base with my "other part." Visiting Africa afforded me the opportunity to see, feel, live and experience—first hand—the culture, the land, and the people who are the [offspring] of "The Motherland," the cradle of all mankind. In retrospect, my Nigerian experience was the most enlightening of my life; I came to know a warm, creative, spirit-filled people who love and live life.

Everywhere we travelled, we were greeted with the words, "You are welcome" spoken with heartfelt sincerity. As guests in many homes, businesses, educational, and political institutions, we met Nigerians of all walks of life who were delighted to share their country with us.

I was astounded at the courtesy, the national pride, and the genuine respect for life and people all so pervasive throughout the society.

I marvelled at the strength of the family unit and its many successful undertakings—religious, moral, and academic teaching; security for the aged; training grounds in marriage and parenthood for the youth.

I envied the enthusiasm for learning displayed by teachers and students alike. I applauded the high priority given education by the government.

I delighted in the artistic nature of the people most evident in the beautiful wares displayed in the open markets. What many Nigerians can do with a piece of leather, or some beads, or seeds, or a piece of cloth in a dye pit, or a weaving loom, or with butterfly wings . . . is phenomenal. Their ability to maximize usage of their environment with little waste is praiseworthy.

I respected the fervor with which the Nigerians adhered to their commitments. The deep sense of loyalty to religion, to

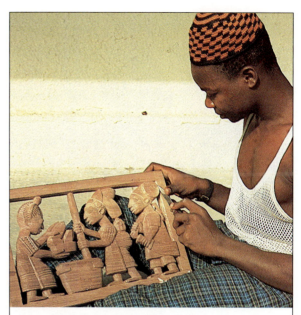

The Yoruba are well-known for their artistry in wood. Here, a young woodcarver creates a scene from daily life. What is another source of inspiration for Nigerian artists?

family, to country, to self, is in all aspects of the society.

My impressions of Nigeria? It is a land growing, developing, inhabited by a vibrant people who have customs, traditions, and values that they live and teach daily. It is an artistic culture. It is a land of many hues of skin color, many languages, and many lifestyles, all of which seem to respond to a common throbbing pulse that sets the pace for creating, learning and living.*

1. How many different ethnic groups live in Nigeria? What are the four major ones?
2. Why has ethnic identity remained important to many Nigerians?
3. What religions are practiced in Nigeria?
4. What are some of the traits of Nigerians that impressed their American visitor?

---

*"Some Thoughts on Nigeria" by June Grundy in "Nigeria," 1981, Department of Curriculum and Instruction, University of Kentucky.

TRADITIONAL DRESS

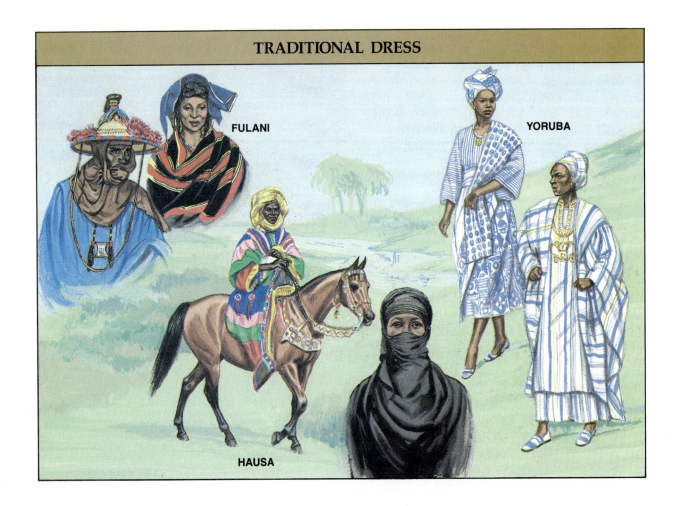

HISTORICAL PERSPECTIVE

The Nok culture of central Nigeria was one of Africa's earliest civilizations. Over 2000 years ago, it mastered the use of iron. Today's Nigerians are proud of the Nok and of the other early societies that gave them their rich history and heritage. That history is taught in school and celebrated through religious festivals, poetry, drama, dance, music, art, and storytelling. Many customs and religious traditions practiced today can be traced to the societies and states that flourished in Nigeria hundreds and even thousands of years ago.

THE EARLY YEARS

Around 1000 AD, the powerful Hausa states of Kano, Katsina, and Zaria arose in northern Nigeria and established long-distance trading ties with the Mediterranean world. The Hausa states remained powerful until the nineteenth century, when they were defeated by the Fulani in a series of *jihads*, or Islamic holy wars. As a result of the Fulani victory, most of northern Nigeria became part of a vast Islamic empire.

In the early 1600's, the Yoruba settled the present-day capital of Lagos. It became the southernmost outpost of the Benin Empire. During the era of the slave trade, human cargo was shipped from the Lagos port to Brazil, the Caribbean, and North America.

CHAPTER 3 NIGERIA

It was also in the 1600's that European explorers, sailing the inland areas along Nigeria's major rivers, discovered many products valuable for trade. Shortly after, traders and missionaries began to arrive. By the mid-1800's, with the seizure of Lagos, the British began their takeover of the country. In 1914, they declared all of Nigeria a British colony.

Nigerians resisted British rule of their country for decades. Finally, on October 1, 1960, Nigeria gained its independence, and Nnamdi Azikiwe became the new nation's first president.

CIVIL WAR

For a time after independence, there was peace. But before long, tension began to grow among various groups. The northern region, which had the largest population, controlled the federal government. Fearful that the Northerners would ignore their needs and concerns, Ibo military leaders seized control in January 1966. Anti-Ibo rioting broke out in the north, leading to the death of many Ibos. Then, in July, northern army officers staged a coup and set up a military government headed by General Yakubu Gowon. In an attempt to avoid domination of the federal government by any one ethnic group, Gowon's government divided the country into 12 states.

This reform, however, came too late. In May 1967, Ibo leader Lt. General E.O. Ojukwu took over the Eastern Region and

This exquisite terra-cotta (clay) head, produced by people of the Nok culture, is among the oldest known examples of African sculpture. Besides clay, what other natural material did the Nok master?

Nigerian police in colonial uniforms observe the 1960 Independence Day celebrations. Although the police are federally controlled, each state has its own chief officer. How many states are in Nigeria?

Although Nigerian forces were strengthened with British, Soviet, French, and Spanish arms, these Ibo soldiers fought courageously for Biafra's independence. What last-minute action did the Nigerian government take in an attempt to avert civil war?

declared it the independent Republic of Biafra. The result was full-scale civil war, which lasted for 30 months. General Gowon's federal forces crushed Biafra's movement for **secession,** or withdrawal from a national union. Thus, Nigeria's territorial unity was preserved.

One of the many Nigerians caught in the war was the novelist Elechi Amadi. Separated from his family for two years, he spent much of the war in prison. Below, in an excerpt from his diary, Amadi talks about the end of the war and his efforts to be reunited with his family:

By November 1969 it was clear that [the Biafrans] were in serious trouble. . . . Refugees streamed in, bringing tales of sinking rebel morale, but the rebel radio never relaxed. It seemed to grow more confident. . . .

Christmas passed almost unnoticed, so tense with expectation was the atmosphere. People were busy fishing out their relations from various refugee camps.

. . . [On] 11 January 1970, Ojukwu made his last broadcast. I listened to it in bed. The moment he said he was going out of the country 'in search of peace', I knew it was all over. The next day Lt-Col. Phillip Effiong renounced secession. The war was at an end.

I rushed to Igwuruta, from where the bulk of refugees seemed to be streaming in. A fantastic sight greeted me. Sprawled in the school compound and all around were over ten thousand refugees. And the number was increasing every minute. . . .

I moved through the seething sea of humanity, trying to trace my family. It was not easy. At every step someone hugged me, weeping with joy.

'They said you were dead. We had given up all hope.'

'Well, I am alive. Please, where is my family?'

'Your mother is on the way, a few miles back, maybe. I saw her.'

'And my wife?'

'I didn't see her. They say she is at Ata. I doubt if she has started moving.'

'And my father?'

'At Mbaise.'

I rushed away in search of my mother. I picked her up at Umuechen—a dirty, emaciated and utterly miserable woman, mourning for her only child. She could not hug me at first because my uncle and other relations carried me shoulder high, weeping like children. I could not stop my tears either. . . .

. . . Our search led us to Owerri. There was a large refugee camp there. . . . Many of my relations were there, and hell broke loose when they saw me. They hugged me fiercely. I could hardly breathe. I tried to peer around to look for my wife and children. I could not, so great was the crush on me. In the end I actually cried out:

'Where is my wife?'

'She has just left for Port Harcourt,' someone said.

'My children?' I gasped again.

'They are clinging to you.'

I looked down. Two of my children were clinging to my feet. After much struggling I bent down and picked them up. I was afraid to ask for the rest, but one by one I fished them out. I took them to the car along with other relations, and stuffed them with food. I arrived at Port Harcourt late in the evening. I rushed into the house, and my mother heaved a sigh of relief.

'Your wife arrived a short while ago. I have had considerable difficulty stopping her from doubling back to Owerri to look for you.'

Then Dorah came rushing at me. We wept.

I picked up my father the next day just four miles [6.4 kilometers] from home. Clad in a tattered ancient black overcoat, and with a white beard, he was pushing his bicycle along. . . . He did not weep as he hugged me, but I knew he felt more than everybody else.*

1. Who were the Hausas? What was the result of their defeat by the Fulani?
2. For how long was Nigeria under British rule? Who was its first president as an independent nation?
3. What was the basic cause of Nigeria's civil war? What was the final result?

NIGERIA TODAY

In the 1970's, huge oil reserves were discovered in Nigeria. The discovery led to a boom period that reshaped the economy. Practically overnight, the country became the eighth largest producer of petroleum in the world and a member of the Organization of Petroleum Exporting Countries (OPEC). In an effort to build a strong industrial base and expand the economy, the government went on a spending spree.

Until this time, Nigeria's economy had been based largely on agriculture. But during the oil boom, many farmers abandoned their fields and moved into the cities looking for jobs. The result was a decline in agricultural production so great that, for the first time, Nigeria was forced to import food.

The boom did not last long, however. In the 1980's, there was a **glut,** or oversupply,

---
Sunset in Biafra: A Civil War Diary by Elechi Amadi, 1973, Heinemann Educational Books Ltd., pp. 181–184.

in the world's oil market. Nigeria, meanwhile, had come to depend on oil **revenue,** or income. Lower oil prices meant less revenue for the government. This, coupled with high government spending, greater transportation costs, and wage increases led to economic problems.

In December 1983, the civilian government was overthrown by Major-General Mohammed Buhari. Buhari promised to correct the sluggish economy and set the country on a course to prosperity. Like other administrations before his, Buhari's government focused on **diversifying,** or varying, the economy. A major goal was to make Nigeria self-sufficient in agriculture once again.

In August, 1985, Buhari's government was overthrown by the Nigerian army, and General Ibrahim Babangida was made president. Like Buhari, his goal was to end corruption and improve the economy.

WAYS OF LIFE

Over three-fourths of the Nigerian people live in rural towns and villages. Most of these people make their homes in enclosed **compounds,** or homesteads, in mud, wood, or cement houses with garden plots and yards. The majority of them earn their living raising such crops as cotton, cocoa, yams, cassava, sorghum, corn, rice, peanuts, rubber, palm oils, and kernels. Some engage in fishing, herding, small-scale industry, and craft production. The food and manufactured goods they produce are sold locally or transported to larger markets in the cities. As one author explains, although many Nigerians end up leaving their village or town of birth, they do not forget their roots:

Workers on this oil rig at Port Harcourt drill a well to tap the country's clean-burning, low-sulphur oil. How did the oil boom of the 1970's affect Nigeria's ability to feed its people?

NIGERIA

Sun-dried bricks and thatch are used in the construction of the houses and storage buildings of this compound in northern Nigeria. What percent of the Nigerian population live in rural towns and villages today?

Attachment to one's home village is striking in Nigerians of all groups. Everyone knows where he or his parents came from. Even if he seldom goes there, it is where he belongs; he has title to land there and can farm if he wants. . . . He usually knows where everyone else from his village has gone and very many areas have associations of local sons and daughters who keep in touch wherever they may be.

The home town or village matters most where marriage is concerned. Most Nigerians marry someone not only from the same ethnic group, but from a nearby area. . . .

Attachment to the home village means attachment to tradition, including traditional authority.*

In recent years, however, many Nigerians have left their rural homes to find work and a better standard of life in the cities. This **urban migration,** or flow of people to the cities, has resulted in overcrowding and a decline in city services. This has been the case in Lagos, the largest of Nigeria's cities. Below, a Nigerian journalist describes the day-to-day struggle to survive in Lagos:

Life in Lagos spells problems. Traffic jams, power cuts, police checks, street traders, armed robbers, open drains, underemployment, exhorbitant rents, shortages of all kinds, corruption, frustration and heat.

Talking to a group of young Lagos city dwellers . . . —the single most time-consuming occupation is generally agreed to be that of solving your problems before they swamp you. . . .

Lagos is now a sprawling metropolis, a hotch potch of unplanned growth. The only recognisably residential areas remain the former government reserved areas of the colonial days. . . . Corner shops and roadside stalls springing up every day— nothing in Nigeria succeeds like trade.

That is the one instinct that unites all the different groups . . . —the language of commerce, the competitive urge to sell and make as much profit as you can with the minimum outlay. . . .

---

*"The Peoples of Nigeria" by John Harris in *New African Survey,* August 1983, p. 63.

The city vibrates with energy during the day—the constant movement of people determined to surmount as quickly as possible all obstacles that stand in their way of a search to a more comfortable standard of living.

The Nigerian market is a seller's paradise. There are profits to be made hand over fist, providing you have either the means, or the import licences or the foreign experts to do the work for you.

The ban on luxury "imported" items . . . has led to . . . street traders who convert streets and pavements into shopping precincts and make brisk business during traffic jams. . . .

As you walk the streets hawkers bombard you. The import ban has not only heightened the taste for imported goods, it has provided thousands with employment. . . .

The average Lagosian has little time for people who cannot keep up with the mainstream and the attitude of the Lagos taxi driver sums it up. He stops for you if you are going his way, and only if you can shout loud enough for him to hear as he tears past. . . .

. . . there are laws to regulate rents but demand so far exceeds supply that a landlord can ask for anything and get it. . . .

It all depends though on how high you want to live. The low, low cost areas . . . are where the young men and women, the airport [peddlers], construction workers, petty traders, messengers and clerks live and suffer the deprivations of incessant power cuts and water shortage.

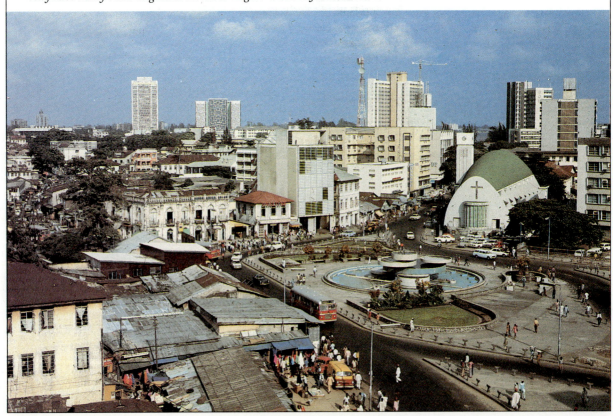

Tununbu Square appears to be a relatively peaceful island in the midst of hectic downtown Lagos, whose busy port handles more cargo than all other West African ports put together. Why have many rural Nigerians moved to Lagos in recent years?

These children are among the nearly 5 million who are benefiting from the Nigerian government's free elementary school education program, which was begun in 1975. How do Nigerians feel about the education of their youth?

Next come the bright young men and women: architects, advertising reps, public relations types, young lawyers, with their eyes on the top, hustling to seize a share of the market. . . .

From the ranks of the company executive and foreign consultant who can conclude their interim negotiations in soundproof air-conditioned comfort, down to the messengers and clerks . . . , the game is basically the same. . . .

Tempers are shortened by the wear and tear of trying to make a living in Lagos, but along with the constant grind and toil that exists for the majority . . . there is an abundance of initiative and zest for life that keeps the city throbbing.*

---

*"This Is What Keeps Lagos Throbbing" by Amma Ogan in *West Africa*, 16 November 1981, pp. 2694–2696. Reprinted by permission.

For many, the problems they face in Lagos and other large cities are well worth it. An example is Efiong Udoh, a father of four who left the palm-producing area of Calabar to find work in Lagos. Although his family is barely making ends meet, he intends to stay in Lagos because "there is a chance to make a substantial life here, and our children, by going to school, can do even better."

NIGERIAN YOUTH

Nigerians believe that the future of their country depends on the young people, that "our children are our wealth." For this reason, the government has made education a top priority. It also has initiated the National Youth Service Corps, which requires young Nigerian men and women to spend a year

These young workers are developing a tree nursery as part of a government program to reforest land damaged by soil erosion. Why has the Nigerian government made education of youth a top priority?

doing community service. The reasons are explained in the excerpt below from the Corps handbook:

> The objectives of the National Youth Service Corps Scheme are clearly spelt out in Decree No. 24 of 22nd May, 1973, as follows:
> (a) to inculcate discipline in our youths by instilling in them a tradition of industry at work, and, of patriotic and loyal service to the nation . . .;
> (b) to raise the moral tone of our youths by giving them the opportunity to learn about higher ideals of national achievement and social and cultural improvement;
> (c) to develop in our youths attitudes of mind, acquired through shared experience and suitable training, which will make them more amenable to mobilisation in the national interest;
> (d) to develop common ties among our youths and promote national unity by ensuring that:
> (i) as far as possible, youths are assigned to jobs in states other than their states of origin;
> (ii) each group, assigned to work together, is as representative of the country as possible;
> (iii) the youths are exposed to the modes of living of the people in different parts of the country with a view to removing prejudices, eliminating ignorance and confirming at first hand the many similarities among Nigerians of all ethnic groups.
> (e) to encourage members of the Corps to seek, at the end of their Corps service, career employment all over the country, thus promoting the free movement of labour;
> (f) to induce employers . . . to employ more readily qualified Nigerians irrespective of their states of origin; and
> (g) to enable our youths to acquire the spirit of self-reliance.*

1. On what was Nigeria's economy largely based before the oil boom? What effect did the boom have on the economy?
2. Why is their home town or village important to Nigerians?
3. What is the driving force of life in Lagos?
4. What are the main objectives of the National Youth Service Corps?

National Youth Service Corps Handbook, 1986, Directorate Headquarters, National Youth Service Corps, Lagos, pp. 3–4. Reprinted by permission.

INSIGHTS ON PEOPLE
AFRICA

FLORA NWAPA

Among the Yoruba, it is said that "a wise man who knows proverbs, reconciles difficulties." The dramatic art of storytelling, often punctuated with proverbs and morals, is one way in which elders have passed on knowledge, recounted historical epics, and given advice to the younger generation. Storytelling is a popular form of literary expression in Nigeria.

Over the past few decades, Nigerian novels and plays written in English have been well received outside the country. These works, however, represent only a fraction of those actually being produced in Nigeria. Most are written in Nigerian languages. Two of the most respected Nigerian authors who have written for English-speaking audiences are Chinua Achebe and Wole Soyinka.

Although in Nigeria female novelists are less common than male ones, over the years some females have achieved recognition. One such female is Flora Nwapa, an Ibo teacher and administrator. Nwapa was the first Nigerian woman to have a novel published. She began writing in the early 1960's. Her first novel, *Efuru*, was published in 1966. Married and the mother of three children, Nwapa believes that most women feel a need to work outside the home and to be financially independent. Although a successful novelist and businesswoman, she continues to work full-time because, in her words, "when I was left at home all day to write, I found I couldn't do it without having a full-time job as well."

In her books, Nwapa often focuses on the problems women face in marriage and with children. In Nigeria, children are very important to a marriage, and women who cannot bear them tend to be treated with less respect. Nwapa maintains, however, that she has no desire to change society's attitudes towards the role of women, that she simply wants to record the lives of the women of her society. The women she writes about are independent and take charge of their own lives.

Nwapa's second book, *Idu*, was published in 1970. Her third work, a collection of short stories entitled *This is Lagos and other stories*, was published in 1971. This was followed in 1976 by *Never Again*, which was about the Biafran War. Her treatment of the subject won her acclaim from critics for her forthrightness and honesty.

In 1977, Nwapa set up her own publishing firm—Flora Nwapa and Company—and her own printing firm—Tana Press. Her goal was to publish well-illustrated books for children about Nigerian life, books that incorporated folklore and fantasy. By 1984, she had published 12 stories, 7 of which she had written herself. Her latest novel, *Once is Enough*, was published by her company. It is about a woman with no children caught in a bad marriage. Once again, the critics praised her skill in presenting her women as individuals and dealing with their special burdens.

Nwapa would like to have one of her titles accepted in schools. She believes that this would not only help her but also would encourage other Nigerians to set up their own publishing firms. At present, three large companies dominate the publishing market in Nigeria. She also believes that although there are few women writers in Nigeria at present, this will change. Slowly, women's literature and women's involvement in the publishing industry will grow.

1. Who is Flora Nwapa? What are some of her major accomplishments?
2. If you were a woman in Africa, would Nwapa's accomplishments influence you in any way? How?

CHAPTER 3 REVIEW

POINTS TO REMEMBER

1. Nigeria is Africa's most populous state and is known as the "giant of Africa" because of its rich historical tradition and its economy.
2. Ethnic identity is important in Nigeria. The four major ethnic groups are the Hausa, the Fulani, the Ibo, and the Yoruba. Islam, Christianity, and traditional religions all are practiced.
3. Nigerians are proud of early societies such as the Nok, Hausa, and Yoruba, which gave them their rich history and heritage.
4. In 1914, after a gradual takeover, the British declared all of Nigeria a British colony. In 1960, it became independent and Nnamdi Azikiwe became the first president.
5. Tension among ethnic groups led to a military takeover in 1966 and the division of the country into 12 states.
6. In 1967, a move to declare the independent Republic of Biafra led to a civil war in which the movement for secession was crushed.
7. In the 1970's, the discovery of huge oil reserves led to a boom period that resulted in a decline in agricultural production. Economic problems brought about a military government whose goal was to make Nigeria self-sufficient in agriculture once again.
8. While the vast majority of Nigerians live in rural towns and villages, urban migration has increased in recent years. It has led to overcrowding and a decline in the standard of living in urban areas.
9. Because Nigerians believe that the country's future depends on the young people, the government has made education a top priority. It also has initiated the National Youth Service Corps.

VOCABULARY

Identify

Nigeria	Nok	Benin Empire	OPEC
Hausa	Kano	Nnamdi Azikiwe	Mohammed Buhari
Fulani	Katsina	Yakubu Gowon	Ibrahim Babangida
Ibo	Zaria	E. O. Ojukwu	National Youth Service Corps
Yoruba	Lagos	Republic of Biafra	Flora Nwapa

Define

jihads	glut	diversifying	urban migration
secession	revenue	compounds	

DISCUSSING IMPORTANT IDEAS

1. Do you think it is important for Nigeria to form a national identity? Why or why not? What obstacles must Nigerians overcome to do this?

2. Christianity and Islam have led to a departure from many traditional ways. What reasons can you give for this? How do you think it affects Nigeria as a nation?
3. The oil boom of the 1970's brought many changes to Nigeria. Do you think the changes were beneficial? Explain.
4. The youth of Nigeria are required to spend one year doing community service. Do you think this will have very much impact on the country's future? Explain. Do you think that your country would benefit from such a system? Why or why not?

Developing Skills

CREATING A TIME LINE

Events take place in a certain order. One happens, then another, and so on down through time. A *time line* is a graphic representation of events in *chronological order*, arranged in the order of time of occurrence.

The following will show you how to create a time line about events in Nigeria:

1. Read the subsection, "The Early Years," on pages 42 and 43. As you read, list the major events mentioned. In this case, they will already be in chronological order. Your list should include: 1000 AD—Hausa states arise in northern Nigeria; early 1600's—Lagos settled by the Yoruba, valuable products for trade discovered by European explorers, traders and missionaries arrive; mid-1800's—Lagos taken over by the British; 1914—Nigeria declared a British colony; 1960—Nigeria becomes independent.
2. Decide what time scale to use. In this case, the time period begins in 1000 AD, with the creation of the Hausa states, and ends in 1960, with independence.
3. On a piece of paper, draw a straight horizontal or vertical line. Using slashes, divide the first part of the line into two equal sections. Each section represents the same period of time —50 years. The first section represents the period from 1000 to 1050; the second, 1050 to 1100. Then, erase a part of the line. This break in the line represents the period from 1100 to 1600, a time when no entries need to be made. Divide the remainder of the line into eight equal sections. Each section represents 50 years, beginning with 1600 and ending with 2000. In a time line, each section should cover the same time span.
4. In the appropriate time period, place a dot or some other symbol to represent each event. Enter the information about the event next to the symbol. You may keep your time line simple. Or, you may make it more elaborate by using different colors to represent different periods of time or by adding photographs or drawings to illustrate different events.

For further practice in this skill, read the material on pages 43 to 46. Then, following the steps given above, use the events discussed to make a new time line or expand the one you already have.

CHAPTER 4
SOUTH AFRICA

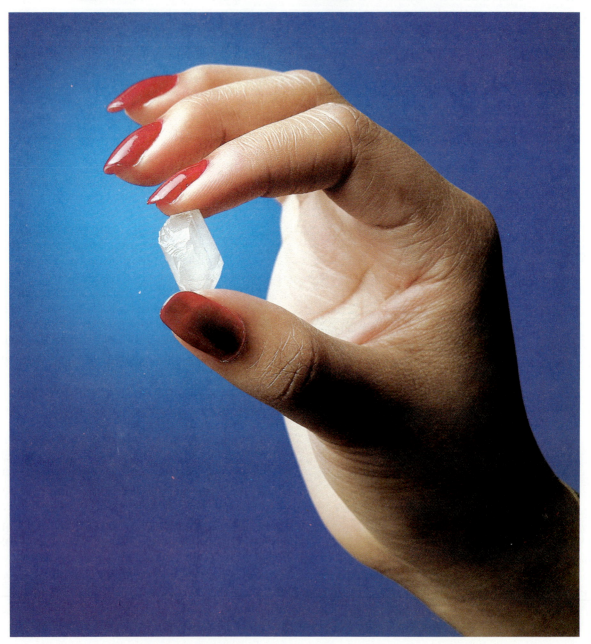

1. Why has there historically been conflict between Europeans and Africans?
2. How does apartheid affect the way Africans live?

We, the people of South Africa, declare for all our country and the world to know:

—that South Africa belongs to all who live in it, black and white, and that no government can justly claim authority unless it is based on the will of all the people; . . .

—that our country will never be prosperous or free until all our people live in brotherhood, enjoying equal rights and opportunities; . . .

The people shall govern!

Every man and woman shall have the right to vote for and to stand as a candidate for all bodies which make laws; . . .

The rights of the people shall be the same, regardless of race, colour or sex; . . .

All national groups shall have equal rights! . . .

All people shall have equal right to use their own languages, and to develop their own folk culture and customs; . . .

The people shall share in the country's wealth! . . .

The land shall be shared among those who work it! . . .

Freedom of movement shall be guaranteed to all who work on the land;

All shall have the right to occupy land wherever they choose; . . .

All shall be equal before the law!

No one shall be imprisoned, deported or restricted without a fair trial; . . .

All shall enjoy equal human rights! . . .

There shall be work and security! . . .

The doors of learning and of culture shall be opened! . . .

There shall be houses, security and comfort! . . . There shall be peace and friendship! . . .

Let all who love their people and their country now say, as we say here:

'These freedoms we will fight for, side by side, throughout our lives, until we have won our liberty'!*

The above declaration is part of the "Freedom Charter" adopted unanimously at a "Congress of the People" in 1955. The close to 3000 delegates from all over South Africa who attended the Congress were protesting the official policy of **apartheid,** or "separate development" of the races. The white South African government, however, responded by calling the charter a treasonable document and arresting 156 of the people involved in its creation.

Apartheid remains the policy of the South African government today. Under this system, the nation's white minority, which accounts for 16 percent of the population, rules the non-white majority.

The history of South Africa shows that both whites and non-whites have fought stubbornly to preserve what they have or to gain that which they do not have. As a result, while the country has one of the strongest economies in Africa and an enormous wealth of natural resources, it continues to suffer intense political strife.

---

*"The Freedom Charter of South Africa," The United Nations Centre against Apartheid, 1979, pp. 3–7. Reprinted by permission.

THE EARLY YEARS

The original inhabitants of South Africa lived in the region as early as 6000 BC. One of the earliest groups, the San, lived in small communities, hunting game and using the skins and furs for clothing. Another group, the Khoikhoi, were nomadic herders who kept large flocks of sheep and herds of cattle.

Later, Bantu-speaking people skilled in making iron farm tools and weapons began moving into the area. Before long, kingdoms and states grew up where there were minerals, fertile land, and opportunities for industry or trade. Trade served to stimulate growth. Some communities traded among themselves. Others engaged in long-distance trade, transporting their gold, copper, ivory, and slaves from the interior to the east coast to be traded overseas.

Nelson Mandela, South Africa's foremost black leader, describes what life was like before the Europeans came:

Khoikhoi homes of bent saplings and woven grass mats were waterproof and easily transportable. They were often arranged in a circle to form livestock corrals. Why did the Khoikhoi resist the Dutch settlers?

Then our people lived peacefully, under the democratic rule of their kings . . . , and moved freely and confidently up and down the country. . . . Then the country was ours, in our own name and right. We occupied the land, the forests, the rivers; we extracted the mineral wealth beneath the soil and all the riches of this beautiful country. We set up and operated our own Government, we controlled our own armies and we organized our own trade and commerce. . . . The names of Dingane and Bambata, among the Zulus, . . . and others in the north, were mentioned as the pride and glory of the entire African nation.*

THE EUROPEANS

In 1652, the Dutch East India Company established a supply base at the Cape of Good Hope. Before long, European settlers began arriving and setting up businesses and farms, and the supply base became a thriving settlement known as Cape Colony.

At first, the San and the Khoikhoi were willing to trade with the settlers, who called themselves Afrikaners or Boers. But when the settlers began to demand more animals than the Africans were willing to part with and to take over Khoikhoi grazing land, the Africans rebelled. As the leader of the original Dutch expedition noted in his diary:

(The Khoikhoi) strongly insisted that we had been appropriating more and more of their land, which had been theirs all these centuries, and on which they had been accustomed to let their cattle graze, etc. They asked if they would be allowed to do such a thing supposing they went to Holland and they added: It would be of little consequence if you people stayed here at the fort, but you come right into the interior and select the best land for yourselves.†

---

*No Easy Walk to Freedom by Nelson Mandela, 1965, Heinemann Educational Books Ltd., p. 147. Reprinted by permission.

†Jan Van Riebeek, as cited in Apartheid, The Facts, 1983, International Defence & Aid Fund for Southern Africa, p. 9. Reprinted by permission.

In this late 1800's photo from the Transvaal, white prospectors and African workers are shown outside a mine dug into the 62-mile (100-kilometer) long, gold-bearing rock formation known as the Witwatersrand. The Witwatersrand gold fields remain the world's richest today. What resource first attracted white prospectors to the Transvaal?

The Africans were no match for the settlers' guns. They were forced to earn their livings as laborers for the Boers or to leave the area entirely.

Then, in 1806, the Dutch lost control of Cape Colony to the British. The Boers, who wanted to preserve their religion, culture, and way of life, resented the British and the changes they made. Much of the Boer way of life depended on slave labor. When the British abolished slavery, many Boers were financially ruined.

In 1836, to rid themselves of British rule and preserve their Afrikaner culture, thousands of Boers headed northeast into the interior of the country. On their journey, known as the Great Trek, they met with strong resistance from several African peoples who resented their trying to take over African land. In some cases, the competition for land turned into war. Although some African groups, like the Xhosa and the Zulu, fought fiercely, by the mid-1850's, the Boers were able to establish two independent republics—the Transvaal and the Orange Free State.

DIAMONDS, GOLD, AND WAR

In 1879, diamonds were discovered in the Transvaal, and Africans were recruited to work in the diamond fields. Life in the fields was hard. Below, a European describes conditions at the time:

> Hardly a more dreary existence can be imagined than that of the early days. . . . Not a single substantial dwelling afforded shelter from the burning sun: men lived under canvas, and the owner of an iron or wooden shanty was looked upon as a lord. . . . The dust and the flies, and worse, pervaded everywhere; they sat down with you to meals and escorted you to bed. The want of good food and pure water brought on disease, and many a poor fellow . . . succumbed to the fever. . . . Today [1875] all this is changed. . . . Kaffir [insulting name for Africans] labour is mainly employed in all the less responsible operations of the mines: in drilling holes for the dynamite cartridges, in picking and breaking up the ground in the claims and *trucking* it away. . . . For every three truckloads of ground daily hauled

This 1901 illustration depicts a Boer surprise attack on British supply wagons during the Anglo-Boer War. The Boers used daring raids such as this because the British forces outnumbered them by some 500,000 to 88,000. Not until late in the war did the British gain the upper hand. What was the result of the Anglo-Boer War?

out of the mine there is on an average one Kaffir labourer employed, and to every five Kaffirs there is one white overseer or artizan.*

In 1886, gold was discovered in the same region. Suddenly, the territory became a valuable prize, and thousands of British colonists rushed in to stake their claims. The discoveries led to increased hostilities between the Boers, who ruled two territories, and the British, who also controlled two territories. In 1899, the hostility erupted into the Anglo-Boer War, which placed various African groups between the warring whites as both sides demanded aid and cooperation. The war, which lasted until 1902, resulted in the loss of many British, African, and Boer lives.

The British won the war, and in 1910 they combined the two Afrikaner republics and their two colonies into the Union of South Africa, a self-governing country within the British Empire.

---

*"Diamond Mining at the Cape" by Theodore Reunert, as cited in *Colonial Rule in Africa*, edited by Bruce Fetter, 1979, The University of Wisconsin Press, pp. 62–64. Reprinted by permission.

1. What role did trade play in early South Africa?
2. How did the Africans react to the coming of the Europeans at first? Later?
3. What effect did the discovery of diamonds and gold have on South Africa?

APARTHEID

Many Afrikaners believed in the superiority of the white race and culture. When the British took control in 1910, they included clauses in their constitution that supported that belief. As a result, conditions for non-whites—especially blacks—worsened.

In 1912, in an effort to better their condition, blacks established the African National Congress (ANC). Under the slogan "We are one people," it worked to unite Africans around the country. But, despite the ANC's efforts, laws continued to be passed that were designed to separate the races and restrict the activities of non-whites.

In 1948, the Afrikaner Nationalist Party won control of the government. During the

CASE STUDY
AFRICA

THE WHITES OF SOUTH AFRICA

The white community of South Africa is divided into two main groups—Afrikaners and English-speakers. Although the two groups have worked together to consolidate their control over the country, feelings between them often are strained. As can be seen in the comments below—the first by an Afrikaner and the second by an English-speaker—their differences are deep-rooted in history:

One of the events that most affected our lives was the Anglo-Boer War. . . . My dad and twenty-two pals started a little army up in the north and pinned down ten thousand British troops. . . . My dad and his men knew the country . . . , and they knew the farmers who lived in the area. The farmers were all on their side. Their fathers and grandfathers had trekked—many of them had died on the trek—and now they were not about to give up what their fathers and grandfathers had died for. My dad and his pals were finally captured. . . . My dad spent the last six months of the war in a British jail. When he was about to be released, the commanding officer said, 'Let's forgive and forget, Mr. van der Merwe.' My dad looked at him for a long time and finally said, 'Forgive, I can. Christ taught us to forgive. Forget, I can't. It's history.' And that's what he told us, his three sons.

When my eldest brother went off to varsity [college], my dad told him, 'You grew up in an Afrikaans area. You have learned to hate the English, but they are here to stay. My job was to shoot them. Your job is to live with them.'*

I lived in the eastern Transvaal for five years before I married Duncan. It was the loneliest time in my life, but I got to know the Afrikaans mentality. They talk about the trek and the 1900 war and the Zulu Wars and the suffering of the Afrikaans people as though no one else has ever suffered.

I was a young girl then, living alone, and not once . . . was I invited to an Afrikaans home. I was the outsider, the enemy, I suppose. They have never forgiven us for winning the Boer War, and I don't think they ever will. It runs in their blood. You can't understand them without understanding the war. It has given them an inferiority complex. They don't like us. They blame us for their problems. They don't consider us true South Africans. They say we always call England home. That makes me mad. . . .

. . . I have a strong feeling for England, but I have never been there and I do not consider England my home. I am a South African, and my children are South African. I love my country.*

1. What two groups make up South Africa's white community?
2. What lasting effect has the Boer War had on white South Africans?

---

*Hennie, as quoted in *Waiting: The Whites of South Africa* by Vincent Crapanzano, 1985, Random House, p. 48. Reprinted by permission.

*Carol Reid, as quoted in *Waiting: The Whites of South Africa* by Vincent Crapanzano, 1985, Random House, pp. 55–56. Reprinted by permission.

election campaign, its leader, D. F. Malan, had promised that if he won, he would preserve a "pure white race." In his victory speech, he proclaimed, "Today, South Africa belongs to us once more, for the first time since Union. May God grant that it will always remain so."

After the election, apartheid became official government policy. The population was divided into four racial categories, which still exist today—Africans, Whites, Coloreds (those of mixed European and African descent), and Asians. Under apartheid, most whites have enjoyed a high standard of living, while most non-whites have suffered from poverty and discrimination.

POLICY AND PRACTICES

Apartheid is particularly harsh on blacks. They cannot vote or participate in the political processes of their own nation. They cannot travel freely. Until 1986, under a series of **pass laws** dating back to the early 1900's, all black South Africans the age of 16 or older had to carry passbooks that indicated such information as place and date of birth, race category, place of employment, and tax records.

The pass laws also restricted where Black South Africans could work and live. Living restrictions came into being in 1913 with the Native Land Act. It prevented Africans from buying or owning land outside small areas known as **reserves.** Thirty-seven years later, the Group Areas Act was passed. It divided 13 percent of South Africa's land into 10 **homelands,** or *bantustans,* for the black population. The rest of South Africa was reserved for whites. Asians and Coloreds were allowed to live in segregated areas within "white" South Africa.

Blacks already living in urban areas were removed to locations outside the cities, known today as **townships.** Until 1985, the townships were viewed by the government as stopping places for Africans until they were moved to the homelands. But, by the mid-1980's, they were home to more than one-half of the black population of South Africa. This led the government to recognize that townships were there to stay.

The government's goal was to have each homeland become an independent nation. Beginning in 1976, it declared four of them independent states under the leadership of selected black chiefs. Although no country in the world recognized their independence, the Africans living in them lost their South African citizenship. This caused serious repercussions in the African community.

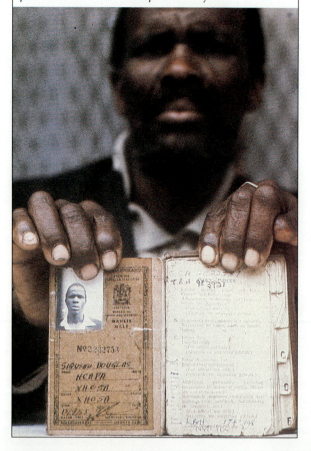

A Xhosa worker displays the passbook that he was required to carry with him at all times. Hundreds of thousands of blacks were arrested each year for violating pass laws. When were the pass laws lifted?

The man shown here being carried off in a truck is one of about 3.5 million black South Africans who were forcibly relocated by the government between 1960 and 1985. What law established the homelands?

The Africans living in all the homelands have had to learn to overcome many problems. For example, although black workers are the backbone of the South African economy, most economic activity takes place in white areas. This forces those who live in the homelands to become migrant laborers. This, in turn, creates a problem for the families they leave behind. Below, a woman who lives in the Lebowa homeland, about 300 miles (480 kilometers) from the city of Johannesburg, comments:

> We were brought here by my husband Obed. He works in town, in Johannesburg. He only sends me 40 rand [South African money] because where he works he doesn't get enough money. . . . Then I go to the store. I buy a big bag of mealie meal [corn meal] for 15 rand and I buy three bags of coal. I buy sugar and soap and that's the end of that money. If the children get sick then I go outside to borrow money from neighbours. Here there's no work, we just sit around.
>
> It's very bad here, nothing grows. It doesn't rain. When you have planted nothing grows. We don't know what to do. I don't like it here but I stay because I don't know where to go. Here there is no food. . . .
>
> . . . [Obed] only comes once a year. . . .
>
> When he comes everybody's so happy. The children run to meet him at the bus-stop. Some of them cry and when he asks why they are crying they say it is with joy. They never know when he is coming. We wish that we can just stay with him, if the white people wouldn't refuse me, staying with him for about three months to be able to talk and plan things and discuss everything together.*

In some homelands, the women have tried to improve life by working together and by pooling their meager resources. Below, a black social worker from the township of Soweto discusses the efforts made in the homeland of Gazankulu:

> I got there [Gazankulu] in the drought season. *Two of every three children were stricken with kwashiorkor* [disease caused by malnutrition]. There was gastroenteritis [disease of the stomach and intestines]. . . . I didn't know where to start. . . . I plunged in, talking nutrition to people who had no food. They were lost, but so was I at first. . . . I got there and I said, "Look ladies, maybe we should start by growing vegetables . . . here are

---

*Letitia Mogabe, as quoted in *We Make Freedom: Women in South Africa* by Beata Lipman, 1984, Pandora Press, pp. 60–61. Reprinted by permission.

REPUBLIC OF SOUTH AFRICA

seeds...." They said, "There's no water"—they were drawing water from a dam a mile to half-a-mile [1.6 to .8 kilometers] away.... This was not clean water and yet they used this water for drinking too..., the goats were a menace to whatever they were going to grow. We had to sit down and devise a means—we said, "Look, we can get some bush and use it as a fence." Very few responded at first... we put our seeds in and, strangely enough, the crops came up. It was like a dream; it was like a miracle during that time. We started talking about preparation, about eating tomato raw and preparing the spinach; and then we talked about powdered milk—the only thing that we could get at that time. We clubbed together as women and went on bulk buying

SOUTH AFRICAN HOMELANDS

and we got milk through these clubs; . . .

Then I realised there was potential for hand work. One of the women just decided one day: she said, "Ellen Khuzwayo, I'm going to school." I said, "To do what?" She said, "To do weaving. I'll come back and teach them here." When she came back she didn't have the equipment, but she didn't stop. I've never seen somebody so resourceful. . . . I saw the women working with combs they made out of reeds from the river. The evenness of the comb surprised me; that it could comb and make a perfect article.

These are the kind of groups that are now growing in Soweto; and each new one helps others get going. The groups are fully co-operative: before you produce anything, you don't earn. You get free tuition, but as soon as you finish an article; it could be on the knitting machine, the sewing machine, weaving, pottery, handwork, patchwork—once you produce something you begin to earn.*

RESISTANCE

Black African resistance to white encroachment on African land and infringement of African rights has existed since Europeans first settled on the Cape. Although the strategies have changed over the years, the goal —basic rights for all—has not. Below, an African explains the reason his people have been discontent:

> The white oppressors have stolen our land. They have destroyed our families. They have taken for themselves the best that there is in our rich country and have left us the worst. They have the fruits and the riches. We have the backbreaking toil and the poverty.
>
> We burrow into the belly of the earth to dig out gold, diamonds, coal, uranium.

This home in the white suburbs of Cape Town reflects a standard of living that contrasts sharply with that of most South African blacks. How have the black women of Gazankulu tried to improve their standard of living?

> The white oppressors and foreign investors grab all this wealth. It is used for their enrichment and to buy arms to suppress and kill us.
>
> In the factories, on the farms, on the railways, wherever you go, the hard, dirty, dangerous, badly paid jobs are ours. The best jobs are for whites only.
>
> In our own land we have to carry passes; we are restricted and banished while the white oppressors move about freely.
>
> Our homes are hovels; those of the whites are luxury mansions, flats, and farmsteads.
>
> There are not enough schools for our children; the standard of education is low, and we have to pay for it. But the government uses our taxes and the wealth we create to provide free education for white children.*

---

*Ellen Khuzwayo, as quoted in *We Make Freedom: Women in South Africa* by Beata Lipman, 1984, Pandora Press, pp. 20–22. Reprinted by permission.

Africa Contemporary Record, Annual Survey and Documents, 1968–1969, edited by Colin Legum and John Drysdale, by permission of Africana Publishing Corporation, New York, N.Y. Copyright 1969, Africana Publishing Corporation, New York, N.Y. Reprinted by permission.

Sharpeville The struggle over land and political rights has led to social unrest and violence. In 1960, blacks in the township of Sharpeville demonstrated against the pass laws. The demonstration, which resulted in the death of 69 blacks, led the government to pass harsher laws, jail people without trial, and outlaw such anti-apartheid organizations as the ANC. These actions convinced many blacks that their goals could not be achieved peacefully or nonviolently.

The following year, the ANC, which had gone underground, formed a military wing called *Umkhonto We Sizwe,* "Spear of the Nation." Led by activist lawyer Nelson Mandela, it swore to oppose the government by violent means. Following his arrest, Mandela explained why *Umkhonto* had been formed:

> How many more Sharpevilles would there be in the history of our country? And how many more Sharpevilles could the country stand without violence and terror becoming the order of the day? And what would happen to our people when that stage was reached? In the long run we felt certain we must succeed, but at what cost to ourselves and the rest of the country? And if this happened, how could Black and White ever live together again in peace and harmony? These were the problems that faced us, and these were our decisions.
>
> Experience convinced us that rebellion would offer the Government limitless op-

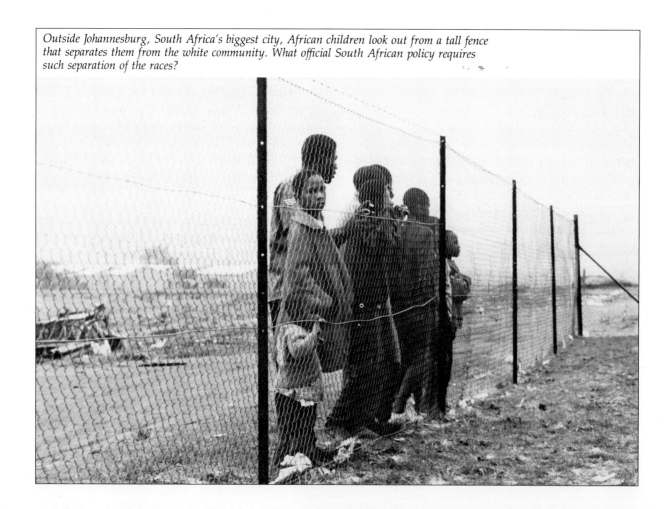

Outside Johannesburg, South Africa's biggest city, African children look out from a tall fence that separates them from the white community. What official South African policy requires such separation of the races?

portunities [to] . . . slaughter . . . our people. But it was precisely because the soil of South Africa is already drenched with the blood of innocent Africans that we felt it our duty to make preparations . . . to use force in order to defend ourselves against force. If war were inevitable, we wanted the fight to be conducted on terms most favourable to our people. The fight which held out prospects best for us and the least risk of life to both sides was guerrilla warfare.*

Soweto In 1976, thousands of students in the township of Soweto peacefully protested a new regulation that made Afrikaans the language of instruction in school. When the unarmed students were fired upon by the police, hundreds were killed. This led to more protests, which, over the next 16 months, left hundreds more dead and forced many young Africans into exile. Below, an African woman describes the effect the situation had on her family:

> In 1976 I had three children in high school in Soweto: two were doing their final year . . . and when everything got disrupted, they just couldn't stay on. The boy was very active—politically active; the girl in a smaller way. . . . We, as parents, got no sleep—the police came at eight, or at ten, at twelve or even at three in the morning: all this just to look for him. . . .
>
> They would ransack the house every time, looking for him: they'd look under the bed, even in the fridge. Everyone would be woken—it was terrible. So many children were arrested but mine never were. The boy was being sought, but he was just elusive; then he disappeared completely. We only realised when I was called to the police station to be questioned: they knew that he had gone away—they wanted to know if I had relatives in . . . Zimbabwe or other places. When I said I didn't have any they said that as soon as I heard from him I must come and let them know. As a mother I too was concerned, so I said, "You people, too, if you hear about him, I also would want you to come and let me know."
>
> Eventually I heard from a friend that they'd gone: it took over six months before we knew where they were. We were relieved that they had gone—if they'd stayed around we might have buried them a long time ago. . . .
>
> It's heartbreaking to lose your children. Each time you dish up, you find that you're missing two plates on the table. I used to bake their favourite cakes when they first went, . . . now I can't bear to do it anymore . . . ! I'm only hoping that one day, somehow, somewhere, I'll be able to see [them].*

1. Why was the ANC established? Despite its efforts, what happened?
2. How did apartheid become official government policy? Into what categories did it divide the population of South Africa?
3. What are some of the restrictions apartheid placed on black South Africans? How have Africans reacted to these restrictions in recent years?

A FUTURE IN QUESTION

The banning of anti-apartheid organizations in the 1960's led to the emergence of new organizations. Their emphasis on the pride and cultural heritage of the African people led them to be known as the Black Consciousness Movement. When in 1977, Steve Biko, one of the movement's leaders, died at the hands of police, the outraged international community condemned the

---

No Easy Walk to Freedom by Nelson Mandela, 1965, Heinemann Educational Books Ltd., pp. 173–174. Reprinted by permission.

*Mavis Thatlane, as quoted in *We Make Freedom: Women in South Africa* by Beata Lipman, 1984, Pandora Press, p. 24. Reprinted by permission.

South African government. It responded by banning two newspapers and 18 Black Consciousness organizations.

Since that time, increased internal demonstrations and protest, greater pressure from other nations, and economic necessity have led the government to make some reforms. People no longer are removed by force to the homelands. The law against interracial marriages has been repealed. Some blacks are allowed to own their own homes, have their families live with them, and change jobs. A new constitution was approved. Although it allowed Coloreds and Asians limited representation in the government, it continued to exclude blacks, who made up 72 percent of the population.

In 1985, on the twenty-fifth anniversary of the Sharpeville shootings, thousands marched to protest rising unemployment and exclusion from parliamentary representation. When police opened fire on the crowd, killing 19 demonstrators, more violence erupted. This led to a July 20 presidential declaration of a "state of emergency," the first since Sharpeville. Since then, the situation has grown more volatile and many hundreds more blacks have been killed.

Apartheid, and the restrictions it imposes, continue to be at the heart of the unrest that plagues South Africa. Not all South African whites however, support government policy. Some agree with the view expressed below by an Afrikaner farmer:

> God put us all on this earth to live together, . . . and that means we'll have to learn to do it or perish. 'Apartheid' is an evil because it sets men against men, builds barriers where there were none and gets in the way of natural processes of change and growth that, prior to 1948, were well on their way to creating a new kind of society in this country. Now I don't delude myself that I have to love the black man or the Colored. Liking him will do. Because if I want respect for myself and my own kind then I must give it to others. It's that simple. During the Second World War, . . . I learned . . . that men of all kinds can live and be together, regardless, and like each other. Death taught us a lot about valuing life and its variety, you see, so to come home from a war like that to find hate and separation preached in my own country disgusted me. And to see a country as gifted as this turned into a fortress of race sickens me. No—it's wrong, this business of 'apartheid.' Wrong because it's unnatural. And unless we take down within the next few years the whole ugly structure it has taken thirty years to build up, it will destroy everything we have managed to create here and with it, South Africa.*

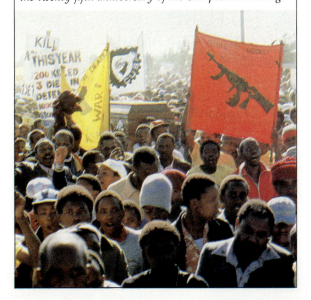

During the 1980's, despite frequent bans by the authorities, funeral processions often became mass demonstrations against apartheid. What happened on the twenty-fifth anniversary of the Sharpeville shootings?

1. What led to the Black Consciousness Movement? What did it emphasize?
2. What reforms has the South African government made in recent years?

---

*Blood River by Barbara Villet, 1982, Everest House/Dodd, Mead & Company, Inc., pp. 56–57. Reprinted by permission.

EXPLORATION
AFRICA

Apartheid has been the way of life in South Africa for many years. Over this time, it has affected the sentiments and attitudes of the South African people—both white and black. This can be seen in comments below. Read the comments, and answer these questions:

1. How do some white South Africans regard blacks?
2. How do some black South Africans regard whites?

We have to civilize and uplift them. Without us, they would have nothing. We are giving them the right to develop in their own way, in their homelands, under our guidance.

These white people are rock-hard—they will never change. Why is there separation here? If I touch you, you don't turn brown.

You see, the black man has a different idea of violence. It does not mean that much. Human life, or life in general, does not mean that much, or does not have the same value to them that it has to a white man.

The Afrikaners think they are liberal if they just say hello to a black.

Kaffir politics are simple: 'Be against whatever the white man is for.' The outside world will always stick up for the white man in the end.

Everywhere in the world the kids hear their fathers complaining about the boss. But in South Africa the boss is always the white man. How do you expect them to grow up believing in racial harmony?

Keeping in mind the sentiments expressed in the quotes, read the following statements made by a black and a white South African regarding the future of their country. Which view do you support? Why? Would you support the same view if you were an Afrikaner? An African? Explain. What do you think South Africa's future will be?

Our program is clear. . . . It is based on three principles:
1. *A unified South Africa—no artificial 'homelands.*
2. *Black representation in the central parliament—not membership in the kind of apartheid assemblies that have been newly established for the Coloreds and the Asians.*
3. *One man, one vote."**

Nelson Mandela, African Leader

We cannot achieve majority rule on the basis of one man, one vote—not only because the whites are against it, but because all moderates [of any race] are against it. If you could remove all the whites tomorrow from the face of South Africa, you would be no nearer to a political solution, because there is no way you are going to force the various black peoples into a unitary system. . . . [Majority rule would] force the strongest group to the top, which would then discriminate against and dominate all the other groups.†

Roelof F. Botha, Foreign Minister

---

*Nelson Mandela, as quoted in "A Rare Talk with Nelson Mandela" by Samuel Dash in *The New York Times Magazine*, July 7, 1985, p. 22. Copyright © 1985 by The New York Times Company. Reprinted by permission.

†Roelof F. Botha, as quoted in "Two Views of the Future," in *Newsweek*, March 11, 1985, p. 32. Copyright 1985 by Newsweek, Inc. All Rights Reserved. Reprinted by Permission.

AFRICA UNIT 1

CHAPTER 4 REVIEW

POINTS TO REMEMBER

1. African societies lived in South Africa from as early as 6000 BC. States and kingdoms grew up and flourished where there were minerals, fertile land, or opportunities for industry or trade.
2. In the 1600's, European settlers began arriving and setting up businesses and farms. The settlers, who became known as Afrikaners or Boers, soon were in competition for land with African groups, who resented their encroachment.
3. Discovery of diamonds and gold made South Africa a valuable prize, attracting thousands of British colonists and increasing existing hostilities between the Boers and the British.
4. The Anglo-Boer War, which erupted in 1899, ended in a British victory and resulted in the establishment of the Union of South Africa, a self-governing country within the British Empire.
5. Many Afrikaners believed in the superiority of the white race and culture. When their party won the national election in 1948, apartheid became official government policy.
6. Apartheid prohibits Africans from voting and from participating in government. It also imposes working and living restrictions on all non-white groups.
7. Because most of South Africa's economic activity takes place in white areas, blacks who live in the homelands are forced to become migrant laborers. This places added hardships on their families.
8. The struggle between the government and Africans over land and political rights has led to the rise of the many movements of resistance and to social unrest and violence in South Africa.
9. Heightened internal unrest, increased pressure from other nations, and economic necessity have influenced the South African government to make some minor reforms. These, however, have not been far-reaching enough to end the turmoil.

VOCABULARY

Identify

Freedom Charter
Congress of the People
San
Khoikhoi
Cape Colony
Boers
Afrikaners

Great Trek
Transvaal
Orange Free State
Anglo-Boer War
Union of South Africa

African National Congress (ANC)
Afrikaner Nationalist Party
Native Land Act
Group Areas Act

Sharpeville
Umkhonto We Sizwe
Nelson Mandela
Soweto
Black Consciousness Movement
Steve Biko

Define

apartheid
pass laws

reserves

homelands

bantustans
townships

Discussing Important Ideas

1. How would you explain the statement, "The discovery of gold and diamonds changed South Africa's history"?
2. The Freedom Charter was viewed by many as a major political event in the "life" of South Africa. Why do you think they viewed it this way? Do you agree or disagree with them? Explain.
3. An African chief once referred to the homelands as "the white man's garbage can." Do you think this is a fair appraisal? Why or why not?
4. If you were an Afrikaner, why would you want things to remain the way they are in South Africa? If you were a black African, why would you want them to change?

Developing Skills

RECOGNIZING FALLACIES IN A LINE OF REASONING

Put yourself in this situation: A classmate borrows your notes to study for a test. The classmate flunks the test and argues that the only reason he or she failed was that your notes were no good. Do you accept this or not?

Your notes may not have been the best, or they may have been perfectly acceptable. It does not matter, however, because, more likely than not, there was more than one reason why your classmate did not pass the test. The situation is an example of a *fallacy*, a false notion or error, in a line of *reasoning*, the process by which one judgment is deduced from another or others that are given.

A fallacy in a line of reasoning, then, is an error in thinking something out. The fallacy may be an unsupported or unsound argument or a mistaken conclusion. Asking yourself the following questions about a statement will help you recognize such fallacies in both spoken and written material.

1. What is the main idea of the statement?
2. What is the conclusion?
3. How was the conclusion reached?
4. Are there any fallacies in the line of reasoning? If so, what are they?

Read the three statements that follow, asking yourself for each the four questions indicated earlier.

a. *These white people in South Africa are rock-hard. They will never change.*
b. *Without the white South Africans, the black South Africans would have nothing.*
c. *The black South African has a different idea of violence. Human life, or life in general, does not mean that much, or does not have the same value to them that it has to the white man.*

Each of the statements contains a fallacy. In each, the conclusion is in error because it is based on an assumption or an unsound or unsupported point or argument. For example, the reasoning in the second statement is that black South Africans do not have the ability, intellect, or will to achieve and that, therefore, they must be directed by whites. This is an unsound and unsupported statement, a fallacy in the line of reasoning.

For further practice in recognizing fallacies in a line of reasoning, read the statements in italics in the Exploration for this chapter. For each, ask yourself the four questions suggested earlier.

CHAPTER 5
KENYA

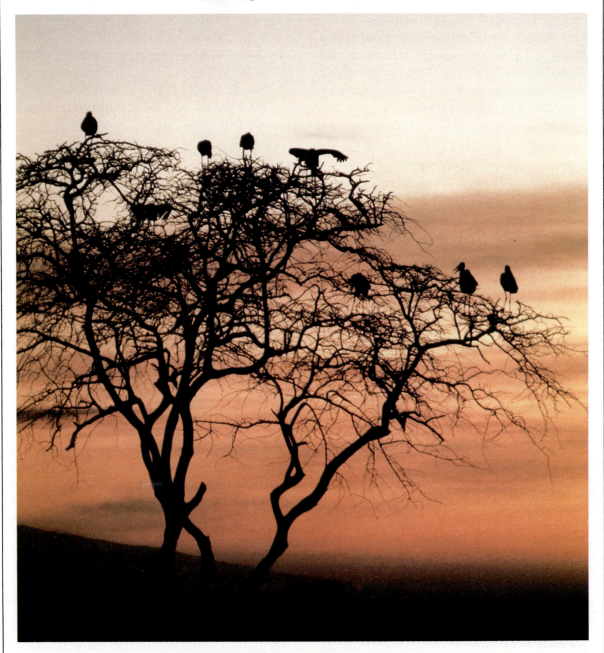

1. How did colonialism affect the Africans of Kenya?
2. How have Kenya and the ways of life of its people changed since independence?

"Where did the land go?...."

I am old now, but I too have asked that question in waking and sleeping. I've said "What happened, O Murungu [African god], to the land which you gave to us? Where, O Creator, went our promised land?" At times, I've wanted to cry or harm my body to drive away the curse that removed us from the ancestral lands. I ask, "Have you left your children naked, O Murungu?"

I'll tell you. There was a big drought sent to the land by evil ones who must have been jealous of the prosperity of the children of the Great One.... The sun burnt freely. Plague came to the land. Cattle died and people shrank in size. Then came the white man as had long been prophesied by Mugo wa Kibiro, that Gikuyu seer of old. He came from the country of ridges far away from here. Mugo had told the people of the coming of the white man.... So the white man came and took the land. But at first, not the whole of it.

Then came the war. It was the first big war.... All of us were taken by force. We made roads and cleared the forest to make it possible for the warring white man to move more quickly. The war ended. We were all tired. We came home worn out but very ready for whatever the British might give us as a reward. But, more than this, we wanted to go back to the soil and court it to yield, to create, not to destroy. But ng'o! The land was gone.

My father and many others had been moved from our ancestral lands.*

In the above excerpt from the work of a Kenyan author, an elderly man laments the loss of African land and asks the god Murungu why this has happened. His question is the same one asked by Kenyans for many years. Land has been an important issue for the 42 black ethnic groups that make up nearly 99 percent of the nation's population. This is especially true for the Kikuyu, the majority ethnic group.

The East African nation of Kenya has had a long and rich history. As early as about 1000 BC, there was farming and domestic herding in the highlands. By the fourth century AD, the Africans who lived along the coast were trading spices, ivory, and rhino horn with merchants from Arabia, Persia, and India. Then came the Europeans and colonial rule. Finally, in 1963, Kenya gained its independence, and its president set a goal—"a single Kenya in which all races, white and black, Arabs and Indians, could live and work in peace alongside each other."

Since then, Kenya has prospered economically and has raised the standard of living of the people. Although the path has not always been smooth, today Kenya is a symbol of African freedom, pride, and self-reliance. One observer refers to it as a kaleidoscope of "varied and attractive images" in which "there is an impressive *uhuru* or independent spirit among the people, but also an astonishing *haram-bee* or pulling together spirit."

Weep Not, Child by Ngugi wa Thiong'o, 1964, Heinemann, p. 25. Reprinted by permission.

From Foreign Rule to Independence

By the eleventh century, foreign influence was being felt in East Africa as Arab traders introduced their religion of Islam and its customs to the Bantu-speaking people who lived along the coast. In time, some of them married Africans, and eventually a new people and culture known as Swahili emerged. Their language, a mixture of Bantu and Arabic, became a *lingua franca,* or common language, that was used for trade up and down the coast. It also was used in the Swahili cities that flourished until the 1300's.

The next group of foreigners to show interest in the coastal areas was the Portuguese, who wanted a port of call on the way to India. By 1507, they had taken the coastal cities, wrested the gold trade from the Swahili, and established supply posts. By the late 1600's, however, their power had declined, and they were defeated by Arabs from Oman, an area of the Arabian Peninsula. The Arabs kept control of the coast for close to 200 years.

The Arabs, the Swahili, and the Portuguese all had confined their control to the coastal areas. None of the three had tried to move into the interior of the country. In 1895, however, the British penetrated the interior. Within two years, they had control of most of present-day Kenya. Believing there was great wealth in Uganda, which they also controlled, they set out immediately to build a railway from there to the coast. Much of the work on the railway was done by laborers recruited from India, and after it was completed, 7000 of them stayed in Kenya. The railway headquarters was established in a few tents about halfway between the port city of Mombasa and Lake Victoria. In later years, because of its location, Nairobi came to be known as "the place of cold waters."

After the Portuguese seized the Swahili island-city of Mombasa, they built the fortified town pictured in this early French drawing. Mombasa became the central base from which the Portuguese controlled the coastal Indian Ocean trade. Who defeated the Portuguese?

The British soon realized that not enough trade goods were coming out of Uganda to make the railway profitable. So they recruited British settlers to raise coffee and tea for export and to turn Kenya into a "white man's country." For years to come, the millions of acres of fertile highlands that they staked out for their plantations were known as the "White Highlands."

The settlers used African labor to work their plantations. Most Africans had no choice but to leave their own farms and go to work for the British. The British government had levied a tax on them. Since they were not allowed to compete with the plantation owners by growing **cash crops,** crops raised for sale, they had to work the plantations in order to earn the money to pay the tax.

EARLY NATIONALIST MOVEMENT

By the 1920's, the Europeans not only controlled the government but owned the best farmland as well. The Africans, meanwhile, grew more and more dissatisfied. Finally, in 1929, a young Kikuyu leader named Jomo Kenyatta went to Great Britain to argue on behalf of the Africans.

Kenyatta remained in England off and on until 1946, when he returned home to assume the leadership of the Kenya African Union (KAU), a political party that had been formed two years earlier. One of the KAU's chief goals was to gain Africans access to their original land in the highlands. Below, an African whose family's lands had been taken over by the British, tells about the first KAU rally he attended and the effect it had on him:

> It was July 26, 1952 and I sat in the Nyeri Showgrounds packed in with a crowd of over 30,000 people. The Kenya African Union was holding a rally and it was presided over by Jomo Kenyatta. He talked first of LAND. In the Kikuyu country, nearly half of the people are landless and have an earnest desire to acquire land so that they can have something to live on. Kenyatta pointed out that there was a lot of land lying idly in the country and only the wild game enjoy that, while Africans are starving of hunger. The White Highland, he went on, together with the forest reserves which were under the Government control, were taken from the Africans unjustly. . . .
>
> . . . He asked the crowd to show by hands that they wanted more land. Each person raised both his hands. And when he asked those who did not want land to show their hands, nobody raised. . . .
>
> The other point that Jomo Kenyatta stressed . . . was African FREEDOM. He raised the KAU flag to symbolize African Government. He said Kenya must be freed from colonial exploitation. Africans must be given freedom of speech, freedom of movement, freedom of worship and freedom of press. Explaining this to the people, he said that with the exception of freedom of worship, the other freedoms are severely limited with respect to the Africans. . . .
>
> I was struck by . . . [the KAU's flag's] red colour in the middle of black and green, which signified blood. . . .
>
> When Kenyatta returned on the platform for the third time, after a few other speakers, he explained the flag. He said, 'Black is to show that this is for black people. Red is to show that the blood of an African is the same colour as the blood of a European, and green is to show that when we were given this country by God it was green, fertile and good but now you see the green is below the red and is suppressed.' I tried to figure out his real meaning. . . . Special Branch [government] agents were at the meeting . . . so Kenyatta couldn't speak his mind directly. What he said must mean that our fertile lands (green) could only be regained by the blood (red) of the African (black). That

After Jomo Kenyatta's release from prison in 1959, he was sent to a remote desert location in northern Kenya. Two years later, members of the KAU party won control of the legislative council. When they refused to serve without Kenyatta, the British finally agreed to free him. What position did Kenyatta hold in the new republic of Kenya?

was it! The black was separated from the green by red: the African could only get to his land through blood.*

RESISTANCE AND REVOLT

As more and more African farmers lost their land, a group of Kikuyu decided to take action. They formed a secret movement, which the Europeans called Mau Mau. The movement's chief goal was to gain back the ancestral lands of the Kikuyu. Those who wanted to join the movement and fight for freedom had to take an **oath**, or pledge, like the one that follows:

If I reveal our secrets, let this oath
turn against me;

If I spy falsely, let this oath turn
against me; . . .
If I leave any comrade in danger, let this
oath turn against me;
If I kill a leader to gain promotion or a
higher post, let this oath turn
against me;
If I surrender before we have gained our
Independence, let this oath turn
against me;
If I see a weapon of the enemy and fear to
take it, let this oath turn
against me;
If I hand over my gun or our books to the
enemy, let this oath turn
against me;
If I kill a fellow soldier out of enmity,
let this oath turn against me;
If I betray our country or our
nationalists, let this oath turn
against me.*

**Mau Mau From Within: Autobiography and Analysis of Kenya's Peasant Revolution* by Donald Barnett and Karari Njama, pp.73–75, copyright ©1966 by Donald Barnett and Karari Njama. Reprinted by permission of Monthly Review Press.

*Mau Mau General by Waruhiu Itote (General China), 1967, East African Publishing House, pp. 275–276. Reprinted by permission.

CHAPTER 5 KENYA

KENYA

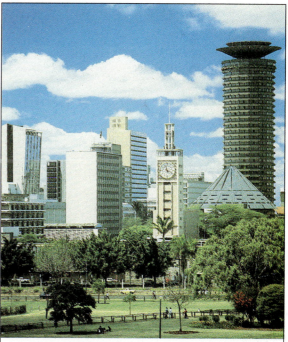

The Parliament Building (with clock tower), Kenyatta Conference Center, and Hilton Hotel are identifiable landmarks of downtown Nairobi. Why was Nairobi first settled?

In 1953, the colonial government declared a state of emergency and asked the British government for military help. All Kikuyu were forced to move into the Central Province, and nearly 80,000 were put in detention camps. Kenyatta was accused of leading the resistance movement and was sent to jail.

This did not bring an end to African resistance. Finally, in 1956, the government gave in to the pressure and allowed greater African representation in the legislative council. More reforms followed. By 1961, Africans held the majority in the council. Two years later, following free elections, Kenya became independent. The following year it became a republic. Shortly after, Jomo Kenyatta became president.

1. Who were the first foreigners to influence the people of Kenya? What was their relationship to the Swahili?
2. Why did the British recruit settlers to come to Kenya? How did their coming affect the Africans?
3. What was the goal of the KAU? Of the Mau Mau? How successful was each group?

THE WAY OF LIFE

Today, the Kenyan population is a mixed one made up of people of many different heritages and backgrounds. As in the past, the largest ethnic group is the Kikuyu, followed by the Luyia, the Kamba, the Luo, and the Kalenjin. More than one-half of the people are Christians, and about 40 percent practice traditional religions.

THE CITIES

Kenya has a number of major cities. The largest and most important is Nairobi, which has been the nation's capital since 1905. It serves as the Africa headquarters for many international organizations and businesses. With the following words, a visitor gives her impressions of this city whose diversity mirrors that of Kenya itself:

These giant "tusks" form arches over the main thoroughfare of modern Mombasa, Kenya's second largest city and East Africa's main port. Many tourists from around the world are attracted each year to the city's resort hotels and white sand and coral beaches. What is Kenya's largest city?

. . . Nairobi: full of vitality, international, intercultural, interreligious, interracial. . . . A city where an American Indian from Oklahoma meets Asian Indians at church; where one meets a couple of Asian extraction (who formerly lived in Uganda and are now living in Canada) at the home of a man from Goa and a woman from the Seychelles; where Protestants and Catholics share in a worship service with an Egyptian Coptic priest as speaker; where a Chinese professor from Taiwan, but recently moved from Australia, is found teaching at the University of Nairobi; where the landscape is silhouetted by Protestant church spires, Anglican, Catholic or Legio Maria cathedrals, Moslem mosques, Hindu or Sikh temples.

Take a look at the skyline of downtown Nairobi: round-tepee roofed Kenyatta Conference Center; the luxurious modern Hilton Hotel in the round; elegant history-filled Norfolk Hotel . . . ; the University of Nairobi; Parliament Building; Maridadi Fabrics Center; Mathare Valley with its thin paper huts; the Indian dukas and curio shops of Biashara Street; the country bus station. . . .

The fantastic flora: flame trees; blue jacaranda; many varieties of hibiscus; the violet/blue/white yesterday, today and tomorrow shrub; the yellow cassias and coral flames; beautiful paper-like bougainvillea at all seasons; hoop pines and she oaks (look like weeping willows); orchids and passion flowers.

The weather: near perfect. It is warm and sunny in the middle of the day with generally cool nights. There are rains in November–December and March–June with sufficient in between to keep lawns lush and blossoms blooming.

The green groceries: shelves lined with pineapples, papayas, bananas, coconuts, mangoes, limes, tomatoes, avocados, plums (in December), rhubarb and green vegetables.

This is Nairobi—city of the sun, city of flowers, plus a national museum, a national park with wild animals five minutes away from the business section, Leakey Institute, the Bomas depicting traditional life styles and dances. . . .*

---

*"Kenya Kaleidoscope" by Lucile Peak Wardin in *The Bridge*, Fall 1980, p. 14. Reprinted by permission.

CHAPTER 5 KENYA

THE COUNTRYSIDE

Although Kenyan cities have grown in recent years, about four-fifths of the people still live in rural areas and make their livings from raising crops or livestock. Prime farmland, however, is very scarce. Most of it lies in the southwestern highlands, which straddle the Great Rift Valley. Below, a tea-picker on a small farm in Kaptel in Kenya's Nandi District talks about his life and the role tea plays in the Kenyan economy:

> Kenya is famous for its good tea. Its flavor is popular with tea drinkers in Europe, North America and the Middle East. Most of Kenya's tea is grown in twelve districts, stretching from Kitale to Meru. There is also a tea belt running about 160 kilometers (100 miles) along the eastern slope of the Aberdares, from Limuru to Nyeri. The big plantations are found to the east of the Rift Valley and on the western slopes of the Mau Escarpment.
>
> A lot of tea is grown around Kericho. That's where the large plantation companies are located. . . . In Kericho there's the old Tea Hotel, which serves what must be the freshest tea in the world! The tea estates (plantations) around the town are delightful to see: vast fields of shiny-leaved, green bushes growing in neat rows.
>
> Tea-picking goes on throughout the year. It's amusing to see the rows of tea-pickers on the estates with their bright-yellow, plastic aprons. They carry baskets on their backs. We pick "two-and-a-bud." That's two leaves of the tender shoot of a tea plant. I get paid 150 shillings a month, about a third of what I could get working as a laborer in the town.
>
> The tea-growing areas lie at an altitude of between 1,800 and 2,400 meters (6 to 8,000 feet). Kericho, known as "the most fertile tea area in the world," has an ideal climate for tea growing. It gets plenty of rain for most of the year. There are also hailstorms occasionally, which harm the tea buds and leaves. It can also get very cold. So it has an ideal climate for drinking tea as well!
>
> There are about 138,000 small-sized tea "farms" in Kenya, each averaging less than a hectare [2.5 acres]. Together they grow 36 percent of Kenya's tea. In all, they cover 53,586 hectares (133,965 acres), producing about 146,000 tons of green tea leaf, or about 33,000 tons of ready-made tea. . . .
>
> Kenya has many tea factories. . . . A factory . . . is supplied by about 3,400 growers. The factories are about 11 kilometers (7 miles) apart. Leaf-collecting centers are located between them. Tea farmers don't have to carry their crop for more than two kilometers (1.5 miles).*

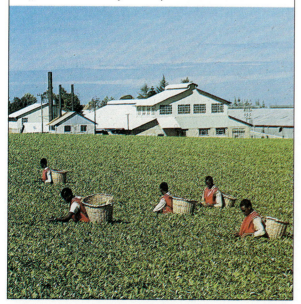

Tea-pickers often work part-time, spending most of the year raising corn, beans, and other crops for their own families. Tea is Kenya's most important cash crop after coffee. Where is Kenya's best farmland located?

1. What are some of the major characteristics of Nairobi?
2. Where in Kenya is tea grown? Why is tea important to the economy?

---

*"Kenya is famous for its good tea" in *We Live in Kenya* by Zulf M. Khalfan and Mohamed Amin, 1984, The Bookwright Press, pp. 26–27. Reprinted by permission.

PATTERNS OF CHANGE

Since independence, Kenya has undergone a great deal of change. With that change has come many problems. These include rising unemployment, the highest rate of population growth in the world, and a failed attempt to overthrow the government. In spite of its problems, however, Kenya remains one of the more politically and economically stable nations of Africa.

A NEW GOVERNMENT

Today Kenya is a democratic republic under whose constitution national elections are held every five years. In 1982, the National Assembly, the country's single-chamber Parliament, amended the constitution to make Kenya a **one-party state,** a nation that consists of a single political party. Phoebe Asiyo, one of Kenya's few female Members of Parliament (MP), describes the challenges of public office this way:

I became the MP for Karachuonyo in 1979, defeating four men in the elections! Being on the shores of Lake Victoria, my constituents are mainly fishermen and farmers. Peanuts and cotton . . . are the main crops around here. Unfortunately, my constituency has the highest infant mortality rate in the whole of Kenya: 246 babies die out of every 1,000 born—that's almost 25 percent. Waterborne diseases and malaria are the main causes of this. The government is trying to improve things by making people more aware of the importance of hygiene and a clean environment.

People have high expectations of an MP. They see us as providers; people who should help to supply them with their basic needs—jobs, food, good health and shelter. I believe in motivating people to help themselves. They must not expect the government to provide them with everything on a plate. I'm encouraging the government to set up more *Harambee* projects.

In this government poster, below words that mean "All the Kenyan People," are figures representing some of the different ethnic groups of Kenya. The poster symbolizes the "pulling together" of all the people to form a united nation. What do Kenyans call this "pulling together spirit"?

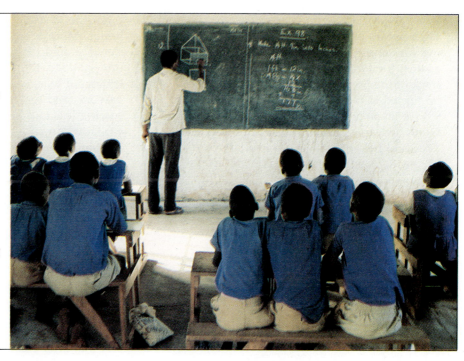

Since independence, Kenya's government has built many new schools. Today, about 80 percent of Kenyan children obtain at least a grade school education. In areas where the government has not yet established schools, some villages have set up their own, such as this one in southern Kenya. Why do you think village-run schools are called haram-bee *schools?*

Harambee is Kenya's motto. It means "pulling together" or "self-help."

I visit my constituency every week. I have a head office there and twenty-nine "mini offices." I try to visit them all regularly, either to discuss problems with people or to address meetings. But getting around can be a bit of a problem. Some areas of my constituency have poor roads and cannot be reached by car, so I have to use a bicycle—or my feet!

I enjoy meeting people and helping to solve their problems. I was a social worker before entering politics, which prepared me for the work of an MP. As an MP, I'm trying to improve the status of women in Kenya, an issue that has interested me for a long time. . . . I wish more women in Kenya would accept challenges. A woman has to work three times harder than a man to get anywhere. But once you've got a responsible position, men accept you and appreciate your capabilities.*

---

*"246 babies die out of every 1,000 born" in *We Live in Kenya* by Zulf M. Khalfan and Mohamed Amin, 1984, The Bookwright Press, pp. 6–7. Reprinted by permission.

LEARNING TO ADAPT

For some Kenyans, the changes that have taken place have been hard to accept. One such group is the Maasai, pastoralists of the southern Kenyan plains and the Great Rift Valley. Most like their traditional way of life and do not want to change it. For years, they have resisted government efforts to make them into farmers. One Maasai elder explained the reason for their opposition with these words: "Before, it was a sin for us to cultivate the land; it was bad to show God that you had turned the land upside down." Below, a journalist doing research in East Africa tells the story of a Maasai named James Morinte:

> Five years ago, when he was a Maasai *moran* [warrior], James Morinte and his six fellow [*morani*] set off to fight the lion. They'd sung songs together around their fire the night before, working up their bravery. . . . Now they trotted together, single file through the forested glades of Kenya's Isuria Escarpment which rises

above the Maasai Mara Game Reserve. Their spears gleamed sharply in the morning sun, and their red robes looked bright against the forest green. They followed the track of the lion until he tired. Then, . . . he turned to face them.

"We made a circle around the lion and when he leaped at me, I dropped to my knee and held my shield, like so, above my head," said Morinte, demonstrating as he walked along the escarpment heading toward his brother's *manyatta* (home). "I kept my spear upright and plunged it into his heart. And so I became 'the one who killed the lion.'"

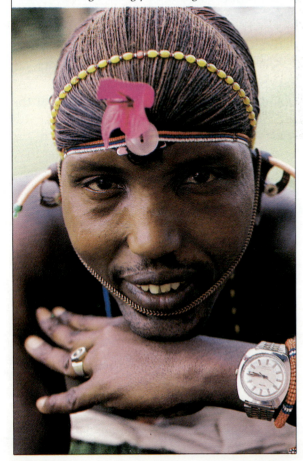

The modern watch and traditional jewelry of this member of the Bomas, a Kenyan dance troupe, point up the mix of new and old in much of Africa today. What are some changes taking place among the Maasai?

For the Maasai, . . . there is no greater honor. Morinte's action signified all that a *moran* should be: strong and brave while under attack, the coolheaded defender of cattle and village. Yet the need for such bravery, and for the warriors at all, is becoming less and less apparent as the Kenyan government—as well as educated Maasai leaders—moves to encourage the . . . [Maasai] to set aside their spears and wandering ways. . . .

. . . when European explorers first came to East Africa, they found the Maasai occupying . . . some 12 percent of the land. . . . [They] had a social system centered on a privileged class of young warriors, the morani. These young men defended the [group] from wild animals and added to its wealth by raiding other [peoples] for their cattle. (Maasai legends assert that after creating the world, God gave them "all the cattle upon Earth," so that cattle seen in the possession of other [groups] were presumed to be either stolen or lost.) They were the dominant [group] of East Africa, proud and certain of their ways. But by the time of Kenyan independence . . . , the Maasai had been, in the words of Ole Hassan Kamwaro, the Narok County Council Chairman, "left far behind."

"Today, however, we are on the run," he said. "We are retaining some traditions, like the respect for our elders. But other things are changing. For example, the morani will disappear. We don't want our young men to go about roaming, stealing cows, wasting their time. Instead, they should go to school. . . ."

. . . At his grandmother's insistence, Morinte went to school and learned English, and now, rather than tend his cattle, he works as a tour guide . . . in the Mara. Although he has given up many of his Maasai ways, and wears cut-off Levis and a digital watch, Morinte retains an intimacy with the land and animals. He knows how to follow the faint tracks of a dik-dik,

CHAPTER 5 — KENYA

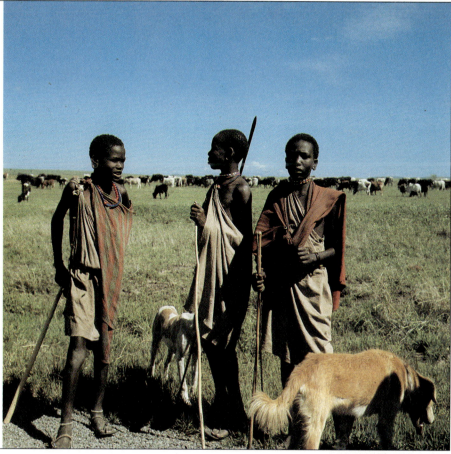

As more land goes into agricultural production, and animals on the Maasai Mara Game Reserve increase their numbers and spill over the reserve's boundaries, it is becoming more difficult for Maasai like these to find adequate grazing land for their cattle. Of what importance are cattle to the Maasai?

find the scat of a leopard and use the trees and shrubs that provide the Maasai with everything from toothbrushes to poisons. He clearly likes being out among the animals, both wild and domestic, and stops to carefully examine his brother's flocks of goats and sheep. Even though he earns a daily wage from his work as a guide, Morinte's real wealth—these flocks and his cattle—are sequestered here on the Isuria escarpment.

"You cannot be a Maasai unless you have cattle," he explained. . . .

From the bushes, two small Masai boys appeared. They were smiling . . . , and carried long switches for tending their flocks. Morinte greeted them. . . .

"This is how I spent my childhood," he said with a shy smile. "We spent our days with the herds, running here and there, watching out for lions. If we saw a lion, then we ran home to tell our fathers, so the morani could hunt it. But these boys, I think, will not be *morani*. They will . . . learn the traditions. But they will not hunt the lion."*

1. What kind of government does Kenya have today?
2. What are some of the tasks performed by Kenyan MP's?
3. Who are the Maasai? What does the government want them to do? Why do many of them oppose this?

---

*"Masai!" by Virginia Morell copyright 1985 by The National Wildlife Federation. Reprinted from the May–June issue of *International Wildlife Magazine*.

Exploration
Africa

When the Europeans first came to Kenya, the Kikuyu believed they were wanderers who would soon tire of Africa and return to their own country. So they welcomed them and gave them the right to build on African land. After a while, however, it became evident that the Europeans were there to stay. The following Kikuyu tale illustrates how the Kikuyu perceived the relationship between themselves and the Europeans. Read the tale. Then, in a short essay, explain in your own words how, according to the tale, the Kikuyu and the Europeans viewed each other. Conclude the essay with a discussion of how the Kikuyu thought they could solve the problem of the Europeans and why they felt justified in doing so.

. . . once upon a time an elephant made a friendship with a man. One day a heavy thunderstorm broke out, the elephant went to his friend . . . and said to him: "My dear good man, will you please let me put my trunk inside your hut to keep it out of this torrential rain?" The man, seeing what situation his friend was in, replied: "My dear good elephant, my hut is very small, but there is room for your trunk and myself. Please put your trunk in gently." The elephant thanked his friend, saying: "You have done me a good deed and one day I shall return your kindness." But what followed? As soon as the elephant put his trunk inside the hut, slowly he pushed his head inside, and finally flung the man out in the rain, and then lay down comfortably inside his friend's hut, saying: "My dear good friend, your skin is harder than mine, and as there is not enough room for both of us, you can afford to remain in the rain while I am protecting my delicate skin from the hailstorm."

The man, seeing what his friend had done to him, started to grumble; the animals in the nearby forest heard the noise and came to see what was the matter. All stood around listening to the heated argument between the man and his friend the elephant. In this turmoil the lion came along roaring, and said in a loud voice: "Don't you all know that I am the King of the Jungle! How dare anyone disturb the peace of my kingdom?" On hearing this the elephant, who was one of the high ministers in the jungle kingdom, replied in a soothing voice, and said: "My lord, there is no disturbance of the peace in your kingdom. I have only been having a little discussion with my friend here as to the possession of this little hut which your lordship sees me occupying." The lion, who wanted to have "peace and tranquillity" in his kingdom, replied in a noble voice, saying: "I command my ministers to appoint a Commission of Enquiry to go thoroughly into this matter and report accordingly." He then turned to the man and said: "You have done well by establishing friendship with my people, especially with the elephant who is one of my honourable ministers of state. Do not grumble any more, your hut is not lost to you. Wait until the sitting of my Imperial Commission, and there you will be given plenty of opportunity to state your case. I am sure that you will be pleased with the findings of the Commission." The man was very pleased by these sweet words from the King of the Jungle, and innocently waited for his opportunity, in the belief that, naturally, the hut would be returned to him.

The elephant . . . got busy with other ministers to appoint the Commission of Enquiry. The following elders of the jungle were appointed . . . : (1) Mr. Rhinoceros; (2) Mr. Buffalo; (3) Mr. Alligator; (4) The Rt. Hon. Mr. Fox to act as chairman; and (5) Mr. Leopard to act as Secretary to the Commission. On seeing the personnel, the man protested and asked if it was not necessary to include in this Commission a member from his side. But he was told that it was impossible, since no one from his side was well enough educated to understand the intricacy of jungle law. Further, that there was nothing to fear, for the members of the Commission were all men of repute for their impartiality in justice, and as they were gentlemen chosen by God to look after the interests of races less adequately endowed with teeth and claws, he might rest assured that they would investigate the matter with the greatest care and report impartially.

The Commission sat to take the evidence. The Rt. Hon. Mr. Elephant was first called. He came along with a superior air . . . , and in an authoritative voice said: "Gentlemen of the Jungle, there is no need for me to waste your valuable time in relating a story which I am sure you all know. I have always regarded it as my duty to protect the interests of my friends, and this appears to have caused the misunderstanding between myself and my friend here. He invited me to save his hut from being blown away by a hurricane. As the hurricane had gained access owing to the unoccupied space in the hut, I considered it necessary, in my friend's own interests, to turn the undeveloped space to a more economic use by sitting in it myself; a duty which any of you would undoubtedly have performed with equal readiness in similar circumstances."

After hearing the Rt. Hon. Mr. Elephant's conclusive evidence, the Commission called Mr. Hyena and other elders of the jungle, who all supported what Mr. Elephant had said. They then called the man, who began to give his own account of the dispute. But the Commission cut him short, saying: "My good man, please confine yourself to relevant issues. We have already heard the circumstances from various unbiased sources; all we wish you to tell us is whether the undeveloped space in your hut was occupied by anyone else before Mr. Elephant assumed his position?" The man began to say: "No, but—" But at this point the Commission declared that they had heard sufficient evidence from both sides and retired to consider their decision. After enjoying a delicious meal at the expense of the Rt. Hon. Mr. Elephant, they reached their verdict, called the man, and declared as follows: "In our opinion this dispute has arisen through a regrettable misunderstanding due to the backwardness of your ideas. We consider that Mr. Elephant has fulfilled his sacred duty of protecting your interests. As it is clearly for your good that the space should be put to its most economic use, and as you yourself have not yet reached the stage of expansion which would enable you to fill it, we consider it necessary to arrange a compromise to suit both parties. Mr. Elephant shall continue his occupation of your hut, but we give you permission to look for a site where you can build another hut more suited to your needs, and we will see that you are well protected."

The man, having no alternative, and fearing that his refusal might expose him to the teeth and claws of members of the Commission, did as they suggested. But no sooner had he built another hut than Mr. Rhinoceros charged in with his horn lowered and ordered the man to quit [leave]. A Royal Commission was again appointed to look into the matter, and the same finding was given. This procedure was repeated until Mr. Buffalo, Mr. Leopard, Mr. Hyena, and the rest were all accommodated with new huts. Then the man decided that he must adopt an effective method of protection, since Commissions of Enquiry did not seem to be of any use to him. He sat down and said: "Ng'enda thi ndeagaga motegi," which literally means "there is nothing that treads on the earth that cannot be trapped," or in other words, you can fool people for a time, but not forever.

Early one morning, when the huts already occupied by the jungle lords were all beginning to decay and fall to pieces, he went out and built a bigger and better hut a little distance away. No sooner had Mr. Rhinoceros seen it than he came rushing in, only to find that Mr. Elephant was already inside, sound asleep. Mr. Leopard next came in at the window, Mr. Lion, Mr. Fox, and Mr. Buffalo entered the doors, while Mr. Hyena howled for a place in the shade and Mr. Alligator basked on the roof. Presently they all began disputing about their rights of penetration, and from disputing they came to fighting, and while they were all embroiled together the man set the hut on fire and burnt it to the ground, jungle lords and all. Then he went home saying: "Peace is costly, but it's worth the expense," and lived happily ever after.*

---

*Facing Mt. Kenya: The Tribal Life of the Gikuyu by Jomo Kenyatta, 1965, Vintage Books, pp. 47–51. Reprinted by permission.

AFRICA

CHAPTER 5 REVIEW

POINTS TO REMEMBER

1. Between the eleventh and nineteenth centuries, the Arabs and the Portuguese exerted influence over Africans who lived along the East African coast. Intermarriage between Arabs and Africans resulted in a new people, culture, and language known as Swahili.
2. In 1895, the British penetrated the interior of East Africa. Within two years, they controlled most of present-day Kenya. Before long, they recruited British settlers to raise export crops and turn Kenya into a "white man's country."
3. By the 1920's, much to the dissatisfaction of most Africans, the Europeans controlled the government and owned most of the farmland of Kenya.
4. In 1946, Jomo Kenyatta, who had tried for years to negotiate with the British on behalf of his people, became the leader of the Kenya African Union (KAU), a new political party whose goal was to gain access for Africans to their original land in the highlands.
5. In response to continued loss of African land to Europeans, the Kikuyu formed a secret movement known as Mau Mau. The chief goal of the Mau Mau was to gain back the ancestral lands taken from the Kikuyu.
6. In 1963, Kenya became independent. The following year, it became a republic with Jomo Kenyatta as its president.
7. Today, although Africans are in the majority, the Kenyan population is made up of people of many different heritages and backgrounds.
8. One of the largest and most important cities of Kenya is Nairobi. It serves as the Africa headquarters for many international organizations.
9. Although about four-fifths of the Kenyan people live in rural areas and make their living from raising crops or livestock, prime farmland is scarce. One of the major crops is tea.
10. Today Kenya is a democratic republic and a one-party state.
11. Certain African groups, such as the Maasai, are having difficulty adapting and are resistant to some of the changes taking place in Kenya.

VOCABULARY

Identify

Kikuyu
Bantu-speaking people
Swahili
Nairobi
White Highlands

Jomo Kenyatta
Kenya African Union
Mau Mau
Luyia

Kamba
Luo
Kalenjin
Kericho

National Assembly
Phoebe Asiyo
MP
Maasai

Define

uhuru
haram-bee

lingua franca

cash crops

oath
one-party state

REVIEWING IMPORTANT IDEAS

1. What part do you think history has played in making Kenya a multi-racial society?
2. What did the KAU and the Mau Mau have in common? Given the circumstances, which group, if any, would you have joined? Explain.
3. In what ways does Nairobi reflect Kenya itself? Do you think this is true of most capital cities? Give examples.
4. Kenya is a democratic republic. At the same time, however, it is a one-party state. Do you think this is a contradiction? Explain.

DEVELOPING SKILLS

RECOGNIZING UNSTATED ASSUMPTIONS

Very often, you read or hear something that seems perfectly clear at first. Then, you realize that you did not really understand it. This may be because it was based on *unstated assumptions*, information an author or speaker assumes is already known and, therefore, does not explain.

There are three basic steps you can follow to help you recognize unstated assumptions in written material. First, read the material. Second, as you read, note point by point the information the author is presenting. Third, for each point, ask yourself what terms or statements you do not understand because the author has not explained them. For example, look at the following statements, and use the steps given above to determine if they contain unstated assumptions:

1. The White Highlands, together with the forest reserves under government control, were taken from the Africans.
   (It is assumed that the reader knows what the White Highlands are, what forest reserves are in the hands of the government, and what government is in control.)
2. The other point that Jomo Kenyata stressed was African freedom. He raised the KAU flag to symbolize African government.
   (It is assumed that the reader knows who Jomo Kenyata is and what KAU means.)
3. The man, having no alternative and fearing that his refusal might expose him to the teeth and claws of the Commission, did as they suggested.
   (It is assumed that the reader knows who the man is, what situation he is facing, what the Commission is, who "they" are, and what they suggested.)

For further practice in this skill, read the following paragraphs, and, using the three steps indicated earlier, determine if they contain unstated assumptions:

In 1953, the colonial government declared a state of emergency and asked the British for help. All Kikuyu were forced to move into the Central Province.

This did not bring an end to African resistance. In 1956, the government gave in to the pressure and allowed greater representation in the legislative council. In 1963, following free elections, the country became independent.

Today, the country is a democratic republic. In 1982, the National Assembly amended the constitution to make the nation a one-party state.

CHAPTER 6
THE ARTS IN DAILY LIFE

1. What are some major African art forms?
2. How are the arts linked to everyday life in Africa?

December, dry and beautiful, the season of the rice harvest, always found me at Tindican, for this was the occasion of a splendid and joyful festival, to which I was always invited, and I would impatiently wait for my young uncle to come for me. The festival had no set date, since it awaited the ripening of the rice, and this, in turn, depended on the good will of the weather. Perhaps it depended still more on the good will of the genii [spirits] of the soil, whom it was necessary to consult. If their reply was favorable, the genii, on the day before the harvest were again [asked] to provide a clear sky and protection for the reapers, who would be in danger of snakebite.

On the day of the harvest, the head of each family went at dawn to cut the first swath in his field. As soon as the first fruits had been gathered, the tom-tom [drum] signaled that the harvest had begun. This was the custom; . . .

Once the signal had been given, the reapers set out. With them, I marched along to the rhythm of the tom-tom. The young men threw their sickles into the air and caught them as they fell. They shouted simply for the pleasure of shouting, and danced as they followed the tom-tom players. . . . [It] would have been impossible for me to have torn myself away from their spirited music, from their sickles flashing in the rising sun, from the sweetness of the air and the crescendo of the tom-toms. . . .

When they had reached the first field, the men lined up at the edge . . . , their sickles ready. My uncle Lansana or some other farmer . . . then would signal that the work was to begin. Immediately, the black torsos would bend over the great golden field, and the sickles begin to cut. Now it was not only the morning breeze which made the field tremble, but also the men working. . . .

"Sing with us," my uncle would command.

The tom-tom, which had followed as we advanced into the field, kept time with our voices. We sang as a chorus, now very high-pitched with great bursts of song, and then very low, so low we could scarcely be heard. Our fatigue vanished, and the heat became less oppressive. . . .

. . . They sang and they reaped. Singing in chorus, they reaped, voices and gestures in harmony. They were together!—united by the same task, the same song. It was as if the same soul bound them.*

In the above excerpt, a writer from Guinea remembers the rice harvests of his youth. The image he recalls is a mixed one in which the heat, men, and music are blended into one. It is hard to separate the music from the rest of the image. This often is true in Africa. In the nations of this continent, the arts are interwoven with many aspects of everyday life. Music, drama, dance, poetry, sculpture, storytelling, and other art forms are a common denominator of life and very much a part of the African heritage.

---

*Excerpt from *The Dark Child* by Camara Laye, translated by James Kirkup and Ernest Jones. Copyright © 1955, renewed 1982 by Camera Laye, pp. 55–57, 61. Reprinted by permission of Farrar, Straus and Giroux, Inc.

MUSIC

In Africa, music is a major art form that serves many functions. It accompanies other art forms and is a vital part of many traditional religious ceremonies. In villages, where many activities are performed by groups, music often provides the motivation and rhythm for such tasks as felling trees, pounding millet, or harvesting a crop.

MUSICAL INSTRUMENTS

African music, which has spread to other parts of the world, is known for its **polyrhythm,** or use of two or more rhythm patterns at once. For example, while one instrument or singer is using a pattern of three beats, another may be using a pattern of five. Then there is the drum music of West Africa, which often uses overlapping polyrhythms.

There is a great variety of African musical instruments. In the words of a Ghanaian scholar, "Almost anything that resonates [vibrates] can be pressed into musical service in Africa. The inventory of musical instruments is breathtaking." Some instruments, like the drums, gourd xylophone, and thumb piano, are found throughout the continent. Instruments such as drums, horns, bells, xylophones, and whistles traditionally have been used to send special signals or messages.

Of special interest are the **talking drums** of West Africa. They are unique because they imitate speech. This is possible because many African languages are **tonal.** This

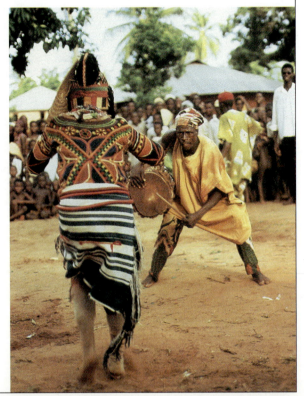

The women pounding grain to a steady rhythm and the man dancing to the beat of a drum provide two examples of the use of music in African life. For what type of rhythm pattern is African music known?

means that different words are made by raising or lowering the pitch of one's voice while pronouncing the same syllable. The word *tsó* for example, when spoken at a high pitch, means "stand." But, when spoken at a lower pitch, *tsò* means "cut." By using different types of drums and special techniques of playing, the drummer can produce the various tones of the language and, thus, understandable words and sentences.

In the past, the talking drums were used to relay messages about warfare, call people together, report special events, praise gods and royalty, and communicate with the supernatural world. Although today they still are used at ceremonies of the royal court, they generally are used more in musical performances than for communication.

PROTEST SONGS

In Africa, as elsewhere, music is more than just the sound of instruments. It also is the sound of the human voice raised in song. Through song, emotions can be expressed and people can be inspired and united. This has been the case in many African nations during their struggles for independence. In these nations, protest songs have played a vital role. In the words of the president of Zimbabwe, "The *Chimurenga* [war of liberation] songs helped to instill grim determination among all actors in the revolutionary process." He went on to explain that whenever the freedom fighters "lost hope, were starving, wounded or subjected to surprise attacks by the enemy, they did not give in. Instead, they turned to the revolutionary songs to refurbish their spirits." Below is an excerpt from one of their songs:

> Let the precious blood of our heroes flow like the raging Falls.
> My mind cannot rest,
> I am constantly thinking about the Welfare of the masses.
> Our precious blood is being spilled
> For the people's freedom.
> The liberation of the masses
> Will flow from the sacrifices we are making.
> Freedom will crown our efforts in the struggle for Zimbabwe. . . .
>
> Our determination to free the Motherland, has brought us face to face with death.
> In the mountains.
> In the raging waters of flooded rivers.
> But together, with the comradeship
> Cemented by mutual love,
> We come to each other's rescue in the hour of need,
> And together overcome the problem.
>
> Zimbabwe is now a sacred country
> Because it has been anointed with the blood of her children.
> Our titular spirits, please protect us from the enemy,
> Protect us from the enemy, who would destroy us.
> We pray to you our guardian spirits
> Please guide our steps.
>
> If death should come today,
> I would accept it with every part of my body;
> I shall have satisfied myself that
> I've fulfilled my solemn undertaking to die for Zimbabwe.
> My body will have performed my duty to my nation,
> The duty which is mine this side of the grave.
> My body will have performed my duty to my nation,
> The duty which is mine this side of the grave. . . .*

1. What are some of the functions performed by music in Africa?
2. What makes the talking drums unique? For what have they been used?
3. What role have protest songs played?

---

*"All the Peoples of Africa" in *Songs that Won the Liberation War* by Alec J.C. Pongweni, 1982, The College Press, pp. 62–63. Reprinted by permission.

INSIGHTS ON PEOPLE
AFRICA

MIRIAM MAKEBA

One of the best known musical artists to come out of Africa is the South African singer Miriam Makeba. Her songs of protest against apartheid earned her permanent exile from her country as well as large numbers of supporters throughout the world. In addition to singing songs about South Africa, Makeba has given benefit concerts for victims of African famine and for world peace. Not too long ago, Makeba was the focus of an article in *Africa* magazine. The following is an excerpt from that article:

Miriam Makeba, the 'Empress of African song', celebrated her fifty-third birthday last month with a gala performance. But it was far away from the place she would have loved to be most, her native South Africa. Still the Royal Festival Hall in London provided her with a large and eager audience for her performance, the first in Britain for more than a decade.

Asked why she had stayed away from Britain for so long, the exiled singer . . . said: 'Nobody ever asked for me. I thought that the English public had forgotten me or probably didn't care.'

A lot of the British did . . . care, as was demonstrated by the numerous standing ovations Makeba received. But more important, perhaps, the people of Africa and particularly South Africa also did care. That fact was driven home by the impromptu appearance . . . by Adelaide Tambo, wife of the president of the African National Congress of South Africa. . . . Adelaide did not only bring a bouquet of flowers, but also a message of celebration and struggle from the dispossessed Black majority in South Africa. . . .

Miriam Makeba was born on March 4, 1932 in Johannesburg, but spent her formative years in Pretoria. It was there . . . that she performed in public for the first time, singing with the school choir. . . .

. . . Makeba is completely self-taught. She began travelling with small groups from village to town, and then city to city. Her break came when she was invited to join a group called the 'Black Manhattan Brothers'.

. . . By 1957 she was appearing as a soloist in a musical revue which toured Africa. . . . She then received the lead in the controversial jazz opera, 'King Kong'. . . . She quickly became South Africa's top recording star.

This period was to be a turning point in Miriam Makeba's life. She was featured as a singing lead in American film-maker Lionel Rogosin's semi-documentary film, Come Back Africa, an exposé and attack on South African apartheid. . . .

. . . In November of 1959 Miriam Makeba was featured on American television, and later at the famous New York jazz spot, the Village Vanguard. As her success began to burgeon in Europe and America she received word that the Pretoria government had revoked her citizenship.

. . . She presently carries passports from eight countries. . . . She has been received by, and sung for the Heads of State of most independent African countries.

Makeba has played peace concerts in Germany, in Martin Luther King's memory in Brooklyn, and most recently in Oslo for Ethiopia's famine relief. 'It is very important for artists to know where they come from, where they are, and where they are going,' Miriam Makeba said. 'And it is very important that they care about what surrounds them, and about what is around them because they are influential. I have not tried to change with the fashions that come in and out, I have always sung the way I feel.'*

1. Who is Miriam Makeba?
2. What does her success and international renown indicate to you about the role and importance of the arts?

---

*"Legend of the Empress of African song" by L.A. Goffe in *Africa*, No., 164, April 1985, p. 87. Reprinted by permission.

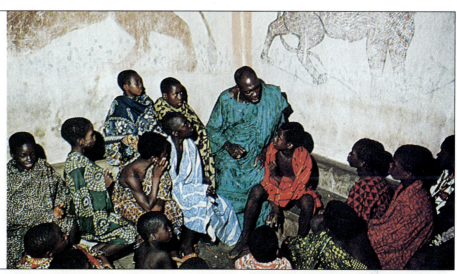

A village elder tells traditional stories to a group of boys in an Ivory Coast village. The children are encouraged to memorize these stories, which are often creation myths about the beginnings of their people. What is oral literature?

ORAL LITERATURE

Another African art form is oral literature, which has been passed down from generation to generation. Often used in religious ceremonies and recited to music, oral literature records the past and teaches traditions and values. Myths, legends, histories, stories, fables, poems, riddles, songs of praise for deities and royalty all are forms of oral literature. So are **proverbs,** short sayings that express a well-known truth or fact. Proverbs are especially common throughout Africa. Almost every African group has its own proverbs that take in nearly every situation and point of view. Below are some examples:

Swahili (East Africa):
"A bad brother is far better than no brother." (Blood is thicker than water.)

"The axe forgets, the tree does not forget." (The one who inflicts the insult may forget, but the one insulted will not.)

"A loud drum will soon split." (Loud promises are hollow.)

"The one with the sharp knife will eat meat." (The alert and ready person gets the job.)

"Why should the hot peppers you have not eaten burn you?" (If you have no secrets what have you to fear?)*

Yoruba (Nigeria):
"He fled from the sword and hid in the scabbard." (Out of the frying pan into the fire.)

"Mouth not keeping to mouth, and lip not keeping to lip, bring trouble to the jaws." (Talk is silver, silence is gold.)

"One who does not understand the yellow palm-bird says the yellow palm-bird is noisy." (Men are prone to despise what they do not understand.)†

Hausa (West Africa):
"Even the Niger [River] has an island." (The mightiest things do not have it all their own way.)

"God made beautiful the silk cotton tree, the rubber tree must cease being angry." (Quarrel not with what God ordains.)

---

*From "Politics in Swahili Proverbs" by Albert Scheven in *Curriculum Materials for Teachers 1983*, African Studies Program, University of Illinois, pp. 212–214, 216, 218. Reprinted by permission.

†"Yoruba Proverbs" in *The Horizon History of Africa*, Volume I, 1971, American Heritage Publishing Co., Inc., p. 207. Reprinted by permission.

Anti-bird Ghost spirit figure, drawn in ink by Nigerian artist Taiwo Olaniyi.

Woman weaving a traditional African basket.

Young Yoruba woman with a contemporary hairstyle.

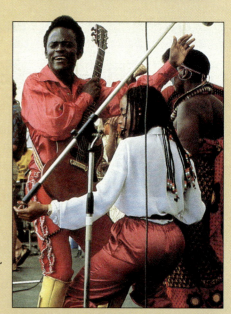

Contemporary African band performing popular African music.

West African beaded bracelets and Maasi watch.

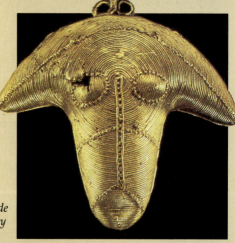

Gold pendant mask made by the Baule of the Ivory Coast.

CHAPTER 6 THE ARTS IN DAILY LIFE

"If music changes so does the dance." (One must move with the times.)*

Zulu (Southern Africa):
"He cries with one eye." (He pretends to be sorry when he is not.)

"The sheep has killed an elephant." (The impossible has happened.)

"One does not follow a snake into its hole." (It is not wise to take unnecessary risks.)†

1. What is considered oral literature?
2. Of what value is oral literature?

VISUAL ARTS

A third important African art form is **visual arts,** or art that appeals to the sense of sight. From ancient times to the present, Africans have used visual arts in many different forms and materials from bronze statues to elephant-hair bracelets. The elaborately carved staff of a chief, the colorful paintings splashed on the side of a bus, the president's portrait stamped on a piece of cloth, and the elegantly designed gold necklace all are visual arts created over the centuries by Africans and enjoyed today by people the world over.

Today, there are thousands of artists in the towns and cities of Africa fashioning pots, carving wooden masks, designing buildings, sculpting statues, and weaving and dyeing cloth. Although these works of African art are being sought increasingly by collectors around the world, for most Africans they are everyday articles used for generations for practical and religious purposes. An example is *Adire* cloth, an indigo-blue printed fabric traditionally produced by the Yoruba of Nigeria. Below, a writer describes the work of two young Nigerian women who create modern versions of this traditional cloth:

> The achievement of two female artists from Oshogbo, Senabu and Kikelemo . . . is unique and exciting. . . .
>
> Senabu and Kikelemo were both trained in the production of *adire eleko* cloth, a starch-resistant technique . . . patterned on only one side of the cloth. A paste is made of cassava [a tropical plant], water and various local chemicals, which is applied in streaks onto a plain white cloth. After dying with one or two colours, the parts treated with the cassava 'gum' emerge darker than the other areas, and with a different texture.

In Nigeria, cloth dyeing is an art form often used by women. Traditional Adire *cloth, shown here, is made in set patterns by an* Aladire, *or cloth-dyeing expert. What African ethnic group produces* Adire *cloth?*

---

*"Hausa Proverbs" in *The Horizon History of Africa,* Volume I, 1971, American Heritage Publishing Co., Inc., p. 248. Reprinted by permission.

†"Zulu Wisdom" in *The Horizon History of Africa,* Volume II, 1971, American Heritage Publishing Co., Inc., p. 428. Reprinted by permission.

Where the two women depart from tradition is that they create strong integrated pictorial images like paintings, exclusive to one length of cloth. These can be hung as tapestries, because each is a 'picture' on its own, with a focal point. Even when their cloths are made up into caftan-styled dresses, each length is a unique piece. Although they employ many of the same design motifs as the *Adire Eleko*, such as animals, certain symbols, kings and queens, their imagery also goes far beyond the stylised, formal, almost abstract effect of the *Adire*. The Oshogbo womens' cloths tell a story, often with stunning emotional impact. . . .

. . . Senabu creates scenes and tells stories on her cloths; . . . the cloths give one the feeling of a lively but ordered world. . . . Her complex cloths incorporate many different elements, which build up to a total picture of Yoruba life. . . . [Her work] is free, energetic, rhythmic and sensual. . . . [She uses] trees as a foil for her figures. Her real and mythical animals are particularly beautiful. . . .

Senabu's use of colour is more experimental than that of Kikelemo. Both use the traditional blue-black indigo a great deal, and the classic *Adire* method in which the finished design is re-dipped in indigo to turn the blue and white to a softer, richer monochrome [painting done in different shades of one color]. Both women also use sharp greens, blue-greens and rich ochre; but Senabu also works with sumptuous purples and subtle purple-browns, pinks and yellows, colours which she softens and which seem to float into each other.

Though Kikelemo too sometimes departs from the indigo, when she does, it is with a great bold statement of colour—brilliant deep red or a massive purple. Her images are much heavier, more sculptural. . . .

The overwhelming impact of Kikelemo's work is carried by wide sweeping lines and bulky forms. Her mask-like figures have considerable depth. Though she is working on a flat surface, her images are sculptural in concept. . . . This is the territory of imposing gods and menacing animals. . . . Within her god's mask-like face, she will often leave areas of pure colour, but the heavy bodies of the animals are usually filled in with surging pattern. . . .

Both women . . . successfully combine the stimulus of contemporary Oshogbo life with the richness of an ancient feminine craft.*

1. What are some of the art forms considered visual arts?
2. How do Africans tend to view most visual arts?
3. What makes the cloths of Senabu and Kikelemo different from most traditional Adire cloths?

MASKS

Still another African art form is the mask, which generally is carved out of wood and worn with a ceremonial costume that covers the entire body. Although masks are used in a variety of ways, they generally are associated with religious ceremonies or rituals.

In some religious ceremonies, masks symbolize the respect a community has for its ancestors. The carving of the masks and the performing of dances while wearing them symbolize the link between the living and the dead. Those who wear the masks and perform the songs and dances are acting not as themselves but as spirits. In this role, they show people what their ancestors wish for them. On the next page, two journalists who visited an Ivory Coast village describe what they saw and what they learned:

---

*"Daughters of Oshogbo" by Chandana Juliet Highet in *New African*, October 1984, pp. 50–51. Reprinted by permission.

CHAPTER 6 THE ARTS IN DAILY LIFE

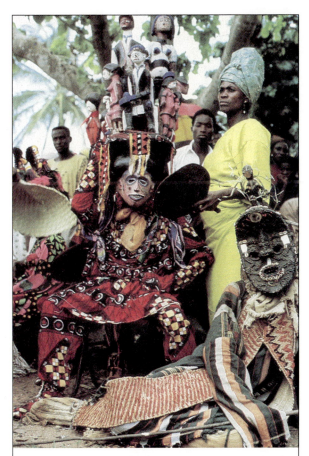

These masks of the Okpella, a northern Edo people of Nigeria, appear during Olimi, a festival held annually to honor ancestors and to "purify" the community. How do some masks link the living and the dead?

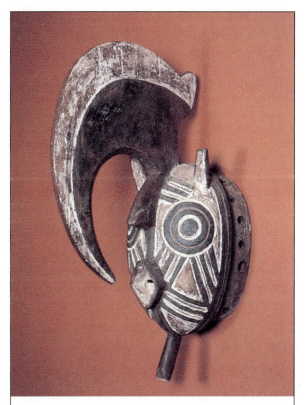

This rooster mask is used in storytelling by the Kô of Burkina Faso. It represents the history of a family and provides continuity with the present. How are masks important to village life?

After dinner a small figure covered with grasses ran into the compound, surrounded by chanting children. "The apprentice masks are bidding you welcome," Albert informed us. "They are in training to be important masks some day."

Ivoirians [people of the Ivory Coast] refuse to acknowledge the human behind the mask, so one never says "masked man," or "masked figure," only "mask." Masks are integral to peasant life—divine, visible links to the ancestors, serving different social roles. There are comedians, dancers, singers, storytellers who amuse and beguile. There are warrior masks who keep order and punish offenders of tribal law. There are masks of wisdom, whose powers are called upon only rarely.

Aubine and I were invited to a great feast day for masks by Dao Bonnot, mask chief at Bangolo in Wè country. "We have chosen our century man," he informed us. "He is the oldest man in the region. We will now give him a wonderful funeral while he is alive."

He added that after this supreme recognition, the century man must live out the remainder of his days as a nonentity, inside his compound. "The mask of masks, Nanh-Sohou, who was never born and is as old as the earth, will watch over him till he dies."

We were warned not to talk directly to masks, or approach too close. We listened as the village chief intoned the mask call.

"We have offered 3 cows, 20 sheep, 20 roosters, and 10 hens. The masks are satisfied!"

Then we heard a jingling noise. Through the winding alleys between [houses] moved a procession of perhaps 200 dancing men and women, surrounding numerous fearsome masks. Each mask walked slowly, pompously. At the end of the line stood an all-white, lion-faced mask, taller than the others, who would take a step only every 15 seconds or so. At each step, his white-costumed [attendants kneeled], rang little bells, and cried out praise to the mask.

"Nanh-Sohou is called only once every eight years," whispered Bonnot. "He gives us great delight in coming."

We were humbled by the sacredness, the solemnity, of the event.*

1. With what are masks generally associated in Africa?
2. What does the carving of masks and dancing while wearing them symbolize?
3. What are some of the social roles masks can represent?

FILMS

Over the past few decades, African films have grown into an important and popular art form. The films are welcomed in the continent because, unlike many imported films, they portray the real problems and life styles of African people. Below, a prominent Malian filmmaker named Souleymane Cissé, tells how he became interested in films and what he sees as the future of African films:

During my infancy I was always fascinated by cinema. I went as often as possible to the movies, without really realising at the time that I could make a career out of the profession. When I was 18 years old I started gradually to become conscious of my affinity to the movie industry. At that time I was a member of a Malian youth group and I became a film projectionist. It was only in 1961 when I received a three-month scholarship to study this profession in the Soviet Union that I became fully cognisant of my love for the Seventh Art. After returning to Mali, I received another scholarship to study film camera work for a year in the Soviet Union. Later I requested, and received, a longer scholarship in the Soviet Union to study cinema. . . .

I started [my cinema career] by realising current affairs films for the Ministry of Information and doing short documentaries on Malian subjects. I managed to complete some small feature films which attracted the attention of film critics abroad. This gave me the opportunity to push forward. I was able to finish a full-length feature film entitled *Den Muso* (The Young Girl). . . . For the first time the film attempted to show daily life in contemporary Mali. A broad public of all ages went to see the

Recently, Malian filmmaker Souleymane Cissé was made an Officer of Arts and Letters by the French government in recognition of his contributions to the film industry. Where was Cissé trained in filmmaking?

---

*"The Ivory Coast—African Success Story" by Michael and Aubine Kirtley in *National Geographic*, July 1982, p. 123. Reprinted by permission.

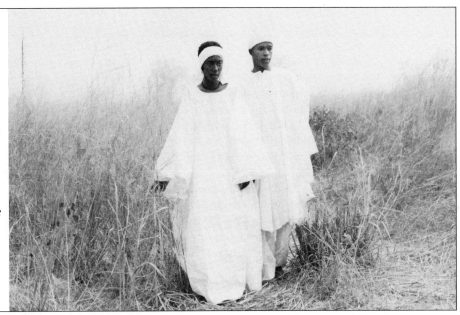

This is a scene from Souleymane Cissé's most successful movie to date, Finyé (The Wind), which is about a young man and woman who fall in love during a student rebellion in an African city. Finyé was presented at the 1986 New York and Cannes film festivals, where it received high marks from critics. A new film, titled Yeelen (The Light), is in production. What obstacles confront African filmmakers?

film. Then I realised that it was possible to move into . . . films of fiction. . . .

For me cinema is an art which is meant to have an impact on life, and it is in this precise framework that I produced *Baara* [a film about the condition of African workers in urban areas]. After independence, Mali . . . opened up factories and started large construction schemes requiring a plentiful labour force. I said to myself that now that this working class is being formed it should also learn to organise itself in defence of its interests. Since the working class in Mali and Africa has little in common with working classes in developed countries, I had to pinpoint an original angle for the film. That is why *Baara* takes at the beginning a young porter as its principal protagonist [hero]. He is a young man from the rural area who drifts into town in search of work. . . . The film also focuses on an executive, the type of person who in independent Africa has become rich because of his relations in the state apparatus instead of by the fruit of his labour. . . .

I would say . . . that African cinema is not properly understood by African leaders. When this finally does occur, and I hope it will be in the near future, it will be an important step forward. In addition, African businessmen have no notion of the possibilities of African cinema. . . . I am sure that if African film makers in five years' time are able to produce films superior in quality to *Finyé*, [one of Cissé's latest films] then foreign businessmen will "discover" African cinema to the detriment of our own businessmen, who will probably regret the missed opportunities. Much depends on the will of African film makers. Our films are also poorly distributed in Africa and elsewhere around the world. A film which is not properly distributed cannot be profitable. This is a situation which must be overcome, though these problems do not mean that one should be pessimistic about the future of African cinema.*

1. Why are African-made films welcome on the continent?
2. What does Souleymane Cissé think is the role of films? The future of African films?

---

*"People's film-maker" by Howard Schissel in *West Africa*, May 7, 1984, pp. 973–974. Reprinted by permission.

EXPLORATION
AFRICA

In recent years, African arts of all types have become sought after by collectors all over the world. As a result, some of the great treasures of Africa's cultural heritage are no longer found in Africa. This worries some people in many African nations. They stress that African art is not separate from life and is not something normally produced as an object to be sold. They point to the fact that for most of the buyers, the value of the art is a material one, which is not so for the African. This contrast is highlighted in the account that follows. After reading the account, answer these questions. Then explain in your own words the point of the account.

1. How does the American businessman perceive the value of the Dogon doors?
2. How does the Dogon chief perceive the value of the Dogon doors?
3. What is meant by the phrase, "the secret of abundance is of a nonmaterial nature"?
4. Do you agree with Ibrahima's assertion that the main problem with Westerners is that they turn everything into money? Explain.

One of the most beautiful lessons [Ibrahima] and my African friends have taught me . . . is that the greatest abundance, that which lights the clearest flame of joy in one's heart, is of a nonmaterial nature. I'll never forget a discussion I had on this theme with Ibrahima, his son Ali, and Thelonius, a black American anthropologist, during a moonlit night in Kinkiliba, Ibrahima's village. Thelonius was telling us how rich Western businessmen touring the Dogon region in Mali (world famous among art connoisseurs for its sculpture), had come upon a superb pair of sculptured doors which hung in a village chief's house.

"He immediately asked the chief, through an interpreter . . . if he could buy them," said Thelonius, who at that time was living in the Dogon village.

At first the chief was indignant. "Why do you want my doors?" he asked. "Don't you have a door on your house?" Thelonius had inwardly chuckled: he knew the businessman had a large mansion with full-time day and night guards, burglar alarms and watch-dogs. "I am just asking you if you'll sell me your doors," the man repeated, "for 50,000 Malian francs." And he waved 10 5,000Fr bills in the chief's face. The chief was visibly taken back: that was at least a year's income for him. He hesitated. These "toubabs" (white men) were hard to comprehend. But he had not paid his taxes because the harvest had been very poor . . . "75,000." The industrialist added five more notes to the wad.

"It was the most obscene thing I had ever seen in my life," Thelonius added. "This foreigner with 2 cameras at his belt and an embarrassed interpreter, adding bill upon bill until the chief said, 'Come into my hut,' because the whole village was by then assembled."

He gave in at 150,000Fr, that is, at $300, a small, dry crumb for the businessman. The next day a Land Rover came from the capital—300 miles [480 kilometers] away—to fetch the century-old doors while gaping villagers watched. So their doors were as precious as that? Their doors were really money?

Today, in the businessman's home country, these doors are insured for $15,000. Today also, in the Dogon country, you will not find any more original carved doors. These century-old symbols —literally priceless, for how do you fix a price on beauty, on memories, on symbols?—have been turned into money. They are no longer valued as expressions of beauty or of culture. They have become things. We Westerners have turned thoughts into things to be possessed. . . .

"That's the main problem with you Westerners," Ibrahima interjected, "you turn everything into money. Everything you touch. It's as if you had big paintbrushes and went round the world painting large DM, $, Fr or [pound] signs onto everything you see. . . ."

Ali said slyly, smiling, "'Time is money' you say. But doesn't that sum up the spiritual misery of a civilization? Real time is the occasion, renewed day after day, to start living. Time is a pair of cupped hands that you lift up towards heaven that they may be filled with beauty and joy, friends and parents, love and gentleness, courage and trust, children of your hopes, dreams of holiness and adventure. Real living destroys time, and hence the pursuit of money and the belief that money can buy joy. . . ."

It must be true that real abundance is not material, for everything beautiful I have ever seen, every courageous act I've ever witnessed, every gesture of love I've ever admired, every friend I've cherished, I carry around with me, every day, every hour, not as memories of the past or hopes of the future, but as examples and realities to be enjoyed and treasured now.

Sometimes I think I am the richest person on earth.*

---

*"The richest person on earth" by Pierre Pradervand in *The Christian Science Monitor*, May 11, 1977, p. 28. Reprinted by permission.

CHAPTER 6 REVIEW

POINTS TO REMEMBER

1. In Africa, the arts are interwoven with many aspects of everyday life. Music, drama, dance, poetry, sculpture, and other art forms are a common denominator and very much a part of the African heritage.
2. In Africa, music is a major art form that serves many functions. African music is known for its polyrhythm.
3. The talking drums of West Africa, originally used for communication, are unique because they actually imitate speech.
4. Protest songs have served many African nations during their struggles for independence by inspiring and uniting the African people.
5. Oral literature has been passed down from generation to generation in Africa. This type of literature, often used in religious ceremonies and recited to music, records the past and teaches traditions and values.
6. Visual arts have been used by Africans in many forms and materials from ancient times to the present. For most Africans, works of art of most forms and materials are everyday articles that have been used for generations for practical and religious purposes.
7. The mask is another African art form. Although masks are used in a variety of ways, they generally are associated with religious ceremonies or rituals.
8. Over the past few decades, films have become an important and popular African art form.

VOCABULARY

Identify

Adire cloth	Kikelemo	Nanh-Sohou	Souleymane Cissé
Senabu			Miriam Makeba

Define

polyrhythm	tonal	proverbs	visual arts
talking drums			

DISCUSSING IMPORTANT IDEAS

1. Songs are important to liberation movements in Africa. Do you think this is unique to Africa? Why or why not?
2. If there were no oral literature, the lives of many Africans would be different. Why and in what ways?
3. Miriam Makeba made this statement about artists: "It is very important that they care about what surrounds them, and about what is around them because they are influential." Do you agree or disagree with this statement? Give examples from your knowledge of artists and their activities to support your answer.
4. How would you explain the statement, "In Africa, art is not separate from life"?

Developing Skills

CLASSIFYING INFORMATION

Most texts are designed to provide you with a great deal of information. Often, to better understand such a large quantity of material, it helps to *classify* the information—separate and arrange it into related groups. One way to classify information is to put it into a table or a *chart*. A chart is a graphic representation of written information set up in columns and rows.

There are several different ways to set up a chart. The two charts below are used to classify information presented in this chapter. The same information is classified in both charts but in different forms. The following steps, used for this example, may be used to set up charts in general.

1. Read the sections "Oral Literature," on pages 91 and 93, and "Visual Arts," on pages 93 and 94.
2. Determine what information you want or need to classify; write the major categories across the top of a piece of paper; and write the information from the section material under the proper heading. Your charts for this example should look like the ones below.

For further practice in classifying information, read the material on Africa's music (pages 88 and 89), masks (pages 94, 95, and 96), and films (pages 96 and 97). Then, using the steps provided above, make a chart.

Chart 1: Characteristics, Uses, and Examples of African Art Forms

ART FORMS	CHARACTERISTICS	USES	EXAMPLES
oral literature	recited, sometimes to music; passed from generation to generation; found in nearly every African group	record past; teach values and traditions; praise deities and royalty	myths, legends, praise songs, and proverbs
visual arts	practical as well as decorative; appeal to the sense of sight; made by traditional methods; use traditional as well as modern symbols	for beauty's sake; show rank or office; record the past and keep traditions; in daily tasks and for religious and other purposes	sculpture, clothing, jewelry, carvings, pottery, cookware, tapestries, utensils, tools

Chart 2: Characteristics, Uses, and Examples of African Art Forms

ORAL LITERATURE	VISUAL ARTS
recited, sometimes to music; passed from generation to generation; found in nearly every African group	practical as well as decorative; appeal to the sense of sight; made by traditional methods; use traditional as well as modern symbols
record past; teaches values and traditions; praises deities and royalty	for beauty's sake; to show rank or office; to record the past and keep traditions; to use in daily tasks and for religious and other purposes
myths, legends, praise songs, and proverbs	sculpture, clothing, jewelry, carvings, pottery, cookware, tapestries, utensils, tools

CHAPTER 7
CHALLENGES TO DEVELOPMENT

1. What are some of the challenges facing Africa today?
2. What are some of the steps being taken to bring about African development?

The United Nations has proclaimed 1985 International Youth Year. The major themes chosen for celebrating this year are: Participation—Development—Peace. No time could have been more fitting than this year for reflecting on the situation of youth, in particular African youth. . . . Indeed, as this twentieth century draws toward a close, Africa is passing through one of the most crucial periods of its existence. The fall-out from the worldwide economic crisis is felt more painfully in our continent, where 30 million people are in danger of dying of hunger and thirst. Young people directly or indirectly suffer the consequences of this situation.

Everywhere from Senegal to Ethiopia, including the Ivory Coast, Benin, Mali, and others, they [young Africans] are anguished and puzzled about their future. In rural areas the persistent drought has brought impoverishment of the countryside, and young people, faced with unemployment, have found no other solution than to migrate to the cities, where they meet with nothing but difficulties and pitfalls.

Urban youth is in equally difficult straits. The poor match between training and employment has resulted in chronic underemployment among young graduates. . . .

The proclamation of International Youth Year will enable all these young people to take stock of all their problems with a view to seeking the most suitable remedies. It is fitting in this connection that youth feel concerned and participate actively in the building of their future. The development of our continent will not be without the full participation of its youth, who represent the hope of all Africa.

But development must first pass through the establishment of genuine peace, the sole guarantee of a real unfolding. . . .

. . . We have felt it necessary to stress agricultural activities as a solution to unemployment in rural areas, but also because they are an illustration of the fight to control the drought and achieve food self-sufficiency. For that is where the future lies. The future of our continent is in our hands. We have yet to take on the responsibility for our destiny if we do not wish to be the victims of a hardly enviable fate.*

This editorial, written by a Senegalese, makes it clear that Africans are faced with many problems today. It also makes clear the fact that African governments and leaders are aware of the problems and want to resolve them. Complicating the matter is the fact that there are as many theories on the origin of the problems as there are suggested solutions.

One Nigerian economist maintains that development has been pursued "with a confusion of purposes and interests." He believes that "the problem lies with the major agents of development. Each of them propagates an idea of development corresponding to its interests and images of the world." While all Africans do not agree with this, they do agree that the continent is experiencing severe hardship and that steps must be taken to intensify development and to change the present state of affairs.

---

*"Let's be practical" by Ousseynou Gueye in *Forum du Developpement*, June 1985. Reprinted by permission.

THE NEED TO DEVELOP

In African nations, as in other nations of the world, the basic aim of development is to improve the quality of life. Most nations pursue this goal by developing their natural resources, industrializing, and modernizing agriculture. For many African nations, however, this has proved to be a difficult task.

Much of the difficulty stems from the colonial period. For example, the present-day boundaries of most African nations are the same as those set up by the colonial powers. Because little consideration was given to ethnic groups at the time, today most African nations are made up of various ethnic groups that may not speak the same language or may be former rivals. In addition, many ethnic groups are divided among several nations. Such conditions make it very hard to create the sense of national identity that is needed for a nation's people to work together toward common development goals.

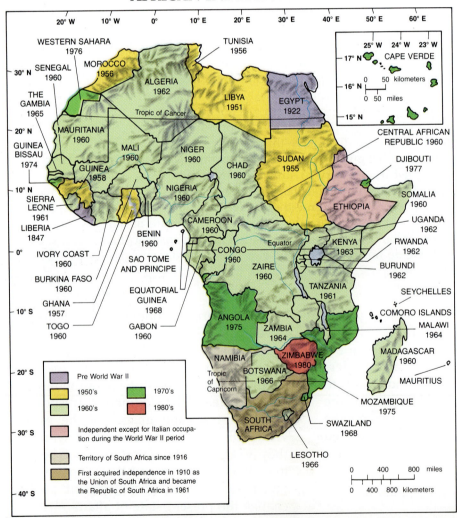

AFRICAN INDEPENDENCE

CHAPTER 7 — CHALLENGES TO DEVELOPMENT

Cattle and goats (above, left) forage in a field littered with abandoned engine parts. Participating in a development project, a farmer (above, right) tries out a new planting technique. Why did some past development projects not have the desired results?

A DECLINING ECONOMY

Following independence and throughout the 1970's and early and mid-1980's, the new African governments worked to develop their economies. Their goal was to export enough manufactured goods, minerals, and cash crops to earn the income needed. While some of the nations tried to do this on their own, several looked to such international agencies as the World Bank for funding and technical assistance.

During this period, some progress was made. Factories and roads were built and farm machinery was brought in. But the methods used were not always appropriate to local conditions and the degree of development hoped for did not come about. There were several reasons for this. One was that there was not enough money, or spare parts, or trained people to operate and maintain the new systems. Another was that the production gains made by some farmers were cancelled out by the high rate of population growth. A third was that not enough research was done before some of the development projects were put into effect. The result of this is described in the newspaper article that follows:

> Down in the rice paddies [in Nigeria], the idea seemed good. So the visiting experts explained it to . . . attentive local farmers.
>
> One way of producing more rice per paddy, the scientists suggested, was to plant rice closer together. Why not try it?
>
> They did—and the rice was planted in a new, close-rowed pattern. But in time it became apparent that one small factor . . .

had been overlooked: Farmers' hoes were too wide to push between the now closely-spaced plants. They could not cultivate properly. And, since they were poor farmers, they weren't able to buy other, narrow-bladed hoes. . . .

On the banks of Lake Turkana in Kenya, a Norwegian aid group decided several years ago to bring Norwegian expertise to bear on the local needs of the Turkana . . . for food and cash. Their plan was to build a fish freezing and processing factory.

Up went the factory walls. In went the first freezer equipment. And along came the problems . . . the Norwegians hadn't realized that it was the Luo people, not the Turkana . . . , who did most of the fishing. But the Luo . . . began using illegal fine-mesh nets to catch large amounts of fish. The Turkana looked for jobs on the land.

Apparently unknown to the Norwegians, the Kenyan government had actually been trying to keep the Luo away from fishing to give the Turkana a chance to develop such skills.

The money the Turkanas did make doing odd jobs was used to buy cattle, which began to overgraze local lands, turning them into arid wastes. A shantytown of workers grew up near the freezer factory, bringing beggars and other problems.

Then the Norwegians found that to freeze the fish would require such large quantities of electricity that none would be available for other uses in the area.

The factory was never completed. Today the building is used for storing dried fish —the same kind of fish local [ethnic groups] have always handled.*

The disappointing rate of development also was due to unfavorable global economic conditions. During the oil shortage of the 1970's, many African countries had to use their limited export earnings to buy high-priced oil from other countries. During the worldwide decline in economic activity of the early 1980's, the prices of the goods that Africa exported fell. During the mid-1980's, the overabundance of oil caused oil prices to drop, which hurt the economies of oil-producing African nations.

These conditions, combined with others such as political unrest, have taken their toll on African nations. Many governments find that they cannot pay back the money they borrowed from international banking agencies. Although they continue to sell cash crops and market their minerals and other goods, the prices they receive in the global marketplace are low. This greatly reduces earnings. At the same time, they are forced to borrow more money to buy food to feed their growing populations. This only increases their debt more.

DROUGHT

In the early and mid-1980's, some countries of Africa experienced one of the worst droughts of the century. One of the nations most severely affected by the drought and the famine that followed was Ethiopia. Its plight did not go unnoticed by the rest of the world, and massive emergency relief campaigns soon got underway. But Ethiopia is only one of 22 African nations that will suffer from the long-term effects of drought. The Republic of Chad, for example, has been suffering not only from drought and famine but civil war as well. Below, an African describes what life has become for many of the people of Chad:

> In an excruciating 12-hour drive to the town of Ati in central Chad, I appreciated the full scope of the drama unfolding in this central African country—dusty tracks littered with thousands of animal carcasses; miles of cultivated fields filled with burnt crops; thousands of displaced persons. . . .

---

*"Tailoring development aid to Africa's needs" by David K. Willis. *The Christian Science Monitor*, August 5, 1985, pp. 11–12. Reprinted by permission from © 1985 The Christian Science Publishing Society. All rights reserved.

CHAPTER 7 — CHALLENGES TO DEVELOPMENT

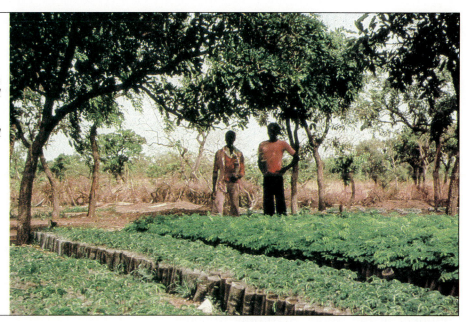

As in other parts of the world, forests in many parts of Africa are being destroyed at an alarming rate because of the collection of firewood, the expansion of agricultural fields, soil erosion, and drought. Here, forestry agents in Burkina Faso examine tree saplings that will later be planted to combat this loss of forests. What other factors besides the loss of forest have made the African drought worse?

We reached Ati late at night and slept in the open air in a compound near Camp One. This is the largest camp for drought victims in Ati. . . .

"I am starving, I have not eaten for 10 days. My 15-year-old daughter starved to death a fortnight [2 weeks] ago," says Hawa Abdel Banat. She arrived in Camp One last September, with seven starving children. Her husband died just before she left her village. "Everything we planted this year died. We were eating . . . wild fruits . . . and wild grass. At 50, I am no longer strong enough to work" she says. Her story is similar to that of the other 12,000 people in this camp. They have exhausted their last resources and are now in extreme desperation. . . . Most people live in makeshift tents made of straw mats, rags and old sacks; but Hawa did not even have a tent. She spent the night on the ground with her children. And the nights are cold in Ati at this time of the year.

The biggest problem is the shortage of food supplies. . . .

Malnutrition is rampant among the children. . . . The worst affected children are taken out to a nutrition centre which is part of Ati's hospital. They are kept until they gain sufficient weight and then they are discharged. Unfortunately, as soon as they come back to the camp they relapse since their parents have no food for them.

Most of the people here, as well as those who were trekking to N'djamena came from the sub-district of Kunjuru. So we decided to go there. . . . The Sultan who received us told us that this used to be the "bread basket" of the region. Not only did Kunjuru once grow sufficient food for its inhabitants but it also fed other less fortunate regions of Chad. This is one of the most worrying aspects in the current Chadian crisis: the fact that the drought has also hit people in the more prosperous parts of the country. . . .*

The drought of the mid-1980's was caused not only by the absence of rainfall. Intensive agricultural use, overgrazing, ill-advised development programs, and population pressures were contributing factors as well.

---

*"Can Chad be saved?" by Djibril Diallo in *West Africa*, December 3, 1984, pp. 2438–2440. Reprinted by permission.

POPULATION GROWTH

Although the African continent is enormous, there are vast areas of desert and rain forest where people generally cannot live. The amount of land available for agriculture and herding, therefore, is not that great. Over the past few decades, Africa's population has begun to catch up with the available land. Farm plots are smaller, which makes it harder for farmers to produce enough to feed their own families let alone raise export crops. In rural areas, there are not enough schools, health clinics, social services, or jobs. This has led many young people to look for work in the already overcrowded cities.

The 2.9 percent yearly population growth rate of Africa is currently the highest of any continent in the world. According to some experts, if the population continues to grow at this rate, it will double in 23 years. Some African countries have tried to resolve the problem by encouraging **family planning**, the use of methods to control and space the number of births. But, as indicated in the newspaper article below, there are some large obstacles to overcome before family planning can have a major impact:

> When delegates from around the world gather in Nairobi this month for the United Nations Women's Decade Conference, Dora Ayonga will be hoeing weeds for six hours in a cornfield. With her day's pay, 48 cents, she will walk to the village market here to buy the beans and corn that keep her husband and children alive.
>
> As the U.N.'s Decade for Women . . . draws to a close, Ayonga is looking for a way not to have another baby. The 23-year-old woman has been pregnant five times in the past five years. Her four children (one baby died) are malnourished. . . . Her husband, Silas, who is out of work, wants another child.
>
> The cost of not getting pregnant—the price of a round-trip bus ticket to a family-planning clinic . . . is $2.50, the equivalent of more than five days of hoeing weeds, a week's food for Ayonga's family, . . .
>
> After thousands of women from around the world have come to Nairobi . . . , assessed the progress of womankind and gone home, Ayonga will, in all likelihood, get pregnant again. And the growing family she wishes would stop growing will be hers to support for another decade or two of 15-hour days. . . .
>
> . . . "If you haven't got children," says Chrispus Ashioya, who grew up in the village [of Ebulakayi] and now lives in Nairobi, "you are nothing in my village. You cannot be recognized as a responsible person. If you speak, people will not listen to you."
>
> Women, who usually do not inherit property, create long-term security by creating children, who one day can take care of them. Deprived of job opportunities and averaging about half the formal education of men, a Kenyan woman's one

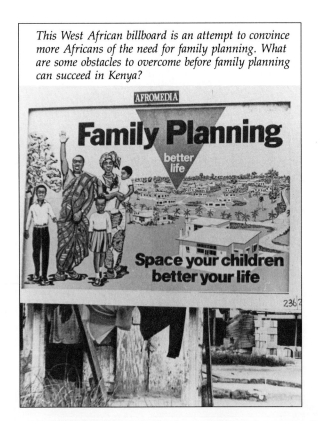

This West African billboard is an attempt to convince more Africans of the need for family planning. What are some obstacles to overcome before family planning can succeed in Kenya?

major route to respectability is to be a . . . mother. . . .

The catch in all this . . . , for Kenyan women, is that they, not their husbands, end up caring for and supporting the [growing] number of babies. . . .

Mikola Sanda, 31, who . . . now lives in the seaport city of Mombasa, says that male attitudes about children have not changed at all in western Kenya despite the government's mandate for family planning. "They hear it as a song that the government sings, they hear it on the Voice of Kenya radio," she says. "But they still believe that to have many children . . . gives them a big name."

1. What were some of the factors that affected African economic development after independence?
2. How has drought affected some African nations?
3. What has happened to Africa's population over the past few decades? What effect has this had?

FACING THE CHALLENGES

Some African nations are joining together to try to solve their problems. This is being done not only on a nation-by-nation basis but also through regional and continent-wide cooperation. One of the foremost cooperative agencies is the Organization of African Unity (OAU), founded in 1963. It promotes economic cooperation among members, tries to settle political disputes, and strongly supports African liberation movements.

In 1980, OAU leaders drew up a blueprint for economic revival of Africa that called for self-sufficiency in food production and in-

*"African Women: Still Exploited On Eve of U.N. Conference" by Blaine Harden in *The Washington Post*, July 6, 1985, pp. A1, A16. Reprinted by permission.

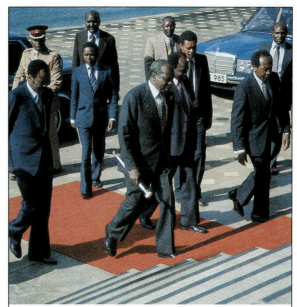

Some of the leaders and officials of the 50 member nations of the OAU are shown arriving for a meeting in Kenya. What did OAU leaders request from lenders in 1985 to ease Africa's debt crisis?

dustrial development by the year 2000, the construction and expansion of transcontinental highways and railroads, the increase of intra-African trade, and the creation and strengthening of regional economic organizations.

Five years later, the OAU reaffirmed and modified its plan but admitted that Africa was near "economic collapse." Pointing to an unjust world economic system, natural disasters, and some domestic policy shortcomings, they called for lenders to ease the debt crisis somewhat by extending the time for repaying the loans. At the same time, however, they insisted that "the external debts are obligations that our member states . . . have to honor."

The efforts by the OAU are not the only ones being made toward African development. Inroads also are being made both jointly and individually in the areas of education, literacy, health care, and self-help programs, to name a few.

CASE STUDY
AFRICA

WOMEN AND DEVELOPMENT

Women in Africa share a common desire for a better life for themselves and their children. They are concerned about many of the same problems as women elsewhere. In addition, as they make up over 70 percent of the agricultural workforce, they are concerned about the demands made on them. In 1984, 40 delegations from all over Africa met "to review and appraise the integration of African women into development, and to come up with a plan of action for the future." In the magazine article below, their findings are discussed:

The delegations agreed . . . that some positive steps have occurred for the advancement and integration of women in African development. But many obstacles still hinder the full integration of women into development and African women have not achieved full equality with men.

"The role of women in the future of Africa is . . . important . . . because women constitute one of the most valuable and dependable resources which Africa cannot afford to waste," Mrs. Shahani [Assistant Secretary-General of the UN Centre for Social Development and Humanitarian Affairs] said.

However, delegates noted that to develop African women, many of the obstacles to Africa's own development . . . must be removed.

"The greatest burden of poverty in Africa is carried by women. They suffer first and the most by the absence of technology and other developments in Africa," said [Tanzanian] President Julius Nyerere. . . .

"We must first alleviate poverty to provide services needed for the emancipation of women in Africa," he said. But President Nyerere also noted that economic development alone will not totally solve the plight of African women.

"Economic development is essential to women's development but does not necessarily mean women's development. In the country where there is wealth women do not benefit from that wealth," he said.

The major obstacle to African women's development in the areas . . . cited by the African delegations was the problem of tradition and social attitudes. These traditions and attitudes often conflict with laws for equality and are the hardest to combat within African societies.

Nawal el Saadawi, an Egyptian medical doctor . . . defined the problem of African women in a different light.

"The unequal distribution of wealth is the main obstacle not only to women but to the development of African countries," she said. . . .

. . . Ms Saadawi also said that the concept of development must be viewed differently when one talks about African women. "African women work and they are integrated in development. But they don't receive wages and they have double work. Women must be given rights, not more work," she said. . . .

"Africa is still very dependent on the west. . . . [We] must redefine development as it relates to Africa's political and economic independence and as it relates to women . . .," she explained.

"Women have to redefine what they mean by development in an African and Arab context," Ms Saadawi said. "Women must organize themselves and have power politically and economically."

"Women must insist that action takes place for their development," President Nyerere said. "No group can be liberated by others. The struggle for women's development has to be conducted by women not in opposition to men, but as part of the social development of the nation."

1. What did the delegations determine was needed for women's development?
2. What strategies would you suggest African governments implement to further women's development?

---

*"African governments plan strategies for women's development" in *MOTO*, November 1984, pp. 22–23. Reprinted by permission.

LITERACY CHART

This Senegalese literacy chart, on which appear words in the Mandingo language, helps students of all ages learn how to read and write by linking everyday objects with the shapes of letters used to spell their names. This modern literacy training method ties together the learning of reading and writing with a person's cultural, economic, technical, and political environment.

					word						word
		C	c	c	cakka				O	o	xooda
		e	e	e	kande				P	p	tepu
		g	g	g	tiga				r	r	fúníír
		J	j	j	jambangine				W	w	ewela
		n	n	n	siine				Y	y	yoot

EDUCATION

During the colonial period, most Africans were denied access to education. As a result, after independence, African governments made it a priority to educate their young people. Many parents believe that education is "a passport to life."

While most Africans are pleased about the emphasis on education, some experts say that schools should be more practical and should teach subjects more relevant to such current national needs as farming and industry. Pointing out that today's educated young people want to work in offices, not in fields, they want the schools to prepare them to live in and develop the rural areas.

One nation making a special effort in education is Zimbabwe. There, the government has set up a special school for young Zimbabweans disabled in the struggle for the nation's freedom. Several of the veterans tell why they feel their education is important to them and to their country:

". . . We fought this liberation war to its end, till we came back here. Then I thought the most important thing I could do was to go back to school. I'm disabled so I thought: 'If I learn, then I can work with my head.'" (Lovemore Choromari, 22)

". . . In 1980 we were taken to a rehabilitation camp where I met a number of other ex-combatants who were disabled. Some had amputated legs or arms, some had different wounds. We didn't know what we were going to do in Zimbabwe since we were all disabled. A good number of us . . . started to have meetings about going to school." (Josephat Zenda, 26)

"I'd gone as far as Grade 7 in 1974, when I started having difficulty in getting finance to further my studies. . . . There was nothing for me to do, so in 1975 I joined the revolution. But my mind never changed about the subject of education. All the time I was fighting, because without it you can't contribute anything of importance to the nation. So as soon as the war was over, I was desperate to get back to school." (Edmund Manyange, 23)*

HEALTH CARE

Health care is another area in which strides are being made. This is essential because the tropical environment of much of Africa plays host to a variety of serious diseases. Because these diseases are found to the greatest degree in rural areas, many African governments are trying to shift the emphasis in health care from urban hospitals and clinics to rural health programs. These programs, which are community-based, stress both prevention and cure. Included are sanitation education to help control waterborne diseases and the training of traditional health-care workers to help offset the shortage of formally trained doctors and nurses. Below, a journalist offers an example of the benefits of such training in Somalia:

The French words on this poster in Burkina Faso read, "For our health, drink water from a properly managed well." Why is the African continent host to a variety of serious diseases?

> Batula Hassan . . . lives and works in a tiny fishing village called Gizera. . . . She is the village midwife, a member of that caste of women who throughout countless generations have learned from mother and grandmother the mysteries of how to tend a woman in labour and bring a newborn baby into the world. . . .
>
> Batula first began to help the women of Gizera deliver their babies at the age of eleven, when her grandmother who used to be the midwife . . . became old and weak. . . . For some years after her grandmother died, there was another midwife in the village called Mumena, whom she also helped. Neither of them ever had any formal education, or any professional medical training, but they had good hands and success with most of the deliveries. If there was a crisis, or diseases set in after the birth, mother or child or both might die. At that stage the only known cause was Allah's [God's] displeasure.
>
> The nationwide literacy campaign . . . , launched in 1973, was a turning point for Batula. Four students were sent to Gizera to teach the people how to read and write and . . . Batula made sure that one of them became a guest in her house. "I was always keen to learn what I could about health and how to prevent disease. Also to read and write because I couldn't read the labels on medicine bottles or health posters. . . ."
>
> Once Batula had mastered a little learning, she offered herself as a volunteer assistant at the dispensary [clinic] nearby. The nurse himself called on Haji Ali and persuaded him to allow Batula to go for

---

*"Disabled fighters set on self-reliance" by Biddy Partridge in *MOTO*, November 1982, pp. 28–29. Reprinted by permission.

training at the health centre in Afgoi town, the district headquarters. . . .

The course lasted four months. Batula learnt first aid and hygiene, and how to use forceps . . . and sterilized scissors. . . . She learnt how to give injections and how to sterilize the needle to avoid infection. . . . Proudly she displays her certificate from Afgoi Health Centre: "Umuliso. Midwife BATULA HASSAN has qualified in First Aid and General Hygiene."

Batula is certain that her techniques have improved. . . . Since 1975, no woman in Gizera has died in childbirth. . . .

. . . Batula is quietly unstoppable. "I enjoy my work. Even when I am tired I think about the ones who need my help, and I see that it is something for the community."*

SELF-RELIANCE

Many people in Africa believe that the keys to development and a more prosperous future lie in self-reliance and economic cooperation. As a result, in many African nations, self-help programs are encouraged. One such nation is Tanzania. Below, a Norwegian journalist describes what he found when he visited a Tanzanian village:

> In the small village of Saja in the Southern Highlands of Tanzania, only a few people were around. The village seemed silent, the place deserted. We stopped the car to look around and soon discovered why.
>
> Down in a hollow there were hundreds of people, all of them busy making bricks. Thousands of bricks were lying around drying in the sun. In a few weeks they would be ready for use.
>
> "This is the result of our policy of self-reliance", said Saja's village chairman.
>
> Saja's village is located in Iringa District, in one of the most underdeveloped parts of Tanzania where disease and malnutrition are common. The soil is thin, the crops are poor. It does not often rain. The only source of water is a swamp below the village. The water is polluted, and the swamp dries out in the dry season.
>
> "The bricks have to be made in the rainy season when we have enough water", says the chairman.
>
> We were surprised at the sight which met our eyes. Never before had we seen bricks being made with such energy, and without the advantage of any special tools or equipment. Each brick is made separately by hand. Men, women and children, almost the whole village, join in. But why the enthusiasm?
>
> "We have got to believe that we ourselves can change our lives for the better", says the village chairman.
>
> The people . . . have already built a school from hand-made bricks. There it is, a monument to their hard work, surrounded by neatly-planted flower-beds.
>
> "We began to make bricks for a dispensary when we were told that if we built the building, equipment and staff would be provided". . . .
>
> Tanzania's Minister of State . . . explains: "We advise villagers that if they construct a building, with UNICEF's help we will equip it. We do things this way around because we want the villagers themselves to lead the way in their development. Central authorities and international aid organizations cannot develop people. People can only develop themselves".*

1. For what does the OAU blueprint for Africa's revival call?
2. Why have some African nations made education a priority?
3. Why are many African nations stressing rural health programs? What do these programs involve?
4. Why are self-help programs being encouraged in many African nations?

---

*"A member of one of the oldest professions" by Maggie Black in UNICEF NEWS, pp. 10–11. Reprinted by permission.

*"Building bricks for progress" by Arild Vollan in *Development Forum*, January–February, 1980, UN Division for Economic and Social Information, p. 10. Reprinted by permission.

EXPLORATION
AFRICA

For there to be development and progress in African nations, there must be unity among the people. Most African governments recognize that a single common language would greatly reduce misunderstanding and help to unite their people. But choosing a language that would be acceptable to everyone is not an easy task. Within the borders of each nation, hundreds of languages may be spoken, and across the continent, there are more than 1500 separate languages.

Some Africans have suggested that Swahili, also known as Kiswahili, be adopted as the common language for the continent. It is estimated that about 50 million people in the world can communicate in Kiswahili today. In the newspaper interview that follows, a Ghanaian student studying Kiswahili at the University of Dar es Salaam in Tanzania explains why he thinks more countries should make Kiswahili their national language. Read the interview, and study the map that accompanies it. Then defend or refute the following statements:

1. The nations of Africa should have a single common language.
2. Kiswahili is an ideal choice for a single common language for Africa.
3. A foreign language would be a better choice than Kiswahili for a single common language for Africa.
4. Most people in Africa will be receptive to a national language.

. . . Kiswahili is the most widely spoken language in the eastern part of Africa. For the people of western Africa, learning and knowing Kiswahili, therefore, brings them closer to their brothers in eastern Africa. . . .

I think you will also agree that Kiswahili is on the way of becoming one of the major world languages. A knowledge of two or three such languages puts one at an advantage. Wherever he goes, he can communicate with less problems. It is like having an international currency in one's pocket. . . .

. . . Some African countries have adopted French and English as their official national languages. Of course, if the French and the British had not come and colonized, such a strange thing as having French as a "national language" of an African state would be unheard of.

Declaring a foreign language a "national language" when less than 10 per cent of the population are conversant with that language is nothing but the height of absurdity. It is only a handful [of] educated elite who use such an alien "national language."

What makes matters complicated is the fact that however committed you are in trying to spread and popularize such languages to the masses, it becomes very difficult for the majority to grasp them. There is no relationship at all between these alien languages and the vernaculars [local languages].

If, on the other hand, a language like Kiswahili is introduced in Ghana or in Nigeria and efforts are made to popularize it, after a few years you are likely to have more people capable of speaking at least broken Kiswahili as compared to those capable of speaking English. . . .

To most Africans, Kiswahili is easier to learn compared to alien languages. This is explained by the fact that it is predominantly a Bantu language, and therefore has a close relationship with other Bantu languages. My experience is that even before I grasped the ABC's of Kiswahili, I could not be lost completely when listening to people conversing in the language. You at least get a vague idea of what the speakers are talking about, though you are unable to participate in the conversation.

With a completely alien language like English, things are different. You have to go through a rigorous study in order to be conversant with the basics of it. . . .

Another advantage of Kiswahili is that it is likely to be acceptable among different [ethnic groups]. In Africa there are [ethnic group] rivalries. . . . Given such a situation, picking one of the

THE KISWAHILI LANGUAGE

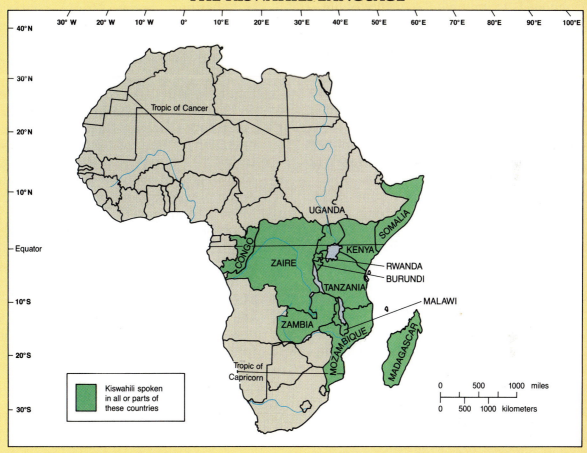

vernaculars and declaring it a national language will not only be scratching a healing wound, but the exercise will also fail. Some people will not accept the proposal, even if they have no strong reasons for their refusal.

In Ghana, for example, the major vernaculars include Akan, Ewe, Nzema, Dagbani, Hausa and Ga. If you suggest that one of these languages be adopted as a national language, you will be inviting trouble. The same problem would arise in Nigeria, Kenya, Uganda, Tanzania, etc, if one dares to suggest that one of the major vernaculars be adopted as a national language.

Fortunately, a good number of people in most of the African countries look at Kiswahili as a neutral African language. They are ready to adopt it as a national language without feeling that a certain [ethnic group] has been favoured and honoured.

Frankly, African states—consisting of different ethnic groups (most of them are)—will have no choice but to adopt Kiswahili, if at all they are determined to settle the national language question once and for all. People capable of seeing decades ahead have no doubt about this.*

*"Kiswahili is spreading" by Henry Muhanika in the *Tanzanian Sunday News*, March 30, 1980, p. 5. Reprinted by permission.

AFRICA

CHAPTER 7 REVIEW

POINTS TO REMEMBER

1. The basic aim of development in African nations is to improve the quality of life.
2. For most African nations, development has been made more difficult by decisions made during the colonial period.
3. Following independence and throughout the 1970's and early and mid-1980's, African governments worked to develop their economies. Although progress was made, the degree of development hoped for did not come about, partly because of unfavorable global economic conditions.
4. In the early and mid-1980's, some countries of Africa experienced one of the worst droughts of the century. The drought was caused not only by the absence of rainfall but also by intensive agricultural use, overgrazing, development programs that were ill-advised, and population pressures.
5. Over the past few decades, Africa's population has begun to catch up with the amount of land available for agriculture and herding. Some African countries have tried to resolve the problem by encouraging family planning.
6. Some African nations are joining together on a nation-by-nation, a regional, or a continent-wide basis to try to solve their problems. One of the foremost agencies promoting economic integration and cooperation is the Organization of African Unity.
7. African governments have made the education of young people a priority.
8. Many African governments are trying to shift the emphasis in health care from urban hospitals and clinics to community-based rural health programs that stress prevention and cure.
9. Most Africans believe that self-reliance and economic cooperation are the keys to development and to a more prosperous future.

VOCABULARY

Identify

World Bank   Organization of African Unity (OAU)   Swahili   Kiswahili

Define

family planning

DISCUSSING IMPORTANT IDEAS

1. Do you think the statement, "The future stems from the past," relates to African development? Give examples to support your answer.
2. The state of the global economy has had a great influence on economic development in Africa. What does this indicate to you about the interdependence of nations?

3. The huge amount of aid that has been provided to the drought-stricken areas of Africa is for some a controversial issue. They say that although the aid is appreciated, it is not the solution to the problem. What do you think the problem is? Do you agree or disagree that aid is not the solution? Explain. What do you think has to be done to solve the problem?
4. Do you agree with the view that for Africans self-reliance and economic cooperation are the key to development and to a more prosperous future? Explain your answer.

DEVELOPING SKILLS

IDENTIFYING THE MAIN IDEA

The object of most written material is to inform the reader about someone or something. Generally, the material is divided into paragraphs, each of which contains at least one sentence that presents the *main idea,* or principal focus, of that paragraph. The other sentences explain or give detail or description about the main idea.

When the main idea is expressed in the first sentence, it is known as the *topic sentence.* It provides focus for the entire paragraph. If the main idea is expressed in the last sentence, it is known as a *summary sentence.* It sums up what the paragraph is about. At times, however, the main idea is stated in a sentence in the middle of the paragraph or is not stated directly in one sentence at all.

The following steps will help you identify the main idea of a paragraph:

1. Read the paragraph carefully, and determine the general focus or subject.
2. Read the paragraph again, sentence by sentence. For each, ask yourself what would happen if that sentence were not in the paragraph. Would the rest of the sentences tie together and make sense? If the answer to the question is no, you probably have identified the sentence that contains the main idea. In that case, identify the idea.
3. Check the remaining sentences to determine if they support the idea put forth in the sentence you have just chosen. Do they describe, explain, or give details about what you have identified as the main idea?

Look, for example, at the following paragraph about Africa:

In African nations, as in other nations of the world, the basic aim of development is to improve the quality of life. Most nations pursue this goal by developing their natural resources, industrializing, and modernizing agriculture. For most African nations, however, this has proved to be a difficult task.

In this example, the second sentence speaks of a goal and explains how that goal is achieved. You have to refer to the first sentence, however, to know that the paragraph focuses on development and that the goal or aim is to improve the quality of life. The third sentence explains that the task is difficult. But, once again, you have to refer to the first sentence to determine what that task is. The second and third sentences, then, give more information about, or support, what is presented in the first sentence. Thus, the sentence beginning with "In African nations" is the topic sentence, stating the main idea that the basic aim of development in Africa is to improve the quality of life.

For further practice in this skill, apply the three steps suggested earlier to the first paragraph under the heading "Facing the Challenges" on page 109.

AFRICA

UNIT 1 REVIEW

SUMMARY

Africa stretches across the equator. It spans nearly 60 lines of latitude and has climates and physical features as varied as its peoples. Rain falls too little or too much, and the varied landscape has long challenged human settlement. Also, each of Africa's 54 nations has had to adapt to many different ethnic groups, languages, religions, and customs.

For a great many years, Westerners mistakenly thought that Africans were isolated and unenlightened. But the peoples of Africa have a rich historical tradition. Long before Greece or Rome existed, Ethiopia had conquered Egypt and was leading the civilized world in culture and conquest. Until recently, many parts of the African interior had little or no contact with the non-African world. Although many early Africans were farmers who lived in small communities, some Africans between the west coast and the interior of the continent actively traded with one another. In East African and Madagascan ports, Africans also exchanged goods with Greeks, Romans, Chinese, Indonesians, and Indians. Many of these commercial contacts, contributed to the rise of early African city-states and empires that in time became centers of commerce and learning. Later, Western merchants sought trading privileges in southern and eastern African ports and in the Suez.

The Atlantic slave trade and Europe's discovery of Africa's vast natural resources had a major impact on the economies and social structures of Africans. By the 1800's and early 1900's, Europeans had colonized most of the African continent. In time, many Africans came to resent European rule. Their resistance finally resulted in independence for most African countries.

Today Africa is beset with many problems. Of major concern is economic development. Africa's goals are to become more self-sufficient in food production and less dependent on goods from other countries. To this end, many African nations have joined together to bring about change.

REVIEW QUESTIONS

1. How have physical environment and history influenced African life?
2. In what ways are Nigeria, South Africa, and Kenya the same? Different?
3. How is the political and economic independence of Africa related to the political and economic independence of Africa's girls and women?

SUGGESTED ACTIVITIES

1. Working in a small group, create a series of collages on outline maps of Africa to illustrate physical environment, history, the arts, language, dress, and family.
2. Listen to and compare music and songs from African countries with songs from different regions of your country.
3. Working in a small group, make a file of articles about Africa and Africans. Compare the topics and themes.
4. Write to United Nations representatives of two or more African countries. Ask them to reply to these questions: What do you consider your country's major achievements in the past 25 years? Its major problems? What do you think is the role of your country in the continent? In the world? What is your hope for the future of your country? Share the replies with the class, discussing reactions to them.

AFRICA

COMPARING CULTURES

Every people and culture is different. At the same time, every people and culture is the same in many ways. Very often, however, people from outside a culture view it more in terms of the ways in which it is different from their own than the ways in which it is the same. This view often is the result of false impressions gained from movies, television, the print media, and beliefs put forth by others.

The chart that follows lists the images some Africans have of the United States and Americans and those that some Americans have of Africa and Africans. Compare and contrast the two sets of images. Then answer these questions:

1. From where do you think each image came?
2. Which images differ from the reality as you know it? How does each differ?
3. What do you think can be done to avoid false images from being formed?
4. What do the images tell you about the culture that holds them?

Some Africans Believe That:	Some Americans Believe That:
1. All Americans are rich.	1. Africa is a country.
2. America is a land of academic opportunities for everyone.	2. All Africans speak "African."
3. All Americans are hard working.	3. Africans do not eat meat.
4. America is an "old" nation.	4. The English language is rarely spoken in Africa.
5. America is technologically advanced.	5. Africa has no urban areas.
6. Americans are free to do whatever they want.	6. Africa has no history.
7. Most Americans mind their own business, and no one interferes in their lives.	7. Africa is still "uncivilized."
8. Most Americans have guns.	8. Most African men have more than one wife.
9. Americans always disagree with Soviets.	9. African females are not educated and have no place in African society.

Unit Two

China, the world's oldest living civilization, probably always has been the most populous nation on earth. In addition to its long history and large population, it always has had a rich and varied culture. While in the past the Chinese preferred to develop their land and their culture without foreign influence, in recent years they have opened the door to other nations and other peoples. China has modernized and industrialized and rapidly is becoming an important part of the world community. For these reasons, it is of value to see the Chinese as they see themselves, to understand how they have reached the point where they are today, and to become aware of where they want to be tomorrow.

CONTENTS

8	THE LAND UNDER HEAVEN	122
9	THE MANDATE OF HEAVEN	140
10	THE FEW AND THE MANY	156
11	THE CHINESE HERITAGE	172
12	THE CHINESE REVOLUTION	186
13	CHINA AFTER MAO	202
14	DAILY LIFE IN MODERN CHINA	218

CHINA

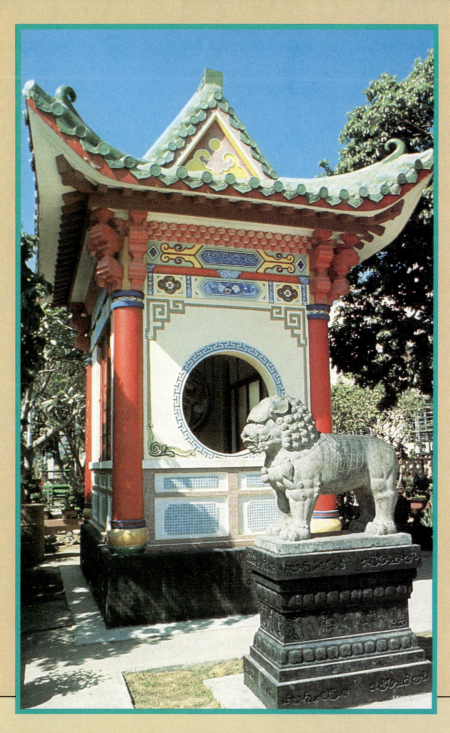

CHAPTER 8
THE LAND UNDER HEAVEN

1. What is the Chinese attitude toward the natural environment?
2. What are the major physical features of China?

> In far-off times the Universe . . . was an enormous egg. One day the egg split open; its upper half became the sky, its lower half the earth, and from it emerged P'an Ku [Pan Gu], [the first] man. Every day he grew ten feet [3.05 meters] taller, the sky ten feet [3.05 meters] higher, the earth ten feet [3.05 meters] thicker. After eighteen thousand years P'an Ku [Pan Gu] died. His head split and became the sun and moon, while his blood filled the rivers and seas. His hair became the forests and meadows, his perspiration the rain, his breath the wind, his voice the thunder—and his fleas our ancestors.*

This legend of Pan Gu was developed by the early Chinese to explain the origins of China. The huge egg symbolized **yang and yin,** the major forces of life. From the union of yang and yin, Pan Gu was born.

Belief in yang and yin was important to the people who lived in the Land Under Heaven, the term the early Chinese used to describe the territory on which they built their settlements. The Land Under Heaven was centered at first in the valley of the Huang He, or Yellow River, of East Asia. Here, the first Chinese settlements developed more than 4000 years ago. In time, the people of the valley expanded their control into neighboring areas and formed the land of China. They brought together a number of **ethnic groups,** social groups each having its own culture. By 2200 BC, the population may have been close to 13,500,000.

In spite of their conquests, the Huang He people, who became known as Chinese, were mostly cut off from other civilizations, largely because of such geographic factors as seas, mountains, and rain forests. This lack of outside contacts, however, aided in the formation of a common culture throughout China. With little outside interference, the Chinese were able to develop a unique civilization that had a strong sense of its own identity.

These early Chinese felt deeply about the land, and their way of life was rooted in the natural environment. They viewed Heaven and Earth as one and believed that each influenced the other through the activity of yang and yin.

The workings of nature were observed carefully. Astrologers and recordkeepers studied and noted the movement of stars and planets as well as any natural occurrences. They held that such happenings were **portents,** or hints of future changes. These changes might include a military victory, a new government, or bad economic times.

It also was believed that human behavior had an effect on nature. If human actions, especially those of the ruler, were in harmony with nature, the portents would be favorable. But if human actions upset the balance of nature, such natural and human disasters as floods and political chaos would follow. Thus, the early Chinese made every effort to live in accord with their surroundings.

---

*_The Arts of China_ by Michael Sullivan, 1977, University of California Press, p. 13.

VARIETY OF THE LAND

Today China has a total area of nearly 3.7 million square miles (9.62 million square kilometers). It is the second largest nation in Asia and the third largest in the world. Few nations have as diverse a natural environment. This can be seen below as a Chinese author describes a railway journey from Guangzhou in southern China to the capital, Beijing, in northern China:

> The first part of [Chu Pin's] journey took him northward through his own province of [Guangdong]. . . . The province was separated from central China by high mountain ranges. . . .
> . . . [Chu Pin's] train took him across the mountain range and plunged into the valley of Hunan. Everything changed: the climate, the language, the people's dress, and the flora—the fruit trees and flowers. . . . [Guangdong] was subtropical, with palm trees, pomelos (a kind of grapefruit), and Chu Pin's favorite fruit, the leechee.
> . . . Hunan was the rice bowl of China. As the train hurtled past the mountainous region he saw tall bamboo forests, vast green hillsides with luxuriant vegetation, and cataracts [waterfalls] and winding torrents. Everywhere he saw terraced rice fields. The air was fresh and cool, but as soon as the train descended to the plains, Chu Pin felt hot, for summer was beginning.
> Most impressive was the number of streams and canals, for this was the basin of the [Dongking] Lake, the biggest lake in China. . . . The lake was just south of the great Yangtze River. . . . The land was flat and level, and the great river bent and curved in its meanderings. . . .
> . . . Chu Pin took the train right through [Henan]. He was in North China now. . . .
> . . . Chu Pin noticed that the Northern Chinese were taller in stature than the Southern Chinese. They also seemed poorer, for instead of the brick houses of South China, he saw principally mud houses. The water buffalo of the South had disappeared, and the beasts of burden now were mules, donkeys, and horses. Instead of the rice paddies covered by water, he saw wheat fields standing in dry land, and instead of sugar cane, he saw corn. . . . And everywhere, he saw a grayish dust, and denuded hills . . . , so different from the generally red soil of the hills in the south.*

1. Where were the first Chinese settlements centered?
2. How does modern-day China compare in size to other nations?

MOUNTAINS

Mountains cover one-third of China, including the southeastern coastal region and inland areas of the northeast and west. These mountains have always fascinated the Chinese. In the past, they held that the mountain ridges were the creation of a magic dragon. Only the dragon could shake and change mountain ridges and make them run in all directions.

Of the 14 highest mountain peaks in the world, nine are in China or on its borders. The highest mountain ranges are concentrated in the west. They include the Altai, Tianshan, Qilian, Kunlun, Karakorum, Tanggula, Hengduan, Gangdise, and Himalayas. Below, a Chinese explorer describes his travels in China's mountainous west:

> Driving northwest from Kangding, we climbed steeply among breathtaking snow-clad mountains that seemed to continue forever. . . . We set out amid pines and birches, which gradually gave way to juni-

---

The Chinese Way of Life by Lin Yutang, 1959, World Book Inc., pp. 10–15.

pers and rhododendrons. Below 4,000 meters (13,000 feet) above sea level the trees ended and there were only low shrubs, grasses, and a profusion of blue and yellow poppies. . . .

On July 6, near Nam Co, Zhang [one of the author's companions] came down with mountain sickness. . . . We rushed Zhang to the nearest hospital. . . .

There we learned . . . that mountain sickness, caused by insufficient oxygen, is common among drivers along the Lhasa-Golmud road. When their trucks are stuck at such high elevation, the drivers strain themselves in freeing the vehicles, at the same time suffering from the hostile weather that can aggravate mountain sickness or cause pneumonia or both. . . .

But miraculously Zhang began to recover, and within days he was well enough to travel. . . .

On the road once more we continued north, climbing higher and higher until we arrived at Tanggula Pass—at 5,300 meters (17,388 feet) the highest point we were to reach during our expedition. . . . From here we had 600 kilometers [360 miles] to go before we reached Golmud, only 3,200 meters [10,560 feet] above sea level. Slowly, then, we descended from the roof of the world to what were merely the eaves.

Over the next day or two we saw many antelopes, a few wolves, and a lot of emptiness. There were practically no settlements along this stretch of road save occasional highway maintenance and military stations.*

In eastern China, mountains are generally lower than in the west, and there are many highland regions. Northeastern China, also known as Dongbei (Manchuria), is partly composed of mountains that are heavily forested and highlands. In southeastern and south central China, the 3000-to-4000-foot

---

*"People of China's Far Provinces," by Wong How-Man in *National Geographic*, Vol. 165, No. 3, March 1984, pp. 291–293, 294, 300.

The Great Wall of China, begun in the third century BC, was built to protect China from invaders from the north. What type of protection from foreign invaders does the environment provide?

(914.4-to-1219.2-meter) peaks are favorite tourist spots because of their lush vegetation, wide variety of animal life, and the many ancient temples and monasteries studding their slopes.

1. How much of China is mountainous? Where are the tallest peaks located?
2. How did the Chinese regard their mountains in the past?
3. Why are the mountains of southeastern and south central China a favorite tourist spot?

DESERT, STEPPE, AND PLAIN

China has desert areas, as well as mountains, in the northwest. North of the Kunlun Mountains is one of the world's largest and driest deserts—the Takla Makan. Farther north along China's border with Mongolia is the Gobi Desert. Both the Takla Makan and the Gobi are rich in mineral resources, but few people live in either place.

South and east of the deserts is the **steppe,** or generally treeless grasslands. The nomadic herders known as Mongolians who live in the steppe use it as grazing land for their sheep and ponies. Since the area gets relatively little rainfall, there is little agriculture. Below, a writer describes the life of two young people and their families who live on the steppe:

> Sugula's and Drol's families belong to the same work team. Each family is in charge of a thousand sheep. When the pasturage in one area is exhausted, Sugula's and Drol's families move on to new grazing grounds. Because they have to roam about so much, they live in tents which are called yurts. The tents are shaped like great mushrooms. . . .
> Whenever the pasturage in one area is exhausted, Sugula and Drol help their families pack their belongings in carts. They take down the yurt felts. . . . Then they take apart the framework of the yurts and strap the individual pieces of wood to the sides of the carts. . . . With the herders on horseback driving the flocks, and the older people and the children taking turns guiding the plodding oxen or getting a ride on the carts, they set off for greener pastures. . . .
> [Sugula's] grandparents live in a three-room brick and stone house in the headquarters town. . . .
> Most of the other people who live in the little town belong to a work team that builds sheds, pens, and kunluns. A kunlun is an enclosure protected by low walls to keep the cattle out. The grass in the kunluns is cut periodically and stored away in the sheds. It will be used to tide the livestock over the leanest winter months.
> Then there are snows and blinding blizzards, and the bucket-shaped stoves in the

This photograph of the dunes of the Takla Makan desert was taken from a National Aeronautics and Space Administration (NASA) satellite with a special camera. Many of the dunes are curved, and some run for up to 20 miles (32 kilometers). In the upper right portion of the photo, part of the desert shown is covered by snow. What other deserts are there in China?

CHAPTER 8   THE LAND UNDER HEAVEN

Most nomadic herders who live on the steppes of China live in yurts like the one pictured here. These portable dwellings can house entire families and protect the occupants from snow and other harsh weather. Warmth generally is provided by bucket-shaped stoves. Why do nomads find this type of housing convenient?

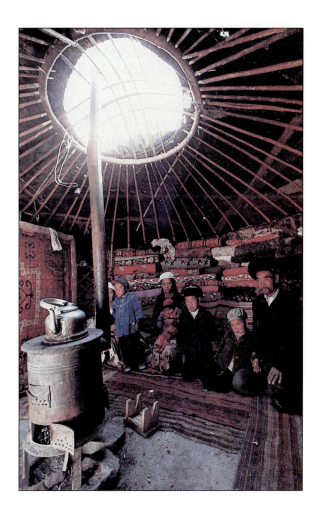

yurts glow red with burning chips of dried cattle dung. The chips . . . serve for fuel here, as wood is so scarce. Meals are hearty, consisting of steamed millet and noodles and hard cheese and great hunks of . . . barbecued mutton. All is washed down with strong tea and fiery drafts of liquor. . . . This food fuels the herders, who must wander far and wide searching for scant pasturage for their gaunt flocks, and who must mount long night watches against the ravenous wolves whose howling floats over the steppelands. . . .

But in this land not all is harsh. Winter gives way to the green loveliness of spring, spangled with flowers, melodic with the song of the lark. It is a time of plenty. The rich lushness of the following summer draws the nomads north again until the chill of early autumn drives them south once more.*

---

*From *Holding Up the Sky: Young People in China,* copyright ©1983 by Margaret Rau. Reprinted by permission of the publisher, E.P. Dutton, Inc.

South of the steppe are the plains of northern China. In the far northeast is the Manchurian Plain, which is almost totally surrounded by mountains. In the south of the Plain, where there is an opening that provides an outlet to the sea, are some of China's best harbors. Farther inland, the Plain has fertile soil and large deposits of coal and iron. These deposits have made the Manchurian Plain the leading industrial area of China.

South of the Manchurian Plain lies the flat, wide North China Plain, most of which is covered with **loess.** This fertile, yellow soil carried in by the wind from the Gobi Desert makes the Plain a rich farming area. It also is an industrial area of coal mines, steel and cotton mills, chemical plants, and factories. Most of these industries are centered around the large cities of Beijing, Tianjin, Xi'an, and Taiyuan.

1. Where are China's desert areas located? In what resources are they rich?
2. Where is the steppe located? Who lives there?
3. How do the people of the plains make a living?

RIVERS

China is a land of rivers. Most of the major rivers begin in the mountainous west and run through China's north, central, and southern regions. Of the northern rivers, the Huang He is the longest. It flows slightly less than 3000 miles (4800 kilometers) before emptying into the sea. Because it often floods over a large area, it has been called "China's Sorrow."

The longest river in Asia, and the third longest in the world—the Yangtze (Chang Jiang)—is in central China. In many areas, its valley is agricultural. In addition, it contains nearly half the industry of south China. Most of the industry is concentrated around the large cities of Shanghai, Wuhan, and Changsha. Below, a passenger on a boat trip describes a journey on the Yangtze:

> Mottled hills appeared in the mist on both sides of the river, and here, just above Chang Shou, the river narrowed to about seventy-five feet [22.9 meters]. The ship slowed to negotiate this rocky bottleneck and gave me time to study the hills. . . .
>
> . . . every inch of these hills was farmland. . . . On the steepest slopes were terraces of vegetables. How was it possible to water the gardens on these cliff-faces? I . . . saw a man climbing up the hillside, carrying two buckets on a yoke. He tipped them into a ditch and . . . started down the hill. No one is idle on the Yangtze. In the loneliest bends of the river are solitary men breaking rocks and smashing them into gravel. . . .
>
> One day I was standing at the ship's rail. . . . We saw some trackers . . . pulling a junk [Chinese boat]. The men skipped from rock to rock, they climbed, they hauled the lines attached to the junk, and they struggled along the steep rocky towpath. They were barefoot. . . .
>
> The junks and these trackers will be on the river for some time to come. Stare for five minutes at any point on the Yangtze and you will see a junk sailing upstream with its ragged, ribbed sail; or being towed by yelling, tethered men. . . . There are many new-fangled ships and boats on the river, but I should say that the Yangtze is a river of junks and sampans [Chinese boats], fuelled by human sweat. . . .
>
> In the days that followed we passed through the gorges. . . . The gorges are wonderful, and it is almost impossible to exaggerate their splendour; but the river is long and complicated, and much greater than its gorges. . . .
>
> [As] soon as we left [Bai De] the mountains rose—enormous limestone cliffs on each side of the river. There is no shore: the sheer cliffs plunge straight into the water. . . . Looking ahead through the gorges you see no exit, only the end of what looks like a blind canyon. . . .
>
> The wind blows fiercely through the gorges. . . . On the day that I passed through, the sky was leaden, and the wind was tearing the clouds to pieces, and the river itself was yellow-brown or viscous and black, a kind of eel-color. It is not only the height of the gorges, but the narrowness of the river . . . which makes it swift. . . . The scale gives it this look of strongness, and fills it with an atmosphere of ominous splendour. . . .*

---

*From *Sailing Through China* by Paul Theroux. Text copyright ©1983 by Paul Theroux. Reprinted by permission of Houghton Mifflin Company.

CHAPTER 8   THE LAND UNDER HEAVEN

The Yangtze, the longest river in Asia, has served as a major trade route for centuries. Gorges, like the ones above, often make the Yangtze impossible to navigate. Through what part of China does the Yangtze River flow?

Next to the Yangtze in volume of flow is the Zhu Jiang. In many ways, it is one of the most important rivers in the country. In its humid valley are produced about 50 percent of China's grain, 20 percent of its jute, and such other products as rubber, oil palm, coffee, cocoa, and sisal hemp. About 95 percent of the valley is hills and mountains which contain many valuable minerals. In addition, most areas in the upper reaches of the river are rich in limestone.

The rivers of China, however, also have a destructive side. Over the centuries, the Chinese often have faced the destruction of their land by floods, which they blamed on the "wild rivers." Chinese tradition states that around 200 BC a man named Da Yu was the first to tame the rivers. Three days after Da Yu got married, he left his new bride to help people cope with the constant flooding. He labored for 13 years without returning home. Finally, his efforts were successful. Nine rivers were dredged, and the flooding was stopped.

Da Yu also had the people build embankments and dikes along the Huna He River. Then his son and grandson directed the building of the Dujiangyan irrigation system on the Min River in central China. The system, which has been adapted and modernized over the years, is still in use as one of China's largest water control projects. It not only serves agriculture, but it also controls water for industry, towns, and cities.

1. Through what regions of the country do most of China's major rivers run? What are some of the major ones?
2. Why is the Zhu Jiang an important river?
3. What did Da Yu contribute to the development of China?

CASE STUDY
CHINA

NORTH, SOUTH, EAST, WEST, AND CENTER

The Chinese who lived in the Land Under Heaven developed their land and led their lives in accordance with a set of structured beliefs. For them, certain forces were sacred and were related to the general pattern of human existence.

One force was cardinal directions. There were five of these—north, south, east, west, and center. Each was associated with a season of the year. North represented winter, and south represented summer. East symbolized spring, and west symbolized fall. Center represented all seasons. Each direction and season, in turn, was related to and described in terms of another force—color. North was black, and south was red. East was green, and west was white. Center was yellow, the color of the soil of the valley where Chinese civilization began.

Each cardinal direction, season, and color also was symbolized by and related to an "activity," or element. There were five activities—water, fire, wood, metal, and soil. Each was related to the other, and each was a power in the world. Water was associated with north and fire with south. Wood symbolized east, and metal symbolized west. Earth represented center. Tradition stated that "[The nature of] Water is to moisten and descend; of Fire, to flame and ascend; of Wood, to be crooked and straighten; of Metal, to yield and to be modified; of Soil, to provide for sowing and reaping."

Still another force was five sacred animals. Like seasons, color, and elements, each of the animals was related to a cardinal direction. The tortoise symbolized north and the bird south. The dragon symbolized east and the tiger west. Symbolizing center was man.

Belief in these forces and in their relationship one to the other was so strong that the Chinese built their royal cities in accordance with them. Each city was laid out in the form of a square. In the center was the palace. To the north was the marketplace, while to the south was the sacred place. The emperor entered the city by the south gate and faced south to receive officials and conduct public business. The temples where most religious services were held were located near the south central gate. Thus, the Chinese showed that the forces had to be taken into account.

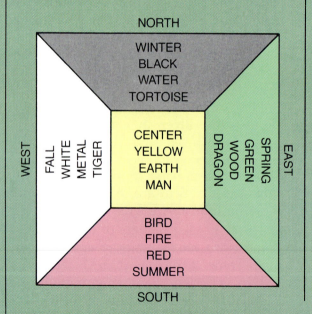

1. What were the five cardinal directions? With what forces was each associated?
2. How did the various forces in which the Chinese believed affect the way in which the people lived?

CHAPTER 8 THE LAND UNDER HEAVEN 131

CITIES AND VILLAGES

Experts believe that for a long time China has had more people than any other country in the world. Today, more than 1 billion people—about one-fourth of the world's population—live in China. Most of these people live under crowded conditions. About 95 percent live on only 45 percent of the available land. While the mountainous west has few people, the eastern part of China has a high **population density,** or number of people per square mile or square kilometer. It is in this area that the major cities and farming areas of the country are located.

CITIES

In old China, there were two different kinds of cities. One was the **royal,** or political, **city.** This was where the capital and the home of the ruler were found. The other was the **commercial city.** This was the home of merchants, skilled workers, and businesses. Each type of city prompted emotional responses by the people who lived there.

A royal city was laid out in a square. At the center was the palace, to the north the marketplace, and to the south the sacred place. The ruler entered the city through the south gate, while officials entered through the east and west gates. Each side of the city was associated with a season—the north with

This photograph of Beijing was taken from a National Aeronautics and Space Administration (NASA) satellite. In the far right center of the photo, the Great Wall of the old city can be seen. What could one find inside the walls of a royal city?

winter, the south with summer, the east with spring, and the west with fall. Below, an observer describes Chang-an, a major royal city during the early Middle Ages:

> The city wall enclosed an area of some 30 square miles [78 square kilometers], divided by a grid of broad avenues. . . . Nearly one million people lived within the walled compound. . . . Walls . . . were [everywhere]. Gates and doors closed at sunset and opened at sunrise. Private life of the well-to-do was private indeed. Rooms opened to interior courts and gardens. Beauty was hidden from the public eye which, from the lanes and streets, could see only blank walls. . . .
>
> . . . The great avenues, though carefully maintained, were quiet. Footpaths, drainage ditches, and fruit trees lined the principal carriageways. . . . These avenues . . . were not so much passageways that linked the people in different sections of the city as open spaces that kept the people apart. If the daytime traffic on these avenues was small, it became nonexistent after dark. With the closing of the gates life withdrew into the intimacy of the houses.*

In contrast to the quiet order of a royal city was the loosely planned commercial, or trading, city. Here the incentive was profit and enjoyment of life. Not content with life in a royal city, the ruler at times moved the capital to a commercial city. One ruler, for example, moved the capital to the city of Hangzhou. Below, an observer gives his account of that major commercial city:

> The walls of [Hangzhou] were irregular in shape. It had thirteen unevenly spaced gates. . . . The principal pig market . . .

---

*Topophilia: A Study of Environmental, Perception, Attitudes, and Values by Yi-Fu Tuan, 1974, George Allen & Unwin Ltd., pp. 176–177.

CASE STUDY
CHINA

YANG AND YIN

The divided circle in the photograph to the right is the symbol of yang and yin. The eight **trigrams,** or figures of three, that surround it are the *pa kua* said to hold the key to knowledge. Many centuries ago, Chinese philosophers identified yang and yin as the major forces, or energy modes, in life. The Chinese believed that the two forces were within every natural object and that the activity of one or the other controlled the universe. The two were constantly interacting. In a process that never ended, they produced each other, influenced each other, and destroyed each other. Thus, any single object could show the characteristics of yang at one moment and the characteristics of yin at another moment.

Yang was the positive force and was masculine in character. It was active, warm, dry, bright, and aggressive. The sun and Heaven were yang. So was fire, the south side of a hill, and the north bank of a river. Horses were yang because they rose front-end first. The *shen,* or good spirits, were yang. Men, too, were predominantly yang. They were celestial and of great worth.

Yin was the negative force and was feminine in character. It was dark, cool, wet, mysterious, secret, and submissive. Shadows and Earth were yin. So was the north side of a hill and the south bank of a river. Camels were yin because they rose hind-end first. The *gui,* or evil spirits, were yin. Women, too, were predominantly yin. They were earthy and of no great worth.

As legend goes, either yang or yin controlled the seasons and life. To achieve the perfect life, the correct balance had to be maintained between yang and yin. Care had to be taken not to upset the harmony of the two forces. If it were upset, the result could be a change in the natural order of things. Too much yang in a person's acts, for example, might cause drought and fire. Too much yin, on the other hand, might bring out-of-season rains and floods. Life for the Chinese, then, was a constant striving to achieve harmony with nature and not upset the balance of yang and yin.

1. What were the characteristics of yang? Of yin?
2. In what ways do you think belief in yang and yin reflected the Chinese feeling for land and nature?

In China's Gansu province, farmers grow an herb called "rape-seed." They often carry their crop to market in horse- and donkey-drawn carts. What is life like in the Chinese countryside?

occupied the city's center. . . . [The avenues] teemed with pedestrians, horse-riders, people in sedan chairs and in passenger carts. Besides roads the city was served by canals, with their heavy traffic of barges loaded with rice, boats weighed down with coal, bricks, tiles, and sacks of salt. More than one hundred bridges spanned the canal system within the city walls, and where these were humpbacked and joined busy arteries they caused traffic to congest. . . . [The streets] were lined with shops and dwellings that opened to the traffic. . . . The [lack] of land forced the buildings to go up to three to five stories. Commercial activity permeated the city and its suburbs. . . . The principal pig market was not far from the main artery. Several hundred beasts were butchered every day in slaughterhouses that opened soon after midnight and closed at dawn. . . . City life in . . . [Hangzhou] continued . . . late into the night.*

Today in the People's Republic of China, many people continue to live in commercial and political cities. The cities themselves, however, have changed in a great many ways. The largest city is Shanghai, with over 10 million people. The capital city of Beijing is home to about 9 million people. In these and in other cities, the old is mixed with the new.

COUNTRYSIDE

While the cities of China remain important, more people today live in the countryside. About 80 percent of China's 1 billion people live in rural villages where most of the houses are built tightly against each other and there are few backyards or gardens. Many Chinese share a special feeling for the countryside. In the past, even those officials who had to live in the city escaped whenever possible to the countryside. "All I ask," said one second-century city dweller, "is good lands and a spacious home, with hills behind and a flowing stream in front, ringed with ponds or pools, set about with bamboos and trees, a vegetable garden to the south, an orchard to the north."

---

*Topophilia by Yi-Fu Tuan, p. 178, in Daily Life in China on the Eve of the Mongol Invasion 1250–1276 by Jacques Gernet, 1962, Translation George Allen & Unwin Ltd., pp. 22–55.

CHAPTER 8   THE LAND UNDER HEAVEN

Eighteen centuries later, many Chinese still feel the same about rural life. Below, a 23-year-old Chinese city dweller tells about his "escape" to the countryside outside of Beijing for a holiday weekend:

Once again I feel the autumn wind, gentle but warmer, as I walk along the road. . . . A beautiful road. . . . It is margined with poplar trees and curves off the main road amid far rice fields.

I hear the jingle of harness bells! I turn around and see a cart pulled by three horses coming my way. As it draws closer, I can hear the carter's humming. I summon up my courage. "Hey, Grandpa, can you give me a lift?"

"Hop on." I try to thank him but he doesn't seem much encouraged with words. He sings away. . . .

We approach the village. . . . He points out where I can do some fishing.

It is a typical north China village. Very tall trees. Low houses. They are separated by dwarf mud walls, grey, about a hundred. The main street is a mud path casually winding in this maze. At each of the numerous turns awaits a surprise: a giant of an ox grazing sullenly, a few idling chickens cackling at the sight of me, a dog recoiling then following me, at times a pig swaggering and grunting in my way.

It is hard but I find the village store. It sells books, tobacco and cigarettes, clothes, farm tools, fresh meat and food. I don't know what kind of store to call it. . . . On the counter I find steamed buns filled with vegetables and fried fish, rather crudely prepared but a banquet for a starving man.

With my stomach full, I stroll outside the village toward a pond. My dream of fishing consists of shady trees, a windless day and green water with a lot of weeds.

A boy of about 16 is standing at the pond looking as if he's at the end of his patience. . . . I offer conversation by asking about himself. He is a native of the village, attending high school and helping his parents with the housework and farming. . . .

The boy seems to enjoy my company. We talk and fish. . . . Judging by the light, it is about two o'clock now, and all we have caught are three small ones. Another half hour goes by. . . . "Is there an empty house somewhere?" I ask him. He thinks of the chicken farm. . . .

I am prepared for the enormous hospitality of the country people, but even so the warm welcome of the head of the production team [of the chicken farm] surprises me. . . . When I introduce myself . . . , the man, in his forties . . . looks astonished. He drags me down to a seat and prepares me a cup of tea. . . .

New friends, but we feel like old ones. He is happy to have me. . . . Usually he works in the production team office, but also helps his wife in the fields. . . .

Soon the wife comes in with her sickle and straw hat. She has been cutting rice all day long, but when she sees her husband talking with me, she starts cooking. . . .

Her parents, having a different schedule, are already finished and are watching a TV program. The food is delicious. The wife has cut fresh leeks from their private plot and done them up with eggs from their own hens. There is a big fried carp deep in sauce. . . .

In the night I sleep soundly. No street lamps, no city noise. The faint whistle of a distant train seems to emphasize the depth of darkness. It is a night one searches for all one's life. . . .*

1. What kinds of cities were there in old China? What was the major difference between them?
2. Where do most of the people in China live today?
3. How do most Chinese people regard the countryside?

---

*"Getting Away From the City" by Xu Xaoping in *China Reconstructs*, Vol. 23, No. 2 February, 1984, China Books & Periodicals Inc., pp. 66–67.

Exploration
China

Based on the information in the four maps that follow and in the chapter, present an argument to defend these statements:

Few nations have as diverse a natural environment as China.

Climates in China are as varied as those of the continental United States.

In China, the pressure on the land to produce is great.

Most of the people of China live under crowded conditions.

NATURAL REGIONS

CLIMATE

LAND USE

POPULATION DENSITY

CHINA

CHAPTER 8 REVIEW

POINTS TO REMEMBER

1. The people of the Land Under Heaven, which began in the valley of the Huang He [Yellow River] about 3500 years ago and then expanded into neighboring areas, felt deeply about the land, and their way of life was rooted in the natural environment. They viewed Heaven and Earth as one and believed each influenced the other through yang and yin. They also believed that natural happenings and human actions influenced each other.

2. Today China is the second largest nation in Asia and the third largest in the world.

3. Few nations have as diverse a natural environment as China. One-third is mountainous, while the rest of the country is made up of fertile river basins and plains. Certain areas of the northwest consist of desert and steppe.

4. Most of China's major rivers begin in the mountainous west and run through the north, central, and southern regions of the country. To cope with the flooding that often destroyed their land, the Chinese have developed technology to control the rivers and to make use of the fertile land.

5. China, with about one-fourth of the world's population, is the world's most populous country. Most of the people live in the eastern half of the country where the major cities and farming areas are located.

6. Cities have played an important role in China as political and commercial centers. Most of the population, however, live in rural areas, and even those people who live in cities share a special regard for the countryside.

VOCABULARY

Identify

Pan Gu
Land Under Heaven
Huang He
Beijing

Takla Makan
Gobi
Manchurian Plain

North China Plain
Yangtze
Zhu Jiang

Da Yu
Chang-an
Hangzhou
Shanghai

Define

yang and yin
ethnic groups
portents

steppe
loess
population density

royal city
commercial city
trigrams

pa kua
shen
gui

DISCUSSING IMPORTANT IDEAS

1. Do you agree or disagree with the early Chinese belief that human behavior has an effect on nature and can upset its balance? Explain.

2. How have China's physical features aided in the development of Chinese civilization? How do you think they have posed problems?

3. Do you think the early Chinese concept of two totally different types of cities—political and commercial—is practical today? Explain.

4. How do you think the distribution of China's population has affected the development of the natural environment? Give examples to support your answer.

Developing Skills

TAKING NOTES

Experts agree that one of the best ways to remember something is to write it down. *Taking notes*—writing down information in an orderly and brief form—not only helps you remember. It also makes your task easier.

There are many different styles of notetaking. All clarify and put material in order. This order may be chronological, based on the importance of the events, or based on the relationships among parts of the material.

When taking notes, it will help to keep in mind these guidelines:

1. Paraphrasing the information—putting the information in your own words—will make you think about what the author or speaker meant.
2. Your notes should be legible and neat so that you will be able to understand them when you read them again.
3. You do not have to use complete sentences. Abbreviations may be used.

One of the most common methods of taking notes is in outline form. To do this, follow the steps in this example:

1. Read the last three paragraphs on page 121, and decide on a heading under which all the material could fall. In this case, since all three paragraphs are concerned with the Chinese and the natural environment, the title could be *The Early Chinese and the Natural Environment*.

2. Read the first two paragraphs again, one at a time, and determine a heading for each. Remember that in most writing, each paragraph has a main idea, which may be used as the heading. The headings for the two paragraphs could be *Chinese way of life rooted in the environment* and *Workings of nature carefully observed.*

3. For each paragraph, determine how the sentences relate to each other and to the main idea. List the information in the order in which it appears, placing it in order of importance, according to the way the points relate to each other, or by category. Leave out any material you do not think is important. You should now have a set of notes like these:

*The Early Chinese
and the Natural Environment*

A. *Way of life rooted in the environment*
   1. *Deep feelings about the land*
   2. *Belief that Heaven and Earth are one*
      a. *influence of yin and yang*
B. *Careful observation of workings of nature*
   1. *Studied by astrologers and recordkeepers*
      a. *noted movements of stars and planets and natural occurrences*
         1. *hints of future changes*

For further practice in taking notes, continue the outline, working the last paragraph on page 121. Then, using a note taking form of your own, take notes on the Case Study on page 128.

CHAPTER 9
THE MANDATE OF HEAVEN

1. *How was traditional China governed?*
2. *How did the Chinese view themselves and foreigners?*

> [The ceremony] was held at dawn, and I had to get out of my bed at two A.M.—how willingly you can imagine. For most of the long ride to the temple I felt very sorry for myself. Gradually, however, the impressiveness of the situation and the magnificence of my surroundings took me out of myself. The sky was a deep, luminous blue that was quite unbelievable. The temples and the pine trees had indeed passed before my eyes on other occasions, but my senses were so sharpened by the dawn that I now realized that I had never before really seen, much less appreciated them. After many years I can still see the details of that ceremony much more clearly than I see the room about me. And I now understand why the Chinese held court at dawn. If it had been my business to deliberate upon affairs of states, I would have done a far better job of it that morning than I could ever do over a luncheon table, or drowsing in midafternoon.*

In these words, a Westerner described a visit to the court of the ruler of China. To the Westerner, dawn seemed an odd time to begin a day of government business. But in traditional China, the official day began at dawn. The time of day and the journey to the temple impressed visitors with the ruler's authority.

The Chinese regarded their ruler as the Son of Heaven. According to tradition, the Son of Heaven governed on the basis of a principle known as the Mandate of Heaven. If he were just, the Son received a **mandate,** or right to rule, from Heaven, the supreme ruler. If he did not govern properly, he lost the mandate, and someone else became the Son of Heaven.

For a great many years, China was governed by a series of **dynasties,** or ruling families. Each dynasty consisted of a line of rulers from the same family. Nineteen dynasties ruled China before the dynastic system came to an end in 1912.

Until 1912, Chinese history was divided into periods based on the reigns of the dynasties. During each period, dynastic government was the same whether the times were good or bad, and one ruler was followed by another from the same family. The central government usually was strong, and there was unity throughout the country. To justify its authority, each dynasty promoted an **ideology,** or political philosophy, among the people. Each new dynasty retained some elements of the dynasties that had gone before it.

Sometimes, rulers faced threats of internal rebellion and foreign invasion. When these challenges became overwhelming, they often led to the collapse of the dynasty and to the onset of chaos. To establish order and reunite the country, a new dynasty would emerge.

Chinese Thought from Confucius to Mao-Tse-Tung by H. G. Creel, 1953, The University of Chicago, p. 261.

Dynastic Government

The first dynasty was the Xia. Although the origins of the Xia are shrouded in legend, scholars today believe that the dynasty came to power about 4000 years ago. It was followed by the Shang, which, in turn, was followed by the Zhou. Below, a twentieth-century historian notes what happened when the Shang was replaced by the Zhou:

> The Duke of [Zhou] tirelessly lectured the conquered Shang peoples about the Mandate of Heaven. He told them that [Zhou] leaders had no selfish wish to glorify themselves by attacking Shang. He said that they had no choice in the matter once Heaven commanded them to punish Shang. He advised the newly conquered peoples to abide by Heaven's decision. He pointed out to them firmly that he was prepared to make them do so if need be. The Duke of [Zhou] understood the double-edged [meaning] of the new doctrine. [Zhou] could not retain its rule unless its kings ruled in such fashion as to remain in Heaven's good graces. To do that they must rule fairly and kindly. Thenceforth no Chinese ruler was above challenge. Any challenger proved the point of his claim merely by succeeding. The doctrine of the Mandate of Heaven was solidly established before many decades had passed. It remained thereafter the cornerstone of all Chinese political theory.*

In 221 BC, the Zhou dynasty was replaced by the Qin dynasty. The Qin was the first dynasty to unite China under one ruler. Its first—and only—ruler, Zheng, named himself Shi Huangdi, or First Emperor. A strong ruler, Shi Huangdi acted cruelly toward his subjects and tried to end freedom of thought. In time, his harsh policies led to a civil war. His dynasty was overthrown, and a new dynasty called the Han came to power.

The Han dynasty expanded China's borders and set up a national capital at Changan. One of its greatest accomplishments was the establishment of a stable government. The government was made up of four main parts—a single ruler, government officials, a system of laws, and an official ideology.

The single ruler was the emperor. He made laws, took charge of the government, and interpreted the ideology. When he wanted to change a law, he had only to issue a new order. Below, a concerned guest discusses the attitude toward the law with a Chinese official:

> You are supposed to be dispenser of justice for the Son of Heaven, and yet you pay no attention to the statute books, but simply decide cases in any way that will accord with the wishes of the ruler. Do you really think that is the way a law official should be?
>
> [The official replied:] And where, may I ask, did the statute books come from in the first place? . . . Whatever the earlier rulers thought was right they wrote down in the books and made into statutes, and whatever the later rulers thought was right they duly classified as ordinances. Anything that suits the present age is right. Why bother with the the laws of former times?**

An emperor who ruled for many years was considered a good ruler. Many Chinese believed that "the people are like grass, the ruler like the wind. As the wind blows, so the grass inclines." Others said that "when a prince's conduct is correct, his government is effective without issuing orders. If his per-

---

*China's Imperial Past by Charles O. Hucker, 1975, Stanford University Press, p. 55.

*China in Crisis Vol. I: China's Heritage and the Communist Political System, translated by Ping-ti Ho, 1968, University of Chicago, pp. 18–19.

CHAPTER 9 THE MANDATE OF HEAVEN 143

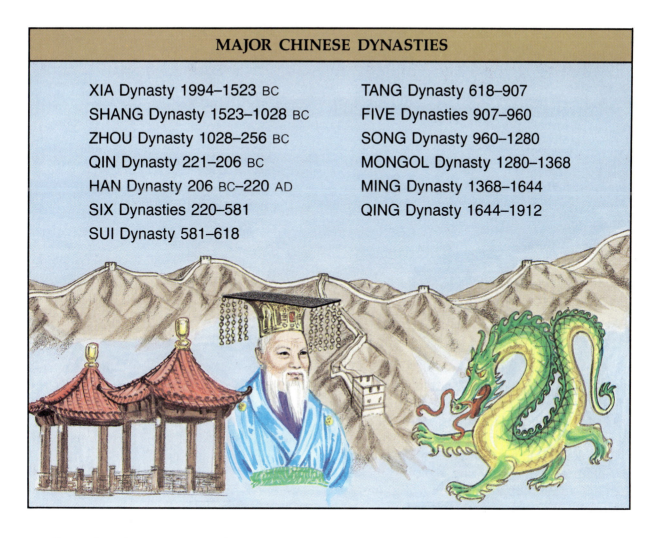

MAJOR CHINESE DYNASTIES

XIA Dynasty 1994–1523 BC
SHANG Dynasty 1523–1028 BC
ZHOU Dynasty 1028–256 BC
QIN Dynasty 221–206 BC
HAN Dynasty 206 BC–220 AD
SIX Dynasties 220–581
SUI Dynasty 581–618
TANG Dynasty 618–907
FIVE Dynasties 907–960
SONG Dynasty 960–1280
MONGOL Dynasty 1280–1368
MING Dynasty 1368–1644
QING Dynasty 1644–1912

sonal conduct is not correct, he may issue orders but they will not be followed."

The emperor was aided by many **bureaucrats,** or government officials, who were appointed to office on the basis of examinations that tested their knowledge of Chinese literature, philosophy, and affairs of state. Some bureaucrats reported directly to the emperor. To make sure that no official became too powerful, the emperor did not allow officials to stay in one place for long or serve in their home provinces. Sometimes he gave an official several jobs to do at the same time so that the official could not master any one. At other times, he gave one job to several different officials.

The bureaucrats were organized into six ministries—civil service, revenue, public works, ceremonies, punishments, and war. Each province also had its own network of officials. A post office handled official correspondence, and business was passed up through the ranks to the emperor for his decision. There were nine ranks of officials. Each rank wore special clothes and caps with a different color badge.

The system of laws was strict and enforced with heavy penalties. The effects of the law were changed by legal opinions given by the more humane officials. Most officials were Confucians, followers of the teachings of the philosopher Confucius. The Confucians did

The Forbidden City, which served as the emperor's residence, was located within the Imperial City. A screen of nine dragons, one of which is pictured here, protected the entrance to the royal palace. Why did the emperor live in a special place?

not often challenge a law when it had to do with a peasant. But when it had to do with a member of the upper class, they might try to have it changed. Some emperors did not like the changes made by the Confucians and tried to keep them out of government. One Han emperor, upon hearing a plea to make the law more humane by allowing more Confucians in government, said:

> The . . . dynasty has its own laws and institutes, which embody and blend the principles of realistic statecraft as well as those of ancient sage-kings. How could I rely entirely on moral instruction which [is alleged to have] guided the government of the [Zhou] dynasty? Moreover, the ordinary Confucians seldom understand the needs of changing times. They love to praise the ancient and to decry [condemn] the present, thus making people confused about ideals and realities and incapable of knowing what to abide by. How could the Confucians be entrusted with the vital responsibilities of the state?*

*China in Crisis Vol. I: China's Heritage and the Communist Political System, translated by Ping-ti Ho, 1968, University of Chicago, pp. 12–13.

1. What were the major contributions of the Qin dynasty? Of the Han dynasty?
2. Under the Han, how was the government set up? What was the role of the emperor? How did he keep the bureaucrats from becoming too powerful?
3. How was the system of laws determined under dynastic government?

DYNASTIC CHANGE

When the Han dynasty ended about 220 AD, China entered a period of division and disorder. It lasted until the late 500's. From then until the early 1100's, a series of strong dynasties—the Sui, the Tang, and the Song—ruled China. These dynasties restored China's greatness as a leading world civilization.

One of the most noted rulers during this period of dynastic strength was Wendi, the founder of the Sui dynasty. To display his power, Wendi began many projects. One was a new city of Chang-an. Another was a canal connecting Hangzhou on the lower Huang He to Lo-yang in the northeast, and eventually, Beijing in the north. Later, this system of canals and rivers was called the Grand Canal. It became an important route for shipping products between north and south China and for sending troops to guard China's northern frontier.

About 1126, China entered another period of dynastic decline and became prey to invaders from the north. The most successful of these invaders were the Mongols, a group of peoples from the steppe region of what is now Outer Mongolia. The Mongols, led by Genghis Khan, conquered an empire that stretched across Asia, from Korea to eastern Europe in the north, and from south China to Asia Minor in the south.

Genghis Khan's grandson, Kublai Khan, founded a Mongol dynasty in China. Although he adopted aspects of Chinese culture and government, he did not allow the Chinese to take part in the government. Under Kublai Khan, China became known for its splendor and culture. Below, Marco Polo, a western merchant and traveler, describes the rules followed when Kublai Khan held court:

> When his Majesty holds a grand and public court, those who attend it are seated in the following order. The table of the sovereign is placed on an elevation, and he takes his seat on the northern side, with his face turned towards the south; and next to him, on his left hand, sits the Empress. On his right hand are placed . . . persons connected with him by blood. . . . The other princes and the nobility have their places at still lower tables; and the same rules are observed with respect to the females, the wives of the . . . relatives of the Great Khan being seated on the left hand, at tables in like manner gradually lower; then follow the wives of the nobility and military officers: so that all are seated according to their respective ranks and dignities, in the places assigned to them, and to which they are entitled. . . .
>
> Officers of rank are . . . appointed, whose duty it is to see that all strangers who happen to arrive . . . and are unacquainted with the etiquette of the court are suitably accommodated with places. . . . At each door of the grand hall, or of whatever part the Great Khan happens to be in, stand two officers . . . , one on each side, with staves in their hands, for the purpose of preventing persons from touching the threshold with their feet, and obliging them to step beyond it. . . . But, as strangers may be unacquainted with the prohibition, officers are appointed to introduce and warn them. This precaution is used because touching the threshold is regarded as a bad omen. . . . The numerous persons who attend at the sideboard of his Majesty, and who serve him with [food] and drink are all obliged to cover their noses and mouths with handsome veils or cloths of worked silk, in order that his [food] or his wine may not be affected by their breath. . . . When the [meal] is finished, and the tables have been removed, persons of various descriptions enter the hall, and amongst these a troop of comedians and performers on different instruments. Also tumblers and jugglers, who exhibit their skill in the presence of the Great Khan. . . . When these sports are concluded, the people separate, and each returns to his own house.*

Mongol rule in China began to decline during the 1300's. The Chinese resented Mongol controls and wanted their own dynasty. After a series of rebellions finally drove out the Mongols, a peasant rebel leader named Zhu Yuanzhang became emperor. Zhu reunited the country and established a

---

*The Travels of Marco Polo, The Marsden Translation revised and edited, 1933, Liveright, Inc., From Book II, Chapter 13. Copyright 1933 by Horace Liveright, Inc. Copyright renewed 1955 by Manuel Komroff.

CHINESE DYNASTIES 1994 BC–1912 AD

capital at Nanjing in southern China. There, he founded the Ming dynasty.

Early Ming rulers introduced government reforms and promoted economic prosperity. But, in time, a series of weak emperors came to the throne, and by the 1600's, the Ming dynasty was near collapse. In 1644, invaders from the north known as Manchus captured China, overthrew the Ming ruler, and established a new dynasty called the Qing. Like the Mongols, the Qing were foreigners who borrowed aspects of Chinese culture and government but kept themselves apart from the Chinese.

1. How did Wendi show his power?
2. What foreign dynasty ruled China from the 1100's to the 1300's? What was its attitude toward the Chinese?
3. Who established the Qing dynasty? What did the Qing have in common with the Mongols?

China and the Outside World

Under Qing rule, the Chinese maintained their traditional belief that China was the "Middle Kingdom," the center of the world. In spite of contacts with foreigners through trade, the Chinese did not borrow new ideas and practices. They believed that their culture was superior to all others and wanted to protect their civilization from foreign influences. To the Chinese, foreigners were **barbarians,** or uncivilized people.

The Chinese viewed the world in terms of five zones of culture, each of which stood for a particular cultural level. Differences between each zone were based on level of culture rather than on power or wealth. At the center was the emperor. Next to him, in the first zone, was the royal family, the highest level of culture. In the second zone were lords who paid tribute to the emperor. In the third were the people who lived on the borders of China and who tended to adopt Chinese culture. In the fourth were barbarians, those uncivilized people who were partners of China. In the fifth zone, the lowest level of culture, were the barbarians who viewed China as a strange land.

The Chinese thought that barbarians would want to "come and be changed," to become more like them, and expected their emperor to welcome them. The emperor's feelings were to be a "tender cherishing" of those from afar. To show respect and that they recognized the superiority of the Chinese, visiting barbarians were expected to bow down before the emperor, present gifts, and perform certain ceremonies.

The cash value of the gifts was not important, but the gift-giving ceremony was. Ambassadors to the Chinese court were expected to perform the *kowtow.* Upon command of a lowly usher, the ambassador would kneel three times before the ruler and touch his head to the ground three times.

FIVE ZONES OF CHINESE CULTURE

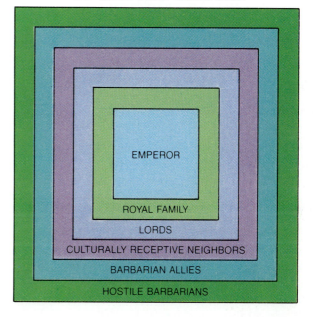

INSIGHTS ON PEOPLE
CHINA

KANG XI

Kang Xi ruled China from 1662 to 1722. A gifted ruler, Kang was very interested in the arts, literature, and science. In a final order given in 1722, he talked about his role as emperor. Part of what he said is noted below:

All the Ancients used to say that the emperor should concern himself with general principles, but need not deal with the smaller details. I find that I cannot agree with this. Careless handling of one item might bring harm to the whole world, a moment's carelessness damage all future generations. Failure to attend to details will end up endangering your greater virtues. So I always attend carefully to the details. . . .

When I had been twenty years on the throne I didn't dare [think] that I might reign thirty. After thirty years I didn't dare [think] that I might reign forty. Now I have reigned fifty-seven years. The ["Five Classics"] says of the five joys:

The first is long life;
The second is riches;
The third is soundness of body and serenity of mind;
The fourth is love of virtue;
The fifth is an end crowning the life.

The "end crowning the life" is placed last because it is so hard to attain. I am now approaching seventy, and my sons, grandsons, and great-grandsons number over one hundred and fifty. The country is more or less at peace and the world is at peace. Even if we haven't improved all manners and customs, and made all the people prosperous and contented, yet I have worked with unceasing diligence and intense watchfulness, never resisting, never idle. So for decades I have exhausted all my strength, day after day. . . .

I am now close to seventy, and have been over fifty years on the throne—this is all due to the quiet protection of Heaven and earth and the ancestral spirits; it was not my meager virtue that did it. Since I began reading in my childhood, I have managed to get a rough understanding of the constant historical principles. Every emperor and ruler has been subject to the Mandate of Heaven. Those fated to enjoy old age cannot prevent themselves from enjoying that old age; those fated to enjoy a time of Great Peace cannot prevent themselves from enjoying that Great Peace.

Over 4,350 years have passed from the first . . . Emperor to the present, and over 300 emperors are listed as having reigned. . . . In the 1,960 years from the first year of [Zheng] . . . to the present, there have been 211 people who have been named emperor and have taken era names. What man am I, that among all those who have reigned long . . . , it should be I who have reigned the longest?

1. To what does Kang Xi attribute his success as emperor? How does he view the Mandate of Heaven?
2. Judging from Kang Xi's description, do you think he had the Mandate of Heaven? Do you think it can be said that every emperor had the Mandate of Heaven? Explain.

*Emperor of China: Self Portrait of K'ang Hsi by Jonathan D. Spence, 1974, Alfred A. Knopf, Inc., pp. 144–145, 146, 147.

CHAPTER 9   THE MANDATE OF HEAVEN   149

This seventeenth-century scroll painting depicts a royal family, which represents the highest level of culture in traditional Chinese thought. What activities do you see in the painting that would support this belief?

CHINA AND GREAT BRITAIN

During ancient and medieval times, most barbarians were willing to go along with such Chinese customs as the *kowtow*. During later times, however, ambassadors from some western countries refused to do so. When the British ambassador visited in 1793, he agreed to kneel only on one knee rather than perform the full *kowtow*.

The western countries, who wanted a part in the China trade, forced themselves on the Chinese. They got special treatment for themselves and became unwelcomed partners in China's trade with the world. They also backed missionaries who were trying to convert the Chinese to western ways. A Chinese emperor explained how he felt about this in the following letter to King George III of Great Britain:

> Let us consider the teachings of Christianity which are upheld in your kingdom. They are merely the teachings which have been fostered until now by the different countries of Europe. The Sacred Emperors and Illustrious Rulers of the Celestial Empire [China] have, ever since the creation of the world, handed down their own teachings from time to time. The earth's millions have a standing guide provided for them to follow and would not seek to be led astray by outlandish doctrines.
>
> The Europeans who have accepted service in Our capital city live within the Palace grounds and are not allowed to establish relations with Our subjects. They are forbidden to preach their faith. The distinction between Chinese and barbarian is thus strictly maintained. The wish of your envoys that barbarians be allowed to preach their faith as they wish is even more impossible to grant than anything else.*

Finally, the emperor gave the following warning:

> We now set forth once more Our meaning for your instruction, O King. We trust that you will share Our views and forever be obedient. You will thereby continue to enjoy your due share of the blessings of peace.

---
*"The Emperor of China to King George the Third," translated by E. H. Parker, in *Nineteenth Century*, Vol. XL, No. 233, July 1896, pp. 48–53.

After Our clear pronouncement, you, O King, should be careful not to heed the misguided words of your subjects. . . . Do not allow your barbarian merchants to send their ships to forbidden places in search of trade. Know that the laws of the Celestial Empire are very strict and that the civil and military officers in charge of each place will do their duty faithfully and will not allow your ships to proceed there. They will at once drive them away and out to sea so that the barbarian merchants of your kingdom will have gone to all their trouble in vain.

Do not say that you were not warned! Tremble and obey! Do not ignore our commands!*

CHINA AND THE UNITED STATES

The United States tended to follow the leadership of Great Britain in regard to China. When American traders first came to China in the 1780's, they accepted the dominance of Great Britain. While some criticized the British attitude, most found the British banks useful for trade.

In the 1840's, the United States took its first official step toward making a treaty with China. The American president sent the following letter to the Chinese emperor:

I, John Tyler, President of the United States of America, . . . send you this letter of Peace and Friendship, signed by my own hand.

I hope your health is good. China is a Great Empire, extending over a great part of the World. The Chinese are numerous. . . . The rising Sun looks upon . . . rivers and mountains equally large, in the United States. Our Territories . . . are divided from your Dominions . . . by the Sea. . . .

Now, my words are, that the Governments of two such Great Countries, should . . . respect each other, and act wisely. . . .

The Chinese love to trade with our People. . . . Let the people trade . . . make a Treaty with [the representative of the president] . . . so that nothing may happen to disturb the Peace, between China and America. . . .

And so may your health be good, and may Peace reign.*

The American ambassador brought President Tyler's letter to China. The Chinese emperor gave the following answer to the president:

The Great Emperor presents his regards to the President and trusts He is well.

I the Emperor having looked up and received the manifest Will of Heaven, hold the reins of Government over . . . the [Middle Kingdom], regarding all within & beyond the border seas as one and the same Family.

Early in the Spring the Ambassador of Your Honorable Nation . . . arrived from afar. . . .

Moreover, [my representative] took [your] Letter and presented it for My Inspection, and Your sincerity and friendship being in the highest degree real, . . . my pleasure and delight were exceedingly profound.

All, and every thing, they had settled regarding the [treaty]. . . .

. . . I trust the President . . . to be extremely well satisfied and delighted.*

THE CHINESE RESPONSE

Soon, the United States shared the same status as Great Britain. Unlike China, both had gone through an industrial revolution. With their new technology, they developed strong military forces. Taking advantage of

---

*"The Emperor of China to King George the Third," translated by E. H. Parker, in *Nineteenth Century*, Vol. XL, No. 233, July 1896, pp. 48–53.

**Treaties and Other International Acts of the United States of America*, Vol. IV, edited by Hunter Miller, 1934, Government Printing Office, pp. 660–661.

*‡*Ibid.*, pp. 661–662.

CHAPTER 9 THE MANDATE OF HEAVEN

During the nineteenth century, Chinese emperors had many visits from western ambassadors who came to get trading privileges for their countries. Each ambassador wanted to make sure no other country got more in the way of trading concessions. Which western powers were among the first to send ambassadors to China?

China's technological weakness, the western countries increased their power and areas of influence in China.

Many westerners, however, did not understand the Chinese way of life and looked down on the Chinese. As western power grew over the years, more and more Chinese began to resent the foreigners and their role in China. In the 1900's, a Chinese leader asked:

> In the world today, what position do we occupy? Compared to the other peoples of the world we have the greatest population and our civilization is four thousand years old; we should therefore be advancing in the front rank with the nations of Europe and America. . . . Today we are the poorest and weakest nation in the world, and occupy the lowest position in international affairs. Other men are the carving knife and serving dish; we are the fish and the meat. . . . As a consequence China is being transformed everywhere into a colony of the foreign powers.*

---
*Sun Yat-sen as quoted in *Modern China: The Story of a Revolution* by Orville Schell and Joseph Esherick, 1972, Alfred A. Knopf, Inc., p. 48.

1. How did the Chinese view the world?
2. How did the Chinese emperor feel about western traders and missionaries? What warning did he give the British?
3. What did the United States hope to gain in China?

THE END OF DYNASTIC RULE

During the second half of the 1800's, famine and rebellions weakened China's government. Below, an opponent of the Qing dynasty describes the hardships experienced in Sichuan province during the 1890's and the effect on the peasants there:

> There was no rain, and only a light flurry of snow that winter, so the winter crops were poor. The next spring rains failed. . . . In the hot summer months that followed, the grain bins of the Ting [a powerful landowning family] remained full from previous harvests, but the peasants began

to starve. Drums rolled in the villages as the people sacrificed to the Rain God. Long processions moved along the country roads, carrying the Rain God in an open litter to soften the heart by a sight of the suffering people. Yet the King of Hell [head of the Ting family] summoned his tenants as usual to transport his family to his cool mountain home. . . .

In the second summer of the drought the people lost all faith in the Rain God, and haggard members of the ancient Ko Lao Hui, or Elder Brother secret society, began whispering in the villages. Peasants arose from their beds at night to mutter against the merciless skies and the blank moon.

One early summer day . . . , someone lifted his head and cried out: "Listen!"

Old Three heard a strange sound. . . . [The] strange sound grew louder, coming from the north where a cloud of dust was rising along the Big Road.

From the dust cloud there soon emerged a mass of human skeletons, the men armed with every kind of weapon, foot-bound women carrying babies on their backs, and naked children. . . .

. . . The avalanche of starving people poured down the Big Road, hundreds of them eddying into the Zhu courtyard, saying: "Come and eat off the big houses!" . . .

Blessed rain fell during the late summer and autumn that year and the famine ended. By then many landowning peasants had sold everything and sunk into the ranks of tenants. Tenants had become coolies or soldiers or labourers on the landed estates. And all were in debt to moneylenders.*

Empress Cixi, pictured below, was one of the most powerful women in Chinese history. Known also as the Dowager Empress, she ruled for nearly half a century during the 1800's. What did Cixi oppose?

In addition to the famine and peasant uprisings, the Qing dynasty suffered the loss of territory to Japan and the western nations. Many Chinese came to believe that if China were to meet the "foreign threat," it had to acquire the advanced technology of the west. Conservative supporters of the dynasty did not agree. They continued to oppose reforms and became more and more corrupt and backward-looking.

In 1908, the Qing empress Cixi died. She had been a powerful ruler, but opposed to reform. Her death further weakened the government. In 1911, there was a widespread national uprising. Cixi's successor, the young emperor Xundi, was forced to **abdicate,** or give up, his throne. In the following year, the "Middle Kingdom" officially became known as the Republic of China.

1. What factors weakened the Qing dynasty and led to its downfall?
2. What form of government did China have after 1912?

The Great Road: The Life and Times of Chu Teh by Agnes Smedley, ©1956, Monthly Review Press, pp. 40–42.

Exploration
CHINA

As can be seen on the map in this Exploration, in the 1800's, a number of western nations were making their influence felt in China. At the same time, some Chinese emigrated to the United States.

To many Chinese, the westerners were barbarians with little culture or learning. To many westerners, it was the Chinese who were the barbarians. Each believed the other was prejudiced against them. Each was right. Two examples of this prejudice can be seen in the excerpts that follow. The first excerpt describes some of the regulations that were imposed on the British merchants and their families who were living and working in China in the 1800's. The second excerpt is a report on incidents involving Chinese working in mining regions in the United States in the 1800's.

*... no foreign devil could stay in Canton [Guangzhou] the year round, or any time except the season, from September to March, when tea and raw silk were brought down to the coast for sale. For the rest of the year the merchants must withdraw to Macao, which the Portuguese occupied not quite independently of Chinese supervision.... in the Canton factory [the foreigner] was practically in prison. He could not stray outside the factory [trading post] limits, though on three days of the year, ... he might visit one of the islands nearby. But even there he must not [mix] with the [Chinese]. Foreign devils could not keep arms, nor must their warships enter the Pearl [Zhu Jiang] River. Wives and families must not ever visit the factories. No women at all were permitted.**

At least as early as 1852, widespread agitation and harassment of the Chinese was occurring in the mining regions of [California]. By 1862, the California Legislature's Joint Select Committee on the Chinese population was itself reporting that

*China Only Yesterday 1850–1950 by Emily Hahn, 1963, Brandt & Brandt, pp. 13–14.

SPHERES OF INFLUENCE

"Your committee were furnished with a list of eighty-eight Chinamen, who are known to have been murdered by Collectors of the Foreign Miner's License Tax—sworn officers of the law. But two of the murderers have been convicted and hanged. Generally, they have been allowed to escape with the slightest punishment."

"The above number of Chinese who have been robbed and murdered comprise, probably, a very small proportion of those who have been murdered...."*

1. Based on the map, what western nations had gained a foothold in China?
2. Why do you think the Chinese tried to impose strict rules of behavior on the British in Guangzhou?
3. How do you think the Chinese in China felt about what happened to the Chinese in California?
4. Based on the information in the chapter, what led to much of the prejudice of the Chinese? Of the westerner? Explain your answers.

*"Teaching the Asian-American Experience" by Lowell K. Y. Chun-Hoon in *Teaching Ethnic Studies*, 1974, National Council for the Social Studies, pp. 128–129. Reprinted with permission of the National Council for the Social Studies.

CHINA

CHAPTER 9 REVIEW

POINTS TO REMEMBER

1. Chinese rulers claimed that their authority came from the Mandate of Heaven. According to tradition, a ruler lost the mandate and fell from power if he ruled unjustly. In fact, a ruler ruled until he was overthrown.
2. Until 1912, China was governed by a series of dynasties.
3. To make sure their dynasty succeeded, government officials took up laws of the previous dynasty and proclaimed an official ideology.
4. The Qin was the first dynasty to unite China under one ruler and to establish the title of Emperor.
5. The Han dynasty expanded China's territory, encouraged trade, and established a stable structure of government consisting of the emperor, bureaucrats, a system of laws, and a political ideology.
6. From the late 500's until the early 1100's, three Chinese dynasties—the Sui, Tang, and Song—ruled. They secured the loyalty of the people and made China an important center of civilization.
7. In the 1100's, the Mongols conquered China. Under their leader, Kublai Khan, they founded a dynasty which adopted aspects of Chinese culture and government.
8. After the overthrow of the Mongols, a Chinese dynasty known as the Ming came to power and reunited the country.
9. The Ming were overthrown in 1644 by foreign invaders called Manchus. They established the Qing dynasty.
10. The Chinese believed that their country was the "Middle Kingdom" and that they were superior to all other cultures.
11. In the 1700's and 1800's, western countries forced the Chinese to trade with them and tried to convert the Chinese to western ways. This caused resentment among the Chinese.
12. Following a national uprising in 1911, the Qing emperor abdicated. A year later, the dynastic system was replaced, and the country officially became known as the Republic of China.

VOCABULARY

Identify

Son of Heaven
Mandate of Heaven
Xia
Shang
Zhou
Qin
Shi Huangdi

Han
Chang-an
Confucians
Sui
Tang
Song

Wendi
Grand Canal
Mongols
Genghis Khan
Kublai Khan
Zhu Yuanzhang

Ming
Manchus
Qing
"Middle Kingdom"
Xundi
Kang Xi

Define

mandate
dynasties

ideology
bureaucrats

barbarians
kowtow

abdicate

CHAPTER 9   THE MANDATE OF HEAVEN

DISCUSSING IMPORTANT IDEAS

1. What is meant by the statement, "For both the ruled and the ruler, the Mandate of Heaven was a two-edged sword for stability and change"?
2. What were the strengths of the dynastic system in China? What were the weaknesses? Do you think China could have been governed better under another system of government? Give examples to support your answers.
3. What factors promoted the Chinese attitude of superiority? Did westerners hold a similar attitude about their own culture? Explain.
4. What basic cultural differences separated China and the West?

DEVELOPING SKILLS

IDENTIFYING CAUSE AND EFFECT

Everything that happens does so because something makes it happen. What happens is called the *effect*. The person, condition, or event that makes the thing happen is called the *cause*. The relationship between what happens and what makes it happen is known as a *cause and effect relationship*.

The following guidelines will help you identify some instances of cause and effect in written material:

1. Often, statements carry "clue words" that will alert you to cause and effect. Look for such words and phrases as *led to, brought about, produced, because, as a result of, so that, thus, outcome, as a consequence, resulted in, gave rise to,* and *therefore*.

   For example: *In time, Shu Huanodi's harsh policies led to a civil war.*

   (The "clue" is "led to." The cause is Huanodi's harsh policies. The effect is civil war.)

2. At times, there are no "clue words." In their place, however, may be the word "and" or a comma.

   For example: *Many westerners did not understand the Chinese way of life and looked down on the Chinese.*

   (If the sentence is reworded—"Because many westerners did not understand the Chinese way of life, they looked down on the Chinese"—it becomes clear that the cause is the westerners' lack of understanding of the Chinese way of life and the effect is westerners looking down on the Chinese.)

3. Cause and effect does not always appear in the same sentence. It is not unusual for several sentences or paragraphs to be involved in stating an effect and explaining the cause or causes.

   For example: *The central government usually was strong. There was unity throughout the country.*

   (In this case, the effect—unity throughout the country—appears in the second sentence. The cause—a strong central government—appears in the first sentence.)

For further practice in this skill, find at least six examples of cause and effect in the material in this chapter. In each case, identify the cause and the effect and explain on what you have based your decision.

CHAPTER 10
THE FEW AND THE MANY

1. What social groups existed in traditional China?
2. What kinds of art and literature flourished in traditional China?

The ancients who wished to be [greatly] virtuous throughout the kingdom, first ordered well their own states. Wishing to order well their states, they first regulated their families. Wishing to regulate their families, they first cultivated their persons. Wishing to cultivate their persons, they first [made right] their hearts. Wishing to [make right] their hearts, they first sought to be sincere in their thoughts. Wishing to be sincere in their thoughts, they first extended to the utmost their knowledge. Such extension of knowledge lay in the investigation of things.

Things being investigated, knowledge became complete. Their knowledge being complete, their thoughts were sincere. Their thoughts being sincere, their hearts were then [made right]. Their hearts being [made right], their persons were cultivated. Their persons being cultivated, their families were regulated. Their families being regulated, their states were rightly governed. Their states being rightly governed, the whole kingdom was made tranquil and happy.*

In traditional China, students carefully studied teachings such as the one above. These teachings illustrated a "chain of reasoning" argument. Students had a program of study that included the memorization and analysis of books known as the Confucian classics, the writing of essays, and the appreciation and writing of poetry. Many years of study were necessary to complete the program, and a large number of students never reached their goal.

The few students who did reach their goal became members of the upper class and served as China's rulers and leaders. As members of the upper class, they valued close family ties and followed set rules of behavior in human relationships. They considered themselves superior to those of the lower classes. They firmly believed that it was their natural right to rule.

The life styles of the upper class were supported by the hard work of the lower classes. Expected to respect and obey those of the upper class, the members of the lower classes received little reward for their efforts. Despite this, they endured and, during the twentieth century, emerged as the new leaders of China.

Women formed their own distinct group in traditional Chinese society. Whether members of the upper class or the lower classes, as females they were considered inferior to males. Not until the twentieth century were they able to change their status and increase their influence.

Great Learning by Confucius as quoted in *The United States and China* by John King Fairbank, 1971, Harvard University Press, pp. 68–69. Adapted by permission.

THE UPPER CLASS

The upper class of traditional China consisted for the most part of three distinct categories of people. One was the **gentry**, wealthy landowning families. Another was government officials. The third was the *literati,* or scholars. It was not unusual for an individual to belong to all three categories.

THE GENTRY

Most members of the gentry owned vast rural estates. Most often, however, they lived in large, high-walled urban **compounds,** enclosed yards with many buildings, in homes with tiled roofs, courtyards, and gardens. The rooms of these homes were filled with fine furniture and carpets. The occupants, who were clothed in silk tunics and jackets, feasted on a variety of foods.

The gentry played an important role in local affairs. They rented their land, loaned money, collected taxes, served as judges, and led the militia. Respected for their influence and wealth, they also were social leaders in local communities. The ladder of success was easier for their sons to climb than for the sons of other social groups. In the words of one Chinese historian:

> The gentry of old China were a special group. They had political, economic, and social privileges and powers and led a special way of life. The gentry stood above the large mass. They dominated the life of Chinese communities. They provided the rules of society and of man's relation to man. During the later years [of the dynastic period], the gentry's position and qualifications became formalized. A ring of formal privileges relieved them from physical labor and gave them prestige and a special position in relation to the government.*

*Adapted from *The Chinese Gentry* by Chang Chung-li, 1955, University of Washington Press, p. xiii.

GOVERNMENT OFFICIALS

Until the twentieth century, China's political leaders and government officials came from the ranks of the gentry. In early times, they controlled China's central government, holding most government posts and making government appointments on the basis of family ties.

This changed, however, when the Han emperors created a **civil service,** a bureaucracy in which officials were hired on the basis of examinations rather than on birth. The examinations tested candidates on their knowledge of Chinese literature and philosophies. To pass them, it was necessary to write with style as well as understanding.

During ancient and medieval times, members of the lower classes were not allowed to take the examinations. In time, however, this changed. "In education," said members of the upper class, "there is no difference between social classes." Despite this, the upper class still had the advantage—they had the wealth that was needed to help their sons study for the examinations.

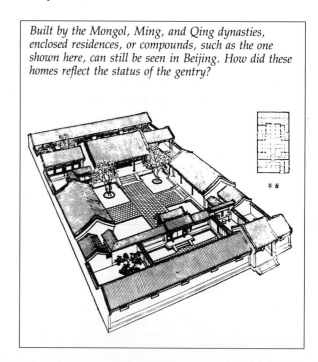

Built by the Mongol, Ming, and Qing dynasties, enclosed residences, or compounds, such as the one shown here, can still be seen in Beijing. How did these homes reflect the status of the gentry?

This copper engraving shows a government official of traditional China with his family. They enjoyed the good life and prestige of the upper class. Who held most government posts before the Han dynasty?

There were four levels of examinations—local, provincial, imperial, and those given by the emperor. Passing a local examination meant that a person could go on to take the more difficult provincial test, which most often required three days of writing during a week. The one in twenty who passed this test could then take the imperial test, which was given every third year in the capital city. The one in two hundred who passed the imperial examination was allowed to take the test given by the emperor. No one failed this test. It served only to rank the order of excellence of the officials.

With each level of examination an official passed, he gained higher status and new privileges. Below, a Chinese author discusses the prestige accorded government officials and the reaction of the Chinese to the examination system:

> The official's status is exalted, his name distinguished, his power great, and his prestige incomparable. . . . In ancient times the commoners were divided into four major . . . orders, namely, scholars, peasants, artisans [skilled laborers], and merchants, each engaging in its own occupation and each performing its own function. . . . Since the introduction of the examination system . . . scholars have forsaken their studies, peasants their ploughs, artisans their crafts, and merchants their trades; all have turned their attention to but one thing—government office. This is because the official has all the combined advantages of the four without requiring their necessary toil. . . .*

SCHOLARS

Those who passed all four levels of the civil service examinations became known as *literati*. Generally, there were more *literati* than there were government jobs.

In later years, in an effort to earn more income, the government began to sell jobs. The result of this was more jobs for the wealthy and fewer for the *literati*. Some *literati* became teachers for very little pay and "plowed with the writing brush." Few were able to climb the ladder of success. An exception was the scholar Tang Gui, whose story is told below:

> T'ang Kuei [Tang Gui] was born in a poor family. His father, being an invalid, could not earn a living. T'ang Kuei never wanted to be anything but a scholar, al-

---
*The Ladder of Success in Imperial China, translated by Ping-ti Ho, ©1962, Columbia University Press, p. 46. By permission.

Insights on People
CHINA

The Wang Clan

The Wang clan, one of the most successful families of traditional China, was rich and well-known. Below, a Chinese author explains how and why it attained such success:

The Wang clan has for generations risen to fame. This success is due to its strict family instruction. At times of family gatherings, such as weddings and funerals, new years and festivals, or ancestral worship, each member of the family must wear clothes proper to his status before the ceremony is held. Those who have attained official ranks are splendid in official hats and sashes. Those who have failed the tests are doomed to wear short commoners' jackets. This sharp contrast in status makes the slow ones ashamed. Therefore, the father instructs his son, the wife urges her husband that everyone must study hard and make good in examinations and officialdom. This is why the Wang clan has produced so many holders of higher degrees and officials and has become a clan of national renown.*

Then the Wang clan began to lose prestige. Soon it became poor and forgotten. Some neighbors gave the following reasons for this:

World affairs constantly change. Nowadays people often think that in view of their present prosperity they should have nothing to worry about for the rest of their lives. In truth many of them sink in almost no time. Almost always, human fortunes are bound to change.

The ancestor's wealth and honor were first obtained by serious studies. The descendants, being used to a life of ease, looked down upon studies. If a family acquired its fortune through hard work and saving, its descendants, with a fortune at their disposal, in most cases forget about industry and thrift. This is the basic reason the clan declined.

Generation after generation, each son got an equal share of inheritance. Each generation was

larger than the one before it. Each share of the inheritance became smaller and smaller.

Wang VI was by nature extravagant. He built a huge home to house all of his females, and when his children went out they were followed by tons of servants. His jewels, curios, ancient bronzes, porcelains, and paintings were without price. At a New Year's Eve feast he always hung up a lantern made of pearls. All wine cups were very old and made of jade. When he returned home, his sedan chair was first placed in front of the middle gate. After the gate was opened, it was carried inside by women servants. He was almost always surrounded by some twenty women, each of whom was waited upon by two maids. When he went to bed, an orchestra led the way to an inner room.

1. Why did the Wang clan remain rich and famous for so many years? What do you think led to its fall?
2. Was the Wang clan more interested in money or in education? Explain.
3. How do you think the Wang clan could have avoided its fall?

**The Ladder of Success in Imperial China*, translated by Ping-ti Ho, ©1962, Columbia University Press, p. 130. By permission.

though the family had not produced any degree holder. In the last half of the fifteenth century, essays by successful candidates were not yet compiled and printed for sale. T'ang Kuei saw the chance of making a living by selecting and editing them for sale. In order to support his parents, younger brothers, and sisters, he sometimes went to neighboring counties to sell his collections of winning test essays. Once he sighed: "If I cannot achieve success, my parents will someday be buried in a ditch."

When he was sixteen, he passed the local examination. He was therefore hired by a local family as a teacher. After placing first in the reviewing tests that followed, he became better known. His salary was increased. Not until then could he provide proper food and basic necessities for his parents and pay for his brothers' and sisters' weddings.*

1. What groups made up the upper class of traditional China?
2. What was the role of the gentry?
3. How did a person become a government official?
4. Why were few *literati* able to climb the ladder of success?

THE LOWER CLASSES

Like the upper class, the lower classes consisted of several different groups of people. The largest group was the peasants, who made up 80 to 90 percent of the population. They lived in the country and provided the food that China needed to survive. Then there were the scientists, merchants, and soldiers. Despite the many contributions they made to China, they were considered third-class citizens.

---

*The Ladder of Success in Imperial China, translated by Ping-ti Ho, ©1962, Columbia University Press, pp. 269–270, adapted. By permission.

PEASANTS

Peasant life styles varied in traditional China, depending on the local climate, landscape, and customs. Common to most peasants, however, were values learned from stories passed down from one generation to another. Also common were small families of four to six persons.

If they could afford it, peasants were allowed to own land. Few, however, could do so because they had to spend most of their income for food. The little left over was spent on clothing, recreation, and housing. Their homes usually were made of brown sun-dried brick, bamboo, or stones and had stone or earth floors and paper windows. What land a peasant did own was divided among the sons of the family. As a result, the amount of land for any one family was small.

The peasants' survival depended on the harvest. In most cases, good harvests yielded enough to meet the basic needs of their families. Bad harvests brought debts

In traditional China, peasants spent the greater part of their lives doing back-breaking work to grow rice, the main crop. How did peasants spend the income they earned from selling their harvests?

and famine. Because of these conditions, peasant rebellions against the local gentry and government were not uncommon. In most cases, however, the rebellions failed, and conditions did not change.

To survive in bad times, peasants could rent or sell their land or leave their village. Some, unable to endure any more, killed themselves. Others ended up selling one of their children to work as a servant under terms much like those stated in the medieval contract below:

> Contract agreed on the third day of the 11th moon of the year.... The monumental-stonemason Chao Seng-tzu, because ... he is short of commodities and cannot procure them by any other means, sells today, with the option of repurchase, his own son Chiu-tzu to his relation ... the lord Li Ch'ien-ting. The sale price has been fixed at 200 bushels of corn and 200 bushels of millet. Once the sale has been concluded, there will neither be anything paid for the hire of the man, nor interest paid on the commodities. If it should happen that the man sold ... should fall ill and die, his elder brother will be held responsible for repaying the part of the goods [corresponding to the period of hire which had not been completed]. If Chiu-tzu should steal anything of ... value from a third person, ... it is Chiu-tzu himself [and not his employer] from whom reparation will be demanded. ... The earliest time-limit for the repurchase of Chiu-tzu has been fixed at the sixth year. It is only when this amount of time has elapsed that his relations are authorized to repurchase him.*

Another option open to the peasant in need was to obtain a loan. Interest rates, however, were very high. An interest charge of 20 percent per month for a cash loan or 50 percent for grain at harvest time was not unusual. Loan contracts like the medieval one that follows were common:

> On the first day of the third moon of the year . . . , Fan Huai-t'ung and his brothers, whose family is in need of a little cloth, have borrowed from the monk Li a piece of white silk 38 feet [11.6 meters] long and two feet and half an inch [0.61 meters, 1.25 centimeters] wide. In the autumn, they will pay as interest 40 bushels of corn and millet. As regards the capital, they will repay it [in the form of a piece of silk of the same quality and size] before the end of the second moon of the following year. If they do not repay it, interest equivalent to that paid at the time of the loan ... shall be paid monthly. The two parties having agreed to this loan in presence of each other shall not act in any way contrary to their agreement.*

SCIENTISTS

Chinese scientists gave the world paper and printing, chemical explosives, the mechanical clock, the compass, canal locks, the crossbow, the kite, cast iron, watertight compartments, and certain drugs. They also contributed a system of measures, irrigation techniques, flood control devices, canals, and military defenses. It was their skill that was responsible for the Grand Canal, the Great Wall, and the superiority of Chinese ships and sails.

The scientists also accomplished much in the field of medicine. Chinese doctors, for example, developed **acupuncture,** a method of treating pain by piercing the skin at vital points with needles. They were vaccinating people for smallpox 700 years before the Europeans began to do so. They also showed that stomachaches, fevers, colds, malaria, and other ailments could be eased or cured by using ginseng and other roots. Another

---

*Quoted in *Daily Life in China in the 13th Century* by Jacques Gernet, 1962, Macmillan Publishing Co., Inc., pp. 103–104.

Ibid., p. 103.

CHAPTER 10 THE FEW AND THE MANY

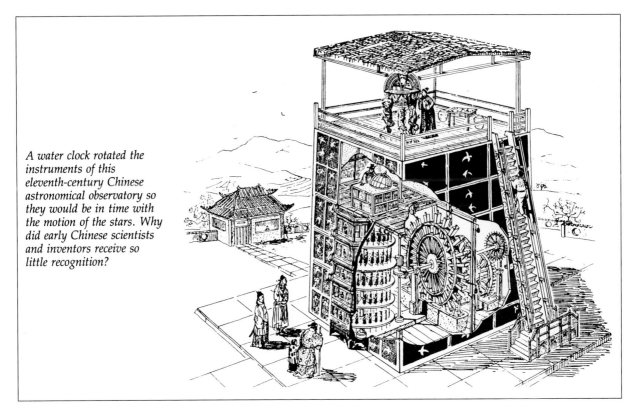

A water clock rotated the instruments of this eleventh-century Chinese astronomical observatory so they would be in time with the motion of the stars. Why did early Chinese scientists and inventors receive so little recognition?

example of early scientific advances in medicine is the operation described below, which was performed in the third century AD:

> Finding that the arm . . . had been pierced to the bone by a poison arrow, the sensible doctor told his adult patient precisely what he was about to do to him: "In a private room I shall erect a post with a ring attached. I shall ask you, sir, to insert your arm in the ring, and I shall bind it firmly to the post. Then I shall cover your head with a quilt so that you cannot see, and with a scalpel I shall open up the flesh right down to the bone. Then I shall scrape away the poison. This done, I shall dress the wound with a certain preparation, sew it up with thread, and there will be no further trouble."
>
> The tough old veteran in fact played a game of chess while the surgeon performed his operation, a young boy holding a basin under the arm. "Although your wound is cured," the doctor admonished him later, "you must be careful of your health, and especially avoid all excitement for a hundred days. . . ."*

Although the scientists made these and other significant contributions and seldom used their skills for profit or to gain power, they were given little recognition by the upper class. Because China had so many workers, there was little incentive to invent anything to save labor, and the government was not very interested in the invention of technology with wide application.

MERCHANTS

Merchants received even less attention than scientists in traditional China. Since they did not work with their minds like scholars or with their hands like laborers, the

---

*The Chinese Looking Glass by Dennis Bloodworth, 1966, 1967 by Dennis Bloodworth, pp. 230–231. Reprinted by permission of Farrar, Straus & Giroux, Inc.

Peasants in traditional China relied on knickknack peddlers such as this one to supply articles that they could not make themselves. Why were wealthy merchants feared by members of the upper class?

Some merchants were generous to the poor. According to one visitor, in bad weather merchants would go from door to door "to find out which families are the worst off, take note of their distress, and when night falls, push through the cracks in their doors some scraps of gold or silver, or else cash coins or notes."

The merchants helped China's economic development by exchanging different products both inside and outside of China. They opened trade routes between China and the rest of the world. Along the Silk Road between China and Europe, they exchanged Chinese silk, lacquerware, and porcelain for ivory and glass. During medieval times, they sparked a "commercial revolution" in China that encouraged a flow of new technology and ideas.

SOLDIERS

Like scientists and merchants, soldiers were largely neglected in traditional China —except during times of crisis. Many Chinese believed that "good iron is not used to make a nail nor a good man to make a soldier." In general, soldiers were thought to be needed—rather than respected—members of society. The one exception to this was generals.

Although seldom praised, soldiers were important to China's survival. They secured the borders and kept peace within those borders. This included protecting the people from the attacks of outlaws, rebels, and invading barbarians. During medieval times, the soldiers expanded China's borders to Afghanistan and Korea.

According to an ancient Chinese army manual, the highest skill of the soldier was to "subdue the enemy without fighting." Soldiers were to make people obey without resorting to physical violence. Violence was to be used to keep the peace only after all else had failed. War tactics were based on

upper class placed them at the bottom of society. As one Chinese historian noted:

> . . . the law despises merchants, but the merchants have become rich and noble; it esteems the farmers, but the farmers have become poor and humble. What is esteemed by the people is despised by the ruler; what is scorned by officials is honored by the law.*

Many merchants were among the richest people in China. It was this wealth that members of the upper class feared because they knew that it could be used to destroy them. To limit the merchants, the government forbade them to deal in certain goods, such as salt and iron.

Others, however, often had a different view. A peasant father thought himself lucky if he married a daughter to a rich merchant.

---

*Quoted from the *Han Shu* in *Han Social Structure* by Ch'u T'ung-tsu, 1973, University of Washington Press, p. 111.

"tricks." According to one Chinese strategist, who lived about 500 BC:

> All warfare is based on deception.
> Therefore, when capable pretend incapacity; when active, inactivity.
> When near, make it appear that you are far away; when far away, that you are near.
> Offer the enemy a bait to lure him; pretend disorder and strike him.*

1. What groups made up the lower classes of traditional China?
2. What was the status of peasants in traditional China? What steps did they take to overcome their difficulties?
3. What did scientists, merchants, and soldiers contribute to China's development? How were their contributions regarded?

WOMEN

In traditional China, women of all classes were considered inferior to men. The Chinese view of a woman's ideal role is evident in the following sayings:

> *A woman from a wealthy family dresses simply so that she can match the level of her poorer husband.*
>
> *A woman is nice to her sister-in-law and obeys her mother-in-law without question.*
>
> *Husbands and wives do not sit together, nor do their hands touch when giving or taking things.*
>
> *A woman's place is in the kitchen. The affairs of government do not concern her.*

Women were expected to yield to, rather than exercise, authority. In the following excerpt, a prominent author of traditional China offers advice to Chinese women on how they should conduct themselves:

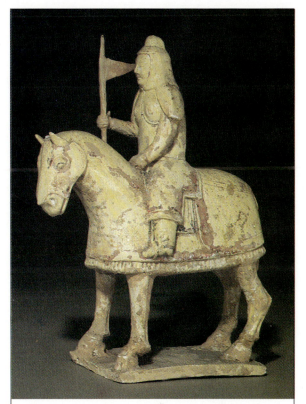

The use of long stirrups, shown in this Tang pottery figure of a mounted warrior, gave a steadier ride at a full gallop, making the Tang cavalry a superior force. How did Chinese soldiers try to make people obey?

> Let a woman modestly yield to others; let her respect others; let her put others first, herself last. Should she do something good, let her not mention it; should she do something bad, let her not deny it. Let her bear disgrace; let her even endure when others speak or do evil to her. Always let her seem to tremble and fear.*

In the husband and wife relationship, the husband was the authority. The wife had little income and few property rights. If she did not bear a son, her husband might bring another wife into the family. If her husband died, it was not easy for her to remarry.

There were many restrictions on women outside the home as well. They could not be

---
*Adapted from *The Art of War* by SunTzu, translated by Samuel B. Griffith. Copyright ©1963 by Oxford University Press. Used by permission.

Pan Chao: Foremost Woman Scholar of China by Nancy Lee Swan, 1932, reprinted in 1968 by Russell and Russell Publishers, p. 32.

political leaders, government officials, or soldiers. Despite this ban, however, some women did manage to become powerful in government. Some, such as the Empress Wu, ruled in their own right. Others, such as the empresses Cixi and Lu, served as **regents,** temporary rulers who acted on behalf of a young or sickly ruler.

1. How were women regarded in traditional China?
2. What restrictions were placed on women?

THE ARTS

In traditional China, the upper class had the time, education, and wealth to pursue an interest in the arts. Even though many of the lower classes did not, they still managed to enjoy some of the many artistic forms and styles. Chinese art included bronze vases; bowls and plates; carved jade jewelry and religious objects; glazed pottery and stone sculptures; painting and lacquerware; rubbings of tombstones; woodcuts; ceramics; and decorative arts. There also was dance, opera, architecture, and writing and painting with a brush.

Although art was enjoyed for art's sake, it usually was enjoyed most for its attempts to achieve spiritual meaning. Elements of nature, such as flowers, birds, and animals, appeared often. Each carried symbolic meanings. The plum blossom, for example, stood for courage, hope, and purity. Geese were a symbol of happy married life. The tiger represented energy, strength, and cunning.

One of the most important symbols was the dragon. While to a foreigner the dragon seemed to be an interesting fantasy, to some Chinese it was a symbol for an emperor, a sign of the zodiac, or a hero in a folktale. To others, the dragon's claws "are in the forks of the lightning," its scales "begin to glisten in the bark of rain-swept pine trees," and its voice "is heard in the hurricane which, scattering the withered leaves of the forest, quickens the new spring."

WRITING WITH A BRUSH

In traditional China, writing was an important art form that a young man "on the way up" had to learn. This was a difficult process for the Chinese writing system was based on a system of "pictures," or symbols called **characters,** rather than on an alphabet. A literate person would know about 3000 characters, an educated person about 7000.

When the characters were written with a brush and ink, they became an art known as **calligraphy,** which allowed the "painter," or calligrapher, to express ideas and reveal inner feelings and emotions. With nature as their inspiration, calligraphers made up different styles called **scripts.** To many Chinese, the flowing strokes of the brush revealed true beauty.

Calligraphy was a valued activity that contributed to such other areas of Chinese culture as painting, drama, and literature. Chinese poets, in particular, aimed to recreate mood and atmosphere in their works. Many of their poems described brief moments of intense feelings such as those expressed in the poem below by Yen Shu, who lived about 1000 AD:

> Among green willows and fragrant grass
>   along the road of post stations
> Youth discards you and slips away
> In the tower the fifth watch bell
>   shatters what's left of dreams
> Beneath the blossoms, the sorrow of
>   parting and March rain
> More bitter to love than not—
> One inch unravels to a thousand, ten
> thousand threads
> Somewhere is an edge of heaven, an end
>   of earth
> But to longing, there is no end.*

---

*"Mu-lan Hua" by Yen Shu, from *Tz'u Poetry*, translated by Julie Landau in *Asia*, July/August 1983, p. 42.

CHAPTER 10 — THE FEW AND THE MANY

1. All Chinese characters are written using one or more of eight basic strokes.

Stroke	Name		
丶	点	diǎn	dot
一	横	héng	horizontal
丨	坚	shù	vertical
丿	撇	piě	left-falling
乀	捺	nà	right-falling
丶	提	tí	rising
亅	钩	gōu	hook
乙	折	zhé	turning

2. The strokes must be written in a certain order.

Rule	Example	Stroke order	
First the horizontal, then the vertical	十	一	十
First left-falling, then right-falling	人	丿	人

"The Writing of Chinese Characters," *China Reconstructs*, June 1977, p. 51.

From top to bottom	京	亠 亠 京
From left to right	你	亻 亻 你
First outside, then inside	月	丿 几 月
Finish inside, then close	国	门 囗 国
First center, then the two sides	小	亅 小

3. Often the difference of one stroke produces an entirely different character with a different meaning. For example, in 大 **dà** (large), if a dot is added at the bottom, it becomes 太 **tài** (too much); if a dot is added at the top-right corner, it becomes 犬 **quǎn** (dog); if a horizontal line is added at the top, it becomes 天 **tiān** (sky); and if the left-falling and right-falling cross each other, it becomes 丈 **zhàng** (a length of ten feet).

Note the following characters which look almost alike:

千 **qiān** (thousand) —— **gàn** (to do) 干

八 **bā** (eight) —— **rén** (person) 人

早 **zǎo** (early) —— **hàn** (drought) 旱

住 **zhù** (to live) —— **wǎng** (to go) 往

刀 **dāo** (knife) —— **lì** (strength) 力

PAINTING WITH A BRUSH

Chinese artists who painted with a brush also were inspired by nature. Their works expressed feelings and were not meant to be accurate or lifelike. Human life was less important than nature.

By the 900's AD, a unique form of landscape painting was developed in which the artists tried to capture the special quality of the environment. Their works reflected the view that nature dominated humanity. When people were portrayed, it was only as part of a scene. The scene itself was more an arrangement of mountains and water than a view of the land. Often, vertical calligraphy that expressed an appropriate thought was part of the painting. Thus, to appreciate fully most landscapes, the viewer needed some knowledge of calligraphy and Chinese life.

One of the most famous painters was Tao Chi, who lived from 1641 to 1720. His painting, "Waterfall on Mount Lu," is a hanging scroll about seven feet (2.1 meters) long and two feet (0.61 meters) wide. On one side of the painting is a poem by Li Bo, part of which appears below:

1. What are some forms of traditional Chinese art?
2. What themes inspired traditional Chinese artists?

> I am the madman of the Ch'u country
> Who sang a mad song disputing Confucius.
> . . . Holding in my hand a staff of green jade,
> I have crossed, since morning at the Yellow Crane Terrace,
> All five Holy Mountains, without a thought of distance,
> According to the one constant habit of my life.
> . . . Lu Mountain stands beside the Southern Dipper
> In clouds reaching silken like a nine-panelled screen,
> With its shadow in a crystal lake deepening the green water.
> The Golden Gate opens into two mountain-ranges.
> A silver stream is handing down to three stone bridges
> Within sight of the mighty Tripod Falls.
> Ledges of cliff and winding trails lead to blue sky
> And a flush of cloud in the morning sun,
> Whence no flight of birds could be blown into Wu.*

*From *The Jade Mountain: A Chinese Anthology*, translated by Witter Bynner from the texts of Kiang Kang-Hu. Copyright 1929 and renewed 1957 by Alfred A. Knopf, Inc. Reprinted by permission of the publisher.

EXPLORATION
CHINA

Many years ago there was an old man who lived in Northern China. People called him the Foolish Old Man of North Mountain. His house faced south and beyond his doorway stood the two great peaks, Taihung and Wangwu, which blocked his view.

So one day he called his sons together and told them he wanted to get rid of the mountains. They each took a shovel and with great determination, they began to dig up the mountains.

A Wise Old Man saw them busily digging away and he laughed at them. "How silly of you to do this," he told them. "It's impossible for you few to dig up these two high mountains."

The Foolish Old Man replied, "When I die, my sons will carry on; when they die, there will be my grandsons, and then their sons and grandsons, and so on until the job is done.

"High as they are, the mountains cannot grow any higher and with every bit we dig, they will be that much lower. You see, we will clear them away."

So, having answered the Wise Old Man, the Foolish Old Man and his sons went on digging.*

1. Chinese leaders use the tale of the foolish old man who moved mountains in their speeches. What would you say is the most important value held by the foolish old man? The wise old man? Which value would Chinese peasants have been more likely to have held? Why?
2. What do you think is the point or moral of the tale? Do you think the peasants of traditional China would recognize the moral? Explain.
3. Why do you think rulers in old China would have wanted their people to know this folktale? Why do you think modern Chinese leaders would want their people to know it?

The Foolish Old Man Who Moved Mountains by Marie-Louise Gebhardt, 1969, Friendship Press, pp. 100–101. Used by permission.

CHINA

CHAPTER 10 REVIEW

POINTS TO REMEMBER

1. In traditional China, society was made up of the "few"—the upper class—and the "many"—the lower classes. The "few" set up the rules of behavior and considered themselves superior. The "many" were expected to be obedient.
2. Women formed their own distinct group in traditional Chinese society.
3. The upper class included the gentry, government officials, and scholars, or *literati*.
4. Government officials were chosen on the basis of civil service examinations. There were four levels of examinations—local, provincial, imperial, and those given by the emperor.
5. The lower classes included peasants and scientists, merchants, and soldiers, who were considered third-class citizens. Although ignored or looked down upon by the upper class, each made significant contributions both to China and the world.
6. Women of all classes were considered inferior to men and were expected to yield to male authority.
7. The arts of traditional China were diverse and included writing and painting with a brush.
8. Nature was a common source of inspiration for most Chinese artists.

VOCABULARY

Identify

Tang Gui   Tao Chi   Li Bo   Wang clan
Yen Shu

Define

gentry   civil service   regents   calligraphy
literati   acupuncture   characters   scripts
compounds

DISCUSSING IMPORTANT IDEAS

1. In traditional China, members of the upper class said, "In education there is no difference between social classes." Based on the information in the chapter, do you think the upper class really believed this? Give examples to support your answer.
2. If you were a peasant in dynastic China, how would you face the choice of selling your child or letting your family starve? How would you react if you were the child being sold?
3. Third-class citizens were looked down upon in traditional China despite their many accomplishments and contributions. In what ways do you think Chinese society and China might have been different had there been no scientists, merchants, or soldiers? If they had been more honored members of society?
4. What do the traditional arts of China indicate to you about traditional Chinese and their beliefs and values?

DEVELOPING SKILLS

IDENTIFYING THE VALUES OF A CULTURE

Most Americans, as well as many people of other cultures, have at one time or another read or heard the following lines from the Declaration of Independence of the United States:

We hold these truths to be self-evident, that all men are created equal, that they are endowed by their Creator with certain unalienable rights, that among these are life, liberty, and the pursuit of happiness. . . .

These words reflect the authors' *values*, ideas or beliefs about which a person (or group of persons) feels so strongly that he or she is willing to act upon them and live by them. The founders of the United States believed so firmly that all people are entitled to the same treatment under law and have the right to live in freedom and seek happiness in life that they chose these values for their nation.

Each individual has his or her own set of beliefs or values that he or she puts into practice in relationships with others. Some of these values are personal, unique to the individual or to a small group of individuals. Others, however, are the same as those held by most, if not all, members of that individual's society or culture. These are the beliefs that make an individual part of a certain culture and express the values of his or her society.

Each culture, then, has its own set of values. Sometimes, these values are the same as those of other cultures. Sometimes, they are not. The values of any culture are expressed in many ways and forms—in its arts, religion(s), politics, and history. Above all, they are reflected in the ways of life of the people who make up the culture.

There are two simple methods you can use to help you identify the values of a culture. One is to examine your sources—text, library books, interviews, and the like—and note the practices of the people of the culture. From these, you can determine important values of the culture as a whole. For example, in traditional China, there was an upper class and a lower class. The upper class made the rules, and the lower class obeyed them. The upper class lived lavishly, and the lower class did the physical labor. From these practices, it becomes clear that the traditional Chinese did not believe that all people were created equal. Some people were superior to others. This belief, because it was practiced daily by the Chinese, was a value of traditional Chinese society.

The other method of identifying cultural values is to examine your sources for the expression of a belief or idea and then check for evidence that these ideas are important enough to the people to put into practice continually. For example, on page 155 of the text it says that as members of the upper class, the gentry valued close family ties, followed set rules of behavior, considered themselves superior to those of the lower classes, and believed that it was their natural right to rule. Statements such as the following, found on page 156, indicate that the gentry acted on these beliefs: "The gentry played an important role in local affairs. They rented their land, loaned money, collected taxes, served as judges, and led the militia."; "Until the twentieth century, China's political leaders and government officials came from the ranks of the gentry." In early times, they controlled China's central government, holding most government posts and making government appointments on the basis of family ties." These actions indicate that the beliefs represent the values of the upper class society of traditional China.

For further practice in this skill, read the chapter, and using each of the two methods described, determine the major values of traditional China.

CHAPTER 11
THE CHINESE HERITAGE

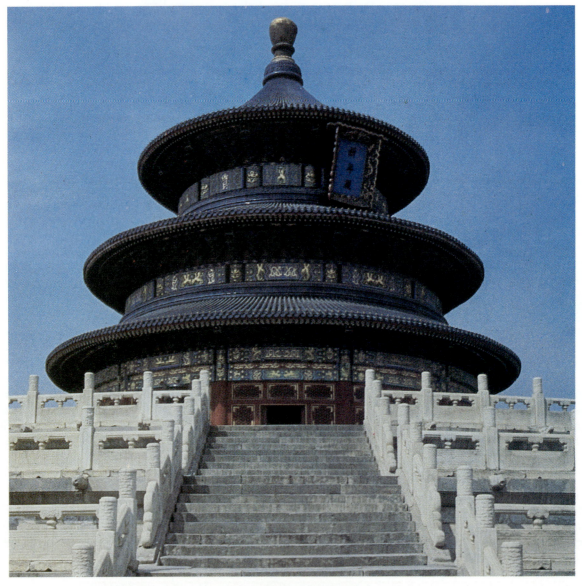

1. What beliefs developed in traditional China?
2. How did philosophy and religion shape the development of Chinese civilization?

1. The Master said, It is Goodness that gives to a neighbourhood its beauty. One who is free to choose, yet does not prefer to dwell among the Good—how can he be accorded the name of wise?
2. The Master said, Without Goodness a man
    Cannot for long endure adversity,
    Cannot for long enjoy prosperity.
The Good Man rests content with Goodness; he that is merely wise pursues Goodness in the belief that it pays to do so.
3, 4. Of the adage Only a Good Man knows how to like people, knows how to dislike them, the Master said, He whose heart is in the smallest degree set upon Goodness will dislike no one.
5. Wealth and rank are what every man desires; but if they can only be retained to the detriment of the Way he professes, he must relinquish them. Poverty and obscurity are what every man detests; but if they can only be avoided to the detriment of the Way he professes, he must accept them. The gentleman who ever parts company with Goodness does not fulfil that name. Never for a moment does a gentleman quit the way of Goodness. He is never so [worried] but that he [clings] to this; never so tottering but that he [clings] to this.*

"The Master" who spoke these thoughts was Confucius, whom many consider China's greatest philosopher. He was one of a number of important thinkers in traditional China. Despite the differences in their teachings, all were more concerned about life in this world than in the supernatural and devoted themselves to **ethics,** or the study of moral principles. Ethics, they believed, provided a key to understanding the workings of nature. If humans adapted to nature rather than try to change it, a harmonious balance would be achieved in human affairs.

These thinkers shaped China's beliefs and values for centuries. They passed on to the Chinese a high regard for education and the use of knowledge to guide conduct. Learning was an exercise in moral development, and to order their lives, the Chinese sought examples of moral living in their past. They believed that any problem could be solved by heeding more closely the wisdom of the past.

Over time, this heritage of thought and practice underwent important changes. The wisdom of such **sages,** or wise teachers, as Confucius became mixed with earlier religious beliefs and superstitions. Foreign religions entered the country and gained Chinese converts. Most Chinese soon found it easy to believe in more than one religion at a time. From this diversity of philosophy and religion, the Chinese developed a unique pattern of faith and practice that has continued into modern times.

---

*The Analects of Confucius, translated and annotated by Arthur Waley, 1938, George Allen & Unwin Ltd., pp. 102–103.

Traditional Chinese Beliefs

In traditional China, the people believed that many gods, goddesses, and spirits ruled the universe. To gain the approval of these deities and to ward off evil, they offered sacrifices of animals and grain. In the spring and fall, Chinese emperors performed sacrifices to the two chief deities—the gods of the Heaven and the Earth. They did this to insure the fertility of the soil and a plentiful harvest.

Another characteristic of traditional Chinese religion was **filial piety,** or reverence for parents and ancestors. Children were expected to take care of their elderly relatives, to obey them, and to bury them properly after death. Departed ancestors and their deeds were to be remembered, and sacrifices were to be offered to them. It was believed that such prayers and sacrifices joined together the worlds of the living and the dead.

The Chinese also held that, because of their contact with the gods, goddesses, and spirits, dead relatives were able to help living family members. Any Chinese who forgot to honor their ancestors were viewed with extreme disfavor. An old belief held that neglected ancestors wandered about as "homeless ghosts," punishing those family members who had abandoned them. The offenders, in turn, would become "homeless ghosts" after death.

Because of the importance of ancestors, each Chinese home had a small altar. There, the names and deeds of deceased family members were remembered, and small sacrifices of wine and rice were offered. In the 1800's, a western scholar described in this way the altar of one wealthy Chinese family and the ceremony its members performed to honor their ancestors:

This seventeenth-century painting shows a family giving thanks before the family shrine for the harvest. What did the Chinese believe happened to family members who forgot to honor their ancestors?

> At the back of the room, standing against the wall and taking up almost the whole length of it, a long table of varnished wood forms the altar. On this altar are stands holding small lacquered tablets, chronologically arranged, on which the names of the ancestors are inscribed. Hanging at the very top of the wall is the sign of the deity; and in front of the tablets are lights and incense burners. Lastly, at some distance from the altar, there is a common square table with chairs round it, and in the middle of the table a register with books on each side of it.
> Everybody has put on his best clothes and is waiting. The father and mother . . . enter, followed by two acolytes [worship assistants], and take their places in front

of the altar. They address a short invocation [appeal] to Heaven, and those present chant the ancestral hymn. . . . A variety of things are offered: . . . a pigeon or a chicken, fruits, wine and grain, either rice or wheat, whichever is grown in the district. Or wine alone, with rice or wheat, may be offered. The two acolytes go to fetch these offerings, the wife takes them from their hands and gives them to her husband, who lifts them above his head, his wife standing beside him, and places them on the altar in sign of thanksgiving. The father then reads the names of the ancestors inscribed on the tablets, and recalling them more particularly to the memory of the family, he speaks in their name. . . . The corn and wine that he has just consecrated [dedicated] to them, which are a symbol of the efforts made and the progress realized, he now returns, on behalf of the ancestors, to those present, in token of their [unbreakable] union. Lastly, the officiator [leader] exhorts the family to meditate on the meaning of this true communion, on the engagements that it implies, which all present swear to carry out and then, after a last prayer, a meal is served, in which the consecrated offerings are included.*

In addition to reverence for ancestors, the Chinese believed in **divination,** or the foretelling of the future. It was used to decide the place for a building, the time for religious services, or the outcome of a battle. To determine the future, fortune-tellers used such techniques as studying lines in stalks of grain or analyzing cracks on bones and shells. They also practiced **geomancy,** or the reading of such signs in nature as the flow of water or the surface of the landscape. In time, most of the principles and techniques of divination were recorded in a book called *Yi Jing,* or the *Book of Changes.*

*La Cité Chinoise by G. E. Simon, as quoted in China by L. A. Lyall, 1934, Charles Scribner's Sons, pp. 28–30. Reprinted by permission.

The zodiac, a band of stars believed to influence people's lives, is used in a form of divination known as astrology. The Chinese zodiac, shown here, has a different animal sign for each of its 12 parts. Each new Chinese year is represented by one of these signs.

1. In what did the people of traditional China believe?
2. How did the Chinese honor their deities and ancestors?
3. What methods did the Chinese use to predict the future?

DAOISM

Between 700 BC and 300 BC, China went through a period of political turmoil. During this time, the first great Chinese thinkers appeared, each with his own answer to China's problems. Among the earliest of these thinkers were the teachers of a philosophy known as Daoism, which means the "Way of Nature." Although scholars know very little about the origins of Daoism, they believe that in its earliest form, it was a philosophy of nature that stressed humanity's need to adapt to its natural surroundings.

The founder of Daoism supposedly was named Lao-zi, or "the Master." According to one tradition, he began his career as a record keeper in the court of the emperor. But he came to dislike the corruption of court life and finally retired from his post to seek peace of mind in nature. While wandering throughout the country, Lao-zi may have written some of Daoism's principal book, the *Dao De Jing*, or *The Way and Its Power*.

The *Dao De Jing* eventually became one of the **classics,** or major and lasting works, of Chinese literature. It is made up of only a few thousand words contained in 81 chapters written in poetic form. Its major themes are the corruption of civilization and the need for human simplicity and closeness to nature.

TEACHINGS

The early Daoists taught that the universe was united by **Dao,** a mysterious force which determined the destiny of all things and could not be changed. Therefore, if they were not in harmony with *Dao*, all human ambition and achievement were in vain.

The Daoists held that people should detach themselves from personal gain and possessions, which were the sources of human conflict. They should reject society, live simply in harmony with nature, and reflect on the meaning of *Dao*. The Daoists also believed that people who truly seek *Dao* should not worry about life. Instead, they should let events take their natural course and not interfere. The Daoist poem below illustrates this teaching:

> Nature does not have to insist,
> Can blow for only half a morning,
> Rain for only half a day,
> And what are these winds and these rains but natural?
> If nature does not have to insist,
> Why should man?*

The Way of Life by Witter Bynner, 1944, John Day Co., p. 38 (XXIII).

Although Daoist teachings focused chiefly on the individual, they also included views on society and government. The Daoists strongly opposed the existence of a large powerful government with a bureaucracy and many laws. Their vision of an ideal society was carefully explained in the following manner in the *Dao De Jing:*

> Let there be a small country with a few inhabitants. Though there be labor-saving [devices], the people would not use them. Let the people mind death and not migrate far. Though there be boats and carriages, there would be no occasion to ride in them. Though there be armor and weapons, there would be no occasion to display them.
>
> Let people revert to the practice of rope-knotting [instead of writing], and be contented with their food, pleased with their clothing, satisfied with their houses, and happy with their customs. Though there be a neighboring country in sight, and the people hear each other's cocks crowing and dogs barking, they would grow old and die without having anything to do with each other.*

RELIGION

As a philosophy little concerned about gods, rituals, and the afterlife, early Daoism appealed only to the educated few. It had little to offer the uneducated masses. But by the 100's AD, Daoism had undergone a major change. Without denying its original beliefs, it gradually became a religion complete with deities, priests, temples, and sacrifices.

The change from a philosophy to a religion was encouraged by Daoism's stress on the importance of life. The Daoists had always taught that a person who faithfully followed *Dao* would enjoy a long life. To carry this

---
*From the *Tao Te Ching*, as quoted in *Sources of Chinese Tradition* compiled by William Theodore de Bary, Wing-tsit Chan, and Burton Watson, ©1960, Columbia University Press, pp. 63–64. By permission.

belief further, scholars and priests sought ways to master the body and prolong life indefinitely. Some Daoists practiced gymnastics and breathing exercises. Others followed strict diets that banned rich foods. Still others practiced **alchemy,** or the effort to change inferior materials into gold. They believed that human flesh could be preserved by drinking liquid gold and other ingredients. Soon, a variety of magical practices developed that were accompanied by elaborate rituals and festivals.

The Daoist religion won wide appeal among the masses and became one of the major faiths of China. Its chief support came from the peasants, who lived and worked close to the soil. At the same time, Daoist philosophy continued to attract the more educated. It influenced poets and artists who sought inspiration in natural beauty and led to studies of plants, animals, and minerals.

1. What were the basic principles of early Daoism?
2. How did Daoism change over the centuries in China?

CONFUCIANISM

In spite of Daoism's widespread popularity, the most important ethical philosophy of traditional China was Confucianism. It was based on the teachings of Kong-fu-zi, better known to westerners as Confucius.

The teachings of Confucius respected the traditional wisdom and beliefs of the Chinese and were intended to be a guide to conduct, not a religion. Confucius himself showed little interest in the deities and seemed to approve of religious rituals chiefly as a means of uniting the people. In time, however, his philosophy, Confucianism, became a religion, and Confucian ethical values became the foundation of traditional Chinese society and government.

This rubbing of a stone engraving, thought to reproduce a Tang painting, shows Confucius as a court official. The verse on the right refers to his achievements and virtue. What were Confucius's teachings intended to be?

CONFUCIUS

Confucius was born in 551 BC to a noble family that had lost its wealth during the Zhou dynasty. Because his parents died when he was young, he had to make his own way in the world. A talented student, he developed an interest in the workings of society and searched for the factors that contributed to good government.

After Confucius completed his studies, he entered government service. He also served as a teacher and attracted a great number of students. In his teachings, Confucius revealed his concern about the poor condition of the Chinese government. He pointed out to his students that government existed for the well-being of the people, not for the enrichment of the rulers. He urged China's leaders to put aside military conquests and to work for the good of the country. He also criticized the appointment of government officials on the basis of family ties rather than ability. He believed that only well-educated officials should serve in the government.

Confucius' views gained him many enemies, and he was forced to resign his government post. During the final years of his life, he spent his time teaching and studying Chinese literary classics. After his death in 479 BC, his followers worked to carry out his political and social aims.

Beihai Park in Beijing, its gardens often compared to a three-dimensional traditional landscape painting, was a retreat for scholar-officials. Who was known as the "Supreme Sage"? The "Second Sage"?

TEACHINGS

Confucius' followers recorded his teachings in a work known as the *Analects*. The work, which later became one of the Chinese classics, stressed several themes. One was described by the word *li*, the outward practice of doing the right thing. Confucius taught that society functions smoothly when it follows *li*. People know their place in society and act for its welfare rather than for their own selfish interests.

Another theme was *ren*, or the inner attitude of being humane, loving, and good. According to the *Analects*, Confucius explained the meaning of *ren* to his students in the following way:

> When Fan Ch'ih asked about *jen* [ren], the Master said: "Love people."
> When Yen Yüan asked about *jen*, the Master said: "If you can control your selfish desires and subject them to the rules of propriety [being proper] and if you can do this for a single day, it is the beginning of *jen* for the entire world. *Jen* is self-sufficient and comes from your inner self; it requires no outside help." Yen Yügan asked for more details. The Master said: "Don't see the improper; don't hear the improper; don't talk about the improper; and don't act improperly."
> When Chung Kung [Zhong Gong] asked about *jen*, the Master said: "When you meet a person outside of your house, greet him as if he were a great noble. If, as a government official, you have to impose . . . duties on the people, you should approach your task with the same seriousness that you would use in performing a religious ritual. Don't do to others what you yourself do not desire."*

Confucius believed that *ren* and *li* should determine all human relationships. In his view, there were five important relationships

---
*Dun J. Li, "Analects of Confucius" from *The Ageless Chinese: A History*, (3rd edition). Copyright ©1978, 1971 Charles Scribner's Sons. Reprinted with the permission of Charles Scribner's Sons.

—ruler and ruled, father and son, husband and wife, older brother and younger brother, and friend and friend. In defining these relationships, he laid stress on the importance of rank. Rulers, for example, were above the ruled, men were superior to women, and the older was ahead of the younger. Only friends enjoyed a position of social equality, but they were expected to treat each other with respect and courtesy. Each person in an inferior position owed respect and obedience to those above him or her. On the other hand, those in a superior position were expected to care for and set a good example for those below them. If the "proper" conduct were carried out in each of the five relationships, the requirements of *ren* and *li* would be fulfilled and a just society would result.

Confucius also taught that for the people to act morally, a good government was necessary. He felt that poor government with tyrannical rulers and bad laws influenced people to do wrong, while conscientious rulers and good laws encouraged them to do good.

CONFUCIAN SCHOLARS

After Confucius' teachings became more widely known, he was given the title of "Supreme Sage and Foremost Teacher," and some of his ideas were taken up by other prominent scholars.

One of these scholars was Mencius (372 BC–289 BC). Mencius, who was born and raised near Confucius' home province and was a student of Confucius' grandson, came to be known as the "Second Sage." In time, his teachings were recorded in the book *Mencius*. Below, in a conversation recorded in *Mencius*, a critic and Mencius discuss human nature:

"Human nature is like water current," said [the critic]. "If it is led to the east, it flows eastward; if it is led to the west, it

In this eighth-century painting, a servant prepares ink as two scholars appear to be contemplating the composition of a poem. With what did Mencius compare human nature? Why?

flows westward. Like water which can be led to either of the two directions, human nature is neither good nor bad. It depends upon the direction towards which it is led."

[Mencius said,] "The goodness of human nature is like water's natural inclination to move downward. As water is inevitably moving downward, there is no man in the world who is not good. If you beat water hard, it jumps up and can rise higher than your forehead. . . . But, is this the nature of water? It acts contrary to its nature because it is given no other choice. If a man does bad things, he, like water, has been forced to do them and has not been given a better choice. His wrongdoing has nothing to do with his inherent nature which is good."*

Another later follower of Confucius was Zhu Xi (1130 AD–1200 AD), who combined teachings of Confucius and others into a

---

*Dun J. Li, "Mencius" from *The Ageless Chinese: A History* (3rd edition). Copyright ©1978, 1971 Charles Scribner's Sons. Reprinted with the permission of Charles Scribner's Sons.

simpler version known as the "Four Books." As a unit, the "Four Books" was so brief that any gentleman could master it. For the next 700 years, the "Four Books" were studied, read aloud, and memorized. They became the basis of the civil service examinations, which continued to be given until 1905.

Confucianism, regarded as a philosophy by scholars, gradually became a religion for the Chinese masses. By 500 AD, shrines and temples had been built to Confucius throughout China, and many Chinese came to look on him as a god. Although periodically certain government officials made an effort to discourage the worship of Confucius, the practice continued well into the twentieth century.

1. What were some of Confucius' teachings? How did they influence government?
2. How did Mencius view human nature?
3. Why were the "Four Books" important?

OTHER FAITHS AND VIEWPOINTS

Although Confucianism emerged as the dominant influence in Chinese life, it was not without rivals or critics. An important critic was Mo Zi, who lived from 480 BC to 400 BC. Mo Zi shunned the Confucian devotion to learning and the arts and urged people to follow more practical pursuits. He also criticized the Confucian emphasis on social rank and duties. Instead, he called for an end to the privileges of the wealthy and the creation of a new society in which all people would be loved and treated equally. Below, Mo Zi presents his view of the ideal society:

> . . . What is it like when righteousness is the standard of conduct? The great will not attack the small, the strong will not plunder the weak, the many will not oppress the few, the cunning will not deceive the simple, the noble will not disdain the humble, the rich will not mock the poor, and the young will not encroach upon the old. And the states in the empire will not harm each other with water, fire, poison, and weapons. Such a regime will be auspicious to Heaven above, to the spirits in the middle sphere, and to the people below. Being auspicious to these three, it is beneficial to all.*

BUDDHISM

One rival to Confucianism was the foreign religion of Buddhism, which merchants from India brought to China during the first century AD. The first Chinese converts to Buddhism came from the upper class, who were attracted by the religion's complex philosophy and elaborate ceremonies. Later, it spread among the lower class, who hoped for release from their poverty in Buddhist afterlife.

By the 300's AD, Buddhist beliefs were seen in Chinese religious practices, literature, scholarship, art, and architecture. At the same time, traditional Chinese beliefs and ways influenced the teachings and practices of Buddhism in China. For most Chinese, Buddhism, Daoism, and Confucianism complemented each other, and they combined the practices of all three.

ISLAM

Another foreign religion that influenced China was Islam, which began in the Middle East during the 600's AD. It was first brought to China a century later by traders. These Muslims, or followers of Islam, lived in their own settlements apart from the Chinese.

Then, in the 1200's, when the Mongols invaded China, they brought with them

---

*Mo Tzu as cited in *Sources of Chinese Tradition* compiled by William Theodore De Bary, Wing-tsit Chan, and Burton Watson, ©1960, Columbia University Press, p. 49. By permission.

many Muslim soldiers who settled in China and married Chinese women. For the first time, Islam spread to the general population. The largest number of converts, however, was among the non-Chinese minorities in the western part of the country. This area remains a stronghold of Islam today.

CHRISTIANITY

Christianity was less successful than Islam in establishing a foothold in China. The first Christian missionaries from Western Europe were Franciscans, a group of Roman Catholic clergy, who reached China during the Mongol period.

Later, during the 1500's, another Roman Catholic group called Jesuits headed a more successful missionary effort. Jesuit priests shared their skills in mathematics, astronomy, and clockmaking with Chinese scholars and won the respect of the Chinese by adopting Chinese dress and customs. As a result, in 1692, the Chinese emperor allowed Chinese converts to Christianity to practice their faith freely. The Catholic Pope in Rome, however, blocked the Jesuit effort to adapt Christianity to Chinese ways. The Chinese emperor viewed this as foreign interference in Chinese affairs and banned the practice of Christianity in China.

In the 1800's, under pressure from the western powers, the Chinese government allowed Christian missionaries to enter China once again. Many of the new missionaries were from the Protestant churches of North America and Western Europe. With the backing of their governments, they preached Christianity and built mission schools, hospitals, and universities throughout China. Many Chinese, however, viewed Christianity as a foreign religion linked to the western powers and to western efforts to impose their ways on China. As a result, antiforeign attacks against missionaries and Chinese Christians were common.

Jesuit priests were admired more for their knowledge of science than for their Christian beliefs by the Chinese, who accepted them as literati *from abroad. Why did a Chinese emperor ban Christianity?*

Although only a small minority of Chinese accepted Christianity, those who did had a noticeable impact on China. A number of Chinese Christians became well educated in western ways and supported efforts to modernize their country. Many backed the revolutionary movement that led to the overthrow of the Qing dynasty in 1911. Although today Christianity is still an important minority religion in China, it has little or no impact on the social and political life of the country.

1. For what did Mo Zi criticize Confucian teachings?
2. What foreign religions gained a foothold in China? In what ways did they influence China and the Chinese?

Exploration
CHINA

For hundreds of years, Confucianism has been one of the world's major religions. Like other religions, it has provided guidelines for its followers. Listed below are guidelines for Confucianism and some other religions as well. After reading the guidelines and studying the chart, answer the following questions:

1. Compare and contrast the Confucian guideline with the others. Based on the information in the chapter and in the chart, how do you think a follower of Confucius would respond to each guideline? Give reasons for your answers.
2. Using your knowledge of Confucianism and other world religions, how is Confucianism similar to other faiths? How is it different? What effect do you think Confucianism and other religions have had on the development of China?

First put yourself in order, then be sure you act justly and sincerely towards others. Then you will find happiness.
—The Analects of Confucius

Perform right action, for action is superior to inaction.
—The Bhagavad-Gita of India

The world is a divine vessel:
It cannot be shaped;
Nor can it be insisted upon.
He who shapes it damages it;
He who insists upon it loses it.
Therefore the sage does not
*   shape it, so he does not*
*   damage it;*
He does not insist upon it,
*   so he does not lose it.*
—The Dao De Jing

Devoutly trust the law of love;
Do not denounce the creed of others.
Devoutly promote the sense of equality;
Do not arouse discriminatory feelings.
Devoutly awaken the sense of compassion;
Do not forget the sufferings of others.
Devoutly cultivate a [friendly manner]; . . .
—Ippen Shonin Goroku of Japan

Decay is (found) in all . . . things.
Work out your salvation with diligence.
—Dialogues of the Buddha

. . . what is good; and what does the Lord require of (you), but to do justly, and to love mercy, and to walk humbly with (your) God.
—The Bible (Micah)

Love your enemies, bless them that curse you, do good to them that hate you, and pray for them which despitefully use you, and persecute you, that you may be children of your Father . . . in heaven.
—The Bible (Matthew)

Those who believe and do deeds of righteousness, and perform the prayer, and pay the alms—their wage awaits them with their Lord, and no fear shall be on them, neither shall they sorrow.
—The Koran (Sura II)

Be kind to parents, and the near kinsman,
and to orphans and to the needy,
and to the neighbor who is of kin,
and to the neighbor who is a stranger,
and to the companion at your side,
and to the traveller, and to that your
right hand owns.
—The Koran (Sura IV)

CHARACTERISTICS OF THE MAJOR PHILOSOPHIES/RELIGIONS OF CHINA

PHILOSOPHIES/RELIGIONS	DAOISM	CONFUCIANISM	BUDDHISM
ORIGIN	Based upon the teachings of Lao-zi, "The Master."	Based upon the teachings of Confucius.	Imported from India and based upon the teachings of Siddhartha Gautama (the Buddha).
MAJOR BELIEFS	Civilization is corrupt and humanity has a need for simplicity and closeness to nature. The origin of creation and its force is the Dao (The Way). The Way can be found by reinterpreting ancient traditions of nature worship and divination. A life lived according to the Dao is a healthy human life.	The moral understanding "What you do not wish for yourself, do not do to others," is at the foundation of social institutions. Everyday life is the arena of religion. All human relationships should be determined by *li, ren,* and the Five Relationships. In a well-disciplined society ceremonies, duties, and public service are emphasized daily.	Life is suffering. Suffering is caused by desire for things to be as they are not. Suffering, however, has an end. The means to the end are the Middle Way of moderation and the Eightfold Path—Right Views, Right Intentions, Right Speech, Right Action, Right Occupation, Right Effort, Right Concentration, and Right Meditation.
CHARACTERISTIC	Adherents vary in beliefs. Some seek immortality through the arts of magic, breath control, and alchemy; offers an alternative to Confucianism.	Confucian ethical values became the foundation of Chinese society and government.	Has split into several branches, virtually extinct in India by the 12th century AD, although influential in China and Japan.

CHAPTER 11 REVIEW

POINTS TO REMEMBER

1. Traditional Chinese thinkers, devoted to ethics, shaped China's beliefs and values, encouraging education and promoting knowledge as a guide to conduct.
2. The Chinese believed that many gods, goddesses, and spirits ruled the universe. They also believed in filial piety, divination, and geomancy.
3. Daoism at first stressed humanity's need to adapt to its natural surroundings. It taught that the universe was united by a mysterious force called *Dao* that determined the destiny of all things and could not be changed. Its stress on the importance of life encouraged its change from a philosophy of the upper class to a religion of the lower class.
4. The most important ethical philosophy of traditional China was Confucianism, which was based on the teachings of Confucius. Confucian ethical values such as *li, ren,* and the five relationships became the foundation of Chinese society and government.
5. Some of Confucius' teachings were developed further by such prominent Chinese scholars as Mencius and Zhu Xi.
6. A major critic of Confucianism was Mo Zi, who urged the Chinese to follow more practical pursuits than learning and the arts and called for the creation of a new society in which all people would be loved and treated equally.
7. Several foreign religions also influenced the Chinese. These included Buddhism, which came from India; Islam, which came from the Middle East; and Christianity, which came from Western Europe and North America. All were an influence on China and the Chinese.

VOCABULARY

Identify

Confucius	*Dao*	Mencius	Buddhism
Yi Jing	Confucianism	Zhu Xi	Islam
Daoism	Kong-fu-zi	"Four Books"	Muslims
Lao-zi	*Analects*	Mo Zi	Franciscans
Dao De Jing			Jesuits

Define

ethics	divination	classics	*li*
sages	geomancy	alchemy	*ren*
filial piety			

DISCUSSING IMPORTANT IDEAS

1. Traditional Chinese thinkers encouraged a high regard for education. In what ways do you think China would be different if education had not been a priority?

2. Which beliefs of Confucianism and Daoism do you think are valuable in today's world? Give reasons for your answers.
3. A critic of Mencius states that "Like water which can be led to either of the two directions (east or west), human nature is neither good nor bad. It depends upon the direction towards which it is led." Do you agree with him? Use examples to support your argument.
4. In what ways can traditional China be considered a "melting pot"?

Developing Skills

HYPOTHESIZING

At one time or another, you may have read a statement and wondered about what you read. Then, in your own mind, you may have begun to form explanations about the material, explanations that you may or may not have been able to prove. What you did was to *hypothesize*. You formed one or more *hypotheses*, assumptions that offer a possible answer or answers to a problem or provide an explanation for an observation and often may be tested to determine whether or not they are correct or true.

The steps in the following example will help you hypothesize:

1. Read this statement:

   The largest number of converts to Islam in China was among the non-Chinese minorities in the western part of the country, which remains a stronghold of Islam.

2. Ask yourself what the statement is actually saying. To do this, put the statement in your own words. For example:

   The people in the western part of China who were not Chinese made up the majority of converts to Islam in China. Islam is still strong in western China.

3. Determine what you might logically assume from these facts. For example:

   a. Since non-Chinese minorities in western China continue to identify culturally with the Middle East, today most converts to Islam in China are found among non-Chinese in western China;
   b. Islam in China has been practiced mostly among the non-Chinese minorities in western China because certain geographical features of China isolated these people from the rest of the country.

4. Test each hypothesis to determine whether or not it is correct or true. Often, this can be done by asking yourself questions that relate to your hypotheses and then researching the answers. In this case, you might want to find information on the history of Islam in China and on the geographical features of China. You also might want to determine where Islam is practiced in China, by whom it is practiced, and how many people practice it.

5. Finally, based on your research, determine which hypothesis, if any, provides an explanation for or supports the statement in step 1.

For further practice in hypothesizing, apply the five steps to the following:

1. Filial piety was practiced for centuries in traditional China.
2. Christianity has little impact on the social and political life of China.
3. The first great Chinese thinkers appeared between 700 BC and 300 BC, each with his own answer to China's problems.

CHAPTER 12
THE CHINESE REVOLUTION

1. What were the major phases of the Chinese Revolution?
2. How did the Chinese Revolution contribute to the emergence of modern China?

We hail from all corners of the country and have joined together for a common revolutionary objective. And we need the vast majority of the people with us on the road to this objective. . . . In times of difficulty we must not lose sight of our achievements, must see the bright future and must pluck up our courage. The Chinese people are suffering; it is our duty to save them and we must exert ourselves in struggle. Wherever there is struggle there is sacrifice, and death is a common occurrence. But we have the interests of the people and the sufferings of the great majority at heart, and when we die for the people it is a worthy death. Nevertheless, we should do our best to avoid unnecessary sacrifices. Our cadres must show concern for every soldier, and all people in the revolutionary ranks must care for each other, must love and help each other.

From now on, when anyone in our ranks who has done some useful work dies, be he soldier or cook, we should have a funeral ceremony and a memorial meeting in his honour. This should become the rule. And it should be introduced among the people as well. When someone dies in a village, let a memorial meeting be held. In this way we express our mourning for the dead and unite all the people.*

The above speech was given by Mao Zedong, China's major twentieth-century revolutionary leader. Mao's achievements were the high point of a long period of revolution in China that began about 1840 and lasted well into the 1970's. The Chinese Revolution went through several phases of development. It began with peasant rebellions against the corrupt Qing dynasty and foreign powers. Later, it spread to the small and western-educated middle class, which wanted a democratic republic and an end to foreign controls.

In 1911, the ruling dynasty was overthrown and a republic established. This, however, did not bring to an end dissatisfaction among students, workers, and peasants. Leadership of the revolution then passed from the middle class to Communist **intellectuals**, or thinkers, and their allies in the poorer classes.

In 1949, after two decades of upheaval, the Communists, led by Mao Zedong, established the People's Republic of China. Mao remained the major leader of the People's Republic until his death in 1976. While in power, he taught his people that the Chinese Revolution was a continuing struggle against old ways.

*"Serve the People" by Mao Zedong in *Selected Works of Mao Tse-tung*, Vol. III, 1967, Foreign Language Press, pp. 177–178.

BEGINNINGS

The roots of the Chinese Revolution date back to the 1800's. At the time, China was in decline, beset by famine, drought, and violence. The ruling Qing emperors lacked the vision and leadership skills of earlier Chinese rulers, and many government officials opposed reforms. Even those officials who favored change did not want to give up the traditional system completely.

CHINA AND FOREIGN POWERS

During the 1800's, China became involved in a series of humiliating wars with the technologically stronger western countries whose governments used force to open China for trade. The United Kingdom, the most powerful western nation, sold the Chinese **opium,** an addictive drug made from poppies. When, in 1839, the Chinese government tried to stop its sale, the British made war on China.

The Opium Wars, which occurred during the 1840's and 1850's, resulted in the first of many **unequal treaties** between China and the West. These treaties treated China as an inferior nation and opened it to further western influence. The 1842 Treaty of Nanking, for example, made China pay money and surrender Hong Kong to the British. It also forced the Chinese government to grant **extraterritoriality** to British merchants in China. This meant that they no longer were under the control of Chinese law. Following Britain's lead, other western nations soon began to demand and receive similar or even greater privileges.

China's greatest setback, however, came not from the West but from Japan, its Asian neighbor. Unlike China, Japan had modernized its society and by the 1890's was challenging China's dominance in the Far East. In 1894, the two rivals went to war over Korea. When China lost the war, it was forced to recognize Korea's independence. It also had to give the island of Taiwan and the Liaotung Peninsula to Japan. In addition, Japan gained even more trading privileges than the trading privileges won by the western nations.

When British merchants turned to smuggling, the Chinese cracked down and began to rigorously enforce their trade ban on opium, leading to the break-out of the Opium Wars. A fierce naval battle fought at Cheunpu in 1841 is depicted in this painting. What was China forced to do under terms of the treaty that ended the wars?

PEASANT REBELLIONS

At the same time China was battling foreign powers, it had to contend with problems within its own borders. From 1850 to 1900, a wave of peasant rebellions swept through China.

The Taiping Rebellion The longest and most violent was the Taiping Rebellion, which lasted from 1851 to 1864. It began in the South of China and spread throughout the country. The Taiping rebels developed an ideology that combined Christianity and traditional Chinese beliefs. They sought to overthrow the Qing dynasty and create a new society based on equality and shared property. In 1853, they stated their goals in the following declaration:

> The distribution of land is made according to the size of the family, irrespective of sex, with only the number of persons taken into account. The larger the number, the more land they shall receive; the smaller the number, the less land they shall receive.... All lands under Heaven shall be farmed jointly by the people under Heaven. If the production of food is too small in one place, then move to another where it is more abundant. All lands under Heaven shall be accessible in time of abundance or famine. If there is a famine in one area move the surplus from an area where there is abundance to that area, in order to feed the starving. In this way the people under Heaven shall all enjoy the great happiness given by the Heavenly Father, Supreme Lord and August God. Land shall be farmed by all; rice, eaten by all; clothes, worn by all; money, spent by all. There shall be no inequality; and no person shall be without food or fuel....
>
> Everywhere in the empire mulberry trees shall be planted beneath the walls. All women shall raise silkworms, spin cloth and sew dresses. Every family in the empire shall have five hens and two sows, without exception.... For under Heaven all belongs to the great family of the Heavenly Father, Supreme Lord and August God. In the empire none shall have any private property, and everything belongs to God, so that God may dispose of it. In the great family of Heaven, every place is equal, and everyone has plenty....*

The Taiping Rebellion almost toppled the Qing dynasty, but divisions among the rebel leaders weakened rebel efforts. With the backing of the gentry and the western powers, the dynasty was able to organize effective armies that eventually defeated the rebels.

The Boxer Rebellion In 1900, another rebellion broke out. It was led by a secret society called the Society of Righteous and Harmonious Fists. Known in English as the Boxers, it's members believed that their country's problems could be solved if foreigners and their "evil influences" were expelled from China. The Boxers were violently anti-Christian and killed western missionaries and thousands of Chinese who had converted to Christianity. The Qing dynasty secretly supported the Boxers and refused to take measures against them. Eventually, military forces from eight foreign nations defeated them, forcing China to pay $333 million and make more concessions.

Following the Boxer Rebellion, the Qing dynasty set out to reform Chinese society. It promised to adopt a democratic constitution and introduce a western-style educational system and army. But these efforts came too late. In 1905, the middle class and students began to turn to revolution. At first, the Qing managed to put down the revolts. But, in October 1911, the revolutionaries received the backing of the army. By the end of the year, all of China had renounced the rule of

---
*"The Land System of the Heavenly Dynasty" in *Chinese Sources for the Taiping Rebellion, 1850–1864* by J.C. Cheng, 1963, Oxford University Press, pp. 39–40.

In this photo taken in 1912, Sun Yat-sen is shown presiding over China's first parliament. The details of parliamentary procedure were considered important to Sun, who described them in his Plan for National Reconstruction. This plan, together with the "Three Principles," summarize Sun's key political doctrines. How did Sun propose to improve China's industry?

the Qing, forcing the emperor to give up the throne.

1. What led China into war with the United Kingdom? With Japan? What was the result of the wars?
2. What were the goals of the Taiping rebels? The Boxers? Why did their rebellions fail?

A DIVIDED CHINA

After the downfall of the Qing in 1911, the leaders of the revolution met in the southern Chinese city of Nanching and proclaimed China a democratic republic. Dr. Sun Yat-sen, a leading revolutionary leader, was named **provisional,** or temporary, president. Sun realized that he had a difficult task ahead of him. Although officially a democracy, China lacked a sense of national unity. Most Chinese could not read or write and had no experience in self-government. Also, the Chinese economy was largely agricultural. As goals for the new republic, Sun announced "Three Principles of the People" —Nationalism, Democracy, and Livelihood —which he described as follows:

> [Nationalism]. . . . For the most part . . . the people of China can be spoken of as completely . . . Chinese. With common customs and habits, we are completely of one race. . . . But the Chinese people have only family and clan solidarity; they do not have national spirit. Therefore even though we have . . . people gathered together in one China, in reality they are just a heap of loose sand. . . .
> [Democracy]. . . . For it is our plan that the political power of the reconstructed state will be divided into two parts. One is the power over government; that great power will be placed entirely in the hands of the people. . . . The other power is the governing power; that great power will be placed in the hands of the government.
> . . . [Livelihood]. . . . Our first method consists in solving the land question. . . . The plan which we are following is simple and easy—equalization of landownership. . .
> [Our second method consists of solving the industrial problem. To promote industry], we must build means of communica-

tion, railroads and waterways, on a large scale . . . we must open up mines. . . we must hasten to develop manufacturing.*

Sun, however, did not have the power to achieve his goals. Failing to get the full support of the army, he stepped aside in favor of General Yuan Shih-k'ai. Yuan cared little for Sun's "Three Principles" and tried to reestablish the monarchy with himself on the throne. Because military leaders opposed him, the republic continued. But it was in the form of a **dictatorship**, or one-person rule, under Yuan. Meanwhile, Sun's supporters had formed a political party known as the Guomindang, or Nationalist party, and most went into exile.

CIVIL WAR

When Yuan died in 1916, the national government had no real power, and political turmoil swept China. Local military leaders known as **warlords** fought each other for control of the provinces. Sun and his Guomindang followers established a base of power in Guangzhou in southern China. Their aim was to reunite China under one republican, democratic government.

Sun realized that he needed a strong army to defeat the warlords. To achieve this goal, he sought help from the West but was refused. Sun then turned to the Soviet Union, which promptly gave him aid. With the help of Soviet advisers, a Guomindang army was organized in 1924. Sun appointed a young military officer named Chiang K'ai-shek to head the new army.

Like Sun, Chiang was influenced by western ways. He married Soong Meiling, the American-educated daughter of a Chinese businessperson. Chiang, however, gave less support to the democratic values that had inspired Sun. When Sun died in 1925,

Chiang became the new leader of the Guomindang. The following year, he won a major victory against the warlords.

CHINESE COMMUNISM

In his efforts to gain control of China, Chiang had to deal with a rival political organization—the Chinese Communist party. Organized in 1921, the party appealed to students, intellectuals, and urban workers unhappy with the failure of the 1911 revolutionaries to meet the needs of the lower classes and to remove foreign influences.

The Communists wanted to carry the revolution forward. They planned to introduce radical social changes that would remove influences of the past, end reliance on foreign powers, and transform China into a modern industrialized nation. In the hope of spreading revolution, many joined the Guomindang, formed their own army, and supported Chiang in his struggle against the warlords.

Soon, however, the Communists and the Guomindang began to fight each other. In 1927, fearing a Communist takeover, Chiang directed a campaign against urban Communists. More than 3000 Communists were killed during this campaign. The Communist leaders who survived fled to the hills of southern China, where they set up Communist local governments.

In 1928, Chiang eliminated the last of the warlords and was elected president of the republic. After a decade of violence, most of China seemed to be united under Chiang's government.

1. What were Sun Yat-sen's "Three Principles"? Why did he initiate them?
2. What happened when General Yuan Shih-K'ai took over the government?
3. What were the goals of the Chinese Communists? Why did the Communists join the Guomindang?
4. How did Chiang K'ai-shek become president of the republic?

---
*Sun Yat-sen, as cited in *Sources of Chinese Tradition*, edited by William Theodore de Bary, ©1960, Columbia University Press, pp. 768–769, 772–773,776,778. By permission.

GUOMINDANG, COMMUNISTS, AND THE JAPANESE

Once in power, Chiang worked to strengthen his government and control the spread of communism. He relied largely on force, abandoning the democratic principles of the early Guomindang. Under his leadership, China gradually became a dictatorship, and such social reforms as equality for women and land reform for poor peasants were neglected.

Instead, Chiang stressed social discipline through a return to Confucian values. This won him the support of the rural gentry and the western-educated middle class, both of which were against any social reforms that would endanger their privileges. At the same time, Chiang worked to promote industrial growth, sponsoring the building of roads, railroads, waterways, and ports. These changes helped tie China more closely to the capitalist economies of western nations.

Meanwhile, in their rural retreats, the Communists rebuilt their leadership and army. One of their most influential members was Mao Zedong, a former librarian, teacher, and union organizer. Under his direction, the Communists gained widespread support in rural areas. Mao declared that peasants, not urban workers, would lead a future Communist revolution in China.

THE LONG MARCH

Before Mao's ideas were accepted by the party, the Communists faced a series of military attacks from Chiang's forces. To escape the Guomindang armies, 90,000 Communists, including Mao Zedong, retreated from southern China and headed to northwestern China. Their retreat, known

CASE STUDY
CHINA

WOMEN AND THE REVOLUTION

One of the goals of the Chinese Communists was to improve the status of women. As a result, women were encouraged to play an important role in the Communist phase of the Revolution. They served in many ways, some as soldiers and medical personnel, others served as teachers and speakers. In the following excerpt, Deng Ying-chao, the wife of Zhou En-lai, explains the role she and other women played in the May Fourth Movement, the opening event of the Communist revolutionary struggle:

> I was a sixteen-year old student . . . when the May Fourth Movement began in 1919. . . .
> On May 4, . . . the students in Peking [Beijing] staged a massive demonstration. . . . [Shortly afterwards] such organizations as . . . the Association of Patriotic Women . . . came into existence. Most members . . . were actually women students. . . . Simple and uncomplicated we relied heavily on our selfless patriotism for our strength. . . .
> We . . . stressed the importance of propaganda work. Many oratorical teams were organized, and I was elected captain of speakers for the Association. . . . My duty was to provide speakers in different areas on a regular basis.
> At the beginning we, as female students, did not enjoy the same freedom of movement as our male counterparts, insofar as our speaking tours were concerned. According to the feudal custom of China, women were not supposed to make speeches in the street; we, therefore, had to do our work indoors. We gave speeches in such places as libraries and participated in scheduled debates, all inside a hall or room. . . .
> Besides making speeches, we also conducted house-to-house visits which often took us to more remote areas of the city and also to the slums. . . .
> In addition to speaking tours and house-to-house visits, we also paid great attention to the use of written words as a means of spreading the patriotic sentiments. . . . The Association of Patriotic Women . . . published a weekly. [It] reported foreign as well as domestic news, with particular emphasis on the students' patriotic movement then conducted all over China. . . .
> In the wake of the May Fourth Movement came the feminist movement which was in fact one of its democratic extensions. Among the demands we raised at that time were sexual equality, abolition of arranged marriage, social activities open to women, freedom of romantic love and marriage, universities open to women students, and employment of women in government institutions. The first step we took toward sexual equality was to merge the associations of male and female students . . . to form a new organization which students of both sexes could join. . . .
> As pioneers in the feminist movement who had had the rare opportunity to work side by side with men, we female students in the merged association were conscious of the example we had to set so that no man in the future could deny women the opportunity to work on the ground of alleged incompetence. In short, we worked doubly hard. . . . Each department . . . was always headed by two chairpersons, one male and one female, and the female chairperson had as much authority as her male counterpart. The merger was such a success that the students in Peking [Beijing] decided to follow our example.*

1. How did the revolutionary movement affect the status of Chinese women?
2. Do you think most Chinese women of the time would have supported Deng Ying-chao and her colleagues? Explain.

---

*Dun J. Li, "My Experience with the May Fourth Movement" from *Modern China: From Mandarin to Commissar*. Copyright ©1978 Dun J. Li. Reprinted with the permission of Charles Scribner's Sons.

later as the Long March, took two years and covered over 6000 miles (9600 kilometers). Below, a Communist soldier who took part in the march describes what happened:

> . . . our forces were confronted with desperate odds. The enemy gave us no rest. We had some kind of skirmish at least once a week. . . . At night we dared not sleep in towns or villages for fear of surprise attack. We had to make our beds in the forests of the mountains. For nearly two years I never undressed at night, but slept with even my shoes on. So did most of our men. . . .
>
> We never had enough to eat. Had it not been for the help of the people we would have starved. . . . The farmers gladly shared with us what rice they had. . . . The farmers hated the thought of the landlords returning and to them our defeat meant the return of the landlord system. . . .
>
> We lost all contact with the outside. We were like wild men, living and fighting by instinct. Many of our best commanders were killed, or died of disease. We had no medicines and no hospitals. Our ammunition ran very low. Many of our guns became useless. . . .
>
> At times we retired into the uninhabited forests. We learned the trails . . . foot by foot. We knew every corner of the mountains. We learned to fast with nothing to eat for four or five days. And yet we became strong and agile as savages. Some of our lookouts practically lived in trees. Our young men could go up and down mountains with incredible speed.*

Although only a few thousand Communists survived the Long March, the ordeal proved that the Communists were strong and dedicated enough to successfully resist Chiang. As a result of the march, support for the Communists increased throughout China, and Mao Zedong emerged as the major leader of the party.

WAR WITH JAPAN

While the Guomindang and the Communists were fighting each other, the Japanese expanded into China. In 1931, the Japanese occupied the northern Chinese province of Manchuria. Six years later, they extended their invasion southward into the rest of China. In spite of their differences, Mao and Chiang now had a common enemy in the Japanese. This forced them into an uneasy alliance.

The Chinese Communists fought with the Japanese in the countryside, while the Guomindang led the resistance in the urban areas. Chiang's troops, however, were no match for the Japanese. In the end, the Guomindang government retreated to the interior of China, leaving the Japanese in control of eastern China.

During World War II, China helped the western nations in the Pacific War. In return, the western nations ended the last of the "unequal treaties." The United States, in particular, sent aid to Chiang's forces. But the cost of the war imposed hardships on the Chinese people and weakened support for the Guomindang government. In addition, the growth of corruption among Chiang's

THE LONG MARCH 1934–35

---

*Han Ying, as related in *The Battle for Asia* by Edgar Snow, 1941, Random House, pp. 131–132. Reprinted by permission.

On the Long March, the Communists suffered heavy losses from daily bombings by Chiang K'ai-shek's air force. Though he was seriously ill with a fever, Mao Zedong (center) led the Communist retreat. He and his followers were plagued by heavy rains and flooded rivers on the first half of their journey. Many did not survive the 18 mountain crossings and the bitter cold. What happened as a result of the Long March?

advisers heightened public distrust of Chiang.

COMMUNIST ADVANCE

As discontent grew, the Chinese Communists increased their power and influence. After gaining control from the Japanese of large areas of northern China, they made radical changes in the countryside. They divided the property of landlords among the peasants, introduced medicine and education, and raised the status of women. All of these changes further weakened the Guomindang's hold over the people.

After the defeat of Japan by the Allies in 1945, the Communists and the Guomindang once again faced each other. In order to avoid a civil war, the United States tried to bring the two groups together. The Communists, however, accused the United States of backing the Guomindang while pretending to take no sides. Although the United States insisted that its aid to Chiang was not intended for use in a civil war, Chiang believed that the aid would help him win back China.

In the civil war that followed, Chiang was defeated. He took his followers to the island of Taiwan, where he continued the Republic of China. The Communists, meanwhile, ruled mainland China, where, in 1949, they formed the People's Republic of China. Since then, both governments have claimed to be the true government of China.

1. How did Chiang govern China during the 1930's and 1940's?
2. What was the Long March? What did it prove?
3. What effect did World War II have on China?

THE PEOPLE'S REPUBLIC

The government of the People's Republic of China was influenced by three dominant groups—the Communist party, the bureaucrats, and the army. The party made policy. The bureaucrats carried it out, and the army enforced it. Almost all of the leaders in the military and the bureaucracy held high positions in the party. Mao Zedong served as chairman, while Zhou En-lai, a noted thinker and revolutionary leader, served as prime minister.

Upon taking power, the Communists enjoyed wide support in China. Those Chinese who opposed the new government were either jailed, sent to labor camps, or executed. Such nationwide mass organizations as labor unions, youth groups, and women's associations assisted the party in furthering public support for its policies. In addition, the government strengthened support for communism by introducing long-awaited reforms. Public sanitation and health were greatly improved. Education was stressed and illiteracy reduced. Women were given full equality with men.

ECONOMIC POLICIES AND FOREIGN AFFAIRS

The Communist government worked to transform China from a technologically backward nation into a modern industrial-agricultural state. To develop rural areas, it completed the seizure of land from landlords and redistributed it among the peasants. In time, however, the peasants were required to combine their individual plots into agricultural **cooperatives,** or units in which the land is jointly owned. With Soviet aid, industrial production was increased, and in 1953, the first Five-Year Plan for economic development got underway. The plan stressed such heavy industry as coal, iron, and steel production. It also brought commerce, banking, and industry under government control.

In 1958, a more ambitious economic program known as the Great Leap Forward was launched. Under it, rural cooperatives were merged into larger government-controlled units called **communes.** In industrial production, human labor, rather than complex technology, was stressed. Factory workers were forced to work long hours to meet production goals.

Within two years, it became clear that the Great Leap Forward was in trouble. Food shortages, industrial mismanagement, and peasant resistance to communes brought the program to a halt. Even so, China did make significant economic gains under Communist rule. By the mid-1960's, it was ranked among the ten leading industrial nations in the world.

At the same time China was developing its economy, it also sought to increase its influence overseas, especially among the newly independent states of Asia and Africa. By the late 1950's, however, its ties to the Soviet Union began to weaken. The two nations soon became involved in a bitter feud over their mutual borders and over Communist ideology. In 1960, the Soviets withdrew their economic support from China, forcing the Chinese to forge ahead on their own as a military power. Four years later, the Chinese exploded their first atomic bomb.

This modern machine tools plant in Wuxi uses equipment and technology acquired since 1969. How did China's government seek to acquire new technology after the Great Cultural Revolution of the late 1960's?

GREAT CULTURAL REVOLUTION

The failure of the Great Leap Forward and the Chinese-Soviet split led to a deep division within the Chinese Communist party. Moderates, headed by Lin Shao-qi and Deng Xiaoping, wanted less stress on revolutionary ideas and more on practical reforms. Radicals, led by Mao and his wife Jiang Qing, insisted on strict obedience to revolutionary principles. To end the influence of the moderates, Mao began a movement known as the Great Cultural Revolution. Moderates, accused of betraying communism, were removed from office, while students loyal to Mao formed groups called Red Guards. Below, a Chinese journalist sympathetic to Mao and the Red Guards comments on activities in Beijing:

> During the past week and more Red Guards have scored victory after victory as they pressed home their attack against the decadent [corrupt] customs and habits of the exploiting classes. Beating drums and singing revolutionary songs, . . . Red Guards are out in the streets doing propaganda work, holding aloft big portraits of Chairman Mao, extracts from Chairman Mao's works, and great banners with the words: "We are the critics of the old world; we are the builders of the new world." They have held street meetings, put up big character posters, and distributed leaflets in their attack against all the old ideas and habits of the exploiting classes. As a result of the proposals of the Red Guards and with the support of the revolutionary masses, shop signs which spread odious feudal and bourgeois ideas have been removed, and the names of many streets, lanes, parks, buildings, and schools tainted with feudalism, capitalism, or revisionism [moderate communism] or which had no revolutionary significance have been replaced by revolutionary names.*

*"Red Guards Destroy the Old and Establish the New," *Peking Review*, September 2, 1966, as cited in *Changing China*, edited by J. Mason Gentzler, 1977, Praeger Publishers, p. 351.

The Great Cultural Revolution was a time of disorder and confusion throughout China. Schools closed, factory production dropped, and violence erupted. Finally, in 1968, Mao and Zhou En-lai called on the army to restore order. Although in the next few years Chinese political and social life quieted, the conflict between moderates and radicals within the Communist party continued.

TOWARD CHANGE

By 1969, China had entered a more moderate period. To offset the growing feud with the Soviet Union and to acquire the technology to build their economy, Chinese leaders sought to improve relations with western nations. In 1972, United States President Richard Nixon visited China. At the end of his visit, he and his Chinese hosts pledged to work toward the improvement of relations between their countries. Soon, leaders of other western nations were visiting or hosting Chinese officials.

On January 8, 1976, Zhou En-lai died. Many observers expected the moderate Deng Xiaoping to become Zhou's successor. But Mao, too, was dying, and the radicals gained influence in the government. In February, it was announced that a lesser-known leader, Hua Guofeng, would serve as prime minister. When, on September 9, Mao died, an era of Chinese history came to an end. Although there was uncertainty about China's future, Mao's place in history seemed assured. Friends and enemies alike recognized him as the most influential Chinese leader of the twentieth century.

1. What three groups influenced the Communist government of the People's Republic of China?
2. What was the purpose of the Great Cultural Revolution? What impact did it have on China?
3. Why did the Chinese seek to improve relations with western nations?

EXPLORATION
CHINA

Below are contrasting views on the death of Mao Zedong. One expresses the opinion of the Chinese Communist party, which rules mainland China. The other expresses the opinion of the Guomindang, or Nationalist, government of Taiwan. Read each viewpoint, and then answer the following questions:

1. What is the Chinese Communist view of Mao Zedong's life and career? What is the Guomindang's view?
2. Which viewpoint do you accept? Explain. How do you feel history will judge Mao Zedong?

At 12:10 AM, September 9, 1976, Comrade [Mao Zedong], the esteemed and beloved leader of

our party, armed forces, and nation, the great teacher of international [workers], and the champion of all the oppressed people and nations, passed [away], despite all meticulous medical care after he had fallen ill.

Chairman [Mao Zedong] was the founder and long-time leader of the Chinese Communist Party, the Chinese People's Liberation Army, and the People's Republic of China. He led our party, our armed forces, and all the Chinese people in waging a successful struggle against imperialism, feudalism, and bureaucratic capitalism. This great victory has not only liberated the Chinese people and improved the situation in the East but also raised new hope for all the oppressed people and nations in the world that wish to be free.

The death of Chairman [Mao Zedong] is a great loss to our party, our armed forces, and all the people in the nation. It is a great loss to the international [workers] and all the revolutionary people in the world. The grief over his death is bound to be immensely felt by all the revolutionaries both at home and abroad.

The Central Committee of the Chinese Communist Party calls upon the Party, the armed forces, and all the people in the nation to transform their grief into strength. It calls upon them to carry on the cause left behind by our great leader and teacher Chairman [Mao Zedong].

Eternal glory to our great leader and teacher Chairman [Mao Zedong]!*

[Mao Zedong], the bandit chieftain of the CCP [Chinese Communist Party], finally died early yesterday morning.

A brutal, treacherous psychopath, [Mao Zedong] embodied the worst in human nature. His career was a career of [unending] betrayal of his nation and immeasurable harm to his own people.

---

*Dun J. Li, "People's Daily," from *Modern China: From Mandarin to Commissar*. Copyright ©1978 Dun J. Li. Reprinted with the permission of Charles Scribner's Sons.

His crime was a crystallization of all the crimes committed by the most wanton traitors and bandits. He was in fact the number one tyrant in history, unprecedented both here and abroad.

After the CCP's illegal occupation of the Chinese mainland in 1949, [Mao Zedong], by invoking the excuse of a "proletarian [working class] dictatorship," conducted a systematic campaign of murdering the Chinese people. According to evidence provided by a variety of sources, the people whom he had murdered numbered no less than 60 million between 1949 and 1976. During his whole career that covered a period of fifty years, the number of people who had died because of his rebellion and violence came close to 100 million. No one, not even Hitler and Stalin, could match him in bloodthirstiness.

To maintain his tyrannical rule, he did not hesitate to declare as his enemy the five-thousand-year-old civilization of China and all the noble values that formed part of this civilization. He opposed heavenly reason as well as the humanity of man. What was objectively right became wrong to him, and vice versa. . . . Now that he is dead, it is most natural that all of us shall rejoice.

The death of [Mao Zedong] marks not only the end of the darkest period in Chinese history but also the beginning of a new era when the Republic of China will rise to restore the mainland and to save all the people therein.*

*Dun J. Li, "Central Daily News" from *Modern China: From Mandarin to Commissar.* Copyright ©1978 Dun J. Li. Reprinted with the permission of Charles Scribner's Sons.

CHAPTER 12 REVIEW

POINTS TO REMEMBER

1. The roots of the Chinese Revolution date back to the 1800's when China became involved in a series of wars with western countries and with its Asian neighbor, Japan.
2. Internal strife also contributed to the Chinese Revolution as a wave of peasant rebellions swept through China. The longest and most violent was the Taiping Rebellion. It was followed by the Boxer Rebellion.
3. After the downfall of the Qing in 1911, the leaders of the revolution proclaimed China a democratic republic and named Dr. Sun Yat-sen as provisional president.
4. In 1924, Chiang K'ai-shek was appointed to head the new Guomindang, or Nationalist, army. In 1925, he became the leader of the Guomindang.
5. The Chinese Communist party was organized in 1921 by students, intellectuals, and urban workers who wanted to continue the Chinese Revolution. In 1927, the Communists and the Guomindang clashed.
6. In 1928, Chiang K'ai-shek was elected president of the republic. He stressed social discipline through a return to Confucian values.
7. Chiang's forces attacked the Communists and forced them to retreat in the Long March, from which Mao Zedong emerged as the major leader of the Communist party.
8. After being defeated by the Communists in a civil war, Chiang took his followers to the island of Taiwan, where he and his followers continued the Republic of China. The Communists ruled mainland China and in 1949 formed the People's Republic of China.
9. The Communist government of the People's Republic of China was influenced by the Communist party, the bureaucrats, and the army. The government worked to transform China from a technologically backward nation into a modern industrial-agricultural state.
10. The government initiated the first Five-Year Plan for economic development, the Great Leap Forward, and the Great Cultural Revolution, which was a time of disorder and confusion throughout China.
11. In 1969, China entered a more moderate period, and, in order to offset its growing feud with the Soviet Union, sought to improve relations with the western nations.
12. When Mao Zedong died in 1976, an era of Chinese history came to an end. Mao was recognized as the most influential Chinese leader of the twentieth century.

VOCABULARY

Identify

Mao Zedong
People's Republic of China
Opium Wars

Taiping Rebellion
Boxer Rebellion
Dr. Sun Yat-sen

"Three Principles of the People"
General Yuan Shih-k'ai

Guomindang
Chiang K'ai-shek
Chinese Communist Party

CHAPTER 12   THE CHINESE REVOLUTION   201

Long March   Zhou En-lai   Great Cultural   Red Guards
Republic of China Great Leap Forward Revolution   Hua Guofeng

Define

intellectuals   extraterritoriality dictatorship   cooperatives
opium   provisional   warlords   communes
unequal treaties

Discussing Important Ideas

1. If you were a Chinese who lived in China at the time of the Boxer Rebellion, would you have been sympathetic to the Boxer's cause? Why or why not? Would you have joined the Boxers? Why or why not?
2. Do you think Sun Yat-sen's "Three Principles of the People" were realistic goals at the time? Explain. Do you think they would be realistic today? Explain.
3. Why are there "two Chinas"?
4. Mao Zedong taught the Chinese people that the Chinese Revolution was a continuing struggle against old ways. What do you think he meant by the "old ways"?

Developing Skills

USING A TIME LINE

A *time line* is a visual representation of a series of events or periods of history, showing them in the order in which they happened. Time lines can be used to help you identify and compare dates and events, form a clear idea of the passage of time in relation to events, and keep important events in proper order. The following steps, which will help you use the time line on page 192 as a study tool, can be applied to any time line:

1. Study the time line to determine into how many time periods it is divided. *(13)* Since intervals of time on a time line may change, determine if the length of the periods of this time line changes. *(Yes. One period, 1860–1900, is 40 years, while all the rest are 10 years.)* Note how the change is indicated. *(A break in the vertical bar.)*

2. Focus on the kinds of events listed. This will tell you the general topic of the time line. *(All the events have to do with the Chinese Revolution.)*

3. Determine how the events are indicated. For example: How are the special periods shown? *(By different color bars)* Which special period, or event, was the longest? *(Opium Wars)* The shortest? *(Mao Zedong elected leader)*

4. Look at the order in which the events occurred. Which conflict was the first? *(Opium Wars)* Which happened nearest the middle of the revolutionary period? *(Conflict between Guomindang and Communists)*

5. The time line has achieved its purpose. You have identified and compared the dates and events of the Chinese Revolution, have a clear idea of the passage of time in relation to the events, and know the proper order of the events.

CHAPTER 13
CHINA AFTER MAO

1. What political, economic, and social changes took place in China after the death of Mao Zedong?
2. What was China's foreign policy during the late 1970's and early 1980's?

In the once sleepy fishing village of Shenzhen, a new golf course stretches out from the Honey Lake Country Club. High-rise apartment buildings tower above newly created avenues, and a 48-story trade center is nearing completion. Scores of foreign-owned operations, including those of such giants as PepsiCo, Citibank and Sanyo, have streamed into the area, where a . . . billboard exhorts, TIME IS MONEY! EFFICIENCY IS LIFE! In the midst of those developments, many peasant families own three-story houses furnished with stereo systems, refrigerators and color TVs. . . . When Deng Xiaoping, China's *de facto* [actual] leader, paid a visit . . . , he asked one resident how much he earned. Upon hearing the reply (more than $300 a month), the leader observed, with as much amusement as amazement, "You make more than I do."

In the outskirts of Canton [Guangzhou], the ballads of Country Singer Kenny Rogers boom across a small store where four youngsters are huddled over a Space Invader screen. In the streets of Peking [Beijing], long-haired young men in dapper trenchcoats walk arm in arm with their girlfriends in high heels. Near by, in neon-lit consumer emporiums, grizzled countryfolk peel off huge sheaves of banknotes to buy TV sets to take back to their villages. The Jianguo Hotel is a replica of the Holiday Inn in Palo Alto, Calif. Not far away, Maxim's de Pékin serves *haute cuisine* [gourmet food] at $70 a head. The regiments of bicycles that clog the streets have been joined by Mercedes sedans and Japanese-made Hino tourist buses. Earlier this month, the Peking [Beijing] *Daily* . . . ran a photo of an attractive woman and her family standing next to a new Toyota. Thanks to an income of more than $18,000 a year, chicken farmer Sun Guiying had just become the first peasant in the . . . history of the People's Republic to buy a private car.*

---

*"Capitalism in the Making," *Time*, April 30, 1984, pp. 26–27. Copyright ©1984 Time Inc. All rights reserved. Reprinted by permission from TIME.

These are just a few examples of some of the more dramatic changes that have taken place in some areas of China since the death of Mao Zedong in 1976. Not all of China has experienced such great change. The changes are the result of an ambitious plan begun by Mao's successors to modernize the country without following Mao's strict revolutionary course. As part of the plan, they have permitted greater freedoms and have borrowed capitalist ideas and practices from the West to strengthen the economy. Greater **incentives,** or encouragements, have been given to peasants and workers to work harder and to produce more. Although these policies have begun to have an impact on China, it is difficult to tell how successful they will be. In addition, there are vast areas of the country, especially in central China and in the west, that are still far behind in their economic development.

POLITICAL CHANGE

During the late 1970's, China went through a period of political chaos that prepared the way for the new turn in its social and economic policies. Following Mao's death, moderates and radicals engaged in a power struggle for control of the country. The moderates favored practical economic and social reforms. The radicals, led by Mao's widow Jiang Qing and three of her supporters, wanted to return to the policies of the Cultural Revolution. Later known as the "Gang of Four," they tried to seize power from Hua Guofeng, the acting premier. But their plot failed, and all four of them were arrested.

By the end of 1976, Hua seemed to be firmly in control. As the new chairman of the Chinese Communist party, he led a national campaign against the "Gang of Four." At an agricultural conference in December, he gave the following speech in which he stated the objectives of the Chinese government:

> . . . [Prospects] are very bright for a rapid development of the national economy. We must . . . bring into full play the initiative of both central and local authorities, mobilize the masses, make determined and maximum efforts first to run agriculture well and also to run light industry well and organize the market well. Meanwhile we must do a good job in transport and communications and in heavy industries that produce fuel, electricity, petrochemicals, iron and steel, and other raw and semi-finished materials, so as to ensure the smooth operation of industry as a whole. We must launch a major drive to increase production and practice economy, set up technical innovations, tap production potential, lower costs. . . . We must pay attention to the well-being of the masses and raise the living standard of the people step by step. . . .*

Although Hua favored economic reforms, he refused to make any major break with Mao's policies. The moderates wanted to continue to honor Mao as a great revolutionary leader, but, at the same time, end many of his policies. In 1977, they won control of the Communist party and the government and restored Deng Xiaoping, the leading

A skit making fun of the "Gang of Four" expresses the bitterness many Chinese felt toward the Great Cultural Revolution. Who brought the "Gang of Four" to trial after they tried to seize power?

---

*"Outline for a New Future," speech made by Hua Guofeng at the Second National Conference on Learning from Tachai in Agriculture, December 25, 1976, as quoted in *Changing China*, edited by J. Mason Gentzler, 1977, Praeger Publishers, pp. 393–394.

moderate, to high office. Deng brought the "Gang of Four" to trial and reduced the radicals' influence in China.

From 1977 to 1980, Deng further strengthened his hold over the country and became the real ruler of China. He replaced Hua Guofeng as head of the Communist party with a supporter of his and installed another supporter as premier. Under Deng, the Communist party remained in firm control of China and continued to deny freedom of speech to Chinese it believed were anti-Communist. In making economic policy, however, Deng placed practical goals ahead of revolutionary idealism. His statement, "I don't care if a cat is white or black, as long as it catches mice," indicated that he was even willing to learn from the capitalist West if it could contribute to China's well-being.

In 1978, under Deng's direction, the Chinese Communist party announced a plan to modernize China by the year 2000. Known as the Four Modernizations, it stressed the need for major improvements in agriculture, industry, science and technology, and the military. During the next two decades, the Chinese hoped to increase national productivity and make their standard of living equal to that of the industrialized West.

1. What were the goals of the "Gang of Four"? The moderates?
2. What steps did Deng Xiaoping take after gaining control?

AGRICULTURE

The first goal of Deng's reform program was to revive agriculture, which had been neglected in favor of such heavy industry as coal and steel production. This had caused food production to fall behind the enormous growth in population. Fears of a food shortage forced the government to take action to increase food supplies.

Construction team members from Henan province in eastern China used profits from their work to purchase these new motorcycles. What did the Chinese hope to do by the year 2000?

Instead of relying on the communes, China's leaders turned to the individual peasant households that make up the communes. To boost food production, the government provided a number of incentives that would appeal to the peasants' desire for profits and greater personal freedom. Although this new agricultural policy seemed to be a turn toward capitalism, Chinese leaders believed that, in the long run, it would not only improve the economy but benefit the Communist system as well.

In the excerpt on the following page, a visitor to China describes how the government's plan is carried out in a village in the western province of Sichuan. The village is

Peasants of Xiaotian, a village in Shandong province in eastern China, constructed a new school with the extra money they were able to earn under the Family Responsibility System. How did the Family Responsibility System change things at the village level?

the home of a young couple named Yang Hungniao and Ligong:

> The Yangs' village is one of several that have been united into a commune. . . .
>
> The commune provides overall management and services for the villages under it. . . .
>
> Local affairs are handled by the villages. Each has its own governing committee which has been elected by the villagers themselves. Ligong is a member of his village committee and has been chosen to represent it at the Commune Congresses. . . . At the congresses, government representatives present the yearly production quotas for the commune.
>
> Commune officials discuss the quotas with the representatives of the villages. The quotas are divided among them according to fertility and amount of land each village tills. The representatives then go home and divide the village quota among the individual families, every one of which is responsible for a particular section of land.
>
> After the harvest is in, the family sells its quota to the government . . . and keeps the proceeds for itself. If the crop surpasses the quota, the family may sell the surplus as it pleases—either to the state or on the open market—and keep these proceeds also. In return, the family pays a low tax to the government and other small amounts to the village and commune. This money goes to building up reserves for such services as schools, health clinics, and hospitals.
>
> This is a new way of doing things in China and is called the Family Responsibility System. It was inaugurated in 1981. Formerly, everyone tilled the land together and received points for the amount of work each did. When the harvests were sold, the proceeds were paid out according to work points. There was little incentive in this way of doing things, and some people didn't even try to meet the quotas.

In addition to the money they get for their grain crops, the peasants have private plots on which they can grow vegetables either for their own use or to sell on the open market. They're also allowed to raise livestock for themselves or for sale. . . .

The government is encouraging the peasants to earn more money by doing handicrafts or making simple utility articles. . . . The products can be sold on the free market and at county fairs for extra income. This raises the peasants' standard of living. . . .

Twice a week the village committee meets with the villagers. They take up business matters and discuss politics. Then the talk centers around the part the peasants should play in bringing about Modernization of Agriculture. . . .

But modernization in the countryside means something quite different from modernization in the city. In the Yangs' little village, there is still no running water. Modernization means being able to draw it from a faucet in the village square instead of having to go down to the irrigation canal to get it. It means electricity on a modest scale—one small light bulb in the kitchen, that is used as little as possible. It means a bicycle, and rubber tires on carts.*

The agricultural reforms put into effect by the government have been very successful. Between 1978 and 1982, agricultural production steadily rose. At the same time, the average annual income for peasants doubled from $65 to $135. Some peasants can now afford consumer goods, such as radios and TV's, that were once luxuries beyond their reach. Pleased by the plan's success, the government has promised to continue the Family Responsibility System until the end of the century.

*From *Holding Up the Sky: Young People in China*, copyright ©1983 by Margaret Rau. Reprinted by permission of the publisher, E. P. Dutton, Inc.

1. Why was the first goal of Deng's reform program to revive agriculture?
2. How does the Family Responsibility System work?

INDUSTRY

Following the agricultural successes, the government began working to improve China's industries. Since the early 1950's, government-owned industries had guaranteed workers their jobs and pay no matter how they performed. As a result, there was little incentive to increase production.

In the fall of 1984, in the hope of making industry more efficient and productive, Deng announced a series of reforms. Under them, the government reduced its role in industrial planning. Factory managers could now decide to produce many goods on the basis of supply and demand rather than government decree. Profits no longer had to be handed over to the government. Instead, a tax was paid on earnings, and the remainder was used to pay workers or to buy modern equipment. Factory managers were allowed to hire and fire workers and determine differences in pay among them. Workers were allowed to move from job to job and could receive bonuses for good work.

A change in the price system was the most controversial reform. The government had kept the prices of such items as food and housing low through **subsidies,** or payments for support. The reforms allowed the cost of many items to rise or fall based on supply and demand. As a result, prices have risen steadily. Communist "hardliners," however, fear that the new pricing policy and other reforms will divide China into rich and poor classes and eventually will turn it into a capitalist nation.

SMALL BUSINESS

Even with the reforms, the Chinese government still owns all major industries and remains responsible for the overall performance of the economy. Chinese leaders, however, have encouraged ambitious and talented individuals to form their own small businesses. Below, a reporter describes the life of and talks with one such business person:

It is shortly before 8 A.M. in Harbin, a city of 2 million in northern China. Bai Shiming, 29, an energetic young bachelor, is preparing to open his shop, the Xiurong photographic studio. Bai sports a gray, Western-style suit and light tan shirt but no tie. . . .

Bai is of a rare breed: an urban entrepreneur working in direct competition with the state. With the help of a brother and sister, Bai handles 80 to 100 customers a day in his neat, red-painted studio, which he keeps open until 8 P.M. seven days a week. He works in the darkroom until midnight. . . . "I don't rest," Bai says. "Even during festivals, I never close." Bai usually charges less than one yuan (50¢) for a portrait, undercutting prices at the state-run photographic studio up the street. After paying rent, salaries and buying supplies, Bai nets between 180 and 200 yuan ($90 to $100) a month. . . . As Bai is quick to note, it is . . . higher than the wages of each of his three other brothers, a boilermaker, a security guard and a storekeeper. Bai . . . enjoys being his own master. Says he: "We can work, or we can stop working. . . ."

Despite his pride in being the first member of his family to achieve such success, Bai remains pessimistic about the future of free enterprise in China. He believes that while private ownership may be an immediate necessity, state control will provide more economic growth in the long run. "As a theory, private enterprise is opposed to Marxism," he explains. "But in China at this stage, we need all sorts of forms of production. As socialism develops toward Communism, my job will be less and less important." What will Bai do then? "With the development of bigger factories run by the state," he responds, "I can get a job there."*

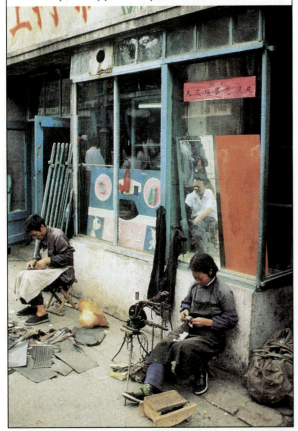

Millions of enterprising individuals in China, like the man and woman shown here, recently have begun their own businesses. How does business owner Bai Shiming view the future of free enterprise in China?

WOMEN

Women also have gained some benefits from the industrial reforms. Today, more than 40 million work in a variety of occupations, many in industrial trades. The number

---

*"Making Free Enterprise Click," *Time,* April 30, 1984, p.30. Copyright 1984 Time Inc. All rights reserved. Reprinted by permission from TIME.

who hold top-level positions, however, is still very low. Below, a Chinese writer comments on the changing role of women:

> Zhao Changbai has just been promoted from chief controller to deputy general manager of production at the Shoudu Iron and Steel Co. of Peking [Beijing], one of China's largest firms. She is responsible for orchestrating a workforce of 110,000 and seeing that production quotas are met. Ms. Zhao, who is admired by her colleagues for "her professional proficiency," says that her managerial experience has provided knowhow in productivity, establishing a clear line of authority, and improving efficiency.
>
> Another woman, Zuo Hong, has helped make a restaurant chain a brilliant success in Shenchen [Shenzhen]. . . . After only two and a half years, the Friendship Restaurant Chain shows a profit of eight times its initial investment. Among the 800 people on the staff, 85 percent are women —including six of eight department heads.
>
> These are only two examples of the opportunities open to Chinese women. . . .
>
> . . . In fulfilling their career aspirations, [women] have had more difficulties than their male colleagues have, reports Zhang Guoying [vice president of the All-China Women's Federation].
>
> Foremost is the burden of housework and children. Ms. Zhang, who worked . . . for ten years, had to rely on her mother-in-law to keep her home in order. She placed her three young children in a nursery school. "Women who want to achieve should face up to the difficulties and learn to do more," she advises. . . .
>
> An educational campaign is currently under way to promote the rights and welfare of women and children. . . . In a month-long campaign last February [1984], women were told that the government and the law are on their side. Arranged marriages and the maltreatment of wives (considered a husband's perogative [right]), were criticized. . . .

A female train conductor waits to assist boarding passengers. Today, women represent over 36 percent of China's total work force. What are some of the needs of Chinese working women?

> . . . There are many other needs to be addressed, according to Zhang Guoying. She notes that women account for 70 percent of China's illiterates and semi-literates, and she calls for higher educational standards. She also cites the need for day-care centers.*

1. What changes were brought about in industry in 1984?
2. How is free enterprise regarded in China today?
3. What effect has industrial reform had on Chinese women?

---

*"Women Progress" by Yi Shui, Depthnews Asia, reprinted in *World Press Review*, October 1984, p. 58.

CASE STUDY
CHINA

CHINA'S REVOLUTIONARY DRAMA

In present-day China, the government is actively involved in the arts. It believes that all art comes from the people and must help in building a Communist society. Many artists receive government financial support.

Since the 1950's, Chinese artists have staged dramas presenting the revolutionary struggle that led to Communist rule in China. Below, a Chinese newsmagazine writer reviews one of these works, *Song of the Chinese Revolution:*

Across a darkened misty lake, lights appear, gradually moving together until they take the shape of a pleasure boat. A fishing girl looks toward the boat, where the inaugural meeting of the Chinese Communist Party is being held. A look of hope crosses her face and she begins to sing with deep feeling. Dawn breaks and the boat hoists a giant sail and begins to move. The Chinese revolution is sailing forward.

This symbolic beginning of the revolution is a scene from the epic Song of the Chinese Revolution. *Combining dance, music and a series of dramatic scenes, the production depicts the more than a century history of the Chinese people making revolution and reconstructing their socialist country. With a cast and supporting crew of 1,000, the epic is magnificent.*

In two and a half hours, Song of the Chinese Revolution *depicts almost all the major political events of the revolution on stage....*

Qiao Yu, one of the directors, said the artists made great efforts to tell the extraordinary story in an artistic way. In depicting the setbacks and sacrifices of the early revolution in 1927, the artists considered many images, but settled on one: In a dark jail, a woman covered with cuts and bruises kisses her new-born baby as she hugs it to her bosom. She sings a final song of farewell, "Mummy is leaving, but a new world is coming."

To fill the music and dance with the flavour of life and the characteristics of the time, the artists spent several months working and living among people at the grass-roots level and talking to people who lived through the events so they could understand and experience the feelings.

Song of the Chinese Revolution *also makes use of the folk song and dance styles of various nationalities of China. "Lantern Fair" shows the people in Hubei Province celebrating the victory of the revolutionary army in driving out the feudal landlords. Carrying decorative lanterns—some resembling clouds, flowers, carps, and others with five stars, axes, and sickles symbolizing revolution —dancers perform the traditional local lantern dances....*

Speaking of the significance of the production, Zhou Weizhi, Vice-Minister of Culture, said that the epic will not only educate young people about history, but will also arouse the enthusiasm of the elderly for today's revolutionary cause through reviewing their past experiences.*

1. What does *Song of the Chinese Revolution* reveal about the relationship of politics and the arts in modern China?
2. How do the arts in modern China compare/contrast with the arts in your country?

**"The Song of the Chinese Revolution" by Gong Yuan in* Beijing Review, *Vol. 27, No. 40, October 1, 1984, pp. 29–30. Reprinted by permission.*

SCIENCE, TECHNOLOGY, AND THE MILITARY

Under the Four Modernizations, China also hopes to develop its science and technology. To this end, the government has invited foreign capitalist companies to open plants and offices in China. It also has developed its own industries based on foreign models.

One area to which the government under Mao and under his successors has given a special priority is the production of radio and television sets. Unlike other consumer goods, they are considered vital because of their value as instruments of propaganda and indoctrination. Below, Huang Zonghan, the manager of a television factory in Beijing, discusses the efforts made to develop this technology:

> Saturday night is TV night at our house, with a dozen local kids joining my wife and me for an evening in front of the tube. Recently we watched the British series, *David Copperfield*.
> These evenings mean more to me than to most other Chinese people because our fourteen-inch (355 mm) color set was made at the factory where I'm manager. It gives me a sense of pride.
> China began making TV sets in 1958, and in the first year produced 215 sets. They were hand-made and very complicated, with 600 parts in a twelve-inch (304 mm) black-and-white set. They were also very expensive.
> Since the 1970s, China has imported sophisticated production equipment and today we have 53 TV factories that make more than two million TV sets. My factory made 200,000 of them and they're reliable, attractive—and have only 249 parts.
> As China modernizes, the demand for TV sets will rise. Today there are about seven million private sets in China, but don't forget we have about 200 million families.
> China relies on her own efforts for most things and so we're going to make these sets ourselves, but with imported equipment for the time being.
> The same is true in factories and farms in various parts of the country that are using the world's latest technology. . . .
> Managing my factory covers everything from production to housing for 1,700 workers. Every Chinese factory is responsible for the welfare of its workers —housing, medical care, night schools, and day-care centers.
> Another of my jobs is to get workers to master new techniques. I encourage them by telling them how important TV is to the country for mass education.
> We pay bonuses out of the ten percent of profits retained by the factory. . . . So with a basic pay of fifty yuan ($25) a month and a bonus of twenty yuan ($10), the workers do quite well . . . .*

This new technological knowledge also is being used to improve the People's Liberation Army (PLA), China's armed forces. The PLA serves not only in China's defense but also in instilling patriotism and promoting political and cultural activities. Below, Liu Yongshe, a 23-year-old soldier, relates his view of life in the Chinese military:

> The name People's Liberation Army is misleading because it also includes the airforce and the navy. But, whatever branch it might be, the PLA provides a rigorous military life for several million men and women.
> You know, eighty percent of all the Chinese people live in the countryside, so most soldiers are from the peasantry. I was born in a little village in Shanxi Province, north China.

---

*"Recently we watched David Copperfield on TV" in *We Live in China*, 1984, The Bookwright Press, pp. 32–33.

The instrument capsule of a military rocket is being unloaded from the helicopter that successfully recovered it in the Pacific Ocean. The communications satellite, which the rocket carried into orbit, and others like it are expected to revolutionize both military and civilian communications systems. What are some activities undertaken by the military to "keep alive" their link with the people?

Before the People's Republic was founded in 1949, the PLA lived among the country people "as a fish in water." Now our officers teach us to keep alive the link between the PLA and the people. We help the farmers with planting and harvesting. And every New Year's Day and Chinese Spring Festival we help the city street-sweepers and the loaders at the food markets, and we carry passengers' luggage at the railway stations.

These activities not only benefit the people but also remind us that we belong to the people.

Other units, stationed in the city [Beijing] itself, undertake some civilian duties like patrolling the streets and guarding public buildings. . . .

But soldiering and garrisoning of Beijing are our main jobs, and most of our day is spent in weapons training. Apart from things like parade drill, we practise marksmanship, bayonet techniques and defense against atomic, chemical and bacteriological warfare.

The day begins with reveille at 5:30 in the summer and 6:20 in the winter. And we must be ready at any time to be in formation in a few minutes in full battle gear. . . .

China doesn't have compulsory military service, but anyone who is fit and over eighteen is urged to join the PLA. The term of service for an infantryman like me is at least three years.*

1. What has China done to develop its science and technology?
2. How is the Chinese military organized? What role does it play in Chinese society?

FOREIGN POLICY

To ensure the success of the Four Modernizations, China's leaders have sought to improve relations with other countries. If there

---

*"We soldiers belong to the people" in *We Live in China*, 1984, The Bookwright Press, pp. 30–31.

is stability abroad, Chinese leaders will be freer to concentrate more on reforms at home. As a result, since the late 1970's, China has greatly expanded trade and cultural contacts with other lands. In 1984, 1600 foreign specialists were working in China, and 10,000 Chinese students were studying at foreign universities, colleges, and technical schools.

Chinese leaders are aware that they can modernize the economy more quickly with technical help from the capitalist West. To this end, they have looked to the United States, from which they hope to obtain most of their high technology skills. In 1979, after nearly 20 years of official diplomatic isolation, the two nations established full diplomatic relations. That same year, Deng Xiaoping became the first high official of the People's Republic to visit the United States. In 1984, American President Ronald Reagan paid an official state visit to China. Yet, in spite of these moves toward friendship, China and the United States still differ greatly over certain issues. The major one is Taiwan, which is claimed by China, but is under Guomindang government.

In spite of their improved relations with other countries, the Chinese stress that they follow an "independent" foreign policy. In pursuing this course, they often criticize the conduct of both the United States and the Soviet Union. In 1984, Huang Hua, a noted Chinese diplomat, gave a speech that defined China's view of its role in the world. Below is part of that speech:

> . . . China's general task in foreign relations has always been to unite with all the friendly countries and people and to strive for a peaceful international environment in order to build a strong socialist China and at the same time to promote the cause of peace for all mankind. . . .
>
> . . . We will continue to strive to build up an equal and just new international order together with the majority of the developing countries. China has taken the initiative to lessen the tense international situation and prevent war, and has declared that in no time and under no circumstances will China ever be the first to use nuclear weapons. Basing ourselves on realities, we have proposed reductions of armaments, resumption of Soviet-U.S. talks and [ending] of the arms race, the nuclear arms race first of all. . . .
>
> As everybody knows, the main obstacle to relations between China and the United States is the question of Taiwan—a question purely of China's internal affairs. . . . [Chinese]-American relations can endure and develop only when both sides act in accordance with the principles of mutual respect for sovereignty and territorial integrity and mutual non-interference in each other's internal affairs.
>
> As for [Chinese]-Soviet relations, the obstacles affecting their normalization are the great number of Soviet troops stationed along the . . . borders; Soviet support for Vietnamese occupation of Kampuchea and Soviet support of Vietnamese armed provocation on the Chinese border; and the Soviet occupation of China's neighbor Afghanistan. All these pose a threat to the safety of China as well as of Asia. . . . The Soviet Union should stop supporting the Vietnamese occupation of Kampuchea, and withdraw its troops from Afghanistan, from the [Chinese]-Soviet border. . . . This would not only be beneficial to the normalization of [Chinese]-Soviet relations but also would accord with the fundamental interests of both countries, and others in Asia.*

1. Why have Chinese leaders sought to improve relations with other countries? What has been the result of their efforts?
2. What kind of foreign policy do the Chinese follow? What do they see as the main obstacles to relations with the United States? The Soviet Union?

---

*"The Five Principles and China's Foreign Policy" by Huang Hua in *China Reconstructs*, October 1984, pp. 16, 18–19.

Exploration
CHINA

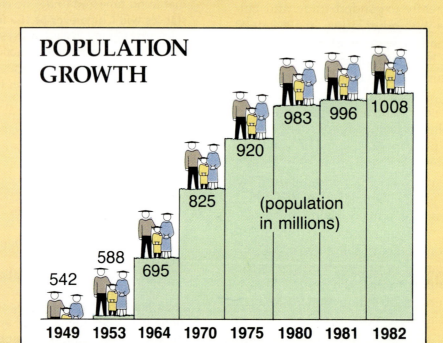

With over 1 billion people, China today faces the problem of **overpopulation,** or having more people than an area has resources to support. This enormous population growth has been due in part to a high birth rate during most of this century. According to population experts, if the average Chinese family continues to have as many as three children, in a century China's population could be as great as that of the world today—4.5 billion. This will lead to a shortage of jobs, food, housing, and social services.

To slow population growth, Chinese leaders are trying to convince young couples to have only one child. They hope to get 80 percent of the newlyweds in the cities and 50 percent of those in rural areas to agree. To win acceptance of this "one family-one child" policy, the government uses a system of rewards and punishments. Couples who promise to have **only** one child are given monthly cash bonuses and free medical care. They also receive special benefits in education, housing, and jobs. Those who break their promise must face fines and reduction in pay and loss of benefits.

Although the policy has gained widespread support, it is difficult to tell what its long-term results will be. Many experts claim that the government's goal of limiting the population to 1.2 billion by the end of the century is not realistic. They explain that the high cost of the benefits offered to one-child families is an obstacle as is the traditional Chinese regard for large families and preference for sons.

The government insists that it has to push for its plan in spite of obstacles. Otherwise, it claims, living standards will not improve and the drive toward modernization will fail.

Study the graphs in this Exploration on China's population. Then, based on the graphs and the other information on these two pages, answer these questions:

1. What was China's population in 1949? in 1975? By how much did the population increase from 1975 to 1982?
2. How large will the population of China be in the year 2070 if China's families were to average one child? Two children? Three children?
3. Why does the Chinese government want to control population growth? How is it trying to achieve this goal?
4. Do you agree or disagree with the government's population policy? Explain your answer. Do you think that such a policy could work in your country? Why or why not?
5. What other methods do you think the Chinese government could take to reduce population growth?

215

CHAPTER 13 REVIEW

POINTS TO REMEMBER

1. Following Mao Zedong's death in 1976, moderates and radicals engaged in a power struggle for control of China. The moderates favored practical economic and social reforms, while the radicals wanted to return to the policies of the Cultural Revolution.
2. The moderates won control of the Communist party and announced the Four Modernizations, a plan to modernize China by the year 2000 by stressing improvements in agriculture, industry, science and technology, and the military.
3. To boost food production, the government provided a number of incentives that would appeal to the individual peasant's desire for profits and greater personal freedom. In 1981, the Family Responsibility System was initiated.
4. To make industry more efficient and productive, the government reduced its role in industrial planning, changed the price system, and encouraged individuals to form their own small businesses. After paying taxes on earnings, companies now had control of profits.
5. Industrial reforms also benefited women, more of whom began to work in industrial trades.
6. In order to develop science and technology, the government invited foreign capitalist companies to open plants and offices in China. At the same time, it developed its own industries based on foreign models.
7. To ensure the success of the Four Modernizations, China has greatly expanded trade and cultural contacts with other lands. The government stresses an "independent" foreign policy and often criticizes the conduct of the United States and the Soviet Union.

VOCABULARY

Identify

Jiang Qing   Hua Guofeng   Four Modernizations   People's Liberation Army
Gang of Four Deng Xiaoping Family Responsibility System   Huang Hua

Define

incentives   subsidies   overpopulation

DISCUSSING IMPORTANT IDEAS

1. Now that China has opened its doors to western thought and culture, do you think the West will influence China? If so, how? Do you think China will influence the West? If so, how?
2. Modernization is the main goal of China, yet it means something quite different in the countryside than in the city. What do you see as the main differences? What would you do to bridge the gap?

3. In China, every factory is responsible for the welfare of its workers, including housing, medical care, night schools, and day-care centers. What advantages do you see in this type of program? What disadvantages? Would you like the factories of your country to take on this kind of responsibility? Why or why not?
4. Chinese leaders stress that their country follows an "independent" foreign policy. What do you think they mean by the word "independent"?

Developing Skills

MAKING GENERALIZATIONS

If you say to a friend, "My dad is a great cook," you are making a *generalization*, a general statement, about your father. If you go on to say that your father has a diploma from the Cordon Bleu cooking school in Paris and is a chef for a famous restaurant, you have provided evidence to support your generalization.

In many fields of study, such as the social sciences, it often is necessary to put together bits and pieces of information in order to find out, for example, about past events or what a culture was or is like. Just as you put together the pieces of a jigsaw puzzle to arrive at a complete picture, you can put together pieces of written information to arrive at a general statement—a generalization—about a topic.

In some cases, authors will provide you with both generalizations and supporting statements that give evidence to the generalizations. In other cases, however, the supporting statements are given, but you must make the generalizations on your own. The most important thing to keep in mind when doing this is that the supporting statements must be directly related to the topic. Otherwise, your generalization might well be in error.

In the following examples, a series of statements are given. Read each carefully, and based on their content, arrive at a generalization:

Example A:

1. Mao Zedong's successors began an ambitious plan to modernize China without following Mao's strict revolutionary course.
2. Mao Zedong's successors borrowed capitalist ideas and practices from the West to strengthen the Chinese economy.
3. Since the death of Mao Zedong, Chinese workers and peasants have been given greater incentives to work harder and produce more.

(Based on the three statements, a logical generalization is "Since the death of Mao Zedong, changes have taken place in China.")

Example B:

1. Between 1978 and 1982, agricultural production rose steadily in China.
2. Between 1978 and 1982, the average annual income for Chinese peasants doubled.
3. Today, many Chinese peasants can afford consumer goods that at one time were considered luxuries.

(Based on the three statements, a logical generalization is "Recent agricultural reforms in China have proved to be successful.")

For further practice in this skill, make a generalization based on the following statements:

1. In the 1980's, China greatly expanded trade and cultural contacts with other lands.
2. In 1984, 1600 foreign specialists were working in China.
3. In 1984, 10,000 Chinese students were studying at foreign universities, colleges, and technical schools.

CHAPTER 14
DAILY LIFE IN MODERN CHINA

1. What role does the Communist party play in Chinese life?
2. How do the Chinese live in the city? In the country?

The little city of Guilin (Kweilin) is a good place to watch the Chinese day unfold, for there city and country are very close. Here in Guangxi (Kwangsi) province, on one side of the Li River, near Liberation Bridge, patchwork fields stretch in front of hills as jagged as pieces of rock candy. On the other side, dusty concrete streets swarm with bell-ringing bicyclists. Morning is the time when Chinese city folk seem closest to their country brethren, getting up with the sun.

You must be up by five or five-thirty or miss the first rush of bicycles, buses and sidewalk vendors jamming the streets. At summer's dawn in Guilin, a thousand miles [1600 kilometers] south of Peking [Beijing], everyone appears to be eating something. Workers in faded blue pants and short-sleeved shirts hold chunks of steamed bread as they walk toward bus stops. From dank, dark little noodle shops along the avenue come sounds of enthusiastic slurping and clicking of chopsticks. City people linger over their dinners at night, but in the morning fast food is a habit—factory supervisors expect their people at work on time. The commuter bus on Guilin's main street begins to pull away from the curb. Half a block away a woman clutching a cylindrical lunch pail begins to run and yell frantically, "Don't go! Don't go!" She chases the bus for a block, but it does not stop.

In similar summer morning heat, we once walked down Liberation Road in Canton [Guangzhou], several hundred miles to the southeast, passing dozens of houses with doors left wide open to let in fresh air. Residents performed their morning chores—combing hair, eating breakfast, checking bicycle tires—oblivious to the glances of curious people passing by the small wooden storefrontlike houses. One small boy, about seven, was laboriously copying his homework. He could barely see what he was doing; the tiny room had no lamp, only weak morning light coming through the doorway.*

This description by an American couple presents the beginning of a "typical" day in modern China. Since the Communist drive for modernization began in 1949, the Chinese have seen many changes in their daily lives. The country has become more industrialized, the cities have grown in size and population, and the standard of living is better. At the same time, however, the people have had to endure a series of rapid shifts in government policy.

In spite of the benefits and problems brought by modernization, certain elements of the Chinese past remain. The Chinese continue to hold to their traditional arts and festivals and to maintain a high regard for family life and education. These traditions have helped bolster Chinese morale during recent trying periods.

Because of the upheavals of the past few decades, it is difficult to say what the future holds for China. Throughout their long history, the Chinese have faced many uncertainties. Yet they have managed to meet each crisis with self-confidence and to make significant contributions to world civilization. Many experts believe that, whatever lies ahead, the Chinese will continue to do so.

One Billion: A China Chronicle by Jay and Linda Mathews, 1983, Random House, pp. 39–40.

THE COMMUNIST PARTY

The Chinese Communist party, which is the largest such party in the world, has a dominant role in the lives of the people. Its 35 million members, however, make up only 4 percent of the population of the People's Republic. In theory, the party's most powerful institution is the National Party Congress, whose 2000 representatives meet periodically. The Congress elects the Central Committee that oversees party activities between meetings. But in practice, party policies are set by the Politburo, a group of about 25 top party officials within the Central Committee. The Politburo also exercises strict control over government.

In its methods of operation, the Chinese Communist party is **totalitarian.** That is, its control extends beyond strictly political affairs to almost all major areas of life. Its most direct impact on the average citizen is at the local level. Government and powerful party committees run the provinces, counties, and townships. **Cadres,** trained personnel who serve on government and party committees, are responsible not only for political matters but also for solving many of the practical, everyday problems of the people in their areas. On the next page, a Chinese journalist describes the work carried out in Shanghai's Huangpu district, which is home to 620,000 people. The system, however, does not always operate as smoothly as it does in the cases he describes:

> ... Huangpu's leading party and government members have adopted a policy of meeting problems squarely in the face. Nothing, no matter how trifling, remains long on the agenda without a responsible member personally taking this task in hand. Dealing with housing, employment, and food problems—or even buying a hat for a widower—are just a few of the concerns.
>
> In 1979 the Huangpu district decided to establish a reception system. Since then, every Thursday all of its 18 leading Party and government cadres take turns receiving visitors and listening to their opinions and demands.
>
> When we arrived one Thursday morning at the reception room . . . , we found district Party Committee Secretary Li Donglu with an old man who had come to ask him to help get a job for his daughter because his three sons were in the army. Li supports this Thursday "air-your-complaints" policy: "For us it's a convenient way to get in contact with the masses and to learn what's happening at the grass-roots level."
>
> To crack the really "hard nuts," the district cadres call together the units involved and put forward their proposals for a solution. Many problems have been solved this way.
>
> But they do not sit around and wait for problems to come to them. In fact, they go out of their way to look for "troubles," shuttling by bike along the Huangpu River banks to make calls and inquiries.
>
> After this type of investigation, they immediately begin to work on 20 "priority" items which often include housing, tailoring, nursery, and breakfast problems.
>
> To alleviate the acute housing shortage in the western Huangpu district and improve the living conditions of the eastern Huangpu district residents, the government constructed 140,000 square meters [168,000 square yards] of housing last year. A gas station, shopping center, water mains, and public telephone booths were also built.
>
> Letters are also an important way to uncover problems. The district government receives an average of 1,000 letters every month. Those containing more weighty matters or addressed to the district leaders are forwarded to them directly. For example, last June Xu Jian addressed a letter to Zhang Zhengkui complaining that because of the light flow of tap water, he was unable to take a bath until after midnight. Inquiries showed that more than 400 families in the neighborhood were suffering from a similar problem. Zhang paid a call to six families living in the same building and discovered that small water pipes and increased water consumption were causing this difficulty. After consulting with the water company, new pipes were laid.
>
> Caring for elderly widows and widowers has always been a priority among the district cadres. Every time Zhang Zhengkui visits them on the eve of a festival he warmly welcomes them to consider him "one of the family!"
>
> In spite of their successes, the Huangpu district cadres do not rest on their laurels. Said Li Donglu: "If we just sit around and do nothing, what are we here for?"*

1. How is the Communist party organized? Which body actually has the most power?
2. What responsibilities are carried out by cadres?

IN THE COUNTRYSIDE AND THE CITY

Most Chinese live in rural areas and work as farmers. Although many of the farmers still rely largely on human and animal labor, recent government reforms have enabled

---

*"Problem Solving From Behind a Desk or on a Bicycle," *China Pictorial*, September 1982, pp. 18–19.

On the outskirts of Luda, a city in Liaoning province in northeastern China, 26 peasant families of the Hanjia Production Brigade have built themselves new houses, thanks to an increase in their incomes. One of these houses, shown here, contains six rooms, a kitchen, three storerooms, and has indoor plumbing. Why do some Chinese peasants in rural areas now live as well or better than some urban residents?

them to buy farm machinery and consumer goods. As a result of increased production and income, Chinese peasants in some areas now live as well as—or even better than—urban residents. Zhou Jincai, the middle-income farmer who is discussed below, is an example:

Zhou Jincai lives in the Taihang Mountains. Last February at Spring Festival time, when the Chinese people celebrate their traditional new year, he took 1,500 yuan out of his savings account and asked a friend to buy him a color TV set in Beijing. For some years in the past, he had often gone to Beijing for financial help from a relative, earning the nickname, the "poor villager. . . ."

He was lucky to get the TV, for color sets were out of stock in the capital. His friend delivered it to him, taking the winding highway directly to Zhou's mountain village. . . .

South of the brick road, several young couples were playing on Lake Yueya, the result of an irrigation project. Rows of new grey brick houses lined the north side. Flowers in full blossom grew in each courtyard. For Chinese peasants, building a new house is the most important thing in their lifetime. So it was with Zhou, the "poor villager." All the houses were built under village planning with the peasants' own funds, and all have running water and sewers.

Zhou lives in the middle of the village in a big courtyard with a dark, painted gate and a long flowerbed centered in the yard, on the east side a brick chicken coop and rabbit hutches, on the west side a big kitchen, and bright and comfortable rooms on the north side.

There are eight rooms for Zhou's family of four—three bed-sitting rooms, others used as storerooms, a reading room and a living room. All are neat and clean. The color scheme is mostly light yellow. The living room has a sofa and armchairs, a wardrobe, cupboard, TV set, tape recorder, console, and an electric fan. There are beautiful brocade quilts on the beds and white nylon mosquito nets.

The village has become prosperous. In the past, agricultural policy required that they plant grain, but the crops grew badly in their barren hilly area, and income stayed low. Today farm production has been allowed to develop according to local conditions and things are different. Roads came first because the increasing quantities of local products needed to be transported. Second, they developed small-size coal mines from local deposits, and brick kilns to broaden their side-line production. In only three years every home had a much higher income.

The "poor villager" and 20 other peasants contracted to run the local brick factory, each of them making more than 2,000 yuan a year. To this, Zhou's wife added 700 yuan from breeding pigs, chickens and rabbits, cultivating 0.2 hectares [.5 acres] of contracted land, and selling surplus vegetables grown in their private plot. The family's bank savings grew. Nevertheless, the family is in the village's middle-income group, for 16 other households have bought tractors (5000 yuan in China).*

The cities of China have changed as much as the rural areas in the past few decades. Before 1949, most urban residents were poor and lived in dirty, overcrowded conditions. Many suffered from unemployment and died from hunger and disease. Today China's cities, especially in coastal areas, are the centers of the country's industry and commerce. Although the cities are still crowded and new housing is in great demand, life is very different. Streets are kept clean of dirt and trash. Most people have jobs and are better fed and clothed. This is illustrated below as a Chinese journalist describes the life of Chen Tianlin, a 47-year-old engineer who is now the director of the Haimen Rubber Sealing Materials Factory in Zhejiang province on China's east coast:

> After passing through broad streets bustling with new construction projects, our bus entered some narrow, twisting lanes. On either side were old houses, groceries, pastry shops and stalls. Crowds of buyers jostled one another in goodnatured disorder. . . .
>
> . . . Since 1949 Haimen's old houses have been refurbished and modernized, but they retain a simple and unsophisticated charm. Our bus stopped near a dark-red wooden gate by a crossroads—Chen's home. Inside the courtyard is an old two-story wooden house with a tile roof and double-tiered eaves. . . .
>
> The house, which Chen shares with his wife, parents and three children, has nine rooms, including a kitchen and toilet. Its floor space of 150 sq. m. [180 sq. yds.] is not very spacious for seven people, but is not bad by Chinese city standards, for urban areas still have housing problems. Like other old houses in Haimen, Chen's is a bit . . . dark without full sunlight.
>
> The living room and bedroom are furnished with high-backed chairs, tables, bookcases, wardrobes and beds, all in traditional Chinese style: elegant, exquisitely made and simple in structure. On the walls hang copies of paintings and calligraphy by well-known artists. . . .
>
> After showing me around the house, Chen led me to the living room, where his wife Luo Meiqin served me tea. On the wall were a dozen certificates testifying to Luo's athletic progress while she was still in school. She actually met her husband on the track and field ground. An engineer herself, Luo is still vigorous and strong in her mid-40's.
>
> Chen, meanwhile, had tied an apron around his waist and was heading for the kitchen. . . .
>
> "When we first got married," Chen said with a sidelong teasing glance at his wife, "she couldn't cook a thing and left it all to me. Now here I am a patriarch, and still chief cook."
>
> "But I've looked after our parents and the children, and done all the laundry!" Luo broke in with a spirited smile.
>
> "That's right, we share the work," her husband agreed.
>
> Soon delicious smells were coming from the kitchen, where the daughter of the house helped her father by washing and slicing vegetables. In no time at all we were sitting down to a tasty meal. I particularly liked the cold lobster and pickled

---

*"Three Chinese Families" by Liu Hongfa, *China Reconstructs*, July 1984, p. 15.

mustard greens cooked with wine, vinegar, salt, and ginger. Unlike the spicy pickled mustard greens of Sichuan province, the Haimen-style dish was fresh, crisp and slightly tart. . . .

Even though Chen was elected director of his factory last year and has heavy responsibilities, he has not given up doing chores around the house. "Families are important," he says. "Look at a man who really loves life, and you'll usually find he has a good relationship with his wife, children, and parents. People express their love in different ways, and one of mine is to do as much around the house as possible."

Chen's three-generation family is a happy and harmonious one. Each member has his or her interests—angling, raising chickens, reading, and good conversation. Early every morning the courtyard is crowded with different activities: Chen works out with dumbbells; Luo does *taijiquan* exercises; their daughter practices martial-arts swordplay; the elder son does *baguaquan,* a kind of Chinese shadow-boxing; and the younger son lifts weights. Chen's elderly parents water the flowers and feed the chickens.*

1. How has life changed for many Chinese peasants since 1949?
2. How has life in China's cities changed since 1949?

YOUNG PEOPLE

In China, young people are regarded as "the wealth of the country," and since 1949, the government has made great strides in advancing their education. Today, children begin elementary school about the age of 6 or 7. Five years later, they take an exam to go to high school, where they are separated into groups based on a particular field of study, such as science or the arts. Some schools teach technical subjects to prepare young men and women for factory or farm work.

UNIVERSITY LIFE

After graduation from high school, most young people start work in a factory, farm, or shop. A few, however, go on to university studies. To enter a university, a candidate must pass a difficult examination. Competition is fierce since there are more people who want to enroll than there are places. Lu Mei, a 19-year-old student, was one of those who passed the exams. Below, she talks about life at Beijing's Qinghua University:

> I'm in my third year in the radio department of Qinghua University, researching the potential of laser beams to transmit information.
>
> Qinghua has 6,000 students. There are 3,700 teachers, including professors and assistant professors, and many other workers, including laboratory technicians, doctors and cooks. The teacher-student

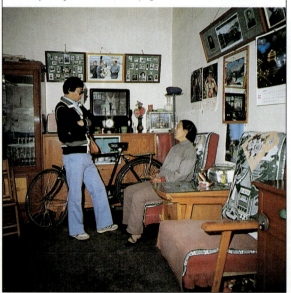

The furnishings of this farm worker's living room and his western-style clothing reflect China's modernization. How do this room's furnishings compare to those of the Chen family, described on page 223?

---

*"Life and Work of an Engineer" by Li Chaochen, *China Reconstructs,* September 1984, pp. 26–27.

CHAPTER 14 DAILY LIFE IN MODERN CHINA

Modern Chinese medicine includes both traditional and western-style practices. Here, at the Herbal College of Guangzhou, a teacher explains to her students the healing properties of various plants and herbs. Once in danger of being lost, the knowledge and practice of herbal medicine is now being revived. How is it decided who may be admitted to a Chinese university?

ratio is very favorable now, but the enrollment is expected to reach over 10,000 in one or two years.

All schools and universities are run by the state. We pay no fees, and at Qinghua seventy-two percent of the students receive grants of up to twenty-two yuan ($11) a month for food and pocket money.

I live at home, but most students live in dormitories with five or six students to a room. The government has a program to build more accommodation. Students can always go to the library to study—the library has more than two million books. . . .

I don't have any boyfriends, although relationships between boy and girl students are very good. The university leadership would strongly advise a student to leave if he or she wanted to marry before the age of thirty. Studies come first.*

RECREATION AND SPORTS

Although Chinese students work hard at their studies, they still find time to participate in a variety of activities outside of school. Many young people are involved in either the Young Pioneers or the Communist Youth League. The Young Pioneers is a children's organization which meets two or three hours a week and to which about 50 percent of China's children belong. Its purpose is to train children to be good citizens. To this end, it sponsors many community service projects, such as planting shrubs and cleaning streets and parks. The Communist Youth League, on the other hand, is an honor organization for high school students. To become a member, a student must be at least 15 years of age and have an excellent academic and political record. The League prepares a select number of distinguished candidates for eventual membership in the Communist party.

Chinese young people also enjoy such sports as ping pong, basketball, soccer, and gymnastics in their leisure time. In recent years, young Chinese athletes have been enthusiastic and talented competitors in international sporting events. In 1984, China participated in its first Olympics at the XIVth Summer Games in Los Angeles, California,

---

*"Students should not marry before the age of 30" in *We Live in China*, The Bookwright Press, 1984, pp. 20–21.

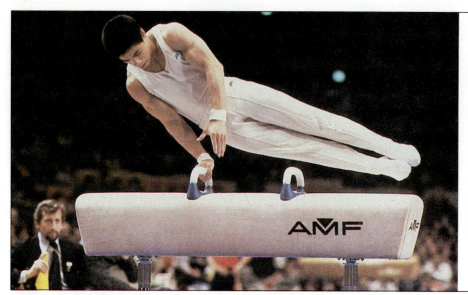

Olympic champion Li Ning concentrates as he circles the pommel horse in his gold-medal winning performance at the 1984 Summer Olympics. Li's flawless routine, in which he achieved extraordinary height with each movement, stunned the audience. For what other reason was Li's Olympic performance on the pommel horse significant?

and won 15 gold medals. One of the outstanding athletes at the Games was the gymnast Li Ning, who won six medals—three gold, two silver, and one bronze. Below, a Chinese journalist describes what happened:

> Li Ning is a vivacious youngster with a sense of humour, but he had become silent in the last few days. Now, with the prospect for his team brightening up, a smile beamed over his countenance when he stepped forward on to the mat and raised his hands in salutation to the spectators. He started his programme with a "double saltos with double twists" which immediately captivated the crowd. . . . His fantastic flair . . . held the spectators in a state of trance. Following a double salto he landed firmly at a corner of the mat. The whole house roared. . . . Li flung up his arms in an ecstasy of delight, then turned and ran to his coach Zhang Jian. . . .
>
> The heart-stirring moment came when Li Ning was awarded full marks by four judges, thus winning the first gold for China in the gymnastics competition. He felt his eyes swimming with tears and so did Coach Zhang. . . .
>
> Zhang's conviction [regarding Li's success] was confirmed by Li's performance . . . in the pommel horse [an event in which the performer has to support his or her whole body with his or her arms]. . . .
>
> Another gold!
>
> When [Li] stood on the victor's podium, he was already turning his mind to his next change—the rings. . . .
>
> Unlike the floor exercise and the pommel horse, the rings are done in slow motions. Li gathered himself and concentrated on each of his movements. He executed a "rear circle in hang" which no one had ever performed at a world competition. His movements were so vigorous and yet so well controlled that the rings, otherwise ready to sway at a mere touch of the hand, remained stockstill throughout. His perfect landing was immediately greeted by a long, deafening ovation. In spite of himself, he jumped high into the air to salute the spectators, with an elation he rarely displayed, not even when he bagged six golds at the Sixth World Cup.*

1. What educational opportunities are open to Chinese children?
2. What do some Chinese youngsters do for recreation?

---

*"Li Ning: A Triple Win" by Chen Shao, *China Sports*, December 1984, pp. 36–37, 40.

CASE STUDY
CHINA

THE OTHER CHINA

Since 1949, there have been two Chinas. In that year, the Communists won mainland China and set up the People's Republic at Beijing. The Guomindang, under Chiang K'ai-shek, fled to the island of Taiwan, 100 miles [160 kilometers] off China's southeast coast. They also acquired 78 smaller islands in the area. The official name of the Guomindang government in Taiwan is the Republic of China; its capital is the Taiwanese city of Taibei.

Taiwan's climate is subtropical with hot summers, mild winters, and a great deal of rainfall. Shaped like a tobacco leaf, the island is about 250 miles [400 kilometers] long and 60 to 90 miles [96 to 144 kilometers] wide, three-fourths of which is steep, forested mountains. On the western third of the island, where most of the people live, the land is suitable for farming. With close to 19 million people, Taiwan is one of the most densely populated islands in the world.

About 16 million of the people of Taiwan are Taiwanese Chinese whose ancestors came to Taiwan from the Chinese mainland around 1600. Another 2.5 million are Guomindang immigrants who fled the mainland in 1949. In addition to these two groups, about 100,000 Malay-speaking groups live in the mountains. While the Taiwanese Chinese control business, the "mainlanders" dominate the government. Although this led to much tension in the past, as a new generation replaces the old, the conflict has eased somewhat. More Taiwanese are entering the government, and the "mainlanders" are adopting Taiwanese ways.

Both the Communists and the Guimindang consider Taiwan and the other islands a part of China. Each claims to be the legal government of all China, and each has declared its aim to obtain the other's territory. Since 1949, the Guomindang government has kept Taiwan and the islands under a state of emergency. Today, it supports a combat-ready army of more than 550,000 soldiers. Political power remains largely in the hands of the Guomindang party leadership. After Chiang K'ai-shek's death in 1975, his son, Chiang Ching-kuo, succeeded him as party leader. In 1978, he became president. Although some limits have been placed on freedom of speech and press under the two Chiangs, the system never became totalitarian. Individuals in Taiwan enjoy more personal freedom than those living on the mainland.

Recently, the government of Taiwan has begun to take a more relaxed attitude. One reason for this is the booming economy, which experts have called one of Asia's "economic miracles." Along with South Korea, Hong Kong, and Singapore, Taiwan is considered a "little tiger" of international economics. The government of Taiwan allows farmers to own their own land and provides them with technical assistance. Over the past 30 years, the farmers have increased their yields so much that Taiwan now can produce 85 percent of its food. With both the government and business people fostering the growth of manufacturing and foreign trade, Taiwan now exports a variety of goods ranging from food to textiles and electronic equipment.

As a result of this economic growth, Taiwan has one of Asia's highest standards of living. Many Taiwanese believe that no matter what the People's Republic of China says, their strong economy will ensure the continued survival of the Republic of China.

1. What is meant by the term "the other China"?
2. If you were a Chinese Communist, how would you react to the statement that Taiwan is one of Asia's "economic miracles"? Why would you react this way?

EXPLORATION
CHINA

Some facts about the "two Chinas" are noted in the charts below. In the first chart are facts about the People's Republic of China. In the second chart are facts about the Republic of China. Which of these facts do you consider most important as shapers of development? As barriers to development? Explain each of your answers.

People's Republic of China

Land Area: 9.56 million square kilometers (3.7 million square miles)
Population: 1.1 billion (80% rural)
Major Cities: (over 2 million)
Shanghai (12)   Beijing (8.5)   Tianjin (7)
Chongquing (6)   Guangzhou (5)
Shenyang (5)   Dalian (4)   Wuhan (4)
Nanjing (3)   Chengou (3)   Jilin (3)
Jinan (3)   Lanzhou (2)   Xi'an (2)   Harbin (2)
Changsha (2)   Zibo (2)   Nanchang (2)
TV Stations: 42 (government)
Radio Stations: 114 (government)
TV Receivers: 5.5 million
Radio Receivers: 40.5 million
Gross National Product: $472,000 million
Per Capita Gross National Product: $436

*1981–1983 Estimates

Republic of China

Land Area: 35,979 square kilometers (13,892 square miles)
Population: 18.7 million (33% rural)
Major Cities: (1 million and over)
Taibei (2)   Kaohsiung (1)
TV Stations: 24 (private and commercial)
Radio Stations: 146 (private, commercial, and government)
TV Receivers: 5.1 million
Radio Receivers: 8.4 million
Gross National Product: $49,810 million
Per Capita Gross National Product: $2679

*1983 Estimate

Both the People's Republic of China and the Republic of China have constitutions. Below are several articles of each. After reading the articles, describe two ways in which the Communist government is constitutionally different from the Nationalist government. Based on what you have read in this chapter, do you think each constitution gives a true picture of how government operates in each China? Give examples to support your answers.

Based on the information in the charts, the articles of the constitutions, and the chapter, what similarities can you find between the two Chinas? What do you view as the most striking differences? In each case, explain your answer.

People's Republic of China

Article 1. *The People's Republic of China is a socialist state under the people's democratic dictatorship led by the working class and based on the alliance of workers and peasants. The socialist system is the basic system. . . .*

Article 2. *All power in the People's Republic of China belongs to the people. The organs through which the people exercise state power are the National People's Congress and the local people's congresses at various levels. . . .*

Article 3. *The state organs of the People's Republic of China apply the principle of democratic centralism.*

The National People's Congress, and the local people's congresses at different levels, are instituted through democratic election. . . . *

---
*Keesing's Contemporary Archives: Record of World Events, Volume XXIX, No. 2, February 1983, Longman, p. 31954.

Republic of China

Article 1

The Republic of China, founded on the Three Principles of the People [Nationalism, Democracy, Livelihood], shall be a democratic republic of the people, to be governed by the people and for the people.

Article 2

The sovereignty of the Republic of China shall reside in the whole body of citizens.

Article 25

The National Assembly shall, in accordance with the provisions of this constitution, exercise political powers on behalf of the whole body of citizens. *

---
*China Yearbook 1976, China Publishing, 1976, pp. 669, 671. Reprinted by permission.

CHAPTER 14 REVIEW

POINTS TO REMEMBER

1. Since the Communist drive for modernization began, China has become more industrialized, its cities have grown, and the standard of living is better.
2. In spite of modernization and change, many Chinese hold to traditional arts and festivals and maintain a high regard for family life and education.
3. The Chinese Communist party, the largest such party in the world, has a dominant role in the lives of the people. The party consists of the National Party Congress, the Central Committee, and the Politburo.
4. The Communist party is totalitarian. Government and powerful party committees run the provinces, counties, and townships, while cadres are responsible for political matters and solving everyday problems.
5. Although most Chinese live in rural areas and work as farmers, China's cities, especially in coastal areas, are the country's centers of industry and commerce. In both areas, the standard of living has improved in recent years.
6. Young people are regarded as "the wealth of the country," and since 1949, the government has made great strides in advancing their education. Most find time, however, to participate in a variety of activities outside of school.

VOCABULARY

Identify

National Party Congress	Zhou Jincai	Young Pioneers	Taiwan
Central Committee	Chen Tianlin	Communist Youth League	Taibei
Politburo	Lu Mei	Li Ning	Chiang Ching-kuo

Define

totalitarian   cadres

DISCUSSING IMPORTANT IDEAS

1. What benefits do you think modernization has brought to China? What problems? Explain your answers.
2. Would you like to live in a totalitarian society like that of China? Why or why not?
3. Is there any group or groups in your country equivalent to the Chinese cadres? What are they? In your view, how do their responsibilities compare with those of the cadres?
4. How does the life of the young people of China compare with that in your country? If you were to go to China to live for a year, do you think you could "fit in" with the Chinese students? Why or why not?

DEVELOPING SKILLS

ANALYZING PRIMARY AND SECONDARY SOURCES

In written material, *primary sources* are first-person accounts by someone who actually saw or lived the experience being described. Diaries, autobiographies, journals, eye-witness reports in newspapers and magazines, and oral interviews generally are primary sources. *Secondary sources* are second-hand accounts by someone using information taken from something or someone else. Textbooks, biographies, histories, or stories in which a person gives information about an event he or she did not actually witness generally are secondary sources.

In other words, if you witness a fire or live through a great storm and then write about your experiences, you are creating a primary source of information. If your friend experiences the fire or storm and tells you about it, or if you read about the fire or storm in the newspaper, and then you write about it, you are creating a secondary source of information.

When you read primary or secondary sources, it is helpful to be able to analyze them in order to know if they are dependable. The steps provided in this example will help you do this:

1. Read the selection about Lu Mei on pages 224 and 225.
2. Based on the definitions given above, determine if what you have read is a primary source or a secondary source. *(Primary source)*
3. Determine how long after the experience being described took place the primary source was written. If a lot of time has passed, the author may not be able to recall the event or experience as it truly was. *(Lu Mei actually was a student when she wrote the article.)*
4. Determine what the person writing the account sees as the main idea. *(University life at Qinghua University)*
5. Decide whether or not the account has been influenced by emotion, opinion, exaggeration, or some other special purpose. *(No. In some cases, however, two people may write about the same event or experience and give differing versions. Then, you must ask yourself why the accounts are different and determine which is more accurate.)*
6. Look for good *documentation*, information that tends to support the interpretation given. *(Lu Mei provides statistics and facts that can be verified in other sources.)*
7. Take into account the writer's background and credibility. Ask yourself: Is he or she a person who would know about university life? Is he or she being truthful? Is his or her account written in a convincing manner?

Other steps you might want to take to help analyze some sources include:

1. Identify the causes and effects described.
2. Read or interview more than one source to see if they agree. If they do, the account probably is true or authentic.
3. If you are using a secondary source, try to find a primary source against which to compare and contrast it.

For further practice in this skill, compare the narrative paragraph, a secondary source, on page 223, with the description by the Chinese journalist of Chen Tianlin's family, a primary source, on pages 223 and 224. Determine if the primary source indicates that the comments made in the secondary source are accurate.

CHINA

UNIT 2 REVIEW

SUMMARY

China, which Chinese called Land Under Heaven, is the world's oldest living civilization. In the distant past, the Chinese believed that they were superior and that all foreigners were inferior and uncivilized. So, the Chinese developed their culture, government, and laws as they saw fit with no concern for the outside world. Traditionally, China was ruled by dynasties supported by a privileged class of scholarly bureaucrats, and most Chinese were poor peasants who often suffered many injustices. The importance of family ties, a closeness between people and nature, and the need for learning to guide behavior were stressed for all Chinese. Ethical systems such as Confucianism shaped Chinese life.

In time, foreign influences began to penetrate China. The entrance of these foreign influences and the dissatisfaction that had built up among the peasants led to revolt and revolution.

In the early twentieth century, the last dynasty of China was overthrown, and the Land Under Heaven became the Republic of China. Despite its efforts, the new Guomindang government could not solve China's many problems. Chinese Communists took over the government and set up the People's Republic of China. The Guomindang leaders fled to the island of Taiwan, where they continued the Republic of China.

On the mainland, the Communists worked to create a modern industrial state. Almost all aspects of Chinese life changed. Over time and with shifts in government policy, the People's Republic of China has become more urbanized and industrialized. Still, most Chinese continue to live in rural areas and work as farmers. However, they and many Chinese now enjoy a higher standard of living than they or their ancestors did in the past.

REVIEW QUESTIONS

1. How do the traditional beliefs and practices of Confucianism and Daoism compare with those of modern Chinese communism?
2. In what ways has the Communist revolution transformed the way the Chinese live?
3. In what ways have family life and the role of women changed in China over the centuries? What factors were responsible for these changes?
4. What are some of the similarities and the differences between the attitudes the Chinese traditionally held about themselves and the outside world and the attitudes they hold today?

SUGGESTED ACTIVITIES

1. Draw or make a map of China showing such geographical and physical features as plains, deserts, rivers, mountains, and major cities.
2. Read English translations of several ancient and modern Chinese poems and short stories. Report to the class on the differences and similarities of their themes.
3. Working with several classmates, prepare a time line showing the major events in the development of China.
4. Working with several other classmates, write a play that focuses on a traditional or a modern Chinese belief or event. Present the play to the class.

COMPARING CULTURES

An important part of any culture is food. The foods people eat reflect their land, beliefs, and life styles. Read the articles below on the foods of China and the United States. Then contrast and compare the kinds of foods and the eating habits of the two cultures.

FOODS OF CHINA

In China, foods vary from region to region. In the north, the people eat foods made of wheat flour, such as noodles, steamed bread, and dumplings. In the south, rice is the basic food. People throughout the country enjoy pork, chicken, fish, cabbage, cucumbers, tomatoes, and eggplant. Most rely more on vegetables than on meat. Dishes of both are seasoned differently from region to region. People from the Hunan region of central China, for example, prefer their food hot and spicy, while those from the Guangzhou region of the south specialize in lightly seasoned dishes.

The Chinese buy their food fresh daily in the local market place. Because China has a large population and little farmable land, the Chinese traditionally place a high value on food, seldom waste it, and have developed efficient ways to prepare it. One method of preparation is steaming. Another is the stir-fry technique in which the ingredients are cut into small pieces and cooked rapidly in hot oil. This is generally done in a wok, an all-purpose metal pan with a rounded bottom and sloping sides. These methods require little fuel, are quick, and preserve the food's flavor and nutritional value.

The Chinese enjoy few desserts. Pastries and sweets are made only for festivals and other special occasions. Usually a meal ends with fresh fruit—bananas and oranges in the south and apples and peaches in the north. Appetizer-like snacks, although not eaten before or during meals, also are enjoyed. These include egg rolls, fried wontons, shrimp balls, dumplings, pressed noodles with honey, baked wheat cakes, and deep-fried dough cakes.

For more than 4000 years, the Chinese have used chopsticks, generally made from bamboo or plastic lacquered wood, to eat their food. The food is served from a large platter placed in the center of the table. Each person takes what he or she wants and fills his or her own bowl. The bowl is held close to the mouth, into which the food is scooped with the chopsticks. Although special spoons may be used for soups and juices, most often they are drunk directly from the bowl.

FOODS OF THE UNITED STATES

In the United States, turkey, hamburger, steak, corn on the cob, and mashed potatoes are regarded as national foods. Most Americans also enjoy such regional dishes as Southern-fried chicken, New England corned beef and cabbage, Texas-style barbecued beef, and Florida key lime pie. In addition, many dishes, such as egg rolls, pizza, sausage, tacos, and *shish kebab*, have spread from particular ethnic groups to the general population. Meat has always been an important part of the American diet, and most Americans delight in snacks, sweets, and pastries.

In the United States, food-shopping patterns differ. Some people shop each day, while others shop only once a week or once a month. Food is readily available in grocery stores and supermarkets in fresh, canned, and frozen form. To visitors from some foreign countries, the variety and abundance is staggering. Because of this abundance, Americans often are criticized for taking food for granted and for wasting it.

There also is variety in the choice of cooking appliances and methods of preparation. Foods are boiled, baked, fried, steamed, grilled, broiled, and roasted—all according to the taste and mood of the cook and the person eating. The prepared food generally is eaten from individual plates with forks, knives, or spoons.

Unit Three

Less than 50 years ago, Japan was a nation devastated and defeated by a world war. Today, it is the leading economic power in Asia. The economic success of the Japanese, along with other aspects of Japanese culture, have been shaped in a special way by geography and history. Throughout the centuries, the Japanese have been skillful in borrowing from other peoples while still keeping their own traditions and national identity. Today, they are trying to reach their national goals while maintaining close ties with the United States. They also are trying to determine whether their country should play a more active role in world affairs, especially in promoting peace in Asia, which is home to nearly two-thirds of the world's population. What they decide will affect not only the Japanese but many other peoples as well.

CONTENTS

15	THE GREAT ISLAND COUNTRY	236
16	TRADITIONAL JAPAN	252
17	MODERN JAPAN	268
18	RELIGION AND THE ARTS	284
19	JAPANESE SOCIETY	300
20	WORK AND LEISURE	314

JAPAN

CHAPTER 15
THE GREAT ISLAND COUNTRY

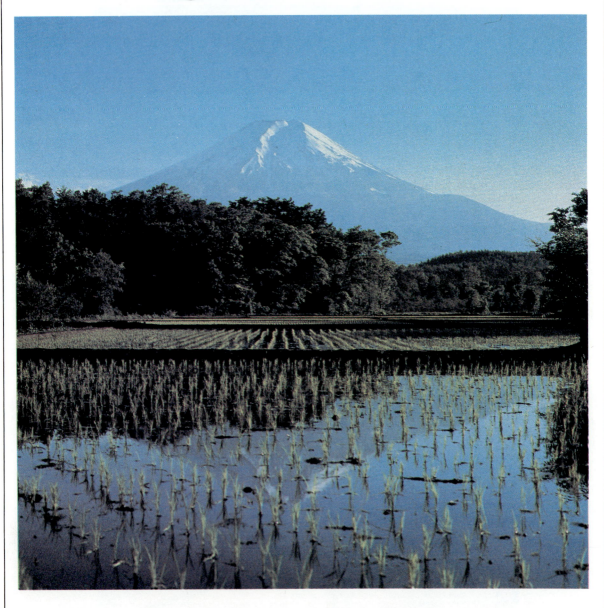

1. What are the major physical features of Japan?
2. How do the Japanese regard their natural environment?

Long centuries ago, when the world was a shadowy mist, the Islands of Japan were born of the sea. Among the many gods inhabiting this misty abode were Izanagi and Izanami. One day, while they were standing on the Floating Bridge of Heaven, talking with each other, Izanagi said: "I wonder what is down below us?" This aroused Izanami's curiosity, and they began to think how they might find out. Taking the Jewel-Spear of Heaven, Izanagi lowered it into the air and swung it around in an effort to strike something, for he could not see through the dense mist. Suddenly the spear touched the ocean. When Izanagi raised it, salty water dripping from it was dried by the wind, becoming hard, and forming an island in the middle of the sea.

"Let us go down and live on the island," said Izanagi. And so they descended from the Floating Bridge of Heaven to live on the island. Soon they had created the Great-Eight-Island-Land and given birth to three noble children: the Sun Goddess and her brothers the Moon God and the Storm God. The Sun Goddess, whose name was Amaterasu-Omi-Kami, also had a family. Her [great-great-great] grandson Jimmu became the first Emperor (Tenno or Mikado) of Japan.*

This **myth,** or traditional story, about the origin of Japan comes from an eighth-century Japanese work called the *Kojiki*, or *Records of Ancient Matters*. In this and such other early works as the *Nihonji*, or *Chronicles of Japan*, were some of the first descriptions of Japan and its environment. The descriptions referred to a land of mountainous islands surrounded by an ever-present ocean. The land had numerous clear streams and was favored with a temperate climate.

Today, the Japanese **archipelago,** or chain of islands, is 145,000 square miles (376,000 square kilometers) in area. It forms a curve off the coast of East Asia. There are four main islands—Hokkaido, Honshu, Shikoku, and Kyushu—and thousands of smaller ones. Honshu is the largest and most populated island and is a leading cultural center of Japan.

The people of Japan have always made love of their environment a major characteristic of their way of life. In early times, the sun, mountains, and the sea were especially important. Standing on the summit of a mountain, the people were awed by the glow of the sun as it rose from the Pacific Ocean. They expressed their love of the land in poetry, in prose, and in painting—a tradition still carried on by the Japanese today.

---

*Vanishing Japan by Morton Wesley Huber. Copyright ©1965 by Morton Wesley Huber. Reprinted by permission of AMPHOTO.

IN THE BEGINNING

The first mention of Japan in written history was in a dynastic history of China compiled about 297 AD. The Chinese did not think that the people of the land they called Wa were especially important, except for trade and occasional military threat. In their history, the Chinese wrote the following about their "barbarian" neighbors:

> The people of Wa . . . dwell in the middle of the ocean on the mountainous islands southeast of . . . Tai-fang. . . . Today, thirty of their communities maintain [communication] with us through envoys and scribes. . . .
>
> The land of Wa is warm and mild. In winter as in summer the people live on raw vegetables and go about barefooted. They have (or live in) houses; father and mother, elder and younger, sleep separately. They smear their bodies with pink and scarlet. . . . They serve food on bamboo and wooden trays, helping themselves with their fingers. . . .
>
> . . . In their meetings and in their deportment, there is no distinction between father and son or between men and women. . . . The people live long, some to one hundred and others to eighty or ninety years. . . . There is no theft, and litigation is infrequent. In case of violation of law, the light offender loses his wife and children by confiscation; as for the grave offender, the members of his household and also his kinsmen are exterminated. There are class distinctions among the people, and some men are vassals of others. Taxes are collected. There are granaries as well as markets in each province, where necessaries are exchanged under the supervision of the Wa officials.*

The people of Wa did not agree fully with the Chinese view. They felt they were equal —and perhaps even superior—to the Chinese. One Japanese ruler wrote to a Chinese emperor, "The Son of Heaven [the ruler] in the land where the sun rises addresses a letter to the Son of Heaven [the emperor] in the land where the sun sets." The Chinese emperor was not amused by the Japanese ruler's attitude and issued a strong rebuke.

Despite the rebuke—and the strong Chinese influence on their lives—the people of Wa continued to develop their own way of life. They displayed an unusual ability to adapt other ways of life to their particular environment.

1. How did the Chinese feel about the people of Wa?
2. What were several features of life in Wa?

MOUNTAINS

One important aspect of Japan's environment is mountains. Nearly 70 percent of the landscape is covered by rugged mountain ranges and steep hills. The mountains,

Hokkaido and Akan Lake, shown here, reflect the ancient description of Japan as a land of mountainous islands with clear streams and a temperate climate. What special ability did the early Japanese display?

Sources of Japanese Tradition compiled by Ryusaku Tsunoda, William Theodore de Bary and Donald Keene, ©1958, Columbia University Press. Reprinted by permission.

CHAPTER 15 THE GREAT ISLAND COUNTRY

On their way to the summit of Mount Fuji, summer hikers climb along a steep trail over loose lava ash. Located on Honshu, about 60 miles (97 kilometers) west of Tokyo, Fuji, which rises to 12,388 feet (3776 meters), is Japan's highest mountain and one of the world's most perfect volcanic cones. Why is Fuji considered an inactive volcano?

which are divided by rocky gorges and narrow valleys, have thick forests on their lower slopes. Flowing through them are swift, shallow rivers and thundering waterfalls.

The Japanese archipelago itself is the upper part of a great mountain range rising 20,000 to 30,000 feet (6000 to 9000 meters) from the floor of the Pacific Ocean. The archipelago lies on the Pacific's "rim of fire," where the earth's crust is not stable and is shifting constantly. As a result, earthquakes and volcanic eruptions are common.

Of the more than 190 volcanoes in Japan, one of the most famous is Mount Fuji. Most Japanese consider Fuji a sacred symbol of their country. Since Fuji has not erupted since 1707, it is considered an inactive volcano. Every July and August, some 300,000 Japanese climb to the top of Fuji.

Mountain climbing is popular throughout Japan and is undertaken in all seasons. Many climb the Japan Alps, which include all of the country's highest peaks except Mount Fuji. Below, visitors describe their initial impressions of a climb they made in September:

A typhoon had passed over the Japan Alps the day before, and its boisterous afterwinds jostled and taunted us as we climbed the flank of Tateyama (9,892 feet) [2967.6 meters]. Thick clouds boiled around our booted feet. A sheet of cold rain streamed over the ridge, twisting and flapping like laundry pinned to a line.

With gruff impatience . . . , the wind picked up our guide, a . . . young fellow named Hidehiko Noguchi, and blew him against a large rock. The same gust filled my rain jacket like a sail and knocked me down. . . .

"*Gambare!*" cried Noguchi-san. The word means, roughly, "Show your spirit!" A favorite saying of Japanese mountaineers, it is a jovial, all-purpose exhortation [plea] to laugh at discomfort and try your best.

Invigorated by the stinging rain and buffeted by the gale, we pushed on and arrived at the crest of the ridge. Suddenly the clouds were parted by fingers of sunlight. Beyond the ridge lay the silvery Sea of Japan. In every other direction the jagged peaks of the Japan Alps soared as high as 10,000 feet [3048 meters]: Yari—"spear," Tsurugi—"sword," Yatsu—"eight peaks."

In early September some of these summits were already dusted with snow. . . . [all] were touched by the tantalizing mystery of mountains we had yet to climb. In the weeks ahead, we would stand on many of these summits. For now, though, we were content with what we had found on our very first climb—the serenity and beauty of a unique region of Japan, a place so little known to the outside world that we would encounter . . . Japanese who had never before met a foreigner. . . .

Why "Alps"? In Tokyo, before we set out for the mountains, Dr. Yasuo Sasa, president of the Japanese Alpine Club, explained how these mountains, which are so bound up with the Japanese spirit, happen to bear such an un-Japanese name.

"We Japanese always revered our high mountains and made pilgrimages to them," said Dr. Sasa, "but it had never occurred to our ancestors to climb them for sport. Then, in the latter part of the 19th century, English climbers saw them for the first time. The meadows and crags, the wildflowers and highland animals of our mountains reminded them of the European Alps—and so they got their name. . . ."

Certainly the mountaineering spirit is in evidence on the mountains. Sometimes, at a place where a wayfarer has been moved by the splendor of the scenery, one will find a homely little shrine—a cone of rocks with a flower or a gift of chocolate or cigarettes laid beside it.

On almost every high summit, pilgrims have built a shrine. Here, it is traditional to leave a five-yen coin, called a goen, a word that also means "bond" or "close relationship" and implies that he who leaves the offering will remember the place and be remembered by it—and, with luck, return.

At the summit of Tateyama's Oyama peak, on a shaft of rock not much larger at the tip than a dining-room table, stands a famous shrine. Thousands of small flat stones form the pavement of its tiny courtyard; on each pebble, a pilgrim has written, with ink and brush, his name and the date on which he visited the summit.*

---

*"The Japan Alps" by Charles McCarry in *National Geographic*, August 1984, pp. 240, 242. Reprinted by permission.

1. Why are mountains an important aspect of Japan's environment?
2. How do the Japanese regard Mount Fuji?
3. How did the Japan Alps get their name?

THE SEA

Just as important to the Japanese as the mountains is the sea. The sea plays a vital role in Japan's climate, which ranges from warm subtropical in the southernmost islands to cool in the north. Northern Japan is influenced by the cool Oyashio Current and southern Japan by the warm Japan Current. Hokkaido has a continental climate with warm summers and cold winters. Northern Honshu, on the other hand, is more temperate. Southern Honshu and the other two major islands have a subtropical climate. **Monsoons,** or seasonal winds, blowing across the seas also influence the climate. They bring rain in summer and, in the north, snow in winter. Each year, **typhoons,** severe tropical hurricanes, strike the country, generally in late summer and early fall.

The sea is important to the Japanese commerce as well as for its effect on the climate. Because Japan has limited natural resources, the people must depend on sea trade. They import most of their raw materials for manufacturing and then send the finished goods to other countries. The Japanese also rely on the sea for food. Japan has one of the largest fishing fleets in the world, contributing about 15 percent of the world's catch.

No part of Japan is more than 70 miles (112 kilometers) from a seacoast. The Japanese coastline, which totals over 17,000 miles (27,200 kilometers), is rough, craggy, and highly irregular. All along it are capes, headlands, peninsulas, islands, and bays. Many of the bays offer good harbors and ports, through which pass the country's vital sea trade.

CHAPTER 15 THE GREAT ISLAND COUNTRY

Off the northernmost tip of Hokkaido lies Rebun Island, whose terrain is typical of much of the rugged natural beauty of coastal Japan. This photo, taken in spring, shows the island's steep grassy hills, which rise above narrow plains and scenic bays. What is the greatest distance one would need to travel in Japan to reach a seacoast?

One of the most famous seacoast areas is in southern Japan along the Inland Sea, which separates Honshu and Shikoku. Below, a passenger on a boat describes the calm and gentle appearance of the thousands of small islands which dot the Inland Sea:

> A typical island of the Inland Sea, as you pass in the boat, consists of: a village clustered on the beach, one road along the shore, others—alleys—running back to the hills then stopping, sometimes a wide road going over the mountains to the other side, sometimes a sea road continuing around the island. Then, in the middle, as seen from the water, near the shore a temple in a grove, often the only grove on the island, or a stone torii, a shady walk, a shrine in the shade. Near it the largest building, the general store; on either side of it black houses, roofs of cemented gray tile—black and white, salt and pepper. Then the yellow or green iron-roofed ticket-house and, much farther away, a red torii for the fishermen, for the goddess. And then—on a spit—the graveyard, the gravestones high, rectangular, like teeth. Then seaweed racks, an overturned boat or two, and the island slides down and back into the sea it came from.*

In direct contrast to the islands of the Inland Sea is the wild, untamed, and unspoiled coastal area in the northern part of Hokkaido. Below, a voyager gives her impressions of Hokkaido's Shiretoko Peninsula:

> The early boat left at 5:30 AM, just as a catch of flounder was being unloaded at the fishermen's cooperative. The sun soon warmed the damp air and the scent of resin from the thickly forested hills and mountains beyond came drifting out to sea where it mingled with the smell of the tide. . . .
>
> . . . Nakamura [the guide] pointed to the shore, where strips of level ground at the water line afforded space for a few scattered huts. The huts, he told me, are used by fishermen . . . in the short summer season when the harvest of giant kelp, *konbu*, is on. *Konbu* is a sort of sea vegetable with thick, wide leaves—dark green in its natural state, but almost black

---
*The Inland Sea by Donald Richie, 1971, Weatherhill, p. 134.

and stiff as leather when it is dried and cut into sheets. It is an important ingredient in many Japanese recipes and is a basic element in soup stock.

I marveled at the vegetation. The hills were bright with . . . flowering plants. To think that this rugged horn-shaped peninsula—surrounded by ice floes all winter—could burst into such bloom come spring! . . .

Nakamura was looking forward to the coming season: "A few more months, and we'll be out there at the huts. We work all day, everybody together, gathering and drying—we dry it here, even though the sun isn't too hot, and the air isn't too dry—and at night everybody drinks by lantern light. At other times of the year, there's not a soul around that place." . . .

Finally, the cliffs of the northwest coast loomed into sight, rising to heights of two hundred meters [660 feet] and extending unbroken for ten-kilometer [6-mile] stretches, relenting only occasionally. . . . These cliffs, with their black and white horizontal stripes, are a striking phenomenon: molten lava spread in sills through fossil-rich, sedimentary rock while the mass was still submerged; then volcanic activity beneath the ocean floor pushed the whole out of the sea, creating these massive cliffs.

Volcanic activity was not, however, the only force involved in the creation of these cliffs. The wind and sea have shaved them into fantastic shapes. . . . The Ainu, as well as the Japanese, have given names to some: Penguin-no-hana (Penguin's Nose), Shishi-iwa (Lion Rock), Tako-iwa (Octopus Rock). . . . It is a sea-bird's paradise. . . . Narrow rivers, whose sources are in the mountains sixteen hundred meters (5280 feet) up above, fall in cascades of white over the dark cliffs. In winter they freeze solid. Foliage tops the cliffs, and beyond them rise the Shiretoko range.*

---

*Taken from *NATIONAL PARKS OF JAPAN* by Mary Sutherland and Dorothy Britton, published by Kodansha International ©1981.

1. Why is the sea important to the Japanese?
2. What are some of the characteristics of Japan's coastline?

THE PLAINS

Narrowly squeezed between the seacoast and the base of the mountains are the plains areas of Japan. Although they make up only one-eighth of the total land area, most of the 120 million Japanese live on them.

The plains have profoundly shaped Japanese life and culture. Living in such small crowded areas has led the Japanese to develop an elaborate system of **etiquette,** or manners, to reduce social tensions and make human relationships easier to manage. The influence also can be seen in other areas. Japanese gardeners, for example, have become known for their skill in reproducing nature on a small scale. They often grow **bonsai,** or dwarfed trees, and arrange miniature gardens. In many ways, bonsai reflects the Japanese spirit. In the passage that follows, the meaning that bonsai holds and the role it plays is described:

> Japan . . . is a relatively small country. For most of its recorded history it has been heavily populated. Virtually every inch of available land is settled or under intensive cultivation. There are few places where a person can get away from all other people for very long. . . .
>
> Through bonsai, the city dweller, who daily sees concrete and steel, can have a bit of greenery to himself. Though enclosed by four walls, he can escape in his imagination into a natural world that exists in his little trees. For a few minutes, walls can be made to vanish, an inch-high mound of moss can become a green meadow, a small rock a mountainside, a few seedlings an entire forest. This is the magic of bonsai.*

---

*Reprinted by special permission.

CASE STUDY
JAPAN

EARTHQUAKES IN JAPAN

Among the most striking of Japan's natural phenomena are earthquakes. The archipelago has about 1500 a year—an average of 20 a day. In most cases, they are minor and cause little damage. But every few years, severe earthquakes occur, causing loss of life and property. Great waves called **tsunami**, set off by vibrations of the earth, are particularly destructive, creating much damage along Japan's Pacific coast.

One of the worst earthquakes occurred in 1923 in the Tokyo area. Whole villages were buried, many city buildings were destroyed, and close to 100,000 people died. Midori Yamanouchi, a survivor of that disaster, tells what it was like:

I was a girl living on the outskirts of Tokyo. . . . My best friend and I had just learned to sew new-style Western dresses for our dolls instead of old-style Japanese kimonos, and I had gone to her house to show her a doll's hat I had just made.

Suddenly her garden fence fell over. Then the dishes in the kitchen crashed to the floor, and the grandfather clock tipped over onto the floor right next to where we were sitting. We ran outside, and as the shaking stopped a little, I started home.

All around, the bamboo was trembling and rustling. I was afraid. Bamboo is supposed to be a safe place during an earthquake because its roots twine together so tight that the earth can't split open beneath you and the trees can't fall on you. But it was shaking so much I wasn't sure. When I got to our house, I found all the neighbors in our backyard because we had the best bamboo grove anywhere around. Everybody stayed right there from noon, when the earthquake began, until almost midnight.

All afternoon we watched black smoke billow up from the city, and when night came we saw the sky glow red. Someone said that a new volcano had erupted in downtown Tokyo, but later we learned that the smoke and red glow came from fires. People were cooking lunch when the earthquake started, and they ran outside without thinking to turn off the gas or put out the charcoal. Kitchens caught fire, and from them, whole houses. Soon the city was flaming. Waterpipes broke so the firemen couldn't do much.

My mother carried our brazier outside the house and started cooking rice enough to last for days and days. She said that it would be a long time before everything would be normal again, and she was right. Twelve relatives came to live with us because their homes were ruined, and the whole neighborhood used our well for a week. It was the deepest one around, and everyone was afraid that water from shallow wells might be unsafe to drink until we could clean up the the debris. . . .

My father was away on a hiking trip at the time, so Mother and my three sisters and I had to get along without him. No trains were running so he could not get home, and lines were down so it was several days before he could even send a telegram to let us know that he was all right.*

1. What impact have earthquakes had on Japan?
2. Do you think you would react as calmly as Midori did? What would you do?

*"The Tremor Next Time" by Hermann Schreiber in *Geo*, July 1981, Vol. 3 pp. 127, 128–129. Copyright ©1981 Knapp Communications Corporation. Reprinted by permission.

The plains areas are important for other reasons as well. The country's major industries, most of its important cities, and its best farmland are on the plains. For this reason, the plains support not only a great number of people but also a wide variety of life styles.

URBAN LIFE

Located on the plains of Honshu are the cities of Tokyo, Yokohama, Osaka, and Nagoya. These four metropolitan areas are home to more than one-third of the urban population of Japan. The largest of the cities is the capital—Tokyo—which is made up of a number of districts, cities, localities, and villages. Below, a frequent visitor to Japan gives his impressions of the capital city:

> From my ninth-floor hotel room I can see for miles and miles across parks and palaces, all the way to the hazy horizon, with its bulky new police headquarters and its faithful replica of the Eiffel Tower. Tokyo is stirring for another day.
> Tokyo: one of the largest, most crowded, most chaotic cities in the world; the center of a breathlessly expanding industrial power, computer capital of the world, megalopolis. There are 11.5 million souls in metropolitan Tokyo; 8.5 million of them live in the city proper. . . . Average living space: just under six square yards [4.8 square meters] per person. Green space: a bit more than one square yard [.8 square meter] per person. There are 98,500 factories and 683,000 businesses. And 39,000 of the city's telephone subscribers are named Suzuki.
> But Tokyo doesn't even exist. People who live here never use the name but speak instead of Shinjuku and Shibuya, Akasaka and Roppongi, Asakusa and Ueno. Tokyo exists only in its parts, and they by no means constitute a whole. At most, what we call Tokyo is a conglomerate, a gigantic accumulation of onetime villages that continue to be quite self-sufficient and that have little to do with one another.
> The villages begin just a hundred yards away from any of the celebrated avenues. There, in the shadows of high-rise buildings, are countless tiny plots, some enclosed by walls six feet high. The little houses often have patches of startling green between them, and they are all connected by a web of alleyways much too narrow for anything but local traffic. At the center of each community there is invariably a shopping street, an open-air treasure trove of mom-and-pop stores that do business whenever there is demand. And in among the shops are thousands of tiny restaurants where you can get a decent meal even at three in the morning.
> Tokyo contains 23 districts, 26 cities, 6 localities and 9 villages in a total of 827 square miles [2150 square kilometers]. That area is only the so-called metropolitan region. . . . Those are the statistics —and they are meaningless.
> It is impossible to get an overview of this city. . . . One perceives Tokyo in pieces, in a sequence of unconnected images and metaphors, in conflicting rhythms with a kind of accidental rhyme.
> The city has no past either architecturally or psychologically. Twice in the first half of this century Tokyo was leveled and then rose from its ashes in totally unplanned, rampant growth. . . .
> . . . In such a place, what matters most is survival. And what could be more important for people . . . than the basic securities provided by life on the land? . . .
> Tokyo should have collapsed into utter ruin long ago. After all, no human concentration of this magnitude and density can reasonably be expected to function. But it works—and it works much better than many other cities.
> In Tokyo, for example, you can walk alone in back streets at night without fear. . . . There is no appreciable drug problem

CHAPTER 15 THE GREAT ISLAND COUNTRY

Crowded with tall office buildings, busy streets, and freeways, Tokyo is the fifth largest city in the world. In addition to its reputation as a world leader in business and industry, Tokyo is also recognized for its art galleries, museums, concert halls, and other cultural attractions. What are some major characteristics of life in Tokyo?

in Tokyo. . . . and the possession of handguns is forbidden.

Tokyo's inhabitants—millions of them—are almost constantly on the move. It is miraculous that they can get to their destinations, but they do. Tokyo provides a model for mass transit that functions—though not, to be sure, on the streets. Tokyo's inhabitants travel by rail, both above and below the ground. The tram, subway and train cars may be densely packed, but the system performs with a punctuality, safety and cleanliness unparalleled anywhere else.

I have a quick lunch in one of the countless small snack bars that line the network of corridors of the large subway stations. I am fascinated by these catacombs of gleaming tile, where you can walk for miles—but never for more than a hundred yards free of the temptation to buy something. The tunnels are a true-to-life replica of the city aboveground, and they're even more confusing. Otemachi, the subway stop near my hotel, has 18 exits. A wrong turn could take me so far in the wrong direction that I'd need a taxi to reach my destination. . . .

In the afternoon I head for Shinjuku, a new high-rise area that serves as a commercial center. . . . There are six skyscrapers and, it seems, five thousand bars. The skyscrapers are monumental in style and tower over electronic game palaces, roving fortune-tellers, Turkish baths and baseball batting ranges on fenced-over rooftops.

Here the merchant is king. The architecture of the shops consists of concrete bunkers with neon facades that seem to shout, "Buy, people, buy!" Wherever you see color, it is because someone wants to sell something. All that glitters is either a commercial product or advertising. . . . In the shopping arcades at the base of the skyscrapers are copies of the boutiques that are found in other downtown department stores—most of them named after European designers. . . .

Prosperity now! That is the slogan.*

Japan: Crossroads of East and West by Ruth Kirk, 1966, Thomas Nelson and Sons, pp. 33–34

A tea farmer inspects the quality of his growing crop. In Japan, most tea is grown in Shizuoka and Uji, outside the city of Kyoto. Tea-drinking, introduced to Japan from China in the twelfth century, has become an important Japanese tradition. Besides tea, what other important crops are grown in the Japanese countryside?

RURAL LIFE

Today, about 24 percent of the Japanese people live in the countryside. But, for hundreds of years, Japan was largely a rural society. Most of the people who still live in rural areas are farmers and their families. Most grow rice, wheat, fruit, vegetables, tobacco, and tea. The majority own their own land and are very productive. The life these people live is described below by an American journalist who traveled through the countryside with a Japanese friend from the city:

> ... The train chugged upcountry, passing through hot-spring villages.... The railroad paralleled the Himekawa, a river that seemed to flow granite, so stony and gray it was. The dark, snowy Hida peaks had gone into another weather, but in the valley the day was warm....
>
> At last the incline leveled to a high flatness split by the Azusa River and surrounded by the mountains called the roof of Japan. Even at this elevation, rice fields lay in all directions....
>
> At Misato, a farm village ..., we left the railroad and headed west up into the foothills, where we took a room at a mountain inn.... We were the last to sit down at the long tables already laid with the meal....
>
> We drank Kirin beer, but the farmers ... drank sake [Japanese liquor made from fermented rice] from bottles the size of a short boy. They drew the corks with their teeth and looked down the slopes onto their fields with satisfaction. But they speculated, too, about weather and the harvest. Bound tightly around their temples were *hachimaki*, small towels to absorb sweat and aid concentration....
>
> From our room, Tadashi and I watched dusk come down the valley to conceal smoke from burning rice straw of last year and only then to reveal the orange fires....
>
> All night long the birds struck their calls against the dark. Toward dawn the cuckoos got into it with their ceaseless two notes, then a rooster, and finally the chirping small ones....
>
> Michisada-san was waiting in the big hot communal bath, and we soaked together with a grower of mulberry leaves and watched through a somewhat steamy window the fertile plain....

CHAPTER 15 THE GREAT ISLAND COUNTRY

Instead of the road, Tadashi and I followed the shortcut under the big pines into the valley orchards and vineyards. The rocky soil was fertile once it got water, so, although too far above the river here for paddyfields, it produced fruit, melons, and chestnuts through a computer-controlled sprinkler system. Down the dusty road until we reached a farmhouse. Tadashi knew the son and his bride.

The Misawa family had lived in Nagano, which means long field, for a thousand years, most of the time as rice growers. After the war, . . . Daimaru Misawa bought land inexpensively on the dry slope. He cleared mountain pine and, with other villagers, put in a cooperative irrigation system. In the '50s he built a home, then a larger one ten years ago. His 4.4-acre [1.8-hectare] farm is about twice the average acreage here, and his grapes, apples, peaches and melons have done well. The eldest son, Isamu, has just installed a new, promising method for improving grape production with vinyl tents.

Now Daimaru, at 72, had time to build a traditional garden with a small fishpond, and he could watch television documentaries and foreign movies late into the night. . . .

To welcome us, the women, Michiko and Fuyuko, served barley tea, buns stuffed with pigweed, pickles, garden strawberries, and grape juice from the vineyards. We sat on the earth in the orchard under an old peach tree. . . .

The family returned to stripping fruit. From a branch carrying six olive-size young peaches, the women plucked all but the largest so that it might grow to its maximum. This attention to each fruit gave them a good living.

Tadashi and I hiked down lanes lined with mugwort [an herb] smelling like sage, through a bamboo thicket, into a blossoming locust grove, on past rice fields and small houses. The oldest houses had thatched roofs caked with moss, while the newer had synthetic tiles and solar panels. "Japan," Tadashi said, "is always a mixture."

By each home was a garden of leeks, bottle gourds, eggplants, cucumbers, cabbages, tomatoes. Along the lanes ran yew hedges and irrigation troughs rushing a swift, cold water, which sometimes carried clover blossoms that children had tossed in a mile away. Shadows from the wings of circling black kites [birds] sent pigs squealing, and wind from a dark mountain storm set scarecrows to flapping.

Often out of a paddyfield, muddy prints from bare feet walked bodiless up the road to the next plot. . . . Occasionally, unexpected, dark rice-field birds rose screeching into the air like so much winged mud flung upward. In one small plot, full of starlings, it was as if the field itself thought to take flight.

Walking, I began to notice carved stones along the lanes. Dozens of them there were: at crossroads, above fields, at boundaries. Although each white granite rock was unique, every one showed two relief figures cut into a naturally smoothed stone about three feet [.91 meters] high. "*Dosojin*," Tadashi said. "Shinto roadside god. . . ."

On the route back to the farm, Tadashi and I came to a crossroads *Dosojin* carved with compass directions. Most potently of all Japanese symbols, these wayside stones reveal how life is a journey wherein the traveler sees that it is the earth itself on which paths cross and from which journeys proceed toward union with otherness. "*Dosojin* shows us the way," Tadashi said.*

1. In what ways have the plains shaped Japanese life and culture?
2. In what cities does one-third of Japan's urban population live?
3. How are some Japanese farms organized? What crops are grown on them?

---

*"Up Among the Roadside Gods" by William Least Heat Moon in *Time*, August 1, 1983, pp. 80–81. Copyright 1983 Time Inc. All rights reserved. Reprinted by permission from TIME.

Exploration
JAPAN

Based on the information in the four maps, decide whether each of the following statements about Japan is true or false. Give reasons for your choices.

1. The island of Hokkaido has a subtropical climate.
2. Japan's largest cities are located on the island of Kyushu.
3. The nation of Japan consists of four major islands.
4. Japan has few natural resources.
5. The greatest number of Japanese live on the island of Honshu.
6. The Japan Current brings cold moist air to Japan from the North Pacific.
7. Most of Japan's population is in the northern part of the country.
8. Hokkaido receives less rainfall than the other Japanese islands.
9. For the most part, Japan is made up of lowlands and plateaus.
10. Shikoku is the largest of all of the Japanese islands.

CLIMATE

POPULATION DENSITY

LANDFORMS AND NATURAL RESOURCES

AVERAGE ANNUAL RAINFALL

CHAPTER 15 REVIEW

POINTS TO REMEMBER

1. The first descriptions of Japan and its environment came from myths recorded in the *Kojiki* and the *Nihonji*.
2. The Japanese archipelago is off the coast of East Asia. It is made up of thousands of islands, the largest of which are Hokkaido, Honshu, Shikoku, and Kyushu.
3. Nearly 70 percent of the Japanese landscape is covered by mountains and hills. Because of Japan's location on the Pacific's "rim of fire," the country often has earthquakes and volcanic eruptions.
4. There are more than 190 volcanoes in Japan. One of the most famous is Mount Fuji, considered sacred by most Japanese.
5. Japan has a long, ragged, and irregular seacoast. The Japanese have a close relationship with the sea, depending on it for food and trade.
6. The narrow plains areas squeezed between the seacoast and the base of the mountains are where most Japanese live and where the major industries, most important cities, and best farmland are found. The plains have profoundly shaped Japanese life and culture.
7. About 76 percent of the Japanese people live in large urban areas. Japanese urban life is modern but has close ties to the past.
8. Today, about 24 percent of the Japanese people live in rural areas. Most are farm families who own their own land and are very productive.

VOCABULARY

Identify

Izanagi	Honshu	Fuji	Tokyo
Izanami	Shikoku	Japan Alps	Yokohama
Kojiki	Kyushu	Inland Sea	Osaka
Nihonji	Wa	Shiretoko Peninsula	Nagoya
Hokkaido			

Define

myth	monsoons	etiquette	*tsunami*
archipelago	typhoons	bonsai	

DISCUSSING IMPORTANT IDEAS

1. In what ways do you think Japan's geographical location has been both an advantage and a disadvantage?
2. How do traditional Japanese attitudes toward nature differ from the traditional attitudes of the West? Which viewpoint do you prefer? Why?
3. Despite their ruggedness, how might Japan's mountains benefit the national economy?
4. In the final reading of the chapter, Tadashi states "Japan is always a mixture." How does this describe both urban and rural life in modern Japan?

CHAPTER 15 THE GREAT ISLAND COUNTRY

DEVELOPING SKILLS

READING FOR DETAIL

Reading a textbook or research paper is different from reading a novel or short story. You read the latter for diversion. You read the former for information, for detail. *Details* are the individual facts that make up a whole reading. So when you read for detail, you are trying to locate the facts the author presents. The more *detailed*, crowded with facts and information, a reading is, the more care and attention you must pay to it.

There are some general guidelines to keep in mind when reading for detail. They are the following:

1. Be sure you understand the vocabulary. If any words are unfamiliar, look those words up in a dictionary.
2. Do not overlook the punctuation. A pair of commas may introduce a synonym, an explanation, or a series of examples. Semicolons and colons may link ideas.
3. As you read, keep in mind these questions: Who?, What?, Where?, When?, How?, and Why?
4. Read slowly, making outline notes whenever possible. Some information may lend itself to being organized into chart or graph form, making it clearly understood at a glance.

Keeping these guidelines in mind, study the following example. The questions you might ask yourself, and their answers, appear in parentheses. Definitions for more difficult words appear in brackets.

The first time Japan was mentioned in written history was about 297 AD. (When was Japan first mentioned in written history? About 297 AD.) *It was discussed by the Chinese in a dynastic history of their country.* (Where was it discussed? By whom? In a dynastic history of China. By the Chinese.) *The Chinese called the Japanese "the people of Wa" and said they lived on mountainous islands in the middle of the ocean.* (Who were "the people of Wa?" Where did they live? The Japanese. On mountainous islands in the middle of the ocean.) *The Chinese and the people of Wa kept contact through envoys [government representatives] and scribes [professional writers].* (How did the Chinese and the people of Wa maintain contact? Through envoys and scribes.)

According to the Chinese account, the land of Wa was warm and mild year-round. (What kind of climate did Wa have? Warm and mild.) *The people of Wa lived in houses, ate raw vegetables, went barefooted, and colored their bodies pink and scarlet.* (What kind of shelter did the people of Wa have? Houses. What did they eat? Raw vegetables. What did they wear on their feet? Nothing. What did they do to their bodies? Colored them pink and scarlet.)

There were no robberies in Wa and very little litigation [court cases]. (What was the crime rate like in Wa? No robberies and little litigation.) *When the law was violated, the offenders [guilty persons] were punished.* (What happened when the law was broken? Offenders were punished.) *For a minor violation, the offender's wife and children were taken away from him.* (What was the punishment for a minor violation? Loss of wife and children.) *For a major offense, the members of the offender's household and his kinsmen [relations by marriage] were killed.* (What was the punishment for a major offense? The death of the members of the offender's household and of his kinsmen.)

For further practice in this skill, read for detail the section on the plains on pages 242 and 244. When you have completed the reading, you should know where the plains are located, how large an area they cover, how much of the population lives on them, how they have influenced Japanese life and culture, and why they are important to Japan.

CHAPTER 16
TRADITIONAL JAPAN

1. How did the Japanese organize their society before modern times?
2. What foreign influences shaped the development of traditional Japan?

After living in Japan for a while, Izanagi and Izanami returned to heaven. There they created many other gods and goddesses, including a sun-goddess called Amaterasu and a storm-god called Susanowo.

Amaterasu was a gentle, lovely goddess. She gave life to everything around her. But Susanowo was wild and fierce. He stormed around causing trouble.

One day Susanowo visited Amaterasu. He behaved so badly that she hid in a cave. The other gods and goddesses had to play a trick with a mirror to get her back out.

Another day Susanowo killed an eight-headed dragon who was about to eat a young girl. In the dragon's tail he found a sword. Susanowo gave the sword to Amaterasu to make up for his bad behavior. Then he married the girl he had saved.

Susanowo and his wife had many children. But none of them was good enough to rule Japan. So Amaterasu sent her grandson, Ninigi, to rule. She gave him three [items] to take with him. One was the mirror that had brought her from the cave. The second was jewel[s] from inside the cave. And the third was [a] sword from the dragon's tail.

"Use these to rule Japan," said Amaterasu. "you and your descendants will rule forever."

Ninigi married and had three sons. One of them, Hoori, married the daughter of the sea-god. They had one son, who married and had four children. And one of those children was Jimmu Tenno, the great-great-great-grandson of the sun goddess and the first human emperor of Japan.*

This legend describes what the people of traditional Japan, Japan before 1868, believed about the beginnings of the Japanese monarchy. Like most legends, it has its basis in fact. For example, although the origins of the three items described in the legend are unknown, the items known as the Regalia probably did exist. A replica of the mirror is housed in a palace shrine. Replicas of the sword and the jewels are in the Imperial Palace in Tokyo. The Regalia symbolize Japan's imperial family, one of the oldest royal families in the world.

Historians trace the origins of Japanese royalty to the 500's AD, a period when history began to be recorded in Japan. At that time, the country was controlled by warring **clans,** or groups based on family ties and headed by a chief. Before long, the Yamato clan emerged as the most powerful and extended its rule over most of the country. Its leaders later became emperors of Japan.

Enchantment of the World: Japan by Carol Greene, 1983, Children's Press, pp. 51–52. Reprinted by permission.

An Emerging Civilization

The Japanese monarchy helped unite the country. At the same time, its military exploits helped bring the Japanese into contact with other peoples on the Asian mainland. One of these peoples was the Chinese, who had the most advanced civilization in East Asia at the time. The Japanese soon developed close ties with the Chinese. In time, they modeled their society on the Chinese way of life. They also borrowed the Chinese system of writing and accepted the Buddhist religion brought by Chinese missionaries.

SHŌTOKU'S CONSTITUTION

About 587 AD, the Japanese empress, Suiko, and her adviser, Prince Shōtoku, encouraged their people to accept Chinese political ideas based on Confucianism. They believed that by adopting the Chinese system of strong centralized imperial rule they could increase the power of the dynasty. The Confucian values of orderly society and obedience to authority were especially stressed.

LEADERS OF TRADITIONAL JAPAN

Prince Shōtoku Taishi (574–622)
Established law and order throughout Japan; encouraged Buddhism; sought diplomatic relations with China.

Empress Jitō (645–703)
Enacted first set of administrative and penal laws; was the author of *Man'yō-shū*.

Minamoto Yoritomo (1147–1199)
Established shogunate in Japan; reorganized local government; strengthened judicial system.

Nichiren (1222–1282)
Founded Buddhist religious sect known as Lotus; combined religion and patriotism.

Oda Nobunaga (1534–1582)
Became skilled at politics and warfare; beginning in 1568, made great strides toward national unity.

Shōtoku Taishi

Family crest of Oda Nobunaga

Minamoto Yoritomo

This can be seen below in an excerpt from Shōtoku's constitution:

> . . . Harmony is to be valued, and an avoidance of . . . opposition to be honored. All men are influenced by [self-interest], and there are few who are intelligent. Hence there are some who disobey their lords and fathers, or who maintain feuds with the neighboring villages. But when those above are harmonious and those below are friendly, and there is [agreement] in the discussion of business, right views of things spontaneously gain acceptance. Then what is there which cannot be accomplished? . . .
>
> . . . When you receive the imperial commands, fail not . . . to obey them. The lord is Heaven, the vassal is Earth. Heaven overspreads, and Earth upbears. When this is so, the four seasons follow their due course, and the powers of Nature obtain their [fulfillment]. If the Earth attempted to overspread, Heaven would simply fall in ruin. Therefore is it that when the lord speaks, the vassal listens; when the superior acts, the inferior yields.
>
> . . . Consequently when you receive the imperial commands, fail not to carry them out [carefully]. Let there be a want of care in this matter, and ruin is the natural consequence.
>
> . . . The ministers and [civil servants] should make [proper] behavior their leading principle, for the leading principle of the government of the people consists in [proper] behavior. If the superiors do not behave [properly], the inferiors are disorderly: if the inferiors are wanting in proper behavior, there must necessarily be offenses. Therefore it is that when lord and vassal behave . . . [properly], the distinctions of rank are not confused; when the people behave . . . [properly], the government of the commonwealth [works properly].*

The Seventeen-Article Constitution of Prince Shōtoku in *Sources of Japanese Tradition,* compiled by Ryusaku Tsunoda, William Theodore de Bary, and Donald Keene, ©1958, Columbia University Press, pp. 50–51. By permission.

TAIKA REFORMS

Almost 50 years later, another Japanese emperor, Kotoku, and his advisers began the *Taika*, or "Great Change," Reforms, which introduced the Japanese to more features of the Chinese style of government. These included proclaiming the emperor ruler and landlord of all Japan, establishing a bureaucracy to carry out government duties, and putting into effect a central system of taxation and a land distribution program. The reforms divided the country into provinces, districts, and villages whose government was run by officials who reported to the emperor.

In 710, to provide a setting for the government, a capital city called Nara was built. With its broad streets and rows of wooden homes, palaces, and Buddhist temples, it soon became the political and religious center of Japan. The construction of Nara symbolized Japan's emergence as an important Asian civilization.

1. What principle did the Shōtoku constitution stress?
2. What features of the Chinese style of government did the *Taika* Reforms bring to Japan?
3. What did the construction of the capital city of Nara symbolize?

THE HEIAN PERIOD

In the 790's, a new capital was built. Called Heian, later it was renamed Kyoto. This marked the beginning of Japan's Heian period, which lasted until the late 1100's. During this period, a powerful noble family named Fujiwara gained power over the emperor and his court and actually ruled the country. Along with other noble families, the Fujiwaras acquired much of the countryside. There they created large, private, rice-growing estates that were worked by peasants.

In this scene of court life in early Japan, three warriors, known as samurai, *are eating main dishes of rice while a woman prepares to serve them a rice liquor known as* sake. *The robes worn by* samurai *were characterized by V-shaped necklines and signified the* samurai *position in society. By what was court life symbolized during the Heian period?*

Since the emperor and court officials had little political authority, they used their time to develop elaborate court ceremonies and to support the arts. Before long, court life was symbolized by elegance, manners, and love of natural beauty. Court officials and their wives wrote poems, stories, diaries, and essays. The selection below from a young woman's diary reveals the importance of the romantic and the artistic to members of the court:

> . . . On a very dark night . . . when sweet-voiced reciters were to read Sutras [Buddhist scriptures] throughout the night, another lady and I went out towards the entrance door of the audience room to listen to it, and after talking fell asleep, listening, leaning, . . . when I noticed a gentleman had come to be received in audience by the Princess.
>
> 'It is awkward to run away to our apartment to escape him. We will remain here. Let it be as it will.' So said my companion and I sat beside her listening.
>
> He spoke gently and quietly. . . . 'Who is the other lady?' he asked of my friend. He said nothing rude or amorous like other men, but talked delicately of the sad, sweet things of the world, and many a phrase of his with a strange power enticed me into conversation. He wondered that there should have been in the court one who was a stranger to him, and did not seem inclined to go away soon.
>
> There was no starlight, and a gentle shower fell in the darkness; how lovely was its sound on the leaves! 'The more deeply beautiful is the night,' he said; 'the full moonlight would be too dazzling.' Discoursing about the beauties of spring and autumn he continued: 'Although every hour has its charm, pretty is the spring haze; then the sky being tranquil and overcast, the face of the moon is not too bright; it seems to be floating on a distant river. At such a time the calm spring melody of the lute is exquisite.
>
> 'In autumn, on the other hand, the moon is very bright; though there are mists trailing over the horizon we can see things as clearly as if they were at hand. The sound of wind, the voices of insects, all sweet things seem to melt together. . . .
>
> 'But the winter sky frozen all over magnificently cold! The snow covering the earth and its light mingling with the moonshine! Then the notes of the *hichiriki* [a pipe made of seven reeds] vibrate on the air and we forget spring and autumn.'

And he asked us, 'Which captivates your fancy? On which stays your mind?'

My companion answered in favor of autumn and I, not being willing to imitate her, said:
Pale green night and flowers all melting into one in the soft haze—Everywhere the moon, glimmering in the spring night. So I replied. And he, after repeating my poem to himself over and over, said:
'Then you give up autumn? After this, as long as I live, such a spring night shall be for me a momento of your personality.'*

1. What did the building of Heian mark?
2. Who actually ruled Japan during the Heian period?
3. What were the major concerns of the emperor's court during the Heian period?

THE SHOGUNS

The rule of the Fujiwaras, who were opposed by several great clans, came to an end in 1185. A dispute had developed between two of the most powerful clans—the Taira and the Minamoto. These families fought for control of the imperial court at Kyoto. Minamoto Yoritomo, the leading member of the Minamoto family, gained support from warriors in the provinces, and in 1185, he and his forces fought and defeated the Taira in the naval battle of Dannoura. Below, a thirteenth-century Japanese writer gives his account of the event:

> . . . the forces of the Genji [Minamoto] went on increasing, while those of the Heike [Taira] grew less. The Genji had some three thousand ships, and the Heike one thousand, among which were some of Chinese build. . . .

Both sides set their faces against each other and fought grimly without a thought for their lives, neither giving an inch. But as the Heike had on their side an emperor endowed with . . . the Three Sacred Treasures of the Realm, things went hard with the Genji and their hearts were beginning to fail them, when suddenly something that they at first took for a cloud but soon made out to be a white banner floating in the breeze came drifting over the two fleets from the upper air, and finally settled on the stern of one of the Genji ships, hanging on by the rope.

When he saw this, Yoshitsune [Yoritomo's brother], regarding it as a sign from the [war god], removed his helmet and after washing his hands did [homage]; his men all followed his example. . . .

As things had come to this pass, Shigeyoshi, who for three years had been a

Minamoto Yoritomo founded the line of feudal lords who ruled Japan for 700 years. Here, he is dressed in the traditional sokutai *costume, worn only by emperors and high officials. Who did Yoritomo defeat in 1185?*

---

*The Sarashina Diary by the Daughter of Takasue, as cited in Anthology of Japanese Literature to the Nineteenth Century, compiled by Donald Keene, 1968, George Allen & Unwin (Publishers) Ltd., pp. 151–152. Reprinted by permission.

The lives of many peasants improved under Tokugawa rule. Using fertilizers and new farm tools, peasants doubled the amount of rice planted and reduced by 20 percent the labor needed to harvest it. Why did the Tokugawa shoguns divide the people into rigid classes?

loyal supporter of the Heike, made up his mind that all was lost, and suddenly forsook his allegiance and deserted to the enemy. . . .

. . . Later on the men of Shikoku and Kyushu all left the Heike in a body and went over to the Genji. Those who had so far been their faithful retainers now turned their bows against their lords and drew their swords against their own masters. On one shore the heavy seas beat on the cliff so as to forbid any landing, while on the other stood the [crowded] ranks of the enemy waiting with leveled arrows to receive them. And so on this day the struggle for supremacy between the Genji and the Heike was at last decided.*

THE KAMAKURA SHOGUNATE

After Yoritomo defeated the Taira, he pledged loyalty to the emperor. In return, the emperor awarded Yoritomo the title of **shogun,** or commander-in-chief. Yoritomo became the real ruler of Japan. He and his warriors left the court at Kyoto and settled in the small seaside town of Kamakura. There, they set up a **shogunate,** or military government, which the Japanese called **bakufu,** or "tent government," after the shelters in which military officers lived. Yoritomo's soldiers took control of government tasks, managed country estates, and replaced the nobles as **patrons,** or supporters, of art and literature.

THE TOKUGAWA SHOGUNATE

Yoritomo died in 1199. After his death, his heirs began fighting among themselves. This weakened the shogunate, and by the 1300's, Japan was divided among rival groups of nobles and warriors. Finally, in 1600, a general named Tokugawa Ieyasu won an important military victory and united all of Japan under a central government. He had the emperor name him *shogun* and took measures to ensure that the title and the power that went with the title stayed in the Tokugawa family. The center of Tokugawa government was the village of Edo, which later became known as Tokyo.

To maintain social stability and to limit rivals, the Tokugawa *shoguns* imposed a rigid social structure. The people were divided into four classes—warriors, artisans, merchants, and peasants. All class positions were **hereditary,** passed from one family member to the next, and members of one

---

*"The Fight at Dan no ura" from *The Tale of the Heike,* as quoted in *Anthology of Japanese Literature to the Nineteenth Century,* compiled by Donald Keene, 1968, George Allen & Unwin (Publishers) Ltd., pp. 173–176. Reprinted by permission.

INSIGHTS ON PEOPLE
JAPAN

TOKUGAWA IEYASU

Known for his strong personality, Tokugawa Ieyasu rose to fame as a soldier and eventually conquered all of Japan. His success as a military commander brought the country the longest period of peace and prosperity in its history as he and his family controlled the office of *shogun* until 1868. The following official Japanese account describes Ieyasu's personality and habits and tells why he achieved such success:

Having lived from boyhood to manhood in military encampments, and having suffered hardship after hardship in countless battles, large and small, His Lordship had little time to read or study. Although he had conquered the country on horseback, being a man of [natural] intelligence and wisdom, he fully appreciated the impossibility of governing the country on horseback. According to his judgment there could be no other way to govern the country than by a constant and deep faith in the sages and the scholars, and as a human being interested in the welfare of his fellow human beings, he patronized scholarship from the very beginning of his rule. Thus, he soon gained a reputation as a great [enthusiast] of letters and as one with a taste for elegant prose and poetry. On one occasion, Shimazu Yoshihisa, whose Buddhist name was Ryuhaku, took the trouble to arrange a poetry composition party in Ieyasu's honor, only to learn that His Lordship did not care at all for such a vain pastime. He listened again and again to discourses on [such Chinese classics as] the Four Books, *the* Records of the Historian *by Ssu-ma Ch'ien, and the* History of the Former Han Dynasty. . . .

. . . He also extolled the spirit of personal sacrifice and the utterances and deeds of loyalty to the state of such [great Chinese statesmen] as T'ai Kung-wang, Chang Liang, Han Hsin, Wei Cheng, and Fang Hsuan-ling. And among the warriors of our country he constantly asked for discourses on the General of the Right of Kamakura (Minamoto Yoritomo). Whatever the subject, he was interested, not in the turn of a phrase or in literary embellishments, but only in discovering the key to government—how to govern oneself, the people, and the country.*

1. Who was Tokugawa Ieyasu? In what skills did he excel?
2. In what ways does Ieyasu embody ideals of traditional Japan?

---

*From *Tōshō-gū go-jikki* by Narushima Motonao, as cited in *Sources of Japanese Tradition*, compiled by Ryusaku Tsunoda, William Theodore de Bary, and Donald Keene, ©1958, Columbia University Press, pp. 340–341. By permission.

class were not allowed to perform tasks that belonged to another class. Below, a Japanese writer of the time recounts Ieyasu's views on the role and tasks of each class:

> Once, Lord Tōshō [Ieyasu] conversed with Honda, Governor Sado, on the subject of the emperor, the shogun, and the farmer. "Whether there is order or chaos in the nation depends on the virtues and vices of these three. The emperor, with compassion in his heart for the needs of the people, must not be remiss in the performance of his duties—from the early morning worship of the New Year to the monthly functions of the court. Secondly, the shogun must not forget the possibility of war in peacetime, and must maintain his discipline. He should be able to maintain order in the country; he should bear in mind the security of the sovereign; and he must strive to dispel the anxieties of the people. One who cultivates the way of the warrior only in times of crisis is like a rat who bites his captor in the throes of being captured. The man may die from the effects of the poisonous bite, but to generate courage on the spur of the moment is not the way of a warrior. To assume the way of the warrior upon the outbreak of war is like a rat biting his captor. Although this is better than fleeing from the scene, the true master of the way of the warrior is one who maintains his martial discipline even in time of peace. Thirdly, the farmer's toil is proverbial—from the first grain to a hundred acts of labor. He selects the seed from last fall's crop, and undergoes various hardships and anxieties through the heat of summer until the seed grows finally to a rice plant. It is harvested and husked and then offered to the land steward. The rice then becomes sustenance for the multitudes. Truly, the hundred acts of toil from last fall to this fall are like so many tears of blood. Thus, it is a wise man who, while partaking of his meal, appreciates the hundred acts of toil of the people. Fourthly, the artisan's occupation is to make and prepare wares and utensils for the use of others. Fifthly, the merchant facilitates the exchange of goods so that the people can cover their nakedness and keep their bodies warm. As the people produce clothing, food and housing, which are called the "three treasures," they deserve our every sympathy."*

THE WAY OF THE WARRIOR

During the period of the shogunates, political power was held by various ranks of warriors. Directly under the emperor and the *shogun* were lords known as **daimyo,** who built castles and controlled vast rural estates. To protect their lands and the peasants who farmed the lands for them, the *daimyo* hired warriors. These warriors were called **samurai.** As the following account shows, even if one was born a *samurai,* one had to endure a great deal of training and adhere to a strict set of rules:

> [Suzuki] Taro was born a samurai. . . . His father had been a samurai. His sons would be samurai. It was far better to be born a samurai than to be born a farmer or a merchant. Only about one person in twenty was a samurai, and only samurai could bear swords or hold administrative office. . . .
>
> From the age of fifteen on, Taro carried two swords: a long sword and a short one. To carry these instruments of death at all times made Taro deeply aware of his mission in life, the mission of all samurai: to serve his lord bravely and loyally, and to set an example for others. Should any situation arise in which dishonor seemed likely, Taro would use the short sword to end his own life, displaying in his ritual suicide his selflessness and devotion to his lord.

---

*The *Koró sodan,* as cited in *Sources of Japanese Tradition,* compiled by Ryusaku Tsunoda, William Theodore de Bary, and Donald Keene, ©1958, Columbia University Press, pp. 338–339. By permission.

The high-ranking samurai, *standing, is being attended by other* samurai, *one of whom is holding his bow and helmet.* Samurai *followed a strict code of honor known as* bushido. *What was a* samurai's *mission?*

To grow up as a samurai meant learning the military arts, so Taro spent many hours wrestling and fencing and riding and studying archery. But Japan had enjoyed . . . peace, and in peacetime one needed other skills as well. So Taro studied reading and writing and, as he grew older, began to read the Chinese classics. . . .

Taro's training was strict, for becoming a worthy samurai was not an easy task. At the age of six Taro began to memorize the Chinese classics. . . .

Taro met his teacher all during the year. Fall and spring were no problem, but the heat of the summer sometimes made him so weak he thought he would faint. The winter cold brought a different kind of suffering. His clothing was not heavy, and the room was unheated. Using a fire simply to warm himself Taro knew was the way of a weakling. When his hands became too cold to hold his writing brush, his teacher would say, "Dip them in that bucket of water." The water in the bucket was ice-cold. When his bare feet became numb, his teacher would say, "Go run around in the snow. . . ."

Samurai were supposed to be above such matters as money and commerce. Ideally, a samurai never handled money. But Taro . . . had no servants, and so he often wound up going to the market himself. To hide his embarrassment, he usually went out after dark. Taro's family and almost all the other samurai families lived near the castle of the lord. . . .

A few temples and a moat separated Taro's neighborhood from the quarter set aside for the [townspeople]—artisans and merchants. No artisan or merchant could live near Taro, nor was Taro permitted to live in their quarter. . . .

Taro had never ventured more than five miles [8 kilometers] away from home. From the top of the hill near his house he could see the ocean, but he had never been in a boat. Nor was it likely that he would travel at all until he was eighteen or twenty. Then his lord might well order him to Edo to serve there as a guard.*

1. How did Minamoto Yoritomo become the ruler of Japan? What form of government did he establish?
2. How did the Tokugawa maintain social stability?
3. Into what classes were the Japanese divided? What was the role of each?

CONTACT WITH THE WEST

Because of their isolated island location, the Japanese felt safe from foreign powers. Then, during the 1500's, the first Europeans —Portuguese and Spanish traders and missionaries—reached Japan's shores. Be-

---

*The Past: The Road from Isolation, Volume I of Through Japanese Eyes, edited by Richard H. Minear, 1974, Praeger Publishers, pp. 42, 43–46, 48. Reprinted by permission.

fore long, they had gained great influence. By 1614, about 300,000 Japanese had accepted Christianity.

Fearing that European ways were a threat to their power, Tokugawa rulers forbade the practice of Christianity and ended Japanese contacts with the European world. All Western Europeans except the Dutch were barred from Japan. Because the Dutch were interested only in trade and not in conquest or conversion, the Japanese were less worried about their influence and allowed them to remain at one isolated port. Through them, however, a small amount of information about the West continued to flow into Japan.

ECONOMIC AND SOCIAL CHANGE

Isolation from the West did not stop the development of Japanese society and Japan's economy. During the 1700's and 1800's, internal trade increased. Merchants grew wealthy and became an important social group. Towns began to play a dominant role in Japanese life. At the same time, ambitious *daimyo* introduced more efficient farming methods on their estates and increased their rice yields. Soon, in the new urban areas, the Tokugawas' rigid social order began to break down, and class divisions blurred.

Gradually, the ban on foreign contacts relaxed, and some Japanese began to read western books and study western ideas. But, most Japanese still did not want foreigners in their country. Below, a prominent Japanese scholar of the early 1800's explains why westerners were not necessary or welcome:

Our Divine Land is where the sun rises and where the [primary] energy originates. The heirs of the Great Sun have occupied the Imperial Throne from generation to generation without change from time immemorial. Japan's position at the

In this seventeenth-century Japanese painting, European missionaries and Japanese converts stroll in front of roadside shops selling wild animal skins, cloth, and other decorative objects. The priests at the left are Jesuits. Those in brown robes are Franciscans. In the scene at the top, Christian samurai *participate in a Catholic mass. Some Christianized* samurai *helped build ties between European traders and Japanese merchants. Why was Christianity banned in Japan?*

Japan's brisk internal trade during the 1700's and 1800's is reflected in this busy street scene at the Edo bridge, the end point for all highways leading into the city. How were the social classes affected by the increase in trade during this period?

[summit] of the earth makes it the standard for the nations of the world. Indeed, it casts its light over the world, and the distance which the resplendent imperial influence reaches knows no limit. Today, the alien barbarians of the West, the lowly organs of the legs and feet of the world, are dashing about across the seas, trampling other countries underfoot, and daring, with their squinting eyes and limping feet, to override the noble nations. What manner of arrogance is this! . . .

Let, therefore, our rule extend to the length and breadth of the land, and let our people excel in manners and customs. Let the high as well as the low uphold righteousness [duty]; let the people prosper, and let military defense be adequate.

If we proceed accordingly and without committing blunders, we shall fare well however forceful may be the invasion of a powerful enemy. But should the situation be otherwise, and should we indulge in leisure and pleasure, then we are placing our reliance where there is no reliance at all. . . .*

PERRY'S MISSION

In 1853, the government of the United States decided to force Japan to end its isolation. It sent Commodore Matthew Perry to

---

New Proposals by Aizawa Seishisai, as quoted in *Sources of Japanese Tradition*, compiled by Ryusaku Tsunoda, William Theodore de Bary, and Donald Keene, ©1958, Columbia University Press, pp. 595–597. By permission.

When Matthew Perry's American vessels steamed into the Japanese harbor at Edo Bay on July 8, 1853, the goal was to reopen Japan to trade after 214 years of isolation. Seven months later, his goal was achieved as the Tokugawa leaders signed a treaty granting the United States trading rights at two Japanese ports. Of what significance to Japan was the reopening of trade with the West?

Japan to demand that the Japanese government grant trading privileges to the United States. In the passage that follows, a Japanese who witnessed Perry's vessels as they steamed into the harbor at Edo describes his reactions:

> ... Some things I still remember. One morning there was a great hubbub. When I asked what it was all about, I was told that in the offing there were ships on fire. I ran to the the top of the mountain to get a good look. There was a crowd of people there, all stirred up and making guesses about the burning ships on the horizon. Then those ships came nearer and nearer, until the shape of them showed us they were not Japanese ships but foreign ones, and we found that what we had taken for a [fire] on the sea was really the black smoke rising out of their smokestacks. When we came down, there was excitement all over town, ... and what with special messengers being sent hurriedly up to Edo, there was a great uproar. Later I learned that even the people in Edo were fussing and excited. ...
>
> "What a joke, the steaming teapot fixed by America—Just four cups [ships], and we cannot sleep at night!"*

Perry told the Japanese that if they did not agree to a treaty within a year, there would be war. The *shogun*, realizing that Japan's defenses could not withstand the military power of the United States, eventually bowed to Perry's demand. By 1858, Japan had signed treaties not only with the United States, but with a number of other western nations as well. This opened Japan to the rest of the world. At the same time, it marked the end to traditional Japan.

1. When did Portuguese and Spanish traders and missionaries arrive in Japan?
2. How did the Tokugawa rulers react to the western powers? Why did they react this way?
3. Why did Commodore Perry go to Japan? What was the outcome of his mission?

---

*Japanese eyewitness, as quoted in *Black Ship Scroll* by Oliver Statler, 1963, Charles E. Tuttle Company, Inc. of Tokyo, Japan, pp. 8–9. Reprinted by permission.

CASE STUDY
JAPAN

THE JAPAN EXPEDITION

Commodore Matthew Perry was sent to Japan to open that country for trade. Many Americans, however, thought that Perry's mission should have other goals as well. They agreed with the views expressed below in a March 17, 1852 editorial in the *New-York Daily Tribune:*

It seems we are to send a fleet to Japan, and to enter the Capital City at all hazards. The interests of American trade require that commercial communication be opened with that recluse region, and a numerous array of armed vessels will proceed to state that fact to the Japanese Government, and to open the gates of its ports. It is a fair suspicion in the premises that the greatness of America is better understood at Washington than at Jeddo [Edo], and that the Japanese will be unable immediately to discern the great advantage of trading with a nation which makes the overture from the cannon's mouth. It may be also presumed that they will decline to accede to such propositions so made, until they have learned, as they infallibly will learn, by much bombarding and battering, that we are determined to give them the benefits of commercial communication with us.

In this state of things, going thus into pagan realms, it behooves us not to lose the opportunity of laboring for the spiritual benefit of the benighted [unenlightened] Japanese. Let not these misguided men, fighting for their own, perish without benefit of clergy. Why should we not combine instruction with mercantile benefit, and while we get from the Japanese such articles as we wish, leave some of our morality in exchange? We might be the gainers in that bargain. To this end, and to impart a moral luster to the expedition, we suggest that some of the many chaplains in the United States now unemployed, be dispatched to Japan with the fleet, and while the ships lie before Jeddo [Edo], bombarding the city, and stray boatsfull of obstinate Japanese are captured and brought on board our ships, the reverend gentlemen might exert all their genius in the conversion of such natives. . . .

We should, indeed, be truly sorry to see the American government engaged in any undertaking of this magnitude to which it would be unwilling to give the [improving] aspect of a [care] for the moral welfare of the people concerned.*

1. What purpose do you think the writer had in mind when he wrote this editorial for the Tribune? Does he really think the expedition was a good idea?
2. What does the editorial reveal to you about American attitudes at the time toward Japan and the Japanese?

---
*"The Japan Expedition," editorial in the *New-York Daily Tribune*, Vol. XI, No. 3,405, March 17, 1852, p. 4. Reprinted by permission.

CHAPTER 16 REVIEW

POINTS TO REMEMBER

1. The Japanese monarchy helped unite the Japanese and bring them into contact with other peoples of Asia.
2. The Japanese modeled their society on Chinese principles, borrowed the Chinese system of writing, and accepted the religion of Buddhism brought by Chinese missionaries.
3. The *Taika* Reforms introduced additional Chinese features of government to Japan, including making the emperor the country's ruler and landlord. Later, a new capital was built at Nara, which symbolized Japan's emergence as an important Asian civilization.
4. The construction of Heian in the 790's marked the beginning of a new period in Japanese history. During this period, the Fujiwara family ruled the country and the emperor and court officials devoted themselves to artistic interests.
5. In the 1100's, the rule of the *shoguns* began in Japan.
6. In 1600, following many years of unrest, Tokugawa Ieyasu became *shogun* and united all of Japan under a central government at Edo. He divided the Japanese into four classes and made class positions hereditary.
7. During the period of the shogunates, political power was held by various ranks of warriors, including *daimyo* and *samurai*.
8. During the 1500's, Europeans arrived in Japan and soon began to influence the Japanese. The Tokugawa rulers, seeing European ways as a threat, soon barred all Western Europeans except the Dutch.
9. During the 1700's and 1800's, Japanese society and the Japanese economy developed steadily. In time, the social order imposed by the Tokugawa rulers broke down, and the ban on foreign contacts was relaxed.
10. In 1853, the government of the United States sent a fleet headed by Commodore Matthew Perry to Japan to demand trading privileges. On threat of war, the Japanese agreed. This opened Japan to the rest of the world.

VOCABULARY

Identify

Izanagi	Yamato clan	Nara	Genji
Izanami	Suiko	Heian	Heike
Amaterasu	Shotōku	Fujiwara family	Kamakura
Susanowo	Kotoku	Taira	Tokugawa Ieyasu
Jimmu Tenno	*Taika* Reforms	Minamoto Yoritomo	Edo
Regalia			Matthew Perry

Define

clans	shogunate	patrons	*daimyo*
shogun	*bakufu*	hereditary	*samurai*

DISCUSSING IMPORTANT IDEAS

1. How would you explain the following statement? "In many ways, the history of traditional Japan is a story of the influence of other cultures."
2. Do you agree with the statement that Japan has been ruled continuously by an emperor since 660 BC? Give reasons for your answer.
3. The Tokugawas divided the Japanese into four classes. To which class would you have liked to belong? Why?
4. Do you think it was wise of the Japanese to shut themselves off from Western contact? Explain. Would it be possible for a nation to do so today? Explain. Would it be desirable? Explain.

DEVELOPING SKILLS

INTERPRETING POINT OF VIEW

"What is your opinion about that?" is a common question. When you ask for someone's opinion, you are asking for a *point of view*, the way a person feels about a situation, event, or topic. Once you determine the person's point of view, it is up to you to *interpret*, or clarify in your own mind, that point of view.

The following steps will help you interpret point of view in written material:

1. Read the material carefully, and identify the main idea or topic.
2. Gather background information on the subject or issue and on the person expressing the viewpoint. This should give you the answers to such questions as "What is the history behind the issue?"; "Who is expressing the point of view, and what are his or her background and credentials?"
3. Determine why the person is making the statement, and, for an issue, whether he or she is for or against it.
4. Determine the tone of the statement. If it is serious, it should have supporting statements, sound sincere, and be a logical opinion for the author to have. If it is sarcastic, the statements should be witty and stinging. If it is humorous, it should make you smile or laugh.

In the example that follows, the above guidelines are applied to a passage about *samurai*:

You may wonder why, when there has been peace in our empire for 250 years, there is still need for the samurai. (Main Topic: Why the *samurai* are still useful) *I am a samurai; my father was a samurai; all our grandfathers back to ancient times were samurai. Our class was created by the emperor to defend him against visible enemies with our swords.* (Background: History of the *samurai* and why they came into being, provided by a *samurai* whose family members have been *samurai* for generations) *Today, our enemies are invisible ones. Without us, righteousness would disappear, and wrong, injustice and other shameful things would prevail. Japan would be thrown into confusion. That is why the samurai are still placed above other classes and are paid great respect.* (Purpose: To defend the existence of *samurai* in peacetime; Tone: Serious)

For practice in this skill, interpret the viewpoint expressed in the Case Study on page 265.

CHAPTER 17
MODERN JAPAN

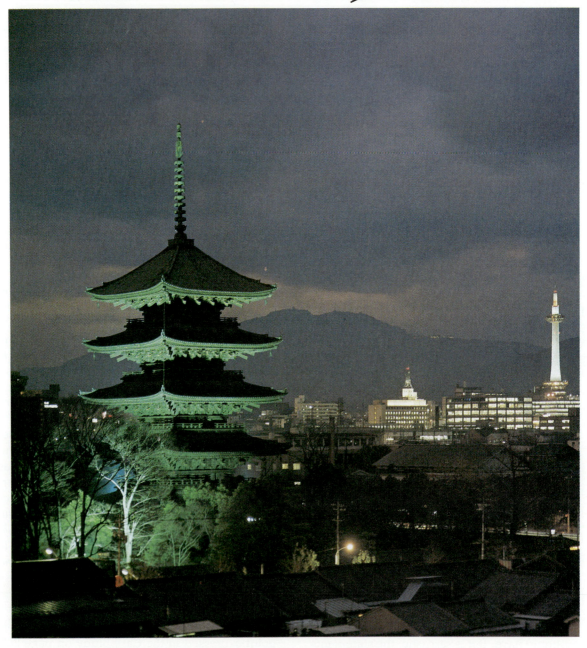

1. *How did the Meiji reforms transform Japan?*
2. *How did the desire for expansion affect Japan and the Japanese?*

It is a winter's evening in Tokyo. In a four-roomed house . . . a family sits after supper enjoying the glow from an electric foot-warmer . . . sunk in the centre of the floor. Over the shallow square pit that contains the heater is a low table. . . . Round the table, sitting on cushions on the floor with their stockinged feet hanging into the pit . . . sit . . . old Mrs. Saito, her son, her daughter-in-law, and favourite grandchild. . . .

In the Saito household there is a reflection of the tensions that afflict Japanese families today—. . .opposition of half-discredited tradition and [tradition-shattering] experiment. Saito Mamoru [the grandson] and his sister . . . are products of the [post-World War II] American Occupation, Japan's fourth and latest cultural invasion. . . .

Near the Shinto God-shelf, a small shrine on the wall . . . , there is a miniature Buddhist temple, a reminder of the first cultural invasion . . . , that of Buddhism from China in the sixth century A.D. In the cramped little kitchen there are the remains of a sponge-cake . . . introduced to Japan by the Portuguese in the sixteenth century, together with Christianity. . . . This second cultural invasion . . . was not substantial. . . .

The third invasion, also from the West, began in the middle of the nineteenth century. . . . It lasted with varying degrees of intensity until the outbreak of the Pacific War [World War II]. Its manifestations in the Saito house are too numerous to be listed; they include . . . every article of Western use in the home—from the strip lighting to the shoes . . . standing in the front porch, from the coathangers in the cupboard to the boy's bicycle pump near the kitchen door. The family now [has] a flush lavatory, refrigerator, washing machine, and fly screens on the windows, so it can be said that the fourth, American, invasion has made a material alteration to the house. And . . . , its non-material effects have been considerable.

. . . [Mingled] with these adaptations and borrowings from abroad are the traditional [items] of Japanese life: the straw *tatami* matting covering the floor; . . . the rice container with its flat wooden server . . . ; the rope sandals in the lavatory; the *geta*, or clogs, by the front door; . . . Mrs. Saito's set of ceremonial tea utensils; the *kakemono*, the hanging scroll, in the recess of the main room; the *sake* (rice wine) bottles and cups; the teapot in the kitchen. . . . Most of them, it is true, derive from China or from Chinese influence. But they have become uniquely and traditionally Japanese.*

This description of a modern Japanese household reveals a major characteristic of Japan and its people—the ability to absorb foreign influences and at the same time keep their own unique traditions. Yet, it cannot be denied that during the past 100 years, the West has had a great impact on Japan. In the late 1800's, Japan adopted western manufacturing methods and became Asia's leading industrial nation. Later, in World War II, it became one of the first Asian nations to use western weapons and technology against the West.

A History of Modern Japan by Richard Storry, (Pelican Books, 1960, revised editions 1961, 1968), pp. 14, 19–20, copyright © Richard Storry, 1960, 1961, 1968. Reprinted by permission of Penguin Books Ltd.

A NEW ERA

Japan's opening to the West in the mid-1800's stimulated the country's modernization. In 1867 and 1868, reform-minded leaders reestablished imperial rule in the name of the young emperor, Mutsuhito. His rule, which lasted from 1868 to 1912, was called *Meiji*, or "enlightened rule." Although Mutsuhito became the symbol of a new era in Japanese history, the real power was held by the *samurai* who had overthrown the Tokugawa shogunate.

MODERNIZATION

Mutsuhito believed Japan had to modernize. He summed up his beliefs in this poem:

May our country,
Taking what is good,
And rejecting what is bad,
Be not inferior
To any other.

Under Mutsuhito's leadership, the Meiji set out to make Japan a modern nation capable of competing with the West. The official capital was moved from Kyoto to Edo, which was renamed Tokyo. A constitution was adopted that set up a new government in which the emperor ruled with the help of a prime minister, cabinet, and **diet,** or legislature. The military ranks of *daimyo* and *samurai* were put to an end and replaced by a modern army and navy. All Japanese were declared equal under the law.

Meiji leaders also encouraged industrialization. To this end, they established a system of universal education designed to produce patriotic, highly skilled citizens and sent people abroad to study and borrow western ideas and methods. In addition, they revised the tax system to raise money for investment, founded a modern banking system, and supported the building of a postal and telegraph network, railroads, factories, and ports. Government-backed **zaibatsu,** large family-owned businesses, soon controlled most of Japan's economy. By the early 1900's, Japanese could look back with pride on what their nation had accomplished during the Meiji period. Fifty years later, a Japanese writer summed it up as follows:

By comparing the Japan of fifty years ago with the Japan of today, it will be seen that the nation has gained considerably in the extent of territory, as well as in population, which now numbers nearly fifty million. The government has become con-

Western fashions, such as the ones in this painting, became very popular among well-to-do Japanese during the late Meiji period, bringing about an early home industry in making western-style dresses. As a result, sewing machines became an important early import. How did Meiji leaders encourage industrialization?

RUSSO-JAPANESE WAR 1904-1905

stitutional not only in name, but in fact, and national education has attained to a high degree of excellence. In commerce and industry, the nation has made rapid strides. The nation's general progress, during the short space of half a century, has been so sudden and swift that it presents a spectacle rare in the history of the world. This leap forward is the result of the stimulus which the country received on coming into contact with the civilization of Europe and America, and may well, in its broad sense, be regarded as a benefit conferred by foreign contacts. It was foreign contacts that brought to life the national consciousness of our people, and it is foreign contacts that have enabled Japan to stand as a world power. We possess today a powerful army and navy, but it was after western models that we laid their foundations. We established a draft in keeping with the principle "all our sons are soldiers." We promoted military education, and encouraged the manufacture of arms and the art of ship building. We have reorganized the systems of central and local administration, and effected reforms in the educational system. All this is nothing but the result of adopting the superior features of western institutions.*

MILITARY SUCCESS

Upon becoming a modern nation, Japan sought the respect of the western powers. In the 1890's and early 1900's, the Japanese began to compete with the nations of the West in establishing overseas empires. Because the Japanese needed more natural resources for their economy, and more room for their growing population they wanted to expand into East Asia and the Pacific Ocean area. As a result, in 1894, they went to war with China for control of Korea. China was defeated easily the following year.

After their victory over China, the Japanese faced growing rivalry with Russia for control of Korea and Manchuria. Finally, in 1904, they declared war on the Russians. Although they won important battles on land and on sea, the fighting exhausted not

*Adapted from *Fifty Years of New Japan, Vol. II* by Okuma Sigenobu, as cited in *Sources of Japanese Tradition*, compiled by Ryusaku Tsunoda, William Theodore de Bary, and Donald Keene, ©1958, Columbia University Press, pp. 698–699. By permission.

only them, but the Russians as well. Within a year, the war was ended, and a treaty was signed. Under its terms, Japan won recognition of its hold on Korea. For the first time in the modern era, an Asian nation had triumphed over a major European one.

Japan's triumph gained it a great deal of prestige as a world military power. At the same time, its military success developed in the Japanese people strong feelings of nationalism. When World War I erupted, the Japanese saw in it the opportunity to further expand their empire and joined the fight against the Germans. After the Germans were defeated, Japan gained a number of islands in the Pacific. Japan's chief interest, however, was in a greater role in China. Of prime concern was the Chinese province of Manchuria, which the Japanese felt they had to dominate for China's sake as well as their own. A prominent Japanese military leader explained the Japanese view in the following way:

> . . . when an ultimatum was sent to Germany [demanding surrender of . . . interests in China] I offered a number of suggestions on the possible aftermath of such a move. Again, this year, I disclosed my frank thoughts to [Foreign Minister] Katō. I told him that if it became necessary to resort to arms . . . I would throw my support to the move immediately. Manchuria is for the Japanese the only region for expansion. Manchuria is Japan's life-line. Thus, we must secure for our people the guarantee that they can settle there and pursue their occupations in peace. If this problem cannot be disposed of by diplomatic means, then we have no other alternative but to resort to arms. . . . The head of the Ministry of Foreign Affairs should go to China when the opportunity presents itself . . . and frankly divulge Japan's true aims and explain Japan's position. . . . I am sure that this would be a step toward [easing] ill-feeling between the two countries.

> . . . Now, are not Japan and China the only true states in Asia? Is it not true that other than these two countries there is no other which can control all of Asia? In short, we must attempt the solution of our myriad problems on the premise of "Asia for the Asians." However, Japan is an island country. She is a small, narrow island country which cannot hope to support within its island confines any further increase in population. Thus, she has no alternative but to expand into Manchuria or elsewhere. That is, as Asians the Japanese must of necessity live in Asia. China may object to the Japanese setting foot in Manchuria, but had not Japan fought and repelled Russia from Manchuria, even Peking might not be Chinese territory today. Thus, while the expansion of Japan into Manchuria may be a move for her own betterment and that of her people, it would also be a necessary move for the self-protection of Asians and for the co-existence and co-prosperity of China and Japan.*

1. What was the goal of the Meiji leaders? What did they do to accomplish this?
2. Why did Japan try to expand overseas? What was the result of their efforts?
3. What reasons did the Japanese offer the Chinese for taking over Manchuria?

DRIFT TO WAR

Although Japan became a world power during World War I, the Japanese still were faced with both foreign and domestic problems. Japan was a member of the League of Nations, a new world organization set up after the war. Japanese interest in the League, however, was slight because the League devoted much of its attention to

---

*San-kō Iretsu by Takahashi, as cited in Sources of Japanese Tradition, compiled by Ryusaku Tsunoda, William Theodore de Bary, and Donald Keene, ©1958, Columbia University Press, pp. 716–717. By permission.

problems of the West. But when the League spoke out against Japan's interest in China, the Japanese turned against it. Eventually, they withdrew completely from the League.

Another source of tension was the restrictions the United States placed on Japanese immigration in 1924. In response, the Japanese staged demonstrations and **boycotted,** or refused to buy, American goods. Japanese bitterness increased even more when western pressure forced Japan to reduce its claims on China and accept western interests there.

At the same time the Japanese were trying to sort out their problems with other nations, they were faced with growing social and economic problems at home. Of major concern was the large growth in population. With emigration cut off to such places as the United States, something had to be done at home to help cope. In the hope that new factories and markets would provide work for large numbers of people, renewed emphasis was placed on manufacturing and foreign trade. This led thousands of Japanese to leave the countryside to find jobs in the towns and cities.

Although working and living conditions often were miserable in the urban areas, those who lived there tended to fare better than those who lived in rural areas. Below, a Japanese writer remembers and comments on life in Tokyo and the role of politicians during the 1920's:

> I doubt that in those years . . . there was anyone even among the most ardent supporters of Tokyo who thought it a grand metropolis. The newspapers were unanimous in denouncing the chaotic transportation and the inadequate roads of "our Tokyo." I believe it was the *Advertiser* which in an editorial [protested] against the gracelessness of the city. Our politicians are always talking about big things, social policy and labor problems and the like, it said, but these are not what politics should be about. Politicians should be thinking rather of mud, and of laying streets through which an automobile can pass in safety on a rainy day. I remember the editorial because I was so completely in agreement. . . . Twice on my way from Asakusa Bridge to Kaminari Gate I was jolted so violently from the cushion that my nose hit the roof of the cab. . . . And so, people will say, it might have been better to take a streetcar. That too could be a desperate struggle. . . . With brisk activity in the financial world, all manner of enterprises sprang up, and there was a rush from the provinces upon the big cities. Tokyo did not have time to accommodate the frantic increase in numbers and the swelling of the suburbs. . . . For the general populace there was no means of transport but the streetcar. Car after car

Japanese women and men make their way down a busy sidewalk in this early 1900's photo of Tokyo's fashionable Ginza district. What was Tokyo like in the 1920's?

In this photo, taken in the 1930's, Emperor Hirohito reviews the Japanese army. Although Hirohito, who became Japan's 124th emperor in 1926, officially headed the armed forces and the government, he had little real power. Late in 1941, the militarists gained complete control of the government under a new prime minister, General Hideki Tojo. Who held the real power in Japan in the 1930's?

would come by full and leave people waiting at stops. At rush hour the press was murderous. Hungry and tired, the office worker and the laborer, in a hurry to get home, would push their way aboard a car already hopelessly full, each one for himself, paying no attention to the attempts of the conductor to keep order. . . . The ferocity in their eyes could be frightening. . . . The crowds, a black mountain outside a streetcar, would push and shove and shout, and we could but silently lament the turmoil and how it brought out the worst in people. . . . They put up with it because they were Japanese, I heard it said, but if a European or American city were subjected to such things for even a day there would be rioting. . . . Old Japan had been left behind and new Japan had not yet come.*

By the 1930's, Japan's leaders had become frustrated both with the difficulties at home and those abroad. As a result, they abandoned the policies of democratic reform at home and cooperation with the West. At the time, political power was largely in the hands of military and urban industrialists. Although the emperor, Hirohito, was a constitutional monarch, he could not control the military.

Finally, those who supported **militarism,** or a war-like policy, removed the **civilian,** or non-military, politicians and took over control of the government. Western cultural influences were limited, and a return to such traditional Japanese values as physical courage and strict obedience to authority were encouraged. The country's military forces were strengthened, and preparations were made for an attack on the Asian mainland.

1. What made the Japanese bitter toward the West after World War I?
2. What problems did Japan face during the 1920's and 1930's?
3. What changes did the new military leadership make in Japan's policies?

---

*Diary of Nagai Kafu, as cited in *Low City, High City* by Edward Seidensticker, 1983, Alfred A. Knopf, pp. 283–284. Reprinted by permission.

JAPANESE EXPANSION

Japan's primary target in Asia was China, which had been weakened by civil war and a backward economy. In 1931, Japanese forces took control of Manchuria. Six years later, they invaded the eastern part of China, forcing the Chinese government to retreat to the interior of the country.

Two years later, World War II broke out in Europe. While the Europeans were busy with the war, the Japanese turned their attention to Southeast Asia which, at the time, was largely controlled by the Europeans. The Japanese needed oil, rubber, and other mineral resources, and Southeast Asia was rich in all of these. The Japanese government announced its plans to create a "Greater East Asia Co-prosperity Sphere" that united all of East and Southeast Asia under Japanese rule. At the same time, it strengthened its ties to Germany and Italy.

WAR IN THE PACIFIC

Japan's expansion in Asia created tensions with the United States, which at the time was the other great power in the Pacific. The United States cut off all exports to Japan. While negotiations between the two powers dragged on, the Japanese government, under General Hideki Tojo, prepared for war. On December 7, 1941, Japanese bombers attacked the large United States military base at Pearl Harbor in Hawaii. The bombing, which took the Americans by surprise, led to the Pacific War between Japan and the United States. Below, a Japanese woman tells how the war affected her family:

> My elder brother was sixteen when the Pacific War started, and Father was very keen that he should join the navy. Right from the day the war broke out, he kept going on at my brother to take the exam for the naval cadets' school. Father, you see, had been turned down for military service in peacetime because he was too short, and I think that had perhaps given him some sort of complex about it. But in fact my brother didn't really seem enthusiastic about the war. In the end, it was decided that his whole class at Middle School should apply to become naval cadets. At that time it was still voluntary in theory, but as all his friends were going to apply, my brother more or less had to try as well. In any case, he failed because his eyesight wasn't up to standard, and later he went off to a pharmacy college . . . , so he never did get [drafted].
>
> But still my father used to go on complaining: 'Isn't anybody in this house going to go and serve their country?' At that time, towards the end of my second year at Girls' School, I'd become friendly with a girl called Okada. . . . Anyway, in the winter of Second Year Okada and I made a vow that we would go every morning to the Kōshū Shrine to pray for victory. It was very, very cold at that time of year, but I would get up early and eat breakfast, and then I would walk up to the shrine through the frost and mist, and meet Okada-san there, and after we'd prayed we would go to school together.
>
> From those early morning meetings we developed another idea. We decided that, by the time we finished school, it might already be too late to offer ourselves for service to our country, so instead we would leave school right away and volunteer for the nursing corps. We told our teacher about the plan, and he must have been quite impressed by our determination, because I remember that he got in touch with a man from the local newspaper, who came and took our photographs and wrote a little article about us, how patriotic we were and so on. For me, I wanted to do it, partly out of patriotism, but partly because, since girls couldn't be [drafted], it seemed like the only way for us to take a main role in the great drama that was taking place. . . .

It's funny, although I knew that being a front-line nurse was very dangerous, I never thought about the danger or the possibility of dying when I went to volunteer. When you are fighting for your country I suppose you don't think about death.*

The Japanese won extensive victories in Southeast Asia and in the Pacific. By 1942, they ruled an empire that stretched from the Aleutian Islands near Alaska south to the Solomon Islands in the western Pacific, and from Wake Island west to Burma. That same year, however, they suffered their first major defeats to the United States, and over the next three years, they were gradually driven from islands they had taken earlier.

THE BOMB AND SURRENDER

By the end of 1944, Japan was being bombed by American planes. But, in spite of the American advance, the Japanese refused to surrender. As a result, the United States decided to end the war by using a new secret weapon—the **atomic bomb**, a bomb whose destructive force is caused by the splitting of atoms of a heavy chemical element. On August 6, 1945, the Americans dropped the first atomic bomb on the city of Hiroshima. Several days later, they dropped a second and larger one on the city of Nagasaki. The Japanese—and the rest of the world—were horrified by the results. Hundreds of thousands of Japanese were killed, many more were maimed, and parts of the cities were reduced to rubble. Below, author John Toland relates the experiences of some Japanese caught by the bombing:

> Hiroshima was serene and so was the sky above it as the people continued on their daily routine. Those who noticed the three parachutes imagined that the plane had been hit and that the crew was bailing out. . . .
>
> Several hundred yards north of Aioi Bridge . . . , Private Shigeru Shimoyama, a recent draftee, looked up and idly peered through his thick glasses at one of the drifting chutes. . . . He had been in Hiroshima four days and was already "bored to death." He wished he were back in Tokyo making school notebooks. All at once a pinkish light burst in the sky like a cosmic flash bulb.
>
> Clocks all over Hiroshima were fixed forever at 8:15.
>
> The bomb exploded 660 yards [594 meters] from the ground into a fireball almost 110 yards [99 meters] in diameter. Those directly below heard nothing, nor could they later agree what color the *pika* (lightning) flash was—blue, pink, reddish, dark-brown, yellow or purple.
>
> The heat emanating from the fireball lasted a fraction of a second but was so intense . . . that it melted the surface of granite within a thousand yards [900 meters] of the hypocenter, or ground zero—directly under the burst. Roof tiles softened and changed in color from black to olive or brown. All over the center of the city numerous silhouettes were imprinted on walls. On Yorozuyo Bridge ten people left permanent outlines of themselves on the railing and the tar-paved surface. . . .
>
> Private Shimoyama was 550 yards [495 meters] north of ground zero. He was not directly exposed to the *pika* flash or his life would have been puffed out, but the blast hurled him into the vast barnlike warehouse, driving him into the collapsing roof beam where five long nails in his back held him suspended several feet off the ground. His glasses were still intact. . . .
>
> A thousand yards [900 meters] on the other side of the hypocenter, Mrs. Yasuko Nukushina was trapped in the ruins of the family *sake* store. Her first thought was of her four-year-old daughter, Ikuko, who was playing outside somewhere. Unaccountably, she heard Ikuko's voice beside her: "I'm afraid, Mama." She told the child they were buried and would die

---

*Tsutsumi Ayako, as quoted in *Shōwa: An Inside History of Hirohito's Japan* by Tessa Morris-Suzuki, ©1984, The Athlone Press Limited, pp. 145–146. Reprinted by permission.

In this photo taken at Hiroshima a few hours after the atomic bomb was dropped, victims wait to receive first aid from medical personnel, who themselves were burned and injured. Today, thousands of people gather at Hiroshima's Peace Memorial Park each year to mark the anniversary of the bombing. Why did the United States drop atomic bombs on Japan?

there. Her own words made her claw desperately at the wreckage. She was a slight woman, . . . but in her frenzy she broke free into the yard. All around was devastation. . . . People drifted by expressionless and silent like sleepwalkers in tattered, smoldering clothing. . . . She watched mesmerized until someone touched her. Grasping Ikuko's hand, she joined the procession. . . .

Half a dozen blocks south, fifteen-year-old Michiko Yamaoka had just left home for work at the telephone office. She remembered "a magnesium flash," then a faraway voice calling "Michiko!" Her mother. "I'm here," she answered but didn't know where that was. She couldn't see—she must be blind! She heard her mother shout, "My daughter is buried under there!" Another voice, a man's, advised the mother to escape the flames sweeping down the street. . . . She was going to die. Then came a shaft of light as concrete blocks were pushed aside by soldiers. Her mother was bleeding profusely, one arm skewered by a piece of wood. She ordered Michiko to escape. She herself was staying to rescue two relatives under the ruins of their house.

Michiko moved through a nightmare world—past charred bodies—a crying baby sealed behind the twisted iron bars of a collapsed reinforced-concrete building. She saw someone she knew and called out.

"Who are you?" the other girl asked.

"Michiko."

The friend stared at her. "Your nose and eyebrows are gone!"

Michiko felt her face. It was so swollen that her nose seemed to have disappeared. . . .

Dr. Fumio Shigeto, head of internal medicine at the hospital, never reached his office that morning. On his way to work, he was waiting for a trolley at the end of a long line which bent around the corner of the Hiroshima railway station, 2,000 yards [1800 meters] east of the hypocenter. The flash seemed to turn a group of girls ahead of him white, almost invisible. . . . As he dropped to the sidewalk, covering eyes and ears, a heavy slate slammed into his back. Whirls of smoke blotted out the sun. In the darkness he groped blindly to reach shelter. . . .

A breeze from the east gradually cleared the area . . . , revealing an incredible scene: the buildings in front of the station

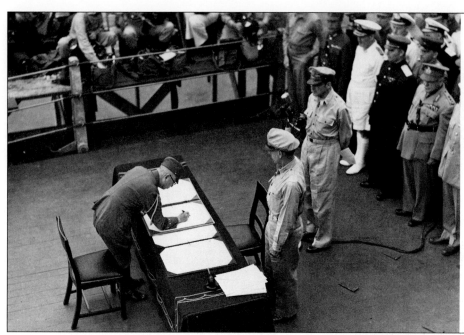

On September 2, 1945, aboard the United States battleship Missouri *in Tokyo Bay, the Japanese formally surrendered. Shown signing for Japan is General Yoshijiro Umezu. Standing at the microphone is General Douglas MacArthur, who signed for the United States and its allies, some of whose leaders are standing behind MacArthur. How was Japan's system of government altered after the war?*

were collapsed, flattened; half-naked and smoldering bodies covered the ground. Of the people at the trolley stop he alone, the last one in line, was unhurt. . . .

Dr. Shigeto started for the hospital but was stopped by an impenetrable wall of advancing flames. He turned and ran for open space. . . .

A nurse approached him. . . . She begged him to help another doctor and his wife lying on the ground. His first thought was: What if this mob of desperate people discovers I am a physician? He couldn't help them all. "Please treat my wife first," said the injured doctor. . . . Shigeto gave the woman a . . . shot. . . . He rearranged the bandages the nurse had applied and then turned to the other wounded, treating them until he ran out of medicine and supplies. There was nothing else he could do. He fled toward the hills.*

The bombings made Japanese leaders realize that the war was lost and that they had to surrender. One Japanese soldier described his reaction to the emperor's announcement of surrender as follows:

> For some reason, on the morning of 15th August our training had taken us outside Kumagaya Air Base. But we had been warned that at midday there would be a very important broadcast which we all had to listen to, so we had gone prepared with our full dress uniforms.
>
> At noon we assembled in the nearest convenient place, which happened to be the village hall of the little village . . . where we had been training. We stood to attention in front of the radio, all in our formal uniforms, with swords at our belts. Unfortunately, the radio in the village hall was very bad, and it was hard to hear what the emperor was saying. Afterwards, we began to argue about what it meant. . . .
>
> In the end, we decided to send someone back to the base to find out what it meant. The hall . . . had a big matted room on the first floor . . . , so while we were waiting for him to come back we all went up there and sat on the *tatami* [straw matting]. Then he returned, and told us that

---

*The Rising Sun, Volume 2 by John Toland, 1970, Random House, pp. 966–971. Reprinted by permission.

the government had accepted the [demand for complete surrender], and that we were all to behave calmly and sensibly. . . .

It was very hot. We all sat collapsed on the *tatami* in our formal uniforms. None of us said anything. I kept thinking: 'What have we been doing for the last year and a half? Every day we've been facing death. So many people have died. What was it all for?'

I felt full of regret and bitterness, but at the same time I also thought: 'Perhaps I am going to survive. Perhaps this thing they call peace is going to come. . . .'

The next day, several things happened almost at once. First, an officer arrived . . . and gave us a speech. He said: 'The broadcast which you heard yesterday was a fake. . . . His Majesty's true wish is that we should fight on to the very last soldier.' When we heard that, most of us felt that it must be true. After all, it fitted in with everything that we had been taught for four years. . . .

But then, soon after, a man from the Imperial Headquarters arrived and gave us another speech, saying that the broadcast was true. The Emperor, he said, was concerned with the fate of future generations. . . . Later that day, one of the lads in the squad . . . took a machine-gun and pointed the barrel into his mouth, and he put his foot against the trigger and fired.*

AFTER 1945

After the war ended, an American army of occupation under General Douglas A. MacArthur was sent to govern Japan. Under MacArthur's rule, Japan was given a democratic constitution. Although the emperor kept his throne, he gave up claims to divine status. To this day, he remains "a symbol of the state and of the unity of the people."

In addition, local government was strengthened. The army and navy were disbanded, and Japan renounced the right to use force in its foreign policy. Women were granted certain rights, including the right to vote. The educational system was reformed along American lines. Economic reforms also were introduced. The large *zaibatsu* were reduced in size, and labor unions were encouraged. Farmers were given the opportunity to own their own land.

In September, 1951, the American occupation came to an end as the Japanese signed a peace treaty with most of the nations they had fought against in the war. Not too long afterwards, tensions that had risen between the Communist and the western nations brought Japan and the United States into an alliance. A security treaty was signed that allowed the United States to have military bases and troops in Japan. With the American military in Japan, the Japanese government saw little need to spend much on defense. As a result, during the 25 years after the Pacific War, the government was able to help rebuild the country's industries.

The Japanese studied modern western technology and became skilled and well-trained. They invested heavily in new factories and developed foreign trade, exporting finished goods in return for energy resources and other raw materials.

Today, Japan has one of the highest rates of economic growth of all industrialized nations. The most developed nation in Asia, it has one of the highest standards of living in the world. As a result of this economic success, many people believe that Japan should play an even larger role in world affairs than it does at present.

1. What were Japan's goals in Asia and the Pacific?
2. What led the Japanese to surrender?
3. In what ways did the American occupation change Japan?
4. Why do many people believe that Japan should have more say in world affairs?

---

*Saito Mutsuo, as quoted in *Shōwa: An Inside History of Hirohito's Japan* by Tessa Morris-Suzuki, ©1984, The Athlone Press Limited, pp. 186–187. Reprinted by permission.

EXPLORATION
JAPAN

Japan has undergone a great many changes since it opened its doors to the West in the mid-1800's. Each of the illustrations on these two pages depicts an important change. Identify each change, and tell what or who helped bring it about.

281

CHAPTER 17 REVIEW

POINTS TO REMEMBER

1. A major characteristic of Japan is its ability to absorb foreign influences and at the same time keep its own unique traditions.
2. Under Meiji rule, strong efforts were made to make Japan a modern nation that could compete with the West.
3. In the 1890's and early 1900's, Japan began to compete with the West in establishing overseas empires. It eventually emerged as the dominant power in East Asia.
4. After World War I, tensions abroad and social and economic problems at home encouraged the Japanese to abandon democratic reform at home and stop cooperating with the West.
5. In the 1930's, the military took control of the Japanese government and began a program of expansion in Asia.
6. Japanese policies in Asia created tensions with the United States. In 1941 the Japanese bombed Pearl Harbor, which set off the Pacific War between Japan and the United States. In August 1945, the Pacific War came to an end after the United States dropped atomic bombs on Hiroshima and Nagasaki. Following the Japanese surrender, the United States military occupied Japan.
7. Today, Japan is the most developed nation in Asia with a high rate of economic growth and a high standard of living.

VOCABULARY

Identify

Mutsuhito Manchuria Greater East Asia Pacific War
Meiji League of Nations   Co-prosperity Sphere Hiroshima
Kyoto Hirohito Hideki Tojo Nagasaki
Edo   Pearl Harbor Douglas A. MacArthur

Define

diet boycotted militarism civilian
zaibatsu   atomic bomb

DISCUSSING IMPORTANT IDEAS

1. The West has had a great impact on Japan. What impact has Japan had on the West?
2. What characteristics in Japan's national character do you think aided the Japanese in recovering from the effects of the atomic bomb?
3. In writing about Japan, an author once said, "Probably no people change so quickly on the surface and so slowly beneath as the Japanese." How would you interpret this statement? Give examples to support your interpretation.
4. What do you think might have happened if the United States had not dropped atomic bombs on Hiroshima and Nagasaki to end the war?

DEVELOPING SKILLS

EXPRESSING AND SUPPORTING A VIEWPOINT

As a student, there are times when you are asked to express your viewpoint. Whether the topic has been chosen for you or you choose it yourself, you are expected to do two things—present your viewpoint clearly and give evidence that supports that viewpoint persuasively. The following guidelines will help you do this:

1. Before stating your viewpoint on a topic, research it thoroughly. Find out what viewpoints others hold on the same topic.
2. Decide what your position is, and develop as many supporting statements as you can. List the statements. Study them to make certain that each relates directly to the topic, to each other, and to the point of view upon which you have decided. Then, check them to make sure they are in a logical, easy-to-follow order and that they support your point of view in a clear enough manner for others to understand. The statements should define, make clearer, explain, give a reason for, or state the consequence(s) of holding your point of view. It also is helpful to include an example or an *analogy*, a comparison with something different but with some of the same characteristics.
3. State your position. Then, present your supporting statements, leaving for last the one that is most impressive and will have the most impact. The last statement might also restate your viewpoint, but in different words than your opening statement.

The author of the statements that follow has followed the guidelines suggested. Read the numbered statements, noting the references to the guidelines that precede them:

Statement of topic and position
1. *Japan owes a great deal to the West.*

Supporting statements that
(1) relate directly to the topic and to the expressed point of view;
(2) are presented in a logical order and are easy to follow and understand;
(3) clarify and explain;
(4) present examples.

2. *Within a period of 50 years, Japan has made more progress than any other nation in the history of the world.*
3. *It has more territory and more people.*
4. *It has a truly constitutional government and an excellent educational system.*
5. *Commerce and industry has grown rapidly.*
6. *This progress is a great achievement, one due mostly to the stimulus Japan received from its contact with the West.*
7. *Its contacts with the West brought to life a national consciousness and made it possible for Japan to become the world power it is today.*
8. *Many of the institutions of which Japan is now proudest were modeled after those of the West—the powerful army and navy, the draft, military education, the reformed educational system.*

Restatement of viewpoint
9. *All of these—and others besides—came about because Japan adopted the superior features of western institutions.*

For practice in this skill, follow the guidelines, and write a paragraph that expresses your viewpoint on the use of the atomic bomb to end the Pacific War.

CHAPTER 18
RELIGION AND THE ARTS

1. How has religion influenced Japanese culture?
2. What art forms have the Japanese developed over the centuries?

> I once felt sadness at the impermanence and constant change of all worldly things. . . . But I finally realized that there is not really anything sad in it at all. Impermanence is, rather, a manifestation of life itself. A flower [always] in bloom would be [empty] of beauty. The knowledge of the shortness of a flower's life, of its fate to soon wither and die, is what makes a flower beautiful. . . .
>
> Encounters with natural landscapes must always be considered once-and-forever affairs. Nature is alive, and constantly changing. The same is true of human beings. We are destined to follow an eternal cycle of growth and decline, life and death. Nature and human beings are forever linked to this cycle.
>
> If flowers and humans lived forever there would be no inspiration in encounters between the two. The brilliance of a flower's existence is manifested in the scattering of its petals. At the root of the sense of beauty felt while viewing a lovely flower is a subconscious joy of an encounter between flower and man, both of whom will exist for but a short time in this world. And this is certainly not limited to flowers; it holds equally true for the smallest blade of grass growing on a dusty road. . . .
>
> I was weak both in body and spirit as a child. I grew up in Kobe, but during my middle school years I spent time in the home of a certain acquaintance near the sea on Awaji Island, close to Kobe. Day after day I would stand facing the sea, my back to the mountains, staring out over the waters. It was during these days that I first sensed the tremendous forces around and within my own existence. Nature, the origin of all life, gave me my initial artistic inspiration. . . .
>
> I scrutinize the wonders of nature, and record these impressions on canvas. The reason I observe things so closely is not to analyze natural phenomena as such, but rather to understand the life therein in clear, accurate terms, without a trace of exaggeration.*

These words, spoken by Kaii Higashiyama, one of the foremost painters of modern Japan, reflect the Japanese appreciation of beauty—both in nature and in the ordinary events of daily life. Over the centuries, the Japanese have developed a variety of beliefs, customs, and art forms to express their delight in plain and simple things.

This trait is one of the many aspects of traditional Japanese culture still very much alive in Japan in spite of modernization. Some of these traditions have been passed on to the West, especially in architecture, literature and film, crafts, and artistic design. At the same time, however, the Japanese have added to their heritage cultural forms of the West. Among these are western entertainment and western-style clothing. In Japan, for example, it is not unusual to see a person dressed in the traditional garment known as a **kimono** walking along talking with another person wearing American-style jeans. In fact, almost nowhere else on earth have the cultures of East and West blended so thoroughly.

---
*Kaii Higashiyama, as cited in *The Dawns of Tradition*, Nissan Motor Co., Ltd., 1983, pp. 82–83. Reprinted by permission.

RELIGION

Japanese culture has been strongly influenced by religion. The Japanese have never held to belief in a single, all-powerful deity beyond time and space. Instead, they looked to the world around them for the meaning of life and, in the beauty of the earth's changing seasons and forms, found a pattern that also applied to human life. As a result, for most Japanese, religion has been directed to worldly, everyday concerns and has stressed each person's duty to live in harmony with nature and to honor family and nation.

Today, many of Japan's population claim to be followers of Shinto. Most Japanese, however, are Buddhists. Because the teachings of Shinto and Buddhism support each other, many Japanese belong to both religions at the same time. In addition, a small minority of Japanese are Christians or members of faiths that combine elements of Shinto, Buddhism, and Christianity.

SHINTO

Early in their history, the Japanese developed a set of religious beliefs and practices that later came to be known as Shinto, or "the way of the gods." At the heart of Shinto is the concept of **kami**, or "divine spirit." Below, a young Japanese student offers his interpretation of the traditional meaning of *kami*:

> I do not yet understand the meaning of the term *kami*. Speaking in general, however, it may be said that *kami* signifies, in the first place, the deities of heaven and earth that appear in the ancient records and also the spirits of the shrines where they are worshipped.
>
> It is hardly necessary to say that it includes human beings. It also includes such objects as birds, beasts, trees, plants, seas, mountains, and so forth. In ancient usage, anything whatsoever which was outside the ordinary, which possessed superior power, or which was awe-inspiring was called *kami*. Eminence here does not refer merely to the superiority of nobility, goodness, or [praiseworthy] deeds. Evil and mysterious things, if they are extraordinary and dreadful, are called *kami*. It is needless to say that among human beings who are called *kami* the successive generations of sacred emperors are all included. The fact that emperors are also called "distant *kami*" is because, from the standpoint of common people, they are far-separated, majestic, and worthy of reverence. In a lesser degree we find, in the present as well as in ancient times, human beings who are *kami*. Although they may not be accepted throughout the whole country, yet in each province, each village, and each family there are human beings who are *kami*, each one according to his own

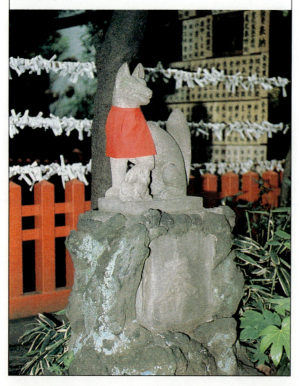

In Tokyo, statues like this one of white, grinning foxes with bushy tails are found in front of shrines devoted to Inari, the popular Shinto rice god. What are the basic beliefs of Shinto?

CHAPTER 18   RELIGION AND THE ARTS   287

CHARACTERISTICS OF THE MAJOR RELIGIONS OF JAPAN	
RELIGIONS	MAJOR BELIEFS
SHINTO	*Kami*, or "divine spirits," can be found in nature and in the processes of creativity, disease, and healing. Shinto emphasizes sacred space and sacred time. Practices vary in local communities and shrines. Rituals often honor ancestors and forces of nature.
BUDDHISM	Existence is a continuing cycle of death and rebirth. The chief obstacle to inner peace lies in one's desires. People can gain *nirvana*, a state of peace and happiness, by ridding themselves of attachments to worldly things. The means to this end include the Middle Way of moderation, wherein one practices restraint and follows the teachings of the Buddha.

proper position. The *kami* of the divine age were for the most part human beings of that time and, because the people of that time were all *kami*, it is called the Age of the Gods (*kami*).*

In 1947, a new democratic constitution ended the ties that had existed between Shinto and the government and granted freedom of religion to all Japanese. Despite this, many Japanese today visit Shinto shrines on birthdays, weddings, and other important family occasions. They value Shinto as an expression of their unique cultural heritage. The centuries-long practice of Shinto rituals in honor of ancestors and the forces of nature have contributed to such Japanese

characteristics as reverence for the natural world, love of simplicity, and concern for cleanliness and good manners.

BUDDHISM

Japanese culture also has been shaped by Buddhism. After Buddhism arrived from China in the 500's AD, it won converts first among the nobles and then among the common people. In Japan as elsewhere in Asia, Buddhists taught about the impermanence of life, the need to seek inner peace, and the unimportance of material goods.

Japanese Buddhism, however, eventually developed into a number of **sects,** or smaller religious groups, many of which linked religion and patriotism and stressed reverence for nature. One important sect was Zen,

*Motoori Norinaga, as quoted in *The National Faith of Japan* by D. C. Holtom, 1938, Routledge & Kegan Paul PLC, pp. 23–24. Reprinted by permission.

which was brought from China in the 1100's. Especially popular among warriors, it taught that the way in which one could achieve inner peace was through bodily discipline and meditation.

Throughout Japanese history, Buddhism sparked cultural awakenings. It had a great influence on the arts. Many artists and writers in traditional Japan were monks who set up libraries of Buddhist writings. In addition, the government built Buddhist temples and shrines that held bronze, wooden, and **lacquer,** or varnished, statues of Buddha as well as religious paintings and other works of art.

Today, most Japanese use Buddhist rituals in funerals and memorial rites for the dead. Like Shinto, Buddhism is used to affirm family ties and to provide continuity with the past. Below, a young Buddhist priest discusses his religion, his role as a priest, and Buddhism's place in the Japan of today:

> I am a priest of the Buddhist Temple, and am called *Obōsan* by people in Japan. . . .
>
> Let me explain in plain language the difference between Buddhism and Christianity. Christ is an absolute being, but the Buddha, who is the equivalent of Christ, is not thought of as divine. He is more of a teacher who taught how people should live harmoniously together, and in this way become closer to God. . . . My job is to teach the ways of Buddha. . . .

This large bronze statue of the Buddha Amitabha in Kamakura, Japan, dates from the thirteenth century. Through time, the original Buddha has become many Buddhas, each with its own special qualities and followers. What are the basic beliefs of Japanese Buddhism?

CHAPTER 18 RELIGION AND THE ARTS

I was born a priest's son and went to a Buddhist university to learn about my religion. After graduation, a student who wishes to become a priest must go through special training before he is allowed to administer a temple. To begin with, he must receive the Buddhist commandments from his master; in my case, my father. Then he must go through a hard period of self-denial, getting up at 4 A.M. every day to learn the duties of being a priest.

The severest training takes place in deepest winter. The young priests shut themselves in the temple for a hundred days, and through a vigorous program of physical self-denial, deepen their understanding of Buddha's ways. Rising at 3 A.M. and not retiring until midnight, they pour cold water on themselves every three hours, seven times a day, to purify their body, and then sit formally reading the *sutras* [lines from the scriptures]. Food is served twice a day, but it is only soft, watery rice. The idea of these trials is to conquer the desires of the body, such as hunger, sleeplessness and pain. I had to endure all this training before attaining my present position as one of the priests administering this temple in Tokyo.

My daily routine begins with the morning service in the temple.... I may conduct several services for the dead during the day. I also have a pastoral role to play —giving advice to runaways and those with domestic problems. I have even been made a godfather to an abandoned baby! The day ends with the evening service and the solemn chanting of the *sutras*.

One of the great problems today is that all over the world religious beliefs are in danger, and Japan is no exception. Yet I believe the spiritual support religion can provide is more important in the modern world than ever before.*

---

*"All over the world religious beliefs are in danger" in *We Live in Japan* by Kazuhide Kawamata, 1984, The Bookwright Press, pp. 30–31. Reprinted by permission.

1. Toward what has Japanese religion been directed?
2. What are the two major religions of Japan? To what Japanese characteristics has each contributed?

CELEBRATIONS AND FESTIVALS

The religions of Japan have encouraged the celebration of many festivals, most of which celebrate the seasons, commemorate family occasions, or honor gods or the spirits of the dead. One of the most popular festivals celebrates the New Year, which is Japan's most joyous, yet most solemn, occasion. The celebration begins on January 1 and lasts for three days. During this time, the people dress in their most colorful and elaborate *kimonos*, visit friends and relatives, and exchange gifts. At home, families enjoy grand feasts and play traditional games.

In addition to the festivals that are held nationally are some celebrated only in certain regions of Japan. Examples are the spring and fall festivals held in Takayama, a small city in the mountains of central Japan. Below, a Japanese journalist discusses the festivities:

> The Spring Festival, which has lasted for 740 years, takes place in the area of Hie Shrine, while the Autumn Festival is held near Sakurayama Hachiman Shrine. Both are extremely popular.... Highlight of the festivals is a gala procession of special floats, which accompanies two ancient dance performances and marionette shows.
>
> Between intervals of the procession, some people dance "Tokeigaku," a unique folk dance of the Hida region, in which young men dance and beat gongs, dressed in white costumes decorated with dragon and feather designs. Ancient *gagaku* music

and the reverberations of the *tokei* [cockfighting] gongs stir up the festival mood to a high pitch. Young men formerly performed this dance at the festivals, but from seven years ago the roles were handed over to children. . . .

All the parents enthusiastically desire to have their children included in this group. While taking a stroll after supper, many grandparents, parents and neighbors come to watch the children practicing earnestly. Everyone is filled with happy anticipation as the festival day approaches.

On the other hand, "Urayasu no Mai" is a solemn dedicatory dance performed by girls in the shrine compound. On the day of the performance, they appear colorfully dressed in their finest clothes. They are very popular and are called out many times . . . to pose for snapshots.

Likewise, Hisamitsu Tsuzuku, 42, a local bus driver and renowned expert of "Shishi-Mai" (Lion Dance), is now training eight primary and junior high students in the hope that at least one or two of them will develop into expert performers.

Finally comes the soul of the festivals: a fabulous procession, led by the Tokeigaku and Shishi-Mai dancers and local residents in ancient ceremonial dress, of three- and four-tier lantern-bedecked floats. These splendid "Ships of the Night" are decorated with elaborate carvings and metal trim, and reach heights of seven meters [23.1 feet].

There are 23 of these . . . floats . . . some featuring open, roofless tops on which are placed huge drums to pound out a rhythm for the handlers. Each of the floats has received official designation as an important cultural property of national folklore so as to be preserved for posterity.

The preservation of this aspect of the festivals is the responsibility of 18 *yatai-gumi* (float groups). Each group includes a number of households, from eight for the smallest float to 269 for the largest. . . . From among the *yatai-gumi* each year are chosen the members of an executive committee which organizes and oversees the entire festival.

Most of the floats were built or reconstructed some 100 years ago, and are today stored in special buildings where they are protected from extreme changes in temperature or humidity. . . . Some of

Crowds of spectators line city streets to delight in the fall festival procession of elaborate floats and costumed participants. What are the highlights of the fall and spring festivals held in Takayama?

the floats were built with donations from wealthy merchants; others constructed painstakingly through the work of poor but expert craftsmen. Each required several years at least to complete, and the attachment of the people of Takayama to these floats is total. They are the key to and major attraction of the twin festivals of Takayama, but more importantly represent the dedication and skills of the traditional Hida craftsman—thus providing a vital link with the heritage of centuries past.*

1. What do many of the Japanese festivals celebrate?
2. What is a typical Japanese festival like?

THE WRITTEN AND SPOKEN WORD

Another link with the heritage of centuries past is the Japanese language, which is distinctly different from other Asian languages. Although the people of early Japan borrowed the Chinese system of writing, the Japanese language has little in common with the Chinese one. The Chinese characters, or picture words, used in written Japanese are known as **kanji**. Although they are still in use today, they are used with symbols called **kana**, which express different sounds rather than entire words. Special forms of *kana* are used in writing. Both *kanji* and *kana* are used in everyday language. It is estimated that in order to read a Japanese newspaper one must know at least 1800 *kanji*.

LITERATURE AND FILM

The Japanese have a rich literary heritage. Two of the oldest surviving Japanese works, probably written in the 700's AD, are legendary accounts found in the *Kojiki* and the *Man'yoshu*, a large collection of poems. The first great prose literature was written around the year 1000 by women of the emperor's court at Heian. One of these women, Lady Murasaki Shikibu, wrote *The Tale of Genji*, which describes the romances and adventures of a Japanese prince. Some literary experts believe the work to be the world's first novel.

In addition to novels, the Japanese developed special forms of poetry. One popular type is **haiku,** which developed in the 1600's. Consisting of three lines and 17 syllables, it usually expresses a mood or feeling. The most noted writer of *haiku* was the seventeenth-century poet Bashō Matsuo. Below are two of his more famous *haiku*:

> The summer grasses—
> Of brave soldiers' dreams
> The aftermath.
>
> Such stillness—
> The cries of the cicadas
> Sink into the rocks.

Many Japanese today learn by heart the *haiku* of Bashō and other poets. They also write their own at special poetry clubs throughout the country.

Literature from Europe and North America began to enter Japan after its opening to the West in the 1800's. Many western books were translated into Japanese, and by the 1900's, Japanese writers were blending western themes with their own. In 1968, Yasunari Kawabata, best known for his works titled *Snow Country* and *1,000 Cranes,* became the first Japanese literary figure to receive the Nobel Prize for Literature.

Many literary themes have been used in Japanese motion pictures. Today, Japan has one of the largest and most productive film industries in the world. Such Japanese film directors as Akira Kurosawa have earned

---
*"Takayama Festival," in *Japan Pictorial*, Vol. 4, No. 2, 1981, pp. 5, 7. Reprinted by permission.

world-wide praise for their work. Many of the films, Kurosawa's *The Seven Samurai* for one, deal with the warriors of the past.

DRAMA

The Japanese also are known for their traditional forms of drama, one of the oldest of which is the **Noh play.** Created during the 1300's, *Noh* plays developed out of religious dances and were used to teach Buddhist ideas. Later, they were based on early Japanese history and legends. There was little plot. The emphasis, instead, was on human emotions and, very often, tragedy. Many *Noh* plays are still performed today. The actors, who wear masks and elaborate costumes, dance, gesture, and chant poetry on a bare stage. They are accompanied by a chorus.

Another form of traditional Japanese drama still performed today is the **kabuki** play. Originating in the 1500's to entertain the common people, *kabuki* was more popular than *Noh* because it was easier to follow and understand. Most *kabuki* themes centered on Japanese history or such domestic events as romances or family quarrels.

Today, as in the past, all roles in *kabuki* drama are played by men who wear heavy, elaborate costumes and mask their faces with thick makeup. Such feelings as joy, anger, and sadness are portrayed in exaggerated form. In recent years, some of the most famous *kabuki* actors have been honored as notable performers. One of the current leading performers is Ennosuke, who is discussed below by a Japanese journalist:

> He is at once direct and retiring, with a small boy's bashful charm. The rigors of a kabuki actor's life have honed him into a single-minded missionary. He is completely dedicated to his art. He does not appear on modern drama stages, in television, films, or commercials. He is unmarried. He has cheerfully admitted that he has no hobbies. "Kabuki is my interest,"

As seen in this photo, traditional Noh *actors wear exquisite, embroidered* kimonos *and wooden masks. Because the masks express little emotion, actors must convey the emotions of their characters through gestures rather than facial expressions. What is emphasized in* Noh *plays?*

Lavish costumes and colorful stage sets characterize kabuki *theater, which has been popular in Japan for centuries. Here, two actors perform a scene in a recent* kabuki *production. Who plays all the roles in* kabuki?

he has said. "I love my job. I'm very lucky." He writes, designs, directs, produces and performs kabuki with that perfectionism only known to one whose art truly is his life.

Zealousness runs in his family. His greatgrandfather, the first Ennosuke, rose from the lowest rank of bit players to establish that branch of the far-flung Ichikawa acting family known by the guild name "Omodaka-ya." After him his son En'ō marched in the vanguard of the sweep toward modern theater in Japan, and forged the *shin-buyō,* "New Dance," revolution in kabuki. En'ō raised and trained his grandson, and the stamp of his eccentric genius was already on the boy when he took the name Ennosuke III in 1963 just weeks before the old man's death. . . .

Ennosuke's life in the theater has perhaps been more rigorous than most. Finding himself head of the Omodaka-ya at barely 24, he [renounced] the usual course . . . of sheltering beneath the wing of an older higher-ranking actor, and struck out on his own. The going was tough. It was this struggle as head of a young group of actors, when he was his own leading man, ticket-seller and press agent, that taught him the techniques of survival, and developed his talent to soar, in the fantastical world of the theater. The many directions in which he now, at 45, is able to stretch himself, are the harvest of this hard apprenticeship thoroughly learning his trade. . . . But with modernity came the severance of kabuki's roots as a . . . theater of the people, and the waning of the influence upon it of single personalities like those of the earlier geniuses. So such artistic independence as Ennosuke's is in many ways harder won for him than it was for his greatgrandfather.

It is precisely Ennosuke's mission to put kabuki back in touch with its roots as a popular theater. His own visionary addition is the idea that today, in the 20th —and 21st—Century, the people to whom kabuki belongs comprise the entire world community. Ennosuke's mission is to make kabuki understandable to everyone and loved by all.*

1. From whom did the Japanese borrow their system of writing?

2. What are Japan's oldest surviving works of literature? What other forms of literature have emerged?
3. What two traditional forms of Japanese drama are still performed today? What are the themes of each?

CRAFTS AND OTHER ARTS

The written and spoken word are not the only forms of artistic expression used by the Japanese. They also have developed a variety of crafts and other arts that express their artistic values. One of these is a form of landscape gardening in which nature is cop-

---
*"Ennosuke's Kabuki: A Very Personal Theater" in *Japan Pictorial*, Vol. 8, No. 1, 1985, p. 9. Reprinted by permission.

ied on a small scale. Japanese gardeners have made an art of building gardens complete with artificial hills and ponds surrounded by trees and flowering shrubs. Some of the gardens, with their carefully placed rocks, raked sand, and a few plants, are centers of meditation and reflect the simplicity of Zen Buddhism.

Other Japanese arts of long standing include ceramics, ivory carving, lacquer ware, silk weaving, embroidery, enameling, and *origami*, the art of folding paper into decorative objects. In the passage that follows, a Japanese woman discusses two other traditional arts—*ikebana,* or flower arranging, and *cha-no-yu,* the tea ceremony—both of which are of special interest to her:

I have always liked flowers, and I first began to practice *Kado* while I was still at school. I have been doing it ever since. *Kado* is the art of increasing the natural beauty of flowers by shaping and arranging them according to set rules.

Sado is the ceremony of drinking tea. It has more difficult rules of movement than *Kado*. In fact to learn how to eat the cake served with the tea properly can take three months of practice, and it takes a year to learn to drink tea correctly. Moreover, to learn all the movements of the ceremony thoroughly—making the tea with a bamboo implement called a *chasen* and serving your guests correctly with tea and cake—takes at least several years.

Both Sado and Kado have a long history which stretches back at least six centuries.

These Japanese women, dressed in formal kimonos, *instruct an audience in the proper ritual of the tea ceremony, once the exclusive privilege of the elite of Japanese society. What are some of the things one must learn to become accomplished at* Sado*?*

An ikebana, *or* Kado, *artist stands beside a flower arrangement he has entered in one of the many ikebana shows held in Japan each year. When selecting the best* ikebana, *judges consider many things, including the quality and attractiveness of the vase and the way the arrangement is displayed. What does the* ikebana *artist try to accomplish?*

The reason why I took up both these arts is because both of them share the same principle—the respect for beauty. Art should not be separate from ordinary life—it is part of it. This is why I enjoy teaching these accomplishments to my pupils.

I worked as a secretary for six years before I became a teacher, and the manners and tact I learned in this job have served me well. Etiquette is very important in *Sado* and *Kado*, so I train my pupils very strictly. I see *Kado* as a hobby, really. It brings great pleasure to gaze at beautiful flowers, and to touch them with your hands. *Sado*, on the other hand, is really part of everyday life. It has its ordinary actions, such as putting on the kettle and cleaning up the tea room, but it also emphasizes the beauty of movement—this is why I spend so much time teaching the correct way to bow or to hold the tea bowl. And of course, my pupils have to practice over and over again before they can make tea correctly. It is not easy. But gradually, after much repetition, they begin to understand the right attitude needed for this ancient ceremony. Good tea utensils are also important for *Sado*. Indeed, some experts say that it is impossible to distinguish between a good and bad tea bowl until one has been practicing this ceremony for many, many years!

In the old days it was compulsory for all Japanese to become accomplished at *Kado* and *Sado*. Times may have changed, but people are still eager to learn. I teach fifteen pupils of all ages. We always finish with a pleasant chat after relaxing our minds with tea and flowers. Many things come and go in this chaotic world, but as long as we still treasure tranquillity of mind, *Sado* and *Kado* will live on among the Japanese.*

1. What are some of the crafts and arts the Japanese have developed to express their artistic values?
2. What are some of the features of Japanese gardens?
3. Why are flower arranging and the tea ceremony important to the Japanese?

---

*"It takes a year to learn to drink tea correctly" in *We Live in Japan* by Kazuhide Kawamata, 1984, The Bookwright Press, pp. 16–17. Reprinted by permission.

Insights on People
Japan

HOKUSAI

In traditional Japan, a popular art form was the printing of illustrations on paper from carved blocks of wood. These prints, which showed scenes of daily life, landscapes, and the theater, are still popular today. They are especially valued for their beautiful designs, fine detail, and bright colors.

One of the most famous print artists was Hokusai. Born in Edo in 1760, he began drawing at the age of 5. Apprenticed to a woodblock engraver when a teenager, he later became a pupil of one of Japan's leading print artists. At the time, Japanese printmakers were interested in showing life as a series of fleeting moments. They called their prints *ukiyo-e*, which means "pictures of the floating world." Although Hokusai adopted their style, he incorporated his own ideas and became known for his individualism.

In many ways, Hokusai broke with the life style that the Japanese of that time expected of their artists. Artists were supposed to become apprenticed to a well-known master, from whom they would receive names. Beginners would learn to work in a traditional style, continue in that style, and pass it on without change to the next generation of artists. Then, like most people of their class, they were expected to live out their lives in their places of birth. Hokusai, however, was different. He changed his place of residence more than 90 times and his name more than 30. Moreover, he ignored Japanese standards of politeness by being rude to patrons, refusing to work for those he did not like, and rejecting gifts in order to avoid future obligations.

Above all, Hokusai broke with artistic tradition and developed his own unique kind of illustrations. He became the first Japanese printmaker to focus on landscapes. Among his most famous works was *Thirty-six Views of Mount Fuji*, a series of prints of the mountain from a variety of locations. Another work, *Great Wave Off the Coast of Kanagawa*, is considered one of the finest examples of Japanese drawing.

After the success of *Thirty-six Views of Mount Fuji*, Hokusai's popularity declined. Although he ended up living in poverty, he continued his work until he died. His last words were:

"If Heaven will give me five more years of life, I will become a real painter."

1. Who was Hokusai?
2. How was Hokusai influenced by the artistic style of his time?
3. How did Hokusai reflect the cultural values of traditional Japan? What did he do to break with tradition?

CHAPTER 18 REVIEW

POINTS TO REMEMBER

1. Japanese religion has had a strong influence on culture. It is directed to worldly, everyday concerns and stresses one's duty to live in harmony with nature and honor family and nation.
2. Shinto is the oldest Japanese religion. It has contributed to such Japanese characteristics as reverence for nature, love of simplicity, and concern for cleanliness and good manners.
3. Buddhism, which came from China, sparked cultural awakenings in Japan. Its various sects all stressed reverence for nature and the need for inner peace. Like Shinto, Buddhism affirms family ties and provides continuity with the past.
4. The religions of Japan have encouraged the celebration of many festivals. Most celebrate the seasons, commemorate family occasions, or honor gods or spirits of the dead.
5. The Japanese language is composed of characters known as *kanji* and symbols known as *kana*.
6. The Japanese have a rich literary heritage of which *haiku* is an important part.
7. Two traditional forms of drama, the *Noh* play and the *kabuki* play, are still performed in Japan today.
8. Over the centuries, the Japanese have developed a variety of crafts and other arts that express their artistic values. These arts include landscape gardening, ceramics, ivory carving, lacquer ware, silk weaving, embroidering, enameling, origami, *ikebana*, and *cha-no-yu*.

VOCABULARY

Identify

Kaii Higashiyama	Takayama	*The Tale of Genji*	Ennosuke
Shinto	*Kojiki*	Bashō Matsuo	*Kado*
Buddhism	*Man'yoshu*	Yasunari Kawabata	*Sado*
Zen	Lady Murasaki Shikibu	Akira Kurosawa	

Define

kimono	lacquer	haiku	origami
kami	kanji	Noh play	ikebana
sects	kana	kabuki	cha-no-yu

DISCUSSING IMPORTANT IDEAS

1. An author made the following generalization about Japan: "That, I was assured, remains the spirit of Japan—love of color and love of nature—cherry blossoms or a mountain in the bright morning—almost a definition, a trademark picture of Japan." Based on the information presented in this chapter, do you think the author has made a valid generalization? Explain your answer.

CHAPTER 18 RELIGION AND THE ARTS

2. In what ways have Japan and the Japanese been influenced by religion? Give examples to support your answer.
3. The Japanese have made many contributions to world culture. What specific examples can you give of these? Do you think these contributions are important? Why or why not?
4. From a religious and cultural standpoint, how do the Japanese view life? In what ways is their view similar to and different from that of your culture?

DEVELOPING SKILLS

MAKING INFERENCES

If you wanted to solve a crime, you would look for clues to the method used to commit the crime and to the identity of the person or persons responsible. Then, based on those clues, you might make an *inference*, a deduction based on facts or circumstances.

People make inferences every day, often without even realizing they are doing so. For example, you know that your grandmother, who is elderly and lives alone, walks to the corner store every day to buy groceries. Today, however, the weather is bad, and the streets are icy. Based on these facts, you infer that your grandmother will not go out today and, unless someone else goes to the store for her, she will not have any groceries.

Or, you and some friends want to go swimming at a lake in the next town. When you ask your friend Mike if he can borrow his father's car to drive there, he tells you he cannot. But he does not tell you why. Then, he tells you that even if you can find someone else to drive, he cannot go with you. Once again, he does not tell you why. You know that Mike has no plans for the day, is not sick, and loves to go swimming in the lake. Based on your conversation with Mike and what you know about him, you make an inference—Mike has done something to make his parents angry and has been grounded.

The following paragraph is about the Japanese artist Hokusai. Read it and the explanation and inference that follow it:

Hokusai adopted the style of other Japanese printmakers. But, at the same time, he incorporated his own ideas into his works. He developed his own unique kind of illustrations and became the first Japanese printmaker to focus on landscapes. Other artists of his time and his class kept the names their parents gave them and lived out their lives in the places where they were born. Hokusai changed his name more that 30 times and moved more than 90 times.
(The paragraph states that Hokusai incorporated his own ideas into his works, developed his own unique kind of illustrations, and changed his name and residence many times. All of these things went against the traditions of the times. Inference: Hokusai was a "rebel" who ignored tradition and did as he pleased.)

For practice in this skill, read the material about Shinto and Buddhism on pages 286 through 289, and explain which of the following inferences seem logical and why.
1. The lack of similarities between Shinto and Buddhism made it hard for the Japanese to accept Buddhism.
2. Both Shinto and Buddhism have had a great impact on the Japanese culture.

CHAPTER 19
JAPANESE SOCIETY

1. How have the roles of family and family members changed in Japan since World War II?
2. How does modern Japanese society reflect a blend of the old and the new?

As soon as Kotaro Nohmura, an executive director of Taiyo Kogyo, an Osaka tent manufacturer, arrives home from work at nearly midnight, he looks in on his four children. They are asleep, just as they were when he left for work at 7:30 that morning. A few fond glances are usually the only contact Nohmura, 37, has with his two sons (7 and 4 months) and two daughters (5 and 9) during the week. Like most Japanese executives, his day starts early and ends only after a long night of business entertaining.

Nohmura earns $51,000 a year before taxes, which enables him to house his family in a four-room apartment in the outskirts of Kobe, a port city. Six days a week, he gets up at 7 and eats a Western-style breakfast. . . . Then he is out the door and into a Toyota . . ., which he drives 40 minutes to his company's head office in . . . Osaka. . . .

Nohmura spends most of his mornings at his desk in a cubbyhole office. He likes his small space, saying, "I can get almost everything I need without having to stand up every time." There he writes reports and discusses new tent designs with engineers. The executive almost never goes to business lunches . . . . He spends the afternoon making the rounds of local customers and inspecting tents being constructed. Then he calls it a day at about 5:30.

But Nohmura's work is far from finished. On a typical recent evening he first went to a meeting of the Osaka Jaycees. . . .

After the Jaycees' session, Nohmura went on to his evening's business entertainment. He escorted a favored client and one of the client's associates to an elegant restaurant . . . where . . . they dined on a twelve-course meal. . . . That contrasted with the group's next stop, a Western-style nightspot. . . . "I don't like entertaining," says Nohmura, "but it has become an institution. . . ."

When Nohmura returned home, his wife greeted him at the door. Then over a quiet cup of green tea, the couple talked about the coming Sunday, when the whole family would be going out to the beach for a picnic. Sunday will constitute Nohmura's one day off.*

Nohmura's busy schedule reflects some of the changes that have taken place in Japan during this century. Changes such as this one have had a great impact on family life. In traditional Japan, the family was the center of national life. Each family member had to follow certain rules of conduct, and all forms of individual expression were discouraged. Grandparents and older aunts and uncles were respected and cared for by the younger family members. The father or the eldest male was the head of the family, supervised its activities, and commanded complete obedience from his wife and children.

In recent years, much has changed. Family ties remain strong, but each family member is allowed more freedoms. Young people often are influenced more by friends than by family. The male's power over family affairs has declined. Since the male now spends more time at work than at home, the wife and mother often becomes the center of the family. For many older Japanese, these changes have been hard to accept.

---

*"A Hard Day's Night" in *Time*, August 1, 1983, p. 42. Copyright 1983 Time Inc. All rights reserved. Reprinted by permission from *TIME*.

MARRIAGE

In traditional Japan, parents played an important role in arranging their children's marriages. Even today, nearly 60 percent of all Japanese marriages are arranged mostly through family and friends, but also through counseling and computer-dating services. At the same time, however, many young people today are choosing their own marriage partners on the basis of common interests and mutual attraction. The average age of the bride and groom also has changed. Japanese men and women are waiting until they are in their late and middle twenties respectively to get married. In addition, the honeymoon, a custom which did not come into being until after World War II, has become very popular. Today, 98 percent of all newlyweds go on a honeymoon for a week or longer.

Regardless of how a couple meets or who makes the marriage plans, in Japan a wedding is an important event. As a Japanese journalist explains below, today most weddings are lavish, costly, and a blend of the old and the new:

A Japanese bride and groom pose for a photograph at a Shinto shrine in Kyoto. She is wearing a traditional wedding dress, while he is attired in western-style formal wear. What is the go-between's role today?

> Weddings in Japan still follow many of the traditions and customs which have been around for centuries, although newer customs are being added. One of the oldest is the formal engagement ceremony, in which a person selected as a "go-between" is dispatched by the parents of the groom-to-be to deliver certain lucky gifts to the household of the betrothed young lady. Packages of dried fish [signifying long life and happiness], kegs of *sake* [rice wine] and other such tokens were sent in days of old. Today, the groom-to-be's family merely writes the names of the gifts on a piece of fine, ceremonial paper.
>
> Cash money also changes hands during the go-between's official call. By custom, the amount should be equivalent to about three months' salary of the groom-to-be. . . . But then, . . . the betrothed girl's family sends the go-between back to the groom-to-be's house to return some of the money. . . .
>
> The old custom of long engagements is still in fashion. . . . How long? In a poll of 1981 newlyweds, the "period of contact before marriage" lasted about a year for some 30 percent, while 57 percent were wed within two years. Go-betweens also continue to play a big role . . . as they have since as long ago as the early 8th century. When a couple decides to "tie the knot," and if all the parents approve, an official go-between is appointed to make the final arrangements. The groom-to-be usually selects a senior employee or executive of his company to do the job. . . .
>
> And still another one of the older customs is picking the most [favorable] date possible for the ceremony itself, and astrology of the ancient Asian kind has a lot

to do with these undertakings. Sundays and holidays in the spring and fall months, when the weather is best, are the most popular. . . . The best day of all is called *taian*, and some believe that marriages . . . on this day are assured of success, happiness and prosperity. . . .

. . . Expenditures [for the wedding] . . . are made without regret, and where large amounts of money are spent, businesses are born. In gross figures, $8.3 billion is spent each year on wedding ceremonies and receptions. . . .

Who pays? By custom, the bride and groom themselves bear about half the costs . . . , while the remainder comes from their parents. . . . This investment naturally strengthens the bond between the two parental households; in view of this, the more elaborate and expensive the wedding, the better it demonstrates the parents' love for their children, and the more effectively it shows neighbors the power and unity of the families involved. . . .

Money saved on the ceremonies is usually spent . . . on the relatively new custom of the honeymoon. Islands are currently the "in" destinations, perhaps because of the image of isolation mixed with tropical luxury. . . .

The honeymoon over, fewer than 12 out of 100 couples return to the groom's (or bride's) former home. Instead, the typical couple moves into a brand-new home, packed full of new furniture, appliances, and clothing. The majority (about 60 percent) of new couples rent their own apartments or houses. . . .

In the old days, a couple was fortunate to begin a marriage with nothing but a few basic possessions—kitchen utensils, bedding and so on. Today, the "basics" include refrigerator, a washing machine, an electric rice-cooker and a color TV. Some young people even list an air-conditioner, a video-tape recorder, an electronic oven and other such goods as "necessities." As a result, yet another "custom" is being added to the wedding scene—starting out on a new life happily in debt to the "buy-now, pay-later" credit merchants.*

1. Who arranged Japanese marriages in the past? Who arranges them today?
2. What are some of the Japanese marriage customs?
3. In what ways are Japanese marriages and weddings a blend of the old and the new?

FAMILY LIFE

Before 1945, many Japanese lived in large family groups with grandparents, parents, and children all in one house. Today, many Japanese live in smaller family groups that consist of only parents and children. Some families, however, have tried to maintain family ties associated with the past. They try, for example, to look after their parents in old age and often set aside a separate area of their homes for them. Below, a Japanese housewife discusses her daily life and the blend of old and new in her household:

I am a housewife living in Saitama, which is a northern suburb of Tokyo. The Saitama area is quite flat and used to be an agricultural area producing mainly rice, but today it has been transformed into suburbs. . . .

My family have been farmers for generations and our house is still surrounded by some rice fields and farmland—though there are more houses than before. My husband is 32 years old and we have three daughters—the eldest one is 7. We live with my parents and grandmother. These days the size of Japanese families has become smaller and smaller, the average size being about four. My family, which consists of eight from four generations, is big by Japanese standards.

---

*"The Romantic World of Weddings" in *Japan Pictorial*, Vol. 7, No. 4, 1984, p. 9. Reprinted by permission.

My husband works in a bank. I worked in the same bank when I left high school. After a few years I met my husband, who was very active and lively. As I have one younger sister but no brothers, my parents adopted him as their heir when we got married.

My house is an old two-story building which was built more than a hundred years ago. It has three traditional Japanese rooms, two Western-style rooms and one kitchen. By Japanese standards the house is big, but as there is not much storage space, we would like to have it rebuilt in the future. In Japan, most families have their own house. The quality of houses has been drastically improved recently, and they can no longer be described as "rabbit hutches" as they were in the past. Nevertheless, they are still not as big on average as European or American houses.

I usually get up at six o'clock and prepare breakfast. Washing, cleaning and shopping are my main chores, which I do after my family leaves for work. In the afternoon, I take my daughters to piano, calligraphy or swimming lessons by car. I start preparing dinner at about half-past six. Each generation likes different sorts of food, so it is difficult for me to satisfy the whole family. For example, my daughters like hamburgers, curry, and corn soup; my husband likes *tempura* (fried fish and vegetables) and meat; and my parents like traditional Japanese stew. After dinner, I wash the dishes and send the children to bed around nine o'clock. After they go to bed I can finally relax watching TV and chatting with my husband and parents. It is not until about half-past eleven that I go to sleep.

One of the things Japanese people are very concerned about is their health. That is partly because the cost of our health care has sharply increased, but a more significant reason may be that the quality of everyday food has got worse, and that they lack physical exercise. I did not bother doing physical exercise, because I thought I was too busy with the housework. However, I realized I needed more exercise so I joined a volleyball club organized by housewives in my town.

Apart from health, what worries me most is our family's living expenses. Although my husband's salary rises regularly, our family's financial situation is deteriorating, because inflation is higher than

This Japanese family, equipped with a tennis racket and bat, is enjoying an outing at a local city park. Picnics and outings such as this one are popular forms of entertainment for many city dwellers. What do some Japanese wives and mothers do during a typical weekday?

pay raises. Therefore, housewives like me have to be thrifty. Despite these financial difficulties my nature is rather optimistic, so I am not too worried. I like to enjoy life.

Our desire in the future is to get our house rebuilt and to give our three daughters a university education.*

1. How have family groups changed in Japan since 1945?
2. How do some Japanese households reflect a blend of old and new?
3. What are some of the concerns of a modern Japanese family?

WOMEN

In traditional Japan, the status of women was lower than that of men. Men led, and women were expected to obey. Their role was to serve their father, husband, or eldest son. But after World War II, Japanese women officially were given equal rights with men in all fields. Today, although most Japanese women still are concerned primarily about a home and family, many are taking jobs outside the home, at least on a part-time basis.

Although Japanese women are better educated than in the past, and many actively participate in political and social life, traditional ideas about their role remain strong. While in the home, many women now tend to manage the family finances and make important family decisions, but they rarely disagree with their husbands in public.

The situation is much the same in the job market, where a wide range of careers are open to women. Yet, although more than half of the medical technicians, teachers, and entertainers in Japan are women, very few females hold leading positions in business, health, government, science, or education.

And, when it comes to pay, job security, or promotions, women are significantly worse off than men in almost any type of job. Below, a Japanese journalist profiles Yuri Kunno, one Japanese woman who overcame the obstacles to achieve a successful career:

There are many career women now around. . . . They are holding executive posts . . . and spreading into . . . heretofore closed fields of work. . . . And they are going into careers without denying themselves the opportunities to get married and bear children. . . .

From among this breed of Japanese women there have emerged into prominence many successful business women. One of them is . . . Yuri Konno, age 42 and married. She came to fame by introducing "telephone answering service" to Japan in 1969. . . .

Born in a small country village . . . , Yuri Konno grew up with a . . . curiosity about life in the city. She became the first woman in the village ever to enter a university. . . . An independent person, she sought work after graduation. . . . She started earning her living as a television interviewer and assistant to a fiction writer.

Then in 1964 she found a job at the New York World's Fair as a companion guide and it was during her stay in New York that she first heard of a telephone answering service, and became enthusiastic about learning more about it. . . . The telephone service was helping numerous local doctors, lawyers and salesmen. . . . The observation soon led to a firm conviction that the system would work in Japan as well, and it would be an area where women could certainly excel.

Upon returning to Japan, she was immediately on the go. She recruited a staff solely of women and proceeded to train them for a full six months before actually establishing a company, Dial Service. . . . Soon the clientele expanded rapidly, presently serving no fewer than 200 lawyers,

---

*"The Japanese are very concerned about their health" in *We Live in Japan* by Kazuhide Kawamata, 1984, The Bookwright Press, pp. 36–37. Reprinted by permission.

businessmen, authors and various other professionals. Her secret? "Enthusiasm," she replies.

Two years later, Yuri Konno was thinking of expanding her operations into a new field where only women could do something for women. Her brainchild was a counseling service for mothers on childcare. . . . The need for such a project was apparent, but it involved financial strain. In order to offer individual counseling free of charge, the program had to be financed by some "goodwill" sponsors. The idea of telephone counseling was still rare, if not unheard of, and few took any interest. Her persistence, however, won the day and sufficient funds began pouring in. . . .

Once the hot-line program, Baby Dial 110 . . . was put into operation, the response was simply enormous. . . .

To the ingenious business woman, however, telephone counseling was just a start in her efforts to discover and create more of the significant jobs for women. . . .

In much the same way, Yuri Konno has continued to organize several other firms and institutions where women can invest their energy, ideas and skills into developing and improving varied consumer goods that are more specifically tailored to meet the needs of women. Among such projects she is currently engaged in is restructuring the design of automobiles, at the request of an automaker, in a way that they will be more comfortable and functional for women drivers.

She intends to continue to encourage women to excel in areas in which they are interested and particularly gifted. Through her experience she knows only too well that it is women who are most qualified to help other women help themselves.*

1. What was the role of women in traditional Japan?
2. What is the status of women in modern Japan?
3. What has Yuri Konno accomplished? What are her goals in respect to other women?

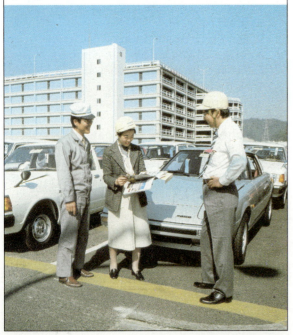

At a Mazda auto plant in Hiroshima, a female member of the management team confers with two other plant employees. Compared to men, how are Japanese women faring in their careers?

YOUNG PEOPLE

The Japanese youth of today enjoy greater freedoms than those of earlier generations. One thing that has not changed, however, is the emphasis placed on education. In Japan, the school year runs from April through March of the following year, with a long vacation break from late June through August. Children start their education at age 6. At 15, they may leave school for work. Most, however, continue their studies at the high school level until they are 18, and then about one-third go on to university.

---

*"A Creative Career Woman" in *Japan Pictorial*, Vol. 3, No. 4, 1980, pp. 3–4. Reprinted by permission.

CASE STUDY
JAPAN

MY RESTAURANT MY LIFE

Although Japanese families enjoy most meals at home, often their homes are too small to entertain a large number of people for dinner or parties. Only a few close friends are invited to such house gatherings. Business associates and acquaintances are invited to a restaurant and, later, to a club for drinks. Restaurants, therefore, are very popular and range from the simple to the elegant. Below, a young Tokyo restaurant owner named Hiroshi Asagi explains how he got interested in his business and what his life is like:

Have you ever tried tempura? *Tempura is one of the most popular dishes in Japan. It is made from different kinds of seafood and vegetables which are coated in a flour mixture and then fried. It sounds easy, doesn't it? But in my opinion to coat the fish and vegetables in the flour mixture requires as much attention and skill as is needed to make a lady's dress. Otherwise, why was it necessary to undergo an apprenticeship [training period] for six long years?*

When I was still at high school, my father's tire business went bankrupt, and although I was able to continue my studies for a while, it soon became obvious that I would have to get a job to help out with the family income. One day I ate a dish of tempura *in a restaurant. It was delicious! The next thing I knew I had got a job as an apprentice at a local restaurant. It had a very good reputation for* tempura, *but the training was old-fashioned and hard.*

I worked from 8 o'clock in the morning until midnight without a break. For the first two years I wasn't even allowed to touch tempura. *Instead I was given all the dirty jobs—cleaning the garbage cans and lavatories and grating vegetables. Later, I was allowed to arrange the food on the dishes, cut up pickles, cook rice, make egg-soybean curd and make up the raw fish dishes. Finally, after three years, I was allowed to fry* tempura.

It was a hard apprenticeship. There was no fire even in winter and the kitchen floor under our work area was frozen. Yet I put up with it. I wanted to have my own restaurant, so I was very eager to learn.

I became independent when I was 24. I had no money to buy my own restaurant so I had to bow my head to the bank and ask them for a loan. With this, I was finally able to open a restaurant called "Tenasa." It is so small that it is full with sixteen customers.

When I first opened I owed so much money that I worked non-stop. I didn't close the restaurant once in a month....

My day starts at 7:30 A.M. when I go down to the local fish market to buy prawns [large shrimp], eels, squid and various kinds of fish I need for my recipes. I return to the restaurant around 10 A.M. and prepare for the lunchtime opening. We are open from 11 A.M. to 3 P.M. We then have our own lunch and prepare for the evening session from 5 P.M. to 9:30 P.M. When business is good we can expect around sixty customers a day, but when it is bad this can fall to around forty. I like my customers. My restaurant is in central Tokyo which is where ordinary people live. Whole families often come to eat with me, and everyone is interesting and friendly.

My dream is to own a restaurant in one of the really smart parts of Tokyo.*

1. What did Hiroshi Asagi have to do to become a cook?
2. How has owning his own restaurant affected Hiroshi Asagi's life style? Would you like to trade places with him? Why or why not?

---

*"I never take extended vacations" in *We Live in Japan* by Kazuhide Kawamata, 1984, The Bookwright Press, pp. 28–29. Reprinted by permission.

EXAMINATIONS

To get into junior high school, high school, and university, Japanese students must pass difficult examinations. Because the number of openings are limited and the educational standards vary, students compete fiercely to do well in the exams and to get into the best schools. They hope that by attending the best schools, they will improve their chances of getting a good job after graduation.

Although Japanese schools have produced a well-educated and highly skilled work force, many Japanese still are critical of their nation's educational system. They feel that the fierce competition that exists has had bad effects on many Japanese youths. Below, a Japanese author discusses this problem:

> Japan's system of education has been reduced to a contest to pass examinations rather than a means by which students are intellectually nourished. Failure at school will influence any child's future so most parents are obsessed with sending their children to "better" schools.
>
> Japan is full of cram schools called "juku" where children are given extra training in how to cope successfully with tests. The juku method is based entirely on memory drills and has nothing to do with understanding a subject. Some of the juku students are as young as three or four years old, and they spend at a minimum two hours a day in order to qualify for acceptance in kindergarten.
>
> Roughly 180,000 juku are in service for five million pupils, aged 7 to 15. This means that at least 30 percent of all children in the compulsory grades from elementary school through junior high school attend extra classes after school. . . . In Japan, . . . a number of children commit suicide every year either before exams or after failing them. . . .
>
> . . . Private schools tend to offer more freedom than the public schools which are run by . . . the Ministry of Education. There are also striking differences between public and private schools because of methods of selecting teachers and textbooks. In public schools, both are rigidly controlled by the government.
>
> Many private schools take children from kindergarten through high school and in a few cases even through university levels.

These Tokyo public high school students attend class 5 ½ days a week and study such subjects as the Japanese language, math, science, social studies, art, music, and physical education. They are also offered job training. Today, nearly one-third of all upper secondary students attend private schools. Why do many Japanese parents send their children to juku?

Like other teenagers in different parts of the world, these Japanese teenage boys are spending part of the afternoon reading their favorite magazines and comics. What do many Japanese youth do for entertainment?

Once accepted, therefore, a student does not have to strive desperately to succeed in examinations since he can move on to the next grade with teachers' recommendations.

Obviously, many parents consider the expensive tuition, entrance fees and huge donations involved in private education all worthwhile. . . .

Some parents, however, strongly support public education. Masanori Iwashita, for instance, sends both of his daughters to public elementary schools near their home in Chofu City. In the public schools, Iwashita says, "children learn automatically that there are very different kinds of people in society; consequently they cope with each situation. Private school is expensive and walled-off and detached from the reality of life."

Whether they are in public or private schools, most students are faced with entrance examinations to universities so every day in high school is spent concentrating on entrance examinations. Once accepted, students can relax since they are virtually assured of passing.

This is only a temporary refuge, however, because soon the students are employed by companies with strict schedules which will continue for the rest of their lives.*

SOCIAL LIFE

Despite the emphasis on education, life is not all work for Japanese youth, who enjoy rock music, modern fashions, motor bikes, television and movies, and comic books. Many young people are members of youth clubs, which meet after school. At these meetings, club members can pursue their personal interests and hobbies. Sports, such as baseball and judo, also are popular. Below, a young Japanese explains how and why he became interested in judo and how it has influenced his life:

> I was born in Kumamoto district of Kyūshū. . . . In traditional Japanese folklore, people from this part of the country have been called *mokkasu,* which means stubborn or hard to please. I'm afraid this is right in my case. From an early age I was unyielding, stubborn and extremely

---

*"Fear of failing crucial exams fills Japan's 'cram schools' with students" by Yoshiko Sakurai in *WorldPaper*, January 1984, p. 13. Reprinted by permission.

A black-belted judo master teaches a young boy one of the methods of throwing an opponent. Judo developed from the ancient martial art known as jujutsu. *How are the martial arts different from modern sports?*

rough. I was big even as a child at kindergarten—as big as children in the second and third grade. . . . Unfortunately my size and muscular power caused some problems in the playground. Sometimes fights would get out of hand, and, without intending it, I would hurt others and make them cry. So when I was 9, my mother decided to send me to the local judo school where I could let off steam.

Judo, like karate and kendo [a Japanese form of fencing], is one of the Japanese martial arts. The big difference between these activities and modern sports is that in the martial arts, the spiritual side is very important. In judo we improve our skills by repeatedly practicing attacking or defending movements, and the aim is not only to increase our physical strength, but our spiritual strength as well. This is the way that the martial arts have been used to train body and soul for centuries. . . .

For someone like me who loved to be active, judo was most suitable. I started to practice enthusiastically and after only four months I won the Kumamoto Judo Tournament. . . . In a few years I became the best in Japan for my age and people started calling me "Monster Child." At about this time I moved to the Kanagawa district near Tokyo in search of the best school to develop my judo. I also enrolled in Tokai University to continue my studies. In my second year here I won the All Japan Judo Tournament. Then in my fourth year all my dreams came true and I won the World Championship title. Since then I have held the All Japan title for six consecutive years, and the World title twice.

It's now fifteen years since I first started judo. It's difficult to continue anything so long, and especially difficult when it is something as demanding as judo. Although practice is important, it is not good enough just to put in a lot of hours. What counts is the amount of mental and physical concentration you put into your practice in a set period of time. It is not possible to win with muscle power alone. To bring one's strength into play one must have physical and spiritual power. This is the fascination and charm of judo and is the reason why I have devoted all my youth to it.

My day begins at 6:30 A.M. and I am hard at work by 7 o'clock. I take a break mid-morning to do my research work at the university and continue my judo practice at 4:30 P.M. for a further three hours. Altogether I suppose I average about five or six hours' practice a day.

I wish to continue judo all my life. And my ultimate ambition? To win a gold medal at the next Olympic Games.*

1. What pressures do Japanese youth face in school?
2. Why do some Japanese prefer private schools to public ones?
3. What are some of the leisure activities enjoyed by Japanese youth?

---

*"Judo develops the mind and body together" in *We Live in Japan* by Kazuhide Kawamata, 1984, The Bookwright Press, pp. 26–27. Reprinted by permission.

EXPLORATION
JAPAN

Over the years, Japanese life styles have undergone many changes. Study the four photographs that appear below. Then explain how each relates to at least one of the following aspects of life style today: marriage, home, family, women, education, leisure activities.

CHAPTER 19 REVIEW

POINTS TO REMEMBER

1. In traditional Japan, the family was the center of national life, and each family member was expected to follow certain rules of conduct. Today, although family ties still remain strong, family members are allowed more freedom and individual expression.
2. Although traditionally Japanese marriages have been arranged by parents, today that is not always the case, and many young people are choosing their own marriage partners.
3. Many Japanese live in smaller family groups today than in the past. They try, however, to maintain family ties associated with the past.
4. While in traditional Japan the status of women was lower than that of men, women today make important family decisions and are better educated than in the past. However, among many Japanese, traditional ideas of the woman's role still remain strong.
5. The Japanese youth of today enjoy greater freedoms than did the Japanese youth of earlier generations.
6. Japanese schools and universities have produced a well-educated and highly skilled work force. Despite this, many Japanese remain critical of the educational system and the competition brought on by examinations because they feel that the fierce competition has had bad effects on many Japanese youths.
7. Despite the emphasis on education, Japanese youth find time to enjoy such activities as music, television, and sports. Most are members of youth clubs, which meet after school.

VOCABULARY

Identify

Kobe   Saitama   Yuri Kunno   Kyūshū

DISCUSSING IMPORTANT IDEAS

1. Do you think the following statement is true? "Even though in today's Japan the roles of individual family members have changed from those of the past, Japan is still basically a male-dominated society." Explain your answer, and give examples to support it.
2. How do marriage arrangements and weddings in Japan compare with those in your country?
3. Young people often are more influenced by friends than by family members. What effect has this had on family life in Japan? What effect do you think it will have in the future on the traditional Japanese concept of family?
4. What has been the result of Japan's emphasis on education? Is the same true in your country? Give examples to support your answers.

Developing Skills

IDENTIFYING TRENDS AND MAKING FORECASTS

Almost any magazine or newspaper you read today will probably have an article that talks about *trends*, general movements in a certain direction or changes or shifts of direction. There are many kinds of trends—weather trends, housing trends, fashion trends, education trends, business trends, political trends. A trend in politics, for example, may be toward more conservative or more liberal policies.

Some trends are *fads*, ideas that take hold for a while and then lose popularity. Other trends, however, remain and become accepted. It is these trends that most often are used in making a *forecast*, or suggestions as to future developments.

Some forecasts are merely "good guesses." Others can be backed up by solid evidence. Even those forecasts supported by the strongest of evidence, however, can be wrong. Weather forecasts are a good example of this. Fronts and systems may become stalled and refuse to move as predicted. A hurricane may take new and unexpected directions. In the same way, trends in society may be stopped or turned toward another direction by new developments.

Using the steps indicated in the following example will help you to identify trends and to make forecasts based on those trends:

1. Read the following passage carefully.

    During the last century, a great many changes have taken place in Japan. One area in which change can be seen is in the attitude toward family and the roles of family members. In traditional Japan, for example, the family was the center of national life. Younger family members respected and cared for grandparents, aunts, and uncles. The father or eldest male was the center of the family and was in charge. He expected—and received—total obedience from his wife and children.

    Today, family ties are still strong. But, at the same time, individual family members have more freedoms. Younger family members tend to be influenced more by their friends than by the members of their family. The male no longer has as much power over family affairs. Since he spends most of his time at work rather than at home, the wife and mother often becomes the center of the family.

2. Identify the trends, and describe them in your own words.

    *(The trends are
    (a) looser family ties;
    (b) fewer restrictions on the activities of individual family members;
    (c) a lessening of the authority of the male as head of a family.)*

3. Ask yourself what might happen in the future if the trends you have identified continue.

    (Family may become unimportant; Individual family members may do exactly as they please without being concerned about what other family members think about their actions or activities; The male may cease to be head of the family and have no say at all about what the members of his family do.)

4. Ask yourself what kind of developments could change the trends you have identified.

    (The work week could become shorter, allowing males more time at home with their families.)

5. Based on the answers to the questions you asked yourself in steps 3 and 4, make your forecast.

    (Forecast: If current trends continue and the work week does not become shorter, the concept of family will be less important to individuals than other things, and the male will lose his dominant status.)

For practice in identifying trends and making forecasts, refer to the material on women on pages 305 and 306, and then use the steps suggested above to identify trends and make a forecast about the future role of women in Japanese society.

CHAPTER 20
WORK AND LEISURE

1. What effect has a prosperous economy had on Japan and the Japanese?
2. What do the Japanese do to enjoy their leisure time?

Some two miles [3.2 kilometers] north of the glittering lights of Tokyo's Ginza district is a lesser-known commercial enclave that, in its way, is every bit as dazzling. Called Akihabara, it is a booming bazaar that spills over 20 blocks and is probably the world's most fiercely competitive market for electrical goods. In hundreds of sprawling stores and cubbyhole shops [decorated] with brightly colored banners proclaiming bargains, customers can buy almost any type of vacuum cleaner or videocassette recorder, refrigerator or radio, humidifier or home computer. Familiar brands such as Sony and Sharp are surrounded by scores of less familiar names: Nakamichi, Denon and Oki. At one store can be found 205 varieties of stereo headphones, 100 different color television sets and 75 kinds of record turntables. While some stores are relatively sedate, others flash lights, blast out rock music and station salesmen on the sidewalk to [pitch for] patrons. . . .

The bedlam at Akihabara goes a long way toward explaining why Japan has conquered consumer electronics markets around the world. For Japanese companies, competition begins at home. To survive and prosper, they must turn out products with exceptionally low prices, outstanding quality, and innovative features. If Japanese firms can outpace their local rivals, foreign competitors often prove to be pushovers. Says a top Japanese electronics executive: "Our target is not some other country; our target is ourselves."*

As can be seen in the above article, business life in modern Japan is hectic. Since the 1960's, the Japanese have been among the world's leaders in technology and trade. Today Japan ranks third, after the United States and the Soviet Union, in the production of goods and services for a worldwide market.

The Japanese have a highly skilled labor force that values hard work, group loyalty, and innovation. In the drive for markets and profits, the Japanese have been willing to learn from other countries and to improve on what they have learned. The result of this is a strong economy known throughout the world for its efficiency, high growth rates, and low unemployment. Many other industrial nations now look to Japan as a model for the improvement of their own economies.

Japan's economic success, however, has not been achieved without some loss. The fast pace of industrialization has made daily life more stressful. Rapid change has undermined many of the traditional ideas and practices that united the Japanese for centuries. Such public services as housing, health care, and pollution control have been neglected. Even so, most experts believe that many of these problems can be solved and that the strengths of the economy far outweigh the weaknesses.

---

*"Fighting It Out" by Charles P. Alexander in *TIME*, August 1, 1983, p. 38. Copyright 1983 Time Inc. All rights reserved. Reprinted by permission from TIME.

WORK— A WAY OF LIFE

Japan's economic success has been aided in great part by the business skills and attitudes of leading Japanese companies. While workers in smaller, less efficient industries often receive low wages and few employment benefits, those in the larger ones generally receive good wages and are guaranteed employment for life. These firms take pride in the quality of their products. To ensure excellence, they promote good working relationships between managers and workers. As a result, although their life styles and daily work tasks may be very different, bosses and employees often view their jobs and work-related issues in much the same way. This is seen below in an article about Toshihiko Yamashita, president of the Matsushita Electric Industrial Company, and Yoshinobu Saito, one of the firm's sales engineers:

> Matsushita President Yamashita earns $330,000 a year, and Saito makes $12,900. But except for age and experience they seem almost interchangeable. The differences between them stem mostly from the less formal, Westernized style of Japan's younger generation.
>
> Yamashita, the soft-spoken chief executive, wears conservative business attire and lives in the rolling hills outside Osaka in a graceful seven-room house with immaculately pruned shrubbery. Trim and athletic, he favors a traditional Japanese diet. His breakfast that day consisted of grilled fish, rice and bean-paste soup.
>
> Saito, the young, eager sales engineer, wears more modish [clothes] and lives three miles [4.8 kilometers] away in a $62,500 four-room house that also has a well-cared-for garden. Saito bought the house two years ago with his own savings, plus loans from his company and bank. Despite monthly house payments of $152 and an additional $1,810 deducted from his yearly bonus to pay off the mortgage, he still saves 15% of his salary. While Saito likes Japanese food, he started his day with a Western-style breakfast of coffee, bread and two hard-boiled eggs.
>
> Both men's fathers were working-class, and both [men] ended their formal educations with technical high school, where

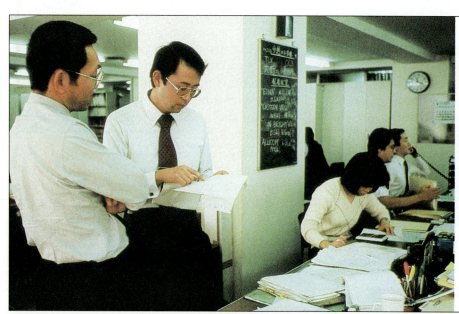

Crowded desks and busy workers attest to the Japanese ethic of hard work, dedication, and loyalty to one's company. What are some of the benefits of working for a major company in Japan?

CHAPTER 20　　WORK AND LEISURE　　317

It is not unusual in Japan for large companies to provide their employees such extra benefits as dormitories and housing, child-care, discount stores, and recreational facilities. In this photo, factory workers play a form of table tennis over a low net on an outdoor court provided by the factory owners. What do Japanese bosses and employees often have in common?

they learned their first phrases in English. After graduation, each went to work for Matsushita—Yamashita in 1938, and Saito in 1970. Neither has ever worked for any other company.

The chauffeur called for Yamashita promptly at 7:50 A.M. in an indigo Mercedes-Benz limousine. His wife Kikuko, 57, accompanied him outside his house and bowed farewell. Acknowledging this ritual with a nod, Yamashita climbed into the back seat. He greeted his driver by saying: "It's going to be another hectic day."

Saito's departure for work at 6:40 A.M. was not quite a photocopy. Etsuko also bowed at the front door, but then Saito hugged her and chased her playfully around his tiny gray Mitsubishi Minica 360. Once in the driver's seat, he called out to his spouse: "Another busy day!"

When they arrived at work, the two men followed entirely different routines. From 8:20 A.M. to 5:30 P.M., Yamashita attended more than a dozen conferences, most of them to hand out citations to the company's most productive employees and to discuss the future direction of the company. Like most Japanese executives,

Yamashita puts a high priority on communications between top management and the rest of the organization. Said the president: "You simply could not or would not make any important decision without first achieving a consensus [general agreement] within your corporation."

So much of Yamashita's day was taken up by discussions with employees that only 32 minutes were left for reading and desk work. . . .

Saito, by contrast, spent much of his day in solitude. Before work began, he sat for 15 minutes in the plant cafeteria drinking coffee and poring over newspapers. Then at 8 A.M. he stood at attention next to his desk and, along with his fellow workers, sang the company song, which begins: "A bright heart overflowing with life linked together, Matsushita Electric." This is an honored tradition in many corporations throughout Japan. Saito's job is to help TV distributors understand the technical details of Matsushita products. . . .

Except for a 45-minute lunch in the company cafeteria, Saito sat at his desk most of the time. But he did not feel isolated. Said he: "Never do I feel like a cog in a

CASE STUDY
JAPAN

SERVICE INDUSTRIES

The prosperity of recent years has encouraged the growth in Japan of **service industries**, industries designed to meet the needs of consumers. These include fast-food chains and amusement parks, many of which are based on models from the United States. Below, a journalist comments on this recent trend:

The Japanese first tasted American fast food —Howard Johnson's and Kentucky Fried Chicken —at the 1970 World Exposition in Ōsaka. At the time, their income per capita [per person] was $1,702. . . . By 1980, that number was $7,672, or close to the $10,094 of the United States, and American-style fast food franchises, as well as amusement parks, supermarkets, and other service businesses, had sprouted from Kyūshū to Hokkaidō.

Indeed, McDonald's (with more than 450 Japanese outlets), Kentucky Fried Chicken (430), and other U.S. fast-food eateries probably owe little of their success to their cuisine; the more than 1,500 take-out sushi [raw fish] outlets run by one Japanese company attest to the superior appeal of native dishes. Both Japanese and American chains, however, have profited from the growth in disposable income and from the fact that 40 percent of all married women now work at least part-time.

Meanwhile, a new breed of "office ladies" —young, single working women living with their parents—has entered the consumer ranks, and the slow spread of the five-day work week has allowed more time for excursions and amusements.

The markets thus created or expanded were made to order for the formula . . . devised by U.S. service companies. One example is Tokyo Disneyland, which opened in April, 1983. While it did not invest in the project, Walt Disney Productions provided the local developer with 300 volumes detailing everything from costume design to crowd control. The result: a 114-acre [45.6 hectares] park identical to its counterparts in California and Florida. In 1983, some 10.4 million Japanese strolled with Mickey and Minnie, rode on the Mark Twain Riverboat, or listened to Slue Foot Sue sing. . . .

Until recently, notes Tokyo economist Kusaka Kimindo . . . , "Japanese companies, bound by a reliance on 'serious' industries, neglected to develop amusements." Now they make and market Windsurfers, hang gliders, and other "fun" items—for home and, of course, export. . . .

The Japanese are also taking service technology a few steps further. Some five million vending units sell everything from shoes to mixed drinks. And at a suburban Tokyo supermarket, robots unload trucks and restock aisles. In Japan . . . , leisure and prosperity are now the mothers of commercial invention.*

1. Why have service industries grown in recent years in Japan?
2. What does the growth in Japan of such industries as fast-food chains and amusement parks indicate to you about the current Japanese attitude toward the West?

---

*"Consumption As Culture" by James Gibney. From *The Wilson Quarterly*, Summer, 1985, p. 61. Copyright 1985 by the Woodrow Wilson International Center for Scholars.

huge impersonal machine." Occasionally he went off to consult with the experts on the assembly line. . . . Then at 4:45 P.M., he and his colleagues stood and again sang the Matsushita song. That was not, however, the end of Saito's day. He returned to the cafeteria for a light supper of grilled fish and then walked upstairs to a 2 1/2-hour English-conversation class. Saito returned home at 9 P.M., when he and Etsuko shared a snack. . . .

Yamashita finished his day at the plant at 5:30 P.M. He did not take time to chant the company song. Instead, he hurried off to entertain a few clients at a restaurant. Such affairs are an integral part of Japanese business life, and Yamashita must often attend them five nights a week. He got home at 10 P.M.

Both men were up early the next morning because, as one old hand at Matsushita says, "Every day is a samurai duel."*

1. What do some Japanese industries do to ensure excellence?
2. What is a typical day like for some company executives? For some employees?

URBAN LIFE STYLES

Seventy-six percent of Japanese live in urban areas. In appearance, these areas closely resemble similar areas in western countries. Office buildings are modern, traffic is heavy, and shoppers and commuters crowd the commercial districts. But, in Japan, the past remains very much a part of urban life. Along the narrow side streets of most cities are small shops that sell such traditional items as straw mats, elaborately dressed Japanese dolls, and the brushes and sticks used in Japanese calligraphy. Parks, gardens, and shrines also are found close to the modern districts.

Since the Pacific War, Japanese cities have grown tremendously because of the large numbers of people who have migrated from rural to urban areas. As a result, like cities in many other parts of the world, cities in Japan are faced with such problems as overcrowding, housing shortages, and air and water pollution. At the same time, however, the crime rate in Japanese cities is lower than that of many large cities in the United States. And, although there are poor neighborhoods, there are few slums. A large number of the city dwellers enjoy a comfortable standard of living.

Most middle-class Japanese live in suburban areas surrounding the city centers. In recent years, these areas have grown in size and importance. As indicated by a Japanese journalist in the article below, some are taking on a personality of their own:

> It's fashionable these days for the young people of Kichijoji, in suburban Tokyo, to call their town "George," an intentional Westernization of the ordinary nickname "Joji." Several of the more trendy tea rooms and boutiques here even have renamed themselves George-this or George-that. The name is symbolic of the changes that have taken place in this once quiet and obscure village in the western reaches of Tokyo: to recall an English-language slang term of bygone days, a term meaning "okay," everything is "George" here.
>
> The renown of Kichijoji as a focal point of fashion and "youth culture" has spread far and wide, to the extent that, indeed, many Tokyoites think it is a city. Actually, it's just the name of a train station, and the square kilometer or so of shopping malls and entertainment parlors around it. . . .
>
> Until some ten years ago, Kichijoji was known, if at all, as merely a part of Musashino City (population 130,000) and shared that community's progressive social

---

*"A Daily 'Samurai Duel'" in *Time*, March 30, 1981, p. 63. Copyright 1981 Time Inc. All rights reserved. Reprinted by permission from TIME.

and political attitudes. The surrounding region was still largely devoted to farming, but as the distinction between city and countryside became less distinct due to the westward expansion of Tokyo's "bedroom towns [towns in which people live but do not work]," long-time residents here came to think of themselves not as hicks but "suburbanites." Gradually their numbers were balanced by newly-arrived, upper-middle-class intellectuals, drawn by Kichijoji's relative closeness to jobs in the center city.

The station is reached in less than 45 minutes by express commuter train from Tokyo on either of two lines. . . . From the train platform, both the southern and northern sides of the station look similarly commercial. But a five-minute walk from the south exit takes you out of the shopping area, through a smattering of attractive private houses, to the edge of Inokashira Park, a haven for mothers and children, sweethearts, artists and nature lovers. The huge park focuses around a large kidney-shaped lake with a small, well-kept, vermilion-painted shrine at one end. Ducks and swans glide freely among the rowers in rented boats, undisturbed by the shiny fat carp swarming beneath them. In cherry-blossom season, the lake is ringed in delicate white and pink.

But this touch of "pretty" Japan is not nearly as interesting as what's happening on the northern side of the station, for it is there that dozens of fashionable boutiques, specialty shops and no fewer than four big-name department stores stand as proof that despite the explosion of Tokyo toward the suburbs, Kichijoji somehow resisted becoming just another "bedroom town."

"Today we might look lots more independent than some of the other little towns out this way," says the manager of a local cinema, a man born and raised in Kichijoji. "But really, we've always been kind of stubborn and conservative in some ways. Our shopkeepers, for instance, stick pretty close together. . . ."

"We did such things as give streets chic names like 'Cherry-nade' and 'Penny Lane'," said the cinema manager, "and did other things to try and make Kichijoji a young spot. We even got teenagers to paint bright pictures on the walls. But we never pretended to be a real culture spot, if you know what I mean."

. . . One by one, as other large department stores announced plans to move into

Typical, tile-roofed, wooden homes line the streets of this suburban working-class residential area. Also visible are modern apartment buildings that have been built in recent years to lessen the severe housing shortage that still exists in most Japanese cities. What other problems face Japanese cities today?

CHAPTER 20   WORK AND LEISURE

In suburban Kichijoji, many middle-class residents live in modern homes like this one with a television and radio (in the corner) and such western-style furnishings as floor-to-ceiling drapes, dining table and chairs, and carpeting. How does Kichijoji differ from typical suburban Japanese "bedroom towns"?

the area, the smaller merchants whose wares included apparel, food, games, records, books, accessories, audio and so forth—items of interest to young people —began to restock and renovate. Sophisticated display techniques were instituted, and establishments that once merely bore the family name of their owners sprouted trendy new names—"boutique," "plaza," "corner" and "live spot." The sons and daughters of middle-class families, born and raised in the economic boom times of the 60s, wholeheartedly supported the changes and felt pride to be a part of it all. News spread about the town's "new look" and before long the district began to draw young shoppers and fun-seekers from neighboring communities.

Kichijoji has turned out to be ideal for those who seek to satisfy their needs for adventure and new things without travelling all the way into (and facing the confusion of) downtown Tokyo itself.*

1. What are some characteristics of Japanese cities? What makes them different from many western cities?

---

*"Kichijoji: Suburbia Comes of Age" in *Japan Pictorial*, Vol. 6, No. 3, 1983, pp. 13–14. Reprinted by permission.

2. How has Kichijoji changed in the last ten years or so?

RURAL LIFE STYLES

The 24 percent of Japanese who live in rural areas is made up chiefly of farmers and their families. Although generally these rural dwellers earn less than city dwellers, their standard of living has improved in recent years. Most have a small house, a color-television set, and modern kitchen appliances. Many have cars.

Almost all Japanese farmers own their own land. Most farms are small—about 20 acres (8 hectares). But because of the use of chemical fertilizers and advanced agricultural methods, crop yields from these farms are among the highest in the world. Since land is scarce, nearly every available piece is farmed. The practices of growing two crops a year and **terracing,** or planting in circular rows on the sloping sides of raised banks of earth, are put into effect whenever possible. In the following passage, a Japanese woman tells what being a farmer means to her:

The district of Nagano where I live lies in the center of Honshū—the main island of Japan. My farm is surrounded by high mountain peaks, and the winters can be very severe, with temperatures dropping well below freezing. Fortunately, my village rarely has a heavy fall of snow, but if there is a freak storm it makes it very hard to get down to the town to buy food. The climate in summer is cool and fresh, and our occasional visitors from Tokyo are always thrilled by the clear mountain air.

So, it is up here in the mountains that I manage my 60 hectares (150 acres) of rice paddies. To be precise I should say *our* rice paddies, but as it happens my father is very old, my husband works at a dam construction site nearby and my son and his wife have moved to Tokyo. So, with the way things are, it's up to me to manage the land of our ancestors as best I can.

Despite mechanization, which has made farm work easier, many people no longer want to work on the land. Young people, especially, reject farm work and leave for the cities. Husbands, too, may earn more in the towns, and this often leaves the housewives like me to do most of the farmwork. This tendency has become a big problem in the farming world.

I'm up by 5:30 at the latest every morning. My husband has to leave for work at 7:00 A.M., so I cook breakfast and do all my cleaning and washing before leaving home for the rice paddies by 8:00 A.M. My rice plants are marsh plants so they always need to be covered with sufficient water. The first thing I do every morning is to check the water level, as the water I let into the fields the previous day often disappears overnight. When this happens I open the sluice gates and get the level back to normal as soon as possible.

The busiest times of the year for rice farmers are at planting time in early summer, at the weeding season in midsummer, and at harvest time in the autumn. During these periods I usually work in the fields right through the day until dark—perhaps stopping once for a chat with neighboring wives over a cup of tea.

In my village, planting time takes place around mid-May. Once we start we cannot stop until it is all done, whatever the weather, or we will miss the right time. After this we work full speed on the weed-

Japanese farmers are among the most successful in the world. Although their farms are generally small, they produce very high yields per unit of land, making the farms very productive. Rice, being harvested here by a farm couple, is Japan's most important crop, occupying better than half of the country's farmland. What has enabled Japanese farmers to be so productive?

ing through June and July. We spray weedkiller, but the weeds seem to emerge as fast as we spray. Still, if we left the weeds and neglected to spray our plants against disease, all our previous hard work would turn into water bubbles! When the plants are ripe we cut off the water supply to the paddies and the harvest begins. With the help of a combine harvester, which is shared by all the farms in the village, we usually finish the harvest in ten days. And that is the end of rice farming for the year.

When the cold winter blows over the land I am free from outside work. Then even I have time to enjoy my hobbies. I knit toys and clothes for my family and it is a great privilege to enjoy a cup of tea sitting round the warm stove with my friends.

I have been living this life ever since I was married. It is certainly true that farming is not an easy life and I cannot blame young people for preferring the bright lights of the city. But I love this land, and wish to continue farming as long as my health permits.*

1. How many Japanese live in rural areas? What do most do to earn a living?
2. What is a typical day like for a Japanese farmer?

RECREATION

Although the Japanese are hard workers, they also enjoy their leisure time. For most, Sunday is the free day of the week—the day they do most of their shopping. On Sundays, and on any other days they have the time, the Japanese enjoy a variety of sports and games. Many practice the traditional martial arts, or go fishing, hunting, jogging, or mountain climbing. People in the cities often play a pinball game called *pachinko.*

BASEBALL

Spectator sports, such as soccer, baseball, and a Japanese form of wrestling called *sumo,* also are popular with Japanese of all ages. As a Japanese journalist explains below, one of the most popular sports of all is baseball:

> Few would argue that the sport most watched by the average Japanese is baseball. At the professional level, the sport consists of two six-team leagues, which battle through 130-game seasons lasting nearly seven months. In terms of sheer popular interest, the nod goes to the national high school tournaments, held each spring and summer. Each and every game is broadcast from start to finish on both television and radio, with no commercial breaks. Seven sports newspapers published in Tokyo focus their coverage on baseball. And, for those who find the lure of the diamond too great to resist, there are many varieties of sandlot baseball (known literally as "grass baseball" in Japanese) to indulge in.
>
> The popularity of sandlot ball may be glimpsed by visiting a local park or river bed any Sunday. From dawn to dusk, teams come and go, playing their games and moving along. There are children's teams with mothers in tow, teams of balding, overweight middle-aged office workers, and lately, many more women's teams.
>
> The craze is no longer limited to weekends. The popularity of "morning baseball" is now on the rise, with teams assembling long before office hours to play. When the games are over, all players depart, naturally, for their respective jobs. . . .
>
> It is difficult to calculate the active sandlot baseball population, because many of the games are played by pickup teams

---
*"It's up to me to manage the land of our ancestors" in *We Live in Japan* by Kazuhide Kawamata, 1984, The Bookwright Press, pp. 24–25. Reprinted by permission.

who gather for a single afternoon's enjoyment. The Leisure Development Center estimates the total at around 12.5 million players—about ten percent of the population. And with almost all male adults having some experience with the sport, the potential roster is certainly much greater. . . .

Although seldom given the attention it deserves, a major factor behind the popularity of baseball among the masses in Japan is a [locally made] ball, invented over six decades ago. The standard baseball has remained basically the same ever since the sport was introduced in Japan in 1872—a cork core, wrapped tightly with leather or horsehide. . . . Whether thrown or batted, such a ball presents a genuine physical threat to anyone untrained in the finer points of the game.

This problem was solved in 1919, when a Japanese developed a hollow rubber "soft-type" baseball. Differing from the larger "softball" pitched underhanded, this ball is the same size as its standard counterpart, and may be gripped and pitched in normal overhand fashion. Even the hardest contact with the body will cause little more than a colorful bruise. The safety of this ball has helped popularize baseball among the masses, as it gives every sandlotter the satisfaction of playing the same basic game as the pros on TV.

Yet, sandlot ball is not without its drawbacks. The greatest is the shortage of fields. Playing time in full-fledged professional stadiums is expensive, and must be booked months in advance. Use of fields managed by local authorities is almost always determined by lottery. The rising population density in urban areas often forces team managers to search out sandlots (real ones) or river beds as game sites.

Over the past few years, the rise in tennis, skiing, golf and other leisure-oriented sports has caused many younger people to lose interest in baseball. But the appeal of the grass diamond is deep-rooted, and is more than capable of weathering this and other challenges.

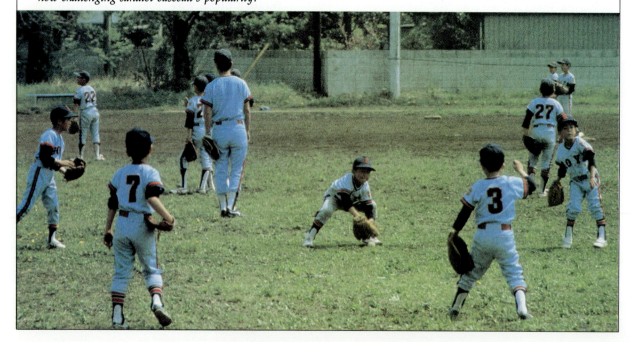

These young players belong to one of Japan's many youth baseball teams. What sports are now challenging sandlot baseball's popularity?

Yet boyhood dreams be as they may, probably the greatest secret behind the popularity of sandlot ball is that it is played primarily for fun. Why, almost all team managers announce to their teams before the game: "All right, get out there and fight. But don't anybody get hurt."*

TELEVISION

Another popular pastime among the Japanese is watching television. In fact, according to a study conducted in 1982 by the Japan Broadcasting Corporation, the Japanese lead the world in the number of hours spent in front of the television set. The study showed that the average Japanese family spent 8 hours and 15 minutes a day watching television. In the excerpt below from a magazine article, a journalist comments on the Japanese passion for television:

> In few countries does television exert as much influence as it does in Japan. As Tokyo critic Satō Kuwashi puts it, "Most Japanese worship TV with blind devotion...."
>
> ... So enamored are the Japanese of the medium that, when polled recently on which one of five items—newspapers, TV, telephones, automobiles, and refrigerators—they would keep if they could have only *one*, 31 percent ... answered "television."
>
> NHK [Nippon Hōsō Kyōkai, or Japan Broadcasting Corporation] spokesman Yoshinari Mayumi asserts that television "fulfills a collective Japanese urge—to be all of a group together, watching TV." Indeed, Japan's "group" mentality has encouraged the medium's rapid growth. In 1959, six years after broadcasting began, networks advertised the marriage of crown Prince Akihito with the slogan "Let's all watch the Prince's marriage on TV." Japanese bought four million sets that year....
>
> During the 1970's, color TVs, cars, and "coolers" (air conditioners) made up the "three Cs"—a trinity of appliances, possession of which signified membership in the middle class. Today, 98 percent of all Japanese households have color sets....
>
> Most Japanese TV sets stay tuned to one of the two channels operated by NHK, a nonprofit network created by the government 32 years ago....
>
> On NHK's Channel One in Tokyo, viewers get a steady diet of news (38 percent of broadcast time), soap operas, sports, variety shows (23 percent), and "cultural" programs (16 percent) such as concerts, local folk festivals, and a recent 30-minute documentary on ancient Chinese caravan routes. Channel Three serves educational fare: high school science courses, music instruction, English, Russian, and Chinese lessons, and the finer points of *Go*, a Japanese game akin to checkers.
>
> Even the NHK programs that fall in the "entertainment" category take pains to promote national values. One of the more successful Japanese soap operas was NHK's "Oshin," the rags-to-riches story of a waif who became a supermarket magnate. From 1983 to 1984, the series ran for a total of 297 episodes....
>
> Japan's five commercial networks ... are far less [educational]. Their most popular offerings are homegrown variety specials hosted by comedians and musicians. ... U.S. imports fill 15 to 20 percent of airtime, but programs such as "Dallas" and "Kojak" seem relatively tame.... Japanese prefer their own samurai dramas, soap operas, and detective stories.... They also enjoy ... sports programs.*

1. What sports and games do the Japanese enjoy in their leisure time? Why is baseball so popular?
2. How do the Japanese regard television?

---

*"Grass Baseball: The Opiate of the Masses?" in *Japan Pictorial*, Vol. 8, No. 2, 1985, pp. 21–22. Reprinted by permission.

*"The Japanese and TV: 'Blind Devotion'" by James Gibney. From *The Wilson Quarterly*, Summer 1985, pp. 72–73. Copyright 1985 by The Woodrow Wilson International Center for Scholars.

CHAPTER 20 REVIEW

POINTS TO REMEMBER

1. The business skills and attitudes of leading Japanese companies have aided Japan's economic success. These companies take pride in the quality of their product and work to promote good working relationships between their managers and their workers.
2. In Japan, the past remains very much a part of urban life.
3. Since the Pacific War, Japanese cities have grown tremendously. Although the cities are faced with such problems as overcrowding, housing shortages, and air and water pollution, the crime rate is relatively low, there are few slums, and a great many city dwellers enjoy a comfortable standard of living.
4. Most middle-class Japanese live in suburban areas which, in recent years, have grown in size and importance.
5. Most of the 24 percent of the Japanese population who live in rural areas farm the land. Although most farms are small, they have high crop yields due to the use of chemical fertilizers and advanced agricultural methods.
6. In their leisure time, the Japanese enjoy a variety of activities, games, and sports. Among the most popular are baseball and television.
7. In recent years, Japan's prosperity has encouraged the growth of service industries, many of which are based on models from the United States.

VOCABULARY

Identify
Akihabara   Yoshinobu Saito   Kichijoji   Nagano
Toshihiko Yamashita

Define
service industries   terracing   *pachinko*   *sumo*

DISCUSSING IMPORTANT IDEAS

1. Since the Pacific War, Japan's productivity has increased a great deal. What reasons can you give for this?
2. Most Japanese work long hours most days of the week. What effect do you think this might have on their family lives? On their regard for and practice of traditional Japanese values and beliefs?
3. In what ways are Japanese suburbs such as Kichijoji similar to those in your country? In what ways are they different?
4. Why do many Japanese no longer want to work on the land? If you were a young Japanese, would you prefer to live and work in the countryside or in an urban area? Give reasons for your answer.

DEVELOPING SKILLS

PREPARING NOTE CARDS FOR A RESEARCH REPORT

At one time or another, every student is asked to write a report. One of the steps involved in doing this is careful *research*, the collecting of information about a particular subject. Another is organizing that research. One way of doing this is to prepare note cards.

Once you have selected or been given the topic of your paper and have determined the order of your main ideas, use the guidelines suggested in the following example to help you prepare note cards. The example is based on using this text as your only resource for a report on Japanese attitudes toward work. The information in parentheses is the information that might appear on your note cards.

1. On the first card, write the title of your report.
   (The Japanese and Work)
2. On the second card, state the principal theme of your report.
   (Statement of Principal Theme: Work is so important to the Japanese that it may be considered a way of life.)
3. On each card on which you write notes, also write the title of the report and the following information about the source you are using: title of work, name of author(s), name of publisher, copyright date, page numbers of pages used.
4. Your notes should consist of the main idea and supporting statements of each paragraph you read. These should be written in your own words rather than be copied word-for-word from the source. Direct quotations should be put in quotation marks.

*(Report Title: The Japanese and Work
Source Title:* Global Insights

*Authors: James Hantula et al.
Copyright Date: 1987
Publisher: Merrill Publishing Company
Page No: 316
Main Idea: Success of Japanese economy is partly due to business skills and big business attitudes
Supporting Statements:*
1. *Large companies pay well, provide job security, take pride in quality of their products*
2. *Good relationships promoted between management and labor*
3. *Attitudes of labor and management toward jobs and work-related issues much the same)*

5. After you have finished taking notes, prepare a summary card on which you state what you have concluded or learned.
   (Summary: Japan has a successful economy largely because of the Japanese attitude toward work. Management and labor work together and have similar views about work.
6. Prepare a separate set of cards to serve as a *bibliography*, a list of sources of information. Make up a separate card for each source you have used. For each source, indicate the following: name of author(s), title of work, location and name of publisher, copyright date, page numbers of pages from which you took notes.
7. Arrange your note cards in the order in which you plan to use the information in your report. You are now ready to draft a rough copy of your report.

For practice in this skill, research and prepare note cards for a report on a Japanese automobile plant or on Japanese martial arts.

UNIT 3 REVIEW

SUMMARY

According to legend, Japan was born of the sea, and throughout its long history, its island location off the coast of East Asia has given its people a sense of identity and protection. The sea, however, did not keep foreigners from influencing the Japanese. During Japan's early history, the greatest influence came from China. In modern times, the influence has been from the West. In both instances, the Japanese borrowed heavily from the cultures with which they came into contact. At the same time, however, they transformed the ideas and practices they borrowed and made them uniquely Japanese. They also passed on to those cultures Japanese traditions, customs, practices, and ideas.

Historians divide Japanese history into two major periods—traditional and modern. Traditional Japan—Japan before 1868—was ruled by warriors under the symbolic authority of an emperor. The Japanese honored the monarchy, which helped unite them as a people and brought them into contact with Asian peoples.

Modern Japan—Japan after 1868—became the leading military and industrial power of Asia. Under the rule of the Meiji, many reforms were introduced and many western institutions were established. At the same time, however, the Japanese experienced problems with foreign powers that led them into war. At the end of World War I, Japan was recognized as a major world power.

Events that took place in the years after World War I led the Japanese to become disillusioned with the West and to turn toward militarism. Before long, they were involved in a war in the Pacific. Following defeat in the Pacific War, Japan became a democracy allied to the United States and began to rebuild its economy. Today Japan is one of the world's great economic powers, and the Japanese enjoy a high standard of living. The people, however, have not allowed the traditional to be completely replaced by the modern. In Japan, the old and the new exist side by side.

REVIEW QUESTIONS

1. In what ways have Japan and the Japanese people been shaped by geography and environment?
2. In what arts have the Japanese excelled? How do these arts reflect the values of the people?
3. What factors distinguish Japan of the 1980's from Japan of the 1930's? Of the 1960's?
4. In what way does life in modern Japan reflect the culture of both the East and the West? Give examples to support your answer.

SUGGESTED ACTIVITIES

1. Draw a map showing the major landforms and population centers of modern Japan. Then, in a short essay, explain how geography has influenced patterns of settlement in the Japanese islands.
2. Working in a small group, construct a vertical or horizontal time line that identifies the major events in Japanese history.
3. Write a *haiku* that expresses a typical Japanese value, idea, or emotion.
4. Working with several classmates, write and present a skit to the class that presents modern Japan as viewed by the following: an 80-year-old farmer, a 50-year-old executive, a 25-year-old industrial worker, and a 16-year-old student.

Comparing Cultures

Language is an important part of any culture. It influences intellectual and artistic life and reflects and shapes a people's basic character. Read the information that follows about the Japanese language and the English language. Then compare and contrast the two.

THE JAPANESE LANGUAGE

Japanese, a language closely related to Turkish, Korean, and Mongolian, is spoken by 120 million people. It is not an easy language even for the Japanese. It is read and written from the top of a page to the bottom and from right to left. It can be written in several different ways. One involves *kanji*, the characters borrowed from the Chinese in the 500's. Each character represents a word; for example:

man,   flower, and   bird
人   花   鳥

The other way of writing involves *kana*, expressions that represent sounds rather than words. For example, to form the word *"kimono,"* three *kana* must be used:

ki,   mo, and   no
き   も   の

Because written Japanese is a mixture of *kanji* and *kana*, the Japanese must memorize hundreds of expressions before they can read and write their language. Although most books, newspapers, and magazines are written in *kanji* and *kana*, Japanese children are expected to learn the language in the alphabet of the West as well.

Spoken Japanese also exists in several forms. The most important are known as the intimate, the polite, and the honorific. The intimate is used in everyday speech, the polite for speaking in well-educated company, and the honorific to show respect for elders and superiors. All forms are spoken with equal stress on all syllables.

The Japanese language tends to express the moods of the speaker. It suggests, rather than states, ideas. For example, the Japanese form of "yes" and "no" actually means "I am hearing you" or "I am not hearing you," rather than "I agree with you" or "I disagree with you." Thus, to avoid confusion, foreigners must understand the way Japanese think and feel as well as the words they speak.

THE ENGLISH LANGUAGE

English, basically a Germanic language, is spoken by about 305 million people. It is an international language of science, of trade, and of diplomacy.

English is a flexible language that allows the speaker to express ideas clearly. With nearly 600,000 words, it has a larger vocabulary than any other language. It absorbs words from other languages. For example, the word "canyon" has its origin in Spanish, while the word "democracy" comes from Greek, the word "sherbet" from Arabic, and the word "restaurant" from French.

New words often are formed by combining existing words. The words "speedboat," "outcome," and "underground," for example, came about in this way. New words also are formed by adding syllables known as prefixes and suffixes to existing words. For example, adding the prefix "pre" (meaning "before") to the word "historic" forms a new word—"prehistoric." In the same way, joining the suffix "ment" to the word "move" creates the word "movement."

English is considered a difficult language to learn, especially for foreigners. It has a large number of exceptions to its rules, especially in regard to spelling and pronunciation. While certain words may have similar sounds, they often are spelled differently. The words "threw" and "through," for example, are pronounced the same way even though they are not spelled the same way. On the other hand, some words, such as "head" and "bead," are spelled similarly but pronounced differently. In spite of these difficulties, however, the language continues to grow and to be used by more people all over the world.

Unit Four

India and several other smaller countries make up the area known today as South Asia. Because of their location in the Indian Ocean, their closeness to the Soviet Union and the People's Republic of China, and the size of their combined populations, these countries are of major importance. India is the largest and most populous country of South Asia. Its ancient and elaborate civilization has spawned two of the world's great religions—Hinduism and Buddhism. Its ideal of nonviolence has been adopted in many areas of the world. Above all, India is a place of contrasts—of new and old, of unity and diversity. It is unique in that it has, in modern times, produced a single nation-state out of one of the most diverse populations in the world.

CONTENTS

21	LAND AND WATER	332
22	THE INDIAN PEOPLE	348
23	RELIGIONS OF INDIA	366
24	AN OLD AND NEW LAND	382
25	DEVELOPING INDIA	400
26	THE ARTS	414

INDIA

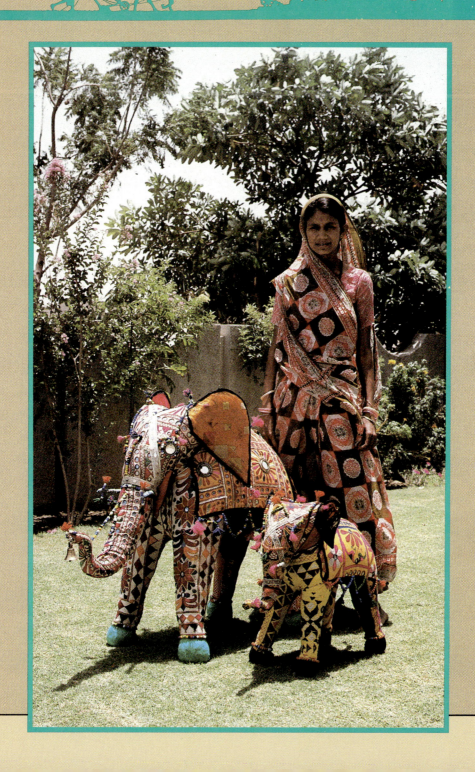

CHAPTER 21
LAND AND WATER

1. What countries, significant natural regions, and climatic features are found in South Asia?
2. How does the natural environment of South Asia affect the lives of its people?

> Mother, I bow to thee!
> Rich with thy hurrying streams,
> Bright with thy orchard gleams,
> Cool with thy winds of delight,
> Dark fields waving, Mother of might,
> Mother free.
>
> Glory of moonlight dreams,
> Over the branches and lordly streams,
> Clad in thy blossoming trees,
> Mother, giver of ease,
> Laughing low and sweet!
> Mother, I kiss thy feet.
> Speaker sweet and low!
> Mother, to thee I bow.
>
> . . . .
>
> Thou art wisdom, thou art law,
> Thou our heart, our soul, our breath,
> Thou the love divine, the awe
> in our hearts that conquers death.
> Thine the strength that nerves the arm,
> Thine the beauty, thine the charm.
> Every image made divine
> In our temples is but thine.*

These are the words of the national song of India. India, along with Pakistan, Nepal, Bhutan, Bangladesh, and Sri Lanka, make up the area known as South Asia. Some geographers also view Afghanistan, the Maldives, and Burma as part of the area. South Asia is a **subcontinent,** a very large landmass smaller than a continent. It extends southward from the Himalaya Mountains to Cape Comerin and Sri Lanka, a distance of about 2000 miles (3200 kilometers). Its **peninsula,** a piece of land nearly triangular in shape and surrounded on two sides by water, juts into the Indian Ocean, which it divides into the Bay of Bengal and the Arabian Sea.

About one-fifth of the world's population lives in South Asia. Of this, almost 76 percent live in India, which is by far the largest country of the subcontinent. India, which takes up about three-fourths of South Asia's total area, is the seventh largest country in the world in area. Until 1947, most of South Asia was known as India and shared a common history.

In the past many of today's national boundaries did not exist. So, people, ideas, and rulers moved freely across South Asia. Even today, many aspects of people's life styles are much the same throughout the subcontinent. So are the problems and possibilities of resources and their use, such as use and control of river water.

---

*"Vande Mataram" translated by Sri Aurobindo in: Sri Aurobindo Birth Centenary Library, Vol. 8, pp. 309–310.

THE HIMALAYAS

The Himalayas, which means "house of snow," are one of the three major environmental regions of South Asia. Rather than being a single mountain range, they are a series of three parallel snow-covered ranges. Separated by canyons and steep valleys, they extend for more than 1500 miles (2500 kilometers) in an east-west arc across the northern part of South Asia. With the Karakorum and Hindu Kush mountains, they form a 100-to-200-mile (160-to-320-kilometer)-thick barrier between South Asia and the rest of the continent.

Below shale and sandstone cliffs, a roadway winds through the narrow, 33-mile (53-kilometer)-long Khyber Pass, which connects northern Pakistan with Afghanistan. Why is the pass historically important?

The southernmost range, which rises abruptly from the plains, is the Siwalik. Next is the Himachal, a range that boasts high, rugged mountains. North of the Himachal are the Great Himalayas, which have the highest peaks in the world. One is Mount Everest, which is 29,028 feet (8848 meters) high. In the west, the Himalayas merge into a lofty plateau known as the Pamir Knot. In the east, they flow southward and form the Naga Hills and the hills of Manipur and Tripura.

The slopes of the Himalayas are steep with few level strips of land. Many glaciers and rushing rivers are found in the mountains. But the soil is poor, and because so many forests have been cut, there is concern about erosion. There are only a few passes through the mountains. One of these is the Khyber Pass in the Hindu Kush Mountains, which stretch across Pakistan. Through the Khyber Pass came great migrations of people and invading armies that in the past pushed their way into the fertile river valleys of northern India.

Most of the people who make their home in the Himalayas live in small valleys and pockets scattered throughout the mountains. Because of the cold and the isolation, life is hard. But there also are several large valleys known for their beauty, such as the Central Valley in Nepal and the Vale of Kashmir. Three relatively large kingdoms can be found in the mountains. They are Nepal, Bhutan, and Sikkim, which is now a part of India. Other small kingdoms also exist. One of these is Zanskar, which was founded in 930 AD. Below, a European traveler in the Himalayas gives his impression of this ancient kingdom:

[My] climb was amply rewarded by the incredible view. I had risen to over one thousand feet [304.8 meters] above the valley and I could now see a new horizon of snow-covered peaks: they formed the tormented sea of the Great Himalayan Chain, in the heart of whose folds I was now standing. Looking at the flat valley beneath me, set in a gargantuan upheaval of tormented ranges, I saw Zanskar for the first time for what it truly was: the lost valley of all dreams. . . . In the setting sun I could see the two rivers glitter where they met, before disappearing to the north down a valley flanked by red, green, and black peaks. There was no natural exit to this little corner of paradise which lay in the heart of the world's most inhospitable mountains. Suddenly I began to feel the cosiness of this enclosed universe, whose splendid peaks would from now on be the constant backdrop to all my activities.

Near the monastery an old man directed me a little further up the mountain where stood three great stones a little over six feet [1.82 meters] tall. . . . They represented three standing Buddhas. . . . Having searched in vain for inscriptions I photographed the stellae [carved stone pillars] and then set off to Lobsang's house.

On the way I passed a group of women busily weeding a field of barley, on the edge of which two long strips of newly dyed woollen cloth were laid out to dry. . . . With their permission I took photographs of them against the staggering background of the fierce Matterhorn-like peaks that rose on the other side of the valley. Then, leaving the girls singing away I walked up a parched, grassless slope and followed a little irrigation ditch that led me to Lobsang's isolated home. . . .

The setting itself is enchanting: a lone house high upon the barren slopes of a great mountain covered with snow and ice. Small and rectangular with a flat roof, fuzzy with great mounds of brushwood, the house overlooked all of Zanskar, moreover it stood surprisingly in an oasis of green fields enclosed by a stone wall. Fast-flowing rivulets ran through the fields, bubbling a constant tune, as beside the house they formed a natural fountain.

Facing south the house had three small, shuttered windows, which turned a blind eye to a sea of summits above the green carpet of the valley beneath, patched with grey and dotted with toy-like villages. In the sunset the peaks glistened with gold while a wind descended the mountain and brought the freezing breath of glaciers. Chattering with the cold, Lobsang directed me to enter his house by a ladder of twisted pieces of wood that led up to the roof.*

1. Where are the Himalayas located? What are the names of the major ranges?
2. Where do most of the inhabitants of the Himalayas live? What makes their life difficult?

THE INDO-GANGETIC PLAINS

A second major environmental region of South Asia is the Indo-Gangetic Plains, a huge crescent-shaped area at the foot of the Himalayas. The plains stretch from the Arabian Sea in the west to the Bay of Bengal in the east. They cover about one-fifth of the area of India, part of Pakistan, and most of Bangladesh. Although there are very few trees on the plains, the soil in most places is rich and fertile. Often it is **alluvial soil,** soil laid down by the rivers when they flood. One traveler reacted to the plains in this way:

Almost as impressive as the Himalayas, the Indo-Gangetic plains have a majesty of their own. Unfolding in seemingly endless flatness and monotony, they stretch on and on for over 1,500 miles [2400 kilometers] from west to east, dotted with village after village of tight clusters of box-like

---

*From *Zanskar: The Hidden Kingdom* by Michel Peissel, copyright ©1979 by Michel Peissel. Reprinted by permission of E. P. Dutton, Inc., and William Collins Sons & Co. Ltd., Publishers, London.

Thousands of Hindus gather to bathe in the sacred waters of the Ganges River in the belief that the waters will make them pure. What part does the Ganges play in Hindu funeral rituals?

mud huts with mud or thatched roofs (or sometimes roofs of handmade tiles). Between the villages lies the same patchwork quilt of tiny fields separated from one another by low mud banks in irregular, haphazard patterns. Along the few roads, bullock carts move with a primeval slowness that itself seems to enlarge the mighty plains. The traveler crossing the plains by car (or even by plane) almost begins to believe that there is no world but this.*

Through the plains run three important rivers. All three begin in the Himalayas. All three supply water for irrigation. In the west is the Indus, which is made up of the waters of five tributaries in the Punjab, a region of Pakistan and northwestern India. This area is very rich agriculturally and sometimes is called "the breadbasket of South Asia." Although wheat is the staple crop, vegetables, some cotton, and **pulses,** or beans, also are grown in this area. Along the lower part of the river's course, however, some of the soil is salty and no longer good for agriculture.

To the east and west of the Indus, the plains are very dry. At the India-Pakistan border is the Thar Desert with its sand dunes, gray-brown and desert soils, and scant scattered vegetation. The desert is about 500 miles (800 kilometers) long and 275 miles (440 kilometers) wide. At its eastern edge, in the Indian states of Rajasthan and Gujarat, it is a little less arid, and some varieties of a type of grain called **millet** can be grown.

The second river, found in the northeast, is the Brahmaputra. It has its source on the Plateau of Tibet and flows through Assam and into Bangladesh. There, not far from the Bay of Bengal, it joins with the Ganges River. A great many people live in the large delta area of the two rivers even though the land, much of it in Bangladesh, is generally flat and can flood easily.

The third river, the Ganges, is fed by tributaries flowing out of the mountains in the north. It runs through semi-arid country there, and then through the rich agricultural area of the Indian state of Uttar Pradesh. Finally, it emerges into the marshy delta area of West Bengal and Bangladesh. Some of the most fertile soil in India is found along the route of the Ganges. Here wheat, rice, jute, sugar cane, pulses, vegetables, and spices are grown. Rice, grown especially along the southeastern part of the river, accounts for 40 percent of the food produced in India. Wheat accounts for another 25 percent.

The Ganges is a very special river for those of the Hindu faith. They believe that it is sacred and can cleanse their souls and make them pure. Many Hindus make long journeys to the river just to bathe in its holy waters. In addition, after the body of a deceased person has been **cremated**, or burned, on a funeral pyre, the ashes are thrown into the river. A visitor to the Ganges describes below what happened when sever-

---

*India—A World in Transition by Beatrice Pitney Lamb, 1975, Holt, Rinehart & Winston, p. 10. Reprinted by permission.

al villagers on a religious pilgrimage encountered the river for the first time:

> Before them was the river. Across it came the yellow dawn, the first dapples of sunlight now at the middle of the river. As one they raised their hands on high and recited the salute to the sun. Then slowly, just as hundreds of others along the bank were doing, they walked down the steps and into the river. With cupped hands they bent and brought the water above their heads, pouring down over their faces. Then each in his own way performed the ritual of washing, watching the priest ahead in the water. When the gestures were finished they stood and watched in awe as the dawn sunshine splashed over them, blessing and warming and greeting them as it had never, quite, done before. Some went out of the water and sat on the steps watching strangers. Others repeated the ritual in the name of someone at home. . . . After a time two long boats, each with a canvas canopy, appeared and pulled in to the shore where they stood. Ashin explained that these boats would take them the length of the city. They boarded them dripping and watched . . . as the boatmen poled out into the current. They turned to look back; for the next hour they were mesmerized by the strange, moving frieze before them.
>
> Up and down and across the ghats [platforms on the bank of the river] moved the crowds. . . . At first it took a moment to realize that the ghat which the villagers had just left was now full of strangers. As the boats swung from the bank and pulled further away the villagers strained to see a group of priests descending a flight of steps in procession. Each carried a furled umbrella, each held his skirts above the damp of the steps, and each walked solemnly directly into the water, the pile of umbrellas mimicking the firewood on the next ghat. This was the central burning ghat where those who died in the city were burned, and their ashes given to the holy river. Already three small family groups were waiting beside their draped corpses. A priest sat near each. Someone was struggling to light the first fire, a body was moved forward. The flames caught and jumped. The villagers sighed.*

1. Where are the Indo-Gangetic Plains located? What crops are grown there?
2. What three rivers flow through the plains? What are their uses?
3. To whom is the Ganges River especially important? Why is it so important?

THE PENINSULA

South of the plains is the Peninsula, the third major environmental region of South Asia. Much of the mineral wealth of India is found in the northeastern part of the Peninsula. The Peninsula begins with rows of hills and low mountains that stretch from east to west. Called the Vindhya Hills, they act as the dividing line between North India and South India. The mountains are very old and greatly weathered.

South of the Vindhya Hills is rolling country, broken occasionally by groups of hills. This is the Deccan Plateau, which is shaped like a triangle pointed south. The plateau takes up the southern two-thirds of India and makes up most of the peninsula. It is bordered on the west and the east by low mountain ranges called the Western Ghats and the Eastern Ghats. Because the Western Ghats are much higher than the Eastern Ghats, the plateau slopes downward from west to east and most of the rivers crossing it flow eastward. The Ghats are fringed by narrow coastal plains which are very fertile and heavily populated. Some of India's largest cities are found here.

Third-Class Ticket by Heather Wood, 1980, Routledge & Kegan Paul, pp. 51–52. Reprinted by permission.

The soils and rainfall patterns of the Peninsula support a variety of crops as well as grazing land for animals. In many of the villages of the area, though, life is hard. Below, an observer describes what life is like for the farmers of Gopalpur, a village located on a plateau cut up by deep river gorges and separated by forested hills and mountains from other parts of India's great central plateau:

> Men and women in Gopalpur rise with the first light of dawn. The woman stumbles into the black interior of the house and brings out cold food left over from the day before.... The farmer wolfs his light breakfast and hurries off to his field, carrying his plow over his shoulder and driving his cattle before him. When the sun becomes warm and the bullocks begin to tire (10:30–11:00 A.M.), the farmer returns to the village....
>
> While the farmer plows, his wife has brought several pots of water from the stream. She has swept the house and the yard in front of the house, and carried the rubbish and manure to the compost heap outside the village. She has dried grain on the roof and ground it, swinging the stone handmill with muscular arms and the weight of her body. She has started a fire in the kitchen using only a few small sticks of wood. Over the fire, she has placed an earthenware pot containing chili, beans, leafy vegetables, tamarind, salt to taste and water to cover....
>
> While the vegetables simmer, the housewife mixes water with sorghum flour, pats the dough into thin cakes of unleavened bread and toasts them over the fire. After pouring water over her husband's arms and legs, she serves his meal, spooning the vegetables onto the bread to make a kind of open-faced sandwich. With this basic meal, people may have a little rice, some mango pickles, or perhaps some yoghurt mixed with water. If the water buffalo is giving milk, *ghi* (clarified butter) is poured over everything that is to be eaten.
>
> After the meal, from about twelve to three, people sit quietly in the shade and gossip. The farmer, if he is tired, sleeps. Younger men and children play games in the shade. At three in the afternoon, nine hours after dawn by the local reckoning, men return to the fields to work until dusk. Women, too, go to the fields during this part of the day to collect grass for the cattle, or to perform light chores connected with weeding or harvesting. At dusk, people return to the village to consume cold meals by the pale light given by cotton wicks placed in clay lamps. If the moon is full, people gather in the streets.
> ... If there is no moon and the night is

Shaded by a thatched roof, these Indian women pound grain into flour, a common practice in many villages of the Peninsula. What do the soil and rainfall patterns of the Peninsula support?

CHAPTER 21   LAND AND WATER

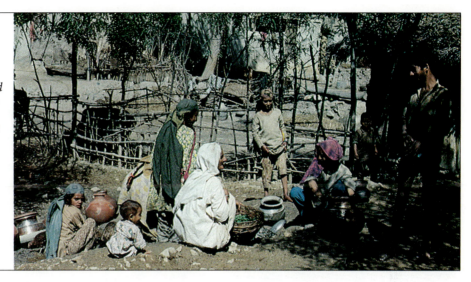

Villagers often use one section of the village compound as a central work and meeting area, where they also visit with friends and share news about the village and the outside world. At what times of year do most villagers spend entire days in the fields weeding and harvesting?

dark, people go early to bed, and by nine o'clock the village is silent.

During the rainy season and the cold season, when such activities as weeding and harvesting are at their peak, people spend the entire day in the fields. The men are joined at noon by the women who had remained home to cook. During the sowing and harvesting seasons in particular, men do not bathe or have haircuts; they live, eat, and often sleep in their fields, taking advantage of every moment of daylight.*

1. What types of terrain make up the region known as Peninsula?
2. What is a typical day like for a farmer in Gopalpur? For his wife?

WATER— THE KEY TO LIFE

Although the land has a very special meaning for most South Asians, water is considered even more crucial. Water is holy and sacred; it purifies. Water also enables

---

*from *Gopalpur: A South Indian Village* by Alan R. Beals. Copyright ©1962 by Holt, Rinehart & Winston. Reprinted by permission of CBS College Publishing.

crops to grow and largely limits what can be grown where.

In South Asia, water is distributed unevenly, both geographically and seasonally. The most rain falls in the Western Ghats, the hills of Assam and nearby areas, and the lands in the southern foothills of the Himalayas. The heavy rainfall in these areas is due chiefly to **orographic lifting.** Moisture-filled clouds reach the mountains and are forced upward, where the cooler and thinner air causes them to drop their moisture. Because the Himalayas are so high, they keep the cold continental winter winds away from the Indian subcontinent and keep the moisture from the southerly winds on the southern side of the mountains.

Although, for the most part, South Asia has three different seasons in a year, almost 80 percent of its rainfall comes during one season alone. The winter, which lasts from October through February, is cool, clear, and relatively dry. The summer, which runs from March to mid-June, is hot and dry. Then, in mid-June, the rainy season sets in.

During the rainy season, seasonal winds called monsoons spread across the continent to water the parched land. One Indian writer describes what happens:

Monsoons, which bring most of the rainfall on which Indian life depends, are welcomed. But too much rain can have serious consequences. Here, a man wades through floodwaters to reach his flood-damaged home in West Bengal. When does most of the rainfall come to South Asia?

[The] people have lost all hope. They are disillusioned, dejected, thirsty and sweating. . . . A hot petrified silence prevails. Then comes the shrill, strange call of a bird. Isn't there a gentle breeze blowing? And hasn't it a damp smell? And wasn't the rumble which drowned the birds' cry the sound of thunder? The people hurry to the roofs to see. The same ebony wall is coming up from the east. A flock of herons fly across. There is a flash of lightning which outshines the daylight. The wind fills the black sails of the clouds and they billow out across the sun. A profound shadow falls on the earth. There is another clap of thunder. Big drops of rain fall and dry up in the dust. A fragrant smell rises from the earth. Another flash of lightning and another crack of thunder like the roar of a hungry tiger. It has come! Sheets of water, wave after wave. The people lift their faces to the clouds and let the abundance of water cover them. . . .

But after a few days the flush of enthusiasm is gone. The earth becomes a big stretch of swamp and mud. Wells and lakes fill up and burst their bounds. In towns, gutters get clogged and streets become muddy streams. In villages, mud walls of huts melt in the water and thatched roofs sag and descend on the inmates. Rivers, which keep rising steadily from the time the summer's heat starts melting the snows, suddenly turn to floods as the monsoon spends itself upon the mountains. All this happens in late August or early September. Then the season of the rains gives way to autumn.*

Manjo Majra by Khushwant Singh, 1956, Grove Press, pp. 90–94. Reprinted by permission.

CASE STUDY
INDIA

"MOTHER EARTH"

Much of South Asia is agricultural, and a large number of people work the land. Below, an Indian farmer speaks for many when he explains how he feels about the land and why:

Bhadre Gowda, the husband of Thayee, was ploughing a millet field, up and down, up and down, turning the soil to catch the next torrent of rain: the bullocks pulled and he pushed as the wooden plough shuddered through the ground. We watched from a bank, and when he stopped for a rest he came and sat beside us. The sun was hot on our backs.

He was a handsome man with the fine features of his sister Bhadramma—the same straight nose, the same delicate eyebrows over bright kind eyes, the same wide mouth expressive of thought and feeling. Small earrings studded his rounded lobes, crystal glass set in a gold trefoil; and tucked on top of each ear was a single pink blossom plucked from a flowering bush.

'Yes, we worship the land,' he said. 'It's our life. It's beautiful. It's always beautiful. But the most beautiful is when it's green, when the crops are large and fruitful. Then it's like a woman. How much more beautiful it is when she wears her jewels, does her hair, wears fine clothes. And when she takes them off, how empty we feel.'

'Yes, when we cut the crops we feel empty. But then we know we'll be starting to plant again, controlling the land, making it bear fruit. And then we feel happy. We feel satisfied in working the land where we grow our life.'

He unwound the small torn scarf from his head and wiped the sweat from his face: his chin was black with stubble, his skin dry and dark from the constant exposure to sun. He looked poor, almost beggarly, with a shirt ripped at the shoulder, and most of the buttons missing.

'You see, we feel the land, just as we feel the rain. We don't see it, splashing down on the paths; we feel it cold on our backs. And the sun—we don't see it, a beautiful sunset as you say. We feel it in the morning when it's cool, when it gives us light to work by; we feel it when it burns our backs and we want the shade of the tree; we feel it in the late afternoon softened by a breeze; and then when it goes down and takes away our light, we feel we've done a full day's work. Then we can sleep in peace.'

He sat quietly, his forehead puckered, his eyes half-closed, and his body began to sway.

"We have great affection and trust for Mother Earth. When we're alive, it's she who gives us rice, gives us food. It's she who takes us in when we're dead. If we don't work the land how will we get food? If we trust her she'll always give. See, this year there was no rain. But now it's come, now we can live and prosper. We should trust her. We should trust her more than our own mother, the mother who's given birth to us."

He closed his eyes; his body was silent now.*

1. How does Bhadre Gowda feel about the land and the elements?
2. Do you agree with Bhadre Gowda that, if you trust Mother Earth, she will always give? Explain.

**Family Web: A Story of India* by Sarah Hobson, 1982, Academy Chicago, pp. 208–209. Reprinted by permission.

Farmers depend heavily on the summer monsoons. If they come in time and bring enough rain, the farmers will have the water they need to make their crops grow. There also will be water to fill storage tanks or basins and canals that have developed over time. During the dry season, this water will be used to irrigate crops. If, however, the monsoons come too late or do not bring enough rain, the crops—and the farmers—will suffer.

The rain also supplies the rivers with water. Too much rain at once, however, causes the rivers to flood. Some rivers, such as the Indus, Ganges, and Brahmaputra, also receive water from melting snow and have it all year long. Some of the rivers of the Peninsula, however, dwindle to a trickle in the dry season. Farmers in this area must catch and store rain water in basins and tanks.

The water in the rivers is used for many different purposes, from transport to irrigation to hydroelectric power. Sometimes, however, the purposes conflict. An example of this is the Bhakra-Nangal, the largest of India's water projects. It is supposed to generate electricity as well as store water for irrigation. But when there is a shortage of water, it means less electricity to run pumps to get water out of wells.

Water, then, is very important in South Asia. The **legend,** or popular story handed down from earlier times, which follows illustrates better than most facts or figures just how important water is to the people of South Asia:

Far away in the Himalaya Mountains in the north of India, the great god Shiva slept. And as he slept, the winds blew and the snow fell and the ice settled on his face and head. But Shiva was weary and continued to sleep as the sun blazed down on the plains and valleys of Hindustan [the Indian subcontinent] and cruelly burned . . . grass and trees. For, at that time, there were no rivers to water the land. The people cried out in their anguish for water but the god, unmoved, slept.

In the mountains there lived a great king called Himavat with his fair wife, Mena, and their lovely little daughter, Ganga. . . .

From time to time, King Himavat would go down into the plains of India, and whenever he returned from a journey, his heart was heavy and his face sad.

"What ails you?" asked Mena, and Ganga clambered upon her father's knee and said, "What is it, father?"

The king said, "The land suffers for want of water; the crops shrivel and die; the cattle waste; men and women go thirsty to give water to their children. But Shiva sleeps and seems not to care for men."

Then Ganga said, "Can no one do anything about this?" The king raised his heavy eyes and looked upon his child.

"Yes, Ganga," he replied, "there is help but it is hard to win. If a girl pure as ice and white as snow would leave her home and go down and dwell forever in the sultry plains, then from her life freely given, would flow life for the perishing people and her name would be sacred and beloved by all in Hindustan."

Ganga, though, was just a young girl and didn't want to leave her beautiful ice cavern. . . .

Then, one day, Himavat came in with a baby, dying in his arms. The soft skin was blistered; the little lips were black and parched; the mouth was open; the eyes, fixed and glassy. Himavat laid the child on Ganga's lap.

"It is dying of thirst," he said.

Ganga bent over the little face and, as she did so, a drop of water fell from her hair on the parched lips. In an instant the flush of life returned to it. The baby opened his eyes and gurgled with joy. Ganga sprang to her feet.

"Father," she cried, "Mother, I will go if I can save children."

And as she spoke she went to the mouth of the ice cavern where she had dwelt in innocent but selfish joy, and there the miracle happened. The beautiful little girl with golden bright hair and white hands vanished and, in her place, a stream of pure soft water, white-flecked with foam, danced on the golden bright sands and the water, as it ran, whispered, "I am Ganga, Ganga, and I go to bless the thirsty plains and to bring water to dying children."

And wherever Ganga turned flowers sprang up to welcome her; stately trees bowed over her waters; fainting cattle grew strong; children played upon her banks; strong men bathed in her torrents and women washed themselves in her pools. Ganga, the Maid, had become Ganga, the Mother, the river of life and joy.

And this is why Ganga has become the symbol of life to Hindustan, and the Ganges the river of life. This is why men think that the Ganga, as she flows, murmurs, "To give oneself for others is duty; to spread happiness around one for others is joy." And this is why the Hindu, dying far from the sacred river, prays that his ashes may be thrown into the Ganga's red-brown depths, so that dying, he may return to the source of life.*

1. Why do the Western Ghats, the hills of Assam and nearby areas, and the lands in the southern foothills of the Himalayas get the most rainfall?
2. What are the monsoons? Why do farmers depend heavily on them?
3. Why is water so important to the people of South Asia?

---

*"Ganga the River Maid—and Other Indian Legends" in *Intercom*, June 1978, Center for Global Perspectives in Education, Inc., p. 8.

Exploration
INDIA

Study the maps that appear in this Exploration. Then, based on what you learn from the maps, defend or present arguments to refute the following statement: *In South Asia, land, water, and survival are linked. Without one, there cannot be the other.*

INDIA UNIT 4

CHAPTER 21 REVIEW

POINTS TO REMEMBER

1. The subcontinent of South Asia is made up of the countries of India, Pakistan, Nepal, Bhutan, Bangladesh, and Sri Lanka. About three-quarters of the subcontinent's total area is taken up by India.
2. South Asia has three major environmental regions—the Himalayas, the Indo-Gangetic Plains, and the Peninsula.
3. The Himalayas are a series of three parallel mountain ranges which serve as a barrier between South Asia and the rest of the continent. The mountains are very steep, and there are few passes through them. Cold and isolation make life difficult for the people who live in them.
4. The Indo-Gangetic Plains cover about one-fifth of the area of India, part of Pakistan, and most of Bangladesh. The Indus, Brahmaputra, and Ganges rivers flow through the plains supplying water for irrigation. Most of the area has fertile soil, and a wide variety of crops are grown there.
5. The Peninsula has a variety of terrains —hills, low mountains, plateau, and coastal plains. Most of the Peninsula is taken up by the Deccan Plateau, which covers the southern two-thirds of India.
6. Water holds special meaning in South Asia. In addition to enabling crops to grow, it is considered holy and sacred by many.
7. Most of the rainfall in South Asia comes during the rainy season, from mid-June through September. Farmers depend on the monsoons to bring them enough rain to water their crops and to save to help them through the dry season.

VOCABULARY

Identify

South Asia	Great Himalayas	Indo-Gangetic Plains	Peninsula
Himalayas	Pamir Knot	Indus	Vindhya Hills
Karakorum Mountains	Khyber Pass	Punjab	Deccan Plateau
Hindu Kush Mountains	Nepal	Thar Desert	Western Ghats
Siwalik	Bhutan	Brahmaputra	Eastern Ghats
Himachal	Sikkim	Ganges	

Define

subcontinent	alluvial soil	millet	orographic lifting
peninsula	pulses	cremated	legend

DISCUSSING IMPORTANT IDEAS

1. What environmental features characterize South Asia as a region of the world and separate it from other world regions?
2. More than one-half of the population of India lives on the Indo-Gangetic Plains. Why do you think this is so?

CHAPTER 21 LAND AND WATER

3. Why do rainfall patterns in South Asia make catching and controlling water so important?

4. Explain: "The monsoons dominate economic life in most of India. They mean life and death to the people of India."

DEVELOPING SKILLS

READING THEMATIC MAPS

Over time, you probably have seen many different kinds of maps on television newscasts and weather reports, in newspapers and magazines, and in textbooks. You also probably have had to use some maps in classroom situations or on vacations or trips with family or friends. You may even have had to draw a map for a class assignment or to show someone where you live or where to meet you.

Even the simplest map can provide a good deal of information—if the person looking at the map knows how to read it. Take, for example, this map of India's agricultural resources, which is a reproduction of the one on page 345.

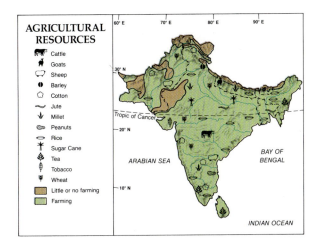

This is a *thematic map*, a map that shows information about a specialized subject. That subject can be economic, political, social, cultural—almost anything that can be expressed geographically.

To read this or any other thematic map, follow the guidelines suggested below:

1. Read the title of the map to determine what the theme is. This is the key to the purpose of the map. (*The title of this map is Agricultural Resources. Therefore, its purpose is to provide information about the agricultural resources of India.*)

2. Locate the *legend*, the list and explanation of the keys that provide information related to the theme of a map. Note on the legend for this map that some of the keys are symbols and others are colors.

3. Study the legend. Ask yourself questions like the following: What resources are identified by symbols? (*Cattle, goats, sheep, barley, cotton, jute, millet, peanuts, rice, sugar cane, tea, tobacco, and wheat*) What do the colors represent? (*Areas where there is farming and where there is little or no farming*)

4. Locate the symbols and colors on the map and, based on their location, determine in which part(s) of the country each resource is found and in which area(s) Indians are or are not engaged in farming. You also will be able to determine which resources are most plentiful and which are least plentiful. From this information, you can hypothesize or make generalizations about such topics as the relationship between environment and way of life.

For further practice in this skill, use the guidelines to read the other three maps on pages 344 and 345.

CHAPTER 22
THE INDIAN PEOPLE

1. How do the Indian people view marriage, the family, and the role of women?
2. What is daily life like in Indian villages and cities?

Listen, friend, for I will talk too long. It is close to my heart. What gives people hope? Is it good harvests? Is it the weddings? Is it a feast? No, these are the pleasures which pass. We hope because we have children and we see again all things new in their eyes. You say that cannot be so for all, since all do not have children, and all who have are not happy? Yes? Is it so? Listen, again. For a nation, for a land of many people, children are the times to come, the lives we have not yet led, the houses not yet built, the pictures not yet made. All that gives us hope, gives us reason to struggle through the illnesses and the loneliness and the years of drought. Why? I shall tell you. Because we are taught by all we know of the past that what each can do becomes greater if his chances become greater. We think we do not know what comes in the future, but we think it will not be the same as the past. There will be other chances and other problems. The fate is not written twice in the same way, you of the villages say. Out of each that is different . . . comes something new which gives another hope. . . .

The power of India lies in the cities, and mostly I think it is wicked. But what endures all powers? The village. . . . That is the memory which India must hope to hold and withstand whatever the powers do. . . .

. . . The village changes whenever there is a new family begun or an old one dies. It is what is kept and how the change is made which you record and which I call the remembering. . . .

. . . As long as there is remembering there is home.*

Indian society is diverse. This diversity is regional, ethnic, cultural, linguistic, religious, educational, rural/urban, and class based. So what is true for one Indian or group of Indians is not necessarily true for another. Children and home, however, are important to all Indians. Through them, the past is carried into the future.

Today, however, India is in a state of change. While traditional beliefs remain important to many, others believe that things cannot stay the same if India is to keep up with the rest of the world. Change can be seen in attitudes about marriage, the family, and the role of women. It can be seen in the villages, where more than three-fourths of India's people live, and in the cities, which comprise the third largest urban population in the world.

**Third-Class Ticket* by Heather Wood, 1980, Routledge & Kegan Paul, pp. 30–31. Reprinted by permission.

Marriage

For Indians, marriage is a process that takes place through time. Generally arranged by the families of the prospective bride and groom, marriage is the special task of a girl's father or brother. Traditionally, the bride had to have a **dowry,** a payment from the bride's father to the groom and his family. It was intended to secure good treatment for the girl, give her a portion of the family wealth, and start the young couple in life. Most brides were very young by western standards and were expected to stay at home, away from men outside the family.

In recent years, changes have taken place. Below, a housewife from Yamunanager talks about some of them:

> It's thirty-eight years since I got married and became a housewife. Mine was a traditional, arranged marriage. In those days, what one calls "love" marriages were almost unheard of. Nobody dared to marry against their parents' wishes or marry out of their caste [social group].
>
> Times are changing slowly and most young people I meet nowadays want to marry somebody of their own choice. But by and large parents still put up terrific opposition if their children want to marry someone they've met and fallen in love with on their own.
>
> We allowed our sons complete freedom to marry whomever they chose. My sons didn't demand any dowry. . . . And their wedding ceremonies were simple.
>
> Hindu weddings are generally very pompous affairs. People tend to treat a wedding as a chance to show off their wealth. The whole house is decked out in multicolored lights. There's a band playing songs from the movies over loudspeakers, and a fireworks display often is thrown in. And the amount of food and sweets and drinks and the number of relatives and guests! You'd have to see it to believe it.
>
> Since my children are abroad, there's not much to do at home. Just the cooking. . . . A woman comes to do the cleaning and washing twice a day. I think we're fortunate to have even this part-time help. In the past, it was easy to hire servants. Now it's becoming more and more difficult to find them. Soon, I think we'll have to do all the housework ourselves. Most households in India don't have gadgets like dishwashers and washing machines or electric stoves.
>
> Gas stoves too, you'll find only in big towns and cities. Most families manage to cook on *chullahs* (charcoal fires) or coal fires or kerosene stoves. For our laundry, we have to depend upon the local *dhobi* (washerman).
>
> Unless we have guests, I have plenty of spare time. So I help my husband in the shop with his filing and typing. . . .
>
> Sitting in the shop and watching customers, I often point out to my husband how customs have changed. . . . When I was young, unmarried girls weren't

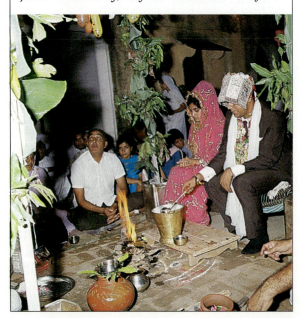

Amidst family and friends, this couple is being married in a Hindu ceremony in the north-central Indian city of Jhansi. Traditionally, why did brides have a dowry?

These photographs were taken from an advertisement in the matrimonial section of an urban newspaper, The Times of India, *which encourages men and women to advertise for their own marriage partners. How do Indian men view arranged marriages?*

allowed to use make-up or even wear jewelry. Now I find married and unmarried girls wearing both.

But change comes so slowly in India. People say, "What has to happen will happen. It's all in our fate, written in our stars," and take things easy. The only things that seem to move fast are prices.*

In 1978, a law was passed setting a minimum marriage age for Indians of the Hindu religion, the major religion of India. Males must be 21 or older and females, 18 or older. The dowry also has been outlawed. But it still remains an important part of many Indian marriages. Today, the bride and groom are likely to have met before the wedding, particularly if they are from the educated middle and upper classes. Even if they cannot select their spouses, they can veto the man or woman who has been chosen for them.

---

*We Live in India *by Veenu Sandal, 1984, The Bookwright Press, pp. 32–33. Reprinted by permission.

It is not uncommon today, especially in the cities, for parents to advertise in a newspaper for matches for their children. Advertisements such as the ones below, from *The Times of India*, are typical:

ALLIANCE INVITED FOR SINDHI GIRL BEAUTIFUL, FAIR, TALL, SLIM, HOMELY [GOOD HOMEMAKER], INTELLIGENT, PRESENTABLE, WORKING, . . . 45 KG [99 LB]. LIBRA ZODIAC. BELONGING TO RESPECTABLE BUSINESS FAMILY. ONLY WELL-SETTLED HANDSOME BOYS WITH SOBER HABITS OF MATCHING AGE FROM RESPECTABLE FAMILY. . . .

For an Oswal Swetamber girl from highly respectable and cultured family, 20 ½ years, 45 kg [99 lb], 156 cms [5 ft. 2 ½ in.], slim, fair, beautiful, sweet natured, active, well versed in household work besides artistic talents, intelligent, convent educated, first class B.S.C. from Rajasthan University, presently residing abroad with parents

—required a suitable vegetarian, non-smoking, smart, educated, Oswal match from any profession/business. Parents and girl shall be in India during September 1984 to finalise match. Advertisement given for better choice. . . .*

Opinions are mixed about marriage customs today. Some Indians see no reason for traditional standards to change. Below, a 28-year-old Senior Research Officer of a large corporation explains why he approves of arranged marriages:

> . . . The mechanics of how you select your wife is of no importance. It would make no difference if you plucked her off a tree. It is the life that comes afterwards. That counts. For example, do you make your own trousers? Why do you go to a tailor without losing face? For obvious reasons. The tailor knows his business whereas if you made your own, it would sit ill on you, that is all. Let someone who knows you deeply and knows the meaning of marriage with some experience in it select a woman for you. She won't kill you I think. On the other hand if you don't believe in anyone because you can't or if no one has earned your faith, choose one yourself. I would, if I believed in no one. Fortunately I am not alone. I have faith, belief, trust and things, in a lot of people around me. So I don't have to go about frantically falling in love.†

Other Indians, however, feel that arranged marriages should be a thing of the past. The bachelor who placed the following advertisement in the "Brides Wanted" column of The *Times of India* makes it clear that he wants to find his own bride:

> A jovial and cheerful but a very lonely young journalist (33) is searching for a real perfect soulmate with true love philosophy view matrimony invites direct correspondence from emotional sentimental, soft-natured, understanding and really good looking girl willing to share my happiness and sorrows, riches and rags, ideals and aspirations. Dowry loathed and severely condemned. No arranged marriages please! Correspondence from parents therefore not solicited. . . .*

1. What are some of the traditional marriage customs in India?
2. What are some of the ways in which marriage customs have changed in recent years?

FAMILY LIFE

Indian families generally are very close, and much of the social life revolves around family activities. Relatives try to live near one another. Those who live in the city go back to visit village relatives. Rural relatives who go to the city to work or go to school often live with their relatives there.

In India, there is a traditional family cycle through time that includes **nuclear families,** a set of parents and their children—and **extended families**—parents, children, and other relatives. For many Indians, the traditional family pattern is the **joint family,** which consists of a husband and wife; the sons and the sons' wives and children; and unmarried daughters. Sometimes it includes other relatives, such as an aunt or cousin. Married daughters live with the families of their husbands. Their children are considered part of the husband's family.

---
*The Times of India, No. 193, Vol. CXLVII, Sunday, August 5, 1984, pp. 3, 4. Reprinted by permission.

‡"A Bride from the Blues" in *They Live in India: Vignettes of Contemporary Indian Lives, Vol. III—The Urban Scene* by Anees Jung, The Educational Resources Center, The University of the State of New York and the State Educational Department of New Delhi, p. 17. Reprinted by permission.

*The Times of India, No. 193 Vol. CXLVII, Sunday, August 5, 1984, p. 2. Reprinted by permission.

CHAPTER 22 THE INDIAN PEOPLE

A joint family, such as this one in Madras, India, shares home and income and cares for the welfare of all its members. Such a family often consists of several generations of family members. Why do many Indians prefer living in a joint family?

The joint family is still strong in India today, although it is more common among the wealthy than the poor. There are a number of reasons why some Indians prefer this type of family arrangement. One is that many members of high status families are bound together by tradition or by the fact that, by staying together, they all can live better. Another is that the members of a joint family often work together. Merchants, for example, may prefer a joint family because family members can pool ideas, labor, money, and risk. Farmers with a lot of land may prefer it because there are more people to work the land. In the interview below, a young woman from Madras tells why she prefers the joint family:

Question: You obviously live in a modern family and have had education. Two years of college, I think you said. As you consider marriage, would you rather live in a traditional joint family or be alone with your husband?

Radha: Oh, the joint family, absolutely. I would never consider anything else.

Question: Why? You would have so much less freedom, so much less opportunity to know your husband and enjoy doing things with him.

Radha: I would be too lonely without the other women, without all the uncles, aunties, and children. Also I would have to do all the housework. . . .

Question: Then, what of your relationship with your husband? Isn't this important to you?

Radha (hesitantly): What is a husband? He goes to work, he sees his friends. He would never discuss things with me, would never take me to the cinema. We would go to visit relatives, but that is all.

Question: Then, what of your relationship with your children? You would have them all to yourself in a separate family.

Radha: It would be too much! I have seen my friend almost crazy because of her children. They haven't other children to play with, aunties to go to, and they are always crying and fighting.

Question: But little children do grow up. Can you think of them as going to school and having school friends?

Radha: That would happen, of course. But mostly I can only think that I would want my son to care for me when I am old. That can only happen in a joint family.*

---

*Voices From India edited by Margaret Cormack and Kiki Skagen, 1972, Praeger Publishers, pp. 243–244. Reprinted by permission of Holt, Rinehart, and Winston and editors.

Joint families, however, are not without problems. Pooling earnings can lead to jealousy and bickering. Family members may want to spend their money as they choose and live independently. Some couples have no children, and all relatives do not get along with one another.

When the father of a joint family dies, the property is divided among the sons. After the division, one son takes over and cares for his mother as part of an extended family. The other sons, with their wives and children, set up separate or nuclear households. In the past, few widows remarried, and some practiced *suttee,* throwing themselves on their husband's funeral pyre to be burned to death. Those who did not stayed with their children. Today, *suttee* is illegal, and many younger widows remarry.

In an Indian family household, the oldest able male is considered the head. He has the authority to make family decisions, market crops, organize household labor for heavier agricultural tasks, and deal with strangers. The oldest able female is in charge of domestic affairs. Generally the mother of the sons or the wife of the eldest brother, she supervises the food, health care, raising of children, and cleaning. Young wives hold the lowest place in the household, especially before they have sons. They are given the least desirable jobs. Their mothers-in-law maintain control and often are quite strict with them. In a joint family, men and women tend to keep their daily activities separate from each other's.

There is great love for children in Indian families, and small children generally are pampered and indulged. In poorer families, however, children five years and older may be expected to help with household labor and the care of their younger brothers and sisters. Children raised in a joint family always have someone to play with them or to comfort and feed them. They learn to get along with many different people living close together. At times, however, they become very dependent on others.

1. What types of families are there in India? Of whom does each consist?
2. What are the advantages of joint family living? The disadvantages?

This man is poling his dugout boat across the smooth waters of Dal Lake, nestled in the mountains near Srinagar in northernmost India. He and other local men earn a portion of their family income by ferrying food and other goods to the many houseboats that line the lakeshore each summer. What is the typical role of the oldest male in an Indian household?

CHAPTER 22   THE INDIAN PEOPLE   355

One of an Indian woman's major household responsibilities is to prepare meals for the family. This woman, cooking on a gas stove and dressed in a colorful traditional garment called a sari, *is making chapatis—flat, round whole wheat flour breads. These are usually served with a bean soup known as* dal, *vegetable curries, and rice. Together,* chapatis *and* dal *make a complete protein. What is the typical role of the oldest able female in an Indian household?*

INDIAN WOMEN

Indian women have a pivotal role in families and households, especially if they are the mothers of sons. Indian men have a great respect for their wives as the mothers of their children. In Indian tradition and belief, women have always been represented as both strong and weak. They are the goddess *Shakti*, the power and energy of the world. The description given below by a Bengali widower after the death of his wife of 50 years explains the traditional Hindu ideal of a woman's role:

> My wife passed away with most of her wishes fulfilled as a Hindu woman. She saw her daughters married and well-established in life. Her only son had a good college career, and she had selected his bride, and her son got his special training in America, and was in a good post. . . . She was quite happy and proud of her position in life, with a husband and a son upon whom she doted and on whom she could also rely. . . . The Sanskrit [classical language of India] adage says that the wife is the Home, and the ideal wife has been characterized . . . as the Mistress of the House, Adviser and Manager of Affairs, Trusted Friend as well as beloved Pupil in the Fine Arts. . . . My wife, born to the tradition [of joint-family living], accepted it as a matter of course and she went on for any amount of sacrifice. . . . She was very much in love with life, and yet she often [showed] in her behavior a strange detachment and objectivity which we frequently see in our Indian womanhood.*

In the past, some Indian women followed the practice of **purdah.** They remained secluded in their homes, kept their faces cov-

---

In Memorium Kamala Devi, 1900-1964: A Husband's Offering of Love and Respect by Suniti Kumar Chatterji, as quoted in *Bengali Women* by Manisha Roy, 1975, The University of Chicago Press, pp. 128–129. Reprinted by permission.

Former prime minister Indira Gandhi addressed this women's convention in the 1970's. Since then, a trade union known as the Self-Employed Women's Association has taught its members, many of whom are among the poorest women in India, how to earn money from their craft and labor skills. The women then use the money to provide necessities for their families and themselves. In what way have most educated middle- and upper-class Indian women changed in recent years?

ered, and were not seen by men who were not close relatives. Today, most educated women of the middle and upper classes no longer lead such structured lives. Many of them have careers and work outside the home. Indian feminists view *purdah* and other Indian customs that limit women and put them under the control of men as restrictive and demeaning. Since 1975, the International Year of Women, Indian feminists have been working to publicize the situations and concerns of Indian women. Upper- and middle-class women especially are pressing for equality and fairness.

1. How was the ideal wife characterized traditionally?
2. How do modern Indian women view some of the traditional customs relating to women? What are they doing to help bring about change?

Village Life

Life styles, including views on marriage, the family, and women, tend to differ throughout India. There are many reasons for this. One of the chief ones has to do with whether a person lives in a village or in the city. There are over 575,000 villages in India. In the state of Bengal, there are so many people that villages are nearly continuous. Some villages, such as the ones on the Gangetic Plains, are clusters of houses with fields lying all around. Others may consist of scattered homesteads.

Although most villages are self-contained and self-sufficient, they are not isolated. Landlords and members of the **panchayat**, the local body of elders elected to office, link villages with the wider society. Village development workers and school teachers bring information to improve living and farming. Villagers often market their crops in towns and cities and travel to, go to school, or visit relatives in other villages and towns. Some villagers also make pilgrimages to temples or holy places. In addition, many city dwellers have village roots and return often to check on their property or to visit relatives and friends.

Many villagers have contact with the outside world via radio or television. Radios have been a feature of village life for several years. Television sets are relatively new. Today, more than 9000 Indian villages have

CHAPTER 22 THE INDIAN PEOPLE 357

government-purchased television sets. Although the government tries to promote educational programming, many villagers prefer to watch movies and such imported programs as *Star Trek* and *I Love Lucy*.

In most villages are brick homes owned by the wealthy and mud houses that belong to the poor. Although homes vary in size according to the wealth of their owners, all have areas for sitting, sleeping, and cooking. In addition, most villages have such public facilities as a community center and clinic, a school, and temples. There also are wells, great shade trees, water tanks, and a grazing area for animals.

The main occupation of most of the villagers is farming. Sometimes a few wealthy landlords own much of the land and hire others to work in the fields. Men, women, and children all may work in the fields. The women play a major role in processing agricultural products. They also prepare much of what is grown for eating or for selling in the market.

Villagers not engaged in farming may produce such items as pots or furniture or provide such services as washing clothes or cleaning drains. Many of the items produced in the village are used by the villagers themselves or by those in nearby villages.

Change is coming slowly to many of the villages. Below, an American author of a book about India discusses some of these changes:

"How," I asked Mihil Lal Shukla [the village priest] . . . "has the village of Chirora [in Uttar Pradesh] changed since your boyhood?" . . .

Shukla rocked on the balls of his feet, scratched his skinny chin and lapsed into silence. He couldn't think of anything. . . .

"What about the dirt road I came in on?" I coached him.

True, said Shukla, that's pretty new. Someone in the crowd of goggling onlookers in the dusty village square volunteered that the road was 15, maybe 16 years old; new enough by Chirora's standards.

What if someone got sick in the old days? Well, said Shukla, they had to carry him out to the main road, and the nearest doctor in those days might be five or six miles [8 or 9.6 kilometers] away. Now the

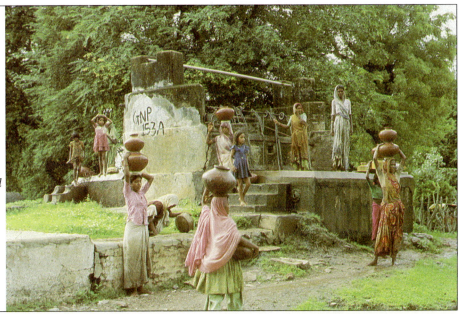

At this "sweetwater," or drinking water, well in a village in western India, women and girls fill jars in which they carry water to their homes. The jars they balance on their heads, sometimes as many as three at once, are made by a local potter. His pots are preferred over tin ones because they keep the water cooler longer. Besides wells, what other public facilities are found in most Indian villages?

doctor is two or three miles [3.2 or 4.8 kilometers] away.

What happened during the rainy season? "We were completely cut off," said Shukla. And if someone got sick then? As often as not they died.

That afternoon . . . I walked through the fields with Indrapal Singh, . . . a "youngblood"—a forward-thinking, model farmer. Indrapal used high-yielding seeds, fertilizer, herbicide. . . .

"Why don't you buy a tractor?" I asked. The Government, which considers the modernization of farming crucial, makes interest-free loans for farm equipment.

Indrapal pondered for a moment. "Why should I go into debt?" he answered. "I have enough to eat and drink, to provide for my family. Why do I need a tractor?" . . .

Chirora looked like most of the other north Indian villages I had seen. Narrow mud alleys snaked among mud houses, leaving the village awash in muck after the rain; cows and bullocks wandered glassy-eyed across . . . courtyards; temples displayed . . . clay idols. . . . We want change, I would be told by old Brahmins [members of the highest Hindu caste] and young farmers alike. But, of course, it will never come, they would add, even though I could see that it had. . . .

When I first arrived in Chirora, I was taken by a group of friendly . . . farmers on a tour of the fields. We wound between tiny plots of a half-acre or less, each with its microenvironment of crops. . . .

We wandered past two shirtless, slender men who were watering a raised field by rhythmically dipping a bucket in an irrigation ditch and depositing the water in another ditch 12 inches [30 centimeters] above. We fetched up at the pump-operated tube well that was supposed to be irrigating the fields, but which received power only between 9 P.M. and 4 A.M. . . . "Power supply," said a well-dressed farmer as we stood around the idle pump, "is *bilkul* bogus"—absolutely bogus.

The speaker . . . turned out to be the owner of the machinery he was cursing. His name was Natwar Singh. . . . Natwar . . . owned 35 *bighas*, or 17½ acres [7 hectares]—a very big farm by local standards. . . .

Natwar . . . had graduated from college and taken a degree in law. Sometimes Natwar talked of finding some clients and doing the work for which he was trained, but he couldn't take his professional ambitions very seriously. "You see," he said . . . , "I am my father's only son. I have to stay in the village. What else can I do?" . . .

Always at the periphery of Natwar's large, cheerful entourage was . . . Guria. . . .

Guria was a member of one of the "backward" castes, a term used in contrast to the "forward" castes, the Brahmins and Thakurs. . . . He had . . . gained a measure of formal political power as the *u-pradhan*, or sub-head, of the . . . *panchayat*. Probably owing to this position, he was able to rent four acres [1.6 hectares] . . . in addition to the . . . half acre [.2 hectares] he owned. Guria's tiny brick home had but one room; here, amid sacks of grain, he lived with his wife and two little children. . . .

On my initial tour of the village, I was surprised to see that perhaps half of the houses were built of brick. . . . But one of the village's neighborhoods . . . was a sea of crumbling mud huts topped by piles of thatch. . . . Here, it turned out, was Chirora's third and lowest caste group, the Untouchables, known in India as Harijans. . . .

Only a few of the families owned enough land to make a living; the rest got by haphazardly. Most of them worked as *mazdoors*, or day laborers. . . .

Wrapped in a sense of defeat, the Harijans were excluded from the life of the village. . . .

Perhaps one can gauge the power of new ideas by the impression they have

MAJOR CITIES OF INDIA

made on Chirora. No one, for example, was embarrassed at the degraded status of their wives and daughters. India's . . . feminist movement had made no inroads at all. Women, especially married women, were invisible. They stayed behind brick walls in their darkened homes. . . . The rule of purdah . . . was complete in Chirora.*

*"A Village in India: Reluctant Progress" by James Traub in *The New York Times Magazine*, September 9, 1984, pp. 106, 129–130, 132–133. Copyright ©1984 by The New York Times Company. Reprinted by permission.

1. What factors help keep villages from being isolated?
2. What are some of the changes taking place in villages? How do some villagers react to them?

CITY LIFE

Millions of Indians, most of them seeking jobs and a better life, have left their villages and are swelling India's cities. In 1881, only 9

CASE STUDY
INDIA

THE OLD AND THE NEW

Many Indians are content with a life style that blends the old and the new. Manubhai, the young stockbroker presented below, is one of those people:

Manubhai works in a square, run-down building on a narrow, noisy street of Bombay's business district.... A row of small rooms, offices of shareholders and stockbrokers, line the passage to the main building. Manubhai conducts his business in one of these rooms.

A short, stocky man with thick round spectacles and a round happy face, he sits behind a desk with two telephones. A radio blares out figures. Portraits of gods with marigolds threaded around their frames, hang behind him and beside him.... "I like my business" Manubhai confided to me in the din. "But my knowledge of the market is not fine, just good. As I am an honest and moral man I am able to earn enough and lead a good life." And these earnings go to share a good life with seventeen other members of his family, six adults and 11 children! The whole bunch turned out to receive me.... They all sat in a circle ... while I shot my questions in different directions....

"I joined the stock business in 1952 ..." said Manubhai. "And I joined the business right after my matriculation," added his older brother. ... "My father was sick at that time and my brother needed an extra hand" continued Manubhai. "We both had it easy compared to our father.... He had struggled for many years in several little businesses ... before he got a job in a brokerage house and moved to Bombay. After ten years he ... had started his own stock business. One was able to live well with very little in those days.... What my father spent in a year, I spend in a day now. But generally we are better off than we used to be," Manubhai added....

Today Manubhai lives in a large apartment in a well-to-do suburb of Bombay, owns a car, eats better and lives better. "My children have a better life than I did as a child. They eat more nourishing food, go to better schools, and know much more about cars and movies than I ever did. They are also more intelligent, ask more questions and argue. Perhaps they see many more things, are open to wider influences and all in all, have better living conditions than I and my brother did," said Manubhai.

Manubhai is aware of this, and he is not averse to his children growing up in a world radically different from his. But he continues to keep his own world intact. His world is built around a joint family and the puja [worship] room. "A joint family has tremendous advantages in business and day to day life. My brother and I are excellent business partners and have never had any differences.... Living in a joint family I can afford to take a month off.... My brother simply takes care of my business and his wife takes care of my children," said Manubhai while the rest grinned approval.*

1. In what kind of environment does Manubhai live?
2. Do you think Manubhai is representative of many Indians today? Explain your answer.

**They Live in India: Vignettes of Contemporary Indian Lives*, Vol. III—*The Urban Scene* by Anees Jung, The Educational Resources Center, The University of the State of New York and the State Educational Department of New Delhi, India, pp. 7-9. Reprinted by permission.

percent of the Indian population lived in cities. By 1981, the number had risen to more than 20 percent. Today, the number is even greater. At least 12 cities—Calcutta, Bombay, Delhi/New Delhi, Madras, Bangalore, Hyderabad, Ahmadabad, Kanpur, Poona, Nagpur, Lucknow, and Jaipur—each are home to more than 1 million people.

Different cities are important for different reasons. Some, such as Varanasi, are important for religious reasons. Others, such as Delhi/New Delhi, serve important functions as political centers. Still others are industrial centers like Ahmadabad or commerce and shipping centers like Bombay, Madras, and Calcutta. The cities are centers from which influence spreads out into the countryside for political and economic control, growth, change, transportation, communication, and education.

Most of the cities have an "old city" area, temples and mosques, bazaars and shopping areas, and commercial areas. Within the city, people with similar backgrounds and wealth tend to live in the same districts. Life styles are very much related to wealth. Nowhere is the contrast greater than in Calcutta. It has elegant boulevards, air-conditioned restaurants, private clubs, and palatial homes for the wealthy. But it also has some of the most crowded slums in the world, with more than 100,000 people occupying each square kilo-

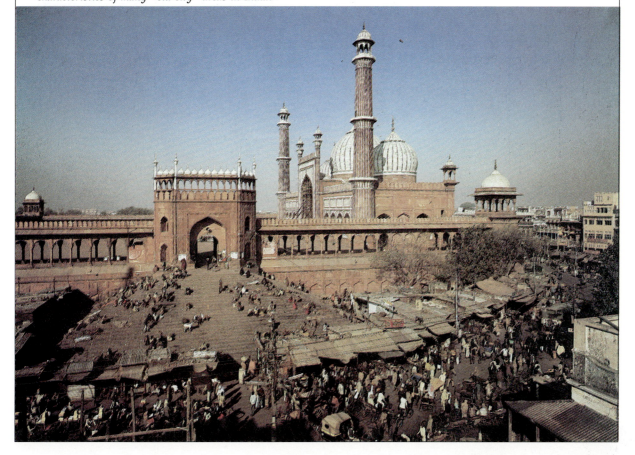

Beyond the market stalls in the foreground, on the steps of one entrance to the Jama Masjid, India's largest mosque, live some of Old Delhi's poorest residents. What are the characteristics of many "old city" areas in India?

meter. Several hundred thousand of the poorest of the poor literally live and die on the streets.

Severe overcrowding has affected other cities as well. One of the hardest hit is Bombay, India's commercial and major international business center. In the words of one Indian, "the millions of hopefuls who stream into the city strain its ability to cope to the breaking point.... The city is on the skids." Below, Bombay—and the life styles of some of its residents—is discussed by an Indian journalist:

> Author V.S. Naipaul once observed that in Bombay you can always find some form of life lower than whatever miserable state you have observed. Today, slum life in Bombay no longer constitutes low life; you are expected to specify what kind of slum, what kind of pavement.... There are slums where dwellers switch on technicolour lights and have ceiling fans, there are others where residents open a refrigerator and offer you a cold drink, there are slums where the only space where women can bathe are two stone slabs . . . screened by tatters of jute and rags. And there are slums where there is nothing—no water or power and virtually no shelter....
>
> In Goregaon East, there is one such slum where recent squatters . . . have made their home in empty plots in a down-at-heel industrial estate. A few scrawny chickens grovel in the filth of the cramped huts; a woman is making rotis [bread] on a fire lit by wood shavings. Her husband, she says, is away at work: he collects cow-dung from stables and sells it as fuel in better-off slums. They came to Bombay two years ago to escape starvation. "If there was food in the village, why would we have come here? There is nothing here...."
>
> ... In another pocket of shanties across the road, . . . a man called Pandhari Tekhade, who arrived in Bombay in the late 1960's . . . , says he still earns his wage in the city doing odd jobs.... "Of course," he agrees, life is worse than in the village. But what is happiness? Happiness is being able to at least eat...."
>
> Life in other slums compares better.... Ovadipada is an example.... It resembles a self-sufficient little township, its boundaries provided with a pan shop, a grocery store and even a kiosk selling cold drinks.

Ocean-going freighters constantly move in and out of the Port of Calcutta, one of the world's busiest harbors. More than one-half of the tea grown in India is shipped through this port, which is situated along the Hooghly River, about 60 miles (96 kilometers) above the river's mouth on the Bay of Bengal. The port also serves as home for thousands of Indian families who live and work on their boats in the harbor. What is the importance of Bombay, India's chief western seaport?

CHAPTER 22 THE INDIAN PEOPLE 363

Inside, the lanes are clean with cement drains, electricity fixtures outside doors and nameplates. A room fifteen feet square [1.35 square meters] here can cost Rs 30.000 [$2565].

N.V. Poojari . . . lives in one such room. When he moved to Ovadipada he bought the place for Rs 11.000 [$940.50]: since then, he has constructed a kitchen at the back, put in a tiled floor, "bought" three electricity connections and his young son now has a proper school desk complete with a table fan. Poojari earns Rs 1,100 [$94.05] a month, but much of it is spent paying off the slum landlord who demands a price for every facility. "You pay Rs 30 [$2.57] a month for living here, another Rs 30 [$2.57] for every electricity point in the room, Rs 20 [$1.71] a month for water. . . . Other residents of Ovadipada complain bitterly. . . . Says one: "You have to pay for every wall, there are different owners for each. If a room has four walls, you have to sometimes end up paying rent to three different owners."

. . . Life for that vast segment of the city population loosely known as the middle class can be as competitive and harrowing especially when they are being driven out to live in the slums. . . . In the thick of the industrial estates of Malad, shanty towns have sprouted on the hilly tracts deep in the hinterland. At the end of a long track with stones sharp as knives, across a dirty stream, and high along a ridge in the hill is . . . Waishet Pada. Living conditions are slightly better than the earlier slums. . . . But the astonishing fact about this slum is that all its 300-odd inhabitants formerly lived in Parel: most of them were textile workers who were slowly forced to move out because of their growing families.

Ramibai is one such immigrant . . . who looks old beyond his 28 years. He was pushed out of his family's one room . . . because the room couldn't accommodate the size of the growing family any more. "This place seemed ideal for me," he says of his perch on the hillside. "It was clean,

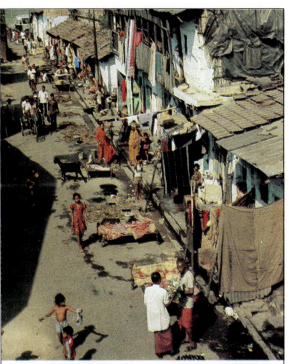

A bike-drawn vehicle moves down the narrow, crowded streets of a Calcutta slum. Slums like this one are home to about 67 percent of Calcutta's population. What are the slums of Bombay like?

uncrowded and cheap." He explains that the slum that has materialised there since he moved in was originally a forest encroachment. "But we've managed everything in six years, a water connection, power connection, everything. You know how Bombay is," he says, making a gesture to indicate money changing hands, "If you grease a few palms, everything works. . . . " For Ramibai there is no alternative to living in Bombay. His job, family and future are here. Like millions of others for whom survival has become a daily battle, Ramibai somehow always manages to find a way of making things work.*

1. What are India's largest cities?
2. What effect has overcrowding had on Bombay and other Indian cities?

---

*"Low Life: A Daily Battle" in *India Today*, November 15, 1983, pp. 58–59. Reprinted by permission.

INDIA UNIT 4

CHAPTER 22 REVIEW

POINTS TO REMEMBER

1. Indian society is diverse. This diversity is regional, ethnic, cultural, religious, educational, rural/urban, and class based.
2. India today is in a state of change. While traditional beliefs remain important to many, others believe that things must change if India is to keep up with the rest of the world.
3. Traditionally, Indian marriages were arranged by the family, a dowry was expected, and most women married at a very early age. While arranged marriages remain common today, the dowry has been outlawed and a minimum marriage age has been established.
4. The traditional Indian family cycle has both nuclear and extended families. Joint families, while providing their members with many benefits, are not completely without problems.
5. In an Indian household, the oldest able male is considered the head of the family. Domestic affairs, however, generally are organized by the oldest able female.
6. Indian women have always had a pivotal role in households and families. In recent years, Indian women have been pressing to change traditional customs that have limited them to households and kept them under the control of men.
7. A majority of the Indian people live in self-contained and self-sufficient villages and follow rural life styles. Contact with the outside world is slowly bringing changes of many kinds to villages.
8. India has one of the largest urban populations in the world. City life styles are very much related to wealth. In recent years, overcrowding has led to serious problems in most of India's urban areas.

VOCABULARY

Identify

Hindu	Untouchables	Madras	Poona
Shakti	Harijans	Bangalore	Nagpur
Sanskrit	Calcutta	Hyderabad	Lucknow
Bengal	Bombay	Ahmadabad	Jaipur
Brahmins	Delhi/New Delhi	Kanpur	Varanasi

Define

dowry	extended families	*suttee*	*panchayat*
nuclear families	joint family	*purdah*	

DISCUSSING IMPORTANT IDEAS

1. What do you consider the pros and cons of arranged marriages? How would you react to marrying someone chosen by your parents? Do you think they would choose the kind of spouse you want? Why or why not?

2. Do you know anyone who lives in a joint family? Would you like to live in a joint family? Why or why not?
3. What do you think accounts for the great difference between rural and urban life styles and attitudes? What would you suggest to alter the situation?
4. Do you think change would come more quickly if there were less diversity in India? Explain.

Developing Skills

DISTINGUISHING RELEVANT INFORMATION FROM IRRELEVANT INFORMATION

In most situations, there are two kinds of information—relevant and irrelevant. *Relevant information* is information related to the topic or main idea of discussion. It defines, explains, illustrates, serves as an example, or describes a cause or consequence of that topic or main idea. *Irrelevant information* is information that does not really relate to the topic or main idea. The following guidelines will help you distinguish the one type of information from the other in written material:

1. Read the material, and determine the topic of discussion.
2. For each statement, determine if it relates directly to the topic by asking yourself if the information in it defines, explains, illustrates, serves as an example, or describes a cause or consequence of the topic.
3. Any statement that does not do one of the things named in guideline 2 is irrelevant.

These guidelines are used to distinguish relevant from irrelevant information in the following paragraph. The topic is Nat and his learner's permit to drive:

Nat is 16 years old. (cause) *He is tall, thin, has blonde hair, plays basketball, and gets good grades in school.* (irrelevant) *In the state in which Nat lives, you can get a driver's learning permit at 16.* (explains) *Nat really likes cars and is thinking of becoming an automobile mechanic.* (irrelevant) *Because he only has a learner's permit, a licensed driver must be with Nat in the car when he drives.* (explains) *Nat's friend Bobby also has a learner's permit.* (irrelevant) *His parents allow him to drive the family car as long as one of his friends who has a driver's license accompanies him.* (irrelevant) *Their family car is a year-old Chevrolet.* (irrelevant) *Nat's family car is a year-old Chevrolet, too.* (irrelevant) *Nat's parents do not care what Bobby is or is not allowed to do.* (explains) *They insist that Nat cannot drive their family car unless one of them accompanies him.* (consequence)

For further practice in this skill, use the guidelines to determine which of the following statements are relevant or irrelevant to the topic "The Slums of Bombay." Give reasons for your decisions.

1. Many Indians are unhappy about having to live in the countryside.
2. Some areas of Bombay have no water or power and too little shelter.
3. Some immigrants arrived in Bombay in 1960.
4. There are different levels of living areas in Bombay.
5. Many poor people live in Bombay.

CHAPTER 23
RELIGIONS OF INDIA

1. What are the major features of Hinduism?
2. How have Hinduism and other religions influenced life in India?

Heart of mine, awake in this holy place of pilgrimage,
In this Land of India on the shore of vast humanity.
Here do I stand with arms outstretched to salute man divine,
And sing his praise in many a gladsome paean [hymn of praise].
These hills that are rapt [enclosed] in deep meditation,
These plains that clasp their rosaries [prayer beads] of rivers,
Here you will find earth that is ever-sacred;
In this land of India, on the shore of vast humanity.

We know not whence and at whose call, these myriad streams
Have come rushing forth to lose themselves in this sea—
Aryan and non-Aryan, Dravidian and Chinese,
Scythian, Hun, Pathan and Moghul, all merged into one body.
Now the West has opened her doors, bringing their offerings,
They will give and take, unite, and will not turn away,
In this land of India, on the shore of vast humanity.

Come O Aryans, come non-Aryans, Hindu, Mussalman [Muslim] come,
Come ye Parsees, come O Christians, come ye one and all,
Come Brahmins, let you be hallowed by holding all by hand.
Come ye all who are shunned, wipe out the dishonour,
Come to the crowning of the Mother, fill the sacred bowl
With water that is sanctified [made holy] by the touch of all
In this land of India, on the shore of vast Humanity.*

The above poem is the work of an early twentieth-century Indian poet named Rabindranath Tagore. In the poem, Tagore expresses love for his land and longs for the unity of its people. At the same time, he recognizes an important fact—India is a land of amazing diversity. The people of India belong to a variety of ethnic groups that together speak 20 major languages and more than 100 minor languages and dialects. India also is a land of many religions. This diversity of ethnic group, language, and belief is the result of many centuries of foreign invasion. With each group of invaders came new ideas and beliefs that often blended with existing ones.

Although modern India has no official religion and religious freedom is guaranteed by law, religion continues to play an important role in daily life. Religious teachings and rules often influence whom one marries and chooses for friends. They also can affect where and at what a person works as well as what he or she eats or wears.

---

*"The Song of India" by Rabindranath Tagore in *Aspects of Indian Culture*, edited by Mahendra Kulasrestha, 1961, Vishveshvaranand V.R. Institute. Reprinted by permission.

Hinduism

The major religion of India is Hinduism, with over 580 million followers known as Hindus. Hindus make up 80 percent of the population and have played a leading role in the development of Indian civilization. Their religion, which is one of the world's oldest, developed gradually over centuries rather than being founded on the teachings of one person.

Hinduism is based on a number of different beliefs and practices. One is the worship of many gods and goddesses. The three most important gods are Brahma, the creator of the universe; Vishnu, its preserver; and Shiva, its destroyer. A number of goddesses, who represent the creative or energetic aspects of life, also are revered. They include Lakshmi, goddess of good fortune, wealth, and prosperity; and Parvati, wife of Shiva, and Mother of the universe, and goddess of life and death.

Hindu thinkers view all of life as sacred and stress the unity of all life. They believe that all living things—gods, goddesses, humans, and animals—have souls that are part of one eternal spirit called Brahman, the world soul. Many Hindus practice *ahimsa*, non-violence to living creatures. They try not to harm animals and do not eat meat.

Closely related to this belief is the concept of **reincarnation,** the belief that a soul continues through a series of lives on the way to union with the eternal spirit. Hindus believe that in each life the soul takes on the form of a human or some other life form. The sum of a person's past lives, which is carried into new lives, is the person's *karma*. People are born who they are because of *karma*. The way in which a person lives in a particular life is determined by how well he or she carried out his or her ***dharma,*** or special moral duty, in past lives. For example, a person who is a street sweeper today may have been, in an earlier existence, a priest who disobeyed his *dharma*. The sweeper, however,

Below left, bedecked in flowers and precious jewels, are the god Vishnu, preserver of the universe, and his wife Lakshmi (also, below right), goddess of wealth and prosperity. The elephant-headed figure, below center, is Ganesa, or Ganapati, god of wisdom and good fortune. Also called the "Remover of Obstacles," Ganesa is prayed to at the start of any undertaking. Why do Hindus practice ahimsa?

by being good and faithful to his *dharma* today may be born a priest in the next life. The goal is to be reborn at higher and higher levels until union is achieved with the eternal spirit. Once this happens, a person ceases being reborn.

Hindus are aided in their spiritual search by **gurus,** or teachers, whom they revere. To discipline both mind and body, some Hindus practice a form of physical exercise and worship known as **yoga.** There also are a number of sacred writings that explain how one should conduct his or her life. One of the most important of these is quoted below. Known as the *Bhagavad Gita,* or *Song of the Soul,* it was written about 500 BC:

> In the bonds of works I am free, because in them I am free from desires. The man who can see this truth, in his work he finds his freedom.
>
> What is work? What is beyond work? Even some seers [wise men] see this not aright. I will teach thee the truth of pure work, and this truth shall make thee free.
>
> He whose undertakings are free from anxious desire and fanciful thought, whose work is made pure in the fire of wisdom: he is called wise by those who see. In whatever work he does such a man in truth has peace: he expects nothing, he relies on nothing, and ever has fullness of joy.
>
> He has no vain hopes, he is the master of his soul, he surrenders all he has, only his body works: he is free from sin. He is glad with whatever God [the eternal spirit] gives him, and he has risen beyond the two contraries here below; he is without jealousy, and in success or in failure he is one: his works bind him not.
>
> He has attained liberation: he is free from all bonds, his mind has found peace in wisdom, and his work is a holy sacrifice. The work of such a man is pure.
>
> Greater is thine own work, even if this be humble, than the work of another, even if this be great. When a man does the work God gives him, no sin can touch this man.
>
> And a man should not abandon his work, even if he cannot achieve it in full perfection; because in all work there may be imperfection, even as in all fire there is smoke.*

PRACTICES

For most Indians, Hinduism is a way of life. The basis of Indian society, law, literature, art, and philosophy, it influences daily life through a number of religious practices. For example, Hindus follow daily rituals of washing and prayer called *puja.* They also follow strict dietary rules. When they die, their bodies are cremated, or burned, and the ashes are scattered over such sacred rivers as the Ganges.

Another Hindu practice is the honoring of deities at public temples. In these temples, which are found all over India, are carved statues of deities, people, and events from Indian religious stories. Worshippers view the statues, pray, and make offerings of food and flowers. Through these actions of *puja,* Hindus believe they are bringing holiness into their lives. The temples are administered by priests, who also perform religious rituals. Priests are expected to be familiar with ancient texts and to know Sanskrit, the ancient language of India. Below, a Hindu priest talks about his role and duties and some of the beliefs and practices of Hinduism:

> My day at the temple begins at half-past four in the morning and ends at eight o'clock every night. It's a long day, but I don't mind one bit, as I devote all the time to the service of God.

---

*The Bhagavad Gita, translated by Juan Mascaró, (Penguin Classics, 1962) pp. 62–63. Reprinted by permission of Penguin Books Ltd.

One of the practices of the Hindu religion is to bathe in the waters of a sacred river. For this reason, each year millions of Hindus will flock to the Ganges River. One of the holiest sites of the Ganges is upriver from Varanasi at Allahabad, where the Ganges and Yamuna rivers come together. It is here that the Kumbh Mela is held. In addition to ritual washing and bathing, what are some other Hindu religious practices?

Which God, you ask? Well, we Hindus have 330 million deities. . . .

It's part of my duty as a priest to offer prayer to the idols, to bathe them with milk and honey, and to dress them. Then, every day, other temple priests and I have to organize the distribution of free food. Our temple feeds about thirty or forty poor people every day. The temple gets its money from donations.

Only a Brahman [high-born person] can become a priest in a temple. He must be learned in the ancient Sanskrit texts known as *Vedas*. He must also know how to conduct weddings, birth and death ceremonies and so on. . . .

There are so many holy cities and places. They're usually on the banks of rivers or up on the snowy mountains. Cities like Hardwar, Rishikesh and Varanasi are on the riverside. Pilgrimage centers like Badrinath, Kedarnath and Amarnath are high up in the mountains. Half the year the pilgrims can't get to them because of the snow.

But I must tell you about the Kumbh Mela, which is held every twelve years and is the world's greatest religious fair. At Kumbh, millions and millions of Hindus gather from all over India to take a bath in the holy Ganges.

With so much going on, life remains busy and full for me. I can't tell you how happy and fortunate I feel serving God and the people.*

Even though there are priests and regular services in temples, Hindu worship is an individual matter. While some **sadhus,** or "holy men", are attached to temples, others wander on their own all over India. Devout Hindus give them food as a good deed. Also, Hindu worship is centered more in the home than in the temple. Every Hindu's home has a spot set aside for worship and **meditation,** or the silencing of thoughts to gain enlightenment. Apart from special acts of worship, Hindus regard ordinary tasks as sacred. They believe that each action, if performed well, will bring a person closer to perfection and union with the eternal spirit.

---

*"We Hindu people have thousands of gods" in *We Live in India* by Veenu Sandal, 1984, The Bookwright Press, pp. 20–21. Reprinted by permission.

CASE STUDY
INDIA

A Hindu Holy City

For Hindus, the fact that the ancient Indian city of Varanasi, also known as Benares and Kashi, is a rail and trade center is secondary to the fact that it is a holy city. Each year, more than 1 million Hindus make pilgrimages to Varanasi to pay homage at one of the city's 1500 temples, palaces, and shrines and to bathe in the sacred Ganges River. They believe that if they die in Varanasi, they will be released from the cycle of rebirths. But, as indicated in the newspaper article that follows, some Indians see the city in a different light:

Benares. Varanasi. Kashi.

These are all names of the same city which, to every Hindu, symbolizes the ultimate destination, the holiest of the holy cities. . . .

Varanasi symbolizes the energy of ancient Hindu learning and art. Situated on the confluence [meeting point] of the Ganges and the Varana River (from which it gets its most common name), Varanasi is one of the few cities in the world that still lives by its ancient traditions—which date from the 6th century BC.

Today, the former Maharajah [princely ruler] of Benares continues to hold a mythical grip on the . . . city. Standing on the breeze-filled verandah of the Ramnagar Fort, his royal residence, he looks out over the Ganges. . . .

"Benares is not a city but a state of mind," he tells me, . . . "If you have reached this . . . city you cannot go anywhere else; you cannot be reborn. When the river washes away the good and the evil, there is no rebirth. Once you know this you can abandon yourself to the freedom of who you are."

"Every Benaresi knows this and indulges in it. You can listen to music all night and wake up early to see the sun rise, have a cold bath in the river and watch it flow, ever changing and yet the same. You rise to see the sun and return to see it set, and you tell yourself that like the sun man too must go. But while he lives in this city he lives fully. . . .

But for one merchant family that has made a fortune from the selling of the legendary saris of Benares, there is another side to the holy city.

Varanasi is decaying, the river is polluted, and the people are decrepit, says the family patriarch. . . . It is a city where trucks honk all night, where streets are filled with nothing but shops whose keepers haggle and sell at all hours, where women buy so many saris, and men do nothing. . . .

The women of this household, dressed in nylon saris . . . sit in wicker chairs on the verandah. . . . The river in this house commands no reverence, just a massive indifference. . . .

What does the city mean to them?

"Nothing," they say. . . .

Do they bathe in the holy river? "No. We take the children to swim when we go for picnics in the summer on the other—the cleaner—side of the ghats."

"We want the city to become modern," says the eldest daughter-in-law. . . . "We have started a ladies club," she continues. . . .

"The club arranges swimming classes in the Ganges. . . ."

As I say goodbye I ask the family patriarch if he ever leaves Benares. "I am an old man and I don't want to go anywhere lest I die in another place and miss out on my 'moksha' [liberation]," he said with a laugh.

His words trail out of the large white house and follow me through the dark lane that leads me back to the ghats and the holy river. *

1. What kind of city is Varanasi?
2. What do the differing views about the city reveal to you about the relationship between religious tradition and modern life in India today?

---

*"The Holy Ganges" by Anees Jung in *The Christian Science Monitor*, June 28, 1985, pp. 18–19. Reprinted by permission.

CELEBRATIONS AND PILGRIMAGES

Hindus celebrate many holidays. One of the most important is Diwali, which marks the arrival of winter and symbolizes the victory of good over evil. Celebrated in both cities and villages, in some areas it is called the Festival of Lights because during the celebrations homes and businesses are aglow with electric lights, candles, and oil lamps.

Another important holiday is Holi. Its purpose is to purify the fields so they will yield good crops. Celebrated in the spring, Holi is regarded as a "fun" festival. On the eve of Holi, bonfires are lit to symbolize ridding the earth of the evils of the past year. The next day, people roam the streets, throwing colored water on each other and painting each other's foreheads. People dye their hair and clothes various shades of red and purple, and children play practical jokes.

Many Hindus consider it their religious duty to make **pilgrimages,** or sacred journeys, to shrines. One of the many pilgrimages takes place at Puri. There, large crowds gather each year to watch an image of the god Juggernaut travel to its summer temple. Below, a visitor to India describes a Puri pilgrimage in which he took part:

> Outside the temple, in the town and on the roads leading to it, there was excitement in the air. There was an increasing noise made by a surging orchestra of creaking, tinkling rickshaws and pilgrims' sandals slip-slapping on the road. Many people peeled away from the main body of marchers and crossed the hot sand dunes to the sea. . . . There were several hundred dunking themselves under the supervision of fishermen. . . .
>
> It would be impossible to say how many were in Puri that day. People talked of a million or more. I guessed there were at least several hundred thousand who had been gathering since long before dawn. . . . People crammed every window, balcony, rooftop, ledge, tree and hoarding [wooden fence], and I paid a few rupees to get onto a roof packed with squirming bodies. There was a strong smell of sweat and camphor and sandalwood. It was . . .

These buildings and images of deities reflected in the river are brightly lit in celebration of Diwali, the Festival of Lights. One of the purposes of Diwali is to honor the goddess Lakshmi. What is the purpose of the Hindu holiday Holi?

hot and humid.... Down in the street cows and bullocks ran amok and people shouted and scattered....

Excitement grew through the afternoon. More pilgrims pressed in, their foreheads daubed with paint. Men jigged incessantly to the beat of drums.... Hundreds of women had cut off their hair and brought their shining tresses in offering. There was a constant cracking and spluttering as people smashed coconuts on the ground and anointed themselves with the milk, falling to their knees in prayer.

All eyes were on three monstrous vehicles standing abreast.... These are great chariots as large as houses, [topped] by decorated pavilions in which . . . three gods ride to their summer house. The largest is Juggernaut's.... It has a red dome and the whole . . . structure is 45 feet [13.5 meters] high....

At about five o'clock long thick ropes were attached to the chariots and men rushed forward to grab them. By tradition, 4,200 men pull each wagon, but there seemed to be more of them than that....

At last, the chariots began to tremble and move. The din was terrific.... The platforms shuddered and the ground shook.... This was no half-hearted carnival, but a [display] of India's religious energy, an event of great power whose participants were singleminded in their devotion and enthusiasm.... The people surged forward and tossed rice, marigolds and coconut shards at the wagons, and scooped up brown dust where the wheels had passed and rubbed it onto their heads. The eyes of men and women were wide and shiny with adoration, tears blobbed their dusty faces. The chariots moved a few yards at a time and then paused while the draggers drew breath. By nightfall they were halfway and the progress stopped while the weary hauliers slept. The journey resumed next morning. This time I watched from the street. I have an indelible memory of the towering mon-

In this painting, a wealthy Kshatriya receives guests at his lavish court. Traditionally, the Kshatriya made up the military or ruling class of Hindu India. In what sacred writing are the Varnas *described?*

sters advancing and people running from the grinding wheels, under which, years ago, some of the devoted used to hurl themselves in sacrifice and to achieve an ultimate bliss.*

THE CASTE SYSTEM

Hindus have traditionally been divided into four categories known as **Varnas.** These categories are Brahmins, or priests; Kshatriyas, or warrior aristocrats; Vaisyas, or farmers and merchants; and Sudras, or servants. Together, they make up the **caste system** of India. The *Bhagavad Gita* describes each of the *Varnas* as follows:

---
*Trevor Fishlock: *Gandhi's Children* ©1983, Trevor Fishlock. Published by Universe Books, New York, 1983.

The works of Brahmins, Kshatriyas, Vaisyas and Sudras are different, in harmony with the . . . powers of their born nature.

The works of a Brahmin are peace; self-harmony, austerity and purity; loving-forgiveness and righteousness; vision and wisdom and faith.

These are the works of a Kshatriya: a heroic mind, inner fire, constancy, resourcefulness, courage in battle, generosity and noble leadership.

Trade, agriculture and the rearing of cattle is the work of a Vaisya. And the work of the Sudra is service.*

Jati The caste groupings to which most Hindus relate and within which they live are called *jatis*. In each area, *jatis* are ranked in order from high to low. Each *jati* is linked to a specific occupation and has its own rules for diet, marriage, and other social practices. A person's social standing often depends on his or her *jati*. Each person is born into his or her *jati* and cannot change *jatis*.

Hinduism and the caste system have been closely tied together. Often, fulfilling one's *dharma* has meant performing one's *jati* obligations. Because strict Hindu social rules require that those of a higher *jati* avoid contact with those of a lower one, members of a *jati* generally live in the same neighborhood and do not mix socially with or marry someone of a different *jati*.

In recent years, the caste system has been challenged. The government, for one, has tried to put an end to the system, whose restrictions it views as barriers to modernizing the country. Government officials claim that because of the system, the poor have had little opportunity to improve their lives. Caste has also been challenged by the recent spread of education and the growth of modern urban industrial life, which have led Hindus of different *jatis* to mix freely in offices, factories, and other public places. As a result, some Hindus now marry outside their *jatis*.

The caste system, however, is an old tradition that yields only slowly to change, and few Hindus are willing to see it end completely. They view it as an important part of Hinduism that links religious belief and social behavior. They point out that *jatis* perform practical functions by passing craft skills from one generation to another and providing social and educational benefits to their members.

Untouchables At least 25 percent of India's population are Sudras, the lowest ranked of all the *jatis*. Some of these Sudras work at the dirtiest jobs, such as handling dead animals or sweeping streets. These people came to be known as **untouchables.** Because they work with dirt, death, or blood, they have been viewed as impure by other Hindus.

The position of untouchables in Indian society has improved a good deal in the last 30 or so years. Since India's constitution outlaws discrimination against them, many untouchables have entered government service. Some have acquired land. Even so, a large number of Hindus still cling to the old traditions that keep some of the untouchables in an inferior status. Below, an Indian journalist discusses the life of some women who are sweepers in private homes:

> The work is very tiring. It involves climbing flights of stairs, carrying garbage on the head for long distances, and working in a bent posture for hours together. Maternity leave is unknown. Most women continue to work almost to the day of childbirth, and they have to provide substitutes for the days they are absent.

---
*The Bhagavad Gita, translated by Juan Mascaró, (Penguin Classics, 1962) p. 119. Reprinted by permission of Penguin Books Ltd.

Their salaries for these days go to the substitutes.

... They are not allowed to enter other rooms in their employers' houses. In many houses, they are not even supposed to touch the tap or bucket in the bathroom, because these would get defiled by their touch. Bimla [a 26-year-old sweeper] says: "Most of my employers address me as Jamadarni (sweeperess). There is no personal relationship with them. I clean the latrine, throw away garbage, sweep the stairs and driveways. I am not supposed to sweep the other rooms, though sometimes when the servant is absent, I am asked to stand in. I get very tired, carrying dustbins and bending over the stairs fifteen times a day."

The older women are more resigned to facing such humiliation but some of the younger ones seethe with indignation, like Kamla, who has been working since the age of 11, and is now a mother of four: "Who says there is no untouchability?

Even after all these years, I am not allowed to go anywhere near the kitchen. I work for Baniyas who are very fussy. There is one relative of theirs—she says she is a school teacher—she lifts up her sari if she has to pass me. When she does that, I feel like throwing acid on her face. Don't we have hearts and bodies just like you?*

1. What are some of the beliefs common to all Hindus?
2. What role do priests play in Hinduism?
3. Why do Hindus make pilgrimages?
4. What are the four main *Varnas*? What is the role of each? Of the untouchables?

ISLAM

After Hinduism, the most important religion of India is Islam. With about 80 million Muslims, followers of Islam, India is the third largest Muslim nation in the world. First preached in the 600's AD by an Arabian religious leader named Muhammad, Islam spread from Arabia to North Africa and eventually to India. Today, some Indian Muslims are descendants of Islamic peoples who invaded and settled India from the eighth to the thirteenth centuries. Others are former Hindus who converted to Islam.

Muslims believe in one God whose teachings are recorded in a holy book called the Koran. They traditionally have opposed the caste system and religious images on the grounds that all people are equal and that God is a spiritual being beyond all forms. Although they eat meat, they do not eat pork, which they regard as unclean.

Although Muslims have played an important role in Indian government, society, and culture for centuries, they have often been in

Street sweepers like this man working in the embassy section of New Delhi are a common sight in India. What kinds of tasks do some of India's female street sweepers perform? What indignities do they endure?

---

*"The 'Unclean' Who Keep the City Clean" by Malavika Karlekar in *Manushi*, July–August, 1979, p. 52. Reprinted by permission.

conflict with the Hindus. In modern India, they officially enjoy equal rights with Hindus. Many live in the cities and are actively involved in government and industry. Others, however, remain in the villages and follow a more traditional life style. Below, a visitor describes the life style of a Muslim family she met in an Indian village:

> Rehana bibi is 30 years old and lives in the Muslim community of Rustampura. She was educated in an elementary school not far from her present home. At 16, she married a local villager named Kolokhan bhai Garashia. They share a house with Kolokhan bhai's elder brother and his family.
>
> Rehana bibi and Kolokhan bhai have three children—two sons and a daughter. They want their sons to be educated so they will have better job opportunities. Their daughter, however, probably will leave school when she becomes a teenager, marry, and assume the role of a housewife. Until she marries, she can help Rehana bibi and Kolokhan bhai in the small shop they rent and run across the street from their home. There, they sell a variety of goods, including vegetables, powders, seeds, slippers, brooms, rubber bands, and soap.
>
> Rehana bibi and Kolokhan bhai are devout Muslims. Every Thursday, Kolokhan bhai spends the entire day at the Darga, a local shrine where pilgrims gather to pray and to receive advice from a "holy man." Rehana bibi stays in the shop and reads her prayer book until there are customers to be served.
>
> In many respects, Rehana bibi's family is different from other Muslim families in the village. Most of the Muslim women spend their days at home and prefer to keep house rather than assist their husbands in their jobs. But Rehana bibi realizes that unless she looks after the shop, her husband would find it difficult to travel to other villages to buy goods. Her strength of character has impressed many of her neighbors, Hindu and Muslim alike.
>
> In keeping with the beliefs of Islam, Rehana bibi and Kolokhan bhai are very generous. They believe that charity and generosity to others is a form of service to Allah [God]. Kolokhan bhai knows what poverty is and that the poor need to have their basic needs met, so he often gives offerings to beggars. He is reluctant, however, to receive financial help from his wealthier in-laws or even from his own brother. He and Rehana bibi usually try to make ends meet through their own efforts. Hopeful about a brighter future, they have made plans to expand both their house and their shop.*

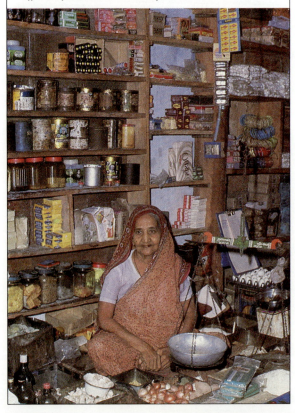

This Muslim woman runs a "provision shop," or general store similar to the one in Rustampura, described on this page. How is Rehana bibi's family different from other Muslim families in Rustampura?

*Adapted from "Case Study of Rehana bibi Garashia" by Sumita Shukla in *Households and Families in Rustampura Village* by Ellen C.K. Johnson and Sumita Shukla, pp. 8–9, 11, 12–13.

1. From whom have many Indian Muslims descended?
2. Why do Indian Muslims oppose the caste system and religious images?

OTHER RELIGIONS

In addition to Hinduism and Islam, India also has a number of other religions. One of these is Sikhism. Founded in the 1500's by a teacher named Guru Nanak, it rejects the caste system and combines the Muslim belief in one God with the Hindu belief in reincarnation. Most of its followers, known as Sikhs, live in the Indian state of Punjab. The rest live in India's major cities. While many Sikhs are business people or farmers, Sikhs generally are known for their military skills. They form one of the largest and best-trained groups in the Indian army.

Another religion of India is Buddhism, which emerged in India during the 500's BC. Its founder, the Indian prince Siddhartha Gautama, wanted to reform Hinduism. Known as Buddha, or "Enlightened One," he disregarded the caste system and taught that anyone could reach spiritual perfection. He knew that suffering was a fact of life. But he taught that it could be overcome by renouncing desires and by finding peace of mind through meditation and good deeds.

In spite of Hindu opposition, Buddhism spread throughout India and later became influential in Southeast and East Asia. Today, although only about 4 million Indians —1 percent of the population—are Buddhists, Buddhism has given to India a rich heritage of art, architecture, and literature.

A third minority religion is Jainism. Like Buddhism, it arose in the 500's BC as a protest against the caste system. Its founder, a *guru* named Mahavira, gave up his wealthy way of life to travel throughout the country to spread his message. Today, Jainism has

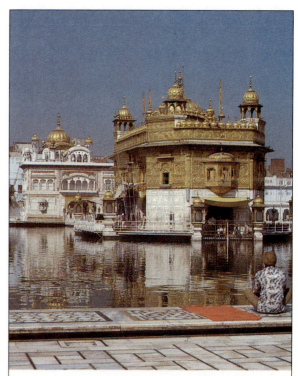

A lone Sikh worshipper meditates in front of the Golden Temple at Amritsar in northwestern India, center of the Sikh faith. What basic Hindu and Muslim beliefs have been combined in Sikhism?

over 3 million followers in India. Known as Jains, they place special emphasis on *ahimsa* and have extended the Hindu ban on killing to include all living things, even insects. Traditionally they have refused to farm for fear of plowing under living things and have devoted themselves to trade and business instead. Today, many are wealthy and have high positions in the Indian economy.

A fourth minority religion in India is Christianity, with about 18 million followers. Most Christians live in the south, where tradition states that an apostle of Jesus named Thomas founded churches in the first century AD. When the Portuguese reached India in the 1500's, they won converts to Catholicism. Two hundred years later, the British brought the first Protestant missionaries to India. Both the Catholic and Protes-

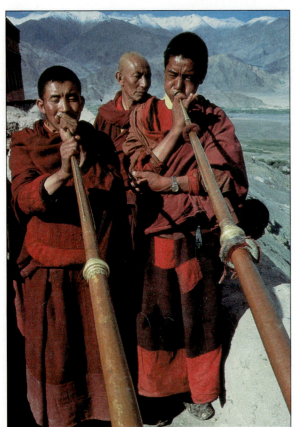

Buddhist monks, like these, play long brass horns and such other instruments as drums, bells, and cymbals to open sacred dances and festivals. How do Buddhists believe the suffering of life can be ended?

tant missionaries built hospitals and schools and won converts among the untouchables.

Still another religion in India is that of the Parsis, a people who came to India from Persia between 700 and 900 AD to escape Muslim persecution. Today, many Parsis live in Bombay and are leaders in industry and in the professions. Their beliefs are based on the teachings of Zoroaster, a Persian religious leader who lived around 1000 BC and who saw the world as a battleground between the forces of good and evil. The Parsis, who have remained separate from other religions in India, are known for their "Towers of Silence" where the dead are placed on platforms for vultures to clean their bones.

They believe that by disposing of the dead in this way, neither the ground nor the fire nor the air will be polluted. Below, an American writer discusses the Parsi influence in Bombay:

> . . . This community of about 80,000—the largest concentration of Parsis in the world—has [had] an influence in Bombay far out of proportion to its numbers. Though . . . businessmen from other groups have now broken the Parsis' near monopoly on wealth in this wealthiest of Indian cities, three Parsi names still stand out: Tata (hotels, steel mills, trucks, chemicals), Wadia (textile mills), and Godrej (typewriters and electric refrigerators among a host of other products).
>
> Philanthropy [the rich aiding the poor] and civic responsibility have been Parsi touchstones for generations. I saw those three names repeatedly as donors to hospitals, schools, Bombay's sparkling new National Centre for the Performing Arts, and the Tata Institute of Fundamental Research. S.P. Godrej, the . . . head of the Godrej organization, sketched a typically Parsi philosophy as he showed me around his company's spacious garden township at Vikhroli, on the edge of Bombay.
>
> "Our workers come to us with only their hands," Mr. Godrej said, as his arm swept a horizon of factories, housing blocks, schools, and—above all, that commodity so rare elsewhere in Bombay—space. "Our job is to give them skills. Today three-quarters of the Godrej working force of 12,000 live here. Their children go to school here. Our idea is to transform the so-called working classes into middle classes."*

1. What are some other religions of India besides Hinduism and Islam? When did each come to India?
2. What has each minority religion contributed to Indian culture?

---

*"Bombay, the Other India" by John Scofield in *National Geographic*, July 1981, pp. 122–123. Reprinted by permission.

EXPLORATION
INDIA

Indians of different religions often live side by side in cities, towns, and villages. In some instances, they have learned to accept their diversity and live in peace. In others, their religious differences have led to conflict and violence. Read the following comments made by Sikhs and Hindus who live in Punjab, where violence has erupted between members of the two religious groups. Then, based on what you have read, answer these questions:

1. How do some Hindus regard Sikhs?
2. How do some Sikhs regard Hindus?
3. What do you think may be some causes of Hindu-Sikh tensions?
4. Do you think the Indian government could take steps to reduce the tension between Hindus and Sikhs? Explain. What steps, if any, do you think the government should take?

"It's the politicians who have created conflict between Hindus and Sikhs. They are after one thing, and that is power. It's people like us who suffer."
— Sikh truck driver

"I am bitter, but not against Sikhs, only against certain sections of the Sikh leadership. Of course, one has become cautious in what one says. It's not easy living in this hostile situation."
— Hindu newspaper editor

"The Government must accept our identity as Sikhs. You must understand that Sikhs don't want to merge into the Hindu mainstream. We must protect our religion."
— Sikh businessman

"You see that it is our duty to spread our faith. You must have heard of the great sacrifices of the Sikh gurus. It is our duty to maintain that tradition. If necessary I will lay down my life to protect my faith."
— Sikh religious leader

"I was uprooted once and made a refugee. I won't let it happen again. And I won't leave because the Sikhs want to set up an independent state here. This is my home and I will fight and die here."
— Hindu textile merchant

"You see this finger. You see the finger-nail here. And you see the skin around it. Now the Sikhs are the finger-nail and Hindus are the skin around. How can you separate the finger from the finger-nail?"
— elderly Sikh

"All the Sikh gurus were Hindus. For 400 years we came of the same stock. We consider the Sikhs our offspring, we're the same family. Now they want to disown their parents."
— Hindu businessman

"What's wrong if Sikhs want a separate, personal law? What's wrong if Sikhs don't want Hindu immigrants to vote in Punjab? Really, the whole thing is rather silly. It's like a younger brother asking an older brother for a chocolate or toffee. And the older one is making such a fuss."
— Sikh housewife

"Punjabi Sikh farmers don't care if Hindu migrant laborers vote or not. They need them to work the fields. Anything that would stop the coming of these laborers would be opposed."
— Sikh university student

"The problem lies in the villages. There's no tension among people like us. Look at the way we joke about each other. Come on, we Sikhs and Hindus have grown up together. There's no social uneasiness."
— Urban Sikh

"No one here knows of Hindu-Sikh troubles. Everyone in this village goes to the Sikh temple— everyone, also the Hindus and Muslims."
— Sikh farmer*

*Adapted from "Journey in Punjab" by Sunil Sethi in *India Today*, September 30, 1983, pp. 98–103. Reprinted by permission.

CHAPTER 23 REVIEW

POINTS TO REMEMBER

1. Modern India has no official religion, and religious freedom is guaranteed by law. Religion, however, plays an important role in daily life.
2. The major religion of India is Hinduism. Hindus worship through many deities, view all of life as sacred, stress the unity of all life, and believe in reincarnation.
3. For most Indians, Hinduism is a way of life. Apart from special acts of worship, its followers regard ordinary tasks as sacred. They have many holiday celebrations and consider it their religious duty to make pilgrimages to shrines.
4. Hindus traditionally have been divided into four *Varnas* and thousands of *jatis*. In recent years, the government has challenged this system.
5. After Hinduism, the most important religion of India is Islam. Muslims believe in one God and oppose the caste system. Over the centuries, they have played an important role in India.
6. Among India's other religions are Sikhism, Buddhism, Jainism, Christianity, and the faith of the Parsis. Followers of each of these have contributed to the culture, economy, and development of India.

VOCABULARY

Identify

Hinduism	Sanskrit	Islam	Jainism
Brahma	Diwali	Koran	Mahavira
Vishnu	Holi	Sikhism	Christianity
Shiva	Brahmins	Guru Nanak	Parsis
Lakshmi	Kshatriyas	Punjab	Zoroaster
Parvati	Vaisyas	Buddhism	"Towers of Silence"
Brahman	Sudras	Siddharta Gautama	Varanasi
Bhagavad Gita			

Define

ahimsa	*gurus*	*sadhus*	*Varnas*
reincarnation	yoga	meditation	caste system
karma	*puja*	pilgrimages	*jatis*
dharma			untouchables

DISCUSSING IMPORTANT IDEAS

1. Do you think that the statement that Hinduism is more than a religion is an accurate one? Explain.
2. Based on what you know about Hinduism, do you think the caste system can be eliminated in India? Explain.

3. What do Islam and the other religions of India have in common with Hinduism? In what ways are they different from Hinduism?

4. What role do you think religious diversity plays in India? Do you think it helps or hinders development? Give examples to support your answers.

Developing Skills

DEVELOPING A GLOBAL POINT OF VIEW

Each person has his or her own *beliefs*, ideas about what is or is not true or real, and *values*, ideas about what is right and wrong, good and bad, beautiful and ugly, important and unimportant, and so on. In the same way, each culture also has its own beliefs and values, which are learned and passed on from generation to generation. These beliefs and values lead to a system of behaviors and practices that become a way of life identified with a particular culture.

There are several points to keep in mind when considering the beliefs and values of a culture. These include the following:

1. Beliefs and values are based primarily on faith and generally develop over a period of time. They cannot be proven or disproven.

2. There is no right or wrong when considering values and beliefs. Because your culture does not hold the same beliefs and values as another culture, it does not mean that the other culture is wrong and yours is right.

3. You must be *objective*, uninfluenced by personal points of view. This means setting aside your own beliefs and values and viewing those of the other culture strictly for what they are and not for what you think they should be.

4. It is important to discover the basis, or reasons for, a culture's beliefs or values. To do this, you may have to spend some time researching the culture's history. Finding out when, why, and how a belief or value came into existence will lead you to a better understanding of its importance to the culture under study.

5. When studying the beliefs and values of more than one culture, look for shared characteristics rather than for differences. If, for example, you are considering different religions within the same culture or of several different cultures, remember that almost every religion has these characteristics in common:

   a. beliefs about a god, be they belief in no god, in one god, or in more than one god
   b. an accepted teaching about *salvation*, the saving of the soul
   c. accepted rules of behavior.
   d. "stories" that explain the founding or beginnings of the religion
   e. religious *rituals*, or ceremonies

Your objective should be to compare the religions, not to judge them. This is true of any beliefs or values you are considering.

The dictionary defines "global" as "of, relating to, or involving the entire earth; worldwide." If, as you learn about other cultures, you put into practice the points discussed above, you come to consider each of them from a *global*, rather than an ethnocentric or judgmental, point of view.

For practice in developing a global point of view, read this chapter, which focuses on the religions of India, applying each one of the suggested points as you go along.

CHAPTER 24
AN OLD AND NEW LAND

1. What groups have influenced the development of Indian civilization?
2. How did India win its independence in modern times?

Ever since I was a boy I've been interested in the culture and people of my land. India is a vast country with many different kinds of people, religions, customs and even weather conditions. . . .

I'm happy to find that once again our educated young are turning to their own Indian culture. It's very rich and varied.

Our Indus Valley civilization, which dates back to the year 3000 B.C., is one of the oldest civilizations in the world. Scholars and archaeologists from all over the world still come to study the mystery of its ruins.

Soon after the Indus Valley civilization, the fair-skinned Aryan race invaded India. They settled in the north and drove the old inhabitants of India, the dark-skinned Dravidians, to the south. Much later, both the races mingled together, but the Aryans remained the dominating group.

It was the Aryans who divided our society into four groups. The Brahmans were considered to be the élite. Then came the warrior class; then the merchants and traders. Butchers, sweepers, and the menial workers were placed in the lowest class and were supposed to be impure and, therefore, untouchable. . . .

Centuries after the Aryans settled in India, the [Muslims] began invading. In the sixteenth century, the [Muslims] founded a great dynasty and ruled over us for a few hundred years. Then the British arrived and became the masters. So India is a mixture of many cultures rolled into one: Hindu culture of the Aryans, [Muslim] culture, and some British habits. . . .*

As indicated above by a present-day Indian scholar, a variety of foreigners have come to India over many centuries. Attracted by its important location and abundance of natural resources, different groups arrived, settled, and ruled all or parts of the country. Each group brought with it a different set of beliefs, customs, and institutions that contributed to the making of Indian civilization, one of the oldest and richest civilizations in the world.

Because of these invasions, India has had many political changes throughout its long history. Powerful empires, as well as small states, rose and fell on Indian soil. Rulers of these territories rivaled each other and outsiders for control of land and trade. At the same time, they supported the arts and enriched the culture.

Present-day citizens of India are proud of their past. At the same time, however, some of them admit that it is a burden. During each period of their long history, their people have faced hunger, disease, and poverty. They have often been at the mercy of strong rulers. They have had little experience in self-government and have found social harmony hard to achieve. Still, they remain hopeful, for today India is a democracy pledging equality for all under the law.

---

*"Our civilisation dates back to 3000 B.C." in *We Live in India* by Veenu Sandal, 1984, The Bookwright Press, pp. 26–27. Reprinted by permission.

EARLY INDIA

The earliest people came to India more than 400,000 years ago. By 2500 BC, there were villages all along the Indus River. The villagers made pottery, built pillars of stone, grew wheat and rice, and herded cattle. They also built such well-planned cities as Mohenjo Daro and Harappa. These cities had two-storied brick houses with built-in trash chutes and bathrooms with running water connected to a city drainage system. Their civilization, known as the Indus River Valley civilization, soon stretched over 1000 miles (1600 kilometers).

Then, around 1000 BC, invaders known as Aryans entered the country through mountain passes in the northwest and spread over North India. They brought with them the Sanskrit language, horses, and iron and copper tools. Over time, their religion of Brahmanism, which honored nature deities, took root, mixed with local religions, and developed into Hinduism.

At first, the Aryans were divided into family groups, each led by the oldest male. Later, kingdoms emerged. The Aryans looked down on the non-Aryans, most of whom were dark-skinned Dravidians. The Aryans were the ruling military class and had the most power. A class of priests dealt with religious rituals and rules. Soon, people with the same kinds of jobs began to group together, and the ideas underlying the caste system began to develop.

MAURYA EMPIRE

About 300 BC, the first great Indian empire arose. Known as the Maurya Empire, it spread over much of northern and central India. Its rulers developed a strong government administration and encouraged the growth of cities and trade.

One of the most famous Maurya rulers was Asoka. After fighting many wars of conquest, he turned against war and devoted himself to the welfare of the people. Under the influence of Buddhism, he issued new laws, which he ordered carved on stone pillars throughout the empire. The laws reflected Asoka's desire to "exchange good for evil and to forsake violence." Declaring that he wanted to establish a reign of "justice, security, peace, and mercy for all," he decreed the following:

> Commendable is the service of the father and mother and so is liberality to friends, neighbors, Brahmans, and sramanas [those who practice self-denial].
>
> It is commendable not to hoard too much gold; to borrow little and to refrain from exploiting [taking advantage of] others.
>
> Benevolence is difficult and he who performs such acts accomplishes a difficult deed.... Reprehensible is he who ne-

Small Harappan seals like this one are thought to have been good luck charms or labels for merchandise. What features of modern cities were present in Harappa and Mohenjo Daro?

CHAPTER 24 — AN OLD AND NEW LAND

INDIAN EMPIRES

ca. 2300 BC Growth of Indus Valley cities
ca. 1200 BC Aryans migrate into India from Central Asia
ca. 1000–300 BC Vedic Period
563–483 BC Gautama Buddha
321–184 BC Maurya Empire

274–236 BC Rule of Emperor Asoka
320–535 AD Gupta Empire—Golden Age of India
ca. 1200 Beginning of Turkish Muslim conquests
1206–1526 Delhi Sultanate
1526–1761 Mogul Empire
1556–1605 Rule of Emperor Akbar

glects acts of benevolence, and it is easy, indeed, to sin.

The king desires that all sects [religious groups] may live [freely] everywhere in the land.

Ceremonies should be performed if they promote morality.

You are true to your own beliefs if you accord kindly treatment to adherents of other faiths. You harm your own religion by harassing followers of other creeds.

Observe dharma; be kind to your parents; be generous to kith and kin; be decent to your slaves.

The sound of the war kettles has been transformed into the call to dharma.*

Asoka the Great by Emil Lengyel, 1969, Franklin Watts, Inc., pp. 91–97. Reprinted by permission.

GUPTA EMPIRE

The Maurya Empire fell apart about 185 BC, and once again all of India was divided into a number of small kingdoms. Finally, around 320 AD, another empire, known as the Gupta Empire, came to power in northern India. The Gupta rulers supported learning and the arts and honored poets, philosophers, and scientists at the royal court.

The period of Gupta rule came to be known as the Golden Age of India. Gupta mathematicians invented the concept of zero and the number symbols 0 through 9, which later reached the West by way of the Middle East. Gupta astronomers studied the heavens. They knew that the world was round and had some knowledge of gravity. Gupta doctors set bones and performed operations. They also invented hundreds of different medical instruments.

1. What contributions did the Indus River Valley people and the Aryans make to early Indian civilization?
2. What were the achievements of the Maurya and Gupta empires?

MUSLIM INDIA

In the late 600's and early 700's, Muslims from the Middle East and Central Asia began moving into India. Some came as scholars to learn about Indian astronomy, medicine, and mathematics. Others came to trade. Still others came seeking riches and converts. By the early 1000's, the entire Indus Valley was under Muslim control.

In the 1200's, Turkish Muslims invaded and conquered northern India. They set up their capital at Delhi and called their ruler the Sultan of Delhi. About 300 years later, the last Sultan of Delhi was defeated by a Turk named Babur. Babur became the new ruler, established a strong central government, and founded the Mogul dynasty. In 1556, Babur's grandson, Akbar, came to power. A skilled warrior and administrator, by 1600 he controlled most of India.

Under the Moguls, the arts thrived. Such local crafts as cotton weaving became important, and luxury goods and precious metals were brought into India. Mogul rulers surrounded themselves with the beautiful and the luxurious. As indicated in the following passage, nowhere was this more obvious than in the court of the Great Mogul, Akbar's grandson—Shah Jahan:

Under the rule of Akbar, shown here receiving visiting princes to his court, Hinduism was tolerated by the Moguls. Who founded the Mogul dynasty in India? From where did he come?

The court of the Great Mogul was situated in three locations; Delhi, Lahore, and Agra. Of his three principal residences, the Red Fort in Agra was the most impressive. Started by Akbar and completed by Shah Jahan, this walled complex of mosques . . . , gardens, and palaces was the pride of the Moguls. . . . The royal apartments were ornamented with ruby-encrusted arabesques [patterns] and crowned with ceilings of solid gold. Musicians were kept performing continuously, even in empty rooms, on the chance that the emperor might pause for a moment's entertainment. In the imperial kitchens, fifteen complete meals were always ready to be served at a moment's notice by a unit of richly dressed kitchen slaves. Embroidered tapestries and choice Persian paintings, enamel lamps that burned scented oil, gold decanters filled with lemonade, a box of pearls, trays of guavas or mangoes, or grapes from Kashmir, pillows, carpets, mirrors, melons, silver goblets filled with night wine or lilacs, seven slender pillars wrapped in satin drapery—all were here. . . . Meanwhile, the emperor, the creator . . . of this garden of earthly delights, bathed . . . in his underground pool, where the light of a thousand candles danced in the reflection of ten thousand mirrors and countless gems encrusted on the walls.

Each day of the week Shah Jahan ruled from a different throne. The greatest of these was the Takht-i-Taus, the Peacock Throne, which was built in 1628 to commemorate his coronation. [It] was the most lavish throne ever made in India. It took seven years to complete and cost a million rupees. . . . The throne itself . . . consisted of an elevated rectangular platform on which twelve emerald-studded pillars were placed, the capitals of each composed of two jeweled peacocks standing on either side of a diamond-leafed tree. These pillars supported a canopy . . . which was covered with [designs] of pearls, emeralds, sapphires, and gold. In order to mount the throne one climbed a staircase of solid silver. "But," wrote a poet much in favor with the emperor, "not because of its gems but because it kisses the feet of Shah Jahan, has the value of the throne ascended to heaven."*

Under the Moguls, social and trade networks tied together villages, towns, and cities, and a culture that was a blend of Muslim and Hindu ways developed. Although the caste system was followed by Hindus and even influenced Muslim social relationships, Mogul leaders after Akbar did not tolerate Hinduism. In some ways, its beliefs were in direct opposition to those of Islam. While Hindus had many deities, Muslims had only one. While Hindus believed one's status was fixed at birth, Muslims believed it could change. The result was conflict between Hindus and Muslims and the breaking up of the Mogul empire into smaller states led by local **rajahs,** or princes. This, combined with political problems and Indian poverty that was the result of heavy taxes, led to the downfall of the Moguls.

1. Why did the Muslims come to India?
2. What did the Moguls contribute to Indian civilization?
3. How did Mogul rule affect Indian society?

BRITISH INDIA

During the 1400's and 1500's, while the Moguls were still in power, Europeans became interested in India. At the time, India was a source of the spices that Europeans used to cook their food and as perfumes. In the 1400's, Portuguese seafarers reached India. They were followed by the Dutch,

---

The Taj Mahal by David Carroll and the Editors of the Newsweek Book Division, 1972, *Newsweek,* pp. 67–68. Reprinted by permission.

French, and British. In time, the British proved to be the most powerful and came to dominate India for nearly 200 years.

THE EAST INDIA COMPANY

In 1600, England's Queen Elizabeth I gave a group of English traders called the East India Company exclusive British trading rights with India. At first, the Company was interested only in securing control of the Indian spice trade and owned no Indian land. Soon, however, it had its own army, which won enough territory in battles with Indian Muslim leaders to make the Company a real power in India.

The Company's policies and the enormous profits it made by taxing the Indians soon led to unrest. By the late 1700's, the situation had become so bad that the British Parliament stepped in. It passed a series of laws that at first gave the British government more control over the Company's actions in India and ultimately made the government responsible for the administration of India.

By the mid-1800's, many Indians found conditions under the British intolerable. In their effort to encourage the spread of western culture, the British had banned Indian customs that conflicted with western values. In addition, some local Indian princes and landowners had lost both their authority and their property. Matters came to a head in 1857, when *sepoys*, Indians who served as officers in the East India Company's army, revolted against their British officers.

The *sepoy* action, called the Sepoy Mutiny by the British, came to be regarded by Indians as their first war of independence against British rule. The revolt came about after a new model rifle was issued to the *sepoys*. The cartridges used in the rifles had to be bitten before they were fired. The *sepoys* believed that the cartridges were greased with cow or pig fat. Putting them in their mouths would violate their religious beliefs, so they refused to accept the rifles. When the British responded by imprisoning *sepoys*, they revolted. In the passage that follows, an Indian officer explains:

The Sepoy Mutiny actually began in the city of Meerut, north of Delhi, when sepoys *who had been jailed for refusing to accept the new, greased rifle cartridges were forcibly freed by their comrades. The* sepoys *then seized Delhi and held it for more than three months before the British finally recaptured it. It took nearly two years to bring the revolt to an end. Why did the sepoys refuse to use the new rifle cartridges provided by the British?*

I have little to say. All you who hear me know why five hundred Brahmins like myself, three hundred Rajpoots of high caste, have been deprived of their daily bread and turned adrift on the world after they had served the English government for many years. . . . Why? Because they would not pollute themselves, because they would not lose their caste—their religion. . . .

All that I have to say to you is this. I have journeyed from Calcutta to here. I have been to every station where sepoy regiments are quartered, been in the lines of thirty or forty regiments. They are all of the same mind. They will not let themselves be the victims. . . . They will not let their caste be [stolen] from them; they will not let their religion be stolen from them. They are firmly of one mind. I have seen many kings and princes and noblemen. . . . They are all of one mind. The reign of the English must cease. I have seen the people in the country and in the towns and cities. They are all of one mind. The reign of the English must cease. . . .

Yes, the whole intention of the English government is to take away our religion and caste, to make us Christians. The new governor-general has come out with . . . orders from the queen to do this. . . .*

A NEW REGIME

The British, however, were stronger than the Indians thought, and in 1859 the *sepoy* revolt was put down. The British government ended the rule of the British East India Company and assumed direct control of Indian affairs. India was divided into provinces, each under a governor. A governor-general, known as a **viceroy,** was sent to India to represent the British monarch. British officers took charge of the Indian army.

Under British rule, all of India was united for the first time under one political system

Littell's Living Age, Vol. 186, by Eliakim Littell, 1890, Littell and Company, p. 808.

The first locomotive entered Indore, in central India, by means of elephant power. By 1900, India's main railway system was completed. How was the Indian economy affected by the railway system?

and set of laws. British writers, educators, and missionaries encouraged Indians to adopt the English language, Christianity, and British-style education. Schools and hospitals were set up in villages, and universities were opened in such major cities as Calcutta and Bombay.

Many British public officials, remembering the Sepoy Mutiny, however, avoided getting involved in Indian cultural and social life. This led to an almost complete separation between Indians and the British living in India. Many of the British thought Indians were culturally and morally inferior. Many Indians thought the British were interested only in power and did not care about India's welfare.

In some areas, however, the British influence remained strong. Roads, seaports, and irrigation systems were improved. An extensive railway system was established that opened the country's interior to the world's markets and made possible the rise of modern industry and agriculture. Fares on the railroads were so low that even poor Indians could travel or send goods. By bringing together people from all over India for the first time, the railroads contributed to a sense of national unity.

These changes, however, largely benefited the British and not the Indians. Improved irrigation, for example, made more land available to grow food. But the British reaped the profits from the land. The British owned the **plantations,** or large farms, and the mines and factories. The Indians provided the labor. They worked long hours under poor conditions and received low wages. In addition, British policies blocked the growth of Indian industries that competed with their own. Below, an Indian leader describes the long-term effect of such British actions and policies:

> The chief business of the East India Company in its early period was to carry Indian manufactured goods, textiles as well as spices, from the East to Europe, where there was a great demand for these articles. With the developments in industrial techniques in England a new class rose there demanding a change in this policy. The British market was to be closed to Indian products. The Indian market was to be opened to British manufactures. To begin with, Indian goods were kept out of Britain by laws. This was followed by attempts to restrict and crush Indian manufactures. At the same time, British goods could enter duty free. The Indian textile industry collapsed, affecting large numbers of weavers and artisans. The process went on during the 1800's, breaking up other old industries also—shipbuilding, metalwork, glass, paper, and many crafts.

The economic development of India was arrested, and the growth of new industry was prevented. Machinery could not be brought into India. A vacuum was created in India which could be filled only by British goods. This led to rapidly growing unemployment and poverty. India became a farming colony of industrial England. It supplied raw materials and provided markets for England's industrial goods.

The destruction of the skilled working class led to unemployment on a huge scale. What were all these scores of millions, who had so far been in industry and manufacturing, to do now?

Cotton had been grown on the Deccan Plateau long before the British came to India, and nearly every village had weavers like this one who turned cotton into cloth on their looms. What are some factors that led to the collapse of the Indian textile industry in the 1800's?

Members of the Indian National Congress posed for this group photo, taken in the 1920's. Twenty months after the shootings at Amritsar on April 13, 1919, the Congress, meeting in Nagpur, voted to adopt Mohandas Gandhi's policy of non-violent, non-cooperation with India's British government. What was the goal of the Indian National Congress in the early 1900's?

All these people had no jobs, no work, and all their ancient skill was useless. They drifted to the land, for the land was still there. But the land was fully occupied and could not possibly absorb them profitably. So they became a burden on the land and the burden grew, and with it grew the poverty of the country.*

1. What first interested the East India Company in India?
2. Why did many Indians come to resent conditions under British rule? How did some of them show their resentment?
3. What changes did the British make in India after 1859? How did Indians react to the changes? Why did they react this way?

INDEPENDENT INDIA

By the late 1800's, anti-British feelings were widespread in India. To improve relations between the British and the Indians, an organization made up of British and Indian members and called the Indian National Congress was formed. Its members wanted to change by peaceful means the government policies that were causing unrest. In the early 1900's, in an effort to please the Congress, the British Parliament allowed more Indians to participate in the Indian government. But, by then, many Indians in the Congress wanted more than greater participation in government. They wanted complete freedom for India.

TOWARD FREEDOM

Tensions continued to rise, and the British took strong measures to keep control. They censored Indian newspapers and ordered punishment of Indians suspected of treason. When British soldiers attacked a crowd of unarmed demonstrators in the city of Amritsar and killed and wounded hundreds of Indians, Indian anger reached a new high.

At this time, a new leader named Mohandas K. Gandhi appeared in the Indian National Congress. Gandhi appealed to the masses, especially villagers and the poor. They called him *Mahatma*, "Great Soul," and

---

*Adapted from *The Discovery of India* by Jawaharlal Nehru, (John Day). Copyright 1946, 1960, by Harper and Row, Publishers, Inc. Renewed 1973 by Indira Gandhi, pp. 210–212. Reprinted by permission of Harper & Row Publishers.

INSIGHTS ON PEOPLE
INDIA

MOHANDAS K. GANDHI

He seemed terribly frail, all skin and bones, though I knew that this appearance was deceptive, for he kept to a frugal but carefully planned diet that kept him fit, and for exercise he walked four or five miles [6.4 or 8 kilometers] each morning. . . . Over his skin and bones was a loosely wrapped dhoti [traditional male garment], and in the chilliness of a north Indian winter he draped a coarsely spun white shawl over his bony shoulders. His skinny legs were bare, his feet in wooden sandals.*

With these words, an American author described Indian leader Mohandas K. Gandhi at age 61. Gandhi, who Indians revere as the father of their country, was born in southern India in 1869 to a middle-class merchant family. Educated in Great Britain, he later went to British-ruled South Africa, where he practiced law. At the time, Indians living in South Africa faced racial discrimination. Gandhi began a campaign for Indian rights, using non-violent methods based on **civil disobedience,** or the refusal to obey unjust laws.

In 1915, Gandhi returned to India, where he became a leader in the Indian independence movement. With these words, he explained his viewpoint:

We believe that it is the inalienable right of the Indian people to have freedom and to enjoy the fruits of their toil and have the necessities of life so that they may have full opportunities of growth. We believe also that if any government keeps a people from having these rights, the people have a further right to change or do away with that government.

We know that the best way of gaining our freedom is not through violence. We will prepare ourselves by withdrawing, so far as we can, all voluntary association from the British Government, and will prepare for civil disobedience. We believe that if we can but withdraw our voluntary help and

stop payment of taxes without doing violence, the end of this rule is assured.*

In 1930, to protest the British government's control of the salt trade, Gandhi led hundreds of followers on a march to the sea, where they made salt from sea water. To show support for the local textile industry, he convinced Indians not to buy or use British cotton goods. He also revived the arts of spinning and weaving as a symbol of national unity.

After India became independent, Gandhi worked for tolerance among the country's many ethnic and religious groups. He was especially saddened by the split between India and Pakistan and the rioting of Hindus and Muslims. In an effort to end the bloodshed, he began a fast. Hindu and Muslim leaders, fearing he would die, agreed to stop fighting. A few days later, however, Gandhi was killed by a Hindu who opposed his peace efforts.

1. How did Mohandas Gandhi seek to end British rule in India?
2. What movements and leaders in your country have used the same methods as Gandhi to bring about change?

**Gandhi: A Memoir* by William L. Shirer. Copyright ©1979, by William L. Shirer, pp. 28–29. Reprinted by permission of Simon & Schuster, Inc.

*Adapted from *Mahatma: Life of Mohandas Karamchand Gandhi*, Vol. III, by D.G. Tendulkar, 1961, The Publications Division, Ministry of Information and Broadcasting, Government of India, pp. 8–9. Reprinted by permission.

In this cartoon, which represents the success of Gandhi's salt march to the sea, the now peaceful lion (British rule) has been tamed by one frail Indian, Mohandas Gandhi. What policy was begun under Gandhi?

he called the untouchables *harijans*, "children of God." Under Gandhi, the Congress began a policy of non-violent resistance to British rule. Millions of Indians joined the movement for independence, staging demonstrations, marches, and hunger strikes.

In 1935, the British responded and granted India limited self-government. But, for most Indians, this was not enough. When World War II started four years later, the Indian National Congress said that unless India received independence, it would not aid the British war effort. When the British refused, Congress leaders in the Indian government resigned their posts. The British arrested them and had them jailed.

After the war ended, the British agreed to give India its freedom. But, while the plans for independence were being worked out, bitterness developed between Indian Hindus and Muslims. This led to the creation of two separate countries out of British India—Pakistan for the Muslims and India for the Hindus. At midnight on August 14, 1947, Pakistan was founded. The following day, India became independent, and Jawaharlal Nehru, the leader of the Indian Congress Party, became India's first prime minister. Three years before, Nehru had made the following prediction:

> India will find herself again when freedom opens out new horizons. The future will then fascinate her far more than the immediate past. . . .She will go forward with confidence, rooted in herself and yet eager to learn from others and co-operate with them. Today she swings between a blind faith in her old customs and a slavish imitation of foreign ways. In neither of these can she find relief or life or growth. She has to come out of her shell and take full part in the life and activities of the modern age. There can be no real cultural or spiritual growth based on imitation. True culture gets its inspiration from every corner of the world, but it is homegrown and has to be based on the wide mass of the people. Art and literature remain lifeless if they are always thinking of foreign models. We have to think in terms of the people. Their culture must be a development of past trends. It must also represent their new urges and creative tendencies.
>
> We are citizens of no mean country. We are proud of the land of our birth, of our people, our culture and traditions. That pride should not be for a past to which we cling. Nor should it allow us to forget our many weaknesses. We have a long way to go before we can take our proper station with others. And we have to hurry for the time is limited and the pace of the world grows ever faster. It was India's way in the past to welcome and absorb other cultures. That is much more necessary today.

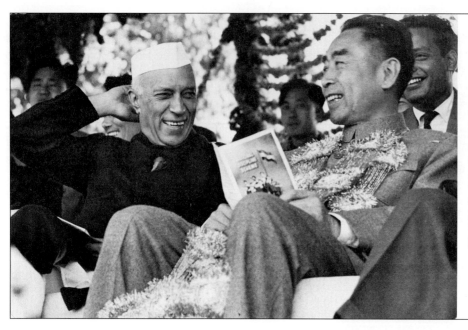

Indian prime minister Jawaharlal Nehru, on the left, and Chinese prime minister, Zhou En-lai, share a light moment during a state visit. Ties between India and the Republic of China were strong during the Nehru years. What predictions did Nehru make in 1944 about India's future?

We march to the One World of tomorrow where national cultures will be mixed with the international culture of the human race. We shall therefore seek wisdom and knowledge and friendship and comradeship wherever we can find them, and cooperate with others in common tasks. We shall remain true Indians and Asiatics, and become good world citizens.*

INDIA SINCE 1947

Upon becoming independent, India faced many problems. The division of British India into two separate nations led to a great migration. Hindus from Pakistan flocked to India, while Muslims from India flocked to Pakistan. This led to violence that resulted in the deaths of about 200,000 people. Yet, despite the problems, India enjoyed political stability and economic progress and became a leader among the **non-aligned nations**, those countries that refuse to side with western or Communist nations.

*Adapted from *The Discovery of India* by Jawharlal Nehru, (John Day). Copyright 1946, 1960, by Harper and Row, Publishers, Inc. Renewed 1973 by Indira Gandhi, pp. 414–417. Reprinted by permission of Harper & Row Publishers.

In 1964, Nehru died. Two years after his death, his daughter, Indira Gandhi, became prime minister. She increased the government's role in the economy, strengthened the hold of the Congress Party on local governments, and continued her father's policy of non-alignment. Relations with Pakistan, however, remained tense. In 1971, India entered a civil war between East and West Pakistan, two disconnected provinces of Pakistan that were separated by 1000 miles (1600 kilometers) of Indian territory. The result was the formation of the independent Republic of Bangladesh in East Pakistan.

Meanwhile, unrest mounted, and new political groups formed to oppose Gandhi's policies. In 1975, a state of emergency was declared, Gandhi's political opponents were arrested, and limits were put on personal freedoms. In 1977, elections were held, and Gandhi and her party lost to the Janata Party, which was made up of groups who opposed Gandhi's policies. The new leadership, however, lost the support of the people, and in 1981, Gandhi and her supporters were returned to power.

INSIGHTS ON PEOPLE
INDIA

INDIRA GANDHI

Indira Gandhi was India's first female prime minister. As the daughter of Jawaharlal Nehru, she became involved in politics at an early age. In 1942, after completing university studies in India and Great Britain, she married Feroze Gandhi. Both she and her husband took an active part in the movement for Indian independence.

In 1947, after her father became prime minister, Gandhi became known as "the nation's daughter." In addition to serving as her father's adviser and accompanying him on official trips overseas, she held posts in the country's ruling Congress Party. In a letter written to a friend in 1955, she talked about her busy life:

> It's certainly true that I have grown enormously since you saw me last. I am confident of myself but still humble enough to feel acutely embarrassed when all kinds of VIPs come for advice and even help in their projects. . . . I still haven't gotten used to being on the Working Committee of the A.I.C.C. (All India Congress Committee)! . . . Can you imagine me being an "elder statesman"?
>
> My duties and responsibilities have also grown enormously. I have my fingers in so many pies that it would take too long even to list them. And if you remember me and what a perfect tyrant of a conscience I have got, you will understand that this does not mean merely lending my name to some association or attendance at committee meetings. It means hard work, planning, organizing, directing, scouting for new helpers, humoring the old and so on, in several fields—political, social welfare and cultural.*

Gandhi's experience in the party gave her administrative skills that proved helpful when she became prime minister, a post she held for nearly two decades. In an interview she gave to an American news magazine in 1982, she talked about some of the problems that were facing India and that, as prime minister, she would have to resolve. As she saw it, the biggest problem was "backwardness," which she described as the differences "between the haves and the have-nots." She denied, however, that the rich were getting richer, while the poor were getting poorer. She went on to point out that, while poverty still existed, the general standard of living had risen and more Indians now belonged to the middle class. Gandhi also acknowledged some of the other problems with which she had to deal. These included urban growth, pollution, environmental and wildlife conservation, and industrial and agricultural development.

Although Gandhi's policies often were controversial, most Indians regarded her as a heroine for her efforts. A few days before her death, she stated, "If I were to die today, every drop of my blood will invigorate the nation."

1. How did Indira Gandhi acquire her political skills?
2. What did Gandhi see as India's greatest problem? Based on what you know about India, do you agree with her? Explain.

---

*From *Indira Gandhi: Letters to an American Friend 1950-1984*, Copyright ©1984 by Dorothy Norman. Reprinted by permission of Harcourt Brace Jovanovich, Inc.

This time, Gandhi faced opposition from regional religious and ethnic groups that wanted more freedom. The most violent opposition came from Sikhs in Punjab. Sikh militants seized the Golden Temple of Amritsar, the holiest Sikh shrine, and used it as a base for terrorist raids. When, on Gandhi's orders, the Indian army stormed the temple and defeated the militants, many Sikhs were angered. Threats were made against Gandhi's life. On October 31, 1984, she was assassinated by two of her bodyguards who were Sikhs.

The assassination touched off four days of anti-Sikh riots all over India. Gandhi's son, Rajiv, who had succeeded his mother as prime minister, called for new elections to bolster his power. An American journalist describes the political situation and mood in India on the eve of the voting as follows:

An engineer, former commercial pilot and member of Parliament, India's prime minister, Rajiv Gandhi, sits beside a statue of his mother, Indira. What became a major issue in Rajiv Gandhi's 1984 election campaign?

Every five years it happens: the world's largest, loudest, most unbridled carnival. . . . It is the greatest show on earth— India's national elections. . . .

From the Himalayas to the Andaman Islands the Indian people, most of them peasants and 65 percent illiterate, will decide the future of the world's biggest democracy. . . .

The governing Congress Party has won every national election but the 1977 vote. . . . The party now holds a two-thirds majority in Parliament. Congress and Mrs. Gandhi's son and successor, Rajiv, are expected to ride a wave of sympathy over her October 31 assassination to another victory this time. . . .

Political analysts say the . . . Congress Party has lost the support of Sikhs and [Muslims] because of violence in Punjab, anti-Sikh riots, and Hindu-[Muslim] riots. Instead it is aiming for the Hindu vote in the northern Hindu-speaking . . . four states. . . .

The . . . seven national parties [have] been unable to field common candidates against the well-oiled Congress machine or agree on a common platform and strategy. The assassination deprived them of their single potent issue: defeat Indira Gandhi. . . .

Prime Minister Rajiv Gandhi . . . will be seeking a mandate to maintain the dynasty begun by his grandfather. . . . He also will seek to carry on his mother's policies. . . .

The campaign has been [empty] of [important] issues and any intense debate on problems such as poverty, unemployment and [religious] violence. But Rajiv Gandhi has made India's unity . . . an issue. . . . He has tarred the entire opposition as unpatriotic . . . and aiding forces bent on violence and dismembering the nation.

"We have to see the powers seeking to weaken and those in the country giving them strength," he said in a speech. . . .

The opposition and many political observers condemn his tactic as irresponsi-

INDIAN STATES AND TERRITORIES

ble, saying the unity of the country should not be made a campaign issue and political rivals should not automatically be regarded as villains.*

Rajiv Gandhi and his Congress supporters won the election by a landslide. Immediately after the election, Gandhi appealed for cooperation. At the same time, he condemned violence. Since then, the Indian government has been working to meet the demands of its peoples and to preserve national unity. Like many Indians, it believes that India's present task is to work for change in a peaceful way that will benefit all of its citizens.

1. Why was the National Congress formed?
2. How did the British respond to the Congress' policy of non-violent resistance?
3. What are some of the problems India has faced since becoming independent?

*"World's Largest Democracy to Elect Parliament" by Victoria Graham in *The Champaign-Urbana News Gazette*, December 23, 1984, p. A-15. Reprinted by permission.

CHAPTER 24 REVIEW

POINTS TO REMEMBER

1. Two of the early civilizations of India were that of the Indus River Valley and that of the Aryans.
2. The first great Indian empire was that of the Mauryas. One of its rulers, Asoka, was influenced by Buddhism and worked to establish a reign that was fair and just to all.
3. A second great Indian empire was that of the Guptas, whose period of rule came to be known as the Golden Age of India.
4. The Mogul Empire of India was founded by a Muslim Turk named Babur. Under his grandson Akbar, all of India came under Mogul control. Under the Moguls, the arts thrived and a culture that was a blend of Muslim and Hindu ways developed.
5. Portuguese seafarers reached India in the late 1400's.
6. In 1600, the East India Company received exclusive British trading rights with India. By the mid-1800's, following the Sepoy Mutiny, the British government had taken control of India. Under British rule, all of India was united for the first time under one political system and set of laws.
7. The Indian National Congress was formed to improve relations between the British and the Indians and to change by peaceful means government policies that were causing unrest. By the early 1900's, the Congress was calling for complete freedom for India.
8. In 1947, British India was divided into two separate and independent nations—Pakistan and India.
9. India faced many problems upon becoming independent, including conflict between Hindus and Muslims. Despite this, India enjoyed political stability and economic progress.
10. In 1966, Indira Gandhi became prime minister of India. She increased the government's role in the economy, strengthened the Congress Party's hold on local governments, and held to the policy of non-alignment. During her last term of office, she was assassinated by Sikhs, who were angered over her policies.
11. Since the election of Rajiv Gandhi as prime minister in 1984, the Indian government has been working for peaceful change and the preservation of national unity.

VOCABULARY

Identify

Mohenjo Daro
Harappa
Indus River Valley civilization
Aryans
Brahmanism
Dravidians
Maurya Empire
Asoka
Gupta Empire
Sultan of Delhi
Babur
Mogul dynasty
Red Fort
Peacock Throne
East India Company
Sepoy Mutiny
Indian National Congress
Mohandas K. Gandhi
Pakistan
Jawaharlal Nehru
Indira Gandhi
Republic of Bangladesh
Janata Party
Golden Temple of Amritsar
Rajiv Gandhi

Define

rajahs viceroy civil disobedience non-aligned nations
sepoys plantations *harijans*

DISCUSSING IMPORTANT IDEAS

1. What did the Aryans contribute to Indian civilization? The Muslims?
2. What do you think were some of the positive effects of British rule in India? Some of the negative effects?
3. Jawaharlal Nehru talked of the "frustration and humiliation" of India's past. To what do you think he was referring? Give examples.
4. Do you think the Indian government can obtain the cooperation of its people and preserve national unity? Why or why not? If you were prime minister, what steps would you take to achieve this goal?

DEVELOPING SKILLS

DETERMINING FACTUAL ACCURACY

It is important to be aware that everything you read or hear is not necessarily *fact*—something known for certain or that can be proven—or *accurate*—correct or without error. The guidelines used in the following example will help you determine if written material is factually accurate:

1. Read this passage, keeping in mind that all the information in it may not be factually accurate.

   I am one of the 500 Brahmins who have been deprived of their daily bread. This happened because we refused to use the cartridges for the new rifles the British gave us. The cartridges, which we had to bite before they would fire, were greased with cow and pig fat. Our religion teaches us that animal fat will pollute us. If we bit the cartridges, we would lose our caste. We will not let the British steal our caste from us. On this, every single sepoy *is in agreement. The British want to take away our religion. They want us to become Christians. That is why they sent us the new rifles in the first place. The British queen and her government do not care about us.*

2. Go through the passage sentence by sentence, pulling out the facts as you go. (*The speaker is one of 500 high-caste Hindus who have lost their jobs because they would not use cartridges given to them by the British. They refused to use them because they were greased with animal fat, which their religion views as polluting. To bite the cartridges would cause them to lose their caste. All* sepoys *in India are united against the British in this issue. The British sent the rifles because they wanted the* sepoys *to convert to Christianity. The British do not care about the* sepoys.)

3. Ask yourself: Does the speaker have a reason to distort the truth? What evidence do I have to support the "facts" presented? (If you do not have the necessary evidence, research the topic.) The answers to these questions will enable you to determine the factual accuracy of the passage.

For further practice in this skill, use the guidelines, and apply them to the passage on pages 390–391 about the effect on the Indian economy of British actions and policies.

CHAPTER 25
DEVELOPING INDIA

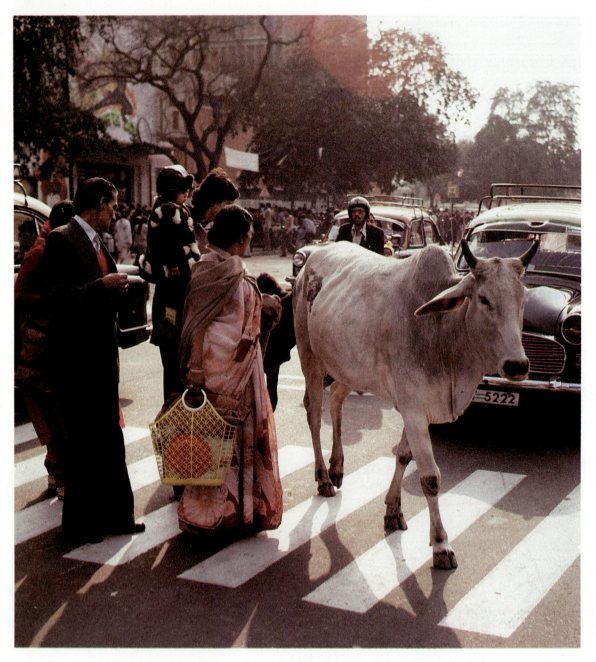

1. How have India's economy and society developed since 1947?
2. What economic and social problems does India face today?

The mention of India immediately brings to the minds of a majority of people a picture of a country filled with poor people, dying of hunger, cows roaming around freely with people looking at them in reverence. Some people perceive India as a romantic land where there are lots of tigers and elephants. And for some, it is a land of mystery.

None of them are correct; they are myths. . . .

On the economic side, while the people know about the poverty, they are largely ignorant of the fact that India is the 10th largest industrial power in the world. It was the 6th country to . . . build a satellite and the 6th country to send a rocket into space.

It is forgotten that India is a young democracy. The state the British left the country in was pathetic. Most commonly used goods were imported, industry was in bad shape. There were acute food shortages and people were dying of starvation. Illiteracy was as high as 90 percent.

In 35 years, India has achieved self-sufficiency in food, and . . . consumer goods are produced in India. It produces 85 percent of its military hardware. Right from a pin to airplanes and ships and computers, they are now produced domestically. It has even started to make its own nuclear power plants. Illiteracy is now about 50 percent and the life expectancy has shot up by 20 years. . . .

After all India has achieved, it would not be true to say that society has no flaws. The country is still beset with problems. India is food sufficient, but the food distribution is not proper. Still millions are undernourished and live on streets. Illiteracy and population [growth] are big problems, and to make things worse, corruption has been growing at a [great] rate. . . .

. . . And despite the constitutional equality, discrimination exists, particularly social. . . .

. . . But, beyond the caste system, people are largely ignorant of some main elements in Indian society like the strong family system and respect given to elders. . . . The family gives warmth to live on and courage and assurance of full backing and help in time of need. No wonder people keep the family above everything.*

---

*"Myths aside, 'true' India merits attention" by Pankaj Jalote in *The Daily Illini*, December 15, 1982, p. 15. Reprinted by permission.

With these words, an Indian graduate student studying computer science in the United States clears up some common misunderstandings about his country. There is no doubt that India has made great economic and social strides since it became independent in 1947. It now has the tenth largest economy in the world in terms of its **gross national product** (GNP), the value of all goods and services produced in a year. It also has growing and prospering upper and middle classes. But, as the student points out, some problems remain. While efforts are being made to resolve these problems, progress is slow.

While most Indians want progress and development, they place a great value on tradition and do not want it to be the price they pay for achieving change. They want to incorporate tradition into change.

AGRICULTURE

The Indian government has worked hard to raise the standard of living of its people. To this end, it set up Five-Year Plans, programs designed to develop the nation over five-year periods in the areas of agriculture, industry, and social welfare. One of the areas targeted by the plans was agriculture, which has been the traditional occupation for most Indians.

Although today almost 80 percent of the Indian people are farmers, India has had a serious food problem. There are a number of reasons for this. For one, Indian farms generally are small—less than 5 acres (2 hectares). For another, many Indians continue to farm the way their ancestors did, using simple tools and sometimes inefficient methods. Still another problem is that crops often are destroyed by diseases and animal pests.

The government has been working since 1947 to overcome these problems and to increase farm production. Some progress has been made. In the past, most farmers expected to do little more than feed their own families and animals. Today, millions of farmers not only can feed their own but have extra left over to sell as well. This change has come about largely because of the Green Revolution, a series of farming improvements introduced in the 1960's. During that time, scientists in different parts of the world developed new types of wheat, rice, and other cereal grain seeds that produced faster-growing crops. To further boost food production, they also developed new kinds of fertilizers.

With the aid of private agencies and foreign governments, the Indian government brought the Green Revolution to India. It provided farmers with the credit they needed to buy the new seeds and to plant such protein-rich crops as soybeans and corn. It promoted increased irrigation and fertilizer use and encouraged farmers to band together to form **cooperatives,** enterprises operated for mutual benefit. The government believed that by working together, farmers could learn better farming methods and be able to use more modern equipment, such as tractors and reapers. In the following passage, an anthropologist describes the im-

In addition to its use for irrigating crops, water from this Indian family's new well also is used for such household tasks as washing laundry, shown here. Financial assistance for wells and other farm projects are offered by the government to help farmers modernize. What did the government expect to accomplish by having farmers form cooperatives?

pact the Green Revolution had in a village in which he had lived more than 10 years earlier:

> Along the thirty-mile [48-kilometer], two-lane, tree-shaded, blacktop road toward the village, everything looked the same, yet slightly different. This late in the hot season the fields should all have been cleared, plowed, and leveled to preserve moisture. Some crops would have been sown; others would await the rains that were due to begin shortly. Yet many of the fields appeared to have been only recently cleared and were yet unbroken by the first summer plowing. Other fields were full of what appeared to be young rice, a crop almost never grown in this area during my first stay. What had been open sky . . . was now laced with electrical wires on concrete poles. Along the road village after village had small sawmills, machine shops, and new retail shops of all kinds. The towns were noticeably larger and busier. The roadside walls, formerly blank and faded, were now often brightly decorated with advertisements for fertilizers, insecticides, and electric fans. On the road itself the confusing assortment of pedestrians, camels, buffaloes, and goats was still there, but it included many more taxis, scooters, motorcycles, and bicycles than I remembered. Everywhere there was activity and animation. Formerly the period between the onset of the hot season and the beginning of the rains had been a time of cautious waiting, a time when the countryside seemed to hold its breath to conserve its strength. . . .
> As we passed through the fields each new thing was pointed out and its origin explained. We rode past cylindrical haystacks . . . of a type I had never seen. They contained wheat straw and the technique for making them had been introduced by Panjab Agricultural University. My impression of the changed agricultural cycle was correct. It was due in part to the fact that the old varieties of wheat, the main winter crop, were no longer grown. They had been entirely replaced by new high-yielding varieties which were harvested later. The . . . Persian wheels [a form of water wheel] that would have been constantly in use at this season, driven by slowing plodding camels or pairs of bullocks, were now almost gone. The few that remained were lying in ruins. Replacing them were mechanized pumping sets in small brick buildings. Small scattered plots of bright green were rice seedlings waiting to be transplanted when the fields were ready—in a few weeks. Overall, it seemed clear that the pattern and rhythm of village agriculture had changed. . . .
> We left the paved road and, after dismounting from the cycles, followed a small dirt path that cut off to the left. The last few dozen yards passed through some work areas to the village houses, grouped within what had once been an almost-continuous rampart of adjoining outer walls. Here again was the familiar and new. The approach route was the same: by a line of trees and some tethered buffaloes, we entered the village center through a farmer's courtyard gate, turned to walk past the old Hindu temple and thence into the bricked lanes within the compact mass of houses and barns. The cool, narrow lanes themselves, between high . . . brick walls, were the same. But there had been new houses near the path on the way in, there were electric lines overhead, and the familiar silence was broken by the chugging of a diesel pump somewhere nearby.*

1. Why did the Indian government set up Five-Year-Plans?
2. What were some of the reasons for India's food problems?
3. Why did the Indian government bring the Green Revolution to India? What are some of the changes it brought?

---

*_Song of Hope: The Green Revolution in a Panjab Village_ by Murray J. Leaf. Copyright 1984, by Rutgers, The State University, pp. 10–11. Reprinted by permission.

INDUSTRY

Another area on which the Five-Year Plans focused was industry and technology. Under the plans, large amounts of money were spent to speed up industrial growth and develop energy sources. Today, India has a **mixed economy,** an economy in which some industries are owned by the government and some by private citizens or groups.

ORGANIZATION

There are three major forms of industrial organization—cottage industries, privately owned small industries, and large-scale industries. **Cottage industries,** a system under which family members use their own equipment to produce goods in their homes, are found mostly in villages. There, generally in an effort to add to their farm income, Indians weave fabrics of cotton, rayon, and silk by hand instead of by machine. They also produce pottery, brassware, jewelry, leather goods, and woodcarvings.

The privately owned small industries generally are plants or factories that employ fewer than 100 workers and use simple machinery. They make such goods as bicycle parts, cardboard boxes, matches, shoes, and carpets. To help these small operations, the government has set up institutes where small-business owners can learn about management, sales, and cost accounting. The

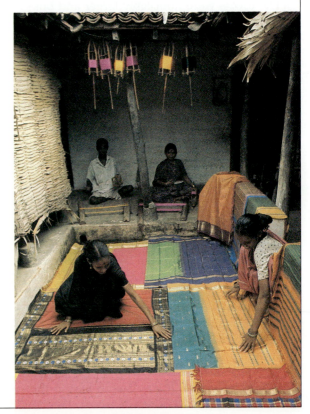

Below left, two Indian women spin yarn in front of their home. Weavers make this yarn into fabrics, which are sold in textile shops like the one shown below right. What cottage industries flourish in India besides spinning and weaving?

Because of India's large, low-cost labor force, most work is still accomplished by human labor rather than by machine. At this gravel pit near Jaipur in northwestern India, workers are collecting rocks to be crushed into gravel for road repairs. Women, as well as men, commonly perform this kind of work. Who owns the industries in India?

government also provides cheap electric power, building space, and training programs for workers.

The large-scale industries are owned solely by the government, jointly by the government and private investors, or solely by private investors. The government-owned industries include mining, heavy tool manufacturing, air and rail transport, nuclear energy, electric power, and iron and steel manufacturing. Among the jointly owned industries is the Tata Iron and Steel Company, whose mills near Calcutta rank among the largest in the world. The private industries produce such products as aluminum, chemicals, fertilizers, and textiles. Below, an Indian industrialist talks about the advances that have been made:

> Life's been good to me. I started this factory six years ago, producing hand tools such as bench vises. Today, I also make brassware such as door-knobs and nameplates. And there's scope to do much more.
>
> I earn about 5,000 rupees ($500) a month. My factory is small compared with the giant industrial complexes at Rourkela and Bhilai. I export my products to the United States, Canada, Germany, Sweden, Australia and the Middle East.
>
> In the last twenty years, our country has advanced tremendously. We are among the top ten industrial nations of the world and we're well on the way to being self-sufficient in making sophisticated machines and gadgets.
>
> We've got our own car factories; and we're making our own aircraft, trains, ships, teleprinters, watches, scooters, motorcycles, drugs, engineering and steel goods. Of course, the cotton textile industry is still the largest single industry in India. There are over 15 million industrial workers in the country.*

In 1985, in an effort to encourage the growth of new privately owned businesses, the government relaxed many of its controls over industry. As a result, investment by foreign businesses and aid from foreign governments and international agencies have increased.

---

*"We have a plentiful supply of cheap labor" in *We Live in India* by Veenu Sandal, 1984, The Bookwright Press, p. 28. Reprinted by permission.

CONSUMER GOODS

Another change that has taken place in recent years is the growth of the consumer goods industry. This is due in great part to the growth of the middle class. Televisions, automobiles, and radios are now being produced in India, while items not made in India are being imported from Western Europe and North America. As the following article indicates, Indians are eager to buy both locally made and imported consumer products:

> When A.S. Bhatia, an [Indian] engineer living in the U.S., returned to India recently for the first time in seven years, he could not believe his eyes. "I would not have thought that Delhi was the same place," he said. "Roadside stalls selling imported goods and television shops everywhere you look."
>
> If he had walked into some middle-class homes he also would have found new stoves, vacuum cleaners, washing machines, vastly superior furnishings, air conditioners, cars, and much else. He would have found a greater tendency to eat out, perhaps in the new breed of fast-food restaurants that recently have mushroomed.
>
> In 1965 only 500 people in India owned TV sets. Now the figure is approaching three million and in three years will reach ten million—equivalent to every household in the country's six or seven biggest cities. Bicycles, radios, refrigerators, and small electrical appliances have had a similar growth.
>
> A broad range of social changes underlies the growth in the market for domestic appliances. Urbanization has brought about a basic change in attitudes to work and leisure, and women who work outside their homes have neither the time nor the patience for laborious domestic chores. Working women also provide the second income that pays for the new gadgets.
>
> The consumer goods boom could hardly have come about without a general increase in prosperity. A study of India's four major [cities] in 1982 showed that 45 percent of the people believed they were better off than five years earlier, and another 42 per cent felt their income level was the same. A majority—54 per cent—felt their spending power would improve over the next five years. Few thought they would be worse off than before.*

1. What kind of economy does India have today?
2. What are the three types of industrial organization in India? What are the characteristics of each?
3. What has brought about growth in the market for consumer goods? What changes have taken place because of it?

NATURAL RESOURCES

Another area in which there has been development is natural resources. India is richer than many other countries in resources suitable for industrial development. These resources include iron ore, manganese, and **mica,** a mineral used in insulation. India also is rich in such energy resources as waterpower, coal, and oil. The country's great river systems supply about 40 percent of the electric power, and several large dams provide electricity to many villages and factories. Below, an Indian engineer explains why he became an engineer and how some of India's resources are being developed:

> I've wanted to be an engineer ever since I was in school. Partly because the pay —1,500 rupees ($150) a month—seemed good, as I belonged to a poor family. Partly because, even then, engineers were in great demand in the country.
>
> Today I have no money problems and

---

*"India's Consumer Boom" by T.N. Ninan and Chander Uday Singh in *India Today*, as quoted in *World Press Review*, May, 1984, p. 68. Reprinted by permission.

An engineer keeps a watchful eye on the control panel of the Tarapur nuclear power plant, India's first such facility. Although the plant, built between 1963 and 1969, is aging and is not run at full capacity, it continues to provide much-needed electric power and is expected to continue to do so into the late 1990's. Recently, the government has built new nuclear power plants at Kota, Bombay, and Madras. What role does India's rivers play in supplying the country's energy?

. . . can keep my family in comfort. I own a refrigerator, TV, and a motor scooter, just like other middle-class families. Besides, my job . . . keeps me on my toes.

What do I mean by power? I'm talking of electric power, thermal power, nuclear power and so on. As a country, I feel we're very fortunate to have more than twenty large rivers. As you know, the Ganga, or Ganges, is not only the holiest river in the land, it's also the most useful.

On these rivers we've set up twenty-eight large dams and we're planning many more. The dams supply water for irrigation, control floods and also provide power. The Bhakra Nangal Dam is India's biggest . . . river valley project so far.

When I look back over the years, I feel good. We've come a long way since the country's first hydroelectric power station was set up in 1900. In addition to so many hydroelectric projects, thermal stations now supply almost 60 per cent of electricity to the country. And since 1969, the nuclear power station at Tarapur has also been functioning.

Our industries alone use almost 65 per cent of the electricity. But it saddens me to think that only about 35 per cent of our villages possess electricity, while the others have to make do with traditional oil lamps, lanterns and candles. It takes time in a vast country like ours. These days, I'm very actively involved in the construction of four World Bank-aided thermal power stations.*

1. In what resources is India rich?
2. What do India's river systems power?

THE QUALITY OF LIFE

Although India has shown economic growth, there still is a great deal of poverty. There are, in effect, two Indias—the India of the prosperous upper urban classes and the India of the urban unemployed and rural poor. Critics claim that while the government stresses the production of more and more goods, it does little to insure that those

---

*From *We live in India* by Veenu Sandal, 1984, The Bookwright Press. Reprinted by permission.

goods are distributed fairly among all the people. They point out that while the rich have become richer, the poor have become poorer. Among the poorest of the poor are women and children. This is especially true in households headed by widows. Below, an Indian woman expresses the frustrations of this group:

>All our life is on fire, all our
>prices rising,
>Give us an answer, O rulers of the country!
>
>A handful of American wheat, a kilo of
>   milo mixed with chaff
>Doesn't our country grow crops
>Or do we have only mud-mixed grains?
>
>Give us an answer . . . . . .
>
>We have forgotten the color of milk
>Coconuts and dried fruits have gone
>   underground
>Our children have only jaggery
>   [unrefined] tea for nourishment
>Sweet oil for cooking is the price of gold
>Coconut oil for our hair is not to be had
>
>Without rock oil for lamps we are
>   familiar with darkness
>We burn in the summer, we are drenched
>   in the rains
>We bear the rigor of winter without any
>   clothes
>Why don't we yet have any shelter?
>
>We toil night and day and sleep
>   half-starved
>While the parasites fill their bellies
>   with butter
>Why does the thief get food while the
>   owner is cheated?
>
>There are pastures for the cattle of the
>   rich
>For forest development land is preserved
>Why is there no land to support living
>   people?
>
>Tall buildings rise before our eyes
>The roads cannot contain these
>   motorcycles and cars
>On whose labor has such development
>   been built?*

In recent years, the government has taken steps to improve the quality of Indian life. It particularly has sought to ease the plight of the poor. Today, unjust treatment of untouchables is illegal, and all professions and trades have been opened to them. Since their living conditions were worse than those of other Indians, the government has given them financial aid to raise their standard of living. But, although their condition has improved somewhat because of these efforts, the acceptance of such change by many Indians has not been easy to achieve.

HEALTH AND EDUCATION

Two major areas of concern are health and education. Experts state that three-fourths of all Indians do not have adequate health care, and nearly 64 percent cannot read or write. In the area of health, the government has begun programs to get villagers to avoid polluted water supplies, practice hygiene, and eat nutritious foods. It also has supported the education of doctors and nurses, built hospitals and clinics, and supported medical research. As a result of these efforts, some progress has been made in eliminating or controlling such diseases as smallpox, malaria, typhoid, and leprosy.

In the area of education, the problems are greater. Although most Indians believe that education is the means to a better life and want the government to make learning available to everyone, this has not been possible. There are not enough schools, books, or trained teachers. In addition, the Indian edu-

---

*"Questions of a woman agricultural worker" by Bhaskar Jadhav in the *Isis International Bulletin No. 11* spring 1979, pg. 9. Reprinted by permission from: Isis-WICCE, PO Box 2471, 1211 Geneva 2, Switzerland and Isis-International Via S. Muria dell'Anima 30, 00186 Rome, Italy.

cational system, which is based mostly on British models, often favors the rich rather than the poor and males rather than females. The system is not suited to the need of most Indians for training in practical skills, and many drop out of school early in order to find work. Below, a journalist provides insight into some of the frustrations and conflicting attitudes in one Indian village regarding education:

> . . . The primary school in the village was more closed than open: the elderly teacher had five miles [8 kilometers] to walk to the school each morning, and the children argued that since he didn't bother to come much, they needn't bother to go. The secondary school at Devarahalli, two miles [3.2 kilometers] away, had better teachers and facilities. The village children wanted to go there, but many did not make it. Either they had insufficient primary schooling, or their labour was needed at home in the fields.
>
> As they always did, when there was no chance of fulfilling their hopes, the family accepted the situation with resignation. If their children could have no education, then they would work in the fields. After all, they were born peasants, and so they would continue as peasants.
>
> Perhaps in a way it was better: the system of education had so little to do with their needs, leading . . . from useful productivity in the village to [unemployment] in the town. Not that the family was seduced by the prospect of urban life, for they understood its economic problems; but they were seduced by the chance of increased status, . . . To them, it meant success to be able to recite by rote, to them it seemed important if a man could write his name even if he could not read the document which he'd signed. They had become part of the text-book system without understanding why.*

Family Web: A Story of India by Sarah Hobson, 1982, Academy Chicago Publishers, pp. 234–235. Reprinted by permission.

POPULATION GROWTH AND CONTROL

Another major challenge is the continuing increase in population. Fifteen percent of the world's population live in India, but India has only 2.4 percent of the world's land area. As a result, even with recent economic gains, the Indian government finds it hard to feed and provide jobs for all its people. For this reason, it is interested in population control and has taken active steps to limit population growth.

India was the first country in the world to set up a national family planning program. The program encourages young couples to limit their families to two children. Social workers show the people how to use modern birth control methods, and loans and housing are made available to those who agree to family planning. Below, an Indian villager explains why he believes population control is important and why some Indians are not interested in it:

The sign draped over this elephant promotes the idea of family planning. It is typical of posters the government has distributed throughout India for years. How does India's national family planning program work?

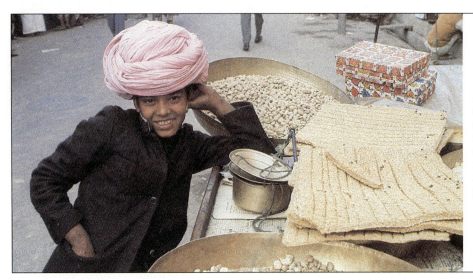

A young Indian boy earns money for his family by selling food at a vendor's market stand in Jaipur, the capital city of the state of Rajasthan. Why do some Indians prefer to have large families?

As time passes . . . you can't say that the Indian nation will remain the same. There might not be room for people even to stand. There mightn't be space to sit down. There mightn't be land to cultivate. So in my opinion it's better to keep the family as small as possible. I give this advice to everybody. If they listen, well and good, otherwise they'll regret it later. See, I can stop, being an educated man. But because my brothers are uneducated, they want boys. Boys will in future—according to Indian custom, somehow according to Indian custom, if we have sons, they can help with the work. If there are girls, they can't do any ploughing—they might do housework or they might tend the cattle. But if there are boys, they can plough the field. What can a girl do? If there's a son, he'll at least plough the field—provided he's not educated. Old age parents—the sons can help.

So many people are born, . . . so many people die. We should leave someone behind to continue the family. And if there are two sons, one can study and the other work in the fields. Even if there are three, they can all work on the land. They can work and get more land. They can do anything.*

Family Web: A Story of India by Sarah Hobson, 1982, Academy Chicago Publishers, pp. 174–175. Reprinted by permission.

Government efforts to limit population can be successful only if the people are willing to cooperate. In India, many still prefer large families. There are several reasons for this. One has its base in religion. Hindus often feel that it is a sign of virtue to be blessed with children. And, a son is needed to light parents' funeral pyres.

A second reason is economic. In rural areas, many children help a poor family get along. In farming families, children earn much more than their keep by caring for the animals, delivering meals to the field workers, collecting manure, and helping with odd jobs. Even those sent to the city contribute. They send home the money they earn, where it may be used to buy fertilizer or farm machinery or to hire farm laborers.

A third reason is social. Parents with many children know that someone will be there to care for them when they get old. Even though the government has offered social security plans to give income to retired people, many Indian families think it wiser to rely on their own children than to trust the government's word about their future.

Some experts believe that many of the reasons Indians give for having children will change in the future and that Indians will

Exploration
INDIA

In India, as elsewhere, development and change go hand in hand. This can be seen very clearly in the countryside. Irrigation, for example, has had a major impact on production. This, in turn, has raised the standard of living for some farmers and their families. Read the following comments by a farmer from Badripur, a village of northern India. Then, based on his comments and on the information in the chapter, do the following: (1) list some major changes that have taken place in India since independence; (2) list problems that still face India today; and (3) offer five suggestions that you think would help India continue to develop in the future:

This has been a fine season for me. Look, there in the distance you can see my sugarcane fields ready for harvesting.

My fields weren't always green and smiling like this. Today, our farm has an ample supply of water from wells, so I can expect good crops. But there was a time not very long ago when I had to rely completely on the rains, as farmers still do in many parts of the country. Of course, a lot still depends on the weather.

The weather gods have been kind to me, but the other day a farmer friend of mine had come from down south and he had a lot of complaints.

"Something or other is always happening," he said. "Sometimes it's too little rain and everything dries up. Other times there are floods and all my labor is washed away. Some years it's a cyclone; other years it's a tornado. Sometimes there are locusts. Nature seems always to be at war with us."

What he said is right to a large extent. But then I say: look at the brighter side. In spite of so many hardships, production has increased remarkably. Take the case of sugarcane. Compared with ten years ago, today we produce more than three times the amount.

You'll find this increase in all the crops —wheat, rice, corn, lentils, cotton, potatoes, vegetables, fruits,—as well as poultry products, tea, coffee, and dairy products, too. Then how is it that almost seventy per cent of my countrymen are poor and don't even get two good meals a day?

Ah, that's the sad part. Our population seems to grow much faster than our production. Don't forget that after China we're the world's second most populous country. . . .

Still, I say hats off to our government and agricultural scientists. Now we have high-yielding varieties of seeds, better fertilizers, special TV programs for farmers. And the government is trying to persuade each family to have only two or three children, instead of the six or nine or more that rural families and the uneducated usually have.

Quite honestly, my wife and I feel that family planning is the answer to all our country's problems. We ourselves have only three children and we're a very happy family. We spend most weekdays at the farmhouse. We have to see that the farm laborers . . . do the work right. Nowadays, we use bullocks as well as the modern tractor for plowing.

Our children stay in an apartment in town. It makes it easier for them to attend college. You see, they don't want to farm. My elder son, Ravindra, wants to do computer programming. The younger one wants to become a geologist. And my daughter wants to teach in a school. My wife and I encourage them, as it would be nice to see somebody in the family breaking away from the tradition of full-time farming.

Sundays we all get together either at the farm or in town. We exchange news and views over a good meal—pulao (rice) and raita (yogurt and salad) followed by lots of fruit: mangos, lichis, oranges or guavas—whatever's in season. We keep a buffalo at the farm, so we get our own milk. . . .

My earnings vary. Last year, I made a profit of about 25,000 rupees ($2,500). It's more than enough for our family. But, as I said, the gods have been kind to me. Not all farmers . . . have it so good.*

---

*"The weather gods have been kind to me" in *We live in India* by Veenu Sandal, 1984, The Bookwright Press, pp. 36–37. Reprinted by permission.

limit their families voluntarily. They say that economic factors will play an important role. Many people are moving from their villages to the cities, where dwellings are crowded and there are fewer jobs for children. In addition, as farming methods become more modern, machines will do a lot of the small jobs now being done by children. Farms are getting smaller, so having many children will mean that when the head of the family dies, the farm will have to be divided among more people. The changing role of women also might mean fewer children in the future.

1. What are the "two Indias"?
2. What is the government doing to bring better health and health care to Indians?
3. What are some of the problems India faces in education?
4. Why is the Indian government interested in population control? Why haven't its efforts been more successful?

CHAPTER 25 REVIEW

POINTS TO REMEMBER

1. To raise the standard of living, the Indian government set up Five-Year Plans to develop the nation.
2. Although India has a serious food problem, the government is working to overcome it and produce more. The progress made has been due largely to the Green Revolution.
3. In India's mixed economy, there are three forms of industrial organization—cottage industries, privately owned small industries, and large-scale industries.
4. In recent years, there has been considerable growth in the market for and the manufacture of consumer goods.
5. India is richer than most countries in resources that are suitable for industrial development.
6. Despite India's economic growth, there is a great deal of poverty. There are, in effect, two Indias. In spite of government efforts, the gap between rich and poor remains, and the poor continue to suffer.
7. Three-fourths of all Indians do not have adequate health care. To solve this problem, the Indian government has begun special health and hygiene programs, has built hospitals and clinics, and has supported medical education and research.
8. Education is of great concern to the Indian government. Although most Indians believe that education is beneficial, the present educational system is not always suited to their needs.
9. Because of the continuing increase in population, the government finds it hard to feed and provide jobs for all its people. Although it has taken steps to limit population growth, many Indians continue to have large families.

VOCABULARY

Identify

Five-Year Plans   Green Revolution

Define

gross national product   mixed economy   cottage industries   mica
cooperatives

DISCUSSING IMPORTANT IDEAS

1. How has development in India been affected by the desire of many Indians to cling to tradition?
2. Although India is a democracy, the government has used strong measures to bring about development. Do you think a government should have such control in a democracy? Explain.
3. According to some, "Indian development will not be the same as western development." What do you think they mean by this statement? Do you think it should be the same? Why or why not?
4. In planning development, decisions must be made on which aspects of development efforts and resources should be concentrated. On which aspects has the Indian government been concentrating? If you were a member of the government, on which would you concentrate? Why?

DEVELOPING SKILLS

PLACING INFORMATION IN ORDER OF SIGNIFICANCE

When you take notes or study, especially for a test, you often have to determine how important one piece of information is compared to others. When you do this, you automatically are performing another skill—placing information in *order of significance,* arranging it in order from the most important to the least important. The following guidelines will help you do this:

1. Find the sentence that expresses the main idea. It is the most important. Without it, none of the other information has anything to which it can relate.
2. Determine which statements support the main idea. These are next in importance. They describe, explain, or give details about the main idea.
3. Determine what information is irrelevant or *incidental,* giving details that may be interesting but are not necessary to understand or support the main idea. This information is the least important. Look, for example, at the following paragraph, each sentence of which is numbered:

(1) With the Green Revolution, the Indian government brought an important program to Indian agriculture. (Main idea; gives meaning to supporting statements) *(2) This program gave farmers credit to buy seeds and fertilizers and to install irrigation systems.* (Supporting statement; explains what the Green Revolution did) *(3) It also encouraged the farmers to form cooperatives.* (Supporting statement; explains what the Green Revolution did) *(4) The farmers planted soybeans and corn.* (Incidental; not needed to understand the Green Revolution)

For further practice in this skill, place the following statements in order of significance. Give reasons for your choices.

1. The major forms are cottage industries; privately owned small businesses; and large-scale industries owned by government, private investors, or a combination of both.
2. The Tata Iron and Steel Company mills rank among the largest in the world.
3. India has a mixed economy in which industries are owned both by the government and the private sector.

CHAPTER 26
THE ARTS

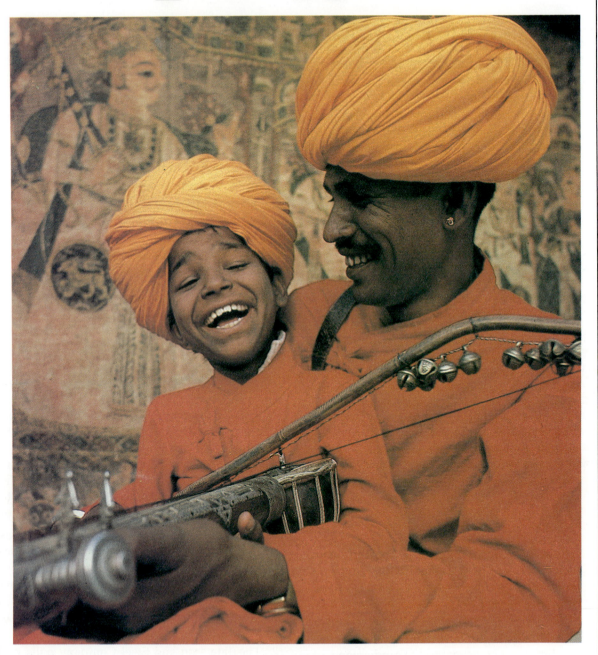

1. What arts have developed in India over the years?
2. What role do the arts play in Indian life?

... Three days into [my] journey, something showed me that, in India, art and life are one. Sometimes Indian art is in a museum. ... Sometimes it is a great monument that has been preserved and guarded. ... But most often it is just there, in the air, on the ground, all over the place, for the taking, and no name is attached to it.

That is what I learned—that art is everywhere in India, if we know how to look, and not only in famous places. It is in the costume ... of a woman working on the road. It is in the fragments of lapis-lazuli mosaic that lie on the ground beside a temple long left for dead. It is in the bracelets (canary yellow, it may be, or emerald green) that we see on the horns of white oxen by the roadside. It is in the ferocious color of the spices in every small-town bazaar, and it is in the celestial spacing of one building after another in the abandoned city of Fatehpur Sikri, near Agra. ...

... [Indians] identify with Indian works of art with an intensity that is almost unknown in the West. To them, they are not works of art at all, ... but objects of worship that happen to be in a museum and not in a temple. To see them lay gifts and offerings at the feet of a figure of dancing Siva [a god] is an experience that has nothing to do with "art appreciation". ... Siva for the Hindu is right there, in person, dancing the universe into being, sustaining it with his perfected rhythms, and finally dancing it out of existence. ...

In India, the art of the past is always relevant. It will tell you how to distinguish the good people from the bad people among the divinities. ... It will tell you what goes on in those tiny, many-storied town houses where everyone knows everyone else's business. It will tell you about gardening, and about hunting, and about how to deal with people great and small.

... Above all, it will give you a whole new set of references by which to judge human motives, human character, human beauty and the interaction between human beings and nature. It will do all this with economy, with subtlety and with wit. You will be lucky to have Indian art as your guide, and its guidance will not fail you when you come home, no matter where "home" may be.*

The above statements by a western art expert reveal the importance of the arts in Indian life. The arts and crafts of India are among the oldest and richest in the world. And, although they differ from region to region and include a variety of forms and styles, they all express a unity in diversity that is typically Indian.

As in other cultures, the traditional arts of India were influenced by religion. Buddhism, Hinduism, and Islam all helped shape the Indian sense and expression of beauty. The rulers who governed India over the centuries also had a major influence. After the 1700's, much of the influence was western. In recent years, however, Indian artists have rediscovered their country's rich cultural heritage and are blending it with western forms to create their own styles.

*"Art and the Life of India" by John Russell in *The New York Times Magazine*, June 2, 1985, pp. 26, 30, 32. Copyright ©1985 by The New York Times Company. Reprinted by permission.

Architecture, Painting, and Sculpture

Until modern times, many Indian artists remained largely unknown and were not individually recognized. Expected to use their talents to glorify deities and rulers, they built and decorated places of worship and public buildings.

ART AND RELIGION

Some of the oldest examples of Indian art still remaining today are temples, monasteries, and shrines built in caves. The earliest of these, built between 200 BC and 600 AD at Ajanta in the Deccan Plateau, was the work of Buddhist sculptors. Out of a 70-foot (21-meter) granite cliff, they cut large chambers in which Buddhist monks set up shrines, monasteries, and temples. Colorful paintings and carvings of the Buddha and other figures lined the walls and ceilings.

Another group of cave temples, which date from the 500's to 700's AD, was created by Buddhists, Hindus, and Jains at Ellora and Elephanta, near the Deccan Plateau. In the large complex at Ellora, carved out of solid rock, is a temple that is over 100 feet (30.5 meters) in height.

In addition to cave temples, early artists also built freestanding religious structures. These included *stupas,* large stone mounds pointing skyward that house sacred Buddhist **relics,** or holy objects, and Hindu temples that were viewed as the homes of specific gods and goddesses. Each temple had a sanctuary that housed a statue or relic, and a large square hall where worshippers gathered. Outside the temple there generally was a porch decorated with life-size **reliefs,** or raised carvings. In the north of India, the temples usually had tall towers with curved sides that met at the top, while in the south most had pyramid-shaped gateway towers with many layers of carved images of gods and goddesses. Below, a journalist describes what she saw and heard when she visited one of the old temples located in southern India:

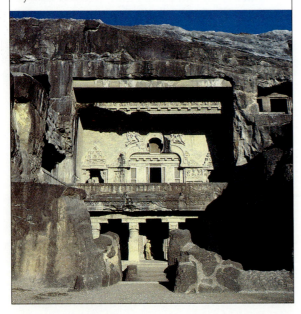

This Hindu temple at Ellora in western India was created by generations of artisans, who carved it in place out of solid cliff walls. What did the early temples of India contain?

> A bell was ringing through the temple, and Sanskrit mantras [chants] echoed the chant of the priest who moved round the inner sanctum, round the idol of Bhadreswami, an incarnation of Shiva. It was dark inside and the flickering light from two small oil lamps shadowed the walls with muted images. The god was barely visible, a blackened statue in a black womb. The chant was constant and repetitious....
>
> The temple was damp and cave-like with its low roof supported by close-set lines of granite [pillars]: there was not the refinement of arches and domes, for this was a temple which came from the earth and gave itself back to the earth, existing for gods not men....

The priest drew down a white curtain in front of the god to hide it while he washed the image with milk, ghee [clarified butter], curds, and coconut water as offering and purification. He also presented food, saying, "Oh God, eat this rice, Oh God, eat this coconut," ringing a bell as he did so. Then he pulled aside the curtain: pink flowers [adorned] the dark stone statue of Bhadreswami, single petals vividly simple against ornate carving. Flames burned, softening the shadows to one complete image, warm and glowing as though caught by the evening sun. The priest swayed beside it, encircling the god with smoke from a wick of camphor. He had washed the god, fed the god, dressed the god in private, and now was the time to show the god and give him light to see.*

The statues found in the temples and other places of worship served as images and helped many Hindus who could not read or write to visualize the gods and goddesses of their religion. This remains true today, making sculpting a widespread artistic activity in India. In the view of many, the best sculptures come from southern India. One of the most common subjects is the god Shiva, who is represented as Nataraja, "the Lord of the Dance," who creates and destroys through his dancing. The stage he dances on is the cosmos. In dancing, he connects heaven and earth and time and space.

THE MUSLIM INFLUENCE

During the rule of the Moguls, the arts of India were influenced by Islam. Muslim styles of architecture were introduced as Mogul rulers built mosques and other buildings of marble that had domes and towers called **minarets.** Since the Muslims were forbidden by their religion to carve the human figure, they decorated their buildings with elaborate designs often inlaid in white marble with semiprecious stones.

One of the leading examples of Muslim art and architecture in India is the Taj Mahal in Agra, built in the mid-1600's by Shah Jahan as a **mausoleum,** or tomb, for his wife. The Taj has been called "a poet's delight." A nineteenth-century English novelist and artist, after seeing the Taj Majal, proclaimed, "Henceforth, let the inhabitants of the world be divided into two classes—them as has seen the Taj Mahal; and them as hasn't." In 1953, Eleanor Roosevelt, a delegate to the United Nations and the wife of an American president visited the Taj Majal. Below, she relates how it affected her:

I must own that by the time we got to Agra I was beginning to feel we had seen a great many forts and palaces and mosques. I realized that I was no longer viewing them with the same freshness of interest and appreciation that I had felt during the early part of my visit. I think the others felt much the same way.... Therefore when we got back to Government House after our visit to Akbar's fort, though we knew we should leave immediately to get our first glimpse of the Taj Mahal at sunset, we all pounced on the letters we found waiting for us, and could not tear ourselves away until the last one had been read. Then, to our dismay, we found we had delayed too long; by the time we got to the Taj—about six-thirty —the light was beginning to fade.

... As we came through the entrance gallery into the walled garden and looked down the long series of oblong pools in which the Taj and the dark cypresses are reflected, I held my breath, unable to speak in the face of so much beauty. The white marble walls, inlaid with semiprecious stones, seemed to take on a mauve tinge with the coming night, and about halfway along I asked to be allowed to sit down on one of the stone benches and

---
Family Web: A Story of India by Sarah Hobson, 1978, John Murray, pp. 83–84. Reprinted by permission.

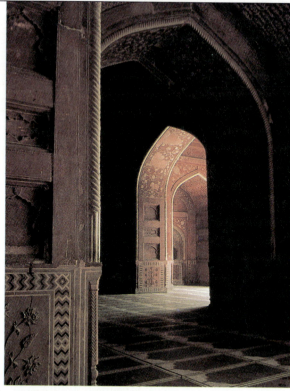

The white marbled Taj Mahal, built between 1632 and 1653, is considered one of the most beautiful buildings in the world. The skill of its artisans is evident both inside and outside of the mausoleum. In what art forms did Mogul artists excel?

just look at it. The others walked on around, but I felt that this first time I wanted to drink in its beauty from a distance. One does not want to talk and one cannot glibly say this is a beautiful thing, but one's silence, I think, says this is a beauty that enters the soul. With its minarets rising at each corner, its dome and tapering spire, it creates a sense of airy, almost floating lightness; looking at it, I decided I had never known what perfect proportions were before. . . .

We returned in the evening to see it in the full moonlight, . . . and though each time I saw it it was breath-taking, perhaps it was most beautiful by moonlight. We could hardly force ourselves to leave, and looked at it from every side, unable to make up our minds which was the most beautiful. . . .

Early the next morning . . . we visited the Taj again to see it in the clear daylight. It was still impressive and overwhelmingly lovely, but in a different way; and the marble looked slightly pinkish, as though it was being warmed by the sun.

As long as I live I shall carry in my mind the beauty of the Taj.*

Muslim artists of the Mogul period also excelled in other art forms. They created detailed miniature paintings of brilliantly colored flowers, animals, and scenes of daily life in a style adopted later by Hindu artists. They also made elaborately designed carpets, painted fabrics, carved jade, and produced works of metal, wood, and ivory.

*Abridged from pp. 168–171 in *India and the Awakening East* by Eleanor Roosevelt. Copyright 1953 by Anna Eleanor Roosevelt. Reprinted by permission of Harper & Row, Publishers, Inc.

THE ARTS TODAY

By the 1800's, European influences could be seen in the arts of India, and soon architects, painters, and sculptors were adopting western styles and techniques. Today, Indian arts reflect a blend of both East and West and old and new. Artisans in towns and villages all over India still carry on many of the traditional art forms. Below, a journalist who visited with a modern Indian artisan relates what he learned:

> In his plain home in the Agra neighborhood called Taj Ganj, Mohammad Husain folded himself into a crouch before a grinding wheel on the floor. As his right hand moved a stick, an attached thong spun the wheel's axle. The fingers of his left hand—long, artistic fingers—applied a sliver of malachite [a bright green stone] to the grinding surface.
>
> Mohammad is certain that his craft has not changed since the 1600s, when Taj Ganj was the home of artisans building the Taj Mahal. He is equally certain that his forebears helped decorate that magnificent mausoleum with bits of turquoise, lapis lazuli, jasper, malachite, coral, and carnelian. These became petals, leaves, and trailing tendrils. Inlaid in marble, the floral displays added delicacy and grace.
>
> In Agra today three thousand men piece semiprecious stones into marble tabletops and boxes. The morning I met Mohammad he was inlaying a rose in a platter.
>
> He has a craftsman's pride in his work, but the pay is meager—five to ten dollars a day. "There is no time for art," he said. "This has become too commercialized."*

1. How did early Indian artists display their talents? What are some characteristics of their work?
2. In what ways did Islam influence Indian art?
3. How have traditional art forms been affected by modern trends?

THE WRITTEN WORD

Like architecture, painting, and sculpture, Indian literature has a long and rich heritage. Today, Indian prose and poetry is written in a variety of languages, including Hindi, Bengali, and Tamil, and is translated into many others as well. But, in the past, most major works of Indian literature were written in the classical languages of Sanskrit and Tami.

THE EARLY YEARS

One of the earliest works of Indian literature is the *Vedas*, a collection of hymns, poems, legends, and religious rituals. The earliest Hindu scriptures, they were repeated for hundreds of years before being written down in 1000 BC. One section of the

This Muslim artisan holding a large goblet, displays the fine copper and enamelled wares he and his family make in Jaipur. What do today's Indian arts reflect?

---

*"When the Moguls Ruled India" by Mike Edwards in *National Geographic*, Vol. 167, No. 4, April 1985, p. 486. Reprinted by permission.

work, known as the *Rig Veda*, is the world's oldest religious text still in use.

Another major work, the *Mahabharata*, is the oldest Indian **epic,** or tale about gods and heroes. It is considered the world's longest poem. If printed in its original form today, it would fill eight large volumes. The *Mahabharata*, which tells the story of a series of battles fought by two warrior families with the help of the gods, includes moral principles and social rules that have shaped Indian civilization for hundreds of years.

Included in the *Mahabharata* is the *Bhagavad Gita,* the most important text of Hinduism. It tells how the god Krishna appeared before the warrior Arjuna just before he went into battle, assured him that all souls survive death, and urged him to fulfill his caste duty as a warrior.

In this painting, based on the Ramayana, *Ram and Sita are being attended by three gods. Ram is himself a god, being one of the countless forms taken by the god Vishnu. What story is told in the* Ramayana?

Another popular epic poem, the *Ramayana*, relates the adventures of a heroic king named Ram. It tells how Ram searched for his kidnapped wife Sita, rescued her, killed her captor, and returned in triumph to his homeland. For centuries, Indians have regarded Ram and Sita as the model of a devoted married couple.

Still another classical work is the *Panchatantra*, a series of short stories, fables, and fairy tales that present moral lessons through animals who act like humans. Many of these stories eventually spread to the Middle East and to the West, where they were retold by other authors. Some of the stories, like the fable that follows, end with a word of advice:

> In the olden days, in Benaras, lived many carpenters. One day a carpenter was planing some wood. His bald head shone like copper. A certain mosquito came and sat on his head and began to bite him again and again.
>
> Becoming vexed, the carpenter said to his son, "A mosquito is biting and biting my head. Get rid of him for me."
>
> The son was sitting behind his father. He said, "I'll do it . . .!"
>
> He picked up a sharp hatchet and with all his strength, drew back and struck his father on the head. The carpenter's head split in two and he immediately died.
>
> At this time, the Bodhisattva [Buddhist religious teacher] was sitting in the carpenter's shop. He spoke: "Verily, a sensible enemy is better than a stupid friend."*

THE TWENTIETH CENTURY

Over the years, Indian literature continued to grow and flourish. During the twentieth century, a number of writers emerged who have received worldwide attention. One of these was Rabindranath Tagore, a Bengali

---

*"Assassination of the Mosquito" from *India: A Teacher and Student Manual,* compiled, edited, and written by Hansen, Mueller and Turkovich, March, 1978. Reprinted by permission.

CHAPTER 26 THE ARTS

Sikh artisan stamping a traditional pattern onto cloth using a hand block and vegetable dyes.

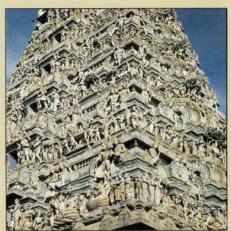

Tower atop a gate to an ancient Hindu temple in Madras, with statues representing Shiva and events in his life.

Miniature painting, developed to a high degree of perfection under Mogul rule.

Ivory carving of a rajah riding in a canopied *howdah* on the back of a royally adorned elephant.

Actors performing the Kathakali.

Lakeside memorial at the University of Chandigarh in Punjab dedicated to Mohandas Gandhi.

poet who won the Nobel Prize for Literature in 1913. Tagore, who wrote in Bengali, Hindi, and English, produced more than 1000 poems, 2000 songs, and a number of novels, short stories, plays, and essays.

Tagore lived at a time when India was awakening from a long period of British rule, and his works expressed the cultural and patriotic ferment that was sweeping the country. At the same time, he believed that India could reconcile the best of its traditional culture with modern times. In the two excerpts that follow, Tagore reveals how he feels:

> Let the earth and the water, the air and
>   the fruits of my country be sweet,
>   my God.
> Let the homes and marts, the forests
>   and fields of my country be full,
>   my God.
> Let the promises and hopes, the deeds
>   and words of my country be true,
>   my God.
> Let the lives and hearts of the sons and
>   daughters of my country be one,
>   my God.*
>
>   Where the mind is without fear and the head is held high;
>   Where knowledge is free;
>   Where the world has not been broken up into fragments by narrow domestic walls;
>   Where words come out from the depth of truth;
>   Where tireless striving stretches its arms towards perfection;
>   Where the clear stream of reason has not lost its way into the dreary desert sand of dead habit;
>   Where the mind is led forward by thee into ever-widening thought and action—
>   Into that heaven of freedom, my Father, let my country awake.†

---

*From "Love's Gift" in *A Tagore Reader*, edited by Amiya Chakravaty, 1961, The Macmillan Company, p. 348. Reprinted by permission.

‡From *Gitanjali* by Rabindranath Tagore, (New York: Macmillan, 1913).

Two other contemporary Indian authors who have won international notice are Salman Rushdie and R. K. Narayan. In a novel called *Midnight's Children*, Rushdie gives a sweeping panorama of life in India from about 1900 to the present. Narayan is known for a number of works that deal with present-day village life in southern India. In the following passage from his short story "A Horse and Two Goats," he describes the life and thoughts of an elderly Indian villager:

> Unleashing the goats from the drumstick tree, Muni started out, driving them ahead and uttering weird cries from time to time in order to urge them on. He passed through the village with his head bowed in thought. He did not want to look at anyone or be accosted. A couple of cronies lounging in the temple corridor hailed him, but he ignored their call. They had known him in the days of [plenty] when he lorded over a flock of fleecy sheep, not the miserable gawky goats that he had today. Of course he also used to have a few goats for those who fancied them, but real wealth lay in sheep; they bred fast and people came and bought the fleece in the shearing season; and then that famous butcher from the town came over on the weekly market days. . . . But all this seemed like the memories of a previous birth. Some pestilence afflicted his cattle . . . , and even the friendly butcher would not touch one at half the price . . . and now here he was left with the two scraggy creatures. He wished someone would rid him of their company too. The shopman had said that he was seventy. At seventy, one only waited to be summoned by God. When he was dead what would his wife do? They had lived in each other's company since they were children. He was told on their day of wedding that he was ten years old and she was eight. During the wedding ceremony they had had to recite their respective ages and names.

He had thrashed her only a few times in their career, and later she had the upper hand. [Children], none. Perhaps a large [family] would have brought him the blessing of the gods. . . . He avoided looking at anyone; they all professed to be so high up, and everyone else in the village had more money than he. "I am the poorest fellow in our caste and no wonder that they spurn me, but I won't look at them either," and so he passed on with his eyes downcast along the edge of the street. . . . Only on the outskirts did he lift his head and look up. He urged and bullied the goats until they meandered along to the foot of the horse statue on the edge of the village. He sat on its pedestal for the rest of the day. The advantage of this was that he could watch the highway and see the lorries and buses pass through to the hills, and it gave him a sense of belonging to a larger world. The pedestal . . . was broad enough for him to move around as the sun travelled up and westward; or he could also crouch under the belly of the horse for shade.*

1. What were some of the earliest Indian writings? Of what did they consist?
2. Who was Rabindranath Tagore? How did he view India?
3. About what does Salman Rushdie write? R. K. Narayan?

THE PERFORMING ARTS

Like the other arts of India, the performing arts have a long and rich history. At their heart are music and dance. Indian musicians play instruments and sing without using chords or other harmonies. A group of musicians starts out with a basic melody called a *raga,* which each player then develops with his or her own **improvisations,** or musical arrangements performed without preparation. The musicians perform on a number of different instruments, including drums, flutes, and a stringed instrument known as a **sitar.** Their performances often go on for several hours at a time.

A more structured art is dance, which has been considered a form of Hindu worship for hundreds of years. With the movements of their hands and bodies and the expressions on their faces, dancers act out stories of Hindu gods and goddesses. Because each step and gesture is important and must be precise, many dances require years of training. One, the Kathakali, is performed only

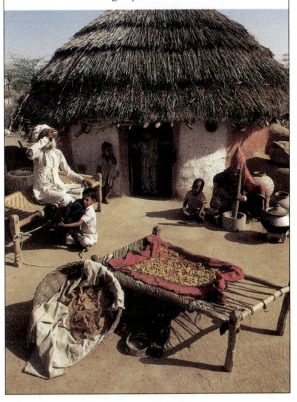

A glimpse of present-day village life is seen in this photo of a family compound in a village near Jodhpur in northwestern India. Which Indian author is known for his works about village life in southern India?

*"A Horse and Two Goats" by R.K. Narayan in *A Horse and Two Goats: Stories by R.K. Narayan,* 1970, The Viking Press, pp. 9–11. Reprinted by permission.

INSIGHTS ON PEOPLE
INDIA

RAVI SHANKAR

Probably the best-known Indian musician in the world today is Ravi Shankar, often called India's "sitar king." Shankar, almost as well known in the West as in India, has brought an appreciation of Indian classical music to western audiences. Below, an Indian journalist discusses Shankar and his career:

Ravi Shankar was clad in a somber off-white kurta and pajama with a touch of embroidered color at the throat. His large, expressive eyes were concealed behind brown-rimmed spectacles. If the sitar had not claimed him at the age of sixteen, he would probably have danced through life in the footsteps of his illustrious brother, the dancer Uday Shankar.

"Music has been the driving force of my life," he says. "What I search for in music is . . . the nerve-center of my being." Shankar has been in the news for four decades. He has been hailed as a "sitar wizard," "musical genius," and "fabulous musician," which undoubtedly he is.

In India, while none doubted his wizardry on the sitar, few appreciated his attempts at bridging the gap between the music of East and West. During the days of the sitar explosion in Britain and the U.S., Pakistani critic Masood Hasan suggested confiscation of all sitars in the two countries and proposed that Shankar be banished to Alaska with a banjo and a mug of coffee. But this piece of unwarranted criticism was overshadowed by violinist Yehudi Menuhin's oft-quoted indebtedness to the maestro "for some of the most inspiring moments I have lived in music."

Born in Varanasi in 1920—the dingy room is now a dilapidated grocer's shop—he received just three years of schooling. His father was the diwan [minister] of the tiny state of Jhalawar. At age ten Shankar joined the dance troupe headed by his famous brother.

He recalls that a trip to Paris "was like going to the moon." He stayed there for eight years. Under his brother's tutelage he was exposed to Western art and culture. . . .

Then in 1935 a chance encounter with Ustad Allauddin Khan . . . transformed his life. . . . Choosing between dance and music was difficult, but Shankar left dance behind and went to Maihar [in India] to become Khan's student. . . .

After practicing the sitar at least fourteen hours daily in Maihar, he spent three years in Bombay, writing music for two ballets and two films, and performing all over India. In 1949 he joined All India Radio as a conductor and director.

In 1956 he embarked on his first major tour abroad and since then has undertaken with passionate sincerity the task of popularizing Indian music in the West. Today Shankar gives about sixty concerts abroad annually. His largest following is in the U.S. . . .

"I have had fame and success," he says, "but I have paid the price. I would like to be like any normal person—have a home, have someone to look after me. But on the whole it has been an extremely lucky, fruitful life."*

1. What contribution has Ravi Shankar made to Indian music?
2. How does Ravi Shankar view his life and career?

*"India's Sitar King" by Lakshmi Mohan, excerpted from "Indian Express" of New Delhi, as cited in *World Press Review*, November, 1984, p. 61. Reprinted by permission.

by men who are dressed in brightly colored costumes and wear heavy makeup. Another dance, the Bharata Natyam, is performed by women. The beauty of the dancing is heightened by the swishing sound of the dancers' colorful silk costumes and the tinkling of small bells fastened around their ankles.

THEATER

Dance and music, along with literature, play an important role in Indian theater. While a variety of plays are produced today, traditional drama remains very popular, especially in rural areas. Below, an Indian actor and director talks about the theater and its history:

> . . . I direct dramas, all sorts of plays. And I find it a great experience. You know, till some years ago, very few people came to see our plays. Without an audience, naturally, our plays didn't last for more than two or three shows.
>
> Now we have an audience of about 300 for each show and there is actually a demand for good plays. There was a play which ran for 100 days. But I'm speaking of urban theater which is professional and has all the modern aids like lighting and sound effects, specially trained actors and good sets. Professional companies, though still few, exist mainly in our large cities.
>
> Theater in India is more than 2,000 years old. In the olden days, groups of actors used to move around the countryside, giving performances in village streets and courtyards. For centuries, most of our rajahs and nabobs [wealthy men] were great patrons of drama. Of course, the themes were mainly religious and dealt with the deeds of our gods.
>
> Even today, if you happen to be in northern India during October or November, you'll find the *Ram Lila* being acted out in every city, town and village. The *Ram Lila* runs continuously for a month. A different scene from the *Ramayana* is enacted every night.

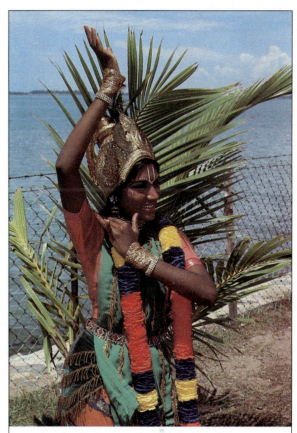

Brightly costumed, a dancer poses in front of a palm tree for a photograph. Dancers must learn 140 different poses in order to perform the Bharata Natyam. Who performs the Bharata Natyam?

> The actors perform on a temporary stage in some open space, with oil lamps providing the light. Entry is free, with everyone sitting in the open on the ground.
>
> At sunset on the last day of the performance, a huge effigy of the many-headed evil God Ravana is burned. This is known as *Dussehra*; thousands come to watch the burning of Ravana.
>
> Like the *Mahabharata*, the *Ramayana* is a great epic and contains the story of Ram and Sita and their fight against the bad Ravana. In every part of the country, people have their own religious dramas in addition to the *Ramayana* and the *Mahabharata*. But in the north, village plays and dance dramas all take their themes

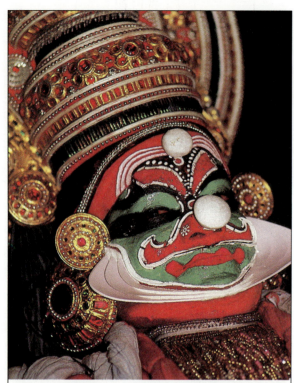

A costumed actor in colorful, grotesque makeup prepares for his role in a traditional drama performance in a local village. What is the status of traditional drama in India today?

from the *Ramayana* and the *Mahabharata*. There are so many, many interesting incidents in them, in which the good always win over the bad.

I don't have time to go see the *Ram Lila* now. *Ram Lila* performances last till around midnight. But many evenings in October and November, when I drive back from my own rehearsals, I'm tempted to step in. Folk theater is really doing very well in India.*

FILMS

Although more Indians than ever before are watching television and listening to the radio, movies are probably the most popular form of entertainment in India today. India's motion picture industry is the largest in the world, with the government supporting training for many filmmakers.

One of the best-known filmmakers is Satyajit Ray, who comes from a distinguished Calcutta family of writers, teachers, and singers. He is especially known for his film *Pather Panchali*, which tells the story of a young Hindu who moves from the village to the city. Ray's films appeal most to intellectuals and film critics, while the general public prefers films filled with action, adventure, and romance. Below, a young Indian actor talks about Indian films and his life as an actor:

> . . . Here in India the public simply idolizes movie stars. You know, only about 36 percent of us Indians can read and write, and turn to books and magazines for knowledge and relaxation. For most people, movies are the only form of relaxation and source of information about fashion, sports, history and the world in general.
>
> In the cities, movies are advertised on huge colorful posters and in the daily papers. But in towns and villages, just to make sure that everybody knows, three or four men go around beating drums and announcing a new movie through loudspeakers. I've signed up for another six movies. But, I don't think of myself as a star—yet. In a country which produces 130 movies in Hindi [the official language] alone every year, six movies make a good beginning, but they don't make a star. . . .
>
> Most of our movies deal with social problems like untouchability, intercaste marriages, family planning, becoming good mothers-in-law and so on. Then there are religious movies, movies for children, and, in recent years, a number of thrillers. In our movies the good guys always win over the bad guys. I prefer to be a good guy in pictures with a social theme.
>
> But I must tell you that, by and large, most movies are made to a set pattern.

---

*"Theater in India is more than 2000 years old" in *We live in India* by Veenu Sandal, 1984, The Bookwright Press, pp. 44–45. Reprinted by permission.

CHAPTER 26 THE ARTS 427

The movie title—"The Companion of the Heart Is the Heart Itself"—on this billboard in New Delhi typifies the love stories told in many Indian films. What kinds of movies do Indian filmmakers make?

The theme has to be set in a love story —but no kissing is allowed. Then there have to be lots of songs—at least five or six per picture, along with a few dance numbers. And a gun- or fist-fight between the hero and the villain. . . .

An actor can earn between 10,000 and 2,000,000 rupees ($1,000–200,000) per picture. I also own a record shop, so I can afford to live a very luxurious life. But my wife and I have simple tastes. Like thousands of others, we still like nothing better than to spend the evenings watching a movie with our kids.

A Hindi film runs for about two and a half hours, but every movie theater in the country has to run a newsreel and a short documentary film before the main film begins. As a form of entertainment, movies are cheap. Tickets range from 2 to 10 rupees (20 cents to $1.00).

Right now, I'm planning to produce a picture myself. It will require a lot of money, certainly, particularly as more and more movies are being made in color. But then look at the export possibilities. Not only does India lead the world in the production of feature films, it also exports them to nearly ninety countries of the world. So if I'm lucky it should turn out to be a worthwhile investment.*

1. What are some characteristics of Indian music? What musical instruments are most common?
2. How are religion and Indian dance linked?
3. What kinds of films do most Indians seem to enjoy?

*"In our movies the good guys always beat the bad guys" in *We live in India* by Veenu Sandal, 1984, The Bookwright Press, pp. 48–49. Reprinted by permission.

CHAPTER 26 REVIEW

POINTS TO REMEMBER

1. Some of the oldest examples of Indian art still remaining today are temples, monasteries, and shrines built in caves. These were created by Buddhist, Hindu, and Jain sculptors.
2. During the rule of the Moguls, the arts of India were influenced by Islam. One of the leading examples of this influence is the Taj Mahal.
3. Today, Indian arts reflect a blend of both East and West, and Indian artisans carry on many of the traditional art forms.
4. Most of the early works of Indian literature were written in Sanskrit and were based on religious teachings and beliefs.
5. Twentieth-century literature is written in various Indian languages. Three writers whose works are recognized worldwide are Rabindranath Tagore, Salman Rushdie, and R. K. Narayan.
6. Performing arts such as music and dance have a long and rich history in India.
7. Dance, music, and literature play an important role in the theater in India, where traditional themes and stories remain very popular.
8. Movies are probably the most popular form of entertainment in India today. Most Indians like movies filled with action, adventure, and romance.

VOCABULARY

Identify

Nataraja	Arjuna	*Panchatantra*	Kathakali
Vedas	*Ramayana*	Rabindranath Tagore	Bharata Natyam
Rig Veda	Ram	Salman Rushdie	*Ram Lila*
Mahabharata	Sita	R.K. Narayan	Satyajit Ray
Krishna			Ravi Shankar

Define

stupas	minarets	epic	improvisations
relic	mausoleum	*raga*	sitar
reliefs			

DISCUSSING IMPORTANT IDEAS

1. An Indian author once stated, "In India, all art is for pleasure." Do you agree or disagree? Explain.
2. In what ways do you think the arts of India have been affected by tradition? By modern trends?
3. In what ways, if any, do the arts help promote Indian unity? In what ways, if any, do they reflect Indian diversity?
4. What do Indian arts tell you about the beliefs, values, and interests of the Indian people?

DEVELOPING SKILLS

DETECTING BIAS

Almost everyone has certain opinions, ideas, or beliefs about particular topics or subjects. For this reason, written material is not always *objective*, free from the influence of a writer's or speaker's personal views or emotions. Sometimes, even if a writer or speaker does not intend it to happen, what he or she writes or says shows *bias*, a set idea or opinion about something or someone. Bias may be in favor of or against an idea or person. Look, for example, at these three sets of statements:

a. *Kate plays soccer.*
b. *Kate plays soccer!*

a. *Zane works after school.*
b. *Poor, tired Zane works long hours at a low-paying job after school.*

a. *The cat sat on the shelf above the girl's head.*
b. *The sneaky feline crouched on the shelf above the unsuspecting girl's head.*

At a quick glance, each of the a. statements seems to be saying the same thing as each of the b. statements. But, if you keep in mind the definition of bias when reading the statements, the differences between the a. and b. statements become clear. Each of the a. statements presents a straightforward fact—by whom soccer is played, what the boy does after school, what the cat is doing. The b. statements, however, reflect the writer's personal feelings. The exclamation point at the end of the b. statement leads you to believe that there is something unusual, different, or special about Kate playing soccer. The words "poor" and "tired" may make you feel sorry for Zane, an emotion that is strengthened by the fact that he works long hours at a job that does not pay well. And, the cat is not just a cat but a "sneaky feline" who appears to be ready to pounce on the poor girl standing under the shelf. All these statements, then, reflect the writer's personal opinion and may make you view the "facts" in the same light.

There are many ways of blending bias into written material. Among these are the use of the following:

1. words or terms that are full of emotion
2. italics or underlining to emphasize certain words or terms
3. *rhetorical questions*, questions that have only one answer or for which no answer is expected

For further practice in detecting bias, read the following passage. As you read, keep in mind the three indicators of bias given above. Upon completing the passage, ask yourself the following questions:

1. Is the material biased?
2. How do I know the material is biased?
3. In whose favor is the material biased?
4. Against whom is the material biased?

One of the most brilliant Indian writers was a Bengali named Rabindranath Tagore. The man wrote in three *languages and produced* thousands *of poems and songs, to say nothing of the novels, short stories, plays and essays he created! Tagore lived and created his magnificent works during the time that long-suffering India was finally getting out from under British rule. As a result, those works reflect the patriotic and cultural ferment that was sweeping his beloved country at that time. He believed that India could blend the best of its traditional culture with modern times. Can one doubt the genius of such a man?*

INDIA

UNIT 4 REVIEW

SUMMARY

India, the largest of the nations that make up the subcontinent of South Asia, is one of the most populous nations of the world today. Its geography and history are as diverse as its people, with traditions and beliefs dating back to ancient times. Incorporated within its civilization are Dravidian and Aryan ideas, Mogul styles and practices, and British organization and institutions.

One of the chief influences on India and on Indian life has been the religion of Hinduism. Unlike Buddhism, Islam, and Christianity, Hinduism was not based primarily on the beliefs and teachings of a single individual. The caste system generated under Hinduism has had a lasting impact on the area and its inhabitants.

When India came under British rule, a great many changes took place. Most Indians were not pleased with many of these changes. They felt that the British were interested only in their own personal gain. Strong Indian leaders, such as Mohandas K. Gandhi and Jawaharlal Nehru, emerged to unite their people and finally gain independence.

Since India became independent from Great Britain in 1947, the government has made an enormous effort to modernize and develop the country and to improve the lot of the poor. At the same time, it has worked to govern and integrate into one nation a great diversity of peoples speaking many different languages and living in many different environments.

As a result of government efforts, today there is new technology as well as new understandings and life styles for many. There has been improvement and development in agriculture, industry, communications, and education. But much still remains to be done. Great gaps continue to exist between the rich and the poor and among those who live in the city and in the country. There is also tension between different ethnic groups, which at times has erupted into violence. And there is a population problem, with too many people and too many births.

REVIEW QUESTIONS

1. How do you think geography and climate have influenced the ways of life in India?
2. In what ways has religion influenced the growth and development of India?
3. What impact did British rule have on India? Do you think that India would be the same today if it had never been a British colony? Explain.
4. India possesses within itself numerous contradictions. What are some of those contradictions? How do you think each affects the nation's future development?

SUGGESTED ACTIVITIES

1. Working in small groups, consult an Indian cookbook, and prepare a menu for a typical Indian meal. Cook the meal for the class.
2. Create a poster that includes a time line and shows the great empires and periods of Indian history. Include the important developments that took place under each empire and during each period.
3. Working with several other classmates, read one of the classical fables or short stories of Indian literature. Make puppets or role play the story for the rest of the class.
4. Research and write a report about one of the great historical rulers or important modern leaders of India. Present the report to the class.

COMPARING CULTURES

An important part of any culture is clothing. The clothes people wear reflect more than their sense of style. They reflect customs and environments as well. Below is information on the clothing of India and of the United States. Read the information, contrast and compare the kinds of clothing worn, and indicate what the dress habits of each people suggest about their culture.

INDIA

Because of the hot climate, Indians often wear lightweight, loose clothing, some of which is homespun. Dress varies from region to region, and while some urban Indians prefer western-style clothing, many Indians in both urban and rural areas still wear traditional garments.

One traditional type of clothing for Indian men is the *dhoti*, a piece of white cotton cloth wrapped around the waist and between the legs, which resembles a pair of loose trousers. In the north, men may also wear a tight cotton coat buttoned to the neck and trousers that fit tightly from the knees to the ankles. Many Indian men wear turbans of various shapes and colors.

A traditional garment for Indian women is a brightly colored piece of clothing called a *sari*. It consists of a piece of cotton or silk cloth that is wrapped around the body to form a long, flowing dress. The loose end of the *sari* is placed over the shoulder or draped over the head to form a hood. At times, a blouse is worn under the *sari*. Such jewelry as bracelets and earrings are also worn, and some women apply a *tilak*, a round dot made with red or black powder, to the middle of their foreheads.

THE UNITED STATES

In the United States, styles of clothing are as varied as the people themselves. Most, however, are designed according to western standards. Although some people wear tailor-made clothing, the great majority wear ready-to-wear clothes that have been mass produced and are available in most stores. Styles change rapidly, often from season-to-season or year-to-year.

Most Americans dress according to their sex, occupation, age group, or the activity in which they are participating. Although men's clothing is more colorful today than it was a few decades ago, women generally wear brighter colors than men. While both men and women tend to dress conservatively on the job, they often are more informal at home. Sportswear and leisure clothing, including jeans, are the preferred dress for many whenever possible.

In the 1960's and 1970's, most Americans seemed to have an "anything goes" attitude toward clothing and dress. In recent years, however, there has been a return to elegance in fashion. But, whatever the fashion trends, Americans probably display one of the greatest varieties of clothing styles of any people in the world.

Unit Five

In the 1500's, Spanish and Portuguese explorers encountered new lands rich in gold and other resources. They conquered the peoples living in the lands and built huge colonial empires. In effect, they created a "Latin" America. Today, Latin America encompasses 23 different nations on several continents and embraces political systems ranging from democracy to communism. While each nation has its own government, mix of peoples, and ways of life, all have a common heritage that unifies them. Politically, the Latin American nations play a significant role in world affairs. Their growing populations and strategic location help make them of major interest and concern to both the United States and the Soviet Union. For these reasons alone, it is important to gain an understanding of Latin America and its people.

CONTENTS

27	VAST AND VARIED ENVIRONMENT	434
28	THE HUMAN DIVERSITY	450
29	THE SOCIAL FABRIC	464
30	PRAYER AND POLITICS	482
31	CHANGE TAKES MANY FORMS	496
32	DICTATORSHIPS AND DEMOCRACIES	516

LATIN AMERICA

CHAPTER 27
VAST AND VARIED ENVIRONMENT

1. What are the major physical characteristics of Latin America?
2. What are the advantages and disadvantages of Latin America's environmental diversity?

Clickety-clacking its way down the track . . . , the train chugs off due east toward Ochomogo, the continental divide. Soon thereafter, mighty Irazú Volcano, a barely sleeping 11,262-foot [3432.6-meter] giant looms off to the left as the train glides into Cartago, the country's former colonial capital. . . .

Winding around lush farmlands and stately forests, small, rounded hills and gently sloping valleys, the train snakes its way through the mountains, leaving the Central Plateau behind. Evergreen farms and forests form a patchwork quilt of varying hues. . . .

This is prime coffee-growing country. . . . Along the tracks the ripening red beans, framed by shiny emerald leaves, seem to beckon the riders to reach out and pluck them. . . .

After the second stop at the small lively town of Paraíso, the spectacular Orosí Valley . . . slips into view. Farmhouses dot the landscape while a hundred shades of green carpeting the valley floor compete for the viewer's attention. The train creeps over an aged, open-slatted bridge spanning a deep gorge. . . .

As the train gently rocks on, it begins its love affair with the Reventazón River. . . . Swirling and thundering toward the sea, the white ribbon of water slices through the fertile valley below. . . . As the train continues its descent, coffee plants are replaced by sugar cane and bananas, and the Cachí Lake and dam come into view. . . .

Passengers and vendors mob the train at Turrialba, the last major stop before the lowlands. . . .

As Turrialba fades into the distance, the train once again parallels the swiftly moving Reventazón. . . . The vegetation becomes denser as the landscape flattens out and the temperature inches up. Squat cacao trees, graceful palms and ferns, and hardy bananas crowd around the tracks. The train breezes through several tunnels hewn from solid rock only to burst out again into the lush tropical foliage. . . .

From Siquirres to Limón the countryside is completely flat and tropical, and the climate hot and steamy.

Toward dusk, giant palms fill the sky and the sparkling Caribbean finally bursts into view. . . . The air is filled with ocean smells. . . .*

The seven-hour, 101-mile (161.6-kilometer) trip on Costa Rica's narrow gauge railroad takes a person through a varied landscape. Such variety is characteristic of Latin America, the name given to a vast region that spans more than one continent.

Latin America stretches from the Río Grande in North America to the southern tips of Argentina and Chile in South America. It covers some 8,500,000 square miles (22,100,000 square kilometers), 16 percent of the earth's surface. It includes Mexico and most countries of Central America and South America. It takes in some of the island-nations of the Caribbean—Cuba, the Dominican Republic, Haiti, and Puerto Rico. It is a complex area in which the environment greatly influences the way people live and what they expect out of life.

---

*"Costa Rica's Jungle Express" by Veronica Gould Stoddart in *Américas*, Vol. 34, No. 6 Nov/Dec 1982, pp. 42–47.

MOUNTAINS

Huge mountain ranges dominate much of Latin America. In Mexico, for example, the Sierra Madre Occidental, which runs along the west coast, and the Sierra Madre Oriental, which runs along the east coast, join around Mexico City to form the Sierra Madre del Sur. From Mexico, mountains run south through much of Central America. Still more mountains are found throughout the Caribbean islands. The largest mountain range, however, is found in South America. There, the Andes, the longest continuous mountain chain in the world, forms the backbone of the continent.

The Andes stretch almost 4000 miles (6400 kilometers) from northern Colombia and Venezuela to the southern tip of South America. Below, their vastness and grandeur is described by a traveler flying over them in Chile:

> Five, six, seven thousand feet [2134 meters] and we turned eastward over the broad valley of the Juncal River and toward the mountains. We gained on them. At first they looked like colossal gobs of sponge cake sprinkled with a thin coating of powdered sugar. In another moment they were beneath us, or I thought so. . . . The great gobs of sponge cake were not the Andes at all. They were only the foothills of the Andes. We hadn't started to climb. . . .
>
> The poppies and hayfields gave way to jagged, contorted cliffs and rocks, around and over which wound and twisted the Aconcagua River. . . . All the time we were climbing up—eight thousand feet, nine, ten [3048 meters]—two miles [3.2 kilometers]. The sponge cake became a coconut cake. It was all solid white, completely iced over. This, I thought, is the Andes proper. But as I looked ahead a wall loomed still higher, so high that it seemed to have no top. . . .
>
> Up and up, nineteen, twenty thousand feet, twenty-one thousand, twenty-one thousand five hundred feet [6553 meters]. What an altitude! . . .
>
> . . . It was like going to heaven in an airplane. We were just above the cordillera, the central range of the mighty mountains. Beneath us, jagged peaks . . . seemed to reach up threateningly. All around were countless slender snowy peaks. To the north, the granddaddy of them all . . . Aconcagua, [22,835] feet [6960 meters] high, looked calmly and silently down upon the whole continent. To the south, Aconcagua's companion, Tupungato, only a hundred feet [30.48 meters] lower. Two giant sentinels of this fantastic garden of the gods.
>
> As we cleared the western edge of the central range and hung . . . between these two magnificent peaks, the morning sun splashed its first yellow rays over the mountains and the great white world became a solid mass of glittering gold. Then it changed. It became a mass of shimmering silver. The rearing peaks looked like great foaming bubbles. I looked south at Tupungato, then north to Aconcagua. They wore crowns of sparkling diamonds, so bright from the light of old Sol [the sun] that it hurt my eyes to look.*

The mountains, however, have created problems. One problem is that they block communications. Most people who live in the mountains are in scattered, isolated villages. Travel is difficult, and many villagers have limited contact with other areas. For this reason, their loyalties and ties often are to their region rather than to their nation. There has been talk about developing more and better transportation systems, but construction work in the mountains is hard, costly, and time-consuming.

Another problem is that the mountains are young geologically. Volcanic eruptions, ava-

---

*Edward Tomlinson, excerpted from *The Other Americans*. Copyright 1943 Edward Tomlinson; copyright renewed 1971. Reprinted with the permission of Charles Scribner's Sons.

CHAPTER 27 VAST AND VARIED ENVIRONMENT

The Andes run parallel to the Pacific shoreline and dominate the landscape of western South America. Like these in Peru, most of the peaks are covered by snow year-round, and, in their shadow, are vast snowfields and glaciers. The melted snow feeds rivers that water the arid coastal plains. What is the largest mountain range in Latin America?

lanches, and earthquakes are not uncommon. Neither are **seaquakes**, or underwater earthquakes. In the past, seaquakes have caused tidal waves that have damaged and even leveled coastal towns.

One of the worst disasters in recent Latin American history took place in March and April of 1982 in Chiapas, a state in southern Mexico. At that time, a series of eruptions blew away the dome of a volcano called El Chichón. Below, a visitor to the area describes what he saw and heard:

> I stood atop El Chichón and peered at the seething mass below, at what was left after the volcano blew.
> It had been a steep climb to the edge of the crater from the helicopter's landing point. The grayish black slope was scarred by deep gashes cut through compacted ash by heavy rains.
> A hundred meters [330 feet] below me lay overlapping lakes of dark blue and green water (above), their temperature an estimated 200°C (nearly 400°F). In one spot, water bubbled as though fed by an underground spring; in another, a black object—a tree?—bobbed up and down, hurled to the surface again and again.
> Steam rose from the water in heavy clouds. . . . Steam seeped from the crater walls, the sulphur content turning them yellowish green and then rust colored as it mixed with oxygen. . . .
> Few gave the mountain any thought. And why should they have? It was well away from most other Mexican volcanoes. . . .
> Oh, sure, some of the Zoque Indian farmers and some local ranchers had been complaining of earthquakes since last November, and a . . . geologist . . . reported he felt tremors and heard rumbling noises the winter before that. The water in nearby rivers was warming and emitting a sulfurous smell. And there was always a cloud of steam over the mountain.
> But that was precisely the point, officials said later. That steam cloud had always been there, and there had always been reports of rumbling in the ground in these mountains. . . .
> Nevertheless, as seismic activity [vibrations from earthquakes that travel through the earth] intensified late in March, the

government prepared to dispatch scientists to the scene. . . .

Before the scientists could arrive, however—at 11:32 P.M. on March 28, a Sunday—there was a local earthquake that registered 3.5 on the Richter scale [device used to compare the size of earthquakes]. The eruption that followed ejected a column of ash, rock, and gases, sending ash hurtling 17 kilometers [10.2 miles] into the sky. . . .

The next Saturday, April 3, seismographs in six locations around El Chichón recorded more than 500 seismic events. They climaxed with a powerful eruption at 7:32 P.M., then scaled down again until the major blast at 5:20 the next morning, Palm Sunday. . . .

After those two weekends, the map, the entire landscape, had changed. Villages, ranches, communal farms no longer existed. . . .

Many people were dead. The exact toll will never be known; . . .

Even two months after those terrible weekends, the signs of destruction were chilling. Four of us . . . rode muleback

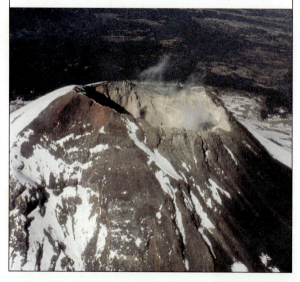

Overlooking the historic Valley of Mexico, rising 17,887 feet (5452 meters), is this sometimes steaming volcano known as Popocatépetl, "Smoking Mountain." Why have Latin America's mountains been so important?

Clinging to the side of an 8000-foot (2400-meter) Andean mountain in Chile are the town and operations plant of El Teniente, the world's largest underground copper mine. What else is mined in the Andes?

for six grueling hours . . . to survey the desolation.

Ten kilometers [6 miles] from the summit, as we entered the restricted zone . . . , we saw a stone marker: a skull and crossbones and the words, *"peligro: volcán*—danger: volcano."

Abandoned clothing lay strewn on barbed wire, mute signs of the desperation felt by the Zoque Indians as they fled along the mountainous path to the relative safety of the highway.

Along our route: crushed roofs, trees turned to charcoal, rocks that had fallen from the sky, and the daytime quiet, so devoid of life that the whinny of an abandoned mule was startling. What had been a fertile valley was now a dead, gray, barren desert.*

Still, people are drawn to the mountains. Some come to mine the rich deposits of copper, iron, silver, tin, lead, and other

---

*"The Disaster of El Chichón" by Boris Weintraub in *National Geographic*, Vol. 162, No. 5 November 1982, pp. 660–661, 664, 666–667.

minerals. Others come to raise livestock or to grow grain and coffee in the rich soil of the valleys and plateaus. It was in such mountains that the great Indian civilizations of Mexico and Peru rose. Today these areas are among the most important and most heavily populated in Latin America.

1. What are some of the major mountain ranges of Latin America?
2. What problems do the mountains create?
3. What draws people to the mountains?

PLAINS

Another feature of the Latin American landscape is plains areas. Coastal plains, seldom more than 50 miles (80 kilometers) wide, extend along the coast of Mexico, through the Yucatán Peninsula, and into Guatemala, Honduras, and Nicaragua. In addition to these, broad inland plains spread over southern Brazil, Paraguay, Uruguay, Argentina, Venezuela, and Colombia. Two of the most interesting of these are the *pampas* of Argentina and Uruguay and the *llanos* of Colombia and Venezuela.

The Argentine *pampas* spread almost 500 miles (800 kilometers) north to the Salado del Norte River and south to the Colorado River. Only a few trees dot the flat surface of the area. It is broken only by a few low mountains in the southeast and northwest. In the east, the *pampas* are hot; in the west, they are dry.

Until the 1800's, the *pampas* were the domain of the **gaucho**, a person who worked the cattle that roamed the vast area. By the late 1800's, the gauchos and their way of life had begun to disappear, pushed out by railroads, immigrants, and farming. This fact is lamented in the following epic Argentine poem about the life of a *gaucho* named Martin Fierro:

A son am I of the rolling plain,
   A gaucho born and bred;
     For me the whole great world is small,
     Believe me, my heart can hold it all;
The snake strikes not at my passing foot,
   The sun burns not my head.

I was born on the mighty Pampas' breast,
   As the fish is born in the sea;
     Here was I born and here I live,
     And what seemed good to God to give,
When I came to the world; it will please him too,
   That I take away with me.

And this is my pride: to live as free
   As the bird that cleaves the sky;
     I build no nest on this careworn earth,
     Where sorrow is long, and short is mirth,
And when I am gone none will grieve for me,
   And none care where I lie.

. . . .

There was a time when I knew this land
   As the gaucho's own domain;
     With children and wife, he had joy in life,
     And law was kept by the ready knife
Far better than now; alas, no more
   That time shall come again.

. . . .

Ah, my mind goes back and I see again
   The gaucho I knew of old;
     He picked his mount, and was ready aye,
     To sing or fight, and for work or play,
And even the poorest one was rich
   In the things not bought with gold.

The neediest gaucho in the land,
   That had least of goods and gear,
     Could show a troop of a single strain,
     And rode with a silver-studded rein,

To many Latin Americans, the gaucho *is a living symbol of freedom. Though not a frequent sight today, some* gauchos, *like this one riding across the* pampas, *continue to follow tradition and live and work on the small number of large* estancias, *or ranches, still found in the Argentine interior. Of what economic importance are the* pampas *today?*

The plains were brown with the grazing herds,
    And everywhere was cheer.

. . . .

There was work for all—or rather play,
    For a goodly game was yon;
        The plain below, and the sky above,
        A horse and a thatch and a bit o'love,
And a nap in the shade in the heat of day,
    And a dram from the demijohn [large bottle in a wicker holder].

. . . .

There was porridge of corn in steaming pots,
    And fresh-baked bread galore,
        And broth and stew, and a barbecue,
        And caña [drink made from sugarcane]
           or wine as it suited you,
No wonder I sigh for the days gone by,
    The times that shall come no more,

When by favour of none the gaucho rode
    O'er the rolling pampas wide;
        But now alas, he grows sour and grim,
        For the law and the police they harry him,
And either the Army would rope him in,
    Or the Sheriff have his hide.*

Today the *pampas* are the economic heart of Argentina and one of the breadbaskets of the world. Although they make up less than one-fifth of Argentina's territory, almost 40 percent of all Argentines live on them. The rich soil makes the area one of the best in the world for farming. Over 80 percent of Argentina's cereals, 65 percent of its cattle, and 75 percent of its pigs come from the *pampas*.

The other great plains area of Latin America, the *llanos*, stretches from the delta of the Orinoco River in Venezuela westward into southern Colombia. The areas along the rivers are level, but the rest is rolling plains and low **mesas**, broad and flat elevated areas. Here cattle-raising has been the major economic activity since the 1500's. In the past, the climate kept the cattle industry from

---
*From *The Gaucho Martin Fierro* by José Hernández. Translated by Walter Owen. Copyright 1936, ©1964 by Holt, Rinehart, and Winston. Reprinted by permission of Holt, Rinehart and Winston, Publishers.

developing as it should have. Below, a Venezuelan author describes the effect the weather had:

> It rained, and rained, and rained. For days nothing else happened. The cattlemen who had been outside their houses had returned to them, for the creeks and streams would flow over into the prairie and there would soon be no path to use. Nor any need to use one.
>
> The marsh was full to overflowing, for the winter had set in with a will. One day the black snout of a crocodile rose to the surface, and soon there would be alligators too, for the creeks were filling fast and they could travel all over the prairie.
>
> Rain, rain, rain! The creeks had flowed over and the pools were full. The people began to fall ill, . . . They became pale, and then green, and crosses began to spring up in the Altamira cemetery.
>
> But the rivers began to go down at last, and the ponds on the river banks to dry up; the alligators began to abandon the creeks, to gorge themselves on the Altamira cattle. The fever was dying out.
>
> The drought had begun to hold sway. It was now the time for driving to the water holes the cattle who had never known them, or had forgotten them in the agony of thirst. The rutted beds of creeks long dried up ran here and there through the brownish weeds. In some marshes there still remained a little oozy, warm water in which rotting steers, who, crazy with thirst, had leaped into the deepest part of the holes and there, swollen with too much drinking, had been trapped and had died. Great bands of buzzards wheeled above the pools. Death is a pendulum swinging over the Plain, from flood to drought and from drought to flood.*

In recent years, things have changed. A dam has been built across the Guárico River to help protect the *llanos* against floods and to provide irrigation for farmers and ranchers. Thousands of acres which, during the dry season, used to be wasteland now are well watered, fertile pasture. Other forms of economic development have come to the *llanos* as well. Iron deposits in the area, for example, support a steel mill in Ciudad Guayana, a city of about 250,000 people.

1. Where are the *pampas* located? The *llanos*?
2. What was the life style of the *gaucho*? What changed it?
3. Why was a dam built across the Guarico River? How did it change the *llanos*?

RIVERS

In addition to soaring mountains and flat plains, Latin America has a number of river systems. In South America, for example, there are five major river systems. They are the Magdalena in Colombia; the Orinoco in Venezuela; the Río de la Plata, formed by the Paraná and Uruguay rivers and flowing through Argentina, Uruguay, and Paraguay;

A seaplane nears Iquitos on the Amazon River in northeastern Peru. Once a busy export port for raw rubber, today Iquitos thrives on the export of oil. In what countries do the five major rivers flow?

---

*Adapted from *Doña Bárbara* by Rómulo Gallegos, translated by Robert Malloy, 1931, Peter Smith Publisher, Inc. (Gloucester, MA), pp. 291–294, 432–433.

and the São Francisco and the Amazon in Brazil.

The Amazon is one of the most important systems. It is the longest river in the Western Hemisphere. It stretches for about 4000 miles (6400 kilometers) across South America—from the Peruvian Andes eastward across Brazil to the Atlantic Ocean. About 2300 miles (3680 kilometers) of the river—from the east coast of Brazil to Iquitos, Peru—is navigable. With its more than 200 branches and tributaries, it drains some 2,700,000 square miles (7,020,000 square kilometers) of land—more than any other river of the world. Two North American journalists described their reaction to the river and to the Amazon port city of Belém in this way:

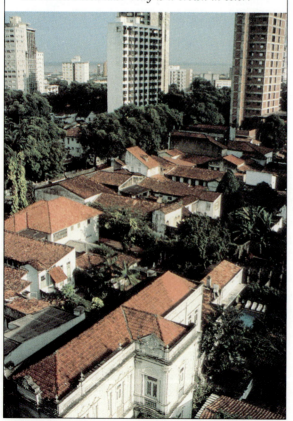

Modern Belém, Brazil, is a study in contrast, of old and new. A gateway to the Atlantic, it is the largest port city on the Amazon River. At Belém, what does the Amazon look like? Why is it brown in color?

We awoke early the next morning still tired yet like schoolchildren on their first day back. We had an appointment that we had been looking forward to for a long time. It was with the Amazon River. That we had spent so long in the Amazon jungle without seeing the lifeline itself was testimony to the river system's breadth and influence.

Walking through the quiet, littered streets of Belém we felt the heat begin to rise. . . .

The main avenue of the town spills out into a dock area, and it was there that we first saw the river, brown and wide. "River Sea" is its common nickname and it is deserved. The water is colored with silt it has carried nearly 4,000 miles [6400 kilometers] in its journey from the Andes. Its brownness is not a sign of pollution, but strength, proof that the river can still alter the topography [features] of the continent. For the next 150 miles [240 kilometers] far out into the Atlantic, the ocean itself is stained brown because of the power of this river.

At Belém the Amazon looks like an ocean. We were unable to follow the shoreline on the other side. From some angles it appeared there was no shoreline; no doubt, it had once been there until it gave way to the incessant flow of the river. *The Mighty, Mighty Amazon* is the title of a book about the river, and it was easy to appreciate that homage to the river's power. We felt its calm omnipotence: "I am the mighty, mighty Amazon, and I go wherever I wish and take with me what and whom I desire." . . .

We watched the tide surge in, jostling the 40,000-ton [36,000-metric ton] *Benedict* visiting from Liverpool as easily as it rocked the two-man *Esperança* carrying fish to market. The port for the *Esperança* and the other fishing boats of the area is upriver from the large commercial docks, a sprawling fish market whose very name, *Ver-o-Peso*, is a warning to consumers: "Watch the weight." To get there we had to slink through a ribbonwide opening between lines of rickety wooden stalls. . . .

Into the small slip at the Ver-o-Peso came boats providentially named, like the *Esperanca* which means Hope, *Sonhos* (Dreams) and *Life Is Tough For Him Who Is Soft*. From these ships tumbled a potpourri of the remarkably varied fish life of the river—small silvery piranhas with sharp deadly teeth; shiny pirarucu, at 6 feet [1.8 meters] long the largest freshwater fish in the world; tambaqui, tucunare—delicious fish with beautiful names. We watched men with towels curled on their heads balancing wood cartons of fish, crossing back and forth from boats to the market. . . .

This place which sells crazy ornaments and exotic fish was, for that morning at least, the real Belém to us. The highway from Brasilia, the airplanes flying overhead, and the apartment houses we had walked by could not distract this town from the real source of its life. The Amazon River did not disappoint us.*

1. What are five major river systems in Latin America?
2. What is the longest river in the Western Hemisphere? Where is it located?

RAIN FORESTS AND DESERTS

Still another feature common to Latin America is the tropical rain forest, the heavily wooded area found in warm, humid regions mostly near the Equator. These forests, which stay green year-round, are rainy and hot all the time and may have thunderstorms several hundred days out of the year. They have more kinds of trees than any other area of the world. More species of animals live in them than anywhere else.

*Excerpted from *Amazon*, copyright ©1983 by Brian Kelly and Mark London. Reprinted by permission of Harcourt Brace Jovanovich, Inc.

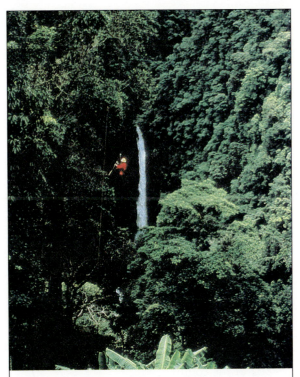

A climber ascends into the interlocking treetops, or canopy, of a tropical rain forest above the Sarapiquí River gorge in Costa Rica, Central America. Where are the tropical rain forests of Latin America found?

The largest, and probably the oldest, tropical rain forest is in the Amazon basin. It covers about one-third of South America. It is not, however, the only such forest in Latin America. There are rain forests along the eastern coast of Central America and in some islands of the Caribbean as well. One of these is El Yunque, "the anvil," a mountain in Puerto Rico with a rain forest on its slopes. Part of the Caribbean National Forest, El Yunque covers 28,000 acres [11,200 hectares]. The entire forest is a bird sanctuary. Below, a visitor to El Yunque describes what she saw there and how she felt about it:

There are nearly 200 species of trees shading the mountains. The palms and tree ferns give it an airy feeling in sharp contrast to the montana thickets of gnarled and twisted trunks. Some such trees are a thousand years old. When you see the pink and white begonias coloring the forest floor, you believe the saying, "Toss a seed into the ground and overnight a garden springs up." Air plants abound, dozens of varieties of tiny orchids snuggling against the trees. . . . If you take one of the side roads or one of the 29 miles [46.4 kilometers] of trails that wind through the forest, you will be in a bamboo forest and you will have the feeling of being in a private cathedral with the wind singing through the leaves in a wayward tune, like the wispy, tuneless song of a child.

There is another song in the air. I hear it again and again, tremulous and piercing sweet. It must be a species of bird. But I am wrong. What I see, after careful inspection, is the coqui—a tree toad—tiny as the fingernail on your smallest finger. . . . Her song is a mother's, her body all throbbing voice. . . . The sound of the katydid is like rock and roll compared to the aria of the coqui.

The flowers at El Yunque are particularly rich in color protected as they are with shade. The heliconias are everywhere. You will know them immediately with their orange lobster-claw flowers. Moss hangs from the trees like an old man's beard. Everywhere are varieties of bromeliads (the pineapple plant is one) with pointed leaves beautiful and shiny, almost artificial looking in their severe perfection. The fruit trees are repeated over and over, with the breadfruit tree a curiosity. That brilliant streak of color is a Puerto Rican parrot, green, blue, and red, a full foot tall. He is at home in the forest along with the tanager, the owl, the pigeon, the quail-dove. There is a thrush flying overhead and somewhere a woodpecker is in the distance with its familiar rat-tat-tat. There are no poisonous snakes to mar this paradise, but lizards are common.

Is there any place in the world more beautiful than El Yunque? I would have to be convinced. If you find it, bring me to it!*

In direct contrast to the green and moisture-laden rain forests are the dry lands of northern Mexico and northeastern Brazil and the Patagonian and Monte deserts of southern and northwestern Argentina. Drier still is Peru's narrow coastal region. A desert of stone and sand dotted by irrigated farmlands, it stretches for close to 1400 miles (2240 kilometers). This region is the northern extension of Chile's Atacama Desert, one of the driest areas of the world.

The Atacama runs south from Chile's northern border with Peru for more than 600 miles (960 kilometers). A thick fog called a *camanchaca,* which rolls in over the coastal mountains, often covers the area. Almost no vegetation grows on the Atacama, and some of its towns never have recorded rainfall. Below, a passenger traveling through the Atacama by train gives her impression of it:

> The scenery looks as though one is on some bizarre planet where centuries ago life was sucked off into a black hole, leaving only dusty specters and eidolic [phantom-like] mountains. In spite of, or perhaps because of, the starkness a hypnotic beauty emanates from this wind-swept land. Strange hues wreathe the mountains and swirl the sands. The nuances of color—the rose, turquoise, gold —are disconcerting and eerie.
>
> For the entire day the train presses across the desert. Borax lakes, resembling late spring snow patches, dot the vast land. Volcanoes creep up the horizon, livid lake beds spring into sight then disappear. Foothills of the Andes form a forlorn backdrop for the desert, slowly fading into the night.*

1. What are some of the characteristics of tropical rain forests? Where is the largest one located?
2. Where are the dry lands located? What and where is the largest and driest?

Come Along to Puerto Rico by Princine Calitri, 1971, T. S. Denison & Company, Inc., pp. 144–146.

*"The Andes by Train" by Sally Wyche as printed in *Américas,* vol. 31, no. 2, February 1979, p. 30.

CASE STUDY
LATIN AMERICA

THE DIMINISHING RAIN FORESTS

In recent years, the tropical rain forests of Latin America, like those of other parts of the world, have become a subject of controversy. In Central America, nearly two-thirds of the primary forests have been cleared to make room for cattle ranches. In Mexico, only one rain forest remains. And that is slowly being encroached on by farmers, ranchers, and timber companies. In the Caribbean, on most islands, only small tracts of the once-large forests remain.

Only in South America do large portions of rain forest remain untouched. But no one knows for how much longer this will be the case. Many industries want to tap the forests for various organic compounds. Some governments look to them for the mineral wealth they need to bolster their poor economies. Some Latin Americans, like the Peruvians in the following account, see the forest as their hope for the future:

In the agricultural ministry office, men fresh from the slums of Lima extolled their projected cooperative—50,000 acres [20,000 hectares] four hours away by boat. "The possibilities are tremendous," said one. "We'll sell wood, we'll have lots of rice, pineapples, coffee."

The agricultural official said the soil isn't that good.

"Then we'll get tourists. We'll sell little monkeys to them."

The official said that would be illegal.

"All right, we'll let them take pictures."

Other Latin Americans, however, oppose development of the rain forests. They argue that development will destroy the lives of the peoples who make their home in the forest. In addition, many scientists view the rain forests as "the world's largest reservoir of genetic traits." They warn that clearing them will result in a loss of "irreplaceable sources of medicines and germ plasm important to agriculture; also much of the world's most remarkable wildlife, all the way up to the orangutan." They also fear that large-scale burning of the forests eventually will result in changes of climate all over the world.

After discussing the matter with different scientists, one journalist summed up their fears as follows:

I was beginning to understand. That the tropical rain forest may well be nature's chief library of experience from which humanity can learn, not only how to do things but also what vast variety of things may be possible. And why the environmental crusader Norman Myers was moved to say that doing away with it would be like burning the ancient library of Alexandria—that if present patterns of converting tropical rain forest persist, it may be the worst biological debacle "since life's first emergence on the planet 3.6 billion years ago."*

1. Why have tropical rain forests become a subject of controversy?
2. Do you think tropical rain forests should be cleared and used for other purposes? Give reasons for your answer.

---

*"Tropical Rain Forests: Nature's Dwindling Treasures" by Peter T. White in *National Geographic*, Vol. 163, No. 1 January 1983, pp. 9, 24, 31–32.

EXPLORATION
LATIN AMERICA

The geographic environment of Latin America differs from country to country and from area to area. So do climate, resources, land use, and population density. The four maps that follow illustrate this. Study the maps, and answer the following questions:

1. What are the seven major landforms of Latin America?
2. What are the major types of climate of Latin America? What effect, if any, do you think altitude has on temperature?
3. What are some of the major resources of Mexico? Of Central America? Of South America? Of the Caribbean? For the most part, how is the land used in each area?
4. In what areas is the population the most heavily concentrated? The least?
5. Based on the information in the chapter and in the maps, what relationship do you see between physical environment, climate, and resources and population density and economic life style?

LANDFORMS

CLIMATE

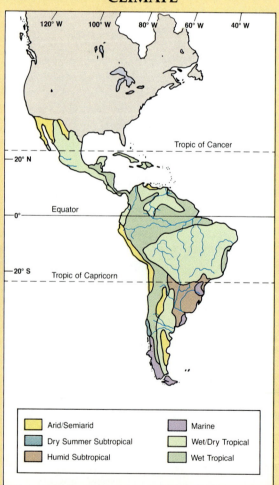

LAND USE AND RESOURCES

POPULATION DENSITY

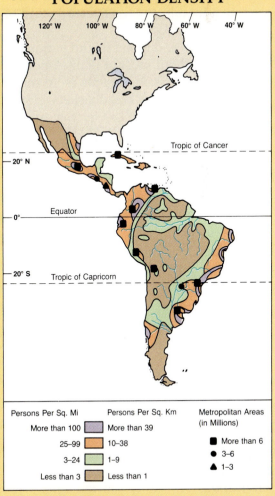

CHAPTER 27 REVIEW

POINTS TO REMEMBER

1. The name "Latin America" refers to Mexico, the countries of Central and South America, and the Caribbean island-nations of Cuba, the Dominican Republic, Haiti, and Puerto Rico.
2. Huge mountain ranges, the largest of which is the Andes, dominate Latin America. The mountains can block communications and be the source of such natural disasters as volcanic eruptions, avalanches, seaquakes, and earthquakes. Many people come to the mountain areas to mine minerals, to raise livestock, and to grow grain and coffee.
3. Coastal plains and broad inland plains are found throughout most of Latin America. One plains area is the *pampas* of Argentina. It is one of the breadbaskets of the world. Until the late 1800's, the *pampas* were the domain of the *gaucho*. Another plains area is the *llanos* of Venezuela and Colombia. It has been a prime cattle-raising territory of Latin America since the 1500's.
4. Latin America has a number of river systems. There are five major ones in South America—the Magdalena, the Orinoco, the Río de la Plata, the São Francisco, and the Amazon. The Amazon, known as the "River Sea," is the longest river in the Western Hemisphere.
5. Tropical rain forests abound in Latin America. The largest, and probably the oldest, is in the Amazon basin and covers one-third of South America.
6. Latin America also has dry lands. One of the driest areas of the world, the Atacama Desert, runs through Peru and Chile.

VOCABULARY

Identify

Latin America
Sierra Madre Occidental
Sierra Madre Oriental
Sierra Madre del Sur

Andes
El Chichón
Guárico

Magdalena
Orinoco
Río de la Plata

São Francisco
Amazon
El Yunque
Atacama

Define

seaquakes
pampas

llanos

gaucho

mesas
camanchaca

DISCUSSING IMPORTANT IDEAS

1. Latin America often is referred to as a land of geographic vastness and great environmental variety. Do you agree with this? Explain.
2. What advantages do you see in the great diversity of geographical environment of Latin America? What disadvantages do you see?

3. Life in Latin America exists on many different levels. In what ways do you think the land's vastness and geographical diversity might influence the people's life styles and expectations?

4. How do the size and geography of Latin America compare with those of your country? What effect do you think your country's size and geography has had on the people's life styles?

Developing Skills

WRITING DESCRIPTIVELY

When you write something, it generally has a purpose. In one case, for example, your purpose may be to give information or explain. In another, it may be to provide a simple, straightforward account of something. And, in still another, it may be to describe a scene or event in a way that will make the reader feel that he or she is sharing the experience with you. This is known as *descriptive writing*.

When you write descriptively, your goal is to create vivid images that give a sense of personal participation to the reader. These guidelines will help you achieve this goal:

1. Include as many aspects of the five senses —sight, sound, taste, smell, and touch—as possible.
2. Create mental images by using:

    (a) *analogies,* comparisons between things that, although different, are similar.
    (Example: He was a bear of a man.)

    (b) *metaphors,* words or phrases that suggest likenesses between things that are really not the same.
    (Example: Vicki was swimming in money.)

    (c) *similies,* figures of speech that compare two unlike things and that often are introduced by "like" or "as."
    (Example: After climbing the hill, he was puffing like a steam engine.)

3. Find and use the most descriptive, imaginative adjectives you can. For example: instead of "the happy dolphin," "the smiling dolphin;" instead of "fine, cotton lace," "cobwebby lace;" instead of "a water fountain," "a leaping, crystal fountain."
4. Use verbs in imaginative ways that will create a vivid image. For example, instead of merely stating that a town came into view, say that it "slipped" into view.

These guidelines have been followed in the description of El Yunque on pages 443 and 444. Note how some of them have been applied to create vivid, sensory images:

1. ... tiny orchids *snuggling* against the trees. (*imaginative use of verb to create a visual image*)
2. ... you will have the feeling of being in a *private cathedral* with the wind *singing* through the leaves in a *wayward* tune *like the wispy, tuneless song of a child.* (*use of analogy to create a visual image; use of unusual but appropriate verb and adjective to create a sound image; use of simile, which also contains the imaginative use of the adjective "wispy," to create a sound image*)
3. Moss hangs from the trees *like an old man's beard.* (*use of simile*)

For practice in writing descriptively, use the guidelines to write a first-person account of a trip down the Amazon or a visit to the *llanos*.

CHAPTER 28
THE HUMAN DIVERSITY

1. In what ways is Latin America a melting pot?
2. What contributions have the various peoples made to the development of Latin America?

Harbor cities are never provincial, and Salvador, one of Brazil's great ports, is no exception. Under constant siege from the foreign, its horizon bustles with the coming and going of ships. Each day's breeze brings exotic shipments, strange customs and foreign garb. The docks throng with humanity, the air is pierced with a gibberish of tongues.

In Salvador—once called São Salvador or Bahia—these ingredients have simmered for hundreds of years. . . .

Salvador is located a thousand miles [1700 kilometers] northeast of Rio de Janeiro. The first Portuguese settlement in the New World, Salvador is perched on a high bluff overlooking the Atlantic Ocean and the . . . Todos os Santos Bay. . . .

History remains alive in Salvador. A city of over a million inhabitants, Salvador maintains a face as colorful as its past. Between the 16th and 19th centuries four million slaves were brought to . . . work the large-scale sugar plantations of Bahia. . . . While the plantation owners grew wealthy and built magnificent churches and mansions, the influx of Africans was forever changing the character of Bahia. Today, . . . [Salvador's] culture is a colorful hybrid of Indian, Portuguese and African traditions.

The Indian influence remains in the decorative arts and some architecture, in the burnished skin tones and high cheekbones of the people, and in the words the Tupi language has given the world. "Cashew" and "tapioca" are only two words from this musical language to be incorporated into dozens of tongues.

The African influence is widespread and fascinating. The depth of its penetration into Bahian life makes the area different from any other in Brazil.*

As stated above, the culture of Salvador "is a colorful hybrid of Indian, Portuguese and African traditions." In this sense, Salvador is typical of all Latin America, where the over 370 million people are of a variety of ancestries. There are Indians, Europeans, Asians, Africans, and mixtures of all these. Over one-half are of mixed heritage. **Mestizos,** persons of European and Indian ancestry, form the largest single group. There are also about 20 million **mulattos,** persons with one black and one white parent.

Each country is different. In Argentina, for example, there are few Africans. Across the border in Brazil, however, there are many. Then again, in Bolivia, Peru, and Mexico, Indians and *mestizos* far outnumber other groups.

The same is true of the language of Latin America, which most people think is Spanish. But the people of Brazil speak Portuguese, not Spanish. In addition, each nation has its own dialects and Indian languages. In Paraguay, for example, there is Guaraní; in Peru, Quechua; and in Bolivia, Aymara. For these reasons, Latin America can be called a "melting pot" of the Western Hemisphere.

---

*"Saucy Salvador" by Carrie Topliffe in *Américas* magazine, published by the organization of American States (OAS), Volume 36, No. 1, January/February 1984, pp. 15–16. Reprinted by permission.

INDIANS

The first Americans were the Indians, who are thought to have come to the Western Hemisphere across the Bering Strait thousands of years ago. By the time Christopher Columbus arrived in the New World in 1492, Indians called Mayas, Incas, and Aztecs already had had their own great civilizations for many years. The Mayan Empire extended through Central America and Mexico's Yucatán Peninsula. The Incan Empire took in Ecuador, Peru, Bolivia, and most of Chile. The Aztec Empire enveloped Mexico. In fact, present-day Mexico City is built on the site of the ancient Aztec capital.

THE AZTECS

In 1520, the Spanish *conquistador,* or conqueror, Hernán Cortés, described the Aztec capital city of Tenochtitlán to King Charles I of Spain. The following is part of that description:

The pyramid-shaped Great Temple at Tenochtitlán, shown in this model, was a dual monument to the Aztec gods of rain and war. What happened to much of what the Aztec and other Indian civilizations built?

The great city of Tenochtitlán is built in the midst of this salt lake, and it is two leagues [about six miles or ten kilometers] from the heart of the city to any point on the mainland. Four causeways lead to it, all made by hand and some twelve feet [3.6 meters] wide. . . . The principal streets are very broad and straight, the majority of them being of beaten earth, but a few and at least half the smaller thoroughfares are waterways along which they pass in their canoes. . . .

The city has many open squares in which markets are continuously held and the general business of buying and selling proceeds. One square . . . is . . . completely surrounded by arcades where there are daily more than sixty thousand folk buying and selling. Every kind of merchandise such as may be met with in every land is for sale there. . . .

There are a very large number of mosques [temples] or dwelling places for their idols . . . in the chief of which their priests live continuously, so that in addition to the actual temples containing idols there are sumptuous lodgings. . . . Among these temples there is one chief one . . . whose size and magnificence no human tongue could describe. For it is so big that within the lofty wall which entirely circles it one could set a town of fifteen thousand inhabitants. . . .

The city contains many large and fine houses. . . . All possess in addition to large and elegant apartments very delightful flower gardens of every kind, both on the ground level and on the upper storeys.*

Much of what the Aztecs and the other Indian civilizations had built was destroyed by their European conquerors, who needed —and used—the Indians. They relied on the Indians to do manual labor, be it building or working the land or digging for treasure.

---

*Hernando Cortéz, *Five Letters, 1519–1526,* pp. 86–93, Routledge & Kegan Paul.

Insights on People
Latin America

MOCTEZUMA

When Hernán Cortés invaded the Aztec Empire of Mexico, it was a highly developed civilization that was ruled by a mighty emperor called Moctezuma. In one of his letters to his king, Cortés described the power and grandeur of Moctezuma and his court in the following manner:

His service was organized as follows: at dawn every day, six hundred lords, and men of rank, came to his palace. Some of these sat down, and others walked about in the halls and corridors of the palace, talking and passing the time, but without entering the room where he was; the servants and retainers who accompanied them filled two or three great courts, and the street, which was very large. They remained in attendance until night. When they served food to Moctezuma, they likewise served all those lords with like profusion, and their servants and followers also received their rations. The larder and the wine cellar were open daily to all who wished to eat or drink. The way they served the meals is this: three or four hundred youths carried in countless dishes, for, every time he wished to dine or sup, they brought him all the different dishes, not only meats, but also fish, and fruits, and herbs, to be found in the land; and as the climate is cold they brought, under each plate and dish, a brazier of coals, so that the food should not get cold. They placed all the dishes together in a great room where he dined, which was almost filled; its floors were all very well covered and very clean, and he sat on a small cushion of leather, beautifully made. Whilst he was eating, there were five or six elder lords standing a short distance from him, to whom he offered from the dishes he was eating. One of the servants waited to bring and remove the dishes for him, which were passed by others, who stood further off as the service required. At the beginning and end of each meal, they always brought him water for his hands, and the towel once used, he never used again; nor were the plates and service in which a dish was served ever brought again; and it was the same with the braziers.

He dressed himself four times every day, in four different kinds of clothing, all new, and never would he be dressed with the same again. All the lords who entered his palace came barefooted, and when those whom he had summoned appeared before him, it was with their heads bent, and their eyes on the ground, in humble posture; and, when they spoke to him, they did not look him in the face, because of respect and reverence. I know they did this out of respect, for certain lords reproved the Spaniards, saying, that when these latter spoke to me, they would behave with a lofty demeanour, looking me in the face, which seemed to them disrespectful and shameless. When Moctezuma went out, which happened rarely, all those who accompanied him and those whom he met in the street, turned their faces aside, and in no wise looked at him, and all the rest prostrated themselves until he had passed. One of the lords, who carried three long thin rods, always went before him, and I believe this was done to give notice of his approach. When he descended from his litter, he took one of those rods in his hand, and carried it as far as he went. The ceremonies which this sovereign used in his service were so many, and of such different kinds, that more space than I have at present would be required to relate them, and even a better memory to retain them; for I believe none of the Sultans, or any infidel sovereign of whom we have had information until now, has ever had such ceremonial in his court.*

1. What were some of the ways in which Moctezuma's subjects showed their respect for him?
2. What was Cortés' reaction to Moctezuma's way of life? How would you have reacted and why?

**Letters of Cortés to Charles: The Five Letters of Relation from Fernando Cortés to the Emperor Charles V*, Volume One, translated and edited by Francis Augustus MacNutt, 1908, G. P. Putnam's Sons, pp. 267–268.

In the process, many Indians were mistreated or killed. Over the years, millions died of diseases brought to their land for the first time by the Europeans.

THE PLIGHT OF THE INDIAN

In time, many Indian words became part of the Spanish and Portuguese languages, and many European men married Indian women. Out of the mixed marriages came a new ethnic group—the *mestizo*.

Over the years, marriage between Indians and Europeans became so extensive that in many areas of Latin America, the distinction between ethnic groups now rests upon cultural rather than physical distinctions. This, however, has not prevented discrimination against Indians in some areas. Below, a journalist discusses the situation in Guatemala, which is home to more than 4.5 million Indians—60 percent of the country's total population:

> . . . Recognizable by their colorful, intricately woven clothing, Indians can be seen all over the country, though most of them live in the . . . barely arable midsection. There, most of them eke out a living farming tiny, mountainside plots.
>
> The Ladinos [non-Indians], in contrast, live in the larger towns, hold higher-paying jobs, wear Western attire and speak only Spanish. They usually stay in school longer than Indians, who are put to work by age six. . . .
>
> . . . centuries of intermarriage among Indians, Europeans, and mixed-blood *mestizos* have blurred physical distinctions; all of them tend to have dark eyes and swarthy complexions. In fact, many who pass for Ladinos are full-blooded Indians who have discarded their Indian language, clothing, and customs. But physical similarity hasn't wiped out discrimination by Ladinos, Indians say.
>
> "Racism is expressed in subtle ways here . . . ," says an Indian schoolteacher. . . . He adds: "It is still humiliating. Ladinos laugh at our names, they refuse to call us 'sir,' and they won't hire us or rent us a home if we wear our traditional clothes. . . ."
>
> Language probably is the biggest obstacle to bringing the Ladinos and the Indians closer together in Central America. . . . [Although] most Indians know enough Spanish to conduct simple business transactions, most can't read or write it or hold much of a conversation.
>
> Moreover, Indians often resist attempts to teach them Spanish. "They realize that to lose their language is to lose their culture," says a Roman Catholic priest who has worked in Guatemala for 30 years. . . .
>
> For the Indians of Guatemala, . . . the path to social acceptance and self-respect

ETHNIC DIVERSITY IN LATIN AMERICA (in percentages)

Country	African	Asian	European	Indian	Mestizo	Mulatto	Other
Argentina			97				2, 1
Bolivia			5	70	25		
Brazil	15		60		4	21	
Chile			20		77		3
Cuba	26	1	73				
Ecuador	5	5	10	40	40		
Guyana	32	61					6, 1
Mexico			5	25	70		
Peru			15	45	37		3

CHAPTER 28   THE HUMAN DIVERSITY   455

This colorful mural, a traditional art form in Latin America, depicts the people and life styles of various Latin American ethnic groups. What have the Indians of Latin America done to preserve their own cultures?

seems to . . . involve . . . forsaking, at least for a while, their own culture. In fact, many Indians who have "made it" in the Ladino world have had to leave their homelands before they could become proud of their heritage.

"It wasn't until I went to medical school in Mexico that I stopped being ashamed of being an Indian," says a 39-year-old doctor from Quetzaltenango, Guatemala. "It is a depressing thought, but now that I'm back, I can see that going abroad was the only thing that cured me."*

A DYING WAY OF LIFE

Today, the Indian may be a farmer high in the Andes or a hunter in the Amazon. Wherever Indians survive in large numbers, they have tried to preserve their own culture. In Bolivia, Ecuador, Mexico, Peru, and Guatemala, Indians have kept their own dress, language, and social structure. Often they prefer to keep apart from the rest of the nation. They use their own ways of farming, live in small villages, and, according to tradition, divide their work among their people. They may even use tools like the ones their ancestors used.

Even when their religion and dress show a western influence, the Indians try to keep enough of their own culture to make them a little different from the rest of the country. Yet, despite their efforts, the Indian way of life is slowly declining in many parts of Latin America. As discussed below, this is especially true in the case of the Indians of the Amazon Basin:

> The great dying has been a quiet affair for the Amazon's [Indian] cultures. No Indian wars, no historic treaties—just a steady attrition [reduction in numbers] from exploitation, disease and occasional small slaughters.
> The million Indians who peopled the Amazon in 1900 now number around 100,000. As many as 80 distinct cultures may have been lost.
> No Indian wars could have been a more potent killer than disease. A single cold could turn to pneumonia, even death, for

---
*"In Central America, Centuries of Racism Still Haunt the Indians" by Brenton R. Schlender in *The Wall Street Journal*, September 15, 1983, pp. 1, 13. Reprinted by permission of *The Wall Street Journal*, ©Dow Jones & Company, Inc., 1983. All Rights Reserved.

CASE STUDY
LATIN AMERICA

THE INDIAN TODAY

The Diaguita Indians have for centuries lived in the Andes Mountains in Argentina. Traditionally, they earned their living farming. While many continue to farm today, their ways of life have changed somewhat. Like many Indian groups of Latin America, they have learned to adapt their lives to modern times while still maintaining many of their age-old traditions. Below, a Diaguita woman talks about her people and their life today:

Diaguita Indians have lived in this region for generations. Life has never been easy for us at this altitude—3,000 meters (9,800 feet). There is less oxygen up here than at sea level, and the variations in temperature are more extreme. It can get very hot during the day, and yet be very cold at night. Also, the soil is of very poor quality. . . .

We are mainly a farming community. We grow beans, corn and potatoes on the mountain slopes. To irrigate these crops, we still use the channels built centuries ago by our ancestors. We also breed llamas. The llama is a very useful animal which provides us with wool, meat, and a means of transportation. Animals like sheep and cattle cannot survive at this altitude. In our community, the more llamas you own, the richer you are.

Our life styles have altered a little since tourists started coming here. The looms in our homes used to be used only for weaving clothes for the family, using wool from llamas. Nowadays, many of the clothes are for selling to tourists. We always go down to the station to meet the Tren a las Nubes *(Train to the Clouds). . . . Many tourists travel on it and we sell them things like blankets, socks, scarves and sweaters. The income we get from this trade is used to buy things we cannot produce ourselves—everything from radios to a small truck.*

Our homes are houses made with stones, held together with a mixture of straw and clay. We live in small, independent communities. Each community has its own leader, . . . usually one of the respected elder members. You can tell to which community someone belongs by the way they dress, the color of their clothes, and the hairstyle of the women.

We consider ourselves Argentines, although we have kept many of our ancestral customs. Religion for us is a mixture of Christianity and our own beliefs. Inti *(the Sun),* Mama Hilla *(the Moon) and* Pacha Mama *(the Earth) are our main gods. We also have minor gods for thunder, rain and lightning. There are festivals throughout the year which are dedicated to our gods. During them, our community organizes huge parties with music, singing and dancing, and lots of food! The most important festival is the one for* Inti.*

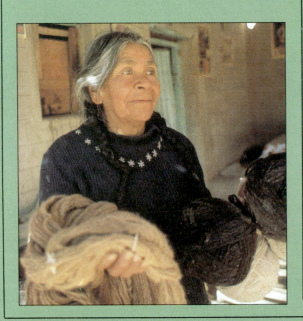

1. Who are the Diaguita Indians? What is their life like today?
2. Do you think that in the future the Diaguitas can continue to adhere to their traditions yet still contribute to their country? Explain your answer.

---

*"The Sun, the Moon and the Earth are our main gods" in *We Live in Argentina* by Alex Huber, 1984, The Bookwright Press, pp. 16–17.

the Indian, whose long evolution in isolation afforded little or no resistance.

In modern times, the risks to Indians of total contamination have been increased by the building of new roads for development and massive colonization. In some instances, Indians even die from the immunizations, which work by injecting small amounts of the disease-bearing organism into the body to make it form resistance to future exposures.

The other major factor in the Indian's decline has been the loss of his traditional lands. . . .

[An] . . . Amazon Indian tribe without the proper amount of jungle is a culture as good as doomed, anthropologists say.

There always were a few places where the Indian could live best—principally along the rivers, with their cooler, drier climates, access to fish and annually renewed fertile floodplain soils.

Forced [today] into areas less favorable for hunting, gathering of forest foods and shifting agriculture, the Amazon's Indians have lost a nutritional base that, along with lack of disease, was the envy of early explorers.*

1. What does Cortés' letter suggest about the level of development and wealth of the Aztec Indian civilization?
2. What has been the result over the years of the intermarriage that has taken place between Indians and Europeans?
3. Why is the Indian way of life in decline?

THE EUROPEANS

Until the early 1800's, when the Latin American colonies won their independence, about 2000 Spanish and Portuguese immigrants landed in Latin America each year. Later, even more than ever arrived. From the

*"The Great Dying Comes Quietly to Amazon Indian Cultures" by Tom Horton in *The Baltimore Sun*. Reprinted by permission.

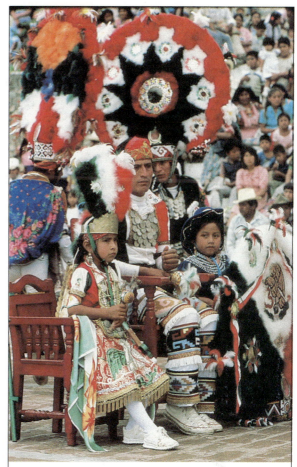

The exotic costumes worn by the people taking part in this festival in Oaxaca, Mexico, reflect Mexico's largely Indian and European heritage. Where did most European immigrants settle in Latin America?

middle of the 1800's until World War I, 12 million Europeans flocked to Latin America. Although most were Spanish and Portuguese, a great many others were Italian, British, and German. Most of the immigrants settled in Argentina, Chile, Uruguay, and the extreme southern part of Brazil.

The European settlers did a great deal to shape the vast area south of the Rio Grande. The Portuguese in Brazil and the Spaniards in the other regions tried to pattern life in their new land after the life they had known in Europe. They introduced new grains and fruits, horses, as well as other domesticated animals. They also brought many kinds of technology, and took advantage of the mineral wealth they found in their new land. Over the years, they contributed greatly to the economic progress of the areas in which they settled.

Today, European immigrants and their descendants make up a large part of the population of Argentina and Uruguay. For this reason, these countries are known as "immigrant nations." Below, an Argentinian of Welsh descent, who owns a cafe in Gaiman in the Patagonian region of Argentina, talks about why his ancestors came to Argentina and how he and his wife feel about the country:

> I'm a direct descendant of one of the 153 Welsh people who landed in Port Madryn in 1865. They were poor people who were escaping from the crowded mining valleys and from an English Parliament which had banned Welsh from being taught in schools and opposed a Welsh independence movement. They chose Patagonia because it was far away from English people! The Argentine government gave the settlers some land along the River Chubut, 64 km (40 miles) across the desert from Port Madryn. The immigrants were very friendly with the Indians and opposed the so-called "War of the Desert," during which the Indians were almost exterminated by the Argentine Army from Buenos Aires. My ancestors began farms and were soon growing good-quality wheat. They also started breeding sheep in the sheltered valleys. Patagonia's *estancias* [ranches] now have the majority of the country's 46 million sheep and help to make Argentina the world's fourth largest wool-producing nation. In the warmer, northern parts of Patagonia, apples, pears and grapes are grown with the help of irrigation projects.
>
> This cafe was opened by my wife's aunt, who thought that the farmers visiting Gaiman for their shopping would like somewhere to have a drink and a bite to eat. It was a great success and other people soon copied her. We serve tea and homemade biscuits, bread and jam. We're very busy on weekends when whole families come to Gaiman to do their shopping.
>
> In 1981, my wife and I went to Wales for the first time. The countryside was beautiful and everyone was very friendly, but

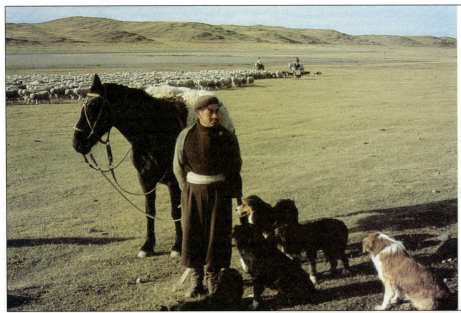

A shepherd takes a break from herding a large flock of sheep across a broad valley in the Patagonian region of Argentina. Why did Welsh immigrants leave their homeland and settle in Argentina in 1865?

we would never leave here. This is our home. We're Argentine, not Welsh. Many of the people of my generation still speak Welsh, but our grandchildren aren't interested in learning it.*

1. From where did many of the immigrants who settled in Latin America come?
2. What did the European immigrants contribute to Latin America?

THE AFRICANS

In the 1500's, European settlers began to bring black slaves from Africa to the New World. Large numbers ended up in Latin America working on plantations. Of the more than 15 million African slaves brought to the New World between the 1500's and the 1800's, more than 12 million were imported into Brazil.

As slaves, and later as free people, Africans, most from West Africa, played an important part in the development of Latin America. It was their labor that made possible the raising of sugar in the West Indies, cocoa in Venezuela, and sugar, cotton, and coffee in Brazil. It was their hand labor that produced much of the farming wealth of the islands of the Caribbean and parts of Brazil. In addition, Africans have served Latin America as skilled craftspeople, fishers, miners, domestic servants, stevedores, soldiers, writers, artists, and musicians.

Like the Europeans, the Africans infused their heritage into many aspects of the Latin American way of life, including music, religion, and, as indicated below, the very foods many Latin Americans eat:

> . . . the strongest ethnic imprint of the Brazilian cuisine is African. African slaves brought to Brazil to work in the sugar plantations of Bahia [a state in northeast-

In the city of Salvador on the east coast of Brazil, an African-descended member of the national police force stands guard. What are some other occupations represented among Latin Americans of African descent?

ern Brazil] enlivened the local cuisine with *dendê* (a thick, pungent, golden oil extracted from a particular African palm), *malagueta* (peppers, ginger and other spices, coconut milk) and their version of the North African dish couscous, known to Brazilians as *cuscuz*.

But the African influence on Brazilian cooking goes far beyond transported ingredients. As creative African cooks put their hands to such Portuguese dishes as *fritada*, they substituted *dendê* for the traditional olive oil, the meaty and plentiful cashew nuts for codfish, and added coconut milk. *Voilà!* A new taste sensation was born.

African cooks experimented freely in a land of tropical plenty. They put the [ever present] banana, pumpkin, and okra to a dozen uses. They took Indian dishes and expanded them, adding pepper and ginger freely, wrapping diverse foods in banana and other wide, flat leaves, then roasting them in charcoal ashes.

A visitor to Rio de Janeiro or São Paulo will find that dishes of African origin such

---

*"Patagonia is a cool desert" in *We Live in Argentina* by Alex Huber, 1984, The Bookwright Press, pp. 14–15.

as *vatapá* (a rich stew made in dozens of variations with smoked dried shrimp, fish, coriander, onion, garlic and other seasonings, cooked in *dendê* and coconut milk), and *caruru* (ground shrimp, coconut oil, cassava meal, onion, green peppers, tomatoes, okra and other vegetables in a thick stew) are standards of Brazilian cuisine.

Another dish with African origins, *feijoada*, is considered Brazil's national dish. A complex [mixture] of many ingredients, *feijoada* usually contains black beans, various types of sausage, pork, jerked beef, bacon and tongue as well as pig's foot, ear and tail. Saturday is the traditional day when *feijoada* is served, though it is always included at a festival or special affair.*

Today there are about 25 million Latin Americans of African descent in Latin America. Some are in trade and commerce, while others are prominent military and political figures. Many own their own businesses or are artists or musicians. Yet, despite their rich heritage and many contributions, in some areas of Latin America the opportunities open to many Africans remain limited.

1. Why did so many Africans settle in Latin America?
2. In what ways did the Europeans depend upon the Africans?
3. What are some of the contributions Africans have made to Latin America?

THE ASIANS

In recent years, Asians have added a new dimension to the varied ethnic composition of Latin America. One group, the Chinese, have made their homes in large numbers in Peru, Cuba, and Panama and in smaller numbers in almost every other Latin American country. First brought to Peru, Cuba, and Panama as laborers, today most are merchants with shops and restaurants in many Latin American cities.

Another group, the Japanese, have settled for the most part in Brazil. The 750,000 Japanese living there today are descendants of the 250,000 Japanese who immigrated to Brazil originally to work on the coffee plantations. There they introduced **jute,** the material used in the bags that hold Brazilian coffee. The jute industry provides a cash crop for individuals who at one time eked out a meager living gathering Brazil nuts and rubber.

Today, the Japanese citizens of Latin America are engaged in such activities as farming, fishing, trade and commerce, and manufacturing. Below, a Japanese woman who settled in Brazil more than 25 years ago discusses her life there and her feelings about the country:

> My husband and I came to Brazil after World War II, which was fought from 1939 to 1945. It was difficult to make a living in Japan and when we heard that Brazil was a land of opportunity, we decided to move. We left our home in Hokkaido in the cold north of Japan for the warm weather of southeastern Brazil.
>
> We settled in the town of Atibaia about 66 kilometers (40 miles) from the big industrial city of São Paulo. Atibaia is famous for growing fruit and flowers. As we are experienced gardeners, we were able to find work quite easily.
>
> It wasn't difficult to get used to Brazil, apart from learning the language. I found Portuguese was very hard to learn, especially because we lived among Japanese people who make up 20 percent of Atibaia's population.
>
> The cold weather in Japan meant we could only plant for six months in each year, but here we can work all year round. In Atibaia, we have a garden full of

---

*"Brazilian Cuisine" by Patricia Brooks in *Américas*, reprinted from *Américas* bimonthly magazine published by the General Secretariat of the Organization of American States in English and Spanish.

CHAPTER 28 THE HUMAN DIVERSITY 461

Like other Brazilian teenagers, these young Japanese wear jeans and are avid fans of popular rock singers and movie stars. Proud of its cultural heritage, the local Japanese community of almost every city in Brazil offers young people instruction in the Japanese language. Why did Japanese immigrants come to Brazil originally?

plants, pine trees and **bonsai,** a traditional Japanese art of growing dwarf trees. On Sundays, we load up our van with plants and go to the Oriental Fair held in the district called Liberdade in the center of São Paulo. We set up a stall on the main street and sell our plants. Liberdade is full of people like ourselves from the Far East, including Chinese and Koreans.

Selling plants is a good business so long as we do not get caught in a downpour! Last year ferns were very popular. This year we sell more climbing-type plants, called *trepadeiras* in Portuguese. On a good day, we earn the equivalent of U.S. $150–U.S. $200.

My husband is one of the few gardeners at the fair who practice *bonsai.* By controlling the pruning and fertilization of trees, they come to look like small versions of big, ancient trees. We only have a few of these trees for sale. They are expensive and cost about U.S. $500. Besides gardening, I work during the week at the Ceasa market-place in São Paulo, selling fruit and vegetables.

When my husband and I were settled in Brazil, we started a family. We now have five children. The oldest daughter is a dentist, the second-oldest girl won a scholarship to study in Tokyo in Japan and our two younger daughters and son are students in Brazil.

I like my life here. Brazilians are good people and we are seldom made to feel like strangers. The Japanese living in Brazil make up the largest community of Japanese outside Japan. There are 750,000 Japanese in Brazil, with 125,000 of us living in the state of São Paulo. Even after visiting Japan two years ago, and seeing how beautiful and modern it is, I don't want to return there to live. Brazil is my home.*

1. In what countries of Latin America have most Asians made their homes?
2. What contributions have the Japanese made to Brazil?

---

*"We heard that Brazil was a land of opportunity" in *We Live in Brazil* by Patricia Robb, 1985, The Bookwright Press, pp. 48–49. Reprinted by permission.

CHAPTER 28 REVIEW

POINTS TO REMEMBER

1. Latin America is known as a "melting pot" of the Western Hemisphere because of the blending of diverse ethnic groups and languages found within its borders.
2. Maya, Inca, and Aztec Indians established their own civilizations long before Christopher Columbus discovered the New World. Much of what the Indians had built was destroyed by their European conquerors.
3. Over the years, mixed marriages between Indians and Europeans became so extensive that, in many areas, the distinction between ethnic groups now rests upon cultural rather than physical distinctions. Despite the Indians' efforts, their way of life is slowly declining.
4. The millions of Europeans who flocked to Latin America from the mid-1800's until World War I contributed greatly to the economic progress of the areas in which they settled.
5. Africans were brought to the New World first as slaves. Later, more came as free people. They have played an important part in the development of Latin America, contributing much to the region's farming wealth. Their heritage has become infused into the Latin American way of life.
6. In recent years, a large number of Asians have settled in Latin America. They are engaged in and have contributed greatly to agriculture, trade and commerce, and manufacturing.

VOCABULARY

Identify

Gauraní	Incas	Tenochtitlán	"War of the Desert"
Quechua	Aztecs	Ladinos	Bahía
Aymara	Hernán Cortés	"immigrant nations"	Moctezuma
Mayas			Diaguita Indians

Define

mestizos	mulattos	*conquistador*	jute

DISCUSSING IMPORTANT IDEAS

1. How do you define the term "melting pot"? Based on your definition, do you consider Latin America a true "melting pot"?
2. If you were an Aztec, Inca, or Maya Indian during the time of the conquistadors, how would you have reacted? Would you have adapted to or resisted your conquerors? Explain.
3. In what ways do you think Latin America would be different had the Europeans not settled there? The Africans? The Asians?

4. What are some ways in which the various groups of Latin Americans can continue to perpetuate their ethnic heritage without endangering national unity?

DEVELOPING SKILLS

SUPPORTING GENERALIZATIONS

People make generalizations all the time, often without even realizing it. Some are *sweeping generalizations,* statements so broad and applied to so many cases or people that most people hearing or reading them generally recognize that they are not logical and probably are false. Generalizations of this type often are applied to a culture. For example:

All Germans like to work hard every day.
All Americans are inventive.

Surely, there are some Germans who would prefer to spend the day hiking through a forest rather than working in an office or factory. And, just as surely, there are some Americans who are not creative thinkers.

It is important, therefore, when making generalizations to be able to back them up with supporting evidence. When, for example, you tell a friend that your dog and all the dogs that graduated from his obedience school are intelligent, you have made a generalization. If, when your friend asks how you know all the dogs are intelligent, you tell him that the dogs that could not learn the commands had to drop out and did not graduate, you have supported your generalization. You have shown that it has a logical basis in fact.

As indicated in the following examples, to truly support a generalization, a statement must (1) relate directly to the generalization, (2) be logical, and (3) have a basis in fact:

Generalization:
European settlers did a great deal to shape the area south of the Rio Grande.
Statements:
1. They brought many kinds of technology.
2. They introduced new grains, fruits, and horses.
3. A large number of immigrants settled in Argentina and Uruguay.
4. The Welsh chose to live in Patagonia because it was far away from English people.

(Only statements 1 and 2 are supportive. Although statements 3 and 4 both give information about immigrants, neither relates directly to what Europeans did to shape the area south of the Rio Grande.)

Generalization:
Africans played an important role in the development of Latin America.
Statements:
1. African labor made possible the raising of many crops.
2. Africans use a thick, pungent oil in many of their dishes.
3. Opportunities for Africans remain limited in some areas.
4. The hand labor of the Africans produced much of the farming wealth in the Caribbean and in parts of Brazil.

(Only statements 1 and 4 are supportive. Although statements 2 and 3 both provide information about Africans, neither relates directly to why Africans played an important role in the development of Latin America.)

For practice in supporting generalizations, write four supporting statements for this generalization: Latin America is a "melting pot."

CHAPTER 29
THE SOCIAL FABRIC

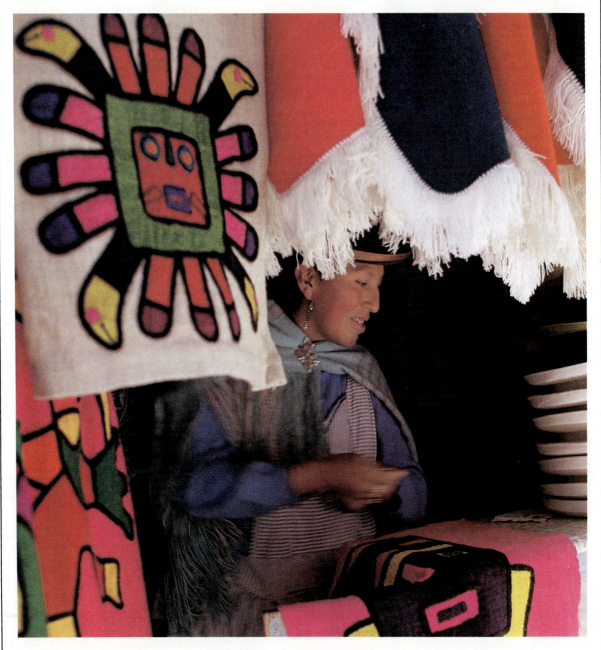

1. *How does social class affect the Latin American family?*
2. *How do Latin Americans view life?*

Juan, his mother and father, and four brothers and sisters live in a house that has grown over the years. It started out as a one-room adobe brick home that measured about 20 feet by 20 feet (6 meters by 6 meters). The family has since built an additional room of wooden stakes and corrugated aluminum. Many of Juan's neighbors live in houses constructed entirely of scrap lumber, packing boxes, and corrugated aluminum. Despite being in the middle of a dismal slum, Juan's mother keeps her house remarkably clean. The outside walls are lined with shelves holding potted plants and flowers.

Juan attends school, but wants to drop out to look for a job. Both his parents insist that he stay in school. At Juan's school, the children sit two at a desk and share textbooks. There are sixty students in his classroom. Juan's teacher is a nineteen-year-old girl who just finished normal school (teacher's school). . . .

Juan's family came to the Mexico City area ten years ago from a . . . farm. . . . Juan's father works as a helper on a truck that delivers soft drinks to stores. He is paid by the driver at the end of the day. Often the driver decides he needs no help. Then Juan's father earns no wages. Juan's mother embroiders potholders which she tries to sell at the market. Juan sells newspapers. Sometimes he wanders the streets with an armload of papers until ten or eleven at night. The Rivera family has a used gas stove but no refrigerator. At one time they owned an old black-and-white television set but had to sell it for food money. The family eats mainly tortillas, beans, and rice. Chicken on a Sunday is a very special treat.

About once a year, the Rivera family scrapes together enough money to take a bus to their old village in the country. There Juan . . . feels he is rich. Juan's country cousins live in homes with dirt floors. They have to walk half a mile to get a bucket of water. There is no electricity. But the air is clean, and Juan can dash about as he pleases without worrying about the speeding cars and trucks. . . . On one visit to the country, Juan began teaching one of his cousins to read. He is Juan's age, but has never gone to school.*

Juan Rivera, whose way of life is discussed above, is 12 years old. The life he and his family lead is not that different from the one led by members of the lower class throughout Latin America. For, in Latin America, social class is a determiner of daily life. Life style generally hinges on wealth, and in most of Latin America, the gap between the rich and the poor is great. The wealthy tend to be very wealthy, and the poor tend to be very poor.

---
*Mexico by R. Conrad Stein, 1984, Children's Press, pp. 105–107. Reprinted by permission.

SOCIAL CLASS

In most Latin American nations, there are three social classes—the upper class, the middle class, and the lower class. The upper class is made up of the **aristocracy** and the *nouveaux riches.* The aristocracy are, for the most part, those people descended from the wealthy landowners of the past. The *nouveaux riches* are those people who have made their fortunes in this century through their own efforts and hard work.

The middle class is largely a product of the twentieth century and is growing rapidly.

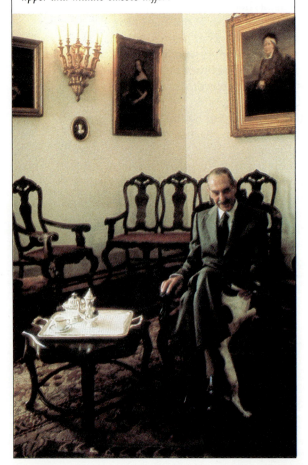

North along the coast from São Paulo live most of Brazil's aristocracy, like this Brazilian who owns a large family estate near Rio de Janeiro. In what ways do the upper and middle classes differ?

The growth is due to the changes that have been taking place in Latin America in recent years. As industry has grown, more white-collar jobs have opened up. As government has expanded, more civil servants, teachers, and different kinds of experts are needed. As more educational opportunities have become available, more people have been able to prepare for careers in medicine, law, and journalism.

The lower class is made up of the rural poor and the urban poor. In most of Latin America, the lower class far outnumbers the middle and upper classes.

HARD WORK, LITTLE REWARD

Within the rural lower class, the biggest group is composed of peasants. Some peasants own and work their own small plots of land. Others work on **haciendas,** large estates owned by the wealthy. In return for tilling the fields, they receive a small plot of land for themselves and their families. Often this is the same land their fathers and grandfathers worked during colonial times.

Another group of the rural lower class is made up of wage hands who generally work on large commercial farms that raise such

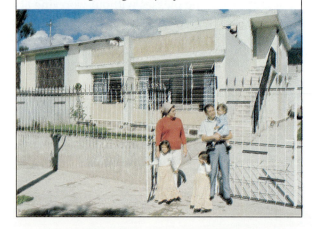

A middle-class family in Quito, the capital of Ecuador, stands proudly in front of their modern home in the northern section of the city. Why is Latin America's middle class growing so rapidly?

CHAPTER 29 THE SOCIAL FABRIC

High in an Andean village in Ecuador, an Indian mother walks with her children in front of the family home, which is made of adobe bricks for protection from the cold. What groups make up the rural lower class? How do they support themselves?

export crops as sugarcane, cotton, coffee, and bananas. Their wages are low, and more often than not their work is seasonal.

Of those who work their own land, some can barely eke out enough for themselves and their families because the land is so poor. This is the case of the Mayan Indian family discussed below:

> The hut of Luz and Trini is between two masonry buildings. . . . It is an old hut, which gave me a happy, cozy feeling. It always seemed to be the center of some activity. On the ceiling are streamers of soot from the fire hanging down like black mobiles. It is fairly small; at one end is the kitchen area run by Doña Luz. There is the typical three-stone hearth, with an iron *comal* [flat dish] where tortillas are cooked. Behind the hearth are earthen jugs for the many necessary pails of water. There is also a sideboard of small logs held up by forked saplings, which is always covered with many jugs, pots and pans. . . . Around the hearth there also are hanging baskets of dried herbs and spices. . . . The table where the tortillas are made is a large circular piece of mahogany, with another smaller circle jutting out from one side. . . . The three legs are removed daily for the scrubbing down of the table with ashes and *zocil* (a leaf that very much resembles brillo), after which it is set on its side to drain. There is another small table . . . that is used either as a stool or a place for the children to eat. The women eat at the table where they make tortillas, sitting on logs. . . . The men usually eat at a regular table, using handmade straight-backed chairs. At the back of the hut is an area about the size of a shower stall that is set out from the oval of the hut; this is where the family bathes. One at a time they sit with a pail of water beside them on a chair or a stool, with their feet on a stone to keep them from getting muddied. The rest of the hut is the living and sleeping area, where the hammocks are pulled down for sleeping or as extra chairs for guests, and thrown up over the rafters during the day. Luz has complete charge of the kitchen where she and Don Trini, Don Trini's son Antonio and his family, her only son by Don Trini, Jorge, and his wife and son, eat. It is also a kind of restaurant for any visitors who

happen to be in town. . . . Flora (Antonio's wife), her two girls, and Ana help out washing, cleaning, and preparing food, but it is clear that Luz is the one who runs things and does much of the work.*

Although there still are more poor people in the country than in the city, the number of urban poor is on the increase. This is due mostly to the millions of people who have migrated from the country to the cities in search of jobs and a better life. Jobs in the city, however, are hard to find, especially for those who are **illiterate,** cannot read or write, or have no skills. Some never find a regular source of work and have to depend on part-time jobs as construction laborers or as firewood or water carriers. Those who fail to find even this type of work may become beggars.

The poverty of the people of the lower class has a strong influence on their way of life. Many marriages, for example, are what is known by some as **common-law unions,** or unofficial marriages without legal or religious ceremony. These marriages are accepted for several reasons. One is that the cost of a formal wedding and the celebration that follows it could force a bride's family into debt for many years. Another is the problem of divorce. If a common-law marriage does not work out, the couple can break up without being concerned about legal or religious problems.

Because there is so little money, young children often are expected to forget about school and go to work. In the country, most boys probably will be working in the fields before they are in their teens. In the city, many boys are expected to have a part-time or fulltime job by the time they are eight years old. In both the country and the city, girls must begin at a very early age to do household chores and take care of the younger children. These are the luckier ones. As can be seen in the newspaper article below about Colombia, poverty can have a devastating effect on the children of the lower class:

> Ten-year-old Jaime Carvajal sat on a downtown curb as he gnawed on one of the chicken bones piled in front of him.
>
> The bones came from an apartment building garbage bag and were a better breakfast than usual.
>
> "Often the rats have gotten everything worth eating," he said.
>
> Colombia's future may depend on what it can do for the thousands of homeless young people like Jaime Carvajal. . . .
>
> The most visible products of the poverty are the estimated 3,000 children, some as young as five, who live on the streets. They are called gamines. . . .
>
> The children are regularly picked up and placed in centers where they are bathed, fed, clothed and offered a chance to learn a trade. Police say most take the free clothes and meals and hit the streets again.
>
> In Bogota, they are differentiated from the children sent out by parents to beg and steal. The gamines wear rags and often go barefoot. Many have open sores, deep coughs, sunken eyes and distended bellies.
>
> At night they sleep in doorways, covering themselves with cardboard or newspapers as temperatures fall to the 40s.
>
> Less visible but more numerous are the tens of thousands of children who work for pennies a day in factories or doing manual labor. A government study . . . found at least 3 million children 14 or younger have adult jobs, earning as little as 50 cents a day. The law allows them to work, although not at night.
>
> Hundreds of children work in outdoor brick factories on the outskirts of this capital city. Boys groan under the weight of shovels of coal that they toss into blazing

---

Nine Mayan Women: A Village Faces Change by Mary Elmendorf, 1976, Schenkman Publishing Company, Inc., pp. 26–27. Reprinted by permission.

CHAPTER 29 THE SOCIAL FABRIC 469

This young child sitting outside her makeshift home in El Salvador is not unlike many of the children of the urban poor, who know only a life of extreme poverty. What happens to many Latin Americans who migrate from the country to the cities in search of a better life?

furnaces. The heat leaves their bodies glistening in sweat. They walk bent, like old men.

Other children carry up to 120 pounds [54 kilograms] of bricks in a sling that falls down their backs.

In factories, the children sew shoes, help make clothes and assemble products. The working places are often dimly lit and cold.*

AN EASIER LIFE

Things are very different for those of the upper class. The aristocracy is, for the most part, well-educated and cultured. While in the past most of its prestige and wealth was based on old family names and the ownership of large rural landholdings, today many aristocrats make most of their money from business holdings. The life led by the young Salvadoran and her family and discussed below is typical of that still led by many of the aristocracy:

Ana's ancestors have lived at the family hacienda near Ranchador for generations, ever since the first Spanish families settled in the area. Today Ana and her father and mother and brothers and sisters occupy the large comfortable farm estate inherited from their ancestors. They are proud of their pure Spanish heritage.

Because of the vast inherited land holdings and his good business ability, Ana's father is very wealthy. . . . The family lives on a lavish scale, entertaining many house guests and enjoying a great deal of activity around the swimming pool. . . .

There are numerous household servants, and Ana has no idea how many people are employed on her father's fields. . . .

Ana's mother is interested in helping the poorer people of the tiny town of

---
*"What of Childhood? . . . In Colombia, It Can Hurt" in *Omaha World-Herald*, December 14, 1980, p. 13A. Reprinted by permission of the *Omaha World-Herald* and The Associated Press.

The designs of Venezuelan socialite and business owner Carolina Herrera have made her well known in the world of high fashion. In general, how do aristocrats and the nouveaux riches *differ in Latin America?*

Ranchador, which is the nearest community near the estate, and also the unfortunate people of Santa Ana, just a few miles to the southwest. . . . Ana's mother has worked to help set up free health clinics at Santa Ana. She and her friends hope to open a training school for nurses. . . . They also want to provide housing for the elderly poor of the area.

Ana does not attend a school; she studies under the watchful eye of tutors employed by her parents. In addition to her regular studies, she is given training in art, ballet, and music. . . . She loves to ride her pony about the estate and play games with her brothers. . . .

The principal crop grown by Ana's father is coffee. His trips to [the port city of] Acajutla are generally to see about the shipment of his crop from the port. However, he owns an interest in the large modern cement factory in the port city, as well as its oil refinery and its fertilizer and sulphuric acid plants.

Ana's father also has an interest in the largest coffee mill in the world. . . .

Ana is not terribly interested in school. She will probably continue her education . . . taking many general college courses and looking forward to marriage. Her mother would like her to think of a career of social service.*

The *nouveaux riches* do not have the background and, in some cases, the culture of the aristocracy. But, as evidenced below, their wealth allows them to lead comfortable lives:

Maria Valdez is thirteen and lives in a section of Mexico City called *Las Lomas de Chapultepec* (the Hills of Chapultepec). It is an area of sturdy single-family homes near Mexico City's famous Chapultepec Park. Maria's father is a dentist. Her mother runs a small shop downtown that caters to American tourists. Maria works part-time in the shop. She enjoys her work because it gives her a chance to practice English. English is her favorite subject at school. Maria attends a private school for which her parents pay about fifty dollars a month. Classroom size averages twenty students per teacher, and the teachers are all experienced professionals.

In Maria's house there is a color television, a stereo, and a piano. The Valdez family also owns a car and uses it to escape Mexico City's smog for weekends in the country. When Maria was a little girl, her family visited her uncle in the United States. Maria still has exciting memories of her one and only trip to *Disneylandia* [Disneyland]. . . .

Maria's family has both a maid and a gardener. All of her neighbors have servants too. Domestic help is still cheap for well-to-do Mexicans. Both of Maria's parents come from prominent Mexico City families. Her oldest brother is now attending medical school. Despite the collapse of the peso, Maria's family and her neighbors continue to prosper.‡

---

*El Salvador by Allan Carpenter and Eloise Baker, 1971, Children's Press, pp. 25, 27. Reprinted by permission.

‡Mexico by R. Conrad Stein, 1984, Children's Press, pp. 103–104. Reprinted by permission.

There is little contact between the social classes in Latin America. This comfortable middle-class home in the capital city of Bogotá, Colombia, contrasts sharply with those in which most of the city's residents live. What are some of the modern conveniences of a middle-class home in Nicaragua?

A NEW GENERATION

In Latin America, it is difficult to determine at times exactly who is a member of the middle class. Incomes range from those of well-to-do bankers to those of poorly paid civil servants or clerks. Housing ranges from high-priced homes in the "better" parts of town to lower-cost ones in less desirable areas. What is considered middle class in one country may well be considered upper class in another. Below, a Nicaraguan talks about the "typical" middle-class family and its life style in his country:

> In Nicaragua, a middle class family generally consists of parents with three to six children. Most often they live in the suburbs just outside cities. Their home usually has many family rooms, including three or four bathrooms, a living room, dining room, kitchen, and terrace as well as one or two rooms with baths for servants. Outside are gardens and patios, enclosed by a high hedge or fence made of blocks or bricks.
>
> The houses are of adobe brick or cement block with roofs of zinc sheeting. The ceilings are wood and the floors cement or ceramic brick. Because of the heat, there are a lot of large glass windows. Most of the houses of the neighborhood are of approximately the same value. Apartments are not very popular because people prefer to live in family groups and do not want to live alone or independently.
>
> Each home generally has a refrigerator, washing machine, stereo, radios, toaster, blender, and oven. There generally are two televisions—one color and one black and white. Most people do not have central air conditioning because power is very expensive, but they do have window air conditioners imported from the United States or Japan. Freezers are not very common, because most people prefer to eat fresh food. The same is true of dishwashers. It is cheaper to hire a servant.
>
> Most middle-class families have two or three cars, generally four-cylinder, including a family car and a jeep or pick-up truck to use in their businesses. Big American cars are not popular. Not many families can buy a car every year.
>
> About 90 percent of the young people of middle-class families are fulltime students.

When they work, it is in the family business, so they can learn early to administer what will later become theirs. Most of the women do not work outside the home but dedicate themselves to taking care of their families. The few who do work have their own business or profession. They never work for someone else.*

1. What groups make up the lower class? What do they have in common?
2. What groups make up the upper class? What do they have in common?
3. What are some characteristics of the middle class? Why is it hard to tell who belongs to it?

THE FAMILY

Latin Americans of all classes have a strong sense of family. For them, "family" includes mother, father, children, grandparents and great-grandparents, uncles and aunts, nieces and nephews, and distant cousins. It also includes **godparents,** people chosen by a mother and father to sponsor their new baby. Godparents are concerned with the child's religious and moral training and help take care of the child if something happens to the parents.

For the most part, the Latin American family is large and closely knit. Even if family members cannot live near one another, they try to keep in constant contact. The family is the center for most social activities, and everyone gathers together to celebrate birthdays, weddings, and other events. Family members are expected to help one another when there is a problem and share any good fortune that may come their way. As indicated in this newspaper article, the importance of family remains strong even for those Latin Americans who have emigrated:

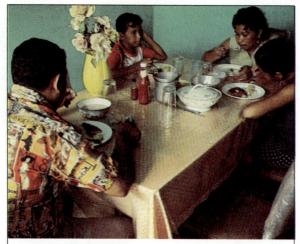

This family in Managua, the capital of Nicaragua, enjoys a Sunday midday meal of rice, fried beans, cheese, and bananas. To Latin Americans, what are some of the advantages of a close-knit family?

A 40-year-old Colombian salesman, who has lived in New York City 10 years, said: "As a father, I see my children as a work of art which I have to present to society. Just as the sculptor shapes the marble until he perfects his work, I have to correct my children and teach them good ways. . . ."

Persons of all ages among the Hispanics interviewed described the family as a major source of personal fulfillment, a precious aspect of Hispanic life. . . .

The words "family unity" were employed by four out of 10 respondents when they were asked to describe traditions that are especially important. . . .

Also mentioned were the "extended family," "fiestas and reunions for unity" and "family meetings. . . ."

A 60-year-old man, whose professional life involves helping Puerto Rican families to stay intact, said: "The concept of the united family is our contribution we can make to this country."*

While family ties continue to remain especially important among the wealthy and the poor, many members of the growing urban

---

*Interview with Plutarco Pasos, April 1985. Reprinted by permission.

*"U.S. Influence Is Seen as Erosive to Cherished Family," *The Omaha World-Herald,* May 30, 1980, p. 13. Copyright ©1980 by The New York Times Company. Reprinted by permission.

CASE STUDY
LATIN AMERICA

WOMEN

Traditionally, Latin American women were under the control of their husbands or fathers and had few legal rights. Today, they have the vote in every nation of Latin America. Each year, more and more attend universities and hold jobs in all of the professions, and many have been elected to national legislatures and as mayors of large cities. One woman, Isabel Perón, served as president of Argentina.

But progress has been slow and uneven, and in practice women's legal rights are often not observed. This is especially true when it comes to equal pay for equal work. Progress tends to be limited to urban areas. In the countryside, change comes slowly. Women themselves have conflicting opinions about their roles. Below, Peruvian women from Mayobamba, a village of 450 people, comment:

There's a great deal of difference in marriage patterns between the coast and the sierra. Men who migrate usually adapt to the coastal pattern. On the coast, both spouses express opinions about life in their home. Men begin to leave behind the authoritarian practices of Mayobamba, where women are not allowed to offer opinions. In Lima, the man is still dominant, but less so because of the change in the social atmosphere. Also on the coast, women's work is less demanding and women can improve themselves through education. Women have jobs and they still do the work in the home. Women don't have to go to the fields; they don't have to do all the spinning and make all the clothes. The work in the sierra is physically much more difficult and takes much more time to accomplish.

The man always has to be on top, has to order, to command. The man has to give ideas to women. He has to take care of the children, to sustain them and his wife. Men know more; women don't know anything.

Men may cook for a day or two, and women may go to the fields for a while, but each has his separate place. If both cooked, who would work in the fields?

It is still the case that here a woman is calculated to be an inferior being, a less competent thing that cannot participate. She is only fit to help at home, not publicly.

Some women get accustomed to the fact that their husbands are the heads of everything; others want to participate. But the majority give up leadership to their husbands.

They say the men . . . prefer to marry women who can't read, because if a man receives a letter or a document from someone and the woman can read it, the woman might want to get involved in the matter. She might cause a fight, and that would be very objectionable.

1. In what ways have women's roles changed in Latin America in recent years?
2. What response would you give to each of the Mayobamba women?

Women of the Andes: Patriarchy and Social Change in Two Peruvian Towns by Susan C. Bourque and Kay Barbara Warren, 1981, The University of Michigan Press, pp. 35, 163, 195. Reprinted by permission. Copyright ©1981 The University of Michigan.

middle class are finding it harder to maintain them. In the past, most young people of all classes remained in their parents' homes even after they married. So, it was easy to keep close contact with relatives. Today, many young people move away from home looking for better educations or jobs. For those who are illiterate or are too poor to use the telephone regularly, it becomes especially hard to keep in touch.

The changed attitude of business and the expansion of government also have had an effect. While at one time Latin Americans could count on family ties to help get them a job, today ability is more important as a basis for hiring. At the same time, welfare and education that once were the responsibility of the family are becoming more and more the responsibility of the state.

1. How do most Latin Americans of all classes view family?

2. Why is the influence of the traditional family beginning to lessen?

LIVING LIFE TO THE FULLEST

Most Latin Americans, regardless of background or class, also agree that in order to live life fully, one must feel deeply and strongly about an idea or a person. They have, however, managed to combine with this belief the idea that one should enjoy life today and think about tomorrow when it comes.

There are several reasons for this philosophy. One has to do with physical conditions. Many poor people, for example, believing that they will never escape poverty, see no reason to save for a rainy day. For them,

The marchers in this parade in Rio de Janeiro, Brazil, are "kicking off" the traditional four-day festival of Carnival. Rio's Carnival unites all the social, musical, dance, and other artistic features of the country. Its spirit is reflected in the lively dance called the samba, which is said to have originated at the Rio Carnival. What commonly held Latin American belief does Rio's Carnival demonstrate?

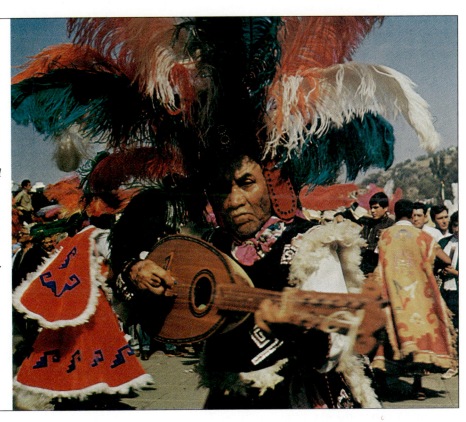

Beginning and ending with fireworks and ringing bells, a Mexican fiesta *is a happy event, filled with music, dancing, and bright, colorful costumes. During a fiesta, people enjoy themselves at parades, bullfights, on carnival rides, and at other special attractions. Many also pray at churches that have been gaily decorated for the occasion. What purpose do* fiestas *serve besides enjoyment?*

every day is a rainy one. Another reason has to do with geographical location. Much of Latin America is in the tropics, where food must be bought daily and eaten right away or it will spoil. Still another reason relates to the economy. Many Latin American nations are not yet stable economically, and when inflation increases, money is worth less. Therefore, it is wiser to spend it while it is worth more.

FIESTAS

Perhaps because of these attitudes, Latin America often is thought of as a land of continuous **fiestas,** or parties. The *fiestas,* however, do not occur very often, and when they do, they serve a purpose. They are a day of relief from the toils and cares of everyday life, a time when the individual can drop many of the restraints of daily life and have a good time.

There are many kinds of *fiestas*. Some last a day and are held in small villages, while others go on for several days and draw tourists from all over the world. One of the most famous *fiestas* is Carnival, which marks the beginning of the Christian Lenten season. Below, a Uruguayan reminisces about Carnival in Montevideo, the capital city of Uruguay:

> . . . a Carnival group going into the night, was a dazzling journey unknown to tourist brochures. Corn husk cigarettes in our mouths, tattered slippers, striped trousers. Sweating brows, shuffling along, eyes fixed above, taking in the window where a generous neighbor threw us flowers, or a lovely dark woman sent us back, in her smile, the ragged crescent moon that led our march.
> How happy we were. Under our oft-mended banners we were like a ship with a hull of Brazilian pine and all sails flying.

Playing in front of a large crowd of soccer fans, Brazilian soccer star Pelé takes the ball down the field, while members of the opposing team scramble to overtake him. How successful have Brazil's soccer teams been in world competition?

The old women working with their fans, the herb doctors . . . looking epileptically into the night to discover the star of happiness, the magnificent sweepers throwing their Guinea brooms higher than the balcony to sweep the sky of evil goblins. The street ran along with us, at times ahead of us. Sometimes we felt as if we were floating on a magic carpet bordered with geraniums and cretonnes and paving stones.

Drum and streets were born together. As we went along the houses made way for us as if made of cardboard, and we were proud to be playing, shaking and waking the night of the neighborhoods. We went along there . . . , expressing our love, leaving it there, sown in the long passages or at the mercy of the corner-crossing currents.*

SPORTS

At one time, bullfighting was considered the most popular sport of Latin America. In recent years, however, its popularity has dwindled while that of *fútbol*, or soccer, has taken its place. Soccer leagues are organized along both professional and amateur lines, and Latin American children play in leagues while still in grade school.

In Brazil especially, *fútbol* is the national passion and a common ground for most Brazilians. In 1970, Brazil became the first country to win the world soccer championship three times. Every village has some kind of soccer field, and the larger cities have stadiums. In Rio de Janeiro, the stadium can seat 220,000 fans. As with all popular sports, soccer has produced many stars. First among them is the Brazilian known as Pelé, whose story is told below:

As a professional soccer player for 18 years, Pelé made more goals than any other player—1,284—and accumulated titles that included highest scoring player for all the São Paulo area championships between 1957 and 1965, two-time world club champion for the Santos team, three-time world champion, and athlete of the century. Embraced by kings and presidents, applauded in stadiums the world over and received by Pope Paul VI, he was even responsible for a temporary halt in the Biafran War in 1969 when the oppos-

---

*"I Miss You, Mediomundo" by Carlos Paez Vilaro reprinted from *Américas*, Volume 33, No. 5, May 1981, p. 43, a bimonthly magazine published by the General Secretariat of the Organization of American States in Spanish and English.

ing troops stopped fighting to watch him play. . . .

His story began on October 23, 1940. The son of a soccer forward . . . and his wife . . . , Pelé moved with his family to Belo Horizonte when he was barely two. Later they returned to Tres Coraçoes because his father had injured himself seriously . . . ; the injury ruined his playing career. The family moved to Bauru where Dico (the nickname Pelé comes from his soccer days . . .), the oldest son, took up his father's career. . . .

Pelé's rise in the soccer world happened almost overnight. His mother had him turn down an invitation to play in Rio de Janeiro when he was 15. . . . Later on he was able to accept an invitation from the city of Santos, where he began to train among the best on the first team. . . . His mother and grandmother didn't want him to go, but his father and brothers favored the move. Pelé resisted, cried and ended up signing the contract. . . . In 1956 he won the first of a seemingly endless series of city championship titles for Santos. The next year, in June, he was visiting Bauru when he heard over the radio that he had been chosen for the national team.

Pelé played 91 games and scored 76 goals for the Brazilian national team. . . . He stopped playing for the team in 1971 and refused to play in the 1974 World Cup in Germany. That same year . . . he retired and left Santos, but he returned to the game to play in the United States for the New York-based Cosmos from 1975 to 1977.

Pelé is the only soccer player to have won three world championship games. In addition, he won two world club championships for Santos. . . . Pelé won international matches all over the world. . . . In total, in Santos and on the national team, he earned 52 titles. His entire star-studded career was a great show that continues today off the playing field. . . .

Pelé, back on the playing field in 1980 for the Beckenbauer farewell game at Giant Stadium, soon became such a focus of general attention that the French newspaper *L'Equipe* declared him the athlete of the century.*

These children are enjoying a warm, sunny afternoon netting crabs in the sparkling, clear waters of the Caribbean Sea. What other recreational sport, besides fishing, is popular in the Caribbean region?

Other sports, while not as popular as soccer, attract supporters as well. Latin Americans have gained world reknown as tennis, golf, and baseball players. Baseball is especially popular in the islands of the Caribbean and in the nations that touch upon the Caribbean. In the Andean areas of Chile and Argentina, skiing is enjoyed by many. In Brazil, the beaches of Rio de Janeiro draw people from all over the world.

FUN AND GAMES

Like other young people all over the world, those of Latin America find many different activities to fill their leisure time.

---

*"Pelé" by Rodolfo Konder reprinted from *Américas,* Volume 35, No. 5, September/October 1983, pp. 9–11, a bimonthly magazine published by the General Secretariat of the Organization of American States in Spanish and English.

In Hernández, Mexico, these young adults occupy some of their leisure time by gathering on the stairs of a public building to listen to a friend play songs on his guitar. What other activities do many of the young people of Latin America, such as María Catalina Paz, enjoy?

Below, a Colombian high school student talks about what she and her friends do:

My name is María Catalina Paz. I am 18 years old and was born in Popayán, a very small city where everyone knows everyone else.

The young Popayanese is very fun-loving, very studious, and very conservative. I say conservative because for generations they have done what their ancestors did. They are fun-loving because they are always looking for something to amuse themselves, and Popayán, being a small city, does not have a lot of diversions for *cocacolos,* young people between the ages of 12 and 20.

Generally there are groups made up of high school girls and university boys, who are four or five years older. Each weekend we meet to do something. We go to parties, which we have often. They begin between 9 or 10 P.M. and end about 2 or 3 A.M. We dance *cumbia* or *salsa,* which always helps animate everyone. When there are no parties, we meet at someone's house and sing, talk, play roulette, or tell scary stories. These last activities are the most common and the most enjoyable.

During the day, we walk to different places. We enjoy this a lot because during these walks we talk with each other and see everyone. Other times we go to the farms of some of our friends, where there is a lot to do. We can go horseback riding, walk, have water fights, or go swimming in the river or a swimming pool with our shoes and all our clothes on. When it begins to get dark, we almost always have hot chocolate with cheese and sit around a bonfire. We play the guitar and sing and watch the moon.

I have four best friends. We have been together since first grade and are very close. We always study together, talk to one another on the telephone, and exercise, shop, and go to the movies together. As we all go to the same girls' school, we are together a lot, talking and helping each other.

At times, when I am alone, I read or study because I am interested in learning more about cultures in general. Sometimes, I like to do things with my hands, like knit, cook, or sew. But what I always try to do is be active and be sure that I am very happy.*

1. Why do Latin Americans believe that life should be enjoyed today?
2. What are some common forms of recreation in Latin America?

---

*Interview with María Catalina Paz, student, April 1985. Reprinted by permission.

EXPLORATION
LATIN AMERICA

Read the discussion of *personalismo* that follows. Based on it, the accompanying photographs, and the information in the chapter, answer the following questions:

1. How do you interpret the concept of personalism? In what ways is your interpretation different from the Latin American one? In what ways is it the same?
2. In what ways do you think *personalismo* is reflected in Latin American class structure? Family life? Leisure activities? Attitudes about the role of women?

One of the principal themes the Latin Americans inherited from their Iberian ancestors is **personalismo**, or personalism. They believe strongly that each individual is unique and has an inner dignity and personality. A strong sense of personal honor and sensitivity to praise, insult, and slight is just part of *personalismo*.

Personalismo is not concerned with outward signs of equality, such as equality before the law, but with a person's inner qualities.

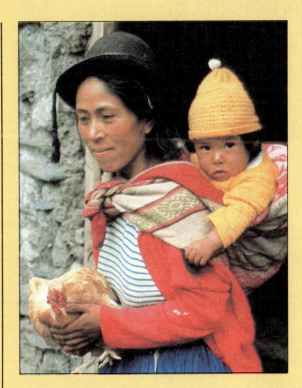

Social standing has no influence on *personalismo*. Every person has inner qualities that he or she can fulfill. A boss, for example, is expected to respect the personalism of each employee and show an active concern for him or her. The boss, therefore, may treat an employee as an employee, but never as a nonentity.

At times, personalism discourages involvement with large numbers of people. The individual is somewhat reluctant to form close associations with persons who are not relatives or close friends. Among family and friends, there is no need to maintain defenses. One can just relax and be the way he or she wants to be. Thus, a friend is an **hombre de confianza,** a person with whom one has an intimate and well-defined friendship, a person in whom one has complete confidence. Only with relatives and close friends can one discard formal manners for informal ones.

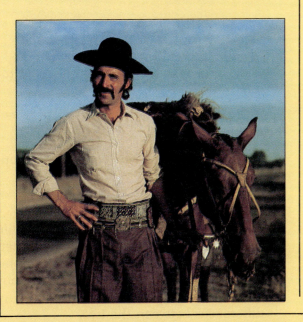

CHAPTER 29 REVIEW

POINTS TO REMEMBER

1. In most Latin American nations, there are three social classes—the upper class, the middle class, and the lower class. There are great contrasts in life styles and wealth among the three.
2. The rural lower class is composed of peasants and wage hands, all of whom work the land. For all members of the lower class, be they in the countryside or the city, poverty is a way of life.
3. Members of the upper class—the aristocracy and the *nouveaux riches*—lead comfortable lives because of their wealth.
4. The middle class is largely a product of the twentieth century and is growing rapidly. Often it is difficult to determine who is a member of the middle class because of the great variance in income.
5. Latin Americans of all classes have a strong sense of family. Families generally are large and closely knit, and serve as the center for most social activities. Family members are expected to help one another.
6. Most Latin Americans agree that in order to live life fully, one must feel deeply and strongly about an idea or person and enjoy life today and think about tomorrow when it comes.
7. During their leisure time, Latin Americans enjoy fiestas, sports, and other forms of recreation.

VOCABULARY

Identify

Pelé Eva Perón Isabel Perón

Define

aristocracy illiterate godparents *fútbol*
nouveaux riches common-law unions *fiestas* *personalismo*
haciendas *hombre de confianza*

DISCUSSING IMPORTANT IDEAS

1. Many Latin American children never go to school and begin working when they are eight years old or younger. In what ways do you think your life might be different today if you were one of these children?
2. Social class is very important in Latin America. What do you think will happen to the distinctions between the classes if the middle class continues to grow? How do you think this will affect the development of the region?
3. How does the Latin American concept of family compare with yours?
4. Latin Americans believe in enjoying life today and thinking about tomorrow when it comes. Compare and contrast this philosophy with the one prevalent in your country. Give possible reasons for any differences between the two.

DEVELOPING SKILLS

PREPARING A RESEARCH REPORT

The first two steps in preparing a research report are taking notes and preparing note cards. The next step is writing a rough draft of the report. Start by writing down your thesis statement or main topic as part of the first paragraph. Then, using your note cards as an outline, continue writing the rest of the draft in your own words. The chapters in this text follow the general form of a report and may be used as a guide.

Look, for example, at page 465, and locate the thesis statement. (. . . *in Latin America, social class is a determiner of daily life.*) This is followed on pages 466 to 471 with a main heading *(Social Class)* that relates to the thesis statement and subheadings *(Hard Work, Little Reward; An Easier Life; A New Generation)* that relate to the main heading. Each paragraph contains a main idea. *(Paragraphs 1 and 2, page 466: In most Latin American nations, there are three social classes—the upper class, the middle class, and the lower class.; The middle class is largely a product of the twentieth century and is growing fast.)* Each paragraph also has supporting statements. *(Paragraph 2, page 466: As industry has grown, more white-collar jobs have opened up.)* Under each subheading, the daily life of a social class is explained, showing that the material is written in a logical sequence.

As you write the draft, be sure that each time you refer to or quote directly from a source, you prepare a footnote based on the information listed on your bibliography note cards. The footnotes, numbered in order, should appear at the bottom of the same page as the references or quotes, separated from the main body of the report by a line drawn partway across the page.

When you are ready to bring your rough draft to an end, refer to your summary note cards for help in preparing a "last" paragraph that recalls your thesis statement, summarizes what you have learned, and/or expresses any conclusions you may have reached.

The fourth step in preparing a research report is to check over your rough draft, asking yourself questions like these:

1. Will the person who reads this report understand it?
2. Are more or better facts needed to support the thesis statement and main ideas?
3. Do the main headings relate to the thesis statement? Does each subheading relate to the main heading?
4. Does each paragraph have a main idea?
5. Are there supporting statements for each main idea?
6. Is the information presented in a logical order?
7. Are the paragraphs indented; correct capitalization, grammar, and punctuation used; and all words spelled correctly?
8. Are all direct references and quotes footnoted correctly?

After you have answered these questions and have made any necessary corrections or changes, you are ready to prepare the final draft of the report. It should include a cover page with the title of the report, your name, and, in some cases, the date, name of the course, and class period for which the report was written. It also should include a bibliography.

For practice in this skill, use the material in this chapter and in two other sources of your choice to prepare a report on family life in Latin America.

CHAPTER 30
PRAYER AND POLITICS

1. What factors have shaped the religious life of Latin America?
2. In what ways does Catholicism influence life in Latin America?

The pilgrimage had been described as a "purely pastoral" visit. But as Pope John Paul II's eight-day trip to Central America and Haiti drew to a close . . . , the dividing line between religion and politics seemed to have all but disappeared. . . . Said a Vatican official traveling with the Pope: "Even when he says Mass it seems to have political implications. . . ."

John Paul's visits to Guatemala, Honduras, Belize and Haiti drew enthusiastic crowds in the hundreds of thousands. Laboring well into the night, Guatemalans laid an 8 1/2-mile [13.6-kilometer] carpet of colored sawdust and grass, decorated with pictures of doves and brilliant floral designs for the papal motorcade. . . .

. . . Speaking to a crowd of about 500,000 gathered for Mass at a military parade ground in [Guatemala City], the Pope stressed that the government still had to improve its human rights record. . . .

John Paul traveled by helicopter to Quezaltenango, some 100 miles [160 kilometers] northwest of the capital, for a meeting with Guatemala's Indians. . . . Demanding legislation to protect the Indians, John Paul told a crowd dressed in bright colored handwoven outfits that "the church is aware of the discrimination you suffer and the injustices you must put up with, the serious difficulties you have in defending your lands and your rights, the frequent lack of respect for your culture and customs."

[In neighboring Honduras] . . . the Pope used every opportunity to preach his message of justice. He told 200,000 people gathered for Mass in front of a church in Tegucigalpa built to honor the country's patron saint, the Virgin of Suyapa, that it was not possible "to invoke the Virgin as Mother while maltreating her sons." In San Pedro Sula, the country's second largest city, he urged workers in newly industrialized areas to form trade unions and called for a wage system that took account of each laborer's needs.*

Pope John Paul II's visit to Central America, discussed above by a North American journalist, demonstrates the influence of the Roman Catholic Church in Latin America. Here, Catholicism is more than a religion. It is a way of life. Crosses and small chapels dot the countryside, and each village has a patron saint whose name it often bears. Each family and family member also has a patron saint. So do such groups as truck drivers, labor unions, and childless women, among others. The Roman Catholic Church is so much a part of everyday life that even those who do not attend services still consider themselves "faithful Catholics."

The influence of the Church, however, has its limits, and even Catholic priests can be found in political parties and movements that range from one end of the political spectrum to the other. In Latin America, where today political and social turmoil affect more than one country, the Church has found that while it can have a strong influence on political life, it cannot decree the path political life will follow.

---

*Excerpted from "'Things Must Change Here'" by John Kohan in *Time*, March 21, 1983, pp. 38–39. Copyright 1983 Time Inc. All rights reserved. Reprinted by permission from TIME.

THE CHURCH IN THE NEW WORLD

The influence of Roman Catholicism in Latin America dates back to the Spanish conquest of the New World in the 1500's, for with the sword came the cross. The priests who came to the New World with the *conquistadores* soon took charge of the spiritual needs of the Spanish and Portuguese settlers and tended to the needs of the African slaves. They also worked to convert the Indians to Christianity.

THE RIGHT TO RULE

The Spanish conquest led to a great controversy over the legality of the conquest itself and the right of the Spaniards to convert the Indians living in the conquered lands. Many Spaniards agreed with the Spanish writer and court historian, Juan Ginés de Sepúlveda. He argued that Indians were ignorant barbarians filled with vices, unable to take charge of their own lives. For this reason, the Indians had to accept rule by their superiors—the Spanish—who would civilize them and bring them religion. If they did not accept willingly, the Spanish had the right to conquer and rule them. In this way, the superior civilization and the Catholic faith of the Spaniards could be imposed on the Indians.

Some Spaniards, however, favored the point of view of Father Bartolomé de las Casas, who maintained that the Spaniards had no right to convert the Indians by force. De las Casas' ardent defense of the Indians made him unpopular with many Spaniards. Below, he explains why the Indians should not be forced to accept Spanish rule or the Catholic religion:

> [The Indians] . . . have a lawful, just, and natural government. Even though they lack the art and use of writing, they are not wanting in the capacity and skill to rule and govern themselves, both publicly and privately. Thus they have kingdoms, communities, and cities that they govern wisely according to their laws and customs. Thus their government is legitimate and natural. . . . From these statements we have no choice but to conclude that the

In this painting of Spanish conquistadores, Hernán Cortés, the bearded figure third from right, is leading the 1519 Spanish expedition to the Aztec Empire, 400 miles (640 kilometers) inland from the Atlantic Ocean. Cortés is accompanied by soldiers, Indian porters, and the young Indian woman Malinche, who served as one of his interpreters. What role did Catholic priests play in the Spanish and Portuguese conquest of the New World?

rulers of such nations enjoy the use of reason and that their people and the inhabitants of their provinces do not lack peace and justice. Otherwise they would not be established or preserved as political entities for long. . . . Therefore not all barbarians are irrational or natural slaves or unfit for government. . . . Now if we shall have shown that among our Indians . . . there are important kingdoms, large numbers of people who live settled lives in a society, great cities, kings, judges, and laws, persons who engage in commerce, buying, selling, lending, and the other contracts of the law of nations, will it not stand proved that the Reverend Doctor Sepúlveda has spoken wrongly and viciously against peoples like these. . . . From the fact that the Indians are barbarians it does not necessarily follow that they are incapable of government and have to be ruled by others, except to be taught about the Catholic faith. . . . They are not ignorant, inhuman, or bestial. Rather, long before they had heard the word Spaniard they had properly organized states, wisely ordered by excellent laws, religion, and custom. They cultivated friendship and, bound together in common fellowship, lived in populous cities in which they wisely administered the affairs of both peace and war justly and equitably, truly governed by laws that at very many points surpass ours. . . .

The second argument is that since the Church . . . never forces unbelievers who are its subjects in law and fact . . . to hear the word of God, the conclusion is inescapable that unbelievers who are not subject either in law or fact must not be forced to hear the word of God.

The third argument is the fact that Christ commanded only that the gospel be preached throughout the world. So wherever the gospel is preached, Christ's command is considered to have been carried out. . . .

Note that Christ did not teach that those who refuse to hear the gospel must be forced or punished. Rather, he will reserve their punishment to himself on the day of judgment. . . .

Now since Christ's words and actions should be examples for us, I do not know if anything more express or certain can be discovered than the fact that, in instructing his disciples, he taught them that men must not be forced to listen to the gospel. . . .

. . . Let us represent our teacher and savior by our deeds, and then those who have been ordained to go from paganism to eternal life will hasten of their own free will to the sheepfold of Christ. . . . The most effective solution is for them to see the Christian life shine in our conduct. But to advance the power of arms is not Christian example but a pretext for stealing the property of others and subjugating their provinces. . . .

From the foregoing it is evident that war must not be waged against the Indians under the pretext that they should hear the preaching of Christ's teaching, even if they may have killed preachers, since they do not kill the preachers as preachers or Christians as Christians, but as their most cruel public enemies, in order that they may not be oppressed or murdered by them.*

WEALTH AND POWER

In time, the Church grew in wealth and power. Although there were many reasons for this, a major one was that in order to serve the needs of everyone in the colonies, priests had to carry their religion outside their churches and missions.

Religion quickly became a part of all aspects of community life. An unsafe passage across a mountain was marked by a cross or a small chapel. Each ranch had its own

---

*Quoted from Bartolomé de las Casas, *In Defense of the Indians*, ed. Stafford Poole, C.M. (DeKalb: Northern Illinois University Press, 1974), pp. 9–11, 12, 13, 14. With permission of the Northern Illinois University Press.

chapel and each village and family its own patron saint. Even the church bell played a role in the community. It rang out the start and finish of each day. The Church—and the Church alone—provided the people with the schools, hospitals, orphanages, and welfare services they needed.

Much of the Church's power and wealth came from its close ties with the government. Religious and political life in the colonies was controlled by whoever sat on the Spanish and Portuguese thrones. These rulers delegated a great deal of authority to Church leaders. As a result, Church leaders played an important part in almost everything that happened.

Favors from the State and offerings from faithful worshipers, including large pieces of land, added up to great wealth for the Church. In addition to this were the large profits from the Church's many business interests, which included ranching, farming, commerce, mining, and banking.

1. When did Catholicism come to Latin America?
2. What arguments did Father Bartolomé de las Casas offer for not conquering the Indians and forcing them to convert to Christianity?
3. How did the Church become so wealthy and powerful in colonial Latin America?

THE NATIONAL PERIOD

In time, many of the colonists, discontent with foreign rule, sought independence. Most Church leaders, content with life as it was, backed the European rulers. When independence came, the new political leaders began to question the Church's power. They were joined by **anticlericals,** people who felt that the Church had too much social, economic, and political power. The anticlericals, most of whom were Catholics, were not anti-Catholic. They simply believed that the Church should be less worldly and more spiritual and should be put under State control and its involvement limited to religious matters.

The anticlericals did not like the fact that Church-owned lands and businesses were not subject to taxation. They felt that this gave the Church an unfair advantage and deprived the government of badly needed funds. They also objected to the Church's large landholdings, which, according to Church law, could not be sold. In Mexico, for example, before land reform became law, the Church owned one-half of the country's most valuable land. This greatly reduced the amount of land available to the people.

One of the most outspoken and determined anticlericals was Benito Juárez, who, in the mid-1800's, served as deputy in the national legislature, governor of the state of Oaxaca, and president of Mexico. With these words, Juárez explained why he believed the Church's power had to be curbed:

> . . . I returned to Oaxaca and dedicated myself to the exercise of my profession. The clergy still found themselves in full possession of their exemptions and prerogatives, and their close alliance with the civil power gave them an influence that was almost omnipotent [all powerful]. The exemption that removed them from the jurisdiction of the common courts served them as a shield against the law of safe-conduct, so that they could indulge . . . in every excess and every injustice. The taxes that were the rights of the parishes were a dead letter, and the payment of the perquisites [special fees] was determined in accordance with the greedy wills of the parish priests. There were . . . some honorable and upright priests who limited themselves to charging what was just, and who did not rob the faithful; but these . . . were very rare, and their example, far from deterring the evil ones from their

Many Catholic holidays, festivals, and saint's days are celebrated with processions like this one in Nicaragua, in which men are carrying a statue of Christ and the cross through their rural village. Some worshipers join the procession, while others show their respect by kneeling in prayer as the procession passes. How has the separation of Church and State affected the traditional role of the Catholic Church in Latin America?

abuses, resulted in their own censure, on the ground that they were misleading the people. . . . Meanwhile, the citizens groaned in their oppression and misery, because the fruit of their work, their time, and their personal services was entirely devoted to the satisfaction of the insatiable greed of their so-called shepherds. Justice, if they took steps to seek it, was usually deaf to them, and commonly they received as their own answer scorn or imprisonment. . . .*

Bit by bit, the anticlericals made their reforms. The Church lost many of its property holdings and had to give up many business activities. This led the Church to lose much of its wealth and be short of money.

1. What did the anticlericals want? Why did they want these things?
2. What effect did the anticlericals have on the Church?

*Specified excerpts from *Viva Juárez!: A biography* by Charles Allen Smart. (J.B. Lippincott Co.) pp. 64–65, 67. Copyright ©1963 by Charles Allen Smart. Reprinted by permission of Harper & Row Publishers, Inc.

THE CATHOLIC CHURCH TODAY

During the colonial period, non-Catholics were not welcome in most of Latin America. But by the 1900's, the number of Protestants there had started to grow. Much of the growth has been due to the efforts of Protestant missionaries who have worked to help the poor and have built hospitals, schools, and colleges. Yet, despite this growth, Catholicism remains the major religion of Latin America today.

Although the number of Roman Catholics remains large, the influence of the Church is not as strong as it was in some areas in earlier years. Today, about one-half of the countries of Latin America have ordered the separation of Church and State. In the countries where this separation has taken place, religious marriage ceremonies no longer are considered legal and must be accompanied by a civil ceremony. Religious instruction no longer is allowed in public schools, and the State has taken over most educational, health, and welfare services.

There are several other reasons for the decline of the Church's influence. Two major ones are the lack of priests and the lack of funds. Although there are over 100 million more people in Latin America today than there were 15 years ago, there are only about 12,000 more priests. That translates to one priest for every 6000 Catholics, whereas in the United States, for example, there is one for every 700 Catholics. The lack of funds is just as serious. Most of the ornate churches, pieces of art, and elaborate altars date back to the times before the Church lost its wealth, and they cannot be sold to raise funds. Although Western European and North American Catholic churches are providing both priests and financial assistance, there still are too few clergy, too little money, and too much to be done.

FAITH AND REFORM

Despite its problems, the Church is not completely removed from politics and continues to have influence. Members of the clergy continue to take a public stand when an issue involves matters of faith and reform.

One of the clergy's main concerns today is **agrarian reform,** the more equal division of land among the people. In recent years, priests have organized credit unions and cooperatives that buy and sell at fair prices for members. They also have helped Church lay people form labor unions and political parties that point out the need for social justice in keeping with Catholic teachings and democratic principles. Efforts being made in Haiti, discussed in the newspaper article below, are an example of the Church's political involvements:

> He is a young Roman Catholic priest ministering in the eastern hills. . . . His parish lies in a dry coffee-growing region a half-day's walk from the nearest road passable by bus or car. More specific identification would endanger him, for he and a hundred other priests are attempting the forbidden: to change the politics of President-for-Life Jean-Claude Duvalier's Haiti.
>
> "I help them to ask questions," the priest says of his work with the peasants. "We are still in discussion. We don't know where we are going. . . ."
>
> Traditionally as quiescent as the peasants themselves, the Catholic Church of Haiti has emerged . . . as the first broad-based group to mount sustained criticism of the quarter-century-old Duvalier regime. . . .
>
> An international official [says], "They don't have the concept here that the government belongs to the people. It's more

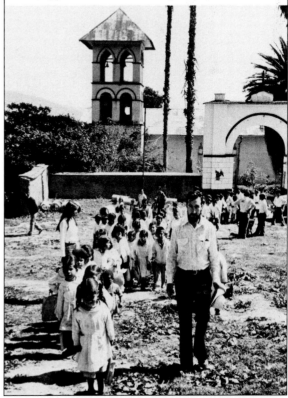

In Bolivia, a Catholic priest, dressed in street clothes, leads Indian children to a mass held in a courtyard outside the church. What is one of the main concerns of the clergy in Latin America today?

that the people belong to the government. . . ."

But if the nation has long suffered under the Duvaliers, its priests have only recently begun to call much attention to the situation. When, during the mid-1960s, a few clerics attempted mild criticism of [Haitian dictator] "Papa Doc," he responded by expelling the country's five foreign bishops and exiling a number of Haitian priests.

Ironically, those expulsions . . . cleared the way for today's clerical activism. Until the mid-1960s, about two-thirds of the Catholic clergymen in Haiti were foreigners. . . . Today, more than half —and perhaps two-thirds . . . —of the approximately 550 priests are Haitian.

That may seem a small number to affect a nation of over five million. But, as the Haitian government knows, a parish led by one or two priests may have as many as 2,000 committed members of lay groups such as Catholic Action or Catholic Volunteers. . . .

Most foreign priests fought voodoo, the native folk religion. The new priests are trying to assimilate it into Catholicism. And . . . "the liturgy went into the vernacular, Creole, which is what 90% of the people speak," says the Rev. Thomas Wenski. . . . "The drum was brought in, and Haitian songs." These innovations, Father Wenski says, "brought about a renewal of the church."

With these changes, priests here say, the newly nationalistic church of Haiti gained in confidence and closeness to the people. Many priests feel the church is strongest—perhaps even more influential than the government—in the back country, where once it was remote and weak. "The church has been doing a lot of work at the base, in little groups," says a priest familiar with the peasant education programs. . . .

"We have an understanding with the other religious orders," says one priest. "If one of us is touched, we will react in solidarity." On the other side of the country, another priest promises that a [government] crackdown would be met with a shutdown of churches, the many church-run schools and even some hospitals. . . . Priests here reply that this is a time of firsts. "I don't think there's a church anywhere that's more unified than the church in Haiti is now," says a cleric in the north. "It'll be an interesting evolution to watch over the next three or four years. It might even point the way for some other countries."*

HELPING THE NEEDY

All of the Church's political efforts are not as effective as it would like. In some countries, divorce laws have been passed and birth control programs established in spite of Church resistance. In several countries, a fear of eventual socialism and communism has undermined the Church's efforts to bring about agrarian reform.

But even with such setbacks, the Church continues in its efforts to bring about change and reform. Many of the clergy have begun to live and work directly with the most needy. Padre Jaime Hilgeman, an American Maryknoll missionary priest, is one of those clergy. Below, he talks about his life and his work in Jardim Veronica, a community on the outskirts of São Paulo, Brazil:

> When I was a boy, I used to dream of traveling to Brazil and paddling a canoe up the Amazon River. My dreams changed when I became a missionary. I wanted to be able to work with the poor people in Latin America. For ten years I worked in Mexico before moving to Brazil in 1978.
>
> I chose Brazil because Maryknoll missionaries were already doing exciting work there and also I wanted to learn a new

---

*"Defying Duvalier, The Pope Visits Haiti Just as Church There Is Challenging Regime" by Thomas E. Ricks in *The Wall Street Journal*, March 9, 1983, pp. 1, 21, 22. Reprinted by permission of *The Wall Street Journal* ©Dow Jones & Company, Inc. 1983. All Rights Reserved.

language. Brazilians speak Portuguese whereas . . . other Latin Americans speak Spanish.

I am a Roman Catholic priest and Brazil has the largest Catholic population in the world. Many years ago, priests came to Brazil after the Portuguese conquest and converted the local Indians to Catholicism. Today, the vast majority of a total population of 120 million people are baptized Catholics. We no longer have to convert people to Catholicism, so we are more concerned with improving the social conditions of the poor.

When I arrived in Brazil, I spent four months in Rio de Janeiro learning Portuguese. After that, I visited the slum districts of São Paulo, which is the biggest city in Brazil. It looks like a rich and prosperous city, but there is great poverty in many areas. São Paulo reflects the great contrast between the rich and the poor which is such a problem in modern Brazil.

I particularly liked one of our communities in São Paulo called Jardim Veronica . . . I rented a simple three-room stucco house close to the *favela* (shanty town) that comes within the boundary of our community. For three years I've been sharing the house with Lucas, a twenty-year-old Brazilian friend.

In Jardim Veronica, I spend my days working with needy people to build a small Christian community which the Maryknolls call a "base" community. By living with the poor, I can understand their problems better and work toward solving them. The community needs paved streets, running water, regular waste disposal, schools, and medical services to fight such diseases as polio which still afflict Brazilian children.

Most of the neighbors work at the nearby glass and chemical factories. In some plants, working conditions are bad and wages low, the equivalent of about U.S. $200 per month. In the evenings, we hold neighborhood meetings at the homes of the workers to discuss what we can do to

Safe water and sanitation are desperately needed in Brazilian slums like this one. What are the problems of the poor in São Paulo, Brazil? How are priests and nuns trying to help?

improve the working situation. We encourage our people to get involved in the development of their country. Very slowly, small improvements are being made.

I work with three other priests and seven nuns in an area which houses 170,000 Catholics. Four priests for all these people are not enough—like the rest of Brazil we need many more priests. Brazil has only 12,000 priests to serve some 98 million baptized Catholics. We divide up our area so that each community has a priest to say Mass at least twice a month. When I say Mass in church, I use the traditional vestments of a priest. But when I'm working with the people in the *favela*, I'm one of them and dress like everyone else.*

1. What factors led to an increase in the Protestant population of Latin America?
2. In what ways has the influence of the Catholic Church declined since the 1900's? What are some reasons for the decline?
3. In what ways does the Church continue to make its influence felt?

---

*"The largest Catholic population in the world" in *We Live in Brazil* by Patricia Robb, 1985, The Bookwright Press, pp. 50–51. Reprinted by permission.

EXPLORATION
LATIN AMERICA

Although many Latin American Indians and blacks are Catholics, their Catholicism often is blended with their own age-old religious beliefs and customs. Read the articles that follow, and comment on this statement:

Some people believe that the Christian elements of the Indian pilgrimage and Candomblé are "merely a thin veneer of Catholicism pasted over ancient Indian and African beliefs." Yet, almost all those who practice these beliefs feel they are true Catholics. What is your opinion? Explain.

Pilgrimage to the Sky

I climbed one last rise and then stopped, stunned by an explosion of color and reverberating music. In an isolated valley beneath glistening glaciers, costumed figures danced among thousands of pilgrims. They would spend the night here, at the concrete-block sanctuary of this sacred place called Qoyllur Riti (Star of the Snow). This days-long Peruvian pilgrimage, held . . . after Easter . . . commemorates a miraculous appearance of Christ in 1780. . . .

To arrive at this spot . . . , I had accompanied Indians on a frigid moonlight trek through the rugged Andes. As I watched the pageant, my companions put on the feathered costumes of the

chunchos . . . , representing jungle Indians. They believe that the creation of the sun drove the precursors of these jungle people—who lived in a world illumined only by the moon—into the rain forests, where light could not penetrate. . . .

A wooden cross was set into the snow . . . , as an Indian friend scooped a hollow in the ice, lit candles and prayed. . . . by climbing up the sacred mountain, he links the people of his community with the gods.

After prayers [they] began their descent. At the base of the glacier they stopped, cut chunks of ice, and slung them on their backs. . . . The Indians believe that ice from the mountain has healing powers. As they snaked down the mountain . . . , morning sunlight glinted blindingly off their frozen burdens.

[They] returned to the sanctuary and distributed the ice to the people of their villages, who melted it. Some of the liquid was mixed with barley to make a warm drink; the rest would be carried home in bottles. . . .

At the sanctuary the dancing and praying continued. The sanctuary contains a rock bearing the image of Christ. It commemorates the miraculous appearance of the Christ child to a young herdsman named Mariano in these mountains two centuries ago.

I joined the crush of pilgrims inside. The light from hundreds of candles burnished the faces of those who cried and prayed in front of the sacred rock.

"They cry," I was told, "for the sufferings of El Señor, The Lord."

"Give me your blessing, Señor de Qoyllur Riti, so that I can return to my home." I heard the final Mass said at the sanctuary after the . . . return.

Then the crowds dispersed, except for a group of a thousand or so who headed out for the trek to the village of Tayankani. . . . Many dancers . . . were going, and I joined them. Near the sanctuary we saw a tiny stone house and corrals . . . built by pilgrims who were asking the mountain god for the fertility of their livestock. We walked all day to arrive at a small hamlet where we rested until moonrise. Then we continued—a long single-file line serpentining over the moonlit mountain trails. Along the way stops were made for prayers at various shrines. With the light of dawn the image of Christ was placed at one last chapel . . . before being carried down to Tayankani.*

Candomblé

Most people find it difficult to understand my religion. They think it's some kind of voodoo brought from Africa to Brazil as far back as the sixteenth century, but that isn't correct. . . . Among the various cults that exist today in Brazil, Candomblé *comes closest to maintaining its pure African form. The others, called* Macumba, Umbanda *and* Quimbanda, *are similar but they have been adapted to modern times.* . . .

My father came from Africa and set up a terreiro *(temple), where he practiced* Candomblé. He was a Pai de Santo—*father of the gods. Because of his influence, I became an active participant in* Candomblé *and after fulfilling the necessary obligations, became a* Maē de Santo [mother of the gods]. I practice my religion at a terreiro run by a Pai de Santo. He is the most important person and oversees the ceremonies.

According to our religion, each person is under the protection of an orixa *or god.* Ogum, *who is represented as Saint Anthony, is one of my gods and acts as a father symbol.* Yansā, *who is Saint Barbara, is the goddess who assumes the role of mother to me. Some of our other gods are* Yemanjá *(the Blessed Virgin Mary),* Oxalá *(Jesus Christ),* Omolú *(Saint Lazarus), and* Exu, *who is the devil.*

When we hold a ceremony, we call on the gods and spirits of Africa to descend into the bodies of their children. We beat drums, chant, dance and meditate as our ancestors did so that the gods will come. Certain privileged members called Filho de Santo *(son of the gods) are mediums who are prepared . . . to receive the gods. During a ceremony, a* Filho de Santo *will go into a trance as a god takes possession of his body. As a* Mãe de Santo, *I must watch over the mediums until the god leaves, calm the god if he becomes too violent and see that he receives his favorite food. Each god has his own personality. For example,* Ogum *likes to eat beans, yams and the bull's liver, heart and lungs. He is the divine blacksmith and the war god. He dwells in the forest, and when he dances he triumphantly waves a sword and has a ferocious look on his face.*

During the ceremony, I wear white clothes in honor of Oxalá. My beaded necklace is blue because that's the color of my orixa, Ogum. *I wear a turban before the gods descend. Once they are amongst us, I exchange it for a festive headdress symbolic of the* orixa *whose day we are commemorating.*

I've been a Mãe de Santo *for fourteen years. My religion is very important to me: it's a source of personal strength through union with natural forces and psychic energies. But, besides being a* Mãe, *I'm an ordinary Brazilian.**

---

*"Peru's Pilgrimage to the Sky" by Robert Randall in *National Geographic*, Vol. 162, No. 1, July 1982, pp. 60, 65, 67, 69. Reprinted by permission.

*"We call on the gods and spirits of Africa" in *We Live in Brazil* by Patricia Robb, 1985, The Bookwright Press, pp. 44–45. Reprinted by permission.

CHAPTER 30 REVIEW

POINTS TO REMEMBER

1. The great majority of all Latin Americans are Catholic. Catholicism is more than a religion. It is a way of life.
2. Although the influence of the Catholic Church is great in Latin America, it is not unlimited. The Church cannot decree the path political life will follow.
3. The Spanish conquest led to controversy over the legality of the conquest and over the right of the Spaniards to convert the Indians who were living in the conquered lands.
4. Over the years, the Church grew in power and wealth. Much of the power and wealth came from the Church's close ties with the government and from offerings made by faithful worshipers.
5. Anticlericals, most of whom were Catholic, made reforms in which the social, economic and political power of the Church was reduced.
6. In recent years, the influence of the Church has declined in some areas. This is due in great part to the separation of Church and State and the lack of priests and funds. It is still active, however, in agrarian reform, aid for the needy, and other related areas.

VOCABULARY

Identify

Pope John Paul II
Juan Ginés de Sepúlveda
Father Bartolomé de las Casas
Maryknoll
Jardim Veronica
Candomblé
Benito Juárez

Define

anticlericals
agrarian reform

DISCUSSING IMPORTANT IDEAS

1. If you were a Catholic living in Latin America today, what role would you want the Church to play? Why do you think it should play that role?
2. Do you think the Spaniards had the right to convert the Indians? Give reasons for your answer.
3. Do you think priests in Latin America should try to assimilate voodoo and native folk religion into the Church? Why or why not? If they do, what effect do you think it will have on other Latin American Catholics?
4. Based on what you have read in this chapter, what do you think the role of the Catholic Church will be in Latin America 10 years from now? Give reasons to support your answer.

DEVELOPING SKILLS

SUMMARIZING

At one time or another, most people have found themselves attending a lecture, a class, or a meeting during which the speaker bores everyone by *rambling on*, giving information that is irrelevant, uninteresting, and unnecessary. Some members of the audience probably wonder why the speaker does not *summarize*, recap the main ideas by bringing together the major points and excluding the minor ones.

Knowing how to summarize is a useful skill not only for speakers but for students who have to answer essay questions, take notes, or write research papers. The guidelines provided in the following example will help you to summarize written material:

1. Read this written material carefully.

    During colonial times, the Roman Catholic Church in Latin America grew in wealth and power. There were many reasons why this happened. One of the major reasons was that when priests tried to serve the needs of everyone in the colonies, they found that they had to carry their religion outside their churches and missions.

    As a result, before long, religion became a part of every aspect of community life. An unsafe passage across a mountain was marked by a cross or a small chapel. Each ranch had its own chapel. Each family had its own patron saint. The start and finish of each day was marked by the ringing of church bells. It was the Church that provided the schools, hospitals, orphanages, and welfare services.

    A great deal of the Church's power and wealth came from its close ties with the government. The religious and political life of the colonies was controlled by whoever sat on the thrones of Spain and Portugal. These rulers delegated a great deal of authority to Church leaders. As a result, Church leaders played an important part in almost everything that happened in the colonies.

    Favors from the State and gifts from faithful worshipers added up to great wealth for the Church. In addition, the Church had many business interests, including ranching, farming, commerce, mining, and banking. The profits from these added to the Church's wealth.

2. Locate and list in order of appearance the main ideas expressed in the material. (1. During colonial times, the Roman Catholic Church in Latin America grew in wealth and power; 2. Before long, religion became a part of every aspect of community life; 3. A great deal of the Church's power and wealth came from its close ties with the government; 4. [Spanish and Portuguese] rulers delegated a great deal of authority to Church leaders; 5. Favors from the State and gifts from faithful worshipers added up to great wealth for the Church; 6. The profits from [the Church's many business interests] added to the Church's wealth.)

3. Summarize by rewriting the main ideas in your own words. (The wealth and power of the Catholic Church in Latin America increased as religion became a part of all aspects of community life. The Church's power came from the Spanish and Portuguese rulers who delegated authority to Church leaders and with whom the leaders maintained close ties. The Church's wealth came from favors from the State, gifts from faithful worshipers, and profits from the Church's many business interests.)

For practice in this skill, read the section on the National Period on pages 486 through 488. Following the guidelines suggested in the example, write a short summary of the material in the section.

CHAPTER 31
CHANGE TAKES MANY FORMS

1. What are some of the changes taking place in Latin America?
2. What problems has change brought to Latin America?

Once regarded as South America's miracle nation, Brazil is watching in despair as dreams of a golden future evaporate under the weight of economic crisis and social unrest.

Brazilians normally are the most optimistic of people, with high confidence in themselves and their country.

But today they are struggling for survival, faced with the world's largest foreign debt . . . soaring inflation and unemployment, labor unrest, bankruptcies and violence in the streets. . . .

. . . Nature has added to the misery, unleashing the worst floods in a century on Brazil's southern states while searing the Northeast with a drought that is now in its fifth year.

These hard realities have shattered ambitions—nearly achieved —to make Brazil a model for economic and industrial development in the Third World.

What happened to that vision? Brazilian officials contend that the shocks of oil-price increases in the 1970s started the economic slide. . . .

The jump in oil costs was followed by a surge in international interest rates on the vast amount of money Brazil had borrowed to finance development during the boom years. . . .

Adding to the nation's woes was a sharp deterioration in markets for some of Brazil's key agricultural exports, particularly coffee, that provided a firm foundation for the economy. . . .

How Brazil was transformed in only a decade from a nation with tremendous potential to a country facing financial disaster may be a case history of ambitious development plans gone awry. . . .

Despite widespread pessimism, there are some in Brazil who see better times down the road. Says . . . [the] director of the respected newsletter *Suma Econômica:* "Despite difficulties, the nation has prospects for accelerated growth in the near future. . . . A management class exists, and there is a relatively well-trained working class. Besides, the mineral and agricultural frontiers are expanding."*

In the early 1970's, Brazil was considered an "economic marvel." Industrial growth, long a dream of most of Latin America, was becoming a reality. As the magazine article above states, Brazil was well on its way to becoming an example of economic and industrial development that other developing countries all over the world could imitate. But by the early 1980's, the situation had changed, and Brazil was in deep trouble.

What happened to bring about the drastic change in Brazil is important. But even more important is that in one respect or another, to one degree or another, Brazil mirrors changes that are taking place throughout Latin America. These changes are affecting every Latin American and every facet of life.

---
*"Brazil: A Giant Reeling on the Ropes" by Steve Yolen in *U.S. News & World Report,* August 22, 1983, pp. 28–29. Reprinted by permission.

THE PEOPLE EXPLOSION

Until a short time ago, population growth was thought to be an important part of a country's economic and political strength. More people meant more workers to help raise the standard of living. This, in turn, meant more prestige for the country. But in recent years, some people have begun to question this line of thinking. They believe that the world is reaching the point where there are too many people in it. With so many people, large numbers cannot be properly fed, clothed, schooled, housed, or given adequate medical services.

In Latin America, the population is expected to double in the next 25 years or so. Traditionally, Latin America had both a high birthrate and a high death rate, and the one offset the other. But, by the 1900's, the death rate had begun to decrease. Immunization against certain diseases and improved sanitary conditions made it possible for people to live longer.

While the death rate decreased substantially, the birthrate did not. Most Latin Americans continued to have large families. One reason for this is the stand taken by the Catholic Church. In Latin America, the Church is opposed to birth control. Another reason is tradition. It has long been the belief of many Latin American men that one way to demonstrate how *macho,* or masculine, they are is to father a lot of children. A third reason is that in some areas there is a lack of information about family planning.

Many people believe that conditions will not improve in Latin America until the birth-

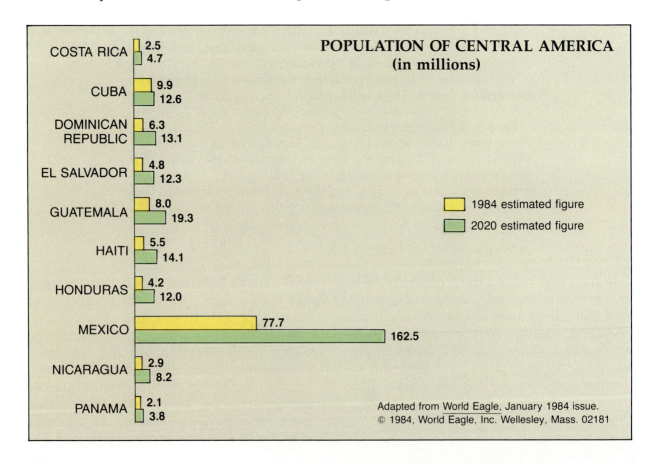

POPULATION OF CENTRAL AMERICA (in millions)

Country	1984 estimated figure	2020 estimated figure
COSTA RICA	2.5	4.7
CUBA	9.9	12.6
DOMINICAN REPUBLIC	6.3	13.1
EL SALVADOR	4.8	12.3
GUATEMALA	8.0	19.3
HAITI	5.5	14.1
HONDURAS	4.2	12.0
MEXICO	77.7	162.5
NICARAGUA	2.9	8.2
PANAMA	2.1	3.8

Adapted from World Eagle, January 1984 issue.
© 1984, World Eagle, Inc. Wellesley, Mass. 02181

rate decreases and that the population will continue to grow at a rapid rate. Others do not agree. They believe that by the end of the century, as Latin America becomes more urban and industrialized, the birthrate will slow down.

URBANIZATION

Some experts also believe that the problem in Latin America is not the number of people but how those people are distributed. Although there is a great deal of land, most of it is forest, mountain, or desert. As a result, most people have settled in the coastal regions, leaving many of the other areas sparsely populated.

The never-ending flow of people from the countryside to the cities adds to the problem. Each year, thousands flock to the cities in hope of finding a better education, higher-paying jobs, broader markets, and decent medical care. Whether they do well or not, almost all the migrants tend to stay in the city, making urban populations soar. This has placed heavy demands on the people and the government. Public services must be expanded continuously. For the most part, these services are ample only in the central part of the cities where the better housing areas are found.

This one-way migration has led to overpopulation, more people than resources available to fill their needs. Four of the largest urban areas in the world— São Paulo, Rio de Janeiro, Buenos Aires, and Mexico City—are in Latin America. At present, greater Mexico City is the fourth largest urban area in the world after New York, Tokyo, and Shanghai. Population experts predict that by the year 2000 it will be the

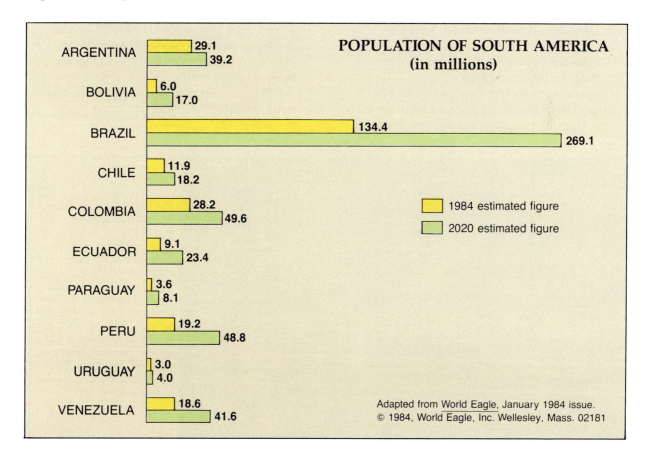

largest urban area in the world. Below, a North American journalist visiting Mexico City gives his impressions:

> Stewing, steaming, sinking, straining, striving, smoking and choking, Mexico City is the ultimate city of too much and too little.
>
> There is no other place quite like this runaway colossus. Here is future shock jammed atop centuries of past shock.
>
> . . . The population of greater Mexico City may be 16 million, 17 million, or 18 million, depending on who is counting or when.
>
> The figures "are out of date by the time they are collected," said . . . the city's beleaguered planning director.
>
> Population has increased sixfold in the last 35 years and has doubled in the last decade. . . .
>
> Mexican land reform has fizzled, and many peasants are hungry. Thousands of them squeeze in here every week, quitting the land for slums that stretch for miles and embrace millions of people.
>
> More than one-fifth of the entire country lives in this metropolis.
>
> Squatter towns and shantyvilles—"lost cities," as they are called—huddle in garbage dumps, virtually next door to mansions and leafy upper-class neighborhoods. . . .
>
> Squatters and beggars are a common . . . sight. But for every beggar, there are a thousand street vendors. . . .
>
> The country has no welfare or food stamps, and the streets consequently are full of people hustling anything—gum, candy, tortillas, bracelets, dolls, shawls, toys. . . .
>
> At traffic stops, youngsters rush up and wipe windshields for a penny tip. Others try to sell motorists a puppy, a blanket, a newspaper with giant headlines. . . .
>
> In this airy center of outdoor selling, the air is blinding and choking, possibly the worst of any great city.
>
> Every morning, motorized Mexico City awakens under a hood of gray smog that hides its once-familiar crest of mountains and clogs its once-clear air. Sometimes nothing can be seen 100 yards [90 meters] ahead. . . .
>
> And yet a surprising number of neighborhoods retain a colonial charm. Some streets even remain free of the hideously noisy, choking traffic.
>
> Parks are generally clean, and workmen weed superhighway strips. Corner bakeries sell crusty . . . rolls. . . .

The layer of grayish brown smog that hangs over Mexico City is clearly visible in this photograph. At least 70 percent of the smog comes from the city's more than 3 million automobiles. Much of the rest is due to smoke from the city's 30,000 factories. The poor air quality harms the health of many of the people who live and work in the city. What are some other characteristics of Mexico City?

The front walls of the Children's Library of Managua, Nicaragua, are decorated with this bright mural that shows students using the library's resources to learn about the world in which they live. Murals are a common sight in many Latin American cities, including those of Mexico. What are some other artistic features of Mexico City?

Markets brim with fruits and vegetables, although stores may be short of toothpaste or milk. . . .

And museums, shops, historic ruins and architecture, murals and the lavishly decorated university are facets of a vivid supercity.

Business growth has brought with it an expanding middle class and clouds of skyscrapers that defy earthquakes and the city's steady slippage into the muck that it is built on. Everyone complains about crowding, noise, and dirty air, but for people earning, say, the equivalent of $30,000 a year, the city offers the sweet life, or at least the bittersweet.*

SHANTYTOWNS AND SLUMS

Most of the people who migrate from the countryside to the cities do not find what they seek. The majority cannot read or write and do not have the skills needed for the kinds of work available. As a result, they end up in the very poverty they hoped to escape, trading their huts in the countryside for old, run-down houses or shantytowns at the outskirts of the city.

All major Latin American cities today have their slums or shantytowns. In Rio de Janeiro and São Paulo, Brazil, they are called *favelas.* In Buenos Aires, Argentina, they are known as *villas miserias.* In Caracas, Venezuela, they are *barrios,* and in Bogota, Colombia, they are *barriadas.*

Although conditions in the shantytowns and slums are far from good, some experts defend the existence of such settlements. They argue that, for all their problems, the settlements provide the poor with free or inexpensive housing. And, since they pay little or no rent, some shantytown dwellers use what they can save to improve their houses and buy things they need. The *pueblos jóvenes,* or young towns, that surround Lima and other Peruvian cities, are an example. To some, these settlements, which are home to about half of Lima's 4.5 million people, are "rings of misery," where no person should have to live or die. But, as the

---

*"Mexico City's Population May Top 30 Million by Year 2000" by M.W. Newman in *The Omaha World-Herald,* September 11, 1983, p. 6A. Reprinted by permission.

newspaper article below reveals, to others they are the "birthplaces of communities":

> Marsha Parades, an American who has studied the pueblos jovenes for years, said, "Maybe I have been here too long, but I think there are many positive aspects about these towns."
>
> Until about 30 years ago, Peru was a rural society. But with changes in the economy combined with cultural and social factors, a major movement of people occurred, and now 70 percent of Peru's 18 million people live in cities.
>
> The urban centers were not prepared, so the migrants began building squatter communities—the pueblos jovenes.
>
> A group of people, usually from the same village or province, would select an empty plot of land and simply occupy it, often gaining government acquiescence.
>
> "But it was more than just squatting," Miss Parades said. "It was a real community effort. The first thing that they would do would be to build a school and a market. Then they would build a police post."
>
> The government would not or could not afford to build the facilities, but it would provide teachers and policemen.
>
> The American and other experts agree that, as bad as things look in the pueblos jóvenes, life was usually worse in rural areas.
>
> "These are not shiftless, lazy people trying to live off handouts. There are no handouts," Miss Parades said.
>
> "They are ambitious people with hopes for themselves and their children. They are very conservative. What they want is to own a home and educate their kids."
>
> After the schools and police stations were built, a typical family head would erect a temporary shelter and begin collecting and saving bricks.
>
> When he had enough, "the man, and sometimes it is a single woman, will build a wall. From there it is a progression of walls and rooms until there is a house," Miss Parades added.
>
> What a stranger sees may look like an unfinished shack, but it is still being built and it will eventually be completed. "It may look odd, but it will be a house," she said.
>
> The problems of overcrowding and lack of sanitation develop after the original settlements are built, according to experts. Then strangers start drifting in and the cohesiveness of the original town breaks down.*

This hillside shantytown on the outskirts of Lima, Peru, is typical of the pueblos jóvenes *that surround Lima and other Peruvian cities. What are some positive features of Lima's* pueblos jóvenes?

1. What factors have contributed to rapid population growth in Latin America?
2. What effect has overpopulation had on the cities of Latin America and the people who live in them?

IN THE COUNTRYSIDE

Although about one-half of the people of Latin America live in the countryside and are farmers, Latin America does not produce enough food to feed its people. Nor are enough earnings brought in through exports

---

*"Peru's Slums: Birthplaces of Communities or 'Rings of Misery'?" by Kenneth Freed in *The Omaha World-Herald,* November 9, 1980, p. 8A. Reprinted by permission.

to pay for the imported food and industrial goods that are needed. With the expansion of farm products slow, the need for imported foods has been rising rapidly, and nearly 75 percent of all manufactured goods must be imported.

In the past, *campesinos*, people who live and work in the countryside, stayed close to home. But in recent years, improved roads and bus service have allowed them to travel to large urban areas. These trips, along with radio, television, and movies, have given the *campesinos* a glimpse of a different life, better than their own. They hope to gain this life through agrarian reform. To this end, *campesinos* in many parts of Latin America have taken part in strikes and have taken over large estates.

HACIENDAS AND COMMERCIAL FARMS

In most Latin American countries, a few people—some 10 percent—own 90 percent of the land, and even today *haciendas* still account for a large part of the big landholdings. Most of the work is done by peasant sharecroppers, who generally keep one-third or one-half of the crop and give the rest to the ***hacendado***, or *hacienda* owner. The *hacendado* provides the sharecroppers with a hut, a small piece of land, seeds, simple tools, and at times, work animals and a small wage. A store and religious and social activities also may be provided.

Most work on the *hacienda* is done by hand, and the amount produced per acre is quite low. Most *hacendados* plant only about 10 to 15 percent of their land at one time, and much is not farmed at all. With taxes on the land low and labor cheap, most *hacendados* feel no need to provide up-to-date machinery or training, to push to produce more, or to sell some of the land to a tenant farmer.

The *hacienda* system allows the *hacendado* to dominate the local area and discourages

On this Honduran hacienda, *children and adult workers are cutting tobacco leaves that will be stored and cured in the drying barns in the background. How does the* hacienda *system work?*

peasants from trying to improve their lot. In the end, it holds back economic progress. Because the peasants get little or nothing for all their work, most do not have enough money to buy many manufactured goods. This means that there is a lack of consumers, which, in turn, keeps new industry from growing and new jobs from opening up.

Some peasants continue to work on the *hacienda* because of tradition. They believe that leaving the land that their ancestors tilled would be desertion. Others are held by the debts they owe the *hacendado*. Still others stay because they feel that they have no other choice. They cannot expect to acquire their own land, and moving to another *hacienda* will not improve their lives. Their only hope for a better life lies in the city. But that would mean adapting to urban life, and many are afraid or unwilling to do so.

Today, many of the large landholdings are commercial farms that produce bananas, sugar, coffee, meat, cereals, and wool for sale on the world market. A great deal of money is spent on machines, fertilizer, and insecticides to help the farmer use the land to the fullest. While most workers labor only during the four-month harvest season, they receive fixed wages and, in some cases, medical and educational services.

Commercial farms are important to the Latin American economy because their products are needed for both export and domestic use. Such farms produce more than half the export earnings of Argentina, Brazil, Colombia, the Dominican Republic, Ecuador, Guatemala, Honduras, Nicaragua, and Uruguay.

EJIDOS AND MINIFUNDIOS

Not all landholdings in Latin America are large. In Mexico, for example, there are many *ejidos,* small farms owned by a community of people. There are two types of *ejidos.* One is the individual *ejido,* which is a piece of land the community gives a farmer for personal use. The farmer must agree not to sell or mortgage the land and to cultivate it for two years. Failure to meet the terms of the agreement means loss of the land. The other is the collective *ejido,* a farm on which the members work together. Each member's share of the harvest depends on how much labor he or she has contributed.

The most common type of Latin American landholding, however, is the **minifundio,** a 2- to 15-acre [.8–6 hectare] farm. Most *minifundios* are too small and their soil too poor to provide a decent living for the family that owns or works them. This often forces these people to find other ways to earn additional income. Some sell produce in the marketplace or run small stores. Others make handicrafts to sell. Still others go to work for larger landowners. But, even when they do this, very often they still do not earn enough for more than the barest essentials.

The life of these peasants is hard. Below, a Chilean woman tells her story. Like that of many others, hers is really not a story of a woman or of family life, but of work:

> I was born and grew up in Reinoso, and I came to San Felipe when my father died. My birth had never been registered, so when I applied, the Civil Registrar asked me, "Do you want to be registered as born in 1915?" I said yes, so that makes me sixty-nine years old. My mother left me with my grandmother and some aunts when I was seven months old; when my grandmother died, I was eight years old, and I had to go to live with my stepmother. That is when I went to work.
>
> My father was given a small piece of land, and I worked it with him planting garlic, peppers, and tobacco for sale in town. At home we also had a garden, where we planted beans, potatoes, and other things to be kept for winter use. Sometimes the house got real crowded in the winter as we kept three or four sacks of wheat to make flour or *harina tostada* [toasted wheat]. Then we had boxes of things like tallow to be stored there also.
>
> I worked all year round, in the winter because that's when garlic was planted. What I earned, I had to give to my stepmother. She was in charge of the money. I didn't know what shoes were until I was

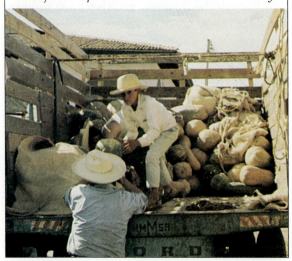
Fresh produce is brought to towns from commercial farms by the truckload. Because refrigeration is not common, the produce must be sold quickly. Why are these farms important to the Latin American economy?

Above 11,000 feet (3300 meters), in the Andes, is the bleak plateau known as the Altiplano, which extends from Peru through Bolivia and Argentina into Chile. In this photo, a woman watches her sheep grazing on the sparse vegetation of the Bolivian Altiplano. Her life, like that of many other poor Latin Americans, is one of long days and hard work. What role does work play in the life of the Chilean woman from San Felipe?

ten years old. The first time I used them, I fell down and finally had to take them off so that I could walk. Lots of times I walked to town with my shoes in my hands.

I also had to help in the house; I came in from the field, got washed, and then I had to clean, scrub, or do other things. By the time I was nineteen, I began to work as a cook in a house in town. But I always went out to pick beans and do field work in season.

When I was twenty-six, I got married, but that didn't work out. My husband ran off with someone else, and I was left alone with three children. Two died; the oldest, Carlitos, went into the hospital when he was twelve. He had heart trouble and died after five years. Then I had a daughter, Carmen. She died, too. That left me with one child, Juan.

When I was young, I never wanted to work at daily wages but always worked on contract because I worked hard. I worked as hard as two men. It was never too cold or too wet for me to work. I could always put food on the table for my family.

In this area, women usually work in the fields. I couldn't get used to being in the house, I had to go out to work. I never had the chance to go to school. I learned to read by myself. I can read anything, but I don't know how to write. I learned to sign my name when I was already a woman. I found out then how to take care of my own money, that I earned by the sweat of my brow.

Then, when I was 38 years old, I got together with Abel. After that I worked in the stables; in the summer cutting beans; and then picking and taking apart nuts; in the winter I picked onions. I always worked, whether it was raining or not. Abel didn't work if it was raining.

Well, I'm old now. It's been eight years since I have gone into the fields. There is not enough work for everyone, and they say, "Let the young ones work to feed their families." Work is all I have ever done. Now, I have to wait for someone to take care of me. I know that I could still work harder than some of them, if they would only let me. *Qué puedo hacer?* What can I do?*

1. What do *campesinos* hope to gain through agrarian reform?
2. What kinds of landholdings are there in Latin America today? In what ways are they the same? Different?

---

*Doña Juana as cited in *Y los campos eran nuestros*, Vol. II *La Realidad* by María Elena Cruz and Rigoberto Rivera, 1984, Study by el Grupo de Investigaciones Agrarias de la Academia de Humanismo Cristiano, pp. 29–32. Special adaptation and translation by Donald W. Waddell.

CASE STUDY
LATIN AMERICA

UNRESOLVED PROBLEMS

While industrialization has brought many positive changes, it has not solved some of the problems plaguing many Latin American nations. Chief among the problems that still exist is hunger. Below, a Brazilian journalist describes how some Brazilians living in large cities are coping with the problem.

Every afternoon at 1:30 a siren in São Paulo signals that it is time for fruit and vegetable dealers to take down their stands on the city's streets. The siren also alerts people in the slums, middle class neighborhoods, and some wealthy areas to begin their hunt for what no one was willing to buy: wilted lettuce, rotten tomatoes, overripe bananas, scraps of meat. The scene is repeated in Rio de Janeiro and every other large Brazilian city. The crowd that assembles to fight over this garbage includes not only the ragged poor, who have always come, but also the well-dressed—some with metal carts in which to take it home.

Two thirds of the population of Brazil eats fewer calories daily than the UN Food and Agriculture Organization considers necessary. In the poor Northeast, even before the present drought, only two out of every ten individuals had been getting enough food to be well nourished. In the developed South and Southeast, less than half the population has been eating an adequate number of calories. Of every thousand Brazilians born alive, 82 per cent die before their first birthday, for reasons related to malnutrition. . . . Brazilians now pay 250 per cent more for rice, beans, milk, sugar, and soybean oil than they did last November. Wages have risen only 90 per cent during the same period. . . .

Even the millions of Brazilians who still go to the markets to buy rather than to pick through the remains have had to learn to eat less. They now drink tea rather than milk, buy chicken necks rather than breasts, fry with lard rather than soybean oil. They buy a minimum of coffee, butter, eggs, fruit, and chocolate. Shops in the slums around São Paulo report that they sold 30 per cent less food in August than in July—even though, like the supermarkets outside Rio, they offer credit.*

1. What do some Brazilians living in large cities do to combat hunger? What Brazilians do this?
2. Does the situation discussed above occur in your country? If so, in what areas? What do you think could be done to improve the situation?

*"The Hungry of Brazil" by Isto, E, reprinted in *World Press Review*, November 1983, p. 55. Reprinted by permission.

THE STATE OF DEVELOPMENT

Many Latin Americans believe that industrial development will take care of most of their problems, make them self-sufficient, and provide them with the higher standard of living they desire. Although in recent years there have been great increases in the production of electrical energy, steel, automobiles, oil, cement, paper, and other products, it has not been enough to meet the needs of the growing population.

There are many reasons why industry has not grown as fast as some would like. Included are lack of money and of skilled labor and too few transportation systems. Most Latin Americans just do not have enough purchasing power to support rapid industrial expansion. Still, some Latin American countries are making headway. As discussed in the magazine article below, Puerto Rico is one of these:

> Puerto Rico's industrial revolution —Operation Bootstrap—has drawn nearly 2,600 plants to the island since the early 1950's. . . . But today there are mixed feelings about Bootstrap's effects.
>
> "It gave us more than we had, which was nothing," said Jose R. Madera, Puerto Rico's economic-development administrator. But most of the new plants were subsidiaries of off-island companies with limited capital investment in Puerto Rico. Many took advantage of the benefits, then left when wages rose. . . .
>
> Puerto Rico is now going through a painful rebuilding of its industrial dream. Fomento, as Madera's agency is called, is wooing drug and high-technology companies to build and invest here and create a skilled work force, which will tie them firmly to the island. As we clattered by helicopter across the cordillera [chain of mountains], he pointed out new industrial buildings that had sprung up in the mountain valleys. In all, 87 pharmaceutical plants are now operating on the island, producing everything from artificial kidneys to most of the world's supply of Valium.
>
> At Humacao, a small east coast town, we landed near a modern one-story building that draws ailing pilgrims from all over

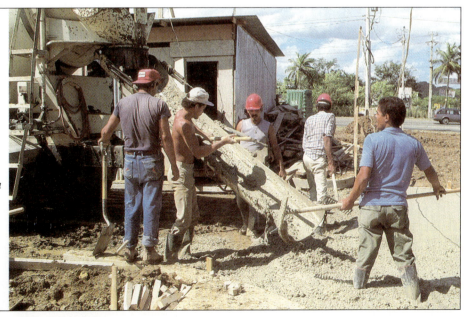

In many Latin American countries, more and more emphasis is being put on development. In recent years, workers like these, who are pouring and spreading wet cement at a large construction site in Puerto Rico, are becoming a common sight. How do many Latin Americans expect industrial development to help them?

the world. This is no religious shrine but Medtronic, Inc., a Minnesota-based firm that makes heart pacemakers here. . . .

Inside a large sterilized room I watched Puerto Rican technicians in surgical gowns assemble the devices. Medtronic has produced 150,000 pacemakers here since 1978. . . .

Thirty-five years of industrial growth has pushed development into nearly every corner of the island. Operation Bootstrap has spread factories into many formerly unspoiled areas and has built up population in previously low-population regions.*

Another Latin American country making industrial and economic progress is Paraguay. Below, a journalist discusses some of the changes taking place there:

Long one of the poorest nations of the Western Hemisphere, . . . the country now boasts one of the fastest growing per capita incomes in Latin America. . . . Traditionally reliant on cotton, cattle, tobacco, and citrus for foreign exchange, it will soon lead the world as an exporter of hydroelectric power.

A decade ago the city of Asunción was focused on its port facilities. . . . No longer. The action now has moved inland to the downtown area. Tall office buildings are sprouting there by the dozens, and fast-charging automobile traffic only grudgingly shares the city streets with antique yellow trolley cars. . . .

With its stable currency and a quarter century of comparative order . . . , Asunción has become a banking center. . . .

. . . In a chartered plane I flew over [Guaira Falls], marveling at the sight of a slow-moving river suddenly roaring into life. . . .

Not much longer will anyone witness the sight; soon the Paraná [River] will back up behind the giant Itaipu Dam, and rising waters will drown the spectacular falls.

We flew on to Itaipu, . . . one of the mightiest construction projects on earth. From above it was an ugly landscape of red earth and raw gray concrete. But to most Paraguayans it surely must be beautiful, for it symbolizes an economic future filled with promise.

I toured the project with . . . an engineer on the technical control staff. "It's the largest hydro dam in the world," he stated proudly. "After it goes fully on stream in 1988, it will produce 12,600 megawatts, six times as much electricity as Egypt's Aswan High Dam."

In addition to the 18 giant turbines at this site, which are shared with Brazil, two other dams, in partnership with Argentina, will harness the Paraná farther downstream. . . .

Though Argentines began buying Paraguayan properties heavily in the 1880s, there was little investment from overseas. "Businessmen just didn't trust a country that changed governments as often as we did," he said. "But Stroessner [the president] has brought us more than a quarter of a century of stability. Europeans, North

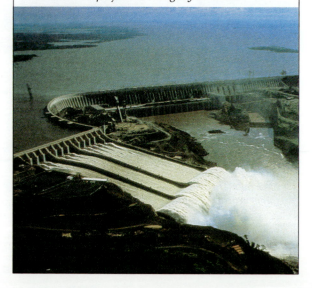

Dams, such as the Itaipú Dam, owned jointly by Paraguay and Brazil, are converting Latin America's water power into electricity. In what other industrial and economic projects is Paraguay involved?

---

*"The Uncertain State of Puerto Rico" by Bill Richards in *National Geographic*, Vol. 163, No. 4, April 1983, pp. 531–532. Reprinted by permission.

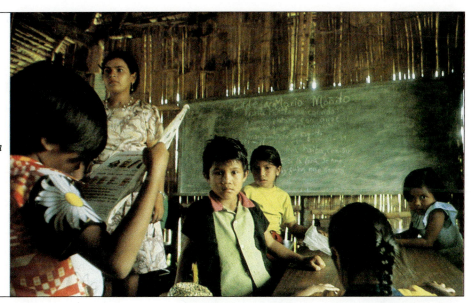

In a bamboo schoolroom in rural Nicaragua, which is not unlike rural classrooms in other Latin American countries, a student reads a lesson aloud to his classmates. Who controls public school education in most Latin American countries?

Americans, and Japanese are interested now. . . ."

He waved toward a sea of new houses and barracks that flowed up the hills ahead of our car. "Workers' quarters. Close to 40,000 people have worked on the Paraguayan side of the dam. It wiped out unemployment and turned Puerto Presidente Stroessner . . . into a boomtown. . . ."*

1. What industrial and economic progress has been made in Latin America in recent years?
2. What problems do Latin Americans face in striving for industrialization?

THE STATE OF EDUCATION

For many years, large numbers of Latin Americans could not afford to go to school, and many were illiterate. Today, education is free in most of Latin America. This, however, has not solved all the problems. The literacy rate remains low in many countries, and there are too few schools and teachers. More than half the teachers, especially in rural areas, do not have teaching degrees. All have little prestige and are paid very poorly.

In most countries, public schools are controlled by the government, which decides when and where to build schools, what teachers to hire, what courses to teach, and what books students will use. Often, the officials responsible for these decisions have had little or no experience as educators. As a result, education remains an important issue in Latin America today.

PUBLIC AND PRIVATE SCHOOLS

In Latin America, children generally start school at the age of six or seven and spend about six years in grade schools and six in secondary school. Some go on to college. Below, a teacher discusses the system in her home—Puerto Rico:

In Puerto Rico, there are elementary, intermediate, and high schools. There also are colleges and universities. Everyone has

*"Paraguay, Paradox of South America" by Gordon Young in *National Geographic*, Vol. 162, No. 2, August 1982, pp. 240, 242–244, 250. Reprinted by permission.

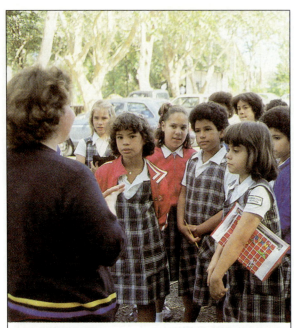

Uniformed private school students on a field trip listen to their teacher explain the day's lesson. What are some of the differences between public and private schools in Latin America?

the right to a public school education, and elementary and intermediate schooling are obligatory. High school and college are not.

In addition to public schools, we have two kinds of private schools—secular and parochial. Although most of the parochial schools are Catholic, there are some Lutheran, Baptist, and Episcopalian ones as well. The private schools generally are called *colegios*, a term also used at times to refer to universities. Entrance requirements and fees for the private schools depend on the school and where it is located.

Parents pay for their children's schooling. In both the public and the private schools, the students wear uniforms, for which parents also pay. In the public schools, the books are free, but in the private schools, parents have to pay for them.*

---
* Interview with Wanda I. Feliciano, teacher, April 1985. Reprinted by permission.

Most of the countries of Latin America have both public schools and private schools. In most cases, those people who can afford it prefer to send their children to private school. As a Brazilian journalist indicates below, in her country, private school vs. public school education has become a major issue:

During the 1970s, the "economic miracle" fed the illusion that the sons and daughters of the middle class could go to private schools, and they virtually abandoned the public school system. Now that it is clear that the "miracle" was but a farce, the situation is being reversed at an alarming rate.

Without the means to pay tuition at private schools, these families now are looking for refuge in the public school system, an institution that shows the classic symptoms of underdevelopment: low salaries for the teachers, inadequate classrooms and insufficient teaching materials.

In the past three years, the public school system in São Paulo . . . grew by between 2 and 3 percent a year. At the same time, the private school network began to shrink. One pessimistic estimate put its loss of students at around 10 percent.

This means that as many as 50,000 students will be descending on the public schools which . . . are unable to provide the quality and variety of education that the middle class is accustomed to receiving in private schools.

In a 1982 survey of 400 housewives in five large Brazilian state capitals, 25 percent said they had been forced to put their children in public schools. For the middle-class family that traditionally considers "a good education as our most important legacy to our children," such a move carries with it connotations of social decay.

Only one of the housewives whose children had transferred to public school said that "it was wonderful." All the others admitted to being worried and apprehensive. . . .

Distant from . . . ideological, political and philosophical discussions, Brazilian children deal with the situation the best they can. Such is the case of the Ribeiro do Valle family. The father, Jaime, is a 45-year-old architect. . . . The mother, Cecilia, 35, is a fashion designer for a São Paulo boutique. . . . The couple has two children: Luciana, 5, and Marcos, 12. Until last year, the children attended a private school. . . .

"It was too much for our budget," says Jaime Ribeiro do Valle. . . . Adds Cecilia: "I know its risky, but there is no other way. If they had stayed at private school we would have had to cut our food expenditures."

Luciana . . . has no idea of what the change means. For her it is simply a matter of new friends, a new environment. . . . Such is not the case for her brother Marcos, today in the fifth grade of a public school. "I don't like it at all," he says. "The teachers give no attention to us, and besides I'm learning things I already know."*

VOCATIONAL AND AGRICULTURAL SCHOOLS

The aim of vocational schools is to train students to be skilled and technical workers, which are in short supply in Latin America. Although some Latin American countries actively promote this type of education, there is not always enough financial support to maintain the schools.

Less than 40 percent of Latin American students take such courses as industrial arts, home economics, and agriculture. One reason for this is that by the time they are 12 or 13 years old, the age required to take part in vocational training, many of them no longer are in school. In addition, vocational training and many of the jobs to which it leads are associated with manual labor, which traditionally has been looked down upon by Latin Americans.

At an adult level, however, vocational and agricultural training has met with success in some countries. As the article below indicates, this is the case in Honduras:

Nearer to Tegucigalpa on the route from Las Manos, I met . . . men uniformly dressed—students in denim. They planted bananas, sacked seed corn, and sprayed insecticide. The Pan-American Agricultural School at El Zamorano believes in getting dirt under the fingernails.

"The trouble with most agricultural schools in Latin America is that they produce *agrónomos* who don't know what to do when they hit reality," said Dr. Simon E. Malo, the school's director. "You don't learn farming just by reading books."

At the urging of Samuel Zemurray [a U.S. planter], . . . the United Fruit Company founded this school in 1942; it is independent of the government.

No agricultural school in Latin America enjoys a better reputation. Students work hundreds of hours on its 12,000-acre [4800-hectare] farm, besides going to classes. This labor helps the school earn half a million dollars a year from vegetables and seed. Some 15 nations . . . are represented among this year's 425 students. . . .

Food production lags in Honduras and other Latin American nations, which import much of what they eat. "There aren't nearly enough trained men to take information to the farmer," Dr. Malo said. He hopes the school can find funds to quadruple enrollment.*

1. What problems does education face in Latin America today?
2. What role do vocational and agricultural schools play in Latin America?

---

*"Brazil's recession forces parents to pull their children from private schools" by Regina Echeverría in *WorldPaper,* January 1984, p. 12. Reprinted by permission.

*"Honduras: Eye of the Storm" by Mike Edwards in *National Geographic,* Vol. 164, No. 5, November 1983, pp. 631–632. Reprinted by permission.

EXPLORATION
LATIN AMERICA

Despite its current economic difficulties, the economies of Latin America have changed significantly over the past 50 years. Therefore, to gauge the economic situation in Latin America, one must look beyond the present into the future. Read the article that follows, in which an author predicts the economic future of Latin America. Then, based on the information in the chapter and in this Exploration, answer these questions:

1. What factors cause the author to predict a brighter economic future for Latin America?
2. How do you think events in other parts of the world affect the economic growth of Latin America?
3. What factors within Latin America do you think will aid economic growth?
4. Do you agree with the author's appraisals and predictions? Why or why not?

. . . Enormous Brazilian state-run companies are now driving U.S. and Japanese companies out of Third World markets, showing that state-owned corporations can out-compete privately managed firms. . . . In short, some highly significant changes are occurring in Latin America that the rest of the world has hardly noticed. But as Europe stagnates economically, and as Japanese products lose some of their faddish attractiveness, the economic potential of Latin America will become more apparent.

Many problems plague the region. Increasingly vulnerable national and world economic systems, an atmosphere foreboding violence and disorder, and a widening gap between rich and poor all lead to a feeling that the next 20 years in Latin America will be difficult. . . .

However, other trends lead to a more positive outlook for the next 20 years. For example, the most dynamic centers of world economic growth are likely to shift from today's advanced capitalist nations to emerging middle-income countries like Mexico and Brazil. Latin America's rapid economic development can be viewed as a positive step toward bringing Latin America into the arena of world trade and attention. Certainly, Latin America possesses the human and natural resources to take advantage of its increasing scientific and technological sophistication.

Several trends in Latin America are likely to affect the way the region fits into the broader pattern of world developments. . . .

. . . population will continue to increase sharply in most Latin American countries compared with the rest of the world. Significant economic growth and investment will be required just to maintain per capita income and the general well-being of the population.

Urbanization is certain to increase. Labor-force size will increase more rapidly than population growth, which will tend to depress wages. . . .

Another likely consequence of rapid population growth in Latin America will be increased pressure to emigrate. . . . In the 1980s and 1990s, there will be sharp increases in an undocumented immigration into the United States far beyond anything so far seen, which will bring on new tensions and political disputes. . . . [However,] uncertainty about Europe's economic and political future, coupled with the desire for new opportunities and markets, could cause a flood of European "refugees" into Latin America. . . .

During the next 20 years, the developed world will slow its rate of economic growth considerably, but the lesser-developed world (particularly the middle-income nations) will continue its high rate of development. This trend will profoundly affect the future of Latin America in that the dynamic growth and center of world economic activity (and, perhaps, cultural and political activities as well) will shift away from the developed nations. . . .

. . . Especially in Mexico, Brazil, Venezuela, Colombia, Argentina, and Chile, the next 20 years could see an economic dynamism that is part of a shift of world growth to undeveloped regions. To a great extent, Latin America and southern Europe would be picking up the slack in world economic *activity that will not be met by the United States and northern Europe.*

This trend probably means change in the kind of economic activity that occurs in Latin America. Increasingly, production and trade in finished manufactured products and processed minerals, rather than in agricultural resources and raw materials, will make up the bulk of export commerce. The emergence of large domestic markets will support this trend, with effects that will transcend economics and reach into education, self-image, and politics. . . .

The most significant trend identified by most business visitors to Latin America is the highly volatile inflation rate found in many of the nations. The natural question to ask is whether this state of affairs can possibly continue. . . .

Argentina has lived with an average annual inflation rate of more than 40% since the late 1940s, while Brazil has lived with inflation in excess of 30% since 1974. But what is worse than high inflation is its explosiveness: Brazilian inflation has topped 100% over the past few years, while Argentina reached nearly a 350% rate in 1976. . . .

. . . The first reaction of most North American businessmen to this seemingly unpredictable environment is that any type of long-term planning is almost impossible in Latin America. Yet many large projects have been completed, demonstrating that long-term planning is quite possible. Successful corporations match the administrative structure of business to the changeable environment, and work within a more flexible, decentralized organization that is capable of making rapid decisions based on knowledge of local conditions. . . .

The vulnerability of Latin America to foreign oil cutoffs is now realized by all governments in the region. Truly massive energy-development projects are under way to exploit regional resources. Colombia, Paraguay, Brazil, and Argentina are now undertaking vast hydroelectric projects that will ease their dependency on oil. Although the full extent of these conversion programs is not certain, enough steps are being taken that by the late 1980s a much more significant use of clean hydroelectricity is certain. To supplement this, both Brazil and Argentina are also embarking on major nuclear-power programs. Many spinoff effects will result from these ventures; perhaps most significantly, by the early 1990s either nation may be a leading Third World exporter of nuclear-power technology and components. This particular example highlights a neglected aspect of the energy crisis: the response of nations to energy problems can produce many exciting new industries and opportunities that would not otherwise occur.

Similar programs to lessen dependence on oil are taking place throughout Latin America. Nonetheless, for at least the next 10 years, the fear that sudden changes in the world oil system could produce large-scale damage to the economies of Latin American nations will be one of the leading threats to orderly growth in the region.

A very positive trend has been . . . agreements . . . to provide aid to some of the poorer nations of the Caribbean. . . .

An especially exciting prospect is that major energy discoveries will occur in Latin America. The region has great, untapped potential, as the Mexican oil discoveries indicate. Offshore explorations for oil and natural gas may be especially likely, and may result in intense political disputes over ownership rights. . . .

Taken together, trends in the areas of population, world economics, business, and energy will be a major force pulling Latin America into a more dynamic leadership role in the world. Much greater use of information-based industries will be commonplace, and vast project undertakings will inevitably capture public and world attention.

No one will call Latin America the "sleeping giant." That is the main lesson for the next 20 years, because Latin America is no longer just coping with and reacting to events in the world. In the future, Latin America will be initiating many of the changes for the rest of the world to follow.*

---

*"The Next 20 Years in Latin America" by Paul Bracken in *The Futurist*, April 1982, pp. 5–11. Reprinted by permission.

CHAPTER 31 REVIEW

POINTS TO REMEMBER

1. The population of Latin America is expected to double in the next 25 years or so. While the area's death rate has declined, the birthrate remains high due to the Catholic Church's opposition to birth control, the *macho* philosophy of many men, and the lack of information in some areas on family planning.
2. Some experts believe that the population problem in Latin America is one of distribution. The endless flow of people from the countryside to the cities especially has resulted in overpopulation of urban areas.
3. Most of the people who migrate from the countryside to the city end up living in poor conditions in slums and shantytowns. Some experts, however, do not think this is all bad and defend the existence of the settlements, arguing they are the "birthplaces of communities."
4. In recent years, Latin American *campesinos*, in search of a better life, have pressed for agrarian reform. In the meantime, many *campesinos* continue to live and work on large landholdings like the *hacienda* or the commercial farm or on small landholdings like the *ejido* or *minifundio*. In almost all cases, the life is hard, and it is almost impossible for the *campesino* to make a decent living.
5. Many Latin Americans believe that the solution to most of their problems lies in industrial development. Although industrial and economic progress has been made in some areas in recent years, it has not been enough to meet the needs of the growing population.
6. Although today education is free in most Latin American countries, it still faces many problems. These include too few schools and teachers, preference for private schools, and lack of funds for and interest in vocational and agricultural schools.

VOCABULARY

Define

macho
favelas
villas miserias

barrios
barriadas

pueblos jóvenes
campesinos

hacendado
ejidos
minifundio

DISCUSSING IMPORTANT IDEAS

1. What relationship do you see in Latin America between rapid population growth, slum conditions, and poverty? Give examples.
2. With whom do you agree—those who argue that no one should have to live or die in Latin America's shantytowns and slums, or those who argue that the settlements have positive aspects? Defend your answer.
3. Do you think, as do many Latin Americans, that industrialization can solve most

problems, make a country or region self-sufficient, and provide the people with a higher standard of living? Why or why not? What examples can you give to support your argument?

4. Why do you think education is such an important issue in Latin America today? Are any of the educational problems confronting Latin America issues in your country as well? Which ones?

Developing Skills

INTERVIEWING

Most people prefer to hear or read about an event directly from a person who has actually experienced or witnessed it. Often, this information is obtained through *interviews*, conversations or reports of conversations between two people, one seeking facts or statements from the other. There are three parts to effective interviewing—preparation, interviewing, and reporting. The following guidelines will help you execute each of these procedures:

Preparation

1. Identify the topic of the interview, and determine who can provide reliable information about it.
2. Research the topic and the person(s) you are going to interview. You will base most of your interview questions on what you learn from your research.
3. Arrange the interview by writing or telephoning the person(s) you plan to interview. Identify yourself, and request an interview. Explain the purpose of the interview, specifying the kind of information you need. Set up an appointment, indicating how long the interview will take. Ask permission to take notes or record the interview.
4. Prepare appropriate questions. Each question should have a specific purpose and lead logically from one to the other.
5. Assemble tools and equipment, such as a notebook, pens and pencils, a dictionary, and a cassette recorder. If you plan to use a recorder, check to make sure that it works properly, that you have enough cassettes to last the length of the interview, and that there is an electrical outlet into which to plug it.

Interviewing

1. Introduce yourself, and explain again the purpose of the interview.
2. Ask your questions slowly and clearly. Listen carefully to the responses, keeping in mind that you must be prepared to ask logical follow-up questions. Ask for clarification of points you do not understand and the spellings of unfamiliar names or terms. Record direct quotations exactly.
3. End the interview by asking for and recording accurately the person's name; position, occupation, or title; and location or place of business. Ask permission to use direct quotes. Thank the person for the interview.

Reporting

1. Based on the information in your notes and/or on your recorder, write up the interview.
2. Read what you have written to determine if you have covered the topic thoroughly, clearly, and accurately. Make the necessary changes or corrections.

For practice in this skill, follow the suggested guidelines, and interview one of your classmates about his or her views on the population explosion as discussed on pages 498 through 502.

CHAPTER 32
DICTATORSHIPS AND DEMOCRACIES

1. What were the characteristics of traditional Latin American politics?
2. What are the characteristics of modern Latin American politics?

Since our independence we Argentines have always believed that we have inherited a culture and a body of ideals centered on the dignity of the human being.

But we also belong irreversibly to Latin America. . . . From this region of the world, together with other Latin countries, we have been developing a universe of values and aspirations that define a particular way of belonging in the world. . . .

Let me state clearly: I hold democracy to be the only form of social organization that allows man his dignity. . . .

[Alexis de]Toqueville [French writer] knew that a country would be strong only if it was based on the liberty and well-being of its people and that peace is prerequisite for greatness and prosperity. We Argentines, as do all Latin Americans, perceive these words to be a precise statement of our predicament. We know only too well of our own efforts to consolidate democracy and dissipate . . . suspicion and mistrust of one another. . . .

Our America needs democracy, development and security. Two fundamental causes conspire today against achieving these objectives: the situation in Central America and the social and economic conditions in Latin America. . . .

How can we break the cycle of violence that has bled the continent over the last decades? . . . Experience shows us that the strengthening of democracy, progress, and the prosperity of our peoples and the peace and security of the continent . . . are intimately intertwined. Starting from this premise, we must find the practical solutions to immediately address the two problems that we face today. . . .

The peace and prosperity of the people of Central America, the consolidation of the democratic processes throughout the continent and the security of a hemisphere that wants to preserve its style of life, depend on adequate solutions. . . . More than one hundred years ago a great Argentine intellectual and politician, Juan Bautista Alberdi, who established the foundations of our constitution said:

". . . The time of the heroes has passed, we enter today the age of common sense. Greatness in America is not the greatness of Napoleon, it is the greatness of Washington who does not represent military victory but rather prosperity, growth, organization and peace. He is the hero of order in liberty." It is this thought today I make my own.*

In the above speech, Argentine president Raul Alfonsín spoke of the need for democracy in Latin America and of the "causes" that had to be resolved to achieve that goal. But, even as he spoke, much of Latin America was in a state of political turmoil, and the practice of democracy was unknown to many Latin Americans.

Political instability is not a new development in Latin America. Revolution, dictatorships, and military takeovers are an integral part of the Latin American political tradition.

---

*"Argentina: Understanding Reality," speech delivered by Raul Alfonsin, President of the Argentine Republic, before a Joint Meeting of Congress, Washington, D.C., March 20, 1985, as cited in *Vital Speeches*, April 15, 1985, pp. 395–397. Reprinted by permission.

THE OLD TRADITION

In the 1800's, political affairs in most of Latin America were controlled by a small group made up of rich landowners, army officers, clergy, merchants, intellectuals, and professionals. Most of the rest of the people failed to vote, were denied the vote, or voted as they were told to by those in power. Generally, they accepted the rule of the minority. For the most part, the Latin American minority who were involved in politics were divided into two separate groups —**conservatives** and **liberals**. The conservatives consisted mostly of the upper class and the clergy. The liberals consisted mostly of merchants and professionals. Both groups were satisfied with life as it was and had little or no interest in helping the lower class. Their major concerns were form of government and Church-State relations.

The conservatives, who wanted to keep the social system as it was, favored a strong central government, a powerful president, and a weak legislature. The liberals, who wanted changes that would bring them greater wealth, social status, and political power, sought local self-rule, a weak president, and a strong legislature. The liberals especially wanted to curb the influence of the Church and the army. Their attacks on the Church met with a fair amount of success. Their attacks on the army, however, had little effect, and it was not uncommon for the military to step in and take over a government. Most of the soldiers who gained control were more interested in personal gain and power than in helping the people or instituting change. An example, described below, was Mariano Melgarejo, who ruled Bolivia from 1864 to 1870:

> Melgarejo . . . was a man without the most basic notion of government. He did not even represent any political belief. He was not supported by anyone who, on his own, could have raised a banner that would have captured the sympathies of the masses. For the moment there was

Military leaders of the 1800's, known as caudillos, *included (left to right) Mexican presidents General Antonio López de Santa Anna and General Porfirio Díaz, and Argentinian ruler General Manuel de Rosas. What role did the military play in politics in the 1800's?*

only one sure fact. Melgarejo had engineered a revolution. But for whom?

A man of humblest origin, his education was the training he had in the barracks. Melgarejo's whole life was made up of treason and crimes.

Before it had been in power a month, the new government issued two decrees. By a stroke of the pen, they did away with the Constitution of 1861.

The country began to show alarm. It plainly saw that this soldier would trample underfoot all its institutions. Armed protests broke out, in the name of upholding the Constitution.

After Melgarejo put down the revolts, the whole country gave up. And the same men who in secret talked against using force yielded too and forsook their principles. They even went further. Many rushed to offer their services to the victor, who found himself surrounded, through fear, by the best elements in the country.

At this time, it was very fashionable to drink many toasts at the palace banquets. Each of the guests was eager to show his allegiance.

When his turn came, one of the guests spoke in words of praise of the new charter which would surely govern the acts of Melgarejo.

Melgarejo's instant response was brutal.

"I want the gentleman who has just spoken and all the deputies gathered here to know that I have put the Constitution of 1861, which was very good, in this pocket" (pointing to his left trouser pocket) "and that of 1868, which is even better in the opinion of these gentlemen, in this one" (pointing to his right pocket). "Nobody is going to rule Bolivia but me."*

Not all political leaders of the era, however, were in the military or like Melgarejo. Some, like liberal Benito Juárez, who served

Visitors to the birthplace of Mexican president Benito Juárez view a large mural depicting important events in his life. Why did many Mexicans think Juárez was a good governor?

as president of Mexico from 1858 to 1872, cared about the people and wanted reforms. Below, an author provides some insights into the life and goals of Juárez:

> Benito Juárez . . . was the first Indian ruler since Cuauhtemoc [the Aztec ruler]. Benito grew up in the . . . southern town of Oaxaca, where he lived in the streets most of the time, more often hungry than not. . . .
>
> As Benito grew older, a priest noticed the thoughtful black eyes under shaggy hair and offered to teach him. The boy learned quickly. He went to school and later studied law. And then, while still a young man, he became Governor of Oaxaca.
>
> Benito Juárez was a good governor. People talked to him with respect because he was honest, and he saw that those who worked under him were honest. Where so

---

*Adapted from "Los caudillos bárbaros" by Alcides Arguedas in *The Green Continent*, edited by Germán Arciniegas and translated by Harriet de Onís, 1944, Alfred A. Knopf, Inc., pp. 205–207, 222. Reprinted by permission.

many officials accepted bribes and made fortunes one way or another while in office, Juárez was never known to have taken a centavo beyond his salary. . . . He said little, but when he spoke, people listened.

Years before, . . . Juárez was imprisoned for opposing [the dictator Santa Anna]. He soon escaped to New Orleans, however, where he made cigars for a living. He returned to Mexico . . . and was named Minister of Justice. His new laws provided for the sale of church property not used for worship and restricted the political power of the Catholic Church. Soon the church sympathizers revolted and civil war broke out. Juárez and his companions were hunted from town to town and many people were killed. It was at this point that his opponents imported Emperor Maximilian and the troops of Napoleon.

For several years, Juárez lived near the northern border of Mexico, going from place to place in his black carriage. In the resistance to the French, it was he who held out and finally defeated Maximilian. . . .

After the war with the French, Juárez undertook many reforms. He started schools to educate Indian children and reduced the size of the army. This angered the officers who tried to start revolts. Juárez also met resistance from the church. He was so opposed by powerful landowners that he was unable to give out much land to the people who needed it. . . .

Even though Juárez had little time to carry out his plans for his country—he died shortly after he was re-elected to the presidency in 1871—he was greatly loved and mourned.*

1. What groups controlled Latin American politics in the 1800's? Why were they so powerful?

2. What did conservatives and liberals have in common? In what ways were they different?
3. What were Melgarejo's ideals and actions in regard to political rule? What were Juárez's?

THE NEW TRADITION

By the end of the 1800's, some Latin Americans felt there was a need to modernize. They believed that to accomplish the needed social and economic changes, the traditional style of politics had to be destroyed. In some countries, labor began to organize, and the middle class began to voice its political opinions. The workers supported the middle class in its efforts to gain free elections. In return, the middle class worked to pass social welfare laws.

Today, the desire for social change dominates Latin American politics, and the few conservative parties that remain active are not strong. In recent years, pressure groups have become common. Among these are the

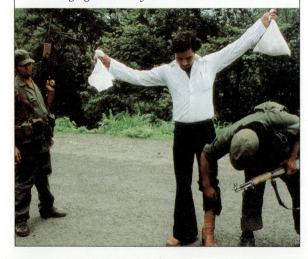

Armed Nicaraguan soldiers search a man at a checkpoint during a raging civil war in 1979. How have the goals and attitudes of the military in Latin America been changing in recent years?

---

*From *The Mexican Story* by May McNeer Ward and Lynd Ward. Copyright 1953 by May McNeer Ward and Lynd Ward. Copyright renewed ©1981 by May McNeer Ward. Reprinted by permission of Farrar, Straus, and Giroux, Inc.

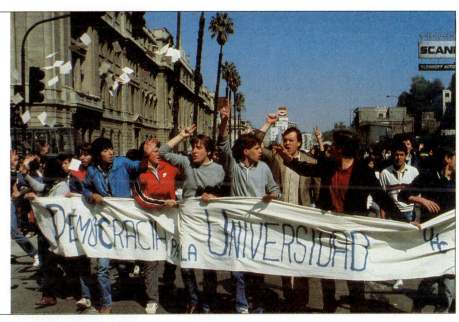

College students, carrying a banner calling for "Democracy for the University," stage an anti-government demonstration in Santiago, Chile, to protest government control of university life. Besides students, what other pressure groups exist in Latin American politics? Which is by far the most important?

Catholic Church, wealthy landowners, organized labor, and college students. But by far the most powerful pressure group is the army. It has the deciding voice in almost every Latin American country and has seized power on a regular basis in the region. At any one time, one-half of the Latin American nations may be ruled by the military.

Although in most cases today's military shows little concern for democracy, it does not have the same goals or attitudes of the military of the past. The strongest branch of the military remains the army. Most of its officers favor economic development, and many support social reform. There are several reasons for this change of attitude. One is that today most Latin American military officers come from the middle or lower class. Therefore, they tend to be favorable to the middle-class outlook and support the middle-class desire for economic modernization. Another reason is that today a professional outlook dominates in the military, and great stress is placed on producing an officer corps thoroughly trained in all aspects of military life. Officers must receive the equivalent of a college degree at a military academy and receive their promotions on the basis of examinations.

The new professionalism of the military has not lessened its intervention in politics. In most cases, as part of their training, members of the military are taught that economic modernization is important to their country, and many have come to believe that the government should make extensive use of its power to stimulate this modernization. For many, this means starting government-owned industries.

As in the past, the military will not hesitate to intervene in and even overthrow governments that pursue policies of which it does not approve. In some cases, this action is brought on by a fervent concern for economic development. In others, it is the result of dissatisfaction with the ineffectiveness, unconstitutionality, corruptness, or weakness of a civilian government. And in still others, it is seen as a solution to unresolvable power struggles between civilian powers.

In most cases, military interventions have at least some civilian support. Some civilian groups believe they will profit from a military intervention, while others believe that the military is the only group strong enough to maintain internal order or keep unprincipled politicians in line. Regardless of the reason for the intervention, once in power, most military governments rarely establish a better record than civilian governments when it comes to solving economic problems or battling corruption.

1. Why did some Latin Americans want to destroy the traditional style of politics?
2. What dominates Latin American politics today?
3. What is the role of the military in Latin American politics today?

REACTION TO CHANGE

Since the 1800's, all of Latin America has undergone some form of change, and different governments have responded in different ways. Some nations have experienced radical change in which efforts were made to alter the socio-economic structure on a drastic scale. Others have experienced more conservative change in which the government has tried to halt or slow down socio-economic change. While both types of response have been successful in some Latin American countries, in others they have led to a loss or abandoning of democratic practices, power struggles, and war. Three nations that have undergone or are undergoing major change are Cuba, Nicaragua, and El Salvador.

CUBA

In 1959, Fidel Castro took power in Cuba and made it the first Marxist nation in the Western Hemisphere. He promised the Cuban people much-needed reforms and a better standard of living. Today, more than 25 years since he took power, Castro remains

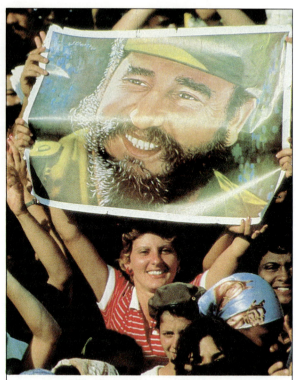

A jubilant crowd in Havana, the capital of Cuba, carries aloft a larger-than-life poster of Fidel Castro during a recent celebration to honor Cuba's war dead. When did Castro come to power in Cuba?

firmly in control. In the article below, a journalist tells what life is like under the Castro government:

> It is true that tough Communist control directs virtually every segment of Cuban life and shows no sign of easing.
> It is also true that about 1 million Cubans have fled since Castro seized power . . . and that up to 500,000 more would leave the island if given the chance. Yet most of the nearly 10 million Cubans know no rule but Communism. They support and admire Castro. . . .
> Even the most skeptical foreign residents of Havana admit that life today for the average Cuban is better than when Castro took over. Luxuries may be few, but the state satisfies the basic needs of the people for food, clothing, housing, education, medical care and jobs.

The quality of daily life is rising slowly, although Cubans still must queue up to board crowded buses or to enjoy restaurant meals that are better and more varied than their rationed fare at home. . . .

A senior Cuban official claims that the purchasing power of the people is "high and rising." He reports that 2.9 million Cubans, 40 percent of them women, have jobs. . . .

In a major revision of economic policy, the government has abandoned the Communist tenet that all citizens should share equally for their labors. . . .

In this revolutionary nation, virtually everybody wears jeans either locally made or provided by relatives abroad. Designers stage shows of Cuban fashions for women. . . .

With some relaxation of Communist control over the economic system, a new affluent class is emerging—electricians, plumbers, painters, and mechanics. After work at state enterprises, they are permitted to moonlight as private entrepreneurs. . . .

Day-to-day life may be improving on the island, but the cost of creating Castro's Communist society has been high for the Cuban people.

The majority of Cubans were born after 1959 or were under 21 when Castro took over. They have no knowledge or memory of personal liberties, and they are inured to a Communist state that systematically directs their lives. . . .

Everything that Cubans see on television, hear on the radio or read in their newspapers has been carefully chosen and edited by their Communist government. . . .

Cubans understand full well the rules laid down by their leaders, and most obey unquestioningly. . . .

Communist indoctrination is found everywhere. At their recent graduation to become officers in the armed forces, smartly uniformed men and women vowed—each on bended knee—never to surrender to American imperialism. . . .

Cubans are grateful for the Soviet aid they receive—more than 4 billion dollars a year in economic help and about 1 billion in military assistance. But they also make it clear that they hold no great love for the Soviet people, and they resent any

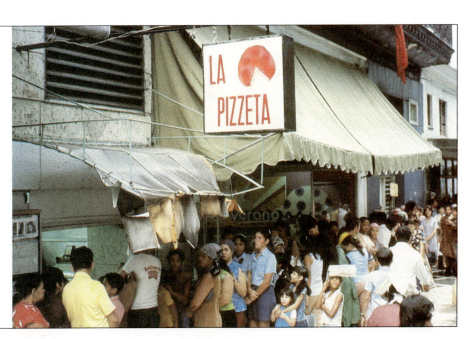

Cubans have become accustomed to waiting in lines for service. Here, customers wait to be seated in a pizza parlor in downtown Havana. How has daily life improved in Cuba in recent years?

Many Nicaraguan youths, like this 14-year-old soldier, are routinely rounded up by the Sandinista National Liberation Front (FSLN) to fight the Contras. *How did the Sandinistas come to power?*

suggestion that Moscow is being generous. "It's their Communist duty to help us," a senior official insists.

In contrast, warmth toward the U.S. pervades, even among Communists. Despite years of indoctrination, most Cubans still respect America. . . .

Restoration of relations with the U.S. —without renouncing the Communist system—has been a Castro dream. . . .

Castro has not abandoned his dream even after 25 years in power. . . .

Talks with other Cuban leaders confirm their hope that the next 25 years of Cuban development will be linked to the U.S. as well as to Moscow. They believe that the economy is ready to take off. Soviet aid is a must, they say. Yet officials note how much more "flexible" Cuba could be with U.S. technology, financing and markets.

If peace replaces confrontation, they say, Cuba could cut military spending and make its Communist system more democratic. "There would be risks," one leader concedes, "but we cannot remain forever a closed society."*

NICARAGUA

In 1979, after 40 years of rule by his family, Nicaraguan dictator Anastasio Somoza Debayle was overthrown and replaced by the Sandinista National Liberation Front. The Sandinistas promised to put an end to the civil war that was raging, revive the economy, and hold free elections. By 1984, however, conditions had worsened rather than improved, and a rebel group known as *Contras* were trying to overthrow the Sandinista government. Below, a renowned Peruvian novelist talks about the conflict and conditions there:

> Although the Sandinistas may be prepared to make almost any concession to restore peace to their country, they are obdurate about one point: They will not relinquish power. The desire to hold on to power is, of course, not peculiar to the Sandinistas. It characterizes totalitarian and authoritarian regimes. . . .
>
> Most of the opposition, however, respond angrily to any suggestion that the ruling Sandinista Front is less than totalitarian. . . .
>
> There are capable and highly intelligent men among the opposition leaders, but their overall political activity is impractical. . . .
>
> . . . they preach a legalism and an orthodox liberal democracy that Nicaragua has never had. . . .
>
> The Government and the opposition versions of the war with the contras are so

---

*"Castro's Cuba: Progress, but at a High Price" by Carl J. Migdail in *U.S. News & World Report,* August 20, 1984, pp. 33–35. Reprinted by permission.

contradictory that trying to see the two sides clearly often leads to confusion. But one point is clear: The "bourgeoisie" is not at the front. This is a war between poor men. Most of the contras . . . are peasants. . . .

The groups that have been effective in forcing the Sandinistas to modify their Marxist-Leninist intentions are the farmers and industrialists. . . .

Enrique Bolaños Geyer, a prosperous industrialist, rancher and farmer, is a steadfast critic of Sandinism. He is also president of the Superior Council of Private Enterprise (known as Cosep), the country's largest business federation. . . .

According to Cosep, the private sector is a fiction in Nicaragua. "What kind of landowners are we?" its members ask. "The state decides what we should plant and when we should plant it. We can sell only to the state, only at the price it sets. It pays in córdobas and decides when, and in what currency, it will give us money for upkeep and equipment. With the banks nationalized, we have to depend on the state for credit, too. And we live with the threat that they'll confiscate our land on the pretext that we're sabotaging the economy."

The Sandinistas' point of view is quite different. "We are saving the private sector in Nicaragua," claims Commander Wheelock [the Minister of Agrarian Reform]. . . .

"The peasant masses were hungry and angered by the exploitation they had suffered," Wheelock continues. "They were pressing for the lands, and there were many unjustified takeovers. But thanks to agrarian reform . . . and because the peasants trust us, we have avoided widespread expropriation of private holdings. We are slowly rectifying whatever abuses may have taken place. . . ."

The newspaper La Prensa is the voice and catalyst of the anti-Sandinista opposition. I attended an independent-union meeting of its employees in Managua, which had been called because the Government censor suppressed 60 percent of their copy the day before and the newspaper could not be published.

All copy must be presented to the Ministry of the Interior by midmorning. Three or four hours later, the Director of Media . . . returns the materials . . . that must be excised. . . .

Despite all this, and despite the fact that the paper comes out as late as 6 or 7 in the evening in order to comply with the censorship procedures, La Prensa sells all of the 70,000 copies permitted under the paper quota. On days La Prensa cannot publish, its readers send in the price of the paper as a token of solidarity and in recognition of La Prensa's symbolic value. . . .

Total censorship, however, is difficult to achieve. Photocopies of suppressed texts

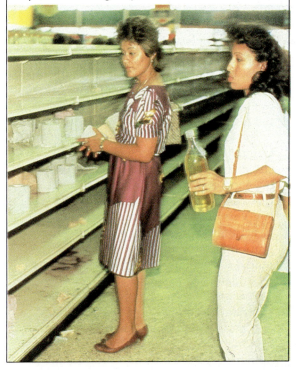

Nicaraguan shoppers like these often find empty shelves in the state-run grocery stores. A thriving black market fills the gap with imported goods. What restrictions are imposed on Nicaraguan farmers?

This 80-year-old man is working with an instructor in a literacy class in Managua. He reflects the Nicaraguan people's great desire for educational programs for themselves and their children. The government reports that 400,000 persons learned to read and write in a 1980 mass literacy campaign. What do the Sandinista Defense committees do besides support literacy campaigns?

circulate from hand to hand; people discuss them on the street and read them to each other on the telephone. And the anti-Sandinista stations . . . are heard everywhere. But the most serious consequence of censorship is the impoverishment of political debate in the news media. There is, in fact, no debate. . . .

The Sandinistas boast of having received 67 percent of the vote in the recent elections, but the organizational structures in Nicaraguan society make it difficult to determine if the figure is a real reflection of the regime's popularity.

The Cuban-style Sandinista Defense Committees organize the populace by street and district. Anyone who does not belong is an outcast, since it is through these committees that one receives the coupons to buy rationed and subsidized basic commodities. The committees also grant the certificates of good conduct required for obtaining passports, state jobs or student scholarships.

The committees have made a valuable contribution to the campaigns for literacy and mass vaccinations, and they played an important role in the success of police operations against crime and drug traffic. . . .

The war, contra sabotage, the Government's totalitarian measures, a weakening economy—all of these factors have cooled the once almost-universal support for the regime. However, broad segments of the population, especially the poor, still favor the Government.*

EL SALVADOR

In 1984, following years of political and social unrest and civil war, José Napoleón Duarte became president of El Salvador. He promised to negotiate with the leftist guerrillas who opposed the government in an attempt to bring the civil war to an end. In the article below, a journalist tells what he saw during a visit to the war-ravaged country:

There is no quiet in El Salvador because of the triki-traki [a toy that makes a staccato sound], and there's no peace because of those . . . automatic weapons . . . —the M16. You see M16s everywhere, in the markets of downtown San Salvador, on the sides of every highway, above every

---

*"In Nicaragua" by Mario Vargas Llosa in *The New York Times Magazine*, April 28, 1985, pp. 39, 41–43, 81, 92–93. Copyright ©1985 by The New York Times Company. Reprinted by permission.

bridge, atop almost every hill, and often, in the arms of mere 14-year-olds—though they are 14-year-olds in uniform. . . . El Salvador is a boy soldier, an M16 strapped to his back, a cone of coconut ice cream or a triki-traki in his hand. . . .

One morning, Big Dan, my ex-Marine photographer, and I get into Chino's cab and head out for San Agustín, a little town . . . in G [guerrilla] territory. We are about an hour out into the countryside in an area that is a battle zone. . . .

Up ahead is a once-stately suspension bridge, the Bridge of Gold, across the Lempa, El Salvador's biggest river. But the bridge is buckled and sagging, thanks to a well-placed rebel bomb. . . . We cross the bridge without any hassles from the dozens of troops who stand guard over it.

About five miles [eight kilometers] farther on, we make a turn off the pavement onto a badly washed-out road. A soldier stands on the corner where we turn, watching us. We drive about three miles [4.8 kilometers] and then from behind we hear a shot, very near. . . . A young man stands in the road, a gimme cap on his head, a white, worn-out shirt on his torso. He wears jeans and boots. He's got a rifle in his hands. He's a G.

Chino backs down the road until we come even with the G, a 24-year-old named Francie. He motions to someone in the bushes, and in seconds, we are surrounded by *muchachos*. The newspapers in El Salvador call the guerrillas "subversives" and "terrorists". . . . But the people call them *los muchachos*, the boys. . . . They are boys. The group's commander is 18, but the average age of the bunch—there are six or eight of them—can't be a day over 16.

They are well-armed, but poor. The youngest kids carry . . . M16s. . . . Those a bit older carry . . . G3s, German weapons. . . . The oldest and biggest carry FALs, Belgian automatic weapons that can hit their target with force at 500 meters [1650 feet]. But all their weapons are old by military standards, scratched and pocked with rust. Besides weapons, they don't have anything very serviceable. . . . Each man, I notice, carries a flashlight on his belt, but not all the flashlights have bulbs. Each boy has a grenade holster, but a couple of the holsters are empty. . . . They are ordinary troops of the Farabundo Martí National Liberation Front, generally known as the FMLN.

Little Alfredo, the youngest in the group, carries an M16. He is a round-faced boy of 14 with straight black hair, cut home-style. His boots look heavy; I wonder where he finds the strength to lift them. . . . He is shy. . . .

"Why did you join the revolution?" I ask him.

In the faintest voice, he stutters, "because I saw it was necessary to organize. . . ."

The purpose of the little FMLN band we've encountered is to guard the road to San Agustín. . . . We decide to meet them in the town the following day, and when we arrive, they are waiting. They're wearing the same ragtag outfits they had on the day before, but there are more of them, one of whom wears a Salvadorean navy uniform. . . .

. . . Five years ago, when combat in the area began, the power station serving [San Agustín] was disabled by a bomb. Nobody has repaired it. People in San Agustín, as in most rebel-held areas, don't have electricity anymore. . . .

There's no tap water in San Agustín either: somebody . . . bombed the town's little processing plant. When the town went dark and dry, a lot of its commerce withered. . . . The fields outside of town are sometimes planted and tilled, but agriculture—the sustenance of the whole Salvadorean economy—is a chancy affair these days. Crop-dusting planes, a necessity in the bug-ridden tropics, can't fly safely anymore. The G's shoot them down. Bridges are out and roads are unsafe. Nothing works as it should. That's why the G's, though they control San Agustín, aren't exactly conquering heroes anymore. People keep their distance from them and from us, timid and afraid. . . . They don't defend San Agustín. . . . With arms and ammunition from either side, they could stop all outsiders from entering the town. . . . Their hunger, their lack of light or facilities, their wretchedness—this is the fruit of their neutrality. . . .

A few days after our talks with the *muchachos*, Chino drove Big Dan and me out to see the San Salvador lava flow. There's an inactive volcano on the edge of the city, and on the far side of it, hard, crusted, rust-toned lava stretches for miles. . . . [If] you walk far enough into

Hundreds of Salvadorans rallied at La Palma in October 1984 in a show of support for peace talks between the rebels and the Duarte government. What can be found at the lava flow at the edge of San Salvador?

A young Salvadoran rebel soldier, barely in his teens, poses with his automatic rifle in a small guerrilla-held town. How have the people of San Agustín been affected by El Salvador's civil war?

it, . . . you will see something God and forces of nature did not put there. Bones. Human bones. Stacks of them. . . . The lava flow was a dump for men and women killed by San Salvador's Death Squads. . . . You can pick up the unclaimed bones there and toss them around the lava; they clunk and bounce, like any inert matter. But they're not inert. The history that produces them is still alive. . . . The war in El Salvador isn't going to go away.*

1. What is life like today under the Castro government?
2. What do the Sandinistas say they have accomplished? What does their opposition say in response?
3. What effect has civil war had on the people of El Salvador?

*"The Children's War" by Dick J. Reavis in *Campus Voice*, February–March 1985, pp. 22–23, 34, 36. Reprinted by permission.

EXPLORATION
LATIN AMERICA

Not all Latin American nations have been ruled by strong-arm governments all of the time. Some nations have enjoyed relatively long periods of democratic rule. Chile, for example, had an almost unblemished record of democratic governments until 1973. Uruguay adhered to democracy for most of the twentieth century until the military took over in the early 1970's. Venezuela has been a democratic nation since 1947. But, as a journalist visiting Costa Rica observed in 1981, the best record of democracy in all of Latin America is that of Costa Rica. Based on the information in his article below and in the chapter, compare and contrast Costa Rica with the other nations discussed in the chapter. Give your interpretation of Juan Bazo's statement, "Costa Rica is the land of the happy medium."

This is, I reminded myself, Central America, an isthmus haunted by discord and racked by turmoil. . . .

And yet Costa Rica, surrounded by such havoc, offers itself as a site for a university dedicated to peace. . . .

Consider: In a part of the world where government by coup is the rule rather than the exception, Costa Rica holds the role for democratic transfers of power. Of some 50 presidents since independence from Spain was declared in 1821, only three were military men and only six could be termed dictators.

Costa Rica maintains no formal military establishment; the 1949 constitution forbids it. The country has never suffered a major invasion, or occupation by a foreign power.

A nation of educators and educated, Costa Rica has the highest literacy rate (90 percent) in Central America, and boasts, correctly, of more teachers than policemen.

As close to the classless society as can be found in Latin America, it has few desperately poor and fewer fabulously wealthy citizens. Social and economic mobility in this most prosperous Central American land is possible and commonplace, thus minimizing class bitterness and resentment.

In the words of World Bank official Juan Bazo, a Peruvian, "Costa Rica is the land of the happy medium."*

*"Costa Rica Steers The Middle Course" by Kent Britt in *National Geographic,* July 1981, p. 34. Reprinted by permission.

CHAPTER 32 REVIEW

POINTS TO REMEMBER

1. Political instability is not a new development in Latin America. Revolution, dictatorships, and military takeovers are an integral part of the Latin American political tradition.
2. In the 1800's, political affairs in Latin America were controlled by a small group made up of rich landowners, army officers, clergy, merchants, intellectuals, and professionals.
3. In the 1800's, the few Latin Americans who participated in politics were divided into conservatives and liberals. Both were more concerned about form of government and Church-state relations than about helping the poor.
4. By the end of the 1800's, in an effort to bring about social and economic changes and modernize, some Latin Americans sought to destroy the traditional style of politics.
5. Today, the desire for social change dominates Latin American politics, and pressure groups are common. The most powerful pressure group is the military, which, despite its new professionalism, continues to intervene in and even topple governments. In most cases, military interventions have some civilian support.
6. Latin American governments have responded to change in a variety of ways. Three countries that have been seriously affected politically, socially, and economically in recent years are Cuba, Nicaragua, and El Salvador. Each has been affected in a different way.

VOCABULARY

Identify

Mariano Melgarejo
Benito Juárez
Fidel Castro
Anastasio Somoza Debayle
Sandinista National Liberation Front
José Napoleón Duarte
Contras

Define

conservatives
liberals

DISCUSSING IMPORTANT IDEAS

1. In most Latin American countries, the military always has had an enormous amount of prestige and power. What reasons can you give for this?
2. In the 1800's, an Argentine said that "the age of heroes has passed; we enter today the age of common sense." Do you think this was true in Latin America in the 1800's? Do you think it is true today? Explain your answers.
3. Even the least democratic governments of Latin America often are supported by the poor. Why do you think this is so? If you were a poor Latin American, could you support a government that deprived you of many of your rights? Why or why not?

4. A Nicaraguan conservative and political analyst told a reporter, "Our native Latin American culture is all powerful. It swallows up everything you give it. It assimilates everything and eventually puts its own stamp on it." What do you think he meant by this? Give examples. From what you know about Latin America, do you agree or disagree with him? Explain your answer.

DEVELOPING SKILLS

DISTINGUISHING BETWEEN FACT AND OPINION

At one time or another, everyone is faced with the need to make a decision based on the facts and opinions he or she hears or reads. These decisions may have to do with all sorts of things, ranging from what outfit to wear to a party to what kind of car to buy to which candidate to vote for in an election.

Being able to distinguish between fact and opinion will help you to make many of these decisions more effectively. A *fact* is a statement that can be verified by evidence. An *opinion* is a belief or conclusion that is not supported by proof or evidence. It is based on what someone thinks may be true based on what he or she knows, thinks, or feels. Opinions often contain such terms as *I believe, probably, seems to me, may, might, could, ought,* and *they say*. They also may contain expressions of approval or disapproval; generalizations that include words like *all, none, every,* or *always;* and superlatives such as *greatest, best, biggest,* and *finest*.

Look, for example, at these statements:

1. *Political instability is not a new development in Latin America.*
2. *In 1959, Fidel Castro took power in Cuba and made it the first Marxist nation in Latin America.*
3. *Benito Juárez cared about the people.*

Each of these statements is a fact. None is based on what someone thinks, believes, or feels. Each can be verified through research.

Now, look at these three statements:

1. *We Argentines have always believed that we have inherited a culture and a body of ideals centered on the dignity of the human being.*
2. *Some groups view the military as the only group strong enough to maintain order.*
3. *They say that the private sector is a fiction.*

Each of these statements is an opinion. In the first statement, the Argentines *believe*. In the second, some groups *view*. And, in the third, *they say*. Each of these statements, then, expresses something that a person or a group thinks, believes, or feels.

For practice in this skill, read the following statements, and determine which statements are fact and which are opinion. Give reasons for your decisions.

1. The time of heroes has passed; we enter today the age of common sense.
2. Greatness in America is the greatness of George Washington, who represents prosperity, growth, organization, and peace.
3. The liberals wanted changes that could bring them greater wealth, social status, and political power.
4. Benito Juárez was the first Indian ruler of Mexico since the Aztec Cuauhtemoc.
5. In most cases, today's military seems to show little concern for democracy.
6. In 1959, Fidel Castro took power in Cuba.
7. A senior Cuban official claims that the purchasing power of the people is high and rising.
8. Civil war seems to be coming to an end in El Salvador.

UNIT 5 REVIEW

SUMMARY

Latin America is a diverse area in terms of geography and people. In many ways, this diversity has helped shape the way of life. The different groups of people who make up the population each have something from their rich cultural heritage to contribute. Moreover, all of the people have had to cope with a diversity of geographical environments — plains, fertile valleys, deserts, great river systems, and tropical rain forests. Adapting to these different environments has produced additional cultural diversity in Latin America.

Differences in life style and income often are dramatic in Latin America. The gap between the rich and the poor and between urban dwellers and rural dwellers tends to be great. In addition, social class remains important in many areas. At the same time, however, the people of Latin America share many of the same values and beliefs. Family, for example, is very important. So are a strong sense of personal honor and pride and the desire to enjoy life. Another unifying factor is religion. The great majority of Latin Americans are Catholics. For many centuries, Catholicism has influenced most aspects of daily life. It also has had a strong influence on politics.

Over the years, politics and economics have posed problems for much of Latin America. Traditionally, dictators ruled in many countries. But with modernization came the desire for social change, which included change in government. Today, democratic government is the goal of many. In some countries, however, the political life remains unstable and tense. In most cases, this is because people demand a better way of life, a higher standard of living.

Even though many problems exist in parts of Latin America today, change and progress are taking place. Industrialization and urbanization are becoming a reality. The middle class is growing in size and importance. Education is improving and is available to more people than in the past. These signs and others have led many Latin Americans to be optimistic about their future.

REVIEW QUESTIONS

1. In what ways is Latin American life diverse? What factors provide unity?
2. In what ways has religion been an important factor in the development of Latin America?
3. How have politics changed in Latin America between the nineteenth and twentieth centuries? What factors were responsible for the changes?
4. What factors have contributed to the changes taking place in Latin America today? How have the changes affected the way of life of most Latin Americans?

SUGGESTED ACTIVITIES

1. Working in a group with five other classmates, hold a press conference. Have three members of the group represent three leaders of Latin American nations, each with a different form of government. Have the other three members of the group represent newspaper reporters who question the leaders about the reasons for and the advantages and disadvantages of their forms of government.
2. Select a Latin American country, and construct a chart showing its political development from independence to the present.
3. Working in a group, make a bulletin board display that shows the major features of Latin American life.
4. Make a map of a Latin American country. Indicate major geographical features, cities, industries, and natural resources.

COMPARING CULTURES

All cultures have unwritten rules about what is and is not acceptable behavior in different social situations. But what is proper and acceptable in one culture may not be so in another. An example is the two situations portrayed below. One takes place in Latin America, the other in the United States. Read the material that follows, and compare and contrast the two situations relative to what is and is not acceptable behavior.

IN LATIN AMERICA

Five Latin Americans meet by accident in front of a store. They greet one another with smiles, handshakes, and hugs. The two women in the group clasp each other affectionately and kiss one another's cheeks. The three men slap each other on the back.

The five people stand and talk. They cover a lot of subjects, but none are of a personal nature. Personal matters are to be discussed only with family members, old acquaintances, and close friends. While conversing, the people in the group stand close to one another and touch each other often, especially if someone wants to make a specific point or show a certain emotion. Those not speaking at the moment maintain constant eye contact with those who are.

As the conversation progresses, the volume grows louder. Gestures become more frequent. Often, the speaker is interrupted by someone else in the group. Just as often, several people speak at once. No one is offended. No one suggests that only one person should speak at a time or that the speaker should not be interrupted. Emotion is important, and volume, tone, and gestures all display emotion.

The people continue to talk as they enter the store. The store is crowded, and they brush against and bump into other shoppers as they move forward. There is no reason to apologize or to make excuses to the people with whom they have come into contact accidently. Everyone understands, and constantly saying "Excuse me" or "Pardon me" is a waste of words.

In time, the members of the group go their separate ways. One couple, arms around each other, go off to meet some friends at a nearby restaurant. On the way, they stop several times to kiss. No one comments or frowns at them. After all, in the words of one Latin American, "This way you can tell who's friends and who's a couple."

IN THE UNITED STATES

Five North Americans meet by accident in front of a store. They greet one another with smiles, asking each other "How are you?" Two of the three men in the group shake hands with one another.

The five people stand and talk. Midway in the conversation, one of the women starts to talk about the problems she is having with her family. Several of the others ask questions and offer advice. The woman speaking moves closer to the man standing next to her. Without interrupting the conversation, he slowly backs away, widening the circle they have formed. Those in the group keep eye contact with the person speaking for a short time, look away in different directions, and then resume eye contact again.

As the conversation progresses, the volume grows louder. Passersby turn and look; some frown. One of the men interrupts the woman who is speaking. She tells him that she is still speaking, and he apologizes.

The people in the group continue to talk as they enter the store. The store is crowded, and they apologize as they brush against or bump into other shoppers. At one point, one of the men bumps into an elderly woman. The woman tells him that he is rude and should be more careful.

In time, the members of the group go their separate ways. One couple, arms around each other, go off to meet some friends at a nearby restaurant. On the way, they stop and kiss. Two passersby stare at them and comment on the bad taste of people who put on public displays of affection.

Unit Six

As the birthplace of three great religions, the crossroads for trade between Europe and Asia, and now the source of vital oil supplies, the Middle East has long been one of the most important regions of the world. Today, hardly a day passes without news items from and about the Middle East. Outside nations seek to protect or advance their interests in the region. Numerous internal conflicts also threaten to have wider consequences. Thus, understanding this volatile and vital region is important for economic and political reasons. It also is important because learning about the Middle East helps one appreciate some of his or her own cultural roots and other people's ways of life.

CONTENTS

33	ENVIRONMENT AND PEOPLE	536
34	A MOSAIC OF PEOPLES	554
35	THE WAY OF LIFE	568
36	RELIGION AND STATE	584
37	THE GREAT BITTERNESS	602
38	THE MIDDLE EAST TODAY	616

MIDDLE EAST

CHAPTER 33
ENVIRONMENT AND PEOPLE

1. *What is the physical environment of the Middle East?*
2. *How has physical environment influenced the ways the people of the Middle East live?*

Once it was clear that the Nile would not flood, food prices soared. Those who could afford to leave Egypt did so. Whole families set off for Syria, Yemen, Arabia, and even Morocco. Country people swarmed into Cairo. When the cool winter had passed and the sun had entered Aries (the first sign of the new astrological year), the effects began to show. The poor were forced to eat dead and rotting flesh, dogs, corpses, and even the excrement of beasts. (An alarming diet anywhere, but to Muslims even more so.) Far worse was in store. The sight of unprotected, homeless children began to tempt the hungry. The government had to issue a decree that those who killed children or ate their flesh would be burned at the stake. Many paid no attention to the decree.*

The famine discussed above took place in Cairo, the capital of Egypt, in the year 1200. The famine came about because the Nile River had not risen enough to water the farmers' fields. For the same reason, there were 11 more famines within 50 years.

Water has always been a key factor in people's lives not only in Egypt but in all of the Middle East. Today, this region at the eastern end of the Mediterranean—where Europe, Asia, and Africa meet—includes large countries with many people—such as Egypt, Turkey, Iran, and Iraq. It includes countries with some of the richest oil fields in the world—such as Saudi Arabia and the tiny states of Kuwait, Bahrain, Qatar, and the United Arab Emirates. It includes the small but politically significant nations of Israel and Lebanon. It also includes the countries of Syria, Jordan, the Yemen Arab Republic, the People's Democratic Republic of Yemen, and Oman.

About two-thirds of the Middle East receives less than eight inches (20 centimeters) of rain each year. Eight inches (20 centimeters) is the least amount needed to grow most food crops. Most of the rain that does fall comes during the winter months when the growing season is over. During the traditional growing months of the summer, the skies are clear and temperatures soar over 100° Fahrenheit (38° Celsius). Farmers must raise crops that can survive such difficult growing conditions as these. These crops include barley, wheat, lentils, fava beans, and chickpeas.

Water, then, means life. For centuries, it has determined where people settle and how long they stay there. It also has determined how many people can live in one spot. Because of water, people have fought wars, have moved long distances, and have suffered or prospered.

---

*Adapted from *Kitab al-Ifadah* by Abdul Latif al-Baghdadi, as quoted in *The Eastern Key* by Ivy E. Videan and Sayid Zand, George Allen & Unwin Ltd.

THE REGION

One hundred fifty million years ago, much of the Middle East was covered with dense tropical forests and swamps. Marshes were thick with grasses and ferns, which rotted in slow waters. Today these same areas contain valuable oil fields, and the land and the climate have changed. Coastlines, rugged mountains, rocky hills, deserts, and areas of watered fertile lands now make up much of the landscape.

Running through almost every country and ringing the entire region are mountains. Among others, there are the Taurus Mountains, which run east and west through the southern edge of Turkey. There is Mount Ararat, in northeastern Turkey. There is the Zagros Mountain range which, stretching northwest to southeast, divides the countries of Iran and Iraq. Then there are the Elburz Mountains of Iran, the Asir Mountains of Saudi Arabia, and the Red Sea Mountains of Egypt.

The many mountains of the Middle East block the flow of rain clouds to the inland side of the region. Thus, even though the Middle East is bounded on the west by the Mediterranean Sea, to the north by the Black and Caspian seas, and on the south by the Persian Gulf and the Arabian Sea, fresh water inland is scarce and unpredictable. Only Turkey, northwest Iran, and a narrow rim of land along the seas in the Yemens, Saudi Arabia, Israel, Syria, and Lebanon flourish with regular and adequate rainfall.

Growing and living conditions differ in areas with little water and in those where there are rivers, springs, and **oases,** green spots in dry lands where groundwater comes to the surface. In the watered areas, more crops can grow, and more people tend to settle. The Nile River, for example, flows through Egypt, from its southern border to the Mediterranean Sea. Today the Nile Valley and its delta support almost 40 million Egyptians. Two other major rivers, the Tigris and Euphrates, flow through southeastern Turkey, Syria, and Iraq and empty into the Persian Gulf. In the following passage, a visitor tells what he and his friends found as they rafted down the Euphrates:

These travelers, whose trip down the Euphrates River is described on the next page, appear small in size compared to the steep cliffs that line the river. Today, the Euphrates meets with the Tigris before emptying into the Gulf, but, in ancient times, this was not the case. Why are the Tigris and Euphrates rivers important in early Middle Eastern history?

CHAPTER 33 ENVIRONMENT AND PEOPLE

[In] Ankara we link up, . . . hop a plane to Elazig and take a minibus west to the Keban Dam, which backs up the largest reservoir in Turkey. . . .

By 12:30 we're on the great, green, cold expanse called the Euphrates. It's beautiful, but somehow anticlimactic. It feels no different from the Colorado, the Blue Nile or a dozen other big rivers. I somehow expected a deeper sense of ancient history, ruins at every bend, caravans crossing the shallows. The yellow canyon, illustrated with folding whorls [circular ridges] and faults, is still, save for the sounds of birds. It feels as though we're floating through an empty coliseum . . . punctured with caves and rimmed with winding paths.

At dusk, as we camp, we see two other inflatable rafts drifting toward us. . . . We thought we were the only inflatable for 1,000 miles [1600 kilometers] and at least as many years. The vessels gradually wave into focus as though emerging from a desert mirage. They're jerryrigged rafts, tractor-tire innertubes lashed to planks, piloted by farmers. . . . I remember that farmers and herders along the Euphrates have been using inflatables for millenia. . . .

The next morning I poke my head from my fiberfill sleeping bag and witness, in the flat dawn light, a tractor in the middle of the Euphrates. . . . The river is gone. A tiny trickle remains. . . . They've turned off the dam!. . . . The mighty Euphrates, river of antiquity, . . . reduced to a rivulet, the victim of the flick of a switch at the Keban Dam. . . .

[The] river's still not there the next day. We break the wait by hiking across the ridge behind us, where we discover the real Euphrates rushing by in sizeable volume. We're on an island, . . . and have parked in a channel. . . . We wrestle the boat down to the trickle and proceed to drag it over the rocks downstream. . . . Within hours we've floated . . . to Kale, at the head of the Kermer Khan Canyon. . . .

Through this Grand Canyon of the Euphrates, the river cuts its most imposing course, scything around a lava mass erupted from the Karajali volcano, and stabbing across the . . . Taurus Mountains. Here, too, are the river's biggest rapids. Lulled by days of flat water, we're taken by surprise when we plummet into the first cataract [waterfall]. . . . This is not a complacent river after all. . . .

. . . Beyond the oblique canyon we can sometimes see snow-capped mountains and, at tributary mouths, we occasionally spot Kurdish women fetching water in long-necked clay jugs.

Late on the sixth day we enter a . . . gorge pocked with shallow caves. High on the west bank, fitted into a limestone alcove, sits a remarkable sight—a masterfully constructed, ancient, abandoned Byzantine monastery. . . . Honeycombed with dank passages, festooned with swallow nests, graced with Roman-arched doors, filled with bats and with no easy access to the world beyond the river gorge, the place is a hidden wonder. . . .

On Sunday, after the river has broken from the canyon, dropped off the Adiyaman Plateau and started its long, sluggish journey across the flatlands, we round a bend and see a glint of steel . . .: the Akinjilar Bridge, our takeout. As we pull in under the abutment, some teenagers manning an open-air soda fountain for bus travelers scramble down to meet us.*

The history of the Middle East began in the areas near the Nile River and in the Fertile Crescent. In the valley of the Tigris and Euphrates lies the biggest part of the Fertile Crescent. The Crescent is an arc-shaped area of land that arches from the Persian Gulf north into Turkey and then south along the coast of the Mediterranean Sea. Here began one of the earliest western civilizations. Here and along the Nile were

---

*"Down the Gorge" by Richard Bangs in ARAMCO WORLD Magazine, January–February 1981, p. 32. Reprinted by permission.

Date palms rise above the flat-roofed, mud-brick homes of a village on the Nile River near Luxor, Egypt. The 4000-mile (6400-kilometer) long river begins in the mountains of East Africa, whose rivers and lakes eventually give rise to the White Nile and the Blue Nile. These merge at Khartoum, Sudan, to form the Nile, which cuts a lush, green valley through Egypt's vast desert landscape. Why is the Nile Valley called a "cradle of civilization"?

the "cradles of civilization." Since those early times, the countries that make up the Middle East have shared many cultural, historical, and geographic ties.

1. Where is the Middle East located? Of what countries does it consist?
2. What are some of the physical characteristics of the Middle East?

ON THE DESERTS

The combination of mountains and prevailing winds has created vast deserts in many parts of the Middle East. Not all of the desert lands, however, are the same. One, the Empty Quarter of Saudi Arabia, is made up of trackless, shifting sand dunes on which almost nothing grows. Another, the Negev, which makes up more than half of the land of Israel, is largely barren rock with badly eroded hills. In northern Saudi Arabia, along the border with Iraq and Jordan, the desert is covered with scrubby bushes. When there is rain, colorful wildflowers burst into bloom and dense grasses grow.

One group of people, the Bedouins, has made their homes on the edges and around the oases of such deserts for centuries. Since food and water for their herds are too scarce to allow them to settle permanently in one spot, the Bedouins are **nomads,** people who move from place to place. They do not just wander, however. They know exactly where they are going. A Bedouin clan ranges over the same area each year. Some raise herds of camels, while others tend flocks of sheep and goats. Their life is carefully tuned to catch fleeting rainstorms and to survive in the harshest settings.

In recent years, however, life has changed for the Bedouins, and few remain nomadic. Today, only about 3 percent of the Middle Eastern population is nomadic. Bedouins are settling and living in houses instead of tents. Jeeps and pickup trucks are putting markets within easy reach for Bedouin livestock herders who want to sell their dairy products, wool, hides, and live animals to customers in the cities. Some young Bedouins are going into the army, while others are taking jobs in the oil fields and in other businesses. Even those Bedouins who prefer not to abandon their age-old way of life have had to make some changes. Below, an anthropologist who studied the Āl'Azab, a clan of Bedouins in the Empty Quarter, describes their life today:

> To the Āl'Azab, fall pasturing deep inside the [Empty Quarter] is a time of happiness and contentment. They always say it is the best season. There is the excitement of game to be hunted; there is the absence of the influences of the city, of the oasis, of the central government; there is bound to be relatively good grazing. But by November, the herders begin to scan the northern skies at night in hope of seeing flashes of lightning in the distant skies. *Insh'allah*, If Allah [God] wills, the rains will come.
>
> How long the fall grazing lasts depends on when and what kinds of rains fall in the north. . . .
>
> Throughout the late fall, the herdsmen are keenly interested in news about the rains. Word is brought about once a month by the members of the Reserve National Guard, who travel by truck to . . . the headquarters of the amir [leader]. While [there], they obtain as much precise information as possible from other members . . . who have been in the north or who have been in touch with others . . . in the north. Each person who reports rains is carefully questioned about how he obtained his information, whether it is first-hand or based on the reports of others. If there is any doubt about the reports . . . , they ask the amir for his opinion. He is in a position to hear the reports of a wide range of [Bedouins], and he considers it part of his business to provide information as reliable as possible for the herdsmen. . . .
>
> Any time after the first of December and when reliable news establishes that rains have fallen in the north, each Āl'Azab household changes the rhythm of its movements. Instead of short moves every few days within a given area, the camels are herded . . . in marches that last from about two hours after sunrise until around sunset, with the camels grazing for a few hours near the camp after sunset.
>
> Depending on how cold the weather is, either tents or enclosure walls are set up about an hour before sunset. The herds graze for a couple of hours and arrive just after dark, at which time they are milked. Camp fires glow in the men's sections of the tents or in front of the enclosures, and one hears the ringing beat of coffee beans being pounded into powder in heavy brass mortars. The men and youths gather closely around the fires and talk of what and whom they have seen during the day. . . . The men eat a communal meal of rice about three hours after sunset. They drink milk later on, and most of the youths sit up until well past midnight talking about camels and the state of the grazing, reciting poems, and listening to the Bedouin Hour on Radio Kuwait. All too soon, the

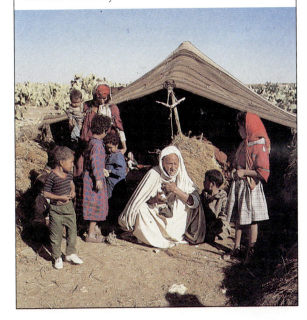

This Bedouin family has pitched its tent near the town of Gafsa on the grassy northern edge of Tunisia's southern deserts. What is fall grazing like among the Bedouin herders of the Āl'Azab clan?

AGRICULTURAL RESOURCES

morning call to prayer comes, just before sunrise, and a new day begins as the march goes on toward the north.*

1. What kinds of desert are found in the Middle East?
2. How has the life of many Bedouins changed in recent years?

ON WATERED LANDS

All of the Middle East is not desert. The region also contains some of the most fertile soil in the world. There is the Nile Valley, which owes its fertility to the build-up of silt left over thousands of years by the annual floods of the Nile River. There is the Fertile Crescent, described in the Bible as "a land of brooks and water, of fountains and depths that spring out of valleys and hills; a land of wheat and barley, and vines, and fig trees, and pomegranates; a land of olive oil and honey." In western Iran, in Turkey, and in the Yemens, there is still more land good for farming.

But even fertile land needs water, and this has always been a problem in the Middle East. Long ago, when the earliest settlers began to spread beyond the fertile areas near the rivers, they found that they had to irrigate the land before crops would grow. Isolated families alone could not build irrigation systems, but groups of families, forming

---
Nomads of the Nomads: The Al Murrah Bedouin of the Empty Quarter by Donald Powell Cole, 1975, Aldine Publishing Company, pp. 43–45.

villages, could. Today about 50 percent of all Middle Easterners are farming peasants who live in villages. Until the 1950's, most of the best farmland was owned by wealthy landlords or by royal families. Now, most of the land is owned by villagers.

All over the Middle East, modern technology and human determination are reclaiming land to support more people. In a process called **desalination,** seawater is made fresh and usable for drinking and irrigation. Huge dams, such as the Aswan in Egypt and the Tabaqa in Syria, harness the great rivers and bring water to millions of acres of thirsty soil. New towns are built where wasteland used to be, and the desert is made to bloom.

THE NILE DELTA

In areas with water and fertile land, Middle Easterners have been able to produce rich harvests. One such area is the Nile Delta. Over the past 100 years, a series of dams, canals, drains, and water pumps have been built in the delta region north of Cairo. These improvements have enabled the *fellaheen,* or Egyptian farmers, to raise three crops a year instead of one. Now the Delta's yields of rice, beans, cotton, sugar, onions, wheat, and corn are among the highest in the world.

The Delta is one of the most densely populated areas of the world with 2300 people per square mile (2.6 square kilometers) living there. Human labor and hard work are responsible for the achievements made. Tractors and mechanization are rarely seen or used. Below, a North American journalist living in the Delta explains how the *fellaheen* keep the land productive:

> Four things in the Delta struck me right away. First, the fierce work ethic; men may spend sixteen or so hours in the fields, and instead of . . . jokes, gossip, and . . . banter, one hears shouts of "Work! Don't speak so much!" "Leave that stubble clean!" . . . and "You work like a boy, not a man!". . . . The Delta *fellaheen* . . . often [stayed] in the fields all day except for an hour's siesta after the noon meal. As I have seen nowhere else, they sometimes harvested wheat by sickle by night as well as day. Most of the time, their long tunics or *galabias* tucked up at the waist, they labored with hoes. . . .

This Egyptian farmer, or fellah, is harvesting wheat by hand with a sickle. This method of cutting grain dates back to the ancient Egyptians and the time when, because of its huge exports of grain, Egypt was known as the granary of the world. What are some other crops grown in the fertile soil of the Nile Delta today?

Second, there were round, cement cisterns in many fields, scattered in long lines a hundred meters [330 feet] apart. These were part of a tile drainage system which is starting to successfully combat the problem of salinity from . . . constant irrigation. . . .

Third, in the Delta one sees a constant procession from fields to the villages and back of men leading camels, donkeys and buffaloes laden with manure or fresh dirt. Great heaps of manure and dirt sit about the edges of the fields; nearly half of the Delta's labor force is engaged in the unceasing task of refertilizing the land with animal manure to replace the minerals and nutrients lost when the Nile stopped flooding the Delta a century ago. . . .

Fourth, Delta women commonly work in the fields, the older ones in the same long black dresses all women in Upper Egypt wear, but in the Delta the younger appear in brightly colored gowns, their heads wrapped in kerchiefs.*

ISRAEL

Much also has been done in Israel. Here, part of the Negev Desert has been reclaimed, and farming settlements called **kibbutzim** have been established. *Kibbutzim* are collective communities in which all members are equal. No one is paid a wage. Instead, everyone shares in the land, labor, and produce. All decisions are made collectively, and children are raised as a group rather than in their own family units. The *kibbutzim* are small in number. There are only about 250, which represents about 4 percent of the Israeli population. Below, a 61-year-old Israeli describes what life was like when his *kibbutz* first began and explains why he is proud of what has been accomplished:

At first, we lived in tents. . . . I didn't even get a bed for myself—I had to share one with another guy for a while after I arrived. Then, during the summer, we built little tree houses in the trees, which was fun. When we moved to our present location, we, as a married couple, had a tent first and a little hut later. The hut was 4-by-6 meters [13.2-by-19.8 feet] and shared by three couples; . . . No restrooms, no showers—nothing. . . .

We had a malaria epidemic at the kibbutz, which was awful. . . . Only about one or two of the men were spared this disease. I caught it, too. We all suffered —malaria is a disease that completely drains you. So we started sleeping under mosquito nets—imagine, in this heat! To sleep under a net was a nightmare. At night I felt as if I would suffocate, and I couldn't escape.

To complete the picture: the food. I can't even start to describe it for you. . . . We had lots of bread, oil, and sugar. Half an egg sometimes. We used to get jam in a tablespoon, smoothed out by a knife so that you wouldn't get too much. Butter appeared rarely. A piece of cake or an egg was a whole day's ration for a working man, a man doing hard physical work outside. . . .

Women, too, had it hard then. . . . They had neither warm water nor heating in the homes. And, worst of all, there were no roads or paved paths within the kibbutz. If you have never experienced rain here, you cannot imagine it. . . . You really cannot walk—and we had just one pair of shoes. Our children grew up on our shoulders. . . . Now, there is no problem. You can wear sandals in the winter and walk on the paved path, and it's fine.

What kept us going (those of us who did) during that period? I really cannot tell you. . . .

Maybe I kept going because of the conviction that we were building something out of nothing. And this is, apparently, something of great significance. The constant planning of what is to come, the ecstasy of the beginning! I remember

---
*Excerpt from *Villages* by Richard Critchfield, pp. 148–149. Copyright © 1980 by Robert Critchfield. Reprinted by permission of Doubleday & Company, Inc.

CHAPTER 33   ENVIRONMENT AND PEOPLE

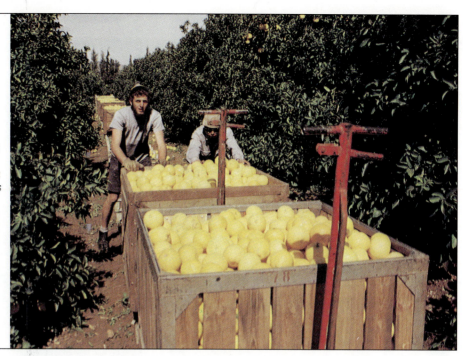

These workers are picking grapefruit at an Israeli kibbutz *in the Negev Desert, where the arid land is often interrupted by the green farms of* kibbutzim *and* moshavim. *Experience on these farms has made Israel a world leader in such desert-farming technology as trickle irrigation, a system by which plastic pipes carry exact amounts of water and nutrients to each individual plant. What have* kibbutzim *and* moshavim *added to their economic activities in recent years?*

when the first buildings, such as our first barn, were erected here. We dug the ground, which is all basalt rocks and heavy soil, with our bare hands. Now we have all the necessary equipment. Yet all of us competed with great enthusiasm to see who would be the first one to reach the basalt, to get deep down to the foundation. This gave all of us tremendous satisfaction.

This stubborn will to build the kibbutz, to settle the area, is what inspired us. And for me, my work kept me going, too. I always loved working in the fields; to this very day I derive a great deal of satisfaction from it.*

More recently, in addition to growing crops, these *kibbutzim*, and another type of cooperative of small individual farms called **moshavim**, have begun to add industries and fish-breeding ponds to their other economic activities.

---

*From *Kibbutz Makom: Report from an Israeli Kibbutz* by Amia Lieblich. Copyright © 1981 by Amia Lieblich, pp. 19–21. Reprinted by permission of Pantheon Books, a Division of Random House, Inc.

1. Where do fertile lands exist in the Middle East?
2. What are four characteristics of farming in the Nile Delta?
3. What conditions characterized early *kibbutzim* life?

IN THE CITIES

Where there was a lot of water, cities grew. Cairo on the Nile River, Baghdad on the Tigris River, Constantinople on the Bosphorus Strait, and Beirut on the Mediterranean Sea all flourished because of their special locations. Some cities have been trade and population centers for centuries. Their streets blend the sites and architecture of several civilizations. Modern boulevards are found next to medieval Islamic buildings and ancient Roman gates and walls.

The early cities were laid out to fit the environment. Narrow streets, for example, were a defense against invaders and against

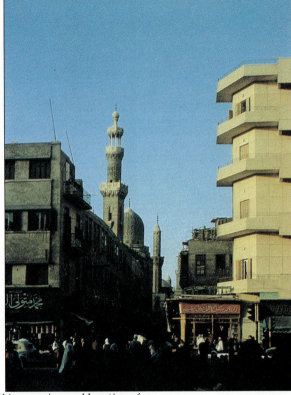

With the exception of mosques, Muslim houses of worship, this scene in an old section of Cairo, above left, contrasts markedly with the modern apartment buildings in the newer section of the city, above right. What was Cairo architecture like in the late 1800's?

the intense rays of the sun. Below, a traveler to Cairo in the late 1800's explains how architecture was adapted to the environment:

> The inner court of the home is almost as silent and deserted as the guarded windows which overlook the street. We shall see nothing of the domestic life of the people who live there. After the bustle of the street this quiet and ample space is very refreshing. One feels that the Egyptian architects have happily realized the needs of eastern life. They make the streets narrow and overshadow them with projecting meshrebiyas (carved wooden screens), because the sun beats down so fiercely. But they make the houses large and surround them with courts and gardens, because without air one could not bear the heat of the rooms in summer. The Eastern architect's art lies in so building your house that you cannot look into your neighbor's windows, nor he into yours. The obvious way is to build the rooms round a high open court, and to closely veil the windows with lattice blinds. This lets in some light and air, and allows an outlook without allowing the passing stranger to see through.*

THE *SŪQ*

At the heart of every Middle Eastern city then—and now—is its ***sūq***, or marketplace. Covering the *sūq* are high-ceiling tentlike arrangements. Windows in the sides allow the air to flow through, while the "roof"

---
*Adapted from *Cairo* by Stanley Lane-Poole, 1898, Virtue, p. 10. Reprinted by permission.

provides people with shelter from the hot sun and the rain. In many modern-day cities, the mall-like *sūq* provides a marked contrast to other areas, some of which may be only a block or two away. This contrast and how one might react to it is described below by a visitor to Bahrain:

> I drifted into a maze of streets on which mine was the only Western face in sight. One narrow alley was full of carpenters and the smell of freshly sawn pine; another was a dazzling canal of brilliant Hong Kong cottons; another, the car-repair zone, was loud with lines of men banging shapeless bits of metal with hammers. . . . The protective labyrinth, in which every trade has its own allocated quarter fixed by use and tradition, is Arabia's strongest bastion [stronghold] against monoculture. Things are kept separate—gold and meat, vegetables and clothing, spices and hi-fi sets . . . every category has at least one street to itself. This separation of objects keeps people apart too; at each turn in the maze one notices a distinct difference in skin color and style of dress. You cannot go more than a hundred yards [90 meters] without trespassing across a clearly defined boundary. A blind man could find his way through the labyrinth by smell alone: machine oil gives way to turmeric and coriander, sweet sawdust to the acrid barnyard odor of live chickens, roast coffee to the oddly musky scent of cheap plastic.

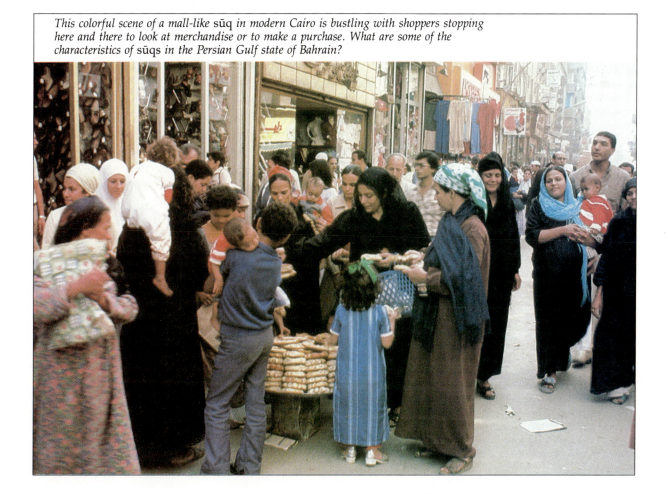

This colorful scene of a mall-like sūq *in modern Cairo is bustling with shoppers stopping here and there to look at merchandise or to make a purchase. What are some of the characteristics of* sūqs *in the Persian Gulf state of Bahrain?*

One of the major features of Istanbul is its mosques. The largest, known as Suleimaniye, viewed here from the Golden Horn harbor, was built between 1550 and 1557 by Sultan Suleiman the Magnificent. A short distance away is the Hagia Sophia, a sixth-century Byzantine Christian church that was later converted into a mosque by the Ottomans. How long has Istanbul been a center for East-West trade?

In one step at the end of a street I crossed from a world of mud and wood to one of marble, glass and concrete. I had been threading my way through a long, rustling procession of black veils; suddenly there were only business suits and sharkskin document cases. The line of banks on Government Road was taller and wider than the lines of spice sellers and carpenters; but it had the same air of being a single specialized component in a labyrinthine system. . . . When I crossed the street and walked behind the back of a great glass investment-company building, money gave way to wood shavings and resin, and two men on a makeshift platform caulking the hull of a dhow [boat used for trade in the Persian Gulf].*

ISTANBUL

The life blood of many early Middle Eastern cities was trade. This has remained true for Istanbul, formerly known as Constantinople. Located at the neck of the Bosphorus, it could control the flow of trade from Russia and the Black Sea to the Mediterranean world. In the mid-1500's, a French visitor to the city wrote, "It seems to me that while other cities are mortal, this one will remain as long as there are men on earth."

Istanbul is the only city that occupies land on two continents. For over 2000 years, it has been a bridge for overland and sea traffic between the East and the West. Below, a visitor to Istanbul paints a picture of the city:

Istanbul is a child of the sea. Few cities are invested so totally, so intimately, by water. It laps the twin shores of the Stamboul peninsula, defines the blunt head of Beyoğlu across the Golden Horn [a harbor], washes the long front of Asian Üsküdar. The sea, perilous and rich with the flux of trade and war, has always been the city's chief highway. As for anchorage, the water is so deep around the city that ocean-going liners berth cheek-by-jowl with streets and markets; and huge freighters, when they need repair, back their sterns without trouble on to shore.

---

*Arabia: A Journey Through the Labyrinth by Jonathan Raban. COPYRIGHT © 1979 by Jonathan Raban, pp. 36–37. Reprinted by permission of SIMON & SCHUSTER, Inc.

CHAPTER 33 ENVIRONMENT AND PEOPLE 549

On most days, the Galata Bridge, shown here, is a hub of activity with a steady flow of pedestrian and motor traffic as well as ferryboats and freighters. What three waterways meet under the Galata Bridge?

The juggling of land and sea plays romantic conjuring tricks with the eye. Lines of smoking funnels glide between landlocked chimneys. Masts linger among rooftops. And the ends of a hundred winding streets are sealed not by suburbs, but by a sparkling curtain of waves. . . .

At the centre of the city's sea traffic is the ramshackle, 70-year-old Galata Bridge, connecting Stamboul to Beyoğlu across the mouth of the Horn. The bridge, floating on half-decayed pontoons, swings open early each morning to usher shipping into the inlet. Closed again, it rocks with the swell of the water and with the flow of the 90,000 cars and 40,000 pedestrians that cross it every day. Beneath the roadway, close above the water, run passageways lined with makeshift stalls and restaurants. But the bridge's days are numbered. Polluted waters, harsh winds, and the endless crash and rub of ferryboats have corroded it to the danger point.

At this bridge, Istanbul's three waterways—the Bosphorus, the Golden Horn and the Sea of Marmara—collide with an eccentric glamour. The sea is ploughed and churned by an embroglio [confused mass] of ships. Hooting, belching, whistling, whooping, groaning, they slide and bump in disorder between one another, miming the insane turmoil of streets not far away. At some moments, in morning or early evening, the whole sea seems to convert itself into a maritime Place de la Concorde or Piazza Venezia, where crashes are avoided only by hard-won expertise and perpetual hornblowing —while overlooking all, as from the tiers of an amphitheatre, the steep shores are thronged with mosques, palaces, banks, offices, bazaars.*

1. Where did cities spring up in the Middle East? In what ways were they developed to fit the environment?
2. How are shopping districts arranged in Middle Eastern cities? Why are they arranged this way?
3. How has location influenced Istanbul?

---

*The Great Cities/ISTANBUL by Colin Thurbron and the Editors of Time-Life Books. © 1978, Time-Life Books Inc. p. 129. Reprinted by permission.

EXPLORATION
MIDDLE EAST

The photographs on the next page were taken from National Aeronautics and Space Administration (NASA) satellites with a special camera. Each color represents a distinct feature: Healthy trees and plants are bright red. Suburban areas with little vegetation appear as bright pink, and barren lands are light gray. Cities and industrial areas show as green or dark gray. Clear water is dark blue or black. Look at the photographs and the maps that precede them, and answer the questions:

1. What geographic features of the Middle East can be seen?
2. Where is there a lot of water? Little water?
3. Where are the areas of the Middle East in which the greatest number of people live? Where are the areas that have permanent settlements?
4. What is the relationship between the red areas on the photographs and the areas of high population on the maps? Between the red areas and the population patterns' map?
5. Based on the information in the chapter and in the photographs and maps, how do you think the environment has helped shape the ways of life of the Middle Eastern people?

POPULATION DENSITY

POPULATION PATTERNS

MIDDLE EAST

CHAPTER 33 REVIEW

POINTS TO REMEMBER

1. Throughout history, water has been a key factor in people's lives in the Middle East, the region located at the eastern end of the Mediterranean Sea and which includes the countries of Egypt, Turkey, Iran, Iraq, Saudi Arabia, Kuwait, Bahrain, Qatar, the United Arab Emirates, Israel, Lebanon, Syria, Jordan, the Yemen Arab Republic, the People's Democratic Republic of Yemen, and Oman.
2. The many mountains of the Middle East prevent adequate rainfall from reaching the inland areas of the Middle East. As a result of this, the countries of the region have only limited areas of fertile watered land.
3. The complexion of the deserts of the Middle East varies, ranging from shifting sand dunes on which almost nothing grows, to barren rock with badly eroded hills, to scrubby bushes and dense grasses.
4. Bedouins make their homes on the deserts, moving their herds to different grazing areas to take advantage of limited food and water supplies. In recent years, the number of Bedouins has decreased, and their way of life has been modified.
5. The Middle East contains some of the most fertile soil in the world. With hard labor and irrigation, fertile lands produce abundantly and support most of the people of the region.
6. Middle Eastern cities developed at locations where there was a lot of water. The layout and architecture of the cities were developed to make trade easy and to fit the environment.

VOCABULARY

Identify

Middle East
Taurus
Ararat
Zagros
Nile
Tigris
Euphrates
Fertile Crescent
Empty Quarter
Negev
Bedouins
Nile Delta
Cairo
Istanbul

Define

oases
nomads
desalination
fellaheen
kibbutzim
moshavim
sūq

DISCUSSING IMPORTANT IDEAS

1. Do any areas of your country have a geography and climate comparable to the Middle East? What areas are they? How do the natural water supplies of those areas compare to the natural water supply of the Middle East?

2. What factors do you think have influenced and led to changes in the Bedouin way of life?
3. Today dams on the Nile and on other rivers keep floodplains dry. Electric fans are used widely, and air conditioning is available. How do you think these changes have altered city architecture and growth in the Middle East?
4. In what ways does water continue to affect the development of the Middle East?

DEVELOPING SKILLS

NARRATIVE WRITING

Many of the books you may have enjoyed when you were younger probably were written in a *narrative style*, a writing style that tells a story. Through narrative adventures, you may have navigated the Mississippi River on a raft with Huckleberry Finn, survived a shipwreck with the Swiss Family Robinson, or crossed the ocean inside a pink snail with Dr. Doolittle.

To tell these or any other stories, real or imaginary, the authors had to include four elements—time, place, people, and events —that together are known as a *story plan*. Most often, the events are told in chronological order —the order in which they happen—using such connecting words and phrases as *next, after, first, the next day*, and *later* to create smooth transitions from one event to the other. Connecting words and phrases do not have to be used with each and every event, but they should be used often enough to relate one event to another and make the narrative flow smoothly.

Look, for example, at the following story, each sentence of which is numbered:

(1) Sada walked down the sandy, palm-lined path to the spring just after the sun rose, while mist still whirled on the banks. (2) Dew sparkled like diamonds glued to the small patches of green on the edge of her village of Tehfa. (3) This was Sada's favorite time of day, and getting water from the spring was her favorite chore. (4) She tucked the hem of her dress into her belt and then waded out into the clear water until it reached almost to her knees, making her legs go numb almost immediately. (5) As she dipped her tin bucket into the water, her gaze rested on the sandy bottom. (6) Suddenly, she saw an enormous head, large black eyes, and a long snout that began to glide toward her with frightening speed, stirring up sandy clouds in the water as it moved closer. (7) Sada flung her arms outward in surprise, sending her bucket flying through the air. (8) She left the water in one leap, and gasping, too frightened to scream, flew along the path back home, heedless now of the beauty of the morning.

To determine if all the elements of the story plan are included, ask yourself these questions:

1. When did the story take place?
2. Where did the story take place?
3. Who are the characters?
4. What happens in the story?

Your answers to these questions, which should be as follows, show that all four elements are covered. Sentence 1 indicates the time as early morning; sentence 2, the place as just outside the village of Tehfa; sentence 3, the people as a girl named Sada; sentences 4–8, the events as a young girl wading into a cold spring to get water, being frightened by a strange animal, dropping her water bucket, and running toward home.

For practice in this skill do as follows:

1. Read about Istanbul on pages 548 and 549.
2. Prepare a story plan for a narrative writing about a walk through the city of Istanbul.
3. Write the story.

CHAPTER 34
A MOSAIC OF PEOPLES

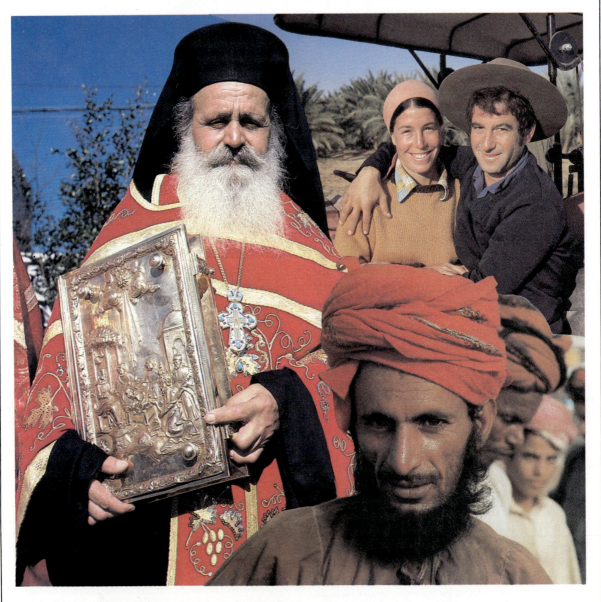

1. What groups of people live in the Middle East?
2. What makes one group of Middle Easterners different from another?

By using . . . service-taxis it was possible to explore most quarters of the town. This was like moving between different countries: from Armenia, to Arabia, to the Maronite people, and then on to the Anglo-Saxons. Seventy to eighty percent of each community lived within its own main quarter, mingling in the Burj, the downtown square, with adjacent sūqs . . . and banking, and in Ras Beirut, the most westernized quarter. . . .

And [there] were the separate schools, separate hospitals, separate churches—the separately formed hearing and seeing. . . . The principal loyalty, the means of self-identification, rested within the primary community.

"What are you, then? Are you Lebanese?

"You see, my family is Armenian. We live here. My brother is in America. My other brother has returned to Russia—do you understand, to Soviet Armenia. We stay inside our history. . . ."

"Yes, yes, I follow your question. In England, of course, I would answer to people that I am Lebanese, but in myself, you know, I am still a Syrian. We are Sunni Muslims; we came from Damascus; we have lived in Beirut for a hundred years."

"Lebanese? Why yes. What else? I am a Christian—that is, I am a Catholic Christian. An Orthodox might answer you differently!"

"Lebanese? You put a difficult question. I am a Druze. We lived here first on the Mountain. I am a Druze. Hah, I am a Druze. *C'est tout!*"*

The above conversation took place in a crowded taxicab in Beirut, Lebanon, in which all but one of the passengers were from Lebanon. Similar conversations, however, could take place in other parts of the Middle East, for the region is not a melting pot. It is a mosaic of many diverse groups.

What sets one group apart from another may vary. The difference may be language, religion, nationality, history, or something else. Each of these will give some clues to a person's background. But questions must be asked to discover to whom or what a person is loyal, and to what roots a person traces his or her identity. In the Middle East, the answers to such questions often are of major importance in understanding the lives of the people and the events surrounding them.

Throughout its long history, the Middle East has been home to many peoples. Some vanished long ago—defeated in wars, wiped out by famines, or absorbed by more powerful groups. Some have survived for hundreds of years and dominate the region today. The Arabs make up the majority in several countries, while groups such as the Iranians, Turks, and Israelis each have their own country. Other groups—such as the Palestinians, the Armenians, and the Kurds —continue to dream of and struggle for a homeland.

**The Mountain Arabs: A Window on the Middle East* by John Sykes, 1968, Chilton Book Company, p. 54. Reprinted by permission.

THE ARABS

More than half the people of the Middle East are Arabs. Their religion of Islam and their culture have had a profound impact on the entire region. Before the spread of Islam in the 600's, Arabic-speaking people lived in Arabia, the Arabian Peninsula, and some areas north of the peninsula. Today, they live in 21 countries in the Middle East and Africa.

But not all Arabic-speaking people trace their roots to Arabia. Many are descendants of such groups as the Canaanites, Philistines, and Egyptians, all of whom became Arabs by learning Arabic. Ninety percent of the Arabs are Muslim. Most of the others are Christians, who live mainly in Egypt, Lebanon, Syria, Jordan, Iraq, and Israel.

A political science professor at a Lebanese university explained that three forces—a belief in Islam, the Arabic language, and Arabic culture—govern the attitudes and actions of all Arabs. Despite this, it is hard to answer the question, "Who are the Arab people?" As one author explains, being an Arab is being part of history:

If you asked one of the world's [160] million Arabs just why he considers himself an Arab, he would answer you immediately that he speaks the Arabic language—a language for which every Arab has great affection and admiration.

Then he would tell you of the more than two thousand years of history shared by the Arab people, and of the Arab Empire which carried the torch of learning and scholarship for six hundred years while Europe was shrouded in the darkness of the Middle Ages.

He would tell you of the two predominant religions of Arab worshipers—Islam, the majority religion; Christianity, the minority—both cradled in Arab lands, both acting as unifying forces.

He would mention some of the great names of the Arab world: the physicians Rhazes [Razi] and Avicenna [ibn Sina]; the great historical philosopher, ibn-Khaldun; the map maker and geographer, al-Idrisi; the philosophers, al-Kindi, al-Farabi, and Averroës; and scores of other scientists, astronomers, mathematicians, musicians, translators, and physicians who made a lasting contribution to world science and scholarship.

Arabs include people from many different lands, such as this Syrian woman dressed in traditional clothes, far left, and this Saudi Arabian man wearing a construction hard hat, left. In the view of Arabs, what is an Arab?

CHAPTER 34 — A MOSAIC OF PEOPLES

Above left, musicians from Kuşadasi, Turkey, entertain their audience with traditional music. Above right, two children from the Iranian capital of Tehran pose for their photograph. How are Iranians and Turks similar to and different from Arabs?

He would recall some of the outstanding Arab monuments: the Alhambra, the Giralda Tower, and the Mosque of Cordova in Spain; the Dome of the Rock Mosque in Jerusalem; the Umayyad Mosque in Damascus; the Ahmed ibn-Tulun and Sultan Hassan mosques and the Citadel in Cairo.

He would remind you of the Arab wood carving, ceramics, inlaid metalwork, weaving, glass, illuminated manuscripts, tiles, and ivory caskets, which are now housed as priceless treasures in leading museums of the world.

It is this heritage of knowledge, history, language, and religion that makes an Arab feel truly an Arab and proud to be one, wherever he may live in the Arab countries.*

1. Where did Arabic-speaking people live before the spread of Islam? Where do most live today?
2. From what groups have Arabs descended? How did they become Arabs?
3. What three forces govern the attitudes and actions of all Arabs?

*The First Book of the Arab World by Ruth Warren, 1963, pp. 1, 4.

THE IRANIANS AND THE TURKS

Two groups of Middle Easterners who have had their own countries for hundreds of years are the Iranians and the Turks. Neither the Iranians nor the Turks are Arab, but, like the Arabs, most are Muslim. Each group, however, has its own language and history.

HERITAGE OF THE PERSIANS

Today more than 40 million people live in Iran, which was called Persia until recent times. The term "Iran" means "land of the Aryans," and many Iranians believe that they are descendants of the Aryans, Indo-Europeans who migrated into the region from southern Russia about 1000 BC. Iranians today speak Persian, or *Farsi*, an Indo-European language that is distantly related to English.

Iranians take pride in their long past, which they trace back 2500 years to the

Persian Empire and the rule of Cyrus the Great. As one author explains below, they also take pride in the fact that their culture has continued to flourish despite periods of **subjugation,** or control, by foreign peoples:

> In the days of Cyrus and Darius, nothing, it seemed, could stop the powerful and confident Persians. In most of the centuries since Alexander, the Iranians have had to accept military defeat and try to turn it into cultural victory, usually with remarkable success. A few years after Genghis Khan conquered and razed [Persia] for example, his descendants had been converted into thoroughly Persian poets and calligraphers. "We were invaded by Greeks, Arabs, Mongols, and Turks, but we did not lose our originality," [a] former Prime Minister . . . pointed out to me. . . . "In Persia, the Bedouins found a richer culture than their own, and the Persians recognized that this more powerful enemy could not be [destroyed]. So we [absorbed him into our culture]." A wry Persian proverb says: "Defeat makes us invincible."*

The early history of Iran is told in the country's national epic poem, the *Shah Namah,* or *Chronicles of the Kings,* written around 1000 AD by the Persian poet Firdausi. In the poem's 40,000 lines, mythological heroes and historical figures show the rise of the Persians and their triumph against evil. Portions of the epic are still memorized by Iranians today and recited in private homes and coffeehouses. As one writer explains below, for many Iranians, history and myth are still linked closely:

> . . . European archaeologists focus on the cliffside tombs of Darius, Xerxes, Artaxerxes I, and Darius II, six miles [9.6 kilometers] from Persepolis, but the Iranians still refer to this place as Naqsh-i-Rustam, or Picture of Rustam [a mythical hero in the *Shah Namah*], simply because they see no objection to confusing history and mythology. Persian parents name their children Kiyumars and Jamshid after the mythical kings as readily as Ardashir and Khosrow after historical kings. Fact and fiction, for the Iranian imagination, seem forms that fit familiarly into the same Persian miniature. This characteristic has moved Sir Roger Stevens to write, . . . "There can be no proper understanding of what underlies modern Iran unless we recognize the significance of this triumph of legend over history, or art over reality, this preference for embellishment as against unvarnished fact, for ancient folk beliefs as against new-fangled creeds."*

A BLENDING OF PEOPLES

The close to 50 million people of Turkey are a blend of the many peoples who have lived for centuries in the area of the Middle East once known as the peninsula of Asia Minor. The original inhabitants, Hittites and Greeks, were absorbed by the Seljuk Turks, who migrated from Central Asia in the 1000's. The Seljuks, who converted to Islam and became some of its fiercest fighters and defenders, were followed by other Turkish groups. The most important of these were the Ottoman Turks, whose empire ruled much of the Middle East, parts of North Africa, and southeastern Europe for over 600 years.

The Turks speak Turkish, which comes from their Central Asian roots but now is written in the Latin alphabet. After World War I, when Mustapha Kemal Ataturk came to power, he called for changes in Turkish customs and traditions. Since then, the Turks have become more and more westernized until today their culture is a blend of Turkish, Islamic, and western elements.

Fall of the Peacock Throne by William H. Forbis. COPYRIGHT © 1980, by William H. Forbis. Reprinted by permission of Harper & Row Publishers, Inc., p. 25.

*Ibid., p. 26

CHAPTER 34 — A MOSAIC OF PEOPLES

These are samples of writing in the four major languages of the Middle East. Arabic, Hebrew, and Persian are written from right to left. Turkish is written from left to right. Each sample is the equivalent of the English phrase "HELLO, HOW ARE YOU?"

ARABIC: مرحباً كيف حالك

HEBREW: מַה שְׁלוֹמְךָ?

TURKISH: *Merhaba Nasılsınız*

PERSIAN (FARSI): سلام حال شما چطور است

Despite their modernization, the Turks have not lost interest in their past. Among the things they treasure are the humor and wisdom of tales like the one below about the folk figure Nasrudin Hodja, a Muslim minister and teacher in whose honor they hold a festival each year:

> Nasrudin heard that there was a banquet being held in the near-by town, and that everyone was invited. He made his way there as quickly as he could. When the Master of Ceremonies saw him in his ragged cloak, he seated him in the most inconspicuous place, far from the great table where the most important people were being waited on hand and foot.
>
> Nasrudin saw that it would be an hour at least before the waiters reached the place where he was sitting. So he got up and went home.
>
> He dressed himself in a magnificent sable cloak and turban and returned to the feast. As soon as the heralds of the Emir, his host, saw this splendid sight they started to beat the drum of welcome and sound the trumpets in a manner consonant with a visitor of high rank.
>
> The Chamberlain came out of the palace himself, and conducted the magnificent Nasrudin to a place almost next to the Emir. A dish of wonderful food was immediately placed before him. Without a pause, Nasrudin began to rub handfuls of it into his turban and cloak.
>
> 'Your Eminence,' said the prince, 'I am curious as to your eating habits, which are new to me.'

These teenage members of Gadna *are working on a project to repair the stone wall of a well located in a remote Israeli village. What does* Gadna *aim to teach Israeli youth?*

'Nothing special,' said Nasrudin, 'the cloak got me in here, got me the food. Surely it deserves its portion?'*

1. From what ancient people do many of the Iranians believe they have descended? What are some of the major characteristics of Iranians?
2. Which ancient peoples blended together to become the Turkish people? What are some of the major characteristics of Turks?

THE ISRAELIS

About 4 million of the people in the Middle East are Israelis, citizens of the country of Israel. Of these, about .6 million are Arab, and most of the rest are Jewish.

The Israeli Jews have come from such places as Europe, the Middle East, North Africa, Asia, and the Americas. They are bound together, however, by their religion and by their long struggle to keep their religion and identity in spite of persecution. In the past, the people were held together by dreams of returning to the land they believe was promised by God to Abraham, the founder of Judaism. In the present, they are held together by the Hebrew language, their past, and their desire to survive as the nation of Israel.

Devotion to country is an important fact of life for Israeli Jews of all ages. Below, a 17-year-old *sabra,* native-born Israeli, discusses the role played by the *Gadna,* the Israeli Youth Corps:

The *Gadna* is the Israeli Youth Corps which began its life ten years before the establishment of the State of Israel. The *Gadna* provides a national framework for teaching young people—high school students and working teenagers—the meaning of national security. It aims to give us information on security matters, to teach us good citizenship, the geography of the country, and to train us in the use and mainte-

---
*"The Food of the Cloak" in *The Exploits of the Incomparable Mulla Nasrudin* by Idries Shah, 1972, A. P. Watt, Ltd., p. 42. Permission of Idries Shah.

nance of arms for when we do our national service. We work solidly day and night for six days a week. It's rough training.

We have six bases between the mountains of Ephriam and the slopes of Carmel. Here at Jua'Ra . . . we have to get up at about 5:00 A.M. and we're then inspected and counted in front of our flag. When we've exercised for half an hour, we have to clean our rooms and be ready for breakfast at 8:00 A.M. sharp.

Usually the first activity of the day for boys and girls alike is the study of weapons. . . . We also have sports and self-defense lessons, with runs and hikes into the nearby countryside. We have to learn about the nature of the country, its flowers and trees.

It's quite relaxing in the midst of all this to learn of our battle heritage, heroic stories that have become legends—Ben Gurion's life story, the War of Independence and so many others. Our field course studies are fun. We set up tents like scouts and learn to find our way around the area at night, using the stars as our guide.

Our morning is quite full. We break for lunch at 12:30, and then have an hour's rest before we continue our activities in the afternoon.

Then we may be taught the basics of security and guarding—how to act in emergencies in both open and closed areas, as well as standard guarding procedures such as patrols, guard duty at a gate, stopping a suspect and searching an area.

In addition to these everyday programs, there are some three-week courses during the school summer vacation. These include navigation; *Gadna* air cadets; corporal course; dog training; and a course which teaches new immigrants our language. Apart from the bases, we have shooting clubs in various cities and sometimes we take part in competitions—even the Olympics.

We really don't have much chance to relax in the evening after a strenuous day. After dinner we have cultural activities. Then we practice night-shooting, go for night hikes, and discuss social problems.

Every high school sends its youngsters to the *Gadna*. The *Gadna* aims to prepare us to be fully active citizens in a country burdened by unique defense problems, but working for peace and a better future. *Gadna* is not an army of youngsters: it is a school of Israel, really a school for the pioneer spirit, where volunteers can learn to serve Israel.*

1. Who are the Israelis?
2. What united Israeli Jews in the past? What unites them today?

THE PALESTINIANS

The pocket of land on the eastern seaboard of the Mediterranean, surrounded by Egypt, Saudi Arabia, Jordan, Syria, and Lebanon, used to be called Palestine, and Muslim and Christian Arabs and Jews lived there. Then, on May 14, 1948, the Jewish state of Israel was created on Palestinian land. The Arabs, however, did not want a Jewish state on land that once belonged to Jews and Arabs, Muslims and Christians, alike. As a result, conflict broke out between the Arabs and the Jews. Below, one Palestinian tells how the conflict broke up her family:

> We were a big family. . . . We were living on a big street. . . . They were shelling. We couldn't leave the house. . . . Our neighbors told us to leave for one week and then come back, for the sake of the children. So we left my father and my two elder brothers, and we came to the south of Lebanon. We couldn't go back.†

The Palestinian woman was one of many who lost their homes, farms, and businesses.

---

*"A school for the pioneer spirit" in *We Live in Israel* by Gemma Levine, 1983, The Bookwright Press, pp. 52–53.

†*The Palestinians* by Frank H. Epp, 1976, Herald Press, p. 57.

Many Palestinians have become permanent refugees, scattered in the countries bordering Israel, with more than 2 million living in crowded refugee camps. Some others, such as the ones discussed below, created new lives. Because of an emphasis on education, they are coming to occupy important posts throughout the Persian Gulf region:

> Many of the Palestinians I had met on the Gulf, . . . who were largely responsible for running [the cities of] Doha and Abu Dhabi, had started out in refugee camps. The doctors and teachers at Marqa Camp were refugees themselves, and the camp schools had a high record of getting students into technical colleges and universities. It was not too improbable that a hungry-looking child with his bowl of slop and paper cup of skim milk might wind up at the Massachusetts Institute of Technology or the London School of Economics. The pressure to succeed was intense.*

More than a half million Palestinians still live in Israel, while another 1.3 million live in the Israeli-controlled West Bank and Gaza areas. Many of these Palestinians are torn by divided loyalties such as the ones described below by a Palestinian living in Israel:

> I feel that I'm an integral part of the country, and I think that I should be loyal to the state of Israel, but still I feel that no power in the world whatsoever can cause me or force me to carry arms and kill my Arab brothers even if I wasn't a pacifist, which I am. And the only thing that I can do is work for peace because my own people, my own nation, is fighting my own state. We Arabs in Israel have quite a dilemma when our own government is fighting against our own people. At the same time our compatriots don't consider us a part of them. Our own people see us as agents and traitors.†

**Arabia: A Journey Through the Labyrinth.* Copyright © 1979 by Jonathan Raban. Reprinted by permission of SIMON AND SCHUSTER, Inc.

†*The Palestinians* by Frank H. Epp, 1976, Herald Press, p. 76.

Many Palestinians feel that their hopes can be fulfilled only by returning to their land and by creating a democratic nonreligious Palestinian state. Many Israelis, however, do not feel that this is workable. They argue that Jews from all over the world have already come and settled in Israel and there no longer is enough room to take back all the Palestinians. This attitude has angered many Palestinians, who agree with one Jerusalem accountant's comment that "the Arabs have been there for hundreds and hundreds of years. The Russian Jew or Polish Jew has never seen or even smelled the Palestine air."

As a result, the Israelis believe that their security would be threatened if they admitted into Israel persons who have been their enemies and who object to the "Jewishness" of the state. As seen below, this attitude, in turn, has increased the resentment of many Palestinians:

> To those . . . Israeli leaders who tell us that they can't trust the Arabs, I tell them that the Arabs feel exactly the same. They can't trust the Jews, who said first of all that they wanted only a national home, they wouldn't throw the Arabs out. . . . They built a state. They threw the Arabs out. Now they say they want a secure state.*

Despite all the difficulties, the Palestinians are sure of one thing—above all else, they are Palestinians. A student summed it up this way: "I am an Arab from the West side but not from Israel. I'm not Egyptian and not Jordanian. I'm a Palestinian."

1. Who are the Palestinians? Why did they leave their land? Where do many of them live today?
2. What is the basis of the disagreement that exists between the Palestinians and the Israelis?

**Ibid.*, pp. 44–45.

CHAPTER 34

THE ARMENIANS AND THE KURDS

Among the many groups living in the Middle East are two large ethnic groups —the Armenians and the Kurds. Although each used to occupy large areas of the region, neither has been able to form its own country.

A STRUGGLE TO SURVIVE

There are 4 million Armenians in the world. About 1 million live in Syria, Turkey, Lebanon, and other Middle Eastern countries, while 3 million live in the Soviet Republic of Armenia, which borders Turkey.

A hundred years ago, most of the Armenians lived in Turkey, the center of the Ottoman Empire. Christians living in a country of Muslims, they had their own culture, language, and alphabet. Then, in the late 1800's, Armenians wanted to break away from the Ottoman Empire and form a separate state. Fearing rebellion, the Turkish sultan, Abdul-Hamid II, ordered the Armenians massacred. As a result, between 1894 and 1896, about 300,000 Armenians were killed.

During World War I, the Armenians, like the Arabs, sought European support for independence. Some Armenians began to aid the armies opposing Turkey. Once again, Turkish anger focused on the Armenians, and in 1915 and 1916, an estimated 1 million were massacred, deported, starved to death, or died of illness. This was more than half of the Armenian people living in Turkey. Many of those who survived fled to Russia, Arab countries, Europe, and America. Most who remained in the Middle East settled in cities, where today they work in business, the trades, and crafts. But for many Armenians, there remain feelings of emptiness and of bitterness. In the poem that follows, an Armenian poet laments the loss of his people:

These Armenian priests are leading a candlelight procession through a Greek Orthodox church in Jerusalem. Where do most Armenians live today?

And I stood up, so that
In keeping with our ancestral laws,
I may read a last prayer
On the hapless victims of my nation,
Who in city and mart,
On hill and plain,
From sea to sea,
Extinguished are,
Dead, strewn, scattered
In their thousands. . . .

I stood there sullen and alone,
Solid like Mount Massis;
I called upon those miserable spirits,
Strewn forever as far as Mesopotamia,
As far as Assyria, the Sea of Armenia,
As far as the Hellespont,
As far as the stony shores of Pontus.

"Rest in peace, my orphans,
In vain are the bitter tears,
In vain and useless,
Man the man-eating beast
Shall remain thus
For a long, long time."*

---

*"Rest in Peace" from *Armenian Folk Festival at the New York World's Fair: 1964–65* by Hovhaness Tourmanian, translated by Zabelle Boyadijan.

This Kurdish woman is spinning yarn in the shade of an open-sided, reed enclosure. What are some of the restrictions that have been placed on the Kurds?

A STRUGGLE FOR SELF-RULE

The Kurds are a minority with a distinct cultural heritage. About 15 to 18 million live in the mountainous border region separating Turkey, Iraq, Iran, Syria, and the Soviet Union. They call their land Kurdistan, but their efforts to establish a nation of their own have been repeatedly put down.

In Turkey, for example, Kurds do not officially exist. Since 1925, it has been illegal for them to speak, read, or write in Kurdish or to wear Kurdish clothing. This has led to the **dual,** or twofold, life style described below:

> Names in Kurdistan have a special significance. The infant mortality rate is high all over Iran, Turkey, and Iraq, but in mountainous Kurdistan it is so high that I once met a Kurd from Turkey who had been named Mewan—"Guest." The local mullah [Islamic religious leader] who was always consulted in these matters suggested the name. Evidently God had been [appeased] by this sign of humility, for the child eventually grew to manhood. But the Turkish government also had to be [appeased]. In Kurdish, "guest" is *mewan;* in Turkish, *misafir.* From the time that this Kurd set foot in a Turkish schoolroom, he was Misafir. Only at home and around his hometown among Kurdish friends did he remain Mewan. The Kurds of Turkey are used to such duality. The town where Mewan was born also had two different names—one imposed by Ankara [the Turkish capital] and one that had been used as long as anyone could remember. In informal conversations out of government and secret police hearing, people always use the old name, even though it has been erased from the official map for years.*

Despite the restrictions placed on them, the Kurds have refused to give up their language. As one author explains below, it is the bond that continues to link them together:

> . . . To a people fighting for their lives and control of their land, their own language is a very precious thing. Not all Kurds are fair with European features; some look like Arabs. Not all Kurds wear their traditional baggy trousers or many-colored dresses; some work in the city and attend universities in Western clothes. But until now, nearly all Kurds, educated or uneducated, fair or dark, living in Turkey or Iran or Iraq or the USSR, have spoken Kurdish.†

The Kurds renew their struggle whenever a central government weakens. Although they have often sought outside help—from the British, Russians, and Americans, among others—they have little to show for their efforts except a very limited self-government in northern Iraq. This has not, however, made them give up their dream of self-rule.

1. Who are the Armenians? How and why did they suffer at the hands of the Turks?
2. Who are the Kurds? Why do they refuse to give up their language?

---

*_Children of the Jinn: In Search of the Kurds and Their Country_ by Margaret Kahn, 1980, Seaview Books, p. 33.

†*Ibid.,* p. xii.

EXPLORATION
MIDDLE EAST

On the map, locate the major groups of people who live in the Middle East. Then, based on the information in the chapter and in the map, discuss each group. Explain the similarities and the differences between each.

Read the quote that follows, and then answer the following questions:

1. What is meant by "Syria is typical"?
2. Based on what you read in the chapter, do you think that many other Middle Eastern countries have the cultural differences that Syria has? Explain your answer.

*Syria is typical. Mostly of Arab-Semitic stock, Syrians speak Arabic. The Muslim majority in Syria is made up of five major sects, and the Christians are split into eight sects. Jews practice their religion as they have done for hundreds of years under Arab rule. The Syrian radio broadcasts in Arabic, French, and English with "foreign" programs in Hebrew, Spanish, and Portuguese.**

*Adapted from "The Arabs: People and Power," Bantam/Britannica Books, p. 16, copyright 1978 by Encyclopaedia Britannica, Inc.

CULTURE–LANGUAGE GROUPS

Legend:
- Arabic
- Greek
- Hebrew
- Turkic
- Kurdish
- Persian, Armenian, Caucasic, Other

MIDDLE EAST

CHAPTER 34 REVIEW

POINTS TO REMEMBER

1. Throughout its long history, the Middle East has been home to many peoples.
2. More than half the people of the Middle East are Arabs, 90 percent of whom are Muslim. They all speak Arabic and are influenced by Arabic culture.
3. Iranians, who believe they are the descendants of the Aryans, take pride in their past and in the fact that their culture continues to flourish despite subjugation by foreign peoples.
4. Turks are a blend of Hittites, Greeks, Seljuk Turks, and Ottoman Turks. Their national language is Turkish, and their culture is a blend of Turkish, Islamic, and western elements.
5. Israeli Jews are bound together by their past, the Hebrew language, and their commitment to survive as a nation.
6. After the nation of Israel was established in 1948, many Palestinians were displaced. Many continue to live in refugee camps and seek creation of a nonreligious state in Palestine.
7. Armenians and Kurds each have their own language and culture. Despite all their efforts, neither has been able to establish a nation of their own.

VOCABULARY

Identify

Arabs	Aryans	Turkish	Palestine
Islam	*Farsi*	Israelis	Armenians
Arabic	Seljuk Turks	Hebrew	Kurds
Persia	Ottoman Turks	*Gadna*	Kurdish

Define

subjugation	*sabra*	dual

DISCUSSING IMPORTANT IDEAS

1. The Middle East is a mosaic of many diverse groups of peoples. Based on the information provided in the chapter and your knowledge of the Middle East, what advantages do you see in having such a diverse population? What disadvantages do you see?
2. Most of the groups mentioned in the chapter have their own languages. Do you think minority groups should be forced or required to adopt the majority's tongue and customs? Explain.
3. If you were a member of a United Nations committee trying to come up with a solution for the dispute between Palestine and Israel, what plan would you submit to establish trust between the two peoples?
4. What elements have created group identity among each of the different peoples of the Middle East? Give examples.

DEVELOPING SKILLS

DISTINGUISHING BETWEEN WARRANTED AND UNWARRANTED CLAIMS

When you buy a major appliance like a television set, you expect a *warranty*, or guarantee, to come with it. The warranty means, in effect, that the manufacturer or the company from which the product is purchased is supporting its statements, or claims, about the product's dependability by promising to fix the product if something goes wrong. In many cases, the terms of the warranty may be a deciding factor in the decision as to which set to buy. You would be more likely to buy, for example, the set whose warranty is in effect for two years than the one guaranteed for only 30 days.

The same holds true in other areas as well. For example, when you make a *claim*, you are stating something as a fact. When you *warrant*, or guarantee, what you say to someone, you are assuring that person of the dependability and truth of what you have said. Therefore, when you make a *warranted claim*, you are stating something as a fact that has a basis in truth and can be proven. An *unwarranted claim*, on the other hand, is a statement that lacks any proof or facts to support it.

Thus, to determine if a claim is warranted or unwarranted, you have to look for supporting proof. Even if a claim is true, if no evidence is presented to back it up, it must be considered unwarranted, and you would be correct to question it. In each case, you must ask yourself, "What evidence is presented to prove the truth of this statement?"

Look at the following examples:

Many Palestinians feel that their hopes can be fulfilled only by returning to their land and by creating a democratic, nonreligious state. Many Israelis, however, do not feel this is workable. They argue that Jews from all over the world have already come and settled in Israel, and there is no longer enough room to take back all the Palestinians.
(While the third statement may be true, no statistics showing the population density of the area or the number of Palestinians who want to return are given. Therefore, in this passage, the claim that there is not enough room to take back all the Palestinians is unwarranted.)

The Israelis believe that their security would be threatened if they admitted into Israel persons who have been their enemies and who object to the "Jewishness" of the state.
(This statement is a prediction that might very well prove to be true. However, since the persons to which the Israelis object have not actually been admitted to the country yet, at this point in time, there is no way of proving if the claim is true or not. Therefore, it is an unwarranted claim.)

The Middle East is not a melting pot. It is a mosaic of many diverse groups. Throughout its long history, the Middle East has been home to many peoples. Some vanished long ago. Others have survived for hundreds of years. Arabs make up the majority in several countries, while groups such as Iranians, Turks, and Israelis each have their own countries. Other groups—such as Palestinians, Armenians, and Kurds—continue to struggle for homelands of their own.
(The claim that the Middle East is not a melting pot but a mosaic of many diverse groups is supported by the statements that follow it, which point out that the Middle East has been home to more than one group or people, that groups formed their own national groups instead of intermixing, and that some groups feel the need to have their own countries rather than mingle with others in different countries. Therefore, the claim made at the beginning of the passage is a warranted claim.)

For practice in this skill, read the primary source reading on pages 370 and 371, and determine if the following claim is warranted or unwarranted: "Three forces—a belief in Islam, the Arabic language, and Arabic culture—govern the attitudes and actions of all Arabs."

CHAPTER 35
THE WAY OF LIFE

1. What is the role of the family in the Middle East?
2. How are traditional roles and patterns changing in the Middle East today?

... coming home one evening you hear the high warbling of the neighborhood women at a distance. Rounding the corner, you see a house draped with lights, strings of them running across the street. There out in front in a large square of light a crowd of men stands in a circle singing choruses to the songs called out from one side by a professional singer and his drummer. The men take their turns, leaping into the center to dance with their knives. Someone is marrying.

The marriage contract was devised, signed, and registered at court days earlier, after months of negotiations between the families. No simple certificate, this. The properties of two families are involved, carefully accumulated over the generations. Too many others are affected by a mismatched marriage; the choice and contract must be sound. Special attention was paid to the [brideprice] due from the groom to the bride; how much is it to be, how paid, and when? Out of that [brideprice] come furnishings for the newlyweds' rooms; perhaps half is held back for support should she be prematurely widowed, or for partial alimony (with additional support payments) should divorce occur.

The men dance before the family house of the groom, where the couple will live. The bride was moved there with great ceremony earlier; now she sits upstairs on a home-made throne in the main reception hall at her own party. She must be a model of demureness and innocence, with little talk and only rare, shy smiles. All of the ladies in the room are watching, thinking of their own weddings with nostalgic tenderness or anticipation. It's a solemn moment; only the occasional laughing glance of the bride's eyes betrays her excitement.

After half an hour has passed, the women usher the bride down from the throne and out to her new rooms. The signal is given; the rhythm of the dance changes. Men on both sides crowd forward; the oval becomes a corridor. The groom, led by the dancers, moves slowly towards the door, encouraged onward by a rapidly chanted cheerful song with the chorus half sung, half shouted; "God bless the Prophet and all of his kin; God bless this house and all within . . . welcome!"*

The wedding described above is a traditional ceremony in the country of Yemen. Most likely, the bride and groom have met only a few times and barely know each other. The marriage is the carefully matched joining of two people and their families. All wedding ceremonies in the Middle East are not like this one. All, however, mark the beginning of a new life for the bride and groom and concern entire families. The family is at the very core of Middle Eastern life. Most socializing centers around it. The roles men and women play in it more often than not mirror their traditions, customs, and values. Although the many changes that have taken place in the area in recent years have created some tensions and strained some family relationships, the family continues to be the most important unit in Middle Eastern society.

*"Impressions from a writer's notebook—At Home in Yemen" by Jon Mandaville in *Aramco World*, Vol. 32, No. 3, May–June 1981, p. 30.

THE FAMILY

Togetherness, love, obedience, mutual help, and respect are the cornerstones of the traditional Middle Eastern family which, for most Middle Easterners, includes grandparents, aunts, uncles, and cousins as well as the immediate family of parents and brothers and sisters. Individuals find their identity through membership in the family group. If one family member does well and is praised, the entire family shows pride. If one family member does not behave properly, the entire family shares the shame.

In the Middle East, then, the proper marriage partner is very important. Marriage generally is a **complementary relationship,** one in which each partner contributes what the other partner may lack or need. Below, Ommohamed, a woman from a village in Egypt, explains to her son what marriage and family mean to her and why:

> "Marriage means you are establishing a household. You must become a real man who looks to the needs of the house and the land, a man who fathers many children and raises them. It means to prosper and lead a decent life so that everyone must respect you." Ommohamed described the kind of marriage she had expected—expected as by right—as a small girl: a husband who would give her love and comfort and an expected place. She knew from hard-earned experience that a villager's freedom and dignity depended upon observing the time-honored codes. The ideal of every *fellah* [farmer] was to own land and a buffalo, marry, father children—especially sons—and prosper. Ommohamed knew young men like Shahhat were ardent, sensual, and romantic, but that the heat of such passion cooled all too soon; after thirty or so it was the children, the household, the needs of the land, and the family's social position within the village that bound a husband and wife together. In her eyes men were kept in place less by their own virtue than by Islamic law and village social pressure.
>
> To the Ommohamed family, property, and social position were everything; the family's task was to uphold such values and work the land, producing children as helpers and eventual replacements in a task that would go on forever. The institutions of family and property had been strengthened by time and tradition, and anyone who lightly violated the customs that supported them would be severely punished and ostracized [excluded].*

Religious teachings and traditional customs have influenced the roles of men and women both in a marriage and in the family. By taking on the responsibilities of their roles, they act to ensure the welfare and survival of their families.

THE MEN

Traditionally, men have held the superior role and have been responsible for the care and protection of their families. Within the family, their word has been law, and it is quite a shock to everyone concerned when something threatens that role. Below, a young Israeli remembers what happened in his family when his father had to resort to doing labor considered beneath him:

> My father believed, he honestly believed, that with Israel's establishment the Messiah was coming. So when Arabs in Tripoli [Libya] burnt our synagogue, we came to Israel with all the rest. I'll never forget that first winter in a tent—mud and cold and meager rations; it was sheer misery. My father and two older brothers finally got jobs, road building. That first evening they came home their backs were breaking. My mother cried, my brothers and sisters cried, we all cried. We wouldn't let

---

*Shahhat, an Egyptian by Richard Critchfield, 1978, Syracuse University Press, pp. 29–30.

CHAPTER 35 THE WAY OF LIFE

The truckers, bus drivers, and other travelers in this drawing, all of whom are male, are relaxing at a truckstop in Bājil, one of a dozen busy crossroads towns in the Yemen Arab Republic. What is the benefit to Middle Eastern families when men and women fulfill their complementary roles?

our father go back to that job, not for anything. You have to understand. Where we came from a Jewish father is a patriarch; he is king of the family. He commanded our absolute obedience and God help us if we ever disobeyed. Our father used to have a small leather shop in the *mellah,* the ghetto. He didn't earn much but he was his own master. Now, here in Israel, he was made into a common laborer—a common laborer! . . . But my father did go back to that job. He had no choice—we had to eat. In my eyes, as a youngster, he was never the same again. He was no longer family king, not to me.*

Young boys learn how to be men by imitating their fathers and by taking over their responsibilities when they are absent. In villages, they help in the fields. They learn how to drive the oxen or the tractor and help

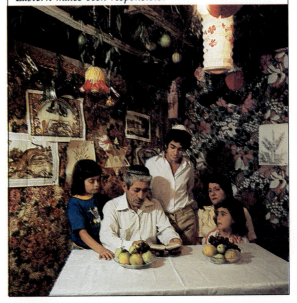

Led by the head of the family, who wears a small black cap called a yarmulke, *this Jewish family celebrates* Sukkot, *the Jewish festival of thanksgiving, which marked the close of harvest season for the Jews of ancient Palestine. Traditionally, for what have Middle Eastern males been responsible?*

---
*Excerpt from *The Young Inheritors* by Yehuda Avner. Copyright © 1982 by Yehuda Avner. Reprinted by permission of Doubleday & Company, Inc.

maintain wells and water lines. In towns and cities, they help in the family shops. In the evenings, boys often sit in on the men's family councils. There they learn such skills as **mediation,** or the settling of disputes. Below, a writer visiting the Yemen Arab Republic comments on this process:

> Seven- or eight-year-old boys sit silently with the men in the family council while business decisions are made. They sit through negotiated land and water disputes with other families, assimilating bargaining postures, the diplomacy of negotiations, preparing for their turn. They learn the usefulness of mediation.
>
> Mediation is critical. In this land, family honor and personal pride can easily drive one and one's family into a struggle which reason knows is foolish. The Prophet Muhammad himself first went out to Medina —then called Yathrib—as a mediator to stop a war long underway there. Many a town has been founded in Yemen as a *hujra,* a place where the mediator, called in from outside, first settled then stayed to guarantee the peace. Watching their fathers, the boys learn this duty early. It is not uncommon to see a passing boy place himself between two angry children, talk their anger down and turn them away from fighting. It's no more than adults do; an argument out of hand demands mediation from the first passerby. Every member of the community must help keep the peace; peace is too fragile to have it otherwise.*

THE WOMEN

In the past, women were considered **subordinate,** or secondary, to men. They were expected to obey and please their husbands and to stay at home and raise their children. *Purdah,* the seclusion or separation of women from men, was practiced by many women. Some extended the concept by wearing veils to hide their faces from men who were not members of their families. In some Muslim homes, women had their own entrances separate from those of the men and ate their meals only in the company of other women.

The ideal Muslim wife and mother was expected to be obedient, quiet, patient, affectionate, self-sacrificing, and devoted to her husband and children. Girls learned these qualities and their roles by imitating their mothers, by helping with household chores, and by listening to what their mothers told them. Girls who had been allowed to attend school as youngsters often were made to stay home once they became teenagers. Their marriages were arranged for them at an early age so that the family honor would not be endangered by a mismatched marriage or the birth of a child out of wedlock.

For most Middle Eastern women, the "proper behavior" has become so ingrained that trying to break the pattern is hard and, at times, embarrassing. As can be seen, an

These Yemeni women and girls mix the modern and the traditional in their clothing. Why is it hard for some Middle Eastern women to break old patterns?

---
*"Impressions from a writer's notebook—At Home in Yemen" by Jon Mandaville in *Aramco World,* Vol. 32, No. 3 May–June 1981, pp. 30–31.

American writer discovered this when she brought her husband with her to lunch with an Iranian Kurdish friend:

> "Would you like to eat with your husband or upstairs with me?" Aisha asked me when Jared arrived.
>
> We were down in the sheikh's sitting room, because the kitchen was also downstairs and Aisha was alternating in her roles as chef and hostess. Sheikh Avdila was leaning back in one of the enormous easy chairs which lined the walls of his sitting room, making small talk in slightly too formal English.
>
> When Jared came to the doorway of the room I looked from him to Sheikh Avdila and back to Aisha. Here was Jared, getting to meet Sheikh Avdila on his first visit to this house, a chance I had waited weeks for. But if I chose to stay with the men, what would Aisha do? She would have to eat alone. Craftily, I appealed to Sheikh Avdila's Western sensibilities.
>
> "Can't we all eat together?" I asked.
>
> "Of course," he said genially, and he instructed Aisha to eat with us. For Sheikh Avdila it was simple. But for Aisha, I saw it was not so easy. She barely touched her food, and I felt badly that my curiosity had outweighed my feelings of consideration for her.*

1. What are the basic values of the traditional Middle Eastern family?
2. What is the role of the man in the family? How do young boys learn this?
3. What is the role of the woman in the family? How do young girls learn this?

SOCIAL LIFE

Socializing is an important part of daily life for most Middle Easterners. They enjoy interacting with other people and, as can be seen below in this description of a crowded working-class Cairo neighborhood, there is constant activity and interchange:

> The household brigade is everywhere —women bringing water; women running errands; women baking bread in ovens beneath the stairways; women washing clothes and hanging them from balconies to drip on the passerby below; women preparing vegetables or picking through rice with keen-eyed inspection; women protecting chickens set free from their coops under the bed to scratch for a few minutes of freedom in the street below; women rocking babies and chatting with their neighbors between tasks. They shout across the alley addressing each other in the traditional way. . . . Other women, usually older ones, take up accustomed spots on street corners, sitting cross-legged to sell the products of their morning efforts: stuffed squash and cabbage, aromatic soups, fried fish, or eggplant. The hours pass in this way, shifting from time to time as quarrels break out, as accidents occur, as sewer pipes burst, as a child needs reprimanding. When women hear news of the death of someone, or a birth, or a marriage in trouble they flock to the scene dropping everything to offer condolence, to give help, and to dispense advice.
>
> As the sun creeps higher in the sky the *muezzin* [Muslim crier who calls the people to prayer] calls the midday prayer, one of the five calls of the day, and mosques fill up with men emerging from workshops, behind counters, and from the ranks of the hard-core coffee shop habituées. Despite their numbers there is no diminution of the bustle outside. The women retire about this time to fill the alleyways with the delicious smells of garlic and frying onions, the poor man's "caviar." Again the [errand runners] emerge with their enamelled bowls bringing back dishes to supplement the family fare or to provide the main dish for families too poor to cook. Their scurryings and the penetrating aromas build anticipation until two or

---

Children of the Jinn by Margaret Kahn, 1980, Seaview Books, p. 140.

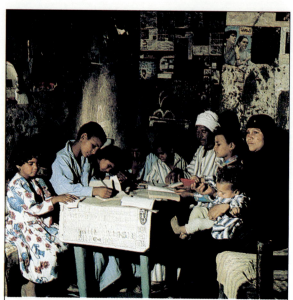

The members of this Egyptian fellaheen *family enjoy reading, writing, and spending time together in their "family circle." What are several characteristics of some middle-class Egyptian social gatherings?*

THE FAMILY CIRCLE

A good deal of the socializing takes place within the family. It is especially important that families and friends exchange visits at times of births, deaths, weddings, and holidays. Social events on these occasions serve to strengthen the bonds of family and friendship. Below, a visitor describes one such event, a seven-day party in celebration of the birth of a son in an Egyptian middle-class family:

> Each person (relatives of the mother and father and some work colleagues of the mother) who came was greeted with kisses and individual attention, even down to the tiniest baby. If anyone was quiet for a while, he or she was drawn into conversation again, regardless of age. The conversations included comments about events that took place on the way to the visit, about events of importance to those assembled, news about persons who were not present. The remarks were normally personal, and the topics rarely touched upon . . . matters beyond the immediate experience of the people present. The host and hostess were active in directing the conversation, asking the critical questions that would bring out each person in turn. There were no long soliloquies [talking by one person] except when a story was told about a sequence of events that everyone could enjoy; more common was rapid-fire comment around the group. The time passed quickly, and the conversation was light and full of jokes. Meanwhile, there was the constant movement of people going and coming, bringing drinks and taking the empty glasses away. It was not easy to distinguish the hosts from the guests; everyone helped out. Age groups were not segregated in different locations nor did they assume special functions at the party. Everyone was included in all aspects of the activity.*

three o'clock when the men return and the family consumes its biggest meal of the day. From then until late afternoon, the pace relaxes as dishes are slowly washed and several of the family members drift off to sleep.

While the adult world runs down, the child's world continues in ever-increasing activity as school children join in the soccer games or general rowdiness of those who stayed at home and now are released from their tasks of the morning. . . .

By late afternoon and evening activity picks up again for the mostly male coffee shop crowd. Women chat quietly in doorways and from the slower pace of their conversations and movements it is clear that the important events of their day are over. They slowly withdraw their children and their attention from the streets to the shuttered interiors of their homes. By ten or eleven the streets are again empty and grown wider as shopkeepers draw in their displays and close up for the night.*

Family in Contemporary Egypt by Andrea B. Rugh, 1984, Syracuse University Press, pp. 18–19.

Family in Contemporary Egypt by Andrea B. Rugh, 1984, Syracuse University Press, p. 150.

PROPER SOCIAL BEHAVIOR

"If people are standing at the door of your house, don't shut it before them." "Give the guest food to eat even though you yourself are starving." These are but two of many Middle Eastern "rules" about social behavior and hospitality. When visiting or entertaining in the Middle East, certain rules set down over time by religious teachings, customs, and proverbs must be followed. As explained below, hospitality of the highest level must be extended and certain rules followed:

> The ultimate aim of civility and good manners is to please: to please one's guest or to please one's host. To this end one uses the rules strictly laid down by tradition: of welcome, generosity, affability, cheerfulness, and consideration for others. . . .
>
> . . . To persuade a friend to stay for lunch is a triumph and a precious honor. To entertain many together is to honor them all mutually.
>
> It is equally an honor to be a guest. Besides the customary obligations of cordiality and welcome, there is the need for the warmth of personal contact and cheerful company, the desire to congregate in groups, and the wish to please. It is common when preparing food to allow for an extra helping in case an unexpected guest should arrive. . . . When a meal is over there should always be a good portion of food left, otherwise one might think that someone has not been fully satisfied and could have eaten more.
>
> The host should set before his guest all the food he has in the house, and apologize for its meagerness, uttering excuses such as: "This is all the grocer had," or "I was just on my way down to the confectioner's," or "For the past two weeks I have been preparing for my niece's wedding and have not had time to make anything else."
>
> If a guest comes unexpectedly, the host must never ask why he has come, but receive him with a smiling face and a look of intense pleasure. After a ceremony of greetings, he should remark on the pleasure of seeing him and the honor of such a visit. The guest should never say right away why he has come, if there is a reason, but first inquire about the family, friends, and affairs of his host. The latter

Although the table at which these two Kuwaitis are seated has been set with eating utensils, they prefer to follow the age-old Arab custom of eating with bread and fingers. Traditionally, only the right hand was used for eating. While rules such as these are still strictly observed in some areas of the Middle East, in others, where western influence is stronger, they are gradually being abandoned. What is the ultimate aim of proper social behavior in the Middle East?

must treat his guests as though he were their servant; to quarrel with them would be a disgrace. He must never argue with them about politics or religion, but should always acquiesce [accept]. He must never ask his guests if they would like food or drink, but provide these automatically, insisting that they have them and ignoring repeated refusals. . . .

A guest, in turn, must also play his role correctly. He should "guard his voice, shorten his sight, and beautify (praise) the food." That is, although he must commend everything, exclaim in admiration, and congratulate, he should not look about too much, nor inspect too closely. The Quran [Koran] advises him to talk nicely and politely: "Sow wheat, do not sow thorns; all the people will like you and love you." "Don't enter other people's houses, except with permission and good manners." "Beautify your tongue and you will obtain what you desire."*

1. What are some of the ways in which Middle Easterners socialize? Why is this socialization important?
2. What are some of the rules of hospitality and social behavior that Middle Easterners observe?

BREAKING WITH TRADITION

Over the past 20 years, broad changes have taken place in the Middle East, upsetting many traditional ideas about the family and the roles of men and women. Increased access to secondary and higher education has led some young men and women to broaden their horizons and, in some cases, to question their traditional roles. Imported television programs and movies have spread western ideas and values about sexual equality and the family. Hard economic times in some countries and new job opportunities in others have brought more and more women into the job market.

FAMILY BONDS

Throughout the Middle East, family bonds have been strained as young people begin to seek less traditional ways of life, forcing parents to develop new outlooks about what is right and proper behavior. A case in point is the reaction of the Shadhad family of Oman to a daughter's choice of a career:

We met the Shadhad family through the police. Oman was the first Gulf state to introduce policewomen, because of the need to search women at the international airport, and among the first [recruits] was Isa's younger sister Fawzia, aged eighteen. The move shocked her family. Her mother was horrified, her uncles, aunts and cousins were scandalized; not that a girl should work, for there is a saying, 'Omani women have the best manners of anybody in the world, and they work for their men like donkeys,' but that she should work with men. The vast majority of girl secretaries are Indian or from other Arab countries. It is now considered all right by many families for an Omani girl to become a teacher, provided she teaches only girls, or a nurse, so long as it is in the women's wards; but to work in the same office as men—and in Fawzia's case, to come into contact with male criminals!

Isa returned home from leading a Boy Scout delegation to Beirut to find his sister missing; she had joined the police and gone to their training school ten miles [16 kilometers] out of Muscat. Being a modern young man, he talked to Fawzia, discovered that her mind was made up, and agreed to support her against family hostility. As soon as their father heard the news, he came to the house and demanded the return of his daughter. He was under the impression that she was

---
*From *A Book of Middle Eastern Food*, by Claudia Roden. Copyright ©1968, 1972 by Claudia Roden. Reprinted by permission of Alfred A. Knopf, Inc.

This Omani policewoman, a radio dispatcher for a large metropolitan police force, reflects the changing role of women in the Middle East. Before 1970, for example, few Omani girls attended school, but in recent years, the government has encouraged education for girls as well as boys. How do some Middle Eastern parents view their children's moves away from the traditional?

working for the money, which reflected badly on his manhood and ability to provide for his family. But when she took her parents to the training school and let them see that she was happy in her job and that she was being well looked after, they agreed to let her stay. It was, in its own way, a dramatic break with tradition.*

It is no easier for young men to break with tradition than young women. Below, a journalist describes the reaction of a family in Yemen to their son's decisions:

> Taha is the result of the new style schools and knowledge. Bright and ambitious, he began as a farmer's son. He knows animals and crops; he knows the land. He also knows literature, and teaches as an instructor at the new University of Sanaa. Back on the farm, his older brother is managing the operation. Taha's father wanted him to come home, but the call of language [studies] and literature led him to refuse. He wants to learn more, research, teach.
>
> It's not that his love for his parents, the land and the village is less. He visits when he can, in breaks between classes and during holidays. Recently he spent three weeks away from the library contracting with a drilling crew to put in a well at the farm. He sits when he can with the family, helping in land dispute matters. I visited the farm with him once, and could see the love shared between him and his parents. I could also see, as the visit progressed, the small signs of growing estrangement.
>
> Two years ago his father in desperation played his last card; he arranged a marriage for Taha with a local village girl.
>
> "My mother says that she's pretty and bright," said Taha. "I'm sure she is. But the point is, she'll never agree to leave the village and father knows this."
>
> The real point was, Taha had already chosen his wife-to-be. This girl, 'Aisha, grew up in the same area as Taha. But like him, she worked her way through the new school system and is in the process of finishing her B.A. in biology at the university. Over this past year Taha has, on his own, negotiated the marriage with her

---

*The Last Corner of Arabia by Michael Darlow and Richard Fawkes, 1976, Namara Publications, pp. 40, 42.

A woman dressed in the traditional black chador peers at western-attired mannequins in the window display of a fashionable clothing store in Tehran. In 1985, 150 imported-clothing stores like this were closed down by the government in an effort to rid the country of western influences. Which Middle Eastern countries have a conservative view toward the changing role of women?

family, negotiations complete with long, serious talks with her father about his future plans. They will be married in June, after she graduates. The house will be finished by then, and waiting.*

CHANGING ROLE OF WOMEN

Change occurs unevenly in the Middle East. Some countries take a conservative view, while others are more liberal. Thus, changes are accepted differently from country to country. This is especially true when it comes to the changing role of women.

In Saudi Arabia, Iran, and the Gulf states, a conservative view is taken toward change concerning women. Saudi women, for example, may attend universities. At the same time, however, strong efforts are made to keep them separated from men. In some universities, female students attend separate classes and may question male professors only over the telephone.

---
*"Impressions from a writer's notebook—At Home in Yemen" by Jon Mandaville in *Aramco World*, Vol. 32, No. 3, May–June 1981, p. 33.

In Jordan, Egypt, Iraq, Syria, Turkey, Lebanon, and Israel, women began entering public life in the 1940's, and a more liberal view is taken. The governments have encouraged women to enter the work force, especially when there has been a shortage of male workers. In Egypt, for example, about 25 percent of the male labor force was working in other countries in 1983. Below, a journalist discusses the impact this has had on the role of Egyptian women:

> . . . as husbands and older sons went off to work in Iraq or the Gulf states, the independence of village women grew enormously. In the Nile Delta and Upper Egypt some villages now have no adult males. Suddenly women have had to learn about buying and selling to get the best prices for their eggs and cows and to make all the decisions about the education of their children.
> Responsibility for their children's schooling has made it much more important for women to learn to read and write. . . . Many women, conscious of their new role, are ashamed to see their children learn the alphabet before they have. . . .

In the cities women who once would not have thought of entering a furniture store or calling a plumber have been forced into the world. A Western visitor to Cairo might take the growing number of long sleeves and veiled faces on the streets as a sign of Islamic fundamentalism on the march. But actually women are breaking down traditional Islamic barriers between the home—traditionally the woman's domain—and the outside world —traditionally the man's. . . .

Another significant change is the increasing representation of women in professional life. Now that the best-trained male teachers, professors, engineers, scientists, and doctors have gone abroad, their places must be filled by women. Women today hold almost half of the jobs in radio, television, and the press, and most of the teaching positions in elementary education. . . .

Even such traditionally male bastions as the army and the police have had to adapt to the exodus of the male labor force, promoting women to higher positions than ever before. Women as traffic officers are no longer the exception in Cairo and Alexandria—handing out tickets to female taxi drivers without a second thought. . . .

The most ambitious women in Egypt have begun to look for work abroad, and many have emigrated to work, for example, in Kuwaiti hospitals as head nurses and in Abu Dhabi as computer operators. Women professors have gone to Riyadh [capital of Saudi Arabia] to teach at the world's first Islamic Women's University.*

Not all Middle Eastern countries are as liberal as Egypt. And, even in Egypt, not all groups have accepted the change. Muslim religious leaders believe that God has ordained that a woman's role is in the home, and some of the more traditional members of the parliament want to pass laws that would ban women from all jobs. Even university women are being pressured to wear the veil, which in recent years has become a symbol of the subordinate role of women.

Resistance to a broader role in society for women is not confined to Islamic countries. In the largely Jewish state of Israel, where there is a tradition of women working outside the home, religious fundamentalists have been calling for laws that would return women to the home and establish separate schools for girls and boys. The greatest acceptance of a broader role for women is found among educated upper- and middle-class people in Istanbul, Beirut, and Cairo. But, even for these groups, when there is a conflict between job and family, obligation to family is expected to come first.

1. What factors have contributed to changing roles for men and women?
2. What did Fawzia and Taha do to cause strain in their families?
3. What are some ways in which the role of women has changed? What has been the reaction to these changes?

*"Egyptian Women Advance" by Harm Botje, translated from "NRC Handelshlad," Rotterdam in *World Press Review*, December 1983.

This Israeli woman is training for army duty. Like other unmarried Jewish women, she must serve two years in Israel's armed forces after reaching age 18. Who opposes a broader role for women in Israel?

EXPLORATION
MIDDLE EAST

Read the following proverbs and indicate what they suggest about the Middle Eastern attitude toward family:

"A house without a child in it is like a room in darkness."

"Children are our hearts walking on earth."

"My brother and I against my cousin; my cousin and I against the strangers."

"To lose one's family is to lose one's dignity."

Read the statements that follow. Then answer these questions:

1. Which statements do you think reflect traditional Middle Eastern views of family and the roles of men and women? Identify the traditional view reflected in each.
2. Which statements do you think show change? Identify each change.

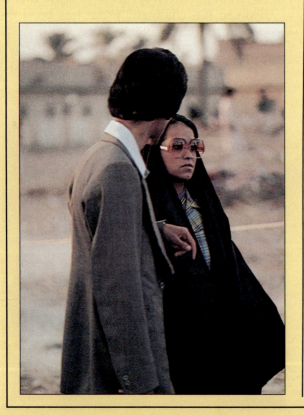

I work all day. Must I fight every night? [My wife] says I don't talk to her. When am I supposed to talk to her? It's part of our way of life to have an open house with friends walking in at any time. I can't lock our door to make time to talk to her. And I don't want to—what else is there that matters in life but your friends and your family?

I don't believe in her covering her face but I wouldn't bring shame on my family by letting her be seen unveiled in daylight. But at night, if we're going by car to friends, I don't even ask that of her. I just ask her to put on her cloak and a thin chiffon scarf. Don't women wear headscarves in Europe? Is that a terrible sacrifice? Ten years ago I couldn't have driven with her sitting beside me in the car, let alone without a veil. I couldn't have let her go to Europe for the summer to get away from the heat. Why won't she see how things have changed for the better?*

I met a teacher who had returned to Syria after a ten-year absence: "I couldn't believe what I found," he said. "Ten years ago the great majority of women went veiled. Now, even in the villages, few do. Most girls wear blue jeans and are really indistinguishable from Europeans or Americans."†

Islamic virtue reigns in every aspect of public life [in Iran]. Alcohol is strictly forbidden, of course, and every woman on the street wears either the traditional chador, . . . or the more practical hijab, a dark scarf pulled over the forehead, a baggy, dark smock and loose trousers. . . . Time, Newsweek and other Western publications are regularly available, but a Government functionary goes through them first, carefully inking over with felt pen all but the face in any woman's picture. . . . An Islamic skiing garment has been designed, at some cost in wind resistance, for women who want to try the

---
*Oil Sheikhs by Linda Blandford, 1976, George Weidenfeld and Nicolson Limited/Arthur Barker Limited, p. 53.

†"Syria" by Howard La Fey in *National Geographic*, Vol. 154, No. 3, September 1978, p. 333.

snow at the ski resorts in the Elburz mountains —separate slopes, of course—and a solid fence is being constructed down the middle of the beach along the Caspian Sea for segregated bathing. . . .

. . . there are patrols of Islamic enforcers in white Nissan jeeps who can grab a woman off the streets if they do not like her garb—perhaps her scarf is set too far back, showing a fringe of hair—and carry her off to Evin Prison, where she is treated as a prostitute.*

My wife must be a Moslem bedouin. My mother will see her first and report back to me —whether she is good-looking; whether the economic situation of her family is good; whether she has gold—and then I decide if I want to marry her. I see her for the first time on our wedding day. . . . Some bedouins still buy their brides with camels. Seven is considered a fair price. . . .†

We live in a large Arab home with a garden full of orange and pomegranate trees. . . . It's normal for a working woman to help her husband pay for the upkeep of the home. The Arabs are very family-minded and since my husband is the only son in the family, he takes care of both his family and me. I find it a bit difficult to live with them; naturally, I'd like complete privacy with my husband. . . .

I work in a pharmacy every day in Afulla until one o'clock. My television job as a news announcer is only twice a week from six o'clock until eight o'clock. My husband drives me down to Jerusalem, and I like that very much; we usually have a meal in Jerusalem or see some friends before returning home. It does make a break for us. So it isn't difficult for me to combine both my jobs.**

---

*"Iran: Obsessed with Martyrdom" by John Kifner in *The New York Times Magazine*, December 16, 1984, pp. 42, 47. Copyright © 1984 by The New York Times Company. Reprinted by permission.

†"Our life is with the sheep and goats" in *We Live in Israel* by Gemma Levine, 1983, The Bookwright Press, p. 15.

**"The Arabs are very family-minded" in *We Live in Israel* by Gemma Levine, 1983, The Bookwright Press, p. 47. Reprinted by permission.

CHAPTER 35 REVIEW

POINTS TO REMEMBER

1. The family, the cornerstones of which are togetherness, obedience, mutual help, and respect, is the most important unit in Middle Eastern society. Family members include grandparents, aunts, uncles, and cousins, as well as the immediate family.
2. In the Middle East, marriage generally has been a complementary relationship in which men traditionally have held the superior position and women were considered subordinate. Men were responsible for the care and protection of their families, while women were expected to obey and please their husbands and to stay at home and raise their children. Children learned these roles by imitating their parents.
3. Visiting, entertaining, and socializing are a part of daily life and serve to strengthen the bonds of family and friendship. These activities are governed by certain rules of etiquette set down over time by religious teachings, customs, and proverbs.
4. The broad economic and social changes occurring in the Middle East are upsetting many traditional values and expectations. This is especially true in regard to the role of women.

VOCABULARY

Define

complementary relationship   mediation   subordinate

DISCUSSING IMPORTANT IDEAS

1. How do you interpret the statement that in the Middle East, individuals find their identity through their membership in the family group? Is this true in your society? Give examples to support your answer.
2. If you were a Middle Easterner of marriageable age, what reasons would you give your family for wanting to select your own husband or wife? What arguments might your parents give you against taking such a step?
3. Middle Easterners see children as "helpers and eventual replacements in a task that would go on forever." Based on the information in the chapter, what reasons can you give for them to have this view? Do you agree or disagree with their view? Explain.
4. During the Egyptian party discussed in the chapter, "age groups were not segregated in different locations nor did they assume special functions at the party." What conclusions can you draw from this as to how Egyptians treat their children? Their elderly? How does this compare/contrast with the treatment of children in your society? With the treatment of the elderly?

CHAPTER 35 THE WAY OF LIFE 583

DEVELOPING SKILLS

ANALYZING PHOTOGRAPHS

Photographs are useful sources of information that can give a sense of people, places, and events. At the same time, however, photographs—and videos as well—can also misrepresent or mislead by omitting things and adjusting where and how objects or people are placed. Therefore, it is important to know how to *analyze* photographs, or view them critically.

The photograph below is a reproduction of a painting that appears on page 572. The guidelines that follow the photo will help you to analyze not only this photo but other ones as well:

1. Look closely at the photograph.
2. Read any accompanying written material. *(Read the caption and the section on women on pages 572 and 573.)*
3. Look at the photograph again, this time for details. List the details you see *(females of different ages; different types of clothing, some dark and some brightly colored; headcoverings on all the females except the younger children).* Describe the content of the photograph, indicating the objects *(none),* people *(females of different ages),* and actions *(none)* you see as well as the location where the photograph was taken *(cannot really tell, but clothing seems to indicate the Middle East).* Determine what the people in the photo seem to be doing *(posing for a painting or photograph)* and what relationship seems to exist between the people or the people and any objects in the photograph *(all female; all from the same culture).*
4. Identify the main idea or purpose of the photograph *(to show women of the Middle East).* At times, it may help to relate the details in the photograph to the information in the available written material. Ask yourself what impression the photograph creates about environment, life style, customs, or beliefs. *(While women in the Middle East have much in common, some hold different views or have different customs from others; little girls are brought up to be like their mothers or other older females.)* Determine what clues or details in the photograph contribute to your impression(s). *(The women are dressed in much the same manner, but the colors of their dress vary from dark to bright; the children are dressed in the same fashion as the older females.)*
5. Determine the accuracy of the photograph by asking yourself what the photograph seems to emphasize *(Women are considered as a group rather than as individuals.)* and what it seems to omit *(women who are westernized).* To help determine what may be left out, compare the photograph with other photographs of the same general subject or with other sources of information on the topic.
6. Determine what generalization(s) or inference(s) you can make based on the photograph. *(While all women are not the same in the Middle East, most tend to be traditional in their dress and manner.)*

For practice in this skill, use the suggested guidelines to analyze the photographs on pages 575 and 578.

CHAPTER 36
RELIGION AND STATE

1. How is Islam related to Judaism and Christianity?
2. What were some of the components and features of the Islamic state?

And We said: O Adam! Dwell thou and thy wife in the Garden, and eat ye freely (of the fruits) thereof where ye will; but come not nigh this tree lest ye become wrongdoers.

O Children of Israel! Remember My favour wherewith I favoured you and how I preferred you to (all) creatures.

And (remember) when We did deliver you from Pharaoh's folk, who were afflicting you with dreadful torment, slaying your sons and sparing your women: That was a tremendous trial from your Lord. And when We gave unto Moses the Scripture and the Criterion (of right and wrong), that ye might be led aright.

(And remember) when the angels said: O Mary! Lo! [God] giveth thee glad tidings of a word from Him, whose name is the Messiah, Jesus, son of Mary, illustrious in the world and the Hereafter, and one of those brought near (unto [God]).

[Muhammad] is but a messenger, messengers (the like of whom) have passed away before him. Will it be that, when he dieth or is slain, ye will turn back on your heels?

Know that [God] is severe in punishment, but that [God] (also) is Forgiving, Merciful.*

Many of these statements may seem familiar. They repeat Jewish and Christian beliefs, and similar ideas can be found in the Bible. Yet they are not from the Bible but from the Koran, the holy book of Islam. The third great religion that began in the Middle East —Islam—has much in common with Judaism and Christianity. All three of these religions share the same roots.

Within 20 years after the death of Muhammad, Islam's founder, in 632 AD, the Muslim Arabs had defeated the armies of the Persian and Byzantine empires and had conquered Syria, Egypt, and Persia. By the early 700's, they had created an empire that extended from the Atlantic Ocean to India and that covered an area greater than any empire that had come before it. The empire was the home of golden ages of achievements and the base of powerful armies that reached into the hearts of Europe, Asia, and North Africa. At different times, the empire was divided into kingdoms and smaller empires. The last of these—the Ottoman Empire—survived until World War I.

---

*The Meaning of the Glorious Koran, translated by Mohammed Marmaduke Pickthall, George Allen & Unwin Ltd., pp. 36–37, 66, 73, 105.

THREE RELIGIONS

In ancient times in the Middle East, there were many religions. People prayed to numerous gods and offered sacrifices to idols. They worshipped the forces of nature, the sun and the moon, the spirits of ancestors, and a goddess of fertility. Each group had its own religion and favorite deity, but belief in many gods was the traditional pattern.

JUDAISM

Then, among the Hebrews, a new and different religion began to emerge. The Old Testament of the Bible tells the Hebrews' story. Abraham, the first in a line of **patriarchs,** or male leaders, urged Hebrews to believe in only one god, an idea known as **monotheism.** God asked Abraham to sacrifice his son Isaac. When Abraham agreed, God made a **covenant,** or agreement, with him. It called for Abraham and his descendants to worship and obey only God. In turn, God would keep the following promise:

> I will indeed bless you, and I will multiply your descendants as the stars of heaven and as the sand which is on the seashore. And your descendants shall possess the gate of their enemies, and by your descendants shall all the nations of the earth bless themselves, because you have obeyed my voice.*

Around 1900 BC, Abraham led the Hebrews to Canaan, where they stayed for about 100 years. Abraham's idea of one god did not take hold at once. Old beliefs were hard to give up, but repeated disasters—periods of war, famine, plague, and enslavement—helped convince the Hebrews to accept God as the only true god.

The Hebrews were forced to leave Canaan by a drought. They went to Egypt where, several hundred years later, they were forced into slavery. They were led out of Egypt by a leader named Moses. During their **exodus,** or escape, Moses made a covenant with God, in which God promised:

> ... if you will obey my voice and keep my covenant, you shall be my own possession among all peoples; for all the earth is mine, and you shall be to me a kingdom of priests and a holy nation. These are the words which you shall speak to the children of Israel.*

God then repeated His promise to the Hebrews to give them "a land flowing with milk and honey."

Over hundreds of years, the Hebrews' beliefs slowly changed. Through a series of **revelations,** or disclosures, they came to believe that God was not theirs alone but of all humanity. But they continued to believe they were "the chosen people." The religion of the Hebrews was called Judaism, and the Hebrews came to be known as Jews.

CHRISTIANITY

A second religion to come out of the Middle East was Christianity, which is based on the life and teachings of Jesus. When Jesus was born, Palestine was ruled by the Romans. According to the Bible, when Jesus was about 30 years old, he began to travel throughout Palestine preaching. He told the people, "Think not that I have come to destroy the law or the prophets; I have come not to destroy but to fulfill them."

Jesus had been born a Jew and had received a Jewish education. The Jews believed that some day a **messiah,** or savior, would come from among them and save them. When Jesus arrived in Jerusalem, many Jews thought he was the messiah. They believed he would defeat the Romans and Jews once

---

*Genesis 22:17–18 (RSV)

*Exodus 19:5–6 (RSV)

This Jewish boy is reading from the Torah, the first five books of the Bible, on the day of his bar mitzvah, *the celebration of a boy's thirteenth birthday, marking his entry into adulthood in the eyes of the Jewish community. After his* bar mitzvah, *a boy is morally responsible for keeping all the commandments of his faith. What covenants did God make with Abraham and Moses?*

more would rule themselves. Jesus, however, was interested only in creating a spiritual kingdom, not in challenging the Romans. He said, "Render therefore to Caesar the things that are Caesar's, and to God the things that are God's."

Jesus taught that God was merciful, loving, and forgiving, and that anyone who was faithful and who lived by His teachings could be **saved,** or rewarded with everlasting happiness after death. He also believed in a **final judgment,** a time when the faithful would be saved while sinners would face eternal suffering and torment. Many people accepted what Jesus taught and became Christians. Most Jews, however, did not view Jesus as their messiah or accept his teachings. Their belief that a messiah was yet to come remains a major difference between Jewish and Christian belief today.

ISLAM

The third religion to come out of the Middle East was Islam, founded by an Arab merchant named Muhammad, who was born in the city of Mecca. Not much is known about Muhammad's early life. An orphan reared by his uncle Abū Tālib, at the age of 25 he married a well-to-do widow named Khadījah.

More is known about the city of Mecca than about Muhammad. It had grown up at the crossroads of two caravan routes, one from the east and the other running north to the Mediterranean. Because there was a constant supply of well water at this spot, Mecca became a regular stopping place for caravans. Some Meccans had become wealthy from serving and helping travelers.

Mecca was also a center of pagan worship. Pilgrims came from far away to pray there, giving Mecca its second largest source of income. Trade fairs, poetry contests, and festivals also attracted people of many talents and beliefs to the city.

In time, Muhammad became troubled by conditions in Mecca and wanted to change them. Members of one wealthy family controlled the city, while most of the townspeople were poor. Drinking, gambling, and corruption were widespread, and the people worshipped idols. Muhammad began to spend time alone, praying and fasting in a cave outside the city. At the time, Muhammad's actions were considered a normal step toward solving problems. Both Moses and Jesus had done the same thing hundreds of years earlier.

According to the Koran, an angel appeared to Muhammad one day while he was fasting. The angel said that God wanted Muhammad to be His messenger and had chosen him to carry His final revelations to the people. At first, Muhammad was terrified, but with the support of his wife Khadījah, he decided to try to do what God wished. Over a period of years, the angel Gabriel spoke God's words, in Arabic, to Muhammad. Muhammad memorized the words and then repeated them to anyone who would listen. Later, the words were written down and became the Koran.

Muhammad tried to make the citizens of Mecca give up their idols and submit to God. He stressed that submission—the word "Islam" in Arabic—should be made to no other god but "Allah"—the word for God in Arabic. Allah, he said, was the same god as the God of the Jews and the Christians.

Muhammad's message was not a popular one with Mecca's business and religious leaders, who feared that the city's economy and their personal prosperity would be ruined. At first, they laughed at Muhammad; later, they became worried and started to threaten him and his followers. Although Muhammad refused to stop spreading the words of God, opposition grew until it became too dangerous for him to stay in Mecca. In 622, he and his followers escaped to Yathrib, a city 250 miles (400 kilometers) to the north. Earlier, pilgrim leaders from Yathrib had been impressed by Muhammad and had invited him to come and settle a dispute in their city. The year of the escape from Mecca was later chosen to mark the beginning of the Muslim calendar.

MAJOR RELIGIONS

CHAPTER 36 RELIGION AND STATE

Calligraphy is one of the highest art forms of the Islamic world. On this panel, a master calligrapher has written an important article of the Islamic faith using 15 different styles of calligraphy. On what were many Islamic beliefs and practices built?

The escape was a turning point in Muhammad's life. Shortly after his arrival in Yathrib, the people accepted him as God's messenger and as the ruler of their city. Yathrib was given the new name of al-Medina al-Munawara, "the enlightened city," and became known as Medina. There, Muhammad continued to teach and to gain many converts. Within ten years, he had defeated the old leaders of Mecca and returned to that city in triumph.

1. What did Abraham urge the Hebrews to believe? How was this different from earlier beliefs?
2. What were some of Jesus' teachings? What did many Jews expect when he arrived in Jerusalem?
3. What did Muhammad stress in his teachings? How did he arrive at his beliefs?

A DIVINE CHAIN

Islam was not an entirely new religion. Many of its beliefs and practices were built on Judaism and Christianity. Muslims believe that the process of divine revelations started with the Old Testament and that Muhammad was the last in a divinely inspired chain of **prophets,** or religious leaders or teachers claiming to have messages from God. According to the Koran, God gave revelation to Muhammad just as He did to Noah and the prophets after him and to Abraham and to Jesus and to others.

As a result, Muslims have great respect for all the prophets as well as for the Bible, Judaism, and Christianity. They call Jews and Christians "People of the Book" and hold Abraham in special esteem. They believe that Arabs are descendants of Abraham through his son Ishmael and Jews descendants of Abraham through his son Isaac. Abraham's act of taking his son to the top of a hill and preparing to sacrifice him is thought to be the first example of complete submission to God's will. Because of this, Muslims consider Abraham to have been a Muslim and the first Muslim prophet. According to the Koran, "Abraham was indeed a model, devoutly obedient to God, true in faith, and he joined not gods with God."

The Koran also repeats many of the events surrounding the birth and life of Jesus. Muslims believe that Jesus was born of the spirit of God and that he transmitted the Lord's message and performed many miracles. As the Koran states:

> And [God] will make him [Jesus] a messenger unto the children of Israel, (saying): Lo! I come unto you with a sign from your Lord. . . .

This engraving shows Jesus preaching the Sermon on the Mount, in which he provided a model for Christian behavior. How do Muslims believe Jesus served God?

Taking their lead from Muhammad, devout Muslims see their lives as a preparation for the Day of Judgment, when people will rise from the dead and be judged according to how they conducted their lives. If they were faithful and obedient to the teachings of the Koran, they will be rewarded with eternal happiness in paradise, a land filled with flower gardens, cool streams, and singing birds. If they were not faithful, they will be damned forever in hell. These and other beliefs are set down in the Koran, which Muslims believe is the direct word of God.

THE KORAN

In addition to containing the basic beliefs of Islam, the Koran tells Muslims in a specific manner how they are to lead their daily lives.

And (I come) confirming that which was before me of the Torah [Jewish law], and to make lawful some of that which was forbidden unto you. I come unto you with a sign from your Lord, so keep your duty to [God] and obey me.*

MUHAMMAD AND GOD

To Muslims, God has no equal and there is no god but God. For this reason, they do not worship Muhammad and object to being called Muhammadans. When Muhammad died, many Muslims were grief-stricken. One of his closest followers comforted them, saying "O, man, if anyone worships Muhammad, let him know that Muhammad is dead. But he who worships God, let him know that God is living and undying."

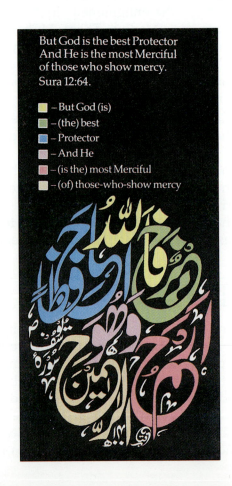

But God is the best Protector
And He is the most Merciful
of those who show mercy.
Sura 12:64.

- – But God (is)
- – (the) best
- – Protector
- – And He
- – (is the) most Merciful
- – (of) those-who-show mercy

---

*The Meaning of the Glorious Koran, translated by Mohammed Marmaduke Pickthall, George Allen & Unwin Ltd., p. 66. Reprinted by permission.

It forbids the eating of pork, the drinking of liquor, and gambling and provides guidelines for marriage and divorce. It also spells out the Five Pillars of faith, the essential religious practices Muslims must fulfill.

The first of the Five Pillars is the confession of faith, or *shahādah.* This requires Muslims to believe and say that there is no god but God and that Muhammad is the messenger of God.

The second pillar involves prayer. Muslims must pray five times a day—at dawn, noon, afternoon, sunset, and evening. Prayers can be offered anywhere—in the fields, in a home, or in an office. To offer a prayer, a worshipper must kneel, bow, and touch his or her forehead to the ground. This is important as a symbol of submitting to God. On Fridays, Muslims usually perform their noon prayers at a mosque. Originally, Muslims faced Jerusalem when they offered their prayers. But ever since they took Mecca and made it the holy city, they have prayed facing Mecca.

The third pillar concerns care for the poor and needy. Any Muslim with an income must give some money, or *zakāt,* to charity each year. For some time, the *zakāt* was set at 2.5 percent of one's income. Muslims who can afford to give more are asked to do so. Government and religious leaders spend some of the money on schooling.

The fourth pillar requires fasting. Once a year, during Ramaḍān, the month in which the Koran was revealed to Muhammad, Muslims must show their obedience to God by fasting every day from sunrise to sunset. Pregnant women, children, travelers, and those who are ill, however, are excused. Those people who do fast generally have big breakfasts before sunrise to help them through the day.

The fifth pillar is the Ḥajj, or pilgrimage to Mecca. All Muslims who are able and can afford it are expected to make the pilgrimage

This Saudi Arabian child reads from Islam's sacred book, the Koran, which many Muslims memorize in its entirety. When do Muslims believe the Koran was revealed to Muhammad? How is this event observed?

at least once in their lifetimes. To be able to do so is the high point in Muslims' lives. When the pilgrims reach Mecca and perform their rites, they feel that they come closest in life to being with God.

Today, more than 1 million people from all over the world come to Mecca each year to fulfill this obligation. The trip has to be made during ʿĪd al-Aḍhā, the Feast of Sacrifice, which commemorates Abraham's offering of his son to God. The pilgrims pray facing the Kaʿbah, a large cubicle that sits at the center of the courtyard of Mecca's Sacred Mosque. Below, a young American woman who became a Muslim gives an account of the Ḥajj as she experienced it:

> I put on the *Ihram* (white robe) and drove along on the road from Jiddah to

Mecca. The road was crowded with cars, buses and trucks. They were all packed with pilgrims chanting the Ḥajj refrain, the *Talbiyah*. . . .

As we drove along I had joined in, "*Labbayk . . . Labbayk!*". . . . a tunnel of sound from Jiddah to Mecca. . . .

At the end of the tunnel the car plunged into busy city streets, crept down the steep side of the bowl that holds the Holy City and stopped at the Mecca Hotel, directly across the street from the Masjid al-Ḥaram, the Sacred Mosque.

Like most pilgrims, I could barely resist the desire to pay my formal respects at the Kaʿbah at once, but the crowds were so thick that I thought it smarter to wait. I stood in the arched cloisters and looked out at the wonderful scene taking place.

The center of it, of course, was the Kaʿbah, draped in black silk, with a wide band of golden calligraphy two-thirds of the way to the top. Just that morning the Kaʿbah had received its ceremonial washing, and the corners of the covering had been raised for the Pilgrimage, showing the dark-gray blocks of Mecca stone of which it is built. . . .

The next day at ʿArafāt I set out at once for Jabal al-Raḥmah, the Mount of Mercy. There, at the foot of a dark granite hill on the edge of the plain, the Prophet had stood to deliver the sermon during his Farewell Pilgrimage. . . .

As I began to climb the Mount a tall African generously shared the shade of his green silk umbrella with me and I remembered the Prophet's word: ". . . Above all else, never forget that each Muslim is the brother of all others: for all Muslims in this world form one race of brothers."

As the sun dropped toward the horizon, the multitude at ʿArafāt began to put their things on top of the buses, to strike their tents and pull up poles and stakes. I took my place again on top of my bus.

To complete the rituals of the Ḥajj I had to perform a sacrifice. . . . I had balked at the idea of the Sacrifice long before being faced with it—and now the time had come to do it. What was I to do? A companion had insisted. "You must do the Sacrifice. There is no question of your not being able to afford it."

Back at our building . . . I turned to the Koran. I found that the Sacrifice has many meanings: it celebrates Abraham's giving in to God's will; it marks the end of idolatry among the Arabs; it is an offering of thanksgiving to the God of Creation.

As I thought about what I had read, a great weight was lifted from my conscience. I saw that the Sacrifice *upholds* the sacredness of life, that it is a pledge by the pilgrim that he will kill for food only. And where I had felt reluctance before I now felt eagerness.

I explained to my friend that I would perform the Sacrifice only if I could arrange to have the animal cooked, eat a part of the meat and give the remainder to

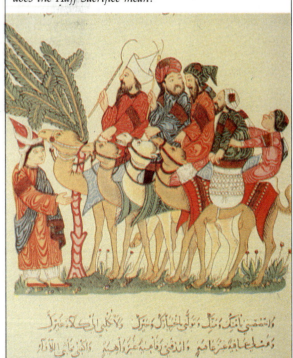

This group of pilgrims, who fulfilled the Ḥajj in 1236, is just one of many that traveled to Mecca bearing palm leaves to show that they were on a pilgrimage. What does the Ḥajj Sacrifice mean?

CHAPTER 36 — RELIGION AND STATE

Considered by Muslims to be the most sacred spot on earth, the Ka'bah, surrounded in this photo by Hajj pilgrims, serves as a visible link between all Muslims and God. Embedded in a corner of the Ka'bah is the holy Black Stone, believed to be a piece of the original Ka'bah built by Abraham. One goal of the Hajj is to touch or kiss the Black Stone. Why did Abraham build the Ka'bah?

someone who was less fortunate than I. We went ahead, therefore, to the Place of Sacrifice, bought a sheep, sacrificed it and took it, cleaned and ready for cooking, to [a shop where the owner] had agreed to cook it for me. . . .

Before I had begun the Pilgrimage its rituals seemed to me just so many curious exercises. But as I took part in the events of the Pilgrimage, the meaning of these rites became clear, my understanding of Islam was deepened and I learned more fully what it meant to be a Muslim. . . .

The courtyard was not crowded as it had been the first day. From the minarets above us the call to prayer pierced the silence of the Sacred Mosque and my guide led us to the edge of the oval floor where we prepared for the congregational devotions of the evening *Salah* (prayer). All of us stood and knelt together round the House built by Abraham to proclaim the oneness of God and the unity of mankind. At that moment I understood why Muslims turn toward this great black cube in prayer.*

*Adapted from "An American Girl on the Hajj" by Michael E. Jansen in *Aramco World Magazine*, Vol. 25, No. 6, November–December, 1974, pp. 32–33, 35–39.

1. Why do Muslims have great respect for the prophets, the Bible, Judaism, and Christianity?
2. Why do Muslims object to being called Muhammadans?
3. What are the Five Pillars?

THE ISLAMIC STATE

While Muhammad was in Medina, he established the basic idea of an Islamic state. He organized the Muslim community and was its religious as well as its political leader. After taking Mecca, he urged all Arabs to accept Islam and required them to swear allegiance to him as their ruler. The Muslim community emerged as a well-organized, religious state.

By the time of Muhammad's death in 632, the Islamic state included nearly all of Arabia. Less than two decades later, after Muslim armies conquered the Persian and Byzantine empires, the Islamic state became a powerful empire in its own right.

Before he died, Muhammad left these words of advice for his followers and the

INSIGHTS ON PEOPLE
MIDDLE EAST

AL-IDRĪSĪ

Commerce and cooperation between the East and the West were of great importance to both worlds. Even when the West was fighting the East and the Christians of Europe were launching the Crusades against the Muslims of the Middle East, the interchange between the East and the West did not really cease. It was during this time that an Arab Muslim geographer and scientist named al-Idrīsī lived and worked in the Christian royal court of King Roger II of Sicily.

Al-Idrīsī, who was a descendant of Muhammad, was born in Morocco and studied at the university in Cordoba, Spain. After traveling in Europe, Africa, and the Middle East, he settled in Sicily under the circumstances described below:

In the year 1138, the royal palace at Palermo, Sicily was the scene of a long-awaited meeting between a Christian king and a Muslim scholar. As his visitor entered the hall, the king rose, took his hand and led him across the carpeted marble to a place of honor beside the throne. Almost at once the two men began to discuss the project for which the scholar had been asked to come: the creation of the first accurate —and scientific—map of the entire known world.

The monarch was Roger II, King of Sicily; his guest the Arab geographer Al-Idrisi.

To carry out the project, Roger set up an academy of geographers, with himself as director and al-Idrisi as secretary, to gather and sort information. The king wanted to know the exact conditions of every area under his rule, and of the world outside. He wanted to know its boundaries, climate, roads, the rivers that watered its lands, the seas that bathed its coasts.

The academy began by studying and comparing the works of earlier geographers. After studying at length the works they had, the king and the geographer saw that they were full of errors. They decided to begin original research.

Finally, the long study was finished and the task of map making began. First, under al-Idrisi's direction, a working copy was produced on a drawing board, with places sited on the map with compasses. Then a great disk almost 80 inches [200 centimeters] in diameter and weighing over 300 pounds [135 kilograms] was made out of silver.

Al-Idrisi explained that the disk merely symbolized the shape of the world: "The earth is round like a sphere, and the waters adhere to it and are maintained on it through natural equilibrium." It remained "stable in space like the yolk in an egg. Air surrounds it on all sides."

On the disk, lines were cut to mark the limits of the seven climates of the habitable world, from the Arctic to the Equator. Following the rough drawing prepared by al-Idrisi, the silversmiths transferred the outlines of countries, oceans, rivers, gulfs, peninsulas and islands to the globe.

To go along with the silver map, al-Idrisi prepared for Roger a book that gave the information gathered by the geographers. Al-Idrisi presented the globe, a silver celestial sphere and the book to his patron in 1154, just a few weeks before Roger died.*

The book was *Nuzhat al-Mushtāq fī Ikhtirāq al-Āfāq (The Excursion of the Eager to Travel Beyond the Horizons),* also known as *The Book of Roger.* It described not only geographical features of the land but cities, communities, and ways of life as well. An important feature of the work were the 70 maps that covered the known world at the time. Translated into several languages, al-Idrīsī's work is considered one of the great achievements in medieval geography.

1. Who was al-Idrīsī?
2. What were some of the major achievements of al-Idrīsī?

---
*Adapted from "Al-Idrisi and Roger's Book" by Frances Gies in *Aramco World Magazine,* Vol. 28, No. 4, July–August 1977, pp. 15–19.

caliph, the leader who would become his successor:

> I charge the Caliph after me to fear God, and I commend the community of the Muslims to him, to respect the great among them and have pity on the small, to honor the learned among them, not to strike them and humiliate them, not to oppress them and drive them to unbelief, not to close his doors to them and allow the strong to devour the weak. . . .
>
> Hear and obey, even if a . . . slave is appointed over you. . . .
>
> He who sees in his ruler something he disapproves should be patient, for if anyone separates himself from the community, even by a span, and dies, he dies the death of a pagan.
>
> Obey your rulers, whatever happens. If their commands accord with the revelation I brought you, they will be rewarded for it, and you will be rewarded for obeying them; if their commands are not in accord with what I brought you, they are responsible and you are absolved. . . .
>
> If you have rulers over you who ordain prayer and the alms tax and the Holy War for God, then God forbids you to revile them and allows you to pray behind them. . . .
>
> Do not revile the Sultan, for he is God's shadow on God's earth.
>
> Obedience is the duty of the Muslim man, whether he like it or not, as long as he is not ordered to commit a sin. If he is ordered to commit a sin, he does not have to obey. . . .
>
> He who commends a Sultan in what God condemns has left the religion of God.*

GOVERNMENT

When Muhammad died, his followers chose as their leader Abū Bakr, a highly respected member of the community and Muhammad's father-in-law. They called him *khalīfah,* or caliph. When he took his place as caliph, he made the following speech:

> . . . O people, I have been appointed to rule over you, though I am not the best among you. If I do well, help me, and if I do ill, correct me. Truth is loyalty and falsehood is treachery; the weak among you is strong in my eyes until I get justice for him, and the strong among you is weak in my eyes until I exact justice from him, if God is willing. Do not refrain from fighting in the name and for the sake of God. God strikes with degradation those who refrain. Obey me as long as I obey God and His Prophet. And if I do not obey God and His Prophet, you do not have to obey me. Come to prayer, and may God have mercy on you.*

The caliph, like Muhammad, was both the religious and the political leader of the state. He chose his own troop commanders and *wazīrs,* or ministers. His power, however, was limited by the Koran and the Ḥadīth, a record of the tradition and teachings of Muhammad. It also was limited by regional commanders and *wālis,* or governors. Nevertheless, he had nearly full power over the management of government affairs.

Caliphs ruled the Islamic Empire in the East until the 900's. With the growth of the empire, however, their duties became so numerous and complex that they began to depend on specialists for important decisions. One group of specialists was the *ulema,* Muslim jurists who explained Islamic laws. The *ulema,* who had to study and train for many years, became very important and had a good deal of power. In later years, some of them were made *muftīs,* officials who made sure the government laws and actions did not violate Islamic teachings.

---

*Abridged from pp.150–151 in *Islam From the Prophet Muhammad to the Capture of Constantinople, Vol. I: Politics and War,* Edited and Translated by Bernard Lewis. Copyright © 1974, by Bernard Lewis. By permission of Harper & Row, Publishers.

*Ibn al-Athīr, al-Kāmil fi Tārīkh, Vol. II, translated by Mounir A. Farah, 1967, Dār al-Kitāb al-ʿArabī, pp. 224–225. Reprinted by permission.

Insights on People

Middle East

MAIMONIDES

Moses ben Maimon, known in the West as Maimonides, was a rabbi, philosopher, physician, codifier of law, and prolific writer. Born in Cordoba, Spain, in 1135, his family left Spain when he was a young man to escape anti-Jewish persecution. After wandering for several years in North Africa and Palestine, the family departed for Egypt, where Maimonides spent the rest of his life.

During those unsettled years of travel and uprooting, Maimonides pursued his study of medicine, ancient Greek and medieval Islamic philosophies, and Jewish law and tradition. In Egypt, he and his family took up residence in Fusṭāṭ, near Cairo. Before long, he became the recognized leader of the Jewish community in Egypt and a court physician for Saladin, the Muslim ruler of Egypt and Syria. His fame as a doctor reached England, whose ruler, King Richard the Lionheart, is said to have invited him to become his personal physician.

Maimonides refused Richard's offer and remained in the service of Saladin. As seen below, in a letter written to a friend, Maimonides' days were full:

> I dwell at Misr (Fusṭāṭ) and the sultan resides at al-Qahira (Cairo); . . . I am obliged to visit him every day, early in the morning; and when he or any of his children, or any of the inmates of his harem, are indisposed, I dare not quit al-Qahira, but must stay during the greater part of the day in the palace. . . . I do not return to Misr until the afternoon. . . . [Then] I find the antechambers filled with people, both Jews and gentiles [non-Jews] . . . who await the time of my return. . . .
>
> . . . I partake of some slight refreshment, the only meal I take in the twenty-four hours. Then I go forth to attend to my patients [who] go in and out until nightfall. . . . On [the Sabbath] the whole congregation [of Jews], or at least the majority of the members, come to me after the morning service; when I instruct them as to their proceedings during the whole week; . . .*

Although Maimonides wrote in both Arabic and Hebrew, most of his medical works after 1190 were written in Arabic. Among these were treatises on asthma, drugs, hemorrhoids, sex, poisons and their antidotes, and symptoms of depression as well as commentaries on the writings of Galen and Hippocrates and a guide to good health. His most distinguished achievements, however, were in the field of Jewish thought. He wrote many volumes, explaining in a systematic way the Jewish tradition. According to the *Encyclopaedia Judaica*, no spiritual leader of the Jewish people of the period has exercised as great an influence as Maimonides.

When Maimonides died in 1204, Jews and gentiles alike observed public mournings. His remains were taken to Palestine for burial. His grave remains an object of pilgrimage even today.

1. Who was Maimonides?
2. What were some of Maimonides' major achievements?

*From a letter to Samuel ben Judah ibn Tibbon, quoted in the *Encyclopaedia Judaica*, *Vol. II*, 1972, Keter Publishing House Jerusalem Ltd., col. 757.

During Ottoman rule, the highest of the *muftīs* was called Grand Muftī or *Sheikh al-Islam*. Even today, most Middle Eastern countries have Grand Muftīs. Other high religious leaders, especially in Iraq, the Yemens, and Iran, are called *imāms*. In Iran, the highest are called *ayatollahs.*

Until recent years, these religious leaders held classes in mosques or special schools and were responsible for education. They also were in charge of orphanages, welfare, and other public assistance projects.

AHL AL-DHIMMA

Non-Muslims who lived under Islamic rule, known as ***ahl al-dhimma,*** were protected and permitted to govern their own internal affairs. Many of them prospered, and some held responsible positions in the government. Many of the famous court physicians, for example, were Christians and Jews. Although *ahl al-dhimma* did not have to serve in the army, they were required to pay a special poll tax called a ***jizyah.***

Under Ottoman rule, non-Muslims lived in communities called **millets.** Each millet had its own schools and ***waqf,*** funds used for charity and to run religious houses. Each also took charge of its own civil affairs, such as marriage and divorce contracts. At first, the government only recognized the Greek Orthodox, Armenian, and Jewish millets. Later, it extended recognition to Catholic and Protestant millets as well.

During certain periods of Islamic rule, non-Muslims in some areas were restricted in their activities and in the way they dressed. This generally happened when there was an invasion by foreigners toward whom local non-Muslims were sympathetic. Below are some of the restrictions detailed in a decree issued in 1354:

These are examples of some of the clothing styles worn by people living in different parts of the Ottoman Empire. How did Islamic law require non-Muslim women to dress in the mid-1300's?

> They shall not build any new church in the lands of Islam, nor rebuild any such building which is destroyed. They shall not harbor spies nor any who are suspect to the Muslims, nor shall they plot against the Muslims. They shall not obstruct any of their relatives who wish to accept Islam. They shall not dress like the Muslims, but shall wear blue and yellow distinguishing dress. They shall not ride on a horse or mule but only on donkeys. They shall not sell intoxicating drinks. They shall keep to their special dress wherever they are. The Christian woman who appears in public shall wear a cotton veil, dyed blue, and the Jewess a yellow veil. . . . They shall not work in the service of our exalted state, nor shall any of them hold a position which would give him authority over any of the Muslims.*

*Abridged and adapted from *Islam From the Prophet Muhammad to the Capture of Constantinople, Vol. II: Religion and Society*, Edited and Translated by Bernard Lewis. Copyright © 1974 by Bernard Lewis. By permission of Harper & Row, Publishers, p. 234.

English Words of Arabic Origin

Arabic	Arabic Meaning	English
dar-es-sina'a	place of industry	arsenal
ka'ba	cube	cube
ta'rifa	fee	tariff
sherab	drink	syrup
githar	guitar	guitar
mosul	city of Mosul	muslin
al-jabr	algebra	algebra
taftah	taffeta	taffeta
ameer-al-bahr	commander of the sea	admiral
e'sar	tornado	hazard
kutn	cotton	cotton
al-kuhul	alcohol	alcohol
sukkar	sugar	sugar
dimashq	city of Damascus	damask
al-'ud	lute	lute

The millet system and *jizyah* were abolished in the 1900's. Today, in the constitutions of the modern states of the Middle East, all citizens are considered equal. In the majority of the states, however, Islam remains the official state religion, and both Muslims and non-Muslims serve in the armed forces.

IMPACT AND ACHIEVEMENTS

The impact of Islamic civilization has been great. Even in a country such as Spain, where the Muslims have not been in power since 1492, hundreds of Spanish words have Arabic roots and Islamic influence abounds in the architecture and music.

The study of sciences, as well as arts, flourished under Islamic rule. In mathematics, the system of Arabic numerals, the zero, and logarithms were developed. In medicine, Muslim doctors such as al-Rāzī and Ibn Sīnā advanced the understanding of the human body and the ways to treat sickness. Al-Rāzī was the first to identify the medical differences between measles and smallpox. Ibn Sīnā was the first to recognize that tuberculosis could be transmitted from person to person. His encyclopedia of medicine, the *Canon of Medicine*, was used in European medical schools for 500 years.

Nor were philosophy and sociology neglected. Not only were the works of such Greek scholars as Socrates and Aristotle translated and studied by Muslims, but the works of such Muslim thinkers as Averröes, al-Ghazzālī, and Ibn-Khaldūn were recognized and discussed by scholars in Europe. Ibn-Khaldūn, thought by many to be the founder of the philosophy of history, became the forerunner of today's sociologists.

1. What advice did Muhammad leave for the caliph? For his followers?
2. As caliph, what did Abū Bakr expect from his people?
3. How were the *ahl al-dhimma* treated?
4. What were some contributions of early Islamic civilization?

Exploration

Middle East

Look at the two photographs. What do they tell you about the level of culture and the achievements of the Islamic state?

The following statements reflect some philosophical views widely held in the Islamic state. Based on the statements and on the information in the chapter, give your impressions of the way of life in the Islamic state.

Govern the best of the people by love; mingle desire and fear for the common people; and govern the lowest by terror.

The hearts of the subjects are the treasure houses of their kings. Whatever they deposit in them, they know it is there.

Fight against those who do not believe in God nor in the Last Day, who do not hold forbidden what God and His Apostle have forbidden, until they pay the poll tax from their hand, they being humbled.

Islam assigns four things to government: a system of justice, booty, the Friday prayer, and the Holy War.

Government and religion are two brothers; neither can stand without the other.

Do not stay in a country which lacks these five things: a strong rule, a just judge, a fixed market, a wise physician, and a flowing river.

CHAPTER 36 REVIEW

POINTS TO REMEMBER

1. Three great religions—Judaism, Christianity, and Islam began in the Middle East. They all share the same roots.
2. Judaism emerged among the Hebrews when Abraham made a covenant with God and urged his people to believe in one god. In time, the Hebrews became known as Jews.
3. Christianity arose out of the teachings of Jesus, who believed that God was merciful, loving, and forgiving. Jesus' followers became known as Christians.
4. Muhammad, who believed in submission to no other god but Allah (God), converted many to Islam, the beliefs and practices of which were built on Judaism and Christianity. According to the Koran, God gave revelation to Muhammad, who was the last in a chain of prophets.
5. The Koran contains the basic beliefs of Islam and tells Muslims how they are to lead their daily lives. It also spells out the Five Pillars, which are the *shahādah*, prayer, almsgiving, fasting, and the Ḥajj.
6. Muhammad established the basic idea of an Islamic state, which, by the mid 600's, became a powerful empire. It was ruled by caliphs who were the religious and political leaders. Although non-Muslims living in the state were protected, they were restricted in their activities at times.
7. The impact of Islamic civilization has been great throughout the world. Islamic influence abounds in the arts and sciences.

VOCABULARY

Identify

Koran	Judaism	Mecca	Ḥajj
Islam	Jews	Allah	Kaʿbah
Hebrews	Christianity	Medina	Abū-Bakr
Abraham	Jesus	Five Pillars	Maimonides
Moses	Muhammad	Ramaḍān	al-Idrīsī

Define

patriarchs	saved	*khalīfah*	*imāms*
monotheism	final judgment	*wazīrs*	ayatollahs
covenant	prophets	*wālis*	ahl al-dhimma
exodus	*shahādah*	ulema	*jizyah*
revelations	*zakāt*	*muftīs*	millets
messiah			*waqf*

DISCUSSING IMPORTANT IDEAS

1. In what ways are Jewish, Christian, and Islamic beliefs alike? Different?
2. What do you see as the purpose of the Five Pillars? Explain.

3. What traits do you think a caliph was supposed to have had in the Islamic State? Give examples from the chapter to support your answer.

4. If you were a non-Muslim living in the Islamic state, how would you have reacted to the restrictions placed upon you? Why would you have reacted this way?

DEVELOPING SKILLS

USING PERSUASIVE ARGUMENTS

The last time your school had an election for the president of your class, why did you vote for the person you did? Was it because he or she was popular? Or, was it because he or she offered the most *persuasive*, or convincing, arguments? Although some people will vote for a candidate because he or she is popular, even the most popular candidate has been known to lose an election to someone who knows how to use the power of persuasion.

The following guidelines will help you write or speak persuasively:

1. Before you write or speak about a subject, do some research. Find out what people think about the subject and why they think that way. This will help you determine what arguments to use to persuade those people who disagree with you to change their minds and those who agree with you to become more secure in their beliefs.

2. Tailor your arguments to your audience. Ask yourself to whom you are speaking, and think about how your presentation will affect the particular group you are addressing. Keep in mind that most people are more likely to share your point of view if they see some benefit in it for themselves.

3. List as many facts and examples as you can to support your viewpoint. Then, go through your list carefully, and discard the least persuasive arguments.

4. Save your most persuasive argument for last. End your presentation by recapping or briefly summarizing your points.

In the following example, in which Muhammad advises his successor how to be a good ruler, several of the guidelines have been kept in mind:

I charge the Caliph after me to fear God, and I commend the community of the Muslims to him, to respect the great among them and have pity on the small, to honor the learned among them, not to strike them and humiliate them, not to oppress them and drive them to unbelief, not to close his doors to them and allow the strong to devour the weak. . . .

Obey your rulers, whatever happens. If their commands accord with the revelation I brought you, they will be rewarded for it, and you will be rewarded for obeying them; if their commands are not in accord with what I brought you, they are responsible and you are absolved. . . .

Obedience is the duty of the Muslim man, whether he like it or not. . . .

After reading the excerpt, it is clear that Muhammad knew the traits, beliefs, and values of his audience—the future Caliph and the Muslim people—and tailored his comments to that audience. He hints as to what might happen if his "suggestions" are not followed and goes on to note how the members of the audience will benefit from following his advice. He sums up by reminding the audience that "obedience is the duty of the Muslim man." Most people would consider Muhammad's argument persuasive.

For practice in using persuasive arguments, keep in mind the guidelines suggested earlier, and write a paragraph persuading a group of Muslims, Christians, and Jews to live together peacefully.

CHAPTER 37
THE GREAT BITTERNESS

1. *What led to colonialism in the Middle East?*
2. *What effect did colonialism have on the Middle East and its people?*

... The position that we occupy in Egypt may be said to be the result of accident. But it has more than accidental justification. Alike by the nature of our interests, by the nature of our power, and by certain special qualities in our national character, we seem marked out for the discharge of this particular duty. Our interests in Egypt are absolutely identical with those of the Egyptian people. We are their principal customers, and they also are very important customers of Great Britain. With the deficiency of outlets which threatens our vast foreign trade, the great and growing market of Egypt is evidently not a thing which we can afford to despise. And if Egyptian prosperity is a British interest, so is Egyptian independence. We have no desire to possess ourselves of Egypt, but we have every reason to prevent any rival power from so possessing itself. . . .

. . . as to the date when our work will be finished and our controlling hand withdrawn, it is simply impossible to give a definite answer. No man can say when, no man can say whether, the attempt to educate the Egyptians in the habits of civilized government is destined to be crowned with success. . . .

. . . The circumstances must decide. As native governing capacity develops, as natives come forward who are fit for responsible posts now held by Englishmen, these posts should be resigned to them. Perhaps some element in the Government would always be necessary. Perhaps the British Minister would always need to exercise some control on the most important questions of policy. But that control might in the end be very light. . . .

Such would be the natural, the wholesome development of British policy in Egypt.*

In this way, the British Under-Secretary for Finance in Egypt justified the 1882 British takeover of the Egyptian government. The British action was prompted by a crisis that threatened to topple Egypt's government, which was controlled by France and Great Britain.

In the Middle East, **colonialism,** foreign occupation of a land with intent to exploit its resources, began in the 1800's when Great Britain, France, and Russia were actively seeking economic **concessions,** or special privileges. The British wanted new markets, raw materials for industry, and control of strategic routes, especially to Asia and the British colony in India. The French wanted control of trade in the Levant, the east coast regions of the Mediterranean Sea.

By 1920, Great Britain and France had gained control of northern Africa and most of the Arab lands of the Middle East. European rule caused frustration and humiliation among Middle Easterners. The colonial territories underwent a great deal of struggle and sacrifice, and many Middle Easterners fought and died for independence. Among the areas affected were Syria and Lebanon, Egypt, Palestine, and the Persian Gulf.

---

*England in Egypt by Alfred Milner, 1892, Edward Arnold, pp. 435–436, 440, 442.

SYRIA AND LEBANON

When World War I broke out in 1914, Syria was part of the declining Ottoman Empire. Arabs in Syria and other Middle Eastern countries saw the war as an opportunity to free themselves from Turkish rule. So when the Turks allied themselves with Germany, the Syrian Arabs asked the British to help them gain their independence.

In the Husayn-McMahon correspondence, an exchange of letters between British diplomat Sir Henry McMahon and Arab leader Sherif Husayn, the British pledged their support for an independent Arab state. Below, in an excerpt from an October 24, 1915 letter, McMahon wrote:

> I have, therefore, lost no time in informing the Government of Great Britain of the contents of your letter, and it is with great pleasure that I communicate to you on their behalf the following statement. . . .
>
> The two districts of Mersina and Alexandretta and portions of Syria lying to the west of the districts of Damascus, Homs, Hama and Aleppo cannot be said to be purely Arab, and should be excluded from the limits demanded.
>
> With the above modification, and without prejudice to our existing treaties with Arab chiefs, we accept those limits.
>
> As for those regions lying within those frontiers wherein Great Britain is free to act without detriment to the interests of her ally, France, I am empowered in the name of the Government of Great Britain to give the following assurances and make the following reply to your letter:—
>
> (1) Subject to the above modifications Great Britain is prepared to recognise and support the independence of the Arabs in all the regions within the limits demanded by the sherif of Mecca.
>
> (2) Great Britain will guarantee the Holy Places against all external aggression and will recognise their inviolability.
>
> (3) When the situation admits, Great Britain will give to the Arabs her advice and will assist them to establish what may appear to be the most suitable forms of government in those various areas.*

A year after this letter was written, the British and the French signed the Sykes-Picot Agreement. It stated that if the Germans lost the war, the Arab territories of the Ottoman Empire would be divided between France and Great Britain. When the Arabs found out about the agreement, they sent Husayn's son, Prince Faisal, to London to ask the British prime minister how the agreement would affect the independent Arab state the British had promised his people.

In spite of Faisal's efforts, the Arab claims for independence were ignored in the World War I peace treaties. Syria was made a French **mandate,** or territory administered by another country. The French established headquarters in Beirut, which at the time was part of Syria. They divided the country into administrative districts, based in part on religious groupings. They added four areas to the district known as Mount of Lebanon and made them the separate country of Lebanon.

For the next 20 years, there were riots and revolts to protest French rule. The following story, which came out of one of these revolts, tells about one group of Syrians' fight for independence:

> "Milk, milk." It was six o'clock in the morning, and I could hear the voice of Abū Hāmid, the milkman. I went down the stairs, picked up the milk jug from the kitchen, opened the door and was greeted with a wide, warm smile from Abū Hāmid. While he poured three cups of milk into the jug, my ten-year-old eyes watched his big gnarled hand with its bent fingers.

---

*The Middle East and North African World Politics, Vol. II, by J. C. Hurewitz, 1979, Yale University Press, p. 50. Reprinted by permission.

CHAPTER 37   THE GREAT BITTERNESS   605

In this photo taken in 1919, troops are shown leaving France to occupy the territory France was given in Syria and Lebanon as part of the peace treaties ending World War I. How was the country of Lebanon created?

While pouring the milk at breakfast, my mother said, "Abū Hāmid is a splendid milkman. God bless him. He never dilutes the milk. He is a man of righteousness."

One day my father left his bed and came down with me when he heard the milkman's voice. In low voices, he and Abū Hāmid discussed the affairs of the revolt in Ghūta, the orchard villages that form a ring on the three sides of Damascus. I could hear references made to battle, to patriots being killed, and to fights against the French.

Abū Hāmid whispered, "But they killed many, many French soldiers before they were killed. They are all young and heading for heaven. I wish I were one of them. But this hand will not permit me. I just can't use a rifle with it."

One wintry day, I heard Abū Hāmid tell my father, "It is getting very cold, sir. Most of the patriots have no ʿabāʾat [heavy robes which can be used as blankets]. Sleeping outdoors without ʿabāʾat is brutal. God help them."

That evening I overheard my mother telling father, "I checked with all the houses on our street and not a single family refused to help. I was able to collect enough to purchase fifty ʿabāʾat."

"It's better that you buy the ʿabāʾat, but buy no more than two from any store. You don't want to draw attention to yourself, the French have traitors and spies everywhere," father cautioned.

The following morning, and every morning thereafter, Abu Hamid would wear one ʿabāʾat that my mother had bought until the stacks of ʿabāʾat were gone.

One dreary morning, our old clock struck six, but I heard no call for milk. I wondered why Abū Hāmid did not come this morning.

Later, after school, some of the students were gathering at the corner. They were repeating the news that some patriots were killed and their bodies were displayed at Marje Square. I joined them, and in a few minutes we were heading there.

We stood frightened, staring at the dreadful sight. There were bodies twisted and broken in torn clothes covered with blood and dirt.

A French officer laughed and pointed at them saying, "Patriots! Patriots!"

I almost screamed when I recognized one of the bodies. It was Abu Hamid. I knew his clothes and his gnarled hand.

We retreated in silence. One boy said, "Those bodies are not of patriots. Those bodies are of poor peasants. The French shot them to scare us."

All of the boys agreed. Each one left for his home wearing a pale face and with a fast-beating heart. I hurried home and went straight to the courtyard. There, my mother was seated and sad-looking, with eyes filled with tears. I rushed to her and asked the whereabouts of my father.

She answered with a trembling voice, "Your father went to the village. He will be back in a few days."

I looked straight into her eyes and replied, "You are not telling me the truth. Father joined the revolt and left us in the care of God."

She hugged me and said, "How did you know that? Don't dare mention anything about it. If the French find out, they will demolish our home immediately."

I slept little that night. As morning drew near, I heard a voice calling "milk, milk." It was my friend Hamid, the milkman's older son. Hamid, one of the best students, will have to quit school and forget his sweet dreams so that he can support a big family. Instead of a book bag in his hand, he will be carrying the big milk can and peddling milk for the rest of his life. Two tears wet my cheeks, and deep inside me I felt a great bitterness.*

---

*Adapted from *Farewell Damascus* by Ilfat al-Idulbi, translated by Mounir A. Farah, 1963, Atlas Publishing and Distribution, pp. 13–22. Reprinted by permission.

The fight for freedom did not end until 1946, when Syria and Lebanon became fully independent. Independence brought to power freely elected democratic governments, and for the next few years, each country experienced rapid social and economic growth.

In Lebanon, democratic governments continued to rule under stable and peaceful conditions until 1958. That year, a civil war broke out between mainly Christian, pro-western forces and anti-western forces that favored stronger ties with Egypt and Syria. After a few weeks of fighting, order was restored, and a new president was elected.

In Syria, the peace did not last as long. In 1949, dissatisfaction over a military defeat at the hands of Israel led to a military coup that replaced the elected government with a dictatorship. Other coups followed until 1958, when the country voted to unite with Egypt and form the United Arab Republic. That union lasted three years.

1. For what did Arabs in Syria ask the British during World War I? What was the British response?
2. What did the Sykes-Picot Agreement state? What effect did it have on Syria?
3. How did the Syrians react to French rule?
4. What happened in Syria and Lebanon after they became independent?

THE SUEZ CANAL

In 1854, a French engineer named Ferdinand de Lesseps traveled to Egypt to seek permission to build the Suez Canal, a 100-mile [160-kilometer] waterway that would link the Mediterranean and Red seas. He told the Egyptian ruler, "I am your friend, I have come to benefit you, and to dig a canal between the two seas for your advantage." Said Pasha, the Viceroy who ruled Egypt for the Ottoman sultan, approved de Lesseps'

CHAPTER 37 THE GREAT BITTERNESS

This old engraving shows some of the laborers who built the Suez Canal digging earth and loading it onto the backs of camels. Most of the canal's excavation was done this way. Earth-moving machinery was not used until the last few years of the project. How did the building of the Suez Canal affect many Egyptian fellaheen *and their families?*

plans and granted him a concession for the project. The concession called for the canal to be built and run by a private international company headed by Ferdinand de Lesseps. At the end of 99 years, however, the canal was to come under the complete control of the Egyptian government.

Work began on the canal in 1859. Ten years later, it was completed—at a cost of $287 million and the lives of a great many Egyptian laborers. The Viceroy had agreed in the concession that Egypt would supply laborers to work on the canal. As a result, thousands of Egyptian *fellaheen* were forced to leave their families and work on the project. In 1863 a new Viceroy came to power, which complicated the already controversial issue of the forced labor. Below, a reporter for *The Times of London* comments on the situation:

> The present Viceroy has not yet announced his final views upon the subject [of forced labor]; but it is very generally believed that he has already arrived at the conclusion that the [Egyptian] Government is bound by the engagements entered into towards the Company by his predecessor. Both labour and money must accordingly continue to be supplied. About 20,000 men are at this moment either engaged upon the works or on their way . . . collected . . . from all parts of Egypt. To each party, as it arrives, a certain portion of the excavations is allotted. . . . The task is usually completed in about a month, when the men are allowed to return to their villages, generally carrying with them the trifling balance of their earnings after paying the cost of the simple food upon which the Egyptian fellahs are content to live.*

By 1875, six years after the canal was completed, the Egyptian ruler was deeply in

---
*From *The Times of London* (1863) as quoted in *Suez: De Lesseps' Canal* by John Pudney, 1968, J. M. Dent and Sons Ltd., p. 100.

debt. To solve his financial problems, he sold the major portion of stock in the canal company to the British government. In 1876, the British, along with the French, took over the financial management of the canal. Six years later, Egyptian nationalists demanded an end to all foreign control.

By this time, the British had become the major user of the canal and relied on it heavily for both strategic and economic purposes. Fearful that they would lose control of the canal, they landed troops in Egypt. In the battle that followed, they defeated the national army led by Egyptian Colonel Ahmad ʿArābī and occupied Egypt.

Although the British claimed that their occupation would be temporary, the last British troops did not leave Egypt until 1956. By that time, Arab nationalism, stirred by Egyptian president Gamal Abdel Nasser, had taken root firmly. Nasser believed that foreigners had no right to control his country or its people. On July 26, 1956, he announced that the canal would be **nationalized,** made the property of the government. He also announced that the money Egypt earned from the canal would go toward building the Aswan High Dam on the Nile River at Aswan. Below, Nasser explains why he nationalized the Canal:

> The Suez Canal Company was formed, and Egypt got 44% of the shares. Egypt undertook to supply labour to dig the Canal . . . , of whom 120,000 died without getting paid. We also paid De Lesseps in order that he might give up some concession. We gave up the 15% of the profits which we were supposed to get over and above the profits of our 44% of the shares. Thus, contrary to the statements made by De Lesseps . . . in which he said that the Canal was dug for Egypt, Egypt has become the property of the Canal. . . .
>
> The result of the words of De Lesseps in 1856, the result of friendship and loans, was the occupation of Egypt in 1882. Egypt then borrowed money. What happened? Egypt was obliged . . . to sell its 44% of the shares in the company. Immediately, England sent out to purchase the shares. It bought them for 4 million pounds. Then, [the Viceroy] gave up his 5% of the company's profits against the ceding of some concessions by the Company which were granted to it.
>
> Then the [Viceroy] was obliged to pay to Britain the 5% profit which he had relinquished. This amounted to over 4 million

Egyptian president Gamal Abdel Nasser waves to crowds in Cairo in 1956 after formally taking control of the Suez Canal in a ceremony at Port Said. After nationalizing the canal, Nasser became a worldwide symbol of the Arab people, and many Arab nations looked to Egypt for leadership and protection. What did Nasser want to do with the money earned from operating the Suez Canal?

pounds. In other words, Britain got Egypt's 44% of the Company's shares free. This was the history which took place a century ago. . . .

Today, the Suez Canal, where 120,000 of our sons had lost their lives . . . and for the foundation of which we paid 8 million pounds, has become a state within the state. It has humiliated ministers and cabinets.

This Canal is an Egyptian canal. It is an Egyptian Joint Stock Company. Britain had forcibly grabbed our rights, our 44% of its shares. Britain still collects the profits of these shares. . . .

The income of the Suez Canal Company in 1955 reached . . . 35 million [English pounds], or 100 million dollars. Of this sum, we, who have lost 120,000 persons, who have died in digging the Canal, take only . . . 1 million [English pounds] or 3 million dollars! This is the Suez Canal Company, which . . . dug for the sake of Egypt and its benefit! . . .

We shall not repeat the past. We shall eradicate it by restoring our rights in the Suez Canal. This money is ours. This Canal is the property of Egypt because it is an Egyptian Joint Stock Company.*

1. What did Ferdinand de Lesseps want from the ruler of Egypt? What was the result of his efforts?
2. Why did the British land troops in Egypt in 1882? How long did they stay there?
3. What reasons did Gamal Abdel Nasser give for nationalizing the Suez Canal?

THE ARAB-ISRAELI CONFLICT

The conflict between Israel and its Arab neighbors has been going on for many years. At the base of the dispute is a disagreement between the Arabs and the Israelis as to who owns the land of Israel, once called Palestine. Both Palestinian Arabs and Israelis claim ownership.

From the early 1500's until World War I, Palestine had been ruled by the Ottoman Turks. Toward the end of the war, it fell under British occupation. The British, seeking support for the war, made conflicting promises to the Arabs and the Jews regarding the area. In the Husayn-McMahon correspondence of 1915, they promised the Arabs an independent state. The Arabs believed that this state would include all of Palestine. Then, in the Balfour Declaration of 1917, the British promised the Jews a home in Palestine. In the words of Lord Balfour:

> I have much pleasure in giving you, on behalf of his Majesty's Government, the following declaration of sympathy with Jewish Zionist [those who want an independent Jewish country] aspirations which has been submitted to and approved by the [British] Cabinet:—
>
> His Majesty's Government view with favour the establishment in Palestine of a national home for the Jewish people, and will use their best endeavors to facilitate the achievement of this object, it being clearly understood that nothing shall be done which may prejudice the civil and religious rights of existing non-Jewish communities in Palestine, or the rights and political status enjoyed by Jews in any other country.
>
> I should be grateful if you would bring this declaration to the knowledge of the Zionist Federation.*

After World War I, however, the British broke their promise to the Arabs for an independent state and occupied and ruled Palestine. Meanwhile, the flow of Jewish immigrants into Palestine continued and

---

*Speech by Gamal Abdel Nasser (1956) in "The Suez Canal Problem," publication 6392, October 1956, U.S. Department of State, pp. 26–27.

*The Middle East and North African World Politics, Vol. II, by J. C. Hurewitz, 1979, Yale University Press, p. 106. Reprinted by permission.

In this cartoon, a dove with an olive branch, a symbol of peace, is shown emerging from a bomb, a symbol of the Middle East embroiled in conflict. What was the Arab reaction when Israel became a state in 1948?

grew until by the late 1930's, Jews accounted for nearly one-third of Palestine's population. The number of Jews continued growing during World War II and after as Jews fled to Palestine to escape Nazi persecution.

So too grew the bitterness between the Arabs and the Jews. Before long, riots and armed conflict broke out. Although the British tried to work out a compromise between the two groups over the future of Palestine, the dissent continued. In 1947, the British referred the matter to the United Nations, which voted to partition, or divide, Palestine into two states—one Arab and one Jewish. The following year, the British withdrew from Palestine, and the Jews set up the new state of Israel on Palestinian soil. The Arabs, however, refused to accept the partition or to recognize the Jewish state of Israel and demanded an election for a government for all of Palestine.

In the spring of 1948, the forces of Egypt, Syria, Lebanon, Trans-Jordan and Iraq invaded Israel, where they were defeated by the Israeli army. By the following year, a cease-fire was in effect. As a result of the war, Israel occupied Arab territory, and nearly three-quarters of a million Palestinian Arabs fled their homeland to become refugees in neighboring Arab countries. The conflict continued to grow and by 1956 erupted into war once more.

1. What is at the base of the Arab-Israeli conflict? What role did the British play?
2. What decision did the United Nations make regarding Palestine? How did it affect Palestinian Jews and Arabs?

THE PERSIAN GULF

As early as the 1500's, Europeans had established strategic and commercial bases in the area of the Persian Gulf. By the 1800's, Great Britain had become the dominant power in the area. India was Great Britain's most important colony, and the Gulf states, located between the Mediterranean region and India, were India's link to Europe.

At first, the British limited their interests in the Gulf to trade and foreign affairs. To protect their interests, they made treaties with the Gulf states. Most of the treaties were written to favor the British. When Russia and other European countries became interested in the area, the British became concerned. To tighten their grip, they concluded many treaties with the Gulf states. To achieve their goals, the British resorted to pressure, force, and bribery. The 1899 secret bond between Great Britain and Kuwait, part of which appears below, was not uncommon:

> The object of writing this lawful and honourable bond is that . . . Sheikh Mubarak-bin-Sheikh Subah, Sheik of Koweit [Kuwait] . . . of his own free will and desire does hereby pledge and bind himself, his heirs and successors not to receive the Agent or Representative of any Power or Government at Koweit [Kuwait], or at any other place within the limits of his territory, without the previous sanction of the British Government; and he further binds himself, his heirs and successors not to cede, sell, lease, mortgage, or give for occupation or for any other purpose any portion of his territory to the Government or subjects of any other Power without the previous consent of Her Majesty's Government. . . .*

When oil was discovered in the Persian Gulf in the early 1900's, the area took on new importance. British companies were quick to gain concessions for exploration and production, and as the world's dependence on oil rose, they made large profits and became even more established in the Gulf. This led many Arabs and Iranians to resent their presence and that of other foreigners. The Middle Easterners particularly resented the fact that while their oil was making other countries more prosperous, it was bringing very little income to them. They wanted a greater financial return for their oil so they could develop their own resources.

Iran took the lead in the move for change. In 1950, the Iranian parliament responded to the widespread anti-British feeling by naming as prime minister nationalist leader Mohammed Mosaddeq. Mosaddeq opposed Iran's ruler, Shah Mohammed Reza Pahlevi, accusing him of dealing too easily with the western powers. On June 21, 1951, with the following statement, Mosaddeq justified the nationalization of Iran's oil industry:

> Our long years of negotiations with foreign countries concerning the legitimacy of our claims to ownership of the industry, which no power in the world can deny us, have yielded no results this far. With the oil revenues we could meet our entire budget and combat poverty, disease, and backwardness among our people. Another important consideration is that by the elimination of the power of the British company, we would also eliminate corruption and intrigue, by means of which the internal affairs of our country have been influenced. Once this tutelage has ceased, Iran will have achieved its economic and political independence.
>
> The Iranian state prefers to take over the production of petroleum itself. The company should do nothing else but return its property to the rightful owners. The nationalization law provides that 25 percent of the net profits on oil be set aside to meet all the legitimate claims of the company for compensation. . . .

---
*"Exclusive Agreement: The Kuwayti Shaykh and Britain" in *The Middle East and North African World Politics, Vol. I,* by J. C. Hurewitz, 1975, Yale University Press, p. 476. Reprinted by permission.

GULF STATES

It has been asserted abroad that Iran intends to expel the foreign oil experts from the country and then shut down oil installations. Not only is this allegation absurd; it is utter invention. The Iranian government has never considered such a step. Rather, it will make every effort to carry out nationalization as smoothly as possible, so as not to interfere with production.*

Fearing the spread of nationalization, western countries responded by **boycotting**, or refusing to buy or sell, Iranian oil. Because Iran had no way to market its oil, the Iranian economy began to suffer. Within two years, the country's oil revenues dropped to almost nothing. As the Iranian people struggled with economic hardship, they became discontent and restless.

In 1953, the Shah, supported by his army generals, took power away from the prime minister and dissolved the government. Nationalization was repealed and the British company restored. A few years later, using pressure and diplomacy, the Shah gained a larger share of the oil profits for Iran.

1. Why was the Persian Gulf important to the British? What did they do to gain control there?
2. Why did many Arabs and Iranians resent the presence of the British and other foreigners in their countries?
3. What action did Iran take to rid itself of foreign control? How did the western nations respond?

The Rise and Fall of the Shah by Amin Saikal, 1980, Bipin Shah Associates, Inc., p. 39.

EXPLORATION
MIDDLE EAST

The two maps that follow show the Sykes-Picot Agreement of 1916 and the British and French mandates in the Middle East. After reading the chapter and studying the maps, answer these questions:

1. Based on the information in the maps and in the chapter, how do you think the British and the French felt about the Middle East? How do you think the Arabs felt about the Sykes-Picot Agreement and colonialism? Why do you think they felt this way?

2. Which Middle Eastern countries were included in the British mandate? In the French mandate?

3. According to the Sykes-Picot Agreement, which countries were to be under British influence? Under French influence?

CHAPTER 37 REVIEW

POINTS TO REMEMBER

1. Colonialism began in the Middle East in the 1800's when the western powers wanted new markets, raw materials for industry, and control of strategic routes.
2. In the Husayn-McMahon correspondence, the British promised their support for an independent Arab state, while in the Sykes-Picot Agreement they agreed with the French to divide the Ottoman Arab territories. After World War I, when Syria became a French mandate and the country of Lebanon was created, Arab riots and revolts resulted. In 1946, Syria and Lebanon became fully independent.
3. Egypt granted Ferdinand de Lesseps concessions to build the Suez Canal, using forced Egyptian labor. Several years after the canal was completed, the British and French took over its financial management. Later, a move towards Egyptian nationalism led the British to occupy Egypt, where they stayed until 1956 when the Egyptian government nationalized the canal.
4. At the base of the Arab-Israeli conflict is the claim of ownership of Israel by both Palestinian Arabs and Israelis. The Arabs base their claim on the Husayn-McMahon correspondence, the Israelis on the Balfour Declaration.
5. In 1947, the United Nations vote to partition Palestine led to the creation of the state of Israel, which most Arabs still refuse to recognize today.
6. By the 1800's, Great Britain was the dominant power in the Persian Gulf. When oil was discovered in the early 1900's, the area took on new importance, and the British tightened their grip. Middle Easterners, who wanted to receive a greater financial return for their oil, protested. In 1951, Iran nationalized its oil industry, leading to a western boycott and hard economic times for Iranians.

VOCABULARY

Identify

Husayn-McMahon correspondence
Sir Henry McMahon
Sherif Husayn
Sykes-Picot Agreement
Prince Faisal
United Arab Republic
Ferdinand de Lesseps
Suez Canal
Said Pasha
Gamal Abdel Nasser
Aswan High Dam
Balfour Declaration
Mohammed Mosaddeq
Mohammed Reza Pahlevi

Define

colonialism
concessions
mandate
nationalized
partition
boycotting

DISCUSSING IMPORTANT IDEAS

1. In the story about Abū Hāmid, the ten-year old Syrian boy ends his narration this way: "Two tears wet my cheeks, and deep inside me I felt a great bitterness." About what do you think he felt bitter? How would you have felt in his situation?

2. Some people feel that the present Arab-Israeli conflict is a direct result of British actions. Do you agree or disagree? On what basis?
3. In 1951, Mohammed Mosaddeq called for the nationalization of Iran's oil industry, and in 1956 President Nasser nationalized the Suez Canal. Do you think government has the right to nationalize industry? Give reasons to defend you answer.
4. Some people believe that colonial rule was beneficial because, among other things, railroads were built and schools were opened. Other people see the colonial period differently. They believe Arab industrialization was blocked and attempts were made to destroy Arab culture. Based on the information in the chapter, what do you think? Give examples to support your answer.

DEVELOPING SKILLS

INTERPRETING HISTORICAL DOCUMENTS

Historical documents include letters, treaties, speeches, agreements, diaries, constitutions, and any other materials written in the distant or recent past. Interpreting such documents can provide clues as to how cultures developed, national character was shaped, or certain events came about.

Some of these documents, however, prove to be difficult to understand. The opening passage on page 603 is a historical document. The following steps will help you interpret it or any other historical document you may encounter:

1. Ask yourself what kind of document you are dealing with *(a written statement)*, when it was written *(1882)*, and why it was written *(to explain the British position regarding their takeover of the Egyptian government)*.
2. Research the event and the period during which the event took place so that you will have the historical background needed to understand the document. *(The two paragraphs at the bottom of page 603 will provide you with the background you need for this particular document.)*
3. Look over the document quickly, scanning for key words and phrases. Read a sentence at the beginning, in the middle, and at the end. Based on this quick review, decide what you think is the main purpose of the document *(to explain why the British were right in taking over the Egyptian government and what control they would exercise in the future)*.
4. Read the document carefully, and determine if your decision about the main purpose of the document was correct. *(It was correct.)* If you no longer believe it was correct, state what you now think is the main purpose.
5. Determine what feelings and opinions are not directly stated but are implied. *(The British considered themselves superior to the Egyptians, a people they saw as incapable of "civilized" self-government.)*
6. Summarize what you have determined. *(In 1882, the British took over the Egyptian government. They felt this was the right thing to do. The British needed to trade with the Egyptians, who they believed were not capable of running their own government. If Egypt did not prosper because of poor leadership, British trade would suffer. The British solution was to take over the Egyptian government and to keep control indefinitely to make sure that no other country interfered with British-Egyptian trade.)*

For practice in this skill, use the suggested steps to interpret President Nasser's nationalization speech on pages 608 and 609.

CHAPTER 38
THE MIDDLE EAST TODAY

1. What major issues challenge Middle Easterners today?
2. What are the people of the Middle East doing to ease their problems?

In my dream, O mother mine,
I saw an angel with wings pure white
Breaking the rifles one by one,
Shattering into pieces each gun,
Which then into the fire he dashes
And turns into smouldering ashes.

In my dream, O mother mine,
I saw an angel with wings pure white
Scattering the ashes clean
Over the glittering scene.
And the ashes turning into a white dove,
Hovering over the East, jubilant above.

In my dream, O mother mine,
I saw an angel with wings pure white
Lifting Moses and Mohammed up to the skies
And demanding they shake hands and be wise.
I heard his voice thunder and echo after them:
Quick, make haste, O sons of Shem—
Behold he is coming, the herald of Peace,
Singing a song of praise to Peace.*

As reflected in the poem above written by a young Israeli, the greatest challenge facing the people of the Middle East today is to bring about peace. It also is their greatest desire. Yet, despite the common desire of the people for peace, the Middle East has been in a state of unrest for many years. Although many factors have contributed to this unrest, one of the most important is conflicts that have not been resolved. Three of these—the Arab-Israeli conflict, the civil war in Lebanon, and the war between Iraq and Iran—already have resulted in the loss of hundreds of thousands of lives and many precious physical resources.

Interwoven with these conflicts—contributing to them and resulting from them—are problems common to many other nations besides those of the Middle East. Governments must find ways to improve their economies—and thus the living conditions of their people. They also must find ways to slow down or put a halt to rising prices and provide for growing populations. In the Middle East, however, many people contend that until the conflicts still raging in the area are resolved, these other problems cannot and will not be dealt with effectively.

---

*"O, Mother Mine" by Gassoub Serhan in *My shalom, my peace*, 1975, Sabra Books, p. 69. By permission of American Israeli Paper Mills Ltd.

THE ARAB-ISRAELI CONFLICT TODAY

The dispute between the Arabs and the Israelis has been going on for more than 40 years. At its core is disagreement over who owns the land of Israel, once called Palestine. After the war of 1948, three other wars broke out between the two groups—in 1956, 1967, and 1973. Instead of solving the existing problems, these wars only created new ones. During the wars, the Israelis occupied new territories, which the Arabs want back. They also want the several million Palestinians who fled during the fighting to have their homes and land returned to them.

A SEPARATE PEACE

Over the years, many efforts have been made to bring about peace between the Arabs and the Israelis. The boldest and most controversial move took place on November 19, 1977, when, at the invitation of the Israeli government, President Anwar el-Sadat of Egypt arrived in Jerusalem to make a speech before the *Knesset*, the Israeli parliament. Sadat was the first Arab head of state to visit Israel. For the first time, the Israelis extended full state honors to a neighboring ruler still at war with them.

About two years later, on March 27, 1979, after much negotiation and with the mediation of U.S. President Jimmy Carter, President Sadat and Israeli Prime Minister Menachem Begin signed the first formal peace treaty between Israel and an Arab country. The Israelis agreed to withdraw over a three-year period from the Sinai Peninsula, which they had occupied after the 1967 war. Egypt agreed to end the state of war and establish normal and peaceful relations with Israel. In addition, elections for local governments were to be held in the West Bank and Gaza, two other territories taken by the Israelis in the 1967 war, and their future was to be decided at a later date.

Reactions to the treaty were mixed. Many Arabs felt that Egypt, once the leader of the Arab world, had deserted the "Arab Muslim family" and should have held out until all outstanding problems, including that of the Palestinians, had been solved. The day the

Israeli Prime Minister Menachem Begin, left, and Egyptian President Anwar el-Sadat, right, are shown at the 1977 session of the Knesset *in which Sadat called for an end to the state of war, a just solution for the Palestinians, and Arab acceptance of Israel as a state. To what did Israel and Egypt each agree under the terms of the 1979 peace treaty?*

Insights on People
Middle East

Anwar el-Sadat

Anwar el-Sadat's childhood was spent in a small, poor village in the Nile Delta. As his father worked for the British army and was away from home much of the time, he was reared by his grandmother.

In 1938, Sadat graduated from the Royal Military Academy in Cairo. During the next ten years or so, his involvement with Egyptian nationalists seeking freedom from British rule led to several arrests and stays in prison. In 1949, he married. His wife, Jihan, did much over time to advance the status of women in Egyptian society.

In 1950, Sadat joined a secret society of army officers which, under the leadership of Gamal Abdel Nasser, overthrew the Egyptian government. Egypt became a republic, and Sadat became a member of the Revolutionary Command Council, which ran the country under Nasser. He then established a newspaper, *al-Jumhūriyah*, and became its editor-in-chief.

For the next 15 years, Sadat held one important government position after another. In 1970, he was elected president of Egypt. He later explained what this meant to him:

I knew that this . . . meant I should have to challenge many conditions and ethical codes in existence at the time; but I believed I had the capacity for this. Indeed, due to the inner power I always felt, I had never been afraid to challenge existing conditions. And now that I was President, I felt I wielded a tremendous real power, which had to be used in doing good. This was my forte, and I proceeded from the ideals I had always adopted, inspired by my love of Egypt and my desire to make the country a happy one. Never had I had a better chance of putting my principles into practice than when the people elected me President.*

Sadat had three goals he wanted to achieve—the return of territory lost to Israel in war, peace in the Middle East, and a just solution to the problem of the Palestinians. In 1977, in an effort to achieve these goals, he accepted an invitation to address the Israeli parliament. The visit ultimately led to a Nobel Prize for Peace, an Egyptian-Israeli peace treaty, and the return of the Sinai Peninsula to Egypt. At the same time, however, the visit also led to resentment and opposition from other Arabs. On October 6, 1981, while reviewing a parade celebrating the anniversary of the 1973 Arab-Israeli war, Anwar el-Sadat was assassinated.

In the following statement, which is part of the prologue to his autobiography, *In Search of Identity*, Sadat tells how he viewed his life and his country:

This is the story of my life, which is at the same time the story of Egypt since 1918—for so destiny has decreed. The events of my life coincided with those which Egypt has lived during that period. I therefore tell my story in full, not merely as the President of Egypt, but as an Egyptian whose life has been intimately bound up with that of Egypt.

It is, I believe, like every man's life, a journey in search of identity. Each step I have taken over the years has been for the good of Egypt, and has been designed to serve the cause of right, liberty, and peace.

This is the image I have had of myself since childhood.*

1. Who was Anwar el-Sadat?
2. What were some of Anwar el-Sadat's major accomplishments?

---

*Specified excerpt, p. 207, from *In Search of Identity* by Anwar el-Sadat. Copyright © 1977, 1978 by the Village of Mit Abul-Kum. English translation copyright © 1977, 1978 by Harper & Row, Publishers, Inc. Reprinted by permission of Harper & Row, Publishers, Inc.

**Ibid.*, prologue.

INSIGHTS ON PEOPLE
MIDDLE EAST

GOLDA MEIR

Born in the Ukranian city of Kiev, Golda Meir immigrated with her family to the United States in 1906 to escape the anti-Semitic feeling and persecution suffered by Jews in Czarist Russia. The family settled in Milwaukee, Wisconsin. In 1917, after studying to be a teacher, Meir married Morris Meyerson, a Jewish immigrant from Lithuania.

Memories of persecution in Russia and reports of anti-Semitic activities elsewhere convinced Golda Meir that the Jews must have their own country. This belief led her to join the Zionist movement, which advocated establishing a Jewish state in Palestine. Years later, Meir stated that "The time hadn't quite come yet for me to decide to live there. But I knew that I was not going to be a parlor Zionist—advocating settlement in Palestine for others."

In 1921, Meir and her husband emigrated to Palestine, where they lived in a *kibbutz* in Merhavia for two years. They then moved to Jerusalem, where she became active in the politics of the Histadrut, the General Federation of Labor. During the next 20 years, she held important posts not only in the Histadrut but in other organizations as well.

In 1948, Meir visited the United States to enlist American support for the creation of the Jewish state of Israel. She also had several meetings in Jordan with King Abdullah in an effort to avoid clashes with the Arabs over the establishment of the new state. During one meeting, to which she had to travel secretly disguised as an Arab, Abdullah asked her to be patient and wait a little longer to declare the establishment of Israel. It is said that she refused, replying "We have been waiting for 2000 years. Is that hurrying?"

After Israel was proclaimed a state, Meir was appointed minister to Moscow. The following year, she was elected to the *Knesset* and became the first woman to hold a seat in the Israeli legislature. For the next seven years, she served as minister of labor, encouraging unrestricted Jewish immigration and initiating public-works projects, which created new jobs and improved living conditions.

In 1956, Meir was appointed foreign minister, a position she held for nine years. In 1969, at the age of 70, she was elected prime minister, an office that she held until 1974. In her autobiography, *My Life*, she talks about her reaction to her election:

> . . . I know that tears rolled down my cheeks and that I held my head in my hands when the voting was over, but all that I recall about my feelings was that I was dazed. I had never planned to be prime minister; I had never planned any position, in fact. I had planned to come to Palestine, to go to Merhavia, to be active in the labor movement. But the position I would occupy? That never. I only knew that now I would have to make decisions every day that would affect the lives of millions of people, and I think perhaps that is why I cried. But there wasn't much time for reflection, and any thoughts I had about the path that had begun in Kiev and led me to the prime minister's office in Jerusalem had to wait. Today, when I can take time for those reflections, I find I have no appetite for them. I became prime minister because that was how it was, in the same way my milkman became an officer in command of an outpost on Mount Hermon. Neither of us had any particular relish for the job, but we both did it as well as we could.*

Golda Meir died in 1978. After her death, her doctors disclosed that she had been suffering from leukemia for 12 years.

1. Why did Golda Meir join the Zionist movement? What did the Zionists want?
2. In what ways did Golda Meir serve Israel?

My Life by Golda Meir, Putnam Publishing Group pp. 364–365. © 1975 by Golda Meir.

This Jewish settlement on the West Bank is one of 135 that have been established by the Israeli government since 1967, when Israel captured the region from Jordan. Over 30,000 Jewish settlers now live on the West Bank, many attracted by low rents and the area's historical significance to their people's early history. Why do the Israelis want to keep the occupied territories?

treaty was signed, many Palestinians and Arabs staged strikes and protest marches, called for Egypt to be punished, and vowed revenge. The next day, foreign and finance ministers of Arab League countries met to discuss what political and economic measures they could take against Egypt.

Most Egyptians and Israelis, however, took a "wait-and-see" attitude. As one Israeli stated, "I would very much like to believe we've fought the last war, at least with Egypt. But I want to see. Sadat may not be around tomorrow. Or he may change his mind." As one newspaper noted, most Egyptians agreed:

> Egyptians shrugged off the start of formal peace with Israel today, treating the day much like any other. . . .
> Interest perked up tonight as families crowded around televisions sets and transistor radios for live broadcasts of the signing ceremony. . . .
> Otherwise, life in Cairo was much as usual. . . .
> "Egyptians are not sure of anything —they are still suspicious," said Khalil el-Mahdi, a mechanical engineer. "The land is not back yet and there have been indications that we will have problems after peace. Egyptians have more pressing problems to think about, even on the day of signing the treaty. . . ."

Nonetheless, virtually everyone interviewed around Cairo today welcomed the end to three decades of belligerency with Israel.*

UNRESOLVED ISSUES

Three major issues were not resolved in the Egyptian-Israeli peace treaty. One was control of East Jerusalem, which the Israelis had taken in 1967, and the Arabs wanted returned. Another was the fate of the million plus Palestinians living on the West Bank of the Jordan River and in the Gaza Strip. A third was control of the Golan Heights. The Arabs wanted, and continue to want, return of all these territories. The Israelis remained opposed to the Arab demands. They felt, and continue to feel, that the occupied land is needed as a security belt around Israel. Some Israelis also want to keep the land because it was once a part of ancient Israel.

---

*"In Egypt, Peace is Welcomed Quietly With Hope for a Better Life" by Christopher W. Wren in *The New York Times*, March 27, 1979, p. A12. Copyright © 1979 by The New York Times Company. Reprinted by permission.

Daily life goes on in West Bank Arab towns such as this one despite the Israeli occupation. How do Israelis and Arabs differ in their views of Arab life under Israeli occupation?

The failure to resolve these issues weakened Sadat's position in Egypt. Boycotts by other Arab countries hurt the Egyptian economy as did the halt of economic aid being provided by oil-exporting Arab states. At the same time, rumors of corruption and mismanagement circulated throughout Egypt, and Muslim religious extremists accused Sadat of betraying his religion. On October 6, 1981, Muslim extremists assassinated Sadat. Vice President Husni Mubarak became the new president of Egypt. Mubarak assured the world community that Egypt would continue to honor its peace with Israel. He also made a strong effort to restore good relations between Egypt and other Arab countries.

Meanwhile, the issues still remain unresolved. As an American reporter indicates below, each side continues to view the issues differently:

> The result [of Israel's 1984 elections], moderates and radicals alike agree, is an atmosphere in which patience and hope have given way to pessimism. Seventeen years after the Israeli military occupation began here [on the West Bank and Gaza Strip], prospects seem further away than ever for a settlement....
> "With every passing day we are losing ground," says Mayor Elias Freij of Bethlehem, considered one of the region's leading Arab moderates. "I believe the situation has reached midnight. In a few years, the people of the West Bank and Gaza may be totally forgotten." By objective measurements, life under occupation constitutes a viable existence. Israeli administrators proudly point out that there is virtually total employment in the region, that its residents are closing the income gap with the Israelis.... Even under occupation, the Israelis argue, the Palestinians here are no less free than their brethren in the rest of the Arab world....
> But by the criteria of those who live here, occupation remains both a hardship and a punishment.... Every Israeli Army traffic checkpoint and every announcement of a new or expanded Jewish settlement becomes a symbol of repression, and every rock-throwing incident a symbol of resistance.
> Seemingly commonplace public events become political battlefields. The Israelis recently announced plans to link this city [Nablus], the West Bank's largest, to Israel's national electricity grid, a move they said would reduce costs and increase efficiency. But the idea was immediately denounced by local Arab leaders as yet another effort to increase Arab dependency.
> "They want to control everything in our daily lives," says former Nablus mayor Bassam Shaka....
> A few blocks north of Shaka's house lie the locked gates of Al Najah, the largest

university in the West Bank. It has been closed since late July. . . .

The Israelis, who agreed to the establishment of four West Bank universities during the last decade, contend the schools have become breeding grounds for radicalism and violence where academic studies have become irrelevant. . . .

But the periodic closings here and at Bir Zeit and Bethlehem universities have become part of the rhythm of life under occupation and have had a depressing effect on radicals and moderates alike. Hikmat Masri, who is chairman of the board and main founder of Al Najah, a former speaker of the Jordanian parliament and a leading Arab advocate of peace talks with Israel, says the Israelis "are punishing the entire university because of a few troublemakers. Education is so important to us, and this closing is a disaster. . . ."*

1. What are the underlying issues of the Arab-Israeli conflict?
2. Why was Anwar el-Sadat's visit to Israel important? To what did it lead?
3. What issues were left unresolved in the 1979 peace treaty? What effect did this have on Egypt and Sadat?

CIVIL WAR

At the same time the Arab-Israeli conflict was brewing, the seeds of a new civil war were growing in Lebanon. Since independence, power in the government had been divided among Christians and Muslims proportionately to their numbers. As Christians were the majority, for many years they had more political power. But by the 1970's, the population had changed, and Muslims were in the majority. When they requested an even sharing of power and were refused, their discontent grew.

*"Palestinians Feel They Lost the Israeli Election" by Glenn Frankel in *The Washington Post National Weekly Edition,* September 24, 1984, p. 13.

Meanwhile, economic problems also were surfacing. Since the increase in oil prices in the early 1970's, a great deal of Middle Eastern oil money had been invested and used in Lebanon. The resulting sudden increase in spending caused prices to rise sharply. The wealthy and the upper-middle class, both of which had benefited from the oil money, were able to keep ahead of the rising prices. The poor, who included the more than 400,000 Palestinian refugees living in Lebanon, could not.

By 1975, the situation had become very tense. As the number of poor Lebanese and Palestinians rose, so did discontent, and revolutionary ideas became popular. Many of the Palestinians were members of the

This 32-year-old Palestinian mother of three became a PLO fighter after her husband was killed during the civil war in Lebanon. What happened in Lebanon as the number of poor Lebanese and Palestinians grew?

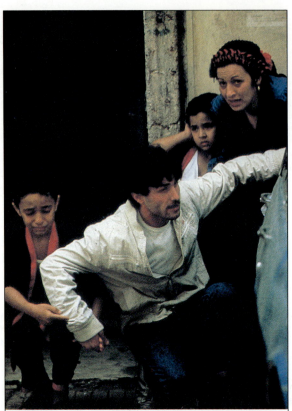

This Lebanese family is hiding in fear behind a car during a battle between two rival Muslim factions. Over 100,000 Lebanese have died in these internal wars. What role did Syria play in Lebanon in 1976?

Palestinian Liberation Organization (PLO), an organization dedicated to regaining Palestinian territory from the Israelis. The PLO was using Lebanon as a base to launch attacks on Israel. While many Lebanese Muslims supported the Palestinians and the PLO, most Lebanese Christians did not. Afraid that a revolution would result that would upset the religious balance of power, political parties formed and trained their own armies. Before long, civil war broke out. While some viewed the conflict as religious, others saw it as a struggle between the "haves" and "have-nots."

In 1976, the Lebanese government and other Arab states asked the Syrian government to help restore peace. Syria sent troops, and order was restored. As one reporter observes below, the city of Beirut, at least, soon seemed to be returning to normal:

> Commercially, the city is fast regaining its old hustle. Rubble has been cleared from most streets; with it went a . . . haze that had shrouded the city. Cement mixers, rather than armored vehicles, rumble through the streets. The port has been restored to 50% of prewar capacity, and once again trucks rattle off the piers and up the winding mountain roads toward delivery points throughout the Persian Gulf. Beirut's airport, the busiest in the Arab world (400 weekly flights) before it was shut down . . . has reopened and handles about 75% of its old traffic volume. The industrial district of Mekhalles . . . is again turning out everything from office equipment to hospital beds.*

But the conditions that led to the war still existed. Clashes with the Israelis continued in southern Lebanon. In June 1982, the Israelis invaded Lebanon. Their goal was to drive the PLO out of southern Lebanon and secure peace for northern Israel. The invasion destroyed many villages and left tens of thousands of Lebanese and Palestinians homeless. Below, Kevin M. Cahill, an American physician, tells what he found when he visited Beirut shortly after the invasion:

> Armenian scholars no longer search for God in the Near East School of Theology in west Beirut. The cool archives room in the cellar is now a blood bank, and the conference hall . . . now contains two operating tables. . . .
>
> This month the Palestinian Red Crescent Society incorporated the School of Theology into one of the most remarkable health-care delivery services in the world, . . . serving a half million people still surviving the air and ground attacks that threaten the existence of west Beirut. . . .

---

*"Beirut: Better, But Not Yet Well". Copyright 1977 Time, Inc. All rights reserved. Reprinted by permission from TIME.

I undertook a tour of the war-ravaged areas of Lebanon.... Square blocks of the ancient biblical cities of Tyre and Sidon have been bombed away. We could not find a single structure intact—nor a single person—in the formerly Christian town of Damur....

... There is no mystery about the scope of this tragedy if one walks the wards of the university hospital or the School of Theology and sees the limbless bodies, the fractured faces, the blind, the burned. These are real people, men and women and children, hundreds of them....

We saw young refugees in Tripoli in the far north of Lebanon who had traveled hundreds of miles over mountains only to find that parents were lost somewhere on the trek.... I met an Austrian woman whose husband and two children were gone when she returned home from her job as a nurse in west Beirut. They lived in a camp that had been destroyed....

Hatred abounds....*

To help restore peace and to observe the withdrawal of PLO forces from Beirut, an international peacekeeping force was sent to Lebanon. The violence, however, never stopped completely. Attacks on the peacekeeping forces cost the lives of several hundred American and French soldiers. In 1984, the peacekeeping forces withdrew. The following year, the Israelis began their withdrawal. The war, however, continues.

1. What were the underlying causes of the civil war in Lebanon?
2. Why did the Israelis invade Lebanon in 1982? What was the result of the invasion?

REVOLUTION AND WAR

Another area where internal conflict broke out in the 1970's was Iran, which had grown wealthy over the years through the sale of oil. The ruler of Iran, Shah Mohammed Reza Pahlevi, was using the money for building programs in the cities, lavish ceremonies, and defense. This displeased many Iranians who argued that while skyscrapers were rising in Tehran and billions were being spent on defense, many villages were without such basic facilities as running water. Hundreds of thousands of peasant farmers left the countryside to seek jobs in the city. Prices went up, and the poor suffered. In addition, in his efforts to modernize and westernize, the Shah often disregarded traditional Iranian and Islamic values.

This tangled mass of concrete and steel rubble in Beirut used to be an apartment building before the city was shattered by invasion and civil war. What happened when peacekeeping forces left Lebanon?

---

*"Beirut's Smell of Death" by Kevin M. Cahill in *The New York Times*, Saturday, July 24, 1982. Copyright © 1982 by The New York Times Company. Reprinted by permission.

When Iranians opposed to the Shah's actions voiced their sentiments, they were stilled by the Shah's secret police. Silent opposition to the Shah grew until 1978, when it broke into strikes, demonstrations, and finally revolution.

A NEW REGIME

In 1979, the Shah fled Iran, and a new government was set up under Ayatollah Ruhollah Khomeini. Khomeini, a Muslim leader who had been living in exile in France, returned to Iran at the request of the Iranian people. His goal was to rid Iran of all foreign influences and make it an Islamic Republic. Below, an American reporter comments on the events that took place in Iran in 1979 and the effects they have had:

Ayatollah Ruhollah Khomeini was returning to the dry, dusty holy city of Qum after 16 years of exile when I first came to Iran in February 1979. Mohammed Reza Pahlevi, Shah of Shahs, Light of the Aryans, policeman of the Gulf and America's best friend in the region, had just departed, taking with him a jar of Persian soil and the dog that revolutionaries delighted in picturing on their posters. . . .

My plane from New York on that day almost six years ago was the first Iran Air flight out following the nationwide strike in Iran that had deposed the hated Shah. As the engine started up . . . , the passengers packing the airliner, many of them newly bearded student exiles returning home in the first flush of the revolution, broke into a chant of prayer for the welfare of the Prophet Mohammed and his family. Sitting next to me was a stocky, well-educated oil engineer who had been stranded . . . in Texas. In excellent English, he talked rapidly of how the Iranians would now control their own oil, would be their own people, their own nation, free of foreign powers. The students gathered around to listen.

"The first thing we need is complete educational reform," he said. "What is going on now is terrible."

"Oh, really?" I asked. "What is to be done?"

"This is just awful," he went on angrily. "These young men come into the classrooms, and all around them are girls with their heads uncovered and even their arms in short sleeves." Around us, the students were nodding in agreement. . . .

Now, six years after the Black Friday massacre . . . , when the Shah's troops opened up with machine guns on demonstrators, that day can be seen as the turning point in the crumbling of the Pahlevi regime. It began the cycle of funeral processions, which led to more deaths, which, 40 days later, led to more processions and still more deaths. Since that revolution, what has come to be called Islamic fundamentalism has grown into a major force throughout the Middle East. . . .

"Death to U.S.A." says the legend greeting travelers in huge letters on the

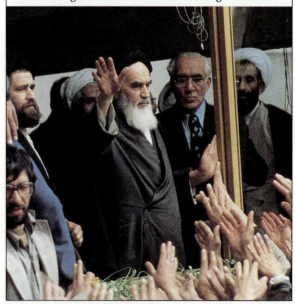

Iranian leader Ayatollah Ruhollah Khomeini greets a crowd of supporters at an Islamic school in Tehran a few days after the Shah was overthrown. What was Khomeini's goal when he took over Iran's government?

These Muslim women in Tehran, clutching their chadors *about them, have gathered for Friday prayers. Under Ayatollah Khomeini's regime, women seen in public must be well covered from head to foot, though their faces need not be veiled. Those who fail to obey this rule may be arrested, whipped, or jailed. Who has been most affected by Iran's brand of Islamic fundamentalism?*

outside wall of the . . . airport terminal at Mehrabad Airport. . . . The procedures are not as stringent as they were a few years ago, when one might expect a body search. . . . Still, it takes three or four hours to get through the airport. . . .

All of the big hotels had coffee lounges in their lobbies, where, even after the revolution, it was fashionable to gather in the late afternoon for pastries. Now, the hotels have family rooms, an area screened off by opaque cloth where accompanied women are allowed to sit. The coffee lounges are for men only. . . .

Still, quirky contradictions continue, including an underlying fascination with America, its things, its popular culture. As the taxi drivers cruise the Islamic streets, they listen to cassettes of the latest American disco hits. . . .

Clerical rule has fallen most harshly on the educated, Western-oriented Iranians, many of whom originally supported the revolution. Women, particularly, smart under the new order. . . .

Diplomats say that the authorities . . . are relaxing somewhat. . . . Some confiscated houses have been relinquished, and the privacy of homes, which once might be raided on suspicion of drinking or other evils, is to be respected. . . .

A European diplomat . . . reflected on the difficulty for a Westerner in understanding Iran. Almost anyone you might have social contact with is critical of the regime, he explained, and this is highly unrepresentative. "The revolution," he said, "still enjoys a vast base of support in a nation overwhelmingly poor and devout, not least because it is seen as trying, whatever the shortcomings, to improve their lives. . . ."*

WAR WITH IRAQ

Khomeini's government called for an Islamic revolution in other Muslim countries, making a special appeal to Muslim leaders in Iraq with whom Khomeini had contact. Iraq had had **secular,** or nonreligious, governments since the 1950's, and its leaders believed firmly in separating state and religion.

---

*"Iran: Obsessed with Martyrdom" by John Kifner in *The New York Times Magazine,* December 16, 1984, pp. 40, 42, 47. Copyright © 1984 by The New York Times Company. Reprinted by permission.

But Iraq and Iran bordered one another and shared much tradition. In addition, half of Iraq's Muslims were Shi'ites, the same sect of Muslims as Khomeini and his followers. Tension mounted between the two countries, and in 1980 Iraq invaded Iran. As a reporter indicates below, the war has become a costly and bloody clash between two opposing views of society:

> . . . The conflict between Iran and Iraq has often been in the shadows of world events, although few, if any, such two-combatant struggles have been so costly. Iran's dead may number 500,000; Iraq's perhaps 70,000. The war is costing the latter country close to one billion dollars a month.
>
> Among other things it is a war of sacred law versus secular, a nasty kidney-blow fight in which child conscripts and outrageous tactics . . . have been employed. . . .
>
> [In Baghdad] there are discos in the new hotels, and there are other nightclubs. . . . Liquor is legally available. There are gambling casinos. The vices are not practiced flagrantly here, but they do taunt the fundamentalist sensibilities of Ayatollah Ruhollah Khomeini in Iran. Probably even more sinful in his eyes are the rights accorded women in Iraq.
>
> Women in Baghdad dress fashionably. They attend universities and hold some of the highest offices in the land. There are women engineers here, and women pilots, doctors, architects, and lawyers. Overall, nationally, women now account for 25 percent of the work force. It is official doctrine . . . that women have full equality with men. On the other side is Iran, where, it is reported, lipstick is removed from women by a swipe of cotton in which a razor blade is imbedded.
>
> "Long ago, in the history of the Islamic world, women worked as traders, and they participated in battles," said Iftikar Ahmed Ayoob. "So what Khomeini is doing today is against Islamic law. He is using Islam as a curtain to hide his illegal and barbarous treatment of women."
>
> Mrs. Ayoob is deputy director of the General Federation of Iraqi Women, an organization of considerable influence.
>
> "When the present government decided to eliminate illiteracy, 1.4 million women went to centers to learn to read and write," Mrs. Ayoob said. "Now we have programs to get them jobs. Many go into factories. Others go on to higher education and the professions. We now have 16 women, including myself, in the National Assembly."
>
> The war accounts in part for the many women in the work force, but the acceptance of equality between the sexes has

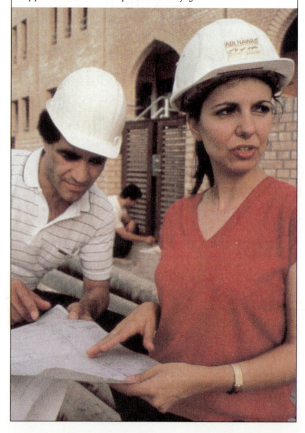

This female electrical engineer, looking over plans with a colleague at a Baghdad construction site, reflects Iraq's policy of equality for women. What rights and opportunities do Iraqi women enjoy?

other strong reflections in the social aspects of life. . . .

The issue of women's rights, as much as anything, is a true measure of the distance between the ideologies of the two warring nations. Iraqi leader Saddam Hussein allows no compromise with the secularism of Iraq, and Khomeini allows none with his interpretation of koranic law.*

1. What were some of the factors that led to the downfall of the Shah?
2. How has Iran changed since under the Khomeini government?
3. What is the major difference in the thinking of the Iranian and Iraqi governments?

A LAND IN TRANSITION

Until recently, much of the Middle East was poor by western standards. Today, however, Middle Eastern countries that export oil do not have to worry as much about money. Instead, their problems center on how much oil to produce, to whom to sell it, and how to manage the money earned. In some of these countries, governments have come under a great deal of pressure from western nations and from their own people. Some western nations want them to produce more oil, but the people want them to cut production and raise prices. Higher prices would mean more money, while producing less would make the oil last longer.

With their added wealth, the people of the oil-exporting countries have been able to buy more food and other goods, which has led to higher prices all over the Middle East. This has created problems in those Middle Eastern countries that do not export oil.

Aggravating the problem of **inflation**, rising prices, is the rapid increase in urban population. Improved health care has reduced infant deaths. But while more babies are surviving and people are living longer, the birthrate has stayed about the same. Many Middle Easterners have large families so as to be sure they will have at least two or three sons to care for them in their old age or in case of emergency. As a result, the population of the Middle East has doubled in the last 30 years.

In addition, the rate of rural to urban migration is very high. The population of the large cities has been doubling every 15 years or so. Many people migrate because they have no room in their villages and the land no longer can support them. When the population of a village increases but the area of cultivated land does not, some villagers must go elsewhere. And that elsewhere is the city. This migration has made it hard for governments to improve living conditions. As a visitor notes below, such is the case in Cairo, the largest city in Africa and the Arab world:

> Just outside the [Egyptian] museum, the full clamor of Cairo. This city that can comfortably hold three million holds almost thirteen million. It shows. There are people everywhere. And cars; crossing the street in Cairo must be like running the bulls in Pamplona. Nobody ever stops. You leap into the crazy lanes and try to make eye contact with the drivers upon whom your life depends. This city is an odd mixture of speed and sloth. Cairenes race by, but the sidewalks are filled with idlers, . . . layabouts waiting to be raised from their economic death to employment. I lose my way to the Sultan Hassan mosque, a severe medieval structure between whose high stone walls serenity may be found, and find myself in a slum that shocks me with its poverty. In Old Cairo, outside the low charcoal walls that enclose small Coptic domes, the poverty is still more shocking. Sewers are now being installed; the heavy pipes are carried, through mud and garbage and flocks of

---

*"The New Face of Baghdad" by William S. Ellis in *National Geographic*, Vol. 167, No. 1, January 1985, pp. 81, 96–97.

Noisy, bumper-to-bumper traffic and crowds of bustling pedestrians combine to form this chaotic street scene in one section of sprawling downtown Cairo. What is one of the major problems confronting urban Egyptians?

lean fowl, by gangs of boys in tattered robes, a method more primitive than the bringing of the blocks to Giza must have been.*

In some areas, housing has become a major problem. In Egypt, for example, one person in three has adequate living accommodations. In the following, the Mideast editor of a large French newspaper comments on the housing situation in Cairo:

*"Cairo Diarist: Ancient Afternoons" by Leon Wieseltier. Reprinted by permission of *The New Republic*, © 1983, The New Republic, Inc.

Many Cairo neighborhoods are without sanitation facilities. The cracked hovels that line the highways often have no drinking water or electricity.

Entire families crowd together in one or two tiny rooms. Lacking separate homes, young people delay marriage and increasingly give up establishing their own families. . . .

Authorities admit that at least three million new dwellings are needed but, lacking the means, they are building only 160,000 a year. In the interim the homeless take refuge in makeshift wood or metal huts in wastelands or fields. They occupy rooftops or sleep under the stars. Cairo has tens of thousands of cemetery squatters.

Real estate promoters used Sadat's credit facilities and tax exemptions to construct not public housing, with rent regulated by the government, but deluxe apartments for the elite. Today Cairo's fancy neighborhoods have some 150,000 unoccupied units.*

Even Turkey, where governments have been trying to modernize and improve living conditions for more than 60 years, has suffered from the rise in urban population. Below, a journalist describes what he found in the capital city of Ankara:

> . . . Peasants just arrived from the bleak, hungry heartland of eastern Anatolia squat in a mess of plastic suitcases and bedrolls bound with cords, on the brink of a new and hopeful urban existence. . . . A decade ago those men in lumpy jackets and women in billowing pantaloons might have begun city life in a shanty tacked to a rocky outcrop on the city's edge, but with the expectation that in a few years they could fill the house with such anchors of modernity as a refrigerator, an electric stove, and even a color TV. They could have hoped to send their sons and daughters on to the university and, if they saved their money, one day to buy a car.
>
> Now when they leave the bus terminal, they walk into a city where every fifth man is unemployed and where the rest are taking home less than half as much in real income as they did five years ago. In the past year alone meat prices have increased by 50 percent and the price of potatoes has tripled. The price of bread, from which Turks get half their calories, has increased by 65 percent. Many urban Turks spend more than half their income paying rents. . . . Although inflation has been cut from a high of 120 percent, it still hovers oppressively at 50 percent a year. The newcomers can see their grim prospects well enough in the picturesque but pathetic vendors who flood the capital's broad boulevards, selling combs, cigarettes, water, gum, tea, stockings, and shoeshines.*

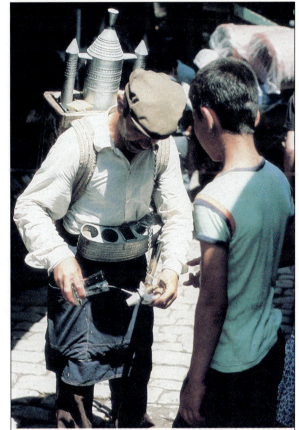

This street vendor in Istanbul pours water for a thirsty patron. His services are much welcomed in cities where running water is still scarce. What conditions can peasant families expect to find when they move to the Turkish capital city of Ankara?

1. What problems has new wealth brought the oil-producing countries?
2. Why is population increasing rapidly in the Middle East?
3. Why is rural to urban migration so great? How has this migration affected large Middle Eastern cities and the people who live in them?

---

*"Egypt's Identity Crisis" by Eric Rouleau as cited in *World Press Review*, November 1984, p. 27.

*"Turkey: From Anarchy to Modernity" by Fergus Bordewich in *The Atlantic*, December 1984, p. 52.

CHAPTER 38 REVIEW

POINTS TO REMEMBER

1. The greatest challenge facing the people of the Middle East today is to bring about peace. To do this, three conflicts—the Arab-Israeli conflict, the civil war in Lebanon, and the war between Iraq and Iran —must be resolved.
2. At the core of the Arab-Israeli conflict is the claim by both the Arabs and the Israelis to ownership of the land of Israel.
3. Egyptian President Anwar el-Sadat became the first Arab head of state to visit Israel. He and Menachem Begin signed the first formal peace treaty between Israel and an Arab nation. Arabs who resented the treaty took revenge on Egypt.
4. Three major issues—control of East Jerusalem, Palestinian self-rule, and control of the Golan Heights— were not resolved in the Egyptian-Israeli peace treaty. All three remain unresolved today.
5. Discontent over distribution of political power between Muslims and Christians led to civil war in Lebanon. The issue was complicated by the growing gap between the "haves" and "have-nots" and the actions of the Palestinians and the PLO.
6. Discontent with the policies of the Shah of Iran led to revolution in Iran and a new fundamentalist Islamic government under Ayatollah Ruhollah Khomeini. When Khomeini tried to convince Muslims in Iraq to overthrow their secular government, war broke out between Iran and Iraq.
7. Added wealth has brought new problems to the Middle East. These problems, concerned with oil production and pricing, are aggravated by inflation, rapid population growth, and a high rate of rural to urban migration.
8. The rapid growth in urban population has made it hard for governments of Middle Eastern countries to improve the living conditions of their people.

VOCABULARY

Identify

Anwar el-Sadat
Knesset
Menachem Begin
Sinai Peninsula

West Bank
Gaza
East Jerusalem
Golan Heights

Husni Mubarak
Palestinian Liberation Organization
Mohammed Reza Pahlevi
Ayatollah Ruhollah Khomeini

Shiʿite
Cairo
Ankara

Define

secular

inflation

DISCUSSING IMPORTANT IDEAS

1. Some Middle Easterners believe that peace between the Arabs and the Israelis may never come. Do you agree or disagree? Why?
2. How has the existence of 400,000 Palestinian refugees contributed to the conflict in Lebanon? What do you think might happen if they all were to leave Lebanon?

3. The establishment of an Islamic republic in Iran has had a major effect not only in Iran but all over the world. Why do you think this is so?

4. If you were the leader of Egypt or Turkey, what steps would you take to raise the standard of living and improve the living conditions of the people?

DEVELOPING SKILLS

INTERPRETING BIOGRAPHICAL ACCOUNTS

At one time or another, you may have been asked to write a *biography*, an account about someone else's life. A biography is a secondary source based on primary sources and other secondary sources. Biographical accounts include information about a person's background; the major events in his or her life; and his or her accomplishments, personality, attitudes, and values. They also help explain a person's significance in the history of a culture or the meaning of a person's place in time.

Some biographies are written in a straightforward manner that is easy to read, understand, and interpret. Others may be a little more difficult. There are some questions you can ask yourself as you read a biography that will help you to interpret it. In the example that follows, those questions have been applied to a biographical sketch of Anwar el-Sadat that appears on page 619.

1. About whom is the account?
   (*Anwar el-Sadat*)

2. What major events occurred in the person's life?
   (*Grew up in small, poor village in Nile Delta; reared by grandmother because father away in British army; graduated from Royal Military Academy; arrested and imprisoned for supporting Egypt's release from British rule; married; participated in overthrow of Egyptian government; member of Egyptian governing body; established and became editor-in-chief of newspaper; held major governmental positions; elected president of Egypt; addressed Israeli Parliament; received Nobel Prize for Peace; assassinated*)

3. What events and persons most influenced the person's life?
   (*Involvement with Egyptian nationalists; Egypt becoming a republic; election as president of Egypt; address to Israeli Parliament*)

4. What attitudes and values did (does) the person consider important?
   (*Freedom from foreign rule; courage to challenge existing conditions; use of power to do good; right, liberty, and peace*)

5. What motivated the person to act as he or she did?
   (*The belief that his personal destiny and identity were intertwined with those of Egypt*)

6. What personality traits or characteristics does the account reveal?
   (*Leadership ability; determination; self-confidence*)

7. On what events or issues did the person have an influence?
   (*Freedom from British rule; overthrow of the Egyptian government; the Israeli-Egyptian peace treaty; the return of the Sinai Peninsula to Egypt*)

8. What are the person's achievements?
   (*Establishment of a newspaper; presidency of Egypt; Nobel Prize for Peace; Israeli-Egyptian peace treaty; return of the Sinai Peninsula to Egypt*)

9. What makes the person significant in history?
   (*His presidency and the peace he brought about between Egypt and Israel*)

For practice in this skill, use the suggested questions to help you interpret the biographical sketch of Golda Meir that appears on page 620.

UNIT 6 REVIEW

SUMMARY

The Middle East was home to the early civilizations of the Nile and the Fertile Crescent as well as being the birthplace of Judaism, Christianity, and Islam. Over the years, many ethnic groups and nationalities have populated the region. Today, more than half its people are Arabs whose language, culture, and religion have been imprinted strongly on the region.

Scarcity of fresh water has made it difficult to live in many areas of the Middle East. In the past, most of the people were concentrated along the fertile river valleys and the seacoasts. But in recent years, modern technology has made it possible to farm and to build cities in some of the most arid areas.

In the Middle East, the family is very important. Togetherness, obedience, love, mutual help, and respect are its cornerstones. In both the family and marriage, religious teachings and custom dictate the traditional roles of men and women. Despite the many changes taking place, the family remains predominant.

The long and rich history of the Middle East includes a period when much of the region was under colonial rule. During this period, the British and the French dominated. The discontent and resentment of many Middle Easterners resulted in long, hard battles for freedom and independence. Some of the decisions made by the colonial powers continue to have an impact even today.

More than anything else, Middle Easterners today desire peace. Although many efforts have been made to achieve this end, unrest continues in many areas. Many people believe that until conflicts like the one between the Arabs and the Israelis are settled, many of the other problems that Middle Eastern governments are facing will not be resolved and the Middle East will not know peace.

REVIEW QUESTIONS

1. How has physical environment affected the course of Middle Eastern history? The ways of life of the people?
2. Why do you think the Middle East is described as a "mosaic of peoples" rather than as a "melting pot?"
3. How have traditional Middle Eastern family values been shaped by Islamic teachings? In what ways and by what factors have these values been challenged in recent years?
4. What factors have contributed to the unrest in the Middle East?

SUGGESTED ACTIVITIES

1. Working in small groups, prepare and present to the class television commercials designed to sell products from your country to Middle Easterners.
2. Participate in a panel discussion on the Arab-Israeli conflict. Take turns role-playing the moderators and the panel members.
3. Select a newspaper or magazine article on a current political issue in the Middle East. Write a background paragraph that will put the article in context.
4. Select a Middle Eastern country, research the status of its major religious and ethnic minorities, and graph or chart your findings.

Middle East

COMPARING CULTURES

Housing, which varies from one place to another, reflects an area's environment and resources and what people can do to adapt to them. Below are descriptions of traditional housing in many rural villages of the Middle East and of housing in winter camps of the Innuits of northern Canada. Based on what the descriptions tell or intimate about housing, geography, climate, and resources, compare and contrast the life styles and environments of the two cultures.

MIDDLE EASTERN HOUSING

Throughout the Middle East, where the days are dry and hot and the nights cool or cold, houses in farming villages are built of sun-dried mud bricks with flat or domed roofs. The walls usually are over two feet (60 centimeters) thick, and the windows are small. The domed roofs are made entirely from mud bricks, while the flat roofs are supported by logs placed horizontally over the walls, then are covered by layers of leaves and mud. In some villages, a grove of trees is planted and carefully tended to provide house-building materials.

The thick walls and roof insulate the inside of the house from the heat of the day and absorb the intense rays of the sun. At night, they slowly radiate their heat into the house, warming the interior. Sometimes the houses of several families who are related are joined and grouped around a courtyard. The rear walls protect the courtyard against wind and sand storms.

INNUIT HOUSING

Although most Innuits today live in more standard housing, some of those engaged in winter hunting in the Arctic, where there are harsh winter winds and subfreezing temperatures, build igloos, snow huts that require no wood or stone. The igloos are made from large, flat blocks of fine-grained compacted snow cut from a snowdrift. The blocks are laid spirally and slope inward to build up a dome. Crevices are packed tightly with snow. The shape of the igloo offers the minimum resistance to the wind and the least surface to its chilling effects.

Sometimes the main room of the igloo is lined with animal skins, and a skin lines the ceiling, leaving a large air space just below the roof. A hole in the roof traps cold air above the ceiling. This insulates the living space and prevents the snow ceiling from melting too much. The only other warmth is that provided by a stone oil lamp fueled by seal blubber.

Unit Seven

Although the Soviet Union is the largest country in the world, very little is known about it. In the words of a British prime minister, Winston Churchill, it is "a riddle wrapped in a mystery inside an enigma." Knowledge of the country's troubled history and appreciation of its geographic remoteness helps one understand Soviet life today. But still, it is a land where inconsistencies and contradictions abound. Despite these contradictions, today the Soviet Union is a foremost superpower and plays a major role in determining world affairs and the destinies of billions of people. Therefore, it is important to know about the Soviet people and to understand how the past has influenced them and shaped the development of their land.

CONTENTS

39	GIANT AMONG THE GIGANTICS	638
40	THE RUSSIAN PAST	654
41	THE SOVIET ERA	672
42	PEOPLES OF THE SOVIET UNION	688
43	CITY AND COUNTRY	704
44	THE ALL-POWERFUL STATE	720
45	SOVIET LIFE	734

SOVIET UNION

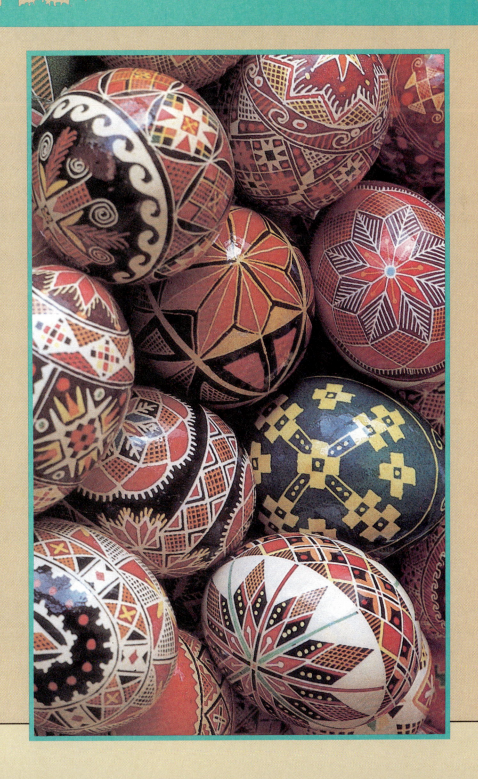

CHAPTER 39
GIANT AMONG THE GIGANTICS

1. Why are the size and global position of the Soviet Union important?
2. What are the major geographical characteristics of the Soviet Union?

I love my country, but my love is strange
And rare, a love that reason cannot change.
It is not my country's victories, nor fame
So dearly bought with blood, nor ancient claim
Of rich tradition, glory, and command
That stir sweet reveries about my native land.

Not these bring quiet joy. I love—I know
Not why—her rivers at the flood like seas,
The voices of her boundless forest trees,
The frozen silence of her plains in snow.
I love to ride for days inside a jolting cart
On dusty lanes, and, searching slow the evening shadows,
To dream of lodgings near and hail with thankful heart
A blur of trembling village light among the meadows.

I love the smell of stubble burning,
The wagons huddled on the plain
At night, a pair of silver birches
Above a field of yellow grain.
With gladness few can share, I see
The grain upon the threshing floor,
The lowly cottage with its trim
Above the window and the door.
I'm glad to watch on holidays
The stamp of dancers on the ground,
And hear until the morning's near
The talk of tipsy peasants round.*

*"My Native Land" by Mikhail Lermontov in *MIKHAIL LERMONTOV The Demon and Other Poems* translated by Eugene M. Kayden, 1965, Kent State University Press, p. 87. Reprinted by permission.

This poem was written by a Russian poet named Mikhail Lermontov almost 150 years ago. The country about which Lermontov is speaking is now known as the Soviet Union and, in many respects, is very different from the Russia Lermontov knew and loved. One thing, however, has not changed over the years. That is the feeling the people have for their land—the land many of them still call "Mother Russia." There are many who say that unless you understand the land, you will not understand the people or the politics.

THE FACTOR OF SIZE

The Soviet Union, with its 8,649,000 square miles (22,487,400 square kilometers) of territory is the largest country in the world. It covers about one-sixth of the entire land surface of the globe. It is more than the size of Canada, the People's Republic of China, and the United States combined. The total length of its frontier is one-and-one-half times that of the Equator.

There is a saying that the sun never sets in the Soviet Union. This is because it encompasses 11 time zones. In the summer, the sun always shines over some part of the country. Geographers include the Soviet Union among the **gigantics,** the eight nations of the world more than 1 million square miles (2.6 million square kilometers) in area. It is, they say, a "giant amongst the gigantics."

The vast size of the Soviet Union has affected the country's development, history, and conduct in domestic affairs and world politics. As discussed below, it also has made the land one of mystery and fascination for many over the ages:

> To the ancients, [today's Soviet Union] was the end of the known world, a land inhabited by Hyperboreans [legendary people of the Far North] and cannibals, by fantastic creatures, half man and half monster. Marco Polo called it the coldest part of the world and the land north of it a region of darkness, with neither the sun, the moon, nor the stars to give it light. Still later, the Europe of the Enlightenment looked with interest and concern on the autocratic treasure-laden Russian empire, trying to guess the intentions of the "Russian bear."
>
> Even the rulers of the land did not know how big it was. In January 1725, Peter the Great sent forth an expedition under Vitus Bering to find the place where Asia and America "meet." It took Bering and his crew three and a half years to reach Kamchatka, from where they sailed on the *St. Gabriel* to reach the straits separating the Chukchi Peninsula and Alaska.
>
> The world has changed much since then. [The Soviet Union] is an industrial power with close ties to other countries. . . . Today, Bering's journey could be made in less than ten hours. The cloak of mystery that at one time had covered this vast country has been lifted, even if not removed altogether.*

1. How large is the Soviet Union?
2. How do geographers view the Soviet Union?

GLOBAL POSITION AND CLIMATE

The Soviet Union spans the two continents of Europe and Asia, or Eurasia. The dividing line between the two is the Urals, a long, low range of mountains running north to south. Below, a Soviet author describes what he sees and feels as he stands along the border:

> Europe and Asia meet on this forest clearing. One fir tree grows in Europe, the other, within sight of it, in Asia. A flock of waxwings rises from an ashberry tree, circles over the clearing and settles on a mountain ash in Asia. The people in the clearing, feeling chilled, run back and forth between Europe and Asia. A bus stops. The passengers read the words "Europe-Asia" on the stone marker, draw a line on the pavement and jump across it into Asia. . . .
>
> . . . In some places the border passes between neighboring villages. When visiting the city of Magnitogorsk you spend the day on the right bank of the Ural River and then take a streetcar to your hotel in Asia. Though the border is of no actual

---

*"The USSR" by Natalya Shemiatenkova in *Russia, the Land and the People of the Soviet Union* by Dieter Blum, 1980, Harry N. Abrams, Inc., p. 20. Reprinted by permission.

CHAPTER 39 GIANT AMONG THE GIGANTICS

The Soviet Union's Ural Mountains, composed of rounded peaks like these, contain rich deposits of oil, iron ore, and other mineral deposits. What two geographic areas do the Urals divide?

significance in everyday life, there is something solemn about crossing the line the first time. Thousands of kilometers lie behind you. Ahead are the frost-tinted crests of the dark forest, yet more thousands of kilometers of your native land stretching endlessly before you. At a moment like this you have a physical sensation of your country's vastness.*

The Soviet Union is one of the northernmost nations on earth. This location influences the country's climate, which has been the most fundamental element in shaping the natural environment. For the most part, the Soviet Union has a **continental climate.** This means short hot summers and long cold winters separated by a very short spring and fall. Global location, distance from great bodies of water, and lack of mountains near lowland areas are three major factors that account for the climate being what it is.

The Soviet Union is not the land of constant cold many people believe it to be. From the Caspian Sea eastward are desert areas

---
*"Europe-Asia" by Vasili Peskov in *This Is My Native Land*, 1976, Progress Publishers, pp. 124–125. Reprinted by permission.

with a hot, dry climate that makes much of the area barren. In the Kara Kum, or "black sand," desert, the temperature has been known to rise above 120° Fahrenheit (48.9° Celsius) in the shade. In the area along the coast of the Black Sea, a favorite vacation spot of the Soviet people, the winters are short and rainy, while the summers are hot and dry. Here, citrus fruit, grapes, olives, and tea thrive.

Much of the country, however, does experience very cold winters, which last for many months. This is especially true in the north of Siberia, a Soviet region in northern Asia. Below, a visitor to the Siberian city of Yakutsk describes how the cold feels and what effects it can have:

> The day I arrived in Yakutsk . . . , it was 46 [-43.3° Celsius] below. When our plane landed, the door was frozen solidly shut, and it took about half an hour for a powerful hot-air blower—standard equipment at Siberian airports—to break the icy seal. Stepping outside was like stepping onto another planet, for at those low temperatures nothing seems quite normal. The air burns. Sounds are brittle. Every breath

Parts of the Kara Kum provide enough vegetation to support herd animals, like this camel, who seems undisturbed by the pumping gas well in the background. Where are the desert areas of the Soviet Union located?

hovers in a strange slow-motion cloud, adding to the mist of ice that pervades the city and blurs the sun. When the breath freezes into ice dust and falls almost silently to the ground, Siberians call it the whisper of stars. Frost as fine as sand shifts into crevices, clings to power lines, coats the scrubby trees along the main avenues until they look like misshapen sculptures. Every few minutes people on the streets put gloved hands over their mouths and noses to keep the flesh from freezing. The smallest children are wrapped in layer after layer so that little more than their eyes are exposed. Buildings have triple windows and triple doors. Private cars are put away for the winter. Taxis are kept in heated garages and are fitted with thick double panes of glass that look like portholes peering into a sea of frost. Trucks for lumbering and other work are kept running constantly through the six months of winter, for to let their engines cool would be to lose the ability to start them again until spring. In this climate, where the low that year was 72 degrees below zero Fahrenheit [-57.8° Celsius], steel cranes can snap, photographic film can shatter like glass, rubber soles on boots can break cleanly in half.*

Siberia is one of the areas of the Soviet Union where a condition known as **permafrost**, permanently frozen ground, occurs. This is because much of the Soviet Union is too far away from the Atlantic Ocean to be influenced by its mild westerly winds.

Permafrost is a problem, especially in Siberia, where soil freezes to a great depth. In some areas, it has not thawed out since the Ice Age tens of thousands of years ago. It makes building roads almost impossible and causes buildings not constructed on piles to sink and tilt in the summer. It also makes extra heat insulation necessary for water mains and sewers and forces steam-heat pipelines to be built aboveground. Above all, it can be ruinous for agriculture.

These warmly dressed passengers are boarding a bus to go to work on a typical, icy-blue morning in Siberia. Why does the condition of permafrost occur in Siberia? What problems can it cause?

In addition to permafrost, Soviet areas north of the Arctic Circle also experience **polar night,** darkness which lasts for more than 24 hours. This occurs during the winter when the northern part of the earth is tipped away from the sun. Below, a reporter describes what happens in the port city of Murmansk when the sun finally appears:

> [After] seven weeks of darkness, the city turned out for a holiday on the last Sunday of January. Signs reading "Zdravstvui sointse" (Hello, sun) went up around town, stalls were raised for amateur skits, and women in folk garb went out with baskets full of oranges, apples and candies. No matter that the sun was still limited to an orange glow through the hazy horizon.
>
> Technically the polar night had ended a week earlier, but because of the rolling hills surrounding Murmansk, it took the sun some time to gain elevation to become visible. The temperature was around zero Fahrenheit [-17.8° Celsius]. . . .

---

*From *Russia: Broken Idols, Solemn Dreams* by David K. Shipler. Copyright ©1983 by David K. Shipler. Reprinted by permission of Times Books, a division of Random House, Inc.

CHAPTER 39   GIANT AMONG THE GIGANTICS

Hazy or cold, it was a day to be out in the streets, to affirm despite evidence to the contrary, that days would get longer and warmer now that the long darkness was at an end. . . .

In Semyonovskioye Lake, . . . a cluster of diehard "morzhi" (walruses) . . . were cavorting in the icy water.

Nearby a stage dominated by a huge smiling sun was set up alongside a bus bursting with children. Groups of these took turns dashing out to perform a skit or a song. . . .

Beyond the stage, women . . . dispensed steaming coffee and cookies. . . .

Similar scenes occurred elsewhere among the concrete housing slabs stretched . . . along Kola Bay. In the Vale of Coziness, a winter sports complex . . . , several hundred young people massed for a cross-country ski race. Downtown, on Kirov Square, sailors joined in an impromptu weight-lifting contest. . . .

The sun is an obsession at these latitudes. Old-timers describe the depressing effect the gloomy polar night has on newcomers, and speak of a drowsiness that afflicts even longtime residents.

"It is an effort to get out of bed in the morning," said a taxi driver. "One feels like a lazy fly, the kind that wanders dazedly into your soup."

To counter the adverse effect of the polar night, powerful sodium lamps bathe thoroughfares in dazzling light, and shops offer more oranges, apples and green onions than those in Moscow. In school, children are given sun-lamp treatment, and school cafeterias have carrots and milk available at all times.

But it is the real sun that people crave. . . .*

The grain kernels this woman is looking at are from plants growing in this experimental Arctic greenhouse at a Moscow agricultural research center. In what ways does climate affect Soviet agriculture?

The climate of the Soviet Union makes it one of the driest countries in the world. This is a major problem in terms of agriculture. Some areas are too cold for productive agriculture. Others do not know how much rainfall they will get during the year. Some years there is a drought, which causes some farm products to be in short supply. As a result, often there is not enough grain and other farm products to feed all the people. Then, the Soviet Union must buy these goods from other countries.

1. What continents does the Soviet Union span?
2. What kind of climate does most of the Soviet Union have? What three factors influence it?
3. Why does the Soviet Union have to depend on other countries for some farm products?

---

*"In Soviet North, a Party Greets the Sun" by Serge Schmemann in *The New York Times*, February 19, 1984. Copyright ©1984 by The New York Times Company. Reprinted by permission.

The Lay of the Land

Like the rest of the land surface of the world, the territory of the Soviet Union has clearly defined climate and vegetation zones. These include expanses of treeless plains called **tundra,** several kinds of forest, steppe, semi-desert and desert areas, and humid subtropical zones. Sprinkled among these are mountains and bodies of water.

TUNDRA

Soviet territory in the far north, along the Arctic shore, consists of hundreds of thousands of square miles of tundra. Here, the low hills and level marshy plains are covered with snow and ice for most of the year, and the ground is almost always frozen. There are no tall trees, only moss, small shrubs, and low grasses.

Not many people live on the tundra. The people who do live there make their living by fishing, hunting, or herding reindeer. Below, a writer who grew up on the tundra talks about the area and its people:

> My birthplace, the settlement of Uelen on the Chukchi Peninsula, is situated on a narrow pebble spit. To the north lies the Arctic Ocean, which came up to our *yaranga*, or family dwelling. During autumn storms, waves often beat against the walrus-skin walls of the hut, while in winter masses of broken ice reached the hole where we kept our winter supplies. . . .
>
> Our whole life was bound up with the sea. Early on summer mornings, the hunters set off from land in their *baydars*, or kayaks, paddling out into the sparkling patches of sunlight among the drifting ice floes to chase the herds of walruses and whales. In winter the men hunted seals on foot, hiding in the light blue twilight among the masses of broken sea ice. . . .
>
> The Chukchi Peninsula, where I was born, is gripped by gale-force winds and severe cold. For all practical purposes there is no summer here, if one excludes the one and a half or two months of relatively warm weather when the temperature rises as high as 21° C (70° F). This is the time when the tundra vegetation blossoms and the midnight sun hardly disappears below the horizon. . . .
>
> Today, . . . many inhabitants of the Soviet Arctic have not only absorbed the ancient heritage that was passed on by their forefathers but also have adopted much of the contemporary outside world. They have shifted from yarangas to modern-style houses furnished with arrays of modern conveniences. . . . Some have exchanged reindeer or dogsleds for snowmobiles or all-terrain vehicles, and they fly from village to nomad camp by helicopter.
>
> But for all their ability to adapt, the native inhabitants of the Soviet Arctic remain inexorably bound to their homeland. They may change, but they will never leave their beloved seacoast or tundra; they will remain hunters and reindeer herders, dwellers amid lands covered for most of the year by ice and snow. . . .
>
> . . . Flying by helicopter from my village of Uelen, I paid a visit to the Chukchi reindeer herders at the state farm known in Russian as Mayak Severa, or "beacon of the north."
>
> Arakamchechen [the island on which the farm is located] is well suited for reindeer farming; in summer the winds blowing across the island sweep the swarms of mosquitoes out to sea, and the pastureland is rich. . . .
>
> Vladimir Tukkay [leader of the farm's reindeer workers] has his own reindeer. . . . His spacious yaranga is packed with recent newspapers and magazines. A powerful all-terrain vehicle with a transceiver stands by his home.
>
> Surveying these comforts, I asked Tukkay if he would live in any other place.

"Any other place?" he pondered. "Most likely not. I was born in the tundra, my parents and forefathers were always reindeer herders. I studied at school, I lived in the dormitory, then served in the army. Could I live in any other place but Arakamchechen? To do that, I would be deprived of a certain part of my very self. Here in the tundra, among the reindeer, . . . I feel the life I was created for."*

FOREST

South of the tundra is forest, which covers more than 30 percent of the country. It constitutes one-fifth of the forest area of the world and contains about one-fourth of the world's supply of timber. Cold climate, poor soil, and a short growing season make most of the eastern forest lands unsuitable for farming. In parts of the western zone, however, trees have been cut down to make room for cities and farms. The soil is good, and rye, barley, and oats grow well.

Most of the forest region is **taiga,** or evergreen forest. The Siberian taiga has so many trees that it is called a "green ocean." Below, a journalist describes his first encounter with the Siberian taiga:

> The taiga is the wellspring of legend and adventure. [The Siberians] go off to hunt, or fish through the open ice, or build a campfire and cook a sumptuous meal in the open, surrounded by the cleanest snow you ever saw. So Yuri and our other guide, Yelena Pankova, . . . were delighted by our interest. And when one day the weather showed the first sign of spring and the temperature rose to minus 20 [-29° Celsius], five of us . . . piled into a four-wheel-drive Gazik, a Soviet version of the Jeep, and headed along a narrow, unpaved road west from Yakutsk. We were going on a picnic.

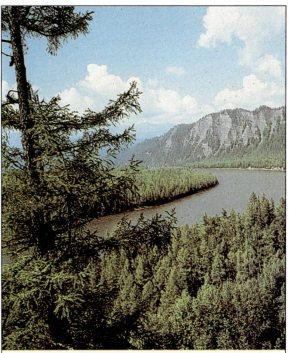

Largest of the Soviet Union's vegetation zones, the thick taiga consists mostly of spruce, larch, and pine trees. Why is the eastern part of the taiga unsuitable for farming?

> About twenty-five miles [40 kilometers] out of town we turned onto a little-used track that led into the forest. The Gazik scrambled through axle-deep snow, wound for miles among the trees, and came to a stop at a flat expanse of pristine woods. The engine was left idling, but we walked up to our knees in snow, back, back into the deep forest where we could hear neither engine nor any other whisper of distant civilization. Within minutes the fluffy snow had been shoveled away from a chosen spot, dry wood had been gathered from dead branches, and a fire was going. A blackened teapot had been filled with snow and was hanging over the flames. A . . . bucket, also brimming with light snow, sat on the logs, the snow melting and sizzling and hurling steam into the icy air. . . .
>
> The first course was then spread out . . . : the *stroganina* [fish], some sliced

---
*"People of the Long Spring" by Yuri Rytkheu in *National Geographic*, Vol. 163, No. 2, February 1983, pp. 206, 209, 212, 214–215. Reprinted by permission.

salami, smoked *omul* [fish] and *ryapushka* [fish], black and brown bread cut into thick slices, and chunks of lightly smoked colt's meat. . . . There were cups of steaming tea. The bread froze, and the apples turned to stone until they were brought close to the fire. Yuri had to keep waving his jackknife through the flames so he could pry it open. The vodka, poured into metal cups, had to be kept close to the heat; otherwise the metal cup would stick to your lips.

After the first course Yelena and Uri turned to making a soup called *ukha*. . . . The soup was done when the fish floated to the surface and the eyes turned white, Yelena said. And she spooned it out. It had a thick, wonderful flavor. And in the woods around the fire, dusk came slowly, turning the snow blue and moving the darkness closer until it pressed against the tight glow of the flames.*

This farmer uses a modern multi-disc tractor to plow the rich soil of this farm and prepare it for a new growing season. Where is the main agricultural area of the Soviet Union found?

STEPPE

South of the forest is the steppe, the main agricultural area of the Soviet Union. This great plain stretches more than 3000 miles (4800 kilometers) from Eastern Europe to Asia. For centuries, it served as an invasion route for foreign armies. Today it is an important industrial area and cattle-breeding zone. In addition, its fertile soil is considered among the best in the world for farming. Below, a Soviet author explains how some of the people who live on the steppe deal with the high temperatures that can occur there:

> The sun is unrestrained and pitiless. It burns you up, it sets the body on fire, making it impossible to think of anything but the heat. "The sun of the steppelands is like a boiling kettle, pouring yellow boiling water over your back," wrote the poet Yuri Pankratov. In this quiet, cozy little town on the steppes, about half the people are Kazakhs, and they have their own way of dealing with the sun.
>
> It is almost unbearable to look at one of them during the hottest time of the day. You will see a man walking in the heat wearing a long, heavy robe and a fur hat. Not a drop of perspiration shows on his bronzed face, and not much more than that of real expression, either. He looks alert but untroubled, in sharp contrast to those who are strange to the area, and who begin to suffer visibly when the thermometer rises menacingly.
>
> The people here assure the visitor that there are two main rules for fighting off the scorching heat: Do not drink, and keep yourself well covered. They always observe these rules, and they never take an afternoon siesta, not even when the temperature is so high that an egg buried in the sand is hard-boiled in a minute. They just go on working their allotted seven hours a day, as they do in any other weather.*

---

*From *Russia: Broken Idols, Solemn Dreams* by David K. Shipler. Copyright ©1983 by David K. Shipler. Reprinted by permission of Times Books, a division of Random House, Inc.

**The Russians* by Leonid V. Finkelstein (Vladmirov), 1968, Frederick A. Praeger, pp. 11–12. Reprinted by permission.

BODIES OF WATER

The Soviet Union also has a great many bodies of water. Two of the world's largest lakes are found here. One is the Caspian Sea, which is really a salt lake. The other is Lake Baikal, which is the deepest continental lake in the world. Both are important as sources of fish.

Then there are the rivers, which have played an important part in the country's trade and development. They are, to a great extent, a product of the climate. The direction in which the rivers flow is determined by the locations of the mountains and the higher elevations. Climate, however, determines how much water each river bears and for how many months of the year each river is frozen.

Most Siberian rivers flow from south to north into the Arctic Ocean and are frozen for most of the year. Because of this, they are not very effective links to the outside world. Most of the rivers in the European part of the Soviet Union, however, are connected to one another and to the seas by a system of canals. This makes possible a continuous flow of river traffic that has helped unify the country.

One of the most important rivers is the Volga, Europe's longest river. Although it is frozen for almost four months of the year, it handles almost half of the country's river-freight traffic. One of the rivers flowing with the Volga is the Kama. Below, a Soviet author explains why the Kama often is described as a "hardworking river":

> Just thirty kilometers [18 miles] from its source the little Kama shoulders its first load: lumber. This load keeps increasing constantly, with lumber, lumber and more lumber from its countless tributaries, down its entire length to the Volga. The Kama has for centuries been a lumber-carrier from the moment the ice breaks up in spring till the river freezes over again. Its small tributaries carry the logs before they are made up into rafts. As seen from above, the logs look like matchsticks someone has dropped on the surface. They are so closely packed that raftsmen can easily run back and forth across them. Sometimes a jam packs the small river bed with logs and then a tractor can roll along the

Some parts of the steppe can be very cold. This is reflected in the warm clothing worn by this family enjoying a meal in their home on the Central Asian steppe. Why is the steppe so important to the Soviets?

This structure stretched across the Kama River is used to catch logs so they can be sorted and lashed into rafts. The lumberjacks who do this work often live with their families in huts aboard the rafts when they are riding their harvested logs to sawmills farther down the river. Besides logs, what other products are transported down the Kama River?

surface. Navigation stops in the upper reaches of the Kama in spring, for then lumber is king. Farther downstream the logs are knocked into rafts. . . . Barriers are set up in the river, and the place where the lumber accumulates makes you think the river is paved with logs. . . .

From above I was now looking at a river covered with an endless string of rafts. . . . Each [raft] resembled a field, for it was about 700 meters [2310 feet] long! A thousand freight cars of lumber were floating down the river. The Kama delivers the rafts to the Volga, and the Volga delivers them to the Caspian Sea or to the Don River. . . .

These giant rafts follow each other in close succession. No sooner does one disappear from view than another appears. There is always a steamer at the head of a raft. Sometimes these are old water-wheel river boats. The rafts once used to float downstream unaided, but the Kama has now overflown its banks like a sea before the dam at the city of Perm, and the current has practically disappeared. This means the rafts have to be towed: six hundred of them each season. . . . The Kama is fondly called the lumber carrier. However, the river carries much more than lumber on its back. Oil from the Kama oil fields is transported by water, as are paper, machinery and chemicals. Salt barges have always gone down the Kama to the Volga. . . . The river demanded that all who traversed it be skilled pilots, which meant one generation handed its knowledge down to the next. There is still an old custom of presenting a bridegroom with an oar in one of the Kama settlements.*

1. What are the major characteristics of the tundra? The taiga? The steppe? How do many people make their living in each?
2. What influence does climate have on the rivers of the Soviet Union?

---

*"Sister to the Volga" by Vasili Peskov in *This Is My Native Land*, 1976, Progress Publishers, pp. 20–21. Reprinted by permission.

CASE STUDY
SOVIET UNION

THE GREEN PATROLS

The government of the Soviet Union has imposed strict laws to protect the environment. Among the Soviet citizens working to help enforce the laws is the Student Scientific Society at Moscow State University. During weekends and holidays, Society members go out to different areas around Moscow in nature protection patrols. Below, a Soviet journalist who accompanied the students on one of their rounds describes the experience:

At 7 P.M. on Friday our motorship left the dock in Pushchino, a town on the Oka River not far from Moscow. Pushchino . . . serves as headquarters for the River Patrol.

The boat was loaded with all kinds of scientific equipment, large rucksacks, rubber boots, two motorboats, my cameras, plus 19 conservation enthusiasts and myself. We were 10 young women and 10 young men. . . . We laughed and joked . . . and told stories about the "exploits" of other Green Patrol members like ourselves. . . .

The long summer day came to an end, and a mist descended over the Oka. The Green Patrol got busy. Night is the time poachers usually operate.

The first group, which I was in, lowered one of the motorboats into the water without making a sound and climbed in. . . . We drifted with the current, paddling occasionally. As our eyes got accustomed to the gloom, we could distinguish the white sand spits and the banks overgrown with osier [willows] and rushes.

We drifted along in complete silence for an hour. I was beginning to think that we'd have to go back empty-handed when suddenly I heard someone whisper: "Two rubber rafts on the starboard side."

"Start the engine!" ordered Andrei Shcherbakov, the leader of the patrol. "We'll see what they're doing."

Our boat shot forward, and in a matter of seconds we were on board the nearest raft. Our flashlight revealed a net lying on the bottom of it.

Amateur fishers are not permitted to catch fish with nets in Moscow Region.

"Volunteer fish warden Shcherbakov," our leader said, introducing himself to the poachers.

While the introductions were being made, the second raft got to shore.

We managed to catch up with its two passengers an hour later while they were transferring their catch into the sidecar of a motorcycle. . . .

Establishing the poachers' identities and drawing up a report of the case required restraint and courage. Caught red-handed, the culprits lied and evaded the questions. After they ran out of words, they started a fight. Our group . . . had to fire an SOS signal, and help arrived immediately.

Day was dawning by the time we returned to . . . the boat. The others were already cooking breakfast over a campfire. It turned out that our group had been the most successful. . . .

"Who are these poachers?" asked Natasha Sidorova, a member of the research group. . . .

"Guys who want to make an easy living," Shcherbakov told her. "They use illegal means of fishing for their own personal gain. In other words, they profit by robbing nature. . . ."

Our Green Patrol combed the area for three days. We detained four groups of poachers and confiscated nine nets, two boats and a large quantity of fish. On the way back I asked Shcherbakov what he thought of the results.

"I would prefer our expeditions to work on scientific problems. Catching poachers is not our sole aim. This expedition is studying the effects of poaching and amateur fishing on the Oka River Basin. . . . Other members of the group are busy banding birds and registering wildlife. . . ."*

1. What are the Green Patrols?
2. Do you have any groups in your country like the Green Patrols? If so, what do they do? How effective are they?

---

*"Students vs. Poachers" by Marina Yurchenko in *Soviet Life*, August 1984, pp. 10, 12–13. Reprinted by permission.

EXPLORATION
SOVIET UNION

There is an old Siberian folktale that says that when God created the earth, he was passing over Siberia carrying a sack of valuable resources. But his hands got so cold that he dropped the sack, leaving in Siberia a wealth of natural resources.

When asked about the resources of her country, a Soviet scientist affiliated with the Central Siberian Museum of Geology had this to say:

"There are great quantities of prospected oil and natural gas from the Urals to the Pacific Ocean, even north to the Kara Sea and the Peninsula of Taymyr. In 1975, a total of 150 metric tons [165 tons] of oil was pumped in western Siberia alone. We also have vast coal deposits. The largest are to be found between the Yenisey and Lena rivers.

*In Yakutia, diamond lodes have been discovered comparable to those in South Africa. The largest stone, found in 1973 and named the Star of Yakutia, weighed 232 carats!"**

Natural resources have been a major factor in the Soviet Union's rise to a leading

---
Journey Across Russia: The Soviet Union Today by Bart McDowell, 1977, National Geographic Society, pp. 335–336. Reprinted by permission.

NATURAL RESOURCES

industrial nation over the past 60 or more years.

Study the maps. Then use the information provided by them to defend or negate the following statements.

1. The natural resources of the Soviet Union are vast and diversified.
2. The Soviet Union has few tracts of fertile soil that, when irrigated, are excellent for farming.
3. Very few natural resources are found in the desert areas and mountain areas of the Soviet Union.
4. At least one-third of the Soviet Union is forest.
5. Timber is one of the major natural resources of the Soviet Union.
6. Almost every major mineral can be found in the Soviet Union.
7. The Soviet Union has very few deposits of coal, oil, and natural gas.
8. Waterpower, which is used to produce electricity, is one of the Soviet Union's main natural resources.
9. One valuable natural resource which the Soviet Union lacks is fish.

NATURAL REGIONS

SOVIET UNION

CHAPTER 39 REVIEW

POINTS TO REMEMBER

1. The Soviet Union is the largest country in the world. Its size has affected its development, history, and conduct in domestic and world affairs.
2. The Soviet Union spans the continents of Europe and Asia. The dividing line between the European part of the country and the Asian part of the country is the Ural Mountains.
3. Climate has been the most fundamental element in shaping the natural environment of the Soviet Union. Three major factors—global location, distance from great bodies of water, and lack of mountains near lowland areas—have influenced climatic conditions.
4. Permafrost and the polar night have greatly affected the economy of the Soviet Union and the ways of life of the Soviet people.
5. The Soviet Union is one of the driest countries in the world. This has had a major impact on the country's agricultural production.
6. The Soviet Union has clearly defined climate and vegetation zones. These include tundra, forest, steppe, semi-desert and desert areas, and humid subtropical zones.
7. Two of the largest lakes in the world—the Caspian Sea and Lake Baikal—are located in the Soviet Union.
8. The rivers of the Soviet Union have played an important part in the country's trade and development. The direction in which each river flows is determined by the locations of mountains and higher elevations. The amount of water rivers bear and how long they remain frozen is determined by climate.

VOCABULARY

Identify

Soviet Union
Eurasia
Urals
Kara Kum
Siberia
Chukchi Peninsula
Caspian Sea
Lake Baikal
Volga
Kama

Define

gigantics
continental climate
permafrost
polar night
tundra
taiga

DISCUSSING IMPORTANT IDEAS

1. In what ways do you think the Soviet Union's vast size has been both an advantage and disadvantage?
2. Because of the Soviet Union's icebound seaports in the north and high mountain ranges in the south, historically it has been thought of as a "landlocked" country. In what ways do you think this may have affected development and national character?

3. In what ways do you think climate has been the most fundamental element in developing the natural environment of the Soviet Union?

4. Three-fourths of the Soviet people live in the Plains area of the country. Why do you think the country's population is so unevenly distributed?

DEVELOPING SKILLS

GAINING UNDERSTANDING THROUGH CONTEXT

How often, when reading something, have you come across an unfamiliar word or phrase? Sometimes, to find out what the word or phrase means, you have to look it up in a dictionary. Other times, however, it is defined, exemplified, or explained in *context*, the part of a written statement that leads up to or follows an unfamiliar word or phrase and provides meaning for it.

Each of the following statements, for example, contains a word or phrase that may be unfamiliar. Read each statement and the explanation directly beneath it that tells how understanding of the unfamiliar word or phrase is provided in context.

1. For the most part, the Soviet Union has a *continental climate*. This means that the region experiences short, hot summers and long, cold winters.
   (The term "continental climate" is explained in the second sentence, immediately after it is introduced.)

2. A flock of *waxwings* rises from an ashberry tree, circles over the clearing, and settles on a mountain ash.
   (That "waxwings" are birds becomes clear because of the clues that there is a flock of them, that they can fly, and that they land on a tree.)

3. The dividing line between the two is the *Urals*, a long, low range of mountains running north to south.
   (The Urals are immediately identified in the same sentence as a mountain range that is long and low and runs from north to south.)

4. Most of the region is taiga, or evergreen forest.
   (The term "taiga" is defined as a certain type of forest immediately after it is introduced.)

5. Geographers include the Soviet Union among the *gigantics*. These are the eight nations of the world that are more than 1 million square miles (2.6 million square kilometers) in size.
   (Most readers will be aware that the term "gigantics" has something to do with an object or person that is very large. But its special meaning in this case is made clear by defining the Soviet Union as one of eight nations of a certain size.)

In each of the statements that follow, one term appears in italics. For practice in gaining understanding through context, read the statements and, in your own words, give the meaning of the term as provided in context.

1. Siberia is one of the areas of the Soviet Union where a condition known as *permafrost*, permanently frozen ground, occurs.

2. Others do not know how much rainfall they will get during the year. Some years *drought* causes farm products to be in short supply.

3. The *vegetation zones* include tundra, forest, steppe, semi-desert, desert, and humid, subtropical areas.

4. They have switched from *yarangas* to modern-style houses filled with modern conveniences.

CHAPTER 40
THE RUSSIAN PAST

1. How did the tsars influence the development of Russia?
2. What differences existed between social classes in tsarist Russia?

We find ourselves in the depths of a thick forest. . . . In a clearing on a steep river bank is a small village. . . . Outside the village is a field. It was no easy matter to work this field. At first all the villagers worked many months to chop down a large patch of forest. . . . Then everything that had been chopped down was burned in big bonfires. With hoes and spades the villagers loosened the earth and mixed it with the ashes. When the time for sowing came, an old man walked into the field and scattered the grain on the loosened earth. . . . Behind him came several younger men who pulled a rope tied around the trunk of a fir tree. . . . This was used to harrow the field and cover the seeds with good earth.

The villagers themselves are slim, fair-haired people. The men wear white linen blouses, tied around the waist with coloured sashes, over linen trousers. The clothes worn by the women are gayer and their dresses are decorated with pretty bright-coloured embroidery. . . .

The ancient Slavs [ancestors of the Russians] were not only farmers. The dense forests were full of birds and animals. . . . [A group of hunters] are carrying a rich trophy, a bear that they have killed. The villagers will now have meat, while the bear skin will make warm winter clothing. Towards evening the shepherd returns with his small herd of cows and flock of sheep and goats. The fishermen also have come back with their catch.

The houses in which the villagers live have been put together with logs and roofed with planks of wood or straw. The tiny windows, which are right down by the ground, hardly let in any light at all. The floor inside is of earth. In one corner a hearth has been built of stones. The smoke from the fire escapes through the doorway, as there is no chimney. Along the walls stand wooden benches. Shelves hold clay and wooden utensils.

Dusk will have fallen when the villagers, tired out after their long day of work, will sit down to eat. Their food is plain and it is almost the same for everyone. There are no poor or rich villagers. They work together and the land and cattle belong to them all.*

This passage from a modern Soviet history book describes the life of the early Russians. Today, the Russians are the largest and most important group in the Soviet Union. They can trace their origins to groups of Slavs who settled in the forests and steppe of southern Russia around the year 500.

At first, the Slavs of Russia were peaceful farmers who lived an isolated life in scattered villages. But, in time, they began to use the rivers in their area for transportation and trade. Before long, they set up trading towns that had contact with places as far away as the Mediterranean, Western Europe, and Scandinavia. In the 800's, they came under the rule of the Varangians, a group of warrior-traders from Scandinavia. A Varangian leader, Oleg, is believed to have set up the first Russian state at Kiev, a trading town on the Dnieper River. Within 100 years, the Varangians had adopted the Slavic language and customs, and Kiev had emerged as the first center of Russian civilization.

*Early Russia—the USSR by T. Golubeva and L. Gellerstein, 1976, pp. 7, 10–11. Reprinted by permission.

EARLY RUSSIA

By the year 900, the Russians had organized into a **confederation,** or loose union, of city-states and **principalities,** territories ruled by princes. Although each region enjoyed self-government, all paid special respect to the ruler of Kiev, known as the Grand Prince. To support his court and army, the Grand Prince collected tribute from the local princes. The local princes administered justice and defended the frontiers. They were aided by councils of wealthy merchants and landed nobles called **boyars.** Together, the upper classes ruled over the vast majority of people—peasants who farmed the land.

The interests of both the peasants and the ruling classes were represented in the *veches,* or assemblies. Made up of all free, adult male citizens, the *veches* handled daily affairs. They also had the power to remove uncooperative princes.

CHRISTIANITY

Until 987, the Russians worshipped many gods representing the forces of nature. That year, Vladimir, the Grand Prince of Kiev, converted to Eastern Orthodox Christianity —a move that decisively influenced Russia's future politically and culturally. Vladimir made Eastern Orthodoxy the official religion and required all of his subjects to become Christians. The *Russian Chronicles*, an early collection of Russian history and legends, records Vladimir's actions as follows:

> When the prince arrived at his capital, he directed that the idols should be overthrown and that some should be cut to pieces and others burned with fire. . . .
> Thereafter Vladimir sent heralds throughout the whole city to proclaim that if any inhabitant, rich or poor, did not betake himself to the river [to be baptized], he would risk the prince's displeasure. . . .
> . . . Having spoken thus, [Vladimir] ordained that churches should be built and established where pagan idols had previously stood. He thus founded the Church of St. Basil on the hill where the idol of Perun [the god of thunder] and the other images had been set, and where the prince and the people had offered their sacrifices. He began to found churches and to assign priests throughout the cities, and to invite people to accept baptism in all the cities and towns.
> He took the children of the best families, and sent them to schools for instruc-

The early Russians' skill in wood construction is evident in this church, still standing centuries after being built. What ruler made Eastern Orthodox Christianity the official religion of Russia?

CHAPTER 40   THE RUSSIAN PAST

This panel from a fifteenth-century icon tells of a struggle in 1169 between two rival Russian cities. Carrying a cross and an icon of the Virgin Mary, nobles and priests of Novgorod, right, force the prince of Vladimir-Suzdal to retreat. What factors other than internal conflict led to Kiev's decline and fall?

tion in book learning. The mothers of these children wept bitterly over them, for they were not yet strong in faith, but mourned as for the dead. When these children were assigned for study, there was thus fulfilled in the Russian land the prophecy which says: "In those days, the deaf shall hear the word of Scripture, and the voice of the stammerers shall be made plain" (Isaiah, 29:18; 32:4).*

Vladimir's acceptance of Eastern Orthodoxy gave the Russians a sense of belonging to the civilized world and strengthened Russia's ties with its powerful neighbors, the Byzantine Empire and the kingdom of Bulgaria. Soon, the Byzantine and Bulgarian influence could be seen in many areas. Byzantine priests introduced the Russians to colorful religious rituals and taught them the art of painting **icons,** or sacred pictures. Byzantine architects helped build stone cathedrals and churches with onion-shaped domes. The Bulgarians gave the Russians a Slavic alphabet on which to base a written language. Known as the Cyrillic alphabet in honor of Cyril, a Byzantine missionary to the Slavs, the alphabet is still in use today.

*The Russian Primary Chronicle, from Medieval Russia's Epics, Chronicles, and Tales, edited and translated by Serge A. Zenkovsky. Copyright ©1963 by Serge A. Zenkovsky. Reprinted by permission of the publisher, E. P. Dutton, a division of New American Library.

MONGOL RULE

During the 100 years after Vladimir's death in 1015, Kiev had several Grand Princes who were strong rulers. Under their rule, the Russians expanded their territory, increased trade, and advanced culturally. Then other Russian princes began to challenge the power of Kiev. Weakened by continual conflict and by interruption of trade with Constantinople, Kiev began to decline. In 1240, Mongol invaders from central Asia captured and destroyed the city. For the next 200 years, all of Russia was part of a vast Mongol domain that stretched from Eastern Europe to China. Although the Mongols allowed the Russians to practice Christianity and to govern their local affairs, they made the Russian princes pay tribute to their leader, the ***khan.*** During this time, Moscow emerged as the most important Russian city.

Because the Russians banded together as a defense against Mongol tyranny, the period of Mongol rule gave them a sense of unity. At the same time, however, they became largely isolated from the outside world, especially from Western Europe, which was entering a period of great artistic and scientific achievement. As a result, the Russians developed their own unique civilization based on the values of the Eastern Orthodox

RUSSIAN EXPANSION 1000 AD–Present

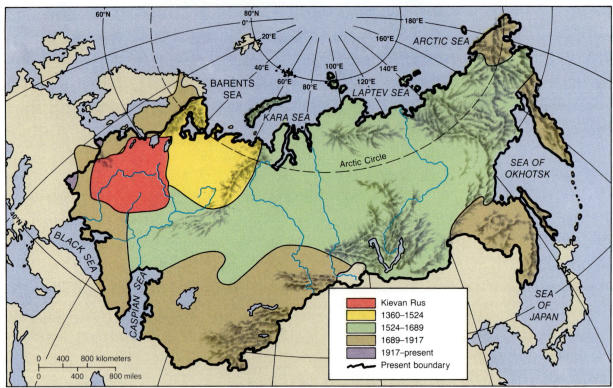

Church, the Byzantine Empire, and the Mongols. This civilization stressed obedience to authority and placed the community's rights ahead of those of the individual. In this way, it was believed, Russia's unity would be preserved against outside threats.

1. How and by whom was early Russia ruled?
2. What impact did Vladimir's conversion to Eastern Orthodoxy have on the Russians?
3. In what ways did Mongol rule affect the Russians?

THE FIRST TSARS

In the mid-1400's, a new form of government emerged. Monarchs known as **tsars** ruled the country. Over time, the tsars became **autocratic,** or all-powerful, rulers who crushed their opponents. They were so powerful that the Church, the nobles, and the townspeople, groups that posed repeated opposition to royal power elsewhere in Europe, never had a chance to pose the same challenge in Russia.

IVAN III

The first tsar of Russia was Ivan III. When he was Grand Prince of Moscow, Ivan centralized the Russian state by conquering other Russian princes. Then he challenged Mongol rule by refusing to pay taxes. In 1462, after defeating the Mongols, Ivan took the title of tsar. Later, he became known as Ivan the Great.

The Russian Orthodox Church gave its full support to a strong Russian monarchy. An important church official during Ivan the Great's reign stated that "although the [ruler] was like other men in his physical characteristics, in his power he was similar to God...." Under Ivan's rule, Moscow became known as the "Third Rome." The "First Rome" was the capital of the long vanished Roman Empire. The "Second Rome" was Constantinople, the capital of the recently fallen Byzantine Empire.

To emphasize Russian ties to the heritage of empire, Ivan married the niece of the last Byzantine emperor and introduced Byzantine rituals into the court. He also encouraged the development of a unique national style of icon painting and building construction. He had Moscow's Kremlin, or fortress, rebuilt and filled it with onion-domed churches and ornately decorated palaces.

IVAN IV

Ivan III's grandson, Ivan IV, became the most powerful of the early tsars. Known as "the Terrible" or "the Awesome," he ruled from 1533 to 1584. Ivan IV was learned, pious, and cruel. Because he suspected the *boyars* of disloyalty, he seized their lands and placed them under his direct control. At the same time, he set up the *Oprichniki*, a secret police force that terrorized the common people into submission.

Under Ivan IV, Russia expanded its territory and increased contacts and trade with Western Europe. One western nation that traded with Russia was England. In 1583, the English ambassador visited Ivan's court. The following is an account of that visit:

Ivan the Great (below left), who ruled until 1505, established a new class of landowning nobles who received land in return for service to the tsar. His grandson, Ivan IV (below right), took land away from the boyars. *What did the two Ivans do for the development of Russia?*

The family life of the peasants shown here revolved around the large fireplace of their one-room home. The infant in the family sleeps in a suspended cradle near the fireplace, while the older children make their beds on a ledge atop the warm fireplace oven. How did the lives of many Russian peasants change during the 1600's?

When the ambassador had been in Moscow for some days . . . he was sent for to go to court. He was accompanied there by about forty gentlemen, richly dressed and well mounted. . . . At the entry into the court he was met by four noblemen dressed in cloth of gold and rich furs, their caps embroidered with pearls and precious stones. They took him toward the emperor until he was met by four others of a higher rank who led him still further on his way. In the corridor there stood along the walls, or sat on benches and forms in rows, seven or eight hundred noblemen and gentlemen. . . .

These four noblemen accompanied him to the Emperor's [tsar's] chamber door, where the Emperor's herald met him. With him were all the great officers of the chamber and they all led him to the place where the emperor sat in state. He had three crowns by him, . . . and he was attended by four young noblemen. . . . When the ambassador had been brought to the Emperor in this way to kiss his hand . . . the Emperor commanded him to sit down in a place provided for him, some ten paces away. From here the Emperor wanted him to hand over the Queen [of England's] letters and present, but the ambassador thought this unreasonable and stepped forward toward the Emperor. The chancellor then came to meet him and wanted to take the letters, but the ambassador told him that the Queen had not sent any letters to him, and went on to give them to the Emperor himself.*

TIME OF TROUBLES

After Ivan IV's death in 1584, a series of weak rulers and false tsars quarreled over who would rule Russia. During this time, the country was torn apart by foreign invasions, famine, plague, and peasant revolts. Finally, in 1613, Michael Romanov was chosen as tsar, and order was restored. This was the beginning of the Romanov dynasty, which ruled Russia until 1917.

Accompanying the political changes taking place after Ivan's death were social and

---

*Excerpted from the book *The Making of Russia* by Joan Hasler. Copyright ©1969 by Joan Hasler. Reprinted by permission of Delacorte Press.

economic changes. Until the late 1500's, *boyars* and peasants both owned their own land. There was a small but prosperous middle class of townspeople. Then, over the next century, the freedoms enjoyed by these groups gradually were destroyed. The *boyars* were replaced by a new group of nobles known as the ***dvorianie***, who were tied to the tsar and served as officials in the growing state bureaucracy and in the army. The influence of the townspeople declined, and many peasants became **serfs,** laborers owned by landowners and bound to the land. The serfs, who worked in the palaces and on the estates of the tsars and nobles, had to pay taxes to the government and serve in the army.

As government controls tightened, many Russian peasants escaped to the borderlands south of Moscow. There, they formed into groups of pioneers known as Cossacks. The Cossacks set up self-governing communities and became skilled fighters. At the same time, other Russian pioneers moved eastward into Siberia, some of them reaching as far as the coast of the Pacific Ocean.

1. How did Ivan III become tsar? What changes took place under his rule?
2. What changes took place in Russia under the rule of Ivan IV?
3. What changes occurred in Russian life during the late 1500's and the 1600's?

THE "REFORMING" ROMANOVS

During the late 1600's and the 1700's, the Romanov tsars tried to make Russia into a Western European nation. They expanded Russian territory, increased their own powers, and placed additional burdens on the Russian people.

PETER THE GREAT

In 1689, a Romanov became Tsar Peter I. A towering, muscular figure, nearly seven feet (2.1 meters) tall, Peter had large ambitions, boundless energy, and strong emotions. Early in his reign, realizing that Russia was

The luxury enjoyed by Russian nobles is reflected in this etching of a Russian gentleman's carriage sleigh, being pulled by a team of horses, ridden and tended by servants. Standing at the rear of the sleigh are regally attired footmen. What roles did nobles play in the court of Ivan IV?

far behind Western Europe in learning and technology, he decided to end Russia's isolation and bring it into the mainstream of European civilization. To this end, he and a group of assistants visited Western Europe. There they toured shipyards, factories, mills, and laboratories, learning first-hand how to handle ships and machines and how to use such tools as charts, maps, and compasses.

When Peter returned home, he forced a series of changes on his people in an effort to adapt them to western ways. He reorganized the government along the lines of the Swedish one and created a regular army and navy like those of the Germans and the Dutch. He founded the first modern industries and tried to introduce western-style forms of education. He also brought the Church under his direct authority. The most controversial change came when he demanded that members of his court wear Western European clothing and that men entering Moscow shave their beards. He also ordered women, who had always been excluded from social gatherings, to attend parties.

Peter wanted to secure land along the Baltic Sea so that Russia could have access to major sea routes. To this end, he fought a series of wars. In 1703, on land won in a war with Sweden, he founded Saint Petersburg, his new capital and "window to the West." As noted below, his "window" was carved out of the wilderness at a high price:

> Peter's first exploration of the site of Petersburg would have discouraged most men. Soundings taken down the channel of the Neva [River] showed only eight feet [2.44 meters] of water—not enough to float full-size frigates. Digging along the marshy shores struck water at two feet [.61 meters]. Still Peter insisted. Stones gathered into massive crates were sunk into the marshes, and piles driven, to serve as foundations for buildings. Building stone was transported by water from the Volga, and good timber from Kazan.
>
> For in this undertaking Peter followed the advice of no one. Here was a port free from ice six months in the year, opening into the Baltic—the sea upon which, at whatever hazard, his fleet-to-be could sail.
>
> Winds from the west drove the gulf waters into the Neva's mouth, flooding and destroying the works around Petersburg. There was no stopping such floods. Peter ordered the shore works rebuilt and town dwellings reinforced. . . .
>
> Work upon [Peter's] paradise was carried on "by a vast number of hands." Actually it was done by human hands. Tools lacked. Dirt was carried in coats or kaftans [traditional robes worn by Russian males].
>
> Finns of the countryside, peasant soldiers and prisoners, slaved. Their bodies strained against ice and wind and water.

Under Peter the Great, a split began between the few who accepted western ways and the many who did not. Why did Peter want Russia to adopt western ideas?

RUSSIAN PROVERBS

- The burden is light on the shoulder of another.
- Fear the goat from the front, the horse from the rear, and man from all sides.
- Pray to God, but keep rowing to the shore.
- Don't be so smart; smarter ones than you are in jail.
- A bad peace is better than a good war.

- Life is unbearable, but death is not so pleasant either.
- Marriage is like sneezing: even when you feel it coming on, you can't stop.
- Happiness is not a horse; you cannot harness it.
- Be friends with the wolf, but keep one hand on your ax.
- Make peace with men and quarrel with your faults.

They died from typhus and from starvation, and their bodies were shoved into the swamps. No one kept count of the bodies.

When a flood came the survivors grieved more for the cattle that had been lost than for the humans, because the cattle had meant food. . . .

Peter talked only of roads to be opened, iron to be found, stones to be cut for the new council house to be called the Admiralty.

Petersburg meant to him not merely access to the sea but the building of a city for the future. This was to be the ground on which he would stand. It was to be in fact the ground of conflict between Peter and the majority of his own people.

For no nation until then had tried to thrust its capital city out into foreign territory.*

*Excerpt adapted from *The City and the Tsar* by Harold Lamb. Copyright ©1948 by Harold Lamb. Reprinted by permission of Doubleday & Company, Inc.

CATHERINE THE GREAT

After Peter's death, one weak tsar after another came to the throne until 1762, when Catherine II took control. During her reign, Catherine expanded Russia's territory and made it a leading country in European affairs. Because of her successful foreign policy, she became known as Catherine the Great.

To strengthen Russia, Catherine built up the army and navy, both of which had declined following Peter's death. Like Peter, she favored western culture and wanted to westernize Russia. She bought huge collections of French, English, and Dutch paintings and followed French fads and fashions.

Under Catherine's influence, wealthy Russians imitated French ways. Some of them even went to France as part of their education. As a result, the ruling classes drew apart from the masses of ordinary Russians, who remained loyal to traditional Russian culture.

Catherine studied the works of the leading Western European thinkers of the time and corresponded with some of them. While visiting Catherine, the French philosopher Denis Diderot encouraged her to make reforms to help her people. But Catherine did not listen. When peasant rebellions threatened her rule, she turned to the nobles for support. She allowed the nobles to treat their serfs as they pleased. As a result, more peasants were forced to become serfs than ever before, and their conditions worsened. By 1800, the common people of Russia had fewer rights than those in any other part of Europe.

1. What were the goals of Peter the Great? Catherine the Great?
2. How did the actions of Peter the Great affect the Russian people?
3. How did the actions of Catherine the Great affect the Russian people?

THE LAST OF THE ROMANOVS

The Romanovs remained in power for 121 years after the death of Catherine the Great. During that time, there were six different Romanov tsars, each of whom faced opposition to the power of the Russian throne.

ALEXANDER I

The reign of Alexander I, from 1801 to 1825, was marked by war with such foreign lands as France and the Ottoman Empire. From these conflicts, Russia gained more territory and much international prestige. Internally, however, the country was in a state of unrest. Alexander was a weak ruler who called for reforms but failed to honor his word. Educated Russians wanted more personal freedoms, and the serfs were no better off than they had been under earlier tsars. The nobles, trying to preserve their privileges, did little to encourage change.

In June of 1812, all talk of reform came to a halt as Russia was invaded by the French Emperor, Napoleon Bonaparte, and an army of 600,000 soldiers. Although the Russians were the final victors in the struggle with the French, they paid a high price for their victory. They lost a great part of their population. In addition, to keep the French from advancing, they had set fire to Moscow. Despite their losses, most Russians were proud of the part their country played in the defeat of Napoleon. The war had made their country one of the great powers of Europe. But at the same time, educated Russians were disappointed because the reforms they

In an effort to gain needed support from Russian nobles, Catherine the Great allowed them to draw up a constitution, which, however, was never implemented. What was Catherine's attitude toward reform?

St. Petersburg, pictured in this etching, remained an important city during the time of the reign of Alexander I. For three centuries after its founding, Russian rulers continued to enhance the city's beauty by adding palaces, cathedrals, parks, and public squares. What other Russian city played an important role during Alexander's rule? What happened to it?

expected after the war did not come. Below, a Russian soldier explains how many Russians felt:

> The war was still on when the soldiers, upon their return home, for the first time [broke up] grumbling among the masses. "We shed blood," they would say, "and we are forced to sweat under feudal obligations. We freed the Fatherland from the tyrant, and now we ourselves are tyrannized over by the ruling classes." The army, from generals to privates, upon its return did nothing but discuss how good it is in foreign lands. A comparison with our own country naturally brought up the question, "Why should it not be so in our own lands?"*

DISCONTENT AND REFORM

Throughout the 1800's, as Russia grew in size and strength, the feelings of discontent increased. As Russia slowly industrialized, new classes of business people and factory workers developed in the cities. Many of these people felt uncomfortable with the traditional social order and wanted Russia to modernize more quickly. At the same time, a movement for revolution arose among the **intelligentsia,** or the educated people. Made up chiefly of students, writers, and artists, the intelligentsia soon became the leading opponent of the government.

In spite of the pressures for change, Nicholas I, who had become tsar in 1825, opposed any limits on his power by either a constitution or a parliament. Even though free workers were needed in the country's small but growing industries, he refused to free the serfs. To eliminate opposition to his government, he set up a secret police force.

In 1854, the Russians went to war against Britain and France. Two years later, Russia lost the war. That same year, Nicholas died, and his son became Tsar Alexander II. Alexander recognized Russian weaknesses and wanted to make Russia into a major industrial power. To this end, he and his advisers began a series of reforms that eased restrictions on the people, improved government services, and promoted education. In 1861, Alexander freed the serfs.

---

*Michael Bestuzhev-Ryumin, as quoted in *Russia in War and Peace* by Alan Palmer. (Copyright ©1972 by Weidenfeld & Nicolson Ltd.) p. 199. Reprinted by permission.

For the serfs, freedom was a mixed blessing. By law, they were personally free and had the right to obtain land the government had purchased from the nobles. In reality, however, the great majority of the newly freed serfs became dependents of the government that had freed them. In return for their land, the peasants were expected to make payments to the government. To insure that this debt was paid, the government bound individual peasants to **mirs,** or local village organizations. Officials in each *mir* made sure the peasants worked the land and paid the government from their earnings. One peasant explained why, even after receiving his freedom, his life was hard:

My grandfather, my father, and I have paid so many taxes for our five desiatinas [13.7 acres] here, that the land could be quite covered with the money that we gave for it. My father and I were made to pay thirty-six roubles [Russian unit of currency] every year, and to get that money in the old days cost us plenty of sweat and blood.

There was scarcely a week in all the year that we were not working hard. All through the summer we worked on the farm. From October until May, we fished and logged on the river. And when there was no other work to do, we used to drag sunken logs from the river bottom. That was a slow, hard job. On a freezing winter morning we would take two boats out on

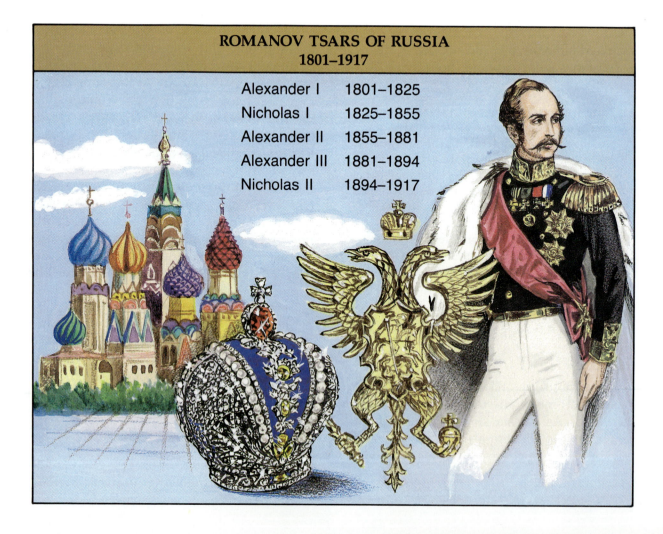

ROMANOV TSARS OF RUSSIA
1801–1917

Alexander I   1801–1825
Nicholas I   1825–1855
Alexander II   1855–1881
Alexander III   1881–1894
Nicholas II   1894–1917

CHAPTER 40 THE RUSSIAN PAST

Alexander III encouraged gangs, like this one beating an elderly Jew, to attack Jews and to destroy their shops and homes. Any person who did not speak Russian or who followed a religion other than Eastern Orthodoxy was considered disloyal to the state. Why did Alexander III rule harshly?

the ice. With our axes we would chop through the ice and make a space as big as this hut. Into the space we would shove the two boats and fill them with water. Then with spiked poles we would feel for the logs on the bottom twenty feet [6.1 meters] below. We would drive four poles into a log and fasten the poles by chains to the boats. Then we would bail the water out, and the boats would rise because they must—as you might say, by the will of God. And as they rose, with the spiked poles they would pull the log loose from the mud below. It took nearly a day to get one log; and for this we received between one and two roubles.*

TOWARD REVOLUTION

The peasants were not the only Russians disappointed with Alexander II's reforms. The growing numbers of unskilled laborers in urban factories complained about long hours and poor working conditions. At the same time, the intelligentsia continued to press for revolution. Many members of the intelligentsia were attracted to **socialism,** a philosophy that called for total ownership of land and factories by peasants and workers. They wanted an end to the tsar's power and the formation of a new society based on social equality.

In 1881, when Alexander II was killed by young revolutionaries, the throne passed to his son, who became Alexander III. Believing that his father's reforms had brought chaos to Russia, Alexander III ruled harshly. He limited freedom of speech, gave nobles control over the peasants, and persecuted non-Russian minorities, especially the Jews. Alexander's government managed to silence its critics, but it could not completely crush them. By the time Alexander's son, Nicholas II, came to the throne in 1894, the end of the tsarist form of government was near, and Russia was about to enter a period of revolutionary change.

1. What did the Russian people expect to happen after their defeat of Napoleon? What did happen?
2. What changes took place in Russia in the 1800's? What impact did they have on the Russian people?

---
*The Village: Russian Impressions by Ernest Poole, 1918. Courtesy of The Macmillan Company, pp. 93–94.

EXPLORATION
SOVIET UNION

During the 1800's, Russian writers reached a level of achievement that won them and their country an esteemed place in western culture. In their works, these writers presented in vivid detail various aspects of daily life which often depicted the gap in living standards between the upper and lower classes. The accounts which follow, the first by Ivan Turgenev and the second by Leo Tolstoy, are examples of this literature. Read the two excerpts, and answer the questions that follow:

1. Based on the accounts by Turgenev and Tolstoy, how would you describe the type of life led by peasants? By the upper class?
2. Do you think that these two literary accounts are accurate and reliable in their presentation of nineteenth-century Russian life? Give reasons and/or examples to support your answer.

Whoever may have chanced to make his way from the district of Bolkhov to that of Zhizdra has, most probably, been struck by the sharp contrast between the breed of men in the Orlovskaya province and that in the Kaluzhskaya. The Orlov muzhik [peasant] is of no great stature, is squat, glum; he eyes you from under his brows, lives in wretched little huts of aspen wood, does compulsory labor for his masters, doesn't go in for trading, eats poorly, wears bast [tree bark] sandals. The Kaluzhsk muzhik pays quitrent to his masters, dwells in roomy huts of pine, is tall of stature, eyes you boldly and cheerfully, is clean-shaven and white of face, trades in butter and birch tar and, of Sundays, goes about in boots.

The Orlov village . . . is usually situated amid plowed fields, near some gully which has been haphazardly turned into a muddy pond. Outside of a few willows, which are always ready to oblige by growing almost anywhere, and two or three scraggly birches, you won't see as much as a sapling for miles around; hut clings to hut, their roofs strewn, rather than thatched, with fusty straw. The Kaluzhsk village, on the contrary, is in most cases surrounded by woods; the huts have more space around them and stand more uprightly; they are roofed with hewn timbers; the gates shut snugly; the wattle fences toward the back aren't all broken and crawling apart, aren't extending an invitation to every passing swine to drop in and visit awhile. . . .

While visiting the Zhizdra district as a hunter, I met in the field and became acquainted with a certain small Kaluzhsk landowner, Polutykin, a passionate hunter and consequently, an excellent fellow. . . .

We rode off at a walk; beyond the village a man of about forty, tall, thin, with a small head tilted backward, caught up with us. This was Kalinych. His good-natured, swarthy face, pockmarked in spots, proved to my liking at first sight. Kalinych . . . went out hunting with his master every day, carrying the latter's gamebag and, at times, his gun as well, noting where the birds alighted, procuring water, gathering strawberries, putting up tepeelike shelters of branches, trotting after the droshky [sleigh]—Polutykin could not take a step without him. Kalinych was a man of the merriest, the meekest nature; he hummed incessantly, kept glancing on every side of him in a carefree way, spoke somewhat through his nose, puckered up his light-blue eyes when he smiled, and frequently put his hand up to his scanty, wedge-shaped beard. His walk was unhurried, but he took big steps, leaning a trifle on a long and slender stick.

During the course of the day he got into talk with me more than once, waiting on me with servility; when it came to his master, however, he kept an eye on him as if the latter were a baby. When the unbearable noonday sultriness compelled us to seek shelter he led us to his beehives, in the very heart of the forest. He opened for us his tiny hut, which was hung about with bundles of dry, fragrant herbs, bedded us on fresh hay, and putting over his head a sort of a bag with netting, took a knife, a pot, and a firebrand and set out for his beehives, to cut a honeycomb for us. We ate the transparent warm honey, chasing it down with water out of a wellspring, and dozed off to the monotonous buzzing of the bees and the gossipy babble of the leaves.*

Natasha had not had a moment to herself since early morning, and had not once had time to think of what lay before her.

In the damp, chill air, and the confined semi-darkness of the swaying carriage, for the first time she vividly pictured what was in store for her there at the ball, in those brightly lighted halls—the music, the flowers, the dancing, the Tsar, all the dazzling young people of Petersburg. The prospect was so splendid, and so incongruous with the chill darkness of the cramped carriage, that she could hardly believe it would come true. She only realized what was before her when, after walking over the red baize at the entrance, she had entered the hall, taken off her fur cloak, and, with Sonya at her side, preceded her mother up the lighted staircase between the flowers. Only then did she remember how she would behave at a ball, and tried to assume the stately air she considered indispensable for a girl on such an occasion. . . . Before and behind them other guests were entering, also in ball gowns, and talking in low tones. The mirrors along the staircase reflected ladies in white, pale blue, and pink gowns, with diamonds and pearls on their bare arms and necks.

Natasha looked in the mirrors and could not distinguish herself from the others. All blended into a shimmering procession. On entering the ballroom the steady hum of voices, footsteps, and greetings deafened Natasha; the light and glitter blinded her. The host and hostess, who had already been standing at the door for half an hour repeating the same words to each arriving guest, "Charmé de vous voir," [So nice to see you], greeted the Rostovs and Peronskaya in the same manner. . . .

There was a sudden stir; a murmur ran through the crowd as they surged forward then fell back, leaving a passage down the middle of which walked the Tsar to the strains of the orchestra that struck up as he entered. Behind him came the host and hostess. He walked in rapidly, bowing to right and left, as if anxious to get through the first formalities as quickly as possible. The orchestra played a polonaise in vogue at the time. . . . The Tsar passed on to the drawing room and the crowds made a rush for the doors, several persons dashing forward and then back again, their faces transformed. The wave receded from the doors of the drawing room, at which the Tsar reappeared in conversation with the hostess. A young man, looking distraught, bore down on the ladies and begged them to move aside. Several of the ladies, with expressions that betrayed a total obliviousness to the rules of decorum, pressed forward to the detriment of their attire. The men began to choose partners and take their places for the polonaise.*

---

*"Hor and Kalinych," From *The Hunting Sketches* by Ivan Turgenev, translated by Bernard Guilbert Guerney. Copyright ©1962 by Bernard Guilbert Guerney, pp. 7, 8, 11, 12. Reprinted by arrangement with New American Library, New York, New York.

*From *War and Peace* by Count Leo Tolstoy, translated by Ann Dunnigan, Copyright ©1968 by Ann Dunnigan, pp. 551, 552, 554. Copyright ©1968 by New American Library. Reprinted by arrangement with New American Library, New York, New York.

SOVIET UNION

CHAPTER 40 REVIEW

POINTS TO REMEMBER

1. Early Russia was a confederation ruled by princes supported by *boyars*. The acceptance by Vladimir, Grand Prince of Kiev, of Eastern Orthodox Christianity gave the people a sense of belonging to the civilized world and strengthened Russia's ties with its neighbors.
2. In 1240, Russia was made a part of the Mongol Empire. Mongol rule gave the Russians a sense of unity but also isolated them from the outside world.
3. In the mid-1400's, the tsarist system of rule emerged under Ivan III, or Ivan the Great, who emphasized Russian ties to the heritage of empire. His grandson, Ivan IV, or Ivan the Terrible, became the most powerful of the early tsars. After his death, Russia suffered a period of political, social, and economic change.
4. The Romanov tsars restored order to Russia and tried to westernize it. Peter I founded Saint Petersburg as a "window to the West" and made massive reforms designed to bring Russia into the mainstream of European affairs. Later, Catherine the Great made it a leading country in European affairs.
5. The six Romanov tsars who followed Catherine all faced opposition to the power of the Russian throne. As Russia grew in size and strength, so did the discontent of the people. Even the reforms of Alexander II—which included freeing the serfs—did not improve the situation.
6. By the time Nicholas II came to the throne, Russia was about to enter a period of revolutionary change.

VOCABULARY

Identify

Slavs	Eastern Orthodoxy	Michael Romanov	Alexander I
Varangians	Ivan III	Cossacks	Nicholas I
Oleg	"Third Rome"	Peter I	Alexander II
Kiev	Ivan IV	Saint Petersburg	Alexander III
Vladimir	*Oprichniki*	Catherine II	Nicholas II

Define

confederation	icons	autocratic	intelligentsia
principalities	*khan*	*dvorianie*	*mirs*
boyars	tsars	serfs	socialism
veches			

DISCUSSING IMPORTANT IDEAS

1. During its early years, Russia was rather isolated. Yet it developed a rich and unique heritage. What explanation can you give for this?

2. Do you think the tsarist system aided or hurt the growth and development of Russia? Of the Russian people? Explain.
3. All reform in Russia came from the top, brought into being by the tsars. Why do you think this was so?
4. What reasons can you give for the great gap between the peasants and the other classes of Russia? Do you think the educated elite of a country have any responsibility to those less fortunate? Why or why not?

DEVELOPING SKILLS

USING LITERATURE AS A CULTURAL SOURCE

Literature is imaginative or creative writing that can be prose or poetry, fiction or nonfiction. Regardless of its form, literature can transport you back in time or into the future. It can take you across continents to places you would not have been able to visit and introduce you to people you might never have met. Literature provides many insights into a culture. Through its story-telling quality, you can acquire detail and knowledge about and identify with people and their culture.

The reading that begins on page 668, written by Ivan Turgenev, is an example of Russian literature. By asking yourself questions like the ones that follow, you can use it—or any other literature—as a cultural source. If you were to use the questions when reading the passage by Turgenev, you would receive answers like the ones that appear in italics.

1. What is the theme of the work? (*the attitudes of and types of life led by the Russian peasant in the 1800's*)
2. Is the work fiction or nonfiction? (*fiction*)
3. In what time period is the story set? (*1800's*)
4. Where is the story set? (*Orlovskaya and Kaluzhskaya provinces of Russia*)
5. Who is the author? (*Ivan Turgenev*) What in his or her background qualifies him or her to write on the theme of this work? (*He lived during the period of time the work covers and was familiar with the provinces where it is set.*)
6. Who are the main characters? (*a hunter who is telling the story, a Kaluzhsk landowner named Polutykin, and a peasant named Kalinych who serves Polutykin*) How do they relate to the culture being presented? (*They form part of the culture.*)
7. Are any historical figures or events portrayed? (*No*) If so, is the portrayal accurate and true-to-life, or is it the product of the author's imagination?
8. Is the work a good source of cultural information? In other words, does the author present descriptions or details that give you a "feel" or understanding that goes beyond mere facts and leads you to believe that you are experiencing the culture firsthand? (*Yes, because the author describes the people, their houses, clothing, life style, character, actions, and attitudes in such vivid detail that the reader feels as if he or she is actually part of what is going on.*)
9. What have I learned from this work about a particular people or culture? (*that the Russian peasant of the 1800's lived in a certain way and had certain characteristics and attitudes that varied according to the area in which he or she lived*)

For further practice in using literature as a cultural source, read the excerpt by Leo Tolstoy on page 669, using the suggested questions as a guide.

CHAPTER 41
THE SOVIET ERA

1. What led to the creation of a Communist government in Russia?
2. What changes have taken place in the Soviet Union since 1917?

It has been Russia's lot to see most clearly, and experience most keenly and painfully the sharpest of sharp turning-points in history as it swings round from imperialism [the control of foreign lands] towards the communist revolution. In the space of a few days we destroyed one of the oldest, most powerful, barbarous and brutal of monarchies. In the space of a few months we passed through a stage of collaboration [cooperation] with the bourgeoisie [the middle class] and of shaking off petty-bourgeoisie illusions, for which other countries have required decades. In the course of a few weeks, having overthrown the bourgeoisie, we crushed its open resistance in civil war. We passed in a victorious triumphal march of Bolshevism [the early Communist movement] from one end of a vast country to the other. We raised the lowest strata of the working people oppressed by tsarism and the bourgeoisie to liberty and independent life. We established and consolidated a Soviet Republic, a new type of state, which is infinitely superior to, and more democratic than, the best of the bourgeois-parliamentary republics. We established the dictatorship of the proletariat [working class] supported by the poor peasantry, and began a broadly conceived system of socialist reforms. We awakened the faith of millions upon millions of workers of all countries in their own strength and kindled the fires of enthusiasm in them. Everywhere we issued the call for a world workers' revolution. We flung a challenge to the imperialist plunderers of all countries. . . .

Russia will become mighty and abundant if she abandons all dejection and all phrase-making, if, with clenched teeth, she masters all her forces and strains every nerve and muscle, if she realizes that salvation lies *only* along that road of world socialist revolution upon which we have set out. March forward along that road, undismayed by defeats, lay the firm foundation of socialist society stone by stone, work with might and main to establish discipline and self-discipline . . . such is the way to build up military might and socialist worth.*

These words were spoken in 1918 by Vladimir Ilyich Ulyanov, revolutionary leader and founder of the Union of Soviet Socialist Republics, commonly known as the Soviet Union. Ulyanov, better known to the world as Lenin, and his followers were part of a revolutionary movement that began in Russia during the 1800's. They blended a Russian sense of outrage against tsarism with the thinking of a nineteenth-century German named Karl Marx.

Karl Marx had predicted that a workers' revolution would begin in industrialized Europe and spread socialism throughout the world. Lenin believed that, even though Russia was backward economically, it could become the starting point of the revolution predicted by Marx. In 1917, much sooner than even he had expected, Lenin's goal was achieved, and the world's first socialist state was established in Russia.

*"The Chief Task of Our Day" by V. I. Lenin in *The Lenin Anthology* edited by Robert C. Tucker, 1975, W. W. Norton and Co., Inc., pp. 434, 435. Reprinted by permission.

THE DOUBLE REVOLUTION

In the early 1900's, revolution was a dominant feature of Russian life. In 1905, peasants, workers, and the small middle class forced reforms on the tsar, Nicholas II. But Nicholas ignored the changes and continued to act as an absolute ruler, carrying out harsh measures against anyone who criticized the government.

Nicholas' efforts to silence the opposition were fairly successful for a time. Then, in 1914, World War I broke out. When the conflict began, the Russians were confident of a rapid victory over the Germans. But they were ill-prepared for war, and their poorly trained and equipped army suffered heavy losses in Eastern Europe. In 1915, they were pushed back by a German-Austrian attack, and Russian land was conquered and occupied. The Russian economy could not meet the needs of soldiers and civilians, both of whom needed food, clothing, and fuel.

THE FIRST REVOLUTION

Most of the Russian people were against the war and wanted to withdraw. Nicholas, however, refused to do so. Meanwhile, the people grew more discontent. The educated classes had been unhappy for a long time. The peasants wanted land still held by the wealthy. The people in the cities resented being without food and fuel because of the broken-down transportation system. The situation continued to worsen until finally, as described below, dissatisfaction grew into revolution:

> On the eighth of March, 1917, a hundred thousand striking factory workers, men and women, jammed the streets of Petrograd [Saint Petersburg] demanding bread and freedom. It was International Women's Day, February 23, in the old calendar. This was the day that marked the beginning of the February Revolution and the downfall of the Russian Emperor. The next day and the day after, despite the absence of plan or leaders, the demonstrations snowballed. Crowds of workers

Nationwide strikes and demonstrations protesting Russia's poor domestic conditions, like this women's march held in 1905, were sparked by "Bloody Sunday," a Sunday in June 1905 when striking workers were killed in a confrontation outside the tsar's palace in St. Petersburg. What did the factory workers who took part in the March 1917 strike demand?

surged across the ice on the Neva and into the center of the city. The Tsar's police could not contain the demonstrators, and the soldiers had to be called out as the workers offered themselves to be shot at.

It was Saturday, February 25, when Tsar [Nicholas II] decided that the situation had gotten out of hand and wired the Petrograd commander General Khabalov, "I command you to put an end as of tomorrow to all disorders in the streets of the capital."

The next day, Sunday the 26th, several units opened fire on the crowds, and scores of demonstrators were killed, but at this point the troops rebelled at the further prospect of cutting down their own compatriots. In a matter of hours almost all the soldiers had joined in with the mobs, and the people went wild. Jails, courts, police stations—all the physical symbols of the old rule—were broken into and burned. In the twenty-third year of his reign, the authority of [Nicholas] Romanov, [Tsar] of All the Russias, ceased to be.*

Nicholas' government fell because it could not govern the country. The troops most loyal to the tsar were still at the front. Except for a small group of conservative nobles, there was no one willing to defend the monarchy. War and social turmoil toppled the government, and the revolution destroyed the tsarist system.

THE SECOND REVOLUTION

After Nicholas gave up power, liberal nobles and middle-class politicians set up a provisional, or temporary, government under Alexander Kerensky. The new government wanted to continue the war with Germany and to wait to distribute land to the peasants. The government, however, did not

*Robert V. Daniels, excerpted from *Red October*. Copyright ©1967 Robert V. Daniels. Reprinted with the permission of Charles Scribner's Sons.

Nicholas II, shown here with his wife and children, believed God had chosen him to rule Russia. On July 16, 1918, he and his family were murdered by Bolsheviks. Who ruled after Nicholas' government fell?

really rule Russia. Instead, it was ruled by **soviets,** councils formed by Russian revolutionaries to represent workers, soldiers, and peasants. Closely linked all over the country, the soviets spoke for the people and were the only ones who could sway the disorganized soldiers and the unruly crowds in the streets. At the heart of the soviets was the Petrograd Soviet in the capital city.

A group of revolutionaries known as Bolsheviks knew that the soviets were the key to power in Russia and set out to control them. They wanted to make peace with Germany at once and encouraged the peasants to seize landed estates and the workers to manage factories. Within nine months, under the leadership of Vladimir Lenin, they were in the majority in the Petrograd Soviet.

In November 1917, the Bolsheviks took over the city of Petrograd and proclaimed a socialist revolution. Once they seized power, they made Lenin the head of a new revolutionary government. Lenin had a long record as a revolutionary. In 1887, when he was 17, his older brother had been put to death for

This painting shows Vladimir Lenin, the head of Russia's new Bolshevik government, captivating his audience in a 1920 meeting of a group of his youthful followers. In what ways did Lenin want Russian society to change?

trying to kill the tsar. His brother's death led him to join the revolutionary movement to overthrow the monarchy.

While in exile because of his revolutionary activities, Lenin developed political ideas based on Marxism, or the teachings of Karl Marx. Like Marx, he believed that the **proletariat,** or working class, would end **capitalism,** the system in which the means of production are privately owned and operated for profit. The workers would overthrow the rule of the **bourgeoisie,** the owners of the factories and the members of the government, and set up their own system under which they would own the factories and produce the goods. There would be no upper or lower classes. All the people would be workers in a classless society. Below, a well-known journalist describes Lenin and the impact he had on his followers:

> It was just 8:40 when a thundering wave of cheers announced the entrance of the presidium, or executive committee, with Lenin—great Lenin—among them. A short, stocky figure, with a big head set down on his shoulders, bald and bulging. Little eyes, a snubbish nose, wide, generous mouth, and heavy chin; clean-shaven now, but already beginning to bristle with the well-known beard of his past and future. Dressed in shabby clothes, his trousers much too long for him. Not impressive, to be the idol of a mob. A strange popular leader—a leader purely because of intellect; without color, without humor, uncompromising and detached—but with the power of explaining deep ideas in simple terms.
>
> Gripping the edge of the reading stand, letting his little winking eyes travel over the crowd as he stood there waiting, not seeming to pay any attention to the long-rolling ovation, which lasted several minutes. When it finished, he said simply, "We shall now proceed to construct the Socialist order!" Again that overwhelming roar.*

1. What were some of the factors that led to the first revolution of 1917? What was the result of the revolution?
2. How did the Bolsheviks gain power?
3. What were Lenin's major political ideas?

---

*Adapted from *Ten Days That Shook the World* by John Reed, 1960, Vintage Books, a Division of Random House, Inc., pp. 170–172.

THE COMMUNIST STATE

Lenin became known as the "Father of the Revolution" and the Bolsheviks as Communists. Together, they worked to bring **communism,** the teachings of Marx and Lenin, to Russia.

THE EARLY YEARS

Not all Russians agreed with the policies of Lenin and his followers. Anti-Communist groups called Whites, made up of people ranging from monarchists to moderate socialists, were strong enough to start a civil war. But even with their strength and the military support they received from western governments that feared the spread of communism, the Communist government was able to hold power. There were several reasons for this. For one, while the Whites found it hard to cooperate with each other, a close associate of Lenin named Leon Trotsky had organized Communist forces into an efficient Red Army. For another, most Russians preferred the Communists because many of the Whites wanted to bring back the old ways.

By 1921, the Red Army had defeated the Whites, and all of Russia was under Communist rule. In December of the following year, the government established the Union of Soviet Socialist Republics (U.S.S.R.), a new Soviet state made up of the four republics of Russia, the Ukraine, Byelorussia, and the Transcaucasus.

During the civil war, the government had worked to restore the declining economy. Because peasants were paid so little for grain, they hoarded it, and little food was available in the cities. Factory production had slumped, and there were few manufactured goods for sale. The money system had broken down, and trade was carried on through a barter system of exchanging goods.

To cope with this crisis, the government instituted **war communism,** a policy under which all factories and land were taken over by the government and workers and peasants had to follow government decrees regarding production, wages, and prices. The

As seen in this early photograph, during the civil war, many people were forced to leave their homes and search for food. What did the government do after the civil war to cope with Russia's economic crisis?

policy, however, only added to the chaos. Dissatisfaction among workers, peasants, and soldiers led to revolts and strikes. Hunger and suffering gripped the nation, and it seemed that the government was about to collapse.

Finally, in 1921, Lenin announced the New Economic Policy (NEP), which departed from Marxist theory by encouraging a limited amount of capitalism. Large-scale industries still remained under government control, but small private businesses were allowed to operate and peasants could own land and sell their produce for a profit. Under the NEP, industrial and farm production gradually improved and reached prewar levels.

Meanwhile, Lenin tightened political controls throughout the country. All opposition to the Communist leadership was banned, and anyone suspected of being an "enemy of the Revolution" was imprisoned, shot, or forced into exile. By the end of the 1920's, the Communist party was the only legal political organization in the Soviet Union.

STALIN

Lenin died in 1924, and a power struggle developed within the Communist leadership between Leon Trotsky and Joseph Stalin. Trotsky, who came from a cultured middle-class background, was the Communist party's leading thinker. Stalin, who was the son of artisans from a territory south of Russia called Georgia, was a dedicated administrator who controlled appointments to top party posts. Each had a different outlook regarding the Soviet Union's future. Trotsky wanted to promote a world socialist revolution, while Stalin wanted to postpone world revolution and concentrate instead on building up the Soviet Union.

The Five-Year Plans By 1928, Stalin was able to outmaneuver Trotsky, who fled into exile. Once in power, Stalin's primary goal was to industrialize the Soviet Union as quickly as possible. To this end, he replaced the NEP with the first of a series of Five-Year Plans under which the government controlled all aspects of industrial and farm production. Goals were set over a five-year period to boost production.

Under the plan, primary attention was given to heavy industry, such as the production of machinery. Little importance was paid to the manufacture of consumer goods, such as radios and refrigerators. As a result, many power plants, dams, and factories were built throughout the country, while the average Soviet citizen faced housing, appliance, and food shortages. As the account that follows reveals, great sacrifices were demanded of the Soviet people to fulfill Stalin's first Five-Year Plan:

> As the Arctic winter broke suddenly into spring, Magnitogorsk [a new city which rose in the wilderness] changed beyond recognition. In early April it was still bitter cold; we had had hardly a single thaw; everything was still frozen solid. By May 1 the ground had thawed and the city was swimming in mud. Leaving our barrack we had to wade. Welding became next to impossible, as our ragged cables short-circuited at every step. At about this time I saw that my friend the doctor was very busy. He told me later what it was all about. Bubonic plague had broken out in three places not far from Magnitogorsk. The three villages had been surrounded by soldiers and isolated. All of the medical staff of Magnitogorsk was getting prepared for a possible outbreak in the city. The resistance of the people was very low because of not enough food during the winter and too much overwork. Sanitary conditions, particularly during the thaw, were frightening.
>
> This was Magnitogorsk in 1933. A quarter of a million people—Communists, foreigners, Tartars [Mongols], and a mass of blue-eyed Russian peasants—building the

This old photograph shows mothers on a collective farm going to work in the fields while their children stay behind in a government-run nursery. Which groups opposed the government's policy of collective farms? What was Stalin's response to the opposition?

biggest steel mill in the middle of the barren Ural steppe. Money was spent like water, men froze, hungered, and suffered, but the building went on.*

Opposition and Purges Although Stalin's plans were turning the Soviet Union into a leading industrial power, his forceful methods carried a high price and led to much opposition. Under the Five-Year Plans, farmland was to be owned **collectively,** or jointly, by the peasants. When *kulaks,* or prosperous farmers, refused to give up their land, livestock, and machinery to the collective farm, fighting broke out in the countryside. Thousands of *kulaks* were killed or arrested and sent to labor camps in Siberia. By 1929, the *kulaks* as a group were completely wiped out. Despite the resistance of many peasants, the collective farms—on which the government controlled output—became a permanent feature of Soviet agriculture.

Opposition also mounted among such other groups as writers, scientists, and engineers. This led Stalin to increase the powers of the secret police who, under his direction, used terror to enforce obedience. A climate of fear spread through Soviet society. Soviet citizens accused of disloyalty were shot or sent to labor camps in Siberia, where only the hardiest survived. Even members of the Communist party were not safe. In the late 1930's, Stalin **purged,** or removed, many of Lenin's old associates from their positions and had them tried and executed.

World War II During the 1930's, fearing the rise of Nazi Germany and its eastward expansion, Stalin looked for an alliance with the democracies of the West. When they did not give him a direct or immediate response, Stalin turned to the German leader, Adolf Hitler. In late August, 1939, they pledged that the Soviet Union and Nazi Germany would not attack each other. They also made plans to carve up Poland and other areas of Eastern Europe between them. A week later, German troops rolled into Poland, beginning World War II, and shortly after, Stalin seized his portion of Eastern European territory.

---
*Adapted from *Behind the Urals* by John Scott, 1942, Houghton Mifflin Co., pp. 65–67. Reprinted by permission.

INSIGHTS ON PEOPLE
SOVIET UNION

EUGENIA GINZBURG

One of the 8 million victims of Stalin's terror was Eugenia Ginzburg, a teacher, journalist, and member of the Communist party. Accused of treason, she was arrested in 1937 and spent the next 18 years in prisons and labor camps and in exile in Siberia. After her release, Ginzburg gave an account of her experiences in the book *Journey into the Whirlwind.* Below, she describes her transfer from prison in Kazan to trial in Moscow:

"Bring your things!"
What a lot of meaning was contained in these few words! Once again you are bound to the wheel, spinning and dragging you away at your master's will from everything that's near and dear, toward the unknown. . . .

A fairly large number of people were being sent to Moscow for the session of the military tribunal. Our sharpened hearing told us that they were being collected from several cells. . . .

The idea that membership in the Communist Party was bound to aggravate the defendant's case had by now taken firm root in everyone's mind. How indeed could the situation be explained except as Stalin's death blow to the Party. . . .

The door opened. We were taken out into the corridor and down the stairs. . . .

All four of us were to appear before a military tribunal on a charge of political terrorism. Rimma assured us that we were the only women sent on this grim journey, along with a multitude of men.

All this ought surely to have made us face the likelihood of our being sentenced to death. It would have been only logical. But evidently we, too, must have been influenced by the law of the reversal of logic which ruled in our crazy world, for not one of us would admit the possibility for a moment.

The gates of the ancient prison clanged behind us. The Black Maria [transport truck] had already been filled up. Coughs and sighs came from inside the cells. . . . We could see a little through a crack in the rear door—not, of course, with our ordinary vision but with our practiced, intensely observant and sensitized prisoner's eyes. The senses of smell, hearing, and direction helped as well. . . .

We stopped. There was a smell of hot rails and engine soot, the sound of engines busily puffing, then of their brief, nervous whistles.

"Everybody out!"
It was not the familiar [train] station. . . . [There] was no one on the platform but a large covey of interrogators and guards. . . .

"This way! This way!"
It was an ordinary third-class coach divided into compartments, each seating four. There was a guard at the door of each compartment, except the one in the middle, reserved for the interrogators in charge of the valuable human freight. . . .

A jolt as the engine was coupled on. Another jolt and we were off. . . . I knew what I was leaving behind—my children abandoned to the mercy of fate (if only it were fate! The NKVD [secret police] was much more frightening!), my mother, my university, my books, a clean and happy life full of the consciousness of having chosen the right way. As for our destination—only those who were taking us there could tell.*

1. What was Eugenia Ginzburg's reaction to her situation?
2. How would you feel if you lived in a country where you could be arrested and imprisoned or exiled for a large part of your life with so little say about the matter? What effect do you think this had on the people living under Stalin's rule?

*Excerpted from *Journey into the Whirlwind* by Eugenia Semyonovna Ginzburg, **Copyright** ©1967 by Arnoldo Mondadori Editore-Milano; English translation **Copyright** ©1967 by Harcourt, Brace Jovanovich, Inc. Reprinted by permission of Harcourt Brace Jovanovich, Inc.

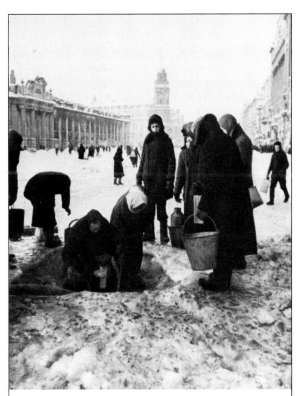

During the German siege of Leningrad (formerly Petrograd), residents had to dig into snowpacked streets to obtain drinking water. Where did the Soviet army succeed in stopping the German advance?

A year and a half later, on June 22, 1941, Hitler launched a surprise attack on the Soviet Union, and German forces drove deep into Soviet territory. They reached the outskirts of Moscow and besieged the city of Leningrad. Below, a Soviet army major describes the ordeal faced by the people of Leningrad during the 900-day siege:

> In those days there *was* something in a man's face which told you that he would die within the next twenty-four hours. . . . I have lived in Leningrad all my life, and I also have my parents here. They are old people, and during those famine months I had to give them half my soldier's ration, or they would certainly have died. As a staff officer I was naturally, and quite rightly, getting considerably less than the people at the front: 250 grams [8.8 ounces] a day instead of 350 [13.3 ounces]. I shall always remember how I'd walk every day from my house near the Tauris Garden to my work in the center of the city, a matter of two or three kilometres [1 or 2 miles]. I'd walk for a while, and then sit down for a rest. Many a time I saw a man suddenly collapse on the snow. There was nothing one could do. One just walked on. . . . And on the way back, I would see a vague human form covered with snow on the spot where, in the morning, I had seen a man fall down. One didn't worry; what was the good? People didn't wash for weeks; there were no bath houses and no fuel. But at least people were urged to shave. And during that winter I don't think I ever saw a person smile. It was frightful. And yet, there was a kind of inner discipline that made people carry on. A new code of manners was evolved by hungry people. They carefully avoided talking about food. . . . Yet we never lost heart. The Battle of Moscow gave us complete confidence that it would be all right in the end. But what a change all the same when February came and the Ice Road [the only supply route] began to function properly! Those tremendous parcels that started arriving from all over the country —honey and butter, and ham and sausages! Still our troubles are not at an end. This shelling can really be very upsetting.*

In spite of the German pressure, the Soviets refused to surrender, and in early 1943, the tide of battle finally turned in their favor at Stalingrad, a port city on the Volga River. There, the Soviets stopped the German advance and destroyed the German army.

After the war in Europe ended, the Soviets joined in the war against Japan, and Soviet armies entered Manchuria, a Japanese-held province in northern China. The war, which the Soviets refer to as the Great Patriotic War,

---

*From *Russia At War: 1941–1945*, copyright ©1964 by Alexander Werth. Reprinted by permission of the publisher, E. P. Dutton, a division of New American Library.

had a profound impact on the Soviet Union and its people. The Soviets suffered more military and civilian casualties than any other country in the war. At least 20 million people lost their lives. In addition, there was widespread destruction throughout the European part of the Soviet Union.

1. What effect did the civil war have on the Soviet economy? What steps did the Lenin government take to bring about change?
2. What was Stalin's goal for the Soviet Union? What methods did he use to realize this goal?
3. How was the Soviet Union affected by World War II?

A NEW SUPERPOWER

After World War II, the Soviet Union emerged as the strongest nation in Europe and Asia—a superpower in rivalry with the United States. In what became known as the "cold war," each sought world influence by means short of total war. In Europe, Stalin moved to strengthen his wartime gains by setting up Communist governments in Eastern Europe. At home, he continued the Five-Year Plans and the drive for industrialization. The war-shattered economy was rebuilt, and great strides were made in heavy industry.

Stalin died in 1953. Several years later, Nikita Khrushchev became the new Soviet leader. He denounced Stalin as a murderer of innocent people, put an end to Stalin's methods of terror, and allowed writers and artists more freedom. Soviet society became more relaxed, but criticism of the party was still forbidden. Although Krushchev sought better relations with the West, he boasted about the superiority of communism over capitalism and vowed that the Soviet Union would surpass the United States as a world power. Khrushchev could be hot-tempered and ruthless. But, as seen in the following excerpt from his memoirs, he also could display shrewd simplicity to make a point:

> I think our foreign policy should be based in part on an old folk custom which I remember from my own childhood. If a housewife went to another village to visit friends or relatives, she would never go without taking a bundle of pastries—or, in our Kursk Province, a dozen eggs—as a house present for her hosts. I think this tradition should be adopted by one state in its dealings with another. This custom should be practiced reasonably and moderately, mind you. It doesn't take much brains or skill to earn the reputation of the kindly uncle who squanders money on gifts for other families without leaving enough to buy groceries for his own family. That's obviously an extreme to be avoided. The policy of giving "house presents" to other countries must be pursued

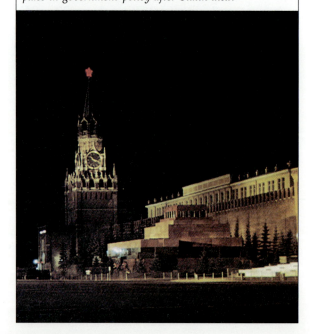

In this late night scene, a bright red star glows atop one of the towers of the Kremlin, which has been the seat of the Soviet government since 1918. What changes took place in government policy after Stalin died?

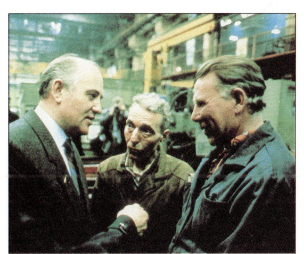

Soviet leader Mikhail Gorbachev, left, a strong supporter of local control of factories, greets workers at a new Soviet manufacturing plant. *What changes did Gorbachev want to make when he came to power?*

intelligently and in moderation so that our generosity will always repay us both economically and politically.

We must never forget that our enemies are always working against us, always looking for a chance to exploit some oversight on our part. There is a battle going on in the world to decide who will prevail over whom: will the working class prevail, or the bourgeoisie? The working class is convinced that the bourgeoisie has exhausted itself, while the bourgeoisie believes it can rule forever. Every right-thinking person can see clearly that the basic questions of ideology can be resolved only by struggle and only by the victory of one doctrine over the other.*

Many of Khrushchev's policies failed. During his rule, Soviet farm production was so low that wheat had to be bought from other countries. Industrial growth slowed, and consumer goods often were in short supply and of poor quality. Ties with the People's Republic of China became strained,

Khrushchev Remembers by Nikita Khrushchev, translated and edited by Strobe Talbott, 1970, Little, Brown and Company, pp. 508–512. Reprinted by permission.

and the United States forced the Soviets to remove missiles from Cuba. In 1964, Khrushchev was removed from office and replaced by a **collective leadership,** or joint rule, headed by Leonid Brezhnev and Aleksei Kosygin.

By the early 1970's, Brezhnev had become the most powerful leader in the Soviet Union. During his rule, the government cracked down on **dissidents,** Soviet citizens who opposed government policies. Although the country's military power was increased, the non-military areas of the economy grew very slowly. Realizing that they needed western technology to make their industries more efficient, the Soviet leaders turned to **détente,** a relaxation of international tensions.

Détente brought about cultural and scientific exchanges between the Soviet Union and western nations as well as treaties that placed limits on the production of nuclear weapons. During the late 1970's, however, relations again grew tense as the two superpowers began a renewed arms buildup and increased their rivalry for influence in various parts of the world.

Brezhnev died in 1982, and the Soviet leadership entered a period of transition. Even though most of the top Soviet leaders were aging, they found it difficult to transfer power to a younger generation. Within a three-year period, the country had two different leaders—Yuri Andropov and Konstantin Chernenko—both of whom died while in office. Then, in the winter of 1985, Mikhail Gorbachev, who was in his fifties, came to power, and the Soviet Union appeared to have a dynamic leader who wanted to reform the Soviet economy and improve relations with the West.

1. How did the world role of the Soviet Union change after World War II?
2. What changes took place in Soviet society following the death of Stalin?

EXPLORATION
SOVIET UNION

During World War II, vast areas of the Soviet Union were destroyed, and millions of people were uprooted from their homes. Almost every family lost someone. Yet, in spite of their enormous suffering, the Soviet people stood united and won.

Today, the Soviet government encourages remembrances of the war to keep patriotism alive and to justify such policies as a strong national defense. The war serves as a popular theme of books, films, and television programs. War veterans meet regularly and swap war stories as if the events had just happened. Every city, town, and village has its war memorial, cemetery, or battle museum.

At the same time, however, the horrors of war have given the Soviet people as a group a fervent desire to avoid a future war. In 1984, a western film crew went to the Soviet Union to make a documentary on the attitudes of Soviet citizens toward peace and the Soviet and American roles in attaining it. After reading some of the comments below, made by Soviet citizens of all different age groups and backgrounds, answer the following questions.

1. What influence do you think World War II has had on present Soviet attitudes about war and peace? Do you think it has the same influence in your country? Explain.
2. Do you think the military position of the Soviet Union relates to its citizens' desire for peace? Explain.
3. Based on the information in the chapter, what influence do you think the Soviet citizens' desire for peace might have had on past government policy? Do you think the same is true today? Give reasons for your answer.

There's very much we'd like to say to America, very much, only we don't believe it will reach them. I wish we could talk together as I'm talking to you right now, simply and as friends. I was a participant in the war. I know what war is. I'm a woman, and I fought. If my words would reach your people, then I'll be happy. That they understand me. All

mothers will understand. Please, I really ask you, make peace with us.

America? Friendship—Peace—The Americans are good people. They helped us a lot during World War II. We fought and they helped us. They gave us food and they sold us trucks. We should be friends. Now why can't we reach an agreement? Ours have made mistakes, yours have made mistakes, am I right or not? It depends not on us—but on the leaders—on the leaders it depends. They have to talk together. And who are we? We're just little people—they tell us go here, we go here. Go there, we go there. Its the same with you, huh?

War has cost us so much. My mother was an orphan, her father was killed in World War I. My father was killed by the Germans in World War II, leaving five of us, with my mother. What hunger we've seen. Such cold! Barefoot and without clothes. We don't want war. We just want peace. I have 4 sons, and grandchildren. And for them I'm afraid. We don't need a war. There should only be peace. War has brought us so much sadness. That's all. I can't talk anymore.

Soon it'll be 40 years without a war. Let there be another without one. Do we remember? We were without clothes. Without bread. We ate grass and thistles. We fought and we defended Soviet power. We didn't eat. We didn't drink. Our husbands put their lives on the line. We lost 20 million, to count

correctly. So, it wasn't easy. They came half way through the Soviet Union, but we beat them. We beat them. That's what.

Many people are not thinking about the military race and so on. They are not thinking about the peace movement, the military race, and so on. They're not thinking about the fighting for peace all over the world. They're thinking how to get things, how to get flats [apartments]. They're thinking about their problems. Many people are sure of the Soviet security. Because sometimes, the Soviet press mentions news about the Soviet rockets. Sometimes it's giving the lectures to the workers at the plants and factories. And those who are giving the lectures are telling that we have such rockets that if the Americans launch rockets to us, we can hit them long before it can reach the territory of the Soviet Union. So we are sure that the rockets will never reach us.

If there'll ever be a war, there'll be no people left afterwards. They won't be people—They'll be radiation struck. People from every walk of life will be affected. Even the bosses won't be saved, ours and yours. I don't know, they say ours are also strong, and America is of course strong, they say on radio and tv all the time. I don't know why it's gotten this way. Who makes these politics? Who can tell?*

---

*"Video from Russia: The People Speak," a 53-minute documentary by Dimitri Devyatkin (producer-director), 134 Haven Ave., New York, NY 10027, 1984. Reprinted by permission.

SOVIET UNION

CHAPTER 41 REVIEW

POINTS TO REMEMBER

1. Revolution was a dominant feature of Russian life in the early 1900's.
2. World War I, from which most Russians wanted to withdraw, added to the discontent already brewing. In 1917, a revolution erupted that toppled the government and destroyed the tsarist system.
3. Although a provisional government was set up after Nicholas gave up power, Russia really was ruled by soviets.
4. In a short time, the Bolsheviks took over Petrograd, proclaimed a socialist revolution, and made Lenin the head of a new revolutionary government. Lenin and the Bolsheviks worked to bring communism to Russia.
5. In 1921, the Communists emerged victorious from the civil war that had broken out between them and the anti-Communist Whites. The following year, they established a new Soviet state made up of four republics and known as the Union of Soviet Socialist Republics.
6. To restore the declining economy during the war, the government initiated the unsuccessful policy of war communism. It was followed by the more successful New Economic Policy.
7. In 1928, Joseph Stalin came to power and began a series of Five Year Plans designed to industrialize the Soviet Union as quickly as possible. To achieve his goal, he resorted to force and terror.
8. Despite Stalin's pact with Nazi Germany, German forces invaded Soviet territory during World War II. The war caused widespread destruction in the Soviet Union and resulted in the loss of millions of lives.
9. After World War II, the Soviet Union emerged as the strongest nation in Europe and Asia and a superpower to rival the United States. Since then, it has undergone various changes in leadership, and Soviet relations with the West have fluctuated.

VOCABULARY

Identify

Vladimir Ilyich Ulyanov
Karl Marx
Nicholas II
Alexander Kerensky
Bolsheviks
Marxism

Communists
Leon Trotsky
Union of Soviet
  Socialist Republics
New Economic Policy

Joseph Stalin
Five-Year Plan
Eugenia Ginzburg
Great Patriotic War
cold war

Nikita Khrushchev
Leonid Brezhnev
Aleksei Kosygin
Yuri Andropov
Konstantin Chernenko
Mikhail Gorbachev

Define

soviets
proletariat
capitalism

bourgeoisie
communism
war communism

collectively
kulaks
purged

collective leadership
dissidents
détente

DISCUSSING IMPORTANT IDEAS

1. What do you think might have happened to the tsarist system if Nicholas II had carried out the reforms the people wanted? Give reasons for your answer.
2. What reasons can you give for the success of Lenin and the Bolsheviks in Russia?
3. Stalin achieved his goal of industrializing the Soviet Union rapidly. Do you think he would have been as successful as rapidly had he used different methods? Explain your answer.
4. What point do you think Nikita Khrushchev was trying to make in his memoirs about Soviet foreign policy? How well do you think the cold war and détente fit in with his strategies? Explain.

DEVELOPING SKILLS

DETERMINING THE RELIABILITY OF A SOURCE

One of the basic ingredients needed to prepare an accurate report or give a convincing speech is supporting evidence from *reliable sources* —books, documents, or other records that supply dependable information. Since not all sources are reliable, when you research a topic, you must be able to determine the worth of the sources you plan to use. The following guidelines will help you to do this:

1. Evaluate the person (or persons) who have supplied the information in the source by considering whether his or her background qualifies him or her to write or speak about the topic. For example, just because someone is an expert in one culture does not mean that he or she is an expert in every culture.
2. Consult more than one source, comparing and contrasting the facts and basic information presented in each. If, for example, upon consulting four different sources, you find that the information in one of them is different from that in the other three, it is likely that the one source is in error and should not be used.
3. Use the skills that you have already learned; ask yourself questions like these:
   a. Is this a primary source—a firsthand account by someone who experienced an event—or a secondary source—information provided by someone who has read or heard about an event?
   b. What is the main idea—major point being stressed?
   c. Is the information factually accurate—well supported by evidence?
   d. Is the information mostly fact—statements that can be verified—or opinion—something someone believes or thinks is true?
   e. Is the information relevant—directly related to the topic or issue?
   f. Is the material biased—slanted in viewpoint?
   g. Does the material contain unstated assumptions—information related to or based on points the author has taken for granted that you already know?
   h. Does the material contain any unwarranted claims—statements that are not supported by facts?
   i. Are there fallacies—false notions and errors in thinking—in the line of reasoning?

For practice in this skill, consider this chapter as a source for a research paper on the Soviet Union in the 1900's. Use the suggested guidelines to determine if the chapter is a reliable source.

CHAPTER 42
PEOPLES OF THE SOVIET UNION

1. What major ethnic groups make up the population of the Soviet Union?
2. How does the Soviet government regard the many peoples of the Soviet Union?

As you travel through the Soviet Union, you will see how the national features change from place to place. Moscow's ancient churches are crowned with round cupolas (domes) of gold, whereas the cupolas in Tbilisi are conical. Pointed. Gothic spires rise above Riga and Tallinn, while Vilnius greets you with its baroque doorways and rounded volutes [curved ornaments]. Of course, modern architecture is more universal, but even our new buildings betray certain national characteristics. In Kiev, for example, you will find Ukrainian ornaments on the walls, and in Baku, the arches and other elements are oriental or what used to be called Moorish architecture.

In Tashkent, you will see people dancing in brightly colored costumes and little hats *(tiubeteiki)* to the rhythmical taps of the tambourine. In the Caucasus, you can see the energetic *lesghinka* performed by fervent dancers in distinctive mountain dress, their daggers in their belts. And take note of the different national cuisines, the various languages on the streets, and the newspapers and books published in diverse languages.

Dress has become more uniform, as everywhere, adapting to the modern urban style. Still, you might be lucky enough to see a Ukrainian girl in an embroidered skirt, an Uzbek in a striped robe, a Turkoman in a huge fur cap, a Caucasian in a wide-shouldered, shaggy sheepskin *burka* [overcoat], or an inhabitant of the Far North dressed in his furs.

But essentially all these different peoples constitute one Soviet nation, a single social structure.*

The Soviet Union often is referred to as Russia. But **ethnic Russians,** Soviet citizens who speak Russian as their first language and follow Russian ways, make up only one-half of the Soviet Union's population of 277 million people. As the Soviet author above indicates, the rest of the people are non-Russians from a variety of backgrounds. Although over the centuries these peoples came under Russian rule, they have kept many of their own customs and languages.

Each of the 15 republics that make up the Soviet Union is based on one of the major **nationalities,** or ethnic groups, in the country. The Soviet Constitution allows the dominant nationality within each republic the right to its own local government, language, and culture. Within the various subdivisions of each republic, minorities also are guaranteed these same rights.

In addition to the ethnic groups concentrated in specific geographical areas, there are many smaller groups scattered across the Soviet Union. The variety of peoples is almost as vast as the land itself. According to the latest Soviet census, there are more than 90 ethnic groups in all. Together, these groups speak about 80 different languages. They write in four different alphabets.

---

*Russia: Land and People of the Soviet Union by Nikolai Nikolaevich Mikhailov, 1980, Harry N. Abrams, Inc., p. 15. Reprinted by permission.

SLAVS

The largest ethnic group in the Soviet Union is the Slavs, who are divided into three groups—ethnic Russians, Ukrainians, and Byelorussians. Together, the three groups account for 72 percent of the Soviet population.

The ethnic Russians, who number 140 million and are the dominant group in the Soviet Union, live for the most part in the Russian Soviet Federated Socialist Republic (R.S.F.S.R.). The R.S.F.S.R. stretches from the Arctic Sea in the north to the Black Sea in the south, and from the Baltic Sea in the west to the Pacific Ocean in the east. It is the largest of the republics, covering three-quarters of the Soviet Union's land area. Over one-half of the population of the Soviet Union live in the R.S.F.S.R. As the ethnic Russian homeland, it is 83 percent ethnic Russian.

West and south of the R.S.F.S.R. is the Republic of the Ukraine, home to 42 million Ukrainians. The Ukraine is the Soviet Union's **breadbasket,** or grain-producing region, and its second most important industrial region. Today, most Ukrainians live in urban areas like Kiev and Odessa. Many, however, continue to make their home in the countryside. The countryside is the leading center of traditional Ukrainian culture, for in spite of years of ethnic Russian influence the Ukrainians remain proud of their Slavic language and customs.

North of the Ukraine is the Republic of Byelorussia. Once ruled by Poland, the 10 million Byelorussians who live there have a strong Polish influence in their culture. In recent years, however, the region has become more industrialized, and the people

UNION OF SOVIET SOCIALIST REPUBLICS

CHAPTER 42 PEOPLES OF THE SOVIET UNION 691

Kiev, pictured here, is the Ukrainian capital city. Like the ethnic Russians and the Byelorussians, the Ukrainians are descended from East Slavs who lived near the Black Sea as early as the sixth century. Some of these East Slavs settled at the Dnieper River trading town of Kiev, which in the 800's became the first Russian state. What does the Ukraine contribute to the Soviet economy?

have adopted many ethnic Russian ways. Below, a Soviet journalist discusses the life of Sergei and Irina Kurbyko, a typical young Byelorussian couple:

> Sergei and Irina Kurbyko were born and grew up in the countryside, in large Byelorussian farm families. Today they live in Minsk, the capital of Byelorussia. Sergei is a construction worker. . . . Irina, his wife, is a house painter. . . .
>
> Sergei had been drawn to city life since childhood, and, after completing eight years of schooling, he set out for Minsk. . . .
>
> In Minsk Sergei graduated from a building vocational school and took a job as an assembler. . . .
>
> Then he joined the navy. When he got out, he returned to Minsk and his job. This time he became the leader of an entire building team (26 men of different ages). . . .
>
> Irina Kurbyko started out on her own in much the same way as her husband. In the beginning she worked at construction sites as an unskilled laborer. She soon discovered that house painting appealed to her more. With the help of her coworkers she mastered her trade on the job, and it wasn't too long before she took her certification exam, which she passed.
>
> At the time Irina was living in a dormitory. One day her girlfriend introduced her to a group of builders, among whom was Sergei. The two . . . were soon married. They now have two daughters —Oksana, aged 13, and Natasha, aged 10. . . .
>
> The Kurbykos live in a cozy two-bedroom apartment. . . .
>
> Sergei's annual leave comes to 24 workdays, while Irina's is 18. They usually take their vacation in the summertime. . . . [Like] most Byelorussians who have grown up on a farm, Sergei and Irina prefer to spend their vacation in their native village. Most of the time they stay at Sergei's mother's place, where the fishing is excellent. The family also likes to take long walks in the woods, pick berries, gather mushrooms, and make preserves and pickles. . . .
>
> On a typical weekend Sergei will spend his time reading. "I feel I have to bone up," he admits, "because next year I want to enroll in a correspondence course at an institute of architecture and building."

This Lithuanian woman expresses the ethnic pride felt by the non-Russian peoples of the Soviet Union. By the fourteenth century, Lithuania had acquired a vast territory extending from the Baltic to the Black Sea. Today, Lithuania is the largest of the three Baltic republics in the Soviet Union. How did the Baltic republics become part of the Soviet nation?

Irina and Sergei may go to the movies or attend a concert once in a while, but more often than not they are at home. . . . The children are quite the opposite and are always raring to go. Oksana is enrolled in two schools—high school and a music school. Natasha goes to elementary school and takes a course in dressmaking at a Young Pioneer Palace [local headquarters of the Communist youth organization].*

1. What is the largest ethnic group in the Soviet Union? Into what three groups is it divided?
2. Who are the ethnic Russians? Why are they important in the Soviet Union?

---

*"A Worker's Family: Everyday Life and Holidays" by Grigori Kolobov in *Soviet Life*, January, 1984, Vol. 328, No. 1., pp. 2, 7. Reprinted by permission.

LITHUANIANS, LATVIANS, AND ESTONIANS

The Lithuanians, Latvians, and Estonians live in three small republics—Lithuania, Latvia, and Estonia—along the Baltic seacoast of the Soviet Union. Although each of these peoples differs from the other in language and religion, all share a common history. For hundreds of years, Russia, Poland, Germany, and Sweden fought for control of their lands. Then, in the early 1900's, their lands became independent nations for the first time. They remained independent until 1940 when Joseph Stalin **annexed,** or joined, them to the Soviet Union.

Apart from geographical closeness, the peoples of these Baltic republics have little in common with their Slavic neighbors in the Soviet Union. Traditionally Western European in outlook, the Baltic peoples use the Latin rather than the Cyrillic alphabet. Most Estonians and Latvians are Protestant and most Lithuanians Roman Catholic, while most of the Slavs of the Soviet Union are Eastern Orthodox. In addition, the Baltic peoples enjoy a higher standard of living than the Slavs of the Soviet Union.

Since 1940, many changes have taken place in the Baltic republics. The Soviet government has actively pushed for increased industrialization in the region. Because the Baltic populations have been barely increasing and the labor force is low, the Soviet government has encouraged a large number of ethnic Russians to move to the Baltic republics to provide more workers. This has drastically changed the area's population. In Latvia, for example, 90 percent of the population was Latvian in 1940. Today, only 55 percent are Latvian, while ethnic Russians make up 30 percent. Ethnic Russians fill a large number of important posts in government and industry in all three Baltic countries. In spite of the growth of ethnic Russian influence, however, the peoples of the Baltic republics continue to cling to their own languages and ways of life.

Estonia is the most prosperous of the Baltic republics. The Estonians are manufacturers and farmers who have close cultural links to Finland, their independent neighbor to the north. Below, an American visitor to Estonia talks about his visit and the people:

> At a textile plant I talked with Luule Allika, the trim woman who directs the 1,800 employees of the enterprise. "About 92 percent of our plant's products stay in Estonia," she said. "Our raincoats are popular because of the weather. All our designs are Estonian, and sizes also differ here—Estonians are slenderer than other Soviet people. Our customers are harder to please. Women here are more fashion-conscious."

The view along any Tallinn [the Estonian capital] sidewalk confirms that fact. The clean blond Estonian girls—with high cheekbones, deep-set eyes, and finely pointed noses—seem leaner, taller, and far more stylish than others in the U.S.S.R. They move like tennis players, as many of them are.

Estonians are also noticeably reticent. When our car was bumped by another one day, the driver got out wordlessly. He inspected our damaged bumper and picked up a broken portion from the pavement. A bit formally, he approached the offending driver. . . . He simply handed the other driver the bumper chunk with a single word: "Souvenir."

Ethnographer [scholar of ethnic groups] Ulo Tedre described his people this way: "Hardworking, perhaps because they were historically oppressed by other nations. Tenacious [tough]. A sense of individuality

This Estonian woman is gathering a bouquet of flowers, which are a popular item at local open-air markets. Why has the Soviet government encouraged ethnic Russians to move to the Baltic republics?

rather than collectiveness [loyalty to a group]."

But . . . [in] song, the Estonian personality makes a sharp turn. Every five years, Estonians gather for a songfest with a choir of 30,000 voices. In two days, they sing dozens of Estonian folk songs —fishermen's songs, harvest songs, songs of love and longing.

Professor Gustav Ernesaks, an Estonian composer . . . described the Estonian spirit this way: "This is a proud nation. . . . You can trust the promises here. A deep sense of humor. Rational, logical people. Good farmers—and patient. . . . We like precision. . . . We have discipline, but the best kind: discipline from within the soul. . . ."

We did attend one folk-dance exhibit— in the rain. No one cared. They got wet and laughed. . . . The dances were prankish and fun. Afterward, Estonians applauded spiritedly—but not in cadenced unison.*

1. What groups make up the Baltic peoples?
2. What are the major characteristics of the Baltic peoples?

GEORGIANS, ARMENIANS, AND AZERBAIJANIANS

South of the Caucasus Mountains, between the Black and Caspian seas, is an area called Transcaucasia that is the home of more than 40 different ethnic groups. For hundreds of years, this region was made up of many separate states that were conquered repeatedly by powerful neighbors. Then, in the 1800's, the states became part of the Russian Empire, and today the Georgians, Armenians, and Azerbaijanians have their own republics within the Soviet Union.

Journey Across Russia: The Soviet Union Today by Bart McDowell, 1977, National Geographic Society, pp. 195–196. Reprinted by permission.

These Georgian sheepherders are preparing to dip their animals in a vat of liquid that will rid them and their wool of harmful parasites. In what ways are the Georgians different from the Azerbaijanians?

Although the Georgians, Armenians, and Azerbaijanians all have cultures similar to those of the Middle East, there still are many differences among them. The 6 million Azerbaijanians who live in an area near the Caspian Sea are Muslims and speak a language related to Turkish. Most live in lowland rural areas and grow corn, cotton, fruits, vegetables, and tobacco. Their major source of wealth, however, is oil, and the Azerbaijanian capital of Baku has many oil refineries.

The 5 million Georgians who live in the Soviet Republic of Georgia have their own language, alphabet, and Christian church. They are known for their business skills, love of festivals, and hospitality to foreigners.

CASE STUDY
SOVIET UNION

LONG-LIFERS

The Soviet Union claims to have some of the oldest living people. These individuals, known as **long-lifers,** have lived to more than 100 years of age. According to Soviet medical experts, there are some 20,000 long-lifers in the U.S.S.R., many living in the Caucasus Mountains. It is stated that their long life is due to their rigorous outdoor life style and simple diet of vegetables, fruits, and milk products.

One of the most publicized long-lifers was Khfaf Lazuria, who reached the age of 139 before her death in 1975. Below, an American author talks about Lazuria and their meeting in Kutol, the Caucasian village where Lazuria was born:

Khfaf Lazuria, according to the official register of her . . . village, . . . was born on October 8, 1835;—in 1974, she was perhaps the oldest woman alive. I was taken to visit Khfaf by her grandnephew. . . . We found Khfaf sitting comfortably in the shade of a large tree in the courtyard of her home. . . .

Although she had not been told of our coming, Khfaf was clearly delighted to have visitors. . . . After warm greetings and introductions, we sat down and I began to question her. Although her Russian was limited, she understood everything I asked, and we communicated with great ease.

She was quite small. . . . She was about five feet [1.5 meters] tall and . . . slender. Her face was astonishingly smooth with few wrinkles. Her eyes were bright, curious, alive—and often full of mischief. She had a keen sense of humor and laughed easily. She responded warmly to me, kissing my cheeks as an expression of her approval. . . . She wore a simple blue-and-white-flowered dress made like a caftan. . . . A white-polka-dotted cotton kerchief was wrapped around her head, and she wore pink slippers over gray stockings.

I told her I'd heard she could thread a needle without wearing glasses. She laughed. "I never had eyeglasses," she said. Would she do it for me? "Oh, yes! . . ."

I asked whether her parents, too, had lived long. She said that her great-grandfather, Dzhadash, had lived to 160, and his grandson, Naruk, to 120. Her mother had also lived long. . . . Khfaf had two brothers and three sisters, some of whom had died when they were "only" ninety or so, because of an epidemic. . . .

Khfaf claimed that . . . measles had been her only childhood disease, and that her health was perfect. I asked her to what she attributes her good health. She told me she eats regularly. . . . She preferred eating small quantities frequently, rather than large meals. . . .

She used to love horseback riding, but gave it up when she was about a hundred because there were too many cars on the road, which frightened the horses. . . .

In her younger days, in addition to working in the collective fields, she was a well-known mid-wife. She proudly announced that she had brought more than a hundred babies into the world. . . .

Everyone respected and liked Khfaf. She played with the great-grandchildren, swept the courtyard daily, took complete care of a good-size vegetable garden, and saw to all of her own needs, including her own laundry. The great respect given to old people allows them to take part in any activity they choose to take part in. It is assumed that people of any age may participate fully in the life of the household—its duties and its pleasures.*

1. Who are the long-lifers? What may account for their long lives?
2. How would you compare Khfaf Lazuria and her life style with that of older people in your country? What do you think accounts for any differences?

*Excerpts from *How to Live to Be 100: The Life-Style of the People of the Caucasus* by Sula Benet, pp. 1–2, 4–5. Copyright ©1976 by Sula Benet. Reprinted by permission of Doubleday & Company, Inc.

Because the country is mountainous, most of the people live in valleys where they grow flowers, tobacco, citrus fruit, and grapes. In spite of its small size, Georgia has had an important impact on the Soviet state. Joseph Stalin, whose real name was Iosif Dzhugashvili, came from Georgia.

The 3 million Armenians who live in the Soviet Republic of Armenia also have their own alphabet and language. Most are members of the Armenian Apostolic Church, one of the world's oldest Christian churches. Although most Soviet Armenians work in industry, many are farmers. No matter what their work, Armenians take particular pride in their history and culture.

In the past, Armenia was an independent kingdom that included part of present-day Turkey as well as the existing Armenian Soviet Republic. Over the centuries, as the Armenian homeland was conquered and invaded, many Armenians were forced to flee their country. As a result, today Armenians live in many different parts of the world, including the United States. Below, an Armenian-American writer describes a visit to a memorial in the land of his ancestors:

> We drove down one of the wide boulevards, a long straight roadway lined with trees, which led toward the semicircle of low hills.
>
> The olive-colored leaves were deep green as we came closer. There were flowers beside the road, and a few houses. . . . There were orange-tiled roofs on the poorish stone houses, red flowers in the skimpy gardens. Some goats wandered beside the road.
>
> . . . Meadows of yellow-green grass extended on all sides. The fields were flat and dry and full of stones. You could see clusters of trees against the horizon, far away, and a few scattered houses, far away—and, yet farther away, the mass of [Mount] Ararat, not quite in front of us but dominating the land, its summit of snow on a level with the clouds.

> "Every Armenian in the world should visit this monument," Sarkis [an Armenian friend] was saying. "Every Armenian should know what it is to stand before it and feel in his bones the tragedy of Armenia." He turned to my wife. "The suffering of the Armenian people has been enormous," he said. . . .
>
> Sarkis said, "To be an Armenian is to have this intolerable weight of sadness on one's soul. . . ."
>
> In a moment, he said, "Armenians can never forget what happened to them. . . . It was a genocide [the planned destruction of a cultural, political, or ethnic group]. Do you know, it was the world's first genocide. . . .
>
> We climbed some stone steps. There was a stone walk. . . . In front of us . . . was an unusual structure. It had the appearance of a kind of Stonehenge—columns, metallic columns rising out of the ground, but angled inward. . . .
>
> In the center of the slanted columns stood a large vessel—a metal bowl—with a flame burning inside it.
>
> We stood beneath the columns looking at the bowl and the flame.
>
> "Think of the Armenians who died," said Sarkis, almost in a whisper. "Think of your martyred countrymen. Think what it is to be an Armenian."*

1. What three ethnic groups have their own republics in Transcaucasia?
2. What are the major characteristics of the Transcaucasian peoples?

CENTRAL ASIANS

Located between the Caspian Sea and China are the Soviet Republics of Kazakhstan, Turkmenia, Tajikistan, Uzbekistan, and Kirghizia. Together these republics, which make up Soviet Central Asia, cover nearly 18

---

*Excerpted from *Passage to Ararat* by Michael J. Arlen. Copyright ©1975 by Michael J. Arlen, pp. 69–72. Reprinted by permission of Farrar, Straus and Giroux, Inc. This material appeared originally in *The New Yorker*.

percent of the Soviet Union's land area. The 35 million or so people who live in the area speak a variety of languages. Most of the languages are related to Turkish, and most of the people are Muslims. Before modern times, many of the people raised animals and roamed the steppe in search of pasture. Others settled in cities and created empires.

In the 1800's, after a period of decline, the Central Asian lands came under the rule of the Russian Empire. In the 1920's, they were made part of the Soviet Union and divided into the present-day republics. The Soviet government built farms, schools, and factories in the region. Today, in addition to being an important agricultural region known for cotton and grain production, Soviet Central Asia also produces such minerals as coal and copper. The resulting prosperity has strengthened the position of the Central Asian peoples in the Soviet Union.

The Muslim population of the Central Asian republics, which already is quite large, is growing faster than that of other ethnic groups in the rest of the country. At the same time, the ethnic Russian birthrate is falling. This worries the ethnic Russians. They fear that they will be a minority in the Soviet Union by the year 2000. The Soviet government has encouraged them to move to Soviet Central Asia, and they now make up a quarter of the region's population. Officially, the relocation policy is designed to speed the region's economic development by providing highly skilled labor. But many experts claim that it also is intended to lessen the influence of the Muslim population.

In spite of modernization, many of the Central Asian peoples still live in rural areas and retain traditional customs. Even in the cities, there is interest in the folklore, dances, and songs of the past. Below, a Soviet author describes a traditional wedding feast in the Soviet Republic of Turkmenia:

Maintaining their religious traditions, these Muslim men attend a Friday prayer service in Tashkent, the Uzbekistan capital. How do the people of Soviet Central Asia contribute to the Soviet economy?

"Attention, folks!" the collective-farm loud speaker blared. It was Mergen-agha, a cotton-grower, speaking over the farm's radio. "Listen carefully. . . . There is great rejoicing in my family. My youngest son, Meret, the agronomist, is to marry the daughter of Murad Dzheren, the teacher. . . . The whole village is invited to the wedding feast tonight, young and old, men, women, and children."

Such is the custom of the Turkmen. When a family has a *toi* (a feast), the whole village helps celebrate it, bringing crockery, sweets, fruits, a lamb or a kid. Every passerby or stranger is welcome. When misfortune befalls anyone, the whole village will pitch in and help or comfort the luckless one. It is an ancient tradition with the Turkmen to lend a helping hand, to face difficulties and misfortunes together and also to rejoice in one's successes together.

... The farmhouses framed in the emerald-green of the orchards made a beautiful picture against the background of yellow dunes. On the collective-farm race course *dzhigits* (skillful horsemen) were caracoling [making turns] on fiery thoroughbred horses. Trails of smoke rose from the fires under the bubbling cauldrons set up in the yard of a big farmhouse. In front of the house were parked ... cars belonging to the guests, the collective farmers.

I arrived on the scene when the games and the dancing were in full swing. *Dzhigits* were showing off their skill. The strongest and the most agile were engaged in *yaglyga tovusmak*, jumping for scarves hanging high overhead, and in *goresh*, a Turkmen form of wrestling.

The large courtyard, the orchard and the six-room house were crammed. On the veranda, decorated with carved woodwork, sat Nobat Odeniyazov, the famous *bakhshi* (singer).... He sat with his legs tucked under him in Turkmen fashion on a bright-coloured rug. He wore a red silk gown with a scarlet homespun sash. On his head he wore a shaggy hat of snow-white sheepskin. That is how the Turkmen dress for a feast.

Watched eagerly by those who had gathered to hear him, Nobat doffed his hat to reveal a skull-cap under it. Then he undid his sash and took his arms from the sleeves of his gown. Sitting there in his white, collarless, embroidered native-style shirt he took up his instrument, the two-stringed *dutar*.

A hush fell on everyone. The *bakhshi* tuned the strings and, as though performing a solemn rite, tested them with strong supple fingers. He started playing slowly, uncertainly it seemed, then faster and faster until it was impossible to follow the movement of his fingers. A song poured forth, resonant and swift, long-drawn and melodious by turns. The *dutar* echoed it with an eagle's cry and the murmuring of streams, the whistle of arrows and the moaning of the wind in the steppes, with a war cry and the whispers of lovers, the cry of a new-born babe and the thunder of cavalry.*

1. What republics make up Soviet Central Asia?
2. What are the major characteristics of the peoples of Soviet Central Asia?
3. Why are ethnic Russians concerned about the Muslim population's rising birthrate?

RUSSIFICATION

When the tsars ruled Russia, they tried to force Russian ways on the non-Russian ethnic groups of their empire. This policy, known as Russification, caused much resentment. After the Revolution of 1917, the non-Russians hoped that the Communists would allow them to determine their own futures. But the new Soviet government was not willing to allow the old Russian Empire to break completely into independent states. Instead, it gave each major ethnic group its own republic within the Soviet Union and kept for itself the power to make important decisions for all.

The government's goal was to end ethnic differences eventually and create a new, united Soviet citizenship under communism. But since ethnic Russians controlled the central government and the Communist party, the interests of the non-Russian groups often took second place. Then, when Joseph Stalin came to power, the government's official policy of tolerance toward the non-Russian groups changed. Stalin was afraid that the non-Russian peoples would cling to their separate national identities rather than re-

---
Turkmenia 1982, Novosti Press Agency Publishing House, pp. 12–13. Reprinted by permission.

gard themselves as Soviet citizens. He believed that the country would be united and strengthened if all Soviets adopted Russian ways. So, while he kept the system of republics, he promoted Russification.

Since Stalin's death, the Soviet government has eased its Russification policies. It still encourages Russian ways, but, at the same time, it works to promote the cultural traditions of all ethnic groups. Still, many problems remain. In spite of the Communist goal of equality for all groups, the ethnic Russians remain dominant. Russian is the official language and is taught in all Soviet schools. Every citizen, regardless of nationality, must speak Russian to get ahead. Some Soviets, like the Kirghiz Communist party official whose comments appear below, approve of the present ethnic policies:

> The Russian language is spoken throughout Kirghizia, and we consider this a great achievement. It helps solve the problem of communication among the various national groups that inhabit the USSR. The mass-scale study of Russian by non-Russian people goes hand in hand with the steady development of the languages of all ethnic groups in our country.
>
> What kind of Russification is it if we, the Kirghiz people, have obtained our own language in written form since Soviet power was established, if we are continuing to develop it all the time, if we are taught in school and write and publish books and newspapers and produce plays in our native language, if 99.6 per cent of the Kirghiz people . . . [mention] Kirghiz as their native language? And please keep in mind that the instruction in 1,060 high schools in the Kirghiz Republic is conducted in our mother tongue. The first Kirghiz book was published in 1926. Since that time 126 million copies of 17,000 Kirghiz books have been published. Sixty republic, regional and district newspapers and 16 magazines are published in the Kirghiz language, and a six-volume encyclopedia of Kirghizia has been published.*

Other non-Russian Soviet citizens, however, do not agree and state privately that the government has a pro-Russian bias. In recent years, **nationalism,** the desire for one's own national identity, has risen in some areas. The nationalist feelings that have surfaced often have had an anti-Russian tone. Although such feelings are strongest in the European part of the Soviet Union, some western experts believe that the possibility of a nationalist awakening also exists in Soviet Central Asia.

1. What did non-Russian groups hope would happen after the Revolution of 1917? What did happen?
2. What was Stalin's attitude toward Russification? What is the government's attitude today?
3. How have non-Russian groups in the Soviet Union reacted to the ethnic policies of the Soviet government?

These children are attending classes at a Russian-language school on a collective farm in Uzbekistan. Why do all Soviet citizens, regardless of ethnic group, have to learn Russian?

*"The Present and Future of Kirghizia," interview with Turdakun Usubaliyev, general secretary of the Communist Party of Kirghizia, in *Soviet Life*, Vol. 343, No. 4, April, 1985, p. 60. Reprinted by permission.

EXPLORATION
SOVIET UNION

As explained in the chapter, a great many different groups of people live in the Soviet Union. The illustrations that follow represent some of these peoples. Based on the illustrations and on the information in the chapter, explain this Russian proverb:

"Russia is not a country; it is a world."

SOVIET UNION

CHAPTER 42 REVIEW

POINTS TO REMEMBER

1. Each of the 15 republics that make up the Soviet Union is based on a major nationality. There are more than 90 ethnic groups in all, speaking about 80 different languages, which are written in four different alphabets.
2. The largest ethnic group in the Soviet Union is the Slavs, who are divided into ethnic Russians, Ukrainians, and Byelorussians. The ethnic Russians are the dominant group in the Soviet Union. They live, for the most part, in the R.S.F.S.R.
3. The Baltic peoples—Lithuanians, Latvians, and Estonians—live in three small republics along the Baltic seacoast. Despite growing ethnic Russian influence, they cling to their own languages and way of life.
4. Transcaucasia is home to the Georgians, Armenians, and Azerbaijanians. While there are many differences between the groups, all have cultures similar to those of the Middle East.
5. The Central Asians live in the Soviet Republics of Kazakhstan, Turkmenia, Tajikistan, Uzbekistan, and Kirghizia. Most are Muslim and speak languages related to Turkish.
6. In 1917, the Soviet government gave each major ethnic group its own republic within the Soviet Union. When Stalin came to power, he kept the system of republics but promoted Russification. Today, although the government promotes the cultural traditions of all ethnic groups, ethnic Russians remain dominant and largely determine policy and culture.

VOCABULARY

Identify

Slavs
Ukrainians
Byelorussians
R.S.F.S.R.
Lithuanians
Latvians
Estonians
Transcaucasia
Georgians
Armenians
Azerbaijanians
Soviet Central Asia
Russification

Define

ethnic Russians
nationalities
breadbasket
annexed
long-lifers
nationalism

DISCUSSING IMPORTANT IDEAS

1. The major ethnic groups of the Soviet Union include the Slavs, the Baltic peoples, the Transcaucasians, and the Central Asians. What are some of the differences between the groups? The similarities?
2. Why is the study of Russian mandatory in all Soviet schools? Do you agree with this policy? Why or why not? How does the diversity of languages in the Soviet Union differ from that in your country?

3. Although many different ethnic groups live in the Soviet Union, a large part of Soviet life is influenced by ethnic Russians. Why do you think this is so? Do you think it would be more difficult for an ethnic group to maintain its own language and culture while living in the land of its ancestors or while living elsewhere as immigrants?
4. The major ethnic groups of the Soviet Union are represented by their own governments within the larger Soviet framework. What kind of recognition, if any, is given to ethnic groups in your country?

DEVELOPING SKILLS

DETERMINING THE STRENGTH OF AN ARGUMENT

Sooner or later, you may find yourself in a position where you have to defend your point of view or convince others to come around to your way of thinking. The best way to do this is to present an *argument,* or a series of reasons, that will support your views. Whether or not you achieve this goal may very well depend on how strong of an argument you present to those persons you wish to sway or who do not agree with you. The same holds true for an argument presented by someone else, be it one with which you want to disagree or one on which you may have to base an important decision.

It is important, therefore, to be able to determine the strength of an argument. Asking yourself questions like the ones that follow will help you to do this:
1. Has the main point or theme of the argument been clearly stated?
2. Do each of the reasons given in the argument truly relate to the issue under discussion?
3. Are the reasons that form the basis of the argument presented in a logical order?
4. Is any evidence given that supports the information offered in the argument?

For practice in determining the strength of an argument, do the following:
1. Read this passage, in which a Soviet citizen presents an argument in favor of the policy of Russification.

Russification is necessary if we want all the many different peoples who live in the Soviet Union to be united and work together for the benefit of the nation. Take, for example, the policy that every citizen must learn the Russian language. The reason for this can be summed up in one word—communication. If each group of people in our vast land speaks its own language, how will the groups communicate with one another? No one has said that each group cannot keep its own language and speak that language at home or publish books, magazines, and newspapers in that language. All that is being asked is that, in addition to its own language, each group learn and speak the Russian language. That way, each group can communicate with other groups. Without communication among its people, a nation cannot be united. A united nation is a strong nation, and the Soviet Union must be a strong nation!

2. Read the passage again, this time seeking an answer to each of the four questions noted earlier. If the answer to all four questions is "yes," then the Soviet has presented a strong argument.
3. Keeping in mind that in a strong argument the main point or theme must be clearly stated, the reasons given must relate to the issue and be presented in a logical order, and evidence must be provided as support, prepare an argument against Russification.

CHAPTER 43
CITY AND COUNTRY

1. What are some major features of urban life in the Soviet Union?
2. How is rural life organized in the Soviet Union?

Moscow's rush-hour traffic fills downtown streets, but keeps moving. To avoid the snarls of other capitals, the mayor said, the city would double its 102-mile [163.2-kilometer] Metro [subway] system by the year 2000. . . .

. . . The system was reaching out toward the new high-rise communities sprouting like mushrooms along the Moscow Ring Road, for it was on the outskirts, the mayor said, that Moscow was building its new housing. "The center of the city must be preserved as it is, for future generations."

I followed the Ring Road south . . . to one of Moscow's typical satellite communities. On one side of a boulevard rose a giant complex: apartment buildings, schools, shopping center, sports field, a hotel. . . .

. . . I saw, across the boulevard, the remains of the village this complex was replacing. I decided to visit it. . . .

. . . A road led down toward what remained of the village: some 40 houses, their blue, green, and ocher. . . . Anna Ivanovna, 51, with a round face and gold teeth, was gathering kindling when I hailed her. She lived with her husband, two sons, a daughter-in-law, and a baby.

She had been born in this village, as had her mother. . . .

"I remember the village was more beautiful; at that time everyone looked after their houses. Each was painted a different color; each had different decorations.

"The cowherd came very early each morning blowing his horn; the housewives would take their cows down to him, and he would lead them to pasture. I remember the cherry trees. We would pick the cherries and put them under our shirts. . . ."

The cherry trees were gone now. "They stopped bearing fruit; in time the villagers cut them down."

Anna was looking forward to moving into a new [apartment]: "In this house you must heat with a coal stove and fetch cold water from the standpipe. The [apartment] will have running water." Some of her friends had already moved into a new building. "They said it should have come earlier, when they were younger."*

This description of a new Moscow suburb and a declining village reveals the changing relationship between city and country in the Soviet Union today. Once largely rural, the Soviet Union now is urban, and twice as many Soviets live in cities and towns as in the countryside. Because of industrial development in urban areas and the higher standard of living it brings, the number of people moving from the country to the city is increasing steadily.

In spite of the dominance of cities, however, rural areas still make an important contribution to Soviet life. Soviet farms still supply much of the nation's food needs. This, coupled with the fact that many city dwellers remain emotionally attached to their rural roots, has led the Soviet government to try to improve the quality of rural life.

---

*"The City Around Red Square: Moscow" by John J. Putnam in *National Geographic*, Vol. 153, No. 1, January 1978, pp. 9, 15. Reprinted by permission.

CITY LIFE

The Soviet government has promoted the growth of the cities. Today, Moscow, the largest city of the Soviet Union, is home to 8.2 million people. The second largest city is Leningrad, with 4.6 million people. Another large city is Novosibirsk, in Siberia, with a population of 1.3 million people. While all three of these cities are rich in tradition, each has its own reason for importance.

MOSCOW

A leading industrial and cultural center, Moscow holds a special place in the hearts of the Soviet people. In tsarist times, Russians regarded it as the center of Orthodox Christianity. Today, they view it as the focal point of world communism. Over the centuries, Moscow has developed like a huge spiderweb fanning out from the center. At its heart is the Kremlin, an old fortress and the seat of the Soviet government. During a visit to this landmark, a young Soviet named Vitaly and his classmates learned the following:

Along one side of the Kremlin walls is Red Square which contains the tomb of Lenin. It is also the place where many great Soviet parades are held.

The Kremlin is a little walled town inside Moscow, with churches and museums of all kinds. Thousands of people visit there every day. The Soviet parliament meets there too, and it has Moscow's biggest theatre, the Palace of Congresses. That building is new compared with all the other buildings in the Kremlin. There were a lot of arguments when it was built about 20 years ago, because people said its straight lines and glass didn't fit in with the ancient churches and cathedrals.

Ekaterina Pavlovna [Vitaly's teacher] loves old buildings, but she doesn't agree. All the other buildings, she points out, are

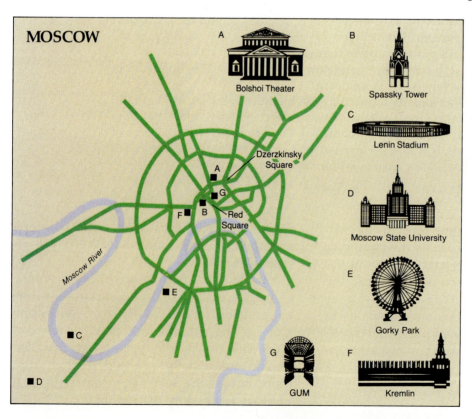

CHAPTER 43 CITY AND COUNTRY

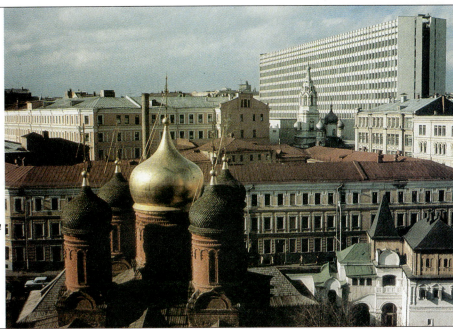

This rooftop view of a downtown section of Moscow contrasts the old architecture typified by the traditional onion-shaped domed cathedral in the foreground with the modern, typified by the office buildings and apartments in the background. Why do many Soviets want to live in Moscow?

in different styles. The theatre is just one more . . . , and it will fit in like the others. She doesn't think that applies to the huge Rossia hotel across Red Square, though. "That monstrosity should be torn down!" she says.

Everyone knows the Spassky Tower, one of many in the Kremlin walls. Its clock is Moscow's Big Ben. Ekaterina Pavlovna says it weighs 25 tonnes [about 27.5 tons].

In the Arsenal building, Vitaly and his classmates see Catherine the Great's crown and Ivan the Terrible's coronet, glittering with diamonds. They also see the Grand Kremlin Palace, where parliament meets, and the Senate where the Council of Ministers holds its sessions. Then they go into the simple office where Lenin worked, when he headed the first Soviet government. The room is as he left it: the pen on his desk looks as if he had just put it down.*

Because of its political importance, Moscow receives more and better goods and services than other Soviet cities. The city continues to grow, and new apartment houses are going up at a rapid rate. Today, special permission is needed to live in Moscow. One way to get that permission is to marry someone who already lives there. One of the reasons so many Soviet citizens want to live in Moscow is that life is better and more goods are available. This is discussed below:

Central Moscow's main underground line stops at Dzerzhinsky Square, a broad plaza of sedate pre-revolutionary buildings that include, among others, the headquarters of the KGB, the internal security police. Few people among the soberly clad multitudes that swarm out of the trains give it much notice, however. They turn instead, shopping bags in hand, to one of the square's largest department stores, Children's World, the Soviet Union's grandest emporium for skates, whistles, prams, volleyballs and dolls.

Inside its doors, long queues [lines] of customers press in upon the sales counters. In one queue, a woman visitor from

---

*Living in Moscow by Ron Harding, 1980, "Living in Famous Cities" series, Wayland Publishers Ltd, pp. 28–29. Reprinted by permission.

These women are looking at items in one of the display windows of Moscow's GUM department store. Completed in 1893, the GUM is a massive glass-roofed three-storied complex with three huge galleries inside. On the average, more than 350,000 shoppers crowd into the GUM each day. How has life changed for Muscovites since the 1940's?

Tbilisi . . . waits to buy a pair of children's long winter underwear—a commodity that is in short supply at home. In another queue, for sledges, [sleds] the wait is six hours. But the sledges are there; a few years earlier, they were not.

The same scene is acted out daily at GUM department store, one of Moscow's largest. . . . Shoppers queue [stand in line] for shaving cream from East Germany and toothpaste from Bulgaria, for cheeses and salamis and rare, smoked sturgeon, for radios and refrigerators, for jumpers from Poland or dresses from Finland. At a necktie display that includes a poster explaining how to tie a cravat, a young man copies down hints; he is about to purchase his first tie. . . .

A Moscow grandmother, recalling the 1940s, describes the living conditions of a family she knew at the time—a near illiterate husband, an overburdened and sickly wife, and 11 children. "All lived in one big, big room—in a barracks, really," with several other families. "They had a curtain which they pulled across it, and they put the beds behind the curtains. They used to sleep in shifts."

Today, she explains, "the children are all grown up and married, and have their own children. Each has a flat [apartment]. Small, only one or two rooms. But with conveniences—a stove, maybe a refrigerator. One of them has a car. They simply can't imagine life any better."*

In spite of material progress, many Muscovites, as well as other Soviets, complain about shortages, shoddy products, and the inefficiency of the state-controlled economy. Because of these, their needs are not always met, and many Soviets turn to the **black market,** a free-enterprise network in which individuals exchange goods and services or carry on private trade using money. While prices usually are higher than in state-run stores, the service is more efficient. Although the black market is illegal, the Soviet government tolerates it in order to keep its citizens contented.

For the *élite,* or privileged members, of Soviet society, living in Moscow has decided

---

*Library of Nations/*The Soviet Union* by the Editors of Time-Life Books ©1984 Time-Life Books Inc.

advantages. The Communist party and government officials, scientists, engineers, and artists who make up the *élite* enjoy such luxuries as cars, comfortable apartments, and **dachas,** or summer houses. They also can get scarce or valuable goods in special shops open only to them. To offset growing dissatisfaction, the Soviet government has extended these privileges to a larger number of people, particularly to those who have faithfully supported and served the Communist system.

LENINGRAD

Leningrad, once known as St. Petersburg, is a leading port and manufacturing center located in the northwest. This northern location gives it very short periods of daylight in winter and **white nights,** prolonged periods of twilight, in the early summer.

Leningrad is spread over 100 islands, which are connected by bridges. Because of its appearance, it is known as the "Venice of the North." Below, an American visitor to the city gives her impressions:

> When we got to Leningrad . . . , the branches of the trees around the Winter Palace were still white with . . . hoarfrost . . . ; above the frozen Neva, in the stunningly clear light of a minus-thirty-degree [−34°C.] morning, the blue-green palace looked like the final step in a theorem proving that cold weather would be the eternal state of the world. As our taxi crossed the bridge to Vasilevsky Island, I saw people strolling on the ice of the river, all of them as bundled up as I was in fur coats and hats and tightly wrapped scarves. . . . Even then, the length of the days betrayed the approach of spring. Every day the twilight comes a bit later. . . . After our arrival the weather swiftly grew warmer, . . . until now the snow has turned to puddles of slush and it is possible to go outside in . . . a wool coat. . . . I paid careful attention to the Neva, so as not to miss the breakup of the ice. . . . [As] I paused one sunny afternoon on the Dvortsovyi Bridge, I heard a light tinkling, like crystals in a chandelier, and looked down to see an open channel . . . in the thick gray ice; inside was a swift eddy of brownish water where dozens of tiny pieces of ice were caught and ringing against one another. . . .

> There is the Leningrad of Rastrelli and the Bronze Horseman, of Nevsky Prospekt and the Winter Palace, and then there is our corner of the city: a working-class neighborhood on Vasilevsky Island. . . . We are staying in a small dormitory . . . that is set inconspicuously among brick apartment buildings and snowy open spaces. . . . Our window looks out on

This dacha *set off by bright pink flowers and hand-carved "gingerbread" window frames belongs to a member of Moscow's* élite. *Besides* dachas, *what other luxuries do the* élite *enjoy?*

These boaters on the Neva River are getting a closer look at some of the cultural heritage of Leningrad. On the right are examples of western architecture, while in the background is a traditional onion-shaped domed church. What made an American visitor decide that the Leningrad neighborhood she was in was not a privileged community?

what seems to be a boys' *gymnasium:* [high school] we often see the boys outside in their school uniforms. . . .

Shopping in the stores in this neighborhood makes it clear that we're no longer in a relatively privileged community. . . . The stores are filled with crowds, strong smells, and puddles of soupy mud near the doors. Entering the *gastronom* . . . where I shop almost daily, [I see] women . . . slice kilos of cheese, weigh butter, and bring out the greenish bottles of *kefir* and acidophilus milk [milk fermented by bacteria]. The people in the endless jostling lines are constantly shouting orders and thrusting out their cashier slips. . . . In the line itself, there is always some nimble old woman who tries, without any subtlety, to dart to the front. . . . In the middle of the crowd, mothers in lacy knitted headshawls try to keep tabs on toddlers bundled in immense wooly coats, with scarves tied around their middles. Workmen . . . line up for salted fish. Behind the welter of bodies, glass sale cases display huge yellowish pigs' heads.

In this uncertain transitional weather between winter and spring, this end of Vasilevsky Island . . . can seem intensely depressing. . . . Yet something of the magic of Leningrad penetrates even to this . . . corner. The early evenings can be lovely. I get off the metro in the middle of a crowd and push my way outside. . . . At this hour dozens of people are waiting for the trolley. . . . Some of the girls and young women have their heads uncovered for the first time since October. . . . The sky . . . is blue-white with a roseate tinge to it; the air is moist and cold, scented with whiffs of cabbage-flavored steam from a nearby cafeteria. By the bus stop stands a small open-air flower market, run mostly by Moldavian women; they sell hyacinths and red tulips, which the crowds carry away like torches.*

NOVOSIBIRSK

Since the 1930's, in an effort to make use of the vast mineral resources of Siberia and promote industrial expansion, the Soviet government has built new cities and developed older ones in the area. So much growth

---

*From *Russian Journal* by Andrea Lee. Copyright ©1979, 1980, 1981, by Andrea Lee. Reprinted by permission of Random House, Inc.

has occurred that Siberia is referred to as "one big construction site." Below, an American talks about his visit to Novosibirsk, one of the oldest and most important Siberian cities:

> Flying into Novosibirsk's busy airport one is impressed by the city's industrial might. Hundreds of food processing plants and light industry buildings come quickly into sight. Three bridges span the Ob [River]. Once landed, a ride through the city's broad boulevards will reveal interesting reminders of what Novosibirsk must have looked like when it was a small town. Wood and log-cabin houses mingle with such modern-day buildings as prefabricated apartment houses . . . , theatres, cinemas, television centers, clinics, and a new sports stadium. And there is a wonderful botanical garden. But most imposing of all is the remarkable tribute the people of Novosibirsk have paid to the 33,000 men and women of the area who made the supreme sacrifice in defense of the motherland from 1941 to 1945. It is a striking monument of successive rows of high white marble slabs on which are inscribed the names of the local war dead. . . .
> Novosibirsk's factories belch smoke and flame. The city's trademark is the smelting and refining of primary metals. Steel, tin and gold works imprint themselves on the senses. So do the chemical plants and flour mills. They can be heard, seen, and smelled. Big locomotive repair and servicing shops, along with shipyards, are evident as well. Novosibirsk's huge biceps and muscular upper arms have been built up by hard work.
> Novosibirsk is Siberia's central transportation hub. Trunk railway lines have played a major part in the city's growth. Local electric commuter trains link the suburbs to the city center. Up to 70,000 passengers move in and out of the city's

MAJOR SOVIET CITIES

New apartment buildings, like these in the city of Bratsk, reflect the rapid growth taking place in Siberia. After a hydroelectric plant was built in Bratsk in the 1960's, many new industries sprang up, creating thousands of jobs and increasing the population tenfold in ten years. Why is Siberia becoming "one big construction site"?

main railway station each day. In the southeast sector of the city, one of the largest railway marshalling yards in the country aligns freight cars twenty-four hours a day for transshipment throughout the Soviet Union. People can get about Novosibirsk on small craft and hydrofoil boats on the Ob River and by bus, streetcar, and trolleybus within the city. Two busy airports service both domestic and international air traffic.

Novosibirsk residents are proud of their big vibrant city. In terms of age, industrial makeup, transportation network, and central location, it is a bit like Chicago. In fact, it is often referred to as the Chicago of the USSR.*

1. Why is Moscow an important Soviet city? What problems does it face?
2. Why is Leningrad called the "Venice of the North?" How does its location affect daily life?
3. Why is Novosibirsk called "Chicago of the USSR?"

---

*Siberia and the Soviet Far East: Endless Frontiers by Abraham Resnick, 1983, Novosti Press Agency Publishing House, pp. 110–111. Reprinted by permission.

RURAL LIFE

About 25 million people—20 percent of the Soviet working population—are employed in agriculture. Although the living conditions of these people have improved in recent decades, they still do not enjoy the same benefits as city workers. As seen in the account below, rural life can be difficult:

Follow the country folk toward home at night, in the railroad stations, and you see what Russians call the *narod*, the masses. They are coarse, raw, simple people, weatherbeaten as the log cabins in which they live, hardy and enduring, made hard by a lifetime of battling the elements. I remember one evening walking through Kazan station. At 11 P.M. the waiting room was overflowing with a couple of thousand people. The peasant women, with broad, flat faces and cheeks worn smooth as the wood of a well-used washboard, were sturdy as work-horses. The shape of their bodies was lost under layers of faded, shapeless clothing. I studied one old woman. Under her worn, black velvet vest-jacket was a gray wool sweater; under

CHAPTER 43   CITY AND COUNTRY

that, an ankle-length housecoat in a flowered print; under that, another sweater, a calico dress and so on. All had long since lost their color, for each piece had obviously been made to survive from harvest to harvest, like the person who wore it. The young, teenage girls in bright jackets and plastic boots or even soldiers in khaki, seemed colorful by comparison. The peasant men were silhouettes of darkness. They wore dark, rumpled, tieless jackets and pants; thick, dark, scratchy wool overcoats; dark workers' caps or fur hats; black rubber boots or black shoes not shined for many, many years.

Follow the *narod* into the country and the modern world peels away. It surprised me to see that just ten miles [16 kilometers] from the Kremlin city life and its modern conveniences just come to an end. New apartment buildings give way to *izbas*, flat, low peasant log cabins. Side roads are suddenly no longer paved but turn to dirt, often no more than two ruts or footpaths dribbling off among garden fences. Thanks to Lenin's belief in electricity, most peasant homes have lights—and television. But plumbing remains a luxury for the future. Each vegetable garden has its outhouse in the corner. Along the roadside every few hundred yards there is a hand pump and a well. In the soft warmth of summer, or in the bitter cold of winter, I have watched country people crank up pails of water and then labor homeward with two buckets balanced carefully on a wooden shoulder-yoke. Off the main highways, I have seen peasant women doing their wash by hand in the fresh cold waters of the country streams, with the onion domes of a church visible over the trees.*

FARMS

Most of the Soviets who live in rural areas work on huge government-controlled farms. There are several types of these farms. One is the ***sovkhoz***, or state farm, which is operated like a government-run factory and whose workers are state employees who receive wages from the government. The first *sovkhozes* were formed in 1918 from land taken from Russian landlords and were to serve as examples of scientific ways of farming. Under Stalin, the *sovkhoz* system became more widespread. Today, *sovkhozes* are the largest and best-equipped farms in the country. Each averages about 112,000 acres (45,320 hectares) and employs about 600 workers. Most are located near large cities, which they supply with milk, eggs, poultry, and vegetables.

The *sovkhozes* are expected to show a profit. Their products are sold to government agencies at prices fixed by the state, and their workers draw monthly wages based on piece-work rates set by the government. The rates vary according to the importance and difficulty of the job. At the end of the farm year, the workers receive bonuses for any production that is higher than the goals set by the state planners.

This peasant woman with her workhorse is in front of a barn on the rural estate that once belonged to Soviet writer Leo Tolstoy. Where do most of the Soviets who live in rural areas work?

The Russians by Hedrick Smith, 1976, Hedrick Smith, p. 269. Adapted and reprinted by permission of Quadrangle/Time Books.

Another type of farm is the **kolkhoz,** or collective farm. On it, the key element is the family. All the families who live and work on the *kolkhoz* share the profits from the sale of grain and animals. While in theory these families run the farms, the government owns the land, chooses the officials, and decides what, where, and how much will be grown.

Although a *kolkhoz* may be made up of as many as several thousand families, in most cases there are about 440 families spread through several villages. Most live in individual cottages that have a fenced-in garden plot at the rear. A *kolkhoznik* is expected to work full-time with a work brigade. To increase production, competition among these brigades is encouraged. In this interview with Nikolai Sobchuk, director of a collective farm in the Ukraine, the problems of collective farm life are described:

Each year, about 40 workers reach retirement, and a somewhat larger number of children complete the 11 years of mandatory schooling. The pensioners stay on —some as consultants—but more than half of the graduates depart for Kiev, the Ukraine's largest city and capital, or elsewhere.

"We encourage them to stay," Sobchuk said, "but life on the soil is difficult, and other professions may appear more romantic."

Those who stay will work six days a week, except in heavier tasks, for which a second day off is given. Milkmaids work three of every four days.

In the Ukraine . . . , young people are finding the choice easy. Since 1970, the number of workers at [the collective farm] has fallen from 1,152 to 910.

Machinery helps to cushion their departure. Sobchuk estimates mechanization has

This collective farm family, dressed in traditional clothing and representing several generations, celebrates a holiday with a lavish meal served in the bright outdoors. What is the key element of the collective farm?

CHAPTER 43   CITY AND COUNTRY   715

The wooden houses of this Siberian village, with their blue and green shutters and planked, pitched roofs, are found throughout rural Siberia. Despite the cold climate and short growing season, many parts of Siberia have fertile soil where wheat and other crops are grown. From where does the Soviet government hope all food supplies will eventually come?

tripled since 1970, and the farm now has 75 tractors and its own workshops and garages.

"We have good machinery for cultivating corn and milking cows," said Sobchuk. "Our greatest need is for more leisure and better working conditions."

These are inducements that might keep more young people down on the collective farm.

Another concern for Sobchuk is budgeting. . . .

Each year, the farm is assigned production targets, which offer an index for measuring the degree of its success. Sobchuk, brisk and forceful, usually exceeds his targets.

"We sometimes discuss whether targets are realistic," he said, "but our positions are not always accepted."

The more Sobchuk exceeds the targets, the more money he has for incentive bonuses. . . .

Normally, drought strikes every other year in the Ukraine. Despite the lack of rain, Sobchuk expects to increase production over last year.*

---

*"Ukraine collective's chairman faces problems common to other farmers" by Watson Sims in *The Central New Jersey Home News*, published at New Brunswick, N.J. September 23, 1984, p. A1, A10. Reprinted by permission.

PEASANT MARKETS

Even with all of its huge farms, the Soviet Union still depends on private garden plots for about 30 percent of its food needs. The workers from state and collective farms who tend these plots keep the money earned from the produce they have grown. The plots may be small, but the produce from them usually is superior to that from the state farm. The land, however, still belongs to the state, and the private farming is done only with government permission. Basically, Soviet leaders dislike the private plots, but because of the country's present food shortages, they allow them to exist.

The Soviet government hopes that eventually all food supplies will come from collective and state farms. Meanwhile, the peasants are allowed to sell their produce in city markets. Below, a writer describes what she found when she visited a peasant market in Moscow:

> We walked toward the entrance of the market, which was ringed with *babushki* and *dyedushki* selling flowers—old women and old men thrusting stalks of red and

These fish vendors in a peasant market in a Siberian city on the Angara River have no problem selling their fresh catch to a throng of eager customers. How do some peasant markets differ from state-run stores?

white gladiolus into the afternoon sun. Russians of all ages and professions were happily inspecting and buying flowers; . . . Inside the market, the scarcity and preciousness of such products were confirmed as we looked at the outrageous prices of vegetables. Three rubles a kilo for carrots, five for apples—and this in summer in a city where an average worker makes about a hundred and fifty rubles a month. The market was a bustling big room filled with tables and with the smell of fruits, meats, and cheeses. . . . Meat and dairy counters lined the walls, and in the center of the room fruit and vegetables were set out in small careful arrangements. I was amazed at the quality and the variety of the produce: peaches, eggplant, lettuce, and squash, as well as the Moscow summer staples of tomatoes, cucumbers, and cabbage.

Behind the counters were not Muscovites, but farmers from the Caucasus and Black Sea regions: Armenians, Georgians, Moldavian women wearing copper earrings and brilliant scarves, Uzbek men in embroidered skullcaps. In the manner of vendors all over the world, they were vocal and dramatic, posturing, cajoling at the top of their lungs. . . . For all their village dress, the farmers looked sleeker than many Muscovites. . . . They come up from the Mediterranean climate of the south carrying fruits and vegetables, which they sell for immense profits; with some of the profits they buy luxuries unattainable in their regions—shoes, fashionable clothes, records—and resell the goods for inflated prices at home. . . .

Later we stood and looked around the room. The pace of the market was picking up as the afternoon wore on. Fruit vendors wheedled and babbled; dairy women slapped huge cream cheeses into shape; from across the room came a dull thudding as a butcher beat a carcass with the blunt end of an ax. . . . These vendors were hustling for themselves, and the result was a nearly complete absence of the shrugging, languid atmosphere that pervades so many state enterprises, where there is no sense of personal gain. . . . My Russian friends complain about the high prices of the peasant markets, but admit that these are the only places where you can find fresh vegetables in winter.*

1. How do many Soviet peasants live?
2. What kinds of farms exist in the Soviet Union? What problems do they face?
3. What role do private plots and peasant markets play in the Soviet Union?

---

*From *Russian Journal* by Andrea Lee. Copyright ©1979, 1980, 1981 by Andrea Lee. Reprinted by permission of Random House, Inc.

Exploration
SOVIET UNION

The four photographs that appear below point up several different aspects of urban life and rural life in the Soviet Union. Study each of the photos and determine what the photographer was trying to show. Then, based on the photographs and on the information in the chapter, compare and contrast urban and rural life in the Soviet Union.

CHAPTER 43 REVIEW

POINTS TO REMEMBER

1. Once largely rural, the Soviet Union now is urban. Because of industrial development in urban areas and the higher standard of living it brings, the number of people moving from the country to the city is increasing steadily.
2. Moscow is the largest city of the Soviet Union and a leading industrial and cultural center, which Russians view as the focal point of world communism. Many Soviet citizens want to live in Moscow because of the better quality of life available there.
3. Many Muscovites, unhappy with shortages, shoddy products, and the inefficiency of the state-controlled economy, turn to the black market to meet their needs. The *élite*, however, can get scarce and valuable goods and enjoy many privileges the average citizen does not.
4. Leningrad is a leading port and manufacturing center that is spread over 100 islands connected by bridges. It is known as the "Venice of the North."
5. Novosibirsk is one of the oldest and most important cities of Siberia. It is Siberia's central transportation hub and often is referred to as the Chicago of the USSR.
6. Soviets employed in agriculture and living in the countryside do not enjoy the same benefits as do city workers. Most work on huge government-controlled farms known as *sovkhozes* and *kolkhozes*. The *sovkhozes* are located near large cities and are the largest and best-equipped farms in the country. The *kolkhozes* are run by families.
7. Thirty percent of the Soviet Union's food needs are met by produce from small private garden plots tended by workers from state and collective farms. Products from the plots are sold in city markets, and the workers are allowed to keep the money earned from the sales.

VOCABULARY

Identify

Moscow   Red Square   GUM   Venice of the North
Kremlin   KGB   Leningrad   Novosibirsk

Define

black market   *dachas*   white nights   *sovkhoz*
élite   *kolkhoz*

DISCUSSING IMPORTANT IDEAS

1. More than 1 million Soviet citizens migrate each year from the countryside to the cities, where they settle permanently. In what ways do you think this will change the character of the Soviet Union and of its people?
2. Although Moscow, Leningrad, and Novosibirsk all are major Soviet cities, each is

very different from the others. In which would you prefer to live? Why?
3. How does rural life compare with urban life in the Soviet Union? How does each compare with that in your country?
4. There is a great disparity between Soviet workers and the Soviet *élite* in life style and material possessions. How would you account for this? What do you think could be done to bridge the gap?

DEVELOPING SKILLS

IDENTIFYING AMBIGUOUS OR EQUIVOCAL STATEMENTS

What might your first reaction be if someone said to you, "With that blonde hair, anyone can spot you from a mile away"? Chances are that you would take the comment to mean that the light color of your hair makes you stand out in a crowd. On second thought, however, you might decide that the comment was not meant as a compliment but as a criticism of your hair color.

Situations such as the one described above are not uncommon. They often happen because someone has made an ambiguous or equivocal statement. An *ambiguous statement* is a statement that is unclear or misleading by accident. An *equivocal statement* is a statement that is unclear or misleading on purpose. Both ambiguous and equivocal statements can be interpreted or understood in more than one way.

Look, for example, at the following statements and the questions in italics accompanying them:

1. Moscow has developed like a huge spiderweb fanning out from the center over the centuries. (*Which fanned out over the centuries, Moscow or the spiderweb?*)
2. Moscow, which is politically important, receives more and better goods and services than other Soviet cities. (*Does the fact that Moscow is politically important have anything to do with it receiving more and better goods and services?*)
3. Long lines of customers press in upon the sales counters inside the doors of Children's World. (*Are the sales counters inserted in the doors, or are they in Children's World itself?*)
4. To keep its citizens contented, even though it is illegal, the black market is tolerated by the Soviet government. (*What is illegal? Keeping citizens contented? The black market? The Soviet government?*)
5. Leningrad's northern location gives it very short periods of daylight in winter and in the early summer, white nights. (*Are the short periods of daylight just in the winter or in the winter and the early summer? When does Leningrad have white nights?*)

On first reading, the five statements may have seemed perfectly clear. However, after reading the questions that follow each of them, you can see why some people might consider them ambiguous or equivocal.

For practice in identifying ambiguous or equivocal statements, read the following passage several times, checking each statement to determine if it is really clear and understandable. Identify those statements that are ambiguous or equivocal.

With a population of 8.2 million people, the Soviet Union's largest city is Moscow. Like Leningrad and Novosibirsk, Moscow is rich in tradition and is important. Moscow is a leading center, industrial and cultural. An old city in the eyes of Russians once the center of Orthodox Christianity, it is viewed today as the focal point of world communism, a city at whose heart is the Kremlin. Moscow is an old fortress and the seat of the Soviet government, which thousands of people visit each day. The Kremlin is a little walled town inside Moscow. Along one side of the walls, where Lenin's tomb is found, is Red Square.

CHAPTER 44
THE ALL-POWERFUL STATE

1. What role does the Communist party have in the Soviet Union?
2. How do Soviet government policies affect the economy, culture, and religion?

Soviet tanks, missiles and artillery paraded through Red Square today in the annual Revolution Day ritual. . . .

. . . Marshal Sergei L. Sokolov . . . said in a keynote speech that . . . "We have never wavered and will never waver in the security of our country and the security of our allies."

The troops, banners snapping in a chilly breeze, answered with deep cries of "Hurrah!" that echoed off the Kremlin's red-brick wall.

Arrayed with Marshal Sokolov atop the Lenin Mausoleum were . . . other members of the civilian leadership, on one side, and the nation's military leaders, on the other side, as some of Russia's weaponry roared past trailing clouds of exhaust fumes.

In the cockpits of tanks and missile launchers, leather-helmeted officers saluted stiffly. . . .

Stamping troops followed in a display of precision-marching that saw elbows rising and falling in unison. . . .

The parade, which marked the . . . anniversary of the Bolshevik Revolution, then gave way to floats bearing political messages, led by a large wheeled portrait of Lenin. . . .

Tens of thousands of people streamed behind the floats through the broad square in an organized parade, carrying balloons, huge crepe-paper flowers and placards with slogans like "Glory to the domestic and foreign policy of the Communist Party."

As loudspeakers switched from Tchaikovsky's martial Fifth Symphony to cries of "Glory, glory, glory!" children ran up the steps of the mausoleum to hand the leaders bouquets of red carnations wrapped in plastic. . . .

With military power at its core, today's parade was a display of the central themes of nationhood stressed by the Soviet leadership.

It included placards bearing catch phrases of industrial and farm production, party loyalty and a foreign policy that is portrayed as defending peace in a world of aggressive forces. . . .

As the parade drew to an end, massed marchers filled the square waving red banners and joined in with recorded cheers:

"Glory to the great Lenin—Glory, glory, glory!

"Glory to the Communist Party of the Soviet Union—Glory, glory, glory!"

"Glory to the great Soviet people, builders of Communism —Glory, glory, glory!"*

Each November 7, the Soviet people celebrate the anniversary of the 1917 Revolution with a big parade on Red Square. The festivities are staged as a display of loyalty to the Soviet state and its leaders. Although during the early years of the Soviet Union, Communist leaders proclaimed that the state eventually would "wither away," today the Soviet state is larger and more powerful than ever. Its control extends to almost every area of Soviet life. Yet, in spite of this, many Soviets quietly look for ways to get around the system's many rules and restrictions.

*"Parade in Soviet Marks Revolution" by Seth Mydans in *The New York Times*, Nov. 8, 1984. Copyright ©1984 by The New York Times Company. Reprinted by permission.

THE PARTY

The power behind the Soviet state is the Communist party, which is set up like a pyramid—with organizations at local, regional, and national levels. The lower levels carry out decisions made by a small number of institutions at the top. One of these is the Central Committee, made up of 500 members elected every five years to represent all areas of the Soviet Union.

Above the Central Committee is the Secretariat, which handles the day-to-day work of the party, and the Politburo, a select committee of about 12 members. The Politburo meets weekly to make the party's—and the nation's—policy decisions. An official known as the General Secretary oversees both the Politburo and the Central Committee. The post of General Secretary, now occupied by Mikhail Gorbachev, is the most powerful office in the Soviet Union.

Since membership in the party opens the way to a good career and many material benefits, the 18 million members enjoy a privileged position in Soviet society. In return, the party expects devoted service. Party activists must attend meetings and perform administrative duties. On any public issue, they are expected to submit to the **party line,** or official viewpoint. In the article that follows, a Soviet reporter describes the work and attitudes of a local party official in Kirghizia:

> Roba Abdusamatova is the first secretary of the local town party committee. She has lived in Kara-Kul since 1977, when it first became a town, but it would be no exaggeration to say everybody in the area knows her. Roba says, "I'd like to have all the people here, young, and old, for friends and comrades."
>
> Her closest aides are those who work side by side with her. One of them is Lyudmila Stefanovich, second secretary of the party committee. It was mere coincidence that the two women arrived in Kara-Kul on the same day. At first Lyudmila did not like Kara-Kul and was homesick. She was unhappy and planning to leave. Roba befriended Lyudmila and convinced her to stay. "And I'm not sorry I did," Lyudmila says. . . .

Soviet youth fill the aisle in this convention hall, joining in the applause being offered by bemedaled Communist party officials and delegates from factories and industries throughout the Soviet Union. What is expected of Soviet Communist party members? What do they receive in return?

The day-to-day business of the town may look insignificant beside the magnitude of the construction work on the [nearby] power station. But they may seem so only to an outsider. Roba thinks differently and devotes an equal share of her energy and time to seemingly prosaic everyday matters. She meets with people who come to talk about the opening of a cafe in the city, about the construction of sports fields or summer camps for children. There is a lot of work to do. "The problem is how to find time for everything," says Roba.*

1. How is the Communist party organized?
2. What are some of the privileges and duties of Communist party members?

THE ECONOMY

The Soviet Union has the world's largest socialist economy. Under this system, the government owns the land, industries, banks, and communication and transportation systems. It organizes and controls the economy through a central planning authority known as *Gosplan*. It develops a Five-Year Plan in which production targets are set, prices and wages are fixed, and labor and raw materials are distributed over periods ranging from one month to five years.

Traditionally, the Plans set forth by *Gosplan* have emphasized heavy industry and military needs, but today increased attention is being given to consumer goods and agriculture. *Gosplan's* priorities are set by the Politburo, and a large, highly centralized bureaucracy exists to carry them out. Widespread corruption and inefficiency in the bureaucracy often has blunted effectiveness in certain areas, such as the quantity and quality of consumer goods.

In spite of such weaknesses, the Soviet economy has expanded rapidly under this system, and the Soviet Union now ranks second only to the United States in overall industrial productivity. Most Soviets take pride in their nation's industrial accomplishments. Certain key economic efforts, known as **hero projects,** are singled out for special attention. One of the most recent is the Baikal-Amur Mainline (BAM) Railway, a 3200 kilometer-(1920 mile-) long railroad that runs through the remote mountainous areas of eastern Siberia. Below, a young construction worker discusses his involvement in the building of the BAM, which has been called the world's largest construction project:

> In 1974, within months of the government announcement that the Baikal-Amur Railroad was to be built in Siberia, literally 200,000 Soviet citizens, most of them young people, declared their willingness to help in its construction.
> I was one of the first lucky ones to receive that coveted assignment to the BAM . . . construction project. . . . I had everything going for me—I loved my job, I had my friends, I was young and I lived on the Volga. . . . But I decided to leave this all behind to become a member of a construction team on the railroad.
> There are eighteen people in my brigade. We had come from all over the country, had all listened to the radio and watched television programs about Siberia's riches, riches still to be procured and turned to the country's benefit. And how could young people like us fail to be inspired to action by the sight and sound of all that natural wealth? This was the job for us—remarkable, worthwhile and tough! Siberia cried out for young people, and we answered that call.
> The distance between Ust-Kut in the west to Komsomolsk-on-Amur in the east is 3,145 kilometers (nearly 2,000 miles). The railroad will travel between them, across areas susceptible to earthquakes

---

*"A Businesslike Woman" by Kadyrkul Omurkulov in *Soviet Life*, December 1981, Vol. 12, No. 303, pp. 33, 35.

With the aid of a crane, these workers are laying a section of ready-made track for the Baikal-Amur Mainline Railroad. Completed in October 1984 at a cost of $14 billion, two-thirds of the railroad track is built over permafrost. What obstacles did the builders of the BAM have to overcome?

and over mountains rising as high as 3,000 meters (9,900 feet). Rivers are another obstacle we come up against. The track goes across more than 3,000 bridges. This is on average one per kilometer (or every half a mile) of track. My friends and I have often joked that building BAM means building bridges and tunnels and joining them up with rails! Experts insist that there is only one other place in the world with a comparably difficult terrain—the basin of the Amazon River. BAM runs through the taiga, across marshes and across areas of permafrost. All of it very hostile terrain.

When I look at a geographical map of Siberia, I see BAM as a trunk from which lesser lines branch out to areas of mineral deposits, toward new villages and new factories. Journalists have dubbed BAM the building project of the century. I'd totally agree with that judgement.

We would like to earn by our work the right to lay the final "golden section" of the Baikal-Amur Railroad. Our brigade is building a tunnel through the Northern Muysk mountain range. This tunnel, over 15 kilometers (9 miles) long, will be the longest on the railway.

I have a dream of traveling along BAM with my son from Lake Baikal to the Pacific coast. We'll sit in a cosy compartment and look out of the window. My son will study the villages, towns, factories and construction sites, that the railroad has made possible, flashing past and exclaim at each one, "You mean there wasn't anything here ten years ago and wild bears used to live in the taiga!"*

1. What kind of economy does the Soviet Union have? How does the Soviet government control it?
2. What are the strengths and weaknesses of the Soviet economy?

THE ARTS

Because the Soviet government believes that culture is an important tool in advancing the goals of communism, it actively controls and promotes a wide variety of cultural activities. As a result, more books are published, more film tickets are sold, and more dance companies are supported in the Soviet Union than in any other nation in the world. Soviet citizens enjoy public poetry readings and ballet as much as sporting events. They are especially proud of their land's cultural heritage, much of which comes from nineteenth-century Russia.

---

*"Siberia cried out for young people" in *We Live in the Asian U.S.S.R*, edited by E. Ryabko, 1985, Bookwright Press, pp. 22–23. Reprinted by permission.

A GOLDEN AGE

During the 1800's and early 1900's, Russia enjoyed a golden age of culture during which musicians, artists, and writers created a large number of outstanding works that captured the admiration of the world. Such composers as Peter Tchaikovsky, Modest Mussorgsky, and Nikolai Rimsky-Korsakov produced many operas, symphonies, and ballets that expressed a deep love for the Russian land and people. Such artists as Ilya Repin and Vasili Perov reproduced on their canvases the serenity of the Russian countryside as well as the often harsh life of peasants and workers.

The highest peak of development, however, was in literature, where Russian writers combined artistic creativity with concern for their country's social and political problems. In the poem, "The Bronze Horseman," for example, the country's first great poet, Alexander Pushkin, wrote about the conflict between the downtrodden individual and the powerful state. In *The Inspector-General*, regarded as one of Russia's greatest plays, writer Nikolai Gogol satirized bad government officials.

Although best known for his long poems, Russian poet Alexander Pushkin (1799–1837) also wrote many plays, short lyrical poems, and short stories. What did Pushkin write about in "The Bronze Horseman"?

The Fair, *a 1906 painting by Russian artist Boris Kustodiev, is a study in contrast with a colorful fair in the foreground set against a subdued background. When was Russia's golden age of culture?*

In the middle and late 1800's, the country's leading novelists—Ivan Turgenev, Leo Tolstoy, and Fyodor Dostoevsky—were dominant. While Turgenev vividly portrayed rural life in *A Sportsman's Sketches*, Tolstoy captured many nineteenth-century historical events, characters, and social customs in his epic novels *War and Peace* and *Anna Karenina*. At the same time, in *Crime and Punishment* and *The Brothers Karamazov*, Dostoevsky focused on human crime and guilt and the need for religious faith. Later, in *The Cherry Orchard* and other plays, playwright Anton Chekov presented the despair and isolation of the declining nobility on the eve of revolution. Another playwright, Maxim Gorky, in *The Lower Depths* described the miserable living conditions of the new urban working class.

CULTURAL FIGURES

Fyodor Dostoevsky (1821–1881)
A writer who focused on crime, guilt, and the need for religious faith. His major works include *Crime and Punishment* and *The Brothers Karamazov*.

Leo Tolstoy (1828–1910)
A writer who captured 19th century historical events, characters, and social customs. His major works include *War and Peace* and *Anna Karenina*.

Peter Ilich Tchaikovsky (1840–1893)
A composer who produced many operas, symphonies, and ballets that expressed a deep love for the Russian land and people. His classic ballets include *Swan Lake*, *Sleeping Beauty*, and *The Nutcracker*.

Ilya Yemovich Repin (1844–1930)
An artist known for the power of his works, which include historical subjects and the serenity of the Russian countryside.

Sergei Prokofiev (1891–1953)
A composer who added modern features to the classical tradition of 19th century Russia. His works include *Romeo and Juliet* and the musical fairy tale "Peter and the Wolf."

Alexander Solzhenitsyn (1918–   )
A writer who won the 1970 Nobel prize for literature. Two of his novels, *One Day in the Life of Ivan Denisovich* and *The First Circle*, reflect his prison and war experiences.

Rudolph Nureyev (1938–   )
A ballet dancer well-known for his exciting stage presence and his strong, expressive dancing.

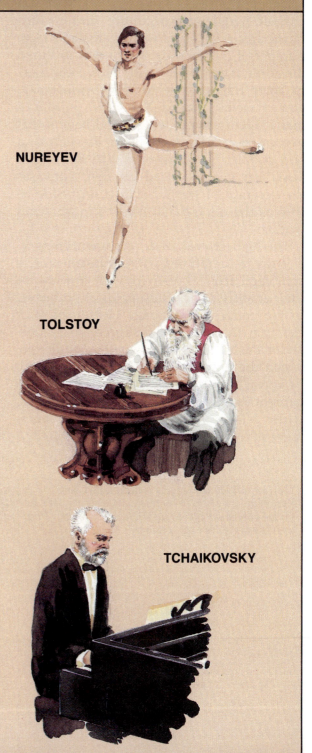

NUREYEV

TOLSTOY

TCHAIKOVSKY

SOVIET CULTURE

Since 1917, Soviet writers, artists, musicians, and filmmakers have continued to make many contributions. Some writers, like Vladimir Mayakovsky, have praised Communist ideals, while others, like Anna Akhmatova, have devoted their works to such personal themes as love and friendship. Still others, like Mikhail Sholokhov, the Soviet Union's first Nobel Prize winner in literature, have written historical novels about the revolution.

Painters like Kazimir Malevich and Lyubov Popova have helped lay the foundations of modern art, while composers like Dmitri Shostakovich, Aram Khachaturian, and Sergei Prokofiev have added modern features to the classical tradition of nineteenth-century Russian music. And filmmakers like Sergei Eisenstein, whose *Battleship Potempkin* and *Alexander Nevsky* were based on Russian history, have made powerful films.

In spite of these accomplishments, the Soviet government often has placed severe restrictions on cultural life. Writers, artists, musicians, and filmmakers opposing government policies have been pressured, ridiculed, imprisoned, or forced to leave the country. Boris Pasternak, for example, won a Nobel Prize in 1958 for his novel *Doctor Zhivago*, but he was not allowed to go to the West to receive his prize. Author Alexander Solzhenitsyn was forced into exile in 1974 after he wrote works critical of the Soviet prison-camp system. And such leading ballet stars as Rudolf Nureyev, Mikhail Baryshnikov, and Natalia Makarova have defected, or fled voluntarily, so that they could develop their talents more fully in the West.

On the other hand, artists willing to work within official limits are rewarded with high government salaries. To comply, however, they must follow a government-imposed style called **socialist realism** in which they must ignore the faults of Soviet society and praise its goals and accomplishments. Although many writers, such as Andrei Voznesensky and Yevgeny Yevtushenko, have been allowed to focus on mildly controversial themes in return for their overall support of government policies, others write secretly. Then they circulate their works underground through a system known as **samizdat,** a Russian word meaning "self-publishing."

In spite of Communist restrictions, both modern and pre-revolutionary theatrical groups like the Moscow Art Theater and the Bolshoi Theater have thrived. Below, a West German journalist describes and comments on a typical theatrical season in Moscow:

> Soviet theatergoers enjoy a wide range of standard fare. They like spectacles that reflect modern life—wives betrayed, citizens corrupted, officials clawing their way to the top, and young people acting out

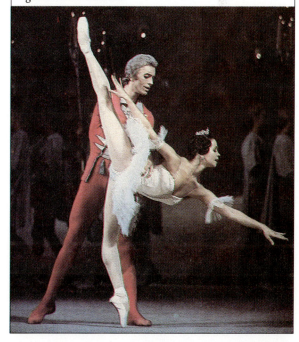

Nadezhda Pavlova and Vyacheslav Gordeyev perform Tchaikovsky's ballet "The Nutcracker" at Moscow's Bolshoi Theater. What must artists do to receive high government salaries?

their aggressions. They also like to laugh at [the seventeenth-century French playwright] Molière's *Tartuffe,* marvel at Tolstoy's *Anna Karenina,* and deplore the decadence revealed in [American playwright] Tennessee Williams' *A Streetcar Named Desire.*

To obtain tickets to such plays, they must stand in line for hours at the box office and pay half a day's earnings. Or they must be willing to spend a week's wages for a black-market ticket.

Getting a ticket to a popular show in Moscow is almost impossible. The city's thirty-three theaters have a total of 35,000 seats, but this does not begin to fill the demand in a metropolis of more than eight million. The prime attraction, the Bolshoi, is known as a "hard-currency" attraction. Most of its tickets go to Western tourists.

In addition, the government daily *Izvestia* has disclosed, there is an "unwritten list" of people who have prior access to coveted Bolshoi tickets. Other theaters give preferential treatment to members of thirty-six organizations, and high-ranking officials get first priority for orchestra and box seats.

When they finally obtain tickets, Soviet citizens regard their evening in the theater as a special occasion. Women wear their best dresses, and men bring out their medals.

The adult puppet theater is especially popular. *Don Juan 85,* a major hit, has been sold out for years. . . .

Moscow's younger audiences want tickets for *Iona and Aula,* a rock opera at the Lenin Komsomol Theater. Its hero is the merchant Nikolai Resanov, who sailed to San Francisco in 1806, fell in love there with the daughter of the Spanish governor, and then died on his journey home, leaving a child.

The conservative party bureaucracy would rather see plays about life on the battlefield, on the assembly line, or at a political meeting. *Pravda,* the Communist Party daily, asks for more government control of what appears on Moscow stages. It prefers "heroes who embody socioeconomic forces" to "family conflicts and antiheroes."

Party-approved fare this season includes *Optimistic Tragedy,* a revolutionary classic in a new production at the Lenin Komsomol. A commissar convinces an anarchist sailor that the Bolshevik cause is the true way.

The Vachtangov Theater is presenting *A Day Longer than Life* by the Kirghiz writer Genghis Aimatov. Its central character is a World War II veteran who made the shameful mistake—for a Soviet soldier —of being captured by the Nazis. . . . After the war . . . , secret police arrest the former soldier, and he dies in a labor camp. But Stalin, the "Great Leader," knows nothing of this injustice. Doubts about such issues are not permitted.

There is little Soviet ideology onstage at the Mayakovsky Theater. *And Fear the Silver Threads* depicts a bitter, elderly writer in his *dacha* near Moscow. "I have never written the truth in my entire life," he declares. His humble surroundings attest that he would have done better to write against the currents.

In a former moviehouse, seating only 200, . . . the innovative Boris Pokrovski, formerly a director with the Bolshoi, is presenting contemporary Western opera with twenty-five mimes and twenty musicians.

The most recent product of the avant-garde [forward-thinkers] is a pair of Chekov plays. In one of them, *The Wedding,* . . . the cast and a small orchestra are crammed into a small space near the audience.
It is theater you can reach out and touch.*

1. What were the main cultural themes during the golden age? What are they today?
2. How does the Soviet government regard cultural activity?

---

*"The Soviets on Stage," excerpted from "Der Spiegel" of Hamburg, in the New York Times Syndication Sales, January, 1985, pp. 59–60. Reprinted by permission.

RELIGION AND DISSENT

Although the Soviet Constitution grants freedom of religion to religious believers, officially the Soviet Union is **atheistic,** disbelieving in the existence of God. Religious beliefs are ridiculed in the press, believers are denied good jobs, and religious activities are forbidden outside of places of worship. The government keeps many religious buildings closed and closely supervises the few religious institutions that are allowed to exist.

In spite of these restrictions, however, about 40 percent of the Soviet people might be considered believers. Estimates place the number of Russian Orthodox at as many as 40 million. There also are about 55 million Muslims, 2 million Jews, and several million Roman Catholics, Evangelical Baptists, and Lutherans.

A great many of those Soviets who are believers do not attend worship services regularly. Those who do generally are elderly, poor, or uneducated. In recent years, however, some reports have indicated that an open interest in religion seems to be growing among some other groups of Soviet citizens. This interest has been noticed even among young people from secular or Communist backgrounds. In the article that follows, an Italian journalist comments on a meeting he had with a young Soviet believer studying for the Russian Orthodox priesthood:

> During an interval between [religious] ceremonies my friends introduced me to a 32-year-old recent seminarian named Alexander Lokhanov. He had been a student at a technical institute but left it when he felt drawn to the Christian faith. He became one of the 1,300 students attending the day or correspondence departments of the Moscow Academy of Theology and the Theological Seminary.

Heading the procession at this Russian Orthodox service is the Patriarch of Moscow. How many Soviets are estimated to be Russian Orthodox?

> Alexander had thought well before deciding to become a priest. Courteous and affable, he told me in almost perfect English about his theological studies and about his study of general problems of philosophy and culture. Like other young people (engineers and technicians, actors and artists, workers and farmers, sailors and fishermen), he had chosen his profession without pressure from anywhere. Probably I shall come here again some day and meet Alexander Lokhanov at one of the monasteries or churches. He will be known by a different name as he will have been ordained [become a priest] by then. I spent about an hour talking with him in the garden of the Academy, which was at a distance from other buildings within the high white walls of the monastery.*

The existence of religion in the Soviet Union after nearly 70 years of Communist rule underlines that fact that, despite its

---

*How I "Discovered" Religion in Russia by Aldo Quinto Lazzari, Novosti Press Agency Publishing House, 1985, pp. 46–47. Reprinted by permission.

great authority, the Soviet state has not been able to impose its views on all its citizens. In recent years, a small group of religious believers and secular human rights activists have joined together to protest Soviet government policies. These dissidents, or government opponents, have been treated harshly by government authorities. Many have been sent to prison camps or forced into exile for supporting greater freedom in Soviet society. The leading dissident in the Soviet Union today is a physicist named Andrei Sakharov. In the following essay, Sakharov discusses his beliefs and his career:

> After 1970, the defense of human rights and of victims of political repression became my first concern. My collaboration . . . on the Moscow Human Rights Committee was one expression of that concern. . . .
>
> After my essay ["Thoughts on Progress, Peaceful Coexistence, and Intellectual Freedom"] was published abroad in July 1968, I was barred from secret work [as a scientist] and excommunicated from many privileges of the Soviet establishment. The pressure on me, my family, and my friends increased in 1972, but as I came to learn more about the spreading repressions, I felt obliged to speak out almost daily in defense of one victim or another. In recent years I have continued to speak out as well on peace and disarmament, on freedom of association, movement, information, and opinion, against capital punishment, on protection of the environment, and on nuclear power plants.
>
> In 1975 I was awarded the Nobel Peace Prize. This was a great honor for me, as well as recognition for the entire human rights movement in the USSR. In January 1980 I was deprived of all my official Soviet awards (the Order of Lenin, three times Hero of Socialist Labor, the Lenin Prize, the State Prize) and banished to Gorky, where I am virtually isolated and watched day and night by a policeman at my door. The regime's action lacks any legal basis. It is one more example of the intensified political repression that has gripped our country in recent years.
>
> Since the summer of 1969 I have been a senior scientist at the Academy of Sciences' Institute of Physics. My current scientific interests are elementary particles, gravitation, and cosmology.
>
> I am not a professional politican. Perhaps that is why I am always bothered by questions concerning the usefulness and eventual results of my actions. I am inclined to believe that moral criteria in combination with unrestricted inquiry provide the only possible compass for these complex and contradictory problems. I shall refrain from specific predictions, but today as always I believe in the power of reason and the human spirit.*

In the early 1950's, Andrei Sakharov helped build the Soviet Union's first hydrogen bomb. Since that time, he has become a strong advocate of world peace. Why is Sakharov considered a dissident?

1. What is the official Soviet policy toward religion? How does the government deal with it?
2. With what is the dissident movement in the Soviet Union concerned?

---

*"An Autobiographical Note" by Andrei Sakharov in *On Sakharov*, edited by Alexander Babyonyshev, translated by Guy Daniels, 1982, Alfred A. Knopf, Inc., pp. xiv-xv. Reprinted by permission.

EXPLORATION
SOVIET UNION

During both the tsarist and Soviet eras, Russian writers have commented on their country's social and political life, as in these two poems, the first by Alexander Pushkin and the second by Yevgeny Yevtushenko. After reading the poems, answer these questions.

1. What is the theme of Pushkin's poem? Of Yevtushenko's?

2. Based on the poems, how would you describe the attitude of Russian writers toward their country, its problems, and its achievements?

3. Based on the poems and the information in the chapter, do you think that writers have the same role in the West as they do in the Soviet Union? Explain.

Rulers! Your crown and throne were given you
By law—and not by nature;
You stand above the people,
But eternally higher than you is the law.

....

And learn this, O rulers:
Neither punishment nor reward,
Neither bloody dungeon nor altar
Will provide you with secure protection.
First place yourselves
Under the protection of trustworthy laws;
And freedom and peace will
Forever stand guard
*Over throne and people.**

Russia has changed, Yesenin my friend,
but, to my mind, shedding tears is purposeless:
I hesitate to say that things are on the mend
—and to say they're worse is dangerous.

There's no end of new buildings and
  sputniks to spare,
but the going was rough and on the way we
  lost twenty millions in the war
—and millions more in war upon the nation.

To forget this we'd have to cut out our
  memories,
but where's the axe to hack off recollection?
No one helps others as much as we Russians
—and no one's so given to self-destruction.

But our ship sails on: though the water's shallow
we haul Russia overland through thick and
  thin. . . .
No matter that there are scoundrels galore—
what's hard to bear is the loss of Lenin.

....

When pink-cheeked Komsomol [Communist Youth
  League] bigwigs
bang their fists and shout at us poets,
hoping to mould our souls like beeswax,
in order to re-create us in their likeness,
their words don't frighten us, Yesenin,
but neither do we find them comfortable,
and, believe me, I do not want to run,
hitching up my breeches, After such a Komsomol.

My Komsomol, with which I march in step,
is building Bratsk and ploughing up the
  Altai steppe;
the Komsomol after which I wish to run
has room for Pushkin, Mayakovsky and Yesenin.

....

But one must live—neither vodka, the rope
nor women can rescue us,
only you, our Russian land, give hope,
only your sincerity, Yesenin, saves us.

....

And the poetry of Russia goes
ahead under suspicion and attack,
yet, with a Yesenin hold it throws
*the West . . . flat upon its back.**

---

*Alexander Pushkin, as quoted in *Years of the Golden Cockerel* by Sidney Harcave, 1968, Random House, Inc., p.53. Reprinted by permission.

*"Letter to Yesenin" by Yevgeny Yevtushenko in *Post-war Russian Poetry*, edited and translated by Daniel Weissbort, 1974, Penguin Books, pp. 161–163. Reprinted by permission.

SOVIET UNION UNIT 7

CHAPTER 44 REVIEW

POINTS TO REMEMBER

1. The power behind the Soviet state is the Communist party, which has organizations at all levels. Its top institutions include the Central Committee, the Secretariat, and the Politburo.
2. While party membership opens the way to a good career and material benefits, party activists must attend meetings, perform administrative duties, and submit to the party line.
3. The Soviet Union has the world's largest socialist economy, which the government organizes and controls through *Gosplan*. In spite of weaknesses, the economy has expanded rapidly under this system, and the Soviet Union ranks high in overall industrial productivity.
4. The Soviet government actively promotes and controls cultural activities to advance the goals of communism.
5. During the 1800's and early 1900's, Russia enjoyed a golden age of culture, during which Russian artists became recognized internationally.
6. In spite of numerous modern-day artistic accomplishments, the Soviet government often has placed severe restrictions on cultural life. Only those artists willing to adhere to socialist realism are rewarded by the government.
7. Although the Soviet Constitution grants Soviet citizens freedom of religion, officially the Soviet Union is atheistic, and close watch is kept on religious institutions and believers.
8. Despite its great authority, the Soviet Union has not been able to impose its views on all its citizens. In recent years, dissidents have joined together to protest government policies.

VOCABULARY

Identify

Central Committee
Secretariat
Politburo
Mikhail Gorbachev
Gosplan
Baikal-Amur Mainline Railway

Peter Tchaikovsky
Ilya Repin
Alexander Pushkin
Nikolai Gogol
Ivan Turgenev
Leo Tolstoy

Fyodor Dostoevsky
Anton Chekov
Maxim Gorky
Vladimir Mayakovsky
Dmitry Shostakovich
Boris Pasternak

Alexander Solzhenitsyn
Mikhail Baryshnikov
Andrei Voznesensky
Yevgeny Yevtushenko
Andrei Sakharov

Define

party line
hero project

defected

social realism

samizdat
atheistic

DISCUSSING IMPORTANT IDEAS

1. In your opinion, what are the "central themes of nationhood stressed by the Soviet leadership?" How do they compare with those stressed by your government?

2. If you were a Soviet citizen, what do you think would be the advantages to being a member of the Communist party? The disadvantages?
3. How do you interpret the statement, "The Soviet government believes that culture is an important tool in advancing the goals of communism." Would you find it difficult to be an artist in the Soviet Union? Why or why not?
4. Considering the Communist party's strong belief in the value of culture, why do you think it places such severe restrictions on cultural life?

DEVELOPING SKILLS

IDENTIFYING EVIDENCE

Not long ago, some high school students formed an organization to fight crime in their neighborhoods. They invited a police detective to speak to them about ways to identify evidence. Although they understood the dictionary definition of *evidence*—"the data on which a judgment or conclusion may be based, or by which proof or probability may be established"—they were not sure how to identify evidence.

To help the students, the detective set up a mock robbery in which a student "stole" a notebook containing a test. Other students acted as eyewitnesses or as friends who were not present at the scene of the crime. One of the witnesses took a photograph of the robbery while it was in progress.

After the robbery, the detective explained that there are two kinds of evidence, that which is *admissible*—allowable or acceptable—and that which is not. For example, a statement by someone who did not actually see the crime committed is not admissible evidence. Only four kinds of evidence are admissible: (1) eyewitness accounts—statements by people who saw the crime in progress; (2) written documents—diaries, letters, memos, statements by an eyewitness, or other such material that is in writing; (3) visual evidence, such as photographs or videos; (4) objects, such as stolen items.

The students submitted the following as evidence: accounts by eyewitnesses and by friends, a note from the robber telling a friend that he planned to steal a copy of the test, the stolen notebook, and a photograph taken by a witness. To determine which of these truly were evidence, they posed these questions:

1. Is this a statement by a witness?
2. Is it a written document?
3. Is it visual evidence?
4. Is it an object related to the crime?

Based on the answers to these questions, the students determined that the only evidence not admissible was the accounts by friends who were not present at the scene of the crime.

The same definitions and questions can help you identify evidence to support your studies. Consider, for example, this statement: "In spite of government restrictions, Soviet culture continues to thrive." If you study the section on Soviet culture on pages 325 and 326 and answer the following questions, you will have identified evidence to support the statement:

1. Are there statements by eyewitnesses? *(yes, a primary source about theater)*
2. Are there written documents? *(Yes, the journalist's account is a written statement by an eyewitness.)*
3. Is there visual evidence? *(yes, photographs of dancers and a chart on cultural figures)*
4. Are there objects? *(No, but a trip to a museum can "provide" such objects as paintings.)*

For practice in identifying evidence, read the section on religion and dissent on pages 327 and 328, and identify the evidence used to support this statement: "The Soviet government has not been able to impose its views on all its citizens."

CHAPTER 45
SOVIET LIFE

1. What is the role of the family in Soviet life?
2. What leisure activities do Soviets enjoy?

Nourouz Ramazonov, 50 years old, works as a machine operator in a Baku oil refinery. His wife Miravid, 45, also works there. The Ramazonovs have four children, three of whom still live with their parents. One son, in his twenties, also works in the refinery.

The Ramazonovs live in a small crowded apartment which they rent from the government. The apartment is located in a multi-storied apartment building, one of many such dwellings in a busy residential area of Baku. It has two small bedrooms, a bathroom, and a tiny kitchen. An adjoining balcony is used for storage space. The center of family activities is the medium-sized living-dining room. The furnishings of this room are very simple: a cloth-covered dining table with a large samovar (urn for making tea), a glass-door china closet, a black-and-white television set, a few chairs, and a couch that also serves as a bed. There is a telephone and a sewing machine. The most outstanding attractions are the hand-made, red oriental rugs that adorn the walls.

Both Nourouz and Miravid were born and raised in poor rural areas of Azerbaijan. After their marriage, they moved to the city and found jobs. They worked hard, and over the years, their standard of living has improved considerably. Today, Nourouz is a distinguished member of the Communist party and serves as a deputy in the Azerbaijan Supreme Soviet (regional parliament). As a result of Nourouz's job and party ties, his family enjoys certain privileges. For example, he has had the opportunity to travel abroad. Despite this, the Ramazonovs still lead a relatively simple life style.

The leisure hours of the Ramazonovs are taken up with a variety of interests. Nourouz and Miravid often entertain relatives and friends at home. At these gatherings, Miravid serves borsch (beet soup), various fish and chicken dishes, cheese, vegetables, matzoni (yogurt), fresh fruit, and honey-nut pastries, such as baklava. The Ramazonovs enjoy watching television or listening to music on the radio or record player. The male members of the family jog, play handball, and attend wrestling matches, while the females sew, read, and clean house. All of the Ramazonovs take turns shopping in neighborhood markets. Once a week, the family goes to a movie or a concert.

During the summer, the Ramazonovs go on vacation. The younger children spend a few weeks at the oil workers' Pioneer Camp, while the older family members often go to Sochi, a famous Black Sea resort.

The Soviet state cares for its citizens by guaranteeing employment, providing free education and health care, and improving the standard of living. At the same time, however, it calls upon the people to work harder, keeps watch over their conduct, and punishes any serious misbehavior. Yet, despite the pressures placed on them to conform, when they are with family and close friends, Soviet citizens like the Ramazonovs find ways to express their "real" selves.

*Interview with the Ramazonov family in Baku, Azerbaijan S.S.R., by Dr. Abraham Resnick, April 1985. Reprinted by permission.

FAMILY

Traditionally, family ties have been strong in Russia and other parts of the Soviet Union. In recent years, however, such pressures of modern life as the growth of industry and cities have strained many family relationships. The urban housing shortage, for example, has forced parents, grown children, and even grandparents to share an apartment. Such crowded conditions often lead to stress and conflict.

As a result, there is a trend toward smaller families, especially among ethnic Russians. Today, the average young Russian couple has only one child. Both the husband and wife usually work because they need two incomes to meet expenses and because communism teaches that all able-bodied people must work to build a socialist society. An elderly relative or social workers in day-care centers take care of the working couple's child.

In Georgia, Armenia, Azerbaijan, and the Central Asian republics, however, larger families still are common. These families often include aunts, uncles, and cousins, all of whom live under one roof. Thus, more people are at home to take care of the children while the parents are at work. Also, a large number of people in these areas still believe that having many children brings honor to a family and guarantees security in old age.

Although many Soviet families live in crowded apartments, some do live in their own homes. One such family is the Platonovas. Below, Nina Platonova, a 28-year-old linen factory worker, describes her family's life style and their home on the outskirts of Smolensk, an old Russian town about 235 miles (375 kilometers) southwest of Moscow:

> [My husband Sergei and I] own our own house, a wooden one which was built by Sergei's parents. It has all the necessary conveniences—electricity, central heating, water, gas and so on. The half-hectare (1-acre) plot that adjoins it is given over to an orchard and kitchen garden. All the family help with those; even our six-year-old, Sasha, putters around there, especially when it's time to pick something.

This Soviet couple is more fortunate than many others since they only need to share their apartment with their two children. The Soviet housing shortage was heightened during World War II when about 6 million houses and apartment buildings were destroyed. Today, the government is building about 2 million new, small housing units each year to try and fill the gap. How has the housing shortage affected many Soviet families?

Sergei's parents live next door and they help us by looking after Sasha while we are out at work.

There are some outbuildings, and we use one of them as a garage. Sergei's parents used to keep a horse; now we "stable" our car, a Lada, there. Another one is used for chickens and ducks, and we have recently added a calf to our livestock. My friends often seem surprised that we have enough money to run such a large household and buy expensive goods at the same time.

My wages depend on the quality of the material I turn out, and there is a bonus for exceeding the quota. Sergei's wages are calculated according to the length of material turned out by the 24 looms he services. On the average, I get 210 roubles ($260) a month and Sergei 270 ($340), which leaves us a total of 426 roubles ($530) a month after deduction of income tax.

How do we spend this money? Our main expenditure is running the car, which, including fuel, costs 100 roubles ($125) a month. Food—cereals, flour, bread, tea, coffee and so on—costs 80 roubles ($100). (Dairy products, some meat and most of our fruit and vegetables come from our own orchard and kitchen garden.) Heating, insurance and telephone bills come to about 6 roubles ($7.50), and newspapers and magazines another 6. Tickets to the theater, the movies, and the sports stadium (Sergei is a football fan) cost 10 roubles, and another 40 goes for all sorts of small household items. Altogether, our basic living expenses come to 242 roubles ($300) a month, which leaves 184 roubles ($230). Some of this goes for clothes and shoes, and I try to put 100 roubles a month in the savings bank. Part of these savings go for vacations—we like traveling by car around the Crimea and Caucasus—and the remainder is set aside for major purchases.*

---

*"Our linen is known as 'northern silk'" in *We live in the European U.S.S.R.* by E. Ryabko, 1985, The Bookwright Press, pp. 22–23. Reprinted by permission.

1. What difficulties do modern Soviet families face?
2. On what items might a Soviet family spend its income?

WOMEN

The 1917 Revolution led to an official declaration of equality that made all Soviet women equal to men. According to the Soviet constitution, both women and men have equal access to education, employment, and other areas of public life. To enable women to work and at the same time raise a family, the law provides such special labor and health services as paid work leaves for expectant mothers and reduced work hours and child-care support for mothers of small children.

The Soviets are proud of their record on women's rights. They point out how Soviet women over the years have made many notable contributions to the nation's growth and security. During World War II, for example, about 800,000 women served as fighter pilots, mechanics, and combat soldiers. After the war, due to the loss of so many Soviet males, women contributed heavily to the rebuilding of the economy.

Today, women make up 51 percent of the Soviet Union's labor force. About 93 percent of working-age women hold full-time jobs. This is the highest percentage of any industrial country. In addition, one-third of the country's lawyers and 70 percent of the doctors are women, and there are more female scientists and engineers in the Soviet Union than in any other country of the world.

Despite this, many Soviet women complain that they often are treated as second-class citizens. Although official policy promises women and men equal pay and working conditions, women rarely are promoted to high-level positions. Many, in fact, hold the

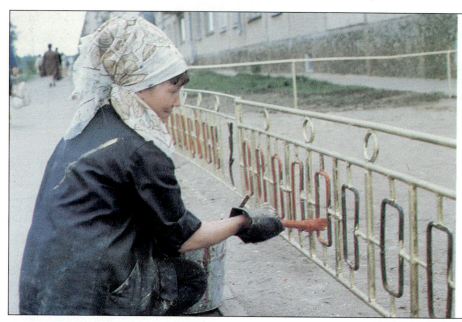

This female worker, in white and brown flowered kerchief and painter's clothes, is putting a fresh coat of red paint on the grillwork fence that surrounds an office building in a Siberian city. Like many other urban Soviet women, in addition to holding a job, she will have to spend an average of 14 hours a week waiting in lines to do her shopping. Besides these responsibilities, what other work do Soviet women routinely perform?

lowest-paying jobs that involve hard manual labor. For example, city streets are cleaned by groups of women with brooms, and potholes are filled by women construction workers using picks and shovels.

Also, women at all levels of Soviet society not only work outside the home but shop, do housework, and tend to their children as well. There are few labor-saving appliances, and Soviet husbands generally refuse to help with household chores. These added burdens leave most women little time or energy to move ahead in their careers or to participate in community activities.

The hectic life of modern Soviet women is revealed in the following excerpt from Alexander Solzhenitsyn's novel, *The Cancer Ward*. It describes the thoughts and actions of Ludmila Afanasyevna, a doctor who works in the cancer ward of a hospital and is on her way home to her husband and son after a day at work:

> . . . The compelling momentum of her work was very difficult to escape. As each day drew to its end she would note with annoyance that once again she hadn't had time to do everything. . . .
> She put out the lamp in her office, but turned back from the door to make note of some things that needed doing next day. . . .
> At last she walked down the steps between the poplars and along the pathways of the Medical Center. Her thoughts, though, remained with her work: she did not even try or want to try to rid herself of them. The weather was nondescript, she didn't notice what it was like. It was just before twilight. . . .
> Once Ludmila Afanasyevna was through the gate, she ought to have made the transition from the working part of her life to the domestic, to her family. But no, her time and energy were not equally divided between work and home. Inside the Medical Center she spent the better and fresher half of her waking hours. Ideas about her work were still circling around her head like bees long after she had left the gates, and in the morning long before she reached them.
> She . . . crossed the road to the streetcar circle. A trolley with the right number

swung round with a slight clank. There was a rush through both front and back doors. Ludmila Afanasyevna hurried to grab a seat—and this was the first tiny thought apart from the hospital that began to transform her from an oracle of human destinies into a simple passenger on a trolley jostled like anyone else. . . .

Many of the women in the trolley, like Ludmila Afanasyevna, were carrying not handbags but big bags like small suitcases that could hold a live piglet or four large loaves of bread. At every stop and with every shop that flashed by the window, Ludmila Afanasyevna's thoughts turned more and more to her housework and her home. Home was her responsibility and hers alone, because what can you expect from men? Her husband and son, whenever she went to Moscow for a conference, would leave the dishes unwashed for a whole week. It wasn't that they wanted to keep them for her to do, they just saw no sense in this repetitive, endlessly self-renewing work.

Today was Friday. On Sunday she absolutely must get through a lot of washing that had piled up. This meant that dinner for the first half of the week had to be got ready and cooked, come what may, on Saturday evening (she prepared it twice a week). As for putting the washing on to soak, that had to be done today, whatever time it meant getting to bed. Even though it was getting late, now was the only time left to go to the main market.

She got out to change trolleys, but, looking through the plate-glass window of a nearby grocery store, decided to go in. . . .

She wanted to get two bottles of sunflower-seed oil . . . and some barley concentrate. From the grocery counter she cut across the quiet shop, paid at the cash desk and went back to collect them. [In Soviet markets, a shopper stands in one line to select goods, another to pay for them, and a third to pick them up.]

She was standing in line behind two men when suddenly there was a hubbub in the shop. People were pouring in from the street, forming lines at the delicatessen counter and at the cashier. Ludmila Afanasyevna started, and without waiting to collect her goods in the grocery department hurried across the line up at the delicatessen counter and at the cashier. So far there was nothing to be seen behind the curved glass cover of the counter, but the jostling women were absolutely confident. Minced-ham sausage was going to be sold, one kilo for each buyer.

What a stroke of luck! It was worth going to the back of the line a bit later for a second kilo.*

1. How did the 1917 Revolution affect the status of Soviet women? What do the constitution and Soviet law provide them?
2. Why do many Soviet women complain that often they are treated as second-class citizens?

YOUTH AND EDUCATION

Soviet youth generally are raised in an atmosphere of loving discipline. At home, they are smothered with attention and protection almost up to their teens. At school, they are taught to be obedient to authority and to place the aims of the group above individual desires.

ELEMENTARY AND HIGH SCHOOL

From ages 6 to 17, Soviet youth are required to attend school six days a week, from September to late May. The educational system is centralized throughout the country. Teachers at each grade level use the same books and teach the same lesson at the same

---

The Cancer Ward by Alexander Solzhenitsyn, 1972, Bantam Books, pp. 90–92. Reprinted by permission.

time. The course of study heavily favors mathematics, science, and foreign languages, and students receive political instruction. At age 15, all students must take an examination that determines who will continue general studies and go on to a university and who will enter a trade or vocational school. Below, in an interview with Sasha Sokolova, a Moscow teenager who lives in an apartment with her mother and another family, an American writer discusses school in the Soviet Union:

"My mother's job takes her out of town on business trips," Sasha tells me, "so I go to a school where I can stay overnight if she is gone. It's called an *internat*. For free, I can stay as many nights as I need to, and have all my meals there as well. My school is specialized in another way: We all study Chinese from the second grade on. It is my hardest subject."

Many schools in the Soviet Union teach a foreign language, beginning in the earliest grades. Only two schools teach Chinese. The most popular language to learn is English.

"All of us students have notebooks, called diaries, where our teachers write in our daily grades for every lesson," Sasha explains. "The highest grade is 5, and 2 is the lowest. If we get too many 2's, we can't go on field trips. We have about three hours of homework every night. . . ."

I ask Sasha what kids wear to school, and she smiles. "We have to wear a uniform to school; it is the same all over the country," she says. "Girls wear dark dresses with white pinafores; boys wear dark pants and white shirts. We all wear red kerchiefs." After school, jeans are among the most popular clothes for kids.

Once a week, Sasha's school holds a dance for students in the sixth grade and up. The most popular musical groups are Abba from Sweden, Boney M from Jamaica, and The Time Machine, a Moscow group. Western records cannot be sold in the Soviet Union. But Western groups are known because tourists bring in tapes and records that are copied and passed on.

After school, kids can take part in activities sponsored by the Young Pioneers, the Soviet youth organization. Students interested in space flight can join the Future Cosmonauts Club. Other students might learn ballroom dancing, put on a play, or raise tropical plants in a greenhouse. Since

These Young Pioneers and others like them spend much of their time at summer camp working. Members of the Young Pioneers range from age 10 to age 15. Younger children, from age 7 to age 9, may join the Little Octobrists, another party-sponsored youth group, while older teens and young adults may join the young Communist League. What other forms of recreation do Soviet young people enjoy?

few Soviet kids hold after-school jobs (they get spending money from their parents), they have time for these activities.

The school year runs from September 1 to May 28. When school lets out for the summer, Sasha goes away for vacation. "Every summer I go stay with my grandmother, who lives in the mountains. There, I work in the garden and go swimming and run around!" But for Sasha, there's no place like home: I'm always happy to come back to Moscow."*

HIGHER EDUCATION

After high school, some young Soviets fulfill their military obligation or enter the work force. Others choose to enter an institute that trains students for technically skilled jobs. Still others try to get into a university. Although higher education is free for those who qualify, only limited space is available at institutes and universities. As a result, the competition is fierce. To be admitted to these schools, students have to pass five difficult qualifying examinations. In the end, only one out of every five students is accepted.

Following graduation, students are assigned jobs by the government for a period of three years. Often, these positions are in places like Siberia, where the state is promoting economic development and labor is scarce. Although students generally are attracted by the extra pay and privileges these positions bring, after the required number of years is completed, many of them look for employment in the more developed areas of the Soviet Union. In the following interview, Timur Khalikov, a 23-year-old student in the Tajik Soviet Socialist Republic, discusses his university life and his future plans:

When I left school the construction of the Nurek hydroelectric plant was in full

It is not unusual for Soviet students like these to have their schoolwork supervised by other students if they do not perform to acceptable standards. What choices do Soviet students have after high school?

swing. . . . Like many others of my age I headed for the construction site. . . .

I worked on the construction site for two years, and then I entered the polytechnic institute [at Dushanbe]. My choice of department at the institute was, naturally, influenced by the job I was doing. I am taking an electrical engineering course. The town where I'm studying lies among mountains. The present population of the town is over half a million. This includes fifty thousand young people studying at the university, the polytechnic, and the agricultural, medical and teacher-training colleges.

Now I'm in my fourth year of studies, and in another year I shall graduate. But at present I'm studying and taking tests and exams. A student doesn't have much free time, but when I can manage some I like going to the movies or a disco. In

---

*"Inside the Soviet Union" by Naomi Marcus in *Junior Scholastic*, March 1985, p. 4. Reprinted by permission.

Soviet senior engineering student Valentina Nikulina, who wants to design engines, is conferring with a colleague at a design office where she is finishing the final work needed for her graduation from a technical institute. Such institutes serve 90 percent of higher education students. While universities generally train students for research, academics, and government work, institutes stress agriculture, medicine, teaching, and engineering. What do many higher education graduates do after completing their required government service?

springtime our town is shrouded in the pink and white haze of flowering trees. Every summer I go off for the long students' vacation to work with construction teams in Siberia, on the Yenisei River, where they're building the Sayan-Shushenskaya hydroelectric station, one of the biggest in the world. When I finish studying I shall go to work in Siberia and will help to build more new hydroelectric stations.*

1. What are elementary and high schools like in the Soviet Union?
2. What qualifications are needed for entry to Soviet higher education? What happens after graduation?

*"A student doesn't have much free time" in *We live in the Asian U.S.S.R.* by E. Ryabko, 1985, The Bookwright Press, pp. 26–27. Reprinted by permission.

LEISURE

The average Soviet citizen works about 41 hours a week. During much of the remaining time, he or she pursues a variety of leisure activities. In most cases, entertaining at home is the major social activity. At these gatherings, there usually is a generous amount of food and drink for the guests. In Russia, for example, the host or hostess begins the feast with *zakuski*, or snacks, which may include smoked salmon, caviar, pickles, and mushrooms. For the main course, there may be black bread, borsch, cucumbers in sour cream, sliced roast, potatoes, and baked pastry pies filled with meat and cabbage. For dessert, there generally is fresh fruit, cheesecake, sweet fruit-filled

CASE STUDY
SOVIET UNION

SOVIET ROCK FANS

Although many young Soviets aspire to be model Communists, others are more interested in pursuing personal goals. They are eager for more and better material goods and show a growing interest in rock music. They form rock bands, attend concerts, and idolize their favorite singers. The newspaper article below describes reactions to pop-singer Alla Pugachova:

Almost daily, young girls cluster around the entrance of an apartment block on [Moscow's] Gorky Street, hoping to catch a glimpse of its illustrious resident, Soviet pop-music queen Alla Pugachova.

These star-struck youths apparently worry authorities because they devote their lives to rock stars, actors or composers and not to the patriotic deeds held up as examples by the Communist Party.

In the past week, two Soviet newspapers have criticized youth organizations for failing to take decisive action against the fans. The daily . . . Sovietskaya Rossiya urged that organized fan clubs be founded quickly to get youths off the streets. . . .

[An] official quoted by Sovietskaya Rossiya suggested premises be made available for fan clubs at which the young Soviets could gather "without their bottles of port wine" and perhaps even meet their idols.

It was not clear, however, how this would lessen the reported obsession of some of the fans. One 19-year-old identified only as Tanya told Mosovsky Komsomolets [another daily] she had seen a film starring Ms. Pugachova 56 times. . . .

Both newspapers suggested that teen-agers turned to pop idols because they led empty lives influenced by . . . "so-called unfavorable families" and what the fans see as "boring, uninteresting" jobs.

Tanya, for instance, said she became a fan five years ago. "I had no understanding with my parents, just like now. I had no close girlfriends. I just felt terribly alone, that no one needed me. And then I heard [Alla Pugachova] on the television. . . ."

"She and her songs are very close to me. . . . I cannot imagine myself without her, life without her. That's everything for me."

Neither newspaper named Ms. Pugachova directly, but made clear the fans were outside her home. The newspapers indicated that the female star herself is not being blamed for the fans' behavior. . . .

At a concert . . . in the Armenian capital of Yerevan, for example, [Pugachova] arrived in the stadium in a gray open limousine, circling around under a spotlight to the cheers of some 50,000 spectators.

Huge letters formed the word Alla in front of the stage and the crowd chanted Ms. Pugachova's name so loudly every time she left the stadium that it took three encores at the end of a two-hour show to get them to leave.*

1. How do Communist officials regard the attitudes of many Soviet youth?
2. How do you think the attitudes of Soviet youth toward rock singers compare/contrast with those of young people in the West?

*"Soviets worry about rock groupies" by Alison Smale. Copyright 1984 by The Associated Press. Reprinted from *The Central New Jersey Home News*, October 10, 1984, Sec. C. p. 8. Reprinted by permission.

Accompanied by his assistant, Snegorouchka, Grandfather Frost appears in a long, white beard and fur-trimmed costume. What are some holidays observed in the Soviet Union?

dumplings, and cream-filled cakes. The most popular beverages are tea, wine, and vodka.

The Soviets especially enjoy these intimate gatherings on birthdays and such public holidays as New Year's Day, International Women's Day, May Day, and Revolution Day. The most festive occasion of the year is New Year's Day, which has replaced Christmas as the major winter holiday. During the New Year's season, indoor and outdoor trees are adorned with colored lights and glittering balls. Gaily decorated stores are busy with shoppers buying gifts and in many public places, Grandfather Frost, the Soviet Santa Claus, hands out toys to children. He usually is assisted by Snegorouchka, or the Snow Maiden, a character from Russian fairy tales.

Quiet activities such as reading and watching television also appeal to many Soviets, and one of the most popular games in the country is chess. On summer evenings and weekends, countless fans gather around the permanent chess tables in city parks to play or to cheer on their champions.

Soviets have a passion for outdoor life and sports as well. Group outings like hiking, cross-country skiing, ice skating, and hunting for mushrooms are very popular. So are spectator sports, which the government uses to arouse patriotic feeling. Soccer matches especially draw large crowds, and fans follow their city teams with great enthusiasm. But ice hockey often is considered the real national game. One of the Soviet Union's greatest ice-hockey players is Vladislav Tretyak. Below, Tretyak discusses the sport, his part in it, and Soviet sports in general:

Ice hockey is one of the most popular sports in the Soviet Union. Much is written about the game and many films and television programs are made about it. Once, on one such program, I was asked why I had chosen to be a goaltender, probably the most dangerous position on the team. The interviewer was very surprised when I replied that I had had little

Children and adults whirl around on a carnival ride at Moscow's Gorky Park, also a favorite haunt of avid chess players. What other forms of recreation are common in the Soviet Union?

Winter is a special delight for children like these who are about to take an afternoon sleigh ride through one of Moscow's many city parks. What other outdoor pursuits do Soviets enjoy?

choice in the matter—it was my mother who made that decision. When I was a boy, she took me down to the ice hockey club, and made sure that I was the goalie. And that's where I've played ever since....

The well-known Canadian goaltender, Tony Esposito, once likened playing goalie to having stones hurled at you for two hours. He was right, I can tell you! An experienced ice hockey player can send the puck flying toward the goal at around 160 kilometers per hour (100 mph). A goaltender wears padding, and that gives some protection, of course. There are times, though, when it's not enough, and some areas of the body have no protection in the first place. I've been hit many times, but other players on the team can find themselves on the receiving end of a fast-flying puck, too. All in all, ice hockey is a tough game, and you have to like living dangerously to enjoy playing it.

The game has increased greatly in popularity here ever since the U.S.S.R. first won the world championships in 1954. During the last 30 years we have been world champions 19 times, not to mention our successes in the Olympics and European championships. There are now more than 10,000 ice hockey rinks in the country, and over 100,000 junior teams compete for the "Golden Puck" prize.

But, of course, mine isn't the only sport that is popular in the U.S.S.R. Soccer, basketball, track, gymnastics, and ice skating also attract many people, both participants and spectators, and more than 80 million people belong to sports clubs and societies. We regularly have great sporting events called "Spartakiads of the Peoples of the U.S.S.R.," where thousands of athletes, men and women, get together to compete in their various sports.

Sports activities in the U.S.S.R. are subsidized by the State and the trade unions. They give grants toward the cost of building new stadiums, ice rinks, and other facilities, and buying equipment.*

1. What is the major social activity for most Soviets? What and how do they celebrate?
2. What sports and outdoor activities are popular in the Soviet Union?

---

*"You have to like living dangerously" in *We live in the European U.S.S.R.* by E. Ryabko, 1985, The Bookwright Press, pp. 48–50. Reprinted by permission.

SOVIET UNION

CHAPTER 45 REVIEW

POINTS TO REMEMBER

1. Although traditionally family ties have been strong in Russia and other parts of the Soviet Union, the pressures of modern life have put a strain on many family relationships.
2. Although there is a trend toward smaller families among ethnic Russians, larger families remain common among other Soviet citizens in certain republics.
3. The 1917 constitution provides Soviet men and women equal access to education, employment, and other areas of public life. Despite this and Soviet pride in the nation's record on women's rights, Soviet women often feel that they are treated as second-class citizens.
4. Soviet youth are protected almost up to their teens. At school they are taught to be obedient to authority and to place the aims of the group above the desires of the individual.
5. The Soviet educational system is centralized. At age 15, all students must take an examination that determines what type of higher education, if any, a student will receive. Following graduation, students are assigned jobs by the government. Often, these positions are in places where the state is promoting economic development and labor is scarce.
6. Soviet citizens pursue a variety of leisure activities, including entertaining at home, reading, watching television, and playing chess. They also enjoy outdoor life and sports and such spectator sports as soccer and ice hockey.

VOCABULARY

Identify

Grandfather Frost   Snegorouchka   Vladislav Tretyak   "Spartakiads of the Peoples of the U.S.S.R."
Alla Pugachova

Define

zakuski

DISCUSSING IMPORTANT IDEAS

1. An ancient philosopher once said that "The root of the state is in the family." Do you think this is true in the Soviet Union today? Explain.
2. Despite laws that guarantee them equality, some Soviet women complain that they are treated as second-class citizens. On what do they base their complaints? How does the situation of the Soviet women compare with the situation of women in your country?
3. Would you like to be a teenager in the Soviet Union? Explain.
4. In what ways is life in the Soviet Union like your own life and that of your family? In what ways is it different?

Developing Skills

USING REFERENCE WORKS IN RESEARCH

Once you have chosen or have been assigned a topic for a report or paper, you will have to decide what sources to use to research the information you need to complete the assignment. In many cases, you will find that you need to use secondary sources.

One type of secondary source that can be of great value when doing research is *reference works*, such as general encyclopedias, biographical dictionaries, guides to periodicals, or books of quotations. All of these generally can be found in a special and separate section of your local public library or your school library.

Some reference works provide information on many different subjects, while others cover only certain subjects. Before you can effectively use any reference work, you must have some idea of exactly what it contains.

A general encyclopedia is a set of books that contains relatively short articles on many subjects and topics. Each book, or volume, of the set covers subjects or topics beginning with a certain letter or letters of the alphabet. Within each volume, articles are arranged in alphabetical order. At the end of each article, there generally is a bibliography, a list of books or other resources from which the information used in the article was compiled. Most general encyclopedias also include aids that will help you locate the information you are seeking. One of the most helpful is an index that covers the material in all the volumes and that is arranged in alphabetical order by subject, topic, theme, and/or proper names. In addition, most general encyclopedias update information by revising the set yearly or by printing yearbooks that contain articles about events that took place during the past year.

A biographical dictionary is a book that contains condensed, or brief, biographies of individuals. The material generally is arranged in alphabetical order by the last names of the individuals covered. Each biography provides such basic data as the individual's date and place of birth, nationality, family affiliations, and occupation, as well as information on the individual's major achievements and accomplishments. Biographical dictionaries are especially useful when you need more information than that provided in an encyclopedia but less than that found in a full biography or autobiography.

A periodical guide, or index, is a book or set of books that catalogues or lists the subjects and topics covered in magazine and newspaper articles. An index of new titles is released each month and then published as a set each year. In this reference work, magazine and newspaper articles are indexed in alphabetical order both by subject and by authors' last names. Each entry under a subject heading generally contains the titles of the article; the name of the author(s); the name, volume number, and publication date of the magazine or newspaper in which the article appears as well as the number(s) of the page(s) on which it appears; and an indication as to whether or not the article is illustrated. All abbreviations used are explained in a key at the beginning of the index. Periodical guides are especially helpful when you need to have very current or up-to-date information.

A book of quotations is a reference work that contains the statements and sayings of famous and not-so-famous individuals about a wide variety of topics. The originator of each quotation is cited along with the quote. In many cases, the date of the quote and the work in which it appeared is noted as well. Some books of quotations are arranged alphabetically by subject, while others are arranged by authors' names or periods of time.

For practice in using reference works, use each of the works that have been discussed to find information about one of the following: Alexander Solzhenitsyn; Education in the Soviet Union; or Soviet gold medalist winners in the Olympic Games.

UNIT 7 REVIEW

SUMMARY

The Soviet Union is the world's largest nation. It occupies one-sixth of the earth's surface and spans eleven time zones. On one hand, its far northern location and sometimes inhospitable environment often have contributed to its isolation from other parts of the world. On the other hand, the land—with its open plains and abundance of natural resources—has been a thoroughfare for foreign invaders from east and west. Throughout their history, the Russians, the dominant nationality of the Soviet Union, have struggled both to gain access to the outside world and to protect their lands.

Russia began 1000 years ago as a small landlocked country. Over the centuries, it expanded its territory and brought neighboring peoples under its rule. Today, Russia is the key republic of the Soviet Union, which includes 14 other republics, each of which is based on a particular nationality. Although officially all the nationalities are equal, Russians remain the dominant group and hold positions of leadership at all levels of government.

Until the twentieth century, Russia was governed by powerful rulers known as tsars. While some of the tsars kept Russia backward and isolated, others worked to increase contacts with the West and to promote reforms. All, however, tried to control every area of Russian life. Then, in 1917, a revolution overthrew the tsarist government and transformed the Russian Empire into the Soviet Union, the world's first Communist nation.

Since the 1930's, the Soviet Union has rapidly built a modern industrial economy controlled by the government. It also has become a major military power and a rival of the West. Although under communism, living standards gradually have improved for Soviet citizens, strict limits are placed on individual freedoms.

REVIEW QUESTIONS

1. In what ways has the environment of the Soviet Union contributed to the nation's successes and failures?
2. In what ways does the Russian and Soviet past influence the attitudes the Soviets have today about the outside world, particularly the West? Give examples to support your answer.
3. What are the similarities and differences between life in Russia under the tsars and life in the Soviet Union under the Communists?

SUGGESTED ACTIVITIES

1. Working in a small group, prepare an illustrated time line that shows significant events in the development of the Soviet Union.
2. Draw or make a map of the Soviet Union. Show each of the 15 republics, their capitals, and their major industrial and agricultural products. Use symbols to represent the products and a legend to explain the symbols.
3. Read a novel or other work that focuses on Russian/Soviet history. Give an oral report highlighting the plot or the central character's life. Explain the view that your reading has given you about Russian/Soviet life.
4. Prepare a list of proverbs and sayings from Russia and other areas of the Soviet Union. Select a few, explain to the class what each means, and have different class members indicate what insights the proverbs and sayings provide into the character of the people of the Soviet Union.

COMPARING CULTURES

A nation's system of government greatly influences the kind of society in which the people of that nation will live. In some nations, like the United States, governmental power ultimately rests with the people. In other nations, like the Soviet Union, it is in the hands of the leaders.

The diagrams that follow illustrate the governmental structures of the Soviet Union and the United States. Study the diagrams and the corresponding paragraphs. Then compare the forms of government and the political values of the two nations.

The Soviet Union officially is a federal union of 15 republics, each governed by soviets, or councils, elected by the people. The Constitution states that all political power belongs to the people and to their elected representatives. In practice, however, the Soviet Union is a highly centralized state under the strict control of the Communist party. No opposition party is permitted. The party makes policy, and the government carries out party decisions.

The United States has a federal system of government in which power is divided between the national, or federal, government and the governments of the 50 states. The United States Government is a democratic republic in which supreme power is held by the people and exercised through elected representatives. Voters usually select officials from candidates named by political parties.

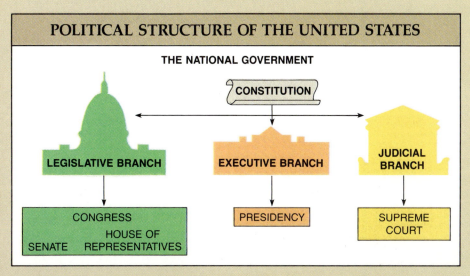

Unit Eight

Although compared to some other areas Western Europe is small in size, it is an influential region of the globe. In ancient times, Greeks and Romans set standards of excellence that dominated the Mediterranean region. In later centuries, in spite of plague, war, and political revolution, a vigorous civilization emerged whose powerful political, economic, social, and religious ideas enabled it to explore and dominate much of the globe.

Today, Western Europe no longer directly controls the greater part of the world. Yet, ideas generated by its civilization continue to shape the thinking and values of many people worldwide. For this and other reasons, understanding Western Europe's past and present is important to understanding ourselves as well as others.

CONTENTS

46	VARIETY IN A SMALL SPACE	752
47	ROOTS OF WESTERN EUROPE	770
48	RISE OF WESTERN EUROPE	790
49	A SENSE OF THEMSELVES	810
50	ARTS AND THOUGHT	828
51	THE WAYS OF LIFE	848

WESTERN EUROPE

CHAPTER 46
VARIETY IN A SMALL SPACE

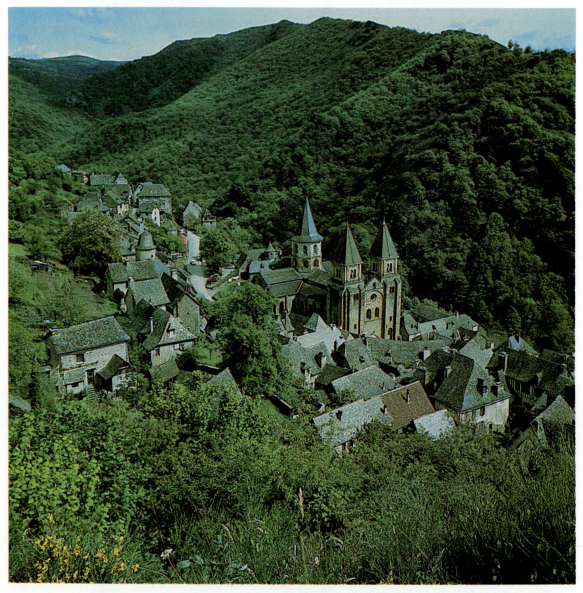

1. What are the physical features of Western Europe?
2. How have climate and physical environment shaped the development of Western Europe?

. . . all experience in Aran [a small Irish island in the Atlantic Ocean] was heightened by the closeness of the community, the long folk-memory that connected present-day happenings with the past and, above all, the physical surroundings. The changing of the seasons was far more dramatic and powerful than it could ever be on a larger mass of land. In winter the Atlantic pounded the high cliffs to the south with great earth-quivering thuds, which vibrated through the soles of the feet on the flat rocks overhead. Great gobbets of spume [foam] were whisked inland from the breakers and made salty the water in the barrels under the eave-shutes. Old men and women leant against the wind as they toiled uphill and stooped to seek the shelter of the stone walls. Such was the force of the elements that even inanimate things were given character and a kind of life. The old [ship] SS *Dún Aengus,* our only link with the mainland, was constantly sought by hundreds of eyes and the people shouted to each other over the howling wind, *'Meastú an dtiocfidh si inniu?'* (I wonder will she come today?) I remember standing behind a huddle of women, enjoying the shelter given by their thick flannel skirts and heavy paisley shawls, as they watched the *Dún Aengus* wallow and plunge toward Kilronan pier, lamenting the severity of the weather. . . .

In spring the light got stronger and although seas still ran high, the shores were now full of men with pitchforks gathering seaweed. It was spread to dry on the foreshore then stacked in great wine-red [stacks] to be burned as kelp [seaweed ashes] in autumn. Broad ribbons of red weed and tufts of tasselated black weed were spread on the greening fields to fertilise them and later men with spades turned the earth over it and planted potatoes.*

The close relationship between the people of Aran and the sea is not unique. It is, in fact, one of the chief characteristics of all of Western Europe. The Arctic Ocean, the Mediterranean Sea, and various extensions of the Atlantic Ocean provide Western Europe with a long coastline. Approximately 80 percent of Western Europe's people live within 100 miles (160 kilometers) of the coast.

The area's deep bays, narrow seas, and well-protected **estuaries,** or inlets, provide many fine harbors. This has encouraged trade with foreign lands and made some Western European countries great **maritime,** or seafaring, nations.

Closeness to the sea also has had a favorable impact on Western Europe's climate. A current known as the North Atlantic Drift brings warm water from the tropical South Atlantic to the western coast of Europe. The water warms the winds that blow across the continent from the Atlantic Ocean. The result is that, despite its northern latitude, Western Europe enjoys relatively mild year-round temperatures.

---

*From 'The 1930 on Aran' by Breandán O'hEithir extract from *Irish Life* by Sharon Gmelch, page 136, The O'Brien Press, Dublin.

THE WESTERN FRINGE OF EURASIA

Western Europe is part of the European peninsula that extends westward from the landmass of Eurasia. The entire continent, which covers about 4.1 million square miles (10.7 million square kilometers), is smaller than any other continent except Australia. Western Europe and its nearby islands take up about 35 percent of the continent. It includes the nations of Iceland, Norway, Denmark, Sweden, Finland, Ireland, Great Britain, France, West Germany, the Netherlands, Belgium, Luxembourg, Switzerland, Austria, Italy, Portugal, Spain, Greece, Malta, and a number of other smaller states. The rest of the continent consists primarily of the Communist nations of Eastern Europe.

Unlike other regions of the world, "Western Europe" often is considered more a cultural or political term than a geographic one. For many years, Western Europeans have been divided into separate **nationalities,** or groups each having its own history, language, territory, and way of life. In spite of recent efforts toward economic unity in Western Europe, many of the people of the region still think of themselves as members of national groups rather than as Western Europeans.

The diversity of the people is related in part to the diversity of the geography—the wide variety of landscapes and climates. Most Western Europeans live in one of three different climates—the Mediterranean in the south, the humid continental in the northwest, and the marine in some parts of the interior. Below, an author who traveled across the continent talks about some aspects of Western Europe's diversity:

> The roofs of Europe, the old roofs at least, . . . have some interesting things to say. . . . They offer a record of how [people] have come to terms with rain and wind and heat and cold and, of course, other people. . . .
> In Normandy [a French province] we saw rooflines of moderate pitch—no need there, evidently, for steep slopes to get rid of heavy rains or snows. Their eaves showed only a moderate overhang—no need for them to be extended to offer shelter, and no need for them to be retracted to avoid ripping winds. . . . The tiles of the roofs looked tightly fitted, and window shutters were closed against the night air. . . . Bent working backs were a part of the landscape. The climate seemed to prevent inhibitions from thawing: we heard no one sing aloud out-of-doors in the day-

These homes, typical of those found in France's northwest province of Normandy, house the many sailors and farmers who live in the area. What do the roofs indicate about the weather in Normandy?

light, and no Normandy child would return our waves. But the wheat with its company of red poppies and cornflowers waved. . . .

Southward from Paris we watched the roofs flatten and broaden, displaying wide eaves that shaded the windows. . . .

Bent working backs were no longer part of the landscape; they were replaced by backs bent to conform to the curve of the chaise lounge. Here a French child might return a friendly wave, people might sing outdoors. . . .

As we continued south into Provence [a French province], we observed one change. . . . Something had happened to the roofs. They had pulled in their eaves. Windows . . . were absent from the north walls of houses, and some roofs had rocks on them.

We were in the area of the mistral, that fearful northwest wind that comes off the Alps each winter and spring, blowing bitter cold for days on end. . . .

As we traveled west into Italy's watery Po Valley, we saw that the tiled roofs of the two-storied farmhouses had extended themselves into L shapes and taken on added responsibilities. One wing of each house . . . accommodated cattle downstairs and the family upstairs. . . . The other wing was open except for its roof and one side, which was built up with openwork brick lattice. . . .

From the productive farmlands spread flat under the sun, we soon turned south. The hill towns and long slopes of olive trees and grape vines beckoned. . . .

The rooflines of Italian cities displayed records of human conflict, pride, and hope. . . . Spires and domes raised bells, and columns raised soldiers and statesmen and wolves and horses and gods. And mingled with these against the sky we enjoyed the lighter note of many dovecotes and decorative chimney pots, and lines of laundry flapping from high balconies.

In southern Italy the roofs became completely flat, and remained that way across

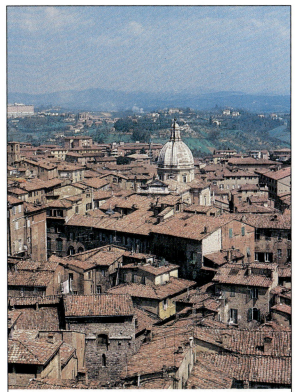

Houses like these are typical in Tuscany, a hilly region in central Italy, where fine wines and olive oil are produced. What are the homes like in the Po Valley region of Italy?

Greece and the Mediterranean countries. In these warm lands, now shorn of all but the most sparse covering of drought-resistant and goat-resistant plants, the flat roofs have long been popular places in the night breeze, places offering unbroken views of the stars over the sea and the treeless hills. . . .

From the flat Mediterranean roofs we turned northward again, and westward, and skyward into the Swiss Alps. The roofs sloped there but shallowly. Thick slabs of slate were used for shingles, and boulders anchored them against the wind. During the winter thick featherbeds of snow provide additional warmth. The eaves were wide and spread like the wings of brooding hens. . . .

For us in our wet raincoats and rainhats it was easy to understand why the roofs

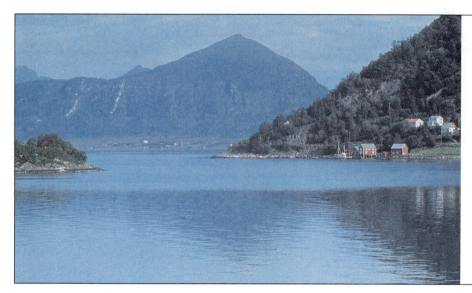

Fjords like the one in this photo are a common sight along the Norwegian coastline. Because of their country's location, most Norwegians live near or along the sea, and fishing is a major industry. When were fjords formed?

had been built so wide, and why porches and balconies were tucked under the eaves.*

1. Where is Western Europe located? Of what nations does it consist?
2. Why is "Western Europe" often considered more a cultural or political term than a geographic one?

COASTLINE AND ISLANDS

The coastline of Western Europe is very irregular and winds into a number of smaller peninsulas. These include the Scandinavian Peninsula, Jutland, the Iberian Peninsula, Italy, and the part of the Balkan Peninsula occupied by Greece. Between these peninsulas lie bays, inlets, and gulfs.

One of the most jagged coastlines is that of Norway. A unique geographical feature of Norway is its **fjords,** long narrow sea inlets cut between mountains and formed during the Ice Age. Below, a traveler describes his impressions of Norway's fjord country:

> . . . my first glimpse of the landscape I'd come . . . to see was in Geirangerfjord, which a poll of the Norwegian crew had ranked as one of the two most impressive among the thousands of fjords along the Norwegian coast. Waterfalls seem to appear all at once, on both sides of the ship, dropping millions of misty gallons hundreds of feet. Rightly the most publicized cascade is the Seven Sisters. They are at their best in early summer when the glaciers and the mountain snows begin to melt.
>
> The cliffs rise abruptly out of the water, and for a view from 5,000 feet [1524 meters] of white peaks and the long-fingered fjords, I joined the ship's first shore excursion. [Norwegian] bus drivers have inherited the Viking sense of adventure. The twists and hairpin turns, at times between walls of snow, must have inspired a roller coaster. . . . From Dalsnibba Observation Point at the top, our anchored ship in the fjord was the size of a pinhead.*

Lying off the Western European coast are thousands of islands. Some are in the North

---

*Pages 1–4, 6–9 from *Reading the Landscape of Europe* by May Theilgaard Watts. Copyright ©1971 by May T. Watts. Reprinted by permission of Harper & Row, Publishers, Inc.

*"Cruising Through the Fjords" by Henry Ehrlich in *Travel and Leisure*, Vol. 12, No. 3, March 1982, p. 54. Reprinted by Permission.

Atlantic—Iceland, the Faeroe Islands, and the British Isles. The British Isles, which include Britain, Ireland, and a number of smaller islands, are the largest of the Western European islands.

Many of the islands are in the Mediterranean Sea. For example, there are the Balearic Islands off the eastern coast of Spain, and Corsica, Sicily, and Malta, which are near France and Italy. Then there are the Ionian Islands off the western coast of Greece and the islands of the Aegean Sea between Greece and Turkey. Below, a writer offers his impressions of some of Greece's Aegean Islands:

> Journeying around the Aegean, I can see how closely these islands, so widely scattered on the map, are linked to mainland Greece. Mainly by big ferries. . . .
>
> The 200-foot [60-meter] *Aegus* crisscrosses the northern Aegean twice a week —Sicathos, Linnos, Samothrace, Lesbos. A steward says his wife brings the baby to the dock at Kavala—he hasn't enough time between trips to go home.
>
> At 2 A.M. in the harbor of Chios the 300-foot (90-meter) *Sappho* arrives . . . three decks for a thousand passengers, two decks for a hundred cars or sixty trucks. Rumbling aboard are double-deck trucks full of goats and sheep. And she's off, to Piraeus [a Greek port]—those animals will go to market in Athens the same day. . . .
>
> In the southern Aegean, at Mikonos, cruise ships disgorge hundreds of tourists into the picturesque harbor, the little lanes between whitewashed walls, the shops with pottery, jewelry, colorful cottons. I join an island cruise.
>
> The sea couldn't be smoother. There's a Greek lesson in the lounge (*efharisto*, thank you; *parakalo*, you're welcome; *yassas* —hello, cheers, good-bye.)
>
> Here's Patmos—picturesque harbor, massive monastery. Rhodes—the castle of the Knights Hospitaler of St. John of Jerusalem. Crete! The palace of the kings called Minos. . . .
>
> On Santorini it's zigzag up the cliff on muleback, take a picture, back to the ship! I stay. . . .
>
> The panorama did it. The half-moon bay is the bluest of blues. In the middle, a little black volcano. The sun sets, the bay turns gold. A man asks, "Can there be anything more beautiful?" I don't see how.*

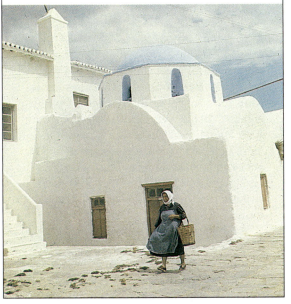

This Greek Orthodox church on the island of Mikonos is typical of Greek island structures, which are white-washed and reflect the brilliant sunlight. In what sea are the islands between Greece and Turkey located?

1. Into what peninsulas does Western Europe's coastline wind?
2. What is the largest island group off the Western European coast? What islands does it include?

MOUNTAIN AREAS

Three major mountain areas mark the landscape of Western Europe. One is the Northwestern Highlands of Iceland, Scandi-

---

*"Greece: Getting the Most Out of Life" by Peter T. White in *National Geographic*, Vol. 157, No. 3, March 1980, p. 387. Reprinted by permission.

navia, Ireland, Scotland, and Wales. Another is the Central Uplands, which stretch from the Iberian Peninsula through central France and Germany to Eastern Europe. A third is the Southern Mountain Ranges, which cross the southern part of the continent from Spain to Eastern Europe.

NORTHWESTERN HIGHLANDS

In the Northwestern Highlands are some of the oldest mountains in Europe. Over the years, many of these have been eroded and smoothed down by ice, wind, and water. The highest peaks, which are about 8000 feet (2400 meters), are in southern Norway.

Compared with other areas of Western Europe, the Northwestern Highlands are sparsely populated. The thin rocky soil and steep slopes of the mountains make large-scale farming difficult. Most of the people who live in the area earn their living from fishing, mining, light industry, and **animal husbandry,** or raising such animals as sheep and cattle.

Forming part of the Northwestern Highlands region are the Scottish Highlands. Below, a British writer reveals the fascination they arouse:

> Coming up from the Border [the region near England], where the land is agricultural, full of grey stone and green hills, dotted with old castles and ruined abbeys, you are presented with the most magnificent scenery in Britain, a landscape dominated by . . . mountain ranges. . . . In the far north are isolated mountains, enhanced and romanticized by a seascape littered with islands. Indeed, this is a truly romantic landscape, snow covered in winter and often seen through driving rain.
>
> The Highland villages are often isolated and old fashioned, with one main street of low whitewashed cottages, a school, post office and shop and perhaps a church. Always one is aware of the mountains, their rounded summits rising above the lochs [Scottish lakes] and tiny crofts [enclosed farmlands]—Glencoe in Argyllshire and Ben Nevis, the highest mountain in the British Isles, formidable both to climb and to contemplate.
>
> But if the landscape of Scotland is the most magical in Britain, it is also the most terrifying. No wonder these mountains were thought to be the haunt of trolls and witches. Ben Nevis could well qualify for such legends. With sublime indifference it rears its head of loose stones and rocks over the loch at its feet. The hazardous precipices on its northeast side are torn by chasms that may hold snow all year round.
>
> The historian Macauley describes Glencoe as 'the most dreary and melancholy of all Scottish passes. . . . ' I disagree with him. Its history may hold sadness, but seen on a summer's day from

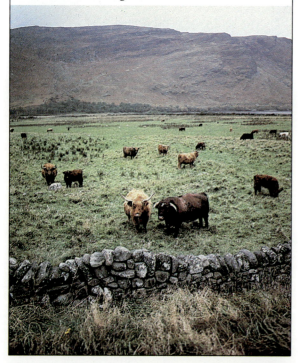

The Scottish Highlands, which cover the northern two-thirds of Scotland, are home to these long-haired Highland cattle. Why is large-scale farming difficult in the Northwestern Highlands?

CHAPTER 46 VARIETY IN A SMALL SPACE

This lush valley is an example of one kind of landscape found in the Massif Central, which covers almost one-sixth of France's surface. What other major area makes up the Central Uplands? Where is it located?

the shores of Loch Leven the great upthrust of the mountain is anything but melancholy.

This is the landscape of peregrines and ravens, which nest in the crags; of wild cats haunting cairns [piles of stones] and forests; of the golden eagle, . . . which soars like a plane over the endless crevices and lochs of the Highlands, . . . above the granite mountains of Inverness-shire, which are the most ancient in Britain.*

CENTRAL UPLANDS

There are several major areas in the Central Uplands. One is the *Meseta,* the high plateau of Portugal and Spain. Another is the *Massif Central,* the central highlands of France. Still another is the Harz Mountains and other uplands of central Germany.

The landscape of the Uplands varies from place to place. In some areas, it is forested, while in others it is rocky and barren. In the passage that follows, a visitor to the *Massif Central* relates what he saw:

---
*Sceptered Isle The Countryside of Britain by James Turner, 1977, Methuen, pp. 28, 30.

I arrived at the village [of Salles-la-Source] early in the morning. . . .

Actually, there are three villages. Below the road in the valley is a cluster of gray-roofed farms and cottages around a rough little . . . church with an octagonal tower. I descended a steep hill, hoping to visit the church, only to find the gate blocked by a self-appointed guard dog. . . .

Higher up on the steeper slopes of the valley is a second cluster of houses around a small château [castle]. They are built of a golden stone . . . that glowed in the early sun, . . . and topped by steep gray-slate roofs. . . .

The main village is perched on the rim of a 300-foot (90-meter) moss-skinned precipice over which streams dribbled. Other springs emerged from the rock itself and splashed into the dark pool. I drove up the hill and found [a] . . . village scattered across a broad green. Sheep were munching the grass at the far side and dozing in fluffy bundles. An English-styled . . . church squatted sedately in one corner, and pigeons swooped over the sycamores. . . . Beyond the green the hill rose steeply. . . . An elderly couple sat together on a rough wood

Cable cars like this one regularly traverse the Dolomite Alps near the Italian ski resort of Cortina d'Ampezzo, transporting tourists, who make up a major portion of the Italian economy. Besides the Alps, what other mountains are part of the Southern Mountain Ranges?

bench outside their cottage, drinking coffee from fat porcelain cups. It was barely 9:00 A.M. and the sun was already hot.

I had expected more dramatic scenery in the southern portion of the Massif Central. . . . To the north I knew lay the arid limestone region of Châtaigneraie, once a well-populated and fertile area. . . . Today it is a vast emptiness of gorse and broom [shrubs], speckled with remnants of villages. To the south lay . . . forests and tight valleys, . . . and far to the east . . . torn gorges. . . . But here, deep in the valley . . . , was all greenery and mellowed woodlands. . . . Dried . . . thistles nailed on doors in the village were the only reminder of the bleak regions beyond.*

SOUTHERN MOUNTAIN RANGES

The mountains of the Southern Mountain Ranges are younger and less eroded than those of the Northwestern Highlands. And, since mountain activity is still continuing, many areas are affected by earthquakes.

The Ranges are made up of several mountain chains—the Sierra Nevada in southern Spain, the Pyrenees along the French-Spanish border, the Apennines in Italy, and the Balkans in Greece. Also in this region are the Alps, which cover part of southeastern France and northern Italy, most of Switzerland, and part of southern Germany and Austria.

In the north of Italy, the Alps curve around the border for about 500 miles (800 kilometers) and separate Italy from France, Switzerland, and Austria. Below, a Norwegian traveler discusses his journey to Cortina d'Ampezzo, a popular Alpine ski resort:

> I drove from Merano to Cortina d'Ampezzo in the heart of the eastern Dolomites [a group of mountains in the Italian Alps]. Cultural borders are so marked that to travel across the Italian Alps is almost like experiencing several different countries. . . .
>
> Cortina is roughly 50 miles [80 kilometers] east of Merano as the jet flies. By car on a good road it takes three to four

---

*Pages 72–74 from *Backroad Journeys of Southern Europe* by David Yeadon. Copyright ©1981 by David Yeadon. Reprinted by permission of Harper & Row, Publishers, Inc.

hours, and you encounter three completely different languages. . . .

Rain cascaded down nearly the whole way to Cortina, and so did a few rocks from the slopes. About 20 miles [32 kilometers] southwest of Bolzano I stopped to see if tiny Lake Carezza would be visible. Just as I walked out to a clearing in the pines, the clouds broke and the sun burst down on this crystal-clear green lake and, behind it at close quarters, the Latermar Range of the Dolomites. . . . For beauty, everyone in Cortina told me, the famous "Tour of the Five Passes" is a must. This route surrounds the Sella Group, with passes at about 7,000 feet [2133 meters] above sea level. Funiculars [cable cars] and lifts offer dizzying rides to perennially snow-clad peaks.

I set off at six o'clock one sunny morning, and when I returned that evening about seven I was astonished to see that my odometer had clocked off only a hundred miles [160 kilometers]—the hairpin curves and sharp turns must have run into thousands. Some of the sharpest are cobbled for better traction, with a speed limit of 7 kilometers [4.2 miles] per hour. The tour resembles a whole day on the world's grandest roller-coaster, among spiraling mountain peaks and deep green valleys.

The first pass, Falzárego, was the scene of bloody battles during World War I. As I reached the crest, the mighty Marmolada, highest of the Dolomites . . . shimmered in the distance. . . .

An hour later, at the Pordoi Pass, I stopped to watch some young Italians at a mountain-climbing lesson. . . .

Approaching the Sella Pass I felt that a few thousand feet of mountains were leaning over me. A sign said: "Danger of Avalanche." Several cars had stopped; so did I, expecting an accident. Everyone was staring up at the Piz Ciavazes. It took me about five minutes to spot two specks—two people climbing. One was inching his way out and up, with nothing but air beneath him, to get around an overhanging bit of rock. I imagined the view these brave souls had—looking 2000 feet [600 meters] straight down—and found my own unnerving enough. Even on the road, even at a pass, you rapidly gain a lot of respect for these mountains.*

1. What are the three major mountain areas of Western Europe? Where is each mountain area located?
2. What are the general physical characteristics of each mountain area?

PLAINS AND RIVERS

In addition to mountains, Western Europe has broad fertile plains. The largest and most important is the Great European Plain. It extends from southern Britain in the west, across northern France, Belgium, the Netherlands, and central Germany to the Soviet Union more than 1800 miles (2880 kilometers) to the east. It is made up of flat rolling land and some hills and is the most heavily populated area of Western Europe. Major cities, as well as most of Western Europe's agriculture and industry, are found on this plain.

Many of Western Europe's rivers flow through the Plain. Until the development of the railroad and the automobile, these rivers were the easiest means of transportation. Even today, rivers and canals play an important role as transportation routes. They also provide water to irrigate farmland and to produce electricity. The Loire, Seine, Rhône, and Garonne rivers, for example, are used extensively in France for irrigation and navigation. Much of the industry and agriculture of northern Italy depend on the Po River. Then there are the Quadalquivir and Tagus

---

*"Italy: Snow-fed Lakes, Majestic Valleys" by Tor Eigeland in *The Alps*, 1973, The National Geographic Society, pp. 144–146. Reprinted by permission.

Rivers of the Iberian Peninsula and the Danube, which begins in the Black Forest of West Germany and flows for 1770 miles (2832 kilometers) through central and southeastern Europe to empty into the Black Sea.

One of the most important and busiest rivers in Western Europe is the Rhine. A major part of the inland waterway system that links many industrial cities, it flows for 700 miles (1120 kilometers) from the Swiss Alps through Germany and the Netherlands to the North Sea. To some, the Rhine is more than just a river. Below, a French writer named Victor Hugo described the feelings the river brought out in him when he visited it early in the 1800's:

> I love rivers. They do more than bear merchandise: ideas float along their surface. Rivers . . . sing to the ocean of the beauty of the earth, the fertility of plains, and the splendour of cities.
>
> Of all rivers, I prefer the Rhine. It is now a year, when passing the bridge of boats at Kehl, since I first saw it. I remember that I felt a certain respect, a sort of adoration, for this old, this classic stream. I never think of rivers—those great works of Nature, which are also great in history—without emotion.
>
> I remember the Rhone at Valserine; I saw it in 1825, in a pleasant excursion to Switzerland. . . . I remember with what noise, with what ferocious bellowing, the Rhone precipitated itself into the gulf. . . . Ah, well! Since that time, the Rhone brings to my mind the idea of a tiger; the Rhine, that of a lion.
>
> The evening on which I saw the Rhine for the first time I was impressed with the same idea. For several minutes I stood contemplating this proud and noble river,—violent, but not furious; wild, but still majestic. It was swollen, and was magnificent in appearance, and was washing with its yellow mane—or, . . . , its ''slimy beard''—the bridge of boats. Its two banks were lost in the twilight, and though its roaring was loud, still there was tranquillity.
>
> Yes, the Rhine is a noble river,—feudal, republican, imperial; worthy at the same time of France and of Germany. The whole history of Europe is combined within its two great aspects,—in this flood of the warrior and of the philosopher; in this proud stream, which causes France to bound with joy, and by whose profound

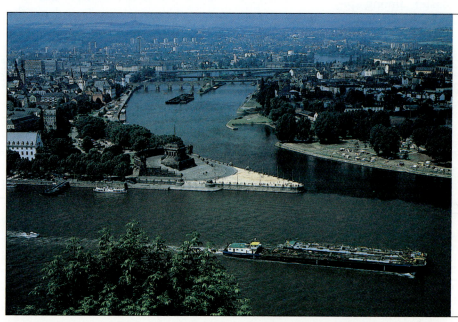

The Rhine, long a river of historical, economic, and cultural influence, flows through one of Western Europe's most heavily populated and industrialized regions. The longest section of the Rhine lies in Germany, whose people view it as a national symbol. What are some of the other major rivers in Western Europe? In what country or countries is each?

murmurings Germany is bewildered in dreams.

The Rhine is unique; it combines the qualities of every river. Like the Rhone, it is rapid; broad, like the Loire; encased, like the Meuse; serpentine, like the Seine; limpid and green, like the Somme; historical, like the Tiber; royal, like the Danube; mysterious, like the Nile; spangled with gold, like an American river; and like a river of Asia, abounding with phantoms and fables. . . .

The Rhine . . . is the great moat which divides the north from the south. The Rhine for thirty ages has seen the forms and reflected the shadows of almost all the warriors who tilled the old continent with that [plow]share which they call sword.

. . . For the thinker, who is conversant with history, two great eagles are perpetually hovering over the Rhine,—that of the Roman legions, and the eagle of the French regiments.

The Rhine—that noble flood, . . . bore at one time upon its surface bridges of boats, over which the armies of Italy, Spain, and France poured into Germany, and, which . . . were made use of by the hordes of barbarians when rushing into the ancient Roman world; at another, on its surface floated peaceably the fir-trees of Murg and of Saint Gall, . . . the marble of Bale, the salt of Karlshall, the leather of Stromberg, . . . the wine of Johannisberg, the slates of Coab, the cloth and earthenware of Wallendar, the silks and linens of Cologne. It majestically performs its double function of flood of war and flood of peace, having . . . upon the ranges of hills which embank the most notable portion of its course, oak-trees on one side and vine-trees on the other,—signifying strength and joy. . . .

The Rhine . . . seems to be a symbolical stream. In its windings, in its course, in the midst of all that it traverses, it is . . . the image of civilization to which it has been so useful, and which it will still serve. It flows from Constance to Rotterdam; from the country of eagles to the village of herrings; from the city of popes, of councils, and of emperors, to the counter of the merchant and of the citizen; from the great Alps themselves to that immense body of water which we term *ocean*.*

1. Why is the Great European Plain important to Western Europe?
2. What role do the rivers play?

DRY LANDS

Another feature of Western Europe is dry lands. The only places in Europe where these barren plains, nearly treeless hills, and hot desert wastes are found are Portugal, Spain, Italy, and Greece—the Mediterranean lands of Western Europe.

About 3000 years ago, the Mediterranean region consisted of thick, well-watered forests. But over time, most of this vegetation disappeared because of changes in climate and careless use of natural resources. Many of the trees were cut, and the land was cleared. With the forests gone, the soil was eroded by wind and rainwater. Goats and other grazing animals ate the young trees before they could grow to great size. Before long, the land was covered by shrubs and gnarled plants like the olive tree, which is able to conserve moisture during the Mediterranean's dry, hot summer months.

One of the driest areas in the Mediterranean is found in Andalucia in southern Spain. Below, a British writer-photographer describes his experiences in the desert there:

> Northwards from the Cabo de Gato on the coast, across the plain of the Campo de Nijar to the southern foothills of the Sierra de los Filabres, the countryside is arid in the extreme, and in the region west of the township of Tabernas it is reduced

---
*derivative*The Rhine*, Volume I, by Victor Hugo, Estes and Lauriat, pp. 130–131, 144–145, 148–149.

to . . . clay. No other part of Spain, no other part of . . . Greece or southern Italy . . . can approach the Tabernas badlands for sheer physical destruction. . . . Such rain as does fall may come in a sudden storm lasting a few hours, when the water runs rapidly off the hills and rushes down the valleys in devastating flashfloods. . . .

. . . when I reached the Tabernas badlands early one morning, it rained. It did not rain much, it is true—but it rained. Where there should have been an incandescent white sky . . . , there were big, blue-grey clouds. . . . Finding a vantage point from which I could see five or six miles [8 or 9.6 kilometers], I looked out across a terrain of hills and deep gullies stretching to the distant mountains. It was a stark, grey-coloured world unrelieved by a single tree, a landscape of mud. . . . "Muy salvaje paisaje," said the local Spaniards. "Very wild country."

And yet, as I found when I entered a maze of deeply eroded gullies that led into the interior of this waste, there was a surprising amount of life. Oleander bushes with brilliant pink flowers and stands of dazzling yellow Spanish broom grew in the gully-beds. Rabbits skittered for cover among the rocks, martins swooped overhead, a crested lark managed a half song. . . .

At the bottom of one of the gullies the ground was covered with a thick salty crust, and to walk on it was like walking on crisp frozen snow. Elsewhere the surface was drier and cracked into pieces of crazy paving the size and convexity of old sandwiches. Withered bushes with brittle twigs and snatching thorns sent tap-roots . . . snaking over the arid ground like hosepipes looking for water. A litter of dried bric-a-brac lay scattered about: dead palm leaves, segments of dead palm trunks, pieces of bleached wood brought down by some sudden flood. . . .

By mid-morning the clouds had blown away and the sun beat down. In the enclosed space of the gully the air soon became stifling and I had become very thirsty by the time I saw signs of human habitation. A village of very old and curiously ramshackle wooden houses lay ahead. . . . I strode into the village. . . . The village looked deserted, as though its wells had dried up. The windows were broken, the planks of the wooden sidewalk were torn loose. I walked up to the swing doors of the saloon . . . and in a trice [brief space of time] stepped through them, back into the desert landscape on the other side. . . . It was a sham. The whole village was a sham—a film set put together . . . for an old Western movie. So hostile was this desert of Almeria, this endless series of grey hills and ragged sierras, that even human influence had dwindled to something barely more substantial than a mirage.*

The part of Andalucia, Spain's largest and most populous region, shown here, is dry and barren. Other parts, however, are green and fertile. Bulls and fine horses are bred here. Where is Andalucia located?

1. Where are the dry lands of the European continent?
2. What factors created the dry lands?

**The World's Wild Places/WILDERNESS EUROPE* by Douglas Botting and the Editors of Time-Life Books ©1976 Time-Life Books Inc.

CASE STUDY
WESTERN EUROPE

LAND FROM THE SEA

According to an old Dutch saying, "God made Heaven and Earth, but the Dutch made Holland." The Dutch, the people of the land known today as the Netherlands, have struggled against the sea for centuries. Their country is a small densely populated nation in northwestern Europe whose flat terrain borders the North Sea. To relieve overcrowding, they have used their skills to obtain new land from the sea. No other people, in fact, have been more successful in increasing their territory at the expense of the ocean.

The Dutch first started to gain land from the sea during the Middle Ages. Around 1000 AD, they began building dunes and **dikes**, or sea walls, to hold back the sea waters. Four hundred years later, they erected windmills. They used the windmills to convert sea winds into energy to pump water from **polders**, land below sea level surrounded by dikes and drained artificially.

Today a large portion of the Dutch countryside consists of polders, and the picturesque, but inefficient, windmills have been replaced largely by electric pumps and other modern equipment. With new technology, Dutch engineers have developed large drainage and flood-control systems. Two projects, in particular, have attracted worldwide attention —the Zuider Zee Project and the Delta Plan.

The Zuider Zee Project was begun in 1920. Its aim was to seal off the Zuider Zee, a large shallow bay stretching deep into the Netherlands, from the North Sea. In 1932, Dutch engineers completed the building of a 19-mile (30-kilometer) barrier dam that succeeded in separating the Zuider Zee from the ocean. In time, the Zuider Zee became a fresh water lake known as the Ijsselmmer.

Over time, parts of the Ijsselmmer were pumped dry and converted into polders. Today, most of the new land that has been created consists of farmland or recreation areas. Although even more sections of the Ijsselmmer are planned for drainage, high costs and disagreements about the use of new land have delayed final completion of the project.

The Delta Plan, a flood-control project, got underway in 1958 as a reaction to a flood five years earlier that killed nearly 2000 people in the southwestern part of the country. To prevent future flood disasters in the region, Dutch engineers began the Delta Plan. It involves a series of dams, barriers, and artificial islands that will prevent the sea from flooding into rivers and inland waterways. It will shorten the coastline by 450 miles (720 kilometers) and reduce the amount of salt in the soil. It also will enable the Dutch to gain 25,000 more acres (10,000 hectares) of land from the North Sea.

1. Why have the Dutch worked to gain land from the sea? What methods have they used in their efforts?
2. What plans, if any, would you devise to gain land from the sea?

Exploration
Western Europe

The phrase "variety in a small space" has been used to describe Western Europe. Explain how the photographs and maps that follow illustrate that description.

CLIMATE

INDUSTRY

POPULATION DENSITY

WESTERN EUROPE UNIT 8

CHAPTER 46 REVIEW

POINTS TO REMEMBER

1. Western Europe is located at the western edge of Eurasia and accounts for about 35 percent of the European continent.
2. The term "Western Europe" is more cultural and political than geographical and refers to the nations of the European continent that are not part of the Communist bloc.
3. Western Europe is largely surrounded by water. It has a long and very irregular coastline that consists of many peninsulas and islands.
4. Western Europe has three major mountain areas: the Northwestern Highlands, the Central Uplands, and the Southern Mountain Ranges.
5. Western Europe has broad fertile plains, the largest of which is the Great European Plain. It contains most of Western Europe's population and natural resources, is the center of the region's industry and agriculture, and is the area through which many of the region's most important rivers flow.
6. Western Europe has the only dry lands found on the European continent. They exist in the Mediterranean countries of Portugal, Spain, Italy, and Greece.

VOCABULARY

Identify

Western Europe
North Atlantic Drift
Scandinavian Peninsula
Jutland
Iberian Peninsula
Balkan Peninsula
British Isles
Northwestern Highlands
Central Uplands
Southern Mountain Ranges
Meseta
Massif Central
Alps
Great European Plain
Rhine River
Andalucia
Zuider Zee Project

Define

estuaries
maritime
nationalities
fjords
animal husbandry
dikes
polders

DISCUSSING IMPORTANT IDEAS

1. How has the sea shaped the development of Western Europe?
2. What are some of the ways in which the natural environment of Western Europe has contributed to the great diversity found in the area?
3. Despite their ruggedness, the mountains of Western Europe have not posed barriers to trade and communication. What reasons can you give for this?
4. In your opinion, why is the European Plain so heavily populated?

DEVELOPING SKILLS

ASKING EFFECTIVE QUESTIONS

Engraved over the door of the library of an American university is this motto: "Half of knowledge is knowing where to find it." Had the stone carver had enough space, he might well have added, "and knowing which questions to ask." A key to acquiring information, or knowledge, is knowing how to ask *effective questions*, questions that serve a specific purpose and provide desired information.

Asking effective questions, be it of people or written sources, cannot be done without preparation. Before you ask the questions, there are four things you should determine—(1) what you want to know; (2) what individuals or written materials you should consult; (3) what questions you should ask; and (4) how you should ask them.

Suppose, for example, that you have been assigned to find out what your classmates think of the food in the school cafeteria. The purpose of your investigation—what you want to know—is student opinion of cafeteria food. From what resource would you be most likely to find out what students think—the school principal, parents, teachers, or students who eat in the cafeteria every day? Since what you need to know concerns the opinion of students, they are the only source mentioned that can give you firsthand, unprejudiced, and unbiased information.

Now that you know what you want to ask and the best resources to consult, you can concentrate on what you need to ask to obtain the information you require. You would not learn what you desire by asking students if they do their homework while they eat or if they have enough time to eat their entire lunch without rushing. You would learn what you want, however, by asking students what cafeteria foods they like best and least; what foods they would like kept on the menu, added to it, or eliminated from it; or what their general opinions are of the food served in the cafeteria. Keep in mind that for a question to be effective, it should be straightforward and not show personal bias. There is a great deal of difference, for example, between asking someone if he or she likes the pizza that is served on Fridays and asking if he or she likes "that tasteless, cardboardy pizza" served on Fridays.

Now that you have determined what you want to know, what or whom to consult, and what questions to ask, you must decide how, or in what form, to ask the questions. Since you are questioning people whom you see every day, you might want to conduct oral interviews. Or, you might prefer to prepare written questionnaires for your classmates to fill out and return to you.

The same steps used for effective questioning about cafeteria food can also be used in other instances. Suppose, for example, you were told to prepare an in-class report on the mountain areas of Western Europe. Using the criteria discussed above, you probably would reason as follows:

1. I want to know what mountain areas are in Western Europe, where they are located, what they are called, and what their general physical characteristics are.
2. Since I have to do this assignment in class, the best source to consult is my text.
3. I should ask questions directly related to what I want to know. For example: How many mountain areas are there in Western Europe? In what country or countries is each found? What is the name of each? How old is each? How high is each? What kind of vegetation is found on and around each?
4. Since I am consulting my text, I can ask myself the questions and write down the answers, or I can write down both the questions and the answers.

As a result of this line of reasoning, your questions will be effective, and you will be able to use the answers as a basis for an effective report.

For practice in asking effective questions, use the suggested guidelines to prepare effective questions on the following topic: "How Geography and Climate Affect the Ways in which People Live in Different Regions of Western Europe."

CHAPTER 47
ROOTS OF WESTERN EUROPE

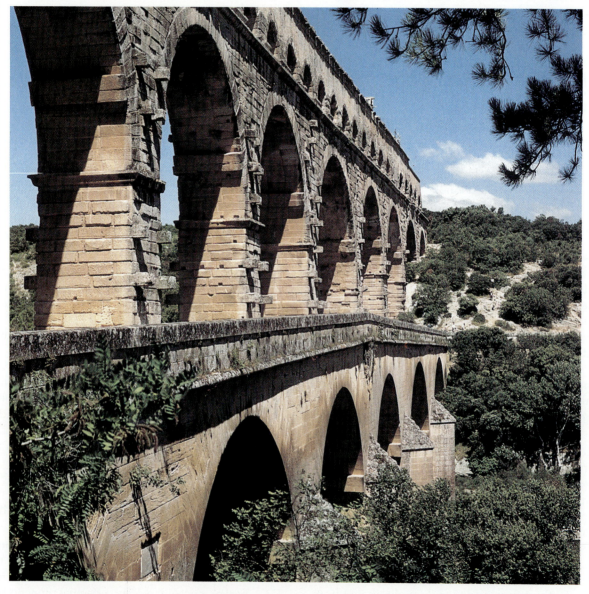

1. *What elements formed the foundation of Western European civilization?*
2. *What are some of the main features of the ancient and medieval civilizations of Western Europe?*

A child tugged at the hand of a guide who was leading visitors through the Palace of the Popes in the [French] city of Avignon. "Sing 'Pont d'Avignon,'" the child begged. He wanted the song about the bridge below the palace.

The guide grinned . . . and . . . , breaking into a few dance steps, began to sing the folk melody with which the twelfth-century tradespeople of Avignon made merry in the shelter of the bridge. . . .

. . . the visitors took up the chorus. . . . Everyone knew the song from childhood.

A moment later the guide was intoning plainsong, rich and plaintive church music that the earliest Christians had inherited from Jews and Greeks. Once it had rolled the length of the audience hall where the group now stood. . . . The echoes of the guide's voice ricocheted from the columned walls and vaulted ceiling, returning eerily to the listeners clustered around him. Most of them were French families. . . .

From the hilltop palace these families had chosen to visit . . . the Popes of the Roman Catholic Church had presided over Christendom for most of the fourteenth century.

The visitors knew this bit of history. It was not the known facts that concerned them. Rather it was the mysteries. How did the Popes of that time . . . obtain this particular site for their palace?

"One of them paid eighty thousand Italian gold pieces," said a visitor. . . .

The guide interrupted: . . . "As you know, the Popes were . . . to the northeast of here. This area was then the Dukedom of Provence, ruled by the aging Duchess Jeanne. She was worried about getting into heaven. . . . Pope Clement VI . . . promised the Duchess to absolve her of all sin if . . . she would make a gift of this site."

"Are you serious?" said one listener. . . . The guide insisted he was, and a lively discussion of his theory followed. . . .

In France, there is nothing unusual about that. At a castle ruin in the country's central region, . . . the ten-year-old granddaughter of the aging guide often takes over for him. She delivers a complete history of the action in every . . . room of the crumbling structure. In the valley of the River Lot, a village librarian moonlights as a guide through a formidable castle-fort, the study of which has been his lifetime hobby. Seated atop the battlements, long white hair disheveled by the wind, . . . he breathes life into the spirits of defenders and attackers alike.*

As indicated above, in France—as in most of Western Europe—history is a part of everyday life. The ancient and medieval structures that still dot much of the countryside represent the common cultural heritage that binds Western Europeans today. That heritage, in which the Western European people have great pride, can be traced to the Mediterranean world of ancient Greece and Rome.

---
*From *France: The Invisible Revolution* by Sabra Holbrook. Reprinted by permission of E.P. Dutton, a division of New American Library.

THE GREEKS

One of the first advanced civilizations on the European continent was developed by the ancient Greeks, who by the 500's BC had many colonies throughout the Mediterranean. To a large extent, the intellectual and artistic achievements of these early Greeks shaped Western European civilization.

THE CITY-STATES

At the heart of Greek civilization were several city-states that traded among themselves, worshipped the same gods and goddesses, and shared a common language and customs. Chief among these city-states were Athens and Sparta.

Athens Athens led Greece into a "golden age" of art and learning. Its government was one of the first democracies in history and its society the freest yet known to the world. Below, an Athenian leader named Pericles explains why, in his view, Athens was unique:

> . . . our government is not copied from those of our neighbours: we are an example to them rather than they to us. Our constitution is named a democracy, because it is in the hands not of the few but of the many. But our laws secure equal justice for all in their private disputes, and our public opinion welcomes and honours talent in every branch of achievement. . . . And as we give free play to all in our public life, so we carry the same spirit into our daily relations with one another. . . . Open and friendly in our private intercourse, in our public acts we keep strictly within the control of law. We acknowledge the restraint of reverence; we are obedient to whomsoever is set in authority, and to the laws. . . .
> Yet ours is no work-a-day city only. No other provides so many recreations for the spirit. . . . Moreover, the city is so large and powerful that all the wealth of all the world flows in to her. . . .
> We are lovers of beauty without extravagance, and lovers of wisdom without unmanliness. Wealth to us is . . . an opportunity for achievement. . . . Our citizens attend both to public and private duties. . . . We differ from other states in regarding the man who holds aloof from public life not as "quiet" but as useless; we decide or debate . . . all matters of policy. . . . We secure our friends not by accepting favours but by doing them.*

Sparta In Sparta, athletic and military feats were glorified, while trade and leisure were discouraged and the arts and intellectual accomplishments ignored. Many of Sparta's laws were the work of a legislator named Lycurgus. Below, an Athenian comments on the laws of Sparta and their effect:

> . . . Throughout the rest of the world the young girl, who will one day become a mother . . . , is nurtured on the plainest food . . . , with the scantiest addition of meat or other condiments. . . . [We], the rest of the Hellenes, are content that our girls should sit quietly and work wools. That is all we demand of them. . . .
> Lycurgus pursued a different path. Clothes were things . . . the furnishing of which might well enough be left to female slaves. And, believing that the highest function of a free woman was the bearing of children, . . . he insisted on the training of the body as incumbent no less on the female than on the male; and in pursuit of the same idea instituted rival contests in running and feats of strength for women as for men. . . .
> . . . Throughout the rest of Hellas . . . as soon as the children are of an age to understand what is said to them they are

---
The History of the Peloponnesian War by Thucydides, translated by Sir Richard Livingstone, 1956, Oxford University Press, pp. 111–114. Reprinted by permission.

immediately placed under the charge of . . . (tutors), . . . and sent off to . . . school. . . . Besides this they are given shoes to wear which tend to make their feet tender, and their bodies are enervated by various changes of clothing. And as for food, the only measure recognized is that which is fixed by appetite.

. . . Lycurgus, instead of leaving it to each member of the state privately to appoint a slave to be his son's tutor, he set over young Spartans a public guardian . . . with complete authority over them. . . .

Instead of softening their feet with shoe or sandal, the rule was to make them hardy through going barefoot. . . .

Instead of making them effeminate with a variety of clothes, his rule was to habituate them to a single garment the whole year through. . . .

Again, as regards food, according to his regulation the . . . head of the flock, must see that his messmates gathered to the club meal, with . . . moderate food. . . .

His belief was that by such training in boyhood they would be better able when occasion demanded to continue toiling on an empty stomach. . . .

Furthermore, . . . he gave to any citizen who chanced to be present authority to lay upon [the boys] injunctions for their good, and to chastise them for any trespass committed. . . .

Furthermore, in his desire firmly to implant modesty in them he imposed a special rule. In the streets they were to keep their hands within the folds of the cloak; they were to walk in silence and without turning their heads to gaze, but rather to keep their eyes fixed upon the ground before them. . . . The plainest answer to the question asked, that is all you need expect to hear from their lips. . . .

There are yet other customs . . . which Lycurgus instituted in opposition to the rest of Hellas. . . . We all know that in the generality of states every one devotes his full energy to the business of making

A goal of the Spartans was to become the strongest people in Greece. To achieve this goal and build physical strength, endurance, discipline, and fighting skills, they promoted physical conditioning, shown here in the form of wrestling. What characteristics did the Spartans scorn?

money. . . . But at Sparta Lycurgus forbade his freeborn citizens to have anything whatsoever to do with the concerns of moneymaking. . . .

. . . We are all aware that there is no state in the world in which greater obedience is shown to magistrates, and to the laws themselves, than Sparta. . . . In Sparta, . . . the stronger a man is the more readily does he bow before constituted authority. . . .

Moreover, he laid upon them . . . the obligation to cultivate the whole virtue of a citizen. Provided they duly performed the injunctions of the law, the city belonged to them, each and all, in absolute possession and on an equal footing. . . . But as for him who . . . shrank from the performance of the law's injunction, the legislator pointed him out as disqualified to be regarded longer as a member of the brotherhood of peers.*

THE ARTS AND SCIENCES

Government was not the only area in which the Greeks made lasting contributions. In the physical arts, for example, they introduced the Olympic Games, a sporting event that drew male athletes from Greece and all its colonies. In the fine arts, they created sculptures, architecture, and other works that incorporated the basic ideals of simplicity, dignity, and proportion. In theater, they developed two types of drama—**tragedies,** plays about human suffering, and **comedies,** plays with humorous themes.

At the same time, the Greeks made history an important part of literature. The first Greek historian, Herodotus, is known today as the "Father of History." Another important historian was Thucydides. In his work on the Peloponnesian Wars, a series of wars between Athens and Sparta, he explained his approach to the writing of history:

. . . I have described nothing but what I either saw myself, or learned from others of whom I made the most careful and particular enquiry. The task was a laborious one, because eye-witnesses of the same occurrences gave different accounts of them, as they remembered or were interested in the actions of one side or the other. And very likely the strictly historical character of my narrative may be disappointing to the ear. But if he who desires to have before his eyes a true picture of the events which have happened, and of the like events which may be expected to happen hereafter in the order of human beings, shall pronounce what I have written to be useful, then I shall be satisfied. My history is an everlasting possession, not a prize composition which is heard and forgotten.*

The Greeks also made many advances in science and laid the foundations for modern western philosophy and thought. The scientist Thales of Miletus, for example, developed the first two steps of what is known today as the **scientific method,** systematic ways to seek knowledge. Another scientist, Hippocrates, concluded that diseases came from natural, rather than supernatural, causes. The code he wrote for doctors, known as the Hippocratic Oath, is still sworn by new physicians today. A philosopher named Socrates developed the Socratic method, a method of teaching by asking questions. Another philosopher, Plato, carried out early studies in **political science,** the study of political systems. One of his students, Aristotle, created the system of reasoning known as **logic.**

---

*"The Constitution of the Spartans" by Xenophon. From *The Greek Historians: The Complete and Unabridged Historical Works of Herodotus, Thucydides, Xenophon, Arrian,* edited by Francis R.B. Godolphin. Copyright 1942 by Random House, Inc. Reprinted by permission of the publisher.

The Peloponnesian War by Thucydides, as translated by Benjamin Jowett. From *The Greek Historians: The Complete and Unabridged Historical Works of Herodotus, Thucydides, Xenophon, Arrian,* edited by Francis R.B. Godolphin. Copyright 1942 by Random House, Inc. Reprinted by permission of the publisher.

END OF EMPIRE

In 338 BC, the Greek city-states were defeated by King Philip II of Macedonia, who believed it his destiny to unify the city-states and spread Greek culture. Two years later, Philip was murdered. His 20-year-old son, Alexander, became king, and, over time, created a vast empire. Below, the Greek biographer Plutarch explains Alexander's motives:

> . . . Alexander . . . did not . . . rule the Grecians like a moderate prince and insult over the barbarians like an absolute tyrant; nor did he take particular care of the first as his friends and domestics, and scorn the latter as mere brutes and vegetables. . . . But believing himself sent from Heaven as the common moderator . . . of all nations, . . . he labored . . . that he might bring all regions, far and near, under the same dominion. And then, as in a festival goblet, mixing lives, manners, customs, wedlock, all together, he ordained that every one should take the whole habitable world for his country. . . .
> . . . It was not his design to ransack Asia like a robber, or to despoil and ruin it, . . . but to subdue all the kingdoms of the earth under one form of government, and to make one nation of all mankind.*

Alexander died at the age of 33, but his Hellenistic civilization, which was a blend of Greek and eastern cultures and customs, flourished long after his death. His idea of a **universal state,** a state that brings all peoples under one government, found new life in later kingdoms and empires.

1. In what ways were Athens and Sparta different?
2. What were some of the major contributions of the Greeks?
3. What changes did Alexander bring to early Western European civilization?

Plutarch's Morals, Vol. I, corrected and revised by William W. Goodwin, 1883, Little, Brown, and Company, pp. 481, 484.

THE ROMANS

Rome began as a small farming settlement on the banks of the Tiber River in central Italy. In 509 BC, the Romans set up a **republic,** a form of government in which people elect leaders to represent them. By 130 BC, they had brought much of the known western world under their rule.

THE REPUBLIC

In the early years, the government of the Roman Republic was headed by two **consuls,** elected officials who ran the city, and a Senate and an Assembly, which made laws and debated issues. Although **plebians,** or common people, could vote, only **patricians,** or aristocrats, could hold public office.

By 451 BC, plebians had forced the patricians to give them more rights, and, for the first time, the laws were put down in written form. Carved on 12 bronze tablets and known as the Twelve Tables, they provided the basic legal code of Rome for nearly 1000 years. As seen below, they dealt chiefly with **civil laws,** rules that apply to the rights and duties of the individual citizen:

> If anyone commits a theft during the day, and is caught in the act, he shall be [whipped], and given up as a slave to the person against whom the theft was committed. . . .
> A father shall have the right of life and death over his son born in lawful marriage. . . .
> No matter in what way the head of a household may dispose of his estate, and appoint heirs to the same, or guardians; it shall have the force and effect of law. . . .
> If a husband desires to divorce his wife, and dissolve his marriage, he must give a reason for doing so. . . .
> If you cause any unlawful damage . . . accidentally and unintentionally, you must

Rome, capital and largest city of the Roman Empire, achieved a size and splendor unequaled in its time. At its center was the Forum, the large open space shown in this photo. Surrounded by government buildings, temples, and markets, the Forum was open to all Romans, rich and poor alike. When did Roman civilization reach its peak?

make good the loss, either by tendering what has caused it, or by payment. . . .

If anyone who has arrived at puberty, secretly, and by night, destroys or cuts and appropriates to his own use, the crop of another, . . . he shall be . . . hung. . . .

When one publicly abuses another in a loud voice, or writes a poem for the purpose of insulting him, or rendering him infamous, he shall be beaten with a rod until he dies. . . .

Anyone who kills a [superior], shall have his head wrapped in a cloth, and after having been sewed up in a sock, shall be thrown into the water. . . .

When a judge, or an arbiter appointed to hear a case, accepts money, or other gifts, for the purpose of influencing his decision, he shall suffer the penalty of death. . . .*

THE EMPIRE

In 27 BC, the Roman Republic came to an end. The Roman Empire came into being, and a Roman named Octavian was declared

emperor. Known as Caesar Augustus, he was the first of a long line of emperors who ruled for the next 500 years.

During the first 200 years of the Empire, known as the Pax Romana, Roman civilization reached its peak. Rome, with a population of about 1 million people, became the largest city in the western world. Below, a modern historian relates what Rome was like at the time:

> . . . Ships from all over the known world fed and clothed and beautified her. Her corn came from Africa, Egypt, Sicily, and Sardinia; her pepper from as far away as India. Her marble came from Africa, Egypt, and Asia Minor; her tin from Britain and Northern Spain. Silk came from China, cotton from India. Linen, embroidery, papyrus, came from Egypt. Her citizens ate meat, poultry and game, and fish imported often at great cost. They ate bread and cakes, olives and fruit of many varieties, and drank various kinds of wine. All classes wore simple gowns and tunics, those of the rich being of fine linen and wool, sometimes of silk, and richer women began to wear fine jewels.

---

*"The Laws of the Twelve Tables," as cited in *The Civil Law*, Vol. I, by S. P. Scott, 1932, Cincinnati, The Central Trust Company, pp. 57, 60, 64, 66, 69, 70, 71, 72, 73, 76. Reprinted by permission.

In appearance Rome became proud and beautiful. . . . The Roman emperors built themselves mighty triumphal arches and victory columns. . . . They built fine temples to the Roman gods, warehouses and offices and shops, often within beautifully constructed arcades. There were government buildings . . . and magnificent palaces for their emperors. . . .

Though the Romans had on the whole little interest in Greek athletics, they were enthusiastic about chariot-racing and built large circuses for the sport. While the charioteers raced around the oval arena spectators watched from tiered seats, as in a theatre.

The theatre itself also developed from the Greek pattern, and the Romans popularized a form of entertainment which had never flourished in Greece—gladiatorial combats between men, and man and animal. Great amphitheatres modeled on the pattern of a theatre were built for these spectacles. . . .

Far more enlightened was the Roman's pleasure in the public bath. This was more than merely bathing or swimming; it constituted a complete social entertainment. The baths were large, and elaborately and beautifully constructed, with mosaic floors . . . and a liberal display of statues. From the ante-room, where he undressed, the

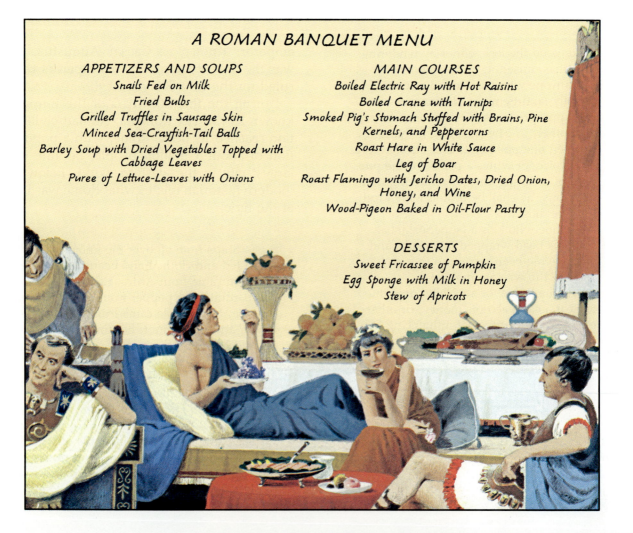

A ROMAN BANQUET MENU

APPETIZERS AND SOUPS
Snails Fed on Milk
Fried Bulbs
Grilled Truffles in Sausage Skin
Minced Sea-Crayfish-Tail Balls
Barley Soup with Dried Vegetables Topped with Cabbage Leaves
Puree of Lettuce-Leaves with Onions

MAIN COURSES
Boiled Electric Ray with Hot Raisins
Boiled Crane with Turnips
Smoked Pig's Stomach Stuffed with Brains, Pine Kernels, and Peppercorns
Roast Hare in White Sauce
Leg of Boar
Roast Flamingo with Jericho Dates, Dried Onion, Honey, and Wine
Wood-Pigeon Baked in Oil-Flour Pastry

DESSERTS
Sweet Fricassee of Pumpkin
Egg Sponge with Milk in Honey
Stew of Apricots

bather went first to the frigidarium for his cold bath. . . . Then he passed through a series of heated rooms and finally relaxed in the caldarium, the hot bath, after which he was massaged with sweet-smelling oils. But the actual bath was only a small part of the entertainment. In all the large public baths was a large open court where he would wrestle, play ball-games, or exchange the gossip of the day.*

At first, the people of the various provinces that made up the Empire were allowed to keep their own languages, religions, laws, and customs. In time, however, the Empire was **romanized,** made Roman in character and style. Roads and bridges were built, making it easier for people to travel and ideas to spread. **Aqueducts,** elevated structures that transported water from distant areas, were erected. Towns and cities modeled after Rome began to spring up. Latin became the official language, and Roman law was enforced throughout the Empire.

THE RISE OF CHRISTIANITY

As the Romans traded with and conquered new peoples, new religions and beliefs mingled with their own. One of these religions was Christianity. At first, Christians were ignored or tolerated. But, in time, they became the target of persecution. They especially angered the Romans by refusing to take part in some rituals dedicated to the emperor. To Christians, observing the rituals meant worshipping the emperor as god, which compromised their religious beliefs. To the Romans, the refusal to observe the rituals was political disobedience.

Christians began to be blamed for all kinds of disasters. When a fire burned much of Rome in 64 AD, the emperor accused Christians and began to put them to death. Although the persecution continued for many

---
The Chain of History by Pauline Gregg, 1958, George G. Harrap & Co. Ltd., pp. 78–83.

Roman guards have discovered Christians worshipping in catacombs, underground passages and rooms like this one, dug by early Christians hoping to escape persecution. Why did the Romans persecute Christians?

years, the religion continued to grow and spread. About 112 AD, a Roman governor named Pliny, concerned about the rapid growth of Christianity in his province, wrote the following letter to the emperor:

> . . . Having never been present at any trials of the Christians, I am unacquainted with the method and limits to be observed either in examining or punishing them. Whether any difference is to be made on account of age . . . ; whether repentance admits to a pardon, or if a man has been once a Christian it avails him nothing to recant; whether the mere profession of Christianity or only the crimes associated therewith are punishable—in all these points I am greatly doubtful.
>
> In the meanwhile, the method I have observed towards those who have been denounced to me as Christians is this: I interrogated them whether they were Christians; if they confessed, I repeated the question twice again, adding the threat of capital punishment; if they still persevered, I ordered them to be executed. . . .
>
> . . . A placard was put up, without any signature, accusing a large number of per-

sons by name. Those who denied they were, or had ever been, Christians, who repeated after me an invocation to the Gods, and offered adoration . . . to your image, . . . and who finally cursed Christ —none of which acts, it is said, those who are really Christians can be forced into performing—these I thought it proper to discharge. Others who were named . . . at first confessed themselves Christians, and then denied it; true, they had been of that persuasion but they had quitted it. . . . They all worshipped your statue and the images of the Gods, and cursed Christ.

They affirmed, however, the whole of their guilt, or their error was, that they were in the habit of meeting on a certain fixed day . . . , when they sang . . . a hymn to Christ, as to a god, and bound themselves by a solemn oath . . . never to commit any fraud, theft, or adultery, never to falsify their word, nor deny a trust. . . . Even this practice, however, they had abandoned. . . .

. . . Persons of all ranks and ages, and of both sexes are, and will be, involved in the prosecution. For this contagious superstition is not confined to the cities only, but has spread through the villages and rural districts.*

By early 300 AD, Christianity was well organized and strong, but the persecution was worse than ever. Then, a new emperor named Constantine came to power in part of the Empire and granted the people in his domain the right to worship as they pleased. In 324 AD, he became the first Christian emperor of the Roman Empire.

1. With what did the Twelve Tables deal? Why were they important?
2. What changes took place in the Roman Empire during the Pax Romana?
3. How were Christians regarded in the Roman Empire?

---
*Pliny, as translated in *Pliny: Letters*, Vol. II, by William Melmoth and revised by W. M. L. Hutchinson, 1963, Harvard University Press and William Heinemann Ltd., pp. 401, 403, 405. Reprinted by permission.

THE MIDDLE AGES

In 476, western Rome fell to German invaders from the north. By the mid-500's, Rome's empire in the west was gone, replaced by large and small Germanic kingdoms. In time, a Germanic people known as Franks built a new empire. It reached its height in the late 700's and early 800's under a leader named Charlemagne. Under his rule, commerce and learning grew, the arts flowered, Christianity spread, and much of Western Europe was united by a common set of ideas and laws. After his death, his empire collapsed, and Western Europe was again divided into many kingdoms.

This was the Middle Ages, a period during which a new civilization emerged in Western Europe. Towns rose and prospered. Commerce grew, and so did the wealth of merchants. **Guilds,** associations designed to protect and regulate a town's trade, became powerful. Western ideas of trade, government, and society began to develop.

FEUDALISM

During the early Middle Ages, a new social and political system took root. Known as **feudalism,** it was based on the ownership of land and on ties of loyalty and duty among nobles. Large landholders, known as **lords,** granted protection and parts of their **fiefs,** or territories, to other nobles, known as **vassals,** in return for loyalty and service. Below, a young man asks a lord to allow him to be a vassal:

> Inasmuch as it is known to all and sundry that I lack the wherewithal to feed and clothe myself, I have asked of your pity, and your goodwill has granted to me permission to deliver and commend myself into your authority and protection . . . in return you have undertaken to aid and sustain me in food and clothing, while I

INSIGHTS ON PEOPLE
WESTERN EUROPE

CHARLEMAGNE

Charles the Great, known as Charlemagne, ruled from 768 to 814. The most powerful leader in Western Europe, the people considered him as important as any Roman emperor. Below, one of his followers talks about the accomplishments of the ruler he called Karl:

The person of Karl was large and robust, and of commanding stature, . . . His walk was firm, and the whole carriage of his body was manly. . . .

He took constant exercise in riding and hunting, which was natural for a Frank, since scarcely any nation can be found to equal them in these pursuits. . . .

In his eating and drinking he was temperate; more particularly so in his drinking, since he had the greatest abhorrence of drunkenness in anybody. . . .

While he was dining he listened to music or reading. . . .

While he was dressing and binding on his sandals, he would receive his friends; and also, if the Count of the palace announced that there was any cause which could only be settled by his decree, the suitors were immediately ordered into his presence, and, as if sitting in court, he heard the case and gave judgment. . . .

He was ready and fluent in speaking, and able to express himself with great clearness. He did not confine himself to his native tongue, but took great pains to learn foreign languages, acquiring such knowledge of Latin that he used to repeat his prayers in that language as well as in his own. Greek he could understand better than pronounce. . . . He was an ardent admirer of the liberal arts, and greatly revered their professors. . . .

The Christian religion, in which he had been brought up . . . was held . . . as most sacred, and he worshipped in it with the greatest piety. . . .

To the Pope he made many and rich presents; and nothing lay nearer his heart . . . than that the city of Rome should attain to its ancient importance by his zeal and patronage, and that the church of St. Peter should . . . not only be in safe keeping and protection, but should also by his wealth be ennobled and enriched beyond all other churches. . . .

Karl . . . went to Rome, and stayed there the whole winter in order to reform and quiet the Church. . . . It was at this time that he received the title of Emperor and Augustus. . . .

After he had taken the Imperial title, he turned his attention to the laws of his people, . . .

He also wrote out and committed to memory the . . . very ancient songs which told . . . of the kings of old. He also began a grammar of the speech of his country. He also gave names in the national tongue to the months of the year. . . .

. . . Above his tomb was erected a gilded monument. . . . His dignity was thus described—

Under this tomb is placed the body of Karl, The Great and Orthodox Emperor, who gloriously enlarged the realm of the Franks, and successfully reigned during forty-seven years.*

1. In what was Charlemagne interested?
2. What contributions did Charlemagne make to the unity and development of Western Europe?

**Life of the Emperor Karl the Great*, translated from Eginhard by William Glaister, 1877, George Bell & Sons, pp. 73–88.

In the early days of feudalism, most nobles and their families lived in one-room manor houses built of wood. By the 1100's, the manor houses were made of stone and were known as castles. During long winter evenings, scenes like this one were common as the lord, his family, friends, and servants gathered together to play chess, listen to music, and talk. Of what did a manor generally consist?

have undertaken to serve you and deserve well of you as far as lies in my power. And for as long as I shall live, I am bound to serve you and respect you as a free man ought, and during my lifetime I have not the right to withdraw from your authority and protection, but must, on the contrary, for the remainder of my days remain under it.*

During this period, much of the land was organized into **manors,** self-supporting estates belonging to one or more lords. Each manor generally consisted of a large house or castle where a noble or a **knight,** or mounted warrior, lived; a home farm known as a **demesne;** and the surrounding fields, woods, and pasture. The estates of some nobles were made up of as many as 20 or 30 manors. Although life for the lords and their families varied according to custom and wealth, most followed the pattern described below:

> As lord of the manor, Robert Fitzralph . . . must see that his estate is kept in good order, that his tenants work hard and pay their rents and that every tenant is treated fairly. He has a large home farm that is managed for him by a bailiff. It is Lord Robert's duty to maintain law and order in the village and to deal with minor crimes and disturbances. . . .
>
> Most of Lord Robert's time is taken up with the day-to-day running of the estate, but sometimes he has to do service directly for the king. Although he no longer has to serve as a knight for so many days a year, he still has certain obligations to the crown. For example, he must give evidence for tax and other financial enquiries. . . . Sometimes he will have to serve as one of the king's tax collectors. . . .
>
> For amusement, Lord Robert enjoys hunting. . . . Hawking is a favourite sport, too, and the ladies can join in. The hawks are very carefully trained to fly after ducks and small animals. . . . One of his tenants looks after them and it is almost a fulltime job. . . . Other amusements are chess, checkers, singing, dancing, and storytelling. Lord Robert also enjoys riding and fencing, which keep him in condition for fighting. . . .

---

*As cited in *Everyday Life in Medieval Times* by Marjorie Rowling, 1968, B. T. Batsford Ltd, pp. 31–32. Reprinted by permission.

Lord Robert's wife is the daughter of . . . a rich man. . . . When she married, the Lady Mathilda brought a 'dowry' of land . . . with her, and, in return, Lord Robert promised her a small house and piece of land on his other estate to support her in her widowhood, should he die first. . . .

Lady Mathilda supervises the household and servants and sees to the running of the manor house. She is in charge of all the stores, including the wine-cellar, and oversees all the baking and brewing for her family. . . . In the little spare time she has, she enjoys embroidery and makes fine belts and ribbons. . . . She also makes vestments for the parish church. . . .

Though their life is easier than the peasants', it is not luxurious and they would be looked down on by the richer nobles, and even some of the wealthier townfolks.*

The land that made up the fields of the manor generally was divided among peasants, most of whom were serfs bound to the land. They could not leave the manor, marry, or inherit land without the lord's permission. Serfs were expected to work three days a week in the lord's fields, perform certain services for and make certain payments to the lord, and carry the manor's produce to fairs whenever the lord ordered. All of their flour had to be ground in the lord's mill and all of their bread baked in the lord's ovens, services for which they were

---

Life in a Medieval Village by Gwyneth Morgan. Copyright 1975, by Cambridge University Press, pp. 36, 38. Reprinted by permission of Cambridge University Press.

expected to pay. As can be seen in the excerpt that follows, taken from a school text written about the year 1000, the life of a serf was hard:

> Now Ploughman, what work do you do?
> I work very hard. I go out at dawn driving oxen a-field and yoke them to the plough. For fear of my lord I dare not stay at home even when the winter is very cold. Every day I must plough a full acre or more.
> Have you any companions?
> I have a boy to threaten the oxen with a goad. He is quite hoarse with the cold and shouting.
> What else do you do?
> I have to get hay for the oxen, water them and clean out the sheds.
> Great is your labor!
> Verily, it is because I am not free!*

THE CHURCH

Life in the Middle Ages revolved around feudalism and the Roman Catholic Church. According to one writer of the time, society could be compared to the human body. Peasants were the feet and legs, because they were the source of the labor on which society depended. Nobles were the hands and arms, because they were the protectors and defenders. Priests and clerks were the head and eyes, because they were the spiritual guides of all the people.

Since the fall of the Roman Empire, the Church had become Western Europe's largest landholder, making it both rich and powerful. All Christians, from the poorest serf to the most powerful noble, belonged to it and were influenced by it. Enemies of the Church were viewed as enemies of God. As seen in this passage, almost every village had a church and a priest:

*From *Aelfric's Colloquies*, as quoted in *The Middle Ages* by Dorothy Mills, © 1935, G.P. Putnam's Sons, p. 174.

> . . . all the land in Christendom was divided up into parishes, which usually consisted of a village, and the farms in neighboring fields. The village . . . boasted two stone buildings. One was the mill to which everyone brought his corn to be ground. The other was the parish church. . . . To one side of the church was the church-yard, . . . and close by was a two-roomed house, which served as a second home to everyone in the parish, for here lived the village priest.
>
> The village priest did not pretend to be a clever man, but he knew more than his neighbors, because he could read and write. . . . He could decline a Latin noun, conjugate a Latin verb, and knew many Psalms by heart. But best of all he knew the hearts of his people, for he had grown up among them, and was a peasant like themselves. Therefore, they trusted him and came to him with their sins and difficulties, certain that he would help them. . . .
>
> In every little hamlet and village the priest was the leader of the people. He christened, married, and buried them. He served them in church on Sundays and holidays. In his sermons . . . , he comforted the heartsore and wretched, and taught all . . . to hold fast to right living. He also taught the children in the shade of the little church porch. . . .
>
> The priest tried to look after his people's bodies as well as their souls, and the old women of the village told him all he did not know about the use of herbs. . . . A sudden pain . . . could be cured by holding a shield of branches over the patient and singing an old heathen chant containing the words: "Flee witch to the hilltop!" But by ending the chant with the words "so be it, Lord," the heathen spell was turned into a Christian one! . . .
>
> But in most things the people obeyed their priest; for to them he stood for the majesty of Rome. Each man set aside a tenth of his goods each year for the Church, and at harvest time one sack of

CASE STUDY
WESTERN EUROPE

THE CRUSADES

In the late eleventh century, the Western Europeans launched the Crusades, a series of holy wars against Muslims who had occupied Palestine. Their intention was to recover Jerusalem and the Holy Land for the Christians. A modern-day author, in the foreword to his work on the Crusades, wrote the following:

It was a migration, and a journey, and war. All kinds of people joined the marchers, lords and vagabonds, weapon men and peasants, proud ladies and tavern drabs. "A thing unheard of," said a chronicler of the day, "that such divers people and so many distinguished princes, leaving their splendid possessions, their wives and their children, set forth with one accord and in scorn of death to seek the most unknown regions."

They were marching out of the familiar, known world into Asia to set free with their own hands the Sepulcher of Christ. They wanted to live there, in the promised land, ruled by no king but by the will of God. On the shoulders of their jackets they wore a cross, sewn out of cloth, and because of this they were called the cruciati, *or cross-bearers. So we, to-day, call them the crusaders.*

Most of them died on the way. But they went on, and after three years some of them reached their destination, Beyond the Sea. Here their journey ended, but other cross-bearers came out to join them. For the first time all the peoples of Christendom, speaking different languages and separated from each other until now, were united in a common enterprise. Christendom had taken up the sword against Islam, and the war went on for more than three centuries and some two million human beings perished in it. *

The Crusades did not achieve their goal. They did, however, have a significant effect on Western Europe and its people. They united Western Europeans under the banner of Christianity and inspired idealism, sacrifice, and chivalry. At the same time, they brought the West and the East into contact with each other and gave each an awareness and knowledge of civilizations and religions different from their own. They also created renewed interest in art, learning, and knowledge. Trade increased and expanded, and money became more important. This led to the growth of towns. These changes, along with others, helped to phase Western Europe out of the Middle Ages into modern times.

1. Why did the Western Europeans launch the Crusades?
2. What effect did the Crusades have on Western Europe and its people?

---

*Excerpt from *The Crusades* by Harold Lamb. Copyright 1930 by Harold Lamb. Reprinted by permission of Doubleday & Company, Inc.

Monasteries, such as this one, considered model centers of Christian living, housed communities of monks who lived under common rules and took vows of celibacy, poverty, and obedience. What duties did the monks perform?

corn from each farmer found its way to the priest's spare room, or into his barn. Each woman brought the first basket of berries she gathered, a fat spring chicken, a dozen eggs, a honeycomb, or a round yellow cheese. One third of these good things had to go to the bishop of the diocese, and another third to the lord of the village, but the rest belonged to the priest.*

The Church also established **monasteries**, places where men called monks withdrew from everyday life to devote their lives to worship and to serving God. The monks worked in the monasteries' fields, cared for the sick and poor, copied ancient manuscripts, and inspired the building of churches and cathedrals. Without their efforts, much land would not have been cultivated, more people would have died of disease or of hunger, and many classics of literature would have been lost.

1. What was the relationship of lord and vassal?
2. What role did the noble play on a manor? What role did the peasant play?
3. What was the role of the Church during the Middle Ages?

---

*_A Picturesque Tale of Progress, New Nations_, Part I, by Olive Beaupré Miller, 1935, pp. 191–194. Reprinted by permission of the United Educators, Inc.

EXPLORATION
WESTERN EUROPE

The quotes that follow are the words of Western Europeans of ancient and medieval times. Based on the information in the chapter, which do you think represent the basic philosophies and values of the ancient and medieval civilizations of Western Europe? Why do you think so? Which philosophies and values do you think endure even today?

United we stand, divided we fall.
—Aesop, Greek fabulist, 620–560 BC

The end and perfection of our victories is to avoid the vices and infirmities of those whom we subdue.
—Alexander the Great, King of Macedonia, 356–323 BC

The law is not made for the just, but for the unjust.
—St. Ambrose, Bishop of Milan, 340–397

Equality consists in the same treatment of similar persons, and no government can stand which is not founded on justice.
—Aristotle, Greek philosopher, 384–322 BC

Philosophy is the best medicine for the mind.
—Marcus Tullius Cicero, Roman orator, 106–43 BC

We must recall that the basic principle [of liberty] is freedom of choice, which saying many have on their lips but few in their mind.
—Dante Alighieri, Italian Poet, 1265–1321

There is nothing, absolutely nothing, which needs to be more carefully guarded against than that one man should be allowed to become more powerful than the people.
—Demosthenes, Athenian orator, c. 385–322 BC

There is written and unwritten law. The one by which we regulate our constitutions in our cities is the written law; that which arises from custom is the unwritten law.
—Diogenes Laërtius, Greek biographer, 200 BC

To the lowly, the powerful and rich are as gods.
—Euripides, Greek dramatist, 485–406 BC

There are two powers by which chiefly this world is ruled: the sacred authority of the priesthood and the authority of kings.
—Gelasius I, Pope, ?–492

Adversity reminds men of religion.
—Titus Livius, Roman historian, 59 BC –17 AD

We should always be disposed to believe that that which appears to us to be white is really black, if the hierarchy of the Church so decides.
—St. Ignatius of Loyola, Spanish founder of the Society of Jesus, 1491–1556

No freemen shall be taken, or imprisoned, or outlawed, or exiled, or in any way harmed, nor will we go upon him, nor will we send upon him, except by the legal judgment of his peers, or by the law of the land.
—"Magna Carta," charter of English political and civil liberties, written 1215

Five great enemies to peace inhabit within us: avarice, ambition, envy, anger, and pride.
—Petrarch, Italian poet, 1304–1374

Man proposes, but God disposes.
—Thomas á Kempis, German Augustinian writer, c. 1380–1471

CHAPTER 47 REVIEW

POINTS TO REMEMBER

1. The ancient Greeks developed one of the first advanced civilizations on the European continent.
2. Athens, which led Greece into a "golden age" of art and learning, was one of the first democracies in history.
3. In Sparta, athletic and military feats were glorified. Trade and leisure, however, were discouraged, and the arts and intellectual accomplishments were ignored.
4. The Greeks made major contributions in government, physical and fine arts, theater, literature, science, and philosophy.
5. In 338 BC, King Philip of Macedonia defeated the Greek city-states. After his death, his son Alexander took control, built a vast empire, and tried to create a universal state.
6. Rome, which began as a small farming settlement, developed into a republic and then an empire.
7. During the period of the republic, Roman laws appeared in written form for the first time. These laws, known as the Twelve Tables, provided the basic legal code of Rome for nearly 1000 years.
8. Roman civilization reached its peak during the Pax Romana.
9. Christians were not accepted in Rome until Constantine came to power and granted the people the right to worship as they pleased.
10. During the Middle Ages, which began after the fall of Rome, a new social and political system known as feudalism took hold, and the manor system became the way of life for Western Europeans.
11. The Roman Catholic Church became Western Europe's largest landholder and very wealthy and powerful. Along with feudalism, it was at the center of life during the Middle Ages.

VOCABULARY

Identify

Athens	Hippocrates	Philip II of Macedonia	Pax Romana
Sparta	Hippocratic Oath	Alexander	Constantine
Lycurgus	Socrates	Hellenistic civilization	Franks
Olympic Games	Socratic method	Rome	Charlemagne
Herodotus	Plato	Twelve Tables	Middle Ages
Thucydides	Aristotle	Caesar Augustus	Crusades
Thales of Miletus			

Define

tragedies	republic	romanized	fiefs
comedies	consuls	aqueducts	vassals
scientific method	plebians	guilds	manors
political science	patricians	feudalism	knight
logic	civil laws	lords	demesne
universal state			monasteries

DISCUSSING IMPORTANT IDEAS

1. Athens and Sparta were in direct contrast in all aspects of life. In which would you have preferred to live? Why?
2. Alexander wanted to spread Greek culture and ideas. At the same time, he wanted to create a universal state. Do you think these two goals conflicted? Explain.
3. Like Pliny, most Roman officials were concerned about the spread of Christianity. For what reasons do you think they feared its spread?
4. Do you think feudalism helped or hindered progress and development in Western Europe? Explain.

DEVELOPING SKILLS

IDENTIFYING VALID ASSUMPTIONS

Suppose that every day after school, you stop in a small store on the way home and buy an ice-cream cone. At first, you bought different flavors of ice cream. For the last few weeks, though, you have been buying chocolate. And, today, you have decided you would rather have strawberry than chocolate. The clerk, however, sees you coming and, without waiting for you to place your order, makes you a chocolate cone. The clerk has made an *assumption*, a decision that something is true without it being supported or proven. Because you ordered chocolate ice-cream cones several times in a row, he *assumed*, took for granted, that you would want it this time as well. The assumption, made without a basis in fact, led him to *conclude*, or reach a decision, that he should make a chocolate ice-cream cone for you.

Assumptions made without a basis in fact, like the one made by the clerk, often lead to wrong conclusions. For this reason, before you can base a conclusion on an assumption or decide if a conclusion is logical or reasonable, you must be able to identify assumptions and determine whether they are valid. The following guidelines will help you do this:

1. Identify the conclusion. It generally tells about or indicates something that is done or is held to be true. The conclusion often is introduced by such terms as *in summary, thus, so, as a result,* and *therefore*. Even if these terms are not actually expressed, they may be understood in the sense of the sentence.
2. Look for the assumption. It generally is in the part of the sentence preceding the conclusion or in a previous, separate sentence.
3. Check to see what facts are provided to support the assumption. If facts are presented, the assumption probably is valid or reasonable and the conclusion acceptable.

Look, for example, at this statement:

And, believing that the highest function of a free woman was the bearing of children, he insisted on the training of the body as no less incumbent on the female than on the male.

In this statement, the conclusion is "he insisted on the training of the body as no less incumbent on the female than on the male." It indicates something that was done. Although the word "therefore" does not actually appear in the sentence, it makes sense when inserted. The assumption is "the highest function of a free woman [is] the bearing of children." No supporting statements are given to indicate whether the assumption is true, and you have no way of knowing whether the person who made the assumption had any facts on which to base it. Therefore, you would be correct to question both the validity of the assumption and the conclusion.

For further practice in this skill, use the guidelines to identify the assumptions and their validity in the passage about Alexander by Plutarch that appears on page 776 of the text.

CHAPTER 48
RISE OF WESTERN EUROPE

1. In what ways did Western Europe change between the 1300's and 1900's?
2. How did development affect the people of Western Europe over the centuries?

But what if our elders, and those who preceded them, had followed simply the same path as did those before them? . . . Nay, on the contrary, it seems good for philosophers to move to fresh ways and systems; good for them to allow neither the voice of the detractor, nor the weight of ancient culture, nor the fullness of authority, to deter those who would declare their own views. In that way each age produces its own crop of new authors and new arts. This age of ours sees art and science gloriously re-risen, after twelve centuries of swoon. Art and science now equal their ancient splendor, or surpass it. This age need not, in any respect, despise itself, and sigh for the knowledge of the Ancients. . . . Our age today is doing things of which antiquity did not dream. . . . Ocean has been crossed by the prowess of our navigators, and new islands found. The far recesses of India lie revealed. The continent of the West, the so-called New World, unknown to our forefathers, has in great part become known. In all this, and in what pertains to astronomy, Plato, Aristotle and the old philosophers made progress, and Ptolemy added a great deal more. Yet, were one of them to return today, he would find geography changed beyond recognition. A new globe has been given to us by the navigators of our time.*

These words were written in 1530 by Jean Fernel, a 33-year-old French doctor and scientist. Like other people of his time, he was looking for "fresh ways and systems." By the time Fernel wrote these words, Western Europe had survived periods of war, plague, and other conflicts and had begun to prosper. Trade had flourished, and towns and cities had begun to grow. Merchants had become more powerful, and banking families had established networks across Europe.

The outburst of learning, scientific advances, and discoveries that took place within Fernel's lifetime stimulated Western European growth and expansion and marked the beginning of modern times. By the 1900's, Western Europe had outdistanced other great world civilizations and had become the most powerful region in the world, controlling the resources and people of many countries. Then, within a period of little more than 20 years, Western Europe found itself embroiled in two world wars. Although it lost its dominant place in world affairs, its ideas continued to lead much of the world.

---

*Jean Fernel, as cited in *The Mapmakers* by John Noble Wilford, 1981, Alfred A. Knopf, Inc., p. 93. Reprinted by permission.

REBIRTH AND REFORM

Beginning in the 1300's, some important changes began to take place in Western Europe in the form of intellectual and religious developments. These developments, which came to be known as the Renaissance and the Reformation, had far-reaching consequences for the region.

THE RENAISSANCE

The Renaissance was a rebirth of learning that began around 1350 in the city-states of Italy. It started with a new interest in the classical writings of Greek and Roman thinkers and soon led to a flowering of the arts and sciences. During the Renaissance, the classical beliefs of intellectual inquiry and the dignity and worth of the individual once again became important. Careful inquiry and experimentation came to be admired, and many old beliefs were challenged.

During this time, the Italian city-states competed with one another for superiority in trade and for artistic and intellectual leadership. The city-state of Florence soon led the others in both areas. Florence was under the rule of Lorenzo de' Medici, the head of a prominent banking family. Many modern historians have come to regard Lorenzo de' Medici as the ideal of the Renaissance man.

RENAISSANCE MANNERS

Do not blow your nose and then open and look inside your handkerchief, as if pearls or rubies had dropped out of your head.

Do not offer anyone a fruit from which you have already taken a bite.

Do not tell sad stories at parties or mealtimes. If someone starts talking this way, gently and politely change the subject and talk about something more cheerful.

Do not brag about honors, wealth, or intelligence.

Do not speak while yawning.

Do not clean your teeth with your napkin or your finger.

Do not lie all over the dinner table, or fill both sides of your mouth with so much food that your cheeks stick out.

Do not undress, comb, or wash your hair in front of others.

Do not stick out your tongue, rub hands together, or groan out loud.

Do not talk too much, especially if your knowledge is small.

Below, an Italian historian of that time provides some insights into the personality of the Florentine ruler:

> Lorenzo was a man of many outstanding virtues. He also had several vices, some of them natural, some the products of necessity. . . . His accomplishments do not shine with the splendor of arms. But we will indeed find in him all those signs and evidence of virtue that are connected with civic life. No one, not even his enemies . . . , can deny that his was a great and singular mind. . . .
>
> His judgment was sound and wise, but not of a quality comparable to his intellect. . . .
>
> He desired glory and excellence more than any man. . . . He wanted to equal and compete with all the princes of Italy in everything. . . . On the whole, . . . his ambition was praiseworthy and brought him glory and fame everywhere, even outside Italy, for it caused him to strive to make the Florence of his time stand out above all other Italian cities in all arts and skills. He had a university founded in Pisa, principally for the study of letters. . . . In his time, all the most excellent and most famous men in Italy taught there and received very high salaries, for he avoided neither expense nor labor to get them. . . . Lorenzo showed the same favor to . . . all the arts of mind and hand, so that the city overflowed with all these exquisite things. And these arts flourished all the more because Lorenzo, a universal man, could pass judgment and distinguish among men, so that they competed with one another to please him. Furthermore, there was his infinite liberality, which provided all talented men with livelihoods and with all the instruments necessary for their work. To give an example: when he decided to establish a Greek library, he sent the very learned Lascaris all the way to Greece to look for good ancient books. . . .
>
> . . . His death deeply grieved all those in Italy who excelled in letters, painting, sculpture, and similar arts, for they had either received highly paid commissions from him, or else they were held in all the greater esteem by other princes, who feared that if they stopped treating them well they would go to Lorenzo.*

THE REFORMATION

The Reformation began as an effort to do away with or reform the abuses of the Catholic Church, which had gained great power in Western Europe. Along with the power had come much corruption. Not only did the Church hold a great deal of land, but it allowed Church positions to be bought and many Church officials to live in luxury. For over 100 years, Europeans who had dared to speak out against the Church were quickly silenced. Then, in the 1500's, a German monk and university professor named Martin Luther denounced certain Church practices. Luther was particularly troubled by the sale of **indulgences,** pardons that freed their owners from time in **purgatory,** a place of suffering after death.

The Church viewed the payments as a sign of repentance for wrong deeds. But Luther believed that **salvation,** forgiveness for sin, could be received only by faith. Because Luther's beliefs directly challenged the authority of the Pope, he was brought before the emperor and asked to take back his teachings. He agreed to retract any passages in his books that proved contrary to the Bible. As can be seen below, this did not satisfy the archbishop questioning him:

> Martin, . . . your plea to be heard from Scripture [the Bible] is the one always made by heretics. . . . Martin, how can you assume that you are the only one to understand the sense of Scripture? Would you put your judgment above that of so

---
**The History of Florence* by Francesco Guicciardini, translated by Mario Domandi, 1970, Harper & Row, Publishers, pp. 70, 71, 72–73, 76. Reprinted by permission.

While a group of nobles looks on, Martin Luther defends his beliefs before the emperor and church leaders. Many of Luther's doctrines found support among the German nobility, while his forceful preaching and writing helped spread his ideas throughout the western world. Why did Luther translate the Bible into German?

many famous men and claim that you know more than they all? You have no right to call into question the most holy orthodox faith, instituted by Christ the perfect lawgiver, proclaimed throughout the world by the Apostles, sealed by the red blood of the martyrs, confirmed by the sacred councils, defined by the Church in which all our fathers believed, . . . and which now we are forbidden by the pope and the emperor to discuss lest there be no end of debate. I ask you, Martin—answer candidly . . . —do you or do you not repudiate [reject] your books and the errors which they contain?*

Thus, the archbishop expressed the view of the Church. Luther, however, stood firm. Believing that the Scripture should be open to everyone, he translated the Bible into German. Before long, others began translating it into the languages of their countries. In time, Luther's efforts to reform the Church resulted in a new form of Christianity known as Protestantism.

―――――――――――
*Here I Stand: A Life of Martin Luther by Roland H. Bainton, 1950, Abingdon Press, p. 185. Reprinted by permission.

1. What were some ideas that became important during the Renaissance?
2. What role did Martin Luther play in the Reformation?
3. Why did the Reformation begin? What was its outcome?

AGE OF DISCOVERY

Beginning in the late 1400's, the rulers of Portugal and Spain, jealous of the great wealth that trade had brought the Italian city-states, became interested in exploration. They saw exploration as a way to put more money in their treasuries and to spread Christianity to new lands.

To these ends, first Portugal, and then Spain, supported a series of voyages to find an alternate route to the East Indies, which were the source of the spices Europeans needed to preserve and flavor their meats. Until this time, Arab traders had brought spices from the Indies by sea and overland to Egypt, where they were sold to Italian merchants for resale in Europe. No other routes were known, nor was the size of the oceans. But Portuguese explorers, using new navigational instruments and improved ships, gradually worked their way down the west coast of Africa. Vasco da Gama capped these voyages in 1497 when he reached India and the islands of the East Indies by sailing around the tip of Africa. Within a few years, Portugal had gained control of the East Indian trade.

In an effort to compete with Portugal, Spain sought a westward route to the Indies. In the late 1400's, an Italian navigator named Christopher Columbus made three westward voyages for Spain, discovering the islands of the Caribbean. Shortly afterward, other explorers flying the Spanish flag found the continents of North and South America.

All the voyages of discovery involved a great deal of risk, but none more so than the one made by Ferdinand Magellan, who set out with five ships and 270 men to accomplish what Columbus had failed to do—reach the East Indies by sailing west. In the account that follows, a member of the expedi-

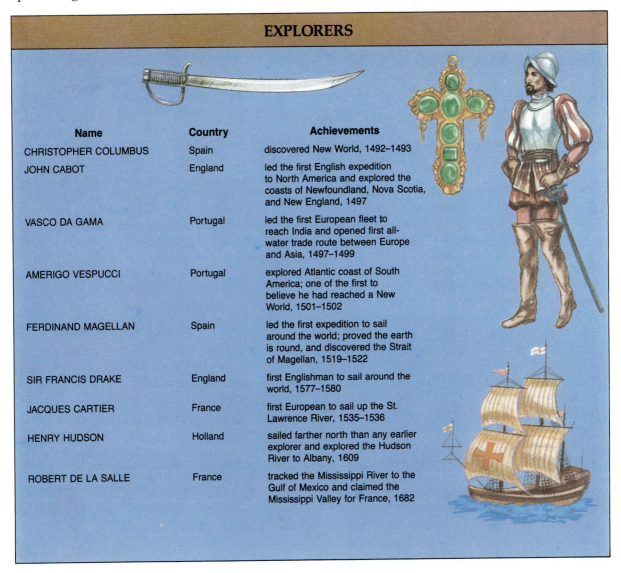

EXPLORERS

Name	Country	Achievements
CHRISTOPHER COLUMBUS	Spain	discovered New World, 1492–1493
JOHN CABOT	England	led the first English expedition to North America and explored the coasts of Newfoundland, Nova Scotia, and New England, 1497
VASCO DA GAMA	Portugal	led the first European fleet to reach India and opened first all-water trade route between Europe and Asia, 1497–1499
AMERIGO VESPUCCI	Portugal	explored Atlantic coast of South America; one of the first to believe he had reached a New World, 1501–1502
FERDINAND MAGELLAN	Spain	led the first expedition to sail around the world; proved the earth is round, and discovered the Strait of Magellan, 1519–1522
SIR FRANCIS DRAKE	England	first Englishman to sail around the world, 1577–1580
JACQUES CARTIER	France	first European to sail up the St. Lawrence River, 1535–1536
HENRY HUDSON	Holland	sailed farther north than any earlier explorer and explored the Hudson River to Albany, 1609
ROBERT DE LA SALLE	France	tracked the Mississippi River to the Gulf of Mexico and claimed the Mississippi Valley for France, 1682

This map of the Pacific Ocean, drawn in 1590, depicts the last surviving ship of Magellan's expedition, the Victoria, with cannon firing, banners flying, and a guiding angel on the prow. The legend in Latin under the ship pays tribute to Magellan and to the ship, the first to sail around the world. Magellan was killed in the Philippines, and one of his captains, Juan Sebastián del Cano, brought the ship home, reaching Spain on September 7, 1522. What problems did Magellan's expedition face?

tion recalls some of the hardships endured by Magellan's crew on the journey home:

> They sailed . . . into the Pacific Sea on the 28th of November in the year 1520, and they were three months and twenty days without eating anything (*i.e.,* fresh food), and they ate biscuit, and when there was no more of that they ate the crumbs which were full of maggots. . . . They drank yellow water, already several days putrid. And they ate some of the hides that were on the largest shroud [a line that supports the mast] to keep it from breaking and that were very much toughened by the sun, rain and winds. And they softened them in the sea for four or five days, and then they put them in a pot over the fire and ate them and also much sawdust. A mouse would bring half a ducat [gold coin] or a ducat. The gums of some of the men swelled over their upper and lower teeth, so that they could not eat and so died. . . . And if God had not given them fine weather, they would all have perished of hunger. . . . And they were certain that such a voyage would never again be made. . . .
>
> . . . And on September seventh [1522] only eighteen men and the most of them sick, all that was left of the sixty that left from the Moluccas [islands in the East Indies], entered the bay of San Lúcar [on the Spanish coast]. Some were dead of hunger, the others killed on the island of Timor for their misdeeds. . . . On the eighth of September they dropped anchor in the port of Seville. And they shot off all the artillery, gave thanks to God in their shirts, barefooted, and with torches in their hands.*

The Spanish conquered the civilizations of the New World they found, spread Christianity, established colonies, and brought great wealth to Spain. Soon, France, England, and Holland were drawn into the competition for colonies and overseas trade. The success of their voyages of discovery had a powerful impact on Europe. The fact that humans could triumph over fear and the

---

*The Voyage of Magellan: The Journal of Antonio Pigafetta, translated by Paula Spurlin Paige, 1969, Prentice-Hall, Inc., pp. 24–25, 148. Reprinted by permission.

CHAPTER 48 RISE OF WESTERN EUROPE

During the late 1500's, the English began to take a greater interest in the New World. By the early 1600's, they had established colonies there. One of these was Jamestown, Virginia, founded in 1607. This was the home of Pocahontas. The daughter of the Indian chief, Powhatan, she is shown here in 1616 being presented at the English court. What countries besides England competed for colonies and trade in the New World?

dangers of the unknown bolstered the confidence of the Europeans and created a new sense of optimism. The many new and different plants and animals brought back by the explorers excited scientists and improved the diet of the Europeans. The wealth obtained from the voyages spurred the economic growth of northern Europe.

1. Why did the Portuguese and the Spanish become interested in exploration?
2. For what were the Portuguese explorers looking? The Spanish explorers?
3. What effect did the voyages of discovery have on Europe and Europeans?

RISE OF THE NATION-STATE

Before 1500, Western Europe was made up of many independent political units whose rulers had little power beyond their own local areas. The people gave their allegiance to these rulers and to the Church.

Gradually, through such means as marriage, flattery, conspiracy, and force, some rulers managed to bring more territory under their control. Their efforts were supported by wealthy merchants and banking families. Finally, between 1500 and 1700, England and France emerged as the most powerful nations in Western Europe. The rulers of both these nations believed in **absolutism,** the concept that monarchs have absolute power and rule by **divine right,** the will of God. In 1609, James I of England explained the belief in this way:

> The state of monarchy is the supremest thing upon earth; for kings are not only God's lieutenants upon earth, and sit upon God's throne, but even by God himself they are called gods. . . .
> Kings are justly called gods, for that they exercise a manner or resemblance of divine power upon earth: for if you will consider the attributes to God, you shall see how they agree in the person of a king. God hath power to create or destroy, make or unmake at his pleasure, to give

The Noble is the Spider and the Peasant the Fly

The more the devil has, the more he wants

This seventeenth-century cartoonist used his art to speak out against the way the nobility treated peasants. How did Louis XIV treat the nobles in his court?

life or send death, to judge all and to be judged nor accountable to none; to raise low things and to make high things low at his pleasure, and to God are both soul and body due. And the like power have kings: they make and unmake their subjects, they have power of raising and casting down, of life and of death, judges over all their subjects and in all causes and yet accountable to none but God only.*

Absolutism in Western Europe reached its peak in France under Louis XIV, who ruled from 1643 to 1715. Louis, known as the Sun King because the government and the nobility revolved around him and he lived in grand style, proudly boasted, *"L'etat, c'est moi"*—"I am the state." He had many different ways of keeping his nobles under his control and making his power known to all. Some of these are detailed below by a French aristocrat named Saint-Simon:

> The frequent entertainments, the private drives to Versailles [a palace in the country], and the royal journeys, provided the King with a means of distinguishing or mortifying his courtiers [followers at court] by naming those who were or were not to accompany him, and thus keeping everyone eager and anxious to please him. He fully realized that the substantial gifts which he had to offer were too few to have any continuous effect, and he substituted imaginary favours that appealed to men's jealous natures, small distinctions which he was able . . . to grant or withhold every day and almost every hour. The hopes that courtiers built upon such flimsy favours and the importance which they attached to them were really unbelievable, and no one was ever more artful than the King in devising fresh occasions for them. . . .
>
> [One] device was the granting of the *justaucorps a brevet*, blue [jackets], lined with scarlet, with scarlet facings and waistcoat, embroidered with gold thread and a little silver in a particular pattern. Only a certain number of these jackets were made. . . . The greatest persons at the Court used to beg one for themselves or another. . . .
>
> He not only required the constant attendance of the great, but was also aware of those of lower rank. . . . He saw and noticed every one of them, marked very well the absences of those usually at Court and even of those who attended more rarely, and took care to discover the reason, drawing his own conclusions and losing no opportunity of acting upon them. He took it as an offense if distinguished people did not make the Court their home, or if others came but seldom. And to come never, or scarcely ever, meant certain disgrace. When a favour was asked

---

*Speech by King James I, as cited in *Pageants of Europe* by Raymond Phineas Stearns, 1961, Harcourt, Brace & World, Inc., p. 216. Reprinted by permission.

for such a one, the King would answer haughtily, 'I do not know him at all,' or, 'That is a man whom I never see,' and in such cases his word was irrevocable [unchangeable].*

The absolute monarchies provided a certain degree of peace and order—enough to allow the economic, artistic, and intellectual life of Western Europe to expand and become great. It was from these monarchies that, in time, the modern nations of Western Europe emerged.

1. How did James I of England and other Western European kings view their roles?
2. What were some of the ways in which Louis XIV kept his nobles under control and demonstrated his power?
3. What effect did absolutism have on growth in Western Europe?

FROM REASON TO REVOLUTION

In the 1600's, some Western Europeans, unhappy with absolutism, began to stress the importance of reason in solving human problems. Using the Renaissance ideals of individual worth and freedom, they developed many new ideas about government and social life, bringing about what came to be known as the Enlightenment or the Age of Reason.

Enlightenment thinkers argued that governments should be based on the consent or agreement of the people. Some, like England's John Locke, believed that people were equal; had natural rights to life, liberty, and property; and had the right to form a new government if the old one was not protecting their rights. In time, some Western European nations began to act on these ideas. In the late 1600's, for example, the English limited the power of their monarchs.

In France, the largest and most advanced nation of Western Europe in the late 1700's, reason turned to revolution. The country was in serious economic trouble, and the government was nearly bankrupt. In 1789, needing approval for new taxes he wanted to impose, the king called into session the Estates-General, the French legislative body. It had been nearly 200 years since the last Estates-General had met.

But, the Estates-General and the king could not come to terms. In the end, the Estates-General, full of Enlightenment arguments, dissolved itself and declared itself a new body called the National Assembly. On August 26, 1789, it stated its goals in the Declaration of the Rights of Man and of Citizens, part of which appears below:

> The representatives of the people of France . . . considering that ignorance, neglect, or contempt of human rights are the sole causes of public misfortunes and corruptions of Government, have resolved to set forth, in a solemn declaration, these natural and unalienable rights. . . .
>
> I. Men are born, and always continue, free, and equal in respect of their rights. . . .
> II. All governments should try to protect man's natural rights. These rights are liberty, property, security, and resistance to oppression.
> III. The nation is essentially the source of all Sovereignty; nor can any INDIVIDUAL or ANY BODY OF MEN, be entitled to any authority which is not expressly derived from it.
> IV. Political liberty consists in the power of doing whatever does not injure another. . . .
> VI. The law is an expression of the will of the community. All citizens have

---

*Saint-Simon At Versailles, selected and translated from the memoirs of M. Le Duc De Saint-Simon by Lucy Norton, 1958, Hamish Hamilton Ltd and Harper & Brothers, pp. 253–255. Reprinted by permission.

On July 14, 1789, an angry French mob, fearing that the National Assembly would be dissolved, stormed the Bastille, a much-hated prison in Paris. What did the National Assembly do the following month?

a right to concur, either personally, or by their representatives, in its formation. It should be the same to all. . . .

IX. Every man [is] presumed innocent till he has been convicted. . . .

X. No man ought to be molested on account of his opinions, not even on account of his *religious* opinions, provided his avowal of them does not disturb the public order. . . .

XI. The unrestrained communication of thoughts and opinions being one of the most precious rights of man, every citizen may speak, write and publish freely, provided he is responsible for the abuse of this liberty in cases determined by the law. . . .

XIII. A common contribution [tax] being necessary . . . , it ought to be divided equally among the members of the community, according to their abilities [to pay].

XIV. Every citizen has a right . . . to a free voice in determining the necessity of public contributions, the appropriation of them, and their amount, mode of assessment, and duration. . . .

XVII. The right to property being inviolable and sacred, no one ought to be deprived of it. . . .*

The result was the French Revolution. Using as their slogan, "Liberty, Equality, Fraternity," the people overthrew the monarchy and took over the country. Their actions inspired peoples of other nations who sought freedom and basic rights. In the view of some historians, the French Revolution had a far greater impact than any other revolution that came before or after it.

1. What did most Enlightenment thinkers believe?
2. To what did Enlightenment beliefs lead in England? In France?
3. What were some of the rights proclaimed in the Declaration of the Rights of Man and of Citizens?

THE INDUSTRIAL REVOLUTION

Meanwhile, in England, a different sort of revolution was taking place. In this case, events happened so gradually that it was 100 years before its developments were given the name Industrial Revolution.

Before this time, goods had always been made by hand. Now, these handcrafted, individually produced items were replaced by machine-made ones. Workers became specialized, with each person making only a portion of an item and then passing it along in a process known today as **mass production.** Workers that had produced goods in their homes came to be employed in large factories.

Rights of Man: Being an Answer to Mr. Burke's Attack on the French Revolution, by Thomas Paine, 1791, J.S. Jordan, pp. 116–119.

INSIGHTS ON PEOPLE
WESTERN EUROPE

NAPOLEON BONAPARTE

In 1796, a young general named Napoleon Bonaparte was given command of the French army in Italy, where he defeated the Austrian and Sardinian armies with whom France was at war. Three years later, he was named the First Consul of the new government of France. In 1804, he became Emperor of the French. Within a few years, he ruled an empire that included much of Europe. The events related below reflect the thinking and style of the man whose power, according to one member of the court, "impressed every one with whom he came in contact.":

... the pope ... is already on the way to Paris. ... But why does he [Napoleon] not go to Rome for his coronation? Why is he not content to be anointed in Rome, as Charlemagne had been, and all the emperors of the west since Charlemagne's day? What does he want a pope for at all?

In this matter, once more, he is trying to harmonise the new with the old. At first he is silent about details, and merely asks the pope "to give the highest religious consecration to the anointing and crowning of the first Emperor of the French." For weeks, letters have been exchanged between Rome and Paris. ... Never before has a pope been summoned in this way. When the Emperor meets the pope at the gate of the city, the Holy Father does not fail to note that Napoleon neither kneels to receive a blessing nor kisses hands in token of fealty. ...

On December 2, 1804, in Notre Dame, an abundance of precious stones reflects the light of a myriad candles, so that the place looks more like a banqueting hall than a church. Everything has been prepared for weeks beforehand. A skillful museum director has even produced a colourful imitation of Charlemagne's sceptre. Ancient parchments ... had been consulted, to ensure that the crowning ... should vie in every respect with that of the legitimate monarchs of France. ...

The Emperor is in a pleasant humour. ... The great procession drives to the cathedral. Napoleon, robed in an antique imperial mantle, strides to the high altar leading the empress by the hand. ... Surrounded by attendant cardinals, the pope is seated, waiting. The organ peals forth.

Then, when the appointed instant has come, and all are expecting this man who has never bowed the knee to anyone, to kneel before the Holy Father, Napoleon, to the amazement of the congregation, seizes the crown, turns his back on the pope and the altar, and standing upright as always, crowns himself in the sight of France. Then he crowns his kneeling wife.

None but the pope had known his intentions. ... Moreover, the crown on the Emperor's head is not a Christian crown at all, but a small pagan circlet of golden laurel leaves. All who describe the occasion agree in saying that the Emperor was pale but handsome. ...

Thus, in this symbolical hour, Napoleon reduces to mockery the legitimate formalities he is affecting to copy. Furthermore, he makes a laughing-stock of the pope, who will not forget the slight. ... [On] the steps of a temple there stands a soldier ... whom a dozen years before this day no one had ever heard of. ...

... When he was seated on the throne, crown on head, ... he said in a low aside to his brother: "Joseph, if only Father could see this! ..."

... As soon as all is over, and, alone with [the Empress] Josephine, he goes in to dinner, he says with a sigh of relief: "Thank God we're through with it! A day on the battle-field would have pleased me better!"*

1. Who was Napoleon Bonaparte?
2. What does the reading indicate to you about Napoleon's personality and power?

*Napoleon by Emil Ludwig, translated by Eden and Cedar Paul, 1926, Boni & Liveright, pp. 225, 226, 227–229.

New towns and cities grew up near the factories, and people left their homes in the countryside to seek work in the factories. New, time-saving inventions bloomed in almost every area—from the textiles industry to transportation to mining to the refining of coal, iron, and steel. With the support of **entrepreneurs,** people who risk their resources for potential profits, new industries were built around the new inventions.

In the 1800's, the pace of change quickened. The development of steam locomotives and railroads opened new possibilities for growth. Poets and writers sang hymns of praise such as the one that follows to the progress brought by machines and to the future they would bring:

> Gather, ye Nations, gather! From forge, and mine, and mill!
> Come, Science and Invention; Come, Industry and Skill!
> Come with your woven wonders, the blossoms of the loom,
> That rival Nature's fairest flowers in all but their perfume.
> Come with your brass and iron, your silver and your gold
> And arts that change the face of earth, unknown to men of old.
> Gather, ye Nations, gather! From ev'ry clime and soil,
> The New Confederation, the Jubilee of toil.*

But, as the Industrial Revolution spread, some people became less sure about its promise. Many had become dismayed by the rapid growth of cities with polluted skies and by the shocking working and living conditions of the new class of factory workers. In 1832, a member of British Parliament conducted an inquiry into conditions of textile workers in his country. Part of what he discovered is revealed in this excerpt:

---
*Quoted in *A Social History of England 1851–1975* by François Bédarida, translated by A. S. Forster, 1979, Methuen, p. 7. Reprinted by permission.

What age are you?—Twenty-two.
What is your occupation?—A blanket manufacturer.
Have you ever been employed in a factory?—Yes.
At what age did you first go to work in one?—Eight.
How long did you continue in that occupation?—Four years.
Will you state the hours of labour at the period when you first went to the factory, in ordinary times?—From 6 in the morning to 8 at night.
Fourteen hours?—Yes.
With what intervals for refreshment and rest?—An hour at noon.
When trade was brisk what were your hours?—From 5 in the morning to 9 in the evening. . . .
During those long hours of labour could you be punctual; how did you awake?—I seldom did awake spontaneously; I was most generally awoke or lifted out of bed, sometimes asleep, by my parents.
Were you always in time?—No.
What was the consequence if you had been too late?—I was most commonly beaten. . . .
In those mills is [punishment] towards the latter part of the day going on perpetually?—Perpetually. . . .
. . . the machine turns off a regular quantity of cardings [combed-out sections of wool], and of course [the children] must keep as regularly to their work the whole of the day: . . . [the overlooker] must keep up with the machine or be found fault with, [so] he spurs the children to keep up also by various means but that which he commonly resorts to is to strap them when they become drowsy. . . .
When you got home at night after this labour, did you feel much fatigued?—Very much so. . . .
What did you do?—All that we did when we got home was to get the little bit of supper . . . and go to bed immediately. . . .

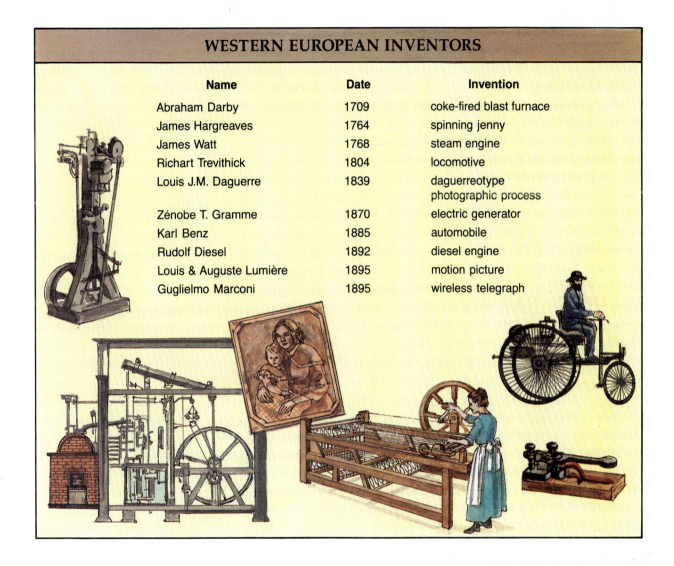

WESTERN EUROPEAN INVENTORS

Name	Date	Invention
Abraham Darby	1709	coke-fired blast furnace
James Hargreaves	1764	spinning jenny
James Watt	1768	steam engine
Richart Trevithick	1804	locomotive
Louis J.M. Daguerre	1839	daguerreotype photographic process
Zénobe T. Gramme	1870	electric generator
Karl Benz	1885	automobile
Rudolf Diesel	1892	diesel engine
Louis & Auguste Lumière	1895	motion picture
Guglielmo Marconi	1895	wireless telegraph

Were the rest of the children similarly circumstanced?—Yes, all of them; but they were not all of them so far from their work as I was.

And if you had been too late you were [afraid] of being cruelly beaten?—I generally was beaten when I happened to be too late; and when I got up in the morning the [fear] of that was so great, that I used to run, and cry all the way as I went to the mill.*

*From "Report of Committee on Factory Children's Labour" in *Parliamentary Papers,* 1831–32, as quoted in *Pageants of Europe* by Raymond Phineas Stearns, 1961, Harcourt, Brace & World, Inc., pp. 493–494.

The Industrial Revolution greatly increased Western European power over other parts of the world. With more accurate and efficient weapons and gunboats, European nations overwhelmed nations that in the past had resisted domination. In time, it became clear that the Revolution raised the standard of living of Western Europeans. Before long, the Revolution had spread to the world beyond Europe, bringing with it social, political, intellectual, and economic change. According to one historian, both the English and the rest of the world knew that the Industrial Revolution "was transforming the world. Nothing could stand in its way. The gods and kings of the past were powerless before the businessmen and steam-engines of the present."

1. How were ways of production changed by the Industrial Revolution?
2. Why did some Western Europeans become unsure about the promise of the Industrial Revolution?
3. What effect did the Industrial Revolution have on Western Europe's power over other parts of the world? On the Western European standard of life?

THE TURMOIL OF WORLD WAR

By 1900, Western Europe was at the height of its power. In the arts and quality of life, it seemed to have reached a "golden age" in which it controlled or influenced the rest of the world. Yet, below the surface, there were troubles. The nations of the region were divided by rivalry and fears. Kings no longer could make foreign policy by themselves. National pride and public opinion had become important factors in international affairs, forcing officials to consider the views of the people when making decisions.

WORLD WAR I

By 1914, the major European powers had grouped themselves into two military alliances with Germany, Italy, and Austria-Hungary on one side and Great Britain, France, and Russia on the other. When, in June of that year, the heir to the throne of Austria-Hungary was assassinated by nationalists who opposed Austrian rule over their land, the result was war between the two alliances. Before long, more nations were drawn into a conflict that lasted four years and was known first as the Great War and later as World War I. This war was different from all those that had gone before it. New techniques of warfare and new weapons increased the terror and the number of casualties. By war's end, more than 8 million soldiers were dead and more than 20 million were maimed or wounded. Germany and its allies were defeated, but Europe was exhausted and nearly bankrupt. The old values of national honor and sacrifice suddenly seemed hollow, and the old way of life was discredited. Below, a British poet who fought in the war speaks out about the horrors of the battlefield and the disillusionment that followed:

Bent double, like old beggars under sacks, Knock-kneed, coughing like hags, we cursed through sludge,
   Till on the haunting flares we turned our backs
And towards our distant rest began to trudge.
   Men marched asleep. Many had lost their boots,
But limped on, blood-shod. All went lame, all blind;
   Drunk with fatigue; deaf even to the hoots
Of tired, out-stripped Five-Nines [gas-shells] that dropped behind.
Gas! Gas! Quick, boys! An ecstasy of fumbling,
   Fitting the clumsy helmets just in time;
   But someone still was yelling out and stumbling
And flound'ring like a man in fire or lime . . .
   Dim, through the misty panes and thick green light,
   As under a green sea, I saw him drowning.
   In all my dreams, before my helpless sight
He plunges at me, guttering, choking, drowning.
   If in some smothering dreams you too could pace

CHAPTER 48 RISE OF WESTERN EUROPE

One of the new techniques of warfare was trench warfare, *shown here, in which ditches protected by barbed wire formed defensive lines to slow down the enemy. One of the new weapons was mustard gas, a colorless, oily liquid, first used by the Germans. Mustard gas bombs, like the one seen exploding here, caused permanent damage to the eyes and lungs of soldiers not wearing gas masks. Why was World War I different from all previous wars?*

Behind the wagon that we flung him in,
And watch the white eyes writhing in his face,
His hanging face, like a devil's sick of sin;
If you could hear, at every jolt, the blood
Come gargling from the froth-corrupted lungs,
Obscene as cancer, bitter as the cud
Of vile, incurable sores on innocent tongues,—
My friend, you would not tell with such high zest
To children ardent for some desperate glory,
The old Lie: *Dulce et decorum est Pro patria mori.* [It is sweet and dignified to die for the fatherland.]*

WORLD WAR II

Most of the people of the world thought that World War I was "the war to end all wars." But, within slightly more than 20 years, a second world war had broken out in Europe, a war even longer and more devastating than World War I.

Germany, humiliated by the treaty that had ended World War I and in grave economic trouble, in 1933 accepted the leadership of Adolf Hitler, who promised to lead the country to a new age of greatness. Taking one bold step after another, Hitler gained territory and power. At first, in the hope of avoiding another war, Great Britain and France did not oppose him. But, in 1939, when Hitler overran Poland, they realized that the only way to stop him was by force. The British were spurred on by their prime minister, Winston Churchill. Below, in a speech he made in 1940 just after France fell to the Germans, Churchill explains why the British must fight:

> What General Weygand called the Battle of France is over. I expect that the Battle of Britain is about to begin. Upon this battle depends the survival of Christian civilisation. Upon it depends our own British life, and the long continuity of our institutions and our Empire. The whole fury and

---
*"Dulce et Decorum Est" in *The Poems of Wilfred Owen,* edited by Jon Stallworthy, 1985, Chatto & Windus: The Hogarth Press, p. 117. Reprinted by permission.

In the shadow of war-damaged buildings, these Berliners are planting vegetable gardens to provide themselves and their families with food. According to Winston Churchill, what would have been the result if Germany had won World War II?

might of the enemy must very soon be turned on us. Hitler knows that he will have to break us in this island or lose the war. If we can stand up to him, all Europe may be free and the life of the world may move forward into broad, sunlit uplands. But if we fail, then the whole world, including the United States, and all that we have known and cared for, will sink into the abyss [pit] of a new Dark Age, made more sinister, and perhaps more protracted, by the lights of perverted science. Let us therefore brace ourselves to our duties, and so bear ourselves that, if the British Empire and its Commonwealth last for a thousand years, men will still say, "This was their finest hour."*

The Second World War: Their Finest Hour by Winston S. Churchill, 1949, Houghton Mifflin Company, pp. 225–226. Reprinted by permission.

Not until 1945 was Germany finally defeated. By this time, between 15 and 17 million soldiers and 12 million civilians were dead. Of the civilians, 6 million were Jews. The war brought to an end Western European dominance in world affairs. After the war, the United States and the Soviet Union emerged as the two most powerful nations in the world. Western Europeans had to look inward and turned their efforts to the long, hard process of rebuilding their war-torn countries.

1. What was Western Europe's role in the world by 1900?
2. What were some of the results of World War I?
3. What were the consequences for Western Europe of World War II?

CASE STUDY
WESTERN EUROPE

THE HOLOCAUST

Adolf Hitler made the Jews the scapegoats for all of Germany's troubles and set out to eliminate them. The result of this was the Holocaust, the mass murder of European Jews and other minorities, during which more than 12 million were killed. The truth about the Holocaust became known when the **concentration camps,** prison camps set up by Hitler for Jews and other minorities, were liberated at the end of the war. The condition of the survivors shocked the liberators. In the words of one medical officer, "They [the survivors] have not yet overcome their fear of authority. It will take them time to become human beings again."

Below, two concentration camp survivors talk of their experiences. The first, Marie Claude Vaillant-Couturier, spent three years in the concentration camps of Auschwitz and Ravensbruck. The second survivor, Franz Blaha, spent four years in the concentration camp of Dachau:

The work at Auschwitz consisted of clearing demolished houses, road building, and especially the draining of marshland. This was by far the hardest work, for all day long we had our feet in the water and there was the danger of being sucked down. It frequently happened that we had to pull out a comrade who had sunk in up to the waist. . . .

The causes of death were extremely numerous. First of all, there was the complete lack of washing facilities. When we arrived at Auschwitz, for twelve thousand internees there was only one tap of water, unfit for drinking, and it was not always flowing. . . .It was therefore almost impossible to wash ourselves or our clothes. For more than three months we remained without changing our clothes. When there was snow, we melted some to wash in. Later, in the spring, when we went to work we would drink from a puddle by the roadside and then wash our underclothes in it. We took turns washing our hands in this dirty water. Our companions were dying of thirst, because we got only half cup of some herbal tea twice a day."*

In 1941 and 1942 we had in the camp [Dachau] what we called invalid transports. These were made up of people who were sick or for some reason incapable of working. We called them Himmelfahrt Kommandos *(suicide squads.) About one hundred or so were ordered each week to go to the showers. There, four people gave injections . . . which soon caused death. After 1943 these invalids were sent to other camps for liquidation. I know they were killed because I saw that their records were marked with a cross and the date of departure . . . One thousand to two thousand went away every three months, so there were about five thousand sent to their death in 1943, and the same in 1944. In April 1945 a Jewish transport was loaded at Dachau and was left standing on the railroad siding. The station had been destroyed by bombing, and they could not leave. So they were left there to die of starvation. . . .*

Many executions by gas or shooting or injection took place right in the camp. . . .

. . . Sometimes prisoners were killed only because they vomited or had dysentery or gave the nurses too much trouble. Mental patients were liquidated by being led to the gas chamber and injected there or shot. . . . Prisoners could be shot just outside the crematorium and carried in. I have seen people pushed into the ovens while they were still breathing and making sounds, although if they were too much alive they were usually hit on the head first.†

1. What was the Holocaust?
2. What was the result of the Holocaust?

---

*Marie Claude Vaillant-Couturier. Reprinted by permission of The Putnam Publishing Group from *Many Kinds of Courage: An Oral History of World War II* by Tichard Lidz, p. 199. Copyright © 1980 by Visual Education Corporation.

†Dr. Franz Blaha op. cit. pp. 218–219.

CHAPTER 48 REVIEW

POINTS TO REMEMBER

1. The intellectual and religious developments of the Renaissance and the Reformation brought important changes to Western Europe beginning in the 1300's.
2. During the Renaissance, which began in the city-states of Italy, the classical beliefs of intellectual inquiry and the worth of the individual became important again.
3. In the 1500's, Martin Luther's efforts to reform the Catholic Church resulted in a new form of Christianity known as Protestantism.
4. In the late 1400's, an Age of Discovery began, during which a New World was found, colonies were founded, and trade flourished.
5. Between 1500 and 1700, England and France emerged as the most powerful nations in Western Europe under monarchs who believed in absolutism.
6. In the 1600's and 1700's, Enlightenment thinkers developed many new ideas about government and social life.
7. The French Revolution had great impact inspiring peoples of other nations who sought freedom and basic rights.
8. The Industrial Revolution, which began in England and spread, increased Western Europe's power and raised the standard of living of Western Europeans.
9. World Wars I and II put an end to Western European dominance in world affairs.

VOCABULARY

Identify

Renaissance
Reformation
Florence
Lorenzo de' Medici
Martin Luther
Protestantism
East Indies

Vasco da Gama
Christopher Columbus
Ferdinand Magellan
Louis XIV
Enlightenment
Estates-General

Declaration of the Rights of Man and of Citizens
French Revolution
Industrial Revolution
Great War

World War I
World War II
Adolf Hitler
Winston Churchill
Napoleon Bonaparte

Define

indulgences
purgatory
salvation
absolutism
divine right
mass production
entrepreneurs
concentration camps

DISCUSSING IMPORTANT IDEAS

1. What relationship do you see between the Renaissance and Reformation and the Age of Reason?
2. What do you think Western Europe might have been like in the 1900's had there been no Industrial Revolution?
3. How has emphasis on the individual and individual rights been important to the rise of European power?
4. In what ways is your life a product of the developments and events discussed in this chapter?

DEVELOPING SKILLS

ANALYZING EDITORIAL CARTOONS

Among the visual materials that may accompany or take the place of written material are cartoons. One type of cartoon that has been popular for several hundred years is the *editorial cartoon*. Also known as *political cartoons*, these drawings, which are often accompanied by words, comment on a topic of public interest. They call attention to important events, problems, issues, or individuals by teaching about or making fun of them. Like written editorials, they encourage the reader to develop an opinion about the topic to which they are devoted.

To express their messages simply and quickly, editorial cartoonists often incorporate in their drawings symbols that the audience they want to reach will recognize easily. For example, a dove may be used to represent peace, a bald eagle or Uncle Sam to represent the United States, or a hammer and sickle to represent the Soviet Union.

Editorial cartoons from the recent or distant past can be used to show how the people of a certain time period viewed the events, issues, or important persons of their era.

Look, for example, at the cartoon, which is a reproduction of the one on page 798:

As you look at the cartoon, ask yourself questions like the ones that follow. They will help you analyze this or any other editorial cartoon.

1. What seems to be the subject?
   (the actions and life style of the nobility)
2. What action is taking place?
   (One man is getting ready to give another man a bag with something in it and a basket with fruit and vegetables in it.)
3. Who are the main characters?
   (a fashionable, elegantly dressed man sitting on a thronelike chair, with his hand resting on a cane or walking stick and a large dog wearing a jeweled collar seated next to him; a simply dressed man who looks like he is getting ready to kneel, holding a sack and a basket, with a large sack holding what looks like grain at his feet between him and the other man)

4. What symbols has the cartoonist used? What does each represent or seem to represent?
   (A spider and its web, and a fly. The spider represents the nobility, and the fly represents the peasantry.)
5. What written messages has the cartoonist provided?
   ("The Noble is the Spider and the Peasant the Fly." "The more the devil has, the more he wants.")
6. Based on what I have observed and read, what do I think is the cartoonist's message?
   (Wealthy nobles take advantage of poor peasants. The peasants are caught with little chance of escape. The more they give, the more the nobles demand and take.)

For practice in this skill, find an editorial cartoon in a current newspaper or magazine, and ask yourself questions about it like the ones suggested.

CHAPTER 49
A SENSE OF THEMSELVES

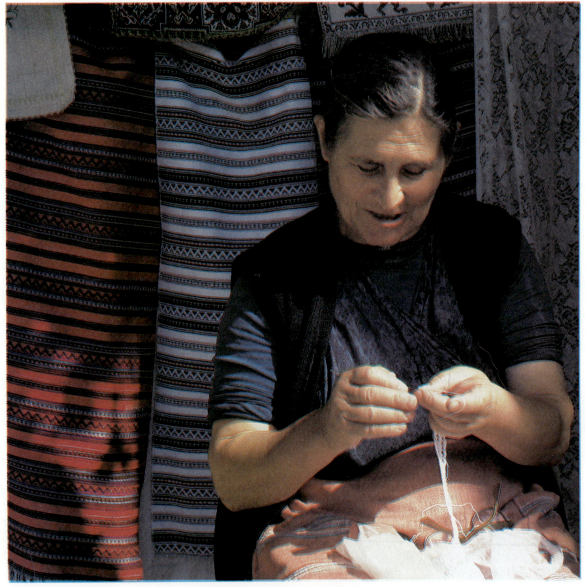

1. What are the sources of Western Europeans' identities?
2. How does sense of identity influence the way Western Europeans live today?

... Hour after hour I can think of Ireland, I can imagine without going far wrong what is happening in any one of the little towns by day or by night, can see the tillage and the walled garden, see the spilt porter [beer] foam along the counters, I can hear argument and ballads, hear the . . . prayers for the dead. I can almost tell what any one of my friends might be doing at any hour so steadfast is the rhythm of life there. I open a book, a school book maybe, or a book of superstition, or a book of place names, and I have only to see the names of Ballyhooly or Raheen to be plunged into that world from which I have derived such a richness and an unquenchable grief. The tinkers [traveling repairpersons] at Rathkeale will be driving back to their settlement by now I say, and the woman who tells fortunes in her caravan will be sending her child down for the tenth loaf of sliced bread, while a mile or two away in her domain Lady so-and-so will tell the groomsman how yet again she got her horse into a lather, and on some door in a town a little black crêpe scarf dangling from a knocker will have on it a handwritten black-edged card stating at what time the remains will be removed. . . . The men will be trying as always to distance their fate either through drink, or . . . stories, and the older women will be filled with the knowledge of how crushing their burdens are, while young girls will be gabbling, to invent diversion for themselves.

It is true that a country encapsulates our childhood and those lanes, byres [barns], fields, flowers, insects, suns, moons and stars are forever re-occurring and tantalising me with a possibility of a golden key which would lead beyond birth to the roots of one's lineage. Irish? In truth I would not want to be anything else. It is a state of mind as well as an actual country. It is being at odds with other nationalities, having [a] quite different philosophy about pleasure, about punishment, about life, and about death.*

This Irish author is like most other Western Europeans in that she has strong feelings of identity. The feelings she shares with her Irish kinspeople and her intimate sense of the Irish landscape and customs set her apart from people of other Western European countries.

Each Western European people has some distinctive qualities that unite them and that, at the same time, set them apart from other Western Europeans. Their particular feelings about family and class, their interaction with their terrain or place, their languages and religious practices, and their historical traditions and experience combine to give each of these peoples an identity, a sense of themselves.

---

*Copyright © 1976 by Edna O'Brien. From *Mother Ireland* pp. 143–144, published by Harcourt Brace Jovanovich, Inc.

FAMILY

Western Europeans value family. But, in some countries, family has traditionally been more important than in others. This has been especially true in Spain, Portugal, France, and Italy. In these countries, family is the primary focus of a person's life. Links with the extended family, with in-laws, grandparents, aunts, uncles, and cousins, provide not only emotional security but financial security as well.

In Italy, for example, family has been a source of strength during times of disorder and outside control. One Italian journalist, who calls the family "a sacred ark in which all Italians put their dearest ideals," explains the traditional view in this way:

> The family extracts everybody's first loyalty. It must be defended, enriched, made powerful, respected, and feared by the use of whatever means are necessary. . . . Nobody should defy it. . . . Its honour must not be tarnished. All wrongs done to it must be avenged. All enemies must be kept at bay. . . . Every member is duty-bound to do all he can for its welfare, give his property if needed, and, sometimes, . . . sacrifice his life. Men have spent their last penny to save a relative from bankruptcy. The family should by every means be safeguarded from runs of bad luck. . . . It must be made to prosper for generations. . . . There must be children, of course, lots of children, especially sons who can carry on the name. Nothing should be spared to produce them. Everything is done for them. . . . Their smallest wishes are satisfied. . . . Humble parents go without food, clothes, and comforts in order to pamper their sons, and to see that they go to school and reach a higher rung in the social ladder. . . .
>
> . . . There is one code valid within the family circle, with relatives and honorary relatives, intimate friends and close associates, and there is another code regulating life outside. Within, . . . they are relatively reliable, honest, truthful, just, obedient, generous, disciplined, brave, and capable of self-sacrifices. They practise what virtues other men usually dedicate to the welfare of their country at large; the Italians' family loyalty is their true patriotism.*

The journalist's comments are reinforced by the ones made below by a young Italian novelist discussing loyalty:

> For the average Italian the first loyalty is to family, then to the region he or she is from, and finally to country. . . . It is very difficult to arouse national interest here. In my lifetime nothing did that so well as Italy's winning of the world soccer championship in 1982. When that happened, everyone was out in the streets, waving Italian flags. And that was a revelation because up to then I don't even think I knew what the Italian flag looked like.†

In Italy, strong family ties are a source of strength and security. Sons, like this one sharing a simple meal with his father, are especially favored. What code do Italians follow within the family circle?

---

*Luigi Barzini, excerpted from *The Italians*, pp 193–194 Copyright © 1964 Luigi Barzini. Reprinted with the permission of Atheneum, Publishers, Inc.

†"Surviving, Italian Style" by William S. Ellis in *National Geographic*, February 1984, p. 185. Reprinted by permission.

In recent years, changes have taken place that have strained the concept of the traditional family, not only in Italy but elsewhere in Western Europe as well. Greater access to education and the need to find work have forced many parents and children to leave their homes. Yet, as one journalist observes below, family ties are not given up lightly, and old values remain strong:

> . . . From the day Isabel Alves' parents went to Paris ten years ago, they have always planned to return home. Meanwhile, Isabel lives with her grandmother and looks forward to her parents' yearly visits. Each time they come, she hopes it will be for good, but at the age of 14 she knows better.
>
> I met Isabel in the north of Portugal, in a region known as the Douro. . . .
>
> . . . northern Portugal has a chronic surplus of people over jobs, a problem facing thousands of families such as that of Isabel Alves. Many solve the problem by emigrating temporarily to one of Europe's more industrialized countries. . . . There they take whatever unskilled jobs are available and save with the one purpose of returning home to retire.
>
> I met Isabel during harvest season. A pretty girl with a quiet manner, she told me her mother and father live and work on the outskirts of Paris. Her father manages three separate jobs. . . . Her mother works full time as a housemaid. . . .
>
> Isabel's situation is common in the Douro. Out of 27 children in her school class, a third have parents who work abroad. I asked when her father and mother plan to come home to stay, and she answered hesitantly, "Perhaps in four or five years. If things go well, they will have saved enough by then to build a house in the Douro and retire."
>
> By that time Isabel will be 19—old enough to marry and, quite possibly, forced to work abroad. I asked if she would mind it.
>
> "Yes," she acknowledged, "but many of my friends will do the same. If I have sons or daughters, my parents will care for them as my grandmother has done for me. I will miss them, but it cannot be helped."*

1. How is family regarded in Italy?
2. What are some of the factors influencing the traditional concept of family today? How great an effect have they had?

SOCIAL CLASS

Class divisions have existed in Western Europe from early times. From the Middle Ages, they were based on ownership of land and having a royal title. First came the upper class, made up of a few titled aristocrats or nobles who owned a great deal of land. Next came a small middle class, at first made up of craftspersons and merchants and later of bankers, lawyers, and doctors as well. Last came the lower classes, the bulk of the population, made up of farmers with small parcels of land, tenant farmers, and day laborers.

For many years, class divisions and barriers were rigid. Sons and daughters learned the same skills as their parents and remained in the same social class. In time, however, some rich merchants and industrialists were able to move into the upper class by buying titles and estates or by marrying their daughters to nobles.

In the twentieth century, the social class structure changed further. Today, for example, though there are titled aristocrats in many countries, for the most part they do not have the economic, social, or political power they had in the past. Even so, in some areas, class divisions and feelings of class identity continue to exist. As explained in

---

*"After an Empire . . . Portugal" by William Graves in *National Geographic*, December 1980, pp. 815, 818, 822. Reprinted by permission.

The way of life of these upper-class Britons enjoying horse racing at Ascot (above left) is very different from that of the working-class Briton selling flowers at an entrance to the underground, or subway (upper right). How do the British "spot" their classes?

the newspaper article below, Great Britain is one of those areas:

"Open-plan offices, that sort of thing," Michael Cookson says in the library of the house built for his great-great-great-grandfather in 1832. . . .

Mr. Cookson stands and puts on his shooting coat, his sharp features backlit against a Regency window [window dating from the period between 1811 and 1820] looking onto his . . . estate. . . .

Beyond the rose garden, a man on a ladder is training a plum tree to grow against a brick wall. . . .

By the [rules] of Britain's bureaucracy, the gardener on the ladder behind Michael Cookson's rose garden belongs to social class "D." Mr. Cookson, "gentleman farmer," belongs in class "A." The gardener may be less poor than his father was; Mr. Cookson is definitely less rich than his.

Mr. Cookson's son might well end up working on that ladder; the gardener's son . . . could end up living in [an elegant] house. But all the cars and open-plan offices in the kingdom wouldn't allow them to trade classes.

. . . the British use clues to spot their classes. The working class plays soccer; the middle class rugby. The working class takes its holidays on the Costa del Sol [Spanish coastal region on the Mediterranean]; the middle class tours France. The working class likes aluminum door handles; the middle class buys brass.

The classes dress differently, comb their hair differently, eat different food at different times of the day. But accent and [dialect] remain the strongest status signals. The middle classes speak alike wherever they live. The working classes speak west country, cockney, geordie, scouse. When they miss a word in conversation, the lower classes say, "I beg your pardon." The upper classes don't beg; they just say, "What?"

Since rising to the top in Britain means playing by the rules, the working classes hug bottom; its members rarely get to find out what the rules are. Working-class youths might succeed in advertising or the media, if they find jobs, but can pretty much forget about big business . . . and the elite civil service. They grow up in separate neighborhoods, go to separate and often unequal schools. . . .

On a back street in Morpeth, one of Northumberland's market towns, the Comrades Club occupies an old house two doors from the unemployment office and next door to a betting shop.

"We provide cheap beer for the working class," says the young man behind the long bar inside. "The middle class go to the Conservative Club. It's jazzier." He draws a pint of strong draught ale and serves it to a long-haul driver in from Manchester.

"It's birds of a feather, isn't it?" the driver says. . . .

"It's a way of life," says Ian Moore, coming up to the bar for a beer with Tommy Hindhaugh. "Some men enjoy a Jaguar. I enjoy a pint and the art of conversation. It's your upbringing." "Class doesn't matter much," Mr. Hindhaugh puts in. "We have a millionaire in town. Self-made. He can come in here anytime."

But would the Duke of Northumberland invite him to tea?

Mr. Hindhaugh's eyebrows shoot up. "Now that's going a bit too far."*

---

*"A Briton Needn't Pay Much Heed to Class; He Knows His Place" by Barry Newman. Reprinted by permission of *The Wall Street Journal*, © Dow Jones & Company, Inc. May 6, 1985, pp. 1, 26. All rights reserved.

1. What used to be the basis on which class membership was determined?
2. What factors divide British social classes today?

PLACE

Before nations were formed in Europe, people identified themselves by the locality or region in which they lived. Each region developed its own character with its own style of architecture, art, and music, its own customs and traditions, and, at times, its own language or dialect. In many of the smaller and more isolated towns and villages, Western Europeans today continue to identify themselves in the same way. As a writer visiting the mountainous nation of Austria discovers, the same is true in some less isolated and more urban areas as well:

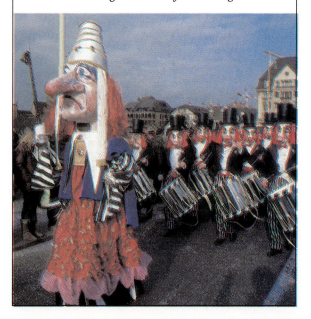

This costumed Swiss drum corps is parading during Fastnacht, a lively carnival celebrated in Germany and Switzerland each year before the religious season of Lent. Where is regional identity still strong?

FOLK COSTUMES OF WESTERN EUROPE

SPAIN PORTUGAL ITALY AUSTRIA SWITZERLAND BELGIUM LUXEMBOURG NETHERLANDS WEST GERMANY

... Would I ever understand these Austrians? Only, I had been told, there was no Austrian character to understand, only a Viennese character, a Tirolean character [of Tirol province], a Styrian character [of Styria province], and so on. "I'll tell you about the Viennese," several Viennese had told me, leaning close as if to disclose a confidence: "Every Viennese has two great ambitions. The first is to be a Vienna Choirboy, and the second—well, when one is older—is to be a Lipizzaner [rider of the performing Lipizzaner horses]!" Laughter, of course, followed; ...

[A doctor said:] "In Vienna you will always find the backward look and the pride of their past. All the things they have come through, and their survival capacity, make them feel great. You may have noticed they have a condescending way of speaking to foreigners. They don't show what they really are. Their friendliness is often a mask; deep down they are very aggressive.

"One of the difficulties of the Viennese character is that the Viennese have ... an outspoken talent for [denying] reality in fantasy. This can be noted in the Viennese saying that the situation is hopeless, but not serious.... This has enabled us, however, to survive a lot: the Turks, Napoleon, the Nazis...."

You could say even that the famous Spanish Riding School reflects the city's taste for fantasy, its capacity for survival. The major led me into the stable. It had a dreamlike quality: a Renaissance building in the heart of the city, dark-painted stalls, 20 grooms, the smell of hay and leather, 60 great Lipizzaner stallions coming and going to and from their exercises. In the half dark, with translucent skin and white hair, they seemed to glow....

I talked with an apprentice rider, 17, from the province of Carinthia. He lived in the palace; the stable, the riding school would be his life.... The major and I watched him lead off a stallion. "He has five years to go before he becomes an assistant rider, and when he has fully trained his first own horse, he becomes a rider. That takes another 10 to 15 years. And then, between 60 and 65, he will retire...."

"It's very simple," the major said with Viennese pride. "You only have to have a nice riding school and more than 400 years of tradition...."

CHAPTER 49   A SENSE OF THEMSELVES

FRANCE   SWEDEN   GREECE   DENMARK   IRELAND   ICELAND   FINLAND   MALTA   NORWAY   WALES

How different the air of Salzburg from that of Vienna: Perhaps it was the mountains, the [closeness] to West Germany. One day I went to a ceremony in the palace of the old prince-archbishops. . . . At the reception afterward I had a chance to put the question to . . . the governor of the province of Salzburg.

"The difference," he said, "lies in the origin. So many of the Viennese people stem from the Slavic regions, Czechoslovakia, Hungary, Poland. This all goes back to the Austro-Hungarian Empire. This changes the mentality. It is not a worse mentality, just a different one.

"We in Salzburg come from the Bavarian regions. We are the more noble Bavarians. The Viennese have also slowly been nobilized by us. Regions, atmospheres, landscapes make the difference."*

In other parts of Western Europe, many local and regional differences have faded. Central governments have required that the national languages be taught in school. Modern transportation and communication systems and work opportunities have broadened people's horizons. As a result, for most people, regional loyalties have been replaced by strong national identities. As he explains in a recent work, this is the case for the president of France, François Mitterrand:

. . . I live France. I have a deep instinctive awareness of France, of physical France, and a passion for her geography, her living body. For it is there that my roots have grown. There is no need for me to seek the soul of France—it lives in me.

I spent my childhood where the Angoumois, the Perigord, and Guyenne [rivers] meet. I need no stories about France. What I feel for her can do without eloquence. I lived whole seasons amid nature, part of a large self-sufficient family. The seasons always return, until the day of our death. Later on I had to get used to other aspects of France—mountains, industry, mining towns, suburbs. I approached them with the same desire to know the country—my country—so diverse, so varied, yet always true to itself, always one. But if I am not to lose my way, I must keep the rhythm of the days, see the sun rise and set, feel the sky above

---

*"Those Eternal Austrians" by John J. Putman in *National Geographic*, April 1985, pp. 410, 418–422, 432, 434. Reprinted by permission.

Many areas of Western Europe carefully preserve their heritages, including their regional languages. European rulers who have tried to unify their countries by suppressing these languages have faced strong opposition and even rebellion. This exceptionally long one-word sign in Welsh over the entrance to a parking area identifies the name of this town in Wales. The sign on the pub to the right announces that coach parties, or bus loads of tourists, are not welcome in that establishment. What are some other regional languages in Western Europe?

my head, smell wheat and oak, feel the hours passing. That is why it is so hard for me to find my way in this land of concrete that France has become. But then, it is still France, so I feel at home there.*

1. Before nations were formed in Western Europe, what distinguished one locality or region from another?
2. According to the governor of Salzburg, what makes its people different from those of Vienna?
3. What factors contributed to the national identity of many Western Europeans?

LANGUAGE

Language is another important part of people's identity. In the words of one Western European writer, the language a person speaks "is a veritable world in which he lives and acts; it is more profound and a more essential part of him than the land and those things he calls his country." Many Western Europeans agree with him. This can be seen in the efforts some groups make to protect their regional and national languages and to have them recognized by others.

In the 1960's, for example, French intellectuals led a movement to ban ***franglais,*** the use of English words in the French language. They feared that the use of such words as *le weekend, le shopping,* or *le jogging,* suggested the French were abandoning their national language.

In other parts of Western Europe, different groups have worked to preserve their local and regional languages. In Wales, a region of Great Britain, groups have established a Welsh-language television channel and have argued for the right to use the Welsh language in schools and government offices. In Catalonia, a region of Spain, there is a similar move underway. As the journalist whose

---

*English language translation copyright © 1982 by Seaver Books/Lattes. Reprinted from *The Wheat and the Chaff* by François Mitterrand, published by Seaver Books, New York, 1982.

CASE STUDY
WESTERN EUROPE

THE ART OF EATING

Each people and nation of Western Europe has its own special foods and dining habits. What and how each group eats reflects its cultural values and traditions. This can be seen in the two articles that follow, the first about the Italian art of eating and the second about the French.

Not everyone in Italy may know how to cook, but nearly everyone knows how to eat. Eating in Italy is one more [illustration] of the Italian's age-old gift of making art out of life.

The Italian art of eating is sustained by a life measured in nature's rhythms, a life that falls in with the slow wheelings of the seasons, a life in which, until very recently, produce and fish reached the table not many hours after having been taken from the soil or the sea.

It is an art that has also been abetted by the custom of shutting down the whole country at midday for two hours or more. Fathers come home from work and children from school, and there is sufficient time for the whole family to celebrate, not just the most important meal, but more likely also the most important event of the day.

There probably has been no influence . . . so effective in creating a rich family life, in maintaining a civilized link between the generations. . . . Eating in Italy is essentially a family art, practiced for and by the family. . . .

The best cooking in Italy is not . . . found in restaurants, but in the home. . . . The finest restaurants in Italy are not those glittering establishments known to every traveler, but the very small, family-run trattorie *of ten or twelve tables that offer home cooking only slightly revised by commercial adaptations. Here the menus are unnecessary, sometimes non-existent. . . . Patrons know exactly what they want, and in ordering a meal they are evoking patterns established countless times at home.**

---

*From *The Classic Italian Cook Book* by Marcella Hazan, translated by Victor Hazan. Copyright © 1973 by Marcella Hazan and Victor Hazan. Reprinted by permission of Alfred A. Knopf, Inc.

. . . Traditional French good eating has suffered many changes in the past decades and has come under various conflicting pressures, . . . On the one hand, bars in central Paris serving le fast-food *and* le hot-dog; *lengthening frozen-food counters in the supermarkets; and restaurant standards . . . now more [irregular]. On the other, much talk of a renaissance of cooking and of the French passion for food; as witness of this, quality restaurants fuller than ever. . . .*

So what is happening? Answer, a curious new [division] of the individual's eating habits. The French, at least in the middle classes, used to eat serenely well as a matter of course every day, especially in their homes. But a modern nation in a hurry no longer has such time or concern for serious daily cooking and eating: both at home and away from it, routine meals have become more simple. . . . And ordinary restaurants, faced with soaring costs, have been cutting corners, . . . and their clients accept it. . . . Yet the Frenchman's [eating] zeal is not dying, it is simply taking a new turn; increasingly he is channelling it towards the once- or twice-a-week occasion. . . . And here he is as exacting as ever. . . . Good eating is becoming less regular, more special. But the change is relative. In the provinces and rural areas especially, with their wealth of tradition, the French still eat far better than any other people; and they still talk and think about food to an amazing extent. . . . The issue today, however, is whether this grass-roots tradition of quality can continue to survive. . . .*

1. How important is eating to the Italians? To the French? Give examples from the excerpts to support your answers.
2. What does the attitude toward food and dining indicate about the values and priorities of many Italians? About the values and priorities of many of the French?

**France in the 1980s* by John Ardagh, 1982, Martin Secker & Warburg, Ltd., pp. 409–410. Reprinted by permission.

writing appears below discovered, for many Catalonians, their language is a unifying force that they believe expresses their soul:

> Hardly a week passed for me without a talk with Sēnora Lourdes [a shopkeeper in Barcelona] about Catalonia, but one day when we were talking about the Catalan language she [hesitated]. It was her mother tongue, she said, but there were others in the barrio [neighborhood] who knew more about it.
> "Oh, mother of mercy," said a woman customer who was listening, "especially Brossa. That Joan Brossa is always publishing poems in Catalan. . . . He only cares about his poetry and his Catalan. People in the barrio take care of him."
> . . . I found him working and holding court in his "atico" room, clogged with volumes and dust.
> He explained that Catalan is a distinctive Romance language also spoken in the Balearic Islands and Valencia [a Spanish province], as well as in a few places in Sardinia and southern France. He cited in some detail the thousand-year history of proud and thoughtful Catalan literature. He cursed those who called Catalan a dialect of French or Spanish, though there are French, Spanish, Italian, and German sounds in his language. . . .
> From a poet's point of view, Brossa said, "Catalan is a marvelous language because it has the ability to grow hard or smooth, with a musicality of many shades. . . . Language is the basic characteristic of Catalonia's personality and the personality of its people. Without my language I have no culture, and culture is the best weapon man has against oppression."*

1. What have the Welsh done to preserve their language?
2. Why do the people of Catalonia want to preserve the Catalan language?

---

*"Catalonia: Spain's Country Within a Country" by Randall Peffer in *National Geographic*, January 1984, pp. 106, 108. Reprinted by permission.

RELIGION

Another powerful shaper of identity and personal outlook in Western Europe is religion. Even where personal faith is not great or is missing, the religious heritages of Western Europe have had an impact, and the cultural aspects of religion are learned as naturally and unconsciously as learning how to speak.

Although people of many different faiths make up the Western European population, the predominant religion is Christianity. Some nations, like Italy, are almost totally Roman Catholic. Below, an Italian priest provides some insight into the role religion plays in his life and in his country:

> I was ordained a priest . . . when I was nineteen. . . . I was a bright child and my parents sent me to the seminary to study when I was ten. In those days it was the best way to give a village boy a good education. . . .
> Today, however, boys begin at the seminary when they're fourteen years old, or even later. . . .
> I never lost touch with my home village of Leonessa. . . . I began taking groups of children from there on camping holidays as soon as I was put in charge of a parish. Later I founded a young people's holiday home near Leonessa. Children come from as far afield as Rome, particularly convalescent children in need of mountain air.
> I get up at 5:30 or 6:00 A.M. . . .
> At 8:30 I'm ready to take my classes at school. A weekly hour of religious education is compulsory in Italian state schools, unless parents ask for a special dispensation. The official religion in Italy is Catholicism. That is not surprising, since the pope . . . lives in Rome, and ninety percent of Italians are baptized Catholics.
> When I've no morning classes, I make my parish calls, visiting those who are too old or sick to move around. I try to keep

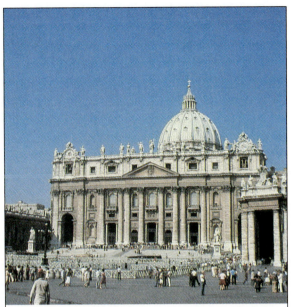

St. Peter's Basilica, in Vatican City in Rome, is of special importance to Catholics because it is the "church of the popes." What role has religion played in Western Europe over the centuries?

in touch, not to let anyone feel forgotten. . . .

On most afternoons, and especially Saturdays, I teach catechism classes in church, instructing children in the principles and mysteries of the Catholic faith. . . .

. . . Once a week we hold a meeting of young people between the ages of fifteen and twenty. I also make a point of talking to the parents of children preparing their First Communion. In Italy it's customary for children to take their First Communion when they're eight years old. This is a very important date in a child's life: he or she becomes a full member of the Church, and it's a first step to growing up.*

Other Western European countries, like Sweden, are largely Protestant. Below, a Lutheran **vicar,** or clergyman, talks about the part the church and religion play in his country:

About 50,000 people live in [my] parish, but unfortunately only a small proportion attend church regularly. My salary is paid by those who live in the parish. Part of their annual taxes are paid to the State Church which then distributes the money to clergymen as a monthly salary. If anyone objects to their taxes being used for such purposes . . . they can apply to have their annual tax contributions reduced.

Religious education is the only subject on the school curriculum in Sweden which is compulsory. Although our state Church is Lutheran, religious education in our schools is not only about the Lutheran Church but about all major world religions. At my parish church we have special children's groups during the week for those especially interested in the Lutheran faith. Because so many people live in the countryside around Falun we found it difficult to collect sufficient children together on Sundays to support a Sunday School. Weekday evenings are much better. . . . We teach them about Christianity, sing songs . . . and spend quite a lot of time outdoors during the summer months, including a summer camp. There's a lot more to being a vicar than working on Sundays. . . . There are weddings, funerals, baptisms and, of course, confirmation classes. In Sweden, confirmation is very important. . . . We even have special confirmation camps in the summer.

There are school visits, hospital visits, and a whole range of church social events. . . . I have fifteen assistants, so I'm also a boss! That means that whenever I want to change someone's job description or hire another person I have to meet and discuss it with the trade unions. Yes, in Sweden we even have trade unions in the Church.*

---

*"Ninety percent of Italians are Catholic" in *We live in Italy* by Tana de Zulueta, 1983, The Bookwright Press, pp. 8–9. Reprinted by permission.

*"Vicars work all week, not just on Sundays" in *We live in Sweden* by Stephen Keeler and Chris Fairclough, 1985, The Bookwright Press, pp. 30–31. Reprinted by permission.

Even though both the Catholic and Protestant faiths have their roots in Christianity, they differ in cultural legacies, teachings, thought, and practices. Over the centuries, religion has often acted to unify the people. At the same time, it also has contributed to division within and between nations.

Today, religion is a factor in the division of the people of Northern Ireland. Below, an Irish clergyman, who finds its hard to understand why the Catholics and Protestants are fighting, offers his views on the subject:

> Most of the main religions are catered for in Northern Ireland, but the vast majority of people are either Roman Catholic or Protestant. The Church of Ireland used to be called the United Church of England and Ireland until it was disestablished in 1870. Like the Church of England it is Anglican. . . .
>
> I think there is too much talk among Christians today of the difference between the separate churches that make up the faith. . . . We all should be working together . . . for a better world in which to live.
>
> If you read the reports in the newspapers or watch the news on TV you would think that Northern Ireland is nothing but a seething mass of sectarian killings, with bombs going off on every street corner. . . .
>
> I have been living at Helen's Bay [near the capital city of Belfast] now for ten years. It is a predominantly middle-class area with both Church of England and Presbyterian congregations. Just 5 km. (3 miles) away is Bangor with a strong Catholic population. If you believe the newspapers we should be fighting in the streets, but instead we are holding fetes together; we work for Christian Aid Week together; and I am just starting a Boy Scout Troop that will have boys from every quarter. . . .
>
> The troubles in Northern Ireland do cast a shadow over our lives, but then we're used to trouble here. There's been fighting in Ireland for hundreds of years. Every so often something happens to make me wonder what the fighting is all about. Some years ago a Roman Catholic woman presented a beautiful stained-glass window to our church in memory of her mother, who was also a Catholic. The window depicts Saint Patrick, the patron saint of all Ireland. He casts his light upon us all—Catholics and Protestants. This present from a Roman Catholic to a Protestant church is indicative of the good faith that still exists in Northern Ireland, despite the last fourteen years of the bomb and the bullet.*

1. What is the predominant religion of Western Europe?
2. What role does religion play in Italy? In Sweden?
3. How does the Irish clergyman feel about religious dissension?

HISTORY AND TRADITION

History is a living part of Western Europeans' sense of themselves. Ancient ruins, cathedrals, monuments, graveyards, museums, and ceremonies testify to earlier times of greatness and pride and of tragedy and sorrow. All of these are visible reminders of a shared past.

With history comes tradition. And a major element of the Western European tradition is the monarchy, which still exists in some Western European countries. Today, the role of Western European monarchs varies from country to country. In Great Britain, for example, even though monarchs have not actually ruled since the 1800's, the monarchy continues to hold the respect and affection of the people. The royal family and its tradi-

---
*"We should be working for a better world" in *We live in Britain* by Chris Fairclough, 1984, The Bookwright Press, pp. 56–57. Reprinted by permission.

CHAPTER 49   A SENSE OF THEMSELVES   823

This parade through the streets of London by the Queen's Household Cavalry, which accompanies and protects members of the royal family as they make the rounds of their official duties, is one of the age-old traditions revered by the British and enjoyed by visitors. What meaning do traditions such as the parade hold for many of the British?

tions provide a colorful tie with the past and are a source of shared values and ideals. As the article below indicates, these qualities are particularly evident in the capital city of London:

> . . . London has a delightful spectacular quality which works its own magic as well. One sees it as one passes through Hyde Park on an early morning: it's there in the scarlet flash of Household Cavalrymen wheeling at the trot, their brilliant capes sending a scarlet shiver through the winter air, their burnished silver breastplates and helmets causing a startle in the mist. Each morning, the Queen's Household Cavalry rides from its new skyscraper barracks at Hyde Park through heavy London traffic, a mounted policeman leading the way; they ride to the old Horse Guards building on Whitehall and their passage evokes a thrill in Londoners as well as foreign visitors. Drivers of motor cars, as they pass the clattering, tinkling troop of cavalrymen, invariably slow down to breathe in the spectacle, for it lifts the heart in a way it is difficult to explain. To think of these soldiers or their counterparts at Buckingham Palace [the Queen's residence] as frozen memorials to some dead past is to miss the point completely: these are working soldiers, guarding the Queen. Like the royal cipher—EIIR—stamped on everything . . . , these soldiers remind one that a Queen reigns in London, that there is continuity, stability and order to be found in ancient institutions. . . . The phrase one often hears elsewhere, that society is coming apart at the seams, is rarely heard in London, for one of the threads that stitches London society together is the tribal magic of the mystic Crown.*

Another element of Western European history is conflict. At times, that conflict has reinforced the Western Europeans' sense of identity. At other times, it has created difficult and painful questions about that identity. This is the case for Germans as a result of World War II and the Holocaust. Some Germans want to forget that part of the past. Others insist that it must be remembered so that a tragedy like the Holocaust never happens again. One such person is the president of West Germany, Richard von Weizsäcker. In a speech Weizsäcker made before the West

---
*From *The Londoners: Life in a Civilized City* by Walter Henry Nelson. Copyright © 1974, by Walter Henry Nelson. Reprinted by permission of Alfred A. Knopf, Inc.

In January, 1984, West German chancellor Helmut Kohl (far left) visited Israel. Here, after laying a wreath on the monument to the unknown soldier in front of the Knesset, *the Israeli parliament, the chancellor is saluted by an Israeli guardsman. What effect has World War II and the Holocaust had on the German sense of identity?*

German parliament in 1985, he pointed out that younger generations of Germans "cannot profess a guilt of their own for crimes they did not commit." He went on, however, to say the following:

   . . . But their forefathers have left them a grave legacy. All of us, whether guilty or not, whether young or old, must accept the past. We are all affected by the consequences and liable for it. The young and old generations must and can help each other to understand why it is vital to keep alive the memories.

   . . . It is not a case of coming to terms with the past. That is not possible. It cannot be . . . modified or made undone. However, anyone who closes his eyes to the past is blind to the present. Whoever refuses to remember the inhumanity is prone to new risks of infection. The Jewish nation remembers and will always remember. We seek reconciliation. Precisely for this reason we must understand that there can be no reconciliation without remembrance. . . . If we for our part sought to forget what had occurred, instead of remembering it, this would not only be inhuman, we would also impinge upon the faith of the Jews who survived and destroy the basis of reconciliation.

   . . . We in the older generation owe to young people not the fulfillment of dreams, but honesty. . . . Hitler's constant approach was to stir up prejudices, enmity [ill will] and hatred. What is asked of young people today is this: Do not let yourselves be forced into enmity and hatred of other people. Let us honor freedom. Let us work for peace. Let us respect the rule of law. Let us be true to our own conception of justice. . . . Let us face up as well as we can to the truth.*

1. What are some of the ways in which history and tradition continue to live in Western Europe?
2. Why is the British monarchy still important to the British people?
3. How has the experience of the Holocaust affected the West German sense of identity and national pride?

---

*Richard von Weizsäcker, as quoted in "Facing Up to Germany's Past" by James M. Markham in *The New York Times Magazine*, June 23, 1985, pp. 25, 30. Copyright © 1985 by The New York Times Co. Reprinted by permission.

EXPLORATION
WESTERN EUROPE

Some people believe that national differences are wearing away in Western Europe. They say that the region is becoming more "homogenized," or blended, and that national identities are being replaced by a Western European sense of identity. In the article that follows, a Western European journalist notes some of the changes he has seen that support this belief. Based on the information in the chapter and in the article, prepare an argument supporting or refuting the belief.

... For the first time in history the British (some of them anyway) speak French, Italian, or German without a condescending heavy accent. More and more people are able to listen to each other's television broadcasts across borders or seas . . . ; more and more people study, work, enjoy life, travel, sightsee, swim, ski, eat, drink . . . in each other's countries. A large number marry other Europeans and raise bilingual children. It is almost impossible to tell what part of Europe the young you meet are from; they appear identical, belonging to the same tribe. (All you can be sure of is that the very blond are probably not Italian or Greek.) It is no longer possible, either, to distinguish one European from another by the cut of his or her clothes. Frenchmen and Germans are almost as elegant, for the first time in more than a century, as only Italians and Englishmen used to be. Germans are thinner than they have ever been. English girls are chic, more so than their mothers and grandmothers, who favored sensible dowdy clothes. Only specialists can tell one country's military uniforms from those of other European countries. Industries merge across frontiers and exchange technical tricks as schoolboys exchange stamps. Merchants flock to each other's fairs. . . . Financiers, film and TV producers, singers, con men, musicians, terrorists, journalists, smugglers, actors, professors who teach with equal skill in their own or other universities, [and] gamblers . . . ignore boundaries and operate easily all over the Continent. At one time, a French citizen was elected leader of an Italian political party. . . . Customs inspectors and border policemen often yawn, play cards, and do not bother to check the passage of fellow European travelers, their passports, and their baggage. High foreign service officials rarely write stuffy . . . notes to each other as they used to, . . . they now consult chattily by telephone as if they were all in one big city . . . , and they call each other by their first names. Staff officers meet informally all the time to exchange ideas and bring plans up to date. The secret services and the police forces have belonged to an imaginary united Europe for years. More and more people are even deserting the last refuge of patriotism, gastronomy [art of eating], and fearlessly eat each other's national specialities. The Germans are spending vast sums to persuade reluctant Italians to eat their sausages and cheeses. Pizza and the little Italian restaurants have conquered Europe; pizza now dominates the Avenue des Champs Elysees [in Paris, France]. . . . Supermarkets are filled with more or less identical products everywhere; only the signs and the prices in local languages and currencies are different.

All this, I admit, is also true almost everywhere else in the world today. . . . Pizza and little Italian restaurants have conquered the globe, not Europe alone. All this is not entirely new either. It was also partly true in the past. . . . Nevertheless, it is evident that these phenomena are now more [widely accepted] than in the past and in Europe more than anywhere else. Exchanges are infinitely easier. Countries being shoulder to shoulder with each other, languages change after but a few hours train or plane ride, and every European must have a working knowledge of his neighbors'. Outside pressures, economic, political, or military, force the people and their governments to stick closer together. . . . What is also true . . . in Europe today is that these trends are accelerating rapidly and no longer involving [a] . . . minority . . . but each year larger and larger numbers of people of all classes.*

---

*The Europeans by Luigi Barzini, pp. 27–29. Copyright © 1983 by Luigi Barzini. Reprinted by permission of SIMON & SCHUSTER, Inc.

CHAPTER 49 REVIEW

POINTS TO REMEMBER

1. Each Western European people has distinctive qualities that unite them and that, at the same time, set them apart from other Western European peoples.
2. In some countries, family has traditionally been more important than in others. In these countries, the family is the primary focus of a person's life.
3. Changes have taken place in recent years that have strained the concept of the traditional family.
4. Although class divisions and barriers, which have existed for many years in Western Europe, have become less rigid, they continue to exist today in some Western European countries.
5. Before nations were formed in Europe, people identified themselves by the region in which they lived. Today, for most Western Europeans, regional loyalties have been replaced by national ones.
6. Because language is an important part of a people's identity, in some areas of Western Europe, groups have sought to preserve local and regional languages.
7. Religion, another powerful shaper of identity and personal outlook in Western Europe, has acted both to unify the people and to divide them.
8. History, tradition, and conflict all have had an impact on the sense of identity of Western Europeans.

VOCABULARY

Identify

François Mitterrand
Catalan

Joan Brossa
Holocaust

Richard von Weizsäcker

Define

franglais

vicar

DISCUSSING IMPORTANT IDEAS

1. Of the various differences that separate one group of Western Europeans from another, which do you think are merely surface differences? Which do you think are deep or fundamental differences? Explain your answers.
2. What does the term "sense of identity" mean to you? Do you think that the elements that contribute to a person's sense of identity are universal? Explain.
3. If you met some Western Europeans who ate and dressed much as you do, would it be reasonable to believe that they also think the way you do? Why or why not?
4. The Catalan poet, Joan Brossa, believes that language is "the basic characteristic" of the personality of his province and its people and that without his language he has no culture. Do you think the same is true of your language? Explain.

DEVELOPING SKILLS

MAKING COMPARISONS

At one time or another, you probably have heard someone say, "You can't compare them. That's like comparing apples and oranges!" What the person is saying is that apples and oranges are two totally different things and cannot be compared. This is not necessarily true.

To *compare* means to examine in order to identify similarities or differences. You can compare, or make comparisons of, things that are very different or that are very much alike. For any comparison to be complete, however, you must note at least one similarity and one difference.

No matter what you are comparing, there are some questions that you can ask yourself to help you make an effective comparison. In the two examples that follow, these questions are used first to compare apples and oranges and then to compare apples and apples.

Example 1:
1. What do I want to compare? *(apples and oranges)*
2. What do they have in common that I can compare? *(size, growing area, growing season, variety)*
3. On which common area do I want to concentrate? *(variety)*
4. What similarities are there in this common area? What differences are there in this common area? *(Similarity: Both apples and oranges come in more than one variety. Difference: There are more varieties of apples than of oranges.)*

Example 2:
1. What do I want to compare? *(apples)*
2. What are the areas on which I could base a comparison? *(size, color, taste, where grown, use, history, variety)*
3. On which area do I want to concentrate? *(variety)*
4. What similarities are there in this area? What differences are there in this area? *(Similarity: All varieties of apples are alike in that they grow on trees and do best in climates that have a cold winter. Difference: The colors of some varieties of apples are not the same as the colors of other varieties.)*

There are some commonly accepted words and phrases that you can use when making comparisons. For example, when indicating similarity, the following may be used:
1. In Western Europe, *both* language and religion *have* contributed to peoples' sense of identity.
2. Attitudes about the importance of family are the *same* in Italy *as* in Portugal.
3. The overall goals regarding preservation of local and regional languages *are identical* in Wales and in Catalonia.
4. Italy and Spain *are similar in that* they are predominantly Catholic nations.
5. The nations of Western Europe *are alike in that they* all have a strong regard for history and tradition.
6. All Western Europeans *have* certain historical traditions *in common*.

When indicating difference, the following may be used:
1. Regional loyalties are strong*er* in some nations of Western Europe than in others.
2. Although regional loyalties still exist in many cities, towns, and villages, they probably are strong*est* in the villages.
3. For some Western Europeans, family loyalty is *more* important *than* national loyalty.
4. For some Western Europeans, the amount of money one has is *less* important *than* one's family background.
5. All Western Europeans *are not alike* in their religious beliefs.
6. The eating habits of the French are *not the same as* those of the Norwegians.
7. Elderly Germans and more youthful Germans often are *different in their* outlooks on World War II and the Holocaust.
8. Scandinavian families generally are *not as large as* Italian families.

For practice in this skill, use the material in this chapter and the suggested guidelines to compare Western European attitudes about sense of identity.

CHAPTER 50
ARTS AND THOUGHT

1. What are some major features of Western European arts and thought?
2. What factors have shaped the development of Western European culture?

I came here to Stratford [England] in February 1982. Prior to that, I'd been on stage . . . and had acted on TV. Although I enjoy TV drama, I find that acting in front of a live audience is much more stimulating and exciting. So when my contract with the TV company ran out I came in search of work back on the stage. Over ninety per cent of all the trained actors and actresses in Britain are out of work at any one time, so I was very lucky to be offered a contract with the Royal Shakespeare Company (R.S.C.).

Shakespeare is Britain's best-known playwright. He . . . wrote thirty-seven plays as well as many poems. Visitors come from all over the world to see his birthplace here at Stratford-upon-Avon in Warwickshire. . . .

The Royal Shakespeare Company itself was formed in 1960, although its history dates back to 1769. In that year a man called David Garrick presented a festival of acting, music and revelry to the local inhabitants of Stratford. Now it is one of the largest and most famous theater companies in the world and plays to an audience of over a million people every year. . . .

Although the R.S.C. probably attracts larger audiences than any theater company in the world, it is impossible to finance the vastly expensive productions that we put on from ticket sales alone. So, like so many of the 270 professional theater companies in Britain, we rely on the Arts Council of Great Britain to provide for a third of our costs. Like other theater companies, too, we receive a certain amount of help through sponsorship from industry and TV coverage of our plays.

I love working as an actress but it is very hard work indeed. I spend a lot of my time learning my lines or rehearsing on the stage. I don't only act in plays by William Shakespeare, though. This year I'll be appearing in *Peer Gynt* by [the Norwegian playwright] Henrik Ibsen and *Lear* by [the English playwright] Edward Bond, as well. . . . Most of the parts are quite small at the moment, but when I'm a little older I hope to tackle some of the bigger and more ambitious parts.*

In the above excerpt, a young British actress talks about her career and theater in Britain. Through her artistry, she, like many others, carries on a cultural tradition of Western Europe—the theater. The theater is an art, as are drama, music, painting, and literature. Each of these arts expresses basic Western European attitudes about truth and beauty. At the same time, each reflects and is shaped by such other aspects of Western European culture as religious faith; scientific inquiry; and social, economic, and political thought.

---

*"Shakespeare is Britain's best-known playwright" in *We live in Britain* by Chris Fairclough, 1984, The Bookwright Press, pp. 28–29. Reprinted by permission.

FROM THE GREEKS TO DICKENS

Like the site of an archaeological dig, Western Europe's culture includes many layers. These layers came about as the contributions of early groups and individuals were enriched and extended by those of later groups and individuals.

AN EARLY LEGACY

The ancient Greeks made one of the first important contributions to Western European culture with their ideas about gods and human beings, which differed sharply from those of earlier peoples. Below, a scholar of Greek mythology explains:

> People often speak of "the Greek miracle." What the phrase tries to express is the new birth of the [western] world with the awakening of Greece. "Old things are passed away; behold, all things are become new." Something like that happened in Greece. Why it happened, or when: we have no idea at all. We know only that in the earliest Greek poets a new point of view dawned, never dreamed of in the

GREEK GODS AND GODDESSES

Name	Realm
ZEUS	ruler of Mount Olympus, king of gods and mortals
HERA	protectress of marriage, children, and the home; wife of Zeus
POSEIDON	god of the sea and earthquakes
APOLLO	god of the sun; patron of truth, archery, music, medicine, and prophecy
ARES	god of war
ATHENA	goddess of wisdom; patron of household crafts; protectress in war; daughter of Zeus
APHRODITE	goddess of love and beauty
DIONYSUS	god of fertility, of joyous life and hospitality, and of wild things
ARTEMIS	goddess of the moon; mighty huntress; guardian of young animals and women; twin sister of Apollo, and daughter of Zeus
HERMES	god of orators, writers and commerce; protector of thieves and mischiefmakers; guardian of way-farers, messenger to mortals; son of Zeus
HEPHAESTUS	god of fire and artisans; maker of the first mortal woman; husband of Aphrodite
DEMETER	goddess of crops, giver of grain and fruit

world before them, but never to leave the world after them. With the coming forward of Greece, [human beings] became the center of the universe, the most important thing in it. This was a revolution in thought. Human beings had counted for little heretofore. . . .

The Greeks made their gods in their own image. That had not entered the [human] mind . . . before. Until then, gods had had no semblance of reality. They were unlike all living things. In Egypt, a towering colossus . . . as fixed in the stone as the tremendous temple columns. . . . Or a rigid figure, a woman with a cat's head. . . . Or a . . . mysterious sphinx, aloof from all that lives. . . .

These and their like were what the pre-Greek world worshiped. One need only place beside them in imagination any Greek statue of a god, so normal and natural with all its beauty, to perceive what a new idea had come into the world. . . .

. . . In Greece alone in the ancient world people were preoccupied with the visible; they were finding the satisfaction of their desires in what was actually in the world around them. The sculptor watched the athletes contending in the [Olympic] games and he felt that nothing he could imagine would be as beautiful as those strong young bodies. So he made his statue of Apollo [god of sunlight, prophecy, music, and poetry]. The storyteller found Hermes [god who served as messenger to the other gods] among the people he passed in the street. He saw the god "like a young man at the age when youth is loveliest. . . ." Greek artists and poets realized how splendid a man could be. . . . He was the fulfillment of their search for beauty. They had no wish to create some fantasy shaped in their own minds. All the art and all the thought of Greece centered in human beings.*

Mythology by Edith Hamilton. Copyright 1942 by Edith Hamilton; copyright renewed © 1969 by Dorian Fielding Reid and Doris Fielding Reid, Executrix of the will of Edith Hamilton. By permission of Little, Brown and Company.

THE MIDDLE YEARS

The ideas set forth by the Greeks were adopted by the Romans, through whose empire they came to Western Europe. Then, after Rome fell, a new layer of culture emerged that was based not only on Greek and Roman ideas, but on those of Christianity as well.

From about 500 to 1700, the church officials, monarchs, and nobles who made up the wealthy upper classes of Western Europe used their riches to support learning and the arts. Acting as **patrons,** or financial backers, they hired artists to carry out different projects, often choosing their styles and dictating their themes. In some cases, this dampened creativity. In others, such as that of Pope Julius II and the sixteenth-century Italian artist Michelangelo Buonarroti, it led to magnificent results. Prodded constantly by his patron, Pope Julius, Michelangelo painted the ceiling of the Sistine Chapel in the Vatican, a task that took him four years to complete. Below, a pupil of Michelangelo talks about the often stormy relationship between patron and artist:

> While [Michelangelo] was painting, Pope Julius often wanted to go and inspect the work; he would climb up by a ladder and Michelangelo would hold out a hand to him to help him up onto the scaffolding. And, being one who was by nature impetuous and impatient of waiting, as soon as the work was half done . . . , he wanted Michelangelo to uncover it. . . .
>
> It is true that I have heard [Michelangelo] say that it is not finished as he would have wanted, as he was hampered by the urgency of the pope, who asked him one day when he would finish that chapel, and when Michelangelo answered, "When I can," the pope, enraged, retorted, "You want me to have you thrown off the scaffolding." Hearing this, Michelangelo said to himself, "You shall not have me thrown off," and he removed himself and had the

scaffolding taken down, and on All Saints' Day he revealed the work, which the pope, who went to the chapel that day, saw with immense satisfaction, and all Rome admired it and crowded to see it. What was lacking was the retouching of the work . . . with ultramarine and in a few places with gold, to give it a richer appearance. Julius, when the heat of his enthusiasm had subsided, really wanted Michelangelo to furnish these touches; but, when Michelangelo thought about the trouble it would give him to reassemble the scaffolding, he answered that what was lacking was nothing of importance. "It really ought to be retouched with gold," answered the pope, to whom Michelangelo responded with the familiarity which was his way with His Holiness, "I do not see that men wear gold." The pope said, "It will look poor." Michelangelo rejoined, "Those who are depicted there, they were poor too." So he remarked in jest, and so the work has remained.*

MASS APPEAL

From the late 1700's to the 1900's, another layer of Western European culture was formed as the middle and lower classes of Western Europe became better educated, experienced a rise in their standard of living, and began to take an interest in the arts. For the first time, great numbers of people of the middle and lower classes began attending concerts, visiting museums, and buying books, sheet music, and paintings. To appeal to this new mass audience, artists developed new styles and themes. The daily lives and personal struggles of common people became acceptable subject matter for paintings, novels, dramas, and other arts. What was known as **mass culture** had emerged.

One of the earliest writers to capitalize on this new market was a nineteenth-century British author named Charles Dickens. Below, a modern British novelist discusses Dickens and the reasons for his success:

> . . . [Dickens'] fame came earlier and more completely than that of any other of the great novelists. By twenty-five he was a national figure and from then on never ceased to be one. This began because of *The Pickwick Papers*. No first novel in any language has made such a stir. . . .
>
> The story was issued in monthly parts. . . . The first numbers didn't sell. [Then] Dickens introduced a comic, clever, witty servant. . . . From that number he was home. The country went mad on *Pickwick*.

In this detail from the Sistine Chapel in Rome, Michelangelo depicts the Old Testament prophet, Zacharias. What reason did Michelangelo give for not retouching his work on the Sistine Chapel?

---

*The Life of Michelangelo by Ascanio Condivi, translated by Alice Sedgwick Wohl, 1976, Louisiana State University Press, pp. 57–58. Reprinted by permission.

CHAPTER 50 ARTS AND THOUGHT

Oil painting, The Hay Harvest, *by Flemish artist, Pieter Brueghel, 1565.*

Illuminated manuscript, from The Book of Kells, *Ireland.*

The Thinker, bronze by French sculptor, Rodin.

Ancient Greek urn, or ornamental vase.

British rock group, the Beatles, from Liverpool, England.

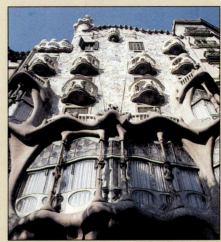

Façade of Casa Batllo in Barcelona, Spain, designed by Spanish architect, Antoni Gaudí.

It was something like the reception today of a supreme hit record. The publishers were made, and so was he. . . .

While *Pickwick* was still in progress, and Dickens having to meet the monthly deadline, he was already building on the success. . . . Plans for new novels!

Oliver Twist, Nicholas Nickleby, Barnaby Rudge beginning to take shape in his imagination! Contracts for the new novels! . . . Work, riches, fame! As for the books themselves, he wasn't yet the conscious artist that he was to become. . . . None of his [early] novels . . . has a coherent theme. They started off with the random eye-flash of a brilliant journalist—the . . . workhouses, juvenile crime in London, the schools in the north for [illegitimate children] whom no one wanted. Everyone knew about these miseries; Dickens knew he could light them up with his spectacular vision.*

1. What important contribution did the ancient Greeks make to Western European culture?
2. What role did church officials, rulers, and nobles play in the development of Western European culture?
3. What effect did the emergence of mass culture have on the styles and themes of Western European artists?

ARTISTIC TRENDS

Traditionally, Western European music, art, and literature have been based on certain rules. Over the centuries, however, as tastes and ideas changed, the rules changed too. Often, what was considered beautiful or important during one period was rejected later, only to be rediscovered and appreciated still later.

During certain periods, for example, Western Europeans, believing that the arts should appeal to the mind's sense of order and balance, followed strict artistic rules. This was known as **classicism.** During other periods, believing that the arts should appeal to the heart, they turned away from the rules. This was known as **romanticism.** These changes in attitude, which reflected a conflict between intellect and emotion, can be seen in all forms of Western European arts, including music, painting, and literature.

MUSIC

Traditional Western European music, which began during the Renaissance, was **monophonic,** made up of a single melody or tune. In time, however, composers found that if they used two or more melodic lines at once, music could be more interesting. This led to what is known as **counterpoint** or **polyphonic music,** a style of music developed to its highest level by an eighteenth-century composer named Johann Sebastian Bach.

Later, another direction was taken by Western European musicians who began to stress harmony. They created their music around a basic melody and **chords,** or several notes played at the same time. Then, to enrich the music further, the solo voice or instrument carrying the melody was accompanied by other voices and instruments. This type of music, known as **homophonic,** became standard for Western Europe during the 1800's as composers such as Ludwig van Beethoven, Felix Mendelssohn, Hector Berlioz, and Johannes Brahms composed symphonies for the larger orchestras with newly developed, stronger pianos and more brass instruments.

Meanwhile, other Western European composers, such as Richard Wagner and Giuseppe Verdi, composed **operas,** stories set to music and performed on stage like a drama.

---
*C. P. Snow, excerpted from *The Realists: Portraits of Eight Novelists.* Copyright ©1978 C. P. Snow, pp. 77–78, 83–84. Reprinted with the permission of Charles Scribner's Sons.

INSIGHTS ON PEOPLE
WESTERN EUROPE

WOLFGANG AMADEUS MOZART

One of the most creative geniuses of Western European music was an Austrian named Wolfgang Amadeus Mozart. Mozart, whose musical talent was discovered at an early age, toured Europe, performing before the pope, monarchs, and nobles, and amazing audiences wherever he went. In 1793, Mozart visited Paris, France. Below, a journalist of the time offers his reactions:

True miracles are so rare that it behoves us to report one when it comes our way. A Kapellmeister [church musician] of Salzburg named Mozart has just arrived here with two children. . . . His daughter, eleven years of age, plays the clavier [stringed keyboard instrument] in the most brilliant manner. . . . Her brother, who will be seven years old next February . . . , is so extraordinary a phenomenon that we can scarcely credit what we see with our own eyes and hear with our own ears. Easily and with utmost accuracy, the child performs the most difficult pieces with hands that are scarcely large enough to span a sixth. . . . The finest conductor has not so deep a knowledge of harmony. . . . Such is his adeptness on the keyboard that if it is covered with a napkin he continues to play through the napkin with the same speed and precision. He has not the slightest difficulty deciphering anything that is put before him: he writes and composes with wonderful ease. . . .

. . . But the following incident, which I witnessed, eludes explanation. A lady asked him casually whether he would accompany her by ear, and without looking at her, . . . She began to sing; the child tried a bass that was formally correct. . . . But as soon as the song was over he asked the lady to begin again from the beginning, and this time he not only played the entire melody with the right hand, but at the same time added the bass with his left without the slightest uncertainty. Then he requested her ten times in succession to begin again, and with each repetition he changed the character of his accompaniment. He would have gone through it twenty times more had he not been asked to stop. It is evident that this child will end by turning my head completely if I hear him more often. I now understand the overwhelming effect of miracles.*

Mozart continued to amaze audiences as he grew older. He produced an enormous amount of music, including the operas *Don Giovanni* and *The Marriage of Figaro*, and wrote symphonies, chamber music, and piano concertos as well. Yet, he could not get a position as composer for a royal court and had many financial difficulties. He died in poverty at age 35 and was buried in an unmarked grave set aside for the poor. Only after his death was his genius rediscovered and was he ranked among the greatest of Western Europe's composers.

1. Who was Wolfgang Amadeus Mozart?
2. What were some of Mozart's major musical accomplishments?

**Mozart: His Life and Times* by Peggy Woodford, 1977, Midas Books, pp. 31–33. Reprinted by permission.

The dialogue of the stories is sung rather than spoken. Many people consider opera one of the greatest musical achievements of Western Europe. In Italy, for example, operatic performances are as popular as sports and are viewed with passion. Below, a Russian-born opera star describes the reaction of many Italians when a famous conductor made some changes in the production of a Verdi opera opening at La Scala opera house in Milan:

Coming into the hotel restaurant on the day of the premiere, . . . I could already detect all the signs of the approaching storm. The level of noise and excitement in the room was extraordinary. Waiters with a warlike air were gathering in groups, shouting something and [gesturing] vigorously. Our waiter came up to us at once, his black eyes flashing threateningly and inquired, "The signora [lady] plans, of course, to be at the opera this evening?" . . .

CULTURAL FIGURES

Johann Wolfgang von Goethe (1749–1832)
German poet, novelist, playwright, and scientist whose works include *Faust* and *The Sorrows of Young Werther.*

Hans Christian Andersen (1805–1875)
Danish novelist, poet, and writer of such fairy tales as "The Ugly Duckling," and "The Emperor's New Clothes."

Simone de Beauvoir (1908–1986)
French author concerned with existentialism, politics, and social freedom, as shown in *The Second Sex.*

Francisco Goya (1746–1828)
Spanish painter and graphic artist, whose works include *Maja Clothed* and *The Caprices.*

Edgar Degas (1837–1917)
French impressionist painter and sculptor whose works include *At the Milliner's* and *Young Dancer.*

Alberto Giacometti (1901–1966)
Swiss sculptor and painter, whose works, mostly of bronze, include *Man Pointing* and *City Square.*

Franz Schubert (1797–1828)
Austrian composer whose works include *Symphony in C Major* and "Ave Maria."

Guiseppe Verdi (1813–1901)
Italian composer of operas, whose works include *Rigoletto, La Traviata,* and *Requiem.*

Jan Sibelius (1865–1957)
Finnish composer and conductor whose works include *Valse Triste* and *Finlandia.*

"The signora absolutely must come! There'll be a scandal the likes of which we've never seen at La Scala. We're all going to be there," he explained . . . : "We won't let him mock our Verdi!" . . .

Before we had a chance to look around, several people had gathered at our table and were vying with one another, trying to explain to me . . . just what was going on.

"We'll teach him to respect our Verdi! We already know what he's been up to. The tempos are all wrong!"

"What do you mean, 'wrong'?" I asked. . . . In the first place, you still haven't heard the performance. In the second place, he is a great conductor, and it wouldn't hurt you to hear his interpretation. His very name is a guarantee of a high-quality performance."

"0 Madonna!" howled our waiter, returning to our table. . . .

"Do you know what you're saying, Signora? He's strangled all the singers. He doesn't let them hold the high notes! . . . He wants to kill our Verdi!"

Unable to go on, he fell silent . . . and wept. . . .

I tried to console him. . . . But around my table the shouting continued. Someone, waving his arms, was singing an aria, trying to prove to me that some note or other must not be cut short, while someone else was explaining how the orchestra should play this or that phrase. . . .

That night the audience came to the theater . . . determined to wreck the performance. . . .

. . . Everyone was . . . busy concentrating on the singing and on the conductor, who, in not permitting the singers to hold the high notes until they were blue in the face, deprived the audience of its usual pleasure. [Fiercely] expressing their opinions, shouting back and forth . . . during the singing, reacting stormily to each imperfect note, the audience grew more and more inflamed. . . . When the curtain finally went down on the first act, people hissed, booed, and swore. Fights even broke out in the gallery. And so on throughout the performance, and then late into the night on the public square. . . .

The next day the scandal carried over into the newspapers. . . . The critics assailed the performers and the co-directors, and tore the whole production to pieces.*

PAINTING

Traditionally, Western European paintings have been concerned with representing scenes, stories, or individuals. Even though styles changed over time, the meanings of the art were easily understood by anyone.

During the Middle Ages, artists devoted themselves chiefly to religious subjects painted in a flat, two-dimensional way. Their goal was to present spiritual truths through symbols. They were not concerned with being realistic. Then, during the Renaissance, ancient Greek and Roman statues were unearthed, and artists developed a new interest in the human form for its own sake. In an effort to show their subjects realistically, artists created rounded, seemingly three-dimensional figures and developed rules for **perspective,** or depth relationships. The sources of light and the way shadows fell were noticed. Nonreligious subjects were undertaken more often.

In the mid-1800's, another change took place when a group of French painters known as Impressionists rebelled against the concern for realism. Rather than portray a scene that was fixed and timeless, the Impressionists tried to capture the fleeting moment. To this end, they painted outdoors, portraying scenes of nature and human activities in the process of change.

In the 1900's, Western European artists developed new styles—styles not concerned

---

*From *Galina: A Russian Story* From English translation copyright © 1984 by Galina Vishnevskaya and Harcourt Brace Jovanovich, Inc. Reprinted by permission of the publisher.

with showing realism but with imparting a feeling, mood, or idea. An example of this style is the work of Spanish painter Pablo Picasso. He believed that nature and art were two different things. In his view, "In art we express our conception of what is not visible to nature." For him, color was a way of expressing emotion rather than of describing reality. Picasso developed a style of art known as Cubism in which objects are reduced into geometrical, unrealistic planes and shapes rearranged into new forms.

Painting and other forms of visual art remain important in Western Europe today. Below, a Spanish artist from the small town of Sitges talks about her life as an artist and about the importance of art in Spain today:

> I started working as an artist when I was 25. . . . I had always enjoyed painting, but until then I had only painted as a hobby. Now I live entirely on what I can get from selling my paintings. It's not very much, but I prefer to live a quiet life in a village rather than get involved with art dealers and galleries in the big cities.

In Spain at the moment there must be at least 500 painters who are internationally recognized, at least in art circles. Spain has given birth to some great masters—Goya, Velazquez, and more recently, Pablo Picasso and Salvador Dali. You mustn't forget, either, that there are many artists who have still to achieve their greatest fame. . . .

Perhaps it is because we have all these famous names as part of our history and our present-day culture, that so many people hope to follow their example. I don't include myself among those painters who dream of fame and fortune. I have never given an exhibition of my paintings in an art gallery, although in Spain there are about 2,500 art galleries, which put on thousands of exhibitions each year. And that's without counting exhibitions that are organized in restaurants, shops and other places from time to time.

Apart from the 500 well-known artists, I think there must be about 10,000 painters like myself, who earn their living through painting. Many put on exhibitions. And many, like myself, take their paintings to

This 1879 oil painting, "Oarsmen at Chatou," by Pierre Auguste Renoir, shows the artistic "shorthand" of the Impressionists, who put small bits of color together side by side and allowed the eye to blend them. Renoir, who liked to paint group studies of middle-class activities, often used his wife, children, and friends as models. What did the Impressionists try to capture in their art?

CHAPTER 50 ARTS AND THOUGHT

This 1940's painting by Pablo Picasso, "Woman in an Armchair," features the geometrical forms and multiple views of the subject typical of Cubism. For Picasso, what was the purpose of color?

one of the *plazas* (squares) in the city, where stalls are set up to sell directly to the public. It's part of Sunday morning routine for people to go out for a stroll before lunch, and they like to wander around looking at the paintings. If I'm lucky they buy one from me. . . .

I live in a small town where the pace of life is pretty slow. . . . I find that the people in small towns like Sitges appreciate artists and welcome them into the community. More than once I've paid for meals with one of my paintings! . . .*

LITERATURE

As with other forms of art, Western European literature evolved and changed over the centuries. While the ancient Greeks and Romans wrote histories, biographies, speeches, epic poetry, tragedies, and philosophical works, Renaissance writers concentrated in great part on drama and poetry. Later, in the 1800's, novelists created fictional worlds with realistic people, and the novel emerged as the favored form of literature.

Over the years, as literary forms changed, so did the use of language. Until after the Middle Ages, Latin and Greek were commonly used by educated people. Then, in the 1300's, writers began using the **vernacular,** the everyday speech of the common people, which later developed into the modern languages of Western Europe. Writing styles also changed. Until the 1900's, writers tended to express themselves in formal and elaborate ways, while in recent times more direct and simplified forms have become typical.

Today, Western European writers observe their societies and comment on current issues. These writers have had a decided impact on modern world literature. One such writer is Claude Simon, who won the 1985 Nobel Prize for Literature. Below, a journalist discusses Simon and his literary works:

The Prize must have caused tumult in the life of this simple, quiet man of seventy-two, who prefers to avoid most social and media contact. He divides his time between his Paris apartment and his vineyard in southern France, where he lives with his Greek wife, Rea. She types his manuscripts and offers discreet opinions on his work. . . .

Simon replies to his mail with perfect courtesy and takes part in the occasional [conference], but his [chief] interest is writing. When he is working on a novel he shuts himself off for months. . . .

His life is paved with noteworthy milestones: his study of mathematics; his involvement in the Spanish Civil War in 1936; his participation in World War II as part of a cavalry regiment; his incarcera-

---

*"I've paid for a meal with a painting!" in *We live in Spain* by Richard Bristow, 1984, The Bookwright Press, pp. 58–59. Reprinted by permission.

tion in a German prison camp and subsequent escape; his travels. Two journeys in particular seem to have left their mark: one to the U.S. and the other to India.

Simon has written eighteen books, fifteen of which are novels. . . . In 1957 he began to be published by *Editions de Minuit*, the home of other writers who had broken with the traditional form of the novel. . . . What they had in common was a break with the traditional novel's emphasis on a story. . . .

[Simon] believes that the *raison d'être* [purpose] of literature is not to represent reality. His motivation to work, he says has "changed greatly over the years." He writes "1) because of a need to do something; 2) in order to represent; 3) in order to communicate; 4) to discover." He continues, "Starting with the order 1, 2, 3, 4 thirty years ago, I have little by little arrived at the order 1, 4, 3—No. 2 appearing more and more dubious to me."

In each work Simon tried a new technique. He used musical forms. . . . He used stream of consciousness. . . . He used sentences five or six pages long, without punctuation.

History is prominent in his novels. The Spanish Civil War and World War II appear in almost all of the books. . . . Simon also weaves the French Revolution and the decades following it into his novels, as he does his own experiences. Many of his works are autobiographical and include personal documents such as postcards exchanged by his parents. . . .

Despite his concern with literary technique Simon's work is not dry or intellectual. . . . Simon touches our sensibility, our imagination, our intellect, and our very inner rhythm.*

1. When did traditional Western European music begin? In what ways did it change over the centuries?

---

*"France's New Nobelist" by Marie-Claudette Kirpalani, *The Statesman* of New Delhi as excerpted in *World Press Review*, December 1985, pp. 58, 60. Reprinted by permission.

2. What were the major characteristics of paintings during the Middle Ages? The Renaissance? The mid-1800's? The 1900's?
3. In what ways has literature changed in Western Europe from the time of the Greeks and Romans to the present?

SCIENTIFIC AND POLITICAL THOUGHT

Another major feature of Western European culture is the development of science and political thought. Both played a major role in the rise and expansion of Western Europe. Both had a major impact worldwide.

SCIENCE

Until the 1500's, Western European thinkers believed that philosophy and **theology,** the study of the nature of God and religious truth, were more important than the natural sciences. For this reason, their views of the universe remained very much the same as those of the ancient Greeks. They believed, for example, that the earth was at the center of the universe with the sun and other heavenly bodies moving around it.

Then, about the 1600's, a number of thinkers began to challenge and disprove the traditional views. Through observation, experimentation, and applied mathematics, they sought to improve knowledge of the universe. Their discoveries seemed to reveal a natural order in the universe that scientific inquiry could describe and explain.

In the 1800's and early 1900's, new discoveries were made; such new disciplines as bacteriology, psychology, chemistry, and physics were created; and the first truly comprehensive theories of science were developed and combined. Science became an important part of the university courses of study, and research laboratories were

CASE STUDY
WESTERN EUROPE

THE AMERICANIZATION OF WESTERN EUROPE

For centuries, Western Europe was the cultural leader of the West. Today, in many ways, the United States has taken over that role, and American cultural influence is strong and growing stronger in Western Europe. As discussed below by a French journalist, not all Western Europeans are happy about the Americanization of their culture:

At one of several rock concerts in Europe by the American rock sensation Bruce Springsteen, 30,000 enraptured youths wear jeans and T-shirts bearing the names of American universities, states, and products. At their feet are thousands of empty Coca-Cola bottles. Springsteen addresses the crowd in English and sings—to roaring applause—his hit, "Born in the U.S.A." . . .

Another development casts an even darker shadow. Hovering high above Europe, a satellite transmits programs made in the U.S. Each hour of broadcasting carries six advertising slots. Four are reserved for the firms that financed the program, and two for Europeans. . . . Consequently, Europe is blanketed in American images, culture, and products.

. . . American films constitute 35 percent of the French market, 50 percent of the Italian, Dutch, and Danish markets, 60 percent of the German market, and 80 percent of the British market.

. . . Most [TV] programming in many countries is nationally produced, and Europe's dominant public stations favor national and European products. But series such as Starsky and Hutch, Dallas, *and* Dynasty *draw the greatest number of viewers.*

In the recording industry U.S. firms supply 50 percent of the global market. It is not by chance that Spaniard Julio Iglesias, an international star, has his headquarters in Miami. . . .

Mickey Mouse and his Disney pals are familiar to Europe's children; the exploits of Superman are well known, as are those of . . . J.R. and Sylvester Stallone's Rambo. The disco beat reverberates through European apartment buildings. Americans are everywhere.

Leaders eager to change all of that are jockeying for position. . . .

Slowly, Europe is realizing that the battle requires new strategies. One is the creation of a European cultural market, advocated primarily by French Minister of Culture Jack Lang. Within the European Economic Community (EEC), Lang has been successful in awakening other leaders to the need for shared strategies and objectives.

The EEC now has a cultural delegate, Carlo Ripa de Maena. At a European Book conference . . . in June plans were made for coordinating translation of European books and for cataloguing the continent's major libraries. De Maena also is trying to establish a "fund to support television and film coproductions of fictional works"—a step toward an eventual European film and TV industry. . . .

Europe has furnished lifestyles, traditions, cultural tools, and language to Americans. It has been like Greece to the Romans. . . . But Europe today is undergoing an economic, technological, and spiritual crisis. It must invent new values and forge new myths that are the leaven of a civilization.

Will Europe be able to create heroes for the children of the 21st century? Cyrano de Bergerac, that tender swashbuckler who seduced the world, claimed to have fallen from the moon. If Europe is to realize its dreams it will be necessary for him to climb back to the stars.*

1. In what ways has Western European culture become Americanized?
2. If you were a Western European, how would you feel about your culture being Americanized? Why would you feel this way?

---

*"Europe Fights 'Americanization'" by Pierre Billard, *LePoint* of Paris, as excerpted in *World Press Review*, October 1985, pp. 34–35. Reprinted by permission.

founded. In the field of medicine, breakthroughs based on research led to the elimination of many diseases. And, just as importantly, for the first time, scientists and inventors realized that science and technology were of use to one another. This realization led to many new inventions and discoveries and increased western status in the eyes of many non-western nations. Below, an Arab born in Sudan and educated in part in the West describes the reaction of some Easterners:

> The mechanical inventions of the West were beginning to invade the Near East. . . . The telegraph and the railway had been there for some time. . . . Now new wonders were appearing. The electric tram, electric light, motor-cars and gramophones. Miracle after miracle, and all invented by Europeans. . . . There were, too, rumours of stranger, more incredible miracles, of motor-cars that could fly, ships that went under the sea, and telegraphy without wire; and all, all invented by the extremely clever Europeans. . . .
>
> I was eleven when I saw the first aeroplane. It was in 1914. . . . Early in the winter rumours began to go round that a French aviator was coming to Khartoum. No aeroplane had yet visited the Sudan, and so everybody was tremendously excited about it. . . . Then the rumours became more and more definite; the name of the aviator was given, the route he was following, the approximate date of his arrival, the place of landing. . . . At last the day and the hour were announced; and the whole population of Khartoum . . . assembled to see the miracle. The landing-place was in a stretch of sand some way outside the town, and we went there by cab. I was consumed with excitement. . . . Impossible that a man, a real man, should come in a machine flying like a bird. Impossible.
>
> 2 o'clock . . . 2:15 . . . 2:30. . . . And then a low distant drone, and a black speck in the sky, there, coming from the north. A hush for a second . . . exclamations, jabberings, strained necks, stretched arms. There he is, there he is! Yes . . . No . . . yes . . . no . . . yes, yes, yes. The noise is louder, the speck is bigger. "What? that thing," said a doubting Sudanese standing next to us. "Why it is a vulture, and the noise is coming from the Power Station." But soon all doubt, all argument ceased. The vulture was above our heads, huge as ten eagles, filling the air with its deafening drone, and as it circled down, a human arm stretched out of it and waved to the crowd. The miracle had come off. . . .
>
> Before the machine reached the ground, the seething crowd, beyond itself with excitement, had broken through the police cordon, and rushed towards the landing spot. The Governor-General . . . had to forget his dignity and advance with hurried steps . . . , while the crowd pushed and jostled in its mad eagerness to see this huge artificial bird, and especially the man in it. Was it really a man, this weird-looking creature with its leather head and huge protruding oval eyes, stepping down on to the ground? See, see he's waving his arm again, he is shaking hands with the Governor-General. *Wallahi zol, zol sahih.* (By God it's a man, a real man!) But even after this, our old Sudanese woman-servant had still some lingering doubts. "Really, Ya Sitt," she asked my mother when we had gone back home, "is it a real man, a *zol* like us, who eats and drinks and gets married?"*

As the 1900's progressed, so did the number of advances. Foremost among these was the **theory of relativity** proposed by a German physicist named Albert Einstein. The theory, which shattered the view of the universe held for centuries, proposed that there were no absolutes in measuring time and space and that time and space depended on the relative motion of bodies in space.

---
*An Arab Tells His Story by Edward Atiyah, 1946, John Murray (Publishers) Ltd., pp. 29–32. Reprinted by permission.

CHAPTER 50 ARTS AND THOUGHT

SCIENCE AND TECHNOLOGY

Date	Event	Date	Event
1859	theory of natural selection developed by Charles Darwin	1904	radium and polonium discovered by Marie and Pierre Curie
1876	germ theory of disease advanced by Louis Pasteur	1905	theory of relativity advanced by Albert Einstein
1900	first rigid airship launched by Count Ferdinand Von Zeppelin	1926	television first demonstrated by John L. Baird
1900	field of psychoanalysis established by Sigmund Freud	1929	first antibiotic drug, penicillin, discovered by Sir Alexander Fleming

After World War II, scientific leadership passed from Western Europe to the United States and the Soviet Union. Still, Western Europeans continue to play an important part in scientific research. Below, a French Nobel Prize winner discusses his schooling and career:

My schooling included the rather weird experience of having to change from my own German language to French when I was sixteen years old. You see, I was born at Guebwiller in Alsace. This region was annexed by France in 1648, ceded to Germany from 1871 until 1918, when it became French again. . . .

My father was a tradesman, and none of my family were particularly brainy. I was about fourteen when my teachers . . . noticed that I had a gift for mathematics.

This enabled me to obtain a scholarship to the École Normale Supérieure in Paris —the leading center for budding scientists, and one of Europe's finest Institutes. A year later, in 1922, I was privileged to meet Albert Einstein on his first visit to Paris from Berlin. . . . Einstein had been awarded the Nobel Prize in Physics the year before, at the age of forty-two. By the way, I was sixty-four when I was awarded mine.

After receiving my science degree, I taught until 1945. I spent most of World War II at the École Normale Supérieure. . . . Obviously little research could be done during the war, so I had to wait until afterwards to build up a research team of ten students to work in my specialized field—the structure of the atom, which should not be confused with nuclear bombs.

I didn't expect to receive the Nobel Prize. . . .

Did the prize affect my life? It's a heavy burden in many ways, because there's a continual call on my time for interviews, or on my support for petitions. I have to refuse many of them.

Many people believe that scientific discoveries come only from hard, logical, reasoned thought. That is so, but it's important to remember that intuition also plays a part. A scientist must also be a poet. . . .

Do I think that any of my work has helped us to understand the universe? No, I don't think so. But the role of science in the world is vital, for good or evil. I believe science has been positive in improving our life, especially in the field of communications. But it is also the cause of a major danger—nuclear war.*

POLITICAL IDEAS AND PRACTICE

During the 1600's and 1700's, revolutions in some Western European lands led to the end of **absolute monarchy,** a government in which a king or queen claims total power. At the same time, new ideas about government came into being. Such thinkers as Britain's John Locke and France's Jean-Jacques Rousseau stressed that government must be based on the consent of the people and must protect individual rights.

Later, during the 1800's, what remained of Western Europe's traditional political system was challenged by three powerful groups —**liberals, nationalists,** and **socialists.** The liberals, most of whom came from the middle class, wanted democratic reforms. They favored voting rights for citizens, protection of private property, freedom of speech, and **capitalism,** the private ownership of business and industry.

The nationalists supported **nationalism,** the idea that all national groups that share the same language, customs, and history should be given political freedom. The nationalists supported the liberals until they failed to realize certain nationalist goals.

The socialists believed that the people as a whole should own all land, factories, and means of production, as well as have the right to vote. Although most socialist ideas came from middle-class thinkers, the movement itself received most of its support from the working class. Many socialists, like the German Karl Marx, believed that a just society could come about only through a worker-led revolution.

In the 1900's, the governments and politics of Western Europe underwent further change. World Wars I and II lessened Western Europe's role in world affairs and forced Western European leaders to settle their differences and work together for greater economic and political unity. A major goal was more social justice and equality at home. In time, full political democracy was achieved in the Western European countries, and social welfare programs that spread a higher standard of living to all of the classes were developed.

Although today the countries of Western Europe share a common commitment to democracy, all the governments are not the same in form or practices. West Germany, for example, is a federal republic in which responsibility is divided between the central government and regional states with the government providing some public services. Its neighbor, Denmark, on the other hand, has a totally different political organization, as explained by the mayor of Køge, a Danish port city:

---

*"A scientist must also be a poet" in *We live in France* by James Tomlins, 1983, The Bookwright Press, pp. 38–39. Reprinted by permission.

This train, which bears the crest of the Danish royal house, is part of Denmark's transportation system. Like other public utilities, it is under government control. What type of government does Denmark have?

As Mayor, I preside over both political and administrative matters, that is to say, I'm the head of the town council and of all the staff employed by it.

The town council of Køge consists of 21 elected members, representing various political parties. The Social Democrats are the largest in the borough—and the largest in the country.

Denmark is a constitutional monarchy: the powers of our sovereign are laid down in our Constitution. Unlike, say, the Queen of England, our monarchs are never crowned, but merely take over from the previous one. . . .

Danish laws are made in our Parliament, the *Folketing*. This is made up of 179 members. . . . Elections to the *Folketing* are by proportional representation. This means that the number of members of each party in Parliament is in proportion to the votes each party receives in the election: the more votes a party gets, the more members it has. The main parties at the moment are the Social Democrats, the Liberals, the Conservatives, and the Progressives. A delegate to the *Folketing* serves for four years. Every Dane over 18 has the right to vote in elections.

All laws enacted in the *Folketing* must get the Queen's consent—usually a formality. They are then implemented by the government of the day. The government is headed by a prime minister, with a cabinet of ministers under him.

In 1970, our local government system was reorganized. The country was divided into 275 municipalities (led by elected municipal boards) and 14 counties (led by elected county councils). The municipalities are in charge of such matters as water, gas and electricity supplies, social welfare, primary schools, libraries and minor roads. The municipalities collect both income and property taxes, and receive grants from the government to help run their services. The county councils are responsible for such things as hospitals, secondary schools, main roads, and conservation of the countryside.

The municipalities have a large degree of self-government, but there are a number of laws from the county level and from central government which they have to administer. Our local government system is also democratic: every fourth year, people can elect whom they want to represent them.

The main task of any municipality, like the one I'm in charge of, is to spend the money it has sensibly, and without waste. Budgets must be drawn up—and kept to. This can often cause a lot of problems, because each party wants money to be used in different ways.*

1. What change took place in Western European scientific thinking in the 1600's? What breakthroughs were made in the 1800's and 1900's?
2. What three groups challenged Western Europe's political system in the 1800's? What views did each hold?

---

*"Housing standards in Denmark are very high" in *We live in Denmark* by Ulla Andersen, 1984, The Bookwright Press, pp. 32–33. Reprinted by permission.

CHAPTER 50 REVIEW

POINTS TO REMEMBER

1. The ancient Greeks made one of the first important contributions to Western European culture. Their belief that human beings were the center of the universe was a revolution in thought.
2. After the fall of Rome, a new layer of culture emerged in Western Europe as church officials, monarchs, and nobles used their wealth to support learning and the arts.
3. From the late 1700's to the 1900's, another layer of culture was formed in Western Europe in an effort to appeal to the tastes of the masses.
4. Traditional Western European music, which began as monophonic, evolved and became more dramatic, and opera became a popular musical form.
5. Like music, traditional Western European painting underwent changes, with less emphasis being put on realism and more nonreligious subjects being portrayed.
6. Over the years, Western European literature also evolved with changes in respect to literary form, the use of language, and writing style.
7. In the 1600's, in an effort to improve knowledge of the universe, Western European thinkers began to challenge and disprove traditional views of science. In the years that followed, new discoveries were made, new disciplines were created, and the first truly comprehensive theories of science were developed and combined. Technology also made great strides as scientists and inventors realized that science and technology were of use to one another.
8. During the 1600's and 1700's, Western Europe's traditional political system was challenged by those who wanted a government based on the consent of the people and that protected individual rights. During the 1800's, it was challenged by liberals, nationalists, and socialists. Today, all Western European governments are not the same, yet they share a common commitment to democracy.

VOCABULARY

Identify

Pope Julius II
Michelangelo Buonarroti
Charles Dickens
Johann Sebastian Bach
Impressionists
Pablo Picasso
Cubism
Claude Simon
Albert Einstein
John Locke
Jean-Jacques Rousseau
Karl Marx
Wolfgang Amadeus Mozart

Define

patrons
mass culture
classicism
romanticism
monophonic
counterpoint
polyphonic music
chords
homophonic
operas
perspective
vernacular
theology
theory of relativity
absolute monarchy
liberals
nationalists
socialists
capitalism
nationalism

DISCUSSING IMPORTANT IDEAS

1. To what extent is present-day Western European culture a product of the past? Explain your answer.
2. Do you agree or disagree with the statement that culture is the mainstay of civilization? Explain.
3. In what ways do you think today's world would be different if scientists and inventors had not realized that science and technology were of use to one another?
4. In what ways are art, science, and political thought linked?

DEVELOPING SKILLS

ANALYZING ART AS A PRIMARY SOURCE

When most people think of primary sources, they think of written or oral material. There is, however, something else that qualifies as a primary source. It is art, which comes in many forms, including sculpture, paintings, collages, cartoons, and etchings. Regardless of the form it takes, art is a statement by an artist of how he or she feels about a subject. In some way or other, art represents the culture and the period from which it comes.

Often, works of art are used as primary sources to accompany secondary source material. This has been done frequently in this text. The guidelines used in the following example will help you analyze a work of art used in this way:

1. Look carefully at the work of art, in this case a reproduction of the painting by Pablo Picasso that appears on page 839.
2. Read the text accompanying the work of art. Based on what you read, determine why this particular piece of art was included with the written material. *(On page 838, you are told that Pablo Picasso developed a style of art known as Cubism. This painting was included as an example of Cubism.)*
3. Determine in what ways the work of art makes clearer or reinforces the written information. *(makes clearer Picasso's comments on page 838 about nature and art; shows how Picasso used color to express emotion rather than describe reality; shows what is meant by "geometrical, unrealistic planes and shapes arranged into new forms")*

For further practice in this skill, use the guidelines to analyze the painting by Renoir on page 838.

CHAPTER 51
THE WAYS OF LIFE

1. What are the major characteristics of urban and rural life styles in Western Europe?
2. How do Western Europeans spend their leisure time?

It's an hour-and-a-half by bus into work every day. I have to be in the café at 7:00 A.M. if I'm on duty for opening time at 8:00. We have to get the coffee machine started, the cups and saucers laid out, and sort out the rolls and sandwiches that the cooks begin to send up. I put on my uniform and white apron, then draw up the steel shutters to let in the crowd of bustling men and women on their way to work.

Most Italians drop into a bar at least once a day. Every day I serve about a thousand cups of coffee! Even when there are two of us behind the counter at peak hours, it's difficult to keep up with the orders. . . .

It's all a matter of practice. I was twelve years old when I started working in a café. . . . It was very hard work, serving at tables and carrying trays of coffee round to the nearby offices from 7:00 in the morning until 10:00 at night—and all for 11,250 lire ($7.70) a month!

Things have improved a lot since then: with overtime and tips I take home about 1,000,000 lire ($684) a month—a fair enough sum! I would say this job is like any other, and the long hours don't trouble me particularly. After seventeen years I'm used to it!

I don't feel particularly tired, but when I get home in the evening I prefer to stay in and play with the children. . . . Sometimes I help my wife in the kitchen. . . . She used to work as an analyst in a medical laboratory, but she gave that up when we got married four years ago. . . .

On my day off my wife and I often take the children into the center of town on the bus; we go for a walk in the park of the Villa Borghese, or around the Spanish Steps. My wife is Roman and so she's used to these beautiful places. . . . But like most of the people living in Rome, I come from the provinces. . . .

This summer I'll be driving the whole family, including my parents, down to our home village. Most of the men there have to travel north to find work . . . , but they all come back in August. The village is very quiet for most of the year, but while we're there it's one long party for everyone, and we have a lot of fun.*

This Italian's life style and attitudes are not unlike those of many other Western Europeans. Yet, although similarities in life style are found throughout Western Europe, ways of life still differ in certain respects from country to country and region to region. The sharpest contrasts are between urban and rural life styles, between the industrialized and agricultural areas of the region.

*"I serve about a thousand cups of coffee each day" in *We live in Italy* by Tana de Zulueta, 1983, The Bookwright Press, pp. 60–61. Reprinted by permission.

THE WAY OF THE CITY

More than one-half of all Western Europeans live in cities. In the northern part of Western Europe, three of the largest cities are London, Paris, and Berlin. In the southern part of Western Europe, four of the largest cities are Madrid, Lisbon, Rome, and Athens. Because a rapid growth of new industries and jobs has drawn many people from rural areas, these cities have become crowded, and new suburbs have grown up around them.

THE WORKING LIFE

Each city of Western Europe is different. At the same time, each has much in common with the other cities of the region. Berlin, for example, is different from most other cities because it is split into two parts—East Berlin, in Communist East Germany, and West Berlin, which although located in East Germany, has ties to democratic West Germany.

Below, an observer comments on attitudes toward work and life in West Berlin:

West Berlin becomes lively very early in the morning. In factories the first shift usually starts at 6:00 A.M. so many workers have to be up and about at 5:00 A.M. if they want to reach their place of work on time. And all of them do. . . .

Office workers usually begin work a little later, most of them have to reach their offices between 7:00 and 9:00 A.M. Nowadays there are flexible working hours in many offices. Most Germans do not mind getting up early, especially as they have most of the afternoon free. The factory worker who starts at 6:00 A.M. will finish at 2:30 P.M., and most office workers are home by 5:00 P.M. So they have more time with their families.

It is difficult in West Berlin to tell what people's jobs are, when seeing them travelling to work. Mechanics and factory workers usually travel to work in their ordinary clothes and change into overalls when they get there.

All factories and large offices have canteens in which the employees can get a

The hectic pace of West Berlin can be seen along the Kurfürstendamm, one of that city's busiest and most popular boulevards. The ruins of the Kaiser Wilhelm Memorial Church, background, and the new church built beside it, are just part of what makes West Berlin a thriving cultural center. Why is Berlin different from most other cities?

CHAPTER 51 THE WAYS OF LIFE

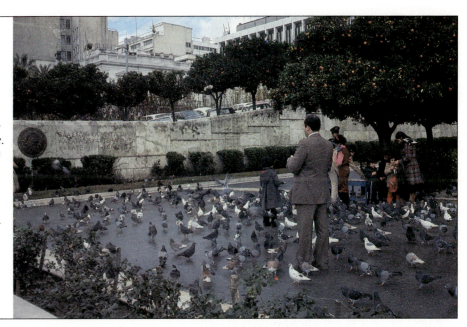

Feeding the pigeons on a square in front of the Greek Parliament Building in Athens is a popular pastime for Greeks and tourists alike. Greeks enjoy being outdoors in the pleasant Mediterranean climate, and Sunday evening walks with family or friends are an important part of Greek life. Why do most Greeks want to enjoy life "right now"?

hot meal at lunch time. Most people eat a big lunch in the canteen and then eat only sandwiches for supper instead of having dinner in the evenings.

Other workers who have to be out and about as part of their job may take sandwiches or eat in one of the numerous pubs [bars] which serve very good meals. Or they may stop at one of the *Würstchenbuden* (sausage stands) to eat a fried sausage or a *Boulette* (fried meat ball) with chips.

Most Germans take their jobs very seriously, and work hard. They do not usually have many tea or coffee breaks. . . . People do their jobs very efficiently but they have less time to talk to and to get to know the people they work with.*

In Athens, Greece, on the other hand, the pace is hectic, but the general attitude is somewhat different from that found in West Berlin. As is explained in the excerpt that follows, most Greeks believe that life should be lived to the fullest:

I hadn't been long in Athens . . . when I was given timetables for getting the most out of life.

Work till 2:30, home for a big meal and into pajamas for a good two-hour sleep. A shower at 6:30—and you have a whole new day! You can go to a second job or to the theater and then, in [warm, friendly] company, to a café or to a taverna [restaurant] for another sizeable meal with music and singing and dancing. To bed around 2, up by 6 or 6:30. . . .

"The only trouble with our two days in one is our four rush hours instead of two."

That was a civil servant talking, but others assured me they kept similar schedules —a factory worker, a newspaperman. A sales manager juggled two additional jobs on alternate afternoons; after midnight I'd find him at a sidewalk table, enjoying the soft breezes of March and the sweetest of pastries, talking to friends about challenging moneymaking ventures. He echoed what I'd been hearing from numerous Greeks: "This country has suffered so much, we want to be as happy as we can, *right now!* . . .

Living in Berlin by Angelika Wagner, 1980, Wayland (Publishers), Ltd., pp. 18–19. Reprinted by permission.

... This is where everybody wants to be, the place for fun and opportunity. And in the center, seemingly incessant noise. I used earplugs to sleep, until the hotel put in double windows.

There's a moving market, each day of the week in a different street—with eggs, flowers, artichokes, 18 kinds of olives. Noon is a good time to go, says a poet; by then they're anxious to get rid of things....

In Athens many a salary earner, risen from his afternoon sleep, [goes] forth to canvass his connections, to see what income-producing activity can be found for the rest of his two-part day. Some short-term job, perhaps, for a flat fee and a share of the profits?... Because of such enthusiastic moonlighting—not just to get by, but to get ahead—men of Athens, so a study shows, devote more time to work than their counterparts do in either Germany or the United States.

Spending is enthusiastic too. An elderly gentleman says he's seen ordinary people in the supermarket load up with things they would never have dared approach twenty years ago. "A feather pillow, Quaker Oats, mustard! If they buy sugar, it's not one little bag but six."

Demand is brisk for bathroom fixtures in blue, black, red, pink. But first comes the automobile, even if import duty and taxes add at least 200 percent.*

INDUSTRY AND UNIONS

Many of the world's leading industrial nations are in Western Europe. In the northwestern part of the region is such heavy industry as coal, steel, and chemical production. In Scandinavia and the Mediterranean lands, the emphasis is on such light industry as the processing of agricultural products, fish, wood, and minerals. Today, more Western Europeans work in manufacturing than in any other economic activity. In an effort to shape business and government policies, many of the workers have joined trade unions. Often, these unions have close links to political parties. Below, a French labor leader talks about his interest in and involvement with trade unions and what they have accomplished for French workers:

I suppose I was destined to become a trade union leader. My father was always talking about unions and I come from Limoges in central France, which has a long tradition of workers fighting for their rights in the shoe, furniture, printing and porcelain factories there.

I was nineteen when I joined the Force Ouvrière (F.O.). It was founded in 1948 after a split in the Communist-led General Confederation of Labor (C.G.T.).

I held a number of jobs in small firms and became a civil servant in the financial section, always organizing my colleagues. Then I was made a full-time F.O. delegate at Paris headquarters.

Today my official title is Confederation Secretary responsible for Press Relations —putting the F.O. on the mass media map. We also have our own weekly and monthly publications.

There's a lot of traveling involved, not only abroad—I've just returned from West Germany and the United States—but also throughout France, keeping in touch with all our 13,000 branches.

We're growing monthly. I think this is mainly because we're non-Communist and we stress the role of negotiation in labor disputes. We don't call our workers out on strike without good reason.

We've taken a leading part in limiting the working week to forty hours, obtaining a month's paid vacation a year, and also additional retirement benefits. All an F.O. member has to pay as his monthly union dues is the equivalent of one hour's pay. He gets a bargain.

---

*"To Be Indomitable, To Be Joyous: Greece" by Peter T. White in *National Geographic*, Vol. 157, No. 3, March 1980, pp. 360, 368, 380, 381. Reprinted by permission.

Manufacturing is an important part of the economy in most countries of Western Europe. This factory in Spain, like many in other areas of Western Europe, is using robots and phasing out old-fashioned equipment and methods of manufacturing in an effort to increase production and make it more efficient. What is a disadvantage to using robots in industry?

Our problems have changed in the past five years. Today they include two new factors—robots and computers. We have to safeguard the jobs of our members, and yet we must show we aren't against progress. After all, they said the steam engine was harmful around 150 years ago. We mustn't make a stand against modern-day "steam engines."

We also face some strange labor paradoxes these days. For example, a man gets paid more according to his qualifications. In other words, the more specialized he is, the better off he is—or was in the old days. But we've found that the greater his specialization, the sooner a man is out of a job because technical progress advances so fast.

France is probably the least trade-union-minded country in Europe, with only about twenty-five percent of the work force organized. Yet unions have brought massive benefits, starting in 1936 with the paid week's annual vacation. There was none before. Today it has gone up to one month.

Most workers have a forty-hour week, and now we're planning a thirty-five-hour week.

French workers have also won agreements guaranteeing them their pay for one year after they've lost their jobs through the economic recession. The first time in the history of the working class movement anywhere in the world that it has obtained such an agreement.

Unemployment benefits are paid partly by the state, and the balance is made up by employers and workers in a four-to-one ratio. After a year on full pay, a worker is paid a percentage until he finds a job.*

1. How do West Berliners view their working life?
2. How do Athenians view their working life?
3. What kinds of industry are found in Western Europe today?
4. Why have many Western European workers joined trade unions? What are some of the benefits gained by trade unions in France?

---

*"No strikes without good reason" in *We live in France* by James Tomlins, 1983, The Bookwright Press, pp. 42–43. Reprinted by permission.

THE WAY OF THE COUNTRYSIDE

About 20 percent of Western Europeans are employed in agriculture or such other rural activities as fishing and hunting. European farmers raise livestock, grow fruits and vegetables, and produce such grain crops as barley, oats, rye, and wheat. Most of the farms in the northern areas use modern equipment and chemical fertilizers and are highly productive. But in the Mediterranean lands, farmers are just starting to use modern machinery and methods, so crop yields are not as high. Below, an observer discusses the effect progress, in the form of a land consolidation program, has had on Santa María del Condado, a small farming village in northern Spain:

> . . . The program's aim is to transform the dozens of tiny fields belonging to a household into three or four larger, more regular plots, as well as to build roads to make the plots accessible. . . .
>
> . . . As I drew closer to Santa María, I could see . . . that the village was exposed, like a sheep just sheared of its wool. Before there had been more trees, more hedges, more gardens. . . .
>
> That things had changed radically, . . . was not simply my own perception; it was also that of the farmers of Santa María. I remember explaining, in 1978, that I had come to Santa María to study the way of life of the village and being told . . . that theirs was a harsh life, for the work they had to do was "brutal, very brutal." A number of times I heard the phrase *la tierra es muy señorita*, "the land is a very spoiled girl"—in other words, the land will not do a thing for you, you have to work and slave "for her." On my return to Santa María, the remark I heard most frequently . . . was that no one wants to work anymore, no one knows *how* to work anymore. . . .
>
> Once I went to observe the irrigation of some hillside lands close to the village dam. . . . There I encountered Felicísimo Llamazares, a farmer in his seventies. . . .
>
> I asked if he was pleased with the consolidation that had been carried out. He

Harvesting machines such as this one are being promoted by the Spanish government and used by Spanish farmers to increase crop yields in order to expand the market and raise the input of agriculture in the Spanish economy. Grain crops, such as the rice being harvested in the photo, are grown mainly in the northern region of Spain. How do the Spanish regard their land?

shrugged his shoulders and said that he thought that in the long run it was for the best. He had owned fifty plots, but his children no longer knew where most of them were; now, with five, they could keep track of their property more easily. Not that his children would ever work the land, he added, but who knows? . . . He explained that you can force water to go in a certain direction, but after a while, if left alone, it reverts to flowing the way it used to. "In other words," he said, "in twenty, thirty, one hundred years, maybe those people who left will return to where they used to be, which is the *pueblos* [villages]. . . ."

Now that every field has access to a road, there is no longer any need or excuse to cross a neighbor's field to reach one's own. In the past there were always problems with teams and carts causing damage to a neighbor's crops. Yet there was a sense that no one, no matter what degree of self-importance he or she possessed, could remain aloof from his or her neighbors. The layout of the land prevented it. Consolidation represents the very opposite of such a conception; it frees the landholder of all servitudes, all ties to the community.

But no change in land tenure can do away at one stroke with the patterns, conceptions, and ideals of the past. Attitudes toward time, work, and the land are changing in Santa María, but these new attitudes have not replaced the old ones; instead, they now coexist . . . with peasant attitudes that have been passed on for generations. Some couples still thresh chickpeas with the threshing sledge, the women winnowing [separating] and sifting the crop with the sieve. Many families still bring the harvest home in their cow carts, and some farmers, long past retirement age, milk their five or six cows by hand every morning and evening. Men still train cows for the yoke, while miniature jewels of gardens are set in fields too large for those accustomed to close contact with the earth.

The common lands have not disappeared. . . . In the summertime, most families still pasture their cows on the communal grazing lands, and participating villagers take turns caring for the communal herd. . . . All the 900 or so sheep belonging to village families are taken to pasture in a single herd by a shepherd from the community.

These are customs that took form in the medieval era. . . . They continue to be practiced today in small communities such as Santa María, where people are linked by kinship and close relations with their neighbors.*

In rural areas of Western Europe, the village often is the center of life. More traditional ways generally are followed than in the cities, and the standard of living usually is lower. One of the more largely rural countries of Western Europe is Ireland. Two-thirds of the country is farmland, and village life remains an important part of the national culture. Below, two visitors to Ballyduff, a small village near the foot of the Knockmealdown Mountains, talk about the village and the life style of one of its inhabitants:

It is seven o'clock in the morning. . . . After breakfast, we set off toward the river. . . .

Ballyduff is slowly coming to life around this time. The few people we see greet us with a smiling, "Good morning." It is heartening to meet people who are so friendly toward perfect strangers.

The small village stores will soon be open, and people are emerging from their houses to collect the milk which has been delivered to their doorsteps. A couple of cars cross the narrow main street, followed by a single tractor. A new day has begun.

Ballyduff has seven stores in all, a restaurant, a lending library, and four pubs.

---

*"Past and Present in the Spanish Countryside" by Ruth Behar in *Natural History*, Vol. 94, No. 11, November 1985, pp. 70, 71, 73, 75. Abridged and reprinted by permission. Copyright the American Museum of Natural History, 1985.

There is also a bank, which is open for just two and a half hours each week. The church is on the edge of the village, and from there it is only a few yards to the bridge over the . . . River Blackwater.

The river runs for 160 kilometers (100 miles), from the hills in the southwest to the southeast coast of Ireland. . . . We walk down to the river bank and see Connie Corcoran [a fisherman] standing a little way out in the water, where it is shallow and foaming—stirred up by the whirlpools over the stony bed. . . .

Connie is 33 years old, and he makes his living fishing for salmon in the Blackwater River. He is what the Irish would call a "gillie": he catches fish for his employer, John McHugh, who is the owner of the fishing rights for this stretch of the river. . . .

Connie is Ballyduff's salmon expert. He can tell exactly where the fish will be, and he knows how changes in the current and water level will affect the day's catch. The Blackwater is one of the best salmon-fishing rivers in Ireland, and people come many miles—even from other countries—to fish in these waters.

Connie is paid a weekly wage by John McHugh, and his services are often hired out to other anglers [people who fish] so that he can give them the benefit of his experience.

When the day's fishing is over, and the tackle has all been packed away, we . . . walk back towards the village. On the way, Connie tells us about his childhood.

"By the time I was 3 or 4 years old, I was already fascinated by the river. I started fishing with a twig and a piece of string, and later I played truant from school to fish. While other boys sat behind desks, I was out providing food for the family. One day John caught me fishing illegally, but to my great surprise, he offered me a job as a gillie! It made sense to him, because he knew that nothing would ever stop me from fishing here: it was my whole life."

The Corcoran family lives on the outskirts of the village in a small, whitewashed cottage which stands in the middle of about half a hectare (1.25 acres) of land. The land is used mainly for growing potatoes and a few other vegetables. There

This Irish father and his children are enjoying an outing in a cart similar to a jaunting car, a light, two-wheeled open vehicle drawn by horses. Once seen frequently on rural Irish roads, today the jaunting car is used mostly by tourists. What role does the village play in many rural areas of Western Europe?

is also room for a goat which stands tethered in the long grass.

Connie's wife, Eileen, is 31 years old, and they have three children. . . .

As we walk up the garden path, we see that the children are waiting on the doorstep for us. Eileen comes out of the kitchen where she has been cooking, to welcome us home. After all Connie has told us, we are not surprised to hear that Eileen is preparing the family's favorite dish—Irish Salmon!*

1. How do most Western Europeans in rural areas make a living?
2. What changes have taken place in some Western European villages in recent years?

EDUCATION

Western Europe, where many of the world's first universities were founded during the Middle Ages, has long been recognized as a center of learning. Today, over 90 percent of the people are literate and have at least a high school education.

The educational systems of Western Europe, however, vary from area to area and country to country. In the northern countries, educational standards generally are high. Young people are required to go to school until they are 15 or 16 years old, at which time they may quit entirely, attend a vocational school to learn a trade, or start preparing for a university education. In the Mediterranean lands, however, the economies are poorer, so less money is spent on education. Although children are required to complete elementary school, afterward many end their formal education and find work on a farm or in industry.

A Family in Ireland by Peter Otto Jacobsen and Preben Sejer Kristensen, 1985, The Bookwright Press, pp. 9–11, 13, 18–19. Reprinted by permission.

This girl of Albanian ancestry is being taught in the Albanian language in her classroom at the Contessa Entillina school in Sicily. Why is less money spent on education in the Mediterranean countries?

In recent years, all Western European countries have tried to improve their educational systems. They especially are concerned about upgrading their scientific, technical, and computer training so they can better compete with the United States, the Soviet Union, and Japan. As reported below, in West Germany, computer education has become a major issue:

A year before he graduated from high school, nineteen-year-old Frank Kardel of Altenholz wrote a program for a secret code on his home computer. He worked on it for two months. The world's largest computers would have to work day and night for eight or nine years to break the West German teenager's code.

Before he started school, four-year-old Jens Niegemann of Saarbrücken wrote his first program, also on a home computer. He tapped a dozen commands on the keyboard, and then his project was finished. He seldom spent more than half an hour at his monitor.

These two programmers illustrate the range of a phenomenon that has sparked a debate throughout West Germany. The debate is underway in classrooms, in livingrooms, and in the offices of the Ministry of Education. The nation must decide whether it is desirable for every student in Germany to learn how to use computers—at school, not at home. . . .

Computer science was introduced to German high schools in 1972. It is now taught in only half of them, usually as an elective. Secondary-school students use computers only for special projects. All of that may change in the near future.

People speak of an "educational crisis," and they use terms such as "computer illiterates" to describe the majority of German high school graduates. They equate knowledge of computers with reading, writing, and arithmetic—a fourth basic skill.

If today's plans materialize it will mean one of the most important changes in German education since World War II. Computer manufacturers already are competing for the educational market. "Never in the history of education," says a Hamburg official, "have we seen as much market pressure on the schools."

Other educators voice other concerns. Ulrich Bosler of Kiel, who has studied computers and their introduction into schools for years, warns that "the school system could lose part of its function." . . .

Students, on the other hand, are enthusiastic about computer training. At both college and secondary school levels, they are choosing computer courses as electives more often than physics, chemistry, or an additional foreign language. "When it comes to computers," says Helmut Mueck, principal of the general high school in Ehringhausen, "you do not have to motivate students."

In high schools in Bonn and Soltau, two thirds of all students in one year have asked for computer courses, and many other schools report similar figures. Despite a lack of computers and a shortage of trained teachers, courses are [growing].

These Scandinavian students are learning to use computers that schools in many countries have recently purchased to aid in their technical education. In Sweden and Denmark, computer courses are integrated with mathematics and social and natural science courses. How are computers being used in schools in Germany?

CHAPTER 51 THE WAYS OF LIFE

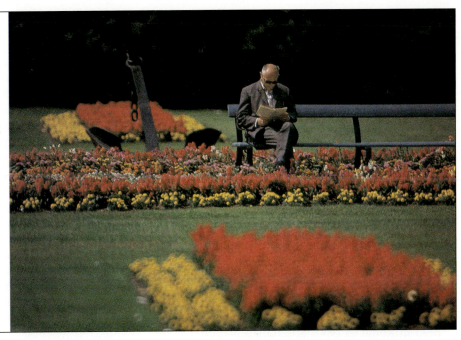

This man enjoys a quiet moment reading in one of Amsterdam's scenic parks. A major port of the Netherlands, Amsterdam is also one of the intellectual, commercial, and artistic capitals of Europe. What are some leisure activities enjoyed by Western Europeans?

Parents often help out when local schools lack money for equipment. A committee of parents in Hesse arranged a contract to lease computers for the school their children attend.

But a growing minority among teachers [strongly] oppose computers in schools. Their bitterness is revealed by Hartmut von Hentig, a professor of education, who says, "A child sits in front of a computer in isolation, sees something, and types in a response. It has no relationship to the rest of his life. Every effort we have made over twenty years to integrate learning with life would be destroyed."*

1. In what ways are the educational systems in northern Western Europe different from those in the Mediterranean area?
2. Why are many Western European countries concerned about improving their scientific, technical, and computer training?
3. What is at the heart of the debate over computers in West German schools?

---
*"Germany Computerizes" as excerpted in *World Press Review*, February 1985, pp. 55–56. Reprinted by permission.

LEISURE ACTIVITIES

During their leisure time, Western Europeans enjoy a wide range of activities. Some people like walking or gardening or reading or other quiet activities. Others like to go to the movies or to the theater. Still others are interested or involved in sports or traditional arts and crafts.

SPORTS

One of the most popular sports throughout Western Europe is soccer, which is called "football" by Western Europeans. Soccer matches draw large crowds, and fans passionately root for their local teams. Soccer, however, is not the only sport enjoyed by Western Europeans. There are skiing, horse racing, and cycling competitions as well as private clubs where people can learn and take part in such activities as judo, karate, horseback riding, and tennis. As discussed in the article that follows, in Rome, Italy, sports and games have become an important part of life in recent years:

Without a doubt, football is the most popular sport in Rome, and indeed in the whole of Italy. The city has two teams both of which have a lively and enthusiastic following, and are given wide coverage in the press and on radio and television. Sunday is the day of the week when most league games are played, and at kick-off time, Roman bars are filled to capacity with supporters who crowd in to watch their team on television.

It is only in the last thirty years that Rome has acquired adequate sports facilities to meet the needs of [its] population. Before then, only a small minority of Romans actually took part in sport. A big boost came when the Olympic games were held in Rome in 1960. The Italian National Olympic Committee promoted the building of sports stadia and gymnasia. The result is that now Rome has ample facilities. There are over 100 public swimming pools, over 100 basketball pitches and more than 300 tennis courts.

Children in Rome are, on the whole, more closely controlled by their families than in some cities. Parks where one can play freely, and purpose-built playgrounds, are few, and the streets are usually too busy to allow for games other than 'hide and seek.' There is plenty of opportunity, however, for games on the sandy beaches of Ostia, the pine woods of Fregene and similar open spaces where people go for picnics in fine weather. Many young people are members of sports clubs and gymnasia. . . .

In the recent educational reforms, sport was at last given consideration as an important part of a child's education. More time is allotted to it in the curriculum and more money is being spent on facilities in schools. An organization of Youth Games . . . has been running since 1969. Teams of children wishing to take part in athletics, gymnastics, swimming, cycling, skiing, ball games or any other sport which an organization wishes to present, are formed on a regional basis, and from these, finalists are chosen to take part in a great annual festival in Rome.

Whether played in a stadium by professionals or on the streets by young Italian boys like these, soccer is a favorite all over the globe. Every four years, 24 nations compete in the World Cup Championship, which Italy won in 1982. What role do sports play in education in Italy?

CHAPTER 51   THE WAYS OF LIFE   861

Every year has brought an increasing number of participants. As the idea behind the games is to involve as many people as possible, the Minister of Education decided to link them with the school system. Since 1977 all those of school age are included.*

FOLK ARTS AND CRAFTS

For many Western Europeans, preserving their heritage is important. As a result, a number of groups have formed throughout Western Europe to preserve traditional arts and crafts and to encourage public interest in them. Some of these groups are devoted to the traditional forms of music and dance that developed over the centuries in farming villages. Below, a member of a local British folk dance club discusses the club and its activities and his and his wife's involvement with them:

There are many different teams of Morris dancers. The costumes, emblems, and hats of these dancers identify them as members of a certain team. What is Morris dancing? With what is it associated?

> Sarah, my wife, and I have been running the folk club in Bracknell since 1975. We sing together regularly in pubs and clubs all over the south of England and are both members of a folk group called "Curate's Egg." Singing is for us though, only a spare-time activity and we both have to earn a living at other jobs during the day.
>
> You don't necessarily need to play a complicated musical instrument to be a folksinger. Sarah and I perform a lot of our songs unaccompanied....
>
> Many of the songs we sing today are English in origin but were collected in America by an English clergyman . . . , who went to the U.S.A. in the late nineteenth century. He came back with the songs taken there by the early settlers....
>
> Folk festivals have become more and more popular over the past few years. The biggest one is held every year at Sidmouth in Devon and attracts many thousands of people. We have one at Bracknell and both Sarah and I get very involved in this. Apart from the singing it's the wonderful social life that goes with the folk scene that Sarah and I enjoy. Over the past few years we have traveled to clubs throughout the country to sing both by invitation, or simply dropping in. We get paid for an invited session, but it's usually only enough to cover our expenses....
>
> English folk music is often associated with a form of dance called a Morris dance. Morris dancing is really an ancient fertility rite to celebrate the coming of spring on 1st May. Originally, the dance was only performed by men, but now there are many Morris teams of men and women throughout the country. Each region

---
Living in Rome by Pamela Carsaniga, 1981, Wayland Publishers Ltd., pp. 40–41. Reprinted by permission.

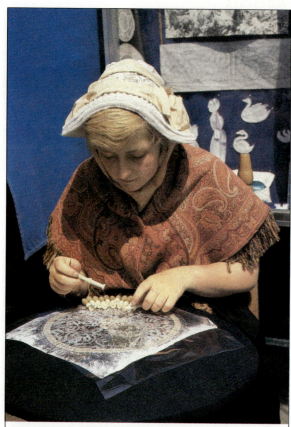

Fine lace like that being made here is a product often associated with Belgium. Traditionally made by hand, today most Belgian lace is machine made. What other goods are still made by hand in Western Europe?

Switzerland, and Austria, for example, woodcarving is still carried out. In Belgium and France, lace is still made by hand. In Spain, sword making remains an important craft. Below, an American journalist visiting the Spanish city of Toledo shares what he learned about this art:

> The sound of hammering led me down a narrow cobblestone street to the forge of Mariano Zamorano, a sword maker, just off the Plaza del Ayuntamiento. On an anvil he was straightening the steel blade of a fencing sword. His face was blackened with soot from the hot coal fire.
>
> "The final quenching—in oil, water, or both—is the most important," said Señor Zamorano, resting his arms. "Oil is a slower process; it makes the blades less stiff, more flexible. Water is faster, and makes them stronger. You see this...." He picked up a discarded blade and thrust it against the wall. It bent out of shape like a coat hanger. "Too weak. I've been doing this for 42 years, and still I sometimes make mistakes."
>
> The [careful work] of Toledan craftsmen was well known in the Renaissance, and their swords, particularly, were highly praised. Sword making has been famous along the Tagus [River] since Roman times. The art had nearly died out, however, when in 1780 the National Arms factory was founded in Toledo. Today the factory produces ammunition and light arms for the Spanish Army, and other Toledan sword makers supply the U.S. Marines, Navy, and Coast Guard with some of their ceremonial swords.*

has its own dances, but the basic idea is similar. Accompanied by drums and accordians, the dancers jump high in the air to make the corn grow and the bells sewn on to their costumes and handkerchiefs they wave ward off the evil spirits of winter, and welcome the good spirits of spring.*

Other groups of Western Europeans are interested in traditional handicrafts and goods. For some, producing these articles is not only an interest but an occupation as well. In the Alpine regions of West Germany,

1. What are some recreational activities enjoyed by Western Europeans?
2. Why are traditional folk arts and crafts important to many Western Europeans? What are some of the folk arts and crafts?

---

*"Settlers kept the traditional folk songs alive" in *We live in Britain* by Chris Fairclough, 1982, The Bookwright Press, pp. 40–41. Reprinted by permission.

*"Toledo—El Greco's Spain Lives On" by Louise Levathes in *National Geographic*, Vol. 161, No. 6, June 1982, pp. 733–734. Reprinted by permission.

CASE STUDY
WESTERN EUROPE

BULLFIGHTING

Some of the people of Spain and Portugal spend part of their leisure time at the bullfights. While outsiders consider bullfighting a sport, Spaniards and Portuguese regard it as an art. In Spain, where most bullfights are held on Sunday afternoon, the bullfighting season begins in early spring and lasts until the middle of autumn. Enrique Molina, a Spanish bullfighter, had the following to say about his life and his art:

> . . . *I was eleven when I saw my first bullfight and decided that I just had to become a* matador. *I entered a competition for budding* matadors—*and won it. My prize was the opportunity to go once a week to the bullring in Malaga and receive lessons from an instructor. Apart from that I spent hours on end practicing with a friend of mine. He would charge at me with a pair of horns mounted on a sort of wheelbarrow. . . .*
>
> *When I was twelve I started practicing with two-year-old bulls weighing about 180 kilos (400 lbs.). . . . About a year later, . . . I made my début in Valencia as a* novillero *(novice bullfighter) in a real bullfight. . . .*
>
> *Although I started bullfighting very early, it took me ten years of hard work to become a* matador. . . . *Lots of experience is essential if you want to stay alive, which is why I was twenty-three by the time I became a* matador. . . .
>
> *Bullfighting originated in Arabia, started by noblemen who would fight bulls with a lance on horseback. . . . Over the centuries things have changed considerably and these days the only person who rides a horse is the* picador. *He enters the bullring in the first* tercio *(third) of the fight and sticks a pike, a lance, into the bull's neck. The second* tercio *is called* banderillas. *Here a man on foot (and with no protection) sticks two* banderillas, *which are decorated barbed darts, into the bull. The third* tercio *is* la muerte *(the death) and this is where the* matador *shows his art with the cape. By now the bull is extremely angry at having things stuck into him—and is ready to kill. The* matador *stands still and goads the bull into charging at him by flapping the red cape. The bull is fooled into running at the cape instead of the* matador, *who sidesteps at the last minute. These passes with the cape go on until the bull begins to tire and the* matador *considers that it is time for the final* estocada *(sword-thrust). This is the* matador's *bravest moment. To kill the bull he must go and lean over its horns in order to plunge the sword into the back of its neck.*
>
> *Many serious wounds are caused by being caught by the bull's horns. . . .*
>
> *These days, bullfighting is not so popular as it was. Everyone talks about soccer instead. Apart from that, many people prefer to spend their free time going off to the country or to the beach.*
>
> *Years ago, becoming a* matador *was a way of escaping from poverty and becoming famous. Nowadays, life is different. Boys think about studying for a career rather than risking their lives in front of a bull.**

1. What is the role of a *matador* in a bullfight? A *picador*?
2. Spaniards and Portuguese regard bullfighting as an art. Do you agree with this interpretation? Explain.

---
*"Nobody was killed last year" in *We live in Spain* by Richard Bristow, 1984, The Bookwright Press, pp. 10–11. Reprinted by permission.

863

WESTERN EUROPE

CHAPTER 51 REVIEW

POINTS TO REMEMBER

1. More than one-half of all Western Europeans live in cities, each of which is different from the others in some way.
2. Attitudes toward work vary from city to city in Western Europe.
3. Many of the world's leading industrial nations are in Western Europe, and more Western Europeans work in manufacturing than in any other economic activity.
4. Many Western European workers have joined trade unions in an effort to shape business and government policies.
5. About 20 percent of Western Europeans are employed in agriculture or such other rural activities as fishing and hunting.
6. In the rural areas of Western Europe, the center of life often is the village, where more traditional ways are followed and the standard of living tends to be lower than in the cities.
7. In Western Europe, long recognized as a center of learning, more than 90 percent of the people are literate and have at least a high school education. Educational systems, however, vary from area to area.
8. The educational systems of Western Europe vary according to country and area. All countries are concerned about improving their educational systems, especially in the areas of scientific, technical, and computer training.
9. Western Europeans enjoy a wide range of activities, including sports and folk arts and crafts, during their leisure time.

VOCABULARY

Identify

Berlin   Santa María del Condado   Ballyduff   Toledo
Force Ouvrière

DISCUSSING IMPORTANT IDEAS

1. Attitudes toward work and life style vary from one urban area to another and one nation to another in Western Europe. What reasons can you give for this?
2. According to the farmer in Santa María del Condado, "in twenty, thirty, one hundred years, maybe those people who left will return to where they used to be, which is the *pueblos*." Do you agree with him? Explain why or why not.
3. In what ways do urban and rural work attitudes and life style differ in Western Europe? What do you think accounts for these differences? Is the same true in your country?
4. "Computer illiteracy" is a topic of debate not only in Western Europe but in many other parts of the world as well. With whom do you agree—those who consider knowledge of computers an important fourth basic skill or those who believe that putting computers in schools will destroy education's attempts to integrate learning with life? Why do you feel this way?

DEVELOPING SKILLS

MAKING DECISIONS

How many questions like these have you asked yourself this week?
1. What should I wear today?
2. If I take time to eat breakfast, will I miss my ride or be late to school?
3. What do I want for lunch—the sandwich I brought with me or the cafeteria special?
4. Which one of the two people who asked me for a date should I go out with Saturday?

The important thing about these questions is not how many are familiar, but that each one requires you to make up your mind about something—in other words, *make a decision*. The following guidelines will help you make decisions more easily:
1. Ask yourself exactly what you have to decide.
2. Determine how the question you want to resolve developed, and list the major factors involved.
3. Examine the *alternatives*— the possibilities from which one has to be chosen—and *consequences*—logical results.
4. Evaluate each alternative and its consequences in terms of your beliefs or values. Most people tend to regret decisions that go against these.
5. Make your decision, and act on it.

The following example shows you how these guidelines can be used to make a decision:

Mario, a young Spaniard from the province of Valencia, must do something that will help his family financially. In the last few years, his parents, with whom he is very close, have had many financial setbacks. Now, they are elderly and are facing poverty. Mario's mother is ill and cannot work. Mario has worked all his life on the family's farm. Life on the farm and in a nearby village is the only one Mario really knows and enjoys. Mario could go to France or Germany, where he could work at a high wage. That way, he could send a lot of money home to his parents. But going abroad to work would mean leaving his family and village for a long time, and there is always the possibility that his mother might not live to see him return. On the other hand, he could take a job in the provincial capital of Valencia. Although it would not pay as much as the one abroad, he would be able to come home frequently, see his family and his friends in the village, and help out on the farm when needed. Then again, he could find several jobs in the village and live there. All the jobs together, however, might not bring in enough in wages to provide for his family. But, he would be where he wanted to be and could see his family every day if he wanted.

(1) Mario had to decide what he should do to help his parents financially. (2) The question developed because his parents had financial setbacks. The major facts are his parents' poverty and his mother's illness. (3) Mario had three alternatives —work abroad, work in the provincial capital, or work in the village. The consequence of the first alternative is being far away from his family and his village for a long time; of the second, earning less money than he would abroad; of the third, not earning enough money. (4) Mario believes in family unity and duty to family. Going far away to work would compromise his belief in family unity. Not earning enough money would compromise his belief in duty to family. (5) Mario decides to work in the capital. In this way, he can help his family yet still maintain family unity and perform his duty as he sees it.

For practice in this skill, do the following:
1. Read the section, "The Way of the City," on pages 850–853.
2. Pretend you have been offered three jobs —one in Germany, one in Greece, and one in France.
3. Using the suggested guidelines, decide which job to take.

UNIT 8 REVIEW

SUMMARY

Geographically, Western Europe is the region located at the western edge of Eurasia. Culturally and politically, however, it is the non-Communist nations of the European continent. The nations and the people that make up this region are as diverse as its geography and natural environment. Yet, there is a common heritage shared by all Western Europeans that stems from the ancient Greek and Roman worlds. From these ancient peoples came Western Europe's principles of democracy and law. From them also came a strong influence still felt today in philosophy, language, religion, and the arts and sciences.

From this ancient base, Western Europe grew and developed over the centuries—from many small kingdoms and feudal rule to nation-states with strong and absolute monarchies to independent nations with democratic governments. In the earlier years, the Catholic Church held the loyalty of all the people and provided a sense of unity. Then, in the 1300's, there began revival of interest in classical learning, in science, in travel, and in trade. This interest remained strong for 400 years. By the 1700's, Western Europe was the dominant region in the world. It remained so through the 1800's, building overseas empires and spreading western ideas to all continents. Not until the mid-1900's, after two world wars, did it lose that dominance.

Throughout the centuries and the many changes and innovations that have marked them, Western Europeans have developed a strong sense of identity and nationality. Life styles vary, but for most, tradition remains important, as does family, class, and culture. In recent years, industrialization, modern technology, and urbanization have brought a higher standard of living to most Western Europeans. Education is improving, and most Western Europeans have had the benefit of at least a high school education. Despite their differences, the nations and peoples of Western Europe retain a unity and continue to grow, develop, and experience change while still maintaining many of the traditions, values, and beliefs that once made Western Europe a world leader.

REVIEW QUESTIONS

1. In what ways have geography and climate influenced Western European history and ways of life?
2. How do you think the political and social changes that have taken place in Western Europe over the centuries affected Western European ideas, arts, and literature?
3. How has religion influenced Western Europe?
4. What role has sense of identity played in the growth and development of Western Europe?

SUGGESTED ACTIVITIES

1. Working in a small group, create two time lines that cover the same period of time. On one, place the major events in Western European history. On the other, place important artists, authors, scientists, and thinkers. Use the time lines to analyze the relationships between historic and cultural events.
2. Read a biography of or a novel about an important Western European. Based on what you have read, write a biography of that person to read to the class.
3. Working in a small group, prepare a series of posters to show the changes that have taken place in Western Europe from the time of the ancient Greeks and Romans to the present.
4. On an outline map of Western Europe, identify each country and the major language(s) spoken in each.

COMPARING CULTURES

Through education, societies transmit their cultures to future generations. In both Western Europe and the United States, schools have been a major means for educating people. Read the following passages, and compare the two. Which system do you prefer? Why?

EDUCATION IN SWEDEN

Sigrid began *grundskola*, primary school, at age seven. During her first three years there, she learned reading and writing and some mathematics, language, science, and art. In the third grade, she began to learn a new language, English.

After six years Sigrid entered secondary school and began choosing classes that would help her later in life. She also began learning a third language and started vocational counseling. A trained teacher gave her and her classmates tests to help them decide in what jobs they would do best. The next year, in the eighth grade, Sigrid began on-the-job training. This helped her in ninth grade, when she had to make a final choice about courses. She could choose from more than 20 programs grouped into three areas—arts and social studies, science and technical studies, economic and commercial studies.

By now, Sigrid was 16 years old and could drop out of school and go to work. She chose to remain in school. Her education—including books, paper, and hot lunches—were free. And, because her parents did not have much money, she also received free transportation and clothing. As long as she stayed in school, her parents were paid an allowance for her.

Sigrid could go to vocational school or to continuation school to learn job skills. She could attend a special school run by certain Swedish companies to train students talented in particular areas. Or, she could plan to go to a university. The government would lend her the money she needed to live on at the university.

Sigrid chose the university. But first she had to attend a *gymnasium* to study social studies, economics, science, art, and another language. Without very high grades, Sigrid would not have been allowed to do this. *Gymnasium* courses are as advanced as those given in the first two years of college in the United States.

When Sigrid finished her third year in *gymnasium*, she became a "student," someone ready for college, and could wear a special cap. She was proud to wear the cap because, like all Swedes, she thinks it is an honor to be educated.

EDUCATION IN THE UNITED STATES

Michael began elementary school when he was six years old. While there, he learned reading and writing, as well as some mathematics, science, social studies, art, music, and health.

After elementary school, Michael entered junior high, where he studied English, social studies, science, and math. In his three years in junior high, Michael also took some electives, or nonrequired classes, in industrial arts, foreign language, and art, was a member of several clubs, and played on the football team.

When Michael graduated from junior high, he was almost 16 years old and could leave school if he wished. But he wanted to go on to secondary, or high school. Now he had to choose between a vocational program, which would prepare him for a job upon graduation, or a college preparatory program, which would give him the background he would need to go on to a college or university.

After discussing the matter with his guidance counselor and his parents, Michael chose the college preparatory program. He took the core courses of the program, which included English, math, science, and social studies, and some electives he thought would help him in a career. He kept his grades high, knowing that good grades were needed to enter college.

At the end of the twelfth grade, Michael graduated with honors and was accepted into the university of his choice. He also won two scholarships—one for high grades, and the other because his parents did not have much money.

APPENDIX

ATLAS
- The World
- Eurasia
- North America
- South America
- Europe
- Africa

GLOSSARY

INDEX

SUGGESTED RESOURCES

I

icons (Ī kahnz) religious images (p. 657)
ideology (id ē AHL uh jē) body of opinions (p. 141)
ikebana (ē ke bah nah) traditional Japanese art of displaying cut flowers (p. 295)
illiterate (i LIT uh ruht) unable to read or write (p. 468)
imāms (i MAHMZ) high Muslim religious leaders (p. 597)
improvisations (im prah vuh ZĀ shuhnz) music performed without practice (p. 423)
incentives (in SEN tivz) actions or policies that motivate people to act in a desired way (p. 203)
indulgences (in DUL jen siz) documents issued by the Catholic Church that freed their owners from time in purgatory (p. 793)
inflation (in FLĀ shuhn) higher price levels (p. 629)
intellectuals (in tuh LEK choo uhlz) people given to study and reflection (p. 187)
intelligentsia (in tel uh JENT sē uh) intellectuals who form an artistic, social, or political élite (p. 665)
Islamic Empire (is lahm ik EM pīr) Muslim nation-states (p. 25)

J

jatis (JAHT ēz) groupings within the Hindu caste system (p. 374)
jihads (ji HAHDZ) wars carried on by Muslims as a religious duty (p. 42)
jizyah (djiz yah) tax levied on non-Muslims by the Islamic state (p. 597)
joint family (joint FAM uh lē) family group in India including parents, children, and adult sons and their spouses and children (p. 352)
jute (jōōt) fibrous material used mainly for sacks, burlap, and twine (p. 460)

K

kabuki (kuh bōō kē) traditional Japanese theater with singing and dancing (p. 292)
kami (kah mē) in Shinto religion, anything with superior power or awe-inspiring (p. 286)
kana (kah nuh) written characters that represent basic sounds in Japanese (p. 291)
kanji (kahn jē) Chinese picture words incorporated into written Japanese (p. 291)
karma (KAR muh) Hindu concept that the total of a person's conduct in past lives determines his or her destiny (p. 368)
khalīfah (kha LĒ fah) religious and political leader of a Muslim state (p. 595)
khan (kahn) Mongol ruler (p. 657)
kibbutzim (ki bŏŏt SĒM) Israeli farm communities in which the land is held in common (p. 544)
kimono (kē mō nō) Japanese outer garment (p. 285)
knight (nīt) medieval gentleman-soldier (p. 782)
kolkhoz (kahl KOZ) Soviet cooperative farm with families who work it sharing in the profits (p. 714)
kowtow (kou tou) kneeling and touching the forehead to the ground to show respect (p. 147)
kulaks (kŏŏ LAHKS) wealthy Soviet peasant farmers (p. 679)

L

lacquer (LAK er) dark, glossy liquid painted on objects (p. 288)
legend (LEJ uhnd) traditional folk tale or myth (p. 342)
li (lē) Confucian principle of proper behavior (p. 178)
liberals (LIB ruhls) persons who believe in individual freedoms and favor political reforms (pp. 518, 844)
lingua franca (LING gwuh FRAHNG kuh) any mixed language used as a means of communication between peoples who speak different languages (p. 72)
literati (LIT uh rah tē) educated class of traditional China (p. 158)
llanos (YAH nōs) grassy, treeless plains of Colombia and Venezuela (p. 439)
loess (lŏŏs) fine-grained silt or clay deposits resulting from wind blown dust (p. 127)
logic (LAHJ ik) science of thinking rationally (p. 788)
long-lifers (long LĪF erz) Soviet people 100 years of age or older (p. 695)
lords (lordz) nobles with great power and authority during the Middle Ages (p. 780)

M

macho (MAH chō) Spanish term for manliness (p. 498)

mandate (MAN dāt) authority to govern (p. 141); region under the administration of another nation (p. 604)

manors (MAN uhrz) areas over which lords had domain during the Middle Ages in Western Europe; also, the lords' residences (p. 782)

maritime (MAR i tīm) relating to navigation or commerce on the sea (p. 753)

mass culture (mas KUL cher) new style of Western European arts, developed between the 1700's and 1900's, that interested people of the middle and lower classes (p. 832)

mass production (mas pruh DUK shuhn) manufacture of goods in large quantities using machines (p. 800)

mausoleum (mo zuh LĒ uhm) tomb built above ground (p. 417)

mediation (mē dē Ā shuhn) settling of disagreements (p. 572)

meditation (med uh TĀ shuhn) deep, quiet thinking (p. 370)

mesas (MĀ suhz) flat-topped hills (p. 440)

messiah (mu SĪ uh) promised savior (p. 586)

mestizos (mes TĒ sōs) in Latin America, persons with one European and one Indian parent (p. 451)

mica (MĪ kuh) mineral used in the outer covering of electric wiring to prevent electric shock (p. 406)

militarism (MIL i tuh riz uhm) policy of aggressive military preparation (p. 274)

millet (MIL it) cereal grain commonly grown in Asia and Africa (p. 336)

millets (MIL ets) non-Muslim communities in the Islamic Empire (p. 597)

minarets (min uh RETS) slender domes and towers of mosques (p. 417)

minifundio (mē nē FOON dē ō) small non-commercial farm in Latin America (p. 504)

mirs (mērz) Russian peasant villages set up during tsarist rule (p. 666)

mixed economy (MIKST ē KAHN uh mē) economic system that is partly capitalistic and partly socialistic (p. 404)

monasteries (MAHN uh stār ēz) houses for persons under religious vows (p. 786)

monophonic (mahn uh FAHN ik) music having only one successive string of tones, or melody (p. 834)

monotheism (MAHN uh THĒ iz uhm) belief that there is only one god (p. 586)

monsoons (MAHN sōōnz) wind system that reverses direction seasonally, producing South Asia's dry and wet seasons (p. 240)

moshavim (mō shuh VĒM) Israeli cooperative farm communities in which farms are individually owned (p. 545)

mosques (mahsks) buildings used for public worship by Muslims (p. 25)

muftīs (MŌŌF tēz) professional jurists who interpret Muslim law (p. 595)

mulattos (muh LAH tōz) in Latin America, persons with one black and one white parent (p. 451)

myth (mith) story that embodies the cultural ideals of a people (p. 257)

N

nationalism (NASH uh nuhl iz uhm) loyalty to a national group or nation (pp. 32, 699, 844)

nationalists (NASH uh nuhl ists) persons devoted to their national group or nation (p. 844)

nationalities (nash uh NAL i tēz) groups who share a common cultural heritage and, in many cases, the same territory (pp. 689, 754)

nationalized (NASH uh nuhl īzd) taken over by a government (p. 608)

Noh play (NŌ plā) traditional form of Japanese dance-drama (p. 292)

nomads (NŌ mads) people who move seasonally within a defined territory to secure a food supply (p. 540)

non-aligned nations (nahn uh līnd NĀ shuhnz) countries allied with neither western nor Communist nations (p. 394)

nouveaux riches (nōō vō RĒSH) people who recently became wealthy (p. 466)

nuclear family (nōō klēr FAM uh lē) family group consisting of a father, mother, and children (p. 352)

O

oases (ō Ā sēz) areas of watered land in arid regions (p. 538)

oath (ōth) solemn promise (p. 74)

one-party state (wun par tē STĀT) nation with only one political party (p. 78)

operas (AHP ruhz) dramas set to music and sung to orchestral accompaniment (p. 834)

opium (Ō pē uhm) drug made from poppy plants on which users become dependent (p. 188)

oral traditions (or uhl truh DISH uhns) stories and history of a group passed from generation to generation (p. 23)

origami (or i gah mē) Japanese art of folding paper (p. 295)

orographic lifting (or uh GRAF ik LIFT ēng) process by which moisture-filled clouds are forced upward and release rain (p. 339)

overpopulation (ō ver pahp yōō LĀ shuhn) having too dense a population (p. 214)

P

pachinko (pah chēng kō) game played in Japan on a pinball machine (p. 323)

pa kua (bah kwā) geometric border around the symbol of yang and yin believed by the Chinese to symbolize the key to knowledge (p. 133)

pampas (PAHM pahs) grassy plains of Argentina and Uruguay (p. 439)

panchayat (puhn CHĪ uht) group of elders elected to govern an Indian community (p. 356)

partition (par TISH uhn) to break into separate parcels (p. 610)

partitioned (par TISH uhnd) broken into separate parcels (p. 610)

party line (PAR tē līn) principles and policies of a political organization (p. 722)

pass laws (PAS loz) former regulations of the South African government that required all black South Africans, age 16 or older, to carry identification cards (p. 60)

patriarchs (PĀ trē arks) male religious leaders or founders; also, male heads of families (p. 586)

patricians (puh TRISH uhnz) rich and powerful upper-class citizens of ancient Rome (p. 776)

patrons (PĀ truhnz) wealthy or influential backers of artists and writers (pp. 258, 831)

peninsula (puh NIN suh luh) long projection of land into water (p. 333)

permafrost (PER muh frost) permanently frozen upper layer of earth (p. 642)

personalismo (pār sō nah LĒZ mō) Spanish term for the belief that each individual is unique and has an inner dignity and personality (p. 479)

perspective (per SPEK tiv) artistic representation of three-dimensional scenes on a one-dimensional surface (p. 837)

pilgrimages (PIL gruhm ij uhz) journeys made by worshippers to religious shrines (p. 372)

plantations (plan TĀ shuhnz) agricultural estates (p. 390)

plebians (pli BĒ uhnz) poor and lower-class citizens of ancient Rome (p. 776)

polar night (PŌ ler nīt) darkness that occurs for 24 hours or longer in far northern and southern latitudes (p. 642)

polders (PŌL derz) tracts of low land reclaimed from the sea; especially in the Netherlands (p. 765)

political science (puh LIT i kuhl sī uhnts) social science that studies political systems (p. 775)

polyphonic music (pahl i fahn ik MYŌŌ zik) music having two or more harmonic melodies at the same time (p. 834)

polyrhythm (PAHL i rith uhm) combination two or more simultaneous beat patterns (p. 88)

population density (pahp yuh LĀ shuhn DEN si tē) average number of individuals per unit of space (p. 131)

portents (POR tents) something that suggests a coming event (p. 123)

principalities (prin suh PAL uh tēz) lands controlled by princes (p. 656)

proletariat (prō luh TĀR ē uht) laboring class (p. 676)

prophets (PRAHF its) persons who foretell future events by divine inspiration (p. 589)

proverbs (PRAH verbz) brief, popular sayings commonly believed to be factual (p. 91)

provisional (pruh VIZH uhn uhl) serving for the time being (p. 190)

pueblos jóvenes (PWĀ blōs HŌ ve nes) Spanish term for certain Peruvian slums and shantytowns (p. 501)

puja (PŌŌ jah) special rites of Hindu worship (p. 369)

pulses (puls uhz) peas, beans, or legumes (p. 336)

purdah (PER duh) seclusion of women from public view (pp. 355, 572)

purgatory (PER guh tor ē) according to Roman Catholic doctrine, place where sinners suffer temporarily in order to become fit for heaven (p. 793)

purged (perjd) got rid of as undesirable or disloyal (p. 679)

R

raga (RAH guh) basic unit of Indian music (p. 423)

rain forest (rān FOR ist) tropical woodland with heavy annual rainfall (p. 8)

rajahs (RAH juhz) traditional Indian rulers (p. 387)

regents (RĒ juhnts) persons who rule when sovereigns are ill, absent, or very young (p. 166)

reincarnation (RĒ in kar NĀ shuhn) Hindu belief of rebirth of a soul in a new body or form of life (p. 368)

relics (REL iks) sacred objects (p. 416)

reliefs (ruh LĒFS) small sculptures carved to stand out from a surface (p. 416)

ren (ren) Confucian principle that goodness comes from one's inner self (p. 178)

republic (ri PUB lik) form of government in which citizens elect their leaders (p. 776)

reserves (ri ZERVZ) portions of land set aside in South Africa for ownership by blacks (p. 60)

revelations (rev uh LĀ shuhnz) communications of divine will or truth (p. 586)

revenue (REV uh noo) taxes and other earnings, usually of a government (p. 46)

romanized (RŌ muh nīzd) made to follow Roman customs and styles (p. 779)

romanticism (ro MAN tuh siz uhm) artistic and literary movement that began in the 1700's, emphasizing imagination and the emotions (p. 834)

royal city (roi uhl SIT e) capital city and home of the ruler of old China (p. 131)

S

sabra (SAH bruh) person born in Israel (p. 560)

sadhus (SAH dooz) male Hindu holy men who deny themselves the comforts of life (p. 370)

sages (SĀ juhz) persons recognized for their wisdom and judgment (p. 173)

salvation (sal VĀ shuhn) deliverance from sin (p. 793)

samizdat (SAH mēz daht) system by which literature banned by the Soviet government is secretly printed and distributed (p. 727)

samurai (sam uh rī) noble and military class of medieval Japan (p. 260)

savanna (suh VAN uh) tropical or subtropical grassland containing scattered trees (p. 8)

saved (sāvd) Christian belief that true believers will have eternal happiness after death (p. 587)

scientific method (sī uhn TIF ik METH uhd) way of seeking knowledge in an orderly fashion (p. 775)

scripts (skrips) styles of handwriting (p. 166)

seaquakes (SĒ kwāks) underwater upheavals of the earth (p. 437)

secession (si SESH uhn) formal withdrawal from an organization or nation (p. 44)

sects (sekts) groups of people who follow a religious doctrine (p. 287)

secular (SEK yuh luhr) lacking religious association (p. 627)

sepoys (SĒ poiz) Indian officers in the British army during the colonial period (p. 388)

serfs (serfs) members of the lowest class, bound to the land and owned by a lord (p. 661)

service industries (SER vis IN duhs trēz) businesses that sell services rather than products (p. 318)

shahādah (shah HAH dah) Muslim pillar of faith that requires Muslims to state their belief in one god and in Muhammad as God's messenger (p. 591)

shen (shen) in old China, good forces associated with yang (p. 133)

shogun (shō gun) military governor in feudal Japan (p. 258)

shogunate (SHŌ guh nāt) government of a military ruler in feudal Japan (p. 258)

sitar (si TAR) Indian long-necked lute (p. 423)

socialism (SŌ shuhl iz uhm) doctrine that calls for the collective ownership of all means of production (p. 667)

socialist realism (SŌ shuhl ist RĒ uhl iz uhm) style of literature, art, and music designed to develop social consciousness along government-imposed lines (p. 727)

socialists (SŌ shuhl ists) individuals who favor collective ownership of land and industry (p. 844)

soviets (SŌ vē ets) committees or councils formed by Russian revolutionaries to represent the people after the fall of the tsar (p. 675)

sovkhoz (soof KŌZ) farm in the Soviet Union owned and run by the state (p. 713)

steppe (step) semiarid grassy plains (p. 126)

stupas (stoo puhz) dome-shaped Buddhist shrines (p. 416)

subcontinent (suhb KAHN tuh nent) landmass of great size but not considered a continent (p. 333)

subjugation (sub juh GĀ shuhn) act of being brought under another's authority (p. 558)

subordinate (suh BOR duh nit) lower in rank (p. 572)

subsidies (SUB suh dēz) government financial aid to individuals or businesses (p. 207)

sumo (sōō mō) Japanese form of wrestling (p. 323)

sūq (sōōk) mall-like areas of shops and vendors in Middle Eastern cities (p. 546)

suttee (suh TĒ) former Hindu custom in which a widow cremated herself with her husband (p. 354)

T

taiga (TĪ guh) subarctic forests, mostly of spruce and fir (p. 645)

talking drums (TOK ēng drumz) West African drums that are used for communication (p. 88)

terracing (TER uhs ēng) planting technique used to prevent hillside erosion (p. 321)

theology (thē AHL uh jē) study of religion (p. 840)

theory of relativity (THĒR ē uhv rel uh TIV i tē) hypothesis that there are no absolutes in measuring time and space (p. 842)

tonal (TŌ nuhl) in a language, having different tones for the same syllable, resulting in different words (p. 88)

totalitarian (tō tal i TĀR ē uhn) government under which the individual is subordinate to the state (p. 220)

townships (toun ships) suburban tracts of land set aside for black South African towns (p. 60)

tragedies (TRAJ uh dēz) sorrowful dramas (p. 775)

trigrams (TRĪ grams) geometric symbols, grouped in three's, that make up the *pa kua* that surrounds the Chinese symbol of yang and yin (p. 133)

tsars (zarz) rulers of the Russian empire from 1547 to 1917 (p. 658)

tsunami (tsōō nah mē) Japanese term for tidal waves (p. 243)

tundra (TUN druh) cold, treeless flatlands (p. 644)

typhoons (tī FŌŌNZ) tropical cyclones that occur in the western Pacific and the China Sea (p. 240)

U

uhuru (ōō HŌŌ rōō) Swahili term for freedom (p. 71)

ulema (ōō luh MAH) Muslim judges (p. 595)

unequal treaties (uhn ē kwuhl TRĒ tēz) nineteenth-century agreements that opened China to unwanted western trade and influence (p. 188)

universal state (yōō nuh VER suhl stāt) state in which all peoples would be under one world government (p. 776)

untouchables (un TUCH uh buhlz) low-ranked Hindus who perform the dirtiest jobs; *harijans* (p. 374)

urban migration (er buhn mī GRĀ shuhn) movement of rural people to cities (p. 47)

V

Varnas (Var nuhz) Hinduism's four categories of society (p. 373)

vassals (VAS uhlz) in medieval Western Europe, persons who owed allegiance to a lord (p. 780)

veches (VYE chez) assemblies of free, adult male citizens in early Russia (p. 656)

vernacular (ver NAK yuh ler) common language or dialect of a region (p. 839)

vicar (VIK uhr) Protestant religious leader (p. 821)

viceroy (VĪS roi) ruling representative of a sovereign (p. 389)

villas miserias (VĒ yahs mē SĀ rē ahs) Spanish term for poor areas in Buenos Aires, Argentina (p. 501)

visual arts (VI zhōō wuhl arts) visible art, such as paintings, sculpture, and woven and dyed cloth (p. 93)

W

wālīs (wāh lēs) regional rulers in some early Islamic states (p. 595)

waqf (wokf) funds and properties earmarked for charity by non-Muslims in the Islamic Empire (p. 597)

war communism (wor KAHM yuh niz uhm) postcivil war Soviet economic policy in which the government controlled production, wages, and prices (p. 677)

warlords (WOR lords) Chinese military commanders who ruled local areas by force in the early 1900's (p. 191)

wazirs (wah ZĒRZ) chief assistants to Islamic rulers (p. 595)

white nights (WĪT nīts) extended nighttime hours with dim daylight (p. 709)

Y

yang and yin (yang and yin) in Chinese philosophy, opposite forces that must be balanced for a perfect life (p. 123)

yoga (YŌ guh) form of Hindu exercise designed to produce complete physical and mental well-being (p. 369)

Z

zaibatsu (Zī baht soo) leading families of Japan who controlled and directed most of the country's industries during Meiji rule (p. 270)

zakāt (za KAHT) money given to charity in accordance with Muslim religious law (p. 591)

zakuski (zah KOOS kē) Russian appetizers (p. 742)

INDEX

A

Abdication of throne, in China, 152
Abdul-Hamid II, 563
Abraham, 586, 589
Absolutism, 797, 798-799, 844
Abū Bakr, 595
Abū Tālib, 587
Acting. *See* Drama
Acupuncture, 162
Adire **cloth,** 93-94
Adulis, 24
Aegean Islands, 757
Afghanistan, 333
    Soviet occupation of, 213
Africa. *See also* individual countries
    adoption of national language, 114-115
    agriculture in, 10, 12-16, 18-19, 24, 106-107
    ancestors, importance of, 40, 94-96
    arts of, 40-41, 87-99
    celebrations in, 87, 94-96
    Christianity in, 34-35, 40, 76
    colonialism in, 16, 30-35, 43, 71, 72-75, 82-83
    dance in, 40, 42, 87, 88, 94-96
    deserts in, 15-16
    development of, 103-115
    drought in, 106-107
    economy of, 55, 105-106, 109, 110, 113
    education in, 65, 111-112
    ethnic groups in, 8, 40-41, 104, 114-115
    health care in, 61-63, 78, 112-113
    herding in, 13-16, 40, 79-81
    history of, 24-29, 42-43, 56, 72
    human fossils in, 23
    Islam in, 25-27, 40, 72
    literature of, 23, 25-27, 44-45, 82-83, 91, 93
    music in, 87, 88-89, 90, 92
    nationalism in, 31-33, 43-44, 71, 73-75
    nations in, 8, 104
    oral literature of, 23, 91, 93
    population growth in, 7, 8, 16-17, 39, 78, 108-109
    religions of, 40, 72, 94
    rural life in, 46-47, 77, 103
    slave trade in, 29, 35, 42
    societies in, early, 23, 24-28
    urban development in, 16-17, 47-49, 75-76, 103
    women in, 18-19, 51, 61-63, 78-79, 90, 93-94, 108-109, 110
African National Congress (ANC), in South Africa, 58, 64
Africanus, Leo, 26-27
Afrikaners, in South Africa, 56-57, 58, 59, 66, 67
Agrarian reform
    in Latin America, 489-490
    in Soviet Union, 665-666
Agriculture
    in Africa, 10, 12-16, 18-19, 24, 45, 46, 73, 106-108
    in China, 127, 128, 151-152, 161-162, 196, 205-207, 221-223
    in India, 335, 336, 338-339, 357, 390, 402-403, 411
    in Japan, 242, 246-247, 262, 321-323
    in Latin America, 466-467, 489-490, 503-505
    in Middle East, 537, 538, 542-545
    in Soviet Union, 645-646, 690, 694, 705, 713-716
    in Western Europe, 758, 761, 765, 854-855
Ahimsa, 368
Ahl al-dhimma, 597
Ahmadabad, India, 359
Ajanta, 416
Akbar, 387
Akhmatova, Anna, 727
Akihabara, 315
Al'Azab, 541-542
Alexander I (Russia), 664-665
Alexander II (Russia), 665-667
Alexander III (Russia), 667
Alexander the Great, 776
Al-Fārābī, 556
Alfonsin, Raul, 517
Al-Ghazzālī, 598
Al-Idrīsī, 556, 594
Al-Kindī, 556
Alluvial soil, in India, 335
Alphabet. *See also* Language and Writing
    in China, 166
    Cyrillic, 657, 693
Alps, 760-761
Al-Rāzī (Rhazes), 556, 598
Amadi, Elechi, 44-45
Amaterasu, 253
Amazon River, 442-443
Amritsar, India, 391
Analects **(Confucius),** 178
Andalucía, Spain, 763-764
Andes Mountains, 436
Anglo-Boer War (1899), 58, 59
Ankara, Turkey, as urban city, 631
Anticlericals, and the Roman Catholic Church in Mexico, 486-488
Apartheid policies, in South Africa, 55, 58, 60-65, 65-66, 67
Apennine Mountains, 760
Aqueducts, building of, 779
'Arabi, Ahmad, 608
Arabia, 537
Arabic language, 556
Arab-Israeli conflict, 609-610, 618-623
Arab League, on Camp David Talks, 619
Arabs
    in Kenya, 72
    in Middle East, 555, 556-557
Akakamchechen, 646
Ararat, Mount, 538
Archipelago, 237, 239, 243
Architecture. *See also* Housing
    in India, 417-418
    Islamic, 25, 417-418
    in Middle East, 545-549
    in Soviet Union, 689, 706-707, 711
Argentina, 435, 439. *See also* Latin America
    Diaguita Indians in, 456
    ethnic diversity in, 451
    gauchos in, 439-440
    government in, 473, 517
    immigrants in, 458-459
    industrial development in, 513
    Pampas in, 439-440

rivers in, 441
women in, 473
Aristotle, 775, 791
Arjuna, 420
Armenian Apostolic Church, 696
Armenians, 563, 694-696, 736
dream of, for homeland, 555
Army. *See individual region or country*
Arts. *See also* Architecture; Painting; and Sculpture
in Africa, 87-99
in China, 166-169, 210
in India, 415-427
in Japan, 285, 288, 291-297
in Latin America, 451, 489, 501
in Middle East, 548, 549, 598, 599
in Soviet Union, 656, 657, 659, 668-669, 697-698, 724-728, 731
in Western Europe, 772, 775, 829, 831-840, 861-862
Aryans, 557
in India, 384
Asir Mountains, 538
Asiyo, Phoebe, 78-79
Asoka, 384-385
Aswan High Dam, 543, 608
Atacama Desert, 444
Ataturk, Mustapha Kemal, 558
Atheism, in Soviet Union, 729
Athens, Greece
ancient, 772, 773-776
democracy in (ancient), 772-773
modern, 851-852
Atomic bomb
in China, 196
dropping of, in Japan, 276-279
Auschwitz, 807
Austria
dress in, 816
national identity in, 815-817
wood carving in, 862
Austria-Hungary, and start of World War I, 804
Autocracy, in Russia, 658
Averroës, 556, 598
Avicenna. *See also* Ibn Sīnā, 556
Axum, 24-25
Ayatollahs, 597
Aymara language, 451
Azerbaijanians, in Soviet Union, 694, 736
Azikiwe, Nnamdi, 33, 43
Aztec Indians, 452, 453, 454

B

Babangida, Ibrahim, 46
Babur, 386
Bach, Johann Sebastian, 834
Baghdad, 545
Bahia, 459. *See also* Salvador
Bahrain, 537, 547-548
Baikal, Lake, 647
Baikal-Amur Mainline Railway, in Soviet Union, 723-724
Baku, Soviet Union, 694
Bakufu, 258
Balearic Islands, 757
Balfour Declaration (1917), 609
Balkan Mountains, 760
Balkan Peninsula, 756
Ballyduff, Ireland, 855-857
Baltic republics, 692-693, 699
Bangalore, India, 359
Bangladesh, 333, 335
formation of, 394
Bantu language, 72
Bantustans, in South Africa, 60
Barbarians
invasion of China by, 147
invasion of Roman Empire by, 780
Baryshnikov, Mikhail, 727
Baseball
in Japan, 323-325
in Latin America, 477
Battuta, Ibn, 25-26
Bazo, Juan, 529
Bedouins, 540-542
Beethoven, Ludwig van, 834
Begin, Menachem, 618
Beijing, China, 124, 128, 134
Beirut, Lebanon, 545, 555, 604
and the Lebanese Civil War, 623
Belém, Brazil, 442-443
Belgium
dress in, 816
lace making in, 862
rule of Congo by, 31-32
rule of Zaire by, 32
Belize, John Paul II's visit to, 483
Benares, India, 371
Bengal, 356
Benin Empire, 42
Berlin, postwar division of, 850
Berlioz, Hector, 834
Bhagavad Gita **(Song of the Soul),** 369, 373-374, 420
Bhakra-Nangal, 342
Bharata Natyam, 425
Bhutan, 333, 334
Biafra, Republic of, 44

Biko, Steve, 65
Black Consciousness Movement, in South Africa, 65-66
Black Forest, 762
Black market, in Soviet Union, 708-709
Black Sea, 641
Blaha, Franz, 807
Boers, in South Africa, 56-57
Bogota, Colombia, 501
Bolivia
ethnic diversity in, 451
government of, 518-519
language in, 451
Bolsheviks, in Soviet Union, 675-676
Bolshoi Theater, 727-728
Bombay, India, 359, 360, 361-363, 389
life in, 361-363
Parsis influence in, 378
Bonnot, Dao, 95
Bonsai, 242, 461
Botha, Roelof F., 67
Bourgeoisie, in Russia, 676
Boxer Rebellion (1900), 189-190
Boyars, in Soviet Union, 656, 661
Brahma, 368
Brahman, 368
Brahmanism, in India, 384
Brahmaputra River, 336, 342
Brahmins, 373
Brahms, Johannes, 834
Brazil, 439. *See also* Latin America
economy in, 497
education in, 510-511
ethnic diversity in, 451
hunger in, 506
industrial development in, 512-513
language in, 451
recreation in, 476-477
rivers in, 442-443
soccer in, 476-477
Brezhnev, Leonid, 683
British. *See* Great Britain
Buddhism
in China, 180, 182-183
in India, 377, 415, 416
in Japan, 254, 287-289, 295
Buenos Aires, Argentina, 499, 501
Buhari, Mohammed, 46
Bullfighting
in Latin America, 476
in Spain, 863
Bureaucrats, in early China, 143
Burma, 276, 333

Byelorussia, 677, 690-692
Byzantine Empire, influence on Russia, 657

C

Cadres. *See also* Civil service in China, 220
Caesar Augustus, 777
Cahill, Dr. Kevin M., 624
Cairo, Egypt, 543, 545, 546
  as urban city, 629-631
Calcutta, India, 359, 389
Calligraphy
  in China, 166
  in Middle East, 589-590
Camanchaca, 444
Campesinos, in Latin America, 503
Candomblé, 492-493
Cape Colony, establishment of, at Cape of Good Hope, 56
Capitalism, 844
Caracas, Venezuela, 501
Caribbean National Forest, 443-444
Carter, Jimmy, 618
Cash crops. *See also* Agriculture
  in Africa, 18, 73
Caspian Sea, 641, 648, 649, 696
Cassava, 12
Caste system, in India, 373-375, 384, 401
Castro, Fidel, 522-524
Catalonia, language in, 818, 820
Catherine II, the Great, 663-664
Cattle industry, in Argentina, 439-441
Cave temples, in India, 416
Central Asian Republics, in Soviet Union, 695-697, 736-737
Central Committee
  in China, 220
  in Soviet Union, 722
Central Uplands, 759-760
Chad, Republic of, drought and civil war in, 106-107
Ch'ang-an, 132, 142, 144
Changsha, China, 128
Cha-no-yu, 295
Charlemagne, 780, 781
Charles I (Spain), 452
Chekov, Anton, 725
Chen Tianlin, 223
Chernenko, Konstantin, 683

Chiang Ching-kuo, 227
Chiang K'ai-shek, 191, 192, 194-195, 227
Chiapas, 437
Chile, 435. *See also* Latin America
  Andes Mountains in, 436-437
  desert in, 444
  government in, 529
Chimurenga songs, 89
China, (People's Republic of), 120
  acupuncture in, 162
  agriculture in, 127, 128, 151-152, 161-162, 196, 205-207, 221-223
  ancestors, religious importance of, 174-175
  arts in, 166-169, 210
  Boxer Rebellion (1900) in, 189-190
  Buddhism in, 180, 182, 183
  celebrations in, 145, 174-175, 210, 212, 222
  Christianity in, 181
  civil service in, 158-159, 220-221
  civil war in, 191
  commerce and trade in, 147, 149-151, 153, 163-164
  communes in, 196, 206
  communism in, 191-197, 204-205, 220-221
  Confucianism in, 143-144, 177-180, 183
  constitution of, 229
  consumer goods in, 211
  cooperatives in, 196
  cultural forces in, 130
  cultural zones in, 147
  daily life in modern, 219
  Daoism in, 175-177, 183
  as democratic republic, 190-191
  deserts in, 125-126
  divination in, 175
  drama in, 210
  dress in, 203, 219
  dynastic government in, 141, 142-147, 151-152
  economy in, 196
  education in, 158, 159, 161, 173, 209, 224-225
  ethnic groups in, 123
  facts about, 228
  families in, 174-175
  family planning in, 214-215
  foods of, 233
  foreign policy of, 212-213
  Four Modernizations in, 205, 211
  gentry in, 158
  geography of, 123-129, 130
  government of, 195-196

  and Great Britain, 149-150, 153, 188
  Great Cultural Revolution in, 197
  Great Leap Forward in, 196
  Han dynasty in, 142, 143, 144
  industry in, 127-128, 207-208
  Islam in, 180-181
  and Japan, 188, 194-195, 238, 254, 271, 272, 273, 275
  literature in, 169, 176
  Long March in, 192, 194
  medicine in, 162-163
  merchants in, 161, 163-164
  "Middle Kingdom" in, 147, 152
  military in, 164-165, 211-212
  Ming dynasty in, 143, 147
  modernization of, 196-197, 203, 219
  Mongol invasion of, 180-181
  mountains in, 124-125
  nationalism in, 190
  Nationalists (Nationalist Party) in, 191
  Opium Wars in, 188
  peasants in, 161-162
  People's Liberation Army (PLA) in, 211-212
  philosophy of, 143-144
  plains in, 127-128
  political structure of, 220
  population of, 131, 134, 214-215
  Qin dynasty in, 142-143
  Qing dynasty in, 143, 151-152, 187, 189
  religions of, 123, 130, 133, 173, 174-183
  revolutionary drama in, 210
  rivers in, 128-129
  rural areas in, 134-135, 221-223
  scholars in, 159, 161
  science and technology in, 162-163, 211-212
  scientists in, 162-163
  Shang dynasty in, 142, 143
  soldiers in, 164-165
  Song dynasty in, 143, 144
  and Soviet Union, 196, 197, 213
  sports and recreation in, 225-226
  steppe in, 126-127
  students in, 157
  Sui dynasty in, 143, 144-145
  Taiping Rebellion (1851-1864), 189
  Tang dynasty in, 143, 144
  traditional beliefs in, 174-175
  and United States, 150, 197, 213
  urbanization in, 131-132, 134, 221-223
  Wang clan in, 160

891

women in, 157, 165-166, 193, 208-209
in World War II, 194, 195
Xia dynasty in, 142, 143
Yang and yin, 123, 133
youth in, 224-226
Zhou dynasty in, 142, 143, 144, 177
China, Republic of, 195. *See also* Taiwan
Chords, music, 834
Christianity
in Africa, 23, 34-35, 40, 43
in ancient Rome, 779-780
beliefs in, 589
in China, 149, 181
in India, 377-378, 389
in Japan, 261-262
in Latin America, 483-491, 493, 498, 518, 521
in Middle East, 555-556, 563, 565, 585, 586-587
missionary activity of, 34-35, 43, 149, 261-262, 389, 490
origins of, 585, 586-587, 779-780
in Soviet Union, 656-657, 658-659, 693, 694, 696, 729
in Western Europe, 792-794, 820-822
Chukchi Peninsula, in Soviet Union, 644-645
Churchill, Winston, 805-806
Cissé, Souleymane, 96-97
Cities. *See* Urban life
Civil disobedience, 392
Civil laws, in Rome, 776-777
Civil service, in China, 158-159, 220-221
Cixi, Empress of China, 152, 166
Clans, Japanese, 253
Classicism, 834
Classics, 176
Clement VI (Pope), 771
Climate. *See also* Geography and Environment
in Africa, 8-10, 12-16
in China, 126, 127
in India, 339, 342
in Japan, 238, 239, 240, 248
in Latin America, 437, 439, 443-444
in Middle East, 537
in Soviet Union, 640-643
in Western Europe, 753, 754
Clothes. *See* Dress
Collective farms, in Soviet Union, 714

Colombia, 439. *See also* Latin America
industrial development in, 513
llanos in, 440
rivers in, 441-443
Colonialism
in Africa, 16, 30-33, 34-35, 43, 72-73, 82-83
in India, 387-391
in Latin America, 452, 454, 457-458, 484-486
in Middle East, 603, 604
Columbus, Christopher, 452
Comedy, Greek, 772, 775
Commerce and trade. *See also* Economy
in Africa, 15, 24-25, 35, 56, 57-58
in China, 147, 149-151, 153, 163-164
in India, 388-391
in Japan, 263-264, 265, 273
in Latin America, 497, 512-513
during Middle Ages, 791
in Middle East, 546-548
in Soviet Union, 659-660, 708-709
in Western Europe, 852-853
Commercial city, 131
Common-law marriage, in Latin America, 468
Communes, in China, 196, 206
Communism
in China, 191-197, 204-205, 220-221
in Cuba, 522-524
in Soviet Union, 676, 677-682, 697, 699, 709, 722-723, 729-730
Communist Youth League, in China, 225
Compounds, as residences
in China, 158
in Nigeria, 46
Computers
impact of, on education, 857-859
industrial use of, 853
Concentration camps, during World War II, 807, 823-824
Confucianism, 143-144, 177-178
founder of, 177-178
and scholarship, 179-180
spread of, to Japan, 254
teachings of, 178-179, 183
Congo, under Belgian rule, 31-32
Congo Free State, 32
Congo River. *See* Zaire River
Congress of the People (1955), in South Africa, 55

Congress Party, in India, 393-394, 395, 396-397
Conquistadores, 452-453, 484
Conservative philosophy, 518
Constantine, 780
Constantinople, 545. *See also* Istanbul
Contras, in Nicaragua, 524-526
Cooperatives, *See also* Collective farms and Communes
in China, 196
in India, 402-403
kibbutzim as form of, 544-545
Corsica, 757
Cortés, Hernán, 452-453, 454
Cortina d'Ampezzo, 760-761
Cosep, 525
Costa Rica
education in, 529
government in, 529
railroads in, 435
Cottage industries, in India, 404
Counterpoint music, 834
Covenant, 586
Cowboys. *See Gauchos*
Crafts. *See* Arts
Cremation, 369
Crime rate, in Japan, 319
Crusades, 785
Cuba, 435
communism in, 522-524
living conditions in, 522-523
and Soviet Union, 523-524, 683
and United States, 524
Cubism, 838
Cyril, 657
Cyrillic alphabet, 657, 693
Cyrus the Great, 558

D

Dachau, 807
da Gama, Vasco, 795
Daimyo, 260, 262, 270
Dali, Salvador, 838
Dannoura, battle of (1185), 257
Dao, 176
Dao-chi, 170
Daoism, 175
teachings of, 176-177, 183
Dao De Jing **(The Way and Its Power),** 176
Da Yu, legend of, 129
Debayle, Anastasio Somoza, 524
Deccan Plateau, 337

Declaration of the Rights of Man and of Citizens, 799
De las Casas, Bartolomé, Father, 484-485
De Lesseps, Ferdinand, 606-609
Delhi/New Delhi, India, 359
Delta Plan, 765
De' Medici, Lorenzo, 792-793
Democracy
    in India, 383
    in Latin America, 517, 521
    in Western Europe, 773, 844-845
Deng Ying-chao, 193
Deng Xiao-ping, 197, 204-205, 213
Denmark, government of, 844-845
    traditional dress in, 817
Desalination, 543
Desert, War of the, 458
Desertification, problem of, in Africa, 18
Deserts
    in Africa, 15-16
    in China, 125-126
    in Latin America, 444
    in Middle East, 540-542
    in the Soviet Union, 641
    in Western Europe, 763-764
Détente, 683
Dharma, 368-369, 374
Diaguita Indians, in Latin America, 456
Diamonds, discovery of, in South Africa, 57-58
Dickens, Charles, 832, 834
Dictatorship, 191
    in Latin America, 517, 522-528
Diderot, Denis, 664
Diet, Japanese, 270
Dissidents, crack-down on, in Soviet Union, 683, 726, 730
Diversification, 46
Divination, in China, 175
Divine right, belief in, 797-798
Diwali, 372
Dnieper River, 655
Dogon, 98-99
Dominican Republic, 435
Dongbei, 125
Don River, 648
Dosojin, 247
Dostoevsky, Fyodor, 725
Dowry, 350, 351
Drama. *See also* Literature
    in ancient Greece, 775
    in China, 210
    in India, 425-426

    in Japan, 292-294
    Shakespearean, 829
    in Soviet Union, 725, 727-728
Dravidians, in India, 384
Dress
    in Africa, 28, 34-35, 80, 92, 93-94
    in China, 203, 219
    in India, 431
    in Japan, 285, 289
    in Latin America, 457, 461
    in Middle East, 556, 571, 572, 578, 580, 597
    in Soviet Union, 712-713
    in Western Europe, 816-817
Drought. *See also* Famine; Hunger
    problem of, in Africa, 15-16, 18, 106-107
Duarte, José Napoleón, 526-528
Dussehra, 425
Dutch. *See* Netherlands
Dutch East India Company, 56
Duvalier, Jean-Claude, 489-490
Dvorianie, in Soviet Union, 661
Dynastic government, in China, 141, 142-147, 151-152

E

Earthquakes
    in Japan, 243
    in Western Europe, 760
Eastern Ghats, 337
East Indies, discovery of, 794, 795
Economy. *See also* Commerce and trade
    in Africa, 55, 105-106, 109, 113
    in China, 196
    in India, 401
    in Japan, 262, 279, 315
    in Latin America, 497, 512-513
    in Middle East, 617, 629-631
    in Soviet Union, 723-724, 737
    in Western Europe, 802
Edo, Japan, 258, 270. *See also* Toyko
Education
    in Africa, 65, 111-112
    in China, 158, 159, 161, 173, 209, 224-225
    impact of the computer on, 857-859
    in India, 408-409
    in Japan, 279, 306, 308-309
    in Latin America, 468, 509-511, 529

    in Middle East, 570-573, 576-579, 628
    roles of monasteries in, 786
    in Soviet Union, 664, 665, 739-742,
    in Western Europe, 843-844, 857-859
Effiong, Phillip, 44
Egypt
    Aswan High Dam in, 543, 608
    and peace talks, 618-619, 621-622
    early society in, 24
    famine in ancient, 537
    fellah in, 570
    as member of Arab league, 621
    under Mubarak, 622
    nationalization of Suez Canal, 608-609
    as part of United Arab Republic, 606
    under Sadat, 618-619, 621, 622
Einstein, Albert, 842-843
Eisenstein, Sergei, 727
Ejidos, in Latin America, 504
Elburz Mountains, 538
El Chichón, 437
Elizabeth I (Queen of England), 388
Ellora, India, 416
El Salvador, government in, 526-528
El Yunque, 443-444
Empty Quarter, of Saudi Arabia, 540, 541
England. *See* Great Britain
English East India Company, 388-389
Enlightenment, 799
Ennosuke, 292-294
Entrepreneurs, and industrialization, 802
Environment. *See also* Geography and Climate
    in Africa, 7-19
    in China, 123-137
    in India, 333-345
    in Japan, 237-249
    in Latin America, 435-447
    in Middle East, 537-551
    in Soviet Union, 639-651
    in Western Europe, 753-767
Equiano, Olaudah, 29
Estates-General, in France, 799
Estonians, in Soviet Union, 693-694
Estuaries, 753

Ethics, in China, 173
Ethiopia, 8, 9, 23, 30
   drought in, 106
Ethnic groups. See this and related headings under individual countries and regions
Etiquette, Japanese system of, 242
Euphrates River, 538
Eurasia, 640
Europe. See individual countries in; Western Europe
Everest, Mount, 334
Exodus, of Hebrews from Egypt, 586
Extraterritoriality, 188

F

Faeroe Islands, 757
Faisal, Prince, 604
Families. See also Marriage
   in Africa, 46-49, 61-63, 65, 87
   in China, 174-175
   extended, 352, 812
   in India, 349, 352-354, 401
   in Japan, 301, 303-305
   joint, 352-354
   in Latin America, 472, 474
   in Middle East, 569, 570-573, 574, 576-578
   nuclear, 352
   in Soviet Union, 690-692, 714, 735, 736-737
   in Western Europe, 812-813
Family planning
   in Africa, 108-109
   in China, 214-215
   in India, 409-410, 411
   in Latin America, 498-499
   in Soviet Union, 736
Family Responsibility System, in China, 206-207
Famine. See Drought and Hunger
Farming. See Agriculture
Farsi **language,** 557
Favelas, in Latin America, 501
February Revolution, 674-675
Fellah, in Egypt, 570
Fellaheen
   and construction of Suez Canal, 607
   in Egypt, 543
Fertile Crescent, 539-540, 542
Festival of Lights, 372

Feudalism
   in Japan, 260-261
   in Western Europe, 780, 782-784
Fiefs, 780
Fiestas, in Latin America, 472, 475-476
Filial piety, in China, 174
Films/Filmmaking
   in Africa, 96-97
   in India, 426-427
   in Japan, 291-292
   in Soviet Union, 727
Finland, 693
   dress in, 817
Firdausi, 558
Fishing
   in Japan, 240
   in Soviet Union, 647
   in Western Europe, 855-857
Five-Year Plans
   in India, 402
   in Soviet Union, 678-679, 723
Fjords, in Norway, 756
Florence, Italy, Renaissance in, 792-793
Flower arranging, in Japan, 295-296
Foods. See individual countries and regions
Football, 859
Force Ouvrière, in France, 852-853
"Four Books," 180
Four Modernizations, in China, 205, 211
France
   absolutism in, 797, 798
   dress in, 817
   and the Enlightenment, 799
   explorations of, 795-796
   family in, 812-813
   foods of, 819
   and the French Revolution, 799-800
   geography of, 754-755, 757, 759-760
   labor movement in, 852-853
   lace making in, 862
   language in, 818
   Middle East, interests of, 603, 604
   under Napoleon Bonaparte, 801
   Napoleonic wars, 664-665
   national identity in, 817, 819
   in World War I, 804-805
   in World War II, 805-806
Franciscans, in China, 181
Franglais, 818

Franks, 780
"Freedom Charter," adoption of, **in South Africa,** 55
French Revolution, 799-800
Fuji, Mount, 239
Fujiwara family, in Japan, 255-257
Fulani, 40, 42
Fútbol, 476

G

Gadna, 560-561
Game reserves, in Africa, 15, 80
Gandhi, Indira, 394, 395, 396
Gandhi, Mohandas K., 391, 392, 393
   memorial to, 421
Gandhi, Rajiv, 396-397
Ganges River, 336, 342, 369
   as sacred in Hinduism, 336-337, 369
"Gang of Four," in China, 204, 205
Garonne River, 761
Garrick, David, 829
Gauchos, in Argentina, 439-440
Gaurani Indians, 462
Gautama, Siddharta, 377
Gaza, conflict over occupation of, 618
Gazankulu, 61-62
Genji, in Japan, 257-258
Gentry, in China, 158
Geography
   of Africa, 8-10
   of China, 123-129, 130
   of India, 333-343
   Islamic study of, 594
   of Japan, 237-244, 272
   of Latin America, 435-445
   of the Middle East, 538-544
   of Soviet Union, 639-649
   of Western Europe, 752-765
Geomancy, in China, 175
George III (King of England), 149
Georgians, in Soviet Union, 694-696, 736
Germany
   Central Uplands of, 759
   education in, 857-859
   government of, 844
   Holocaust, experience of, 807, 823-824
   life style in, 850-851
   music in, 834-835

Rhine in, 762-763
wood carving in, 862
in World War I, 804-805
In World War II, 679-680, 805-806, 807
Geyer, Enrique Bolaños, 525
Ghana
   early society of, 24
   languages in, 115
   nationalism in, 32-33
Gigantics, 640
Ginzburg, Eugenia, 680
Glut, in African oil market, 45-46
Gobi Desert, 126, 127
Gogol, Nikolai, 725
Golan Heights, conflict over control of, 621
Gold, discovery of, in South Africa, 58
Gold trade, in early Africa, 24-25
Golden Temple of Amritsar, 396
Good Hope, Cape of, 56
Gopalpur, 338
Gorbachev, Mikhail, 683, 722
Gorky, Maxim, 725
Gosplan, 723
Gowon, Yakubu, 43
Goya, Francisco, 838
Grand Canal, building of, in China, 145, 162
Great Britain, 757
   and China, 149-150, 153, 188
   colonial interests of, 43, 57, 58, 72-73, 387-391, 603, 604
   exploratory expeditions of, 795-796
   folk arts and crafts in, 861-862
   in India, 388-391
   Industrial Revolution in, 800, 802-804
   literature of, 832, 834
   Middle East interests of, 611-612
   monarchy in, 797-798, 822-823
   Shakespearean drama in, 829
   social class in, 814-815
   and Suez Canal construction, 607-608
   in World War I, 804-805
   in World War II, 805-806
Great Cultural Revolution, in China, 197
Great European Plain, 761
Great Himalayas, 334
Great Leap Forward, in China, 196, 197
Great Patriotic War, 680-681
Great Rift Valley, 8

Great Trek, 57
Great Wall, building of, 162
Great War. *See* World War I
Great Zimbabwe, 24-25
Greater East Asia Co-prosperity Sphere, 275
Greece, 756-757
   arts in, 775
   Athens (ancient), 772-775
   dress in, 817
   government (ancient), 773-775
   Hellenistic, 776
   life in modern, 851-852
   mythology, 830-831
   science in, 775
   Sparta, 773-775
Green Patrols, in Soviet Union, 649
Green Revolution, in India, 402-403
Gross national product (GNP), in India, 401
Groups Area Act (South Africa, 1950), 60
Guaraní language, 451
Guatemala, 439
   John Paul II's visit to, 483
   indigenous population of, 455
Gui, 133
Guilds, in Western Europe, 780
Guinea, life style in, 87
Guomindang, 191, 195, 198-199, 227
Gupta Empire, in India, 386
Gurus, 369

H

Hacendado, in Latin America, 503
Haciendas, in Latin America, 466
Hagashiyama, Kaii, 285
Haiku, in Japan, 291
Haiti, 435
   John Paul II's visit to, 483
   Roman Catholic Church in, 489-490
Ḥajj, 591-593
Han dynasty, in China, 142, 143, 144
Hangzhou, 132-134
Haram-bee, 71, 78-79
Harappa, 384
Harare, Zimbabwe, as urban center, 16
Harijans. See Untouchables
Harz Mountains, 759
Hasan, Masood, 424

Hausa, 40, 42
   oral literature of, 91, 93
Health care/conditions
   in Africa, 112, 113
   in India, 408
   in Japan, 304
   in Latin America, 498
   in Middle East, 629
Hebrews, 586
Heian, Japan, 255. *See also* Kyoto
Heian period, in Japan, 255-257
Heike, in Japan, 257-258
Hellenistic civilization, 776
Heredity, importance of, in Japan, 258, 260
Herodotus, 775
Hilgeman, Padre Jaime, 490
Himachal Mountain Range, 334
Himalayas, 334-335, 336, 339
Hindu Kush Mountains, 334
Hinduism
   and art, in India, 416-417
   beliefs of, 368-375, 410
   and caste system, 373-375
   Ganges River as sacred to, 336-337, 369
   holidays and pilgrimages of, 371, 372-373
   and marriage, 350-352
   Mogul opposition to, 387
   practices of, 369-371
   and *Varnas,* 373-375
Hippocrates, 775
Hirohito, 274
Hiroshima, bombing of, in World War II, 276-278
Histadrut, 620
Hitler, Adolf, 679, 681, 805, 807, 824
Hodja, Nasrudin, 559-560
Hokkaido, 237, 240, 241-242
Hokusai, 297
Holi, 372
Holland. *See* Netherlands
Holocaust, 807, 823-824
Homelands, in South Africa, 60
Homophonic music, 834
Honduras, 439
   education in, 511
   John Paul II's visit to, 483
Hong Kong, British control of, 188
Honshu, 237, 240, 241
Hoori, 253
Horseback riding, 478, 859
Hua Guofeng, 197, 204-205
Huang He, 123, 128
Huang He civilization, 123

Huang Hua, 213
Hugo, Victor, 762-763
Hunger. *See also* Famine; Drought and Poverty
  in ancient Egypt, 537
  as problem in Latin America, 506
Husain, Mohammad, 419
Husayn, Sherif, 604
Husayn-McMahon correspondence, 604, 609
Hyderabad, India, 359
Hydroelectric power
  in Egypt, 543
  in Latin America, 513
  in Soviet Union, 741

I

Iberian Peninsula, 756, 758
Ibn-Khaldūn, 556, 598
Ibn Sīnā, 598
Ibo, 40
Iboland, 40
Ibsen, Henrik, 829
Ice hockey, in Soviet Union, 744-745
Iceland, 757
  dress in, 817
Icons, as art form in Soviet Union, 657
Ieyasu, Tokugawa, 258, 259, 260
Ijsselmmer, 765
Ikebana, 295
Illiteracy. *See also* Education
  as problem in Latin America, 468, 509
Imāms, 597
Immigrant nations, in Latin America, 458-459
Impressionism, 837
Inca Indians (Quechua), 452
India
  agriculture in, 335-336, 338-339, 339-340, 341, 342-343, 345, 357, 390, 402-403, 411
  architecture in, 384, 387, 417-418
  arts in, 415-427
  British in, 388-391
  Buddhism in, 377, 415, 416
  caste system in, 373-375, 384, 401
  Christianity in, 377-378, 389
  early civilization in, 383, 384
  commerce and trade in, 388-391
  consumer goods in, 404-406
  cooperatives in, 402-403
  dance in, 423, 425
  development of, 401-402
  drama in, 425-426
  dress in, 431
  economy of, 401
  education in, 408-409
  family in, 349, 352-354, 401
  family planning in, 409-410, 411
  films in, 426-427
  Five-Year Plans in, 402
  foods of, 350
  geography of, 333-343
  government of, 383, 394, 395, 396-397
  Green Revolution in, 402-403
  Gupta Empire in, 386
  health conditions in, 408
  Hinduism in, 415, 417
  history of, 383-391
  independence of, 391-394
  Indian National Congress, 391, 393-394
  industry in, 401, 404-406
  Islam in, 375-376, 415, 417-418
  Jainism in, 377
  Janata Party of, 394
  life style in, 360
  literature in, 367, 369, 373-374, 419-420, 422-423
  marriage in, 349, 350-352
  Maurya Empire in, 384-385
  medicine in, 386
  music in, 423, 424, 425
  Muslims in, 375-376, 386-387, 394, 396-397
  natural resources in, 406-407
  Parsis in, 378
  pilgrimages in, 370, 371, 372-373
  population growth in, 349, 359, 361-362, 409-410
  population of, 368, 375, 377-378
  poverty in, 301, 401, 407-408
  quality of life in, 360, 361-363, 407-410
  religions of, 367-378, 379, 386-387, 389, 396, 415-417
  rural life in, 356-359
  science and technology in, 386
  sepoys, 388-389
  Sikhs in, 377, 379, 396
  sports and recreation in, 357
  Taj Mahal, 417-418
  urban life in, 359, 360, 361-363
  Varnas, 373-375
  women in, 349, 354, 355-356, 374-375
  post-World War II, 394-397
  Zoroastrianism in, 378
Indian National Congress, 391, 393-394
Indo-Gangetic Plains, 335-337
Indulgences, selling of, by Catholic Church, 793
Indus River, 336, 342
Indus River Valley civilization, 384
Industrial development. *See also* Economy and Urban life
  in Africa, 104, 105
  In China, 127-128, 207-208
  in India, 401, 404-406
  in Japan, 270-271, 273, 279, 315-318, 319
  in Latin America, 506, 507-509, 512-513
  in Puerto Rico, 507-508
  in Soviet Union, 710-712
  in Western Europe, 800, 802-804, 852-853
Industrial Revolution, 800, 802-804
Inflation, as problem in Middle East, 629
Inland Sea, 241
Inlay, art of, in India, 419
Innuit, housing of, 635
Intellectuals, in China, 187
Intelligentsia, in Soviet Union, 665, 667
International Year of Women (UN, 1975), 356
International Youth Year (UN, 1985), 103
Ionian Islands, 757
Iran
  under Khomeini, 626-627
  modernization of, 625-626
  nationalization of oil industry in, 611-612
  Persian heritage of, 557-558
  revolution in, 625-626
  war with Iraq, 627-629
Iraq, war with Iran, 627-629
Ireland, 757, 758, 811
  dress in, 817
  lifestyle in, 855-857
  religious conflict in Northern, 822
Irrigation, in Middle East
  need for, 542, 544
  techniques in, 543-545
Isaac, 589

Ishmael, 589
Islam
  in Africa, 25-27, 40, 42, 72
  Allah, 588
  influence on art and architecture, 25, 417-418
  beliefs of, 589, 591-596, 598
  in China, 180-181
  holy wars of, 42
  impact and achievements of, 598
  in India, 375-376, 386-387, 415, 417-418
  in Kenya, 72
  Koran, as holy book of, 375, 576, 585, 588, 589, 591-594
  in Middle East, 556, 558, 564, 565, 585, 587-589, 590-593, 598
  in Nigeria, 40
  origins of, 595, 587-589
  Shi'ite sect in, 627
Islamic Empire, 25, 593, 594, 595, 597-598. *See also* Muslims
Israel, 537, 544-545
  Arab-Israeli conflict, 609-610, 618-622
  creation of, 561, 609-610, 631
  and Golda Meir, 620
  irrigation techniques in, 545
  kibbutzim in, 544-545
  moshavim in, 545
  population of, 560
  sabra in, 560
  wars with Lebanon, 623-624
  women in, 544, 579
  youth in, 560-561
  and Zionism, 609
Istanbul, Turkey, 548-549
Italy, 756
  dress in, 816
  family in, 812-813
  government (ancient), 776-779
  life style in, 849
  Renaissance in, 792-793, 831-832
  Roman Catholic Church in, 820-821
  in World War I, 804-805
Ivan III, the Great, 658-659
Ivan IV, the Terrible, 659-660, 707
Izanagi, 237, 253
Izanami, 237, 253

J

Jahan, Shah, 386-387, 417
Jainism, in India, 377
Jaipur, India, 359
James I (England), 797-798
Janata Party, 394
Japan
  agriculture in, 242-243, 246-247, 262, 321-323
  ancestors, religious importance of, 286-288, 289
  American postwar occupation of, 279
  arts in, 285, 288, 291-297
  Buddhism in, 287-289
  celebrations and festivals in, 289-291
  and China, 188, 194-195, 238, 254, 271, 272, 273, 275
  Christianity in, 261-262
  climate in, 240, 248
  commerce and trade in, 263-264, 265, 273
  democracy in, 279
  drama in, 292-294
  dress in, 285, 289
  earthquakes in, 243
  economy of, 262, 279, 315
  education in, 279, 306, 308-309
  expansion of, 275-276
  family life in, 301, 303-305
  films in, 291-292
  fishing in, 240
  foods of, 304, 316
  foreign influence on, 269
  geography of, 237-244, 272
  government of, 270-271, 274, 279
  haiku in, 291
  health conditions in, 304
  Heian period, 255-257
  history of, 253-265
  industrial development in, 270-271, 273, 279, 315-318, 319
  judo in, 309, 310
  karate in, 310
  kendo in, 310
  landforms in, 249
  language of, 329
  leaders of, 254
  and League of Nations, 272-273
  life style in, 280-281, 309-312, 319-323
  literature in, 291
  Manchuria, interest in, 271-272, 275
  marriage in, 302-303
  military in, 260-261, 271-272, 274, 279
  modernization of, 269-272, 279
  mountains in, 238-240
  myths of, 253
  Perry's visit to, 263-264, 265
  plains in, 242-243
  population in, 248, 273
  rainfall in, 249
  religions of, 237, 240, 253, 286-289
  restaurants in, 306-307
  rural areas of, 246-247, 273
  science and technology in, 279, 315
  influence of sea on, 240-242
  Shinto in, 286-287
  shoguns in, 257-260
  social life in, 309-310
  and Soviet Union, 271, 680
  Taika reforms in, 255
  and United States, 263-264, 265, 273
  urban development of, 244-245, 273, 318, 320-321
  western influence on, 261-264, 265
  women in, 279, 305, 307, 321-323
  and World War I, 271
  and World War II, 272-279, 680
  writing in Japanese, 291, 329
  Yamato clan in, 253
  youth in, 307-310
Japan Alps, 239-240
Japan Current, 240
Japanese immigration, U.S. restrictions on, 273
Jardim Veronica, Brazil, 490-491
Jen, 178
Jerusalem. *See also* Israel
  conflict over control of East, 621
Jesuits, in China, 181
Jesus, 586-587, 589-590. *See also* Christianity
Jews. *See also* Hebrews; Israel; Judaism; and Holocaust
Jihads, 42
Jimmu Tenno, 253
Jang Qing, 197, 204
Jizyah, 597
John Paul II (Pope), visit of, to Latin America, 483
Joint families, 352-354
Jordan, 537
Juárez, Benito, 487-488, 519-520
Judaism. *See also* Hebrews; Israel; and Jews
  beliefs of, 589
  origins of, 585, 586
Judo
  in Japan, 309, 310
  in Western Europe, 859

Juku, in Japan, 308
Julius II (Pope), 831
Jute, 460
Jutland, 756

K

Kabuki, 292
Kado, 295-296
Kalenjin, 75
Kamakura, Japan, 258
Kamakura shogunate, in Japan, 258
Kama River, 647-648
Kamba, 75
Kami, 286
Kampuchea (Cambodia),
  Vietnamese
  occupation of, 213
Kana, 291, 329
Kang Xi, 148
Kanji, 291, 329
Kano, 42
Kanpur, India, 359
Karakorum Mountains, 334
Kara Kum Desert, 641
Karate
  in Japan, 310
  in Western Europe, 859
Karma, 368
Kashmir, 334
Kathakali, 421, 423, 425
Katsina, 42
Kawabata, Yasunari, 291
Kazakhstan, 696
Kendo, in Japan, 310
Kenya, 8
  agriculture in, 73, 77
  colonization of, by Europeans, 72-73, 82-83
  ethnic groups in, 71, 72, 75, 78
  government of, 78-81
  history of, 71
  languages in, 115
  Maasai in, 79-81
  nationalism in, 73-75
  population of, 71
  religions of, 75-76
  rural life in, 77
  urbanization in, 16-17, 75-76
Kenya African Union (KAU), 73
Kenyatta, Jomo, 73, 75
Kerensky, Alexander, 675
Kericho, Kenya, 77
KGB, in Soviet Union, 707
Khachaturian, Aram, 727

Khadījah, 587, 588
Khalīfah, 595
Khan, Genghis, 145
Khan, Kublai, 145
Khan, Ustad Allauddin, 424
Khoikhoi, 56
Khomeini, Ayatollah Ruhollah, 626-629
Khrushchev, Nikita, 682-683
Khyber Pass, 334
Kibbutzim, in Israel, 544-545, 620

Kichijoji, Japan, 319-321
Kievan Russia, 655, 656-658
Kikelemo, 93-94
Kikuyu, 71, 74-75, 82-83
Kilimanjaro, Mount, 8
Kilwa, 28
Kimono, 285, 289
Kirghizia, 696, 699
Kiswahili. *See* Swahili language
Knesset, 618
Knights, 782
Kojiki **(Records of Ancient Matters),** 237, 291
Koran, 375, 576, 585, 588, 589, 590-593
Korea
  independence of, 188
  and the Sino-Japanese War, 271-272
Kosygin, Aleksei, 683
Kotoku, 255
Kowtow, 147, 149
Kremlin, 706-707
Krishna, 420
Kshatriyas, 373, 374
Kulaks, in Russia, 679
Kong-fu-zi, 177
Kunno, Yuri, 305-306
Kurdistan, 564
Kurds, 564
  dream of, for homeland, 555
Kurosawa, Akira, 291-292
Kush, early society in, 24
Kuwait, 537
  and Great Britain, 611
Kyoto, Japan, 255, 270
Kyushu, 237

L

Labor Unions, in Western Europe, 852-853
Ladinos, in Latin America, 454, 455

Lagos, Nigeria, 16, 42-43, 47-48
Lakshmi, 368
Landscape gardening
  in Japan, 242, 294-295
  practice of, by Japanese in Latin America, 461
Land Under Heaven, 123
Language. *See also* Alphabet and Writing
  in Africa, 72, 114-115
  Arabic, 556
  Chinese, 166, 167, 168, 174-177
  English, 329
  Farsi, 557
  Franglais, 818
  in India, 367
  Japanese, 291, 329
  in Latin America, 451
  in Middle East, 565
  Sanskrit, 369
  in Soviet Union, 689, 690, 692-693, 694, 696, 697, 699
  Swahili, 114-115
  in Western Europe, 818, 820
Lao-zi, 176
Latin America. *See also individual countries in*
  African influence on, 451, 459-460
  agrarian reform in, 489-490
  agriculture in, 466-467, 489-490, 503-505
  aristocracy in, 466, 469-470
  arts in, 451, 489, 501
  Asians in, 460-461
  Candomblé in, 492-493
  celebrations in, 468, 472, 474-476
  Christianity, *See* Roman Catholic Church (below)
  climate in, 439, 440-441, 443-444, 446
  commerce and trade in, 503-504, 507-509, 512-513
  dance in, 474, 478
  deserts in, 444
  dress in, 457, 461, 475
  economy of, 497, 512-513
  education in, 468, 509-511, 529
  ethnic diversity in, 451-461
  European influence on, 457-459
  families in, 472, 474
  family planning in, 498-499
  fiestas in, 475-476
  foods of, 459-460
  geography of, 435-445
  health conditions in, 498

history of, 452-454, 457, 459, 484-485, 518-520
hunger in, 506
illiteracy in, 468
Indians of, 451, 452-457
industrial development in, 506, 507-509, 512-513
languages in, 451
literature of, 439, 518
living conditions in, 471-472
marriage in, 468, 473
middle class in, 520
military, role of, 520-522
mountains in, 436-439
natural resources in, 438-439, 441
pilgrimages in, 492-493
plains in, 439-441
political instability in, 517-529
population growth in, 498-501
population of, 451
Portuguese in, 457-458
poverty in, 468-469, 474-475, 490-491, 500, 501-502, 506
rain forests in, 443-444, 445
religion in, 456, 483-493, 498, 518, 521
river systems in, 441-443
Roman Catholic Church in, 483-491, 492-493, 498, 518, 521
rural areas in, 502-505
social class in, 465, 466-472
Spanish in, 452, 454, 457-458, 484-485
sports and recreation in, 476-478
urban development, 499-502
women in, 473
Latvians, in Soviet Union, 693
Laws, Roman, 776-777
League of Nations, Japan as member of, 272-273
Lebanon, 537
civil war in, 606, 617, 623-625
creation of, 604
independence of, 606
and Palestinian problem, 623-625
Legends, in India, 342-343
Lenin, 673, 675-676, 678, 721
Leningrad, 709-710
Lenin Komsomol Theater, 728
Leopold, King of Belgium, 32
Lermontov, Mikhail, 639
Li, 178
Liaotung Peninsula, Japanese control of, 188
Liberal philosophy, 518, 844
Liberia, 30

Lima, Peru, 501-502
Lingua franca, 72
Li Ning, 226
Lin Shao-qi, 197
Li-Bo, 168
Literati **(scholars),** in China, 158, 159, 161
Literature. *See also* Drama
of Africa, 25-27, 44-45, 91, 93
of China, 169, 176
of India, 367, 369, 373-374, 419-420, 422-423
of Japan, 242, 291
of Latin America, 439, 518-520
of Middle East, 558
of Soviet Union, 639, 668-669, 725, 727, 738-739, 744
of Western Europe, 832, 834, 839-840
Lithuanians, in Soviet Union, 692-693
Llanos, in Latin America, 439-441
Loan contracts, development of, in China, 162
Locke, John, 799, 844
Loess, in China, 127-128
Logic, 775
Loire River, 761
Lokele, 9-10
London, England, 823
Long-lifers, in Soviet Union, 695
Long March, in China, 192, 194
Louis XIV (France), 798
Lu, Empress, 166
Lucknow, India, 359
Lumumba, Patrice, 31-32
Luo, 75
Luther, Martin, 793-794
in Sweden, 821
Luxembourg, 754
dress in, 816
Luyia, 75
Lycurgus, 773

M

Maasai, in Kenya, 79-81
MacArthur, Douglas A., 279
Macho, 498
Madagascar, 8
Madera, José R., 507
Madras, India, 359
Magdalene River, 441
Magellan, Ferdinand, 795-796
Mahabharata, 420, 425-426
Mahatma ("Great Soul"), 391

Mahavira, 377
Maimonides, (Maimon, Moses ben), 596
Makarova, Natalia, 727
Makeba, Miriam, 90
Malan, D. F., 60
Maldives, 333
Malevich, Kazimir, 727
Mali, 7
early society in, 24-26
Malta, 757
dress in, 817
Manchuria, 125
Japanese interest in, 271-272, 275
Soviet invasion of, 681
Manchurian Plain, in China, 127
Manchus, 147
Mandate, 141
Mandate of Heaven, concept of, 141
Mandate system, following World War I, 604
Mandela, Nelson, 56, 64, 67
Manipur, 334
Manors, 782
Mansa Musa, 25
Man'yoshu, 291
Mao Zedong, 187, 192, 194, 196-197, 198, 211
death of, 198, 203
Maritime nations, 753
Marketplace, role of, in Middle East, 546-548
Marriage. *See also* Families
in Africa, 47, 51
in China, 165
in India, 349, 350-355
in Japan, 302-303
in Latin America, 454, 468
in Middle East, 569, 570
mixed, 454
in Soviet Union, 691, 697
Marx, Karl, 673, 676, 844
Maryknoll missionaries, in Latin America, 490
Masks, in Africa, 92, 94-96
Mass culture, emergence of, 832
Massif Central, 759-760
Mass-production, effect of, on industrialization, 800
Matsuo, Bashō, 291
Matsushita Electric Industrial Company, 316, 317, 319
Mau Mau, 74
Mauritania, 9, 12, 15
Maurya Empire, in India, 384-386
Mausoleums. *See* Taj Mahal

Maya Indians, 452
Mayakovsky, Vladimir, 727
Mayakovsky Theater, 728
May Fourth Movement, 193
Mayobamba, Argentina, 473
McMahon, Sir Henry, 604
Mecca, Saudi Arabia, importance of, to Islam, 587-589, 591-593
Medina, Saudi Arabia, 589
Meditation, 370
Mediterranean region, 763-764
Meiji **rule,** in Japan, 270
Meir, Golda, 620
Melgarejo, Mariano, 518-519
Mencius, 179
Mendelssohn, Felix, 834
Meroë, early society in, 24
Mesas, in Latin America, 440
Meseta, 759
Mestizos, 451, 454-455, 457
Mexico, 435
    education in, 465
    ethnic diversity in, 451, 454
    government of, 519-520
    land reform in, 487-488, 500
    living conditions in, 465
    poverty in, 465
    power of Roman Catholic Church in, 487-488
    rain forest in, 445
    slums in, 500-501
    volcanic eruption in, 437-438
Mexico City, Mexico, 452, 499-500
Michelangelo Buonarroti, 831-832
Middle Ages
    and fuedalism, 780, 782-784
    and Roman Catholic Church, 781, 784, 786
Middle class, in Latin America, 466, 471, 520
Middle East. *See also individual countries in*
    agriculture in, 537, 538, 542-544
    and Arab-Israeli conflict, 609-610, 618, 619, 620, 621-623
    Arabs in, 556-557
    Armenians in, 563, 694-696
    arts in, 548, 549, 598, 599
    Christianity in, 556-557, 563, 565, 585, 586-587
    civil war in, 623-625
    climate in, 537
    commerce and trade in, 546-548
    dance in, 569
    deserts in, 540-542
    dress in, 556, 571, 572, 578, 580, 597
    families in, 569, 570-573, 574, 576-579, 580-581
    foods of, 547, 573
    geography of, 538-545
    Hajj in, 591-593
    health conditions in, 629-631
    history of, 556-558, 585-589
    housing in, 546, 629-631, 635
    Iranians in, 557-558
    Iran-Iraq war, 617, 627-629
    irrigation in, need for, 542-544
    Islam, 556, 558, 564, 565, 585, 587-589, 590-593, 598
    Israelis in, 560-561
    Judaism in, 560, 561-562, 565, 585, 586, 596
    Kurds in, 564
    language groups, 565
    Lebanese civil war, 606, 617, 623-625
    literature of, 558
    marriage in, 569, 570
    medicine in, 556, 590, 598
    oil in Persian Gulf, discovery of, 611-612
    problems in modernization, 629-631
    Palestinians in, 561-562
    philosophy in, 598
    pilgrimages in, 591-593
    population of, 538, 543, 555
    religions of, 585-599
    science and technology in, 556, 598
    social customs in, 569-581
    Turks in, 558-560
    urban development in, 545-549
    water in, importance of, 537
    women in, 572-573, 578-579, 580-581, 628-629
"Middle Kingdom," in China, 147, 152
Military. *See individual region or country*
Millet, 336
Millets, 597
Minamoto clan, in Japan, 257
Ming dynasty, in China, 143, 147
Minifundio, in Latin America, 504
Min River, 129
Mirs, 666
Missionaries. *See also* Christianity and Roman Catholic Church
    in Africa, 34-35, 43
    in China, 149, 181
    in India, 377-378, 389
    in Japan, 261-262
    in Latin America, 490
Mitterrand, François, 817, 819
Mixed economy, in India, 404
Moctezuma, 453
Mogul dynasty, in India, 386-387
Mohenjo Daro, 384
Molina, Enrique, 863
Mombasa, Kenya, 72
    early society in, 28
Monasteries, establishment of, by Catholic Church, 786
Mongols
    invasion of China by, 145, 180-181
    in Russia, 657-658
Monomotapa, early society in, 24
Monophonic music, 834
Monotheism, 586
Monsoons
    in India, 339-340, 342
    in Japan, 240
Monte Desert, 444
Morocco, 537
Morris dancing, 861-862
Moscow, Soviet Union
    life in, and around, 705, 706-709
    as the Third Rome, 659
Moscow Art Theater, 727
Moses, 586
Moshavim, in Israel, 545
Mosques
    in Africa, 25-26
    in India, 417-418
    in Middle East, 546, 548-549
Mo Zi, 180
Mountains
    in Africa, 8
    in China, 124-125
    in India, 334-335, 337
    in Japan, 238-240
    in Latin America, 436-439
    in Middle East, 538
    in South Asia, 334-335
    in Soviet Union, 640-641, 694
    in Western Europe, 757-761
Mount of Lebanon, 604
Mozart, Wolfgang Amadeus, 835
Mubarak, Husni, 622
Muftis, 595, 597
Muhammad, 375, 587, 593, 595
    as founder of Islam, 587-589
    relationship to God, 591
Mulattos, 451
Musical Technique and Style
    homophonic, 834
    improvisations, 423
    monophonic, 834

polyphonic, 834
polyrhythm, 88
rock, 740, 743, 841
Muslims. *See also* Islam
   in Africa, 25-27, 40, 42
   in China, 180-181
   in India, 375-376, 386-387, 417-418
   in Middle East, 556, 557, 561-562, 563-564, 565, 588-589, 589-593, 598
   in Soviet Union, 694, 697
Mussorgsky, Modest, 725
Mutsuhito, 270
Myths, 237, 830

N

Naga Hills, 334
Nagano, 322
Nagasaki, bombing of, in World War II, 276-278
Nagoya, 244
Nagpur, India, 359
Naipaul, V. S., 362
Nairobi, Kenya, 72, 75-76
   as urban center, 16
Namibia, 7
Nanak, Guru, 377
Nanh-Sohou, 95-96
Nanking, Treaty of (1842), 188
Napoleon Bonaparte, 664, 801
Nara, Japan, 255
Narayan, R. K., 422
Nasser, Gamal Abdel, 608-609, 619
Nataraja, 417
National Assembly, in Kenya, 78
Nationalism, 844
   in Africa, 31-33, 43-44, 73-75, 89
   in China, 190
   in Europe, 754, 804
   in Middle East, 562, 563-564, 608-609
   in Soviet Union, 699
   in Western Europe, 844
Nationalist party, Chinese, 191
National Party Congress, in China, 220
National Youth Service Corps, in Nigeria, 49-50
Native Land Act (South Africa, 1913), 60
Negev Desert, 540, 544
Nehru, Jawaharlal, 393-394
Nepal, 333, 334
Netherlands
   and Delta Plan, 765

   dress in, 816
   explorations and colonial activities of, 56-57, 262, 796
   and Zuider Zee project, 765
New Economic Policy (NEP), in Soviet Union, 678
Nicaragua, 439
   civil war in, 524-526
Nicholas II (Russia), 667, 674, 675
Nigeria
   agriculture in, 45, 46
   British colonialism in, 43
   civil war in, 43-45
   economic development of, 45-46
   ethnic groups in, 40
   geography of, 39
   history of, 42-43
   languages in, 115
   life style in, 39
   literature in, 44-45, 51
   nationalism in, 33
   oil industry in, 45-46
   population of, 39, 40-41, 47
   present-day life in, 45-49
   religions of, 40
   secession of Biafra from, 44
   urbanization in, 16, 47-49
   village life in, 46-47
   women in, 51
   youth in, 49-50
Niger River, 9
Nihonji (Chronicles of Japan), 237
Nile Delta, 543-544
Nile River, 9, 538, 542
Ninigi, 253
Nixon, Richard, visit of, to China, 197
Nkrumah, Kwame, 33
Noh play, 292
Nok culture, 42
Nomadic people
   Bedouins as, 540-542
   in early Africa, 15, 24
   in Central Asia, 696-697
   in Middle East, 540-542
Non-aligned nations, 394
North Atlantic Drift, 753
North China Plain, 127
Northwestern Highlands, 757-759
Norway, 756
   drama in, 829
   dress in, 817
   fjords in, 756
Nouakchott, 15-16
Nouveaux riches, in Latin America, 466, 470
Novosibirsk, 710-712

Nuclear arms, and China, 213
Nuclear families, 352
Nureyev, Rudolf, 727
Nwapa, Flora, 51
Nyerere, Julius, 110

O

Oases, importance of, in Middle East, 538
Ojukwu, Lt. Gen. E. O., 43-44
Oil industry
   in Africa, 45-46, 106
   discovery of oil in Persian Gulf, 611
   in Latin America, 513
Oleg, 655
Olympic Games
   Chinese participation in 225-226
   in modern Rome, 860-861
   origin of, 775
Oman, 537
   family structure in, 576-577
Ommohamed, 570
One-party state
   development of, in Kenya, 78
   in Soviet Union, 722
OPEC (Organization of Petroleum Exporting Countries), Nigeria as member of, 45-46
Opera, of Western Europe, 834, 835, 836-837
Opium trade, in China, 188
Opium Wars, in China, 188
Oprichniki, in Soviet Union, 659
Oral tradition, in history, 23, 237, 342-343
Orange Free State, 57
Organization of African Unity (OAU), 109
Origami, 295
Orinoco River, 441
Orographic lifting, 339
Orthodox Church, Russian, 656-657, 658-659, 693, 706, 729
Osaka, 244
Ottoman Turks, in Middle East, 558
Overpopulation. *See* Population
Oyashio Current, 240

P

Pachinko, 323
Pahlevi, Shah Mohammed Reza, 611-612, 625-626

Painting. *See also* Arts
  Cubism, 838
  Impressionism, 837
  during the Middle Ages, 837
  during the Renaissance, 831-832, 837
Pakistan, 333, 335
  civil war between East and West, 394
  creation of, 393
Pa kua, 133
Palestinian Liberation Organization (PLO), 623-624, 625
Palestinian Red Crescent Society, 624-625
Palestinians
  dream of, for homeland, 555
  in Middle East, 561-562, 623-624
Pamir Knot, 334
Pampas, in Argentina, 439
Panchatantra, 420
Panchayat, 356
Pan Gu, legend of, 123
Paraguay, 439
  industrial development in, 513
  language in, 451
  rivers in, 441
Paraná River, 441
Parsis, in India, 378
Partitioning
  of Africa, 30-31
  of India, 394
  of Pakistan, 394
  of Palestine, 610
Parvati, 368
Pasha, Said, 606
Pass laws, in South Africa, 60, 64
Pasternak, Boris, 727
Patagonian Desert, 444
Pather Panchali, 426
Patriarchs, 586
Patricians, in ancient Rome, 776
Patrons, during Renaissance, 831
Pavlovna, Ekaternia, 706-707
Pax Romana, 777-779
Peacock Throne, 387
Pearl Harbor, Japanese bombing of, 275-276
Peasants. *See also* Poverty
  in China, 161-162, 205-207
  serfs in Russia, 661, 664, 665-667
Pelé, 476-477
Peloponnesian Wars, 775

People's Liberation Army (PLA),
  in China, 211-212
People's Republic of China. *See* China
Pericles, 773
Perm, Soviet Union, 648
Permafrost, in Soviet Union, 642
Perón, Isabel, 473
Perov, Vasili, 725
Perry, Matthew, 263-264, 265
Persia, 557. *See also* Iran
Personalismo, 479
Perspective, rules of in art, 837
Peru
  ethnic diversity in, 451
  language in, 451
Peter I, the Great, 640, 661-663
Philip II (Macedonia), 776
Philosophy
  in ancient Greece, 775
  in China, 143-144
  in Middle East, 590, 598
  in Western Europe, 844-845
Picasso, Pablo, 838
Plains
  in China, 127-128
  in India, 335-336
  in Japan, 242, 244
  in Latin America, 439-441
  in South Asia, 335-337
  in Western Europe, 761
Plantations, in India, 390
Plato, 775, 791
Plebians, in ancient Rome, 776
Pliny, 779-780
PLO. *See* Palestinian Liberation Organization (PLO)
Plutarch, 776
Poetry. *See* Literature
Pokrovski, Boris, 728
Poland, in World War II, 679, 805
Polar night, in Soviet Union, 642, 643
Polders, in Netherlands, 765
Politburo
  in China, 220
  in Soviet Union, 722
Political science, 775
Political structure
  of China, 220
  of Soviet Union, 749
  of United States, 749
Political thought, in Western Europe, 844-845
Polo, Marco, 145, 640
Polyphonic music, 834
Polyrhythm, 88

Poona, India, 359
Popova, Lyubov, 727
Population/population growth
  in Africa, 7, 8, 16, 39, 108-109
  in China, 131, 134, 214-215
  in India, 349, 359, 409-410
  in Japan, 273
  in Latin America, 498-499
  in Middle East, 538, 543, 629
  in South Asia, 333
  in Soviet Union, 693, 706, 712
  in Western Europe, 753
Po River, 761
Portents, 123
Portugal
  bullfighting in, 863
  dress in, 816
  explorations of, 794-795
  family in, 812
  and India, 377-378
  and Japan, 261-262
  and Kenya, 72
Poverty
  in India, 361, 401, 407-408
  in Latin America, 468-469, 474-475, 490-491, 500, 501-502, 506
  in Soviet Union, 661, 665-667
Pravda, 728
Prokofiev, Sergei, 727
Proletariats, in Russia, 676
Protestantism. *See also* Christianity
  origins of, 793-794
Protest songs, in Africa, 89
Proverbs, in Africa, 91, 93
Ptolemy, 791
Publishing industry, in Nigeria, 51
Pueblos jóvenes, in Latin America, 501
Puerto Rico, 435
  education in, 509-510
  industrial development in, 507-508
  rain forest in, 443-444
Pugachova, Alla, 743
Puja, 369
Pulses, 336
Punjab, 336, 377
Purdah
  in India, 355-356
  in Middle East, 355-356, 572, 627
Purgatory, belief in, 793
Purges, in Russia, 679
Puri, India, 372
Pushkin, Alexander, 725, 731
Pyrenees Mountains, 760

Q

Qatar, 537
Qiao Yu, 210
Qing dynasty, in China, 143, 147, 151-152, 181, 187, 189
Quadalquivar River, 761-762
Quechua Indians (Inca), 462
Quechua language, 451

R

Raga, in India, 423
Rain forests
 in Africa, 8, 12-13
 in Latin America, 443-444, 445
Rajahs, in India, 387
Ram, 420
Ramayana, 420, 425-426
Ram Lila, 426
Ray, Satajit, 426
Reagan, Ronald, 213
Recreation. *See* Sports and recreation
Red Army, in Russia, 677
Red Fort, 387
Red Guards, in China, 197
Red Sea Mountains, 538
Reformation, 793-794
Regalia, 253
Regents, 166
Reincarnation, 368
Relativity, theory of, 842-843
Relics, in India, 416
Reliefs, in India, 416
Religion. *See also individual religions*
 in Africa, 34-35, 40-41, 42, 72, 94-96
 in China, 173, 174-181
 in India, 367, 368-370, 371, 372-375, 375-377, 377-378, 379, 386-387, 389, 415-417
 in Japan, 286-289
 in Latin America, 483-491, 498, 518, 521
 in Middle East, 585-599
 in Soviet Union, 656-657, 658-659, 693, 694, 696, 697, 703, 706, 729-730
 in Western Europe, 779-780, 807, 820-822, 823-824
Renaissance, 792-793
 manners of, 792
 role of patrons in, 831
Repin, Ilya, 725
Reserves, in South Africa, 60
Rhazes. *See* Al-Rāzī
Rhine River, 762-763
Rhone River, 761, 762-763
Richard the Lionhearted, 596
Rig Veda, 420
Rimsky-Korsakov, Nikolai, 725
Rio de Janeiro, 499, 501
Río de la Plata River, 441
Rivers
 in Africa, 8-10
 in China, 128-129
 in India, 342
 in Japan, 239
 in Latin America, 441-443
 in Middle East, 538-540
 in South Asia, 336-337
 in Soviet Union, 647-648, 649, 655, 662, 711, 712, 742
 in Western Europe, 761, 762-763
Robotics, 853
Rock music
 in Soviet Union, 743
 in Western Europe, 841
Roger II, King (Sicily), 594
Roman Catholic Church
 in Africa, 76
 anticlericals in Mexico, 486-491
 and *Candomblé,* 492-493
 in China, 181
 and Crusades, 597, 785
 Franciscan order, 181
 in Middle Ages, 781, 784, 785
 establishment of monasteries, 786
 in Italy, 820-821
 in Latin America, 483-491, 498, 518, 521
 Jesuit order, 181
 missionary activity of, 34-35, 149, 181, 378-379, 389, 490
 and Reformation, 793-794
 selling of indulgences, 793
 in Soviet Union, 693
Romanov, Michael, 660
Romanticism, 834
Rome (ancient)
 Christianity in, 779-780
 empire of, 777-779
 foods of, 778
 Germanic invasions of, 780
 Pax Romana, 777-779
 republic of, 776-777
Rousseau, Jean-Jacques, 844
Royal city, 131
Royal Shakespeare Company, 829
Rural life. *See also* Agriculture
 in Africa, 46-47, 77
 in China, 134-135, 221-223
 in India, 356-359
 in Japan, 246-247, 273, 321-323
 in Latin America, 502-505
 in Middle East, 540-544
 in Soviet Union, 697-698, 712-716
 in Western Europe, 854-855
Rushdie, Salman, 422
Russia. *See* Soviet Union
Russian Orthodox Church, 656-657, 658-659, 693, 729
Russian Soviet Federated Socialist Republic, 690
See also Soviet Union
Russification, 698-699
Rwanda, 15

S

Sadat, Anwar el-, 618, 619, 621-622
 assassination of, 619, 622
 visit to Israel, 618, 619
Sadhus, 370
Sado, 295-296
Sages, in China, 173
Sahara Desert, 15
Sahel, 15
Saint Patrick, 822
St. Petersburg, Russia, 662-663
 See also Leningrad
Saint-Simon, 798-799
St. Thomas, 377
Sakharov, Andrei, 730
Saladin, 596
Salvador, Brazil, 451
Salvation, Christian beliefs regarding, 586-587, 793
Samizdat, 727
Samurai, 256, 260-261, 270
San, 56
Sandinista National Liberation Front, 524-526
Sanskrit, 369
São Francisco River, 442
São Paulo, Brazil, 499, 501

903

São Salvador. *See* Salvador
Sari, 431
Sasu, 24-25
Saudi Arabia, 537
Savanna, in Africa, 8, 13-15
Scandinavian Peninsula, 756
Scholarship. *See* Education
Science and technology
   in China, 162-163, 211-212
   in India, 386
   in Japan, 279, 315
   in Middle East, 556, 598
   in Western Europe, 775, 840, 842-844
Scientific method, 775
Scottish Highlands, 758-759
Scripts, 166
Sculpture. *See also* Arts
   Buddhist, 288
Seaquakes, in Latin America, 437
Seawater, desalination of, 543
Secretariat, in Soviet Union, 722
Sects, 287
Seine River, 761
Seljuk Turks, in Middle East, 558
Senabu, 93-94
Senegalese, 12, 13
Sepoy Mutiny, in India, 388-389
Sepoys, in India, 388
Sepúlveda, Juan Ginés de, 484, 485
Serfs, 664
   in Western Europe, 783-784
   in Russia, 661, 665-667
Service industries, in Japan, 318
Shahādah, as Islamic belief, 591
Shah Mohammed Reza Pahlevi, 611-612, 625-626
Shah Namah (Chronicles of the Kings), 558
Shakespeare, 829
Shang dynasty, in China, 142
Shanghai, China, 128, 134
Shankar, Ravi, 424
Shankar, Uday, 424
Sharpeville, South Africa
   demonstrations in, 64-65, 66
Shen, 133
Shiretoko Peninsula, 241-242
Shi Huangdi, 142
Shi'ite Muslims, 628
Shikibu, Lady Murasaki, 291
Shikoku, 237, 241
Shinto religion, in Japan, 286-287
Shiva, 368, 416-417, 421
Shogun/Shogunates, in Japan, 257-258, 260-261, 264

Sholokhov, Mikhail, 727
Shostakovich, Dmitry, 727
Shotoku, Prince, 254
Siberia, 641-643
   exile of dissidents to, 727, 730
   flow of rivers in, 648
   government employment in, 723, 741-742
   housing in, 641-642
   as labor camp, 679
   life in, 641-643, 710-712
Sicily, 757
Sierra Madra Occidental, 436
Sierra Madre del Sur, 436
Sierra Madre Oriental, 436
Sierra Nevada, 760
Sikhs, in India, 377, 379, 396
Sikkim, 334
Simon, Claude, 839-840
Sinai Peninsula, conflict over occupation of, 618
Sistine Chapel, 831-832
Sita, 420
Sitar, 423, 424
Siva. *See* Shiva
Siwalik Mountain Range, 334
Slave trade, in Africa, 29, 42
Slavs, in Soviet Union, 655, 690-692
Sobchuk, Nicholai, 714-715
Soccer
   in Latin America, 476-477
   in Western Europe, 859
Social class
   in India, 373-375, 375, 377
   in Japan, 258, 260
   in Latin America, 465, 466-472
   in Western Europe, 813-815
Socialism
   and Russian intelligentsia, 667
   in Western Europe, 844
Socialist Realism, 727
Social life. *See also* Families; Social Class; Sports and Recreation
   in China, 225-226
   in India, 349, 357
   in Japan, 239, 309-310, 323-325
   in Latin America, 474-478
   in Middle East, 573-576
   in Soviet Union, 735, 742, 743-745
   in Western Europe, 857-861, 863
Socrates, 775
Sofala, 28
Soldiers. *See* Army
Solomon Islands, 276

Solzhenitsyn, Alexander, 727, 738
Somalia, health care in, 112-113
Song dynasty, in China, 144
Songhai Empire, 26-27
Son of Heaven, concept of, 141
Soong Meiling, 191
South Africa, 7
   Anglo-Boer War in, 58, 59
   apartheid policies in, 55, 58, 60-66, 67
   black resistance movement in, 63-66, 67
   economy of, 55
   education in, 65
   ethnic groups in, 56
   European colonization of, 56-58
   Gandhi, Mohandas, in, 392
   history of, 56-58
   mining in, 12, 57-58
   population of, 55, 66
South Asia, 333
Soviet Union
   agriculture in, 645-646, 690, 694, 705, 713-716
   under Andropov, 683
   architecture in, 689, 706-707, 711
   army in, 661-663, 664-665, 674-675, 677-679, 681-682, 684-685
   arts in, 656-657, 659, 663-664, 668-669, 689, 694, 697-698, 724-728, 731
   black market in, 708-709
   Bolshevik revolution, 675-676
   under Brezhnev, 683
   Byelorussia, 690-692
   under Catherine the Great, 663-664
   celebrations in, 694, 697-698, 722
   under Chernenko, 683
   and China, 196, 197, 213, 683
   Christianity in, 656-657, 658-659, 693, 694, 696, 706, 729-730
   Christians in, 729
   cities in, 711
   civil war in, 677-679
   climates of, 640-643
   commerce and trade in, 659-660, 708-709
   communism in, 676, 677-682, 697, 699, 709, 722-723, 729-730
   Communist party in, 722-723
   constitution of, 689
   Cossacks, 661
   and Cuba, 523-524, 683
   deserts in, 641
   and détente, 683

904

dissidents in, 683, 729-730
drama in, 725, 727-728
dress in, 712-713
economy in, 677-679, 737
education in, 664, 665, 739-742
ending of Romanov dynasty, 664-667
ethnic groups in, 689-699
families in, 714, 735, 736-737
family planning in, 736
February Revolution, 674-675
filmmaking in, 727
fishing in, 647
Five-Year Plans of, 678-679, 723
foods of, 645-646, 742, 744
and France, 664-665
geography of, 639-649
and Germany, 674-675, 679, 681-682
under Gorbachev, 683
Green Patrols, 649
history of, 655-669
housing in, 736-737
industrial development in, 710-712
intelligentsia in, 665, 667
under Ivan III, 658-659
under Ivan IV, 659-660
and Japan, 271, 681
Jewish persecution in, 667
Jews in, 667, 729
KGB in, 707
under Khrushchev, 682-683
Kievan state, 655, 656-658
under Kosygin, 683
Kremlin, 706-707
languages in, 689, 690, 692-693, 694, 696, 697, 699
under Lenin, 673, 675-676, 678
literature of, 639, 668-669, 725, 727, 738-739, 744
long-lifers of, 695
and Manchuria, 681
modernization of, 662-663
Mongol rule of, 657-658
music in, 694, 725, 727, 741, 743
Muslims in, 694, 697
Napoleonic invasion of, 664-665
nationalism in, 699
natural resources in, 650-651
under Nicholas II, 674-675
1917 Revolution in, 698, 721, 737
occupation of Afghanistan, 213
peasant markets in, 715-716
under Peter the Great, 661-663
political structure of, 749

population growth in, 697
population of, 693, 706, 712
pre-revolutionary period, 667
provisional government in, 675
railroads in, 723-724
Red Army of, 677
religions in, 658-659, 693, 694, 696, 697, 706, 729-730
religious dissent in, 729-730
revolutionary period in, 674-676
rural life in, 712-716
Russian Orthodox Church in, 706, 729
secret police in, 659, 665, 675, 679, 680
serfs in, 661, 664-667
Siberia, 641-643, 647, 679, 710-712, 726, 730, 741-742
Slavs in, 655, 690-692
and socialism, 667
sports and recreation in, 735, 742, 743, 744-745
under Stalin, 678-679, 680, 682, 692, 696, 698
steppe region in, 646, 648
taiga region in, 645-646
tundra region, 644-645
Ukraine, 690
urban development in, 705, 706-712
water in, 641, 647-648, 649, 662
white nights in, 709
women in, 680, 737-739
in World War I, 674, 804-805
in World War II, 679, 681, 684-685, 737
youth in, 739-745
Sovkhozes, 713
Soweto, South Africa, 61-63
protests in, 65
Spain
art in, importance of, 838-839
bullfighting in, 863
dress in, 816
exploratory expeditions of, 484-485, 794-796
family in, 812
in Latin America, 484-485
life style in, 854-855
Sparta, 773-775
"Spartakiads of the Peoples of the U.S.S.R.," 745
Spassky Tower, 707
Sports and recreation
in China, 225-226

in ancient Greece, 775
in India, 356-357
in Japan, 239, 309-310, 323-325
in Latin America, 476-478
in modern Rome, 860-861
in Soviet Union, 735, 743-745
in Western Europe, 859-861, 863
Springsteen, Bruce, 841
Sri Lanka, 333
Stalin, Joseph, 678-681, 682, 692, 695, 696, 698
Steppe
in China, 126-127
in Soviet Union, 646
Stupas, in India, 416
Subcontinent, South Asia as, 333
Sudras, 373
Suez Canal
British/French management of, 608
construction of, 606-607
nationalization of, 608-609
Sui dynasty, in China, 143, 144-145
Suiko, 254
Sultan of Delhi, 386
Sumo, 323
Sun Yat-sen, 151, 190-191
Sūq, in Middle East, 546-548
Susanowo, 253
Suttee, 354
Swahili language, adoption of, as national language, 114-115
Swahili, 28, 72
Sweden
dress in, 817
education in, 821, 867
Lutheran Church in, 821
Switzerland,
dress in, 816
wood carving in, 862
Sykes-Picot Agreement, 604
Syria
as French mandate, 604-606
independence of, 606
and Lebanese civil war, 623
as part of United Arab Republic, 606
Tabaqa Dam in, 543

T

Tabaqa Dam, 543
Tagore, Rabindranath, 420, 422
Tagus River, 761-762
Taibei (Taipei), 227

Taiga, in Soviet Union, 645-646
Taika **reforms,** 255
Taiping Rebellion (1851-1864), 189
Taira clan, in Japan, 257
Taiwan, 195, 227
    constitution of, 229
    establishment of Republic of China on, 195
    facts about, 228
    Japanese control of, 188
    and U.S.-Chinese relations, 213
Taiyuan, China, 128
Tajikistan, 695
Taj Mahal, 417-419
Takayama festival, 289-291
Takla Makan desert, 126
Tale of Genji, The **(Shikibu),** 291
Talking drums, 88-89
Tang dynasty, in China, 144
Tanzania
    languages in, 115
    self-help programs in, 113
Tashkent, 689
Tata Iron and Steel Company, 405
Taurus Mountains, 538
Tchaikovsky, Peter, 721, 725
Technology. *See* Science and technology
Television
    in India, 356-357,
    in Japan, 325
Tennis, 859
Tenochtitlán, 452
Terracing, 321
Thales of Miletus, 775
Thar Desert, 336
Theater. *See* Drama
"Three Principles of the People," 190-191
Thucydides, 775
Tianjin, China, 128
Tidal waves, seaquakes as cause of, 437
Tigris River, 538
Tilak, 431
Timbuktu, early society in 24, 26-27
Tojo, Hideki, 275
Tokugawa shogunate, in Japan, 258, 260, 270
Tokyo, Japan, 244-245, 273-274. *See also* Edo, Japan
Toland, John, 276
Toledo, Spain, sword manufacture in, 862
Tolstoy, Leo, 669, 725
Tonal sounds, 88-89

Tocqueville, Alexis de, 517
Towers of Silence, 378
Townships, in South Africa, 60
Trade and commerce. *See* Commerce and trade
Tragedy, Greek, 775
Transcaucasia, 694-695
Transcaucasus, 677
Transportation
    in Europe, 761-763
    in Soviet Union, 711-712
    Suez Canal, 606-609
Transvaal, 57-58, 59
    mining in, 57-58
Trepadeiras, 461
Tretyak, Vladislav, 744
Trigrams, 133
Tripura, 334
Trotsky, Leon, 677, 678
Tsunami, in Japan, 243
Tundra, in Soviet Union, 644, 645
Turgenev, Ivan, 668-669, 725
Turkey
    modernization of, 631
    population of, 558-560, 563, 564
Turkmenia, 696-698
Twelve Tables, 776-777
Tyler, John, 150
Typhoons, in Japan, 239, 240

U

Uganda, 9, 72
    languages in, 115
Uhuru, 71
Ukraine, 677, 690, 701, 714-715
Ulema, 595
Ulyanov, Vladimir Ilyich. *See* Lenin
Umkhonto We Sizwe, 64
Union of South Africa, 58. *See also* South Africa
Union of Soviet Socialist Republics. *See* Soviet Union
United Arab Emirates, 537
United Arab Republic, formation of, 606
United Nations
    proclamation of 1985 as International Youth Year, 103
    role of, in creation of Israel, 610
United States
    and China, 150, 197, 213
    and Cuba, 524
    dress in, 431

    dropping of atomic bomb on Japan, 276-279
    foods of, 233
    and Japan, 263-264, 265, 273, 275, 279
    language in, 329
    political structure of, 749
    in World War II, 275-276
Universal state, 776
Untouchables, in India, 374-375, 393
Ural Mountains, 640-641
Urban life
    in Africa, 16-17, 47-49, 75-76
    in China, 131-132, 134, 223-224
    in India, 359, 361-363
    in Japan, 244-245, 273, 318, 319-321
    in Latin America, 499-502
    in Middle East, 545-549, 629-631
    in Soviet Union, 705, 706-712, 717
    in Western Europe, 850-853
Uruguay, 439
    government in, 529
    rivers in, 441
Uruguay River, 441
Uttar Pradesh, 336
Uzbekistan, 696

V

Vachtangov Theater, 728
Vaillant-Couturier, 807
Vaisyas, 373
Varanasi, India, 371
Varangians, in Russia, 655
Varnas, in India, 373-375
Vassals, 780, 782
Veches **(assemblies),** in early Soviet Union, 656
Vedas, in India, 419-420
Velázquez, 838
Venezuela, 439
    rivers in, 441
Verdi, Giuseppe, 834
Vernacular speech, 839
Vertical calligraphy, 168
Viceroy, 389
Vietnam, occupation of Kampuchea by, 213
Village life. *See* Rural Life
Villas miserias, in Latin America, 501
Vindhya Hills, 337
Vishnu, 368

Visual arts. *See* Arts
Vladimir (Grand Prince of Kiev), 656-657
Volcanoes
  in Japan, 239
  in Latin America, 436-438
Volga River, 647-648
Voznesensky, Andrei, 727

W

Wa, 238
Wagner, Richard, 834
Wake Island, 276
Wales, 758
  dress in, 817
  language in, 818
Wālīs, 595
Wang clan, in China, 160
Waqfs, 597
War communism, 677-678
Warlords, 191
Water needs
  in Middle East, 537, 542-545
  in South Asia, 342-343
Wazīrs, 595
Weizsäcker, Richard von, 823-824
Wendi, 144-145
Wenskei, Thomas, 490
West Bank, conflict over occupation of, 618
Western Europe. *See also individual countries in*
  arts of, 772, 775, 829, 831-840, 861-862
  Americanization of, 841
  animal husbandry, 758
  Christianity in, 791-793, 820-822
  rise of Christianity in, 779-780
  climate of, 753, 754
  democracy in, 773, 844-845
  dance in, 861-862
  diversity of, 754-756
  dress in, 816-817
  education in, 843-844, 857-859
  ethnic groups, *see* diversity (above) and national identity (below)
  explorers from, 794-797
  families in, 812-813
  fishing in, 856-857
  folk arts and crafts in, 816-817, 861-862
  geography of, 753-765
  governments (ancient) of, 773-775, 776-779
  Holocaust, 807, 823-824
  housing in, medieval, 783
  industrial development in, 800, 802-804, 852-853
  inventors in, 803
  labor movement in, 852-853
  languages in, 818, 820
  life styles in, 849-852, 854-857
  literature in, 832-834, 839-840
  and Middle Ages, 780-787
  music in, 834-837
  national identity in, 815-818
  painting in, 837-839
  political thought in, 844-845
  population of, 753
  religions in, 779-780, 820-822
  science and technology in, 775, 840, 842-844
  social class in, 813-815
  sports and recreation in, 859-861, 863
  in World War I, 804-805
  in World War II, 805-807
Western Ghats, 337
West Germany
  dress in, 816
  government of, 844
  life in, 850-851
  post-World War II, 823-824
"White Highlands," in Kenya, 73
White nights, 709
Wildlife, protection of, in Africa, 15, 80
Women
  in Africa, 18-19, 51, 61-63, 78-79, 108-109, 110
  in China, 157, 165-166, 193, 208-209
  in India, 349, 354, 355-356, 374-375
  in Japan, 279, 305-306, 307, 321-323
  in Latin America, 469-470, 473, 504-505
  in Middle East, 544, 572-574, 576-579, 580-581
  in Soviet Union, 680, 737-739
  in Western Europe, 857, 861-862
Woodcuts, in Japan, 297
World Bank, role of, in Africa, 105-106
World War I
  causes of, 804
  effects of, on Middle East, 604, 609
  and Japan, 272
  and Soviet Union, 674, 804-805
  and Western Europe, 804-805
World War II
  American occupation of Japan following, 279
  causes of, 805
  China in, 194-195
  dropping of atomic bomb in, 276-278
  and Holocaust, 807, 823-824
  Japanese bombing of Pearl Harbor, 275
  Japanese surrender, 278-279
  and Jewish migration to Palestine, 610
  Pacific front, 275-276
  and Soviet Union, 679-681, 684-685, 737
  and Western Europe, 805-807
Writing. *See also* Alphabet and Language
  in China, 166, 168
  in Japan, 291, 329
Wuhan, China, 128

X

Xhosa, 57
Xia dynasty, in China, 142
Xi'an, China, 128
Xundi, 152

Y

Yakutsk, Soviet Union, 641
Yamanouchi, Midori, 243
Yamashita, Toshihiko, 316-318
Yamato clan, in Japan, 253
Yangtze River, 128
Yang/yin, 123, 133
Yathrib, 588, 589
Yellow River, 123
Yemen Arab Republic, 537
  family structure in, 577-578
  marriage ceremony in, 569
  use of mediation skills in, 572
Yemen, People's Democratic Republic of, 537
Yen Shu, 166
Yevtushenko, Yevgeny, 727, 731
Yi Jing (Book of Changes), 175
Yin. *See* Yang/yin
Yoga, 369
Yokohama, 244
Yoritomo, Minamoto, 257, 258
Yoruba, 40-41, 51
  oral literature of, 91
  visual arts of, 93-94
Young Pioneers, in China, 225

Youth
  in Africa, 49-50, 103
  in China, 224-226
  in Israel, 560-561
  in Japan, 307-309
  in Latin America, 465, 468-470, 477-478
  in Middle East, 560-561, 571-572
  in modern Rome, 860-861
  in Soviet Union, 739-745
Yuan Shih-k'ai, 191
Yucatán Peninsula, 439

Z

Zagros Mountains, 538
Zaibatsu, in Japan, 270, 279
Zaire, 9-10
  Belgian rule of, 32
  mining in, 12
  nationalism in, 32-33
  rain forest in, 13
Zaire River, 9
Zakāt, as Islamic belief, 591
Zakuski, 742
Zambezi River, 9
Zambia, 9
  mining in, 12
Zanskar, 334-335
Zaria, 42
Zen Buddhism, in Japan, 287-289, 295
Zhou dynasty, in China, 142, 143, 144, 177
Zhou En-lai, 193, 196, 197
Zhou Jincai, 222
Zhou Weizhi, 210
Zhu Jiang River, 129
Zhu Yuanzhang, 145, 147
Zimbabwe, 7, 9, 12
  education in, 111-112
  nationalism in, 89
  protest songs in, 89
  urbanization in, 16
Zionism, 609, 620
Zoroaster, in India, 378
Zuider Zee Project, 765
Zulu, 57
  oral literature of, 93

SUGGESTED RESOURCES

UNIT ONE AFRICA

Africa: Portrait of a Continent. Teaching Resources Films. Sound filmstrips, color. Dispels common stereotypes as it examines the terrain, peoples, and cultures of Africa.

Cambridge Encyclopedia of Africa by Roland Oliver and Michael Crowder, 1981, Cambridge University Pres. Gives an overview of Africa by theme and by country.

Famine in Africa by Lloyd Timberlake, 1986, Gloucester Press. Gives an overview of the problem of African hunger.

Modern Nigeria by Guy Arnold, 1977, Longman Inc. Provides an introduction to contemporary Nigeria.

Move Your Shadow—South Africa, Black and White by Joseph Lelyveld, 1985, Time Books. Traces race and special conditions in South Africa since 1961.

UNIT TWO CHINA

Changing China: Product of Revolution by John Whomsley, 1983, Longman. Depicts contrasting ways of life in different parts of China.

China: The One Billion Society. Current Affairs. Sound filmstrip, color. Focuses on people to introduce the economics, politics, history, and culture of contemporary China.

China in Perspective: Roots of Civilization. Guidance Associates. Sound filmstrips (2), color. Explores the achievements of ancient Chinese civilization as background to modern China.

China in Revolution: A Sleeping Giant Awakes. New York Times. Sound filmstrip, color. Depicts China from the late 1800's to the defeat of the Nationalists in 1949.

China Yesterday and Today, edited by Joel Coye and Jon Livingston, 1984, Bantam. Depicts China from the Shang dynasty to the present and includes the writing of Chinese philosophers, historians, and poets.

UNIT THREE JAPAN

Black Ships and Rising Sun by John G. Roberts, 1971, Julian Messner. Tells how Japan was opened to the West and how it industrialized and modernized.

The Human Face of Japan. Learning Corporation of America. Films (6), color, 28 minutes each. Profiles individuals from diverse socio-economic backgrounds in modern Japan.

Japan: A Historical Overview. Coronet Films. Film, color, 17 minutes. Recounts major events in Japan's history from 800 B.C. to the early 1960's.

Japan: Of Tradition and Change. National Geographic Society. Film, color, 23 minutes. Focuses on the life of a young woman in modern Tokyo whose life demonstrates a harmony of tradition and change.

Japan: A Unit of Study. United Learning. Sound filmstrips (6), color. Traces Japan's earliest beginnings through World War II to the 1980's. Includes on-location photography and interviews with Japanese from different walks of life.

UNIT FOUR INDIA

The Indian Subcontinent. Educational Design. Sound filmstrips (4), color. Examines current social and economic issues in the major geographic areas of the Indian subcontinent.

The Maharajas: Imperialism by Conspiracy. Centron Educational Films. Film, color, 25 minutes. Relates the rise and fall of the maharajas during the period of British imperialism in India.

Through Indian Eyes, Vol. 1: The Wheel of Life, edited by Donald and Jean Johnson, 1981, Center for International Training and Education (CITE), revised edition. Twenty-eight selections describe childhood, education, and other aspects of life in traditional India. From writings of India's people.

Through Indian Eyes, Vol. 2: Forging a New Nation, edited by Donald and Jean Johnson, 1981, Center for International Training and Education (CITE), revised edition. Examines contemporary issues. Selections from fiction, news media, memoirs, and historical documents.

UNIT FIVE LATIN AMERICA

The Ancient New World. Churchill Films. Film, color, 16 minutes. Describes the early cultures of Mesoamerica focusing on the rise and decline of the Maya and the Aztecs.

Latin America: Its History, Economy, and Politics. McGraw-Hill. Film, b/w, 33 minutes. A survey of Latin American history from pre-European conquest until recent times. Focus on struggles for independence and subsequent problems.

Revolution in Central America by Glenn Alan Cheney, 1984, Watts. Revolution and civil war as related to Nicaragua, El Salvador, Guatemala, and Honduras.

The Revolution in Spanish America: The Independence Movements of 1808-1825, by Albert Prago, 1970, Macmillan. A history of the leaders and early events of Latin American independence, and the challenges of establishing independent nations.

UNIT SIX MIDDLE EAST

Arabs and Jews: The Crisis. World Studies. Sound filmstrips (6), color. Summarizes major events from biblical time to the 1967 Arab-Israeli war.

Essence of Israel. Kevin Donovan Films and I.S. Associates. Sound filmstrips (4), color. The history of Jews from ancient times to 1973.

The Middle East: A Unit of Study. United Learning. Sound filmstrips (8), color. Interviews with teenagers from Egypt, Iran, Iraq, Jordan, Lebanon, Yemen, Saudi Arabia, Syria, Turkey, and the United Arab Emirates.

The Palestine Question by Raymond Carroll, 1983, Watts. A land dispute between Israelis and Palestinian Arabs.

The Sword of the Prophet by Robert Goldston, 1974, Dial. A history of the Arab Middle East, including the rise of Islam.

UNIT SEVEN SOVIET UNION

The Byzantine Empire by Robert Browning, 1980, Scribner. The impact of the Byzantine world from about 500 A.D. to the fall of Constantinople in 1453.

Inside the U.S.S.R. New York Times. Sound filmstrips (8), color. A broad view of present-day Soviet life, focusing on the diversity of cultures and peoples.

Russia: A Modern History by David Warnes, 1984, University Tutorial Press. Describes the fall of the tsar in 1900 through political and social developments of contemporary times.

Siberia and the Soviet Far East by Abraham Resnick, 1985, GE McCuen. Highlights the diversity of cultures, peoples, and climates in the area.

The Soviet Union: A Changing Nation. Focus Media. Diskette. Traces changes in Imperial Russia and illustrates other aspects of the USSR, including geography and demographics.

UNIT EIGHT WESTERN EUROPE

The Aftermath. Douglas Botting, 1983, Time-Life Books, Inc. Discusses developments in postwar Europe from 1945 to 1950.

All Quiet on the Western Front by Erich Maria Remarque, 1979, Fawcett. Novel about a young German soldier in World War I.

European Studies: The Southern Nations. Educational Enrichment. Sound filmstrips (4), color. Reviews past history and speculates beyond the present in Spain, Portugal, Italy, and Greece.

European Studies: The Western Nations. Educational Enrichment. Sound filmstrips (6), color. Examines various aspects of France, Belgium, Switzerland, the Netherlands, West Germany, and Austria.

Pioneers in Science by Frank and James M. Siedel, 1968, Houghton. Short biographies of leading scientific figures from the Age of Reason to modern times.

Seven Medieval Queens by Joseph Dahmus, 1972, Doubleday. Brief biographies of such monarchs as Theodora and Eleanor of Aquitaine.

PHOTO CREDITS

COVER: (r to l) David Ryan/Uniphoto, Danielle Pellegrini/Photo Researchers, Robert Frerck/Woodfin Camp & Assoc., Paolo Koch/Photo Researchers, David G. Houser/Uniphoto, George P. Koshollek/Woodfin Camp & Assoc., Bill Weems/Woodfin Camp & Assoc., Gilda Schiff/Photo Researchers.

AFRICA: 5, Brian Brake/Rapho-Guillumete/Photo Researchers; 6, Shostal Assoc.; 8, Syndication International Ltd.; 10, Andy Bonczyk; 11, Louise Gubb/Liaison; 12, Hewett/UNICEF; 14, P. Morris; 15, Georg Gerster/Photo Researchers; 17, David Northrup; 22, Eliot Elisofon/National Museum of African Art/Eliot Elisofon Archives/Smithsonian Institution; 25, E. Streichan/Shostal Assoc.; 27, The British Library; 29, Peabody Museum, Salem; 31, Photri; 32 (l) Jak Kilby, (r) Vivienne Silver/Art Resource; 33, UPI/Bettmann Newsphotos; 34, File Photo; 35, Shostal Assoc.; 38, Jak Kilby; 40, Bruno Barbey/Magnum; 41, Shostal Assoc.; 43, (l) Bruno Barbey/Magnum, (r) Ken Heyman; 44, Historical Pictures Service, Chicago; 46, Robert Harding Picture Library; 47, Marc & Evelyne Bernheim/Woodfin Camp & Assoc.; 48, Shostal Assoc.; 49, Leo DeWys; 50, Ian Steele/International Stock Photo; 54, Tim Courlas; 56, IDAF Publications, London; 57, BBC Hulton/Bettmann Archive; 58, Historical Pictures Service, Chicago; 59, Ian Berry/Magnum; 60, United Nations; 61, Mark Peters/Black Star; 63, AP/Wide World Photos; 64, Pendl/United Nations; 66, Mark Peters/Black Star; 67, Abbas/Magnum; 70, Nancy Adams/EPI; 72, File Photo; 74, AP/Wide World Photos; 75, H. Armstrong Roberts; 76, Anne Martens/Image Bank; 77, Shostal Assoc.; 78, Marc & Evelyne Bernheim/Woodfin Camp & Assoc.; 79, Paolo Koch/Photo Researchers; 80, Dave Bartruff/FPG; 81, W. Shostal/Shostal Assoc.; 86, Tim Courlas; 88, (l) Lois Greenfield/Bruce Coleman, Inc., (r) Jean M. Borgatti (Olimi Festival, May 1973. New Iddo, Bendel State, Nigeria.); 91, Marc Bernheim/Woodfin Camp & Assoc.; 92, (lt) Frank Willett, (lc) H. Armstrong Roberts, (lb) Tim Courlas, (rt) Edward S. Ross, (rc) Jak Kilby, (rb) Lee Boltin; 93, Michigan State University/African Cultural Heritage Program; 95, (l) Jean M. Borgatti (Olimi Festival, May 1973. New Iddo, Bendel State, Nigeria.), (r) Robert Shay; 96, 97, The Christian Science Monitor; 98, Bryan & Cherry Alexander; 99, (l) Lee Boltin, (r) Dave De Roche; 102, Douglas Pike/Bruce Coleman, Inc.; 105, (l) Peter Marlow/Magnum, (r) Steele Perkins/Magnum; 107, Ron Lutz; 108, Maggie Murray/Format Photographers Ltd.; 109, A.L. Hinton/Art Resource; 112, Maggie Murray/Format Photographers Ltd.

CHINA: 121, Frank Lerner; 122, Eugene Gilliom; 125, Leo DeWys; 126, EROS Data Center; 127, (l) Robert Harding Picture Library, (r) Galen Rowell/High & Wild Photography; 129, Sovfoto/Eastfoto; 132, EROS Data Center; 133, Wellcome Institute Library, London; 134, Robert Harding Picture Library; 140, Paolo Koch/Photo Researchers; 144, Stock Concepts; 148, The Granger Collection; 149, Scala/Art Resource; 151, Bettmann Archive; 152, Historical Pictures Service, Chicago; 156, Bibliotheque Nationale, Paris; 158, China Pictorial; 159, Bettmann Archive; 160, The Granger Collection; 161, Brown Brothers; 163, File Photo; 164, National Palace Museum, Taipei; 165, The British Museum; 168, Sekai Bunka Photo; 172, Art Brown/Tom McCarthy Photography; 174, The British Musuem; 177, Museum of Fine Arts, Boston; 178, ZEFA; 179, Freer Gallery of Art; 181, Giraudon/Art Resource; 186, Felix Greene/Hutchison Library Ltd.; 188, New China Photo Service/Historical Pictures Service, Chicago; 190, Bettmann Archive; 195, Rene Burri/Magnum; 196, Historical Pictures Service, Chicago; 198, Xinhua News Agency/UN Bureau; 199, 202, Gwendolyn Stewart; 204, C. Hinton; 205, 206, Beijing Review; 208, Sally & Richard Greenhill; 209, Wolfgang Kaehler; 210, Xinhua News Agency/UN Bureau; 212, Sovfoto/Eastfoto; 218, Anne Rippy/Don Klumpp; 222, Sovfoto/Eastfoto; 224, K. Scholz/Shostal Assoc.; 225, Eve Arnold/Magnum; 226, AP/Wide World Photos.

JAPAN: 235, Burt Glinn/Magnum; 236, S. Vidler/Leo DeWys; 238, J.P. Nacivet/Shostal Assoc.; 239, Michael S. Yamashita/Woodfin Camp & Assoc.; 241, Leo DeWys; 243, Topham Picture Library; 245, Alexander M. Chabe/Worldwide Photo; 246, J.P. Nacivet/Shostal Assoc.; 252, Lee Boltin; 256, Gemini Smith; 257, Sekai Bunka Photo; 258, Gemini Smith; 259, Sekai Bunka Photo; 261, Suzanne J. Engelmann/Shostal Assoc.; 262, 263, Gemini Smith; 264, Eiji Miyazawa/Black Star; 265, Historical Pictures Service, Chicago; 268, Sekai Bunka Photo; 270, Gemini Smith; 273, H. Armstrong Roberts; 274, FPG; 277, US Air Force/DAVA; 278, Navy Dept.; 284, K. Scholz/H. Armstrong Roberts; 286, Dave Wade/Lightwave; 288, F.L. Lambrecht/Berg & Assoc.; 290, Shostal Assoc.; 292, Bruno Barbey/Magnum; 293, Dirck Halstead/Liaison; 295, Ralph Gates; 296, Robert Harding Picture Library; 297, The British Museum; 300, Nik Wheeler/Black Star; 302, File Photo; 304, Norma Morrison; 306, Suzanne J. Engelmann/Shostal Assoc.; 308, Richard Kalvar/Magnum; 309, Michal Heron/Woodfin Camp & Assoc.; 310, Burt Glinn/Magnum; 311, (tl) (tr) Norma Morrison, (bl) J. Messerschmidt/Bruce Coleman, (br) Dirck Halstead/Liaison; 314, H. Armstrong Roberts; 316, Richard Kalvar/Magnum; 317, David Bartruff/FPG; 318, Gil & Ann Loescher/Shostal Assoc.; 320, Shostal Assoc.; 321, Norma Morrison; 322, Nigel Blythe/Robert Harding Picture Library; 324, Nik Wheeler/Black Star.

INDIA: 331, Vincent Rakestraw; 332, Jonathan T. Wright; 334, Vincent Rakestraw; 336, M. Epp/FPG; 338, Jacques Jangoux/Peter Arnold; 339, Vincent Rakestraw; 340, Val Mazzenga/Chicago Tribune; 341, Gemini Smith; 348, Robert Holmes; 350, Tom Hanley; 351, Bennett Coleman & Co. Ltd, Bombay; 353, Jane Richardson/FPG; 354, Vincent Rakestraw; 355, Shostal Assoc.; 356, Volker Corell; 357, 360, Ellen Johnson; 361, Shostal Assoc.; 362, Bury Peerless; 363, H. Armstrong Roberts; 366, Robert Harding Picture Library; 368, (l) Ann & Bury Peerless, (c) (r) Bettmann Archive; 370, Roberto Collier/FPG; 372, Jehangir Gazdar/Woodfin Camp & Assoc.; 373, Ann & Bury Peerless; 375, Vic Cox/Peter Arnold; 376, Ellen Johnson; 377, Patricia G. Foschi/Art Resource; 378, H. Armstrong Roberts; 382, Robert Frerck/Odyssey Productions; 384, Smithsonian Institution; 386, Robert Harding Picture Library; 388, Bettmann Archive; 389, 390, Historical Pictures Service, Chicago; 391, Bettmann Archive; 392, 393, Historical Pictures Service, Chicago; 394, Mark Riboud/Magnum; 395, Jehangir Gazdar/Woodfin Camp & Assoc.; 396, Dillip Metha/Contact; 400, John Hillery; 402, 404, (l) Marc & Evelyne Bernheim/Woodfin Camp & Assoc., (r) Jehangir Gazdar/Woodfin Camp & Assoc.; 405, Bernard Pierre Wolff/FPG; 407, Jehangir Gazdar/Woodfin Camp & Assoc.; 409, Indian Consulate; 410, Marc Bernheim/Woodfin Camp & Assoc.; 414, Tony Heiderer; 416, Patricia G. Foschi/Art Resource; 418, (l) A. Palmer/H. Armstrong Roberts; (r) Raghu Rai/Magnum; 419, Tom Hanley; 420, 421 (l) (rc) Ann & Bury Peerless, (rt) File Photo, (rb) Robert Frerck/Odyssey Productions; 423, Robert Frerck/Woodfin Camp & Assoc.; 424, Geoffrey Hiller/Leo DeWys; 425, Vince Rakestraw; 426, Dillip Metha/Contact; 427, Robert Holmes.

LATIN AMERICA: 433, H. Armstrong Roberts; 434, Loren A. McIntyre; 437, Jack Riesland/Berg & Assoc.; 438, (l) Flora L Phelps, (r) UPI/Bettmann Newsphotos; 440, Editions Vilo, Inc.; 441, Ron Butler; 442, Betty Crowell; 443, James Beach/Donald Perry; 445, David Perry; 450, Elliott Varner Smith; 452, Shostal Assoc.; 455, Norman Prince; 456, Stock Imagery; 457, Bob Thomason/Click, Chicago; 458, Peter Frey/Image Bank; 459, Dave Bartruff; 461, Delfim Martins/F4; 464, Larry Dale Gordon/Image Bank; 466, (l) Bruno Barbey/Magnum, (r) David Mangurian; 467, Wolfgang Kaehler; 469, Victor Aleman/FPG; 470, Co Rentmeester/People Weekly; 471, Robert Hatton; 472, David Mangurian; 473, David Perry; 474, Shostal Assoc.; 475, H. Grathwohl/FPG; 476, Wide World Photos; 477, Rich Brommer; 478, Hernandez/Art Resource; 479, (l) FPG, (r) Eric L. Wheater/Image Bank; 482, Betty Crowell; 484, Biblioteque Nationale, Paris courtesy Newsweek; 488, John Hoagland/Liaison; 489, Marcel Minee/International Stock Photo; 491, UNICEF; 492, Loren McIntyre; 493, Manchete/Pictorial Parade; 496, John Pennington/Picture Cube; 500, Chip & Rosa Maria Peterson; 501, Tom McGuire; 502, Victor Engelbert; 503, Brett-Smith/Bruce Coleman; 504, Rich Brommer; 505, Chip & Rosa Maria Peterson; 506, Tannenbaum/Sygma; 507, Doug Martin; 508, Liaison; 509, Susan Meiselas/Magnum; 510, Doug Martin; 516, Carl Frank/Photo Researchers; 518, Historical Pictures Service, Chicago; 519, Norma Morrison; 520, Alon Reninger/Woodfin Camp & Assoc.; 521, D. Goldberg/Sygma; 522, Claude Urraca/Sygma; 523, Leo DeWys; 524, 525, D. Goldberg/Sygma; 526, Sovfoto/Eastfoto; 528, Daniel D. Morrison; 529, Milton & Joan Mann/Cameramann International.

MIDDLE EAST: 535, George Holton/Photo Researchers; 536, Shostal Assoc.; 538, Richard Bangs/Sobek Expeditions; 540, Ralph Gates; 541, A.F. Kertsing; 543, Fred J. Maroon; 545, Photo Researchers; 546, (l) Magnum, (r) A.F. Kertsing; 547, Marc Bernheim/Woodfin Camp & Assoc.; 548, John Elk III/Bruce Coleman; 549, Fred Adler/Kino Studios; 551, NASA; 554, Vladimir Bibic; 556, Aramco; 557, (l) Shostal Assoc., (r) Roloc Color Slides; 560, Fred Adler/Kino Studios; 563, A. Duncan/MEPhA; 564, Bruce Coleman; 568, Bernard Gerard/Liaison; 571, (t) Aramco, (b) Richard Nowitz/FPG; 572, Aramco; 574, Kurt Scholz/Shostal Assoc.; 575, Christine Osborne; 577, M. Hoare/MEPhA; 578, Gianfranco Gorgoni/Contact; 579, Gordon Gahan/Photo Researchers; 580, Jonathan T. Wright/Bruce Coleman; 581, (t) Amedeo Vergani/Image Bank, (b) John Running; 584, (t) Barbara Pfeffer, (c) James Westwater, (b) Roger Wood; 587, Photo Researchers; 589, Aramco; 590, (l) Bettmann Archive, (r) Aramco; 591, Aramco; 592, Historical Pictures Service, Chicago; 593, Aramco; 596, Robert F. White; 597, Historical Pictures Service, Chicago; 599, (t) The Granger Collection, (b) Pat Lanza Field/Bruce Coleman; 602, 605, Bettmann Archive; 607, Historical Pictures Service, Chicago; 608, AP/Wide World Photos; 610, Atlanta Journal/NEA; 616, Tor Eigeland/Aramco; 618, Jean Gaumy/Magnum; 621, James Nachtwey/Black Star; 622, William Karel/Sygma; 623, AP/Wide World Photos; 624, Aral/SIPA; 625, John Running; 626, Olivier Rebbot/Woodfin Camp & Assoc.; 627, Coyne Productions/Image Bank; 628, Steve McCurry; 630, Leo DeWys; 631, Brian Gibbs/Topham Picture Library; 635, (l) Mike Yamashita/Woodfin Camp & Assoc., (r) Bryan & Cherry Alexander.

SOVIET UNION: 637, James Sugar, Black Star, 638, Tass from Sovfoto/Eastfoto; 641, (l) Sovfoto/Eastfoto, (r) Tass from Sovfoto/Eastfoto; 642, Emil Schultess/Black Star; 643, Magnum; 645, Tass from Sovfoto/Eastfoto; 646, Novosti Press; 647, Entai/Zefa/H. Armstrong Roberts; 648, Progress Publishers, Moscow; 654, Dick Rowen; 656, John Kohan; 657, The Granger Collection; 659, Historical Pictures Service, Chicago; 660, 661, The Free Library of Philadelphia; 662, 664, Historical Pictures Service, Chicago; 665, Hubert Jasse/Editorial Photocolor Archives; 667, Historical Pictures Service, Chicago; 669, File Photo; 672, Historical Pictures Service, Chicago; 674, 675, Brown Brothers; 676, Photri; 677, 679, Bettmann Archive; 681, Sovfoto/Eastfoto; 682, David L. Shearer; 683, 684, Tass from Sovfoto/Eastfoto; 685, (l) Wolfgang Kaehler, (r) Tass from Sovfoto/Eastfoto; 688, Warren Eason; 691, 692, Tass from Sovfoto/Eastfoto; 693, Photri; 694, Burt Glinn/Magnum; 697, Shostal Assoc.; 699, Novosti Press; 704, Shostal Assoc.; 707, Farrell Grehan/FPG; 708, Tass from Sovfoto/Eastfoto; 709, Susanna Pashko/Leo DeWys; 710, Lee Boltin; 712, Jacques Jangoux/Peter Arnold; 713, Alexander M. Chabe/Worldwide Photo; 714, Tass from Sovfoto/Eastfoto; 715, Wolfgang Kaehler; 716, Ralph Gates; 717, (lt) Erevan/Sygma, (lb) Wolfgang Kaehler, (rt) John Launois/Black Star, (rb) Al Michaud/FPG; 720, 722, 724, Tass from Sovfoto/Eastfoto; 725, 727, File Photos; 729, Tass from Sovfoto/Eastfoto; 730, SIPA; 734, A. Borodulin/Leo DeWys; 736, Jacques Jangoux/Peter Arnold; 738, Ralph Gates; 740, Tass from Sovfoto/Eastfoto; 741, Warren Eason; 742, 743, Tass from Sovfoto/Eastfoto; 744, (l) Bea Wagner/Berg & Assoc., (r) Zimmerman/FPG; 745, Bea Wagner/Berg & Assoc.

WESTERN EUROPE: 751, Wayland Publishers; 752, J. Allan Cash, Ltd.; 754, Daudier/Jerrican; 755, 756, Art Directors; 757, 758, Beeldbank en Uitgeefprojekten, Amsterdam; 759, A.G.E. Fotostock; 760, J.R. Livermore/Art Directors; 762, Werner Otto; 764, J. Allan Cash, Ltd.; 765, Fred Salaff/FPG; 767, Betty Crowell; 770, Walter S. Clark/Photo Researchers; 774, Mary Evans Picture Library; 777, File Photo; 779, Mary Evans Picture Library; 781, 782, File Photos; 785, Mary Evans Picture Library; 786, 790, File Photo; 794, 796, 797, The Granger Collection; 798, File Photo; 800, The Granger Collection; 805, Harry S. Truman Library; 806, File Photo; 810, Marcus Brooke/FPG; 812, W. Fischer/FPG; 814, (l) S. Brown/Leo DeWys, (r) Buck Campbell/FPG; 815, Danilo Boschung/Leo DeWys; 818, E. Nagele/FPG; 821, Don Nieman; 823, Dave Bartruff/FPG; 824, AP/Wide World Photos; 828, Travel Pix/FPG; 832, Three Lions/Shostal Assoc.; 833, (lt) (lc) (rt) File Photos, (lb) FPG, (rc) Smithsonian Institution, (rb) Robert Frerck/Odyssey Productions; 835, Mary Evans Picture Library; 838, Oarsmen at Chatou, Auguste Renoir, National Gallery of Art, Washington, Gift of Sam A. Lewisohn; 839, A.G.E. Fotostock; 845, Paul Slaughter/Image Bank; 848, Messerschmidt/Leo DeWys; 850, Zefa/Leo DeWys; 851, Joyce White; 853, 854, A.G.E. Fotostock; 856, Bryan/FPG; 857, Amedeo Vergani/Image Bank; 858, A.G.E. Fotostock; 859, Tom McCarthy/Image Bank; 860, Melchior DiGiacomo/Image Bank; 861, K&G/FPG; 862, G. Ricatto/Shostal Assoc.; 863. K. Reinhard/FPG.